To the researchers, past and present, whose work embodies psychology today, and to the students who will follow in their footsteps to shape the psychology of tomorrow.

Sponsoring Editor: David C. Lee
Senior Associate Editor: Jane Knetzger
Senior Project Editor: Carol Newman
Senior Production/Design Coordinator: Sarah Ambrose
Senior Manufacturing Coordinator: Priscilla Bailey
Marketing Manager: David Lenehan

Cover designed by Harold Burch, Harold Burch Design, NYC.

Anatomical illustrations by Joel Ito

Credits

Chapter opener photos: Ch. 1, p. 2 © Pete Saloutos/Tony Stone Images; **Ch. 2, p. 25** © Mel Digiacomo/The Image Bank; **Ch. 3, p. 46** © Alfred Pasteka/Science Photo Library/Photo Researchers; **Ch. 4, p. 86** © Kindra Clineff/The Picture Cube; **Ch. 5, p. 125** © J. Paul Kennedy/The Stock Market; **Ch. 6, p. 160** © Cathlyn Melloan/Tony Stone Images; **Ch. 7, p. 190** © Kirk Weddle/Sipa Press; **Ch. 8, p. 227** © Paul Conklin/PhotoEdit; **Ch. 9, p. 263** © David Young-Wolff/Tony Stone Images; **Ch. 10, p. 302** © Michael Newman/PhotoEdit; **Ch. 11, p. 336** © Michael Kodas/The Hartford Courant/Image Works; **Ch. 12, p. 381** © William Johnson/Stock Boston; **Ch. 13, p. 428** © Myrleen Ferguson/PhotoEdit; **Ch. 14, p. 457** © T Resource/Tony Stone Images; **Ch. 15, p. 489** © Thomas Kitchin/First Light, Toronto; **Ch. 16, p. 531** © David Harry Stewart/Tony Stone Images; **Ch. 17, p. 568** © Hubert Camille/Tony Stone Images; **Ch. 18, p. 595** © Mark Kelley/Tony Stone Images.

Text Credits

p. 68, *Fig. 3.18:* Reprinted with permission of Simon & Schuster from *The Cerebral Cortex of Man,* by Wilder Penfield and Theodore Rasmussen. Copyright © 1950 Macmillan Publishing Company, Renewed @ 1978 Theodore Rasmussen. **p. 203,** *Fig. 7.9:* From *The Psychology of Learning and Memory* by Hintzman. Copyright © 1978 W. H. Freeman and Company. Used with permission. **p. 247,** *Fig. 8.12:* From *Cognitive Psychology: A Neural Network Approach* by C. Martindale. Copyright © 1991 Brooks/Cole Publishing, Pacific Grove, CA 93950, a division of Thomson Publishing Inc. By permission of the publisher. **p. 290,** *Fig. 9.12:* From *Cognitive Psychology and Information Processing* by Lachman/Lachman/Butterfield, p. 513, figure 13.4, 1979. Copyright © 1979 by Lawrence Erlbaum Associates. Reprinted by permission.

(Credits continue following references)

PSYCHOLOGY

FOURTH EDITION

Douglas A. Bernstein
University of Illinois at Urbana-Champaign

Alison Clarke-Stewart
University of California, Irvine

Edward J. Roy
University of Illinois at Urbana-Champaign

Christopher D. Wickens
University of Illinois at Urbana-Champaign

Houghton Mifflin Company   Boston   New York

BRIEF CONTENTS

CONTENTS

SENSATION

 PERCEPTION

11 MOTIVATION AND EMOTION

12 HUMAN DEVELOPMENT

13 HEALTH, STRESS, AND COPING

14 PERSONALITY

16   TREATMENT OF PSYCHOLOGICAL DISORDERS

15   PSYCHOLOGICAL DISORDERS

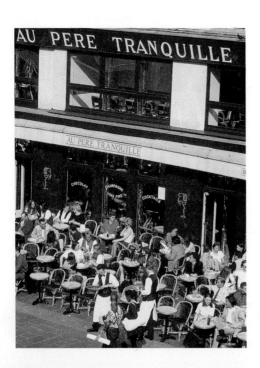

FEATURES

FOCUS ON RESEARCH METHODS

THINKING CRITICALLY

PREFACE

IN REVISING *PSYCHOLOGY* WE have rededicated ourselves to the goals we pursued in the first three editions:

- To explore the full range of psychology, from cell to society, in an eclectic manner as free as possible from theoretical bias.
- To balance our need to explain the content of psychology with an emphasis on the *doing* of psychology, through a blend of conceptual discussion and description of research studies.
- To foster scientific attitudes and to help students learn to think critically by examining the ways that psychologists have solved, or failed to solve, fascinating puzzles of behavior and mental processes.
- To produce a text that, without oversimplifying psychology, is clear, accessible, and enjoyable to read.
- To demonstrate that, in spite of its breadth and diversity, psychology is an integrated discipline in which each subfield is linked to other subfields by common interests and overarching research questions. The productive cross-fertilization among social, clinical, and biological psychologists in researching health and illness is just one example of how different types of psychologists benefit from and build on one another's work.

Preparing the Fourth Edition provided us with new ways to do justice to our goals.

We sought to respond to the needs of instructors who wanted us to reduce or expand coverage of various topics. For example, many instructors asked us to expand our coverage of the history of psychology and to show how scientific research methods appear in all of psychology's subfields. As a result, Chapter 1 now contains a section called "A Brief History of Psychology," and Chapters 3 through 18 each contain a feature called Focus on Research Methods (described in more detail below).

We sought to strike an ideal balance between classic and current research. The important historic findings of psychological research are here, but so is coverage of much recent work. Approximately one-third of the research citations are new to the Fourth Edition, and we have added the latest information on such topics as:

- Methods for evaluating claims for the effectiveness of eye movement desensitization (Chapter 2)
- Action potentials in dendrites as well as axons (Chapter 3)
- Genes for color vision (Chapter 4)
- Auditory scene analysis (Chapter 5)
- Mental processing without awareness (Chapter 6)

- Active learning in the classroom (Chapter 7)
- The repressed memory controversy (Chapter 8)
- The circle of thought (Chapter 9)
- Theories of intelligence (Chapter 10)
- The biological and environmental bases of sexual orientation (Chapter 11)
- Cognitive development (Chapter 12)
- Cynical hostility and health (Chapter 13)
- The big-five model of personality (Chapter 14)
- Child abuse and antisocial personality disorder (Chapter 15)
- Meta-analysis of psychotherapy effects (Chapter 16)
- Subconscious processes and prejudice (Chapter 17)
- Factors affecting helping (Chapter 18)

The Fourth Edition also contains abundant new material on culture and human diversity. Throughout the text students will encounter recent research on multicultural phenomena both domestic and global. We introduce this multicultural emphasis in Chapter 1, and follow it through such topics as:

- Selecting human participants for research (Chapter 2)
- Culture, experience, and perception (Chapter 5)
- Classrooms across cultures (Chapter 7)
- Cultural differences in formal reasoning (Chapter 9)
- Knowledge, language, and culture (Chapter 9)
- Bilingualism (Chapter 9)
- Cultural bias in mental ability testing (Chapter 10)
- Ethnic differences in IQ (Chapter 10)
- Flavor, cultural learning, and food selection (Chapter 11)
- Social and cultural factors in sexuality (Chapter 11)
- Cultural and gender differences in achievement motivation (Chapter 11)
- Cultural aspects of emotional expression (Chapter 11)
- Culture and cognitive development (Chapter 12)
- Cultural background and heart disease (Chapter 13)
- Personality, culture, and human development (Chapter 14)
- Ethnic bias in psychodiagnosis (Chapter 15)
- Sociocultural factors in psychological disorders (Chapter 15)
- Gender and cultural differences in depression and suicide (Chapter 15)
- Cultural factors in psychotherapy (Chapter 16)
- Ethnic differences in responses to drug treatment (Chapter 16)
- Cultural differences in attribution (Chapter 17)
- The roots of ethnic stereotyping and prejudice (Chapter 17)
- Cultural factors in social norms (Chapter 18)
- Culture and social loafing (Chapter 18)
- Cultural factors in aggression (Chapter 18)

We also have increased our coverage of behavioral genetics and evolutionary psychology. These topics are introduced in Chapters 1 and 2 and in a new behavioral genetics appendix. They are also explored wherever appropriate—for example, when we discuss:

- Gene manipulation research on the causes of Alzheimer's disease (Chapter 3)
- Biopreparedness for learning (Chapter 7)
- Genetic components of intelligence (Chapter 10)
- Genetic components of sexual orientation (Chapter 11)
- Evolutionary explanations of mate selection (Chapter 11)
- Innate expressions of emotion (Chapter 11)
- The genetics of prenatal development (Chapter 12)
- The heritability of personality (Chapter 14)
- Genetic factors in psychological disorders (Chapter 15)
- Evolutionary/genetic explanations for aggression, helping, and altruism (Chapter 18)

CHAPTER ORGANIZATION

As always, we have refrained from grouping the book's eighteen chapters into sections. Indeed, we designed each chapter to be a freestanding unit so that you may assign chapters in any order you wish. For example, many instructors prefer to teach the material on human development relatively late in the course, which is why it appears as Chapter 12 in the Fourth Edition. But that chapter can be comfortably assigned earlier in the course as well.

SPECIAL FEATURES

Psychology contains a number of special features designed to promote efficient learning and students' mastery of the material. Most of the features from previous editions have been revised and enhanced in the Fourth; two features are new to the Fourth Edition.

Linkages

In our experience, most students enter the introductory course thinking that psychology concerns itself mainly with personality, psychological testing, mental disorders, psychotherapy, and other aspects of *clinical* psychology. They have little or no idea of how broad and multifaceted psychology is. Many students are surprised, therefore, when we ask them to read about neuroanatomy, neural communication, the endocrine system, sensory and perceptual processes and principles, prenatal risk factors, and many other topics that they tend to associate with disciplines other than psychology.

We have found that students are better able to appreciate the scope of psychology when they see it not as a laundry list of separate topics but as an interrelated set of subfields, each of which contributes to and benefits from the work going on in all of the others. To help students see these relationships, we have built into the book an integrating tool called Linkages. There are four elements in the Linkages program:

1. Beginning with Chapter 2, a Linkages diagram at the top of the second page of each chapter presents a set of questions that illustrate three of the ways in which material in the chapter is related to other chapters in the book. For example, the Linkages diagram in Chapter 3 "Biological Aspects of Psychology" contains questions that show how biological psychology is related to consciousness ("Is there a way to drink alcohol without getting drunk?"), human development ("How do our brains change over a lifetime?"), and treatment of psychological disorders ("How do drugs help people who suffer from schizophrenia?").

2. The page numbers following each question in the Linkages diagram direct the student to pages that carry further discussion of that question. There, the linking question is repeated in the margin alongside the discussion.

3. One of the questions in each chapter's Linkages diagram is treated more fully in a special section later in the chapter entitled, appropriately enough, Linkages.

4. Each chapter contains at least one captioned photo illustrating yet another way in which the content of that chapter is related to the content of another chapter.

The Linkages elements combine with the text narrative to highlight the network of relationships among psychology's subfields. This Linkages program is designed to help students see the "big picture" that is psychology—no matter how many chapters their instructor assigns, or in what sequence.

Thinking Critically

A section in each chapter is called Thinking Critically. We try throughout the book to describe research on psychological phenomena in a way that reveals the logic of the scientific enterprise, that identifies possible flaws in design or interpretation, and that leaves room for more questions and further research. In other words, we try to display critical thinking processes. The Thinking Critically sections are designed to make these processes more explicit and accessible by providing a framework for analyzing evidence before drawing conclusions. The framework is built around five questions that the reader should find useful in analyzing not only studies in psychology but other forms of communication as well. These questions, first introduced when we discuss the importance of critical thinking in Chapter 2, are

1. What am I being asked to believe or accept?

2. What evidence is available to support the assertion?

3. Are there alternative ways of interpreting the evidence?

4. What additional evidence would help to evaluate the alternatives?

5. What conclusions are most reasonable?

Thinking Critically sections new to the Fourth Edition include:

■ Can traumatic memories be repressed, then recovered? (Chapter 8)
■ Do genes determine sexual orientation? (Chapter 11)
■ Is ethnic prejudice too ingrained ever to be eliminated? (Chapter 17)

Focus on Research Methods

This new feature, appearing in Chapters 3 through 18, examines the ways in which the research methods described in Chapter 2, Research in Psychology, have been applied to help advance our understanding of some aspect of behavior and mental processes. By describing in some detail the design and methodology of one particularly interesting research project, the Focus on Research Methods section is designed to help students appreciate the value of a particular research method and the creativity with which psychologists have applied it. Examples of these sections include the use of case-study methods to track the problem-solving methods that led to the invention of the airplane (Chapter 9, Thought and Language), the use of experiments to study attention (Chapter 5, Perception), learned helplessness (Chapter 7, Learning), the development of physical knowledge (Chapter 12, Human Development), and attribution (Chapter 17, Social Cognition). Other sections illustrate the use of quasi-experimental, survey, longitudinal, laboratory analogue, and meta-analytical designs. A full list of topics appears on p. xv.

Behavioral Genetics Appendix

This new feature is designed to amplify the coverage of behavioral genetics methodology that appears in Chapter 2, Research in Psychology. The appendix includes a section on the basic principles of genetics and heredity, a brief history of genetic research in psychology, a discussion of what it means to say that genes influence behavior, and an analysis of what behavioral genetics research can—and cannot—tell us about the origins of such human attributes as intelligence, personality, and mental disorders.

In Review Charts

In Review charts summarize information in a convenient tabular format. We have placed two or three In Review charts strategically in each chapter to help students synthesize and assimilate large chunks of information—for example, on drug effects, key elements of personality theories, and stress responses and mediators.

Future Directions

Each chapter concludes with Future Directions, a section intended to excite and inform students about new trends in psychology. Here we offer our views on the directions that theory, research, and applications are likely to take in future years.

We also suggest courses that an interested student could take in psychology and other disciplines to learn more about the chapter's topic.

Chapter Summaries

These summaries are configured to reflect clearly the heading structure of each chapter. The chapters' key terms are integrated into the summaries rather than set off as a separate list. These terms are defined in the glossary.

TEACHING AND LEARNING SUPPORT PACKAGE

Many useful materials have been developed to support *Psychology*. Designed to enhance the teaching and learning experience, they are well-integrated with the text and include some of the latest technologies. Several components are new to this edition.

Annotated Instructor's Edition

To help instructors coordinate the many print, software, and video supplements available with the text, an Annotated Instructor's Edition shows which materials apply to the content on every page of the student text. These materials include learning objectives, test questions, discussion and lecture ideas, handouts, active learning activities from the study guide, videodisc segments, computer simulations, overhead transparencies, and so forth.

Print Ancillaries

Accompanying this book are, among other ancillaries, a *Test Bank,* an *Instructor's Resource Manual,* and a *Study Guide.* Because these items were prepared by the lead author and his colleagues from the University of Illinois psychology department, you will find an especially high level of coordination between the textbook and these supplements. All three are unified by a shared set of learning objectives. Equally important, all three have been significantly revised and enhanced for the Fourth Edition.

Test Bank The *Test Bank,* by Graeme McGufficke, Sandra S. Goss, and Douglas A. Bernstein, contains more than 3,000 multiple-choice items plus three essay questions for each chapter of the text. Half of the multiple-choice questions are new; in all others, the foils have been scrambled.

All multiple-choice items are keyed to pages in the textbook and to the learning objectives listed in the *Instructor's Resource Manual* and *Study Guide.* In addition, questions that ask students to apply their knowledge are now distinguished from those that require factual recall. More than 1,600 questions have already been class-tested with between 500 and 2,500 students and are accompanied by graphs indicating the question's discriminative power, level of difficulty, the percentage of students who chose each response, and the relationship between students' performance on a given item and their overall performance on the test in which the item appeared.

Instructor's Resource Manual The *Instructor's Resource Manual,* by Joel I. Shenker, Sandra S. Goss, and Douglas A. Bernstein, contains a complete set of lecture outlines, learning objectives, and numerous specific teaching aids—many of them new to the Fourth Edition—including handouts, demonstrations, and classroom exercises. It also contains a new section on active learning techniques and other material that will be useful to teachers of large introductory courses, such as a section on classroom management and administration of large multisection courses, and a discussion of careers in psychology that instructors may want to distribute to students.

Study Guide The *Study Guide,* by Amanda Allman, Bridget Schoppert, and Douglas A. Bernstein, employs numerous techniques that help students to learn. Each chapter contains a detailed outline, a key-terms section that presents fresh examples and aids to remembering, learning objectives, a Concepts and Exercises section that shows students how to apply their knowledge of psychology to everyday issues and concerns, a Critical Thinking exercise, and new Personal Learning Activities. In addition, each chapter concludes with a two-part self-quiz consisting of forty multiple-choice questions. An answer key tells the student not only which response is correct but also why each of the other choices is wrong, and new answer-key tables enable students to track patterns to their wrong answers, either by topic or by type of question—definitional, comprehension, or application.

Succeed in College! *Succeed in College!* is a skills-building booklet containing selected chapters from Walter Pauk's bestselling study skills text *How to Study in College.* This booklet, which offers time-tested advice on notetaking, test-taking, and other topics, as well as a section on Careers in Psychology, can be shrinkwrapped free of charge with new copies of the student text.

Internet Guide for Psychology Houghton Mifflin's *Internet Guide for Psychology,* by David Mahony of St. John's University, is available at no cost to students who purchase *Psychology.* This handy manual introduces students to electronic mail, discussion groups, on-line journals, Usenet newsgroups, the World Wide Web, APA Reference Style for the Internet, and more, and it provides students with step-by-step exercises and a wealth of addresses and sites relevant to psychology.

Electronic and Video Ancillaries

In an effort to keep up with the technological developments on campus in the 1990s, we provide the following electronic and video supplements to *Psychology:*

Power Presentation Manager Software This powerful program allows instructors to create exciting and well-organized classroom presentations. It provides line art, tables, lecture outlines, pre-planned PowerPoint® presentations, and access to *The Psychology Show* videodisc material. Instructors can also add their own PowerPoint® slides and presentations as well as access their own text and image files.

Computerized Test Bank The *Computerized Test Bank* allows instructors to generate exams and to integrate their own test items with those on the disk.

Computerized Study Guide The *Computerized Study Guide* is an interactive program that gives students feedback on incorrect as well as on correct answers.

Psychabilities *Psychabilities,* created by Sarah Ransdell, New College of the University of South Florida, consists of thirteen computer simulations, specially designed for use in either the classroom or the computer laboratory. The simulations illustrate intriguing phenomena and recreate important experiments, and they include a multiple-choice self-quizzing program to test progress and encourage mastery.

The Psychology Show Houghton Mifflin's video supplement for introductory psychology is available in both videodisc and videotape formats to qualified adopters. Containing nineteen motion segments plus nearly one hundred still images, *The Psychology Show* is designed to expand on text coverage and to stimulate class discussion through the length of your course. An accompanying instructor's guide offers information on each motion segment and still image and provides bar codes for videodisc use.

Transparencies The accompanying transparency set contains 100 images from the text, most in full color, plus over 60 images from outside the text.

Other Multimedia Offerings A range of videos, CD-ROMS, and other multimedia materials relevant to psychology are available free to qualified adopters. Houghton Mifflin sales representatives have further details.

ACKNOWLEDGMENTS

Many people provided us with the help, criticism, and encouragement we needed to create the Fourth Edition.

Once again we must thank Katie Steele, who got the project off the ground in 1983 by encouraging us to stop talking about this book and start writing it.

We are indebted to a number of our colleagues for their expert help and advice on the revisions of a number of chapters for the Fourth Edition. These colleagues include, for Chapters 14, 17 and 18, Louis Penner (University of South Florida), for Chapters 5 and 8, Michael Venturino (SUNY-Geneseo), for Chapters 6 and 11, Joel Shenker (University of Illinois), for Chapter 7, Michael Vidulich (Wright State University), for Chapter 9, Gary Bradshaw (University of Illinois), for Chapter 10, John Newman (Mount Saint Mary's College), for Chapter 13, Shelley Taylor (UCLA), for Chapter 15, Connie Hammen (UCLA), for Chapter 16, Michael Lambert (Brigham Young University), and for the behavioral genetics appendix, Robert Plomin (University of London).

Students, friends, and associates who evaluated parts of the Fourth Edition manuscript include Amanda Allman, Linda Bartoshuk, Sandra Goss, Elizabeth Loftus, Michael Nietzel, Peter Ornstein, Astrid Stec, Scott Stoltenberg, and Craig Waldo. We offer thanks also to Duane Jackson, who first suggested the idea of adding a behavioral genetics appendix to the Fourth Edition. Thanks are due as well to the many graduate students who have served as instructors in introductory psychology at Illinois during the creation of the Fourth Edition. Their comments and suggestions about how to make this edition easier to teach from were extremely helpful to us. We also want to offer a special thanks to Diane Weidner who, as Doug Bernstein's assistant, did an outstanding job at a multitude of secretarial and administrative tasks while putting up with us as we struggled to meet deadlines.

We owe an enormous debt to the colleagues listed below, who provided prerevision evaluations of or reviewed the manuscript for the Fourth Edition as it was being developed. Their advice and suggestions for improvement were responsible for many of the good qualities you will find in the book. If you have any criticisms, they probably involve areas these people warned us about.

G. John Andersen, *University of California, Riverside*

Wendy Beller, *Quincy University*

Joseph J. Benz, *University of Nebraska at Kearney*

Lilly Both, *University of Waterloo*

Vic Burton, *Grossmont College*

William C. Calhoun, *University of Tennessee*

J. Timothy Cannon, *University of Scranton*

Rich Carlson, *Pennsylvania State University*

Carroll E. Izard, *University of Delaware*

Alan Childs, *Lafayette College*

Lorry J. Cology, *Owens Community College*

Carol DeVolder, *Augustana College*

Ernest Dzendolet, *University of Massachusetts*

Jeremiah M. Faries, *Northwestern University*

Kathleen A. Flannery, *Saint Anselm College*

Michael Gaynor, *Bloomsburg University*

Janet Gibson, *Grinnell College*

Sallie Gordon, *University of Idaho*

Sandra Kerr, *West Chester University of Pennsylvania*

Kerry Kilborn, *University of Glasgow*

Geoff Kramer, *Indiana University—Kokomo*

John W. Kulig, *Plymouth State College*

Thomas W. Lombardo, *University of Mississippi*

Matthew Margres, *Saginaw Valley State University*

Douglas W. Matheson, *University of the Pacific*

David G. McDonald, *University of Missouri*

Jay Moore, *University of Wisconsin—Milwaukee*

Gerry Mulhearn, *Queen's University, Belfast*

Dean Murakami, *American River College*

Ian Neath, *Purdue University*

Richard Pisacreta, *Ferris State University*

Judith C. Reiff, *University of Georgia*

Edward J. Rinalducci, *University of Central Florida*

Richard Robbins, *Washburn University*

Connie Schick, *Bloomsburg University*

Mark Schittekatte, *University of Ghent*

Beth M. Schwartz-Kenney, *Randolph-Macon Woman's College*

Nancy Simpson, *Trident Technical College*

Alexander A. Skavenski, *Northeastern University*

Susan Smith, *University of Westminster, London*

Jacqueline A. Solfronk, *Joliet Junior College*

Ebo Tei, *University of Arkansas at Pine Bluff*

Anthony P. Thompson, *Lakehead University*

Robert M. Thorndike, *Western Washington University*

David Uttal, *Northwestern University*

Rene van der Veer, *University of Leiden*

Kenneth Wolkon, *Bridgewater State College*

The process of creating the Fourth Edition was greatly facilitated by the work of many dedicated people in the College Division at Houghton Mifflin Company. From the sales representatives and sales managers who told us of faculty members' suggestions for improvement to the marketing staff who developed innovative ways of telling our colleagues about the changes we have made, it seems that everyone in the division had a hand in shaping and improving the Fourth Edition. Seven people deserve special thanks, however. Former sponsoring editor Becky Dudley and senior associate editor Jane Knetzger gave us invaluable advice about structural, pedagogical, and content changes for the new edition, and Jane, especially, acted as the project's main shepherd. Barbara Muller, our developmental editor, applied her editorial expertise and disciplined approach to helping us create this manuscript. She suggested changes based on reviewers' comments and our own goals, and she kept these suggestions and goals in mind as, chapter by chapter, she worked diligently to find ever better ways to organize the book and clarify its content. Carol Newman, project editor on the Second and Third Editions, returned to star in the same role for the Fourth, bringing with her a set of organizational skills and a level of dedication to excellence that is, in our opinion, unmatched in college publishing. Joanne Markow checked and rechecked each stage of proof ensuring its typographical accuracy. We also wish to thank Ann Schroeder and Charlotte Miller for their outstanding work in the creation of the art program for the Fourth Edition. And a great big thank you goes to Christine Arden for once again doing an outstanding job of copyediting the manuscript. Without these people, and those who worked with them, this revision simply could not have happened.

Finally, we want to express our deepest appreciation to our families and friends. Once again, their love saw us through an exhilarating but demanding period of our lives. They endured our hours at the computer, missed meals, postponed vacations, and occasional irritability during the creation of the First Edition of this book, and they had to suffer all over again during the lengthy process of revising it once more. Their faith in us is more important than they realize, and we will cherish it forever.

Doug Bernstein

Alison Clarke

Ed Roy

Chris Wickens

PSYCHOLOGY

INTRODUCING PSYCHOLOGY

CHAPTER **1**

n April 19, 1995, terrorists detonated a truck bomb that destroyed the Alfred P. Murrah federal building in Oklahoma City, Oklahoma. The blast killed 168 people—including 15 children in day care—and injured 400 more. As investigators sought the culprits, everyone sought answers. How could human beings do such a thing, and why? How do terrorists' extreme beliefs develop? Will the survivors' emotional scars ever heal? Why were people so quick to falsely presume that the bombers were from the Middle East?

Psychologists study questions like these because **psychology** is the science that seeks to understand behavior and mental processes, and to apply that understanding in the service of human welfare. Unfortunately, psychologists have still not traced all the roots of violence, nor found ways to prevent it. You will see in later chapters, however, that their research in areas such as motivation, aggression, stress and coping, personality, psychological disorders, and prejudice offers some important clues. That research tells part of the story of psychology, but there is much more. We wrote this book to give you a better understanding of what psychology is, what psychologists study, where and how they work, what they have—and have not—discovered so far, and how their discoveries are being put to practical use.

THE WORLD OF PSYCHOLOGY: AN OVERVIEW

Consider the subject matter of psychology, *behavior and mental processes*. Obvious examples are eating, talking, reading, and thinking, but the realm of behavior and mental processes that psychologists study includes many other phenomena as well. To appreciate just how many, consider how you would answer the question "Who are you?" Would you describe your personality? Your interests? Your aspirations? Your accomplishments? You could mention these and dozens of other things as well, and every one of them would probably reflect some aspect of what psychologists mean by behavior and mental processes. No wonder, then, that the chapters to come cover such a wide range of topics, including some—such as vision and hearing—that you might not have expected in a book about psychology. The topics have to be diverse in order to capture the full range of behaviors and mental processes that make you who you are and that combine in other ways in people of every culture around the world.

The Scope of Behavior and Mental Processes

So who *are* you, anyway? For one thing, you are a collection of cells that make up your bones and muscles, your skin and hair, your brain, liver, and other organs. Part of what we mean by behavior and mental processes is the activity of these cells, especially their ability to communicate with one another (the chapter on biological aspects of psychology describes that process). To illustrate this point, stop reading for a moment and feel your pulse. You stay alive because your heart beats and your lungs breathe—all thanks to the activity of cells in your brain and elsewhere. Further, as shown in the chapter on human development, it was your cells' ability to divide and carry out specific functions that allowed you to blossom from the single fertilized cell you once were into the complex physical being you are now.

Some of your specialized cells make possible another remarkable aspect of behavior and mental processes: your capacity to sense information coming from the outside world and from inside your body. Again, stop reading for a moment and, this time, look left and right. The images of whatever you saw just then, like what you are seeing on this page right now, are the result of an amazing process through which cells in your eyes convert light into nervous activity that reaches your brain. Barring physical disability, cells in your sense organs provide your brain with information that allows you not only to see your world but to hear, smell, taste, and feel it as well. Now snap your fingers, or at least try to. It was cells in your brain and motor system that allowed you to move your fingers as you did, just as they allow you to produce the coordinated patterns of behavior we call walking, dancing, talking, and the like. If you have an impairment in your ability to see, hear, or move, the problem lies somewhere in the structure or function of

THE SCOPE OF PSYCHOLOGY Like other living creatures, humans are biological beings, but they are more than just a collection of specialized cells. Throughout our lives, we develop and display remarkable capabilities to experience the world, to remember and think about it, to make decisions, solve problems, and take actions, to have feelings and strive for goals, to form relationships and attachments, and, unfortunately, to suffer distress and disorder. These are just some of the behaviors and mental processes that psychologists seek to understand. Throughout this book you will see how their research has provided knowledge and insights that are being used every day to promote human welfare.

cells in your brain or in sensory or motor systems. These cells and systems are described in the chapters on biological psychology and sensation.

Are you, then, only a bundle of cells that passively receives information and automatically reacts to it? You know you are much more than that, and we can help you prove it. Look at Figure 1.1. Although the drawing does not change, two different images emerge depending on which of its features *you* emphasize. Obviously, you don't just take in raw information; you also interpret it and give it meaning. This fascinating aspect of behavior and mental processes is discussed in the chapter on perception.

In addition to interpreting information, you can think about it and decide how to respond. Suppose you see someone standing in front of you with a knife. You recognize the knife as dangerous and you understand the meaning of the words "Give me your money," so you decide to comply. However, if the person smiles and says "Happy birthday," you will probably reach for the knife to cut your cake. Your decision about what to do in these two situations is guided not only by immediate circumstances but also by your capacity for learning and memory. If you couldn't understand the words you hear, could not recall the faces of your family or what you have learned about muggers and

Husband and Father-in-Law

This figure is called "Husband and Father-in-Law" (Botwinick, 1961) because it can be seen as two different people, depending upon how you mentally organize the features of the figure. The elderly father-in-law faces to your right and is turned slightly toward you. He has a large nose, and the dark areas represent his coat pulled up to his protruding chin. However, the tip of his nose can also be seen as the tip of a younger man's chin; the younger man is in profile, also looking to your right, but away from you. The old man's mouth is the young man's neck band. Both men are wearing broad-brimmed hats. Your ability to see two different figures in a drawing that does not physically change — and to choose which one to see at any given moment — demonstrates the active nature of your perceptual processes. You manipulate incoming information rather than just passively receiving it.

birthdays, you would be at a loss. You can read more about these aspects of behavior and mental processes in the chapters on learning, memory, and thought and language.

So far, you seem to be an utterly rational being, capable of coolly processing information under any circumstances. But would you experience only logical thought in the knife situations we described? Probably not. Chances are, you would also experience an emotion, maybe fear or happiness. You are capable of feeling many other emotions as well. Where do these emotions come from, and why are they sometimes so difficult to control? You might ask the same questions about your wants and needs. Perhaps you do volunteer work, love to read, compete fiercely, work two jobs, skydive, knit, or eat more than you should. *Why* you behave as you do, how your behavior makes you feel, and how your feelings influence your behavior add yet other dimensions to your being and reflect yet other aspects of behavior and mental processes. They are discussed in the chapter on motivation and emotion.

Above all, you are an individual, in many ways unlike anyone else on earth. You have your own personality, mental abilities, values, attitudes, beliefs, and probably even a special set of problems of one kind or another. Your individuality arises partly from the unique set of physical characteristics and behavioral tendencies you inherited from your parents, and partly from the experiences you have had while growing up in your particular family and culture. The kaleidoscope of individual differences in behavior and mental processes is discussed throughout this book but receives special attention in chapters on mental abilities; health, stress and coping; personality; psychological disorders; and treatment.

Finally, because you are an individual in a social world, your answer to the question "Who are you?" would probably include something about how and where you fit into that world. You might mention the size of your family, your place in organizations you belong to, or your attitudes about the government. Indeed, as described in the chapters on social cognition and on social behavior, no definition of behavior and mental processes is complete without some reference to how people think about, and relate to, other people. And no wonder. Great human achievements—from the performance of a symphony to the exploration of space—can result when people work together. And great human tragedies—from the Holocaust to terrorism and war—can occur when prejudice and hatred turn people against one another.

Research: The Foundation of Psychology

To help face the challenge of understanding these various aspects of behavior and mental processes, most psychologists rely on a philosophical view known as *empiricism.* Empiricists see knowledge as coming through experience and observation, not through speculation. Accordingly, psychologists use the methods of science to conduct *empirical research,* meaning that they perform experiments and other scientific procedures to systematically gather and analyze information about psychological phenomena.

For example, Kenneth Mathews and Lance Canon (1975) were interested in understanding helping behavior, especially the factors governing whether people will help others. They knew from previous research that people are most likely to help when the need for assistance is most obvious—as when they actually see someone fall down. However, the evidence also showed that, especially in cities, people tend to ignore those who appear to have recently had an accident and are, say, sitting on the ground and rubbing an ankle. Why should this be? Mathews and Canon speculated that people tend to ignore the aftermath of urban accidents not so much because the victim's need for help is less obvious, but because there is so much noise and activity in big cities that passersby suffer "stimulus overload." In such situations a person's need for help might simply fade into the background (Milgram, 1970).

To test this "stimulus overload" idea, Mathews and Canon conducted an experiment in which a person "accidentally" dropped several heavy boxes of books on a sidewalk, right in front of a passerby. In half of these staged incidents, the street was quiet; in the rest, a noisy lawn mower added to the passerby's stimulus load. The need for help was

A DISASTROUS MISUNDERSTANDING
Yoshihiro Hattori, a Japanese exchange student living in the United States, was looking for a Halloween party when he knocked on the wrong door. Thinking the student was an intruder, the alarmed homeowner told him to "freeze." Because Yoshihiro only knew this word to mean "cold," he began to enter the house. Interpreting this behavior as hostile, the homeowner fired a shot that killed the young man. Here, Yoshihiro's brother carries his photo in a funeral procession. This tragic case illustrates how easy it is to make bad decisions when people misunderstand the information they receive from one another.

MOTIVATED PEOPLE   Why do people do what they do? Psychologists have discovered that the motivation behind most human behavior stems from a few basic sources. You will have a better idea of what might be motivating these people after you read **Chapter 11** on motivation and emotion.

made obvious in half the incidents by a heavy cast on one of the victim's arms. Figure 1.2 shows what happened. These results—in conjunction with others discussed in the chapter on social behavior—have given psychologists an empirical basis for recommending that, especially in urban areas, you should ask for help when you need it.

In other words, psychologists do more than speculate about behavior and mental processes; they also use scientific methods to test the validity of their theories. They conduct empirically oriented scientific inquiries and draw informed conclusions from their results. Even psychologists who do not carry out research themselves are constantly applying the results of their colleagues' work to enhance the quality, currency, and effectiveness of their own teaching, writing, or service to clients and organizations.

The rules and methods of science that guide psychologists in their research are summarized in the next chapter. We have placed this material about research early in the book in order to underscore the fact that, without scientific methods and the foundation of empirical data they provide, psychologists' statements and recommendations would be no more credible than those of astrologers, the tabloids, or talk-show gadflies who offer empirically unsupported opinions. Indeed, throughout this book, the results of scientific research in psychology shape not only the presentation of what is known so far about behavior and mental processes but also the evaluation of psychologists' efforts to apply that knowledge to improve the quality of human life.

A Brief History of Psychology

The birthdate of modern psychology is usually given as 1879, the year that Wilhelm Wundt (pronounced "Voont") established the first formal psychology research laboratory at the University of Leipzig, Germany. However, the roots of psychology can be traced through centuries of history in philosophy and science. Since at least the time of Socrates, Plato, and Aristotle, there has been lively debate about such topics as the source of human knowledge, the nature of mind and soul, the relationship of mind to body, and the possibility of scientifically studying these matters (Wertheimer, 1987).

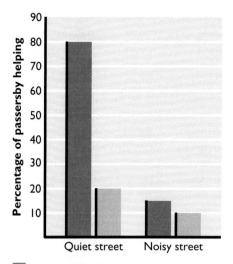

FIGURE 1.2

Helping Under Differing
Noise Conditions

In Mathews and Canon's (1975) experiment, when an unimpaired person
dropped boxes of books, passersby
offered help only about 15 percent of
the time, regardless of the amount of
noise in the situation. When the person's need for help was made obvious
by the presence of a cast on one arm,
passersby helped about 80 percent of
the time, as long as the street was
quiet. However, the needy victim was
ignored 85 percent of the time under
noisy street conditions, thus supporting the "stimulus overload" hypothesis.

WILHELM WUNDT (1832–1920) In one of
his classic experiments on the speed
of mental processes, Wundt (third
from left) first measured how
quickly subjects could respond to a
light by releasing a button they had
been holding down. He then determined how much longer the
response took when subjects held
down one button with each hand
and had to decide—based on the
color of the light—which one to
release. Wundt reasoned that the
additional time revealed how long it
took to perceive the color and
decide which hand to move. You will
see in Chapter 9 on thought and language that the logic behind this experiment remains a part of research
on cognitive processes today.

The philosophy of empiricism was particularly important to the development of scientific psychology. Beginning in the seventeenth century, proponents of empiricism—
especially the British philosophers John Locke, George Berkeley, and David Hume—
challenged the view held by philosophers from Plato to Descartes that some knowledge
is innate. As mentioned earlier, empiricists see everything we know as coming through
the experience of our senses. At birth, they said, our minds are like a blank slate (*tabula
rasa,* in Latin) upon which experience writes a life long story.

Wundt and the Structuralism of Titchener   By the nineteenth century, a number of
German physiologists, including Hermann von Helmholtz and Gustav Fechner, were
conducting scientific studies of the structure and function of vision, hearing, and the
other sensory systems and perceptual processes that empiricism identified as important
to human knowledge. A physiologist, Wundt studied sensory-perceptual systems, too,
but his goal was to use the methods of laboratory science to study *consciousness,* the
immediate experience arising from these systems. In short, with Wundt, psychology
had evolved from the *philosophy* of mental processes to the *science* of mental
processes. Wundt wanted to describe the basic elements of consciousness, how they are
organized, and how they relate to one another (Schultz & Schultz, 1992). He developed
numerous ingenious laboratory methods to study these elements, including the speed
of mental events. In an attempt to observe conscious experience, Wundt used the technique of *introspection,* which means "inward perception." Subjects specially trained in
this method were exposed to a light or sound, for example, and, on repeated trials, tried
to describe the sensations and feelings the stimulus created. Wundt concluded that
"quality" (e.g., cold or blue) and "intensity" (e.g., brightness or loudness) are the two
essential elements of any sensation and that feelings can be described in terms
of pleasure-displeasure, tension-relaxation, and excitement-depression (Schultz &
Schultz, 1992). Edward Titchener, an American who had been a student of Wundt, used
introspection in his own laboratory at Cornell University to study Wundt's basic elements as well as images and other aspects of conscious experience that are harder to

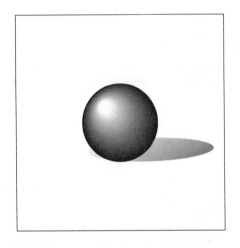

FIGURE 1.3

A Stimulus for Introspection

Look at this object and try to describe, not what it is but only how intense and clear are the sensations and images (such as redness, brightness, and roundness) that make up your experience of it. This was the difficult task that Wilhelm Wundt, and especially Edward Titchener, set for carefully trained subjects in a search for the building blocks of consciousness.

WILLIAM JAMES (1842–1910)   William James, founder of functionalism, saw structuralism as a dead end. In one paper, he noted that trying to understand consciousness by studying its components is like trying to understand a house by looking at individual bricks (James, 1884).

quantify (see Figure 1.3). One result was that Titchener added "clarity" as an element of sensation (Watson, 1963). Though often associated with Wundt, *structuralism* is the name given to Titchener's approach because of his efforts to define the structure of consciousness.

Wundt was by no means alone in the scientific study of psychology, nor was his work universally accepted. In psychology laboratories established by German contemporaries such as Hermann Ebbinghaus, the use of introspection to dissect consciousness was seen as less important than conducting experiments on the capacities, limitations, and other characteristics of mental processes such as learning and memory. Indeed, Ebbinghaus's experiments—in which he himself was the subject—formed the basis for much of what we know about memory today, as you will see in Chapter 8. Another group of German colleagues, including Max Wertheimer, Kurt Koffka, and Wolfgang Köhler, criticized Wundt on the grounds that introspection can be misleading. They pointed to visual illusions of the type shown in Figure 1.1 to support their argument that our experience of the world is more than just the sum of its parts. These Gestalt psychologists (*Gestalt* means, roughly, "unified whole" in German) argued that consciousness can be best understood by observing it as a total experience, not as a cluster of elements.

Freud and Psychoanalysis   While Wundt and his colleagues in Leipzig were conducting scientific research on consciousness, Sigmund Freud (1856–1939) was in Vienna, beginning to explore the unconscious. As a physician, Freud had presumed that all behavior and mental processes have *physical* causes somewhere in the nervous system. He began to question that assumption in the late 1800s, however, after encountering a series of patients who displayed a variety of physical ailments that had no apparent physical cause. Using hypnosis and other methods, Freud found evidence that convinced him that the roots of these people's "neuroses" lay in shocking experiences from the distant past that the patients had pushed out of consciousness (Breuer & Freud, 1896). He eventually came to believe that all behavior—from everyday slips of the tongue to severe forms of mental disorder—is motivated by *psychological* processes, especially unconscious conflicts within the mind. For the next fifty years, Freud revised and expanded his ideas into a body of work known as *psychoanalysis*, which included a theory of personality and mental disorder, as well as a set of treatment methods. As you will see in Chapters 14 and 16, Freud's ideas were controversial (and still are), but they have had an undeniable influence on the thinking of many psychologists around the world.

William James and Functionalism   It was also during the late 1800s that scientific research in psychology took root outside Europe, especially in the United States and Canada. The first U.S. psychology laboratory was founded by William James at Harvard University, at around the same time Wundt established his lab in Leipzig. The first Canadian laboratory was established in 1889 at the University of Toronto by James Mark Baldwin, Canada's first modern psychologist. Like the Gestalt psychologists, William James rejected Wundt and structuralism. Influenced by Darwin's theory of evolution, James was more interested in understanding how consciousness *functions* to help people adapt to their environments (James, 1890, 1892). This idea came to be called *functionalism,* and it focused on the ongoing "stream" of consciousness—the ever-changing pattern of images, sensations, memories, and other mental events. James wanted to know how the whole process works for the individual. Why, for example, do most people remember recent events better than things that happened in the remote past?

The functionalist view encouraged North American psychologists to look not only at how mental processes work in general but also at how they vary from person to person. Accordingly, some psychologists began to measure individual differences in learning, memory, and other mental processes associated with intelligence, made recommendations for improving educational practices in the schools, and even worked with teachers on programs tailored to children in need of special help (Nietzel, Bernstein & Milich, 1994).

JOHN B. WATSON (1878–1958) The founder of behaviorism, Watson argued that, by focusing on observable behavior, psychologists would not have to rely on people's potentially distorted reports about themselves. Here, he observes a baby's grasping reflex.

John Watson and Behaviorism Besides fueling James's functionalism, Darwin's theory led psychologists—especially in North America after 1900—to study animals as well as humans. If all species evolved in adaptive ways, perhaps their behavior and mental processes would follow the same, or similar, laws. Psychologists could not expect cats or rats or chickens to introspect, so they observed animal behavior in mazes and other experimental situations. From these observations, they made inferences about conscious experience, learning, memory, intelligence, and other mental processes.

John B. Watson, a psychology professor at Johns Hopkins University, agreed that overt behavior in animals *and* humans was the most important source of scientific information for psychology. However, Watson believed it was utterly unscientific to use behavior as the basis for *inferences* about consciousness, as structuralists and functionalists did—let alone about the unconscious, as Freudians did. In 1913, Watson wrote an article called "Psychology as the Behaviorist Views It." In it, he argued that psychologists should ignore mental events and base psychology only on what they can actually observe about overt behavior and its response to various stimuli (Watson, 1913, 1919). Watson's *behaviorism* recognized the existence of consciousness but considered it useless as a target of research since it would always be private and unobservable by scientific methods. Preoccupation with consciousness, said Watson, would prevent psychology from ever being a true science. Influenced by Ivan Pavlov's research on classical conditioning in dogs (described in detail in Chapter 7), Watson believed that *learning* is the most important determinant of behavior. He was famous for claiming that, with enough control over the environment, he could create learning experiences that would turn any infant into a doctor, a lawyer, or even a criminal.

American psychologist B. F. Skinner was another early champion of behaviorism. From the 1930s until his death in 1990, Skinner worked on mapping out the details of how rewards and punishments shape, maintain, and change behavior through what he termed "operant conditioning." His *functional analysis of behavior* helped explain, for example, how children's tantrums are sometimes inadvertently encouraged by the attention they attract from parents and teachers, and how a virtual addiction to gambling can result from the occasional and unpredictable rewards it brings.

Many psychologists were drawn to Watson's and Skinner's vision of psychology as the learning-based science of observable behavior. Behaviorism dominated psychological research from the 1920s through the 1960s, while the study of consciousness languished, especially in the United States.

FIGURE 1.4

Visualizing Brain Activity

Technological advances such as magnetic resonance imaging (MRI) allow psychologists and other scientists to study brain activity accompanying various mental processes. This study, for example, found that males (left) and females (right) show different patterns of brain activity (indicated by the brightly colored areas) while reading (Shaywitz et al., 1995).

MARY WHITON CALKINS (1863–1930)
When Mary Whiton Calkins studied psychology at Harvard University with William James, he described her as brilliant. Her research on memory helped her to be named, in 1905, the first woman president of the American Psychological Association. Because she was a woman, however, Harvard refused to grant her a doctoral degree; when they offered her the degree through Radcliffe, an affiliated school, she refused it. Margaret Washburn (1871–1939) encountered similar sex discrimination at Columbia University, so she transferred to Cornell, became the first woman to earn a doctorate in psychology and, in 1921, the second woman president of the APA.

Psychology Today   Psychologists continue to study all kinds of overt behavior in humans and in animals. By the 1960s, however, many had become dissatisfied with the limitations imposed by behaviorism (some, especially in Europe, had never accepted it in the first place). They grew uncomfortable ignoring mental processes that might be important in more fully understanding behavior (e.g., Ericsson & Simon, 1994). The advent of the computer age gave these psychologists just what they needed. Computers provided a new way to think about mental activity—as information processing. They also enabled psychologists to measure mental activity far more accurately than ever before. At the same time, progress in computer-supported biotechnology began to offer psychologists exciting new ways to study the biological bases of mental processes, to literally see what is going on in the brain when, for example, a person thinks or makes decisions (see Figure 1.4).

Armed with ever more sophisticated research tools, many psychologists today are striving to do what Watson thought was impossible: to study mental processes with precision and scientific objectivity. In fact, cognitive and biological factors in psychology are as influential now as behaviorism used to be. So mainstream psychology has come full circle, once again accepting consciousness—in the form of cognitive processes—as a legitimate topic for scientific research and justifying the definition of psychology as the science of behavior *and* mental processes.

A final point about the history of psychology: If you looked only at the photographs on the preceding pages, you might think that psychology was founded and shaped entirely by male Caucasians. It *is* true that, as in many other realms of human endeavor in the nineteenth and early twentieth centuries, white males dominated the world of psychology. But there is much more to the story. Women and people of color made important early contributions to psychology (De Angelis, 1996; Guthrie, 1976; Russo & Denmark, 1987), and throughout this book you will find the work of their modern counterparts.

Indeed, the contributions of women and ethnic minorities in psychology have increased in tandem with their growing representation in the field. In the United States, women now constitute about 38 percent of all psychologists holding doctoral degrees (National Science Foundation, 1994), and they are earning 60 percent of the new doctorates awarded each year (American Psychological Association, 1995a). Moreover, nearly 10 percent of new doctoral degrees are being earned by members of ethnic minorities (American Psychological Association, 1995b). These numbers reflect continuing efforts by psychological organizations and governmental bodies, especially in the United States and Canada, to promote the recruitment, graduation, and employment of women and ethnic minorities in psychology (DeAngelis, 1995b).

GILBERT HAVEN JONES (1883–1966)
When Gilbert Haven Jones graduated from the University of Jena in Germany in 1909, he became one of the first African-Americans to earn a doctorate in psychology. Many others were to follow, including J. Henry Alston (b. 1894) who was the first African-American to publish research in a major U.S. psychology journal (Alston, 1920).

UNITY AND DIVERSITY IN PSYCHOLOGY

Psychologists today are unified by their commitment to empiricism and scientific research, by their linked interests, and by the debt they owe to predecessors whose work has shaped psychology over its nearly 120-year history. However, they approach behavior and mental processes in many different ways. In this section, we review these various approaches and describe the network of linked subfields into which psychology has evolved. We conclude by highlighting psychologists' efforts to ensure that their research is as inclusive of, and as applicable to, as much of humankind as possible.

Approaches to Psychology

Suppose you are a psychologist trying to understand some aspect of the behavior and mental processes we have reviewed. Perhaps, like Mathews and Canon, you are interested in helping behavior; or maybe you want to identify the origins of aggression, pinpoint the causes of schizophrenia, or solve the riddle of drug abuse. Where would you look for answers? In brain cells and hormones? In inherited characteristics? In what people have learned from their parents? The direction of your research efforts will be determined largely by your *approach* to psychology—that is, by the set of assumptions, questions, and methods that you believe will be most helpful for understanding the behavior and mental processes you wish to explore.

Whereas some psychologists adopt one particular approach, many others are *eclectic*, combining features of two or more approaches because they believe that no one perspective can fully account for all aspects of psychological phenomena. Psychologists today no longer refer to themselves as structuralists or functionalists, but the psychodynamic and behavioral approaches remain, along with others known as the biological, evolutionary, cognitive, and humanistic approaches. Some of these approaches are currently more influential than others, but we will briefly review the essential features of all of them in order to give you a better understanding of why psychologists over the years have conducted their research as they have. In later chapters we will examine the value—and the limitations—of each approach for understanding many psychological phenomena.

RECORDING BRAIN WAVES The biological approach to psychology seeks to understand how behavior and mental processes relate to internal bodily events and activities. Here, researchers record the brain waves of a person who is performing a task similar to that performed by an air traffic controller (ATC). Psychologists in the Navy and elsewhere are working on systems that could warn ATCs and radar/sonar operators that they are failing to attend to important information.

EVOLUTION AND BEHAVIOR In animals, such as insects, birds, and fish, species-specific behaviors often appear as relatively rigid rituals, called *fixed action patterns*, which are not altered much by learning and which tend to be triggered by specific cues called *sign stimuli*. Here, a herring gull chick pecks for food in a characteristic way, but only after seeing the red spot on the parent's beak that serves as a target.

The Biological Approach Investigating the possibility that aggressive behavior or schizophrenia, for example, might be traceable to a hormonal imbalance or a brain disorder reflects the biological approach to psychology. As its name implies, the **biological approach** assumes that behavior and mental processes are largely shaped by biological processes. Psychologists who take this approach study the psychological effects of hormones, genes, and the activity of the nervous system, especially the brain. Thus, if they are studying memory, they might try to identify the changes taking place in the brain as information is stored there. Or if they are studying thinking, they might look for patterns of brain activity associated with, say, making quick decisions or reading a foreign language.

Research discussed in nearly every chapter of this book reflects the enormous influence of the biological approach on psychology today. To help you better understand the terms and concepts used in that research, the behavioral genetics appendix discusses some basic principles of genetics and Chapter 3 explains other biological aspects of psychology.

The Evolutionary Approach Biological processes also figure prominently in the evolutionary approach to psychology. The foundation for this approach was English naturalist Charles Darwin's book, *The Origin of Species.* Darwin (1809–1882) argued that the forms of life we see today are the result of *evolution*—of changes in life forms that occur over many generations—and, more specifically, that evolution occurs through natural selection. In *natural selection,* said Darwin, individuals whose appearance and patterns of action allow them to elude predators, withstand the elements, find food, and mate successfully are able to survive and produce offspring with characteristics similar to their own. In other words, the inherited characteristics that allow individuals to remain alive by successfully adjusting, or *adapting,* to changing conditions are likely to survive in the species as well. Other, less adaptive attributes die out of the species along with the unfortunate creatures who carry them.

Scientists who study animal behavior in the natural environment—called **ethologists**—have identified the effects of natural selection not only in inherited physical characteristics, such as the camouflage coloration that helps animals escape predators, but also in instinctive or, more properly, *species-specific* behaviors that aid survival.

In psychology, the **evolutionary approach** holds that the behavior of animals and humans today is the result of evolution through natural selection. Psychologists who take an evolutionary approach therefore try to understand (1) the adaptive value of behavior, (2) the anatomical and biological mechanisms that make it possible, and (3) the environmental conditions that encourage or discourage it. The evolutionary approach has generated a growing body of research (Buss, 1994b, 1995; Buss & Schmitt, 1993; Cosmides & Tooby, 1994). You will read about its influence in later chapters in relation to topics as diverse as helping and altruism, mental disorders, temperament, and interpersonal attraction.

The Psychodynamic Approach The **psychodynamic approach** offers a different slant on the role of inherited instincts and other biological forces in human behavior. Rooted in Freud's psychoanalysis, this approach asserts that all behavior and mental processes reflect the constant and mostly unconscious psychological struggles that rage silently within each person. Usually, these struggles involve conflict between the impulse to satisfy instincts or wishes (for food, sex, or aggression, for example) and the need to abide by the restrictions imposed by society. From this perspective, hostility and aggression reflect the breakdown of civilizing defenses against the expression of primitive urges, whereas anxiety, depression, or other disorders are the overt signs of inner turmoil.

The psychodynamic approach is reflected in a number of the contemporary theories of personality, psychological disorders, and treatment discussed in Chapters 14, 15, and 16. However, the orthodox Freudian perspective is far less influential in psychology now than in the past. Most psychologists today who take a psychodynamic approach prefer one of the many revised versions of Freud's original theories (Youngstrom, 1992).

The Behavioral Approach The **behaviorial approach** to psychology stands in stark contrast to the psychodynamic, biological, and evolutionary approaches. As founded by John Watson, the behavioral approach characterizes behavior and mental processes as primarily the result of *learning*. From Watson's point of view, biological, genetic, and evolutionary factors provide the raw material on which rewards, punishments, and other experiences act to shape each individual. Thus, whether the topic is aggression or drug abuse, self-confidence or helping, behaviorists seek to understand it in terms of an individual's learning history, especially the patterns of reward and punishment the individual has experienced. They also believe that people can change problematic behaviors, from overeating to criminality, by unlearning old habits and developing new ones.

A BEHAVIORAL PREVENTION PROGRAM
The behavioral approach to psychology suggests that most human behaviors are learned and that problematic behaviors can be changed—or even prevented—by the development of alternative responses. In this summer program, for example, youngsters participate in confidence-building exercises and learn the social skills they will need to "say no" to drugs.

COGNITIVE SCIENCE Some psychologists are working on a "computational theory of the mind" in which computer programs model how humans perceive, remember, reason, and otherwise process information. In Chapter 9 on thought and language, we discuss their progress in creating artificial intelligence in computers that can make medical diagnoses, search for mineral deposits, pick stocks, and perform other complex cognitive tasks.

Today, many behaviorists have come to endorse a variation on behaviorism. The *cognitive-behavioral* view adds the study of reportable mental processes to the traditional behavioral emphasis on observable actions (Beck, 1993; Viken & McFall, 1994). The cognitive-behavioral approach explores how learning affects the development of thoughts and beliefs and, in turn, how these learned cognitive patterns affect overt behavior.

The Cognitive Approach Recognition by many behaviorists of the importance of cognitive factors reflects the influence of a broader cognitive approach to psychology. The **cognitive approach** focuses on how people take in, mentally represent, and store information; how they perceive and process that information; and how cognitive processes are related to the integrated patterns of behavior we can see. In other words, the cognitive approach guides psychologists to study the rapid series of mental events—including those outside of awareness—that accompany overt behavior. Consider, for example, how an incident in which one person shoves another in front of a theater might be analyzed cognitively: The aggressor (1) perceives that someone has cut into the theater line, (2) uses stored memories and concepts to decide that this act is inappropriate, (3) attributes the act to the culprit's obnoxiousness, (4) considers possible responses and their likely consequences, (5) decides that shoving the person is the best response, and (6) executes that response.

Psychologists taking the cognitive approach are interested in discovering how people process information in domains ranging from decision making and interpersonal attraction to intelligence testing and group problem solving, to name but a few. Some of them work with researchers from computer science, the biological sciences, engineering, linguistics, philosophy, and other disciplines in a multidisciplinary field called *cognitive science,* which analyzes intelligent systems. Cognitive scientists attempt to discover the building blocks of cognition and to determine how these components produce complex behaviors such as remembering a fact, naming an object, or writing a word (Margolin, 1991).

The Humanistic Approach Another slant on the role of mental events in psychology is provided by the **humanistic approach** (also known as the phenomenological approach). From the humanistic perspective, behavior is determined primarily by each person's capacity to *choose* how to think and act. And humanistic psychologists see these choices as dictated, not by instincts, biological processes, or rewards and punishments, but by each individual's unique perceptions. If you perceive the world as a friendly place, you are likely to feel happy and secure. If you view it as dangerous and hostile, you will probably be defensive and anxious. So, like cognitively oriented psychologists, humanists would see aggression in a theater line as stemming from a perception that aggression is justified.

However, unlike those who take a cognitive approach, humanistic psychologists do not search for general laws that govern people's perceptions, judgments, decisions, and actions. Instead, the humanistic approach celebrates immediate, individual experience. Many of its proponents assert that behavior and mental processes can be fully understood only by appreciating the perceptions and feelings experienced by each individual. Humanistic psychologists also believe that people are essentially good, that they are in control of themselves, and that their main innate tendency is to grow toward their highest potential.

The humanistic approach began to attract attention in North America in the 1940s through the writings of Carl Rogers (1902–1987), a psychologist who had been trained in, but later rejected, the psychodynamic tradition. His views on personality and his methods of therapy are discussed in Chapters 14 and 16. The humanistic approach also shaped Abraham Maslow's (1943) influential hierarchy-of-needs theory of motivation, which is described in Chapter 11. Today, however, the impact of the humanistic approach to psychology is limited, mainly because many psychologists find humanistic concepts and predictions too vague to be expressed and tested scientifically. (For a summary of the approaches we have discussed, see "In Review: Approaches to Psychology.")

IN REVIEW	Approaches to Psychology
Approach	**Characteristics**
Biological	Emphasizes activity of the nervous system, especially the brain; the action of hormones and other chemicals; and genetics.
Evolutionary	Emphasizes the ways in which behavior and mental processes are adaptive for survival.
Psychodynamic	Emphasizes internal conflicts, mostly unconscious, which usually pit sexual or aggressive instincts against environmental obstacles to their expression.
Behavioral	Emphasizes learning, especially each person's experience with rewards and punishments.
Cognitive	Emphasizes mechanisms through which people receive, store, retrieve, and otherwise process information.
Humanistic	Emphasizes individual potential for growth and the role of unique perceptions in guiding behavior and mental processes.

Subfields of Psychology

The world's approximately half-million psychologists are engaged in an amazing variety of jobs related to many aspects of behavior and mental processes (Rosenzweig, 1992). Most have chosen to focus their efforts on one or two of psychology's numerous specialties, or *subfields.* The diversity of these subfields and the career opportunities they offer can be quite surprising to anyone who thinks of psychology only as the study and treatment of mental disorders.

Cognitive Psychology Wundt and other early psychologists called themselves **experimental psychologists** because they wanted to be distinguished from their colleagues in philosophy, who contemplated the nature of mental processes but did not conduct

ENGINEERING PSYCHOLOGY Research by cognitive psychologists whose special interest is *engineering psychology,* also known as *human factors,* has guided the development of realistic computer-controlled flight simulators used in pilot training. Their research also guides the placement of controls, instruments, and warning lights so that pilots will react to them quickly and correctly. Cognitive psychologists' findings are also being applied by engineers and designers striving to create computer keyboards, nuclear power plant control panels, and even VCR remote controls that are logical and easy to use without error (Norman, 1988).

MENTAL PROCESSES AND THE BRAIN
Biological psychologists study differences in the way each half of the brain processes information. Here, in one of her experiments on this topic, Marie Banich explains to a participant that pictures of faces will be flashed to only the left or the right side of his brain.

experimental research on them. Today, psychologists studying mental processes such as sensation, perception, learning, memory, judgment, decision making, and problem solving are still often referred to as experimental psychologists, but the label applies much more widely now. Psychologists in *all* subfields use experiments and other empirical methods in their work. So today, those whose research focuses on basic mental processes and their relation to behavior tend to be known as **cognitive psychologists.**

Biological Psychology   **Biological psychologists,** also called **physiological psychologists,** analyze how biology shapes behavior and mental processes. Their work has helped us understand, for example, how the brain controls physical movements, regulates eating, and receives information from the senses. Biological psychologists address questions such as the role of genetics and brain anatomy in schizophrenia, whether patterns of brain activity can reveal that someone is lying, or how hormones associated with stress can suppress the body's immune system.

Social and Industrial-Organizational Psychology   **Social psychologists** study the many ways in which people influence one another. Among the topics on their research agenda is the effectiveness of social influence strategies such as advertising in promoting safe sex and other behaviors that can halt the spread of AIDS. Social psychologists also seek the roots of ethnic prejudice and ways to help eradicate it. And even more than the rest of us, social psychologists are interested in interpersonal attraction—who we like, and why. **Industrial-organizational psychologists** ask how social factors influence human performance in the workplace. For example, they conduct research on men's and women's leadership styles, and on the effects those styles have on male and female employees' productivity.

Personality Psychology   Whereas some psychologists seek laws that govern the behavior of people in general, **personality psychologists** focus on characteristics that make each person unique. One recently developed test from this subfield measures five dimensions on which most people can be described and which can be used to make predictions about how they will tend to behave (look for the "Big-Five" model in Chapter 14). Personality psychologists also study personality traits in children that might help predict the appearance of alcoholism, drug abuse, aggressiveness, or other problems in later life.

OPPOSING VIEWS   Conflict and harmony, competition and cooperation, are all elements of the social world. Research by social and industrial-organizational psychologists has helped identify some of the principles governing human relations. Their insights are used every day to help groups of people to resolve conflicts, make decisions, and work together more productively.

DEVELOPMENTAL PSYCHOLOGY Ross Parke (shown here with a student in his laboratory) videotapes father-child play to explore how fathers shape their children's social development. He has found that good father-child play helps teach children to regulate and communicate emotion and to read emotion in others. These skills are important for developing good relationships with other children.

Developmental Psychology   Behavior and mental processes change over the life span. **Developmental psychologists** describe these changes and try to understand their causes and effects. They are interested in discovering when children begin to form friendships, whether strict parental discipline leads to conformity or rebellion, and whether a midlife crisis is inevitable. Developmental psychologists also explore the development of thought. In one study, children were asked to draw a picture indicating where they would place a third eye, if they could have one. The youngest children showed they were still in an early stage of cognitive development by drawing the extra eye on their forehead "as a spare." More complex thinking was revealed in slightly older children, one of whom placed the extra eye in his palm—"so I can see what's in the cookie jar better" (Shaffer, 1973).

Clinical, Counseling, and Community Psychology   **Clinical** and **counseling psychologists** conduct research on the causes of behavior disorders and offer services to help troubled people overcome those disorders. **Community psychologists** create systems to ensure that psychological services reach the homeless and others who need help but tend not to seek it. They also try to *prevent* psychological disorders by working for changes in schools and other social systems in hopes of reducing the poverty and other stresses of life that so often lead to disorder.

Educational and School Psychology   **Educational psychologists** conduct research and develop theories about teaching and learning. The results of their work are applied to improving teacher training and—through refinement of school curricula, for example—to helping students learn more efficiently. **School psychologists** specialize in IQ testing, diagnosing learning disabilities and other academic problems, and setting up programs to improve students' achievement and satisfaction in school.

Quantitative Psychology   To what extent is intelligence inherited, and to what extent can it be influenced by environment? As you will see in Chapter 10, on mental abilities, this is one of the hottest topics in psychology, and **quantitative psychologists** are right in the middle of it. They develop ever more sophisticated statistical methods for analyzing the vast amounts of data collected by their colleagues in other subfields (e.g., Hoyle, 1994; Russell, 1995), they evaluate the validity of tests (including tests of mental

HEALTH PSYCHOLOGY   Shelley Taylor *(left)* **was trained in experimental social psychology and now conducts research on how people cope with stressful events.**

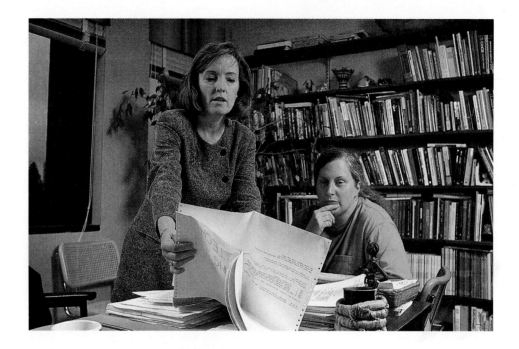

ability), and they seek mathematical methods to tease apart the effects of such closely entwined variables as heredity and environment.

Still other subfields of psychology deal with other aspects of behavior and mental processes. For example, **health psychologists** study the effects of behavior on health and the impact of illness on behavior and emotion, **sport psychologists** search for the keys to maximum athletic performance, and **environmental psychologists** explore the effects of the physical environment on behavior and mental processes. Where do the psychologists in all these subfields work? Table 1.1 summarizes the latest figures on the settings in which they can be found and the kinds of things they typically do there.

Linkages Within Psychology and Beyond

No doubt you noticed that psychology's subfields overlap. For example, we mentioned developmental psychologists who study thought processes, biological psychologists

PLANNING ENVIRONMENTS Environmental psychologists' research on how floor plans, availability of natural light, and a building's other physical features can affect occupants' mood, energy, interaction, stress level, and productivity helps architects create optimal designs for workplaces, nursing homes, schools, prisons, private homes, and even campus residence halls (Stokol, 1995).

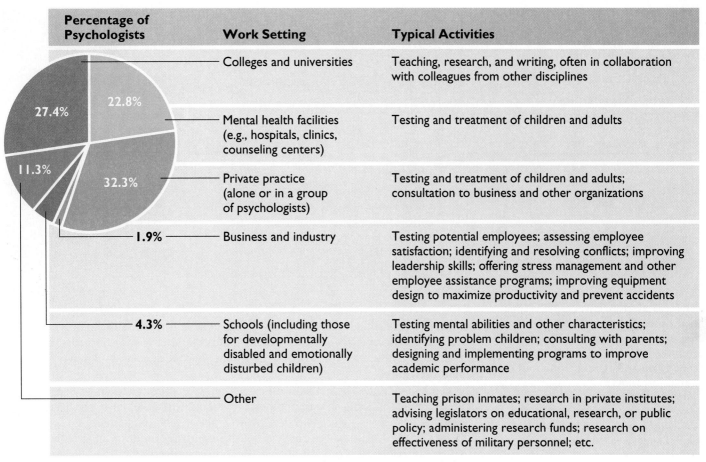

Percentage of Psychologists	Work Setting	Typical Activities
22.8%	Colleges and universities	Teaching, research, and writing, often in collaboration with colleagues from other disciplines
	Mental health facilities (e.g., hospitals, clinics, counseling centers)	Testing and treatment of children and adults
32.3%	Private practice (alone or in a group of psychologists)	Testing and treatment of children and adults; consultation to business and other organizations
1.9%	Business and industry	Testing potential employees; assessing employee satisfaction; identifying and resolving conflicts; improving leadership skills; offering stress management and other employee assistance programs; improving equipment design to maximize productivity and prevent accidents
4.3%	Schools (including those for developmentally disabled and emotionally disturbed children)	Testing mental abilities and other characteristics; identifying problem children; consulting with parents; designing and implementing programs to improve academic performance
	Other	Teaching prison inmates; research in private institutes; advising legislators on educational, research, or public policy; administering research funds; research on effectiveness of military personnel; etc.

Source: Data from the 1993 APA Directory Survey.

TABLE 1.1

Typical Activities and Work Settings for Psychologists

The fact that psychologists can work in such a wide variety of settings and perform such a wide range of functions helps account for the popularity of psychology as an undergraduate major (Murray, 1996). Psychology courses also provide excellent background for students planning to enter medicine, law, business, and other fields (Pauk & Fiore, 1989).

who explore mental disorders, and social psychologists who are concerned with health psychology. The interests of psychologists are linked, in some cases, because they are investigating a common topic, such as violence or language, and in other cases because they are dealing with an overarching issue, such as how biological and cultural influences interact (Plomin & Neiderhiser, 1992).

Even when psychologists do not themselves conduct research that crosses subfields, they often draw on, and contribute to, the knowledge developed in other subfields. Their theories, methods, findings, and applications to daily life are inextricably linked. Recognizing linkages among subfields is an important part of understanding psychology as a whole. At the beginning of each chapter, we illustrate just a few such linkages in a Linkages diagram, similar to the one shown on the following page. Each question in the diagram illustrates a way in which the topics of two chapters are connected to each other; the page numbers indicate where the questions are discussed. To help you keep these linkages in mind as you read, each linking question will appear in the margin next to the major discussion of that question (see, for example, p. 42). By examining the Linkages diagram in each chapter, you can see how the topic of that chapter is related to other subfields of psychology. In each chapter, one of these relationships is given special attention in a section entitled "Linkages." You might find it interesting to identify some of the many other linkages we do not mention.

Much as psychology's subfields are linked to one another, psychology is linked to many other academic disciplines. Sometimes these linkages occur because psychologists and researchers from other disciplines have common interests. Cognitive science, which we described earlier, is one example. Another is *neuroscience,* a multidisciplinary research enterprise that examines the structure and function of the nervous system in animals and humans, at levels ranging from the individual cell to overt behavior. This

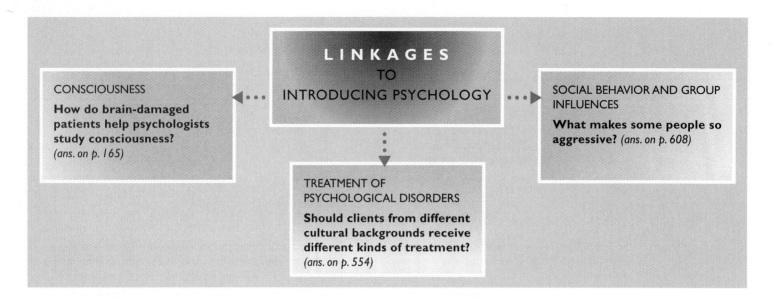

CONSCIOUSNESS

How do brain-damaged patients help psychologists study consciousness? *(ans. on p. 165)*

LINKAGES
TO
INTRODUCING PSYCHOLOGY

SOCIAL BEHAVIOR AND GROUP INFLUENCES

What makes some people so aggressive? *(ans. on p. 608)*

TREATMENT OF PSYCHOLOGICAL DISORDERS

Should clients from different cultural backgrounds receive different kinds of treatment? *(ans. on p. 554)*

The questions in this diagram illustrate some of the relationships between the topics discussed in this chapter and the topics of other chapters. Time and again throughout this book, you will see how psychology's subfields and approaches are linked to one another. Diagrams like this one appear near the beginning of each chapter to illustrate some of these linkages. The page numbers indicating where the questions are discussed follow the questions. Of course, there are many more linkages than could be included in the diagrams. We hope that the diagrams will prompt you to look for these additional linkages. This kind of detective work can be enjoyable and useful. You may find it easier to remember material in one chapter by relating it to linked material in other chapters. You might also want to use the questions as a self-testing device when studying for quizzes and exams. Or you might want to read the discussions of some questions before reading the chapter to clarify how it relates to the rest of psychology. Most of all, by staying alert to linkages as you read this book, you will come away not only with threads of knowledge about each subfield but with an appreciation of the interwoven fabric of psychology as a whole.

integrated field includes biological psychologists as well as specialists in neuroanatomy, neurophysiology, neurochemistry, genetics, and computer science. Someday, biological psychologists, like the colleagues with whom they work, may be known simply as "neuroscientists."

Psychology is also linked with other disciplines because research and theory from one discipline is applicable to another. For example, psychologists are beginning to apply chaos theory—which was developed in physics and mathematics to understand natural systems such as weather—to detect underlying order in apparently random patterns of violence, drug abuse, depression, or family conflict (e.g., Barton, 1994). Similarly, political scientists apply social psychologists' research on cooperation, conflict, and negotiation to help explain international tensions (e.g., Tetlock, 1986; Worchel & Simpson, 1993).

This book is filled with examples of other ways in which psychological theories and research have been applied to fields as diverse as medicine, dentistry, law, business, engineering, architecture, aviation, public health, and sports. Cognitive psychologists' research on memory has influenced the ways in which attorneys question eyewitnesses and judges instruct juries; developmental psychologists' work on understanding the social and emotional aspects of aging is reshaping nursing home policies on sexual behavior; and research by industrial-organizational psychologists is helping budding businesses in Russia and other former Soviet states adjust to and survive in a market-driven economy.

Human Diversity and Psychology

The Soviet example is of more than passing interest because it provides an analogy for another important aspect of the diversity inherent in psychology. Until the Soviet Union dissolved in 1991, most Westerners, and certainly most Americans, tended to perceive it as a single entity and the Soviet people as a relatively homogenous group. But ethnic wars in the former Soviet bloc provided tragic evidence that the old U.S.S.R. was actually a political and economic association of dozens of diverse states, each with distinct traditions, alliances, and animosities.

Similarly, many psychologists once implicitly assumed that all people are essentially the same, and that whatever principles emerged from research with local volunteer subjects would apply to people everywhere. Since about 90 percent of researchers in psychology work at universities in North America and Europe, they tended to study local college students, mostly white and middle-class, and more often men than women (Crawford & Marecek, 1989; Graham, 1992). Most of the psychologists, too, tended to be white, middle-class, and male (Walker, 1991).

From one perspective, studying a narrow sample of humankind need not compromise the generality of psychological research, because, in many ways, people *are* very much alike. They tend to live in groups, develop religious beliefs, and create rules, music, and games. Similarly, the principles governing nerve cell activity or reactions to heat or a sour taste are the same in men and women the world over, as is their recognition of a smile.

But are the forces that motivate people to achieve, or the development of their moral thought, or their patterns of interpersonal communication universal as well? Do the principles derived from research on European-American males living in the Midwestern United States apply to African-American women or to people in Greece, Korea, Argentina, or Egypt? Not always. What people experience and what they learn from that experience are shaped by *sociocultural variables,* which are variations in social identity and background such as gender, ethnicity, social class, and culture. These variables create many significant differences in behavior and mental processes, especially from one culture to another (Berry et al., 1992; Lonner & Malpass, 1994).

Culture has been defined as the accumulation of values, rules of behavior, forms of expression, religious beliefs, occupational choices, and the like for a group of people who share a common language and environment (Triandis, 1994). As such, culture is an organizing and stabilizing influence. It encourages or discourages particular behaviors and mental processes; it also allows people to understand and anticipate the behavior of others in that culture. It is a kind of group adaptation, passed by tradition and example rather than by genes from one generation to the next. Culture determines, for example, whether children's education will focus on skill at hunting or reading, how close people stand when they converse, and whether or not they form lines in public places (Munroe & Munroe, 1994).

Psychologists as well as anthropologists have isolated many respects in which cultures differ (Berry et al., 1992). Table 1.2 outlines one interesting way of analyzing these differences; it shows that many cultures can be described as either individualist or collectivist. *Individualist* cultures tend to accept people who place personal goals ahead of the goals of the collective (such as the family or work group), whereas *collectivist* cultures tend to reject such people and to encourage subordination of personal goals to those of the collective (Guisinger & Blatt, 1994). Cultures also vary in the degree to which they impose tight or loose rules for social behavior, value achievement or self-awareness, seek dominion over nature or integration with it, and emphasize the importance of time (e.g., Triandis, 1995).

Culture is often associated with a particular country, but in fact most countries are *multicultural* (Oyserman, 1993); in other words, they host many *subcultures* within their borders. Often, these subcultures are formed by people of various ethnic origins. The population of the United States, for instance, encompasses African-Americans,

TABLE 1.2

Some Characteristics of Behavior and Mental Processes Typical of Individualist vs. Collectivist Cultures

Cultural factors do not act as cookie cutters that make everyone in a culture the same, but certain broad tendencies in behavior and mental processes have been associated with particular kinds of cultures. For example, many people in individualist cultures, such as those typical of North America and Western Europe, tend to focus on and value personal rather than group goals and achievement. Competitiveness to distinguish oneself from others is common, as is a sense of isolation. Many people in collectivist cultures, such as Japan, tend to think of themselves mainly as part of family or work groups. Cooperative effort aimed at advancing the welfare of those groups is highly valued, and while loneliness is seldom a problem, fear of rejection by the group is common. Though we seldom think about it, many aspects of U.S. culture—from self-reliant cowboy heroes and bonuses for "top" employees to the invitation to "help yourself" at a buffet table—reflect its tendency toward an individualist orientation.

Variable	Individualist	Collectivist
Personal identity	Separate from others	Connected to others
Major goals	Self-defined; be unique; realize your personal potential; compete with others	Defined by others; belong; occupy your proper place; meet your obligations to others; be like others
Criteria for self-esteem	Ability to express unique aspects of the self; be self-assured	Ability to restrain the self and be part of a social unit; be self-effacing
Sources of success and failure	Success comes from personal effort, failure from external factors	Success due to help from others; failure due to personal faults
Major frame of reference	Personal attitudes, traits, and goals	Family, work group

FIGURE 1.5

Cultural Diversity in the
United States

The people of the United States represent a wide array of cultural backgrounds as illustrated in this figure.

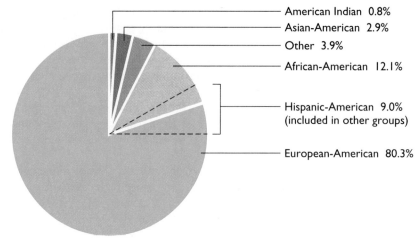

American Indian 0.8%
Asian-American 2.9%
Other 3.9%
African-American 12.1%

Hispanic-American 9.0%
(included in other groups)

European-American 80.3%

Source: Data from U.S. Census, 1990.

Hispanic-Americans, Asian-Americans, and American Indians as well as European-Americans with Italian, German, English, Polish, Irish, and other origins (see Figure 1.5). In each of these groups, the individuals who identify with their cultural heritage tend to share behaviors, values, and beliefs based on their culture of origin and, hence, form a subculture.

Like fish unaware of the water in which they are immersed, people often fail to notice how their culture or subculture has shaped their patterns of thinking and behavior until they come in contact with people whose culture or subculture has shaped different patterns. For example, sending a letter-opener as a birthday gift to a Mexican friend might be a mistake because, to some people in Mexico, the gift of a knife can mean that the sender wishes to sever the relationship. Even some of the misunderstandings that occur between men and women in the same culture are traceable to subtle, culturally influenced differences in their communication patterns (Tannen, 1990, 1994). In the United States, for example, women's efforts to connect with others by talking may be perceived by many men as "pointless" unless the discussion is aimed at solving a specific problem; thus women often feel frustrated and misunderstood by men who, in lieu of conversation, tend to offer well-intentioned, but unwanted, advice.

THE IMPACT OF CULTURE Culture helps shape virtually every aspect of our behavior and mental processes, from how we dress to what we think is important. Because we grow up immersed in our culture, it is easy to forget its influence, until—like these participants at a U.N. World Conference on Women—we encounter people whose culture has shaped them differently.

For decades, psychologists interested in *cross-cultural* research have studied cultural differences (Triandis, 1964), but now the influence of sociocultural variables is of growing interest to psychologists in general (Betancourt & Lopez, 1993; Lonner & Malpass, 1994). As psychology strives to be the science of all behavior and mental processes, its research will increasingly take into account gender and other sociocultural variables (Riger, 1992; Tavris, 1992; Triandis, Kurowski & Gelfand, 1993; Yoder & Kahn, 1993). The trend in this direction will be evident in much of the research described in the chapters to come.

FUTURE DIRECTIONS

Those chapters will also reveal that psychology deals with some of the most interesting subjects imaginable, from subliminal perception, sexual behavior, and love to drug abuse, aggression, and mental disorder. The results of psychological research on these and many other fascinating and important topics constitutes an impressive body of knowledge, but it is only a beginning. Future research in all of psychology's subfields will bring new discoveries about behavior and mental processes. Those discoveries will be applied to help people better understand themselves—and each other—and to improve the quality of human life around the world. We will try to predict some of these developments in a "future directions" section at the end of each chapter.

We hope you will enjoy exploring psychology with us, and that you will find the science of behavior and mental processes to be as interesting and exciting as we do. You can learn even more about psychology by taking additional psychology courses. You might even consider pursuing one of psychology's many career opportunities.

SUMMARY AND KEY TERMS

Psychology is the science that seeks to understand behavior and mental processes, and to apply that understanding in the service of human welfare.

■ THE WORLD OF PSYCHOLOGY: AN OVERVIEW

The concept of "behavior and mental processes" is a broad one, encompassing virtually all aspects of what it means to be a human being.

The Scope of Behavior and Mental Processes
Among the topics studied by psychologists are the activity of individual nerve cells and organ systems, the operation of sensory and perceptual systems, the capacity for thought and decision making, the experience of emotion, the sources and effects of motivation, personality traits and other individual characteristics, and the effects people have upon each other.

Research: The Foundation of Psychology
Psychologists use the methods of science to conduct empirical research. This means that they perform experiments and use other scientific procedures to systematically gather and analyze information about psychological phenomena.

A Brief History of Psychology
The founding of modern psychology is usually marked as 1879, when Wilhelm Wundt established the first psychology research laboratory. Wundt used laboratory methods to study the building blocks of consciousness—an approach later called structuralism. At about the same time, in the United States, William James offered an alternative perspective known as functionalism, suggesting that psychologists should study how consciousness functions to help us adapt to our environments. In 1913, John B. Watson founded behaviorism, arguing that, to be scientific, psychologists should study only the behavior they can see, not private mental events. Behaviorism dominated psychology for decades, but psychologists are once again studying consciousness, now called cognitive processes. Most of the prominent figures in psychology's history were white males, but women and members of ethnic minority groups made important contributions from the start, and continue to do so.

■ UNITY AND DIVERSITY IN PSYCHOLOGY

Psychologists are unified by their commitment to empirical research and scientific methods, by their linked interests, and by the legacy of psychology's founders.

Approaches to Psychology
Psychologists differ in their approaches to psychology—that is, in the assumptions, questions, and methods they believe will be most helpful in their work. Some adopt one particular approach; many combine features of two or more approaches. Those adopting a *biological approach* examine how physiological processes shape behavior and mental processes. Research by *ethologists* helped stimulate the *evolutionary approach*, which emphasizes the inherited, adaptive aspects of behavior and mental processes. The *psychodynamic approach* sees behavior and mental processes as a struggle to resolve conflicts between impulses and the demands made by society to control those impulses. Psychologists who take the *behavioral approach* see behavior as determined primarily by learning based on experiences with rewards and punishments. The *cognitive approach* assumes that behavior can be understood through analysis of the basic mental processes that underlie it. The *humanistic approach* views behavior as controlled by the decisions that people make about their lives based on their perceptions of the world.

Subfields of Psychology
Because the subject matter of psychology is so diverse, most psychologists work in particular subfields within the discipline. For example, *experimental psychologists,* now usually called *cognitive psychologists,* focus on basic psychological processes such as learning, memory, and

perception in both animals and humans; they also study judgment, decision making, and problem solving. *Biological psychologists,* also called *physiological psychologists,* study topics such as communication among nerve cells and the role played by the nervous system in regulating behavior. *Social psychologists* examine questions regarding how people influence one another; *industrial-organizational psychologists* ask how social factors influence human performance in the workplace. *Personality psychologists* focus on characteristics that set people apart from one another. *Developmental psychologists* specialize in trying to understand the development of behavior and mental processes over a lifetime. *Clinical* and *counseling psychologists* provide direct service to troubled people and conduct research on abnormal behavior. *Community psychologists* work to prevent mental disorders, and to extend mental health services to those who need it. *Educational psychologists* conduct and apply research on teaching and learning, while *school psychologists* specialize in assessing and alleviating children's academic problems. Among other things, *quantitative psychologists* develop methods for statistical analysis of research data. *Health psychologists, sport psychologists,* and *environmental psychologists* exemplify some of psychology's many other subfields.

Linkages Within Psychology and Beyond

Psychologists often work in more than one subfield and usually share knowledge with colleagues in many subfields. Psychologists also draw on and contribute to knowledge in other disciplines such as biology, chemistry, physics, anthropology, and political science.

Human Diversity and Psychology

Psychologists are increasingly taking into account the influence of *culture* and other sociocultural variables such as gender and ethnicity in shaping human behavior and mental processes.

RESEARCH IN PSYCHOLOGY

CHAPTER 2

LINKAGES
TO
RESEARCH IN PSYCHOLOGY

BIOLOGICAL ASPECTS OF
PSYCHOLOGY

**How much of our behavior is
due to genetics and how
much to our environment?**
(ans. on p. 42)

SOCIAL BEHAVIOR AND GROUP
INFLUENCES

**Is it ethical to deceive people
in order to learn about their
social behavior?** *(ans. on p. 607)*

TREATMENT OF
PSYCHOLOGICAL DISORDERS

**Is it possible to do experi-
ments on psychotherapy?**
(ans. on p. 548)

Francine Shapiro, a clinical psychologist practicing in northern California, had an odd experience one day in 1987. She was walking in a park, thinking about some distressing events, when she noticed that her emotional reaction to them was fading away. Upon reflection, she realized that she had been involuntarily moving her eyes back and forth. Did the eye movements have anything to do with the change? When she made the eye movements deliberately, the emotion-reducing effect was even stronger. Curious, she examined the effect in others, first among friends and colleagues, then with clients who had suffered traumatic experiences such as childhood sexual abuse, military combat, or rape. She asked these people to think about their unpleasant experiences while following her finger with their eyes as she moved it back and forth in front of their faces. Like her, they said that their reactions to the memories faded. And her clients reported that emotional flashbacks, nightmares, fears, and other trauma-related problems dropped dramatically, often after only one session (Shapiro, 1989a).

Dr. Shapiro eventually called her new treatment *eye movement desensitization and reprocessing,* or *EMDR* (Shapiro, 1991). Today, Dr. Shapiro and other therapists are using EMDR to treat a wide range of anxiety-related problems, from simple phobias to disorders caused by the trauma of military combat (e.g., Wilson, Becker & Tinker, 1995; Spates & Burnette, 1995). But the question remains: Can anxiety be reduced by anything as simple as eye movements?

Psychologists did not know what to make of EMDR (Mueser, 1993). Is it a breakthrough in the treatment of anxiety disorders or a flash in the pan? As when examining any aspect of behavior and mental processes, it was vital for them to determine first what specific questions to ask about this new form of treatment and then how to go about searching for the answers. Determining what questions to ask depends on an ability to think critically about the world; making progress toward answers depends on translating critical thinking into scientific research methods. As described in Chapter 1—and as shown in the Linkages diagram—psychologists use these methods to study a wide range of behavior and mental processes. In the pages that follow, we summarize some of the basic questions that emerge from thinking critically about psychology, describe the methods of science, and show how some of these methods have been applied in evaluating the effectiveness of EMDR.

THINKING CRITICALLY ABOUT PSYCHOLOGY (OR ANYTHING ELSE)

Often, people simply accept what they are told because it comes from a believable source or because "everyone knows" it is true (see Table 2.1). Indeed, some advertisers, politicians, TV evangelists, and social activists hope for this kind of easy acceptance when they seek your money, vote, or allegiance. They want you to believe their promises or claims without careful thought; they don't want you to think critically.

Critical thinking is the process of assessing claims and making judgments on the basis of well-supported evidence (Wade, 1988). Consider Shapiro's EMDR treatment. Does it reduce anxiety-related problems, as reports by Shapiro and others suggest? One strategy for applying critical thinking to this or any other topic is to ask the following five questions:

1. *What am I being asked to believe or accept?* In this case, the assertion to be examined is that EMDR causes reduction or elimination of anxiety-related problems.

TABLE 2.1

Ten Myths About Human Behavior

Myth	Fact
Many children are injured each year in the United States when razor blades, needles, or poison are put in Halloween candy.	Reported cases are rare, most turn out to be hoaxes, and in the only documented case of a child dying from poisoned candy, the culprit was the child's own parent (Brunvald, 1989).
A drunken person can sober up by taking a shower and drinking coffee.	A drunken person who takes a shower and drinks coffee will be wet, awake, and drunk. Neither cold water nor caffeine alters the rate at which the body metabolizes alcohol (see Chapter 6).
If your roommate commits suicide during the school term, you automatically get A's in all your classes for that term.	No college or university anywhere has ever had such a rule.
Shaving makes hair on your face or legs grow back thicker, darker, and faster.	Hair may *appear* denser and darker after the first shave exposes the thicker base of hair shafts, but color and thickness is determined by your genes, and growth rate is unchanged (Margolis, 1994).
People have been known to burst into flames and die from fire erupting from within their own bodies.	People die by fire in many ways, but cases of alleged spontaneous human combustion are traceable to external sources of ignition (Randles & Hough, 1993).
Most big-city police departments rely on the advice of psychics to help them solve murders, kidnappings, and missing persons cases.	Only about 35 percent of urban police departments ever seek psychics' advice, and that advice is virtually never more helpful than other means of investigation (Nickell, 1994; Rowe, 1993; Sweat & Durm, 1993).
As part of their initiation, some urban street gang members in the United States drive with their lights off at night. If you blink your own lights at them, they will follow you home and kill you.	Warnings about this "ritual" were rampant in the summer of 1993, but no police department ever issued them, nor has any such gang rite ever been documented (Brunvald, 1995).
Murders, suicides, and mental disorders are more likely to occur when the moon is full.	Crime statistics and mental hospital admissions data show no evidence to support this common belief (Gorvin & Roberts, 1994; Rotton & Kelly, 1985).
You can't fool a lie detector.	Lie detectors can be helpful in solving crimes, but they are not perfect; their results can free a guilty person or send an innocent person to jail (see Chapter 11).
Viewers never see David Letterman walking to his desk after the opening monologue because his contract prohibits him from showing his backside on TV.	When questioned about this story on the air, Letterman denied it and, to prove his point, lifted his jacket and turned a full circle in front of the cameras and studio audience (Brunvald, 1989).

2. *What evidence is available to support the assertion?* Shapiro began her research on EMDR by gathering information about whether the reduction of her own emotional distress was related to her eye movements or simply a coincidence. When she found the same effect in others, coincidence became a less plausible explanation.

3. *Are there alternative ways of interpreting the evidence?* The dramatic effects experienced by Shapiro's friends and clients might be due not to EMDR but to factors such as their motivation to change or their desire to please her. Even the most remarkable evidence cannot be accepted as confirming an assertion until all equally plausible alternative assertions have been ruled out, which leads to the next step in critical thinking.

4. *What additional evidence would help to evaluate the alternatives?* The ideal method would be to identify three groups of people who are identical in every way except for the anxiety treatment they received. If a group receiving EMDR improved to a much greater extent than those given an equally motivating but inherently useless treatment, or no treatment at all, it would become less likely that EMDR effects could be explained on the basis of clients' motivation or the mere passage of time. The ways in which psychologists and other scientists collect evidence to test alternative explanations constitute the methods of scientific research, which we describe in detail later.

5. *What conclusions are most reasonable?* The evidence available thus far has not yet ruled out alternative explanations for the effects of EMDR (e.g., Lilienfeld, 1996; Lohr et al., 1995; Vaughan et al., 1994), so the only reasonable conclusions to be drawn at this point are that (a) EMDR remains a controversial treatment, (b) it seems to have an impact on clients, and (c) further research is needed in order to understand it.

Does that sound wishy-washy? Critical thinking sometimes does seem indecisive because conclusions must be tempered by the evidence available. But critical thinking also opens the way to understanding. To help you hone your critical thinking skills, we include in each subsequent chapter of this book a section called "Thinking Critically" in which we examine an issue by considering the same five questions we asked here about EMDR.

Critical Thinking and Scientific Research

Imagine that you are Dr. Francine Shapiro. You begin, as scientists often do, with curiosity about a phenomenon. Curiosity frequently provokes stimulating questions, but they may be too general to be investigated scientifically. In Dr. Shapiro's place, you might at first wonder, Can eye movements help with anxiety? However, critical thinking requires that you make your question more specific, in order to clarify the assertion to be evaluated.

Psychologists and other scientists typically phrase their questions about behavior and mental processes in terms of a **hypothesis**—a specific, testable proposition about something they want to study. Researchers state hypotheses in order to establish in clear, precise terms what they think may be true, and how they will know if it is not. In this case, the hypothesis might be: *EMDR treatment causes significant reduction in anxiety.* To make it easier to understand and evaluate hypotheses, scientists employ

operational definitions, which are statements describing the exact operations or methods used in their research. In the hypothesis just stated, "EMDR treatment" might be operationally defined as creating a certain number of back-and-forth eye movements per second for a particular period of time, while "significant reduction in anxiety" might be defined as a certain amount of reduction in clients' self-reported discomfort. The kind of treatment a client is given (say, EMDR versus no treatment) and the results of that treatment (how much anxiety reduction occurred) are examples of research **variables,** specific factors or characteristics that are manipulated and measured in research.

It is all too easy for scientists to look only for evidence that confirms a hypothesis, especially if they expect or hope the hypothesis is true. This common human failing is called "confirmation bias," and it is described in Chapter 9. Scientists have a special responsibility to combat confirmation bias by looking for contradictory as well as supporting evidence for even their most cherished hypotheses. They not only gather evidence but also assess its quality. Usually, the quality of evidence is evaluated in terms of two characteristics: reliability and validity. *Reliability* is the degree to which the evidence is repeatable; the *validity* of evidence is the degree to which it accurately assesses the topic being studied. For example, the initial claims for EMDR stemmed from Dr. Shapiro's use of the treatment with her colleagues and clients. If she had not been able to repeat, or *replicate,* the initial effects, or if only a few clients showed improvement, she would question the reliability of the evidence. If the clients' reports of improvement were not checked for accuracy by, say, corroborating reports from family members, she would doubt the validity of the evidence.

The Role of Theories

After examining the evidence from research on particular phenomena, scientists often begin to favor certain explanations. Sometimes, they organize these explanations into a **theory,** which is an integrated set of statements designed to account for, predict, and even suggest ways of controlling certain phenomena. For example, Dr. Shapiro's theory about the results of her new treatment suggests that the eye movements of EMDR activate parts of the brain where information about trauma or other unpleasant experiences have been stored but never fully processed. EMDR, she says, allows this information to be processed so that the emotional and behavioral problems it had been causing can be resolved (Shapiro, 1994, 1995). In Chapter 1, we reviewed broader and more famous examples of explanatory theories, including Charles Darwin's theory of evolution and Sigmund Freud's theory of psychoanalysis. Throughout this book you will encounter other theories designed to explain phenomena such as color vision, sleep, memory, and aggression.

Theories are tentative explanations that must themselves be subjected to scientific evaluation based on critical thinking. For example, Dr. Shapiro's theory about EMDR was immediately criticized as being vague, lacking in supportive evidence, and having less plausibility than alternative explanations based on the established learning principles described in Chapter 7 (e.g., Steketee & Goldstein, 1994). In other words, theories are based on research results, but they also generate hypotheses for further research. Predictions flowing from a theory proposed by one psychologist will be tested by many other psychologists. If research does not support a theory, it is revised or, sometimes, abandoned. Without research results, there would be nothing to explain; without explanatory theories, the results might never be organized in a usable way. The continuing interaction of theory and research lies at the heart of the process that has created the knowledge generated in psychology over the past century.

As later chapters illustrate, the constant formulation, evaluation, reformulation, and abandonment of theories has generated many competing explanations of behavior and mental processes. A sometimes frustrating consequence of this continuing search for answers in psychology is that we cannot offer as many final conclusions as you might want. The conclusions we *do* draw about many of the phenomena described in this book are tentative and almost always accompanied by a call for additional research.

Indeed, it is rare for a piece of research not to raise more questions than it answers. Keep this point in mind the next time you hear someone confidently regaling a talk-show audience with easy answers to complex problems or offering simple formulas for ideal parenting or a happy marriage. These self-proclaimed experts—called "pop" (for popular) psychologists by the scientific community—tend to oversimplify issues, cite evidence for their views without concern for its reliability or validity, and ignore good evidence that contradicts their pet theories. Psychological scientists must be more cautious—often suspending final judgments about complex aspects of behavior and mental processes until they have acquired better data.

Nevertheless, current knowledge and tentative conclusions can be put to good use. EMDR and many other forms of treatment, for example, are being applied and studied every day. Indeed, psychologists in all subfields are using today's knowledge as the foundation for the research that will increase tomorrow's understanding. In the rest of this chapter, we describe their research methods and some of the pitfalls threatening progress toward their goals.

RESEARCH METHODS IN PSYCHOLOGY

Like other scientists, psychologists strive to achieve four main goals in their research: to *describe* a phenomenon, to *make predictions* about it, and to introduce enough *control* in their research to allow them to *explain* the phenomenon with some degree of confidence. Certain methods are especially useful for gathering the evidence needed to attain each of these goals. Specifically, psychologists tend to use *naturalistic observation, case studies,* and *surveys* to describe and predict behavior and mental processes. They use *experiments* to introduce the control necessary to rule out alternative explanations for the evidence they collect and thus help establish *cause-effect relationships,* in which one variable can be shown to have actually caused a change in another. Thus, Francine Shapiro initially *described* the EMDR effect on the basis of observations of her own reactions; then she tested the *prediction* that similar results might occur in other cases. Later we discuss an experiment designed to introduce enough *control* into the treatment situation to begin evaluating alternative *explanations* for the effect, and thus to explore whether EMDR itself is actually the cause of clients' improvement. Let's look at how these goals and methods are blended in psychologists' work.

[Handwritten margin notes:]
4 main goals:
① describe phenomenon
② make predictions
③ introduce enough control
④ explain the phenomenon.

SCIENTIFIC RESEARCH Mark Johnson studies babies' abilities to remember sequences of color images, as shown here. In the "classic" scientific research sequence, explanations result when initial observations of memory abilities or other phenomena suggest a hypothesis about them. As in Francine Shapiro's case with **EMDR**, these observations lead to predictions, further observations, more precise predictions, and then experiments to eliminate alternative explanations and establish cause-effect relations between variables. However, psychologists follow no fixed sequence in working toward their goals of description, prediction, control, and explanation. Sometimes, for example, explanatory theories spark the curiosity that guides researchers' choices of what topics to explore.

NATURALISTIC OBSERVATION   Observing people in natural settings can provide important clues to understanding social interaction and other aspects of behavior and mental processes.

LINKAGES: AN ETHOLOGIST AT WORK Konrad Lorenz, one of the founders of ethology, used naturalistic observation to describe many examples of inborn but environmentally triggered behaviors, discussed under the evolutionary approach in Chapter 1. One of the most delightful of these is shown here. Baby geese follow their mother because her movement and honking provide signals that are naturally attractive. After Lorenz squatted and made mother-goose noises in front of newborn geese whose real mother was not present, the goslings began following him wherever he went, much to the amusement of his neighbors.

Naturalistic Observation

Sometimes, the best way to gather descriptive data is through **naturalistic observation,** the process of watching without interfering as a phenomenon occurs in the natural environment. This method is especially valuable in cases where other methods are likely to be disruptive or misleading. For example, if you studied animals only by observing them in the laboratory, you might conclude that learning alone determines most of what they do, because you would not see how they normally use cues in their natural environment. In fact, many animals—like the herring gull chicks shown in Chapter 1— display inherited patterns of behavior that are predictable, stereotyped, and triggered automatically by environmental events.

Naturalistic observation of people can also be revealing. For example, as noted in Chapter 12, much of what we know about gender differences in how children play and communicate with one another has come from psychologists' observations of children in classrooms and playgrounds (e.g., Newcomb & Bagwell, 1995). Observations of adults, too, have helped psychologists see that gender differences already evident in childhood might underlie some of the conflict and miscommunication seen in marriages and other cross-gender intimate relationships (Bradbury, Campbell & Fincham, 1995). As they work to alleviate relationship problems, therapists are aided by their understanding of gender differences that first came to light through observational research.

Although naturalistic observation can provide large amounts of rich information, it is not problem-free (Nietzel, Bernstein & Milich, 1994). For one thing, when people know they are being observed (and ethics usually requires that they do know), they tend to act differently than they otherwise would. Researchers typically combat this problem by observing long enough for subjects to get used to the situation and begin behaving more naturally. Observations can also be distorted if observers expect to see certain behaviors. If, in a study of the effects of EMDR on self-confidence, observers know which subjects received treatment and which did not, they might tend to rate treated subjects as more self-confident no matter how they actually behave. To get the most out of naturalistic observation, psychologists must counteract problems such as these.

Case Studies

Observations are often an important part of a **case study,** which is an intensive examination of a phenomenon in a particular individual, group, or situation. Often, case

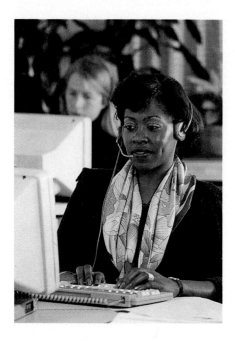

studies combine observations, tests, interviews, and analysis of written records. Case studies are especially useful when a phenomenon is new, complex, or relatively rare. The EMDR method, for example, first attracted psychologists' attention through Dr. Shapiro's reports of cases in which her clients' anxiety was reduced (Shapiro, 1989a).

Case studies have a long tradition in clinical work. Freud's development of psychoanalysis, for example, was based on case studies of people whose paralysis or other physical symptoms disappeared when they were hypnotized or asleep. Case studies have also played a special role in *neuropsychology,* the study of the relationships among brain activity, thinking, and behavior. Consider the case of Dr. P., a patient described by Oliver Sacks (1985). A distinguished musician with superior intelligence, Dr. P. began to display odd symptoms, such as the inability to recognize familiar people or to distinguish between people and inanimate objects. During a visit to a neurologist, Dr. P. mistook his foot for his shoe. When he rose to leave, he tried to lift off his wife's head—like a hat—and put it on his own. He could not name even the most common objects when he looked at them, although he could describe them. When handed a glove, for example, he said, "A continuous surface, infolded on itself. It appears to have . . . five outpouchings, if this is the word. . . . A container of some sort." Only later, when he put it on his hand, did he exclaim, "My God, it's a glove!" (Sacks, 1985, p. 13).

Using case studies like this one, pioneers in neuropsychology noted the deficits suffered by people with particular kinds of brain damage or disease. Eventually, neuropsychologists were able to tie specific disorders to certain types of injuries, tumors, poisons, and other causes. (The cause of Dr. P.'s symptoms was apparently a large brain tumor.) Case studies do have their limitations, however. They may contain only the evidence that a particular researcher considered important, and, of course, they are unlikely to be representative of people in general. Nonetheless, case studies can provide valuable raw material for further research. They can also be vital sources of information about particular people, and they serve as the testing ground for new treatments, training programs, and other applications of research.

Surveys

Case studies provide close-up views of individuals; surveys give broad portraits of large groups. Through interviews or questionnaires, a **survey** asks people about their behavior, attitudes, beliefs, opinions, or intentions. Just as politicians and advertisers rely on opinion polls to gauge the popularity of policies or products, psychologists use surveys to gather descriptive data on just about everything related to behavior and mental processes, from parenting practices to sexual behavior. However, the validity of survey data depends partly on how questions are worded. This point was vividly illustrated in 1992, when the Roper polling organization asked people in the United States, "Does it seem possible or does it seem impossible to you that the Nazi extermination of the Jews

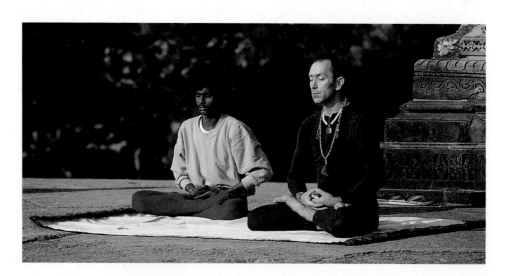

never happened?" Results suggested that 22 percent of the respondents thought the Holocaust might be a myth, but the question was written in such a confusing way that many of these people probably meant exactly the opposite of what they said. Indeed, when the question was stated more clearly in a later survey, only 8 percent of respondents expressed doubt about the reality of Nazi persecution of the Jews (Ladd, 1994). A survey's validity also depends on the representativeness of the people surveyed. If neo-Nazi skinheads had been the only participants in the new survey, doubt about the Holocaust would have appeared rampant; but that result would reflect only the views of extremists, not those of the general population.

Other limitations of the survey method are more difficult to avoid. For example, people may be reluctant to admit undesirable or embarrassing things about themselves, or they may say what they believe they *should* say about an issue. To the extent that such tendencies distort responses, survey results—and the conclusions drawn from them— will be distorted, too (Ottati et al., 1989). Still, surveys provide a relatively efficient way to gather large amounts of data about people's attitudes, beliefs, or other characteristics.

Experiments

Naturalistic observation, case studies, and surveys are valuable for describing and making predictions about behavior and mental processes, but these methods can only offer clues about the reasons behind their results. For example, surveys have described steady increases in both domestic violence and violent street crimes in the United States over the last several decades and predict worsening violence ahead (Koss et al., 1994), but they do not *explain* the upward trend. Perhaps this trend is due not to changes in behavior but to more accurate reporting of violence, made possible by networked police computers, the advent of rape crisis centers, and greater attention to child abuse. And if there *is* more violence, the increase might be due to crowding, frustration, televised violence, air pollution, or other factors discussed in Chapters 7 and 18.

In order to choose among alternative explanatory hypotheses and establish cause-effect relationships, psychologists must exert some *control* over variables, not just describe them. This kind of research usually takes the form of an experiment. **Experiments** are situations in which the researcher manipulates one variable and then observes the effect of that manipulation on another variable, while holding all other variables constant. The variable manipulated by the experimenter is called the **independent variable.** The variable to be observed is called the **dependent variable** because it is affected by, or *depends on,* the independent variable.

Francine Shapiro performed an experiment in an attempt to better understand the effects of EMDR. As illustrated in Figure 2.1, she first identified twenty-two people suffering the ill-effects of traumas such as rape or military combat. These were her subjects, or participants. She assigned the subjects to two groups. The first group received a single session of EMDR treatment for about fifty minutes; the second focused on their unpleasant memories for eight minutes, but without moving their eyes back and forth (Shapiro, 1989b). The experimenter controlled whether EMDR treatment was administered to each subject, so the presence or absence of treatment was the independent variable. The subjects' anxiety level while thinking about their traumatic memories was the dependent variable.

FIGURE 2.1

A Simple Two-Group Experiment

Ideally, the only difference between the experimental and control group in experiments like this one is whether the subjects receive the treatment the experimenter wishes to evaluate. Under such ideal circumstances, at the end of the experiment any difference in the two groups' reported levels of anxiety (the dependent variable) should be attributable to whether or not they received treatment (the independent variable).

1. Preliminary screening of subjects	2. Random assignment to conditions	3. Treatment phase	4. Post-treatment phase
Subjects are interviewed by the researcher, and their baseline anxiety is established.	Experimental group	Receives EMDR treatment	Reports on anxiety
	Control group	No EMDR	Reports on anxiety

The group that receives the experimental treatment is called, naturally enough, the **experimental group.** The group that receives no treatment, or some other treatment, is called the **control group.** Control groups provide baselines against which to compare the performance of others. In Shapiro's experiment, having a control group allowed the experimenter to measure how much change in anxiety could be expected from exposure to bad memories without EMDR treatment. If everything about the two groups is exactly the same except for exposure to treatment, then any difference in anxiety between the groups at the end of the experiment should be due to the treatment. In turn, hypotheses about alternative causes of improvement, such as the passage of time, become less plausible.

The results of Dr. Shapiro's (1989b) experiment showed that subjects receiving EMDR treatment experienced a complete and nearly immediate reduction in anxiety related to their traumatic memories, while the controls showed no change. At this point, you might be ready to believe that the treatment caused the difference. Before coming to that conclusion, however, look again at the structure, or design, of the experiment. The treatment group's session lasted about fifty minutes, but the control group focused on their memories for only eight minutes. Would the people in the control group have improved if they had spent fifty minutes focusing on their memories? We don't know, because the experiment did not compare methods of equal duration.

Anyone who conducts or relies on research must be on guard for such flaws in experimental design and control. Before drawing any conclusions from research, experimenters need to consider other factors—especially variables that could confuse, or confound, interpretation of the results. Any factor that might have affected the dependent variable, along with or instead of the independent variable, may be such a **confounding variable.** When confounding variables are present, the experimenter cannot know whether the independent variable or the confounding variable produced the results. Here we examine three sources of confounding variables: random variables, subjects' expectations, and experimenter bias.

Random Variables In an ideal research world, everything about the experimental and control groups would be identical except for the amounts of the independent variable, such as the presence or absence of treatment. In reality, however, there are always other differences, especially those introduced by **random variables.** Random variables are uncontrolled, sometimes uncontrollable, factors such as differences among the subjects—in terms of their backgrounds, personalities, physical health, or vulnerability to stress, for example—as well as differences in conditions such as the time of day and noise level.

Random variables are so numerous that no experimenter can create groups that are equivalent on all of them. A common solution to this problem is to flip a coin or use some other random process to assign each subject to experimental or control groups. Such procedures—called **random assignment**—tend to distribute the impact of uncontrolled variables randomly (and probably about evenly) across groups, thus minimizing the chance that they will distort the results of the experiment.

Placebo Effects In Shapiro's (1989b) experiment, control subjects, after eight minutes of focusing on negative memories, were asked to begin moving their eyes; then they, too, started to experience a reduction in anxiety. Was this improvement caused by the eye movements themselves, or could it be that the instructions made the subjects feel more confident that they were now getting real treatment? This question illustrates a second source of confounding: differences in what subjects think about the experimental situation. If subjects expect that a treatment will help them, they may try harder to improve than those in a control group who receive no treatment or a less impressive one. Improvement created by a subject's knowledge and expectations is called the *placebo effect.* A **placebo** (pronounced "pla-see´-bow") is a treatment that contains nothing known to be helpful, but that nevertheless produces benefits because a person *believes* it will be beneficial. People sometimes improve after receiving medical or psychological treatment, not because of the treatment itself but because of their belief that it would help them.

How can researchers determine the extent to which a result is caused by the independent variable or by a placebo effect? Often they include a special control group that receives *only* a placebo. Then they compare results for the experimental group, the placebo group, and those receiving no treatment. In one smoking-cessation study, for example, subjects in a placebo group took sugar pills described by the experimenter as "fast-acting tranquilizers" that would help them learn to endure the stress of giving up cigarettes (Bernstein, 1970). These subjects did as well at quitting as those in the experimental group, who received extensive treatment. This result suggests that the success of the experimental group may have been due largely to the subjects' expectations, not to the treatment methods. Research on EMDR treatment similarly suggests that the eye movements themselves may not be responsible for improvement, inasmuch as staring, finger tapping, or listening to rapid clicks while focusing on traumatic memories have also produced benefits (Bauman & Melnyk, 1994; Cocco & Sharpe, 1993; Renfrey & Spates, 1994). However, no placebo-controlled experiments have yet been done, so final conclusions about the value of EMDR must await further research (Tolin et al., 1996).

Experimenter Bias Another potential confounding variable comes from **experimenter bias,** the unintentional effect that experimenters may exert on results. Robert Rosenthal (1966) was one of the first to demonstrate the power of experimenter bias. His subjects were laboratory assistants who were asked to place rats in a maze. Rosenthal told some of the assistants that their rats were bred to be particularly "maze-bright"; he told the others that their rats were "maze-dull." In fact, both groups of rats were randomly drawn from the same population and had equal maze-learning capabilities. But the "maze-bright" animals learned the maze significantly faster than the "maze-dull" rats. Why? Rosenthal concluded that the result had nothing to do with the rats and everything to do with the experimenters. He suggested that the assistants' expectations about their rats' supposedly superior (or inferior) capabilities caused them to subtly alter their training and handling techniques, which in turn speeded or slowed the animals' learning. Similarly, when administering different kinds of anxiety treatments to different groups, experimenters who believe one treatment will be the best may do a slightly better job with that treatment and, thus, unintentionally improve its effects.

To prevent experimenter bias from confounding results, experimenters often use a **double-blind design.** In this arrangement, both the subjects *and* those giving the treatments are unaware of, or "blind" to, who is receiving a placebo, and do not know what results are expected from various treatments. Only the director of the study—a person who makes no direct contact with subjects—has this information, and does not reveal it until the experiment is over. The fact that double-blind studies of EMDR have not yet been conducted is another reason for caution in drawing conclusions about this treatment.

In short, experiments are vital tools for examining cause-effect relationships between variables, but like the other methods we have described, they are vulnerable to error. To maximize the value of their experiments, scientists try to eliminate as many confounding variables as possible, replicate their work to ensure consistent results, then temper their interpretation of the results to take into account the limitations or problems that remain.

Quasi-Experiments Sometimes an experiment is flawed not because the experimenter failed to create the conditions needed to eliminate alternative hypotheses but because it would have been impossible or unethical to do so. Consider the problem of testing the hypothesis that a pregnant woman's use of drugs causes abnormalities in her developing baby. From an experimental design standpoint, it would be ideal to take a large group of newly pregnant women, randomly assign them to either use or not use, say, cocaine, then observe the condition of the babies they deliver. Such an experiment would be unthinkable, however. In evaluating hypotheses like this one, the best psychologists can do is conduct **quasi-experiments,** which are studies whose designs approximate the control of a true experiment (*quasi-* means "resembling") but may not include manipulation of the independent variable, random assignment of subjects to groups, or other elements of true experimental control (Campbell & Stanley, 1966). Even when subjects cannot, for example, be randomly assigned to different conditions, the experimenter can still measure differences in dependent variables between subjects who have or have not been exposed to particular conditions. Thus, a researcher can measure differences in the mental, physical, and behavioral characteristics of children whose mothers did or did not use drugs during pregnancy.

The conclusions that can be drawn from quasi-experiments are usually not as firm as those from true experiments, but, especially when their results are replicated many times with large numbers of subjects, they can inspire considerable confidence. They also allow scientific research to be conducted on topics and in settings that would otherwise be impossible.

Selecting Human Participants for Research

As already mentioned in relation to surveys, the results of naturalistic observation, case studies, and experiments will be limited if they do not include a representative sample of subjects, or participants. (For a review of all these methods, see "In Review: Methods of Psychological Research.") Just as visitors from another galaxy would err wildly if they tried to describe the typical earthling after meeting only George Foreman, Geraldo Rivera, and Madonna, psychologists can wander astray if they do not have access to a sample of participants that provides a fair representation of the population about which they want to draw conclusions.

The process of selecting participants for research is called **sampling.** It is a profoundly important component of the research process. If all the subjects come from a particular subgroup (say, male Asian-American musicians), the research results might apply, or *generalize,* only to people like them. This outcome would be especially likely if the researcher is studying a behavior or mental process that is affected by age, gender, ethnicity, cultural background, socioeconomic status, sexual orientation, disability, or other characteristics specific to the subjects. When, as is often the case, these *subject variables* are likely to have an impact on research results, the sample of subjects studied must be representative of people in general if the researcher wants results that reveal something about people in general (Lips, 1988).

If every member of a population to be studied has an equal chance of being chosen as a research subject, the individuals selected would constitute a **random sample.** If not everyone has an equal chance of participating, those selected constitute a **biased sample.** In reality, no researcher is likely to draw a truly random sample, unless it is from a very restricted population, which might be of very limited interest. The practical alternative is to draw *representative samples,* which contain people who represent significant subject variables in the overall population.

Sometimes representative samples are not necessary, or even desirable. In the area of language development in children, for example, the most valuable case study may be one that examines not the average youngster but the unfortunate child raised in solitary confinement by a parent who provided no language instruction (Rymer, 1992; see also Chapter 12). Further, if you *want* to learn about male Asian-American musicians, or pregnant teenagers, or Hispanic-American women executives, all your subjects should be randomly selected from those groups, not from the general population.

For convenience, researchers often begin their work by studying a particular population, such as local college students or, as in Dr. Shapiro's case, friends and colleagues; then they attempt to replicate their results with broader, more representative samples. If outcomes are consistent across a diverse group of subjects, researchers can more confidently draw future samples from whatever willing group is at hand without worrying too much about subject diversity. However, it is vital to show, rather than merely to assume, that subject variables do not limit the breadth of conclusions that can be drawn from research data.

Psychologists must also guard against allowing preconceptions about gender, ethnicity, and other variables to influence the questions they ask, the research designs they create, and the way they analyze, interpret, and report their data (Denmark et al., 1988;

SELECTING RESEARCH PARTICIPANTS
Obtaining a sample of people that fairly represents a population of interest is a major challenge in psychological research.

IN REVIEW	Methods of Psychological Research		
Method	**Features**	**Strengths**	**Pitfalls**
Naturalistic observations	Observation of human or animal behavior in the environment where it typically occurs	Provides descriptive data about behavior presumably uncontaminated by outside influences	Observer bias and subject self-consciousness can distort results
Case studies	Intensive examination of the behavior and mental processes associated with a specific person or situation	Provides detailed descriptive analyses of new, complex, or rare phenomena	May not provide representative picture of phenomena
Surveys	Standard sets of questions asked of a large number of subjects	Gathers large amounts of descriptive data relatively quickly and inexpensively	Sampling errors, poorly phrased questions, and response biases can distort results
Experiments	Manipulation of an independent variable and measurement of its effects on a dependent variable	Can establish a cause-effect relationship between independent and dependent variables	Confounding variables may prevent valid conclusions
Quasi-experiments	Measurement of dependent variables when independent variables were not entirely under the experimenter's control	Can provide strong evidence suggesting cause-effect relationships	Lack of full control may weaken conclusions
All of the above	Choosing among alternative hypotheses; sometimes generating theories	Can expand our understanding of behavior and mental processes	Errors, limitations, and biases in research evidence can lead to incorrect or incomplete explanations

McHugh, Koeske & Frieze, 1986). When designing a study on gender and job commitment, for example, the researcher must be sure to sample men and women in jobs of equal status. Comparing male executives with female secretaries might create a false impression of greater male commitment, because people in lower-status jobs tend to change jobs more often, regardless of gender. Similarly, researchers who use a male-only sample should give this fact the same prominence in their report as is customarily the case when only females are studied (Ader & Johnson, 1994). To do otherwise would imply that males provide a standard against which females' behavior and mental processes are to be compared. Finally, researchers must report whatever results appear. After all, it is just as valuable to know that men and women, or African-Americans and European-Americans, did *not* differ on a test of leadership ability as to know that they did. Stephanie Riger (1992) suggests that one of psychologists' greatest challenges is to "disengage themselves sufficiently from commonly shared beliefs so that those beliefs do not predetermine research findings" (p. 732).

STATISTICAL ANALYSIS OF RESEARCH RESULTS

Whether psychologists conduct naturalistic observations, case studies, surveys, or experiments, their investigations usually generate a large amount of **data:** numbers that represent research findings and provide the basis for conclusions. *Statistical analyses* are the methods most often used to summarize and analyze data. These methods include *descriptive statistics,* which are the numbers that psychologists use to describe and present a set of data, and *inferential statistics,* which are mathematical procedures used to draw conclusions from data and to make inferences about what they mean. Here, we describe a few statistical terms that you will encounter in later chapters; you can find more information about these terms in the statistics appendix.

Descriptive Statistics

The three most important descriptive statistics are *measures of central tendency*, which describe the typical value in a set of data; *measures of variability*, which describe the spread, or dispersion, in a set of data; and *correlation coefficients*, which describe relationships between variables.

Measures of Central Tendency   Suppose you want to test the effects of EMDR treatment on fear of the dark. Looking for subjects, you collect the eleven anxiety ratings listed on the left side of Table 2.2. What is the typical value, the central tendency, that best represents the group's anxiety level? There are three measures designed to capture this typical value: the mode, the median, and the mean.

The **mode** is the value or score that occurs most frequently in a data set. You can find it by ordering the scores from lowest to highest. On the left side of Table 2.2, the mode is 50, because the score of 50 occurs more often than any other. Notice, however, that in this data set, the mode is actually an extreme score. Sometimes, the mode acts like a microphone for a small but vocal minority, which, though speaking most frequently, does not represent the views of the majority.

Unlike the mode, the median takes all of the scores into account. The **median** is the halfway point in a set of data: half the scores fall above the median, half fall below it. For the scores on the left side of Table 2.2, the halfway point—the median—is 45.

TABLE 2.2				
	Data from 11 Subjects		**Data from 12 Subjects**	
A Set of Pretreatment Anxiety Ratings	*Subject Number*	*Anxiety Rating*	*Subject Number*	*Anxiety Rating*
Here are scores representing peoples' ratings, on a 1–100 scale, of their fear of the dark.	1	20	1	20
	2	22	2	22
	3	28	3	28
	4	35	4	35
	5	40	5	40
	6	45 (Median)	6	45 (Median = 46[*])
	7	47	7	47
	8	49	8	49
	9	50	9	50
	10	50	10	50
	11	50	11	50
			12	100

Measures of central tendency	**Measures of central tendency**
Mode = 50	Mode = 50
Median = 45	Median = 46
Mean = 436/11 = 39.6	Mean = 536/12 = 44.7
Measures of variability	**Measures of variability**
Range = 30	Range = 80
Standard deviation = 11.064	Standard deviation = 19.763

[*]When there is an even number of scores, the exact middle of the list lies between two numbers. The median is the value halfway between those numbers.

THE IMPACT OF VARIABILITY   Suppose you are a substitute teacher who comes to a new school hoping for an easy day's work. You are offered either of two classes. In each, the students' mean IQ is 100. At first glance, there would appear to be no major difference between the classes, but it turns out that the standard deviation (SD) of IQs in one class is 16; the SD in the other is 32. Since a higher standard deviation means more variability, the class with the SD of 32 is likely to be more difficult to teach because its students vary more in ability. The standard deviation is a particularly important descriptive statistic in any data set.

The third measure of central tendency is the **mean,** which is the *arithmetic average.* When people talk about the "average" in everyday conversation, they are usually referring to the mean. To find the mean, add the values of all the scores and divide by the number of scores. For the scores on the left side of Table 2.2, the mean is 436/11 = 39.6.

Like the median (and unlike the mode), the mean reflects all the data to some degree, not just the most frequent data. Notice, however, that the mean reflects the actual value of all the scores, whereas the median gives each score equal weight, whatever its size. This distinction can have a big effect on how well the mean and median represent the values in a particular set of data. Suppose, for example, that you add to your sample a twelfth subject whose anxiety rating is 100. When you re-analyze the anxiety data (see the right side of Table 2.2), the median hardly changes, because the new subject counts as just one more score. However, when you compute the new mean, the actual *amount* of the new subject's rating is added to everyone else's ratings; as a result, the mean jumps 5 points. Sometimes, as in this example, the median is a better measure of central tendency than the mean because the median is less sensitive to extreme scores. But because the mean is more representative of the value of all the data, it is often the preferred measure of central tendency.

Measures of Variability   The variability (also known as spread or dispersion) in a set of data can be quantified by the range and the standard deviation. The **range** is simply the difference between the highest and the lowest value in the data set (it would be 30 for data on the left side of Table 2.2 and 80 for data on the right side). In contrast, the **standard deviation,** or **SD,** measures the average difference between each score and the mean of the data set. The SD for the eleven subjects on the left side of Table 2.2 is 11.06, but it rises to 19.76 once the very divergent twelfth score is added on the right side. Thus, the more variable data are, the higher the standard deviation. In the statistics appendix, we show how to calculate the standard deviation.

Correlation and Correlation Coefficients   Does the number of fears people have tend to decrease with age? In general, yes (Kleinknecht, 1991); but to test hypotheses about questions such as this, psychologists must have a way to measure how, and to what extent, variables such as age and fearfulness are correlated.

Correlation means just what it says—"co-relation"; in statistics, it refers both to how strongly one variable is related to another *and* to the direction of the relationship. A *positive correlation* means that two variables increase together or decrease together. A *negative correlation* means the variables move in opposite directions: when one increases, the other decreases. For example, James Schaefer observed 4,500 customers in 65 bars and found that the tempo of jukebox music was negatively correlated with the rate at which the customers drank alcohol; the slower the tempo, the faster the drinking (Schaefer et al., 1988).

Does this mean Schaefer could wear a blindfold and predict exactly how fast people are drinking by timing the music? Or could he plug his ears and determine the musical tempo by watching people's sip rates? No, and no, because the accuracy of predictions about one variable from knowledge of another depends on the *strength* of the correlation. Only a perfect correlation between two variables would allow you to predict the exact value of one from a knowledge of the other. The weaker the correlation, the less one variable can tell you about the other.

To describe the strength of a correlation, psychologists calculate a statistic called the **correlation coefficient** (shown in the statistics appendix). The correlation coefficient is given the symbol r, and can vary from +1.00 to −1.00. Thus, the coefficient includes (1) an absolute value, such as .20 or .50, and (2) either a plus sign or a minus sign.

The *absolute value* of r indicates the strength of the relationship. An r of +0.01 between people's shoe size and the age of their cars, for example, indicates that there is virtually no relationship between the variables, whereas an r of +1.00 indicates a perfectly predictable relationship between two variables (see Figure 2.2). Unfortunately, the variables of interest in psychology are seldom perfectly correlated. Throughout this book, you will find correlation coefficients whose absolute values range from .20 to .90,

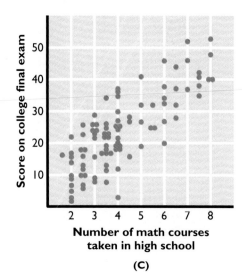

(A)   (B)   (C)

FIGURE 2.2

Three Correlations

The strength and direction of the correlation between two variables can be seen in a graph called a *scatterplot*. Here are three examples. In part (A), we have plotted the cost of a gasoline purchase against the number of gallons pumped. Since the number of gallons is *positively* and perfectly correlated with their cost, the scatterplot appears as a straight line, and you can predict the value of either variable from a knowledge of the other. Part (B) shows a perfect *negative* correlation between the number of miles you have traveled toward a destination and the distance remaining. Again, one variable can be exactly predicted from the other. Part (C) illustrates a correlation of +.81 between the number of high school math courses students had taken and their scores on a college-level final exam in math (Hays, 1981). As correlations decrease, they are represented by ever-greater dispersion in the pattern of dots. A correlation of 0.00 would appear as a shapeless cloud.

reflecting relationships of intermediate strength in which knowing about one variable tells us something, but not everything, about the other.

The *sign* of a correlation coefficient indicates its direction. A plus sign signifies a *positive* correlation between variables; a minus sign indicates a *negative* correlation.

Psychologists use correlation coefficients to help them describe and predict phenomena, to evaluate existing hypotheses, and, often, to generate new hypotheses, but they must be very careful when interpreting correlations. Consider, for example, the positive correlation that has been found between watching violent television programs and behaving violently. Does seeing violence on TV cause viewers to be violent, or does being violent to begin with cause a preference for violent shows? Perhaps neither causes the other; violent behavior *and* TV choices could both be due to a third factor, such as stress. (In Chapter 7, on learning, we discuss how researchers have evaluated these possibilities.) In short, just because two variables are *correlated* doesn't mean that one is *causing* an effect on the other. And even if it is, a correlation coefficient can't say which variable is influencing which. Correlations can reveal and describe relationships, but correlations alone cannot *explain* them (see Figure 2.3).

Inferential Statistics

The task of understanding the meaning of research results summarized in correlations or other descriptive statistics is not an easy one. Is a correlation between college grade-point averages and the consumption of certain foods large enough to support the hypothesis that diet is important for mental functioning? Is the anxiety reduction following EMDR sufficiently greater than that following other treatments to recommend one over the other? The answers to questions such as these are based largely on the results of analyses that use inferential statistics.

Inferential statistics employ certain conventional rules to evaluate the likelihood that a correlation or a difference between groups reflects a relationship to be found in the general population of interest and not just the operation of chance factors on the particular sample drawn from that population. Suppose, for example, that subjects who received EMDR showed a mean decrease of 10 points on a test of fear of the dark, whereas the scores of a no-treatment control group decreased by a mean of 7 points. How likely is it that the difference between 10 and 7 was due to chance alone? Analysis through inferential statistics can provide an answer. When a correlation coefficient or the difference between the means of two groups is larger than would be expected by chance alone, it is said to be **statistically significant.** In the statistics appendix we discuss how the size of mean differences or correlations, the number of subjects studied, and the amount of variability in the data affect statistical significance.

Statistical significance alone does not necessarily constitute final "proof," but scientists pay more attention to correlations or other research findings that are statistically

(A) ICE CREAM CONSUMPTION

(B) DROWNINGS

FIGURE 2.3

Correlation and Causation

These graphs show that, in the United States, ice cream consumption and drownings tend to rise and fall together. However, this positive correlation does not mean that eating ice cream *causes* drownings. A correlation between variables says nothing about whether one variable actually exerts an impact on the other; it would take experiments to confirm that. In this case, the correlation probably reflects a third variable—time of year—that affects both ice cream sales and the likelihood of swimming and boating.

significant, especially when they are replicated (Cohen, 1994; Powell, Nabers & Knight, 1992). Thus, when one is thinking critically about research, part of the process of evaluating evidence about hypotheses requires asking whether a researcher's results are statistically significant and replicated.

ETHICAL GUIDELINES FOR PSYCHOLOGISTS

The obligation to analyze and report research fairly and accurately is one of the ethical requirements that guide psychologists. Preservation of the welfare and dignity of their subjects, animal and human, is another. Although researchers *could* measure severe anxiety by putting a loaded gun to people's heads, or study marital conflicts by telling one partner that the other has been unfaithful, such methods are potentially harmful and, therefore, unethical.

In each of these examples, the ethical course of action is obvious: The psychologist must find another way to conduct the research. In practice, however, ethical choices are often more complicated, and psychologists must decide how to balance conflicting values. Many experiments reflect a compromise between the need to protect subjects from harm and the need to learn about the unknown. In finding ways to help people cope with anxiety, for example, researchers may ask them to try new coping skills while enduring an anxiety-provoking, but not traumatic, situation.

When a study does create risks or discomfort for subjects, researchers must convince a local human-research review committee that the potential benefits of the work in terms of new knowledge and human welfare outweigh any potential harm. They must also minimize the discomfort and risk, and they must act to prevent subjects from suffering any long-term negative consequences from participation. Researchers must inform potential participants about every aspect of the study that might influence their decision to participate and ensure that each subject's involvement is voluntary. But what if a researcher must withhold information about a study because full disclosure beforehand would bias subjects' behavior? Or what if subjects must be given inaccurate information in order to create mild annoyance, a sense of time urgency, or some other temporary condition essential to the study? In such cases, the researcher must "debrief" the participants as soon as the study is over by revealing all relevant information about the research and correcting any misimpressions it created.

The obligation to protect subjects' welfare also extends to animals, which are used in about 8 percent of psychological research (Shapiro, 1991). Psychologists study animals partly because their behavior is interesting in and of itself and partly because research with animals can yield information that would be impossible or unethical to collect from humans.

Contrary to the allegations of some animal-rights activists, animals used in psychological research are not routinely subjected to extreme pain, starvation, or other inhumane conditions (Coile & Miller, 1984; Novak, 1991). Even in the small proportion of studies that require the use of electric shock, the discomfort created is mild, brief, and not harmful. The recently revised Animal Welfare Act, the National Institutes of Health *Guide for the Care and Use of Laboratory Animals,* the American Psychological Association's *Principles on Animal Use,* and other laws and regulations set high standards for the care and treatment of animal subjects. In those relatively rare studies that require animals to undergo short-lived pain or other forms of moderate stress, legal and ethical standards require the psychologist to persuade funding agencies—as well as local committees charged with monitoring animal research—that the discomfort is justified by the expected benefits to human welfare.

The responsibility for conducting research in the most humane fashion forms just one aspect of the *Ethical Principles of Psychologists and Code of Conduct* developed by the APA (American Psychological Association, 1992b). The main purpose of these standards is to protect and promote the welfare of society and those with whom psychologists work. For example, as teachers, psychologists should strive to give students a complete, accurate, and up-to-date view of each topic, not a narrow, biased point of view. Psychologists should perform only those services and use only those techniques

CARING FOR ANIMALS IN RESEARCH
Psychologists are careful to protect the welfare of animal subjects. They take no pleasure in animals' suffering, and besides, inflicting undue stress on animal subjects can create reactions that can act as confounding variables. For example, in a study of how learning is affected by the size of food rewards, the researcher could starve animals to make them hungry enough to want the experimental rewards. But this would introduce discomfort that would make it impossible to separate the effects of the reward from the effects of starvation.

for which they are adequately trained; a biological psychologist untrained in clinical methods should not try to offer psychotherapy. Except in the most unusual circumstances (to be discussed in Chapter 16), psychologists should not reveal information obtained from clients or students, and they should avoid situations in which a conflict of interest might impair their judgment or harm someone else. They should not, for example, have sexual relations with their clients, their students, or their employees.

Despite these guidelines, doubt and controversy arise in some cases about whether a proposed experiment or a particular practice, such as deceiving subjects, is ethical (Christensen, 1988; Fisher & Fyrberg, 1994; Rosenthal, 1994). Indeed, ethical principles for psychologists will continue to evolve as psychologists face new and more complex ethical issues (Anderson & Kitchener, 1996; Gurman, 1994; Fisher & Fyrberg, 1994).

LINKAGES: PSYCHOLOGICAL RESEARCH AND BEHAVIORAL GENETICS

One of the most fascinating and difficult challenges in psychology is to find research methods that can help us understand the ways in which people's genetic inheritance—their biological *nature*—intertwines with environmental events and conditions before and after birth—often called *nurture*—to shape their behavior and mental processes. Questions about nature and nurture surface in relation to perception, personality, mental ability, mental disorder, and many other topics discussed throughout this book. Psychologists' efforts to explore the influences of nature and nurture in relation to these phenomena have taken them into the field of **behavioral genetics,** the study of how genes and heredity affect behavior. In this section, we describe the logic—and some results—of research methods in behavioral genetics. The basic principles of genetics and heredity that underlie these methods are described as part of a more detailed discussion in the behavioral genetics appendix.

LINKAGES How much of our behavior is due to genetics and how much to our environment? (a link to Biological Aspects of Psychology)

Researchers in behavioral genetics realize that most behavioral tendencies can be influenced by many different genes, but also by the environment. Accordingly, they do not expect to find specific genes that control specific behavioral tendencies—such as aggression or shyness—in particular people. Instead, research in behavioral genetics is designed to explore the *relative roles* of genetic and environmental factors in creating differences in behavioral tendencies in *groups* of people.

Early research in behavioral genetics relied on the selective breeding of animals. For example, Robert Tryon (1940) mated rats who were fast maze learners with other fast learners and mated slower learners with other slow learners. After repeating this procedure for several generations, he found that the offspring of the fast learners were significantly better at maze learning than those of the slow learners.

Selective-breeding studies must be interpreted with caution, however, because it is not specific behaviors that are inherited but, rather, differing sets of physical structures, capacities, and the like, which, in turn, make certain behaviors more or less likely. These behavioral tendencies are often narrow, and they can be altered by the environment. For example, "maze-dull" rats performed just as well as "maze-bright" rats on many tasks other than maze learning (Searle, 1949). And, when raised in an environment containing tunnels and other stimulating features, "dull" animals did as well at maze learning as "bright" ones; both groups did equally poorly in the maze after being raised in an environment that lacked stimulating features (Cooper & Zubek, 1958).

Research on behavioral genetics in humans must be interpreted with even more caution because environmental influences have an enormous impact on human behavior and because legal, moral, and ethical considerations prohibit manipulations such as selective breeding. Instead, research in human behavioral genetics depends on quasi-experiments, where control is imperfect. Some of the most important quasi-experimental designs are family studies, twin studies, and adoption studies (Plomin, DeFries & McClearn, 1990; Segal, 1993).

In *family studies,* researchers examine whether similarities in behavior and mental processes are greater in people who are closely related as compared to more distant relatives or unrelated individuals. If increasing similarity is associated with closer family ties, the similarities might be inherited. For example, data from family studies suggest a genetic basis for schizophrenia because this severe mental disorder appears much more often in the closest relatives of schizophrenics than in other people (see Figure 2.4). But family studies alone cannot establish the role of genetic factors in mental disorders or other characteristics, because close relatives tend to share environments as well as genes. Thus, similarities in close relatives might stem from environmental factors instead of, or in addition to, genetic ones.

Twin studies explore the heredity-environment mix by comparing the similarities seen in identical twins with those of nonidentical pairs. Twins usually share the same environment and may also be treated very much the same by parents and others, so if identical twins—whose genes are exactly the same—are more alike on some characteristic than nonidentical twins (whose genes are no more similar than those of other siblings), that characteristic may have a significant genetic component. As we will see in

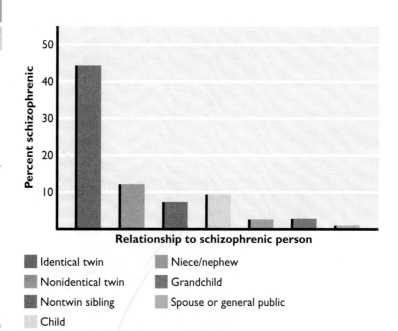

FIGURE 2.4

Family Studies of Schizophrenia

Data from family studies show that the risk of developing schizophrenia, a severe mental disorder described in Chapter 15, is highest for the siblings and children of schizophrenics and decreases progressively with genetic distance; the risk is lowest for people with no genetic relationship to a schizophrenic. Does this mean that schizophrenia is inherited? The data are certainly consistent with that interpretation, but the question cannot be answered through family studies alone. Other factors, including environmental stressors that close relatives share, could also play an important role in the development of the disorder.

Percent schizophrenic

Relationship to schizophrenic person

■ Identical twin   ■ Niece/nephew
■ Nonidentical twin   ■ Grandchild
■ Nontwin sibling   ■ Spouse or general public
□ Child

RESEARCH IN BEHAVIORAL GENETICS
Like other identical twins, each member of this pair has identical genes. Twin studies and adoption studies employ quasi-experimental designs that help illuminate the interaction of genetic and environmental influences on human behavior and mental processes. Cases in which identical twins who had been separated at birth, but have similar interests, personality traits, and mental abilities suggest that these characteristics have a significant genetic component.

later chapters, this pattern of results holds for a number of characteristics, including some measures of intelligence and some mental disorders.

Adoption studies take advantage of the naturally occurring quasi-experiments that take place when babies are adopted very early in life. The logic underlying these studies is that if adopted children's characteristics are more like those of their biological parents than those of their adoptive parents, genetically inherited ingredients in the nature-nurture mix play a clear role in that characteristic. As described in Chapter 14, for example, the personalities of young adults who were adopted at birth tend to be more like those of their biological parents than those of their adoptive parents. Adoption studies can be especially valuable when they focus on identical twins who were separated at or near birth. If identical twins show similar characteristics after years of living in very different environments, the role of heredity in those characteristics is highlighted. Adoption studies of intelligence, for example, tend to support the role of genetics in variations in mental ability, but they show that environmental influences are important as well.

As you read in later chapters about the role of genetics in human development and in differences in personality and mental abilities, remember that research on human behavioral genetics can help illuminate the relative roles of heredity and environment that underlie *group differences,* but it cannot determine the degree to which a particular person's behavior is due to heredity or environment. The two factors are too closely entwined in an individual to be separated that way.

FUTURE DIRECTIONS

Through new technology and new ideas, psychologists are creating ever better ways to manipulate independent variables and measure dependent variables. For example, Joseph Malpeli created a tiny device for use with animals that temporarily deactivates cells in particular parts of the lateral geniculate nucleus (LGN), an area of the brain vital to vision. The ability to "turn off" various parts of the LGN and to observe the effects on vision has greatly enhanced understanding of the visual system (Farrera, Nealey & Maunsell, 1992; Mignard & Malpeli, 1991).

At the same time, standard psychological research methods are being applied to new topics. For example, a few years ago, Douglas Biklen (1990) described a procedure called "facilitated

communication" (FC), which he said could help people with autistic disorder (described in Chapter 15) to use language for the first time. These people, said Biklen, have language and coherent thoughts, but no way to express themselves. He claimed that they can answer questions or convey intelligent messages on a computer keyboard if helped by a "facilitator" who physically supports their unsteady hands. Controlled experiments on this case study–based claim showed it to be groundless (Jacobson, Mulick & Schwartz, 1995). Autistic subjects' alleged communication abilities disappeared under experimental conditions in which the facilitator (a) did not know the question being asked of the subject or (b) could not see the keyboard (Delmolino & Romanczyk, 1995). The discovery that facilitators were—perhaps inadvertently—guiding their subjects' hand movements has helped those who work with autistic patients to see FC in a different light.

As psychologists follow new research directions, they will continue to develop new research designs, methods, and analytical techniques. Each chapter of this book describes research that uses specialized methods for collecting and analyzing data. For example, in Chapter 14 we discuss correlational procedures known as *factor analysis* that help psychologists identify the basic components of human personality. In Chapter 10 we describe *cross-sectional* and *longitudinal* studies of changes in mental ability over the life span. And in Chapter 16 we describe

meta-analysis, a method for evaluating the results of many research studies on many forms of therapy for many kinds of problems.

In each chapter to come, we include a special feature called "Focus on Research Methods," which describes in some detail the specific procedures employed in a particularly interesting research project. We hope that this feature will help you see how the research methods covered in this present chapter are applied in every subfield of psychology. If you would like to learn even more about the principles of psychological research and about methodological innovations that are constantly appearing in psychology, consider taking a course in research methods.

SUMMARY AND KEY TERMS

■ THINKING CRITICALLY ABOUT PSYCHOLOGY (OR ANYTHING ELSE)

Critical thinking is the process of assessing claims and making judgments on the basis of well-supported evidence.

Critical Thinking and Scientific Research

Often, questions about psychological phenomena are phrased in terms of *hypotheses* about *operationally defined variables,* which must be evaluated for reliability and validity.

The Role of Theories

Explanations of phenomena often take the form of *theories,* which are integrated sets of propositions that can be used to account for, predict, and even control certain phenomena. Theories must also be subjected to rigorous evaluation.

■ RESEARCH METHODS IN PSYCHOLOGY

Research in psychology, as in other sciences, focuses on four main goals: description, prediction, control, and explanation.

Naturalistic Observation

Naturalistic observation entails watching without interfering as behavior occurs in the natural environment. This method can be revealing, but care must be taken to ensure that observers are unbiased and do not alter the behavior being observed.

Case Studies

Case studies are intensive examinations of a particular individual, group, or situation. They are useful for studying new or rare phenomena and can also help evaluate new treatments or training programs.

Surveys

Surveys ask questions, through interviews or questionnaires, about behavior, attitudes, beliefs, opinions, and intentions. They provide an excellent way to gather large amounts of data from a large number of people at relatively low cost, but their results can be distorted if questions are poorly phrased or if respondents do not answer honestly.

Experiments

In *experiments,* researchers manipulate an *independent variable* and observe the effect of that manipulation on a *dependent variable.* Subjects receiving experimental treatment are called the *experimental group;* those in comparison conditions are called *control groups.* Experiments can reveal cause-effect relationships between variables, but only if researchers use *random assignment, placebo* conditions, *double-blind designs,* and other strategies to avoid being misled by

random variables, experimenter bias, and other *confounding variables.* When ethics or other concerns prevent full experimental control, researchers sometimes employ *quasi-experiments.*

Selecting Human Participants for Research

Psychologists' research can be limited if their subject *sampling* procedures do not give them a fair cross-section of the population they want to study and about which they want to draw conclusions. Anything less than a *random sample* is said to be a *biased sample* of subjects; but in most cases, a representative sample is adequate.

■ STATISTICAL ANALYSIS OF RESEARCH RESULTS

Psychologists use descriptive and inferential statistical analyses to summarize and analyze *data,* the numbers that represent research findings and provide the basis for conclusions.

Descriptive Statistics

Descriptive statistics include measures of central tendency (such as the *mode, median,* and *mean*), measures of variability (such as the *range* and *standard deviation*), and *correlation coefficients.* Although they can be very valuable, *correlations* alone cannot establish that two variables are causally related; nor can they determine which variable might affect which, or why.

Inferential Statistics

Psychologists employ inferential statistics to guide conclusions about data, especially to determine if correlations or differences between means are *statistically significant*—that is, larger than would be expected by chance alone.

■ ETHICAL GUIDELINES FOR PSYCHOLOGISTS

Ethical guidelines promote the protection of human and animal subjects in psychological research, and set the highest standards for behavior in all other aspects of psychologists' professional lives.

■ LINKAGES: PSYCHOLOGICAL RESEARCH AND BEHAVIORAL GENETICS

Researchers have developed research methods to help them explore how nature and nurture interact to shape behavior and mental processes. This exploration has taken them into the field of *behavioral genetics,* the study of genes' effects on behavior. Behavioral genetics uses family studies, twin studies, and adoption studies to explore the interaction of heredity and environment in shaping human behavior and mental processes.

BIOLOGICAL ASPECTS OF PSYCHOLOGY

CHAPTER **3**

LINKAGES
TO
BIOLOGICAL ASPECTS
OF PSYCHOLOGY

CONSCIOUSNESS

Is there a way to drink alcohol without getting drunk? *(ans. on p. 183)*

TREATMENT OF PSYCHOLOGICAL DISORDERS

How do drugs help people who suffer from schizophrenia? *(ans. on p. 558)*

HUMAN DEVELOPMENT

How do our brains change over a lifetime? *(ans. on p. 74)*

Today millions of people who suffer from depression or anxiety take drugs such as Prozac, because doctors now believe these conditions result from biological imbalances. A grandmother's inability to remember her family could be due to Alzheimer's disease, and Parkinson's disease might be the reason your neighbor can't drink coffee without shaking. Maybe you yourself worry that your body's metabolism is working against your best efforts to lose or gain weight.

These examples of biological explanations for behavior and mental processes reflect the biological approach to psychology discussed in Chapter 1. The popularity and influence of that approach stems from the fact that brain cells, hormones, genes, and other biological factors are intimately related to all behavior and mental processes, from the fleeting memory you had a minute ago to the movements of your eyes as you read this sentence now (see the Linkages diagram). In this chapter, we describe these biological factors in more detail. In the process of reading it, you will enter the realm of **biological psychology,** which is the study of the cells and organs of the body and the physical and chemical changes involved in behavior and mental processes. It is here that we begin to consider the relationship between your body and your mind, your brain and your behavior.

People often assume that if a behavior or mental process has a strong biological basis, it is beyond control, that "biology is destiny." Accordingly, many smokers don't even try to quit because they assume that a biological addiction to nicotine will doom them to failure. This is not necessarily true, as millions of ex-smokers can attest. Indeed, the fact that all behavior and mental processes are *based* on biological processes does not mean that they can be fully understood through the study of biological processes *alone.* Those who would reduce all of psychology to the analysis of brain chemicals vastly oversimplify the interactions between our biological selves and our psychological experiences, between our genes and our environments.

For one thing, just as all behaviors and mental processes are influenced by biology, all biological processes are influenced by the environment. Height, for example, is a biologically determined characteristic, but how tall you actually become also depends on nutrition and other environmental factors (Tanner, 1992). Similarly, a genetic basis for schizophrenia is suggested by the fact that if one member of an identical twin pair displays this serious mental disorder, the other—who has the same genetic makeup—is likely to be schizophrenic, too. Often, however, only one twin is schizophrenic, meaning that environmental as well as genetic causal factors are at work. (The behavioral genetics appendix describes scientists' efforts to explore how hereditary and environmental influences combine in determining height, intelligence, personality, mental disorders, and other characteristics.)

In short, understanding behavior and mental processes requires that we synthesize information from many levels of analysis, from the activity of cells and organ systems to the activity of individuals and groups. This chapter focuses on the biological level, not because it reveals the whole story of psychology but because it tells an important part of that story.

We begin by considering your **nervous system,** a complex combination of cells that allows you to gain information about what is going on inside and outside your body and to respond appropriately. In doing so, the nervous system displays the components of an information-processing system: It has input, processing, and output activities (see Figure 3.1). *Input* occurs in the form of the sensory signals you receive from the world. *Processing* occurs as you integrate the information with past experiences and decide what to do about it. And *output* occurs as your brain activates your muscles to act on the information. It is a fundamental tenet of scientific psychology that every thought, every feeling, every action, is represented somehow in the nervous system and that none of these events could occur without it.

The nervous system is able to do what it does partly because it is made up of cells that *communicate with each other.* Like all cells in the body—indeed, like cells in all life forms—those in the nervous system can respond to outside influences. Many of the signals that cells respond to come in the form of *chemicals* released by other cells. So even as various cells specialize during prenatal development to become skin, bones, hair, and other tissues, they still "stay in touch" to some extent through chemical signals. Bone cells, for example, add or drop calcium in response to hormones secreted in another part of the body. Cells in the bloodstream respond to viruses and other invaders by destroying them. We focus on the cells of the nervous system because their ability to communicate is most efficient and complex.

THE NERVOUS SYSTEM

Scientists are exploring nervous systems at many levels, from the workings of molecules and cells to the wonders of how vast networks of brain cells accomplish such tasks as recognizing visual patterns and learning a language. We begin our exploration of the nervous system at the "bottom," with a description of the individual cells and molecules that compose it. Then we consider how these cells are organized to form the structures of the human nervous system.

Cells of the Nervous System

One of the most striking findings in current research on the cells of the nervous system is how similar they are to other cells in the body, and how similar all cells are in all living organisms, from bacteria to plants to humans. For example, bacteria, plant cells, and brain cells all synthesize similar proteins when they are subjected to reduced oxygen or elevated temperatures. The implications of this similarity are clear: We can learn much about humans by studying animals, and much about brain cells by studying cells in simple organisms. For example, studies of viruses by cancer researchers led to the discovery of proteins that may be involved in the formation of memories in the brain (Morgan & Curran, 1991; Alcantara et al., 1993).

Figure 3.2 illustrates three of the characteristics that cells of the nervous system share with every other kind of cell in the body. First, they have an *outer membrane* that, like a fine screen, lets some substances pass in and out while blocking others. Second, nervous system cells have a *cell body*, which contains a *nucleus*. The nucleus carries the genetic information that determines how a cell will function. Third, nervous system cells contain *mitochondria*, which are structures that turn oxygen and glucose into energy. This process is especially vital to brain cells. Although the brain accounts for only 2 percent of the body's weight, it consumes more than 20 percent of the body's oxygen (Sokoloff, 1981). All of this energy is required because brain cells transmit signals among themselves to an even greater extent than do cells in the rest of the body.

Two major types of cells—called neurons and glial cells—allow the nervous system to carry out its complex signaling tasks so efficiently. **Neurons** are cells that are specialized to rapidly respond to signals and quickly send signals of their own. Most of our discussion of brain cells will be about neurons, but glial cells are important as well. Glial means "glue," and scientists have long believed that glial cells did no more than hold neurons together. Recent research shows, however, that **glial cells** also help neurons communicate by directing their growth, keeping their chemical environment stable,

FIGURE 3.2

The Neuron

Part (A) shows the cell body of a nervous system cell known as a neuron, enlarged from one of the whole neurons shown in part (B). The cell body of a neuron has typical cell elements, including an outer membrane and mitochondria. Part (B) shows some of the shapes neurons can take. The fibers extending outward from each cell body, the axons and dendrites, are among the features that make neurons unique.

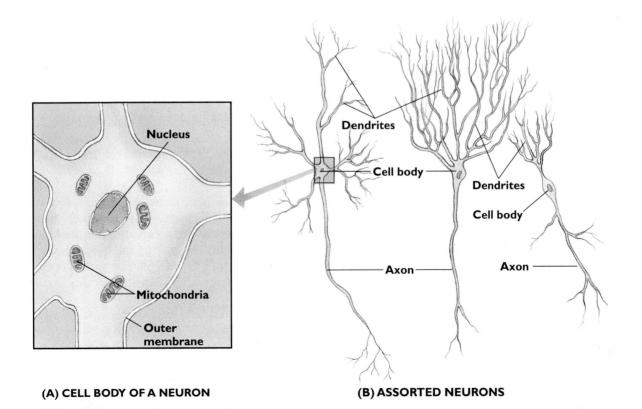

(A) CELL BODY OF A NEURON   **(B) ASSORTED NEURONS**

secreting chemicals to help restore damage, and even sending signals between neurons (Travis, 1994). Without glial cells, neurons could not function.

Neurons have three special features that enable them to communicate signals efficiently. The first is their structure. Although neurons come in many shapes and sizes, they all have long, thin fibers that extend outward from the cell body (see Figure 3.2). When these fibers get close to other neurons, communication between the cells can occur. The intertwining of all these fibers with fibers from other neurons allows each neuron to be in close proximity to thousands or even hundreds of thousands of other neurons (Guroff, 1980).

The fibers extending from a neuron's cell body are called axons and dendrites. **Axons** are the fibers that carry signals away from the cell body, out to where communication occurs with other neurons. Each neuron generally has only one axon leaving the cell body, but that one axon may have many branches. Axons can be very short or several feet long, like the axon that sends signals from the spinal cord all the way down to the big toe. **Dendrites** are the fibers that receive signals from the axons of other neurons and carry those signals to the cell body. A neuron can have many dendrites. Dendrites, too, usually have many branches. Remember that *a*xons carry signals *a*way from the cell body, whereas *d*endrites *d*etect those signals.

The neuron's ability to communicate efficiently also depends on two other features: the "excitable" surface membrane of some of its fibers, and the minute gap, called a **synapse,** between neurons. In the following sections we examine how these features allow a signal to be sent rapidly from one end of the neuron to the other and from one neuron to another.

Action Potentials

To understand the signals in the nervous system, you first need to know something about cell membranes and the chemical molecules within and outside the cell. The cell membrane is *selectively permeable;* that is, it lets some molecules pass through, yet excludes others. Many molecules carry a positive or negative electrochemical charge and are referred to as **ions.** Normally, the membrane maintains an uneven distribution of positively and negatively charged ions inside and outside the cell. The result is that the inside of the cell is slightly negative compared with the outside, and the membrane is said to be *polarized.* Because molecules with a positive charge are attracted to those with a negative charge, a force called an *electrochemical potential* drives positively charged molecules toward the inside of the cell; but many are kept outside by the membrane.

For communication in the nervous system the most important "excluded" molecules are sodium (the same sodium found in table salt), which is symbolized Na^+ when positively charged, and calcium, symbolized Ca^{++}. Sodium and calcium ions are highly concentrated on the outside of the cell and are strongly attracted to negatively charged molecules inside the cell. However, sodium and calcium can pass through the membrane only by going through special openings, or *channels,* in the membrane. These channels are distributed along the axon and dendrites and act as *gates* that can be opened or closed.

Normally the sodium channels along the axon are closed, but changes in the environment of the cell can *depolarize* the membrane, making the area inside the membrane less negative. If the membrane is depolarized to a point called the *threshold,* then the gates swing open (see Figure 3.3). As sodium ions rush in, the adjacent area of the axon becomes more depolarized, thereby causing the neighboring gate to open. This sequence continues, and the change in electrochemical potential spreads like a wild rumor all the way down the axon.

This abrupt change in the potential of an axon is called an **action potential,** and its "contagious" nature is referred to as its *self-propagating* property. When an action potential shoots down an axon, the neuron is said to have *fired.* This is an *all-or-none* type of communication: The cell either fires at full strength or does not fire at all. For many years, scientists believed that only axons were capable of generating action potentials, and that sodium was the ion responsible for them. However, measurement of the

FIGURE 3.3

The Beginning of an Action Potential

This diagrammatic view of a polarized nerve cell shows the normally closed sodium gates in the cell membrane. The electrochemical potential across the membrane is generated by an uneven distribution of positive and negative ions. For example, there are more positive ions, such as sodium (Na^+), on the outside than on the inside. There are also more negative ions, such as negatively charged proteins (Pr^-) on the inside than on the outside. If stimulation causes depolarization near a particular sodium gate, that gate may swing open, allowing sodium to rush into the axon, stimulating the next gate to open, and so on down the axon. The cell is repolarized when the sodium gates are closed and gates are opened for potassium (K^+) to flow out. Calcium gates allow action potentials to spread along dendrites in a similar fashion.

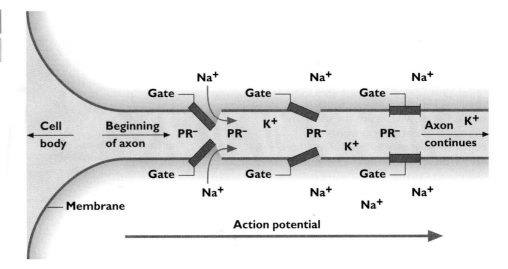

activity of individual gates has recently revealed that action potentials also occur in dendrites (Spruston et al., 1995) and that both sodium and calcium channels are responsible. So action potentials may go in different directions in different neurons. In some, the action potential begins at the axon and shoots down the axon, as already described. In others, action potentials are generated in the dendrites and send a signal into the cell body and on down the axon (Magee & Johnston, 1995). In still others, action potentials beginning in the axon go in both directions—down the axon and also "backward" through the cell body and into the dendrites. Action potentials that spread into the dendrites from the cell body appear to invade some branches and not others, leading scientists to suspect that these messages may be important in strengthening connections between neurons. In Chapters 7 and 8, we discuss how such neural connections might be related to learning and memory, respectively.

The speed of the action potential as it moves down an axon is constant for a particular cell, but in different cells the speed ranges from 0.2 meters per second to 120 meters per second (about 260 miles per hour). The speed depends on the diameter of the axon—larger ones are faster—and on whether myelin is present. **Myelin** (pronounced "my´-a-linn) is a fatty substance that wraps around some axons and speeds action potentials. Larger, myelinated cells usually occur in the parts of the nervous system that carry the most urgently needed information. For example, the sensory neurons that receive information from the environment about onrushing trains, hot irons, and other dangers are fast-acting, myelinated cells. Multiple sclerosis, a severe brain disorder that destroys myelin, occurs because of a virus that is very similar to a component of myelin. When the victim's immune system attacks this virus, it attacks and destroys vital myelin as well, resulting in disruption of vision, speech, balance, and other important functions (Wucherpfennig & Strominger, 1995).

Although each neuron fires or does not fire in an "all-or-none" fashion, its *rate* of firing varies. It can fire over and over because the sodium gates open only briefly and then close. Between firings there is a very brief rest, called a **refractory period.** During this time, gates for positively charged potassium (K^+) open briefly; because of their high concentration on the inside of the axon, these ions flow out of the axon, and the membrane becomes re-polarized. At that point the neuron can fire again. Because the refractory period is quite short, a neuron can send action potentials down its axon at rates of up to 1,000 per second. The *pattern* of repeated action potentials amounts to a coded message. We describe some of the codes used by the nervous system in Chapter 4, on sensation.

Synapses and Communication Between Neurons

How does the action potential in one neuron affect the next neuron? For communication to occur *between* cells, the signal must be transferred across the synapse between

FIGURE 3.4

A Synapse

This photograph taken through an electron microscope shows part of a neural synapse magnified 50,000 times. Clearly visible are the mitochondria; the neurotransmitter-containing vesicles in the ending of the presynaptic cell's axon; the synapse itself, which is the narrow gap between the cells; and the dendrite of the postsynaptic cell.

neurons. Most often, the axon of one cell delivers its signals across a synapse to the dendrites of a second cell; those dendrites in turn transmit the signal to their cell body, which may relay the signal down its axon and thus on to a third cell, and so on. But other communication patterns also occur. Axons can signal to other axons or even directly to the cell body of another neuron; dendrites of one cell can send signals to the dendrites of other cells (Glowinski, 1981). These varied communication patterns allow the brain to conduct extremely complex information-processing tasks.

Neurotransmitters   Unlike the communication down the axon, which uses electrochemical signals, communication at the synapse between neurons relies solely on chemicals. The transfer of information across a synapse is accomplished by chemicals called **neurotransmitters.** These chemicals are stored in numerous little "bags," called *vesicles,* at the tips of axons (see Figure 3.4). When an action potential reaches the end of an axon, a neurotransmitter is released into the synapse, where it spreads to reach the next, or *postsynaptic,* cell (see Figure 3.5).

FIGURE 3.5

Communication Between Neurons

When a neuron fires, a self-propagating action potential shoots to the end of its axon, triggering the release of a neurotransmitter into the synapse. This stimulates neighboring cells. One type of stimulation is *excitatory,* causing depolarization of the neighboring cells. This depolarization, in turn, will cause those neurons to fire an action potential if threshold is reached. New evidence indicates that action potentials can also sometimes occur in dendrites.

1. An action potential shoots down the axon.

2. Neurotransmitters are released into the synapse, changing the membrane potential of the dendrite.

3. If the depolarization is strong enough, it spreads down the dendrite and across the cell body.

4. If the threshold is reached, the cell fires, shooting an action potential down the axon.

FIGURE 3.6

The Relationship Between
Neurotransmitters and Receptors

**Neurotransmitters influence post-
synaptic cells by stimulating special
receptors on the surface of those cells'
membranes. Each type of receptor
receives only one type of neurotransmitter, the two fitting together like
puzzle pieces or like a key in a lock.
Stimulation of these receptors by
their neurotransmitter causes them,
in turn, to either help or hinder the
generation of a wave of depolarization
in their cell's dendrites.**

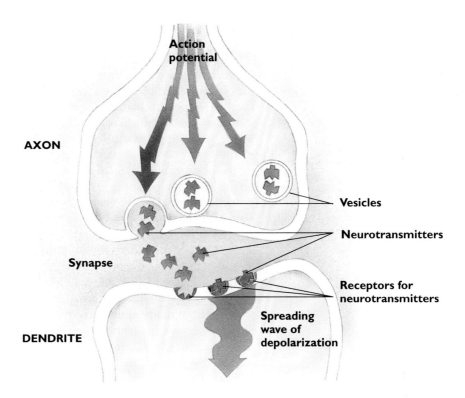

FIGURE 3.7

Electrical Recording of a Single
Sodium Channel

**Scientists are now able to record the
electrical changes that occur when a
single sodium channel opens and
closes. Using a tiny glass tube only
1/25,000th the diameter of a human
hair, they suck up a small "patch" of
cell membrane that contains a channel. When the channel opens, sodium
ions flow through and cause the section of membrane to be less polarized.
Amazingly, when neurotransmitter-
sensitive ion channels are inserted
into non-neural cells, those cells begin
to behave like neurons when neurotransmitters are applied.**

At the postsynaptic membrane, neurotransmitters bind to proteins called **receptors.**
Like a puzzle piece fitting into its proper place, a neurotransmitter snugly fits, or
"binds" to, its own receptors but not to receptors for other neurotransmitters (see
Figure 3.6). The receptors "recognize" only one type of neurotransmitter. However,
each neurotransmitter type can bind to a number of different receptor types. Thus the
same neurotransmitter can have different effects depending on the type of receptor to
which it binds. New receptor types are still being discovered.

The binding of a neurotransmitter to a receptor stimulates channels in the postsynaptic cell to open (much like the sodium channels involved in action potentials),
allowing ions to flow in or out. The flow of ions into and out of the postsynaptic cell
produces a change in its membrane potential; thus, the chemical signal at the synapse
creates an electrochemical signal within the postsynaptic cell.

Excitatory and Inhibitory Signals   Today, scientists can record the extremely small
electrochemical changes that occur as ions flow through a single ion channel, as Figure
3.7 illustrates (Sakmann, 1992). The change in the membrane potential of the dendrite
or cell body of the postsynaptic cell is called the **postsynaptic potential.** It can make the
cell either more likely or less likely to fire. If positively charged ions (such as sodium or

calcium) flow *into* the neuron, it becomes slightly *less* polarized, or *depolarized.* Because depolarization of the membrane can lead the neuron to fire an action potential, a depolarizing postsynaptic potential is called an **excitatory postsynaptic potential,** or **EPSP.** However, if positively charged ions (such as potassium) flow *out* of the neuron (because the concentration of potassium is higher on the inside), or if negatively charged ions flow *in,* the neuron becomes slightly more polarized, or *hyperpolarized.* Hyperpolarization diminishes the likelihood that the neuron will fire an action potential. Thus, a hyperpolarizing postsynaptic potential is called an **inhibitory postsynaptic potential,** or **IPSP.**

The postsynaptic potential spreads along the membrane of the postsynaptic cell. But unlike the action potential in an axon, which remains at a constant strength, the postsynaptic potential fades as it goes along. Usually, it is not strong enough to pass all the way along the dendrite and through the cell body to the axon, so a single EPSP is not enough to cause a neuron to fire. However, each neuron is constantly receiving EPSPs and IPSPs. The combined effect of rapidly repeated potentials or potentials from many locations can create a signal strong enough to reach the junction of the axon and cell body, a specialized region where new action potentials are generated.

Whether or not the postsynaptic cell fires and how rapidly it fires depend on whether, from moment to moment, excitatory ("fire") or inhibitory ("don't fire") signals from many other neurons predominate at this junction (see Figure 3.8). Thus, each neuron constantly integrates or processes information from many other neurons, mediated by multiple neurotransmitters.

Several specific neurotransmitters will be mentioned later in this chapter, and in other chapters as well, because their effects touch on virtually every aspect of psychology. In the next chapter, for example, we describe some of the neurotransmitters used in pathways that convey pain messages throughout the brain and spinal cord. In Chapter 6, we will see that receptors for these neurotransmitters are also the sites at which drugs such as heroin and morphine produce their pain-relieving and euphoric effects. In Chapter 15, on psychological disorders, we discuss the role that neurotransmitters play in schizophrenia and depression. And in Chapter 16, on treatment, we discuss how therapeutic drugs act on neurotransmitters and the cells they affect. Thinking itself requires communication among neurons, and neurotransmitters and their receptors are key links in this vital process.

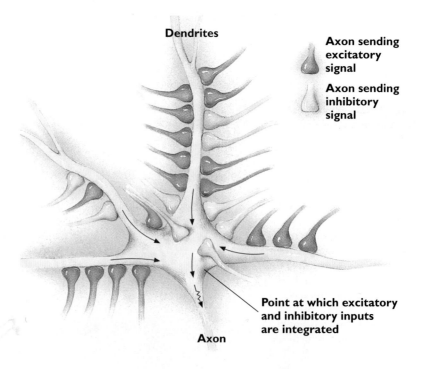

FIGURE 3.8

Integration of Neural Signals

Most of the signals that a neuron receives arrive at its dendrites or at its cell body. These signals, which typically come from many neighboring cells, can be conflicting. Some are excitatory, stimulating the cell to fire; others are inhibitory signals that tell the cell not to fire. Whether the cell actually fires or not at any given moment depends on whether excitatory or inhibitory messages predominate at the junction of the cell body and the axon.

IN REVIEW	Neurons, Neurotransmitters, and Receptors	
Part	**Function**	**Type of Signal Carried**
Axon	Carries signals away from the cell body	The action potential, an all-or-none electrochemical signal, that shoots down the axon to vesicles at the tip of the axon, releasing neurotransmitters
Dendrite	Carries signals to the cell body	The postsynaptic potential, an electrochemical signal that fades as it moves toward the cell body
Synapse	Provides an area for the transfer of signals, usually between axon and dendrite	Chemicals that cross the synapse and reach receptors on another cell
Neurotransmitter	Chemical released by one cell that binds to the receptors on another cell	A chemical message telling the next cell to fire or not to fire its own action potential
Receptor	Proteins on cell membrane that receive chemical signals	Changes in the flow of ions through the cell membrane

Organization and Functions of the Nervous System

Impressive as individual neurons are (see "In Review: Neurons, Neurotransmitters, and Receptors"), an understanding of their functions requires that we look at the organization of groups of neurons. Neurons in the brain and spinal cord are organized into groups called *networks*. Many neurons in a network are reciprocally connected, sending axons to the dendrites of many other neurons in the network. Signals from one network also go to other networks, and small networks are organized into bigger collections. By studying these networks, neuroscientists have begun to see that the nervous system

NERVE CELLS IN THE SPINAL CORD
Neurons in the central nervous system are connected to each other, forming complex communication networks.

FIGURE 3.9

Organization of the Nervous System

The bone-encased central nervous system (CNS) is made up of the brain and spinal cord and acts as the body's central information processor, decision maker, and director of actions. The peripheral nervous system includes all nerves not housed in bone and functions mainly to carry messages. The somatic subsystem of the peripheral nervous system transmits sensory information to the CNS from the outside world and conveys instructions from the CNS to the muscles. The autonomic subsystem conveys messages from the CNS that alter the activity of organs and glands, and sends information about that activity back to the brain.

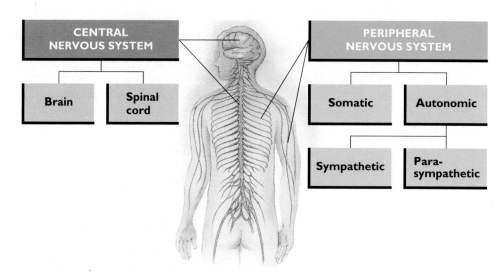

conveys information not so much by the activity of single neurons sending single messages with a particular meaning, but by the activity of *groups* of neurons firing together in varying combinations. Thus, the same neurons may be involved in producing different patterns of behavior, depending on which combinations of them are active. Such combinations have been identified in the simple nervous system of the sea slug (Wu, Cohen & Falk, 1994) as well as in the vastly more complicated brains of rats and monkeys (Schiebera & Hibbard, 1993; Whittington et al., 1995).

The groups of neurons in the nervous system that provide input about the environment are known as the senses, or **sensory systems.** These systems—including hearing, vision, taste, smell, and touch—are described in the next chapter. Integration and processing of information occur mainly in the brain. Output flows through **motor systems,** which are the parts of the nervous system that influence muscles and other organs to respond to the environment.

The nervous system has two major divisions, which work together: the peripheral nervous system and the central nervous system (see Figure 3.9). The **peripheral nervous system,** which includes all of the nervous system that is not housed in bone, carries out sensory and motor functions. The **central nervous system (CNS)** is the part encased in bone. It includes the brain, which is inside the skull, and the spinal cord, which is inside the spinal column (backbone). The CNS is the "central executive" of the body; in other words, information is usually sent to the CNS to be processed and acted on.

THE PERIPHERAL NERVOUS SYSTEM: KEEPING IN TOUCH WITH THE WORLD

As shown in Figure 3.9, the peripheral nervous system has two components, each of which performs both sensory and motor functions.

The Somatic Nervous System

The first is the **somatic nervous system,** which transmits information from the senses to the CNS and carries signals from the CNS to the muscles that move the skeleton. For example, when you lie in the sun at the beach, the somatic nervous system is involved in sending signals from the skin to the brain that become sensations of warmth. The somatic nervous system is also involved in every move you make. Neurons extend from the spinal cord to the muscles, where the release of a neurotransmitter onto them causes the muscles to contract. In fact, much of what we know about neurotransmitters was discovered in laboratory studies of this "neuromuscular junction," especially in the

THE NEUROMUSCULAR JUNCTION When nerve cells (shown here as tan fibers) release neurotransmitters onto muscle tissue, the muscle contracts.

frog's hind leg. At the neuromuscular junction, the action of a neurotransmitter allows a quick response that can mean the difference between life and death, for a frog or anyone else.

The Autonomic Nervous System

The second component of the peripheral nervous system is the **autonomic nervous system;** it carries messages back and forth between the CNS and the heart, lungs, and other organs and glands (Cechetto & Saper, 1990). These messages increase or decrease the activity of the organs and glands to meet varying demands placed on the body. As you lie on the beach, it is your autonomic nervous system that makes your heart beat a little faster when an attractive person walks by and smiles.

The name *autonomic* means "autonomous" and suggests independent operation. This term is appropriate because, although the autonomic nervous system is influenced by the brain, it controls activities that are normally outside of conscious control, such as digestion and perspiration. The autonomic nervous system has two divisions to exercise this control: the sympathetic and parasympathetic branches. Generally, the *sympathetic system* mobilizes the body for action in the face of stress; the responses that result are sometimes collectively referred to as the "fight or flight" response. The *parasympathetic system* regulates the body's functions to conserve energy. Thus, these two branches often create opposite effects. For example, the sympathetic nervous system can make the heart beat faster, whereas the parasympathetic nervous system can slow it down.

The functions of the autonomic nervous system may not get star billing, but you would miss them if they were gone. Just as a race-car driver is nothing without a good pit crew, the somatic nervous system depends on the autonomic nervous system in order to get its job done. For example, when you want to move your muscles, you create a demand for energy; the autonomic nervous system fills the bill by increasing sugar fuels in the bloodstream. If you decide to stand up, you need increased blood pressure so that your blood does not flow out of your brain and settle in your feet. Again, the autonomic nervous system makes the adjustment. Disorders of the autonomic nervous system can make people sweat uncontrollably or faint whenever they stand up; they can also lead to other problems, such as an inability to have sex. We examine the autonomic nervous system in more detail in Chapter 11, on motivation and emotion.

THE CENTRAL NERVOUS SYSTEM: MAKING SENSE OF THE WORLD

The amazing speed and efficiency of the neural networks that make up the central nervous system—the brain and spinal cord—have prompted many people to compare it to the central processor in a computer. In fact, to better understand how human and other brains work and how they relate to sensory and motor systems, *computational neuroscientists* have created neural network models on computers (Koch & Davis, 1994). Figure 3.10 shows an example. Notice that input simultaneously activates several paths in the network, so that information is processed at various places at the same time. Accordingly, the activity of these models is described as *parallel distributed processing*. In the chapters on sensation, perception, learning, and memory, we describe how parallel distributed processing often characterizes the activity of the brain.

However, the flesh-and-blood central nervous system is not neatly laid out like computer circuits or the carefully planned streets of a new suburb. In fact, the CNS looks more like Boston or Montreal, with distinct neighborhoods, winding back streets, and multi-laned expressways. Its "neighborhoods" are collections of neuronal cell bodies called **nuclei.** The "highways" of the central nervous system are made up of axons that travel together in bundles called **fiber tracts** or **pathways.** Like a freeway ramp, the axon from a given cell may merge with and leave fiber tracts, and it may send branches into other tracts. The pathways travel from one nucleus to other nuclei, and scientists have learned much about how the brain works by determining the anatomical connections among nuclei. To begin our description of some of these nuclei and anatomical connections, let's consider a practical example of nervous system functioning.

At 6 A.M., your alarm goes off. The day begins innocently enough with what appears to be a simple case of information processing. Input in the form of sound from the alarm clock is received by your ears, which convert the sound into neural signals that reach your brain. Your brain compares these signals with previous experiences stored in memory and correctly associates the sound with "alarm clock." However, your output is somewhat impaired because your brain's activity has not yet reached the waking state. It directs your muscles poorly: Stumbling into the kitchen, you touch a glowing heating element as you reach for the coffee pot. Now things get more lively. Heat energy activates sensory neurons in your fingers, which generate action potentials that flash along fiber tracts going into the spinal cord.

The Spinal Cord

The **spinal cord** receives signals from peripheral senses, including pain and touch from the fingertips, and relays those signals to the brain through fibers within the cord. Neurons in the spinal cord also carry signals downward, from the brain to the muscles. In addition, cells of the spinal cord can direct some simple behaviors without instructions from the brain. These behaviors are called **reflexes** because the response to an incoming signal is directly "reflected" back out (see Figure 3.11).

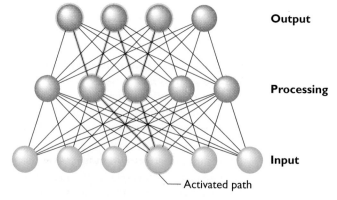

Output

Processing

Input

Activated path

Source: Hinton, 1992.

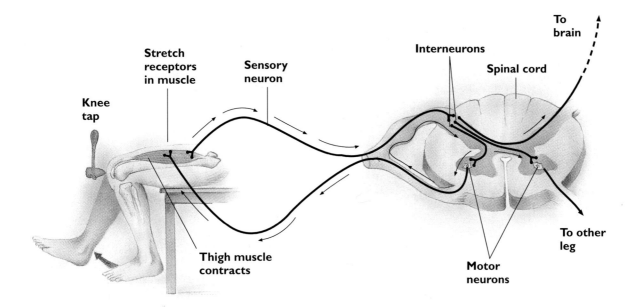

Knee tap

Stretch receptors in muscle

Sensory neuron

Interneurons

To brain

Spinal cord

Thigh muscle contracts

Motor neurons

To other leg

FIGURE 3.11

A Reflex Pathway

A tap on the knee sets off an almost instantaneous sequence of events, beginning with the stimulation of sensory neurons that respond to stretch. When those neurons fire, their axons, which end within the spinal cord, cause interneurons to fire. This in turn stimulates the firing of motor neurons with axons ending in the thigh muscles. The result is a contraction of the thigh muscles and a kicking of the lower leg and foot. Information about the knee tap and about what the leg has done also ascends to the cerebral cortex, but the reflex is completed without waiting for guidance from the brain.

For example, when you touched that heating element, impulses from sensory neurons in your fingers reflexively activated motor neurons, which caused muscles in your arm to contract and quickly withdraw your hand. Because spinal reflexes like this one include few time-consuming synaptic links, they are very fast. And because spinal reflexes occur without instructions from the brain, they are considered involuntary; but they also send action potentials along fiber tracts going to the brain. Thus, you officially "know" you have been burned a fraction of a second after your reflex got you out of trouble.

The story does not end there, however. When a simple reflex set off by touching something hot causes one set of arm muscles to contract, an opposing set of muscles relaxes. If this did not happen, the arm would go rigid. Furthermore, muscles have receptors that send impulses to the spinal cord to let it know how extended they are, so that a reflex pathway can adjust the muscle contraction to allow smooth movement. Thus, the spinal cord is an example of a *feedback system,* a series of processes in which information about the consequences of an action goes back to the source of the action, so that adjustments can be made.

In the spinal cord, sensory neurons are often called *afferent* neurons and motor neurons are termed *efferent* neurons, because *afferent* means "coming toward" and *efferent,* "going away." To remember these terms, notice that *afferent* and *approach* both begin with *a; efferent* and *exit* both begin with *e.*

The Brain

The brain has three major subdivisions: the hindbrain, the midbrain, and the forebrain. Table 3.1 and Figures 3.12 and 3.13 describe and illustrate some of the techniques scientists use to learn about these structures and how they function.

The Hindbrain   Incoming signals first reach the **hindbrain,** which is actually a continuation of the spinal cord. As you can see in Figure 3.14, the hindbrain lies inside the skull. Blood pressure, heart rate, breathing, and many other vital autonomic functions are controlled by nuclei in the hindbrain, particularly in an area called the **medulla.**

Threading throughout the hindbrain and into the midbrain is a collection of cells that are not arranged in any well-defined nucleus. Because the collection looks like a net, it is called the **reticular formation** (*reticular* means "netlike"). This network is very important in altering the activity of the rest of the brain. It is involved, for example, in arousal and attention; if the fibers from the reticular system are disconnected from the rest of the brain, a person goes into a permanent coma. Some of the fibers carrying pain

Technique	What It Shows	Advantages (+) and Disadvantages (−)
EEG (electroencephalogram) Multiple electrodes are pasted to outside of head	A single line that charts the summated electrical fields resulting from the activity of billions of neurons	+High temporal resolution (thousandths of seconds) to monitor stages of cognitive processing −No indication of anatomical source of activity
PET (positron emission tomography) and SPECT (single photon emission computed tomography) Positrons and photons are emissions from radioactive substances	An image of the concentration and localization of any molecule that can be injected in a radioactive form: for example, drugs, neurotransmitters, or tracers for blood flow or oxygen consumption (which reflect local changes in neuronal activity)	+Allows functional and biochemical studies +Concentration is color-coded, making activity easy to visualize −Requires exposure to low levels of radioactivity −Spatial resolution is not as good as with MRI −Rapid changes (faster than 30 seconds) cannot be followed
MRI (magnetic resonance imaging) Exposes the brain to magnetic field and measures radiofrequency waves	An image of structure: fibers appear white and nuclei appear gray	+No radioactivity +High spatial resolution of anatomical details (<1 mm)
FMRI (functional MRI)	Reveals changes in blood flow (which reflect changes in neuronal activity)	+High-speed MRI has higher temporal resolution than PET (<1/10 of a second)

TABLE 3.1

Noninvasive Techniques for Studying Human Brain Function and Structure

Neuroscientists have developed a number of techniques for studying the structure and functions of the brain.

signals from the spinal cord make connections in the reticular formation, which immediately arouses the rest of the brain from sleep. Within seconds, the hindbrain causes your heart rate and blood pressure to increase.

Activity of the reticular formation also leads to activity in a small nucleus called the **locus coeruleus** (pronounced "lo´-kus seh-roo´-lee-us), which means "blue spot" (Aston-Jones et al., 1991a). There are relatively few cells in the locus coeruleus—only about 30,000 of the 100 billion or so in the human brain (Foote, Bloom & Aston-Jones, 1983)—but each sends out an axon that branches extensively, making contact with as many as 100,000 other cells (Moore & Bloom, 1979; Swanson, 1976). Studies of rats and monkeys suggest that the locus coeruleus is involved in the state of vigilance (Aston-Jones, Chiang & Alexinsky, 1991b). In humans, abnormalities in the locus coeruleus have been linked to depression; however, as noted in the chapter on psychological disorders, the exact cause of the disorder is not clear.

The **cerebellum** is also part of the hindbrain. Its primary function is to control finely coordinated movements, such as threading a needle. The cerebellum also allows the eyes to track a moving target accurately (Krauzlis & Lisberger, 1991), and it may be the storehouse for well-rehearsed movements, such as those associated with ballet, piano playing, and athletics (McCormick & Thompson, 1984). Recent work on the function of the cerebellum highlights the fact that there are different ways to think about what various parts of the brain do. You can think of coordinated movements as "motor functioning" or as an example of the more general activity of "sequencing and timing." The importance of sequencing has become increasingly apparent in the study of non-movement activities, particularly language. To speak fluently, you must put together a sequence of words, rapidly and in the correct order. It now appears that the cerebellum plays a vital role in normal speech by integrating moment-to-moment feedback about vocal sounds with a sequence of precise movements of the lips and tongue (Leiner, Leiner & Dow, 1993). When this process of integration and sequencing is disrupted, stuttering can result. Even nonstutterers who hear their own speech with a slight delay begin to stutter. (This is why radio talk-show hosts ask callers to turn off their radios;

FIGURE 3.12

FIGURE 3.12

PET Scans of Brain Activity While Viewing Words and Nonwords

These patterns of brain activity were revealed by **PET** scans as a subject looked at four types of stimuli: a "word" made up of geometrical patterns that resemble letters but are not; a word made of letter patterns that cannot be pronounced; a pseudoword that follows the rules of spelling; and a meaningful word. Note that some areas of the brain are activated by all four tasks, that some areas are activated only by the pseudo-word and the real word, and that the real word creates the most intense activity in these regions (Petersen et al., 1990). Similar studies using auditory (sound) stimuli show that different parts of the brain are activated depending on whether sounds convey words or not, and on whether the listener is trying to decide about the sound of words (for example, was it *pig* or *big*?) or about which of two sounds had a higher pitch (Zatorre et al., 1992).

listening to the delayed sounds of their own voice on the radio can cause callers to stutter.) If, as some have suggested, stuttering is a result of problems in sensory feedback, the cerebellum may be involved.

Reflexes and feedback systems are important to the functioning of the hindbrain, just as they are in the spinal cord. For example, if blood pressure drops, heart action increases reflexively to compensate for that drop. If you stand up very quickly, your blood pressure can drop so suddenly that it produces lightheadedness until the hindbrain reflex "catches up." If the hindbrain does not activate autonomic nervous system mechanisms to increase blood pressure, you will faint.

FIGURE 3.13

Combining PET Scans and Magnetic Resonance Imaging

PET scans provide excellent data about the brain's activity but imprecise information about structures. Much clearer pictures of structures come from magnetic resonance imaging (MRI), which detects the magnetic fields that surround the atoms in brain tissue. Researchers have superimposed images from both techniques to construct a three-dimensional view of the living brain. This figure shows the brain of a young epileptic girl. The picture of the outer surface of the brain is from the MRI; the pink area is from **PET** and shows the source of epileptic activity. The images at the right are the MRI and **PET** images at one plane, or "slice," through the brain (indicated by the line on the brain at the left).

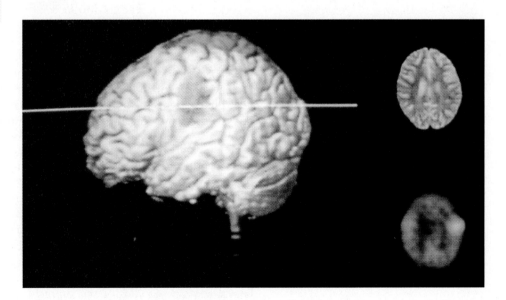

Major Structures of the Brain

This view from the side of a section cut down the middle of the brain reveals the forebrain, midbrain, hindbrain, and spinal cord. Many of these subdivisions do not have clear-cut borders, since they are all interconnected by fiber tracts. Indeed, though beautifully adapted to its functions, the brain was not the work of a city planner. Its anatomy reflects its evolution over millions of years. Newer structures (such as the cerebral cortex, which is the outer surface of the forebrain) that handle higher mental functions were built on older ones (like the medulla) that coordinate heart rate, breathing, and other more basic functions.

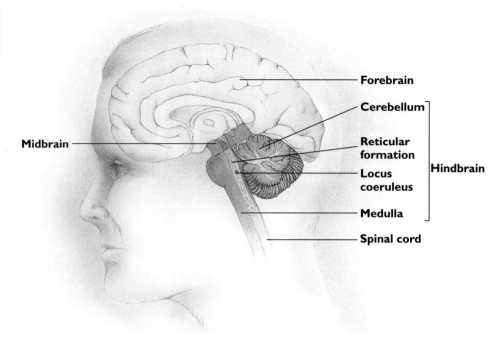

The Midbrain   Above the hindbrain is the **midbrain.** In humans it is a small structure, but it serves some very important functions. Certain types of automatic behaviors that integrate simple movements with sensory input are controlled there. For example, when you move your head, midbrain circuits allow you to move your eyes smoothly in the opposite direction, so that you can keep your eyes focused on an object despite the movement of your head. And when a loud noise causes you to turn your head reflexively and look in the direction of the sound, your midbrain circuits are at work.

One vital midbrain nucleus is the **substantia nigra,** meaning "black substance." This small area and its connections to the **striatum** (named for its "striped" appearance) in the forebrain are necessary for the smooth initiation of movement. Without them, you would find it difficult, if not impossible, to get up out of a chair, lift your hand to swat a fly, move your mouth to form words, or, yes, reach for that coffee pot.

The Forebrain   In humans the **forebrain** has grown so out of proportion to the rest of the brain that it folds back over and completely covers the other parts. It is responsible for the most complex aspects of behavior and mental life. As Figure 3.15 shows, the forebrain includes parts known as the *diencephalon* and the *cerebrum;* the latter is covered by the *cerebral cortex.*

The diencephalon includes two structures deep within the brain—the hypothalamus and the thalamus—that are involved in emotion, basic drives, and sensation. The **thalamus** relays pain signals from the spinal cord as well as signals from the eyes and most other sense organs to upper levels in the brain, and it plays an important role in processing and making sense out of this information. Under the thalamus lies the **hypothalamus** (*hypo-* means "under"), which plays an important role in regulating hunger, thirst, and sex drives. It has many connections to and from the autonomic nervous system and the endocrine system, as well as to other parts of the brain. Destruction of one section of the hypothalamus results in an overwhelming urge to eat. Damage to another area of the male's hypothalamus causes the sex organs to degenerate and the sex drive to decrease drastically. There is also a fascinating part of the hypothalamus that contains the brain's own timepiece: the **suprachiasmatic nuclei.** The suprachiasmatic nuclei keep an approximately twenty-four-hour clock that determines your biological rhythms. Studies of the suprachiasmatic nuclei in animals suggest it is for biological reasons that many people are "morning people" or "night people," with different periods of greatest alertness. This characteristic is stable throughout a lifetime

Some Structures of the Forebrain

The forebrain is divided into the cerebrum and the diencephalon. The structures of the cerebrum are covered by the outer "bark" of the cerebral cortex. This diagram shows some of the structures that lie deep within the cerebrum, as well as structures of the diencephalon.

(Cofer et al., 1992). We discuss the functions of the hypothalamus in more detail in the chapter on motivation and emotion.

The largest part of the forebrain is the **cerebrum.** Two structures within it, the **amygdala** and **hippocampus,** are important in memory and emotion. For example, the amygdala associates features of stimuli from two sensory modalities, such as linking the shape and feel of objects in memory (Murray & Mishkin, 1985). It is also involved in fear and other emotions (Davis, Rainnie & Cassell, 1994; LeDoux, 1995); its activity has been found to be altered in people suffering from posttraumatic stress disorder, which you will read about in Chapter 13. Damage to the hippocampus results in an inability to form new memories of events. In one case, a patient known as R.B. suffered a stroke (an interruption of blood flow to the brain) that damaged only his hippocampus. Although tests indicated that his intelligence was above average and he could recall old memories, he was almost totally unable to build new memories (Squire, 1986). Research using MRI scans and tests of the decline of memory function in normal elderly people suggests that memory ability is correlated with the size of the hippocampus (Golomb et al., 1994). Animal studies have also shown that damage to the hippocampus within a day of a mildly painful experience erases memories of the experience, but that removal of the hippocampus several days after the experience has no effect on the memory. Thus, memories are not permanently stored in the hippocampus but, rather, are transferred elsewhere.

In fact, the way memories are stored, as well as the way they are formed, seems to depend partly on the type of memory involved. For example, the hippocampus is critical in associating an unpleasant experience with a particular *place,* but it is not involved in associating the unpleasant experience with particular *sounds* (Kim & Fanselow, 1992). As described in Chapter 8, your storehouse of memories depends on the activities of many parts of the brain.

The hippocampus and amygdala are both part of the **limbic system,** which is a set of interconnected structures that play important roles in regulating emotion and memory. Among the other structures in the limbic system are the hypothalamus and the septum. Severe degeneration of neurons in the hippocampus and other limbic structures occurs in victims of Alzheimer's disease (see Figure 3.16). Alzheimer's disease is a major cause of dementia, the deterioration of cognitive capabilities often associated with aging. About 10 percent of people over the age of sixty-five, and 47 percent of people

Source: Seab et al., 1988.

FIGURE 3.16

Alzheimer's Disease and the Hippocampus

These magnetic resonance images of living brains show that, compared to the normal person (left), a patient with Alzheimer's disease shows degeneration in the hippocampus (marked *H*). On average, the hippocampus of Alzheimer's patients has been found to be 40 percent smaller than in normal people. Damage to the hippocampus may be responsible for the severe memory impairments in Alzheimer's disease.

over eighty-five, suffer from this disorder (Evans et al., 1989). The financial cost of Alzheimer's disease is more than $80 billion a year in the United States alone (Selkoe, 1991); the cost in human suffering is incalculable.

FOCUS ON RESEARCH METHODS

Manipulating Genes

What causes Alzheimer's disease? Postmortem microscopic examination of the brains of Alzheimer's disease victims reveals features known as plaques and tangles. *Plaques* are deposits of protein and parts of dead cells found between neurons. The major component of plaques is a small protein called *beta-amyloid,* which is produced from a larger protein called beta-amyloid precursor protein. *Tangles* are twisted fibers within neurons; their main protein component is called *tau.*

For years, scientists have worked to discover how beta-amyloid and tau might be responsible for the death of neurons seen in Alzheimer's disease, but their progress has been slowed by the lack of an Alzheimer's-like condition in any species of animal. With an "animal model" of the disease, scientists could study the causes and treatment of Alzheimer's using animals as subjects in experiments that could not ethically be performed with humans. As described in Chapter 2, experiments involve manipulating an independent variable, such as a drug treatment for Alzheimer's, and measuring its effect on a dependent variable—in this case, memory abilities.

Experimental methods are also being used in efforts to create, literally, an animal model of Alzheimer's. If Alzheimer's disease is caused by faulty beta-amyloid precursor protein, inserting the gene for this faulty protein into the cells of mice should cause deposits of beta-amyloid and the loss of neurons in the same parts of the brain as those seen in human Alzheimer's victims. At the same time, there should be no change in a control group of untreated animals. However, finding the desired result is not enough. An experiment's results must be replicable in order to be reliable. Thus, in 1992, one group of scientists reported success in creating a model of Alzheimer's disease in mice, only to retract their statements when they could not repeat their results. More recently, researchers at a biotechnology company have repeatedly succeeded in implanting the faulty protein into mice whose brains then show damage characteristic of Alzheimer's disease (Games et al., 1995). The scientists are now conducting experiments to determine whether these mice show the same kinds of memory impairment seen in human Alzheimer's patients. If they do, an animal model of the disease will finally be available.

Experimental modification of animal genes is a powerful new technique for testing all kinds of hypotheses about biological factors influencing behavior. Besides *inserting*

GENE MANIPULATION IN MICE In one study, the gene for a particular type of neurotransmitter receptor was "knocked out" in these black mice. As shown here, the animals were much more aggressive than a control group of brown mice (Nelson et al., 1995).

new or modified genes into brain cells, scientists can manipulate an independent variable by "knocking out" specific genes, then looking at the effect on dependent variables. One research team has shown, for example, that knocking out a gene for a particular type of neurotransmitter receptor causes mice to become obese, overeating even when given appetite-suppressant drugs (Tecott et al., 1995). Genetic elimination of another type of receptor in mice canceled out the stimulating effects of cocaine (Xu et al., 1994).

The lack of animal models of obesity, drug addiction, Alzheimer's disease, and other problems has impeded progress in finding biological treatments for them. In the case of Alzheimer's, for example, there have been only occasional reports in which drugs had any effect in slowing the progression of the disease or improving its elderly victims' deteriorating memory capacities. Drugs intended to improve cognitive functioning are called *nootropic* drugs (from *noos*, which is Greek for "mind").

In some cities around the world, nootropics are touted as "smart drugs" and sold at "smart bars" in combination with vitamins and other ingredients. Are "smart drugs" really effective, or are they modern-day snake oil, giving no more than the illusion of a sharpened mind?

THINKING CRITICALLY

Are There Drugs That Can Make You Smarter?

What am I being asked to believe or accept?

The belief that certain drugs can enhance memory was popularized in a 1990 book by John Morgenthaler and Ward Dean, *Smart Drugs and Nutrients*. In an interview that year, thirty-one-year-old Morgenthaler said he had been taking "smart drugs" for ten years, about eight pills twice a day. "It's not a scientific study; I may have gotten smarter just from growing up, educating myself and stimulating my brain. But I do stop taking the drugs every now and then, and I know that I have better concentration, attention and memory when I'm on them" (Greenwald, 1991).

What evidence is available to support the assertion?

There is certainly an element of truth to the idea that some of these drugs can improve cognitive performance under some circumstances. Animals given the drugs under controlled conditions show statistically significant improvements in performance on tasks requiring attention and memory. The chemicals used in these drugs include piracetam, vinpocetine, codergocrine (Hydergine), and vasopressin. Pramiracetam and other new variants of piracetam have been shown to be more effective than piracetam itself in facilitating the formation of new memories and the retrieval of old ones (Nicholson, 1990). Consistent with their behavioral effects, these drugs have measurable biochemical effects on the brain. Some have general effects on brain metabolism and also increase blood sugar levels; others affect specific neurotransmitters (Pepeu, 1994; Wenk, 1989).

Do "smart drugs" work with humans? One study of elderly people with general cerebral impairment found significant improvement after twelve weeks of treatment with piracetam. There have also been reports that the drugs have positive effects on memory and cognition in normal persons. For example, tenilsetam, a piracetam-like drug, was associated with improved performance on several tests of cognitive performance by eighteen-year-old college students (Wesnes, Simpson & Kidd, 1987). And vinpocetine has been shown to improve memory in normal volunteers (Subhan & Hindmarch, 1985) as well as in elderly people with memory impairments due to poor blood circulation to the brain (Balestreri, Fontana & Astengo, 1987).

Are there alternative ways of interpreting the evidence?

Glowing testimonials from individuals who feel they are helped by a drug may reflect their *belief* in the drug, not the effectiveness of the drug itself. For example, in 1894, when the scientist Charles Edouard Brown-Sequard was feeling old and tired, he gave himself injections of an extract made of ground-up dog testicles. He reported a return of youthful energy and sharpened cognitive abilities, but it was all a placebo effect. Only carefully controlled double-blind studies can separate the effect of patients' expectancies from the specific effects of drug or other treatments.

Some of those studies show that nootropic drugs have positive effects on memory and other cognitive functions. These effects are statistically significant but tend to be small and inconsistent. Often, the drugs primarily affect attentiveness, and the improvements are no greater than those caused by having a cup of coffee (Service, 1994). Overall, evidence from properly designed studies shows nootropic drugs to be a major disappointment (Bartus et al., 1982; Schindler, 1989). Even their benefits for Alzheimer's patients may be temporary (Claus et al., 1991).

What additional evidence would help to evaluate the alternatives?

Researchers are evaluating several promising new categories of nootropic drugs in animals (e.g., Staubli et al., 1994). It will take years of study to determine which drugs are truly effective for memory enhancement, and under what circumstances. It will also take time to learn whether the drugs affect memory or related processes such as motivation or attention. Research on side effects will also be needed. For example, tacrine, one of the more effective drugs for Alzheimer's, was found to cause serious liver damage in about one-third of those who took it (Molloy et al., 1991). And vasopressin, which has occasionally been found to improve memory in humans, may create nausea and increased blood pressure (Goodman-Gilman et al., 1990).

What conclusions are most reasonable?

In spite of their unimpressive showing overall, nootropic drugs are sometimes used with Alzheimer's patients, mainly for lack of better alternatives (Pepeu, 1994). Currently available drugs for improving memory are limited in effectiveness, but proponents argue that even if the drugs only delay the institutionalization of Alzheimer's patients for several months, the savings to society are substantial. As for the drinks you can buy in "smart bars," be sure they taste good, because their effect on your mental powers is likely to be minimal. Indeed, the memory strategies described in Chapter 8 are likely to be far more effective in helping you remember information and do well in school. Further, educational achievement—and a life of working at a job that engages the mind—has been associated with a lowered risk for, or at least the delayed appearance of, Alzheimer's disease (Stern et al., 1994). We now offer you an opportunity to engage your mind by learning about a few more parts of the brain.

The Cerebral Cortex

So far, we have described some key structures within the forebrain. There are other structures on its surface. The outermost part of the cerebrum appears rather round and has right and left halves that are similar in appearance. These halves are called the **cerebral hemispheres.** The outer surface of the cerebral hemispheres, the **cerebral cortex,** has a surface area of one to two square feet—an area that is larger than it looks because of the folds that allow the cortex to fit compactly inside the skull. The cerebral cortex is much larger in humans than in other animals (with a few exceptions, such as dolphins). It is associated with the analysis of information from all the senses, control of voluntary movements, higher-order thought, and other complex aspects of human behavior and mental processes.

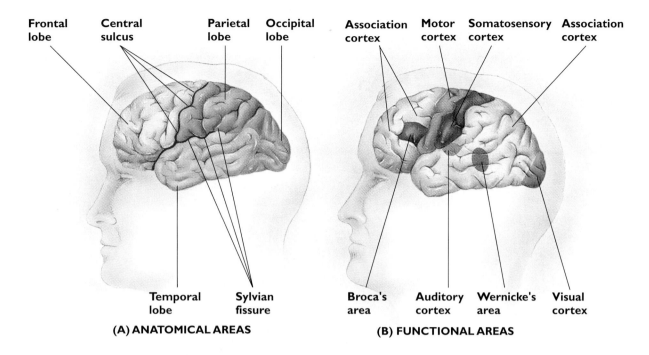

(A) ANATOMICAL AREAS

Frontal lobe · Central sulcus · Parietal lobe · Occipital lobe · Temporal lobe · Sylvian fissure

(B) FUNCTIONAL AREAS

Association cortex · Motor cortex · Somatosensory cortex · Association cortex · Broca's area · Auditory cortex · Wernicke's area · Visual cortex

FIGURE 3.17

The Cerebral Cortex (viewed from the left side)

The ridges (gyri) and valleys (sulci) are landmarks that divide the cortex into four lobes: the frontal, the parietal, the occipital, and the temporal. These terms describe anatomical regions, but the cortex is also divided in terms of function. These functional areas include the motor cortex (which controls movement), sensory cortex (which receives information from the senses), and association cortex (which integrates information). Also illustrated are Wernicke's area, which is involved in the interpretation of speech, and Broca's area, a region vital to the production of speech. (These two areas are found only on the left side of the cortex.)

The folds of the cerebral cortex give the surface of the human brain its wrinkled appearance, its ridges and valleys. The ridges are called *gyri* and the valleys, *sulci* or *fissures*. As you can see in Figure 3.17, several deep sulci divide the cortex into four areas: the *frontal, parietal, occipital,* and *temporal lobes*. Thus, the gyri and sulci provide landmarks for describing the cortex, although the functions of the cortex do not follow these boundaries. Divided according to functions, the cortex includes areas called the sensory cortex, association cortex, and motor cortex.

Sensory and Motor Cortex   Different regions of the **sensory cortex** receive information about different senses. As Figure 3.17 shows, the sensory cortex lies in the parietal, occipital, and temporal lobes. Cells in the occipital lobe receive visual information; information from the ears reaches cells in the temporal lobe. Cells in the parietal lobe take in information from the skin about touch, pain, and temperature; these areas are called the *somatosensory cortex*. Information about skin sensations from neighboring parts of the body comes to neighboring parts of the somatosensory cortex, as Figure 3.18 illustrates. It is as if the outline of a tiny person, dangling upside down, determined the location of the information. This pattern is called the *homunculus*, Latin for "little man."

Neurons in specific areas of the **motor cortex,** which is in the frontal lobe, initiate voluntary movements in specific parts of the body. Some control movement of the hand; others stimulate movement of the foot, the knee, the head, and so on. The specific muscles activated by these regions are linked not to specific neurons but, as mentioned earlier, to the patterned activity of many neurons. Some of the same neurons are active in moving different fingers, for example, but the *combinations* of neurons differ from finger to finger (Schieber & Hibbard, 1993). The motor cortex is arranged in a way that mirrors the somatosensory cortex. For example, as you can see in Figure 3.18, the parts of the motor cortex that control the hands are near parts of the sensory cortex that receive sensory information from the hands.

Controlling the movement of the body may seem simple: You have a map of body parts in the cortex, and you activate cells in the hand region if you want to move your hand. But the actual process is much more complex. Recall again your sleepy reach for the coffee pot. The cortex must first translate the coffee pot's location in space into coordinates relative to your body; for example, your hand must be moved to the right

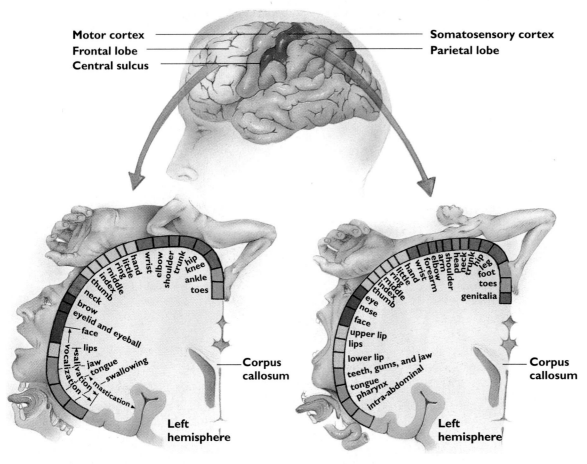

(A) MOTOR AREAS (END VIEW)　　　　　**(B) SENSORY AREAS (END VIEW)**

Source: Penfield & Rasmussen, 1968.

Note: Can you find the error in this classic drawing? (The figure shows the right side of the body, but the left hand and left side of the face.)

FIGURE 3.18

Motor and Somatosensory Cortex

The areas of cortex that move parts of the body (motor cortex) and receive sensory input from body parts (somatosensory cortex) occupy neighboring regions on each side of the central sulcus. These regions appear in both hemispheres; here we show cross-sections of only those on the left side, looking from the back of the brain toward the front. The cross-sections also show how areas controlling movement of neighboring parts of the body, like the foot and leg, occupy neighboring parts of the motor cortex. Areas receiving input from neighboring body parts, such as the lips and tongue, are near one another in the sensory cortex.

LINKAGES　Where are the brain's language centers? (a link to Thought and Language)

or left of your body. Next, the cortex must determine which muscles must be contracted to produce those movements. Populations of neurons work together to produce just the right combinations of direction and force in the particular muscle groups necessary to create the desired effects. Many interconnected areas of the cortex are involved in making these determinations. Artificial neural networks are demonstrating how these exquisitely complex problem-solving processes might occur (Kalaska & Crammond, 1992).

Association Cortex　Parts of the cerebral cortex that are not directly involved with either receiving specific sensory information or initiating movement are referred to as **association cortex.** These are the areas that perform such complex cognitive tasks as associating words with images. The term *association* is appropriate because these areas either receive information from more than one sense or combine sensory and motor information. Association cortex occurs in all of the lobes and forms a large part of the cerebral cortex in human beings. For this reason, damage to association areas can create severe deficits in all kinds of mental abilities.

One of the most devastating deficits, called *aphasia,* involves difficulty in producing or understanding speech. Language information comes from the auditory cortex (for spoken language) or from the visual cortex (for written language); areas of the motor cortex produce speech (Geschwind, 1979). But the complex function known as language also involves activity in association cortex. In the 1860s Paul Broca described the

"Whoa! *That* was a good one! Try it, Hobbs —
just poke his brain right where my finger is."

difficulties that result from damage to the association cortex in the frontal lobe near motor areas that control facial muscles. This part of the cortex on the left side of the brain is called *Broca's area* (see Figure 3.17). When Broca's area is damaged, the mental organization of speech suffers. Victims have great difficulty speaking, and what they say is often grammatically incorrect. Each word comes slowly. One patient who was asked about a dental appointment said haltingly, "Yes . . . Monday . . . Dad and Dick . . . Wednesday 9 o'clock . . . 10 o'clock . . . doctors . . . and . . . teeth" (Geschwind, 1979). The ideas—dentists and teeth—are right, but the fluency is gone. A fascinating aspect of the disorder is that when a person with Broca's aphasia sings, the words come fluently and correctly. Presumably, words set to music are handled by a different part of the brain.

Other language problems result from damage to a portion of association cortex described in the 1870s by Carl Wernicke (pronounced "ver-nick-ee"). Like Broca's area, *Wernicke's area* is also on the left side; it is in the temporal lobe, near the area of sensory cortex that receives information from the ears, as Figure 3.17 shows. Wernicke's area also receives input from the visual cortex. It is involved in the interpretation of both speech and written words. Damage to Wernicke's area produces complicated symptoms. It can leave fluency intact but disrupt the ability to understand the meaning of words or to speak comprehensibly. One patient who was asked to describe a picture of two boys stealing cookies behind a woman's back said, "Mother is away here working her work to get her better, but when she's looking the two boys looking in the other part. She's working another time" (Geschwind, 1979).

It appears that differing areas of cortex are activated depending on whether language is spoken or written and whether particular grammatical and conceptual categories are involved (see Figure 3.12). For example, two women (H.W. and S.J.D.) each had a stroke in 1985, causing damage to different language-related parts of their association cortex. Neither woman has difficulty speaking or writing nouns, but both have difficulty with verbs (Caramazza & Hillis, 1991). H.W. can write verbs but cannot speak them. S.J.D can speak verbs but has difficulty writing them. Furthermore, H.W. had difficulty pronouncing *watch* when it was used as a verb in the sentence "I watch TV" but spoke the same word easily when it appeared as a noun in "My watch is slow." Another person

MOVEMENT AND THE BRAIN Smooth movements require the coordination of neural activity in both the brain and the spinal cord. Without this co-ordination, walking would be a jerky affair, similar to the movements seen when this paralyzed woman receives computer-controlled electrical stimulation of her leg muscles.

with damage in a different language area lost the ability to name certain nouns, specifically fruits and vegetables! He could name an abacus or a sphinx, but when presented with an apple or an artichoke he was dumbfounded (Hart, Berndt & Caramazza, 1985). Another bizarre language abnormality following brain damage is "foreign accent syndrome," as exemplified in a recent report about a thirty-two-year-old stroke victim whose native language was English. His speech was slurred immediately after the stroke, but as it improved, he began to speak with a Scandinavian accent, adding syllables to some words ("How are you today-ah?") and pronouncing "hill" as "heel." His normal accent did not fully return for four months (Takayama et al., 1993). Case studies of "foreign accent syndrome" suggest that specific regions of the brain are involved in the sound of language, while others are involved in various aspects of its meaning.

The Divided Brain in a Unified Self

A striking idea emerged from observations of people with damage to the language areas of the brain. Researchers noticed that damage to limited areas of the left hemisphere impaired the ability to use or comprehend language, while damage to corresponding parts of the right hemisphere usually did not. Perhaps, then, the right and left halves of the brain serve different functions.

This concept was not entirely new. It had long been understood, for example, that most sensory and motor pathways cross over as they enter or leave the brain. As a result, the *left hemisphere* receives information from and controls movements of the *right* side of the body, while the *right hemisphere* receives input from and controls the *left* side of the body. However, *both* sides of the brain perform these functions. In contrast, the fact that language centers, such as Broca's area and Wernicke's area, are almost exclusively on the left side of the brain suggested that each hemisphere might be specialized to perform some functions almost independently of the other hemisphere.

In the late 1800s there was great interest in the hypothesis that the hemispheres might be specialized, but no techniques were available for testing it. Renewed interest in the issue grew out of studies during the 1960s by Roger Sperry, Michael Gazzaniga, and their colleagues.

Split-Brain Studies Sperry studied *split-brain* patients—people who had undergone a radical surgical procedure in an attempt to control severe epilepsy. Before the surgery, their seizures began in one hemisphere and then spread to engulf the whole brain. As a last resort, surgeons isolated the two hemispheres from each other by severing the **corpus callosum,** a massive bundle of more than a million fibers that connects the two hemispheres (see Figure 3.19).

After the surgery, researchers used a special apparatus to present visual images to only *one* side of these patients' split brains (see Figure 3.20). They found that severing the tie between the hemispheres had dramatically affected the way these people thought about and dealt with the world. For example, when the image of a spoon was presented to the left, language-oriented side of patient N.G.'s split brain, she could say what the spoon was; but when the spoon was presented to the right side of her brain, she could not describe the spoon in words. She still knew what the object was, however. Using her left hand (controlled by the right hemisphere), N.G. could pick out the spoon from a group of other objects by its shape. But when asked what she had just grasped, she replied, "A pencil." The right hemisphere recognized the object, but the patient could not describe it because the left (language) half of her brain did not see or feel it (Sperry, 1968).

Although the right hemisphere has no control over spoken language in split-brain patients, it does have important capabilities, including some related to nonspoken language. For example, a split-brain patient's right hemisphere can guide the left hand in spelling out words with Scrabble tiles (Gazzaniga & LeDoux, 1978). Thanks to this ability, researchers discovered that the right hemisphere of split-brain patients has self-awareness and normal learning abilities. In addition, it is superior to the left on tasks dealing with spatial relations, especially drawing three-dimensional shapes, and at recognizing human faces.

LINKAGES **Which parts of the brain control which mental abilities?** (a link to Mental Abilities)

FIGURE 3.19

The Brain's Left and Right Hemispheres

The brain's two hemispheres are joined by a core bundle of nerve fibers known as the corpus callosum; in this figure the corpus callosum has been cut and the two hemispheres are separated. The two cerebral hemispheres look nearly the same but perform somewhat different tasks. For one thing, the left hemisphere receives sensory input from and controls movement on the right side of the body. The right hemisphere senses and controls the left side of the body.

Corpus callosum

Hemispheres

Apparatus for Studying Split-Brain Patients

When the subject stares at the dot on the screen, images briefly presented on one side of the dot go to only one side of the brain. For example, a picture of a spoon presented on the left side of the screen goes to the right side of the brain. Thus the right side of the brain could find the spoon and direct the left hand to touch it; but because the language areas on the left side of the brain did not see it, the subject would not be able to identify the spoon verbally.

Lateralization of Normal Brains   Sperry concluded from his studies that each hemisphere in the split-brain patient has its own "private sensations, perceptions, thoughts, and ideas all of which are cut off from the corresponding experiences in the opposite hemisphere.... In many respects each disconnected hemisphere appears to have a separate mind of its own" (Sperry, 1974). But when the hemispheres are connected normally, are certain functions, such as mathematical reasoning or language skills, lateralized? A **lateralized** task is one that is performed more efficiently by one hemisphere than by the other.

To find out, researchers presented images to just one hemisphere of people with normal brains and then measured how fast they could analyze information. If information is presented to one side of the brain and that side is specialized to analyze that type of information, a person's responses will be faster than if the information must first be transferred to the other hemisphere for analysis. These studies have confirmed that the left hemisphere has better logical and language abilities than the right, whereas the right hemisphere has better spatial, artistic, and musical abilities (Springer & Deutsch, 1989). PET scans of normal people receiving varying kinds of auditory stimulation also demonstrate these asymmetries of function (see Figure 3.21). The language abilities of the left hemisphere are not specifically related to auditory information, since deaf people also use the left hemisphere more than the right for sign language (Corina, Vaid & Bellugi, 1992).

The precise nature and degree of lateralization vary quite a bit among individuals. For example, in about a third of left-handed people, either the right hemisphere or both hemispheres control language functions (Springer & Deutsch, 1989). In contrast, only about 5 percent of right-handed people have language controlled by the right hemisphere. Evidence about sex differences in brain laterality comes from studies on the cognitive abilities of normal men and women, the effects of brain damage on cognitive function, and anatomical differences between the sexes. Among normal individuals there are sex differences in the ability to perform tasks that are known to be lateralized in the brain. For example, women are better than men at perceptual fluency tasks, such as rapidly identifying matching items, and at arithmetic calculations. Men are better at imagining the rotation of an object in space and of tasks involving target-directed motor skills, such as guiding projectiles or intercepting them. As demonstrated in any video-game arcade, however, males tend to practice this type of skill more than females; the performance difference might be reduced if practice effects were equated (Law, Pellegrino & Hunt, 1993). Damage to just one side of the brain is more debilitating to

FIGURE 3.21

Lateralization of the Cerebral Hemispheres: Evidence from PET Scans

These PET scans show overhead views of a section of a person's brain that was receiving different kinds of stimulation. At the upper left, the subject was resting, with eyes open and ears plugged. Note that the greatest brain activity, as indicated by the red color, is in the visual cortex, which is receiving input from the eyes. As shown at the lower left, when the subject listened to spoken language, the left (more language-oriented) side of the brain, especially the auditory cortex in the temporal lobe, became more active, but the right temporal lobe did not; the visual and frontal areas were also active. However, when the subject was listening to music (lower right), there is intense activity in the right temporal lobe but little in the left. When the subject heard both words and music, the temporal cortex on both sides of the brain became activated. Here is visual evidence of the involvement of each side of the brain in processing different kinds of information (Phelps & Mazziotta, 1985).

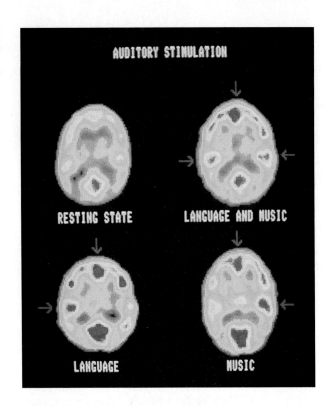

men than to women. In particular, men show larger deficits in language ability than women when the left side is damaged (McGlone, 1980). This difference may reflect a wider distribution of language abilities in the brains of women compared to those of men. When subjects in one study performed language tasks, such as thinking about whether particular words rhyme, MRI scans showed increased activity on the left side of the brain for men but on both sides for women (Shaywitz et al., 1995; see also Figure 1.4 on page 10). Although humans and animals show definite sex differences in brain anatomy and metabolism (Allen et al., 1989; Gur et al., 1995), no particular anatomical feature has been identified as underlying sex differences in lateralization. One highly publicized report claimed that the corpus callosum is larger in women than men (de Lacoste-Utamsing & Holloway, 1982), but nineteen subsequent investigations failed to replicate this finding (Witelson, 1992). Nevertheless, the original report of a sex difference in the corpus callosum continues to be cited in spite of overwhelming evidence against it, suggesting that scientists are sometimes not entirely unbiased.

Having two somewhat specialized hemispheres allows the brain to more efficiently perform some tasks, particularly difficult ones (Hoptman & Davidson, 1994), but the differences between the hemispheres should not be exaggerated. Indeed, the corpus callosum usually integrates the functions of the "two brains." As a result, the hemispheres work so closely together, and each makes up so well for whatever lack of ability the other may have, that people are normally unaware that their brains are made up of two partially independent, somewhat specialized halves. With such efficiency built in, it is no wonder that programs for training one hemisphere or to synchronize the two hemispheres do little or nothing to enhance human performance (Druckman & Swets, 1988).

Plasticity in the Brain

The brain has a remarkable property called **synaptic plasticity,** which is the ability to strengthen neural connections at synapses as well as to establish new synapses. This property provides the basis for the capacity to form memories and learn from experiences, as described in Chapters 7 and 8. However, the brain's plasticity is severely limited when it comes to repairing damage. So while there are heroic recoveries from brain damage following a stroke, for example, more often the victim is permanently enfeebled in some way.

A PATIENT WITH PARKINSON'S DISEASE
Cells from a person's own adrenal gland have been used in place of fetal brain tissue as an alternative transplant treatment for Parkinson's disease. Cells of the adrenal gland may act like neurons when placed in the brain, and people can live with just one adrenal gland. Unfortunately, fewer than 20 percent of fifty-eight patients who receive grafted adrenal cells still exhibited improved conditions after two years; further, a significant number died from surgical complications (Goetz et al., 1991).

Why is it difficult for the brain to repair damage? For one thing, adult animals generally cannot produce new neurons. During prenatal development, neurons divide and multiply as other cells do, but as the brain matures the neurons stop dividing. They can grow new axons, but they cannot produce new cells, even in response to injury. Second, even if new neurons could be grown, their axons and dendrites would have to reestablish all their former communication links. In the peripheral nervous system, the glial cells form "tunnels" that guide the regrowth of axons. But in the central nervous system, reestablishing communication links is almost impossible, because glial cells "clean up" after brain damage, consuming injured neurons and forming a barrier to new connections. Nevertheless, the brain does try to heal itself. For example, healthy neurons attempt to take over for damaged ones, partly by changing their own function and partly by sprouting axons whose connections help neighboring regions take on new functions (Cao et al., 1994). Unfortunately, these changes rarely result in total restoration of lost functions. Indeed, it is the brain's inability to replace dead or damaged neurons that underlies the unremitting progression of disorders such as Parkinson's disease and Alzheimer's disease.

Several new methods are being employed to help people recover from brain damage. One approach is to replace lost tissue with tissue from another brain. Scientists have transplanted, or grafted, tissue from a still-developing fetal brain into the brain of an adult animal of the same species. If the receiving animal does not reject it, the graft sends axons out into the brain and makes some functional connections. This treatment has reversed animals' learning difficulties, movement disorders, and other results of brain damage. The technique has also been used to treat a small number of Parkinson's disease patients, with very encouraging results (Kordower et al., 1995; Lindvall et al., 1992), including maintenance of significant improvement years after the transplant (Hoffer & Van Horne, 1995). Exciting new work with animals has shown that the effectiveness of brain tissue grafts can be greatly enhanced by adding naturally occurring proteins called growth factors, or *neurotrophic factors,* which promote the survival of neurons (Takayama et al., 1995). One of the most effective of these proteins is Glial-cell Derived Neurotrophic Factor, or GDNF (Henderson et al., 1994). The brain tissue transplant procedure is promising, but because its use with humans requires tissue from aborted fetuses, it has generated considerable controversy.

Another approach seeks ways to guide newly sprouted axons in the central nervous system. Researchers have "engineered" cells from rats to produce *nerve growth factor,* a substance that helps stimulate and guide the growth of axons. When the engineered cells were implanted into the brains of rats with brain damage or disease, the cells secreted nerve growth factor. In many cases, brain damage was reversed, with surviving neurons sprouting axons that grew toward the graft (Rosenberg et al., 1988). Based on these animal studies, nerve growth factor has been infused directly into the brain of a person with Alzheimer's disease (Seiger et al., 1993). The results were encouraging, and trials with other patients are in progress. In addition, studies of nerve growth factor led to the discovery of other growth factors (such as brain-derived neurotrophic factor, or BDNF, and neurotrophin-3) that may provide new avenues for treatment. Interestingly, physical exercise increases brain BDNF concentrations in rats (Neeper et al., 1995). While there is no causal evidence for the same effect in humans, physical activity is positively correlated with level of mental functioning as humans age.

Yet another prospect for reversing brain damage was originally suggested by studies of bird brains (Nottebohm, 1985). Each year, the male canary learns new songs, then forgets many of them at the end of the breeding season. Also, each year, a part of his brain related to the learning of songs grows by neuronal cell division! Later, the neurons die, and the cycle repeats during the next season. If scientists could discover what is different about this part of the bird brain, perhaps the same processes could be generated in the human brain, allowing it to heal itself by producing new neurons. Some progress has already been made in discovering factors that might allow the birth of new neurons in adult mammals. For example, cells were taken from the striatum of mice and maintained in a dish with nutrients and oxygen. When the cells were treated with a growth factor known as *epidermal growth factor (EGF),* some of them divided and produced immature forms of neurons and glial cells. Some cells then developed into new neurons (Reynolds & Weiss, 1992), showing that, if conditions are right, the mammalian brain does have the potential to form new neurons. This effect has not yet been produced in an intact brain, but scientists are trying to accomplish that goal. Additional encouraging evidence comes from research showing that, in rodents at least, small parts of the hippocampus generate new neurons into adulthood, and that their formation is partly controlled by stress hormones (Gould, Cameron & McEwen, 1994). Clearly, the time is coming when it will be possible to offer more effective treatment, and perhaps even reversal, of brain damage and degeneration.

LINKAGES: HUMAN DEVELOPMENT AND THE CHANGING BRAIN

How do our brains change over a lifetime?

Fortunately, most of the changes that take place in the brain throughout life are not the kind that produce Parkinson's disease and Alzheimer's disease. What are these changes, and what are their effects? How are they related to the developments in sensory and motor capabilities, mental abilities, and other characteristics described in Chapter 12?

PET scans are one technique that researchers have used to begin to answer these questions. They have uncovered some interesting correlations between changes in neural activity and the behavior of human newborns and young infants. Among newborns, activity is relatively high in the thalamus but low in the striatum. This pattern may be related to the way newborns move: They make nonpurposeful, sweeping movements of the arms and legs, much like patients with Huntington's disease, who have a hyperactive thalamus and a degenerated striatum (Chugani & Phelps, 1986). During the second and third months of life, activity increases in many regions of the cortex, a change that is correlated with the loss of subcortically controlled reflexes such as the grasping reflex. When infants are around eight- or nine-months-old, activity in the frontal cortex increases, a development that correlates well with the apparent beginnings of cognitive activity in infants (Chugani & Phelps, 1986).

These changes reflect brain plasticity, not the appearance of new cells. After birth, the number of dendrites and synapses increases. In one area of the cortex the number of synapses increases tenfold from birth to twelve months of age (Huttenlocher, 1979). In fact, by the time children are six- or seven-years-old, their brains have more dendrites and use twice as much metabolic fuel as those of adults (Chugani & Phelps, 1986; Huttenlocher, 1979). In early adolescence, the number of dendrites and neural connections actually drops, so that the adult level is reached by about the age of fourteen (see Figure 3.22).

(A) AT BIRTH

(B) SIX YEARS OLD

(C) FOURTEEN YEARS OLD

Source: Conel, 1939/1967.

FIGURE 3.22

Changes in Neurons of the Cerebral Cortex During Development

During childhood, the brain overproduces neural connections, establishes the usefulness of certain connections, and then "prunes" the extra connections (Cowan, 1979). Overproduction of synapses, especially in the frontal cortex, may be essential for infants to develop certain intellectual abilities (Goldman-Rakic, 1987). Some scientists believe that the pruning of connections may reflect a process whereby those connections that are used survive, while others die.

Even as dendrites are pruned, the brain retains its plasticity and "rewires" itself to form new connections throughout life. Genes apparently determine the basic pattern of growth and the major lines of connections, the "highways" of the brain and its general architecture. (For a summary of this architecture, see "In Review: Organization of the Brain.") But the details of the connections seem to depend on factors such as how complex and interesting the environment is. For example, researchers have compared the brains of rats raised in individual cages with only a boring view of the side of the cage to the brains of rats raised with interesting toys and stimulating playmates. The cerebral cortex of those from the enriched environment had more and longer dendrites as well as more synapses than the cortex of animals from barren, individual housing (Turner & Greenough, 1985; Volkmar & Greenough, 1972). Furthermore, the number of cortical synapses increased when old animals who had always lived in boring individual cages were moved to an enriched environment (Green, Greenough & Schlumpf, 1983). Environmentally influenced neuronal changes may help explain why, as described in Chapter 2, the maze-learning ability of genetically "maze-dull" rats raised in stimulating cages can equal that of genetically "maze-bright" animals.

Researchers have not yet determined whether an enriched environment stimulates the development of new connections or slows down normal pruning; also not yet known is whether animals will lose synaptic complexity if they are moved from an enriched to a barren environment. To the extent that these ideas and research findings apply to humans, however, they hold obvious implications for how people raise children and treat the elderly. These findings may someday help explain why, as discussed in Chapter 12, children raised in stimulating environments tend to show faster and more extensive cognitive development than those from barren backgrounds.

In any event, this line of research highlights the interaction of environmental and genetic factors. Some overproduced synapses may reflect genetically directed preparation for certain types of experiences. Generation of these synapses is an "experience

IN REVIEW	Organization of the Brain	
Major Division	**Some Important Structures**	**Some Major Functions**
Hindbrain	Medulla	Regulation of breathing, heart rate, and blood pressure
	Reticular formation (also extends into midbrain)	Regulation of arousal and attention
	Cerebellum	Control of finely coordinated movements
Midbrain	Various nuclei	Relay of sensory signals to forebrain; creation of automatic responses to certain stimuli
	Substantia nigra	Smooth initiation of movement
Forebrain	Hypothalamus	Regulation of hunger, thirst, and sex drives
	Thalamus	Interpretation and relaying of sensory information
	Hippocampus	Formation of new memories
	Amygdala	Connection of sensations and emotions
	Cerebral cortex	Analysis of sensory information; control over voluntary movements, abstract thinking, and other complex cognitive activity
	Corpus callosum	Transfer of information between the two cerebral hemispheres

expectant" process, and it accounts for sensitive periods during development when certain things can be most easily learned. But overproduction of synapses also occurs in response to totally new experiences; this process is "experience dependent" (Greenough, Black & Wallace, 1987). Within constraints set by genetics, interactions with the world appear to mold the brain itself.

THE CHEMISTRY OF PSYCHOLOGY

So far, we have described how the cells of the nervous system communicate by releasing neurotransmitters at their synapses, and we have outlined some of the basic structures of the nervous system and their functions. Let's now pull these topics together by considering two questions about neurotransmitters and the nervous system. First, which neurotransmitters occur in which structures? We will see that different sets of neurons use different neurotransmitters; a group of neurons that communicates using the same neurotransmitter is called a **neurotransmitter system.** Second, how do neurotransmitter systems affect behavior? It appears that certain neurotransmitter systems play a dominant role in particular functions, such as emotion or memory, and in particular problems, such as Alzheimer's disease. Our discussion will also reveal that drugs affect behavior and mental processes by altering these systems. Details about how these *psychoactive drugs* work are presented in Chapters 6 and 16 in relation to drugs of abuse—such as cocaine and heroin—and to those used in treating mental disorders.

Chemical neurotransmission was first demonstrated, in frogs, by Otto Loewi in 1921. Since then, about 100 different neurotransmitters have been identified. Some of the chemicals that act on receptors at synapses have been called *neuromodulators*, because they act slowly and often modify or "modulate" a cell's response to other neurotransmitters. The distinction between "neurotransmitter" and "neuromodulator" is not always clear, however. Depending on the type of receptor it acts on at a given synapse, the same substance can function as either a neuromodulator or a neurotransmitter. A more radical modification of the concept of neurotransmitter occurred following the recent discovery that nitric oxide—a toxic gas and a major constituent of air pollution—is also a neurotransmitter (Dawson & Dawson, 1995). When nitric oxide is released by neurons, it diffuses to other neurons nearby and sends a signal that acts on chemical reactions *inside* those neurons rather than on receptors on the surface of neurons. Nitric oxide appears to be one of the neurotransmitters responsible for such diverse functions as penile erection and the formation of memories—not at the same site, obviously.

Seven Major Neurotransmitters

The following sections describe seven of the most important neurotransmitters: acetylcholine, norepinephrine, serotonin, dopamine, GABA, glutamate, and endorphins. Usually the suffix *-ergic* is added to the name of a neurotransmitter to make the word an adjective. Thus, a group of neurons using dopamine as a neurotransmitter is called a *dopaminergic system* and a group using acetylcholine is called *cholinergic*.

Acetylcholine   The first compound to be identified as a neurotransmitter was **acetylcholine** (pronounced "a-see-tull-ko´-leen"), which is used by neurons in both the peripheral and the central nervous systems. In the peripheral nervous system, cholinergic neurons control the contraction of muscles by releasing acetylcholine onto muscle tissues. It is also the neurotransmitter used by neurons of the parasympathetic nervous system to slow the heartbeat and activate the gastrointestinal system. In the brain, cholinergic neurons are especially plentiful in the striatum, where they occur in circuits that are important for movement (see Figure 3.23). Axons of cholinergic neurons also make up major pathways in the limbic system, including the hippocampus, and other areas of the cerebrum that are involved in memory (Bartus et al., 1982). Drugs that interfere with acetylcholine prevent the formation of new memories. In Alzheimer's disease, there is a nearly complete loss of cholinergic neurons in a nucleus in the forebrain that sends fibers to the cerebral cortex and hippocampus (Whitehouse et al., 1983).

Norepinephrine   Neurons that use **norepinephrine** (pronounced "nor-eppa-nef´-rin") are called *adrenergic*, because norepinephrine is also called *noradrenaline*. Like

FIGURE 3.23

Examples of Neurotransmitter Pathways

Neurons that release a certain neurotransmitter may be concentrated in one particular region (indicated by dots) and send fibers into other regions, to which they communicate across synapses (arrows). Four examples are shown here.

(A) ACETYCHOLINE   **(B) NOREPINEPHRINE**   **(C) SEROTONIN**   **(D) DOPAMINE**

acetylcholine, norepinephrine occurs in both the central and the peripheral nervous systems; in both places, it contributes to arousal. Noradrenaline (and the closely related adrenaline) are the neurotransmitters used by the sympathetic nervous system to activate you and prepare you for action. Approximately half of the norepinephrine in the entire brain is contained in cells of the locus coeruleus, which is near the reticular formation in the hindbrain (see Figure 3.23). Because adrenergic systems cover a lot of territory, it is logical that norepinephrine affects several broad categories of behavior. Indeed, norepinephrine is involved in the appearance of wakefulness and sleep, in learning, and in the regulation of mood.

Serotonin   The neurotransmitter **serotonin** is similar to norepinephrine in several ways. First, most of the cells that use it as a neurotransmitter occur in an area along the midline of the hindbrain; the region for serotonin is the *raphe nuclei* (see Figure 3.23). Second, serotonergic axons send branches throughout the forebrain, including the hypothalamus, the hippocampus, and the cerebral cortex. Third, serotonin affects sleep and mood.

Serotonin differs from norepinephrine, however, in that the brain can use one of the substances from which it is made, *tryptophan,* directly from food. As a result, what you eat can affect the amount of serotonin in your brain. Carbohydrates increase the amount of tryptophan getting into the brain and therefore affect how much serotonin is made; so a meal high in carbohydrates produces increased levels of serotonin. Serotonin, in turn, normally causes a reduction in the desire for carbohydrates. Some researchers suspect that malfunctions in the serotonin feedback system are responsible for the disturbances of mood and appetite seen in certain types of obesity, premenstrual tension, and depression (Weltzin, Fernstrom & Kaye, 1994). Serotonin has also been implicated in aggression (Saudou et al., 1994).

Dopamine   Figure 3.23 shows that **dopamine** is the neurotransmitter used in the substantia nigra and striatum, which are important for movement. Indeed, malfunctioning of the dopamine system in these regions contributes to movement disorders, including Parkinson's disease. As dopamine cells in the substantia nigra degenerate, Parkinson's disease victims experience severe shakiness and difficulty at initiating movement. Parkinson's is most common in elderly people, and available evidence suggests that it results from an inherited sensitivity to an as yet unidentified environmental factor or toxin (Payami et al., 1995). Parkinson's has been treated, with partial success, using drugs that enable neurons to make more dopamine, or that stimulate dopamine receptors (Jenner, 1995).

Other dopaminergic systems send axons from the midbrain to the forebrain, including the cerebral cortex. Some of these neurons are important in the experience of reward, or pleasure, which is vital in shaping and motivating behavior (Wise & Rompre, 1989). Animals will work intensively to receive a direct infusion of dopamine into the forebrain. These dopaminergic systems play a role in the rewarding properties of many drugs, including cocaine (Wise, 1988). Malfunctioning of other dopaminergic neurons that go to the cortex may be partly responsible for *schizophrenia,* a psychological disorder in which perception, emotional expression, and thought are severely distorted (Weinberger, 1988).

GABA   Neurons in widespread regions of the brain use **GABA,** which stands for "gamma-amino butyric acid." GABA reduces the likelihood that postsynaptic neurons will fire an action potential; in fact, it is the major inhibitory neurotransmitter in the central nervous system. When you fall asleep, neurons that use GABA deserve part of the credit.

Malfunctioning of GABA systems has been implicated in a variety of disorders, including severe anxiety and Huntington's disease, an inherited disorder that results in the loss of many GABA-containing neurons in the striatum. Normally these GABA systems inhibit dopamine systems, so when they are lost through Huntington's disease, the dopamine systems may run wild. The effects are in some ways the opposite of those of Parkinson's disease: Instead of being unable to begin movements, the victim is plagued by uncontrollable movement of the arms and legs, along with a progressive loss of cog-

IN REVIEW	Major Neurotransmitters	
Neurotransmitter	**Normal Function**	**Disorder Associated with Malfunctioning**
Acetylcholine	Movement, memory	Alzheimer's disease
Norepinephrine	Sleep, learning, mood	Depression
Serotonin	Mood, appetite, aggression	Depression
Dopamine	Movement, reward	Parkinson's disease, schizophrenia
GABA	Movement	Huntington's disease; epilepsy
Glutamate	Memory	Neuron loss after stroke
Endorphin	Modulation of pain	No established disorder

nitive abilities. Woody Guthrie, the legendary folksinger and father of Arlo Guthrie, was a famous victim of Huntington's disease.

Because drugs that block GABA receptors produce intense repetitive electrical discharges, known as *seizures,* researchers suspect that malfunctioning GABA systems probably contribute to *epilepsy,* a brain disorder associated with seizures and convulsive movements. Repeated or sustained seizures can result in permanent brain damage; drug treatments can reduce their frequency and severity, but completely effective drugs are not yet available.

Glutamate The major excitatory neurotransmitter in the central nervous system is **glutamate.** Glutamate is used by more neurons than any other neurotransmitter; its synapses are especially plentiful in the cerebral cortex and the hippocampus.

Glutamate is particularly important because it plays a major role in the ability of the brain to "strengthen" its synaptic connections—that is, to allow messages to cross the synapse more efficiently. This process is necessary for normal development and may be at the root of learning and memory. At the same time, overactivity of glutamate synapses can cause neurons to die. In fact, this overactivity is the main cause of the brain damage that occurs when oxygen is cut off from neurons during a stroke. Glutamate can "excite neurons to death," so blocking glutamate receptors immediately after a brain trauma can prevent permanent brain damage (Faden et al., 1989). Glutamate may also contribute to the loss of cells from the hippocampus that occurs in Alzheimer's disease (Cotman, Monaghan & Ganong, 1988).

Endorphins One family of neurotransmitters was discovered in the 1970s by scientists who were interested in *opiates,* which are substances derived from poppy flowers. Opiates such as morphine and heroin can relieve pain, produce euphoria, and, in high doses, bring on sleep. After marking morphine with a radioactive substance, researchers traced where it became concentrated in the brain. They found that opiates bind to receptors that were not associated with any then-known neurotransmitter. Since it was unlikely that the brain had developed opiate receptors just in case a person might want to use morphine or heroin, researchers reasoned that the body must contain a substance similar to opiates. This hypothesis led to the search for a naturally occurring, or endogenous, morphine, which was called *endorphin,* a contraction of "endogenous morphine." As it turned out, there are many natural opiatelike compounds. Thus, the term **endorphin** refers to any neurotransmitter that can bind to the same receptors stimulated by opiates. Neurons in several parts of the brain use endorphins, including pathways that modify pain signals to the brain. (For a summary of the main neurotransmitters and the consequences of their malfunction, see "In Review: Major Neurotransmitters.")

THE ENDOCRINE SYSTEM: COORDINATING THE INTERNAL WORLD

As noted earlier, neurons are not the only cells that can use chemicals to communicate with one another in ways that affect behavior and mental processes. Another class of cells with this ability resides in the **endocrine system,** which regulates functions ranging from stress responses to physical growth. The cells of endocrine organs, or **glands,** communicate by secreting chemicals, much as neurons do. In the case of endocrine organs, the chemicals are called **hormones.** Figure 3.24 shows the location and functions of some of the major endocrine glands.

Hormones from the endocrine organs are similar to neurotransmitters. In fact, many such chemicals, including norepinephrine and the endorphins, act both as hormones and as neurotransmitters. However, whereas neurons secrete neurotransmitters into synapses, endocrine organs put their chemicals into the bloodstream, which carries them throughout the body. In this way, endocrine glands can stimulate cells with which they have no direct connection. But not all cells receive the hormonal message. Hormones, like neurotransmitters, can influence only those cells with receptors capable of receiving them (McEwen, 1991). Organs whose cells have receptors for a hormone are called *target organs.*

Each hormone acts on many target organs, producing coordinated effects throughout the body. For example, when the sex hormone *estrogen* is secreted by a woman's ovaries, it activates her reproductive system. It causes the uterus to grow in preparation for nurturing an embryo; it enlarges the breasts to prepare them for nursing; it stimulates the brain to enhance interest in sexual activity; and it stimulates the pituitary gland to release another hormone that causes a mature egg to be released by the ovary for fertilization.

The brain has ultimate control over the secretion of hormones. Through the hypothalamus, it controls the pituitary gland, which in turn controls endocrine organs in the

FIGURE 3.24

Some Major Glands of the Endocrine System

Each of the glands shown releases its hormones into the bloodstream. Even the hypothalamus, a part of the brain, regulates the adjacent pituitary gland by secreting hormones.

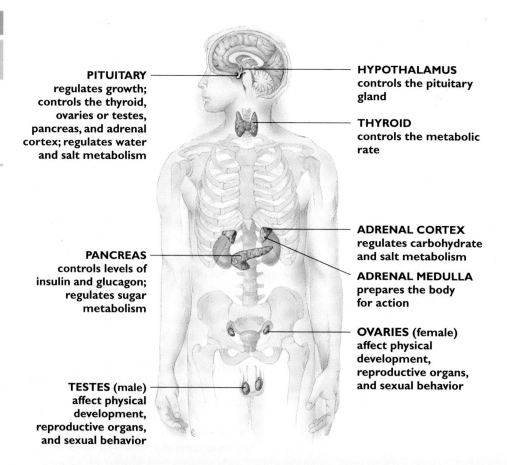

PITUITARY
regulates growth;
controls the thyroid,
ovaries or testes,
pancreas, and adrenal
cortex; regulates water
and salt metabolism

HYPOTHALAMUS
controls the pituitary
gland

THYROID
controls the metabolic
rate

PANCREAS
controls levels of
insulin and glucagon;
regulates sugar
metabolism

ADRENAL CORTEX
regulates carbohydrate
and salt metabolism

ADRENAL MEDULLA
prepares the body
for action

OVARIES (female)
affect physical
development,
reproductive organs,
and sexual behavior

TESTES (male)
affect physical
development,
reproductive organs,
and sexual behavior

body. The brain is also one of the target organs for most endocrine secretions. Thus, the endocrine system typically involves four elements: the brain, the pituitary gland, the endocrine organ, and the target organs, which include the brain. Each element in the system uses hormones to signal the next element, and the secretion of each hormone is stimulated or suppressed by other hormones.

For example, in stress-hormone systems, the brain controls the pituitary gland by signaling the hypothalamus to release hormones that stimulate receptors of the pituitary gland, which secretes another hormone, which stimulates another endocrine gland to secrete *its* hormones. Specifically, when the brain interprets a situation as threatening, the pituitary releases the hormone *ACTH,* which causes the adrenal glands to release the hormone *cortisol* into the bloodstream. These hormones in turn act on cells throughout the body. The combined effects of the adrenal hormones and the activation of the sympathetic system result in a set of responses called the **fight or flight syndrome,** which, as mentioned earlier, prepares the animal or person for action in response to danger or other stress. The heart beats faster, the liver releases glucose into the bloodstream, fuels are mobilized from fat stores, and the organism is generally placed in a state of high arousal.

However, the hormones also provide feedback to the brain as well as to the pituitary gland. Just as a thermostat and furnace regulate heat, this feedback system regulates hormone secretion so as to keep it within a certain range. If a hormone rises above a certain level, feedback about this situation signals the brain and pituitary to stop stimulating its secretion. Thus, after the immediate threat is over, feedback about cortisol's action in the brain and in the pituitary terminates the secretion of ACTH and, in turn, cortisol. Because the feedback suppresses further action, this arrangement is called a **negative feedback system.**

As an additional example of the effect of hormones, consider another class of sex hormones, the *androgens.* Pituitary hormones cause the male sex organs to secrete androgens, stimulate the maturation of sperm, increase a male's motivation for sexual activity, and increase his aggressiveness (Davidson, Camargo & Smith, 1979; Archer, 1991). The relationship between androgens and aggressiveness in humans is complicated and controversial; we discuss it further in Chapter 18.

Can differences between hormones in men and women account for some of the differences between the sexes? During development and in adulthood, sex differences in hormones are relative rather than absolute: Both men and women have both androgens and estrogens, but men have relatively higher concentrations of androgens while women have relatively higher concentrations of estrogens. There is plenty of evidence from animal studies that the presence of higher concentrations of androgens in males during development creates both structural sex differences in the brain and sex differences in adult behaviors. Humans, too, may be similarly affected by hormones early in development. For example, studies of girls who were exposed to high levels of androgen before birth found that they were later more aggressive and showed greater spatial ability than their sisters who had not had such exposure (Reinisch, Ziemba-Davis & Sanders, 1991). And, as shown in Figure 1.4, MRI studies have revealed specific regions of the brain that function differently in men and women. However, such sex differences may not be simple, inevitable, or due to the actions of hormones alone. For example, just the act of practicing finger-tapping for ten minutes a day over several weeks can create alterations in the activity of the motor cortex that are detectable with functional MRI (Karni et al., 1994a). Most likely, the sex differences we see in behavior depends not only on hormones but also on complex interactions of biological and social forces, as described in the chapter on motivation and emotion.

THE IMMUNE SYSTEM: LINKING THE BRAIN AND THE BODY'S DEFENSE SYSTEM

With many similarities to the nervous system and endocrine system, the **immune system** serves as both a sensory system and a surveillance system. It monitors the internal state of the body and detects unwanted cells and toxic substances that may invade the body. It recognizes and remembers foreign substances, and engulfs and destroys foreign cells as well as cancer cells. Individuals whose immune system is under-responsive—AIDS patients, for example—face certain death from invading bacteria or malignant tumors. However, if the system becomes overzealous, the results can be just as devastating: Many diseases, including arthritis and cancer, are now recognized as **autoimmune disorders,** in which cells of the immune system attack normal cells of the body, including brain cells.

The immune system is perhaps as complex as the nervous system, and it contains as many cells as the brain (Guyton, 1991). Some of these cells are in identifiable organs such as the thymus and spleen, and some circulate in the bloodstream and enter tissues throughout the body (see Figure 3.25). In Chapter 13, on health, stress, and coping, we describe a few of the immune system's many cell types and how they work.

The nervous system and the immune system were once thought of as completely separate (Ader, Felten & Cohen, 1990). This view stemmed in part from the fact that various types of immune cells seem to act on their own. However, four lines of evidence suggest important interactions between the nervous system and the immune system (Dunn, 1989).

First, stress can alter the outcome of disease in animals, and, as discussed in Chapter 13, there is growing evidence that psychological stressors also affect disease processes in humans. Second, immune responses can be "taught" using some of the principles of

FIGURE 3.25

Relations Among the Nervous System, Endocrine System, and Immune System

All three systems interact and influence one another. The nervous system affects the endocrine system by controlling secretion of hormones via the pituitary gland. It also affects the immune system via the autonomic nervous system's action on the thymus gland. The thymus, spleen, and bone marrow are sites of generation and development of immune cells. Hormones of the pituitary gland and adrenal gland modulate immune cells. Immune cells secrete cytokines and antibodies to fight foreign invaders; cytokines are blood-borne messengers that regulate development of immune cells and also influence the central nervous system.

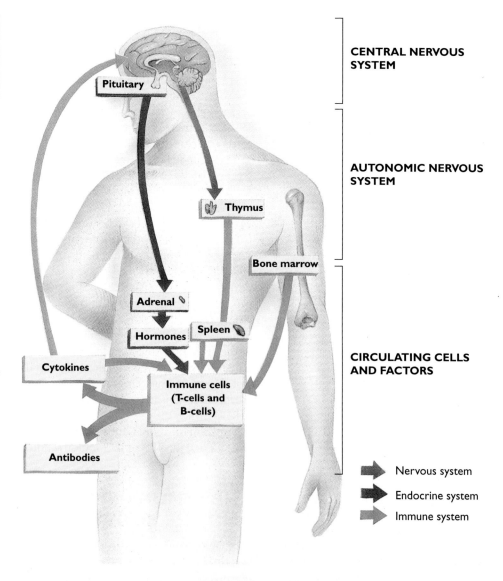

CENTRAL NERVOUS SYSTEM

AUTONOMIC NERVOUS SYSTEM

CIRCULATING CELLS AND FACTORS

Pituitary
Thymus
Bone marrow
Adrenal
Hormones
Spleen
Cytokines
Immune cells (T-cells and B-cells)
Antibodies

Nervous system
Endocrine system
Immune system

LINKAGES: THE COMMON COLD The interaction of the immune system and the nervous system is exemplified by some of the symptoms associated with routine "sickness." Sleepiness, nausea, and fever are actually a result of chemicals released by immune cells, collectively called *cytokines*, which act directly on the brain through specific receptors (Pousset, 1994).

learning outlined in Chapter 7. In one study with humans, for example, exposure to the taste of sherbet was repeatedly associated with an injection of epinephrine, which increases immune system activity. Eventually, an increase in immune system activity could be prompted by the taste of sherbet alone (Buske-Kirschbaum et al., 1992). Third, animal studies have shown that electrical stimulation or lesions of specific parts of the hypothalamus, the cortex, or the brainstem that control the autonomic nervous system can enhance or impair immune functions (Felten et al., 1991). Finally, activation of the immune system produces changes in the electrical activity of the brain, neurotransmitter activity, hormonal secretion, and behavior. Immune cells also produce some of the same substances that are used by the brain as neurotransmitters and by the endocrine system as hormones (Blalock, 1994). These include endorphins, which are the body's natural painkillers, and ACTH, the hormone that stimulates the adrenal gland to produce glucocorticoids during stress.

These converging lines of evidence point to important relationships that illustrate the intertwining of biological and psychological functions, the interaction of body and mind. They highlight the ways in which the immune system, nervous system, and endocrine system—all systems of communication between and among cells—are integrated to form the biological basis for a smoothly functioning self that is filled with interacting thoughts, emotions, and memories and is capable of responding to life's challenges and opportunities with purposeful and adaptive behavior.

FUTURE DIRECTIONS

Today, new information about the brain is increasing at an explosive rate. Medical researchers, biochemists, computer scientists, physiologists, and psychologists are all applying specialized techniques to the study of the nervous system and approaching questions about the brain and behavior from complementary angles (Sarter, Bernston & Cacioppo, 1996).

Technical breakthroughs have allowed a tremendous amount of information to be gathered in an amazingly short time, and each year impressive new research capabilities will

continue to appear. For example, ever-improving PET scans, functional MRI, and other advanced imaging techniques will allow increasingly rapid and detailed monitoring of brain activity (Buonocor & Hecht, 1995). At the same time, techniques from molecular biology will allow the dissection and manipulation of genes that shape behavior.

Some of the most exciting work in coming years is likely to focus on biological factors in diseases. Scientists may soon be able to identify the specific biological processes occurring in

Alzheimer's disease and schizophrenia and to pinpoint genetic differences that can be used to predict who is susceptible to alcoholism and other disorders. At the same time, better ways of treating or even preventing many disorders will be found (Azar, 1996).

Our understanding of the biological aspects of cognitive functioning will also continue to grow. A molecular basis for learning and memory will be identified, although it appears unlikely that a single mechanism will account for all types of memory. The ways in which complex neural networks allow the brain to solve complicated problems will be unraveled, and the principles derived will allow computers to be programmed to do a better job of understanding language. As computer-based models of mental activity more closely approximate the way real brains work, these models will become increasingly useful in understanding normal and abnormal cognitive functions. Neural network models for language abilities have already been shown to learn language in the same way as infants; they even go through a babbling stage (Guenther, 1994). Such models also respond to changes in the computer program in much the same way that human language is affected by brain damage. Indeed, neural network models will lead to theories about how the brain malfunctions in mental disorders such as schizophrenia (Hoffman & McGlashan, 1993).

The larger question of how the functioning of the nervous system translates into what people experience as consciousness will be more difficult to answer. How do all the details fit together? More information than any individual can master is being generated about such questions. It will take some great minds, probably working with great computers, to synthesize this information into a vision of how the brain generates experience and behavior.

If you are interested in taking part in this collective challenge, either as a participant scientist or as an informed spectator, you can prepare yourself by learning more about both the physical and the psychological sciences. Relevant courses offered by most psychology departments include physiological psychology, sensation and perception, learning and memory, motivation and emotion, and abnormal psychology. Many departments now offer courses in drugs and behavior. And courses in chemistry, physiology, anatomy, and computer science are also relevant. Studying the relationships between body and mind is an interdisciplinary adventure, so a broad background will help you greatly.

SUMMARY AND KEY TERMS

Biological psychology focuses on the biological aspects of our being, including the nervous system, which provide the physical basis for behavior and mental processes. The *nervous system* is a system of cells that allows an organism to gain information about what is going on inside and outside the body and to respond appropriately.

■ THE NERVOUS SYSTEM

Much of our understanding of the biological aspects of psychology has stemmed from research on animal and human nervous systems at levels ranging from single cells to complex organizations of cells.

Cells of the Nervous System
The fundamental units of the nervous system are cells called *neurons* and *glial cells*. Neurons are especially good at receiving signals from, and transmitting signals to, other neurons. Neurons have cell bodies and two types of fibers, called *axons* and *dendrites*. Axons usually carry signals away from the cell body, while dendrites usually carry signals to the cell body. Neurons can transmit signals because of the structure of these fibers, the excitable surface of some of the fibers, and the *synapses*, or gaps, between cells.

Action Potentials
The selectively permeable membrane of neurons normally keeps the distribution of electrochemically charged molecules, or *ions*, uneven between the inside of cells and the outside, creating an electrochemical force called a potential. The membrane surface of the axon can transmit a disturbance in this potential, called an *action potential*, from one end of the axon to the other. The speed of the action potential is fastest in neurons sheathed in *myelin*. Between firings there is a very brief rest, called a *refractory period*.

Synapses and Communication Between Neurons
When an action potential reaches the end of an axon, the axon releases a chemical called a *neurotransmitter*. It crosses the synapse and interacts with the postsynaptic cell at special sites called *receptors*, creating either an *excitatory* or an *inhibitory postsynaptic potential* that makes the postsynaptic cell more likely or less likely to fire an action potential. Thus, whereas communication within a neuron is electrochemical, communication between neurons is chemical. Because the fibers of neurons have many branches, each neuron can interact with thousands of other neurons. Each neuron constantly integrates signals received at its many synapses; the result of this integration determines how often the neuron fires an action potential.

Organization and Functions of the Nervous System
Neurons are organized in networks of reciprocally connected cells, forming *sensory systems*, which receive information from the environment, and *motor systems*, which influence the actions of muscles and other organs. The two major divisions of the nervous system are the *central nervous system (CNS)*, which includes the brain and spinal cord, and the *peripheral nervous system*.

■ THE PERIPHERAL NERVOUS SYSTEM: KEEPING IN TOUCH WITH THE WORLD

The peripheral nervous system has two components.

The Somatic Nervous System
The first is the *somatic nervous system*, which transmits information from the senses to the CNS and carries signals from the CNS to the muscles that move the skeleton.

The Autonomic Nervous System
The second is the *autonomic nervous system;* it carries messages back and forth between the CNS and the heart, lungs, and other organs and glands.

■ THE CENTRAL NERVOUS SYSTEM: MAKING SENSE OF THE WORLD

The CNS is laid out in interconnected groups of neuron cell bodies, called *nuclei*, whose collections of axons travel together in *fiber tracts* or *pathways*.

The Spinal Cord

The *spinal cord* receives information from the peripheral senses and sends it to the brain; it also relays messages from the brain to the periphery. In addition, cells of the spinal cord can direct simple behaviors, called *reflexes*, without instructions from the brain.

The Brain

The brain's major subdivisions are the *hindbrain, midbrain,* and *forebrain.* The hindbrain includes the *medulla,* the *cerebellum,* and the *locus coeruleus.* The midbrain includes the *substantia nigra.* The *reticular formation* is found in both the hindbrain and the midbrain. The forebrain is the largest and most highly developed part of the brain; it includes the diencephalon and cerebrum. The diencephalon includes the *hypothalamus* and *thalamus.* A part of the hypothalamus called the *suprachiasmatic nuclei* maintains a clock that determines biological rhythms. Structures within the *cerebrum* include the *striatum, hippocampus,* and *amygdala.* Several of these structures form the *limbic system,* which plays an important role in regulating emotion and memory.

The Cerebral Cortex

The outer surface of the *cerebral hemispheres* is called the *cerebral cortex;* it is responsible for many of the higher functions of the brain, including speech and reasoning. The functional areas of the cortex consist of the *sensory cortex, motor cortex,* and *association cortex.*

The Divided Brain in a Unified Self

The right and left hemispheres of the cerebral cortex are specialized to some degree in their functions. In most people, the left hemisphere is more active in language and logical tasks; and the right hemisphere, in spatial, musical, and artistic tasks. A task that is performed more efficiently by one hemisphere than the other is said to be *lateralized.* The hemispheres are connected through the *corpus callosum,* allowing them to operate in a coordinated fashion.

Plasticity in the Brain

The brain's *synaptic plasticity,* the ability to strengthen neural connections at its synapses as well as to establish new synapses, forms the basis for learning and memory. Scientists are studying ways to increase plasticity following brain damage.

■ LINKAGES: HUMAN DEVELOPMENT AND THE CHANGING BRAIN

A child's growing and changing intellectual abilities are based on changing synaptic connections in the brain, not on an increase in the number of brain cells. The brain produces many more synaptic connections than it needs, pruning extra connections as experience strengthens useful connections. The ability to form new synapses nevertheless continues even into old age.

■ THE CHEMISTRY OF PSYCHOLOGY

Neurons that use the same neurotransmitter form a *neurotransmitter system.*

Seven Major Neurotransmitters

There are seven particularly important neurotransmitters. *Acetylcholine* systems in the brain influence memory processes and movement. *Norepinephrine* is released by a small number of neurons whose axons spread widely throughout the brain; it is involved in arousal, mood, and learning. *Serotonin,* another pervasive neurotransmitter, is active in systems regulating mood, attention, and appetite. *Dopamine* systems are involved in movement and higher cognitive activities; both Parkinson's disease and schizophrenia involve a disturbance of dopaminergic function. *GABA* is an inhibitory neurotransmitter involved in anxiety and epilepsy. *Glutamate* is the most common excitatory neurotransmitter; it is involved in learning and memory and, in excess, may cause neuronal death. *Endorphins* are neurotransmitters that modulate pain pathways.

■ THE ENDOCRINE SYSTEM: COORDINATING THE INTERNAL WORLD

Like nervous system cells, those of the *endocrine system* communicate by releasing a chemical that signals other cells. However, the chemicals released by endocrine organs, or *glands,* are called *hormones* and are carried by the bloodstream to remote target organs. *Negative feedback systems* are involved in the control of most endocrine functions. The brain is the main controller: Through the hypothalamus, it controls the pituitary gland, which in turn controls endocrine organs in the body. The brain is also a target organ for most endocrine secretions. The target organs often produce a coordinated response to hormonal stimulation. One of these is the *fight or flight syndrome,* which is set off by adrenal hormones that prepare for action in times of stress. Hormones also modulate the development of the brain, contributing to sex differences in brain and behavior.

■ THE IMMUNE SYSTEM: LINKING THE BRAIN AND THE BODY'S DEFENSE SYSTEM

The *immune system* serves as a sensory system that monitors the internal state of the body and as a protective system for detecting, then destroying, unwanted cells and toxic substances that may invade the body. *Autoimmune disorders* result when cells of the immune system attack normal cells of the body. There are important relationships among the immune system, nervous system, and endocrine system.

SENSATION

CHAPTER 4

LINKAGES TO SENSATION

BIOLOGICAL ASPECTS OF PSYCHOLOGY

Do both halves of your brain "see" the same world? *(ans. on p. 89)*

CONSCIOUSNESS

Can blind people see without being aware of it? *(ans. on p. 165)*

SENSATION

Are there senses we do not know about? *(ans. on p. 131)*

Before you read the next sentence, look at the background tint of the Linkages diagram. What color would you say it is? Ask someone else the same question. That person will probably say the tint is mainly green because people in the same culture tend to learn the same names for colors. But does the background tint really look exactly the same to others as it does to you? This may seem a foolish question because we assume there exists an objective reality that is the same for everyone. The seat you sit on and the book you are reading are solid objects. You can see and feel them with your senses. But sensory psychologists tell us that reality is not so simple, that the senses do not reflect an objective reality. On the contrary, the senses of each individual actively shape information about the outside world to create a *personal* reality. The sensory experiences of different species—and individual humans—vary, such that you do not see the same world a fly sees, people from California may not hear music quite the same way that British people do, and different people may experience a color differently, even if they give it the same name.

In order to understand how sensory systems create reality, consider some basic information about the senses. A **sense** is a system that translates information from outside the nervous system into neural activity. For example, vision is the system through which the eyes convert light into neural activity. This neural activity tells the brain something about the source of the light (for example, that it is bright) or about objects from which the light is reflected (for example, that there is a round, red object out there). These messages from the senses are called **sensations.** Because they provide the link between the self and the world outside the brain, sensations help shape many behaviors and mental processes (see the Linkages diagram).

Traditionally, psychologists have distinguished between sensation—the initial message from the senses—and *perception,* the process through which messages from the senses are given meaning. Thus, you do not actually sense a *cat* lying on the sofa; you sense shapes and colors—visual sensations. You use your knowledge of the world to interpret, or perceive, these sensations as a cat. However, it is impossible to draw a clear line between sensation and perception. Research shows that the process of interpreting sensations begins in the sense organs themselves. For example, the frog's eye immediately interprets any small black object as "fly!"—thus enabling the frog to attack the fly with its tongue without waiting for its brain to process the sensory information (Lettvin et al., 1959).

This chapter covers the first steps of the sensation-perception process, examining the ways in which the senses pick up information and convert it into forms the brain can use. The next chapter deals with the later phases of the sensation-perception process. Together, these chapters illustrate how human beings, with their sense organs and their brains, create their own realities.

SENSORY SYSTEMS

The senses gather information about the world by detecting various forms of *energy,* such as sound, light, heat, and physical pressure. Specifically, the eyes detect light energy, the ears detect the energy of sound, and the skin detects the energy of heat and pressure. Humans depend primarily on vision, hearing, and the skin senses to gain information about the world; they depend less than other animals on smell and taste. To your brain, "the world" also includes the rest of your body, and there are sensory systems that provide information about the location and position of your body parts.

All of these senses must detect stimuli, encode them into neural activity, and transfer this coded information to the brain. Figure 4.1 illustrates these basic steps in sensation. At each step, sensory information is "processed" in some way: The information that arrives at one point in the system is not the same as the information that goes to the next step.

In some sensory systems, the first step in sensation involves **accessory structures,** which modify the stimulus. The lens of the eye is an accessory structure that changes incoming light by focusing it; the outer part of the ear is an accessory structure that collects sound.

The second step in sensation is **transduction,** which is the process of converting incoming energy into neural activity. Just as a radio receives energy and transduces it into sounds, the ears receive sound energy and transduce it into neural activity that people recognize as voices, music, and other auditory experiences. Transduction takes place at structures called **receptors,** cells that are specialized to detect certain forms of energy. Sensory receptors are somewhat like the neurons that we described in Chapter 3, in that they respond to incoming energy by changing their membrane potential and can release neurotransmitters to send a signal to neighboring cells. Sensory receptors respond best to *changes* in energy. A constant level of stimulation usually produces **adaptation,** a process through which responsiveness to an unchanging stimulus

FIGURE 4.1

Elements of a Sensory System

Objects in the world generate energy that is focused by accessory structures and detected by sensory receptors, which convert the energy into neural signals. As the signals are transferred through parts of the brain, information is extracted and analyzed.

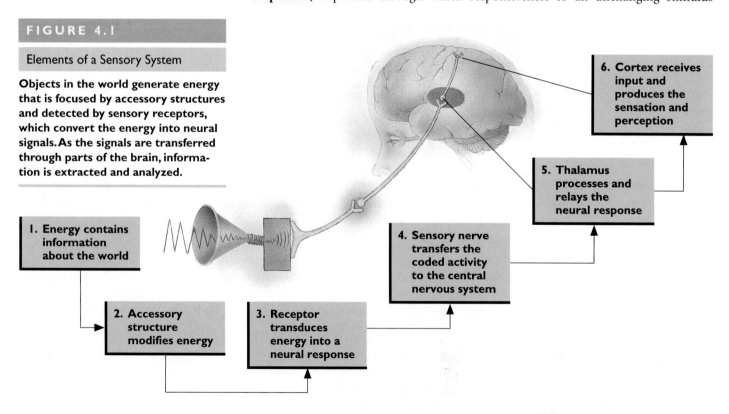

1. **Energy contains information about the world**

2. **Accessory structure modifies energy**

3. **Receptor transduces energy into a neural response**

4. **Sensory nerve transfers the coded activity to the central nervous system**

5. **Thalamus processes and relays the neural response**

6. **Cortex receives input and produces the sensation and perception**

decreases over time. This is why the touch sensations you get from your glasses (or your underwear) disappear shortly after you have put them on.

Next, sensory nerves carry the output from receptors to the brain. For all the senses except smell, the information is taken first to the thalamus, which relays it to the cerebral cortex. It is in the cortex that the most complex processing occurs.

The Problem of Coding

When receptors transduce energy, they must somehow code the physical properties of the stimulus into patterns of neural activity that, when organized by the brain, allow you to make sense of the stimulus—to determine, for example, whether you are looking at a cat, a dog, or underwear. Each psychological dimension of a sensation, such as the brightness or color of light, must have a corresponding physical dimension that is coded by sensory receptors.

As a way of thinking about the problem of coding, suppose that, for your birthday, you are given a Pet Brain, a new product inspired by the people who brought us Ginzu knives and Power Rangers. Your Pet Brain is alive, but it does not respond when you talk to it. You show it a hot-fudge sundae; no response. You show it pictures of other attractive brains; no response. You are about to deposit your Pet Brain in the trash when you suddenly realize that the two of you are not talking the same language. You should be buzzing the brain's sensory nerves to send it messages and recording from its motor nerves to discern its responses.

After having this brilliant insight and setting up an electric stimulator, you are faced with an awesome problem. How do you describe a hot-fudge sundae in terms of action potentials? This is the problem of coding. **Coding** is the translation of the physical properties of a stimulus into a pattern of neural activity that specifically identifies those physical properties.

If you want the brain to see the sundae, you should probably stimulate its optic nerve (the nerve from the eye to the brain) rather than its auditory nerve (the nerve from the ear to the brain). This idea is based on the doctrine of **specific nerve energies:** Stimulation of a particular sensory nerve provides codes for that one sense, no matter how the stimulation takes place. For example, if you apply gentle pressure to your eyeball, you will produce activity in the optic nerve and sense little spots of light.

Having chosen the optic nerve to convey visual information, you must next code the specific attributes of the sundae stimulus: the soft white curves of the vanilla ice cream, the dark richness of the chocolate, the bright red roundness of the cherry on top. These dimensions must be coded in the language of neural activity. As described in the previous chapter, this language is created by the firing of action potentials in nerve cells.

Some attributes of a stimulus are coded relatively simply. For example, a bright light will cause some neurons in the visual system to fire faster than will a dim light. This is a **temporal code,** because it involves changes in the *timing* of firing. Temporal codes can be more complex as well; for example, a burst of firing followed by a slower firing rate means something different than a steady rate. The other basic type of code is **spatial,** in which the *location* of firing neurons relative to their neighbors provides information about the stimulus. For example, neurons that carry sensations from the fingers travel close to those carrying information from the arms, but far from those carrying information from the feet. Information can be recoded at several relay points as it makes its way through the brain. Psychologists are still working on deciphering the codes that the brain uses, so your Pet Brain may have to wait awhile to appreciate that sundae.

LINKAGES: SENSATION AND BIOLOGICAL ASPECTS OF PSYCHOLOGY

Do both halves of your brain "see" the same world?

As sensory systems transfer information to the brain, they also organize that information. This organized information is called a *representation*. If you have read Chapter 3, you are already familiar with some characteristics of sensory representations. In humans, representations of vision, hearing, and the skin senses in the cerebral cortex share the following features:

1. The information from each of these senses reaches the cortex via the thalamus. (Figure 3.15 shows where these areas of the brain are.)

2. The representation of the sensory world in the cortex is *contralateral* to the part of the world being sensed. For example, the right side of the somatosensory cortex "feels" the left side of the body, and the left side of the primary visual cortex "sees" the right side of the world. This happens because nerve fibers from each side of the body cross on their way to the thalamus. Why they cross is still a mystery.

3. The cortex contains maps, or **topographical representations,** of each sense. Accordingly, features that are next to each other in the world stimulate neurons that are next to each other in the brain. There are multiple maps representing each sense, but the area that receives input directly from the thalamus is called the **primary cortex** for that sense.

4. The density of nerve fibers in any part of a sense organ determines its representation in the cortex. For example, the skin on a fingertip, which has a higher density of receptors for touch than the skin on the back, has a larger area of cortex representing it than the back does.

5. Each region of primary sensory cortex is divided into columns of cells that have similar properties. For example, some columns of cells in the visual cortex respond most to diagonal lines.

6. For each of the senses, regions of cortex other than the primary areas do additional processing of sensory information. As described in Chapter 3, these areas of *association cortex* may contain representations of more than one sense.

In short, sensory systems convert some form of energy into neural activity. Often the energy is first modified by accessory structures; then a sensory receptor converts the energy to neural activity. The pattern of neural activity encodes physical properties of the energy. The codes are modified as the information is transferred to the brain and processed further. In the rest of this chapter we describe these processes in specific sensory systems.

HEARING

When Neil Armstrong stepped onto the moon in 1969, millions of people back on earth heard his radio transmission: "That's one small step for a man, one giant leap for mankind." But if Armstrong had taken off his space helmet and shouted, "Whoo-ee! I can moonwalk!" not even an astronaut three feet away could have heard him. Why? Because he would have been speaking into airless, empty space. **Sound** is a repetitive fluctuation in the pressure of a medium, such as air; in a place like the moon, which has almost no atmospheric medium, sound cannot exist.

Sound

The fluctuations in pressure that constitute sound are produced by the vibrations of an object. Each time the object moves outward, it increases the pressure in the medium around it. As the object moves back, the pressure drops. In speech, for example, the vibrating object is the vocal cord, and the medium is air. When you speak, your vocal cords vibrate, producing fluctuations in air pressure that spread as waves. A *wave* is a repetitive variation in pressure that spreads out in three dimensions. The wave can move great distances, but the air itself barely moves. Imagine a jam-packed line of people waiting for a movie. If someone at the rear of the line shoves the next person, a wave of people jostling against people may spread all the way to the front of the line, but the person who shoved first is still no closer to getting into the theater.

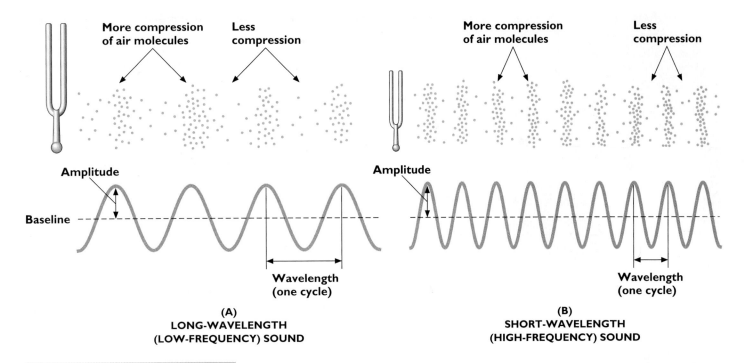

More compression of air molecules | Less compression

More compression of air molecules | Less compression

Amplitude

Baseline

Wavelength (one cycle)

(A)
LONG-WAVELENGTH
(LOW-FREQUENCY) SOUND

Amplitude

Wavelength (one cycle)

(B)
SHORT-WAVELENGTH
(HIGH-FREQUENCY) SOUND

FIGURE 4.2

Sound Waves and Waveforms

Sound is created when objects, such as a tuning fork, vibrate. They create alternating regions of greater and lesser compression of air molecules, which can be represented as a *wave-form*. The point of greatest compression is the peak of the graph. The lowest point, or trough, is where compression is lowest.

Physical Characteristics of Sound Sound is represented graphically by waveforms like those in Figure 4.2. A waveform represents in two dimensions the wave that moves through the air in three dimensions.

Three characteristics of the waveform are important in understanding sounds. First, the difference in air pressure from the baseline to the peak of the wave is the **amplitude** of the sound, or its intensity. Second, the distance from one peak to the next is the **wavelength.** Third, **frequency** is the number of complete waves, or cycles, that pass by a given point in space every second. Frequency is described in a unit called *hertz*, abbreviated Hz (for Heinrich Hertz, a nineteenth-century physicist). One cycle per second is 1 hertz. Because the speed of sound is constant in a given medium, wavelength and frequency are related: The longer the wavelength, the lower the frequency. Likewise, high-frequency sound is short-wavelength sound. Most sounds are mixtures of many frequencies and amplitudes. In contrast, a *pure tone* is made up of only one frequency and can be represented, as in Figure 4.2, by what is known as a *sine wave.*

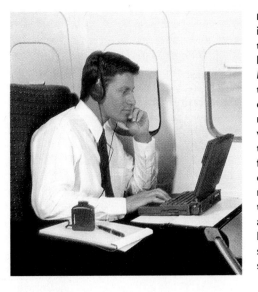

NOISE ELIMINATORS Complex sounds, including noise, can be analyzed into their component, simple sine waves by a mathematical process called *Fourier ("for-yay") analysis.* This technique can be used to eliminate engine, wind, and other repetitive noises in moving vehicles. After the waveforms are analyzed, a sound synthesizer produces the *opposite* waveforms. The opposing waves cancel each other out, and the amazing result is silence. Several versions of these noise eliminators are now sold as consumer products. As music fans know, synthesizers can also *combine* sound waveforms to produce the sound of any musical instrument.

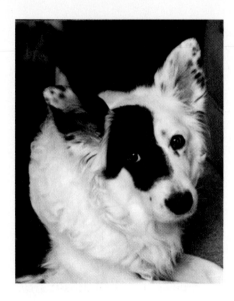

AN ACCESSORY STRUCTURE Some animals have a large pinna that can be rotated to help localize the source of a sound.

Psychological Dimensions of Sound The amplitude and frequency of sound waves determine the sounds that you hear. These *physical* characteristics of the waves produce the *psychological* dimensions of sound known as loudness, pitch, and timbre.

Loudness is determined by the amplitude of the sound wave; waves with greater amplitude produce sensations of louder sounds. Loudness is described in units called *decibels*, abbreviated dB. By definition, 0 decibels is the minimal detectable sound for normal hearing. Table 4.1 gives examples of the loudness of some common sounds.

Pitch—how high or low a tone sounds—depends on the frequency of sound waves. High-frequency waves are sensed as sounds of high pitch. The highest note on a piano has a frequency of about 4,000 hertz; the lowest note has a frequency of about 50 hertz. Humans can hear sounds ranging from about 20 hertz to about 20,000 hertz. Almost everyone experiences pitch as a relative dimension—that is, they can tell whether one note is higher than, lower than, or equal to another note. But almost no one can identify specific frequencies—for example, that a 262 Hz tone is middle C. Adults are unable to learn this skill, so it was once thought that "perfect pitch" occurs only in gifted people. However, we now know that, if they are taught before the age of six, children can learn that specific frequencies are particular notes (Takeuchi & Hulse, 1993).

Timbre (pronounced "tamber") is the quality of sound; it is determined by complex wave patterns that are added onto the lowest, or *fundamental*, frequency of a sound. The extra waves allow you to tell, for example, the difference between a note played on a flute and a note played on a clarinet.

The Ear

The human ear converts sound energy into neural activity through a fascinating series of accessory structures and transduction mechanisms.

Auditory Accessory Structures Sound waves are collected in the outer ear, beginning with the **pinna,** the crumpled, oddly shaped part of the ear on the side of the head. The pinna funnels sound down through the ear canal (see Figure 4.3). At the end of the ear canal, the sound waves reach the middle ear, where they strike a tightly stretched membrane known as the eardrum, or **tympanic membrane.** The sound waves set up vibrations in the tympanic membrane.

Next, the vibrations of the tympanic membrane are passed on by a chain of three tiny bones named for their shapes: the *malleus*, or *hammer;* the *incus*, or *anvil;* and the *stapes*, or *stirrup* (see Figure 4.3). These cleverly named little bones amplify the changes in pressure produced by the original sound waves, by focusing the vibrations of the tympanic membrane onto a smaller membrane, the *oval window*.

Auditory Transduction When sound vibrations pass through the oval window, they enter the inner ear, or **cochlea** (pronounced "cock-lee-ah"), the structure in which transduction occurs. The cochlea is wrapped into a coiled spiral. (*Cochlea* is derived

---

TABLE 4.1		

Intensity of Sound Sources

Because sound intensity varies across an extremely wide range, an unusual scale is used to describe it. A barely audible sound is, by definition, 0 decibels; every increase of 20 dB reflects a tenfold multiplication of the amplitude of the sound waves. Thus at 20 dB a whisper is 10 times as intense as a barely audible sound, and traffic noise at 100 dB is 10,000 times as intense as a whisper.

Source	Sound Level (dB)	
Spacecraft launch (from 45 m)	180	
Loudest rock band on record	160	
Pain threshold (approximate)	140	
Large jet motor (at 22 m)	120	
Loudest human shout on record	111	
Heavy auto traffic	100	
Conversation (at about 1 m)	60	
Quiet office	40	
Soft whisper	20	
Threshold of hearing	0	

Source: Levine & Shefner, 1981.

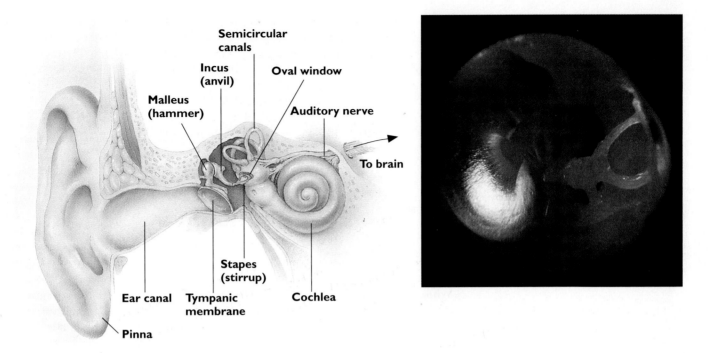

FIGURE 4.3

Structures of the Ear

The outer ear (pinna and ear canal) channels sound waves into the middle ear (shown also in the photo), where the vibrations of the tympanic membrane are amplified by the delicate bones that stimulate the cochlea. In the cochlea the vibrations are transduced into changes in neural activity, which are sent along the auditory nerve to the brain.

from the Greek word for "snail.") If you unwrapped it, you would see that a fluid-filled tube runs down its length. The **basilar membrane** forms the floor of this long tube (see Figure 4.4). Whenever a sound wave passes through the fluid in the tube, it moves the basilar membrane, and this movement deforms *hair cells* of the *organ of Corti*, a group of cells that rests on the membrane. These hair cells make connections with fibers from the **auditory nerve,** a bundle of axons that go into the brain. Mechanical deformation of the hair cells stimulates the auditory nerve, changing the electrical activity of some of its neurons and thus sending a coded signal to the brain about the amplitude and frequency of sound waves, which you sense as loudness and pitch.

Deafness Problems with the three tiny bones of the middle ear are one cause of deafness. Sometimes, the bones fuse together, preventing accurate reproduction of vibrations. This condition is called *conduction deafness*. It may be treated by breaking the bones apart or replacing the natural bones with plastic ones; a hearing aid that amplifies the input can also be helpful.

If the auditory nerve or the hair cells are damaged, *nerve deafness* results. Hair cell damage can be caused by very loud sounds, including intense rock music (see Figure 4.5).

FIGURE 4.4

The Cochlea

The vibrations of the stirrup set up vibrations in the fluid inside the cochlea. The coils of the cochlea are unfolded in this illustration to show the path of the fluid waves along the basilar membrane. Movements of the basilar membrane stimulate the hair cells of the organ of Corti, which transduce the vibrations into changes in neural firing patterns.

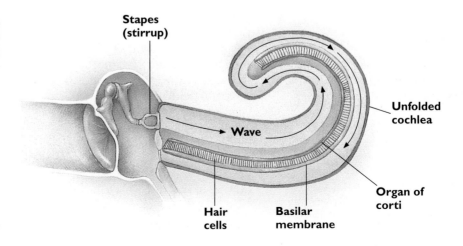

FIGURE 4.5

Effects of Loud Sounds

High-intensity sounds can perma-nently damage the hair cells of the inner ear. Part (A) shows the cochlea of a normal guinea pig. Part (B) shows the damage caused by exposure to twenty-four hours of 2000 Hz sound at 120 decibels. Generally, any sound loud enough to produce ringing in the ears causes some damage. In humans, small amounts of damage can accumulate to produce a significant hearing loss by middle age—as one of your rock-music-fan authors is now learning.

Outer hair cells

Inner hair cells

Scars

(A)   (B)

While hair cells can be regenerated in chickens (who seldom listen to rock music), this was long believed to be impossible in mammals (Corwin, 1992). However, evidence that mammals can regenerate another kind of inner-ear hair cell has fueled optimism about finding a way to stimulate regeneration of human auditory hair cells (Warchol et al., 1993). The feat might be accomplished by treating damaged areas with growth fac-tors similar to those used in efforts to repair damaged brain cells (Staecker et al., 1995; see Chapter 3). Indeed, hair cell regeneration could revolutionize the treatment of nerve deafness because this form of deafness cannot be improved by conventional hearing aids. Scientists are also working on an artificial cochlea that, like the hair cells it replaces, can stimulate the auditory nerve (Mulder et al., 1992).

Coding Intensity and Frequency

People can hear an incredibly wide range of sound intensities. The faintest sound that can be heard moves the hair cells less than the diameter of a single hydrogen atom (Hudspeth, 1983). Sounds more than a trillion times more intense can also be heard. Between these extremes, the auditory system codes intensity in a straightforward way: The more intense the sound, the more rapid the firing of a given neuron.

Recall that the pitch of a sound depends on its frequency. How do people tell the dif-ference between frequencies? Differences in frequency appear to be coded in two ways, which are described by place theory and frequency-matching theory.

Place Theory   Georg von Bekesy performed some pioneering experiments in the 1930s and 1940s to figure out how frequency is coded (von Bekesy, 1960). He opened the skulls of human cadavers, exposed the cochlea, and made a hole in the cochlear wall to observe the basilar membrane. He then presented sounds of different frequencies by mechanically vibrating a rubber membrane that was installed in place of the oval win-dow. With sensitive optical instruments, von Bekesy observed ripples of waves moving down the basilar membrane. He noticed something very important. The outline of the waves, called the *envelope,* grows and reaches a peak; then it quickly tapers off to smaller and smaller fluctuations, much like an ocean wave that crests and then dissolves.

As shown in Figure 4.6, the critical feature of this wave is that the place on the basi-lar membrane where the envelope peaks depends on the frequency of the sound. High-frequency sounds produce a wave that peaks soon after it starts down the basilar membrane. Lower-frequency sounds produce a wave that peaks farther along the basi-lar membrane, farther from the stirrup.

How does the location of the peak affect the coding of frequency? According to **place theory,** also called *traveling wave theory,* the greatest response by hair cells occurs at the peak of the wave. Because the location of the peak varies with the frequency of the sound, it follows that hair cells at a particular place on the basilar membrane respond most to a particular frequency of sound, called a *characteristic frequency.* Thus, place theory describes a spatial code for frequency. One important result of this arrangement

FIGURE 4.6

FIGURE 4.6

Movements of the Basilar Membrane

As vibrations of the cochlear fluid spread along the basilar membrane, the membrane is deflected and then recovers. The point at which the bending of the basilar membrane reaches a maximum is different for each of the three sound frequencies shown in this graph. According to place theory, these are the locations at which the hair cells receive the greatest stimulation.

Distance along basilar membrane from oval window in millimeters

Source: Rasmussen & Windle, 1960.

is that if extended exposure to a very loud sound of a particular frequency destroys hair cells at one spot on the basilar membrane, the ability to hear sounds of that frequency is lost as well.

Frequency-Matching Theory Although place theory accounts for a great deal of data on hearing, it cannot explain the coding of very low frequencies, such as that of a deep bass note, because there are no auditory nerve fibers that have very low characteristic frequencies. Since humans can hear frequencies as low as 20 hertz, however, they must be coded somehow. The answer seems to be **frequency matching,** which refers to the fact that the firing *rate* of a neuron in the auditory nerve matches the frequency of a sound wave. Frequency matching provides a temporal code for frequency. For example, one neuron might fire at every peak of a wave. Thus, a sound of 20 hertz could be coded by a neuron that fires twenty times per second.

In this simple form, however, frequency matching would apply to few sounds, because no neuron can fire faster than 1,000 times per second. A slightly more complicated process can account for the coding of moderate frequencies above 1,000 hertz. These frequencies can be matched, not by a single neuron, but by the summed activity of a group of neurons firing in concert. Some neurons in the group might fire, for example, at every other wave peak, others at every fifth peak, and so on, producing a *volley* of firing at a combined frequency higher than any could manage alone. Indeed, the frequency-matching theory is sometimes called the **volley theory** of frequency coding.

In summary, the nervous system apparently uses more than one way to code the range of audible frequencies. The lowest sound frequencies are coded by frequency matching, whereby the frequency is matched with the firing rate of auditory nerve fibers. Low to moderate frequencies are coded by both frequency matching and the place on the basilar membrane where the wave peaks. High frequencies are coded exclusively by the place where the wave peaks.

Mixtures of frequencies can produce sounds of ambiguous pitch. In fact, the same sequence of notes can sound like an ascending scale to one person and a descending scale to another. Recent work has shown that cultural factors are partly responsible for which way the pitch is sensed; American and British people, for example, tend to hear the ambiguous scales progressing in opposite directions (Deutsch, 1992).

Auditory Pathways and Representations

Before sounds can be heard, the information coded in the activity of auditory nerve fibers must be conveyed to the brain and processed further. (For a review of how changes in air pressure become signals in the brain that are perceived as sounds, see "In Review: Hearing.") The auditory nerve, the bundle of axons that conveys this information, makes one or two synapses and crosses the midline before reaching the thalamus. From there, the information is relayed to the **primary auditory cortex,** an area in the temporal lobe of the brain, close to areas of the brain involved in language perception and production (see Figure 3.17).

Cells in the auditory cortex have preferred frequencies, just as neurons in the auditory nerve do. Neighboring cells in the cortex have similar preferred frequencies; thus,

IN REVIEW	Hearing	
Aspect of Sensory System	**Elements**	**Key Characteristics**
Energy	Sound—pressure fluctuations of air produced by vibrations	Amplitude, frequency, and complexity of the sound waves determine the loudness, pitch, and timbre of sounds.
Accessory structures	Ear—pinna, tympanic membrane, malleus, incus, stapes, oval window, basilar membrane	Changes in pressure produced by the original wave are amplified.
Transduction mechanism	Hair cells of the organ of Corti	Frequencies are coded by the location of the hair cells receiving the greatest stimulation (place theory) and by the firing rate of neurons (frequency matching).
Pathways and representations	Auditory nerve to thalamus to primary auditory cortex	Neighboring cells in auditory cortex have similar preferred frequencies, thus providing a map of sound frequencies.

the auditory cortex provides a map of sound frequencies. However, although each neuron in the auditory nerve has a "favorite" or characteristic frequency, each responds to some extent to a range of frequencies. Therefore, the cortex must examine the pattern of activity of a number of neurons in order to determine the frequency of a sound.

Does the cerebral cortex provide a spatial code for the location of sounds as it does for mapping frequencies? It must provide some kind of code, because you can usually determine where a voice or other sound is coming from even when you can't see its source. The code is not spatial, however, because neurons that respond to sounds from neighboring locations in space are not neighbors in the cortex. Instead, the code that allows judgments of sound localization is a temporal one. The frequencies of firing by neurons in the auditory cortex combine to create a kind of "Morse code" that describes where a sound is coming from (Middlebrooks et al., 1994). A spatial code *is* used in a system of cells in the brainstem that allows you to quickly and automatically turn your head toward a sound. Like other adaptive reflexes, this system helps you react to danger quickly, but it plays no role in conscious judgments about the location of sounds (Barinaga, 1994).

VISION

Soaring eagles have the incredible ability to see a mouse move in the grass from a mile away. Cats have special "reflectors" at the back of their eyes that help them to see even in very dim light. Nature has provided each species with a visual system uniquely adapted to its way of life. The human visual system is also adapted to do many things well: It combines great sensitivity and great sharpness, enabling people to see objects near and far, during the day and night. Our night vision is not as acute as that of some

Wavelength in meters

VISIBLE SPECTRUM

400   450   500   550   600   650   700   750 nm

Wavelength in nanometers

FIGURE 4.7

The Spectrum of
Electromagnetic Energy

**The eye is sensitive to a very limited
range of electromagnetic wavelengths.
To detect energy outside this range,
humans rely on radios, TV sets, radar,
infrared night-vision scopes, and other
electronic instruments that can "see"
their own kind of light, just as the eye
sees visible light.**

animals, but our color vision is excellent. This is not a bad tradeoff, since being able to experience a sunset's splendor seems worth an occasional stumble in the dark. In this section, we consider the human visual sense and how it responds to light.

Light

Light is a form of energy known as *electromagnetic radiation.* Most electromagnetic radiation—including x-rays, radio waves, television signals, and radar—passes through space undetected by the human eye. **Visible light** is electromagnetic radiation that has a wavelength from just under 400 nanometers to about 750 nanometers (a *nanometer* is one-billionth of a meter; see Figure 4.7). Unlike sound, light does not need a medium to pass through; light waves are like particles that pass through space, but they vibrate with a certain wavelength. Thus light has some properties of waves and some properties of particles, and it is correct to refer to light as either *light waves* or *light rays.*

Sensations of light depend on two physical dimensions of light waves: intensity and wavelength. **Light intensity** refers to how much energy the light contains; it determines the brightness of light, much as the amplitude of sound waves determines loudness of sound. What color you sense depends mainly on **light wavelength.** At a given intensity, different wavelengths produce sensations of different colors, much as different sound frequencies produce sensations of different pitch. For instance, 440-nanometer light appears violet-blue, and 600-nanometer light appears orangish-red.

Focusing Light

Just as sound energy is converted to neural activity in the ear, light energy is transduced into neural activity in the eye. First, the accessory structures of the eye focus light rays into a sharp image. The light rays enter the eye by passing through the curved, transparent protective layer called the **cornea** (see Figure 4.8). Then the light passes through the **pupil,** the opening just behind the cornea. The **iris,** which gives the eye its color, adjusts the amount of light allowed into the eye by constricting to reduce the size of the pupil or relaxing to enlarge it. Directly behind the pupil is the **lens.** The cornea and the lens of the eye are both curved so that, like the lens of a camera, they bend light rays. The light rays are focused into an image on the surface at the back of the eye; this surface is called the **retina.** This arrangement of lens and retina is not the only way to create an image; ten distinct types of eyes are found in nature (Land & Fernald, 1992), from simple eyes with a pinhole opening instead of a lens to the compound eyes of flies, which have hundreds of separate eyes.

The lens of the human eye bends light rays from a point source so that they meet at a point on the retina (see Figure 4.9). If the rays meet either in front of the retina or behind it, the image will be out of focus. The muscles that hold the lens adjust its shape so that either near or far objects can be focused on the retina. If you peer at something

FIGURE 4.8

Major Structures of the Eye

As shown in this top view of the eye, light rays bent by the combined actions of the cornea and the lens are focused on the retina, where the light energy is transduced into neural activity. Nerve fibers known collectively as the optic nerve pass out the back of the eye and continue to the brain.

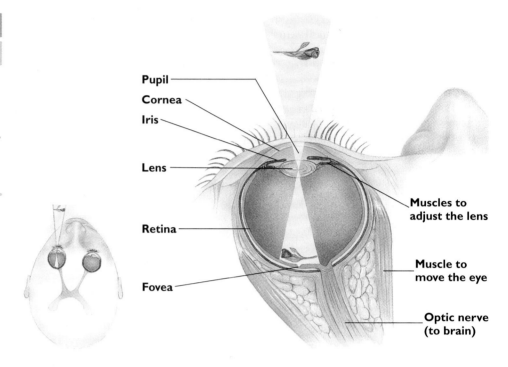

very close, for example, your muscles must tighten the lens, making it more curved, to obtain a focused image. This ability to change the shape of the lens to bend light rays is called **accommodation.** Over time, the lens loses some of its flexibility, and accommodation becomes more difficult. This is why most older people need glasses for reading or close work.

Converting Light into Images

Visual transduction, the conversion of light energy into neural activity, takes place in the retina, which contains neurons that actually constitute an extension of the brain. The word *retina* is Latin for "net"; the retina is an intricate network of cells. Before transduction can occur, light rays must actually pass *through* several layers in this network to reach photoreceptor cells.

Photoreceptors   The **photoreceptors** are specialized cells in the retina that convert light energy into neural activity. They contain **photopigments,** which are chemicals that respond to light. When light strikes a photopigment, the photopigment breaks apart, changing the membrane potential of the photoreceptor cell. This change in membrane potential provides a signal that can be transferred to the brain.

FIGURE 4.9

The Lens and the Retinal Image

Light rays from the top of an object are focused at the bottom of the image on the retinal surface, while rays from the right side of the object end up on the left side of the retinal image. The brain rearranges this upside down and reversed image so that people see the object as it is.

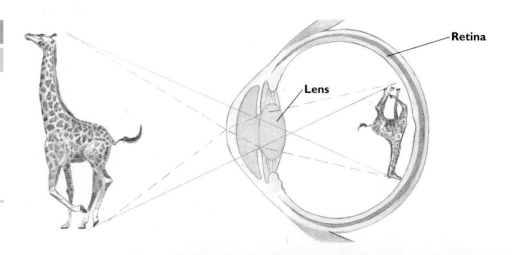

READING AND NEARSIGHTEDNESS
Visual experience can modify the eye, as when large amounts of reading leads to nearsightedness (Young et al., 1969). How? In one study, chickens wore special goggles that caused part of their retinas to receive an unpatterned image; that part of the eyeball became elongated, or myopic (Wallman et al., 1987). Humans may be vulnerable to the same elongation because reading presents areas around the fovea with a constant, relatively unpatterned image. We urge you to continue reading this chapter, but rest your eyes now and then.

After a photopigment has broken down in response to light, new photopigment molecules are put together. This takes a little time, however. So when you first come from bright sunshine into, say, a dark theater, you cannot see because your photoreceptors do not yet have enough photopigment. In the dark, your photoreceptors synthesize more photopigments, and your ability to see gradually increases. This increasing ability to see in the dark as time passes is called **dark adaptation.** Overall, your sensitivity to light increases about 10,000-fold after about half an hour in a darkened room.

The retina has two basic types of photoreceptors: **rods** and **cones.** As their names imply, these cells differ in shape. They also differ in composition and response to light. For one thing, the photopigment in rods includes a substance called *rhodopsin,* whereas the photopigment in cones includes one of three varieties of *iodopsin.* The multiple forms of iodopsin provide the basis for color vision, which we explain later. Because rods have only one pigment, they are unable to discriminate colors. However, the rods are more sensitive to light than cones. Thus, rods allow you to see even when there is very little light, as on a moonlit night. But if you have trouble trying to match a pair of socks in a darkened bedroom, you now know the reason: In dim light you are seeing with your rods, which cannot discriminate colors. At higher light intensities, the cones, with their ability to detect colors, become most active.

The rods and cones also differ in their distribution in the eye. Cones are concentrated in the center of the retina, a region called the **fovea.** This concentration makes the ability to see details, or **acuity,** greatest in the fovea. Indeed, the fovea is precisely where the eye focuses the light coming from objects you look at. Variations in the density of cones in the fovea probably account for individual differences in visual acuity (Curcio et al., 1987). Interestingly, animals who live where the topography is very flat (cheetahs on the plains and sea birds near the ocean, for example) have, not a circular fovea, but a horizontal streak of dense photoreceptors corresponding to the unbroken horizon (Land & Fernald, 1992).

There are no rods in the human fovea. With increasing distance from the fovea, the number of cones gradually decreases and the proportion of rods gradually increases. Thus, if you are trying to detect a small amount of light, such as that from a faint star, it is better to look slightly away from where you expect to see it. This focuses the weak light on the very light-sensitive rods outside the fovea. Because cones do not work well in low light, looking directly at the star will make it seem to disappear.

Interactions in the Retina   If the eye simply transferred to the brain the stimuli that are focused on the retina, the images would resemble a somewhat blurred TV picture.

Instead, the eye actually sharpens visual images. How? The key lies in the interactions among the cells of the retina, which are illustrated in Figure 4.10. The most direct connections from the photoreceptor cells to the brain go first to *bipolar cells* and then to *ganglion cells;* the axons of ganglion cells form the optic nerve, which extends out of the eye and into the brain. However, interactions with other cells modify this direct path. Two types of interactions are especially important.

First, most **bipolar cells** receive input from many photoreceptors, as illustrated in Figure 4.11(a); this arrangement is called convergence. **Convergence** increases the sensitivity of each bipolar cell, because light striking any of the photoreceptors to which the cell is connected will stimulate it. However, convergence reduces acuity, because information about exactly *which* photoreceptor was stimulated is lost. Thus, it is not surprising that there is little convergence among the cones of the fovea, an area that is good at detecting fine details but is not very sensitive to light.

Second, photoreceptor cells make connections to other types of cells in the retina, **interneurons,** which make lateral (sideways) connections between bipolar cells. Through these lateral connections, the response to light by one cell can excite or, more commonly, inhibit the response of a neighboring cell. Figure 4.11(b) illustrates **lateral inhibition.**

Lateral interactions have the important result of enhancing the sensation of *contrast.* Why? Most of the time, the amounts of light reaching two photoreceptors will differ. As Figure 4.11(b) illustrates, through its lateral connections the photoreceptor receiving more light inhibits the output to the brain from the photoreceptor receiving less light, making it seem as if there is less light at that cell than there really is. Therefore, the brain actually receives a *comparison* of the light hitting two neighboring points, and whatever difference exists between the light reaching the two photoreceptors is exaggerated. This exaggeration is important, because specific features of objects can create differences in amounts of incoming light. For example, the visual image of the edge of an object con-

FIGURE 4.10

Cells in the Retina

Light rays actually pass through several layers of cells before striking the photoreceptive rods and cones. Signals generated by the rods and cones then go back toward the surface of the retina, passing through bipolar cells, ganglion cells, and on to the brain. Interconnections among interneurons, bipolar cells, and ganglion cells allow the eye to begin analyzing visual information even before that information leaves the retina.

(A) CONVERGENCE

(B) LATERAL INHIBITION

FIGURE 4.11

Convergence and Lateral Inhibition Among Retinal Cells

Part (A) shows that input from many photoreceptors converges onto bipolar cells in the retina, either directly or by influencing interneurons. As part (B) illustrates, this influence is often inhibitory. The bipolar cell of photoreceptor A makes a lateral connection to an interneuron that synapses on the bipolar cell of photoreceptor B. When A is stimulated, it excites the interneuron, which inhibits the bipolar cell of B.

tains a transition from a lighter region to a darker region. Lateral inhibition in the retina enhances this difference, creating contrast that sharpens the edge and makes it more noticeable.

Ganglion Cells and Their Receptive Fields   Photoreceptors, bipolar cells, and interneurons communicate by releasing neurotransmitters. But, as discussed in Chapter 3, neurotransmitters cause only small, graded changes in the membrane potential of the next cell, which cannot travel the distance from eye to brain. **Ganglion cells** are the cells in the retina that generate action potentials capable of traveling that distance. Ganglion cells are stimulated by bipolar cells and modulated by interneurons, and their axons extend out of the retina to the brain.

What message do ganglion cells send to the brain? The answer depends on the **receptive field** of each cell, which is that part of the retina *and* the corresponding part of the visual world to which a cell responds. Most ganglion cells have a *center-surround receptive field*. That is, most ganglion cells compare the amount of light stimulating the photoreceptors in the center of their receptive fields with the amount of light stimulating the photoreceptors in the area surrounding the center. This comparison results from the lateral interactions in the retina that enhance contrast. Some center-surround ganglion cells (*center-on cells*) are activated by light in the center of their receptive field; light in the regions surrounding the center inhibits their activity (see Figure 4.12). Other center-surround ganglion cells (*center-off cells*) work in just the opposite way. They are inhibited by light in the center and activated by light in the surrounding area.

The center-surround receptive fields of ganglion cells make it easier for you to see edges and, as shown in Figure 4.13, also create a sharper contrast between darker and lighter areas than actually exists. By enhancing the sensation of important features, the retina gives your brain an "improved" version of the visual world.

Seeing Color

Like beauty, color is in the eye of the beholder. Many animals see only shades of gray even when they look at a rainbow, but for humans color is a highly salient feature of

Medium activity (light on center and surround)   **Higher activity** (light on center; dark on surround)   **Low activity** (dark on both center and surround)

| FIGURE 4.12 | Center-Surround Receptive Fields of Ganglion Cells |

Center-surround receptive fields allow ganglion cells to act as edge detectors. An edge is a region of light next to a region of relative darkness. If, as shown at the left, an edge is outside the receptive field of a center-on ganglion cell, there will be a uniform amount of light on both the excitatory center and the inhibitory surround, thus creating a moderate amount of activity. If, as shown in the middle drawing, the dark side of an edge covers a large portion of the inhibitory surround but leaves light on the excitatory center, the output of the cell will be high, signaling an edge in its receptive field. When, as shown at right, the dark area covers both the center and the surround of the ganglion cell, its activity will be lower, because neither segment of the cell's receptive field is receiving much stimulation.

FIGURE 4.13

Visual Effects of Lateral Inhibition

Because of lateral inhibition among retinal cells, dark spots appear at the intersections in this figure, called the Hermann grid. The receptive fields of two ganglion cells projected onto the pattern show why. At the intersection, a center-on ganglion cell has more whiteness shining on its inhibitory surround. Thus, its output is reduced compared to that of the one on the right, and the spot on the left appears darker. When you look directly at an intersection, the dark spot disappears, because ganglion cells in the fovea have smaller receptive fields than those elsewhere in the retina.

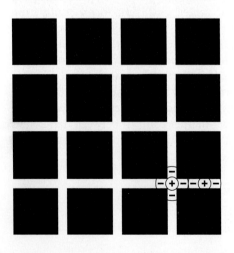

vision. An advertising agent might tell you about the impact of color on buying preferences, a poet might tell you about the emotional power of color, but we will tell you about how you see colors—a process that is itself a thing of elegance and beauty.

Wavelengths and Color Sensations   We noted earlier that, at a given intensity, each wavelength of light is sensed as a certain color (look again at Figure 4.7). However, the eye is seldom if ever presented with pure light of a single wavelength. Sunlight, for example, is a mixture of all wavelengths of light. When sunlight passes through a droplet of water, the different wavelengths of light are bent to different degrees, separating into a colorful rainbow. The spectrum of color found in the rainbow illustrates an important concept: The sensation produced by a mixture of different wavelengths of light is not the same as the sensations produced by separate wavelengths.

Characteristics of the mixture of wavelengths striking the eyes determine the color sensation. There are three separate aspects of this sensation: hue, saturation, and brightness. These are *psychological* dimensions that correspond roughly to the physical properties of light. **Hue** is the essential "color," determined by the dominant wavelength in the mixture of the light. Black, white, and gray are not considered hues because no wavelength predominates in them. **Saturation** is related to the purity of a color. A color is more saturated and more pure if just one wavelength is relatively more intense—contains more energy—than other wavelengths. If many wavelengths are added to a pure hue, the color is said to be *desaturated*. For example, pastels are colors that have been desaturated by the addition of whiteness. **Brightness** refers to the overall intensity of all of the wavelengths making up light.

The color circle shown in Figure 4.14 arranges hues according to their perceived similarities. If lights of two different wavelengths but equal intensity are mixed, the color you sense is at the midpoint of a line drawn between the two original colors on the color circle. This process is known as *additive color mixing*, because the effects of the wavelengths from each light are added together. If you keep adding different colored lights, you eventually get white (the combination of all wavelengths). You are probably more familiar with a very different form of color mixing called *subtractive color mixing*, which occurs when paints are combined. Like other physical objects, paints reflect certain wavelengths and absorb all others. For example, grass is green because it absorbs all wavelengths *except* wavelengths that are perceived as green. White objects are white because they reflect all wavelengths. Light reflected from paints or other colored objects

FIGURE 4.14

The Color Circle

Ordering the colors according to their psychological similarities creates a color circle that predicts the result of additive mixing of two colored lights. The resulting color will be on a line between the two starting colors, the exact location on the line depending on the relative proportions of the two colors. For example, mixing equal amounts of pure green and pure red light will produce yellow, the color that lies at the midpoint of the line connecting red and green.

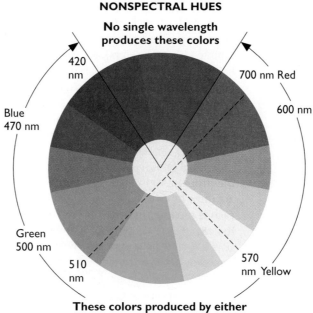

NONSPECTRAL HUES

No single wavelength produces these colors

420 nm

700 nm Red

600 nm

Blue 470 nm

Green 500 nm

510 nm

570 nm Yellow

These colors produced by either a single wavelength or a mixture

SPECTRAL HUES

FIGURE 4.15

Matching a Color by Mixing Lights of Pure Wavelengths

A target color is presented on the left side of this display; the subject's task is to adjust the intensity of different pure-wavelength lights until the resulting mixture looks exactly like the target. A large number of colors can be matched with just two mixing lights, but *any* color can be matched by mixing *three* pure-wavelength lights. Experiments like this generated the information that led to the trichromatic theory of color vision.

is seldom a pure wavelength, so predicting the color resulting from mixing paint is not as straightforward as combining pure wavelengths of light. But if you keep combining different colored paints, all of the wavelengths will eventually be subtracted, resulting in black. (The discussion that follows refers to additive color mixing, the mixing of light.)

By mixing lights of just a few wavelengths, we can produce different color sensations. How many wavelengths are needed to create any possible color? Figure 4.15 illustrates an experiment that addresses this question, using a piece of white paper, which reflects all wavelengths and therefore appears to be the color of the light shined upon it. The answer to the question of how many lights are needed to create all colors helped lead scientists to an important theory of how people sense color.

Color to be matched

Knob to adjust intensity

Blue light   Green light   Red light

Mixture of many wavelengths

Each projector produces one pure wavelength color

COLOR VISION AND COLOR TELEVISION
The discovery of how activity in three types of cones combines to produce color vision was applied in the creation of color television screens, which contain microscopic elements of red, green, and blue. A television broadcast excites these elements to varying degrees, mixing their colors to produce many other colors. You see color mixtures, not patterns of red, green, and blue dots, because the dots are too small and close together to be seen individually.

FIGURE 4.16

Relative Responses of Three Cone Types to Different Wavelengths of Light

Each type of cone responds to a range of wavelengths but responds more to some wavelengths than to others. Thus, it is possible to generate the same pattern of output—and hence the same sensation of color—by more than one combination of wavelengths. For example, a pure light of 570 nanometers (A in the figure) stimulates long-wavelength cones at 1.0 relative units and medium-wavelength cones at 0.7 relative units. This ratio of cone activity (1/0.7 = 1.4) yields the sensation of yellow. In fact, any combination of wavelengths at the proper intensity that generates the same ratio of activity in these cone types will produce the sensation of yellow.

The Trichromatic Theory of Color Vision   Early in the nineteenth century, Thomas Young and, later, Hermann von Helmholtz established that they could match any color by mixing pure lights of only three wavelengths. For example, by mixing blue light (about 440 nanometers), green light (about 510 nanometers), and red light (about 600 nanometers) in different ratios, they could produce *any* other color. Young and Helmholtz interpreted this evidence to mean that there must be three types of visual elements, each of which is most sensitive to different wavelengths, and that information from these three elements combines to produce the sensation of color. This theory of color vision is called the *Young-Helmholtz theory,* or the **trichromatic theory.**

Support for the trichromatic theory has come from recordings of the responses of individual photoreceptors to particular wavelengths of light and from electrical recordings from human cones (Schnapf, Kraft & Baylor, 1987). This research reveals that there are three types of cones. Although each type responds to a broad range of wavelengths, each is most sensitive to particular wavelengths. *Short-wavelength cones* respond most to light of about 440 nanometers (a shade of blue). *Medium-wavelength cones* are most sensitive to light of about 530 nanometers (a shade of green). Finally, *long-wavelength cones* respond best to light of about 560 nanometers (a shade of yellow, although these cones have traditionally been called "red cones").

Note that no single cone, by itself, can signal the color of a light. It is the *ratio* of the activities of the three types of cones that indicates what color will be sensed. Color vision is therefore coded by the pattern of activity of the different cones. For example, a light is sensed as yellow if it has a pure wavelength of about 570 nanometers; this light stimulates both medium- and long-wavelength cones, as illustrated by arrow A in Figure 4.16. But yellow is also sensed whenever any mixture of other lights stimulates the same pattern of activity in these two types of cones.

The Opponent-Process Theory of Color Vision   Brilliant as it is, the trichromatic theory in its simplest form cannot explain some aspects of color vision. For example, it cannot account for color afterimages. If you stare at Figure 4.17 for thirty seconds and then look at the blank white space below it, you will see an afterimage. What was yellow in the original image will be blue in the afterimage, what was green before will appear red, and what was black will now appear white.

This type of observation led Ewald Hering to offer an alternative to the trichromatic theory of color vision, called the **opponent-process theory.** It holds that the visual elements sensitive to color are grouped into three pairs and that the members of each pair oppose, or inhibit, each other. The three pairs are a *red-green* element, a *blue-yellow* element, and a *black-white* element. Each element signals one color or the other—red or green, for example—but never both. This theory explains color afterimages. When one

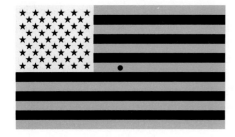

part of an opponent pair is no longer stimulated, the other is activated. Thus, as in Figure 4.17, if the original image you look at is green, the afterimage will be red.

The opponent-process theory also explains the phenomenon of complementary colors. Two colors are **complementary** if gray results when lights of the two colors are mixed together. Actually the neutral color of gray can appear as anything from white to gray to black depending on the intensity of the light. On the color circle shown in Figure 4.14, complementary colors are roughly opposite. Red and green are complementary, as are yellow and blue. Notice that complementary colors are *opponent* colors in Hering's theory. According to opponent-process theory, complementary colors stimulate the same visual element (for example, red-green) in opposite directions, canceling each other out. Thus, the theory helps explain why mixing lights of complementary colors produces gray.

A Synthesis and an Update   The trichromatic and opponent-process theories seem quite different, but both are correct to some extent, and together, they can explain most of what is now known about color vision. Electrical recordings made from different types of cells in the retina paved the way for a synthesis of the two theories.

At the level of the photoreceptors, a slightly revised version of the trichromatic theory is correct. There *are* three types of cones. However, molecular biologists who recently isolated the genes for cone pigments have found variations in the genes for the middle-wavelength and long-wavelength cones. These variants have slightly different sensitivities to different wavelengths of light. Thus, we can have two, three, or even four genes for long-wavelength pigments (Neitz & Neitz, 1995). Individual differences in people's long-wavelength pigments become apparent in color-matching tasks. When asked to mix a red light and a green light to match a yellow light, a person with one kind of long-wavelength pigment will choose a different red-to-green ratio than someone with a different long-wavelength pigment. So the answer to the question of whether a certain color looks the same to everyone is "Not necessarily."

As noted earlier, the output from many photoreceptors feeds into each ganglion cell, and the output from the ganglion cell goes to the brain. Recall that the receptive fields of most ganglion cells are arranged in center-surround patterns. The center and the surround are color coded, as illustrated in Figure 4.18. The center responds best to one color, and the surround responds best to a different color. This color coding arises because varying proportions of the three cone types feed into the center and the surround of the ganglion cell.

When either the center or the surround of a ganglion cell is stimulated, the other area is inhibited. In other words, the colors to which the center and the surround of a given ganglion cell are most responsive are opponent colors. Recordings from many ganglion

---

FIGURE 4.17

Afterimages Produced by the Opponent-Process Nature of Color Vision

Stare at the dot in the figure for at least thirty seconds, then fixate on the dot in the white space below it.

FIGURE 4.18

Color Coding and the Ganglion Cells

The center-surround receptive fields of ganglion cells form the anatomical basis for opponent colors. Some ganglion cells, like G_2, have a center whose photoreceptors respond best to red wavelengths and a surround whose photoreceptors respond best to green wavelengths. Other ganglion cells pair blue and yellow, while still others receive input from all types of photoreceptors.

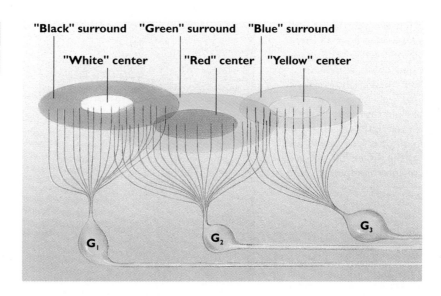

cells show that three very common pairs of opponent colors are those predicted by Hering's opponent-process theory: red-green, blue-yellow, and black-white. Stimulating both the center and the surround cancels the effects of either light, producing gray. Black-white cells receive input from all types of cones, so it does not matter what color stimulates them.

In summary, color vision is possible because the three types of cones have different sensitivities to different wavelengths, as the trichromatic theory suggests. The sensation of different colors results from stimulating the three cone types in different ratios. Because there are three types of cones, any color can be produced by mixing three different wavelengths of light. But the story does not end there. The output from cones is fed into ganglion cells, and the center and surround of the ganglion cells respond to different colors and inhibit each other. This activity provides the basis for afterimages. Therefore, the trichromatic theory embodies the properties of the photoreceptors, while the opponent-process theory embodies the properties of the ganglion cells. Both theories are needed to account for the complexity of visual sensations of color.

Colorblindness   People who have cones containing only two of the three color-sensitive pigments are described as *colorblind* (see Figure 4.19). They are not actually blind to all color; they simply discriminate fewer colors than other people. Two centuries ago, a colorblind chemist named John Dalton carefully described the colors he sensed—to him, a red ribbon appeared the same color as mud—and hypothesized that the fluid in his eyeball must be tinted blue. He instructed his doctor to examine the fluid after he died, but it was clear. However, his preserved retinas were examined recently by molecular biologists. They were not surprised to find that, just as most colorblind people today lack the genes that code one or more of the pigments, Dalton had no gene for medium-length pigment (Hunt et al., 1995).

Visual Pathways

The brain performs even more elaborate processing of visual information than does the retina. The information reaches the brain via the axons of ganglion cells, which leave the eye as a bundle of fibers called the **optic nerve** (see Figures 4.8 and 4.10). Because there are no photoreceptors at the point where the optic nerve exits the eyeball, a **blind spot** is created, as Figure 4.20 demonstrates.

FIGURE 4.19

What Do Colorblind People See?

At the upper left is a photo as it appears to people who have all three cone photopigments. The other photos simulate how colors appear to people who are missing photopigments for short wavelengths (lower left), long wavelengths (upper right), or medium wavelengths (lower right). If any of these photos look to you just like the one at the upper left, you may have a form of colorblindness.

FIGURE 4.20

The Blind Spot

There is a blind spot where axons from the ganglion cells leave the eye as the optic nerve. To "see" your blind spot, cover your left eye and stare at the cross. Move the page closer and farther away, and at some point the dot to the right should disappear from view. However, the vertical lines around the dot will probably look continuous, because the brain tends to fill in visual information at the blind spot. We are normally unaware of this "hole" in our vision because the blind spot of one eye is in the normal visual field of the other eye.

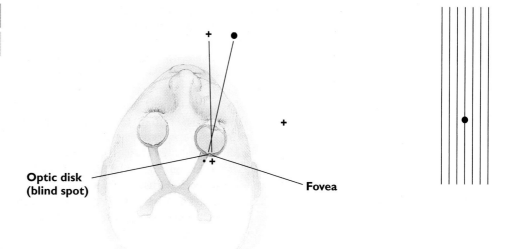

Optic disk
(blind spot)

Fovea

After leaving the retina, about half the fibers of the optic nerve cross over to the opposite side of the brain at a structure called the **optic chiasm.** (*Chiasm* means "cross" and is pronounced "ki-asm"). Fibers from the inside half of each eye, nearest to the nose, cross over; fibers from the outside half of each eye do not (see Figure 4.21). This arrangement brings all the visual information about the right half of the visual world to the left hemisphere of the brain and information from the left half of the visual world to the right hemisphere of the brain.

The optic chiasm is part of the bottom surface of the brain; beyond the chiasm, the fibers ascend into the brain itself. The axons from most of the ganglion cells in the retina form synapses in the thalamus, in a specific region called the **lateral geniculate nucleus (LGN).** Neurons in the LGN then send the visual input to the **primary visual cortex,** which lies in the occipital lobe at the back of the brain. Visual information is also sent from the primary visual cortex for processing in many other areas of cortex. In monkeys, 32 separate visual areas interconnected by more than 300 pathways have been

FIGURE 4.21

Pathways from the Ganglion Cells Into the Brain

Light rays from the right side of the visual field (the right side of what you are looking at) end up on the left half of each retina (shown in red). Light rays from the left visual field end up on the right half of each retina (shown in green). From the right eye, axons from the nasal side of the retina (the side nearer the nose, which receives information from the right visual field) cross over the midline and travel to the left side of the brain with those fibers from the left eye that also receive input from the right side of the visual world. A similar arrangement unites left visual-field information from both eyes in the right side of the brain.

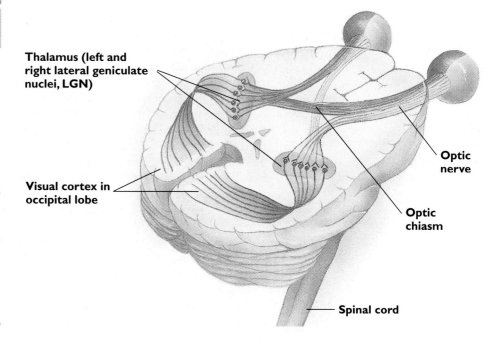

Thalamus (left and right lateral geniculate nuclei, LGN)

Visual cortex in occipital lobe

Optic nerve

Optic chiasm

Spinal cord

identified so far (Van Essen, Anderson & Felleman, 1992). There are also many connections from the cortex back to the LGN in the thalamus. The functions of this cortical feedback to the thalamus are still under investigation. One possibility is that it helps to coordinate, or synchronize, signals from the LGN to the cortex. Whatever the case, it is now clear that the thalamus is not just a simple relay station to the cortex (Sillito et al., 1994).

The retina has a topographical map of the visual world, which means that neighboring points on the retina receive information from neighboring points in the visual world. This topographical map is maintained in the brain, in the primary visual cortex, and in each of the many other visual areas of the cortex. That is, neighboring points in the retina are represented in neighboring cells in the brain: This is a spatial coding system. The map is a distorted one, however. A larger area of cortex is devoted to the areas of the retina that have many photoreceptors. For example, the fovea, which is densely packed with photoreceptors, is represented in an especially large segment of cortex.

Visual Representations

The normally effortless experience of sight provides no clues to the complexities involved as visual sensations are transmitted from the retina through various cortical regions. We can appreciate some of these complexities by considering the receptive fields of neurons at each point along the way. These receptive fields are characterized by *parallel processing of visual properties, hierarchical processing of visual information, and spatial frequency processing of visual information.*

Parallel Processing of Visual Properties   Like ganglion cells, neurons of the LGN have center-surround receptive fields. However, the LGN is organized in multiple layers of neurons, and each layer contains a complete map of the retina. Neurons of different layers respond to particular aspects of visual stimuli. In fact, four separate aspects of the visual scene are handled by *parallel processing systems* that extend into the cortex (Livingstone & Hubel, 1988). The form of objects and their color are handled by one system, while their movement and cues to distance are handled by another system. In primates, there is a separate pathway to the cortex, whose function is still unknown (Casagrande, 1994).

You might expect that somewhere in the cortex the puzzle of these separate sensations would finally be assembled in order to provide the basis for a unified conscious experience. However, there appears to be no one region where the separate streams of processing converge (Engel et al., 1992). Instead, horizontal connections among the regions of cortex that process separate aspects of visual sensation appear to integrate their activity, making possible a distributed but unified experience (Gilbert, 1992).

PET scans provide evidence of these separate processing channels in humans. For example, as shown in Figure 4.22, one area of visual cortex is activated when a person views a colorful abstract painting; a different area is activated by viewing black-and-white moving images (Zeki, 1992). Brain damage may also reveal the separate channels. Damage in one area can leave a person unable to see colors, or even remember them, while still being able to see and recognize objects. Damage in another area can leave a person able to see only stationary objects; as soon as the object moves, it disappears. People with brain damage in still other regions can see only moving objects, not stationary ones (Zeki, 1992). Even in visual imagination, the same separate processing channels apparently operate. Thus, some patients with brain damage can recall parts of a visual image, but not their correct spatial relationship. For example, they may be able to "see" a mental image of a bull's horns and ears, but cannot assemble them mentally to form a bull's head (Kosslyn, 1988).

Another way to think about parallel channels of visual processing is that different parts of the visual system determine the "what is it?" (form and color) and "where is it?" (movement and distance) of a visual image (Mishkin & Ungerleider, 1982). In evolutionary terms, the more primitive "where is it?" systems are critical for being able to *act* on visual information, through avoiding a predator or grasping an object, for example (Goodale & Milner, 1992).

FIGURE 4.22

Separate Processing of Color and Movement

Different aspects of a visual image are processed in parallel by different parts of the visual system. **PET** scans show that a brightly colored image causes activation of one area of the brain, while black-and-white moving images trigger activity in a completely different area. Both types of images activate the primary visual cortex, but within that region the neurons stimulated by each type of image are segregated.

(A) ACTIVATED BY BRIGHTLY COLORED IMAGES **(B) ACTIVATED BY BLACK AND WHITE MOVING IMAGES**

(C) ACTIVATED BY EITHER TYPE OF IMAGE

Source: Zeki, 1992.

Hierarchical Processing of Visual Information Multiple inputs from the LGN converge on single cells of the cortex, as Figure 4.23 illustrates. Cells of the cortex that receive input from the LGN have more complex receptive fields than the center-surround fields of LGN cells. For example, a specific cell in the cortex might respond only to vertical edges, but it responds to vertical edges anywhere in its receptive field. Another class of cells responds only to moving objects; a third class responds only to objects with corners. Because cortical cells respond to specific characteristics of objects in the visual field, they have been described as **feature detectors** (Hubel & Wiesel, 1979).

Feature detectors illustrate how cortical processing is partly *hierarchical* in nature. Complex feature detectors may be built up out of more and more complex connections of simpler feature detectors (Hubel & Wiesel, 1979). For example, several center-surround cells might feed into one cortical cell to make a line detector, and several line

Receptive fields
of ganglion cells

Cortical cell

LGN cells

FIGURE 4.23

Construction of a Feature Detector

Here, output from several center-on ganglion cells goes to cells in the lateral geniculate nucleus (LGN) and is then fed into one cell in the cortex. This "wiring" makes the cortical cell respond best when all of its LGN cells are excited, and they are most excited when light falls on the center of the receptive fields of their ganglion cells. Because those receptive fields lie in an angled row, it takes a bar-shaped light at that angle to stimulate all their centers. In short, the cortical cell responds best when it detects a bar-shaped feature at a particular angle. Rotating the bar to a different orientation would no longer stimulate this particular cortical cell.

detectors might feed into another cortical cell to make a cell that responds to a particular spatial orientation, such as the vertical. With further connections, a more complex detector, such as a "box detector," might be built from the simpler line and corner detectors.

Cells with similar receptive-field properties are organized into columns in the cortex. The columns are arranged perpendicular to the surface of the cortex. For example, if you locate a cell that responds to diagonal lines in a particular spot in the visual field, most of the cells in a column above and below that cell will also respond to diagonal lines. Other properties are represented by whole columns of cells, so, for example, there are columns in which all of the cells are most sensitive to a particular color.

Spatial Frequency Processing of Visual Information   According to the *spatial frequency filter model* of visual representation, the brain analyzes patterns not only by putting together information about lines, edges, and other features but also by analyzing gradual changes in brightness over broader areas. Spatial frequency analysis is a radically different way of describing what the cortex does with visual information.

This model points out that *any* pattern, no matter how complex, can be decomposed into regions of light and dark. These regions can be represented by sine waves (which are shaped like the sound waves depicted in Figure 4.2). Narrow areas of alternating light and dark—like the pin stripes on a dress or shirt—are represented by higher-frequency sine waves, while broader areas of light and dark—like the wide stripes on a big awning—are represented by lower-frequency sine waves. The spatial frequency filter model suggests that the brain does just this kind of analysis. The brain sees the com-

FIGURE 4.24

Spatial Frequency

According to the spatial frequency filter model, the visual system can extract information based on an analysis of visual patterns into their component sine waves. The computer-generated image on the right shows the average light-dark level within each block of Abraham Lincoln's picture on the left. The blocks are a low spatial frequency analysis of the figure, but the edges of the blocks present a high spatial frequency component that interferes with "seeing" the figure. To see just the low spatial frequency components, take off your glasses (if you wear them), and blur your vision by squinting.

Source: Leon B. Harmon and Bela Julesz, *Science,* 180:1194–1197 (1973).

IN REVIEW	Seeing	
Aspect of Sensory System	**Elements**	**Key Characteristics**
Energy	Light—Electromagnetic radiation from about 400 nm to about 750 nm	The intensity, wavelength, and complexity of light waves determine the brightness, hue, and saturation of visual sensations.
Accessory structures	Eye—cornea, pupil, iris, lens	Light rays are bent to focus on the retina.
Transduction mechanism	Photoreceptors (rods and cones) in the retina	Rods are more sensitive to light than cones, but cones discriminate among colors. Sensations of color depend first on the cones, which respond differently to different light wavelengths, and then on processing by ganglion cells. Interactions among cells of the retina exaggerate differences in the light stimuli reaching the photoreceptors, enhancing the sensation of contrast.
Pathways and representations	Optic nerve to optic chiasm to LGN of thalamus to primary visual cortex	Neighboring points in the visual world are represented at neighboring points in the LGN and primary visual cortex. Neurons there respond to particular aspects of the visual stimulus—such as color, movement, distance, or form.

plex visual world as alternating regions of light and dark and, in effect, represents these patterns as a collection of sine waves of many different frequencies. Large areas of uniform light or dark correspond to low-frequency waves; areas of detailed pattern correspond to high-frequency waves (see Figure 4.24).

What evidence is there that the visual cortex might do this complicated processing? For one thing, if you shine differing patterns of light and dark onto the retina, each neuron in the visual cortex will respond best to a pattern that has a particular sine wave frequency; in effect, each neuron has a preferred sine wave (Kelly & Burbeck, 1984). Further, removing one part of the cortex does not eliminate the ability to see a certain type of object. The implication is that a large part of the visual cortex might participate, possibly through spatial frequency analysis, in sensing each object.

Our description of spatial frequency analysis demonstrates that there is still a great deal to learn about the way the brain makes use of visual information. The mysteries are by no means solved, and evidence suggests that two very different processes, hierarchical feature detection and spatial frequency analysis, contribute to how the brain sees things. ("In Review: Seeing" summarizes how the nervous system gathers the information that allows people to see.)

THE CHEMICAL SENSES: SMELL AND TASTE

There are animals without vision, and there are animals without hearing, but there are no animals without some form of chemical sense, some sense that arises from the interaction of chemicals and receptors. **Olfaction** (smell) detects chemicals that are airborne, or *volatile*. **Gustation** (taste) detects chemicals in solution that come into contact with receptors inside the mouth.

Olfaction

People sense odors in the upper part of the nose (see Figure 4.25). Receptors there detect molecules that pass into the moisture lining of the nose, called the mucous. Odor molecules then bind to receptors on the dendrites of olfactory neurons, causing depolarization or hyperpolarization of the membrane, which in turn leads to changes in the firing rates of the neurons. The axons of these olfactory neurons combine to form the olfactory nerve (Dionne & Dubin, 1994). A single molecule of an odorous substance can cause a change in the membrane potential of an olfactory neuron, but detection of the odor by a human would require about fifty such molecules (Menini et al., 1995); the average hot pizza generates lots more than that.

Odor molecules can reach olfactory receptors either through the nose or through an opening in the palate at the back of the mouth that allows us to sample odors from food as we eat. Damaged olfactory neurons are replaced with new ones. Scientists are very interested in this process because, as we mentioned in Chapter 3, most neurons cannot divide to create new ones. An understanding of how new olfactory neurons are generated—and how they make appropriate connections in the brain—may someday be helpful in treating brain damage.

Substances that have similar chemical structures tend to have similar odors, but the precise means by which olfactory receptors in the nose discriminate various smells and code them in ways the brain can interpret is still being debated. We do know that the cells of the nasal cavity have thousands of different kinds of receptors to detect the many different odors that humans can discriminate (Buck & Axel, 1991). This arrangement contrasts sharply with the visual system, where only three different receptors allow the discrimination of hundreds of colors. The code for a particular odor appears to lie in a distributed pattern of both increases and decreases in the firing of a number of neurons in the olfactory system (Hildebrand, 1995).

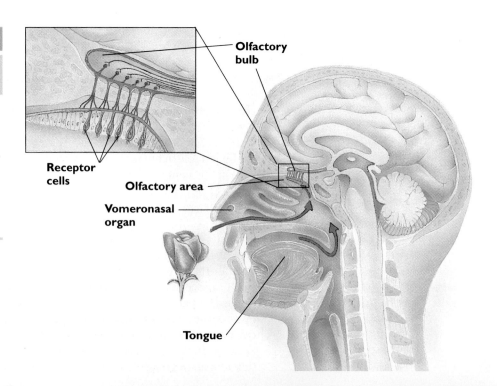

FIGURE 4.25

The Olfactory System: The Nose and the Rose

Airborne chemicals from the rose reach the olfactory area through the nostrils and through the back of the mouth. Fibers pass directly from the olfactory area to the olfactory bulb in the brain, and from there signals pass to areas such as the hypothalamus and amygdala, which are involved in emotion.

Olfactory bulb

Receptor cells

Olfactory area

Vomeronasal organ

Tongue

A "MATING BALL" There is intense competition for females in the snake world—hundreds of males will wrap themselves around a single female in a "mating ball." Snakes' forked tongues allow them to sample airborne chemicals at two different points, and hence to follow an olfactory trail (Schwenk, 1994). Males with the best olfactory tracking abilities are the ones most likely to reach a female first and thus to pass on their genes to the next generation.

Olfaction is the only sense that does not send its messages through the thalamus. Instead, the axons from the nose extend through a bony plate and directly into the brain, where they have a synapse in a structure called the **olfactory bulb.** Connections from the olfactory bulb spread diffusely through the brain, but they are especially plentiful in the amygdala, a part of the brain involved in emotional experience.

These unusual anatomical features of the olfactory system may account for some aspects of the unique relationship between olfaction and memory. For example, associations between a certain experience and a particular odor are not weakened much by time or subsequent experiences (Lawless & Engen, 1977). Thus, catching a whiff of the cologne once worn by a lost loved one can reactivate intense feelings of love or sadness associated with that person. Odors can also bring back very accurate memories of significant experiences linked with them; sights, sounds, and other sensory experiences are less capable of doing this (Engen, Gilmore & Mair, 1991). Yet despite the enduring nature of olfactory memories, people have a curious difficulty in associating a name with a particular odor. They may recognize an odor as familiar but be unable to name it, a phenomenon called the "tip-of-the-nose" state (Engen, 1987).

The neural mechanisms of olfaction are remarkably similar in species ranging from humans to worms. Different species vary considerably, however, in their sensitivity to smell, and in the degree to which they depend on it for survival. Thus, while humans have about 9 million olfactory neurons, there are about 225 million such neurons in dogs, a species that is far more dependent on smell to identify food, territory, and receptive mates. Indeed, dogs and many other species have an accessory olfactory system that is able to detect pheromones. **Pheromones** (pronounced "fer´-o-mones") are chemicals that are released by one animal and, when detected by another, can shape the second animal's behavior or physiology. For example, when male snakes detect a chemical exuded on the skin of female snakes they are stimulated to "court" the female (Mason et al., 1989).

In mammals, pheromones can be nonvolatile chemicals that animals lick and pass into a portion of the olfactory system called the **vomeronasal organ.** In female mice, for example, the vomeronasal organ detects chemicals in the male's urine; by this means a male can cause a female to ovulate and become sexually receptive, and an unfamiliar male can cause a pregnant female to abort her pregnancy (Bruce, 1969).

Although there is not yet any solid evidence that humans give off or can detect pheromones that act as sexual attractants, learned associations between certain odors and emotional experiences may enhance a person's readiness for sex. People also use olfactory information in other social situations. For example, after just a few hours of contact, mothers can usually identify their newborn babies by the infants' smell (Porter, Cernich & McLaughlin, 1983). And if infants are breast fed, they can discriminate their mothers' odor from that of other breast-feeding women, and appear to be comforted by it (Porter, 1991). Indeed, individual mammals, including humans, have a distinct "odortype," which is determined by their immune cells and other inherited physiological factors (Beauchamp et al., 1995). During pregnancy, a woman's own odortype combines with the odortype of her fetus to form a third odortype. Researchers have found that each of these three odors is distinguishable (Beauchamp et al., 1995), suggesting that recognition of odortypes may help establish the mother-infant bonds discussed in Chapter 12.

Gustation

The chemical sense system in the mouth is gustation, or taste. The receptors for taste are in the taste buds, which are grouped together in structures called **papillae** (pronounced "pa-pill´-ee"). Normally, there are about ten thousand taste buds in a person's mouth, mostly on the tongue but also on the roof of the mouth and on the back of the throat.

In contrast to the olfactory system, which can discriminate thousands of different odors, the human taste system detects only a very few elementary sensations: sweet, sour, bitter, and salty. Each taste bud responds best to one or two of these categories, but it also responds weakly to others. The sensation of a particular substance appears to

TASTE RECEPTORS Taste buds are grouped into structures called papillae. Two kinds of papillae are visible in this greatly enlarged photo of the surface of the human tongue.

result from the responses of taste buds that are relatively sensitive to a specific category. A possible fifth taste, called *umami,* enhances other tastes and is produced by monosodium glutamate (MSG), but its status as a separate taste sensation is controversial (Bartoshuk, 1990; Kinnamon & Cummings, 1992).

Scientists are still trying to determine the properties that allow chemicals to stimulate specific types of taste receptors. They do know that sweetness is signaled when a chemical fits into receptor sites (Tinti & Nofre, 1991). Although the sweet properties of saccharin and aspartame (NutraSweet) were discovered by accident (Mazur, 1991), knowledge of the chemistry of sweetness is allowing scientists to design new chemicals that fit the sweetness receptors and taste thousands of times sweeter than sugar (Tinti & Nofre, 1991). Many of these substances are now being tested for safety and may soon allow people to enjoy low-calorie hot-fudge sundaes. The question of whether such low-calorie treats will satisfy hunger is discussed in Chapter 11, on motivation and emotion.

Salty is another important dimension of taste. Most people like a certain degree of saltiness in their food, but excessive salt intake can contribute to high blood pressure and heart disease. In animals, taste responses to salt are determined during early development, before and after birth. If the mother is put on a low-salt diet, the offspring are less likely to prefer salt (Hill & Przekop, 1988). In humans, experiences with salty foods over the first four years of life may alter the sensory systems that detect salt and contribute to enduring preferences for salty foods (Hill & Mistretta, 1990).

Smell, Taste, and Flavor

If you have a stuffy nose, everything tastes like cardboard. Why? Because smell and taste act as two components of a single system, known as *flavor* (Rozin, 1982). Most of the properties that make food taste good are actually odors detected by the olfactory system, not activities of the taste system. The olfactory and gustatory pathways converge in some areas of the brain (Van Buskirk & Erickson, 1977), but no one knows yet how smell and taste come to seem like one sensation.

Both tastes and odors prompt strong emotional responses. For tastes, the repugnance of bitter flavors is inborn, but the associations of emotions with odors are all learned (Bartoshuk, 1991). Many animals easily learn taste aversions to particular foods when the taste is associated with nausea, but humans learn aversions to odors more readily than to tastes (Bartoshuk & Wolfe, 1990).

Variations in one's nutritional state affect taste and flavor, as well as the motivation to consume particular foods. For example, food deprivation or salt deficiency makes sweet or salty things taste better. Intake of protein and fat are influenced more indirectly. Molecules of protein and fat have no inherent taste or smell; the tastes and smells of foods that contain these nutrients actually come from trace amounts of other volatile substances. So adjustments in intake of these nutrients are based on associations between olfactory cues from the volatile substances and the nutritional consequences of eating the foods (Bartoshuk, 1991). These findings have implications for dieting, also discussed in Chapter 11.

Flavor includes other characteristics of food as well: its tactile properties (how it feels in your mouth) and especially its temperature. Warm foods are experienced as sweeter, but temperature does not alter saltiness (Frankmann & Green, 1987). Also, warming releases aromas that rise from the mouth into the nose and create more flavor sensations. This is why some people find hot pizza delicious and cold pizza disgusting. Spicy "hot" foods actually stimulate pain fibers in the mouth because they contain a substance called capsaicin (pronounced "cap-say´-a-sin"). Thus the texture, warmth, and "hotness" of food are detected by nerve endings in the mouth that are sensitive to temperature, touch, and pain—sensations that we examine in the next section.

SOMATIC SENSES AND THE VESTIBULAR SYSTEM

Some senses are not located in a specific organ, such as the eye or the ear. These are the **somatic senses,** also called **somatosensory systems,** which are spread throughout the body. The somatic senses include the skin senses of touch, temperature, and pain as well as kinesthesia, the sense that tells the brain where the parts of the body are. Closely related to kinesthesia is the vestibular system, which tells the brain about the position and movements of the head. Though not strictly a somatosensory system, it will also be considered in this section.

Touch and Temperature

Touch is crucial. People can function and prosper without vision, hearing, or smell. But a person without touch would have difficulty surviving. Without a sense of touch, you could not even swallow food.

Stimulus and Receptors for Touch   The energy detected by the sense of touch is a mechanical deformation of tissue, usually of the skin. The skin covers nearly two square yards of surface and weighs more than twenty pounds. The hairs distributed virtually everywhere on the skin do not sense anything directly, but when bent, they deform the skin beneath them. The receptors that transduce this deformation into neural activity are in, or just below, the skin.

Many nerve endings in the skin are candidates for the role of touch receptor. Some neurons come from the spinal cord, enter the skin, and simply end; these are called *free nerve endings*. Many other neurons end in a variety of elaborate, specialized structures. However, there is generally little relationship between the type of nerve ending and the type of sensory information carried by the neuron. Many types of nerve endings respond to mechanical stimuli, but the exact process through which they transduce mechanical energy is still unknown. These somatosensory neurons are unusual in that they have no dendrites. Their cell bodies are outside the spinal cord, and their axon splits and extends both to the skin and to the spinal cord. Action potentials travel from the nerve endings in the skin to the spinal cord, where they communicate across a synapse to dendrites of other neurons.

People do more than just passively respond to whatever happens to come in contact with their bodies; jellyfish can do that much. For humans, touch is also an active sense that is used to get specific information. In much the same way as you can look as well

THE SENSE OF TOUCH Touch provides information about the world that is vital to survival. Its importance is revealed in many other aspects of behavior as well. For example, this sculptor can create without his sight, but not without touch.

as just see, you can also touch as well as feel. When people are involved in active sensing, they usually use the part of the sensory apparatus that has the greatest sensitivity. For vision, this is the fovea; for touch, the fingertips. (The area of primary somatosensory cortex devoted to the fingertips is correspondingly large.) Fingertip touch is the principal way people explore the textures of surfaces. It can be extremely sensitive, as evidenced by blind people who can read Braille as rapidly as 200 words per minute (Foulke, 1991).

Adaptation of Touch Receptors   Constant input from all the touch neurons would provide an abundance of unnecessary information. Once you get dressed, for example, you do not need to be constantly reminded that you are wearing clothes. Thanks in part to the process of adaptation mentioned earlier, you do not continue to feel your clothes against your skin.

Changes in touch (for example, if your jeans suddenly drop to your knees) constitute the most important sensory information. The touch sense emphasizes these changes and filters out the excess information. How? Typically, a touch neuron responds with a burst of firing when a stimulus is applied, then quickly returns to baseline firing rates, even though the stimulus may still be in contact with the skin. If the touch pressure increases, the neuron again responds with an increase in firing rate, but then it again slows down. A few neurons adapt more slowly, continuing to fire at an elevated rate as long as pressure is applied to the skin. By attending to this input, you can sense a constant stimulus.

Coding and Representation of Touch Information   The sense of touch codes information about two aspects of an object in contact with the skin: its weight and its location. The *intensity* of the stimulus—how heavy it is—is coded by both the firing rate of individual neurons and the number of neurons stimulated. A heavy object produces a higher rate of firing and stimulates more neurons than a light object. *Location* is coded much as it is for vision: by the spatial organization of the information.

Touch information is organized such that signals from neighboring points on the skin stay next to each other, even as they ascend from the skin through the spinal cord to the thalamus and on to the somatosensory cortex. Accordingly, just as there is a topographical map of the visual field in the brain, the area of cortex that receives touch information resembles a map of the surface of the body. (To confirm this, look again at Figure 3.18.) As with the other senses, these representations are contralateral; input from the left side of the body goes to the right side of the brain, and vice versa. In primates, however, touch information from each hand is sent to both sides of the brain. This arrangement appears to amplify information from manual exploration of objects and to improve feedback from hand movements (Iwamura, Iriki & Tanaka, 1994).

Temperature   When you dig your toes into a sandy summer beach, the pleasant experience you get comes partly from the sensation of warmth. Touch and temperature seem to be separate senses, and to some extent they are; but the difference between the two senses is not always clear.

Some of the skin's sensory neurons respond to a change in temperature, but not to simple contact. There are "warm fibers" that increase their firing rates when the temperature changes in the range of about 95° to 115° F (35° to 47° C). Temperatures above this range are painful and stimulate different fibers. Other fibers are "cold fibers"; they respond to a broad range of cool temperatures. However, many of the fibers that respond to temperature also respond to touch, so sensations of touch and temperature sometimes interact. For example, warm and cold objects can feel up to 250 percent heavier than body-temperature objects (Stevens & Hooper, 1982). Also, if you touch an object made up of alternating warm and cool bars, you will have the sensation of intense heat (Thunberg, 1896, cited in Craig & Bushnell, 1994).

Although different patterns of activity in a single nerve fiber in the skin can code different stimuli, no one knows how the different stimuli create different patterns of firing. Thus, scientists have so far been unable to resolve whether each of the skin senses has a separate existence or whether they are just aspects of the touch sense.

Pain

The skin senses can convey a great deal of pleasure, but a change in the intensity of the same kind of stimulation can create a distinctly different sensation: pain. Pain provides you with information about the impact of the world on your body; it can tell you, "You have just crushed your left thumb with a hammer." Pain also has a distinctly negative emotional component. Researchers have focused on the information-carrying aspects of pain, its emotional components, and the various ways that the brain can adjust the amount of pain that reaches consciousness.

Pain as an Information Sense   The information-carrying aspect of pain is very similar to that of touch and temperature. The receptors for pain are free nerve endings. For example, capsaicin, the active ingredient in chili peppers, creates pain in the mouth by specifically stimulating these pain nerve endings. Painful stimuli cause the release of chemicals that fit into specialized receptors in pain neurons, causing them to fire. The axons of pain-sensing neurons release neurotransmitters not only near the spinal cord, thus sending information to the brain, but also near the skin, causing local inflammation.

Two types of nerve fibers carry pain signals from the skin to the spinal cord. *A-delta fibers* carry sharp, pricking pain sensations; they are myelinated to carry the sharp pain message quickly. *C fibers* carry chronic, dull aches and burning sensations. Some of these same C fibers also respond to nonpainful touch, but with a different pattern of firing.

Both A-delta and C fibers carry pain impulses into the spinal cord, where they form synapses with neurons that carry the pain signals to the thalamus and other parts of the brain (see Figure 4.26). Different pain neurons are activated by different degrees of painful stimulation. Numerous types of neurotransmitters are used by different pain neurons, a phenomenon that has allowed the development of a variety of new drugs for pain management (Foley & Macaluso, 1992).

FIGURE 4.26

Pain Pathways

Pain messages are carried to the brain by way of the spinal cord. *A-delta fibers* carry information about sharp pain. Unmyelinated *C fibers* carry several types of pain, including chronic, dull aches. Pain fibers make synapses in the reticular formation, causing arousal. They also project to the thalamus and from there to the cortex.

EASING PAIN Candy containing a substance called capsaicin is sometimes given for the treatment of painful mouth sores associated with cancer chemotherapy (Berger et al., 1995). Capsaicin is what makes chili peppers "hot," but eating enough of it results in desensitization and a corresponding reduction in pain sensations (Bevan & Geppetti, 1994).

The role of the cerebral cortex in experiencing pain is still being defined. Earlier studies of humans undergoing brain surgery for epilepsy concluded that pain has little, if any, cortical representation (Penfield & Rasmussen, 1968). More recently, PET scans of healthy volunteers have compared cortical activity during the experience of "warm" versus "painful but tolerable heat" (Talbot et al., 1991). The scans show activation of the somatosensory cortex under both conditions, and additional activity during pain in the cingulate cortex, an evolutionarily primitive region thought to be important in emotions.

Emotional Aspects of Pain All senses can have emotional components, most of which are learned responses. For example, the smell of baking cookies can make you feel good if it has been associated with happy childhood times. The emotional response to pain is more direct. Specific pathways carry an emotional component of the painful stimulus to areas of the hindbrain and reticular formation (see Figure 4.26), as well as to the limbic parts of cortex via the thalamus (Craig et al., 1994).

Nevertheless, the overall emotional response to pain depends greatly on cognitive factors. For example, experimenters compared responses to a painful stimulus in people who were informed about the nature of the stimulus and when to expect it, and in people who were not informed. Knowing about pain seemed to make it less objectionable, even though the sensation was reported to be just as noticeable (Mayer & Price, 1982). Other factors that affect the emotional responses to pain sensations include whether people use pain-reducing strategies (such as distracting thoughts or mental images of pleasant stimuli) and whether they expect these strategies to succeed (Marino, Gwynn & Spanos, 1989).

Modulation of Pain: The Gate Control Theory Pain is extremely useful, because in the long run it protects you from harm. However, there are times when enough is enough. Fortunately, the nervous system has several mechanisms for controlling the experience of pain.

One explanation of how the nervous system controls the amount of pain that reaches the brain is the **gate control theory** (Melzack & Wall, 1965). It holds that there is a "gate" in the spinal cord that either lets pain impulses travel upward to the brain or

LINKAGES: THE COMPLEX NATURE OF PAIN If pain were based only on the nature of incoming stimuli, this participant in a purification ceremony in Singapore would be hurting. However, the experience of pain is a complex phenomenon that is affected by psychological and biological variables that can make it more or, as in this case, less intense.

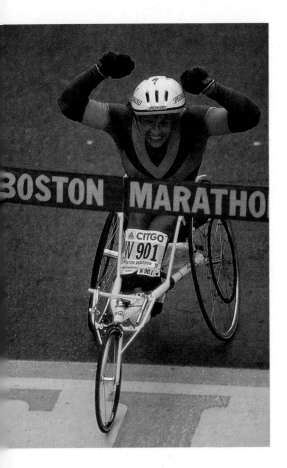

NATURAL ANALGESIA The stress of athletic exertion causes the release of endorphins, natural painkillers that have been associated with pleasant feelings called "runner's high."

blocks their progress. The details of the original formulation of this theory turned out to be incorrect, but more recent work supports the idea that natural mechanisms can block pain sensations (Hoffert, 1992; Yeh et al., 1992).

For example, input from other skin senses can come into the spinal cord at the same time the pain gets there and "take over" the pathways that the pain impulses would have used. This appears to be why rubbing the skin around a wound temporarily reduces the pain that is felt, why electrical stimulation of the skin around a painful spot relieves the pain, and why scratching relieves itching. (Itching is actually low-level activity in pain fibers.)

The brain can also close the gate to pain impulses by sending signals down the spinal cord. The control of sensation by messages descending from the brain is a common aspect of sensory systems (Willis, 1988). In the case of pain, these messages from the brain block incoming pain signals at spinal cord synapses. The result is **analgesia,** the absence of the sensation of pain in the presence of a normally painful stimulus. For example, if part of a rat's brain stem is electrically stimulated, pain signals generated in the skin never reach the brain (Reynolds, 1969). Permanently implanting stimulating electrodes in the same region of the human brain has reduced severe pain in some patients, but unfortunately it also produces a profound sense of impending doom (Hoffert, 1992).

Natural Analgesics   At least two substances play a role in the brain's ability to block pain signals: (1) the neurotransmitter *serotonin,* which is released by neurons descending from the brain, and (2) natural opiates called *endorphins.* As described in the previous chapter, endorphins are natural painkillers that act as neurotransmitters at many levels of the pain pathway, including the spinal cord, where they block the synapses of the fibers that carry pain signals. Endorphins may also relieve pain when the adrenal and pituitary glands secrete them into the bloodstream as hormones.

Several conditions are known to cause the body to ease its own pain. For example, during the late stages of pregnancy an endorphin system reduces the mother's labor pains (Facchinetti et al., 1982). An endorphin system may also be activated by consumption of spicy chili peppers; people who like "hot" foods no longer can tolerate them when they receive *naloxone,* a drug that blocks the action of endorphins (Etscorn, 1992, cited in Stern & Stern, 1992). Further, an endorphin system is activated when people *believe* they are receiving a painkiller even when they are not; this may be one basis for the placebo effect, discussed in Chapter 2. Physical or psychological stress can also activate natural analgesic systems. Stress-induced release of endorphins may account for instances in which injured soldiers and athletes continue to perform in the heat of battle or competition with no apparent pain.

There are also mechanisms for reactivating pain sensitivity once a crisis is past. Studies with animals show that they can learn that certain situations signal "safety," and that these safety signals prompt the release of a neurotransmitter that counteracts endorphins' analgesic effects (Wiertelak, Maier & Watkins, 1992).

*A*cupuncture is an ancient and widely used treatment in Asian medicine that is alleged to relieve pain. The method is based on the idea that body energy flows along lines called *channels* (Vincent & Richardson, 1986). There are fourteen main channels, and a person's health supposedly depends on the balance of energy flowing in them. Stimulating the channels by inserting very fine needles into the skin and twirling them is said to restore a balanced flow of energy. The needles produce an aching and tingling sensation called *Teh-ch'i* at the site of stimulation, but they relieve pain at distant, seemingly unrelated parts of the body.

THINKING CRITICALLY

Does Acupuncture Relieve Pain?

What am I being asked to believe or accept?

Acupuncturists assert that twirling a needle in the skin can relieve pain caused by everything from tooth extraction to cancer.

What evidence is available to support the assertion?

There is no scientific evidence for the existence of energy channels as described in the theory underlying acupuncture. But what about the more specific assertions that acupuncture relieves pain and that it does so through direct physical mechanisms?

In studies of acupuncture, it is very difficult to control for the placebo effect, especially in double-blind fashion. (How could a therapist not know whether the treatment being given is acupuncture or not? And from the patient's perspective, what placebo treatment could look and feel like having a needle inserted and twirled in the skin?) Nevertheless, researchers have tried to separate the psychological and physical effects of acupuncture by, for example, using mock electrical nerve stimulation.

Numerous studies show positive results in 50 to 80 percent of patients treated by acupuncture for various kinds of pain (Richardson & Vincent, 1986). In one controlled study of headache pain, for example, 33 percent of the patients in a placebo group improved following mock electrical nerve stimulation (which is about the usual proportion of people responding to a placebo), but 53 percent reported reduced pain following real acupuncture (Dowson, Lewith & Machin, 1985). Another headache study found both acupuncture and drugs to be superior to a placebo. Each reduced the frequency of headaches, but the drugs were more effective than acupuncture at reducing the severity of headache pain (Hesse, Mogelvang & Simonsen, 1994). Such well-controlled studies are rare, however, and their results are often contradictory (Ter Riet, Kleijnen & Knipschild, 1990).

There is evidence that acupuncture activates the endorphin system. It is associated with the release of endorphins in the brain, and drugs that slow the breakdown of opiates also prolong the analgesia produced by acupuncture (He, 1987). Furthermore, the pain-reducing effects of acupuncture during electrical stimulation of a tooth can be reversed by naloxone, the substance mentioned earlier that blocks the painkilling effects of endorphins (and other opiate drugs). This finding suggests that acupuncture somehow activates the body's natural painkilling system. In the cases where acupuncture activates endorphins, is this activation brought about only through the placebo effect? Probably not entirely, because acupuncture produces naloxone-reversible analgesia in monkeys and rats, who are much less likely than humans to have developed positive expectancies by reading about acupuncture (Ha et al., 1981; Kishioka et al., 1994).

Are there alternative ways of interpreting the evidence?

Yes. Evidence about acupuncture might be interpreted as simply confirming that the body's painkilling system can be stimulated by external means. Acupuncture may merely provide one activating method; there may be other, even more efficient methods for doing so. We already know, for example, that successful placebo treatments for human pain appear to operate by activating the endorphin system.

What additional evidence would be helpful to evaluate the alternatives?

Researchers need to focus not only on the effects of acupuncture but on the general relationship between internal painkilling systems and external methods for stimulating them. Regarding acupuncture itself, scientists do not yet know what factors govern whether it will activate the endorphin system. Other important unknowns include the types of pain for which acupuncture is most effective, the types of patients who respond best, and the precise procedures that are most effective.

What conclusions are most reasonable?

There seems little doubt that, in some circumstances, acupuncture relieves pain. It is even effective for some types of pain that resist other forms of treatment (Terenius,

1988). Acupuncture is not a panacea, however. For example, acupuncture does not appear to be useful for relieving pain following major surgery (He, 1987).

If scientists can determine how natural analgesic systems are activated by acupuncture and other means, the total amount of medication necessary to relieve pain could be reduced. There is certainly a need for better methods of pain control. The pain of arthritis, migraine headaches, back disorders, cancer, and other physical ailments imposes a heavy burden, causing disability for millions and costing more than $70 billion a year in medical and other costs (Bonica, 1992).

Proprioception

Most sensory systems receive information from the external world, such as the light reflected from a flower or the feeling of cool water. But as far as the brain is concerned, the rest of the body is "out there" too. You know about the position of your body and what each of its parts is doing only because sensory systems provide this information to the brain. These sensory systems are called **proprioceptive** ("received from one's own").

Kinesthesia   The sense that tells you where the parts of your body are with respect to each other is **kinesthesia** (pronounced "kin-es-thee´-zha"). You probably do not think much about kinesthetic information, but you definitely use it—as the following exercise demonstrates. Close your eyes, hold your arms out in front of you, and try to touch your two index fingers together. You probably did this well because your kinesthetic sense told you where each finger was with respect to your body. You also depend on kinesthetic information to guide all your movements. Otherwise, it would be impossible to develop or improve any motor skill, from basic walking to complex athletic movements. These movement patterns become simple and fluid because, with practice, the brain uses kinesthetic information automatically.

Normally, kinesthetic information comes primarily from the joints but also from muscles. Receptors in muscle fibers send information to the brain about the stretching of muscles (McCloskey, 1978). When the position of the bones changes, receptors in the joints transduce this mechanical energy into neural activity, providing information about both the rate of change and the angle of the bones. This coded information goes to the spinal cord and is sent from there to the thalamus along with sensory information from the skin. Eventually it goes to the cerebellum and to the somatosensory cortex (see Figures 3.14 and 3.17), both of which are involved in the smooth coordination of movements.

BALANCING ACT   The smooth coordination of all physical movement, from scratching your nose to complex feats of balance, depends on kinesthesia, the sense that provides information about where each part of the body is in relation to all the others.

Oliver Sacks, a well-known neurologist, has described the case of "Christina," a woman who somehow lost her kinesthetic sense (Sacks, 1985). As noted in Chapter 2, case studies sometimes lead to important insights about clinical problems or other phenomena that occur so rarely that they cannot be studied through surveys or controlled experiments. The case report on Christina led to the realization that kinesthesia not only tells us where our body parts are but also plays an important role in our sense of self.

In 1977, Christina was a healthy young woman who entered a hospital in preparation for some minor surgery. Before the surgery could be performed, however, she began to have difficulty holding onto objects; then she had trouble moving. She would rise from bed and flop onto the floor like a rag doll. Assuming that Christina was

FOCUS ON RESEARCH METHODS

A Case Study of Kinesthesia Lost

fearful of her impending surgery, a psychiatrist diagnosed her muscular weakness as *conversion disorder*—a condition described in Chapter 15 in which there is apparent, but not actual, damage to sensory or motor systems. But there *was* damage in Christina's case. Sacks's intense and careful examination of Christina showed that she had lost all sensory feedback about her joints, muscle tone, and the position of her limbs. For unknown reasons, the sensory neurons carrying this information had selectively degenerated. As a result, Christina seemed to have lost her body; she felt disembodied, like a ghost. On one occasion, for example, she became annoyed at a visitor whom she thought was tapping her fingers on a table top. But it was she, not the visitor, who was doing it. Her hands were acting on their own; her body was doing things she did not know about.

In his analysis of this case, Sacks noted that the sense we have of our bodies is provided partly through our experience of seeing it, but also partly through proprioception. Christina put it this way: "Proprioception is like the eyes of the body, the way the body sees itself. And if it goes, it's like the body's blind." With great effort and determination, Christina was ultimately able to regain some of her ability to move about. If she looked intently at her arms and legs, she could coordinate their movement to some degree. Eventually, she left the hospital and resumed many of her normal activities. But Christina never recovered her sense of self. She still feels like a stranger in her own body.

Notice that Christina's case study did not confirm any hypotheses about kinesthesia the way an experiment might, but it did focus attention on the subjective dimension of this relatively obscure sensory modality. It also highlighted a rare condition that, though almost unknown when Sacks reported it, has been observed more often in recent years, especially in people taking megadoses of vitamin B_6, also known as pyridoxine (Sacks, 1985). These high doses—or even lower doses taken over a long period of time—can damage sensory neurons (Dordain & Deffond, 1994).

Vestibular Sense   Kinesthesia tells the brain about where body parts are in relation to one another; the **vestibular sense** tells the brain about the position of the head (and hence the body) in space and about its general movements. It is often thought of as the sense of balance. People usually become aware of the vestibular sense only when they overstimulate it and become dizzy.

Two vestibular sacs and three semicircular canals that are part of the inner ear are the organs for the vestibular sense. (You can see the semicircular canals in Figure 4.3; the vestibular sacs connect these canals and the cochlea.) The **vestibular sacs** are filled with fluid and contain small crystals called **otoliths** ("ear stones") that rest on hair endings. The **semicircular canals** are fluid-filled, arc-shaped tubes; tiny hairs extend into the fluid in the canals. When your head moves, the otoliths shift in the vestibular sacs and the fluid moves in the semicircular canals, stimulating hair endings. This process activates neurons that travel with the auditory nerve, signaling to the brain the amount and direction of head movement.

The vestibular system has neural connections to the cerebellum, to the part of the autonomic nervous system (ANS) that affects the digestive system, and to the muscles of the eyes. The connections to the cerebellum help coordinate bodily movements. The connections to the ANS help create the nausea that sometimes follows overstimulation of the vestibular system—by amusement park rides, for example. Finally, the connections to the eye muscles create *vestibular-ocular reflexes*. For instance, when your head moves in one direction, your eyes reflexively move in the opposite direction. This reflex allows your eyes to fixate on a point in space even when your head is moving around, so you can track a ball in flight as you are running to catch it. You can dramatize this reflex by having a friend spin you around on a stool for a while; when you stop, try to fix your gaze on one point in the room. You will be unable to do so, because the excitation of the vestibular system will cause your eyes to move repeatedly in the direction opposite to that in which you were spinning.

FUTURE DIRECTIONS

In this chapter we have described how sensory systems allow people to make contact with the outside world as well as with what is going on within their own bodies. The study of these systems has been somewhat unusual. On the one hand, it relates to abstract, philosophical issues such as: What is reality, and how do we come to know it? On the other hand, the study of sensory systems has led to some of the most concrete, down-to-earth research in psychology. This work focuses on learning more about just how sensory systems detect energy, transduce it, and send it to the brain in a usable form.

Psychologists have accumulated a vast body of knowledge in these areas, but much remains unknown or poorly understood, and the research goes on. For some senses, such as olfaction and touch, we still need to learn more about transduction. For other senses, the major questions concern how the brain processes the information it receives. When it comes to the transition from sensation to perception, to the means by which the pathways and connections give rise to perception and subjective reality, we still know very little. Nevertheless, our detailed knowledge—of the visual system in particular—has opened the way for new theorizing about the basis of consciousness (Churchland & Sejnowski, 1992; Sperry, 1993).

Research on sensory systems will have many practical applications in the future—contributing, for example, to the design of computers that can see and recognize objects from any angle. Even now, some recently understood principles about the brain, such as its independent processing of several dimensions of visual sensation (including edges, movement, and color), are being applied in computer modeling of vision. Biological principles have also been applied in the development of artificial sensory organs that can be integrated into the nervous system, artificial limbs that stimulate sensory nerves to create feelings of pressure and warmth, and robots that can perform complex sensorimotor tasks (Arbib & Liaw, 1995; Sabolich & Ortega, 1994).

There are many as-yet-unsolved mysteries of sensation and many practical applications of the information to come. For more detailed information on sensory systems and how they work, consider taking courses on sensation and perception, biological psychology, vision, speech and hearing, or computer science.

SUMMARY AND KEY TERMS

A *sense* is a system that translates information from outside the nervous system into neural activity. Messages from the senses are called *sensations*.

■ SENSORY SYSTEMS

The first step in sensation involves *accessory structures*, which collect and modify sensory stimuli. The second step is *transduction*, the process of converting incoming energy into neural activity; it is accomplished by sensory *receptors*, neural cells specialized to detect energy of some type. *Adaptation* takes place when receptors receive unchanging stimulation. Neural activity is transferred through the thalamus (except in the case of olfaction) and on to the cortex.

The Problem of Coding

Coding is the translation of physical properties of a stimulus into a pattern of neural activity that specifically identifies those physical properties. It is the language the brain uses to describe sensations. Coding is characterized by *specific nerve energies:* Stimulation of a particular sensory nerve provides codes for that one sense no matter how the stimulation takes place. There are two basic types of sensory codes: *temporal* and *spatial*.

■ LINKAGES: SENSATION AND BIOLOGICAL ASPECTS OF PSYCHOLOGY

The *topographical representations* of sensory information in the central nervous system maintain the topographical relationships of the stimuli. Information from the left side of the sensory world is represented in the right side of the cerebral cortex, and vice versa. The region of cerebral cortex in which a sense is first represented is called the *primary cortex* for that sense. Neurons in primary cortex are organized in columns that have similar response properties. The density of sensory receptors in an area determines how much of the cortex is devoted to representing that part of the sensory world. There are multiple topographical representations of the sensory world, as well as areas of cortex, called association cortex, that integrate information from more than one sense.

■ HEARING

Sound is a repetitive fluctuation in the pressure of a medium like air; it travels in waves.

Sound

The *frequency* (which is related to *wavelength*) and *amplitude* of sound waves produce the psychological dimensions of *pitch* and *loudness*, respectively. *Timbre*, the quality of sound, depends on complex wave patterns added to the basic frequency of the sound.

The Ear

The energy from sound waves is collected and transmitted to the *cochlea* through a series of accessory structures, including the *pinna, tympanic membrane,* malleus (hammer), incus (anvil), stapes (stirrup), and oval window. Transduction occurs when sound energy stimulates hair cells of the organ of Corti on the *basilar membrane* of the cochlea, which in turn stimulate the *auditory nerve*.

Coding Intensity and Frequency

The intensity of a sound stimulus is coded by the firing rate of auditory neurons. *Place theory* describes the coding of high frequencies: They are coded by the place on the basilar membrane where the wave envelope peaks. Each neuron in the auditory nerve is most sensitive to a specific frequency (its characteristic frequency). Very low frequencies are coded by *frequency matching*, which refers to the fact that the firing rate of a neuron matches the frequency of a sound wave; according to *volley theory*, some frequencies may be matched by the firing rate of a group of neurons. Low to moderate frequencies are coded through a combination of these methods.

Auditory Pathways and Representations

Auditory information is relayed through the thalamus to the *primary auditory cortex* and to other areas of auditory cortex. Sounds of similar frequency activate neighboring cells in the cortex, but loudness is coded temporally.

■ VISION

Light

Visible light is electromagnetic radiation with a wavelength from about 400 to about 750 nanometers. *Light intensity,* or the amount of energy in light, determines its brightness. Differing *light wavelengths* are sensed as different colors.

Focusing Light

Accessory structures of the eye include the *cornea, pupil, iris,* and *lens.* Through *accommodation* and other means, these structures focus light rays on the *retina,* the netlike structure of cells at the back of the eye.

Converting Light into Images

Photoreceptors in the retina—*rods* and *cones*—have *photopigments* and can transduce light into neural activity. Rods and cones differ in their shape, their sensitivity to light, their ability to discriminate colors, and their distribution across the retina. The *fovea,* the area of highest *acuity,* has only cones, which are color sensitive. Rods are more sensitive to light but do not discriminate colors; they are distributed in areas around the fovea. Both types of photoreceptors contribute to *dark adaptation.* From the photoreceptors, energy transduced from light is transferred to *bipolar cells* and then to *ganglion cells,* with *interneurons* making lateral connections between the bipolar and ganglion cells. As a result of *convergence* and *lateral inhibition,* most ganglion cells in effect compare the amount of light falling on the center of their *receptive fields* with that falling on the surrounding area. The result is that the retina enhances the contrast between dark and light areas.

Seeing Color

The color of an object depends on which of the wavelengths striking it are absorbed and which are reflected. The sensation of color has three psychological dimensions: *hue, saturation,* and *brightness.* According to the *trichromatic* (or Young-Helmholtz) *theory,* color vision results from the fact that the eye includes three types of cones, each of which is most sensitive to short, medium, or long wavelengths; information from the three types combines to produce the sensation of color. Individuals may have slight variations in the number and sensitivity of their cone pigments. According to the *opponent-process* (or Hering) *theory,* there are red-green, blue-yellow, and black-white visual elements; the members of each pair inhibit each other so that only one member of a pair may produce a signal at a time. This theory explains color afterimages as well as the fact that lights of *complementary* colors cancel each other out and produce gray when mixed together.

Visual Pathways

The ganglion cells send action potentials out of the eye, at a point where a *blind spot* is created. Axons of ganglion cells leave the eye as a bundle of fibers called the *optic nerve;* half of these fibers cross over at the *optic chiasm* and terminate in the *lateral geniculate nucleus (LGN)* of the thalamus. Neurons in the LGN send visual information on to the *primary visual cortex,* where cells detect and respond to features such as lines, edges, and orientations.

Visual Representations

Visual form, color, movement, and distance are processed by parallel systems. *Feature detectors* are hierarchically built out of simpler units. The visual system also analyzes input into spatial frequencies of light and dark.

■ THE CHEMICAL SENSES: SMELL AND TASTE

The chemical senses include olfaction and gustation.

Olfaction

Olfaction detects volatile chemicals that come into contact with olfactory receptors in the nose. Olfactory signals are sent to the *olfactory bulb* in the brain without passing through the thalamus. *Pheromones* are odors from one animal that change the physiology or behavior of another animal, sometimes acting through the *vomeronasal organ.*

Gustation

Gustation detects chemicals that come into contact with taste receptors in *papillae* on the tongue. Elementary taste sensations are limited to sweet, sour, bitter, and salty. The combined responses of many taste buds determines a taste sensation.

Smell, Taste, and Flavor

The senses of smell and taste interact to produce flavor.

■ SOMATIC SENSES AND THE VESTIBULAR SYSTEM

The *somatic senses,* or *somatosensory systems,* include skin senses and proprioceptive senses. The skin senses include touch, temperature, and pain.

Touch and Temperature

Nerve endings in the skin generate touch sensations when they are mechanically stimulated. Some nerve endings are sensitive to temperature, and some respond to both temperature and touch. Signals from neighboring points on the skin stay next to each other even in the cortex.

Pain

Pain provides information about damaging stimuli. Sharp pain and dull, chronic pain are carried by different fibers—A-delta and C fibers, respectively. The emotional response to pain depends on how the painful stimulus is interpreted. According to the *gate control theory,* pain signals can be blocked by messages sent from the brain down the spinal cord, producing *analgesia.* Endorphins act at several levels of the pain systems to reduce sensations of pain.

Proprioception

Proprioceptive senses provide information about the body. *Kinesthesia* provides information about the positions of body parts with respect to one another, and the *vestibular sense* provides information about the position of the head in space through the *otoliths* in *vestibular sacs* and the *semicircular canals.*

PERCEPTION

CHAPTER 5

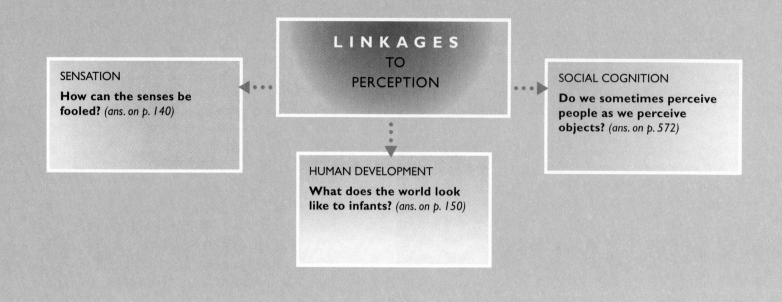

LINKAGES
TO
PERCEPTION

SENSATION

How can the senses be fooled? *(ans. on p. 140)*

SOCIAL COGNITION

Do we sometimes perceive people as we perceive objects? *(ans. on p. 572)*

HUMAN DEVELOPMENT

What does the world look like to infants? *(ans. on p. 150)*

A t a traffic circle in Scotland, fourteen fatal accidents occurred in a twelve-month period, partly because drivers failed to slow down as they approached the circle. When warning signs failed to solve the problem, Gordon Denton, a British psychologist, proposed an ingenious solution. White lines were painted across the road leading to the circle, in a pattern that looked something like this:

/   /   /   /   /   / //

Crossing these ever-closer spaced lines at a constant speed gave drivers the impression that their car was accelerating, and their automatic response was to slow down (Denton, 1980). During the fourteen months after implementation of Denton's idea, there were only two fatalities at the traffic circle. To reach this solution, Denton depended partly on his knowledge of *sensation,* the process (described in Chapter 4) through which energy from outside the nervous system is translated into neural signals that are sent to the brain. He relied even more on his knowledge of the principles of human *perception.*

Perception is the process through which sensations are interpreted, using knowledge and understanding of the world, so that they become meaningful experiences. Thus, perception is not a passive process of simply absorbing and decoding incoming sensations. If it were, people's understanding of the environment would be poor indeed. The visual scene would be a constantly changing, confusing mosaic of light and color. Instead, our brains take sensations and create a coherent world, often by filling in missing information and using past experience to give meaning to what we see, hear, or touch. For example, the raw sensations coming from the stimuli in Figure 5.1 convey only the information that there is a series of intersecting lines. But your perceptual system automatically interprets this image as a rectangle (or window frame) lying on its side.

Perception is so quick and familiar that it is difficult to appreciate the processes that allow you to turn the signals from sensory receptors into your personal experience of reality. By shaping experience, perceptions influence thoughts, feelings, and actions (see the Linkages diagram). In this chapter, we explore the wondrous processes of perception, examining how people detect incoming energy, organize sensations into distinct and stable patterns, and recognize those patterns. We also explore the role of attention in guiding the perceptual system to analyze some parts of the world more closely than others. First, however, we examine the nature of perception itself.

FIGURE 5.1

What Do You See?

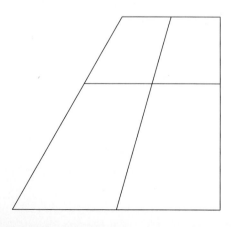

THREE VIEWS OF PERCEPTION

As discovered by drivers who found themselves slowing at Denton's traffic circle, much of our perceptual work is done automatically, without conscious awareness. Other perceptual tasks take attention and effort, as when a young child struggles to recognize printed letters, then mentally organizes them into meaningful words and sentences. There are three major ways of thinking about these complex perceptual processes.

According to the **ecological view** of perception, most of what we perceive is already present in the rich array of stimuli in the environment. Consider the process of landing a plane, for example: A pilot's perceptual system uses information from the landscape below to precisely establish the plane's location and movement through the air (Gibson, 1979). James J. Gibson, founder of the ecological view, argued that the primary goal of perception is to *support actions*, such as walking or driving, by "tuning in" to the part of the environmental stimulus array that is most important for performing those actions (Hancock et al., 1995; Warren & Werthheimer, 1990).

A different view of perception is held by **constructionists,** who argue that the perceptual system must construct a representation of reality from fragments of sensory information, much as a paleontologist constructs an entire dinosaur from a few bits of bone (Rock, 1983). This constructive process, they say, explains how you can perceive the images in Figure 5.2 as a triangle and a face even though the sensory information is incomplete. We know what people will perceive in this display, say constructionists, because perceptual processes do not build reality randomly. The construction is heavily influenced by past experience and knowledge, which create *expectations* of what you will see or hear. These expectations make perception easier, particularly when sensory evidence is weak or ambiguous. For example, suppose you are on the roof of a tall building. Your knowledge about the size of adult humans tells you that the people on the sidewalk below are probably about the same height as the person standing next to you, but appear tiny only because they are so far away. In other words, constructionists argue that most aspects of perception involve *inferences* about sensory information. Accordingly, many constructionist psychologists are less concerned about how perception supports action than about how perception supports people's *understanding* of the world.

The newest approach to perception, called the **computational** view, tries to explain how complex *computations* within the nervous system might turn raw sensory stimulation into a representation of the world (Green, 1991). Through these computations, information from, say, edges, corners, contours, and surface texture are rapidly combined to create a recognizable object or experience (see Figure 5.3). The computational approach is based in part on research in neurophysiology aimed at identifying structures and mechanisms in the nervous system that analyze basic features of the perceptual scene. It also depends on computer models capable of making computations as complex as those carried out by the human brain (Grossberg, 1988).

In summary, to explain perception the ecological view emphasizes the information provided by the environment itself, the constructionist view emphasizes how people

---

FIGURE 5.2

The Constructionist View of Perception

The constructionist view of perception maintains that, when you look at stimuli such as these, you perceive more than the raw sensory information they provide.

FIGURE 5.3

The Computational View of Perception

The experience of three-dimensional depth in this two-dimensional figure is overwhelming. According to the computational view of perception, this experience is the result of your brain's ability to almost instantaneously combine the information presented by each of the drawing's many features.

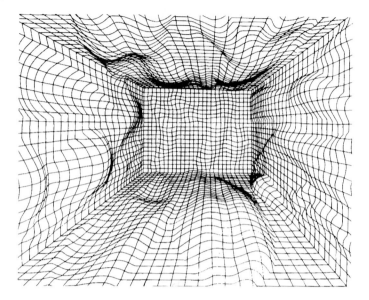

Source: Marr, 1982.

make inferences about that environment, and the computational view focuses on how the nervous system manipulates incoming signals. You will see evidence for each of these views later in this chapter.

PSYCHOPHYSICS

How can psychologists measure people's perceptions when there is no way to get inside their heads to experience what they are experiencing? In one approach to this problem, people are presented with lights, sounds, and other physically measurable stimuli and then asked to report their perception of the stimuli, using special scales of measurement. This method of studying perception, called **psychophysics,** describes the relationship between *physical energy* in the environment and our *psychological experience* of that energy. Psychophysical research focuses on psychological responses to particular *amounts* of energy as well as to changes in that energy.

Absolute Thresholds: Is Something Out There?

How much stimulus energy is needed to trigger a conscious perceptual experience? The minimum detectable amount of light, sound, pressure, or other physical energy is called the *absolute threshold*. This threshold can be amazingly low. Normal human vision, for example, can detect the light equivalent to a single candle flame burning in the dark thirty miles away. Table 5.1 lists absolute thresholds for human vision, hearing, taste, smell, and touch.

TABLE 5.1

Some Absolute Thresholds

Here are examples of stimuli at the absolute threshold for the five primary senses.

Human Sense	Absolute Threshold
Vision	A candle flame seen at 30 miles on a clear night
Hearing	The tick of a watch under quiet conditions at 20 feet
Taste	One teaspoon of sugar in two gallons of water
Smell	One drop of perfume diffused into the entire volume of air in a six-room apartment
Touch	The wing of a fly falling on your cheek from a distance of one centimeter

Source: Galanter, 1962.

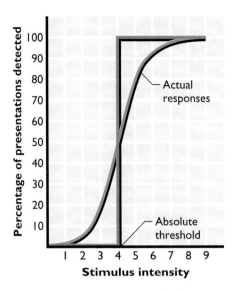

FIGURE 5.4

The Absolute Threshold

The curve shows the relationship between the physical intensity of a signal and the likelihood that it will be detected. If the absolute threshold were indeed absolute, all signals at or above a particular intensity would always be detected, and no signal below that intensity would ever be detected (see red line). Because this response pattern almost never occurs, the "absolute" threshold is defined as the intensity at which the signal is detected with 50 percent accuracy.

If you were participating in a typical experiment on the absolute threshold for vision, you would be seated in a darkened laboratory. After your eyes have adapted to the darkness, brief flashes of light would be presented at varying intensities. Each time, you would be asked if you saw the stimulus. Your responses would probably form a curve like the one shown in Figure 5.4. As you can see, the "absolute" threshold is not an all-or-none phenomenon. Thus, a stimulus at an intensity of 3—which is below the absolute threshold in Figure 5.4—will still be perceived 20 percent of the time it occurs. Because of such variability, psychophysicists have redefined the **absolute threshold** as the minimum amount of energy that can be detected 50 percent of the time. Why should there be variability in an "absolute" threshold? The two most important reasons have to do with internal noise and our response criterion.

Internal noise is the spontaneous, random firing of cells in the nervous system that occurs in varying degrees whether or not we are stimulated by physical energy. This unceasing neural activity is a little like "snow" on a television screen or static between radio stations. If the amount of internal noise happens to be high at a particular moment, our sensory systems may mistakenly interpret the noise as a stimulus. If the level of internal noise is extremely low at the moment a faint light or sound occurs, it may not add enough extra neural activity to make that stimulus noticeable.

The second source of variation in absolute threshold, the **response criterion,** reflects a person's willingness or reluctance to respond to a stimulus. The response criterion is affected by a person's *motivation*—wants and needs—as well as *expectancies*. For example, if you were penalized for reporting that a faint light appeared when it didn't, you might raise your response criterion and report the light only when you are very sure you saw it. Similarly, expecting a faint stimulus to occur lowers the response criterion, making us more likely to detect the stimulus than when it is unexpected.

Overcoming the Threshold Problem: Signal-Detection Theory

In short, whether you detect a stimulus depends not only on its physical energy but also on the effects of neural noise and your response criterion. Because these effects are inherent in human beings, researchers realized that the measurement of absolute thresholds could never be more precise than the 50 percent rule mentioned earlier. Accordingly, they abandoned the effort to determine absolute thresholds and turned instead to signal-detection theory.

Signal-detection theory (Green & Swets, 1966) is a mathematical model of how people's sensitivity and response criterion combine to determine decisions about whether they say that a near-threshold stimulus has occurred. **Sensitivity** refers to one's ability to discriminate a stimulus from its background; it is influenced by neural noise, the intensity of the stimulus, and the capacity of sensory systems. As already noted, the response criterion is the internal rule, also known as *bias,* that a person uses in deciding whether to report a signal. Will a lab technician notice the presence of cancer cells in a pap smear? Will an airport security guard spot the weapon in a passenger's x-rayed luggage? Because it allows precise measurement of people's sensitivity to stimuli of any kind, signal-detection theory provides a way to understand and predict responses in these and many other situations (Swets, 1992).

For example, signal-detection theory can be valuable in understanding why weather forecasters using the latest Doppler radar systems sometimes fail to warn of a tornado that local residents can see with the naked eye (Stevens, 1995). The forecaster's task is not easy because these high-tech systems are so sensitive that they respond not only to dangerous shifts in wind direction (wind shear) and a tornado's spinning funnel but also to such trivia as swirling dust and swarming insects. Thus, the telltale radar "signature" of a tornado appears against a potentially confusing background of visual information. Whether or not that signature will be picked out and reported depends both on the forecaster's sensitivity to the signal and on the response criterion being used. In establishing the criterion for making a report, the forecaster must consider consequences. Setting the criterion too high might cause evidence of a tornado to go unnoticed. Such a *miss* could cost many lives if it left a populated area with no warning

Tornado present?

Forecaster's decision		Yes	No
	Yes	Hit	False alarm
	No	Miss	Correct rejection

(A) POSSIBLE OUTCOMES

Tornado present?

Forecaster's decision		Yes	No
	Yes	Hit 70%	False alarm 30%
	No	Miss 30%	Correct rejection 70%

(B) TORNADO PRESENT IN 50% OF THE STORMS

Tornado present?

Forecaster's decision		Yes	No
	Yes	Hit 90%	False alarm 40%
	No	Miss 10%	Correct rejection 60%

(C) TORNADO PRESENT IN 90% OF THE STORMS

FIGURE 5.5

Signal Detection

Part (A) shows that the possible outcomes of examining a radar display for signs of a tornado include a *hit* (correctly detecting the tornado), a *miss* (failing to detect the tornado), a *correct rejection* (seeing no tornado when there is none), or a *false alarm* (reporting a tornado when none exists). Parts (B) and (C) compare the likelihood of various outcomes when a tornado is present in 50 percent and 90 percent of the radar displays examined.

of danger. If the response criterion is set too low, however, the forecaster might report a tornado when there really is none. This *false alarm* would unnecessarily disrupt people's lives, activate costly emergency plans, reduce the credibility of future warnings, and, if part of a pattern of false alarms, put the forecaster's job in jeopardy (see Figure 5.5A). In short, there is a tradeoff. To minimize false alarms, the forecaster could set a very high response criterion, but doing so would also make misses more likely. Lowering the response criterion to avoid misses, however, would make false alarms more likely.

Let's examine how various kinds of information can change the response criterion, and how those changes might affect the accuracy of a forecaster's decisions. If a forecaster knows it is a time of year when tornadoes exist in only about 50 percent of the storm systems seen on radar, a rather high response criterion is likely to be used; it will take reasonably strong evidence to trigger a tornado warning. The hypothetical data in Figure 5.5B show that, under these conditions, the forecaster correctly detected 70 percent of actual tornadoes but missed 30 percent of them; also, 30 percent of the tornado reports were false alarms. Now suppose the forecaster learns that a different kind of storm system is on the way, and that about 90 percent of such systems spawn tornadoes. This information is likely to increase the forecaster's expectancy for seeing a tornado signature, thus lowering the response criterion. The forecaster will now require less visual evidence of a tornado before reporting one, especially in borderline cases. Under these conditions, the hit rate might rise from 70 percent to, say, 90 percent, but the false-alarm rate might also increase from 30 percent to 40 percent (see Figure 5.5C).

We can estimate a specific forecaster's *sensitivity* to visual signals of a tornado by looking at what happens to the hit rate and false-alarm rate when various response criteria are used. As the response criterion drops (thus requiring less evidence of a tornado to trigger a report), forecasters with the greatest sensitivity will show a hit rate that increases faster than their false-alarm rate. Less sensitive forecasters will show about the same increase in both hits *and* false alarms.

As Figure 5.5 suggests, people do sometimes make mistakes at signal detection, whether it involves spotting tornadoes, inspecting aircraft, diagnosing medical conditions, searching for oil, or looking for clues at a crime scene. Research on limitations and individual differences in these perceptual abilities has led psychologists to suggest ways of improving people's performance on signal-detection tasks (Warm & Parasuraman, 1987; Wickens, 1992b). For example, they recommend that manufacturers occasionally place flawed items into a stream of objects to be inspected. This strategy increases inspectors' expectations of seeing flaws, thus lowering the response criterion and raising the hit rate.

Judging Differences Between Stimuli

Often people must not only detect a stimulus but also determine whether two stimuli are the same or different. For example, when tuning up, musicians must decide if notes played by two instruments have the same pitch. And when repainting part of a wall, a contractor needs to decide if the new paint matches the old.

It turns out that people's ability to judge differences in the amount of a stimulus depends on how much of that stimulus there is to begin with. More specifically, the ability to detect differences declines as the magnitude of the stimulus increases. For example, if you are comparing the weight of two envelopes, you will be able to detect a difference of as little as a fraction of an ounce. But if you are comparing two boxes weighing around fifty pounds, you may not notice a difference unless it is a pound or more.

Weber's Law   One of the oldest laws in psychology gives a precise description of the relationship between the intensity of a stimulus and our ability to detect a change in its magnitude. Named after the nineteenth-century German physiologist Ernst Weber (pronounced "vay-ber"), **Weber's law** states that the smallest detectable difference in stimulus energy is a constant fraction of the intensity of the stimulus. The smallest detectable difference in the stimulus is called the **difference threshold** or **just-**

Stimulus	K
Pitch	.003
Brightness	.017
Weight	.020
Loudness	.100
Pressure on skin	.140
Saltiness of taste	.200

TABLE 5.2

Weber Constants (K) for Different Stimuli

The value of Weber's constant, *K*, differs from one sense to another. Differences in *K* demonstrate the *adaptive* nature of perception. Humans, who depend more heavily on vision than on taste for survival, are more sensitive to vision than to taste.

noticeable difference (JND). The constant fraction, which is different for different types of sensory input, is given the symbol *K*.

In algebraic terms, Weber's law is *JND = KI*, where *K* is the constant fraction and *I* is the amount, or intensity, of the stimulus. For example, the value of *K* for weight is .02. If an object weighs 25 pounds *(I)*, the JND is only half a pound (.02 x 25 pounds). So for 25 pounds of luggage, groceries, or other liftable objects, an increase or decrease of half a pound is necessary before you can detect a change in heaviness. But candy snatchers beware: It takes a change of only two-thirds of an ounce to determine that someone has been into a two-pound box of chocolates! Table 5.2 lists the value of *K* for a variety of human senses. The smaller the value of *K*, the more sensitive a sense is to stimulus differences. For example, *K* for vision is .017, which indicates a high degree of sensitivity; only a small change in the intensity of light is needed for a difference in its brightness to be noticeable.

Weber's law does not hold when stimuli are very intense or very weak, but it does apply to complex as well as simple stimuli. Accordingly, you would surely notice a fifty-cent increase in a one-dollar bus fare; this 50 percent increase is well above the JND for noticing changes in cost. But the same fifty-cent increase in monthly rent would be less than a JND and thus unlikely to cause notice, let alone concern.

Fechner's Law   How much must the volume on a stereo increase before it would seem twice as loud? How many pounds could you add to a package before it seems twice as heavy? Weber's law does not address questions like these, but it helped Gustav Fechner look for an answer. In 1860 Fechner proposed that Weber's law could be used to understand the perception of stimulus magnitude. He applied the concept of a JND in an attempt to describe the relationship between the intensity of a stimulus and the perception of its magnitude.

According to *Fechner's law,* as stimulus magnitude increases, larger and larger increases in physical energy are necessary to obtain equal changes in *perceived* magnitude. For example, it would take only a small increase in volume to make a soft sound seem twice as loud, but imagine how much additional volume it would take to make a rock band twice as loud. To put it another way, Fechner's law says that constant increases in physical energy will produce progressively smaller increases in perceived magnitude. Thus, the perceived difference in brightness between a 75-watt bulb and a 100-watt bulb will be greater than the perceived difference between a 100-watt bulb and a 125-watt bulb.

Fechner's law applies to most, but not all, stimuli. While light and sound must increase more and more to create the same amount of change in perceived magnitude, each successive increase in the perceived intensity of electric shock takes *less and less* increase in physical energy. Thus, it would take a relatively large increase in shock intensity to make a barely noticeable shock seem twice as intense, but if the shock is already painful, it would take only a small increase in intensity before you said it was twice as strong. S. S. Stevens offered a formula (known as *Stevens's power law*) that, like Weber's law, includes a factor that takes into account the differential sensitivity of various sensory systems. You need not be familiar with the mathematics of these laws to realize that they echo an important theme: The perception of magnitude is not absolute but relative. Your experience of one stimulus depends on its relationship to others.

LINKAGES   **Are there senses we don't know about?** (a link to Sensation)

Weber's law is based on the assumption that people experience the world through the sensory systems. Throughout history, however, various people have claimed *extrasensory perception,* the ability to perceive stimuli from the past, present, or future through a mechanism beyond vision, hearing, touch, taste, and smell. Alleged forms of extrasensory perception (ESP) have included *clairvoyance* (perceiving objects obscured from view or out of earshot), *telepathy*

THINKING CRITICALLY

Can People Perceive What Cannot Normally Be Sensed?

AN ESP EXPERIMENT This woman is attempting to use clairvoyance to "see" objects in another room while hearing only white noise and wearing goggles that provide unpatterned visual stimulation. She is unlikely to succeed. Since 1964 James Randi, an expert magician and ESP skeptic, has carried a $10,000 check that he will give to anyone who can perform clairvoyance, telepathy, or any other feat of ESP under scientific conditions (Randi, 1987). After investigating hundreds of claims, he still has his money.

("reading" another person's thoughts, for example), and *psychokinesis* (involving not perception, but the moving or controlling of dice or other objects through mental effort alone). Claims for ESP are widely believed (Alcock, 1995; Lett, 1992). Research on them is called *parapsychology,* meaning an area that alters or "goes beyond" psychology.

What am I being asked to believe or accept?

Proponents of ESP ask you to believe that information can be transmitted from the outside world to the brain (and back again, in the case of psychokinesis) without using traditional sensory receptors.

What evidence is available to support the assertion?

Many apparent parapsychological phenomena are weak and difficult to replicate. Under close scrutiny by outside observers, reported ESP phenomena often fail to occur (Swets & Druckman, 1990). However, several laboratory experiments have apparently demonstrated clairvoyance, telepathy, or psychokinesis (e.g., Rao & Palmer, 1987). Some blindfolded subjects do far better than chance would predict at clairvoyance tasks such as naming the colors of cards by touching them (Youtz, 1968). Others do slightly better than chance at telepathy or psychokinesis tasks such as describing or altering the output of a machine that is generating random numbers in another room (e.g., Honorton & Harper, 1974; Jahn, 1982; Schmidt, 1969).

In one set of experiments, subjects were asked to predict which of four randomly illuminated lights would appear next (Schmidt, 1969). After several thousand trials, a few subjects correctly predicted the illumination up to 26.3 percent of the time, a performance that—statistically speaking—is significantly better than the 25 percent to be expected by chance alone (Rao & Palmer, 1987).

Are there alternative ways of interpreting the evidence?

Consider first the experiments on identifying colors through touch. Different colors give off different amounts of radiant energy. Is it possible that certain subjects' sense of touch is particularly sensitive to differences in heat? Some evidence for this possibility comes from experiments in which color-guessing performance drops to chance levels after heat-blocking filters are placed over the cards. Thus, claims made about color guessing, at least, could be accounted for by extra*sensitive* rather than extrasensory perception.

Many psychologists have also challenged the use of apparent changes in random number–machine output as a measure of psychokinesis. They note that randomness is not an all-or-none concept. If you flip a coin seven times and it comes up heads each time, is the pattern really nonrandom? Does it mean you have psychokinetic ability? A sequence of seven heads in a row is unlikely (it will occur on average only once in 128 tries), but it certainly can happen. Indeed, a seven-heads sequence is just as likely as any of the 127 other possible seven-flip sequences. In other words, it is far more difficult than one might think to determine that something really is "nonrandom" (Hansel, 1980). Thus, a very plausible interpretation of apparently nonrandom events in ESP experiments is that they are random after all.

Finally, some apparently remarkable results of ESP experiments can be attributed to fraud. A few researchers have tampered with their equipment and measurements, thus destroying their credibility and raising suspicions about all parapsychological research.

What evidence would help to evaluate the alternatives?

As a science, psychology depends for evidence on clear, reliable, and replicated observations. Skeptical scientists place the burden of proof for the existence of ESP on parapsychologists, who must be able to show robust, replicable ESP effects that do not depend on interpretations of nonrandomness and that occur under tightly controlled conditions. Until and unless such new evidence becomes available, most scientists will interpret existing evidence as suggesting the operation of factors other than ESP. Claims for ESP would also be more plausible if scientific evidence could be found for a form of energy—and a system for sending it to and from the brain—that could provide the psychophysical basis for ESP (Alcock, 1987).

What conclusions are most reasonable?

Given relatively weak and unreplicated laboratory effects, numerous negative findings in the presence of neutral observers, and the absence of additional supporting evidence, a strong scientific case for the existence of ESP cannot be made.

Does this mean that parapsychological phenomena have been disproven? No. In the first place, scientists in the past have been surprised by the existence of phenomena, such as subatomic particles, that they once believed nonexistent or impossible. It may be that current scientific tools and methods are not sensitive enough to detect the existence of ESP. Furthermore, reputable and honest researchers continue to report phenomena that are not easily explained by known sensory or perceptual mechanisms (Honorton et al., 1990; Bem & Honorton, 1994). A distinguished panel of scientists assembled by the U.S. National Research Council reviewed much of the ESP literature and visited the most respected laboratories (Swets & Bjork, 1990). The panel concluded that the data offered were not convincing enough to warrant efforts to use ESP to improve performance in, say, air-traffic control; but the panel did recognize the possible value of additional research on ESP. Until such research identifies plausible and scientifically respectable mechanisms through which ESP signals could be transmitted, the majority of the scientific community is likely to remain skeptical.

ORGANIZING THE PERCEPTUAL WORLD

Suppose for a moment that you are driving down a busy road while searching for Barney's Diner, an unfamiliar restaurant where you are to meet a friend. The roadside is crammed with signs of all shapes and colors, some flashing, some rotating. If you are ever to recognize the sign that says "Barney's Diner," you must impose some sort of organization on this overwhelming array of visual information.

How do you do this? How do you know where one sign ends and another begins? And how do you know that an apparently tiny sign is not too small to read but is just far away? In this section, we describe some of the organizational processes that allow people to understand which parts of the visual array are objects and which are not, how far away these objects are, how bright or colorful they are, which ones are moving and which are still.

Principles of Perceptual Organization

Before you can recognize the "Barney's Diner" sign, your perceptual system must separate that sign from its background of lights, colors, letters, and other competing stimuli. Two basic principles—*figure-ground perception* and *grouping*—guide this initial organization.

Figure and Ground   When you look at a complex scene or listen to a noisy environment, your perceptual apparatus automatically picks out certain features, objects, or sounds to be emphasized and relegates others to be **ground**—the less relevant background. For example, as you drive toward an intersection, a stop sign becomes a figure, standing out clearly against the background of trees, houses, and cars. A **figure** is the part of the visual field that has meaning, stands in front of the rest, and always seems to include the contours or edges that separate it from the less relevant background (Rubin, 1915). As described in Chapter 4, edges are one of the most basic features detected by our visual system; they combine to form figures.

To illustrate the effect of figure-ground differentiation, look at Figure 5.6. The fact that you can repeatedly reverse its figure and ground to see faces, then a vase, then faces

The deadly couch cobra — coiled and alert in its natural habitat.

The natural camouflage of certain animals works by blurring cues for figure and ground, thus making immobile objects much less noticeable. If the snake depicted here were to move, however, it would stand out more and become much easier to see.

FIGURE 5.7

Gestalt Principles of Perceptual Grouping

We tend to perceive (A) as two groups of two circles plus two single circles, rather than as three groups of two circles or some other arrangement. In (B), we see two columns of X's and two columns of O's, not four rows of XOXO. We see the X in (C) as being made out of two continuous lines—one straight and one curved—not a combination of the odd forms shown. We immediately perceive the disconnected segments of (D) as a triangle and a circle. In (E), the different orientation of the lines in one quadrant of the rectangle makes that quadrant stand out from the others. In (F), we see the same three-dimensional cube from different angles, but the one on the left is normally perceived as a two-dimensional hexagon with lines running through it; the other, as a three-dimensional cube. In (G) we tend to pair up dots in the same oval even though they are far apart.

again, shows that perception is not only an active process but a *categorical* one. People usually organize sensory stimulation into one perceptual category or another, rarely to both or to something in between. You cannot, for instance, easily perceive Figure 5.6 as both a vase and two faces at the same time.

Grouping   Why is it that certain parts of the world become figure and others become ground, even when nothing in particular stands out in the physical pattern of light that falls on the retina? The answer is that certain inherent properties of the stimulus environment lead people to group them together, more or less automatically.

In the early 1900s, several German psychologists described the principles behind this grouping of stimuli. They argued that people perceive sights and sounds as organized wholes. These wholes, they said, are different from and more than just the sum of the individual sensations, much as water is something more than just an assortment of hydrogen and oxygen atoms. Because the German word meaning (roughly) "whole figure" is *Gestalt,* these researchers became known as **Gestalt psychologists.** They proposed a number of principles that describe how the perceptual system "glues" raw sensations together in particular ways, organizing stimuli into a world of shapes and patterns. For example:

1. **Proximity.** The closer objects or events are to one another, the more likely they are to be perceived as belonging together, as Figure 5.7(A) illustrates.

2. **Similarity.** Similar elements are perceived to be part of a group, as in Figure 5.7(B). People wearing the same school colors at a stadium will be perceived as belonging together even if they are not seated close together.

3. **Continuity.** Sensations that appear to create a continuous form are perceived as belonging together, as in Figure 5.7(C).

4. **Closure.** People tend to fill in missing contours to form a complete object, as in Figure 5.7(D).

5. **Texture.** When basic features of stimuli have the same texture (such as the orientation of certain elements), people tend to group those stimuli together, as in Figure 5.7(E). Thus, you group standing trees together and perceive them as separate from their fallen neighbors.

6. **Simplicity.** People tend to group features of a stimulus in a way that provides the simplest interpretation of the world. In Figure 5.7(F), for example, perceiving the image

"Wait! Wait! . . . Cancel that, I guess it says 'helf.'"

The principle of closure allows us to fill in the blanks in what we see and hear. Without it, the world would appear as fragmented images and sounds that would confuse everyone, including would-be rescuers.

on the left as a two-dimensional hexagon with six radii is much simpler than perceiving it as a three-dimensional cube, so the two-dimensional perception usually prevails. For the image on the right, however, it is the two-dimensional perception that is more complex (try describing it in words!), so we are likely to see it as a cube.

7. **Common fate.** Sets of objects that are moving in the same direction at the same speed are perceived together. Thus, a flock of birds, though separated in space, will be perceived as a group. Choreographers and marching-band directors often use the principle of common fate, arranging for groups of dancers or musicians to move identically, causing the audience to perceive waves of motion.

8. **Common region.** Stephen Palmer (1992) has proposed the principle of common region, which holds that elements located within some boundary tend to be grouped together. The boundary can be created by an enclosing perimeter, as in Figure 5.7(G), a region of color, or other factors.

These principles are generally consistent with both the ecological and computational views of perception. The properties of the stimuli can account quite well for most of these principles of perceptual organization, as ecological psychologists have argued. At the same time, research on neurophysiology is demonstrating how neural pathways detect edges, lines, and texture in a way that can allow these organizational processes to be carried out early in perception, in an essentially automatic way.

Auditory Scene Analysis   Gestalt grouping principles such as similarity, proximity, closure, and continuity apply to what we hear as well as to what we see. For example, sounds that are similar in pitch tend to be grouped together (Heise & Miller, 1951), much like sounds that come close together in time. Through closure, we hear a tone as continuous even if it is repeatedly interrupted by bursts of static (Warren, Obuseck & Acroff, 1972). **Auditory scene analysis** (Bregman, 1990) is the perceptual process of mentally representing and interpreting sounds. First, the flow of sound energy is organized into a series of segments based on characteristics such as frequency, intensity, location, and the like. Sounds with similar characteristics are then grouped into separate *auditory streams,* which are sounds perceived as coming from the same source. Thus, the sounds of a musical group combine to form a complex pattern of acoustical information, but you can perceive the melody of the flute, for example, separately from the other instruments because its notes are similar in timbre and come from a particular location. It is through auditory scene analysis that the potentially overwhelming world of sound is organized into separate, coherent patterns of speech, music, or even noise.

Perception of Depth and Distance

We are able to experience the world in three-dimensional depth even though the visual information we receive from it is projected onto two-dimensional retinas. How is this possible? The answer lies in **depth perception,** our ability to perceive distance. Depth perception, in turn, is made possible partly by *stimulus cues* provided by the environment and partly by the properties of our visual system.

Stimulus Cues   To some extent, people perceive depth through the same cues that artists use to create the impression of depth and distance on a two-dimensional canvas. These cues are actually characteristics of visual stimuli and therefore illustrate the ecological view of perception. Figure 5.8 demonstrates several of these cues.

- The two men at the far left of Figure 5.8 illustrate the principle of **relative size:** If two objects are assumed to be the same size, the object producing a larger image on the retina is perceived as closer than the one producing a smaller image.

- Another cue comes from **height in the visual field:** On the ground, more distant objects are usually higher in the visual field than those nearby. The woman near the man at the front of Figure 5.8 therefore appears to be farther away.

- The woman walking by the car in the middle of Figure 5.8 illustrates another depth cue called **interposition,** or *occlusion.* Closer objects block the view of things farther away (see Figure 5.9 to see what happens when interposition cues are reversed).

FIGURE 5.8

Stimulus Cues for Depth Perception

See if you can identify how cues of relative size, interposition, linear perspective, height in the visual field, textural gradient, and shadows combine to create a sense of three-dimensional depth in this drawing.

FIGURE 5.9

A Case of Depth Misperception

The runner in this photo is actually farther away than the man on the pitcher's mound. But because he is lower, not higher in the visual field—and because his leg seems to be in front of, not behind, the pitcher's leg—the runner appears smaller than normal rather than farther away.

- The figure at the far right of Figure 5.8 is seen as very far away, in part because she is standing near a point in the road where its edges, like all parallel lines that recede into the distance, appear to converge toward a single point. This apparent convergence provides a cue called **linear perspective.** The closer together two converging lines are, the greater the perceived distance.

- Notice that the road in Figure 5.8 disappears into a hazy background. Since greater distances usually produce less clarity, **reduced clarity** is interpreted as a cue for greater distance. The effect of clarity on perceived distance explains why a mountain viewed on a hazy day appears to loom larger than the same mountain on a clear day. The haze acts as a cue for greater distance, but the size of the mountain's retinal image is unchanged. The same retinal image accompanied by a greater perceived distance produces a larger perceived size.

- **Light and shadow** also contribute to the perception of three dimensions (Ramachandran, 1988). The buildings in the background of Figure 5.8 are seen as three-dimensional, not flat, because of the shadows on their right faces. Figure 5.10 gives another example of shadows' effect on depth perception.

Two additional stimulus cues for depth come from **gradients,** which are continuous changes across the visual field. A **textural gradient** is a graduated change in the texture, or "grain," of the visual field, as you can see from the sidewalk and the centerline of the road in Figure 5.8. Texture appears less detailed as distance increases; so as the texture of a surface changes across the retinal image, people perceive a change in distance. The second gradient cue is the **movement gradient,** which is the difference in the apparent movement of objects. As you move your head back and forth, things closer to you

Light, Shadow, and Depth Perception

The shadows cast by these protruding rivets and deep dents make it easy to see them in three dimensions. But if you turn the book upside down, the rivets now look like dents and the dents look like bumps. This reversal in depth perception occurs, in part, because people normally assume that illumination comes from above and interpret the pattern of light and shadow accordingly. With the picture upside down, light coming from the top would produce the observed pattern of shadows only if the circles were dents, not rivets.

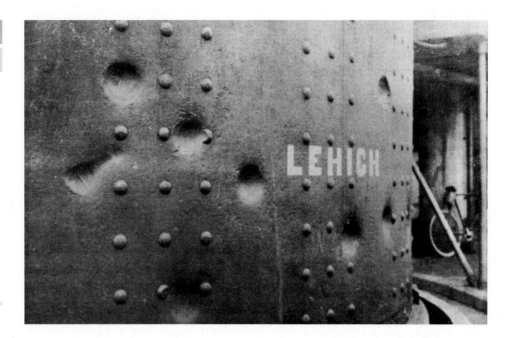

appear to move farther and faster than things farther away. The next time you are riding in a car through an open area, look out the side window. The objects closest to you will appear to fly rapidly across your visual field; in contrast, distant objects will look as if they are motionless or moving along with you. This difference in relative movement, sometimes called *motion parallax,* provides cues to the difference in distance. Faster relative movement across the visual field indicates less distance.

Cues Based on Properties of the Visual System   Several cues to depth result from the way human eyes are built and positioned. One of these cues is related to facts discussed in Chapter 4, on sensation. To bring an image into focus on the retina, the lens of the eye changes shape, or *accommodates.* To accomplish this feat, muscles surrounding the lens either tighten, to make the lens more curved for focusing on close objects, or relax,

TEXTURAL GRADIENT   The details of a scene fade gradually as distance increases. This textural gradient helps us to perceive the less detailed animals in this photo as farther away.

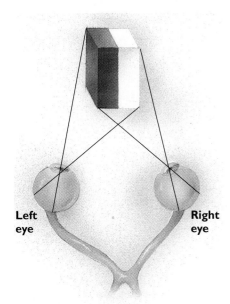

**Left   Right
eye   eye**

**Images go to brain
where they are compared**

Binocular Disparity

**The difference between each eye's
view of the block decreases as distance from it increases. The resulting
reduction in binocular disparity helps
us perceive the block as farther away.
To see how binocular disparity
changes with distance, hold a pencil
vertically about six inches in front of
you, then close one eye and notice
where the pencil is in relation to the
background. Now open that eye, close
the other one, and notice how much
the pencil "shifts." These are the two
rather different views your eyes have
of the pencil. If you repeat this procedure while holding the pencil at arm's
length, you will notice less disparity or
"shift" because there is less difference
in the angles at which the two eyes see
the pencil.**

to flatten the lens for focusing on more distant objects. Information about such muscle activity is relayed to the brain, and this **accommodation** cue helps create the perception of distance.

The relative location of our two eyes produces two other depth cues. One is **convergence:** Because each eye is located at a slightly different place on the skull, the eyes must converge, or rotate inward, in order to project the image on each retina. The brain receives and processes information from the eye muscles about this activity. The closer the object, the more the eyes must converge, and the greater the proprioceptive information going to the brain.

Second, because of their differing locations, each eye receives a slightly different view of the world, as Figure 5.11 illustrates. The difference between the two retinal images of an object is called **binocular disparity.** For any particular object, this disparity decreases with increasing distance. The brain combines the two images, processes information about the amount of disparity, and generates the impression of a single object having depth as well as height and width. Viewmaster slide viewers and 3-D movies create the appearance of depth by displaying to each eye a separate photograph of a scene, each taken from a slightly different angle.

What binocular disparity does for depth perception, the placement of the ears does for auditory scene analysis: It provides a cue for locating the source of sounds. If a sound is continuous, the peak of sound waves coming toward the right side of the head will reach the right ear before reaching the left ear. Similarly, a sound coming toward the right side of the head will be a little bit louder to the right ear than to the left ear, because the head blocks some of the sound from the latter. Thus, the brain can use both the timing and the intensity of sounds as cues to locate their source.

In short, there are a host of cues—some present in the environment and in retinal images, others arising from the structure of the visual system—that combine to give us a powerful and accurate sense of depth and distance.

Perception of Motion

Sometimes the critical property of an object is not its size or shape or distance but its motion—how fast it is going and where it is heading. Usually the perception of motion occurs as visual patterns from objects move across the surface of the retina. As in the case of depth perception, we automatically translate this two-dimensional information into a three-dimensional experience.

One example is the response to **looming,** which is a rapid expansion in the size of an image so that it fills the retina. When an image looms, there is an automatic tendency to perceive it as an approaching stimulus. Furthermore, if the expansion is as fast to the right as to the left, and as fast above as below, this information signals that the object is directly approaching the eyes. In other words: duck! (Regan, Kaufman & Lincoln, 1986).

If movement of the retinal image were the only factor contributing to motion perception, however, turning your head around or even rotating your eyeballs would create the perception that everything in the visual field is moving. This is not the case because the brain also receives and processes information about the motion of the eyes and head. If the brain determines that such bodily movement accounts for all of the movement of light on the retina, then the outside world is perceived as stable, not moving. To demonstrate this, close one eye and wiggle your open eyeball by gently pushing your lower eyelid. Because your brain receives no signals that your eye is being moved by its own muscles, the *world* is perceived as moving.

When you *are* moving, the movement gradient discussed in the section on depth perception can provide another cue to this fact. Imagine driving a car toward the horizon. As you look ahead, objects appear to diverge from the point where the road disappears into the horizon and to move faster as they move away from this vanishing point. You automatically perceive this pattern as the forward movement of your own body toward and past unmoving objects. Further, the magnitude and pattern of texture moving across the retina provide a cue to your speed and to whether you are accelerating, decelerating, or holding a steady rate. (The safety measure at the traffic circle described earlier relied on this phenomenon.) The fact that the accurate perception of self-motion depends greatly on "tuning in" to information already in the environment illustrates the value of the ecological view of perception (Warren & Wertheimer, 1990).

Normally, as you move through an environment, the flow of visual information across the retina combines with information from the vestibular and tactile senses. If you accelerate in a car, you feel pressure from the back of the seat and feel your head tilting backward. When visual flow is perceived without appropriate sensations from other parts of the body, motion sickness may result. This explains why people sometimes feel nauseous while operating motion simulators and playing some video games, especially those employing "virtual reality" technology; the images suggest that the person is in motion when there is no real motion (Andersen, 1986; Azar, 1996).

Perceptual Constancy

Suppose that one sunny day you are watching someone walking toward you along a tree-lined sidewalk. The visual sensations produced by this person are actually rather bizarre. For one thing, the size of the image on your retinas keeps getting larger as the person gets closer. To see this for yourself, hold out a hand at arm's length and look at someone far away. The retinal image of that person will be so small that you can cover it with your hand. If you try to do the same thing when the person is three feet away, the retinal image will now be too large. But you perceive the person as being closer now, not bigger. Similarly, if you watch people pass from bright sunshine through the shadows of trees, your retinas receive images that are darker, then lighter, then darker again. Still, you perceive individuals whose coloring remains the same.

These examples illustrate **perceptual constancy,** the perception of objects as constant in size, shape, color, and other properties despite changes in their retinal image. Without this aspect of perception, the world would be an Alice-in-Wonderland kind of place in which objects continuously changed their properties. Perceptual constancy is created by the combined influence of distance perception and life experience.

Size Constancy   Why does the perceived size of objects stay more or less constant, no matter what changes occur in the size of the retinal image? One view, which emphasizes the computational aspects of perception, suggests that as objects move closer or farther away, the brain perceives the change in distance and automatically adjusts the perception. Thus, the *perceived size* of an object is equal to the size of the retinal image multiplied by the perceived distance (Holway & Boring, 1941). As an object moves closer, its retinal image increases, but the perceived distance decreases at the same rate, so the perceived size remains constant. If, instead, a balloon is inflated in front of your eyes, perceived distance remains constant, and the perceived size (correctly) increases as the retinal image increases.

This computational perspective is reasonably good at explaining most instances of size constancy, but it cannot fully account for the fact that people are better at judging the true size (and distance) of familiar objects than unfamiliar ones. This phenomenon suggests that there is an additional mechanism for size constancy, one that is consistent with the constructionists' emphasis on the knowledge-based aspects of perception. Indeed, it is your knowledge and experience that tell you that most objects (aside from balloons) do not suddenly change size.

The perceptual system usually produces size constancy correctly and automatically, but it can sometimes fail. For example, people may perceive objects with smaller retinal images to be farther away than those with larger images even when the distance is actually the same. This error may explain why, in countries where cars vary greatly in size, small cars have higher accident rates than large ones (Eberts & MacMillan, 1985). A small car produces a smaller retinal image at a given distance than a larger one, possibly causing the driver of a following vehicle to overestimate the distance to the small car and therefore fail to brake in time to avoid a collision. Such misjudgments illustrate the

SHAPE CONSTANCY Trace the outline of this floating object onto a piece of paper. The tracing will be oval-shaped, but shape constancy causes you to perceive it as the circular life ring that it actually is.

inferential nature of perception emphasized by constructionists: People make logical inferences or hypotheses about the world based on the available cues. Unfortunately, if the cues are misleading, or the inferences are wrong, perceptual errors may occur.

Shape Constancy   The principles behind shape constancy are closely related to those of size constancy. To see shape constancy at work, remember what page you are on, close this book, and tilt it toward and away from you several times. The book will continue to look rectangular, even though the shape of its retinal image changes dramatically as you move it. The brain automatically integrates information about retinal images and distance as movement occurs. In this case, the distance information involved the difference in distance between the near and the far edges of the book.

As with size constancy, much of the ability to judge shape constancy depends on automatic computational mechanisms in the nervous system, but expectations about the shape of objects also play a role. For example, in Western cultures, most corners are at right angles, and most curved surfaces are circular or spherical. Knowledge of these facts helps make "rectangle" the most likely interpretation of the retinal image shown in Figure 5.1.

Brightness Constancy   No matter how the amount of light striking an object changes, the object's perceived brightness remains relatively constant. You can demonstrate brightness constancy by placing a charcoal briquette in sunlight and a piece of white paper in nearby shade. The charcoal will look very dark and the paper very bright, even though a light meter would reveal much more light energy reflected from the sun-bathed coal than from the shaded paper. One reason the charcoal continues to look dark, no matter the illumination, is that you know that charcoal is nearly black, illustrating once again the knowledge-based nature of perception. Another reason is that the charcoal is still the darkest object *relative* to its background in the sunlight, and the paper is the brightest object *relative* to its background in the shade. The brightness of an object is perceived in relation to its background (see Figure 5.12).

Perceptual Illusions

It is difficult to appreciate the complexities underlying the normally smooth and automatic functioning of the perceptual system until it fails. One category of perceptual failures, called *optical illusions,* is particularly helpful in revealing the wonders, and vulnerabilities, of your perceptual system. Some of these illusions are shown in Figure 5.13.

For psychologists, some of the most fascinating illusions are those related to depth, distance, and size constancy. These illusions are named for the scientists who first

LINKAGES   How can the senses be fooled? (a link to Sensation)

| FIGURE 5.12 | Brightness Constancy |

You probably perceive the inner rectangle on the left to be lighter than the inner rectangle on the right. But carefully examine the inner rectangles alone (covering their surroundings). You will see that both are of equal intensity. The brighter surround in the right-hand figure leads you to perceive its inner rectangle as relatively darker.

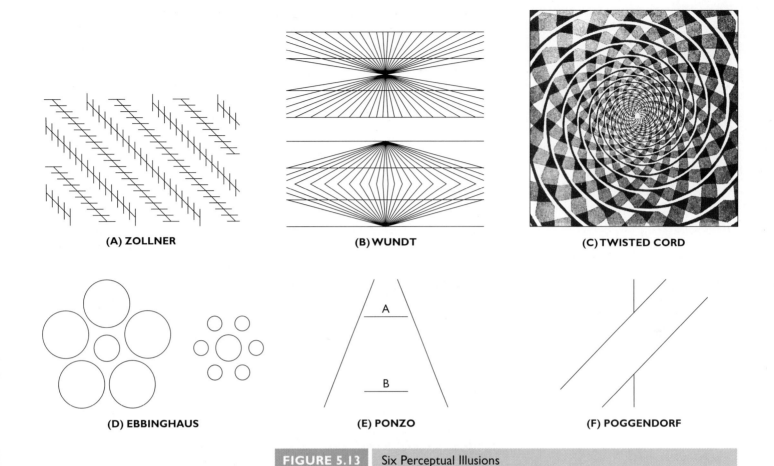

(A) ZOLLNER   (B) WUNDT   (C) TWISTED CORD

(D) EBBINGHAUS   (E) PONZO   (F) POGGENDORF

FIGURE 5.13 | Six Perceptual Illusions

If you focus on a pair of lines in the Zollner illusion (A), you can see that they are parallel; but if you look at the entire figure, you get the impression that they are not. The horizontal lines in the Wundt illusion (B) are actually parallel; and the twisted cord (C) is actually made up of concentric circles. The Ebbinghaus illusion (D) is analogous to the misjudgment of brightness shown in Figure 5.12; the center circle in the pattern on the left probably looks smaller than the one on the right because of the sizes of the surrounding circles. In the Ponzo illusion (E), the two horizontal lines are in fact the same length, and the vertical line in the Poggendorf illusion (F) is actually aligned, not offset.

described them. Consider, for example, the *Ponzo illusion* shown in Figure 5.13(E). Why does line A look longer than line B, even though they are equal in length? The principles behind size constancy provide one explanation. The converging lines provide a strong cue (linear perspective) that tells the perceptual system that A must be farther away than B, but both lines form images of the same length on the retina. Recall the size constancy principle: that when two objects have retinal images of the same size, the one that seems farther away is perceived as larger. Consistent with past perceptual experience and size constancy principles, then, most people perceive A to be longer than B (Rock, 1983). This explanation supports the constructionist view of perception. It also highlights the degree to which depth cues based on linear perspective automatically capture perception and signal a slanting, three-dimensional surface even when it is not there.

Similarly, Richard Gregory (1968, 1973) has argued that the *Müller-Lyer illusion* shown in Figure 5.14(A) represents a misapplication of the depth cue of linear perspective. The convergence of the arrowheads on each side of the shaft on the left makes the shaft appear to be the closest part of the scene—like the outside corner of the house

FIGURE 5.14

Variations on the Müller-Lyer Illusion

Here, the standard Müller-Lyer illusion
(A) is placed in a three-dimensional
context (B) so that the vertical line
forms the outside corner of a house or
the inside corner of a room. The inside
corner looks taller. A two-dimensional
version (C) shows that the illusion
does not require depth cues.

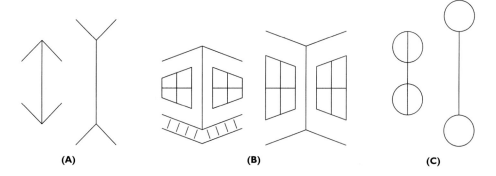

(A)   (B)   (C)

in Figure 5.14(B)—whereas the divergence of the arrowheads on the right makes that
shaft seem to be toward the back. By the logic applied to the Ponzo illusion, the more
"distant" shaft appears to be larger.

The idea that depth cues underlie the Müller-Lyer illusion makes sense, but it cannot account for Figure 5.14(C) in which misperception of length occurs even without
three-dimensional distance cues (Nijhawan, 1991). A possible reason for this misperception is that the perceived length of an object is based on its "frame." When the frame
is perceived as larger, as on the right side of Figure 5.14(C), so is the line segment within

FIGURE 5.15

The Moon Illusion

Some experiments suggest that the
moon appears larger on the horizon
than overhead because the horizon
moon—seen across a space filled with
houses, trees, and terrain—appears to
be farther away than when it is overhead (Kaufman & Rock, 1962). Since
the size of the retinal image of the
moon does not change, the greater
perceived distance causes the horizon
moon to be perceived as larger. This
explanation is probably incomplete,
however, because the horizon moon
sometimes seems larger even when
the observer cannot see the intervening terrain (Suzuki, 1991). A completely satisfying explanation of this
illusion has eluded everyone from the
ancient Greeks to the psychologists of
today (Hershenon, 1989).

IN REVIEW	Principles of Perceptual Organization and Constancy	
Principle	**Description**	**Example**
Figure-ground	Certain objects or sounds automatically become identified as figures while others become meaningless background.	You see a person standing against a building, not a building with a person-shaped hole in it.
Grouping	Properties of stimuli lead us to automatically group them together. These include proximity, similarity, continuity, closure, texture, simplicity, common fate, and common region.	People who are sitting together, or are dressed similarly, are perceived as a group.
Depth perception	The world is perceived as three-dimensional, with help from stimulus cues—such as relative size, height in the visual field, interposition, linear perspective, reduced clarity, light and shadow, and gradients—and from visual system cues, such as accommodation, convergence, and binocular disparity.	A person who looks tiny and appears high in the visual field will be perceived as being of normal size, but at a great distance.
Perceptual constancy	Objects are perceived as constant in size, shape, color, and other properties, despite changes in their retinal images.	A train coming toward you is perceived as getting closer, not larger; a gas station sign is perceived as rotating, not changing shape.

it (Rock, 1978). Indeed, since perception is based on many principles, the Müller-Lyer and other illusions—including one involving the moon (see Figure 5.15)—probably reflect the violation of more than one of them. (For a summary of these principles, see "In Review: Principles of Perceptual Organization and Constancy.")

Culture, Experience, and Perception

So far, we have talked as if all aspects of perception work or fail in the same way for everyone. Differing experiences, however, do affect people's perceptions. To the extent that people in different cultures are exposed to substantially different visual environments, some of their perceptual experiences may be different as well. For example, researchers have compared responses to pictures containing depth cues by people from cultures that do and do not use pictures and paintings to represent reality (Derogowski, 1989). This research suggests that people in cultures that provide minimal experience with pictorial representations, like the Me'n or the Nupa in Africa, have a more difficult time judging distances shown in pictures (see Figure 5.16). These individuals also tend to have a harder time sorting *pictures* of three-dimensional objects into categories, even though they can easily sort the objects themselves (Derogowski, 1989).

Other research shows that the perception of optical illusions varies from culture to culture and is related to cultural differences in perceptual experiences. In one study, researchers enhanced the Ponzo illusion shown in Figure 5.13(E) by superimposing its horizontal lines on a picture of railroad tracks. This familiar image added depth cues for American subjects but not for people on Guam, where railroad tracks were absent at the time of the research (Leibowitz et al., 1969). In short, although the structure and principles of human perceptual systems tend to create generally similar views of the world for all of us, our perception of reality is also shaped by experience, including the experience of living in a particular culture. Unfortunately, as more and more cultures are "westernized," the visual stimulation they present to their children will become less distinctive; eventually, research on the impact of differential experience on perception may become impossible.

Source: Hudson, 1960.

FIGURE 5.16

The Hudson Test

Viewing these pictures from the Hudson Test, people are asked to judge which animal is closer to the hunter. Those familiar with pictured depth cues choose the antelope, which is at the same distance from the viewer as the hunter. Those less familiar with such cues may choose the elephant, which, though closer on the page, is more distant when depth cues are considered. Some have argued that cultural differences in perception might actually stem from differences in attention, experience with test materials, or the like (Biederman, 1987). Still, reported cultural differences in perception are consistent with what we know about the role of experience in perception.

RECOGNIZING THE PERCEPTUAL WORLD

In discussing how people organize the perceptual world, we have so far ignored one vital question: How do people recognize what objects are? If you are driving in search of Barney's Diner, exactly what happens when your eyes finally locate the pattern of light that spells out "Barney's Diner"? How do you recognize it as the place you are seeking?

In essence, the brain must analyze the incoming pattern and compare that pattern to information stored in memory. If it finds a match, recognition takes place and the stimulus is classified into a *perceptual category*. Once recognition occurs, your perception of a stimulus may never be the same again. Look at Figure 5.17. Do you see anything familiar? If not, turn to Figure 5.20, then look at Figure 5.17 again. You should now see it in an entirely new light. The difference between your "before" and "after" experiences of Figure 5.17 is the difference between the sensory world before and after a perceptual match occurs and recognition takes place.

Exactly how does such matching occur? Some aspects of recognition begin at the "top"—that is, at a conceptual level, guided by knowledge, expectations, and other psychological factors. This phenomenon is called **top-down processing** because it involves higher-level, knowledge-based information. Other aspects of recognition begin at the "bottom," relying on specific, detailed information elements from the sensory receptors that are integrated and assembled into a whole. This latter phenomenon is called **bottom-up processing** because it begins with basic information units that serve as a foundation for recognition. Let's consider the contributions of bottom-up and top-down processing to recognition, as well as the use of neural network models to understand both.

Bottom-up Processing

Research on the visual system is providing a detailed picture of how bottom-up processing works. As described in Chapter 4, on sensation, all along the path from the eye to the brain, certain cells respond to selected features of a stimulus, so that the stimulus is actually analyzed into *basic features* before these features are recombined to create the perceptual experience.

What features are subjected to separate analysis? Again, as discussed in Chapter 4, there is strong evidence that certain cells specialize in responding to stimuli having specific orientations in space (Hubel & Weisel, 1979). For example, one cell in the cortex

FIGURE 5.17

Perceptual Categorization

For the identity of this figure, turn to page 146.

FIGURE 5.18

Feature Analysis

Feature detectors operating at lower levels of the visual system detect such features of incoming stimuli as the corners and angles shown on the left side of this figure. Later in the perceptual sequence, bottom-up processing might recombine these features to aid in pattern recognition, as in the examples on the right.

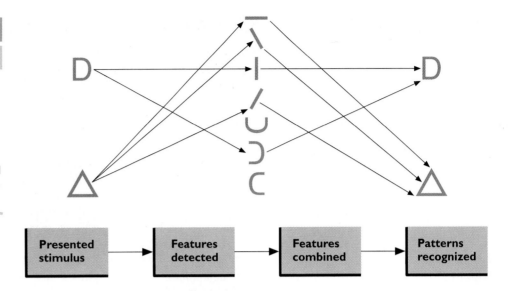

| Presented stimulus | → | Features detected | → | Features combined | → | Patterns recognized |

might fire only in response to a diagonal line, so it acts as a *feature detector* for diagonal lines. Figure 5.18 illustrates how the analysis by such feature detectors, early in the information-processing sequence, may contribute to recognition of letters or judgments of shape. Color and motion are other sensory features that appear to be analyzed separately—in different parts of the brain—prior to full perceptual recognition (Baylis & Driver, 1992; Livingston & Hubel, 1987; Treisman, 1988).

In addition, the brain apparently analyzes *spatial frequencies*—that is, patterns of light and darkness in the visual scene (see Figure 4.24). Analyzing the difference between low and high spatial frequencies may allow you to perceive texture gradients that help in making depth judgments and to recognize the general shape of blurry images or an object's fine details.

How do psychologists know that these kinds of feature analysis are actually involved in pattern recognition? Again, as noted in Chapter 4, recordings of brain activity indicate that the sensory features we have listed here cause particular sets of neurons to fire. Further, as described in connection with the neuropsychology of consciousness in Chapter 6, people with certain kinds of brain damage show selective impairment in the ability to perceive certain sets of sensory features, such as an object's color or movement (Banks & Krajicek, 1991).

Irving Biederman (1987) has suggested that, consistent with research indicating that the features of lines and angles might be used for recognizing letters, a slightly more complex set of features provides the basis for recognizing other objects. He has proposed that people recognize three-dimensional objects by detecting and then combining simple forms, which he calls *geons;* Figure 5.19 shows some of these geons. Evidence

FIGURE 5.19

Geometric Feature Analyzers for Object Perception

In the top row are some of the fundamental features, or *geons,* proposed by Irving Biederman (1987). Biederman's research suggests that our perceptual system detects and combines geons to allow recognition of common geometric objects like those shown in the bottom row.

Source: Biederman, 1985.

FIGURE 5.20

Another Version of Figure 5.17

Now that you can identify a dog in this figure, it should be much easier to recognize when you look back at the original version.

for Biederman's theory comes from experiments in which people must identify drawings when some of the details have been eliminated. Recognition becomes particularly difficult when the geons are no longer intact, as Figure 5.21 demonstrates.

Top-down Processing

Bottom-up feature analysis can explain why you recognize the letters in a sign for Barney's Diner. But why is it that you will recognize the sign more easily if it appears where you were told to expect it rather than a block earlier? And why can you recognize it even if a few letters are missing from the sign? Top-down processing seems to be at work in these cases. In top-down processing, people use their knowledge in making inferences or "educated guesses" to recognize objects, words, or melodies, especially when sensory information is vague or ambiguous (DeWitt & Samuel, 1990; Rock, 1983). For example, once you knew that there is a dog in Figure 5.17, it became much easier for you to perceive one.

Many aspects of perception can best be explained by higher-level cognitive influences, especially by expectancy and motivation. Consider Figure 5.22, for example.

FIGURE 5.21

Recognition of Objects With and Without Their Geons Destroyed

The drawings in columns 2 and 3 have had the same amount of ink removed, but in column 3 the deletions have destroyed many of the geons used in object recognition. The drawings in column 2 are far easier to recognize because their geons are intact.

Source: Biederman, 1987.

FIGURE 5.22

An Ambiguous Figure

Which face do you see in part (A)? Unambiguous portraits of the young and old women are shown in parts (B) and (C).

(A)   (B)   (C)

Source: Rumelhart & McClelland, 1986.

LINKAGES: THE EYE OF THE BEHOLDER
Top-down processing can affect our perception of people as well as objects. As noted in Chapter 17, for example, if you expect everyone in a certain ethnic or social group to behave in a certain way, you may perceive a particular group member's behavior in line with this prejudice. On the other hand, have you ever come to perceive someone as physically more attractive or less attractive as you got to know the person better? This change in perception occurs largely because new information alters, in top-down fashion, your interpretation of the raw sensations you get from the person.

Some people immediately see a young woman wearing a feathered hat and turning her head away. Others see an old woman with a large nose and a protruding chin (Boring, 1930). Which one you recognize first can be influenced by what you expect to see. Robert Leeper (1935) showed people either Figure 5.22(B), in which the young woman is strongly emphasized, or Figure 5.22(C), which makes the old woman stand out. Then he showed Figure 5.22(A), the ambiguous drawing, to everyone. Most of those who had first seen the "young woman" version continued to see her in the ambiguous figure, whereas the old woman was more often identified by those who had first seen the version emphasizing her.

These results illustrate that our experiences create **schemas,** which are mental representations of what we know and have come to expect about the world. Schemas can bias our perception toward one recognition or another by creating a *perceptual set,* the readiness or predisposition to perceive a stimulus in a certain way. Expectancy may also be shaped by the immediate *context* in which a stimulus occurs. For example, people are more likely to perceive the ambiguous drawing in Figure 5.22(A) as a young woman if it appears in a set of unambiguous drawings of young women. Context and expectancy have biasing effects for sounds as well as sights. The raw sound "eye screem" takes on different meanings when heard in the context of "I scream when I am angry" rather than "I love ice cream." Personality characteristics may also predict the kinds of top-down processing that people engage in (King & Sorrentino, 1988).

Motivation is another aspect of top-down processing that can affect perception. A hungry person, for example, might misperceive a sign for "Burger's Body Shop" as indicating a place to eat. Similarly, if you have ever watched an athletic contest, you probably remember a time when an obviously demented referee incorrectly called a foul on your favorite team. You knew the call was wrong because you clearly saw the other team's player at fault. But suppose you had been cheering for that other team. The chances are good that you would have seen the referee's call as the right one.

Top-down and Bottom-up Processing Together

Often, bottom-up and top-down processing work together to aid in recognizing the perceptual world. This interaction is beautifully illustrated by the process of reading. When the quality of the raw stimulus on the page is poor, as in Figure 5.23, top-down processes compensate to make continued reading possible. They allow you to fill in where words are not well perceived and processed, thus giving a general idea of the meaning of the text.

FIGURE 5.23

Interaction of Top-Down and
Bottom-Up Processing

**Top-down processing assists in reading
the obscured text on the top line.
However, in the bottom line, the
words are not coherently related, so
top-down processing cannot operate.**

it is very easy to read this redundant sentence
BUT NOT
better resist reading hist grammatical/saw writing)

You can fill in the gaps left by stimuli because the world is *redundant,* providing multiple clues about what is going on. If you lose or miss one stimulus in a pattern, others can help enough that you still recognize the pattern. There is so much redundancy in written language, for example, that many of the words and letters you see are not needed. Fo- ex-mp-e y-u c-n r-ad -hi- se-te-ce -it- ev-ry -hi-d l-tt-r m-ss-ng. Similarly, vision in three dimensions normally provides multiple redundant cues to depth, making recognition of distance easy and clear. It is only when many of these cues are eliminated that ambiguous stimuli, subject to multiple interpretations, create the sort of depth illusions discussed earlier.

In hearing, too, top-down processing can compensate for ambiguous stimuli. In one experiment, subjects heard strings of five words in meaningless order, such as "wet brought who socks some." There was so much noise in the background that only about 75 percent of the words could be recognized (Miller, Heise & Lichten, 1951). However, when the same words were read in a meaningful order (for example, "who brought some wet socks"), a second group of subjects was able to recognize almost all of them, even under noisy conditions. In fact, it took twice as much noise to reduce their performance to that of the first group. Why? When the words were in meaningless order, only bottom-up processing was available, and recognizing one word was no help in identifying the next. Meaningful sentences, however, provided a more familiar context and allowed for some top-down processing; hearing one word helped the listener make a reasonable guess (based on knowledge and experience) about the others.

Network Processing

FIGURE 5.24

The Object Superiority Effect

**When people are asked to say
whether the feature on the left
appears in patterns briefly flashed on a
computer screen, the feature is more
likely to be detected when it appears
in patterns like those at the top, which
most resemble three-dimensional
objects. This "object superiority
effect" supports the importance of
network processing in perception.**

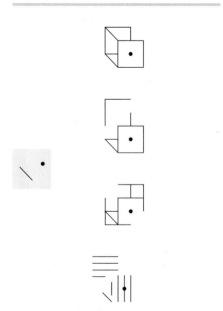

Source: Weisstein & Harris, 1974.

An experiment with visual patterns suggests another way of explaining how recognition occurs. Subjects were asked to say whether a particular feature, like the dot and angle shown on the left side of Figure 5.24, appeared within a pattern that was briefly flashed on a computer screen (Weisstein & Harris, 1974; Purcell & Stewart, 1991). The feature was detected faster when it was embedded in a pattern resembling a three-dimensional object than when it appeared within a random pattern of lines. This result is called the *object superiority effect.* There is also a *word superiority effect:* When strings of letters are briefly flashed on a screen, people's ability to detect target letters was better if the string formed a word than a nonword (Reicher, 1969; Prinzmetal, 1992).

These and related findings appear to be best explained in terms of *network processing,* which involves interaction among the various feature analyzers we have discussed (Green, 1991; Rumelhart & Todd, 1992). More specifically, some researchers explain recognition by **parallel distributed processing (PDP) models** (Rumelhart & McClelland, 1986). As described in Chapter 4, each element in these neural network models is connected to every other element, and each connection has a specific weight or strength. According to PDP models, the units in a network operate in parallel—simultaneously. Connections between units either excite or inhibit other units. If the connection is excitatory, activating one unit spreads the activation to connected units. Using a connection may strengthen it.

How does this process apply to recognition? According to PDP models, recognition occurs as a result of the simultaneous operation of connected units. Units are activated when matched by features in a stimulus. To the extent that features such as the letters in a word or the angles in a box have occurred together in the past, their connective links will be stronger, and detection of any of them will be made more likely by the presence

FIGURE 5.25

Recognizing a Word

The first letter of the word shown in (A) could be *R* or *P*, the second *E* or *F*, and the third *D* or *B*. Yet the pattern is quickly recognized as the word RED. According to PDP models, recognition occurs because, *together*, the letters excite each other's correct interpretation. This mutual excitation process is illustrated in (B) by a set of letter "nodes" (corresponding to activity sites in the brain), surrounded by some of the words they might activate. These nodes will be activated if the feature they detect appears in the stimulus array. They will also be activated if nodes to which they are linked become active. The stronger the link between nodes, the more activation will occur. Thus, all six letters shown in (B) will initially be excited when the stimulus in (A) is presented, but mutual excitement along the strongest links will guarantee that the word *RED* is perceived (Rumelhart & McClelland, 1986).

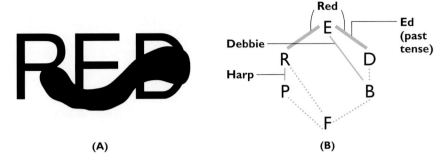

(A)   (B)

Source: Rumelhart & McClelland, 1986.

of all the others. This appears to be what happens in the word and object superiority effects, as illustrated in Figure 5.25.

PDP models, sometimes called *connectionist* models, clearly represent the computational view of perception. Indeed, researchers have achieved many advances in theories of pattern recognition by programming computers to carry out the kinds of computations that neural networks are assumed to perform in the human perceptual system (Grossberg, 1988). These computers have "learned" to read and recognize speech and even faces, in a manner that is strikingly similar to the way humans learn and perform the same perceptual tasks. Research on such *artificial intelligence* is discussed further in Chapter 9, on thought and language.

In summary, we have described three kinds of perceptual processing for pattern recognition (see "In Review: Mechanisms of Pattern Recognition"). Bottom-up processing analyzes and combines raw stimulus features. Top-down processing uses higher-

IN REVIEW	Mechanisms of Pattern Recognition	
Mechanism	**Description**	**Example**
Bottom-up processing	Raw sensations from the eye or the ear are analyzed into basic features, such as color or movement; these features are then recombined at higher brain centers, where they are compared to stored information about objects or sounds.	You recognize a dog as a dog because its physical features—four legs, barking, panting—match your perceptual category for "dog."
Top-down processing	Knowledge of the world and experience in perceiving allow people to make inferences about the identity of stimuli, even when the quality of raw sensory information is low.	On a dark night, a small, vaguely seen blob pulling on the end of a leash is recognized as a dog because the stimulus occurs at a location where we would expect a dog to be.
Network, or PDP, processing	Recognition depends on communication among feature-analysis systems operating simultaneously and enlightened by past experience.	A dog standing behind a picket fence will be recognized even though each disjointed "slice" of the stimulus may not look like a dog.

level knowledge—including past experience, expectations, and context—to guide recognition. Finally, network processing combines aspects of the other two; each feature in a stimulus array is more likely to be perceived as belonging to a particular pattern if it is activated by another feature with which it has been paired in the past.

LINKAGES: PERCEPTION AND HUMAN DEVELOPMENT

What does the world look like to infants?

We have seen the important role that knowledge and experience play in recognition, but are they also required for more basic aspects of perception? Which perceptual abilities are babies born with, and which do they acquire by seeing, hearing, smelling, touching, and tasting things? How do their perceptions compare to those of adults?

To learn about infants' perception, psychologists have studied two inborn patterns called *habituation* and *dishabituation*. For example, infants stop looking when they repeatedly see stimuli that are perceived to be the same. This is habituation. If a stimulus appears that is perceived to be different, looking resumes. This is dishabituation. Using the habituation/dishabituation technique, Russell Adams and his associates (1986) found that newborns could perceive the difference between black-and-white versus colored displays although they could not distinguish between particular hues (Adams, 1987). Other researchers used the same method to show that newborns can perceive differences in the angles of lines (Slater et al., 1991). These and other studies suggest that we are born with the basic components of feature detection.

Do we also have an innate ability to combine features into perceptions of whole objects? Apparently not. At one month of age, infants concentrate their gaze on one part of an object, such as the corner of a triangle (Goldstein, 1989). At two months, however, the eyes systematically scan the perimeter of the object, suggesting that the infant is perceiving the pattern, or shape of the object, not just its component features.

While the ability to recognize complex patterns seems to come only with experience, there is some evidence that infants may be innately tuned to perceive at least one important complex pattern: the human face. In one study of newborns, some less than an hour old, patterns like those in Figure 5.26 were moved slowly past the infants' faces (Johnson et al., 1991). The infants moved their heads and eyes to follow these patterns, but they tracked the facelike pattern shown on the left side of Figure 5.26 significantly farther than any of the nonfaces. The difference in tracking indicates that the infants could discriminate between faces and nonfaces, and are more interested in the former. Why should this be? The investigators suggest that interest in human faces is adaptive, in evolutionary terms, because it helps newborns focus on their only source of food and care.

Other research on perceptual development suggests that our ability to accurately perceive depth and distance develops more slowly than recognition of object shapes. For example, research suggests that infants' ability to use binocular disparity and relative motion cues to judge depth appears to develop some time after about three months

FIGURE 5.26

Infants' Perception of Human Faces

Newborns show significantly greater interest in the facelike pattern at the far left than in any of the other patterns. Evidently, some aspects of face perception are innate.

Face   **Configuration**   **Linear**   **Scrambled**

Source: Johnson et al., 1991.

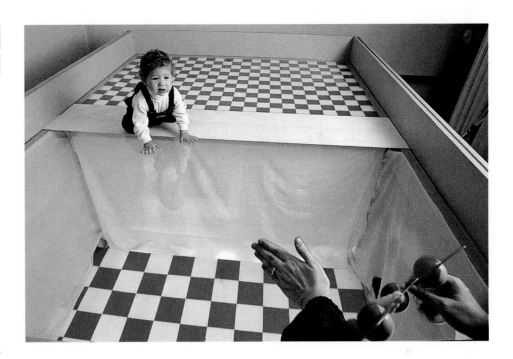

FIGURE 5.27

The Visual Cliff

The *visual cliff* is a glass-topped table that creates the impression of a sudden drop-off. A ten-month-old placed at what looks like the edge will calmly crawl across the shallow side to reach a parent, but will hesitate and cry rather than crawl over the "cliff" (Gibson & Walk, 1960). Changes in heart rate show that infants too young to crawl also perceive the depth, but are not frightened by it (Campos, Langer & Krowitz, 1970). Here again, nature and nurture interact adaptively: Depth perception appears shortly after birth, but fear and avoidance of dangerous depth do not develop until an infant is old enough to crawl into trouble.

of age (Yonas, Artiberry & Granrud, 1987; see Figure 5.27). Infants do not use texture gradient and linear perspective as cues to depth until they are five to seven months old (Artiberry, Yonas & Bensen, 1989).

In summary, there is little doubt that many of the basic building blocks of perception are present within the first few days after birth. The basics include such organ-based cues to depth as accommodation and convergence. Maturation of the visual system adds to these basics as time goes by. For example, over the first few months after birth, the eye's fovea gradually develops the number of cone cells necessary for high visual acuity and perception of fine details (Goldstein, 1989). However, visual experience is also necessary if the infant is to recognize unified patterns and objects in frequently encountered stimuli, to interpret depth and distance cues, and to use them in moving safely through the world. Thus, like so many aspects of human psychology, perception is the result of a blending of heredity and environment. From infancy onward, the perceptual system creates a personal reality based in part on the experience that shapes each individual's feature-analysis networks and knowledge-based expectancies.

ATTENTION

Believe it or not, you still haven't found Barney's Diner! By now, you understand *how* you will recognize the right sign when you perceive it, but how can you be sure you *will* perceive it? As you drive, the diner's sign will appear as but one ingredient in a sensory soup that also includes road signs, traffic lights, sirens, talk radio, and dozens of other stimuli. You can't perceive all of them at once, so to find Barney's you are going to have to be sure that the information you select for perceptual processing includes the stimuli that will help reach your goal. In short, you are going to have to pay attention.

Attention is the process of directing and focusing certain psychological resources to enhance perception, performance, and mental experience. We use attention to *direct* our sensory and perceptual systems toward certain stimuli, to *select* specific information for further processing, to *allocate* the mental energy required to do that processing, and to *regulate* the flow of resources necessary for performing a task or coordinating several tasks at once.

Psychologists have discovered three important characteristics of attention. First, it *improves mental processing;* you often need to concentrate attention on a task to do your best at it. If your attentional system temporarily malfunctions, you might drive right past Barney's Diner. Second, attention takes *effort*. Prolonged concentration of attention can leave you drained, and when you are fatigued, focusing attention on anything becomes more difficult. Third, attentional resources are *limited*. When your attention is focused on reading this book, for example, you have less attention left over to listen to a conversation in the next room.

To experience attention as a process, try "moving it around" a bit. When you finish reading this sentence, look at something behind you, then face forward and notice the next sound you hear, then visualize your best friend, then focus on how your tongue feels. You just used attention to direct your perceptual systems toward different aspects of your external and internal environments. Sometimes, as when you looked behind you, shifting attention involves *overt orienting*—pointing sensory systems at a particular stimulus. But you were able to shift attention to an image of your friend's face without having to move a muscle; this is called *covert orienting*. There is a rumor that students sometimes use covert orienting to shift their attention from the lecturer they are looking at to thoughts that have nothing to do with the class.

FIGURE 5.28

Measuring Covert Shifts in Attention

It took people less time (measured in thousandths of a second) to detect a square appearing at an expected location than at an unexpected location. This result suggests that, even though their eyes did not move, they covertly shifted attention to the expected location before the stimulus was presented.

FOCUS ON RESEARCH METHODS

An Experiment on "Mind Reading"

Everyone knows what it is like to covertly shift attention, but how can we tell when someone else is doing it? As noted in this chapter's Thinking Critically section the answer is not likely to come from telepathy; yet a different kind of "mind reading," made possible by innovative research methods, is helping psychologists to measure where a person's attention is focused.

Michael Posner and his colleagues hypothesized that when people covertly shift their attention to a specific location in space, their perceptual systems should be more sensitive to stimuli at that location than at other locations (Posner, Nissen & Ogden, 1978). To test this idea, Posner asked volunteer subjects to keep their eyes on a fixation point that appeared at the center of a computer screen. One second later, a tiny square appeared at either the right or left edge of the screen. With their vision focused on the fixation point, subjects could see this mark only out of the "corner" of their eye.

The independent variable in this experiment was the type of cue given at the fixation point about where the square would appear; the dependent variable was how long it took subjects to detect the square and press a computer key. One cue was a plus sign (+) at the fixation point, which meant that the square was equally likely to occur at either edge. In this case, the best strategy for quickly detecting the square would be to keep attention centered, with the eyes, in the middle of the screen and to shift it only *after* the square appeared. A second cue was a "right arrow" (→), which signified that eight times out of ten, the square would occur at the right edge of the screen. The best detection strategy with this cue would be to covertly shift attention to the right edge of the screen *before* the square was presented. On 80 percent of the trials, at least, this covert shift would save time in detecting the square. Finally, a "left arrow" (←) meant that eight times out of ten, the square would appear at the left edge, suggesting that the best strategy would be to covertly shift attention to the left side of the screen.

As shown in Figure 5.28, the square stimulus was detected significantly faster when the center cue gave valid information about where the square would appear. In such cases, subjects used the cue to covertly shift their attention to the expected location, thus readying their perceptual system to detect information there. When the cue led subjects to shift attention to the wrong location, their perceptual system was *less* ready to detect information at the correct location, thus slowing their detection.

Experiments such as this not only provide a way to measure where someone's attention is focused at any given moment; they also illustrate some of the methods that psychologists have developed to measure hidden mental events through observation of

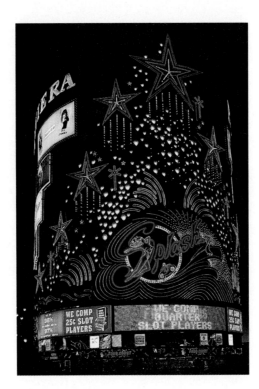

CAPTURING ATTENTION Advertisers use stimulus features such as movement, contrast, color, and intensity to make us involuntarily attend to their products or services. Knowing that attention is selective, magicians use sudden movements or other stimuli to distract our attention from the actions that lie behind their tricks.

FIGURE 5.29

The Stroop Task

Look at this list of words and try, as rapidly as possible, to call out the color of the *ink* in which each word is printed. This *Stroop task* (Stroop, 1935) is not easy because the brain automatically processes the *meaning* of these familiar words, which then competes for attention with the response you are supposed to give. To do well, you must focus on the ink color and not allow your attention to be divided between color and meaning. Children just learning to read have far less trouble with this task, because they do not yet process the meaning of words as automatically as experienced readers do.

BLUE	**GREEN**
GREEN	**ORANGE**
PURPLE	ORANGE
GREEN	BLUE
RED	**RED**
GRAY	GRAY
RED	**BLUE**
BLUE	PURPLE

overt behavior. We describe a number of other examples of this kind of work in Chapter 9, on thought and language.

Allocating Attention

As shown in the experiment on "mind reading" (Posner, Nissen & Ogden, 1978), attending to some stimuli makes us less able to attend to others. In other words, attention is *selective;* it is like a spotlight that can illuminate only a part of the external or internal environment at any particular moment. How do you control, or allocate, your attention?

Control over attention can be voluntary or involuntary (Yantis, 1993). *Voluntary,* or goal-directed, attention control occurs when you purposely focus it in the service of performing a task, such as reading a book in a noisy room or watching for a friend in a crowd. Voluntary control reflects top-down processing because attention is guided by knowledge-based factors such as intentions, beliefs, expectations, and motivation. As people learn certain skills, they voluntarily direct their attention to information they once ignored. For example, the skilled driver looks farther down the road than the novice does. When, in spite of these top-down factors, some aspect of the environment—such as a loud noise—diverts your attention, control is said to be *involuntary,* or stimulus-driven. Stimulus characteristics that tend to capture attention include abrupt changes in lighting or color (such as flashing signs), movement, and the appearance of unusual shapes (Folk, Remington & Wright, 1994).

Using the results of research indicating which stimuli are most likely to attract attention, engineering psychologists have helped design warning systems for airliners, nuclear power plants, and other complex systems (Bettman, Payne & Staelin, 1986; Wogalter et al., 1991). For example, the most effective auditory warning signal in an aircraft cockpit might be a personalized one that calls out the pilot's name.

Divided Attention In many situations, people can divide their attention efficiently enough to allow them to perform more than one activity at a time (Damos, 1992). In fact, as Figure 5.29 illustrates, it is sometimes difficult to keep our attention focused

IN REVIEW	Attention	
Characteristics	**Functions**	**Mechanisms**
Improves mental functioning Requires effort Has limits	Directs sensory and perceptual systems toward stimuli Selects specific information for further processing Allocates mental energy to process information Regulates the flow of resources necessary for performing a task or coordinating multiple tasks	Overt orienting (e.g., cupping your ear to hear a whisper) Covert orienting (e.g., thinking about spring break while looking at the notes in front of you) Voluntary control (e.g., purposefully looking for cars before crossing a street) Involuntary control (e.g., losing your train of thought when you're interrupted by a thunder clap) Automatic processing (e.g., no longer thinking about grammar rules as you become fluent in a foreign language) Divided attention (e.g., looking for an open teammate while you dribble a soccer ball down the field)

rather than divided. People can walk while talking, or drive while listening to music, but we find it virtually impossible to read and talk at the same time. Why is it sometimes so easy and at other times so difficult to do two things at once?

When one task is so *automatic* as to require little or no attention, it is usually easy to do something else at the same time, even if the other task takes some attention (Schneider, 1985). Even when two tasks require attention, it may still be possible to perform them simultaneously, as long as each taps into different kinds of attentional resources (Wickens, 1992). For example, some attentional resources are devoted to perceiving incoming stimuli, while others handle making responses. This specialization of attention allows a skilled pianist to read musical notes and press keys simultaneously even the first time through a piece. Apparently, the human brain has more than one type of attentional resources and more than one spotlight of attention (Navon & Gopher, 1979; Wickens, 1989). This notion of different types of attention also helps explain why a driver can listen to the radio while steering safely and why voice control can be an effective way of performing a second task in an aircraft while the pilot's hands are busy manipulating the controls (Wickens, 1992a).

Attention and Automatic Processing

Your search for Barney's Diner will be aided by your ability to voluntarily allocate attention to a certain part of the environment, but it would be made even easier if Barney's had the only flashing sign on the road (see In Review: Attention). Your search would not take much effort in that case because you could simply allow the most intense stimulus around to attract your attention automatically. Psychologists describe this ability to search for targets rapidly and automatically as *parallel processing;* it is as if you can examine all nearby locations at once (in parallel) and rapidly detect the target no matter where it appears.

Thus, if Waldo—the target to be found in Figure 5.30—were bright red and twice as large as any other character, you could conduct a parallel search and he would quickly "pop out." The automatic, parallel processing that allows detection of color or size suggests that such features are analyzed before the point at which attention is required. However, because Waldo shares many features with the other characters in the figure, you must conduct a slower, serial search, examining each one in turn (Treisman, 1988; Treisman & Gelade, 1980). The more nontarget elements there are in a display, the longer a serial search will take. The "pop out" test offers a good way to determine which kinds of information are processed in parallel, leaving spare attention for use elsewhere, and which require serial processing and thus more focused attention.

Attention and the Brain

If directing attention to a task causes extra mental work to be done, there should be evidence of that work in brain activity. Such evidence has been provided by positron emission tomography (PET) scans, which reveal increased blood flow to regions of the brain associated with the mental processing necessary for the task. In one study, for example, people were asked either to focus attention on reporting only the color of a stimulus or to divide attention in order to report its color, speed of motion, and shape (Corbetta et al., 1991). When attention was focused on color alone, increased blood flow appeared only in the part of the brain where that stimulus feature was analyzed; when attention was divided, the added supply of blood was shared between two locations. Similarly, particular patterns of blood flow have been observed in different areas of the brain involved in different reading processes such as attending to the shape, sound, or meaning of words (Peterson et al., 1990).

Other research using PET scans, surgery on animals, and case studies of humans with brain damage has shown that switching the spotlight of visual attention involves at least three different parts of the brain (e.g., LaBerge, 1991; Posner & Peterson, 1990).

FIGURE 5.30

Where's Waldo?

Find Waldo. (He's the only person wearing a striped shirt and glasses.)

An area in the posterior parietal lobe of the cerebral cortex appears to be responsible for disengaging attention from its present focus. A region in the midbrain's superior colliculus is involved in shifting the focus of attention. (Interestingly, this region is also involved in eye movements.) A third area deep in the thalamus, called the pulvinar, focuses attention on a new location (Posner & Peterson, 1990). Finally, there is evidence that the right cerebral hemisphere, more than the left, is responsible for sustaining or concentrating attention on a particular task (Pardo, Fox & Raichle, 1991). Because attention appears to be a linked set of resources that improve information processing at several levels and locations in the brain, it is not surprising that no single brain region has been identified as an "attention center" (Posner & Peterson, 1990).

APPLICATIONS OF RESEARCH ON PERCEPTION

Throughout this chapter we have mentioned ways in which perceptual systems shape people's ability to handle a variety of tasks, from recognizing restaurant signs to detecting tornadoes. In this section we examine the application of perception research to two areas in which perception is particularly important: aviation and human-computer interaction.

Aviation Psychology

Much of the impetus for research on perception in aviation has come from accidents caused in part by failures of perception (Wiener & Nagel, 1988; O'Hare & Roscoe, 1991). To land an aircraft safely, for example, pilots must make very accurate judgments of how far they are from the ground, and how fast and from what angle they are approaching a runway. Normally, the bottom-up perceptual cues providing this information are rich and redundant, and the pilots' perception is accurate (Gibson, 1979). Further, the ground surface they are approaching matches their expectations based on experience, thus adding top-down processing to produce a correct perception of reality. But suppose there are few depth cues because the landing occurs at night, and suppose the lay of the land is different from the pilot's normal experience. With both bottom-up and top-down processing impaired, the pilot's interpretation of reality may be disastrously incorrect.

If, for example, the runway is much smaller than a pilot expects, it might be perceived as farther away than it actually is—especially at night—and thus may be approached too fast (O'Hare & Roscoe, 1991). (This illusion is similar to the one mentioned earlier in which drivers overestimate their distance from small cars.) Or if a pilot expects the runway to be perfectly flat but it actually slopes upward, the pilot might falsely perceive that the aircraft is too high. Misguided attempts to "correct" a plane's altitude under these circumstances have caused pilots to fly in too low, resulting in a series of major nighttime crashes in the 1960s (Kraft, 1978). Psychologists helped to prevent similar tragedies by recommending that airline training programs remind pilots about the dangers of visual illusions and the importance of relying on their flight instruments during landings, especially at night.

Unfortunately, the instruments in a typical aircraft cockpit present information that bears little resemblance to the perceptual world. A pilot depending on these instruments must do a lot of time-consuming and effortful serial processing in order to perceive and piece together the information necessary to understand the aircraft's position and movement. To address this problem, engineering psychologists have helped to develop displays that present a realistic three-dimensional image of the flight environment—similar in some ways to a video game display. This image more accurately captures the many cues for depth perception that the pilot needs (Lintern, 1991; Haskell & Wickens, 1993; Theunisson, 1994).

Research on auditory perception has also contributed to aviation safety, both in the creation of warning signals that are most likely to catch the pilot's attention and in

AVOIDING PERCEPTUAL OVERLOAD   The pilot of a commercial jetliner is faced with a potentially overwhelming array of visual and auditory signals that must be correctly perceived and interpreted to ensure a safe flight. Engineering psychologists are helping to design instrument displays that make this task easier.

VIRTUAL REALITY In virtual reality systems, the user wears a computer-generated display as a mask that senses head movements. Using this movement information, the computer creates an image of wherever the user looks in the virtual world. The user may also wear "data gloves" that can both sense hand position (and so display a "virtual hand" to the eyes) and provide sensations to the finger tips, creating the perception of touch when the virtual hand makes contact with a virtual object.

efforts to minimize errors in cockpit communications. Air-traffic control communications use a special vocabulary and standardized phrases in order to avoid ambiguity. But as a result, the communications are also usually short, with little of the built-in redundancy that, in normal conversation, allows people to understand a sentence even if some words are missing. If a pilot eager to depart on time perceives an expected message as "take off" when the actual message is "hold for takeoff," the results can be catastrophic. Problems like these are being addressed, "bottom-up," through "noise canceling" microphones and visual message displays (Kerns, 1991), as well as through the use of slightly longer messages that aid top-down processing by providing more contextual cues.

Human-Computer Interaction

The principles of perception are also being applied by engineering psychologists who serve as key members of design teams at various computer manufacturing and software companies. For example, in line with the ecological view of perception, they are trying to duplicate in the world of computer displays many of the depth cues that help people navigate in the physical world (Preece et al., 1994). The next time you use a word-processing or spreadsheet program, notice how shading cues make the "buttons" on the application toolbar at the top or bottom of the screen seem to protrude from their background as real buttons would. Similarly, when you open several documents or spreadsheets, interposition cues make them appear to be lying on top of one another.

The results of research on attention have been applied to your cursor. It blinks to attract your attention, making it possible to do a quick parallel search rather than a slow serial search when you are looking for the cursor amid all the other stimuli on the screen (Schneiderman, 1992). Perceptual principles have also guided creation of the pictorial images, or icons, that are used to represent objects, processes, and commands in your computer programs (Preece et al., 1994). These icons speed your use of the computer if their features are easy to detect, recognize, and interpret (Rogers, 1989). This is why a little trash-can icon is used in some software programs to show you where to click when you want to delete a file; a tiny eraser or paper shredder would also work, but its features might be harder to recognize, making the program confusing. In short, psychologists are applying research on perception to make computers easier to use.

FUTURE DIRECTIONS

We have outlined how perception translates raw sensations into information that is meaningful and useful to the perceiver. The process is elaborate, involving both bottom-up and top-down processing. Many of the principles of perception are well-documented; yet questions and debates remain.

The most active trend in perceptual research, and one that is likely to engage researchers for years to come, is modeling on computers the computational processes thought to be involved in perception. To shed light on human perception, these computational models must work in a way that is faithful to the means by which the brain actually carries out perceptual analysis—relying, for example, on neural networks and parallel distributed processing (McClelland, 1996). This computer modeling will be part of a larger effort to determine which aspects of perception can be explained purely by characteristics of the incoming stimulus array, which can be explained by neural computations, and which must be accounted for by complex cognitive and motivational variables. It will also be critically important to a growing field called machine vision, involving increasingly sophisticated visual capabilities (and

accompanying intelligence) that are being built into robots and other machines.

The issue of attention, too, will continue to intrigue psychologists. They will study its complex relation to the structure of the brain. They will try to clarify exactly which aspects of perception require attention and which do not. And they will seek to identify those forms of automatic perceptual processing which are fundamental to the hardware of the nervous system and those which *become* automatic through experience and practice (Treisman, Viera & Hayes, 1992).

The coming years will also see a new approach to the age-old question of "what is reality?" If reality lies in perceptions of sensory input, it may be possible to manufacture sensory cues that can give people the experience of many different realities, much as an electronic synthesizer creates the sound of many different musical instruments. Capitalizing on recent advances in computer technology, scientists continue to create more and more elaborate examples of *virtual reality,* a set of sensations so compelling that observers perceive themselves as being "in" the computer-generated world, not just looking at an image of it (e.g., Barfield & Furness, 1995). Part of the effect is created by computer graphics, which produce startlingly faithful images. The sense of reality is enhanced by other sensory inputs, such as three-dimensional sound (Cohen & Wenzel, 1995).

Though already being widely used for entertainment purposes, virtual reality technology also has valuable applications in space exploration, medicine, scientific visualization, and other fields. Scientists might explore a "virtual" Martian surface created by data from space probes (McGreevy, 1991). And before actually performing certain operations, surgeons can

now explore relevant anatomical details, and even practice the procedure, using a virtual human body whose characteristics have been digitized on a computer. Chemists and physicists are now able to manipulate virtual images of structures and molecules and thus more easily make new discoveries about them.

If you want to learn more about these and other aspects of perception, consider taking the basic course in the area, which is usually called "Sensation and Perception." Many psychology departments also offer advanced courses in perception. For more on the nature of reality, take some philosophy courses.

SUMMARY AND KEY TERMS

Perception is the process through which people actively use knowledge and understanding of the world to interpret sensations as meaningful experiences.

■ THREE VIEWS OF PERCEPTION

The *ecological* view of perception holds that the environment itself provides the cues that people use to form perceptions. The *constructionist* view suggests that the perceptual system constructs the experience of reality, making inferences and applying knowledge in order to interpret sensations. The *computational* view emphasizes the computations performed by the nervous system.

■ PSYCHOPHYSICS

Psychophysics is the study of the relationship between stimulus energy and the psychological experience of that energy.

Absolute Thresholds: Is Something Out There?
Psychophysics has traditionally been concerned with matters such as determining *absolute thresholds* for the detection of stimuli. *Internal noise* and the *response criterion* being used cause variation in the absolute threshold.

Overcoming the Threshold Problem:
Signal-Detection Theory
Signal-detection theory describes how detection is affected by *sensitivity* and the response criterion. Signal-detection theory has been applied to understanding decision making and performance in areas such as the detection of tornados on radar.

Judging Differences Between Stimuli
Weber's law states that the minimum detectable amount of change in a stimulus—the *difference threshold* or *just-noticeable difference (JND)*—increases in proportion to the initial amount of the stimulus. The less the initial stimulation, the smaller the change must be in order to be detected. Fechner's law and Stevens's power law describe the relation between the magnitude of a stimulus and its perceived intensity.

■ ORGANIZING THE PERCEPTUAL WORLD

Principles of Perceptual Organization
When people perceive objects or sounds, they automatically discriminate *figure* from *ground*. In addition, the perceptual system automatically groups stimuli into patterns on the basis of the *Gestalt* principles of *proximity, similarity, continuity, closure, texture, simplicity, common fate,* and *common region*. The process of mentally representing and interpreting sounds is called *auditory scene analysis*.

Perception of Depth and Distance
The perception of distance, or *depth perception*, depends partly on stimulus cues and partly on the physical structure of the visual system. Some of the stimulus cues are *relative size, height in the visual field, interposition, linear perspective, reduced clarity, light and shadow,* and *gradients* such as *textural gradients* and *movement gradients*. Cues based on the structure of the visual system include *convergence* of the eyes (the fact that the eyes must move to focus on the same object), *binocular disparity* (the fact that the eyes are set slightly apart), and *accommodation* (the change in the shape of the lenses as objects are brought into focus).

Perception of Motion
The perception of motion results, in part, from the movement of stimuli across the retina. Expanding or *looming* stimulation is perceived as an approaching object. Movement of the retinal image is interpreted along with information about movement of the head, eyes, and other parts of the body, so that one's own movement can be discriminated from the movement of external objects.

Perceptual Constancy
Because of *perceptual constancy*, the brightness, size, and shape of objects can be seen as constant even though the sensations received from those objects may change. Size constancy and shape constancy depend on the relationship between the retinal image of the object and the knowledge-based perception of its distance. Brightness constancy depends on the perceived relationship between the brightness of an object and its background.

Perceptual Illusions
Perceptual illusions are distortions of reality that result when principles of perception are applied inappropriately. Many illusions are caused by misreading depth cues and by evaluating stimuli in the context of their surroundings.

Culture, Experience, and Perception
To the extent that the visual environments of people in different cultures differ, their perceptual experiences—as evidenced by their responses to perceptual illusions—may differ as well.

■ RECOGNIZING THE PERCEPTUAL WORLD

Both *bottom-up processing* and *top-down processing* may contribute to recognition of the world. The ability to recognize objects is based on finding a match between the pattern of sensations organized by the perceptual system and a pattern that is stored in memory.

Bottom-up Processing
Bottom-up processing seems to be accomplished by the analysis of

stimulus features, or combinations of features, such as form, color, motion, depth, and spatial frequencies.

Top-down Processing

Top-down processing is influenced by expectancy and motivation. *Schemas* based on past experience can create a perceptual set, the readiness or predisposition to perceive stimuli in certain ways. Expectancies can also be created by the context in which a stimulus appears.

Top-down and Bottom-up Processing Together

Top-down and bottom-up processing commonly work together to create recognition. Top-down processing can fill in gaps in physical stimuli, in part because the environment provides redundant stimuli.

Network Processing

Research on pattern recognition has focused attention on network, or *parallel distributed processing (PDP),* models of perception. These emphasize the simultaneous activation and interaction of feature-analysis systems and the role of experience.

■ LINKAGES: PERCEPTION AND HUMAN DEVELOPMENT

The ability to perceive color, basic shape features, and possibly the human face are present at or near birth. Other abilities, such as recognition of form, are acquired later. Depth is perceived early, but its meaning is learned later. Perceptual abilities are modified by both experience and maturation.

■ ATTENTION

Attention is the process of focusing psychological resources to enhance perception, performance, and mental experience. We can shift attention overtly—by moving the eyes, for example—or covertly, without any movement of sensory systems.

Allocating Attention

Attention is selective; it is like a spotlight that illuminates different parts of the external environment or various mental processes. Control over attention can be voluntary and knowledge based or involuntary and driven by environmental stimuli. People can sometimes attend to two tasks at once, but there are limits to how well they can divide attention.

Attention and Automatic Processing

Some information can be processed automatically, in parallel, while other situations demand focused attention and a serial search.

Attention and the Brain

Psychologists are identifying various brain regions responsible for different aspects of attention. No single brain region has been identified as an "attention center."

■ APPLICATIONS OF RESEARCH ON PERCEPTION

Research on human perception has numerous practical applications.

Aviation Psychology

Accurate size and distance judgments, top-down processing, and attention are all important to safety in aviation.

Human-Computer Interaction

Perceptual principles relating to recognition, depth cues, and attention are being applied by psychologists who work with designers of computers and computer programs.

CONSCIOUSNESS

C H A P T E R 6

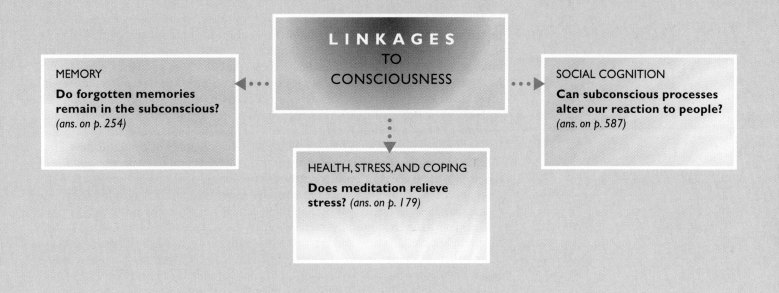

LINKAGES
TO
CONSCIOUSNESS

MEMORY

Do forgotten memories remain in the subconscious?
(ans. on p. 254)

SOCIAL COGNITION

Can subconscious processes alter our reaction to people?
(ans. on p. 587)

HEALTH, STRESS, AND COPING

Does meditation relieve stress? *(ans. on p. 179)*

A s a teenager, Neil developed a brain tumor. Though successfully treated, it caused damage that left him with a set of odd symptoms. For example, Neil could remember his childhood and recall other past events, but he now seemed incapable of forming *new* memories. He was unable to recall what someone had said to him—or what he had read—even a minute earlier. Indeed, within seconds of meeting a new person, Neil would have no memory of having been introduced. Further, although his vision remained normal, Neil had serious perceptual difficulties that left him unable to recognize even familiar objects. Thus, he could define the word *table* and describe what a table looks like, but when actually looking at a table he would be unable to say what it is. Once an excellent student, Neil was no longer able to read words, identify numbers, or even match upper-case letters with their lower-case equivalents. Remarkably, however, Neil could accurately describe recent events and correctly name objects if allowed to do so in *writing*. For example, hours after hearing a taped version of a textbook, he could write his reactions to the book and even quote its content. Yet as soon as he finished writing, he would ask, "What does this say?" He had no memory of having listened to the book on tape, no memory of having written his comments about it, and no idea of what his written words meant (Vargha-Khadem, Issacs & Mishkin, 1994).

Apparently, Neil *could* form memories, recognize visual objects, and read, but he no longer had any *conscious* experience of these abilities, even as he performed them. Cases like Neil's show that people can detect, analyze, and respond to stimuli without being aware of having done so.

Consciousness can be defined as awareness of the outside world and of one's own mental processes, thoughts, feelings, and perceptions. It is a central topic in psychology (see the Linkages diagram). Consciousness is a property of many mental processes rather than a unique mental process in and of itself. Thus, memories can be conscious, but consciousness is not memory; perceptions can be conscious, but consciousness is not perception. In this chapter we consider the nature of consciousness and the ways in which it affects mental activity. We also explore changes in consciousness that occur as people sleep, dream, undergo hypnosis, meditate, or use certain drugs.

ANALYZING CONSCIOUSNESS

As discussed in Chapter 1, the formal psychological study of consciousness began when Wilhelm Wundt founded the first European psychology laboratory in 1879.

Psychologists have been fascinated by the study of consciousness ever since. Some continued to explore its structure and functions even during the decades of the 1920s through the 1960s, when behaviorism's influence made research on mental processes unpopular, especially in the United States. Since the late 1960s, mainstream psychology has again accepted consciousness as a legitimate and compelling research topic. As with other areas of study, psychologists examine consciousness scientifically, using the empirical research principles described in Chapter 2 and the most sophisticated research technologies available.

Three questions dominate the modern psychological study of consciousness. First, like the philosophers who preceded them, psychologists grapple with the *mind-body problem:* What is the relationship between the conscious mind and the physical brain? One approach, known as *dualism,* sees the mind and brain as entirely separate (Maunder, 1995). This idea was championed in the seventeenth century by French philosopher René Descartes. Descartes claimed that a person's soul was separate from the brain but could "view" and interact with brain events through the pineal gland, a brain structure about the size of a grape. In contrast, *materialism* suggests that mind *is* brain. Materialists argue that complex interactions among the brain's nerve cells create consciousness, much as the parts in a television set interact to produce a picture (Sperry, 1993).

A second question focuses on the nature of consciousness. According to the *Cartesian theater* view, consciousness is a single phenomenon, a kind of "stage" where all the different events of awareness converge to "play" before the "audience" of your mind. Those adopting this view note that the subjective intensities of lights, sounds, weights, and other stimuli follow similar psychophysical laws (as described in the chapter on perception), as if each sensory system passes its inputs to a single "monitor" that coordinates the experience of magnitude (Teghtsoonian, 1992). The *multiple-drafts* view sees the mind simultaneously processing many parallel streams of information, each of which can independently contribute to conscious experience (Dennett, 1991, 1993). The multiple-drafts view has become influential due to recent research on *parallel processing,* as described in the chapters on sensation, perception, memory, and thought and language. In the visual system, for example, the identity and location of objects are each processed by separate brain regions, yet there is no brain region in which both streams of processing come together (de Jong et al., 1994).

A third question addresses the relationship between mental activity and conscious awareness. More than a century ago, Sigmund Freud theorized that some mental processes occur without our awareness and that these processes can affect us in many ways. Most aspects of Freud's theory have not been supported by modern laboratory research, but, as described in the next section, the results of that research have shown that the scope of consciousness does indeed go beyond the mental events of which people are normally aware.

THE SCOPE OF CONSCIOUSNESS

Conscious awareness is vital in many situations, of course. As just one example, consider how helpful it is to be aware of your memory's limitations when planning the best strategies for taking notes and studying for tests. Yet many of the processes involved in memory, perception, and thought can occur without your being aware of them.

Mental Processing Without Awareness

A fascinating demonstration of mental processing without awareness was provided by an experiment with patients who were under anesthesia for surgery. While the still-unconscious patients were in a postoperative recovery room, an audiotape of fifteen word pairs was played over and over. After regaining consciousness, these patients could not say what words had been played in the recovery room—or even whether a tape had been played at all. Yet when given one word from each of the word pairs and asked to say the first word that came to mind, the patients were able to produce the other member of the word pair from the tape (Cork, Kihlstrom & Hameroff, 1992).

Evidence for the operation of subconscious mental processing includes research showing that surgery patients may be able to hear and later comply with instructions or suggestions given while they are under anesthesia and of which they have no memory (Bennett, Giannini & Davis, 1985). In another study, people showed physiological arousal to emotionally charged words even when they were not paying attention to them (Von Wright, Anderson & Stenman, 1975).

BLOOM COUNTY   **by Berke Breathed**

Even when people are conscious and alert, information can sometimes be processed and used without their awareness. In one study of this phenomenon, subjects watched a computer screen as an *X* flashed in one of four locations. The subjects' task was to indicate where the *X* appeared by rapidly pushing one of four buttons. The *X*'s location seemed to vary randomly, but the placement sequence actually followed a set of complex rules, such as "If the *X* moves horizontally twice in a row, then it will move vertically next." The subjects' responses became progressively faster and more accurate, but they instantly deteriorated when the rules were secretly abandoned and the *X*s began appearing in *truly* random locations. Apparently, the participants in this study had learned a complex rule-bound strategy to improve their performance. However, even when offered $100 to state the rules that had guided the location sequence, they could not do so, nor were they sure that any such rules existed (Lewicki, 1992).

Information processing without awareness has also been demonstrated in research on *priming*. In a typical priming study, people tend to respond faster or more accurately to previously seen stimuli, even when they cannot consciously recall having seen those stimuli (Schacter & Cooper, 1993; Selco & Cohen, 1996). In one study, for example, people were asked to look at figures like those in Figure 6.1 and decide which of them could actually exist in three-dimensional space and which could not. The subjects were better at classifying pictures that they had seen before, even when they could not remember having them (Cooper et al., 1992b; Schacter et al., 1991).

Similar results occur in experiments on the *mere-exposure effect*, the tendency for people to like previously encountered stimuli more than new ones. In one experiment,

FIGURE 6.1

Stimuli Used in a Priming Experiment

The figures in section **(A)** can actually exist in three-dimensional space; those in section **(B)** cannot.

(A)   (B)

Source: Schacter et al., 1991.

subjects viewed a series of unfamiliar block figures similar to those in Figure 6.1. Then they were shown several *pairs* of figures and asked to say which member of each pair came from the series they had seen earlier. They were also asked to choose the figure in each pair that they liked better. Their choice of the previously seen figure was correct only about half the time (as would be expected by chance alone), but they tended to *like* best the figures they had seen before, even when they did not remember having seen them. In other words, the subjects' responses demonstrated the mere-exposure effect, revealing a memory of their prior experience with the figures that was not reflected in their conscious reports (Seamon et al., 1995).

FOCUS ON
RESEARCH METHODS

Presenting Stimuli Outside of Awareness

The fact that surgery patients can correctly pair up words that had been presented to them while they were unconscious suggests that the entire process of exposure to, and influence by, a stimulus can occur outside of awareness.

To explore this possibility without having to anesthetize people, Mark Klinger and Anthony Greenwald (1995) conducted a two-stage priming experiment. In the first stage, participants looked through a set of viewing tubes that showed each eye its own computer screen. The same pair of words appeared on each screen, and the subjects' task was to press one key if the words were related (as in *eagle-falcon*), and another key if they were unrelated (as in *eagle-polka*). Before the word pairs appeared, a priming word was presented to one eye long enough to be consciously perceived. Sometimes, this priming word was related to one of the words in the pair that followed (for example, *hawk* might appear just before *eagle-falcon* or *eagle-polka*); at other times, the prime was unrelated *(nurse)*. Under these conditions, the expected priming effect occurred: Subjects made faster and more accurate decisions about the word pairs when they were consciously primed by a word that was related to a member of the pair than when primed by an unrelated word.

Would the priming effect occur if the subjects were unaware of being primed? To find out, the researchers had to present the priming word in such a way that a person could mentally process it without being conscious of doing so. But how? The solution is to show the priming word to only one eye while showing a meaningless visual pattern, called a "mask," to the other eye. The longer these stimuli are displayed, the easier it is to see the word, but if this *visual masking* procedure is timed just right, a person will mentally process the priming word without being aware of seeing it.

The researchers determined the best exposure time for each participant during a pretest, in which the participant looked through the viewing tubes described earlier. On some trials, one eye saw a word while the other eye saw a nonsense pattern that acted as a mask. On other trials, the mask was presented to one eye while the other eye saw only a blank screen. The participant was asked to press one key when a mask-plus-word combination appeared and a different key when a mask-plus-blank appeared. The displays were flashed on the screens for periods ranging from 800 milliseconds (eight-tenths of a second) down to 80 milliseconds (eight-hundreths of a second). For each subject, an exposure time was found at which it became impossible to say whether or not a word appeared.

In the second stage of the experiment, the priming task was repeated with a new set of word pairs. This time, however, the priming words were *masked* by the nonsense pattern. As before, the subjects' decisions about the word pairs were faster and more accurate when the priming word was related to the word pairs than when it was unrelated. In other words, the priming effect occurred even when masking prevented the person from consciously perceiving the priming word.

These findings suggest that stimuli can affect us when we are aware of them and—to some extent, at least—when we are not. Researchers are now investigating the differences between such phenomena. As described in Chapter 8, for example, psychologists now distinguish between *explicit,* or conscious, memories and the *implicit* memories whose effects occur even when we are unaware of them.

The Neuropsychology of Consciousness

LINKAGES **How do brain-damaged patients help psychologists study consciousness?** (a link to Introducing Psychology)

Another way to appreciate the scope of consciousness is to observe how brain damage alters conscious experience. Consider the case of Karen Ann Quinlin. In 1975, after drug-induced heart failure starved her brain of oxygen, Karen entered a coma; she was unconscious, unresponsive, and—in medical terms—"brain-dead." Amid worldwide controversy, her parents obtained a court order that allowed them to shut off Karen's life-support machines; but, to everyone's surprise, she continued to live in a vegetative state for ten more years. A detailed study of her autopsied brain revealed that it had sustained damage mainly in the thalamus, an area described in Chapter 3 as a "receiving station" for most sensory signals entering the brain (Kinney et al., 1994). Some researchers have used this finding to argue that the thalamus may be critical for the experience of consciousness (e.g., Bogen, 1995).

Prosopagnosia provides an example of how brain damage can also cause more limited impairments in consciousness. People with prosopagnosia cannot consciously recognize faces—including their own face in the mirror—yet they can still see and recognize many other objects, and can still recognize people by their voices (Young & De Haan, 1992). The problem appears to be relatively specific—one patient who became a farmer could recognize and name his sheep, but never was able to recognize humans! (McNeil & Warrington, 1993). However, when such people see a familiar—but not consciously recognized—face, they show eye movement patterns, changes in brain activity, and autonomic nervous system responses that do not occur when viewing an unfamiliar face (Bruyer, 1991). Thus, some vestige of face recognition is preserved, but it remains unavailable to conscious experience.

LINKAGES **Can blind people see without being aware of it?** (a link to Sensation)

Visual processing without awareness may even occur in certain cases of blindness. For example, when damage to the visual cortex causes clinical blindness, victims say they cannot see anything at all. But if only the primary visual cortex is damaged, nerve fibers from the eyes will still connect to other brain areas that process visual information (see Chapter 4, on sensation). Some of these surviving pathways may permit visual processing, but without visual awareness—a condition known as *blindsight* (Gazzaniga, Fendrich & Wessinger, 1994). Thus, even though such patients say they see nothing, if forced to guess they can still locate visual targets, identify the direction of moving images, reach for objects, and name the color of lights (Weiskrantz, 1995).

Brain damage can also impair conscious access to mental abilities outside the visual realm. Consider *anterograde amnesia,* the inability to form new memories, which often accompanies damage to the hippocampus (Eichenbaum, Otto & Cohen, 1994). Anterograde amnesics seem unable to remember *any* new information, even about the passage of time. One man who developed this condition in 1957 still needed to be reminded more than thirty years later that it was no longer 1957 (Smith, 1988). Yet as Figure 6.2 shows, anterograde amnesics can learn new skills, even though they cannot consciously recall the practice sessions (Milner, 1962). A 1911 case report offers a dramatic, though cruel, example: A doctor hid a pin in his hand while shaking the hand of a patient with anterograde amnesia. The patient quickly lost conscious memory of the episode but thereafter refused to shake anyone's hand, saying only that "sometimes pins are hidden in people's hands" (Cleparede, 1911, cited in Schacter & Tulving, 1982).

Much like the stream to which William James compared it, consciousness is everchanging and multilayered, varying in both quantity and quality. Variations in its quantity—that is, in *how much* awareness one has for mental events—create different *levels of consciousness.* Variations in quality—in the *nature* of the mental processing available to awareness—are called *states of consciousness.* Let's look first at the levels of consciousness.

Memory Formation in
Anterograde Amnesia

In this experiment, a patient known as
H.M., who had anterograde amnesia,
was asked to trace the outline of an
object while using only a mirror
(which reverses left and right) for
visual feedback. H.M.'s performance
on this difficult task improved from
day to day, indicating that he learned
and remembered how to do the task.
Yet he had no conscious memory of
the practice that allowed his skill to
develop (Milner, 1965).

(A) MIRROR-TRACING TASK

**(B) PERFORMANCE OF H. M. ON
MIRROR-TRACING TASK**

Source: Data from Milner, 1965.

Levels of Consciousness

At any moment, the mental events that you are aware of are said to exist at the **conscious level.** For example, look at the *Necker cube* in Figure 6.3. You can hold the cube in one configuration for only a few seconds before the other configuration "pops out" at you. The configuration that you experience at any moment is at your conscious level of awareness for that moment.

Some events, however, cannot be experienced consciously. For example, you are not directly aware of the fact that your brain constantly regulates your blood pressure. Such mental processing occurs at the **nonconscious level,** totally removed from conscious awareness. As described in the chapter on health, stress, and coping, some people can learn to alter a nonconscious process through *biofeedback training,* a special method in which a measuring device tracks and gives information about biological processes like blood pressure; still, the processes themselves remain out of conscious awareness.

Some mental events are not conscious but either can become so or can influence conscious experience; these mental events make up the *cognitive unconscious* (Reber,

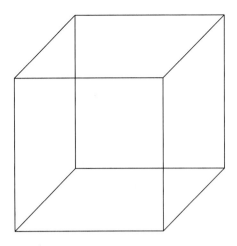

FIGURE 6.3

The Necker Cube

Each of the two squares in the Necker cube can be perceived as either the front or rear surface of the cube. Try to make the cube switch back and forth between these two configurations. Now try to hold only one configuration. You probably cannot maintain the whole cube in consciousness for longer than about 3 seconds before it "flips" from one configuration to the other.

1992), which is further divided into preconscious and subconscious (or unconscious) levels. Mental events that are outside of awareness but can easily be brought into awareness exist at the **preconscious level.** For example, stop reading for a moment and think about last night's dinner. As you do so, you become aware of what and where you ate, and with whom. But moments ago, you were probably not thinking about that information; it was preconscious, ready to be brought to the conscious level. Similarly, in a trivia game you may draw on your large storehouse of preconscious memories to come up with obscure facts.

Other mental activities that can alter thoughts, feelings, and actions are more difficult to bring into awareness (Ratner, 1994). Freud suggested that these **unconscious** activities—especially those involving unacceptable sexual and aggressive urges—are actively kept out of consciousness (see Chapter 14, on personality.) Most psychologists do not accept this Freudian view, however; they use the term **subconscious** to describe the level of consciousness at which mere-exposure effects, priming, and other empirically demonstrable but normally inaccessible mental processes occur.

C an stimuli perceived at a *subliminal* level—that is, below your conscious awareness—affect your thoughts, emotions, and actions? It is said that, in the late 1950s, a New Jersey theater flashed messages such as "buy popcorn" and "drink Coke" on a movie screen, too briefly to be noticed, while customers viewed the movie *Picnic.* The story goes that these messages caused a rise of 15 percent in Coke sales and 58 percent in popcorn sales. Can such "mind control" really work? About 50 percent of Americans seem to think so (Rogers & Smith, 1993), and millions of dollars are spent each year on audiotapes and videos that promise subliminal help to people who want to lose weight, raise self-esteem, quit smoking, make more money, or achieve other goals.

THINKING CRITICALLY

To What Extent Can You Be Influenced by Subliminal Perceptions?

What am I being asked to believe or accept?

The claim underlying the alleged value of subliminal tapes is that stimuli can be detected, perceived, and overtly acted upon without conscious awareness. The strong version of this claim implies that people's buying habits, political decisions, and other actions can be secretly influenced without their awareness or consent.

What evidence is available to support the assertion?

Evidence that subliminal messages can affect conscious judgments is provided by studies that use a *tachistoscope* to present visual stimuli too briefly to be perceived consciously. In one such study, subjects viewed slides showing people performing ordinary acts like washing dishes. Unbeknownst to the subjects, each slide was preceded by a subliminal (9-millisecond) exposure to a photo of "positive" stimuli (such as a child playing) or "negative" stimuli (such as a monster). Later, subjects rated the people on the visible slides as more likable, polite, friendly, successful, and reputable when their images had been preceded by a positive rather than a negative subliminal photo (Krosnick, Jussim & Lynn, 1992). Thus, the subliminal photos not only affected subjects' liking of the people they saw but also shaped beliefs about their personalities.

An earlier study showed that subliminal messages can also affect emotional responses (Bach & Klein, 1957). Subjects saw slides of faces paired with a subliminally flashed word (*happy* or *sad*). Later, subjects described the faces that had been associated with the word *sad* as sadder than those that had been paired with *happy.* More recently, subjects were shown written messages at subliminal (4-millisecond) speed while researchers recorded their *galvanic skin resistance (GSR),* a measure of autonomic arousal. Although the slides were flashed too quickly to be consciously perceived, subjects exhibited higher GSR after messages such as "no one loves me," but not after equally long nonemotional messages such as "no one lifts it" (Masling & Bornstein, 1991). In yet another study, people viewed slides of snakes, spiders, flowers, and mushrooms. Only those who were afraid of snakes or spiders showed increased GSR (and reported fear) in response to snake or spider slides, and they did so even when the visual masking technique described earlier made the slides impossible to perceive at the conscious level (Öhman & Soares, 1994).

The results of studies like these confirm that subliminal information can have an impact on judgments and emotion, but they say little or nothing about the value of subliminal tapes for achieving self-help goals. Indeed, no laboratory evidence exists to support the effectiveness of these tapes; their promoters offer only the reports of satisfied customers (e.g., McGarvey, 1989).

Are there alternative ways of interpreting the evidence?

Many commercial claims for subliminal persuasion—including the New Jersey theater case mentioned above—have turned out to be publicity stunts using fabricated data (Pratkanis, 1992). Other claims may reflect what statisticians call a *Type 1 error*, which occurs when researchers collect so many data sets that the desired result finally appears by chance. Clearly, it is misleading to publicize one positive result without mentioning all the negative results.

Further, testimonials from satisfied customers could be biased by what these people would like to believe about the subliminal tapes they bought. This interpretation is supported by a double-blind, placebo-controlled study in which subjects heard subliminal self-help tapes designed to improve memory. Some heard the standard commercial tapes, while others got "placebo" tapes—identical to the commercial versions, but without subliminal messages. Neither subjects nor researchers knew which individuals heard which kind of tape. The results showed that the commercial self-help tapes were no better than the placebo versions in improving memory (Greenwald & Spangenberg, 1991).

In another study, half the subjects were told they would be listening to tapes containing subliminal messages for improved memory; the other half were told the subliminal messages would promote self-esteem. However, the subjects were not necessarily exposed to the subliminal messages they were expecting; half the subjects in the memory group actually heard self-esteem messages and half of the self-esteem group heard memory messages. Regardless of which tapes they *actually* heard, subjects who *thought* they had heard memory-enhancement messages reported improved memory; those who *thought* they had heard self-esteem messages said their self-esteem had improved (Pratkanis, Eskenazi & Greenwald, 1994). In other words, the effects of the tapes were determined by the listeners' expectations—not by the tapes' subliminal content. This result suggests that customers' reports about the value of subliminal self-help tapes may reflect placebo effects based on optimistic expectations rather than the effects of subliminal messages (see Chapter 2).

What additional evidence would help to evaluate the alternatives?

The effects of subliminal messages must be assessed via controlled experiments like those described in Chapter 2. Those advocating the development and use of subliminal methods must provide supporting evidence based on the kind of double-blind, placebo-controlled studies just described.

What conclusions are most reasonable?

The available evidence suggests that subliminal perception occurs but has no potential for "mind control" (Greenwald, Klinger & Schuh, 1995). Subliminal effects are usually small and short-lived, and affect only general measures of overall arousal. Most researchers agree that subliminal messages have no special power to create needs, goals, skills, or actions (Pratkanis, 1992). Indeed, advertisements, political speeches, and other messages that people can perceive consciously have far stronger persuasive effects.

States of Consciousness

Mental activity is always changing. The features of consciousness at any instant—what reaches your awareness, the decisions you are making, and so on—make up your **state of consciousness** at that moment. Possible states range from deep sleep to alert wakefulness; they can also be affected by drugs and other influences. Consider, for example, the varying states of consciousness that might occur aboard an airplane en route from New York to Los Angeles. In the cockpit, the pilot calmly scans instrument displays while talking to an air-traffic controller. In seat 9B, a lawyer has just polished off her second Scotch while planning a courtroom strategy. Nearby, a young father gazes out a window, daydreaming, while his small daughter sleeps in his lap, dreaming dreams of her own.

All these people are experiencing different states of consciousness. Some states are active and some passive (Hilgard, 1980). The daydreaming father is letting his mind wander, passively noting images, memories, and other mental events that come unbidden to mind. The lawyer is actively directing her mental activity, evaluating various options and considering their likely outcomes.

Most people spend most of their time in a *waking* state of consciousness. Mental processing in this state varies with changes in attention or arousal. Thus, while reading, you may temporarily ignore sounds around you. Similarly, if you are upset or bored, you may miss important environmental cues, making it dangerous to drive a car.

When changes in mental processes are great enough for you or others to notice significant differences in how you function, you have entered an **altered state of consciousness** (Glicksohn, 1991). In an altered state, mental processing shows distinct

ALTERED STATES AND CULTURAL VALUES Different cultures define what altered states of consciousness are approved and which are considered inappropriate. Here we see participants in a Haitian voodoo ceremony reaching an altered state by sniffing fumes and, in India, a religious healer entering a self-induced trance.

changes unique to that state. Cognitive processes or perceptions of yourself or the world may change, and normal inhibitions or self-control may weaken (Martindale, 1981).

The phrase *altered states of consciousness* recognizes waking consciousness as the most common state, a baseline against which "altered" states are compared. However, this is not to say that waking consciousness is universally considered more normal, proper, or valued than other states. In fact, value judgments about different states of consciousness vary considerably across cultures (Ward, 1994).

Consider, for instance, *hallucinations,* which are perceptual experiences—such as hearing voices—that occur in the absence of sensory stimuli. In the United States, hallucinations are viewed as undesirable. Mental patients who hallucinate often feel stress and self-blame; they may avoid reporting their hallucinations and tend to receive poorer prognoses and more drastic treatments than patients who do not hallucinate (Wallace, 1959). Among the Moche of Peru, however, hallucinations have a culturally approved place. When someone is beset by illness or misfortune, a healer conducts an elaborate ritual to find causes and treatments. During the ceremony, the healer ingests mescaline, a drug that causes hallucinations. These hallucinations are thought to give the healer spiritual insight into the patient's problems (de Rios, 1992). In the context of many other tribal cultures, too, purposeful hallucinations are revered, not demeaned (Grob & Dobkin-de-Rios, 1992).

Thus, states of consciousness differ not only in terms of their basic characteristics but also in their value to members of particular cultures. In the sections to follow, we describe some of the most interesting altered states of consciousness, beginning with the most common one, sleep.

SLEEPING AND DREAMING

According to ancient myths, sleepers lose control of their minds, flirting with death as their souls wander freely. Early researchers thought sleep was a time of mental inactivity. In fact, however, sleep is an active, complex state.

Stages of Sleep

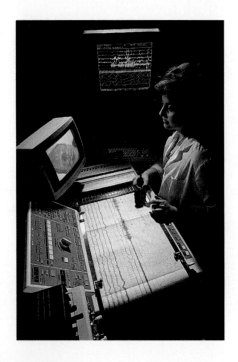

A SLEEP LAB The electroencephalo-gram (EEG) allows scientists to record brain activity through electrodes attached to the skull. The advent of this technology opened the door to the scientific study of sleep.

The brain's electrical activity during sleep can be seen on an *electroencephalogram,* or *EEG.* EEG recordings, often called *brain waves,* vary in height (amplitude) and speed (frequency) as behavior or mental processes change. The brain waves of an awake, alert person have high frequency and low amplitude; they appear as small, closely spaced, irregular EEG spikes. A relaxed person with closed eyes shows *alpha waves*—rhythmic brain waves at speeds of 8 to 12 cycles per second (cps).

During a night's sleep, brain waves show distinctive and systematic changes in amplitude and frequency (Loomis, Harvey & Hobart, 1937; Guevara et al., 1995). These EEG changes, along with changes in muscle activity and eye movement, have been used to describe six sleep stages: stage 0, which is a prelude to sleep, four stages of quiet sleep, and rapid eye movement (REM) sleep (Dement & Kleitman, 1957; Armitage, 1995).

Stage 0 and Quiet Sleep In stage 0, you are relaxed, with eyes closed, but awake. During this stage, EEG activity includes alpha waves; muscle tone and eye movements are normal. The next stages, stages 1 through 4, are called **quiet sleep,** characterized by slower brain waves, deep breathing, a calm heartbeat, and low blood pressure. Because it contrasts with REM sleep, quiet sleep is sometimes called non-REM, or NREM, sleep.

As you enter stage 1 sleep, your eyes start to roll lazily. Rhythmic alpha waves give way to irregular waves similar to those seen in an awake and mentally active person (see Figure 6.4). Minutes later, stage 2 sleep begins. The EEG shows rapid bursts of waves called *sleep spindles,* along with occasional *K-complexes,* waves with high peaks and deep valleys. Stage 3 sleep shows fewer spindles and K-complexes, but it adds *delta waves,* which are much slower (0.5 to 0.3 cps) and larger in amplitude. When delta waves appear more than half of the time, you are in stage 4 sleep, from which it is quite diffi-

FIGURE 6.4

EEGs During Sleep

Notice the regular patterns of alpha waves in stage 0 (relaxed wakefulness), the sleep spindles and K-complexes in stage 2, and the slower delta waves in stages 3 and 4 (Webb, 1968).

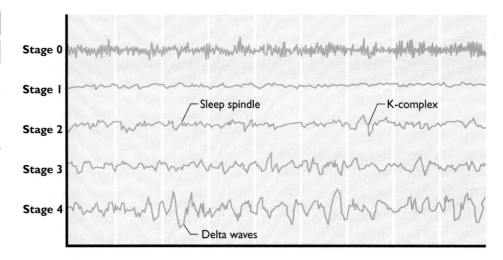

Source: Webb, 1968.

cult to be roused. If you *are* roused from this stage of deep sleep, you tend to be groggy and confused. Your journey from stage 1 to stage 4 has taken about twenty minutes.

REM Sleep. After thirty to forty minutes in stage 4, you quickly return to stage 2 sleep and then begin a special stage in which your eyes move rapidly under closed lids (Jones, 1991). This is called **REM (rapid eye movement) sleep, or active sleep.** As in stage 1, the EEG resembles that of an awake, alert person, but now physiological arousal—heart rate, breathing, blood pressure—also mimics the waking state. Paradoxically, while EEG and other measures resemble those of an awake person, muscle tone falls to the point of near paralysis. Sudden, twitchy spasms appear, especially in the face and hands, as brainstem and spinal neurons control limb muscle movements (Blumberg & Lucas, 1994). Comparisons of reports by sleepers who are awakened during REM versus non-REM sleep suggest that most of a night's dreams occur during REM sleep (Dement & Kleitman, 1957; Stickgold, Rittenhouse & Hobson, 1994).

A Night's Sleep Most people pass through the cycle of sleep stages four to six times each night. Each cycle lasts about ninety minutes, but with a somewhat different itinerary (see Figure 6.5). Early in the night most of the time is spent in stages 3 and 4, with

FIGURE 6.5

A Night's Sleep

During a typical night a sleeper goes through this sequence of EEG stages. Notice that sleep is deepest during the first part of the night and more shallow later on, when REM sleep becomes more prominent.

Source: Cartwright, 1978.

only a few minutes in REM. As sleep continues, though, it is dominated by stage 2 and REM, from which sleepers finally awaken.

Sleep patterns change with age. An average infant sleeps about sixteen hours a day; an average seventy-year-old, only about six hours (Roffwarg, Muzio & Dement, 1966). The composition of sleep changes with age, too (see Figure 6.6). REM accounts for half of total sleep at birth but less than 25 percent in young adults. People may vary widely from these averages, however; some people feel well-rested after four hours sleep while others of similar age require ten hours to feel satisfied (Clausen, Sersen & Lidsky, 1974). There are also wide cultural variations in the tendency to take daytime naps (Cartwright, 1978; Webb, 1968).

Sleep Disorders

The most common sleeping problem is **insomnia,** in which one feels daytime fatigue due to trouble falling asleep or staying asleep. Besides being tiring, insomnia is tied to mental distress. A review of 177 studies covering 7,151 patients found that psychiatric patients sleep less than other patients (Benca et al., 1992). Insomnia is especially associated with depressive and anxiety disorders (Ball, Buchwald & Waddell, 1995); overall, insomniacs are three times as likely to show a mental disorder as those with no sleep complaints (Ford & Kamerow, 1989). It is unclear from such correlations, however, whether insomnia causes mental disorders, mental disorders cause insomnia, or some other factor causes both.

FIGURE 6.6

Sleep and Dreaming Over the Life Span

People tend to sleep less as they get older. There is also a sharp reduction in the percentage of REM sleep, from about eight hours per day in infancy to less than an hour per day by age seventy. Non-REM sleep time also decreases but, compared to the drop in REM, remains relatively stable. After age twenty, however, non-REM sleep contains less and less of the deepest, or stage 4, sleep.

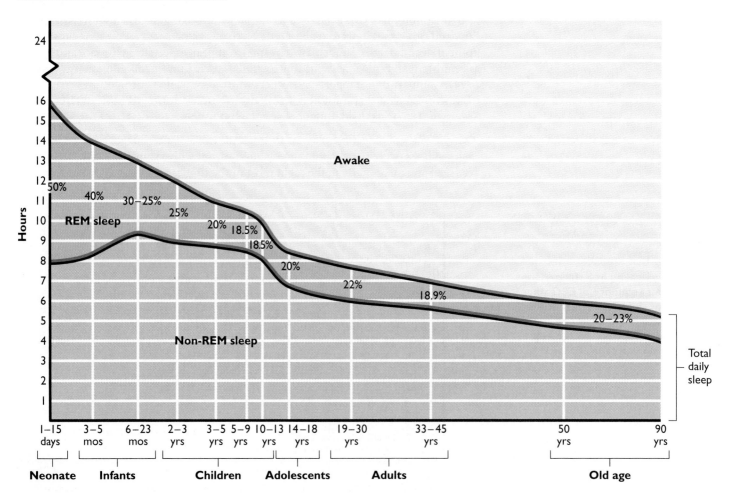

Note: Percentages indicate portion of total sleep time spent in REM.
Source: Roffwarg, Muzio & Dement, 1966 (revised 1969).

Sleeping pills can relieve insomnia, but they interact dangerously with alcohol and may eventually lead to *increased* sleeplessness (Ashton, 1995). In the long run, learning-based methods may be more helpful (Lichstein & Riedel, 1994). For example, stress management techniques such as relaxation training and biofeedback have been shown to help insomniacs reduce unusually strong physiological reactions to stress (Stepanski et al., 1994). Another option is *sleep restriction therapy*, in which the person goes to bed only when sleepy and gets out of bed if sleep does not come (Spielman, Saskin & Thorpy, 1987). The goal is for insomniacs to associate their bed with sleeping, not wakefulness.

Narcolepsy is a disturbing daytime sleep disorder. Its victims abruptly switch from active, often emotional waking states into a few minutes of REM sleep. Because of the loss of muscle tone in REM, the narcoleptic collapses and remains briefly immobile even after awakening. The cause of narcolepsy is unknown, but genetic factors appear to play a role (Wing et al., 1994). Stimulants and napping can be helpful treatments.

Sleep apnea sufferers briefly stop breathing hundreds of times each night, waking up each time long enough to resume breathing. In the morning, victims do not recall the awakenings, yet they feel inadequately rested and tend to show reductions in attention and learning ability (Naëgelé et al., 1995). Apnea has many causes, including obesity and compression of the windpipe. Effective treatments include weight loss and use of a nasal mask that provides a steady stream of air (Chua & Chediak, 1994; Schmidt-Nowara et al., 1995).

In **sudden infant death syndrome (SIDS),** a sleeping baby stops breathing and dies. In the United States, SIDS strikes about two of every thousand infants, usually when they are two to four months old (Hirschfeld, 1995). SIDS is less common in cultures where infants and parents sleep in the same bed, suggesting that sleeping position may be important (McKenna et al., 1993). Indeed, about half of apparent SIDS cases may be accidental suffocations caused when infants lie face down on soft surfaces (Guntheroth & Spiers, 1992). Other SIDS cases may stem from problems with brain systems regulating breathing or from exposure to cigarette smoke (Harper et al., 1988; Klonoff-Cohen & Edlestein, 1995).

Nightmares are frightening REM dreams; **night terrors** are horrific dream images during stage 4 sleep. Sleepers often awaken from a night terror with a bloodcurdling scream and remain intensely afraid for up to thirty minutes, but they may not recall the episode in the morning. Night terrors are especially common in boys, but adults can suffer milder versions. The condition is sometimes treatable with drugs (Lillywhite, Wilson & Nutt, 1994).

Like night terrors, **sleepwalking** occurs in non-REM sleep, usually in childhood (Masand, Popli & Welburg, 1995). By morning, most sleepwalkers have forgotten their travels. Despite myths to the contrary, waking a sleepwalker is not harmful. Drugs help, but most children simply outgrow the problem. One adult sleepwalker was cured when his wife blew a whistle whenever he began a nocturnal stroll (Meyer, 1975).

In **REM behavior disorder,** the near paralysis that normally accompanies REM sleep is absent, so sleepers move as if acting out their dreams (Kempenaers, Bouillon & Mendlewicz, 1994). If the dreams are violent, the disorder can be dangerous to the dreamer or those nearby. Indeed, many sufferers attack sleeping partners. One man grabbed his wife's throat while dreaming he was breaking a deer's neck. The disorder sometimes occurs along with daytime narcolepsy (Schenck & Mahowald, 1992). Fortunately, drug treatments are usually very effective (Bamford, 1993).

Why Do People Sleep?

In trying to understand sleep, psychologists have studied both the functions that sleep serves and the ways in which brain mechanisms shape its characteristics.

Sleep as a Circadian Rhythm   The sleep-wake cycle is one example of the rhythmic nature of life. Almost all animals (including humans) display cycles of behavior and physiology that repeat about every 24 hours in a pattern called a **circadian rhythm** (from the Latin *circa dies*, meaning "about a day") (Kyriacou, 1994). Longer and shorter

DISRUPTED CIRCADIAN RHYTHMS **This Australian diver flew all the way to Spain to compete in the Olympic games. The disruptive effects of international travel or changes in shift work schedules can be reduced somewhat by exposure to bright light during waking hours. This procedure speeds the process of resetting the body's circadian rhythms, possibly by stimulating cells of the brain's suprachiasmatic nucleus (Dawson et al., 1995).**

FIGURE 6.7

Westward/Eastward Travel and Jet Lag

Changing time zones causes more intense symptoms of "jet lag" after eastward travel (when time is lost) than after westward travel (when time is gained). These data show how long it took people flying between London and Detroit (a five-hour time change) to fall asleep once in bed, both on the night before the trip (B1) and on the five nights afterward. Those who flew eastward, from Detroit to London, needed more time to fall asleep than those who flew westward, from London to Detroit (Nicholson et al., 1986).

rhythms also occur, but they are less common. These rhythms are linked, or *entrained*, to signals such as the light and dark of day and night, but some rhythms continue even without such time cues. Volunteers living for months without external cues maintain daily rhythms in sleeping and waking, hormone release, eating, urination, and other physiological functions. Under such conditions, these cycles repeat about every 25 hours (Hillman et al., 1994).

Disrupting the sleep-wake cycle can create problems. For example, air travel across several time zones often causes **jet lag,** a pattern of fatigue, irritability, inattention, and sleeping problems. The traveler's body feels ready to sleep at the wrong time for the new locale. Similar problems affect workers changing between day and night shifts. Because it tends to be easier to stay awake longer than usual than to go to sleep earlier than usual, sleep-wake rhythms readjust more easily when sleep is shifted to a later rather than an earlier time (see Figure 6.7).

Since circadian-like rhythms continue without external cues, an internal "biological clock" must keep track of time. This clock appears to be the *suprachiasmatic nucleus (SCN)* of the hypothalamus (see Figure 6.8). Signals from the SCN reach hindbrain areas that initiate sleep or wakefulness (McCarley, 1987). SCN neurons show a 24- to 25-hour rhythm in firing even when removed from the brain and put in a dish (Gillette, 1986). And when animals with SCN damage receive transplanted SCN cells, the restored circadian rhythms parallel those of the donor animal (Hurd & Ralph, 1992). SCN neurons also regulate the release of the hormone *melatonin* from the *pineal gland*. Melatonin, in turn, appears to be important in maintaining circadian rhythms; timely injections of melatonin reduce fatigue and disorientation from jet lag or other sleep-wake cycle changes (G. M. Brown, 1994).

The Functions of Sleep Examining the effects of sleep deprivation may help explain why people sleep at all. People who go without sleep for as long as a week usually do not suffer serious long-term effects, but sleeplessness does lead to fatigue, irritability, and inattention (Smith & Maben, 1993). Short-term sleep deprivation effects can also take their toll. Most fatal auto accidents in the United States occur during the "fatigue hazard" hours of midnight to 6 A.M. (Coleman, 1992), and fatigue has been implicated as the primary cause of up to 25 percent of all auto accidents (Summala & Mikkola, 1994).

Some researchers believe that sleep, especially non-REM sleep, helps to restore the body for future activity (Adam & Oswald, 1977). They point out, for example, that most people get their non-REM sleep first (Hartman, Baekeland & Zwilling, 1972). After total sleep deprivation, people do not make up lost sleep hour for hour. Instead, they sleep about 50 percent more than usual, then awake feeling rested. But if people are deprived only of REM sleep, they later compensate more directly. In a classic study, subjects were awakened whenever their EEG showed REM sleep. When allowed to sleep

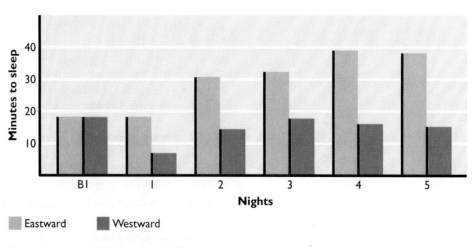

Source: Data from Nicholson et al., 1986.

FIGURE 6.8

Sleep, Dreaming, and the Brain

This diagram shows the location of some of the brain structures thought to be involved in sleep and dreaming as well as in other altered states discussed later in the chapter. Scientists have recently discovered that cells in the ventrolateral preoptic area, a region near the suprachiasmatic nucleus, may act as a "master switch" for sleep by sending signals that shut down arousal systems in the hindbrain (Sherin et al., 1996).

Suprachiasmatic nucleus

Pineal gland

Cerebellum

Hindbrain

Locus coeruleus

uninterrupted the next night, the subjects "rebounded," nearly doubling the percentage of time spent in REM (Dement, 1960). Even after *total* sleep deprivation, the next night of uninterrupted sleep includes an unusually high percentage of REM sleep (Feinberg & Campbell, 1993). This apparent need for REM sleep suggests that REM has special functions.

First, REM may improve the functioning of neurons that use norepinephrine (Siegel & Rogawski, 1988). Norepinephrine is a neurotransmitter released by cells in the *locus coeruleus* (see Figure 6.8) and, during waking hours, affects alertness and mood. But the brain's neurons lose sensitivity to norepinephrine if it is released continuously for too long. Because the locus coeruleus is almost completely inactive during REM sleep, researchers suggest that REM helps restore sensitivity to norepinephrine and thus its ability to keep us alert (Steriade & McCarley, 1990). Indeed, animals deprived of REM show unusually high norepinephrine levels and decreased daytime alertness (Brock et al., 1994).

THE EFFECTS OF SLEEP DEPRIVATION Here, scientists at Loughborough University, England, test the effects of sleep-deprivation on motor co-ordination. Driving while sleep deprived can be dangerous, but some other functions may not suffer as much. One man reportedly stayed awake for 231 hours and was still lucid and capable of serious intellectual work, including the creation of a lovely poem on his tenth day without sleep (Katz & Landis, 1935).

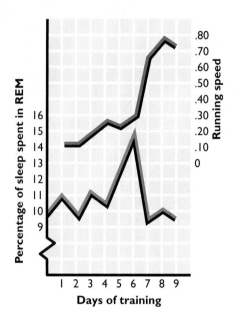

Source: Drucker-Colin & McGaugh, 1977.

FIGURE 6.9

REM Sleep and Learning

The upper curve shows the average running speed of rats as they learned their way around a maze over several days. The lower curve shows the average percentage of REM sleep during the nights between practice sessions. Notice that the rats spent more time in REM on nights during the learning phase than after learning was complete.

**RECALLING DREAMS IN THE LABORATORY
This "flying carpet" image was drawn on a computer by a dream research participant after being asked to recall the previous night's dreams.**

REM may also be a time for developing, checking, and expanding the brain's nerve connections (Roffwarg, Muzio & Dement, 1966). This notion would explain why children and infants, whose brains are still developing, spend so much time in REM (see Figure 6.6). In contrast, guinea pigs and other animals born with well-developed brains spend very little sleep time in REM early in their lives (Cartwright, 1978). REM sleep may also help to solidify and assimilate the day's experiences. In one study, people who were REM-deprived showed poorer retention of a skill learned the day before than people who were either deprived of non-REM sleep or allowed to sleep normally (Karni et al., 1994b). Further, animals that spend daytime hours engaged in learning tasks display more frequent and longer REM episodes than those that spend the day in their cages (Ambrosini et al., 1992; see also Figure 6.9).

Dreams and Dreaming

We have seen that the brain is active in all sleep stages, but **dreams** differ from other mental activity in sleep because they are usually story-like, lasting from seconds to minutes. Dreams may be organized or chaotic, realistic or fantastic, boring or exciting (Hobson & Stickgold, 1994). Sometimes, dreams lead to creative insights about waking problems. For example, after trying for days to write a story about good and evil in the same person, author Robert Louis Stevenson dreamed about a man who drank a potion that turned him into a monster (Hill, 1968). This dream inspired *The Strange Case of Dr. Jekyll and Mr. Hyde.*

Although they often seem bizarre, dreams often contain a certain amount of logic. In one study, for example, when segments from dream reports were randomly reordered, readers could correctly say which had been rearranged and which were intact (Stickgold, Rittenhouse & Hobson, 1994). A second study showed that dream reports commonly describe one person transforming into another or one object turning into another object, but transformation of objects into people or vice versa are rare (Rittenhouse, Stickgold & Hobson, 1994).

Daytime activities can clearly influence the content of dreams. In one study, people wore red-tinted goggles for a few minutes just before going to sleep. Although they did not know the purpose of the study, the next morning they reported more red images in their dreams than people who had not worn the goggles (Roffwarg, Hermann & Bowe-Anders, 1978). It is also sometimes possible to intentionally direct dream content, especially during **lucid dreaming** in which the sleeper is aware of dreaming *while a dream is happening* (LaBerge, 1993).

Research leaves little doubt that everyone dreams during every night of normal sleep. Even blind people dream, although their perceptual experiences are usually not visual. Whether you remember a dream depends on how you sleep and wake up (Cartwright, 1978). Recall is better if you awaken abruptly and lie quietly while writing or tape-recording your recollections.

Why do we dream? Theories abound. Some see dreaming as a fundamental process by which all mammals analyze and consolidate information that has personal significance or survival value. Indeed, research suggests that nonhuman animals do dream. After researchers disabled the neurons that cause REM sleep paralysis, sleeping cats ran around and attacked or seemed alarmed by unseen objects, presumably the images from dreams (Winson, 1990).

According to Freud (1900), dreams are a disguised form of *wish fulfillment,* a way to satisfy unconscious urges or resolve unconscious conflicts that are too upsetting to deal with consciously. For example, sexual desires might appear in a dream as the rhythmic motions of a horseback ride; conflicting feelings about a parent might appear as a dream about a fight. Seeing patients' dreams as a "royal road to a knowledge of the unconscious," Freud interpreted their meaning as part of his psychoanalytic treatment of psychological disorders (see Chapter 16).

In contrast, the *activation-synthesis* theory sees dreams as the meaningless, random by-products of REM sleep (Hobson & McCarley, 1977). According to this theory, hind-brain arousal during REM creates random messages that *activate* the brain, especially the cerebral cortex. Dreams result as the cortex *synthesizes* these random messages as best it can, using stored memories and current feelings to impose a coherent perceptual organization on confusingly random inputs. From this perspective, dreams represent the brain's attempt to make sense of meaningless stimulation during sleep, much as it does when a person, while awake, tries to find meaningful shapes in cloud formations (Bernstein & Roberts, 1995; Rittenhouse, Stickgold & Hobson, 1994).

Even if dreams arise from random physiological activity, their content may still have psychological significance. According to the *problem-solving* theory, dreams give people a chance to review and address some of the problems they face during waking hours (Cartwright, 1993). For example, one study investigated the dreams of divorcing or recently divorced women (Cartwright et al., 1984). Those who were depressed dreamed mostly of the past, but nondepressed women more often had problem-solving dreams as well as dreams spanning the past, present, and future. Thus, the mental style or current concerns of the dreamer can affect the ways in which dreams are organized and recalled (Stevens, 1996).

HYPNOSIS

The word *hypnosis* comes from the Greek word *hypnos*, meaning "sleep," but hypnotized people are not sleeping. People who have been hypnotized say that their bodies felt "asleep," but their minds were active and alert. **Hypnosis** has traditionally been defined as an altered state of consciousness brought on by special techniques and producing responsiveness to suggestions for changes in experience and behavior (Kirsch, 1994a; Orne, 1977). Most hypnotized people do not feel forced to follow the hypnotist's instructions; they simply see no reason to refuse (Hilgard, 1965).

Experiencing Hypnosis

Usually, hypnosis begins with suggestions that the subject feels relaxed and sleepy. The hypnotist then gradually focuses the subject's attention on a restricted, often monotonous set of stimuli while suggesting that the subject ignore everything else and imagine certain feelings.

Not everyone can be hypnotized. Special tests measure **hypnotic susceptibility,** the degree to which people respond to hypnotic suggestions (Gfeller, 1994). Such tests categorize about 10 percent of adults as difficult or impossible to hypnotize (Hilgard, 1982). Hypnotically susceptible people typically differ from others in having a better ability to focus attention and ignore distraction (Crawford, Brown & Moon, 1993), more active imaginations (Spanos, Burnley & Cross, 1993), a tendency to fantasize (Lynn & Rhue, 1986), and a capacity for processing information quickly and easily (Dixon, Brunet & Laurence, 1990). You can become more susceptible by developing a more positive attitude toward hypnosis (Spanos, Burnley & Cross, 1993; Gfeller, 1994). Your *willingness* to be hypnotized is the most important factor. Contrary to myth, you cannot be hypnotized against your will.

The results of hypnosis can be fascinating. People told that their eyes cannot open may struggle fruitlessly to open them. They may appear deaf or blind or insensitive to pain. They may forget their own names. Some appear to remember forgotten things. Others show **age regression,** apparently recalling or re-enacting childhood (see Figure 6.10). Hypnotic effects can last for hours or days through **posthypnotic suggestions**— instructions about behavior to take place after hypnosis has ended (such as smiling whenever someone says "Oregon"). Some subjects show **posthypnotic amnesia,** an inability to recall what happened while they were hypnotized, even after being told what happened.

Ernest Hilgard (1965, 1992) described the main changes people display during hypnosis. First, hypnotized people show *reduced planfulness.* They tend not to initiate actions, waiting instead for the hypnotist's instructions. One subject said, "I was trying to decide if my legs were crossed, but I couldn't tell, and didn't quite have the initiative to move to find out" (Hilgard, 1965, p. 6). Second, subjects tend to ignore all but the

FIGURE 6.10

Hypnotic Age Regression

Here are the signatures of a man and a woman before hypnotically induced age regression (top) and while age-regressed (bottom). Notice that the lower signatures look less mature. In spite of such changes in behavior, however, the things people "recall" during age regression are not especially accurate and are subject to the usual distortions associated with attempts to retrieve old memories (Nash et al., 1986).

Source: Hilgard, 1965.

INDUCING HYPNOSIS   In the late 1700s, Austrian physician Franz Anton Mesmer used a forerunner of hypnosis to treat various physical disorders. His procedure, known as mesmerism, began with patients touching afflicted body parts to magnetized metal rods extending from a tub of water. Upon being touched by Mesmer, the patients would fall into a curative "crisis" or trance, sometimes accompanied by convulsions. We now know that hypnosis can be induced without such elaborate rituals, often simply by staring at an object, as this woman did.

FIGURE 6.11

Can Hypnosis Produce Blindness?

The top row looks like gibberish, but it can be read as the numbers and letters in the lower row if viewed through special glasses *with one eye closed.* Yet when hypnotized subjects who had been given suggestions for blindness in one eye wore the glasses, they were unable to read the display, indicating that both eyes were in fact working normally (Pattie, 1935).

hypnotist's voice and whatever it points out; their *attention is redistributed.* Third, hypnosis enhances the ability to *fantasize,* so subjects more vividly imagine a scene or relive a memory. Fourth, hypnotized people display increased *role-taking;* they more easily act like a person of a different age or a member of the opposite sex, for example. Fifth, hypnotic subjects show *reduced reality testing,* tending not to question if statements are true and more willingly accepting apparent distortions of reality. Thus, a hypnotized person might shiver in a warm room if a hypnotist says it is snowing.

Explaining Hypnosis

Hypnotized people look and act differently from nonhypnotized people (Hilgard, 1965). Do these differences indicate an altered state of consciousness?

In contrast to traditional beliefs, **role theory** maintains that hypnosis is *not* a special state of consciousness. Proponents of role theory argue that hypnotized subjects are merely complying with social demands and acting in accordance with a special social role (Kirsch, 1994b). In other words, they say, hypnosis provides a socially acceptable reason to follow someone's suggestions, much as a doctor's white coat provides a good reason for patients to remove clothing on command.

Support for role theory comes from several sources. First, unhypnotized people sometimes display behaviors usually associated with hypnosis. On television game shows, for example, contestants do lots of odd or silly things, all without benefit of hypnosis. Second, laboratory studies have shown that motivated but nonhypnotized volunteers can duplicate many, if not all, aspects of hypnotic behavior, from arm rigidity to age regression (Dasgupta et al., 1995; Orne & Evans, 1965). In other studies, special tests have shown that people rendered blind or deaf by hypnosis can still see or hear, even though their actions and beliefs suggest that they cannot (Pattie, 1935; Bryant & McConkey, 1989; see also Figure 6.11).

Advocates of **state theory** argue that hypnosis does indeed create an altered state of consciousness. They point to the fact that hypnosis can produce dramatic effects—including insensitivity to pain and the disappearance of warts (Noll, 1994)—that are difficult to attribute to social role-taking. They also note that there are subtle differences in the way hypnotized and nonhypnotized people carry out suggestions. In one study, for example, hypnotized people and those who had been asked to simulate hypnosis were told that they would run their hands through their hair whenever they heard the word *experiment* (Orne, Sheehan & Evans, 1968). Simulators did so only when the hypnotist said the cue word; hypnotized subjects complied no matter who said it. Another study found that most hypnotic subjects passed a traditional polygraph "lie detector" test when answering questions about their hypnotic experiences, while most simulators did not (Kinnunen, Zamansky & Block, 1994).

Hilgard (1979, 1992) has proposed **dissociation theory** to blend role and state theories. He suggests that hypnosis is not one specific state but a general condition in which our normally centralized control of thoughts and actions is temporarily reorganized, or broken up, through a process called *dissociation,* meaning a split in consciousness (Hilgard, 1979). Thus, body movements normally under voluntary control can occur on their own, and normally involuntary processes (such as overt reactions to pain) can be controlled voluntarily. Hilgard argues that this relaxation of central control occurs as part of a *social agreement* to share control with the hypnotist. In other

EHMTWXZMI2ƎTHⓈ∩GⵌMꝹⱲ

FHNV XTMI2 D N 6 NCLⅤ DA

Source: Pattie, 1935.

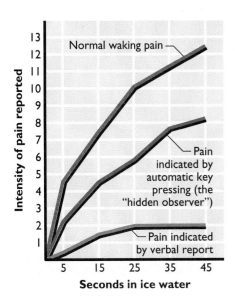

Source: Hilgard, 1977.

FIGURE 6.12

Reports of Pain in Hypnosis

This graph compares the average reports of pain when a person's hand is immersed in ice water. The red line shows the reports by nonhypnotized subjects. The blue line shows the reports by hypnotized subjects who were told they would feel no pain. The purple line shows responses made by hypnotized subjects who were told they would feel no pain but were asked to press a key if "any part of them" felt pain. The key-pressing by this "hidden observer" suggests that under hypnosis the experience of pain was dissociated from conscious awareness.

Does meditation relieve stress?

words, people usually decide for themselves how to act or what to attend to, perceive, or remember—but, during hypnosis, the hypnotist is "allowed" to control some of these experiences and actions. To Hilgard, then, hypnosis is a socially agreed-upon display of dissociated mental functions. Compliance with a social role may account for part of the story, he says, but hypnosis also leads to significant changes in mental processes.

Evidence for dissociation theory comes from a study in which hypnotized subjects immersed one hand in ice water after being told that they would feel no pain (Hilgard, Morgan & MacDonald, 1975). With the other hand, subjects were told to press a key to indicate if "any part of them" felt pain. Subjects' oral reports indicated almost no pain, but their key-pressing told a different story (see Figure 6.12). Hilgard concluded that a "hidden observer" was reporting on pain that was reaching the person but had been separated, or dissociated, from conscious awareness (Hilgard, 1977).

Contemporary research continues to test the validity of various explanatory theories of hypnosis (Bowers, 1992; Green & Lynn, 1995). However, traditional distinctions between state and role theories have become less relevant as researchers focus on larger questions, such as the roles played by social and cognitive factors in hypnotic phenomena, the nature of the hypnotic experience, and the psychological and physiological bases for hypnotic susceptibility (Kirsch & Lynn, 1995). Indeed, there is much yet to be learned about the nature of hypnosis.

Applications of Hypnosis

Whatever hypnosis is, it has proven useful, especially in relation to pain. Hypnosis seems to be the only anesthetic some people need to block the pain of dental work, childbirth, burns, and abdominal surgery (Finer, 1980; Van Sickel, 1992). For others, hypnosis relieves chronic pain from arthritis, nerve damage, migraine headaches, and cancer (Hilgard, 1980; Nolan et al., 1995). Hypnotic suggestion can reduce nausea and vomiting due to chemotherapy (Redd, 1984), and it can help reduce surgical bleeding (Gerschman, Reade & Burrows, 1980).

Other applications of hypnosis are more controversial, especially the use of hypnosis to aid memory. When hypnotized people show age regression, for example, they are probably reconstructing early memories, as well as imagining or acting out past actions (Foenander & Burrows, 1980). Similarly, it is doubtful that hypnosis can help witnesses to recall a crime. Instead, their expectations about and confidence in hypnosis may cause them to unintentionally distort information or reconstruct memories for the events in question (Weekes et al., 1992; Garry & Loftus, 1994; see also Chapter 8).

LINKAGES: MEDITATION, HEALTH, AND STRESS

Meditation provides a set of techniques intended to create an altered state of consciousness characterized by inner peace and tranquillity (Shapiro & Walsh, 1984). Some claim that meditation increases awareness and understanding of themselves and their environment, reduces anxiety, improves health, and aids performance in everything from work to tennis.

In the most common meditation methods, attention is focused on just one thing—a word, sound, or object—until the meditator stops thinking about *anything* and experiences nothing but "pure awareness" (Benson, 1975).

What a meditator focuses on is far less important than doing so with a passive attitude. To organize attention, meditators may, for example, inwardly name every sound or thought that reaches consciousness, focus on the sound of their own breathing, or slowly repeat a *mantra*, which is a soothing word or phrase. During a typical meditation session, breathing, heart rate, muscle tension, blood pressure, and oxygen consumption decrease (Wallace & Benson, 1972). Most forms of meditation induce alpha-wave EEG activity, the brain-wave pattern commonly found in a relaxed, eyes-closed, waking state (see Figure 6.4).

Meditators often report significant reductions in stress-related problems such as general anxiety, high blood pressure, and insomnia (Beauchamp-Turner & Levinson, 1992). More generally, meditators' scores on personality tests indicate increases in general mental health, self-esteem, and social openness (Sakairi, 1992; Janowiak & Hackman, 1994). Exactly how meditation produces its effects is unclear. Many of its effects can also be achieved by biofeedback, hypnosis, and just relaxing (Holmes, 1984).

PSYCHOACTIVE DRUGS

Every day, most people in the world use drugs that alter brain activity and consciousness (Levinthal, 1996). For example, 80 to 90 percent of people in North America use caffeine, the stimulant found in coffee (Gilbert, 1984). A drug is a chemical not usually needed for physiological activity and that can affect the body upon entering it. (Some people use the word *drug* to mean therapeutic medicines, but refer to nonmedicinal drugs as *substances.*) Drugs that affect the brain, changing consciousness and other psychological processes, are called **psychoactive drugs.** The study of psychoactive drugs is called **psychopharmacology.**

Psychopharmacology

Most psychoactive drugs affect the brain by altering the interactions between neurotransmitters and receptors, as described in Chapter 3 on biological aspects of psychology. To create their effects, these drugs must cross the **blood-brain barrier,** a feature of blood vessels in the brain that prevents some substances from entering brain tissue (Sage & Wilson, 1994). Once past this barrier, a psychoactive drug's effects depend on several factors: With which neurotransmitter systems does the drug interact? How does the drug affect these neurotransmitters or their receptors? What psychological functions are performed by the brain systems that use these neurotransmitters?

Drugs can affect neurotransmitters or their receptors through several mechanisms. Neurotransmitters fit into their own receptors, as Figure 6.13 shows. Some drugs are similar enough to a particular neurotransmitter to fool its receptors. These drugs, called **agonists,** bind to the receptor and mimic the effects of the normal neurotransmitter.

FIGURE 6.13

Agonists and Antagonists

In part **(A)**, a molecule of neurotransmitter interacts with a receptor on a neuron's dendrites by fitting into and stimulating it. Part **(B)** shows a drug molecule acting as an *agonist,* affecting the receptor in the same way a neurotransmitter would. Part **(C)** depicts an *antagonist* drug molecule blocking a natural neurotransmitter from reaching and acting upon the receptor.

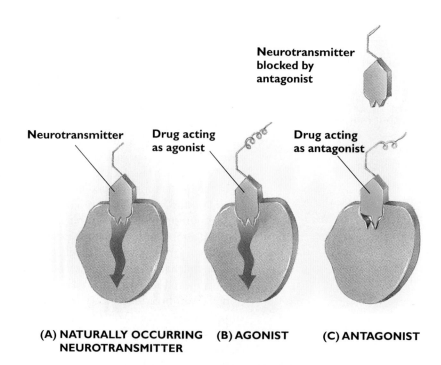

Neurotransmitter blocked by antagonist

Neurotransmitter   Drug acting as agonist   Drug acting as antagonist

(A) NATURALLY OCCURRING NEUROTRANSMITTER   **(B) AGONIST**   **(C) ANTAGONIST**

Other drugs, called **antagonists,** are similar enough to a neurotransmitter to occupy its receptors but cannot mimic its effects; they bind to a receptor and prevent the normal neurotransmitter from binding. Still other drugs work by increasing or decreasing the *release* of a specific neurotransmitter. Finally, some drugs work by speeding or slowing the *removal* of a neurotransmitter from synapses.

Predicting a drug's behavioral effects is complicated by the fact that some drugs interact with many neurotransmitter systems. Also, the nervous system may compensate for a disturbance. For example, repeated exposure to a drug that blocks receptors for a certain neurotransmitter leads to a compensatory increase in the number of receptors available to accept the neurotransmitter.

The Varying Effects of Drugs

Drugs affect biological systems in accordance with their chemical properties. Unfortunately, their medically desirable *main effects,* such as pain relief, are often accompanied by undesirable *side effects,* which may include the potential for abuse. **Substance abuse** is the self-administration of drugs in ways that deviate from a culture's social norms (Gilman et al., 1985).

Substance abuse may lead to psychological or physical dependence. **Psychological dependence** is a condition in which a person continues drug use despite adverse effects, needs the drug for a sense of well-being, and becomes preoccupied with obtaining the drug if it is no longer available. Psychological dependence can occur with or without **physical dependence,** or **addiction,** which is a physiological state in which drug use is needed to prevent a **withdrawal syndrome.** Withdrawal symptoms vary across drugs but often include an intense craving for the drug and effects generally opposite to those of the drug itself. Physical dependence can develop gradually, without awareness. As addiction progresses, drug tolerance may appear. **Tolerance** is a condition in which increasingly larger drug doses are needed to produce the same effect (Gilman et al., 1985). With the development of tolerance, many addicts need the drug just to prevent the negative effects of not taking it. However, most researchers now believe that a craving for the positive effects of drugs is what keeps addicts coming back to drug use (Wise, 1988).

The potential for "normal" people to develop drug dependence should not be underestimated. All addictive drugs stimulate the brain's "pleasure centers," regions that are sensitive to the neurotransmitter dopamine. Neuronal activity in these areas produces intensely pleasurable feelings; it also helps generate the pleasant feelings of a good meal,

CHANGING DEFINITIONS OF ILLICIT DRUGS The definition of inappropriate drug use can vary across cultures and over time (Weiss & Moore, 1990). For example, in the United States cocaine was once a respectable, commercially available drug; today, it is illegal.

Expects alcohol and receives alcohol
Expects alcohol but receives tonic
Expects tonic but receives alcohol
Expects tonic and receives tonic

Source: Lang et al., 1975.

FIGURE 6.14

Expectancy and Alcohol's Effects
on Aggressiveness

**In this experiment, aggression was
measured by the intensity of shocks
that subjects gave to another person.
Those who *thought* they had been
drinking alcohol gave significantly
more intense shocks, whether they
had consumed alcohol or not, than
did subjects who were sober, or at
least thought they were. Here,
aggression was influenced more
by expectancies about alcohol's effects
than by alcohol itself.**

a "runner's high," or sex (Grunberg, 1994; Harris & Aston-Jones, 1995). Thus, addictive drugs have the capacity to create tremendously rewarding effects in most people.

Expectations and Drug Effects   Drug effects are determined by more than biochemistry; *learned expectations* also play a role. In one study (Lang et al., 1975), subjects drank tonic water with or without tasteless alcohol. Those drinking alcohol got enough to make them legally drunk by most U.S. standards. Half of those drinking each beverage were told what they were drinking. The other half were misinformed—wrongly told that they were drinking alcohol or plain tonic water. Then a research assistant, posing as an obnoxious subject, angered the subjects. Subjects later could hurt him with electric shocks (the shocks did not reach the assistant, but he faked pain). As shown in Figure 6.14, the subjects' aggressiveness (measured in terms of the strength of shocks given) depended not on what the subjects *actually* drank but on their *expectations*. Other studies have shown that learned expectancies also contribute to the effects of heroin, cocaine, and marijuana (Goldman et al., 1991; Schafer & Brown, 1991; Stacy, Widaman & Marlatt, 1990).

Expectations about drug effects develop in part as people watch other people react to drugs. Because what they see can be different from one individual and culture to the next, researchers have concluded that drug effects vary considerably thoughout the world (MacAndrew & Edgerton, 1969). For example, the loss of inhibition, increased violence, and sexual promiscuity commonly associated with alcohol use in the United States is partly attributable to custom, inasmuch as these effects are not universal. Consider the contrasting example of Bolivia's Camba culture, in which people drink, in extended bouts, a brew that is 89 percent alcohol (178 proof). During their binges, these people repeatedly pass out, wake up, and start drinking again—all the while maintaining tranquil social relations.

The learned nature of responses to alcohol is also demonstrated by cases in which there are *changes* in the model for appropriate "drunken comportment." When Europeans brought alcohol to Tahiti in the 1700s, the Tahitians' initial response to drinking it was to become relaxed and befuddled, much as when consuming *kava,* their traditional—nonalcoholic—tranquilizing drink. But after years of watching European sailors' drunken violence, Tahitian alcohol drinkers became violent themselves. Fortunately, subsequent learning experiences once again made their response to alcohol more pacific (MacAndrew & Edgerton, 1969).

These examples and experiments show that the effects of psychoactive drugs are complex and variable. In Chapter 16 we discuss psychoactive drugs that are used in the treatment of psychological problems. Here, we consider several major categories of psychoactive drugs that are used primarily for the alterations they produce in consciousness, including depressants, stimulants, opiates, and psychedelics.

Depressants

Depressant drugs reduce activity of the central nervous system. Examples are alcohol, barbiturates, and anxiolytics, all of which increase activity of the inhibitory neurotransmitter GABA. Since GABA reduces neuron activity, enhancing GABA function reduces the excitability of many neural circuits.

Alcohol   In the United States, over 100 million people drink alcohol; it is equally popular worldwide (Korolenko, Minevich & Segal, 1994; Alvarez, Delrio & Prada, 1995). Alcohol's effects involve the neurotransmitters dopamine, endorphins, and GABA (Koob & Bloom, 1988). The GABA effect is notable; drugs that interact with GABA receptors can block some of alcohol's effects, as shown in Figure 6.15 (Suzdak et al., 1986). Alcohol enhances the effect of endorphins (the body's natural painkillers, described in Chapter 4). This action may underlie the "high" that people feel when drinking alcohol and may explain why *naltrexone* and *naloxone,* endorphin antagonists, are better than placebos at reducing alcohol craving and relapse rates in recovering alcoholics (Volpicelli et al., 1992; Nishikawa et al., 1994). Alcohol also interacts with dopamine systems. Prolonged alcohol use can have lasting effects on the brain's ability

FIGURE 6.15

GABA Receptors and Alcohol

Both of these rats received the same amount of alcohol, enough to incapacitate them with drunkenness. The rat on the right then received a drug that reverses alcohol's intoxicating effects and, within two minutes, was acting completely sober. The drug, Ro15-4513, blocks the ability of alcohol to stimulate **GABA** receptors. The company that developed Ro15-4513 discontinued its development because the drug does not reverse the effects of alcohol on hindbrain breathing centers. So if people were drinking to become intoxicated and Ro was frustrating their efforts, they could easily ingest a lethal overdose.

LINKAGES   Is there a way to drink alcohol without getting drunk? (a link to Biological Aspects of Psychology)

LINKAGES: DRINKING AND DRIVING DON'T MIX   Though practice may make it seem easy, driving a car is a complex information processing task. As described in the chapter on thought and language, such tasks require constant vigilance, quick decisions, and skillful execution of responses. Alcohol can impair all these processes—as well as the ability to judge the degree of impairment—thus making drinking and driving a deadly combination that kills tens of thousands of people each year in the United States alone.

to regulate dopamine levels (Tiihonen et al., 1995), and dopamine agonists reduce alcohol craving and withdrawal effects (Lawford et al., 1995).

Alcohol affects specific brain regions. For example, it depresses activity in the locus coeruleus, an area that helps activate the cerebral cortex (Koob & Bloom, 1988). Reduced cortical activity tends to cause cognitive changes and a release of inhibitions. Some drinkers begin talking loudly, acting silly, or telling others what they think of them. Emotional reactions range from euphoria to despair. Normally shy people may become impulsive or violent (Steele, 1986). Alcohol's impairment of the hippocampus causes memory problems, making it more difficult to form memories for new information (Givens, 1995). And its suppression of the cerebellum causes poor motor coordination (Rogers et al., 1986). Alcohol's ability to depress hindbrain mechanisms that control breathing and heartbeat can make overdoses fatal.

As suggested earlier, some effects of alcohol—such as anger and aggressiveness—depend both on biochemical factors and on learned expectations (Chermack & Taylor, 1995). But many effects—especially disruptions in motor coordination, speech, and thought—result from biochemical factors alone (Vuchinich & Sobell, 1978). These biological effects depend on the amount of alcohol the blood carries to the brain. Since the

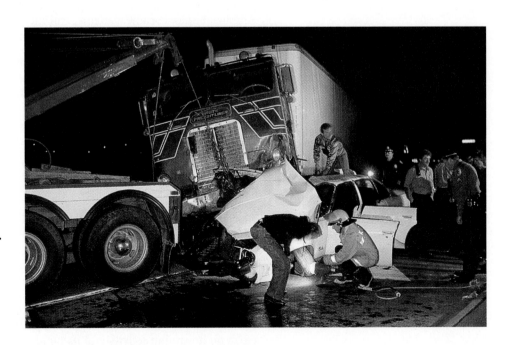

liver breaks down about one ounce of alcohol in an hour, alcohol has milder effects if consumed slowly. Effects increase with faster drinking, or if one drinks on an empty stomach, thereby speeding absorption into the blood. Even after allowing for differences in average male and female body weight, researchers have found metabolic differences that make male bodies able to tolerate somewhat higher amounts of alcohol. Thus, equal doses of alcohol may create greater effects in women compared to men (York & Welte, 1994).

Genetics also seems to play a role in determining the biochemical effects of alcohol. Evidence suggests that some people have a genetic predisposition toward alcohol dependence (Cadoret et al., 1995). Others (the Japanese, for example) may have inherited metabolic characteristics that enhance alcohol's adverse effects, thus possibly inhibiting the development of alcohol abuse (Iwahashi et al., 1995).

Barbiturates   Sometimes called "downers" or sleeping pills, *barbiturates* are very addictive. Small doses cause relaxation, mild euphoria, loss of muscle coordination, and lowered attention. Higher doses cause very deep sleep, but continued use actually distorts sleep patterns (Kales & Kales, 1973). Thus, long-term use of barbiturates as sleeping pills is unwise. Overdoses can be fatal. Withdrawal symptoms are among the most severe for any drug and can include intense agitation, violent outbursts, convulsions, hallucinations, and even sudden death.

Anxiolytics   Once called *tranquilizers* or *anti-anxiety* drugs, *anxiolytics* are used to help patients with anxiety, but they also have sedative properties. For example, the anxiolytic meprobamate (Miltown) can be taken in small daily doses for anxiety, but it has barbiturate-like effects (overdoses can cause sleep or death). *Benzodiazepines* such as Valium are widely used to relieve anxiety but cause less sedation and pose a lower risk of fatal overdose (Serfaty & Masterton, 1993). Like alcohol, benzodiazepines affect GABA receptors, but they do so by causing GABA to bind to its receptors more readily (Barbee, 1993). The result is greater inhibition whenever GABA is released. Benzodiazepines are particularly useful in treating anxiety disorders such as panic disorder and obsessive-compulsive disorder (Marazziti et al., 1994; see Chapter 16).

Unfortunately, psychological and physical dependence on anxiolytics is common; the withdrawal syndrome resembles that of barbiturates (Petursson, 1994). Many long-term users experience panic, confusion, anger, and memory loss. These effects are exaggerated if anxiolytics are used with alcohol, an often fatal combination.

Stimulants

Amphetamines, cocaine, caffeine, and nicotine are all examples of **stimulants,** drugs that increase behavioral and mental activity.

Amphetamines   Also called "uppers" or "speed," the *amphetamines* (Benzedrine, for example) increase the release, and decrease the removal, of norepinephrine and dopamine at synapses, causing increased activity at these neurotransmitters' receptors. It is probably dopamine activity that causes the drugs' rewarding properties, since taking dopamine antagonists reduces amphetamine use (Holman, 1994).

Amphetamines stimulate both the brain and the sympathetic branch of the autonomic nervous system, raising heart rate and blood pressure, constricting blood vessels, shrinking mucous membranes (thus relieving stuffy noses), and reducing appetite. Amphetamines also increase alertness and response speed, especially in tasks requiring prolonged attention (Koelega, 1993), and may improve memory for verbal material (Soetens et al., 1995).

Amphetamine abuse is usually due to a desire to lose weight, stay awake, or obtain a "high." Continued use leads to anxiety, insomnia, heart problems, confusion, paranoia, nonstop talking, and, in some cases, symptoms virtually identical to those of paranoid schizophrenia.

Cocaine   Like amphetamines, *cocaine* increases norepinephrine and dopamine activity, and thus produces many amphetamine-like effects. Cocaine's particularly powerful effect on dopamine activity and its rapid onset may underlie its remarkably addictive

SMOKING CRACK COCAINE Cocaine can be smoked, injected, or inhaled nasally (Gossop et al., 1994). It is addictive, very dangerous and, accordingly, one of the most intensely studied of all psychoactive drugs.

nature (Holman, 1994). Indeed, drugs with rapid onset and short duration are generally more addictive than others (Kato, Wakasa & Yanagita, 1987), which may explain why *crack*—a purified, fast-acting, very potent, smokable form of cocaine—is especially addictive.

Cocaine stimulates self-confidence, a sense of well-being, and optimism. But continued use brings nausea, overactivity, insomnia, paranoia, a sudden depressive "crash," hallucinations, sexual dysfunction, and seizures (Lacayo, 1995). Overdoses, especially of crack, can be deadly, and even small doses can cause a fatal heart attack or stroke (Marzuk et al., 1995). There is now little doubt that a pregnant woman who uses cocaine harms her fetus (Konkol et al., 1994). Exposure to the drug in the womb, and to poverty and neglect after birth, causes severe and lasting behavioral problems in these "cocaine babies" (Snodgrass, 1994; Hurt et al., 1995).

Ending a cocaine addiction is difficult. A possible treatment involves *buprenorphine,* an opiate antagonist that supresses cocaine self-administration in addicted monkeys (Mello et al., 1989). The results of other methods have been mixed; success is most likely if addicts remain in treatment for at least a year (Carroll, Rounsaville & Nich, 1994).

Caffeine   *Caffeine* may be the world's most popular drug (Gilbert, 1984). It is found in coffee, tea, chocolate, and many soft drinks. Caffeine reduces drowsiness, improves problem solving, increases the capacity for physical work, and raises urine production (Warburton, 1995). At high doses it induces anxiety and tremors. Caffeine use can result in tolerance as well as physical dependence (Strain et al., 1994). Withdrawal symptoms—including headaches, fatigue, anxiety, shakiness, and craving—appear on the first day of abstinence and last about a week (Silverman et al., 1992). Caffeine may delay conception in women trying to become pregnant (Alderete, Eskenazi & Sholtz, 1995), but, overall, moderate daily caffeine use appears to have few if any negative effects (Thompson, 1995; Kawachi, Colditz & Stone, 1994).

Nicotine   A powerful stimulant of the autonomic nervous system, *nicotine* is the psychoactive ingredient in tobacco. Nicotine is an acetylcholine agonist, but it also increases neuronal release of glutamate, the brain's primary excitatory neurotransmitter (McGehee et al., 1995). Nicotine has many psychoactive effects, including elevated mood and improved memory and attention (Pomerleau & Pomerleau, 1992). Its ability to create dependence is still being hotly debated. The U.S. Surgeon General has concluded that nicotine, like heroin or cocaine, is physically addictive (USDHHS, 1988; Stolerman & Jarvis, 1995). This claim is supported by evidence of a nicotine withdrawal syndrome, which includes craving, anxiety, irritability, lowered heart rate, and weight gain (Hughes, Higgins & Bickel, 1994). Others see nicotine as creating psychological rather than physical dependence for many people (Robinson & Pritchard, 1995). Whatever blend of physical and psychological dependence may be involved, there is no doubt that smoking is a difficult habit for most smokers to break (Robinson & Pritchard, 1992). It is also clearly recognized as a major risk factor for cancer, heart disease, and respiratory disorders (Doll et al., 1994), as discussed in Chapter 13, on health, stress, and coping.

MDMA   "Ecstasy," or *MDMA* (short for 3,4-Methylenedioxymethamphetamine), has both stimulant and psychedelic effects. It causes visual hallucinations, a feeling of greater closeness to others, dry mouth, hyperactivity, and jaw muscle spasms resulting in "lockjaw." On the day after using MDMA, people often experience muscle aches, fatigue, depression, and poor concentration (Peroutka, Newman & Harris, 1988). With continued use, positive effects decrease but negative effects persist.

Since MDMA increases the activity of dopamine-releasing neurons, it leads to some of the same effects as those produced by cocaine and amphetamines (Steele, McCann & Ricaurte, 1994). At serotonin synapses, MDMA is a receptor agonist and also causes neurotransmitter release, thus possibly accounting for the drug's hallucinatory effects (Green, Cross & Goodwin, 1995).

Although it does not appear to be physically addictive (Peroutka, 1989), MDMA is a dangerous, potentially deadly drug with many negative effects. For one thing, it permanently damages the brain, killing serotonin-sensitive neurons (Green, Cross &

Goodwin, 1995); the damage increases with higher dosages and continued use (Battaglia, Yeh & De Souza, 1988). MDMA users may also develop *panic disorder,* a problem whose symptoms include intense anxiety and a sense of impending death (see Chapter 15).

Opiates

The **opiates** (opium, morphine, heroin, codeine) are unique in their capacity for inducing sleep and relieving pain (Julien, 1995). *Opium,* derived from the poppy plant, relieves pain and causes feelings of well-being and dreamy relaxation. One of its most active ingredients, *morphine,* was first isolated in the early 1800s and is used worldwide for pain relief. Percodan and Demoral are some common morphine-like drugs. *Heroin* is derived from morphine but is three times more powerful, causing intensely pleasurable reactions.

Opiates have complex effects on consciousness. Drowsy, cloudy feelings occur because opiates depress activity in areas of the cerebral cortex. But they also create excitation in other parts, causing some users to experience euphoria (Bozarth & Wise, 1984). Opiates exert many of their effects through their role as agonists for endorphins. When opiates activate endorphin receptors, they are "tricking" the brain into an exaggerated activation of its pain-killing and mood-altering systems (Julien, 1995).

Opiates are very addictive, perhaps because they stimulate a particular type of glutamate receptor in the brain that can bring physical changes in a neuron's structure. As discussed in Chapter 8, such changes may be the physical basis for certain kinds of memories. It may be, then, that opiates alter neurons so that they come to require the drug to function properly. Supporting this idea are data showing that glutamate antagonists appear to prevent morphine dependence yet leave the drug's pain-killing effects intact (Trujillo & Akil, 1991). Beyond the hazards of addiction itself, heroin addicts risk death through overdoses, contaminated drugs, or AIDS contracted by sharing drug-injection needles.

Psychedelics

Pychedelics create a loss of contact with reality and alter other aspects of emotion, perception, and thought. They can cause distortions in body image (one may feel gigantic or tiny), loss of identity (confusion about who one actually is), dream-like fantasies, and hallucinations. Since these effects resemble many severe forms of mental disorder, psychedelics are also called *hallucinogens* or *psychotomimetics* (mimicking psychosis).

LSD   One of the most powerful psychedelics is *lysergic acid diethylamide,* or *LSD,* first synthesized from a rye fungus by Swiss chemist Albert Hofmann. In 1938, after Hofmann accidentally ingested a minuscule amount of the substance, he discovered the drug's strange effects in the world's first LSD "trip" (Julien, 1995). LSD's hallucinations can be quite bizarre. Time may seem distorted, sounds may cause visual sensations, and users may feel as if they have left their bodies. These experiences probably result from LSD's action as a serotonin agonist, since serotonin antagonists greatly reduce LSD's hallucinatory effects (Nielson et al., 1985).

The precise effects of LSD are rather unpredictable. Unpleasant hallucinations and delusions can occur during a person's first—or two hundredth—LSD experience. Although LSD is not addictive, tolerance to its effects does develop. Some users suffer lasting side effects, including severe short-term memory loss, paranoia, violent outbursts, nightmares, and panic attacks (Gold, 1994). Distortions in visual sensations can remain years after the end of heavy use (Abraham & Wolf, 1988). Sometimes flashbacks occur, in which a person suddenly returns to an LSD-like state of consciousness weeks or even years after using the drug.

Marijuana   A mixture of crushed leaves, flowers, and stems from the hemp plant (*Cannabis sativa)* makes up *marijuana.* The active ingredient is *tetrahydrocannabinol,*

IN REVIEW	Major Classes of Psychoactive Drugs

Drug	Trade/Street Name	Main Effects	Potential for Physical/ Psychological Dependence
Depressants			
Alcohol	"booze"		High/High
Barbiturates	Seconal, Tuinal ("downers"), Nembutal	Relaxation, anxiety reduction, sleep	High/High
Anxiolytics (meprobamate, benzodiazepines)	Miltown, Equanil, Librium, Valium		Moderate to high/High
Stimulants			
Amphetamines	Benzedrine, Dexedrine, Methadrine ("speed," "uppers," "ice")	Alertness, euphoria	Moderate/High
Cocaine	"coke," "crack"		Moderate to high/High
Caffeine		Alertness	Moderate/Moderate
Nicotine	"smokes," "coffin nails"	Alertness	High (?)
MDMA	Ecstasy	Hallucinations	Low
Opiates			
Opium		Euphoria	High/High
Morphine	Percodan, Demoral	Euphoria, pain control	High/High
Heroin	"junk," "smack"	Euphoria, pain control	High/High
Psychedelics			
LSD	"acid"	Altered perceptions, hallucinations	Low/Low
Marijuana (cannabis)	"pot," "dope," "reefer"	Euphoria, relaxation	Low/Moderate

or *THC*. When inhaled, THC is absorbed in minutes by many organs, including the brain, and it continues to affect consciousness for a few hours. THC tends to collect in fatty deposits of the brain or reproductive organs, where it can be detected for weeks. The specific receptors for THC include those sensitive to anandamide (from a Sanskrit word meaning "bliss"), a naturally occurring brain substance that research suggests may be a neurotransmitter (Fride & Mechoulam, 1993).

Low doses of marijuana may initially create restlessness and hilarity, followed by a dreamy, carefree relaxation, an expanded sense of space and time, more vivid sensations, food cravings, and subtle changes in thinking (Kelly et al., 1990).

Although it is among the least potent of psychoactive drugs, marijuana can create a number of problems. (See "In Review: Major Classes of Psychoactive Drugs.") It disrupts memory formation, making it difficult to carry out mental or physical tasks (Lichtman, Dimen & Martin, 1995; Pope & Yurgelun-Todd, 1996). And because marijuana disrupts muscle coordination, driving while under its influence is quite dangerous; motor impairment continues well after the subjective effects of the drug have worn off. In one study, pilots had difficulty landing a simulated aircraft even a full day after smoking one marijuana cigarette (Yesavage et al., 1985). Marijuana easily reaches a developing fetus and should not be used by pregnant women (Fried, Watkinson & Gray, 1992). Finally, long-term use can lead to dependence (Stephens et al., 1994), as well as to lasting impairments in reasoning and memory. Research has shown that adults who frequently used marijuana scored lower than equal-IQ nonusers on a twelfth-grade academic achievement test (Block & Ghoneim, 1993).

An intense debate is currently raging over the apparently successful use of marijuana by some doctors in the treatment of asthma, glaucoma, epilepsy, chronic pain, and nausea from cancer chemotherapy (Grinspoon & Bakalar, 1995). Critics argue that medical legalization of marijuana is premature because its medicinal value has not been established by controlled research (Bennet, 1994).

FUTURE DIRECTIONS

Most psychological researchers today view human behavior as guided by both conscious and subconscious mental events. Accordingly, the study of consciousness provides a kind of conceptual meeting place for ideas and findings from many areas of psychology. In fact, as noted in Chapter 1, investigators and researchers from disciplines as diverse as biology, psychology, linguistics, electrical engineering, and computer science—all interested in the broad field called *cognitive science*—are working together to better understand human consciousness. There is a long way to go. Psychologists still do not know where or how self-awareness resides in the brain, and intense research is under way to understand the many ways in which drugs affect consciousness.

One question sure to attract continued scrutiny relates to the "binding problem" (Banich & Shenker, 1994). If, as suggested by the multiple-drafts view of consciousness, the brain processes information in parallel at many physically separate areas, how do these disparate activities bind together into a single, coherent, conscious experience? Part of the answer may lie in synchronous firing frequencies that have been observed in neurons in various parts of the brain (Horgan, 1994), but there is much more to be learned.

Research on other aspects of consciousness has the potential to open the way for significant improvements in the understanding and treatment of various disorders. For example, if investigators find the natural substance that normally fits into the receptors for the benzodiazepines, they may learn more

about the chemistry of anxiety. And the fact that some drugs appear to block the craving for more than one type of abused drug supports the notion that there may be common (and perhaps blockable) mechanisms underlying all drugs of abuse.

Sleep research will continue to push a number of frontiers, including the "final frontier." As humans venture into outer space more often and for longer periods, researchers have begun to study how sleep is affected by weightlessness and the lack of the earth's usual light and dark cues (Polyakov et al., 1994). Another developing line of research focuses on transitions between wakefulness and sleep—the *hypnogogic state* (transition from wakefulness into sleep) and the *hypnopompic state* (transition from sleep into wakefulness). We now know that the images and thoughts that occur in these states differ from those typical of sleep (Cicogna, 1994), but a greater understanding of these transitional periods may help clarify which properties separate sleep from wakefulness. Research on sleep and other circadian rhythms also promises new therapies for mental disorders, such as bipolar disorder, that may be related to disruptions of these rhythms. And if sleep disorders are found to reliably predict psychological disorders, this link may allow early intervention, assuming that better sleep therapies can be developed.

For more detailed information about the study of consciousness, consider taking courses in neuropsychology, cognitive psychology, psychopharmacology, computational neuroscience, and sleep.

SUMMARY AND KEY TERMS

Consciousness can be defined as awareness of the outside world and of one's own thoughts, feelings, perceptions, and other mental processes.

■ ANALYZING CONSCIOUSNESS

Current research on consciousness focuses on three main questions. First, there is the mind-body problem: Is the mind distinct from the brain as dualists claim? Or is the brain the complete basis for the mind, as materialists argue? Second, does consciousness occur as a single "point" in the stream of mental processing or as several parallel mental operations that operate independently. Third, what mental processes are outside awareness and how do they affect us?

■ THE SCOPE OF CONSCIOUSNESS

Mental Processing Without Awareness

Awareness is not always required for mental operations. The priming phenomenon shows that people's responses to stimuli are speeded and improved as stimuli are repeated, even when the people have no conscious memory of which stimuli are old and which are new. In the mere-exposure effect, people tend to judge previously encountered

stimuli more favorably even when they are unaware of having seen the stimuli before.

The Neuropsychology of Consciousness

Brain injuries often reveal ways in which mental processing can occur without conscious awareness. Some blind people are able to "guess" details of visual stimuli, and patients with anterograde amnesia continue to acquire new skills without later awareness of learning them.

Levels of Consciousness

Variations in how much awareness you have for a mental function are described by different levels of consciousness. The *preconscious level* includes mental activities that are outside of awareness but can be easily brought to the *conscious level*. *Subconscious* or *unconscious* mental activity involves thoughts, memories, and processes that are more difficult to bring to awareness. Mental processes that cannot be brought into awareness occur at the *nonconscious level*.

States of Consciousness

A person's *state of consciousness* is constantly changing. When the changes are particularly noticeable, they are called *altered states of consciousness.* Examples include sleep, hypnosis, meditation, and some drug-induced states. Different cultures vary considerably in the value placed on different states of consciousness.

■ SLEEPING AND DREAMING

Sleep is a very active and complex state.

Stages of Sleep

Different stages of sleep are defined on the basis of changes in brain activity (as seen on an electroencephalograph, or EEG) and physiological arousal. Sleep normally begins with stage 1 sleep and progresses gradually to stage 4 sleep. Sleep stages 1 through 4 constitute *quiet sleep,* or non-REM sleep. After passing back to stage 2, people enter *REM (rapid eye movement) sleep,* or *active sleep.* This is when most dreaming occurs. The sleeper cycles through these stages several times each night, gradually spending more time in stage 2 and REM sleep later in the night.

Sleep Disorders

Sleep disorders can disrupt the natural rhythm of sleep. Among the most common is *insomnia,* in which one feels tired because of trouble falling or staying asleep. *Narcolepsy* produces sudden daytime sleeping episodes. In *sleep apnea,* people briefly but repeatedly stop breathing during sleep. *Sudden infant death syndrome (SIDS)* may be due to brain abnormalities or accidental suffocation. *Nightmares* and *night terrors* are different kinds of frightening dreams. *Sleepwalking* happens most frequently during childhood. *REM behavior disorder* is potentially dangerous because it allows people to act out REM dreams.

Why Do People Sleep?

The cycle of waking and sleeping is a natural *circadian rhythm,* controlled by the suprachiasmatic nucleus of the brain. *Jet lag* can be one result of disrupting the normal sleep-wake cycle. The purpose of sleep is much debated. Non-REM sleep may aid bodily rest and repair. REM sleep may help maintain activity in brain areas that provide daytime alertness, or it may allow the brain to "check circuits," eliminate useless information, and solidify learning from the previous day.

Dreams and Dreaming

Dreams are story-like sequences of images, sensations, and perceptions that occur during sleep. Evidence from research on *lucid dreaming* suggests that people may be able to control their own dreams. Some claim that dreams are the meaningless by-products of brain activity, but one's recall of dreams may still have psychological significance.

■ HYPNOSIS

Hypnosis is a well-known but still poorly understood phenomenon.

Experiencing Hypnosis

Tests of *hypnotic susceptibility* suggest that some people cannot be hypnotized. Hypnotized people tend to focus attention on the hypnotist and passively follow instructions. They become very good at fantasizing and role-taking. They may exhibit apparent *age regression,* experience *posthypnotic amnesia,* and obey *posthypnotic suggestions.*

Explaining Hypnosis

Role theory suggests that hypnosis creates a special social role that gives people permission to act in unusual ways. *State theory* sees hypnosis as a special state of consciousness. *Dissociation theory* combines aspects of role and state theories, suggesting that hypnotic subjects enter into a social contract with the hypnotist to allow normally integrated mental processes to become dissociated and to share control over these processes.

Applications of Hypnosis

Hypnosis is useful in the control of pain and reduction of nausea associated with cancer chemotherapy.

■ LINKAGES: MEDITATION, HEALTH, AND STRESS

Meditation is a set of techniques designed to create an altered state of consciousness characterized by inner peace and increased awareness. During meditation, muscle tension and blood pressure decrease, and alpha waves appear. The consistent practice of meditation has been associated with reductions in stress-related problems such as anxiety and high blood pressure.

■ PSYCHOACTIVE DRUGS

Psychoactive drugs affect the brain, changing consciousness and other psychological processes. *Psychopharmacology* is the field that studies drug effects and their mechanisms.

Psychopharmacology

Psychoactive drugs exert their effects primarily by influencing specific neurotransmitter systems and, hence, certain brain activities. To reach brain tissue, drugs must cross the *blood-brain barrier.* Drugs that mimic the receptor effects of a neurotransmitter are called *agonists,* and drugs that block the receptor effects of a neurotransmitter are called *antagonists.* Some drugs alter the release or inactivation of specific neurotransmitters, thus affecting the amount of neurotransmitter available for receptor effects.

The Varying Effects of Drugs

Adverse effects such as *substance abuse* often accompany psychoactive drugs. *Psychological dependence, physical dependence (addiction), tolerance,* and a *withdrawal syndrome* may result. Drugs that produce dependence share the property of directly stimulating certain dopamine-sensitive areas of the brain known as pleasure centers. The consequences of using a psychoactive drug depend both on how the drug affects neurotransmitters and on the user's expectations.

Depressants

Alcohol, barbiturates, and anxiolytics are all *depressants.* They reduce activity in the central nervous system, often by enhancing the action of inhibitory neurotransmitters. They have considerable potential for producing both psychological and physical dependence.

Stimulants

Stimulants such as amphetamines and cocaine increase behavioral and mental activity mainly by increasing the action of dopamine and norepinephrine. These drugs can produce both psychological and physical dependence. Caffeine, one of the world's most popular stimulants, may also create dependency. Nicotine is a potent stimulant. And MDMA, which has both stimulant and psychedelic properties, is one of several psychoactive drugs that can permanently damage brain tissue.

Opiates

Opiates such as opium, morphine, and heroin are highly addictive drugs that induce sleep and relieve pain.

Psychedelics

LSD and marijuana are examples of *psychedelics,* or hallucinogens. Psychedelics alter consciousness by producing a temporary loss of contact with reality and changes in emotion, perception, and thought.

LEARNING

CHAPTER 7

LINKAGES
TO
LEARNING

CONSCIOUSNESS

Can learning shape the effect of a drug on consciousness? *(ans. on p. 199)*

HUMAN DEVELOPMENT

Who teaches boys to be men and girls to be women? *(ans. on p. 413)*

PSYCHOLOGICAL DISORDERS

Are psychological disorders learned behaviors? *(ans. on p. 495)*

Can you recall how you felt on your first day of kindergarten? Like many preschoolers, you may have been bewildered, even frightened, as the comforting familiarity of home or day care was suddenly replaced by an environment filled with new names and faces, rules and events. But, like most youngsters, you probably adjusted to this new environment within a few days.

This adjustment, or *adaptation,* to a changed environment can take many forms. Some are simple, as when once-startling sounds from a balky heating system are eventually ignored. Others are more complex. Ringing bells, roll call, and other strange new events become part of children's pattern of expectancies about the world. Youngsters come to expect that certain events, such as the arrival of the music teacher, signal the likely occurrence of other events that are pleasant or unpleasant. They also develop expectancies about which aspects of their school behavior are likely to be rewarded and which are likely to be punished. Talking at will, for example, may not be as acceptable at school as at home, but enthusiastic finger painting—perhaps forbidden at home—may bring praise at school. Finally, schoolchildren acquire facts about the world and develop skills ranging from reading to kickball.

Adaptation is not confined to school. The entire process of development, from birth to death, involves adapting to increasingly complex, ever-changing environments, using continuously updated knowledge gained through experience. Though perhaps most highly developed in humans, the ability to adapt to changing environments appears to varying degrees in members of all species. According to the evolutionary approach to psychology discussed in Chapter 1, it is individual variability in the capacity to adapt that shapes the evolution of appearance and behavior in animals and humans. As Darwin noted, individuals who don't adapt may not survive to reproduce.

Many forms of animal and human adaptation follow the principles of learning. **Learning** is the process through which experience modifies pre-existing behavior and understanding. The pre-existing behavior and understanding may have been present at birth, acquired through maturation, or learned earlier. Indeed, learning plays a central role in most aspects of human behavior, from the motor skills we need to walk or tie a shoe to the language skills we use to communicate and the object categories—such as food, vehicle, or animal—that help us to organize our perceptions and to think logically about the world. This chapter describes what psychologists now know about the fundamental principles of learning and how these principles operate in arenas such as medical treatment, psychotherapy, and education; many other examples of the pervasive influence of learning on human behavior appear in other chapters. (The Linkages diagram provides just three such examples.)

People learn primarily by identifying relationships between events and noting the regularity in the world around them. When two events repeatedly take place together, people can predict the occurrence of one from knowledge of the other. They learn that a clear blue sky means dry weather, that too little sleep makes them irritable, that they can reach someone on the telephone by dialing a certain number, that screaming orders motivates some people and angers others.

Which relationships do people identify, and how do they do it? What determines whether and how people learn? These and other basic questions about learning are among the most frequently and intensively studied topics in psychology. For several decades, much of the research on learning was guided by the behaviorist approach, which, as described in Chapter 1, stresses the importance of reward and punishment in altering the frequency of observable behavior. That approach was inspired by the hope that all behavior could be explained by a few basic principles of learning and by the idea that all learning amounted to the automatic formation of associations between stimuli and responses. Research on learning, and on the role of cognitive processes in learning, eventually showed that these ideas about unthinking, automatic associations were oversimplified. Still, an understanding of how associations are formed is basic to an understanding of learning. Thus, we first consider two models of how basic associations develop and how cognitive factors can influence them; these models are called classical conditioning and operant conditioning.

CLASSICAL CONDITIONING: LEARNING SIGNALS AND ASSOCIATIONS

At the opening bars of the national anthem, a young ballplayer's heart may begin pounding; those sounds signal that the game is about to begin. A flashing light on a control panel may make an airplane pilot's adrenaline flow, because it means that something has gone wrong. These people were not born with such reactions; they learned them from associations between events in the world. The experimental study of this kind of learning was begun, almost by accident, by Ivan Petrovich Pavlov.

Pavlov's Discovery

Pavlov is one of the best-known figures in psychology, but he was not a psychologist. A Russian physiologist, Pavlov won a Nobel Prize in 1904 for his research on the digestive system of dogs. In the course of this work, Pavlov noticed a strange phenomenon: His dogs sometimes salivated when no food was present—for example, when they saw the assistant who normally brought their food.

Pavlov devised a simple experiment to determine how salivation could occur in the absence of an obvious physical cause. First he performed an operation to divert a dog's saliva into a container, so that the amount secreted could be measured precisely. He then placed the dog in an apparatus similar to the one shown in Figure 7.1. The experiment had three phases.

In the first phase of the experiment, Pavlov and his associates (Anrep, 1920) confirmed that when meat powder was placed on the dog's tongue, the dog salivated, but that it did not salivate in response to a neutral stimulus—a white lab coat or a musical tone, for example. Thus, the researchers established the existence of the two basic components for Pavlov's experiment: a natural reflex (the dog's salivation when meat powder was placed on its tongue) and a neutral stimulus (the sound of the tone). A *reflex* is the swift, automatic response to a stimulus, such as shivering in the cold or jumping when you are jabbed with a needle. A *neutral stimulus* is one that initially does not elicit the reflex being studied, although it may elicit other responses. For example, when the tone is first sounded, the dog pricks up its ears, turns toward the sound, and sniffs around; but it does not salivate.

Apparatus for Measuring
Conditioned Responses

**In this more elaborate version of
Pavlov's original apparatus, the
amount of saliva flowing from a dog's
cheek is measured, then recorded on a
slowly revolving drum of paper.**

**Pen recording
on cylinder**

It was the second and third phases of the experiment that showed how one type of
learning can occur. In the second phase, the tone sounded and then meat powder was
quickly placed in the dog's mouth. The dog salivated. This *pairing*—the tone followed
immediately by meat powder—was repeated several times. In the third phase of the
experiment the tone was sounded and, even though no meat powder was presented, the
dog again salivated. In other words, the tone by itself now elicited salivation, as if the
tone predicted the presentation of the meat powder.

Pavlov's experiment was the first laboratory demonstration of what today is called
classical conditioning—a procedure in which a neutral stimulus is repeatedly paired
with a stimulus that already triggers a reflexive response until the previously neutral
stimulus alone provokes a similar response. Figure 7.2 shows the basic elements of classical conditioning. The stimulus that elicits a response without conditioning, like the
meat powder in Pavlov's experiment, is called the **unconditioned stimulus (UCS)**. The
automatic, unlearned reaction to this stimulus is called the **unconditioned response
(UCR).** The new stimulus after being paired with the unconditioned stimulus is called
the **conditioned stimulus (CS),** and the response it comes to elicit is a **conditioned
response (CR).**

Classical Conditioning

**Before classical conditioning has
occurred, meat powder on a dog's
tongue produces salivation, but the
sound of a tone—a neutral stimulus—
does not. During the process of conditioning, the tone is repeatedly paired
with the meat powder. After classical
conditioning has taken place, the
sound of the tone alone acts as a conditioned stimulus, producing
salivation.**

PHASE I: Before conditioning has occurred

PHASE II: The process of conditioning

PHASE III: After conditioning has occurred

FIGURE 7.3

Changes Over Time in the Strength of a CR

As the CS and UCS are repeatedly paired during initial conditioning, the strength of the CR increases. During extinction, CR strength drops as more trials occur in which the CS is presented without the UCS; eventually the CR disappears. However, after a brief period, the CR reappears if the CS is again presented.

FIGURE 7.4

Stimulus Generalization

The strength of a conditioned response is greatest when the original CS occurs, but the CR also appears following stimuli that closely resemble the CS. Here, the CS is the sound of a buzzer at 1,000 hertz (Hz), and the CR is salivation. Notice that the CR generalizes well to stimuli at 990 or 1010 Hz, but that it gets weaker and weaker following stimuli that are less and less similar to the CS.

Conditioned Responses Over Time: Extinction and Spontaneous Recovery

Continued pairings of a conditioned stimulus (CS) with an unconditioned stimulus (UCS) strengthen conditioned responses (CR). The curve on the left side of Figure 7.3 shows an example: Repeated associations of a tone (CS) with meat powder (UCS) caused Pavlov's dogs to increase their salivation (CR) to the tone alone.

What if the meat powder (UCS) is no longer given? In general, unless the UCS continues to be paired with the CS, at least now and then, the conditioned response will gradually disappear through a process known as **extinction** (see the center section of Figure 7.3). If the CS and the UCS are again paired after the conditioned response has been extinguished, the conditioned response returns to its original strength very quickly, often after only one or two trials. This quick relearning of a conditioned response after extinction is called **reconditioning.** Because reconditioning takes much less time than the original conditioning, extinction must not have completely erased the conditioned response.

Additional evidence for this conclusion is illustrated on the right side of Figure 7.3: An extinguished CR will temporarily reappear if, after some time delay, the CS occurs without the UCS. This reappearance of the conditioned response after extinction (and without further CS-UCS pairings) is called **spontaneous recovery.** In general, the longer the time between extinction and the reappearance of the CS, the stronger the recovered conditioned response. (However, unless the UCS is again paired with the CS, extinction rapidly occurs again.) Thus, when a person hears a song or smells the cologne associated with a long-lost lover, there is a ripple of emotion—a conditioned response. Through its association with that person, the song or fragrance, which once had no particular significance, has become a conditioned stimulus that—even years later—can provoke conditioned emotional reactions.

Stimulus Generalization and Discrimination

After a conditioned response is acquired, stimuli that are similar but not identical to the conditioned stimulus also elicit the response. This phenomenon is called **stimulus generalization.** Usually the greater the similarity between a new stimulus and the conditioned stimulus, the stronger the conditioned response will be. Figure 7.4 shows an example.

Stimulus generalization has obvious adaptive advantages. For example, it is important for survival that a person who becomes sick after drinking sour-smelling milk later avoids dairy products that give off an odor resembling the smell associated with the illness. Generalization, however, would be problematic if it had no limits. Most people would be frightened to see a lion in their home, but imagine the inconvenience if you became fearful every time you saw a cat or a picture of a lion.

Stimulus generalization does not run amok because it is balanced by a complementary process called **stimulus discrimination.** Through stimulus discrimination, organisms learn to differentiate among similar stimuli. Thus, the sound of your own dog barking may become a CS that triggers a conditioned response that wakes you up. That conditioned response might not occur when someone else's dog barks.

The Signaling of Significant Events

Is classical conditioning entirely automatic? Pavlov's research suggested that it is, that classical conditioning allows the substitution of one stimulus (the CS) for another (the UCS) in producing a reflexive response. The animal or person may thus prepare for the arrival of the UCS. It is certainly useful and adaptive for a dog to prepare for the arrival of food; having saliva flowing in advance makes it easier to swallow a meal. For years the study of classical conditioning focused mainly on its role in the control of such automatic, involuntary behavior. However, psychologists have now recognized the wider implications of classical conditioning (Rescorla, 1988; Turkkan, 1989). They argue that organisms acquire conditioned responses when one event reliably predicts, or *signals,* the appearance of another. In other words, they believe that classical conditioning creates, not robot-like reflexes, but a means through which animals and people develop *mental models* of the relationships between events in their environment. These models aid adaptation and survival.

What determines whether and how a conditioned response is learned? Important factors include the timing, predictability, and strength of signals; the amount of attention they receive; and how easily the signals can be associated with other stimuli.

Timing   A signal cannot prepare you for something that has already happened, so it is not surprising that classical conditioning works best when the conditioned stimulus *precedes* the unconditioned stimulus, an arrangement known as *forward conditioning.* *Backward conditioning,* in which the CS signal (the tone) *follows* the UCS (the meat powder), takes place very slowly, if at all. Even *simultaneous conditioning,* in which the CS and UCS arrive at the same time, occurs much less easily than forward conditioning.

Research shows that forward conditioning usually works best when there is a delay of about one-half to one second between the CS and the UCS (Ross & Ross, 1971). Notice that this "optimum interval" makes adaptive sense. Normally, the presence of food, predators, or other significant stimuli is most reliably signaled by smells or growls or similar events that come just before their appearance (Einhorn & Hogarth, 1982). Thus, it is logical that the brain should be "wired" to form associations most easily between things that occur in a tight time sequence.

Predictability   Is it enough that the CS precedes the UCS—that two events are *contiguous* in time—in order for classical conditioning to occur? Think about it. Suppose your dogs, Dashiell and Harley, have very different personalities. When Harley growls, he sometimes bites, but sometimes doesn't. Other times, he bites without growling first. Dashiell, however, growls *only* before biting. Your conditioned fear response to Harley's growl will probably occur slowly, if at all, because his growl is a stimulus that does not *reliably* signal the danger of a bite. But you are likely to quickly develop a classically conditioned fear response to Dashiell's growl, because classical conditioning proceeds most rapidly when the CS *always* signals the UCS, and *only* the UCS. Thus, even if both dogs provide the same number of pairings of the CS (growl) and UCS (bite), it is only in Dashiell that the CS *reliably* predicts the UCS (Rescorla, 1968).

Signal Strength   A conditioned response will be learned more rapidly if the UCS is strong than if it is weak. Thus a predictive signal will be more rapidly associated with a strong shock (a UCS) than with a weak one. As with timing and predictability, the effect of signal strength on classical conditioning makes adaptive sense: It is more important to be prepared for major events than for those that have little impact.

How quickly a conditioned response is learned also depends on the strength or "salience" of the conditioned stimulus (CS). As described in Chapter 5, on perception, louder tones, brighter lights, or other more salient events tend to get attention, so they are most rapidly associated with a UCS—as long as they remain reliable predictive signals.

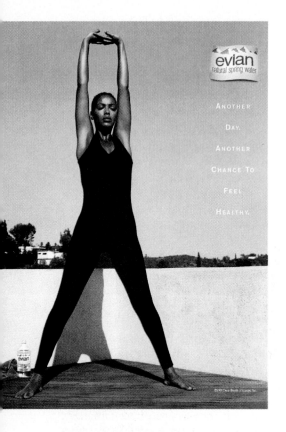

**CONDITIONING CONSUMERS Adver-
tisers commonly link their products
with images of attractive people, or
other stimuli which are likely to
evoke good feelings. Ideally, those
good feelings will be associated with
the products through second-order
conditioning. This strategy can back-
fire, however. In one case, consumers
came to dislike a line of sportswear
because its ads used music that had
already been used in some boring
videos (Blair & Shimp, 1992).**

sour milk

Attention   Attention can also influence *which* CS becomes associated with a UCS. In
the natural environment, more than one potential conditioned stimulus often precedes
a UCS. For example, suppose a person is tasting a sandwich, reading a book, and enjoying the smell of newly mown grass just before being nearly struck by lightning. Which
of these stimuli is most likely to become a conditioned stimulus for fear? It depends in
part on where the person's attention was focused. In line with the principles governing
perception (again, see Chapter 5), the stimuli were probably not receiving equal attention just before the lightning hit. Accordingly, the stimulus most closely attended to,
and thus most fully perceived at that moment, may dominate the others in later triggering a conditioned response.

Doctor's office: child's name - white coat - teeth cleaning

Second-Order Conditioning   Similarly, when a child suffers the pain of an injection
(a UCS) at a doctor's office, salient stimuli—like the doctor's white coat—that precede
and predict the UCS can become conditioned stimuli for fear. Once the white coat
evokes a conditioned fear response, it may take on some properties of a UCS. Thus, at
future visits, the once-neutral sound of a nurse calling the child's name can become a
conditioned stimulus for fear because it signals the appearance of the white coat, which
in turn signals pain. When a conditioned stimulus acts like a UCS, creating conditioned
stimuli out of events associated with it, the phenomenon is called **second-order conditioning.** Conditioned fear, and the second-order conditioning that can be based on it,
illustrates one of the most important adaptive characteristics of classical conditioning:
the ability to prepare the organism for damaging or life-threatening events (a UCS)
when these are predictably signaled by a CS.

Biopreparedness   After Pavlov's initial demonstration of classical conditioning, many
psychologists believed that associations formed through classical conditioning were
like Velcro. Just as Velcro pieces of any size or shape can be attached with equal ease, it
was believed that any conditioned stimulus—such as the taste of food or the sight of a
book in our lightning example—had an equal potential for becoming associated with
any unconditioned stimulus, as long as the two occurred in the right time sequence.
This view, called *equipotentiality,* was later challenged by experiments showing that certain signals or events are especially suited to form associations with other events
(Logue, 1985; Rescorla & Gillian, 1980). This apparent natural affinity for certain events
to become linked suggests that organisms are "biologically prepared" or "genetically
tuned" to develop certain conditioned associations.

The most dramatic example of the *biopreparedness* of organisms is conditioned taste
aversion. Consider the results of a study in which rats were either shocked or made nauseous in the combined presence of a bright light, a loud buzzer, and saccharin-flavored
water. Only certain conditioned associations were formed. Specifically, the animals that
had been shocked developed a conditioned fear response to the light and the buzzer, but
not to the flavored water. Those who had been made nauseous developed a conditioned
avoidance of the flavored water, but showed no particular response to the light or
buzzer (Garcia & Koelling, 1966). Notice that these results are adaptive: Nausea is more
likely to be produced by something that is eaten or drunk than by an external stimulus
like noise. Accordingly, nausea is more likely to become a conditioned response to an
internal stimulus, such as a saccharin flavor, than to an external stimulus, such as a
sound. In contrast, the sudden pain of a shock is more likely to have been caused by an
external stimulus, and so it makes evolutionary sense that the organism should be
"tuned" to associate shock with a sight or a sound.

Notice, too, that conditioned taste aversion violates the usual timing rules of classical conditioning. In taste aversion, strong conditioning develops despite the long delay
between the CS (the taste) and the UCS (the nauseous sensation). Poisons do not usually produce their effects until minutes or hours after being ingested, but people who
experience food poisoning may never again eat the type of food that made them ill—
even though that illness was delayed far longer than the optimal CS-UCS interval of
one-half to one second. In evolutionary terms, organisms that are biologically prepared
to link taste signals with illness, even if it occurs after considerable delays, are more
likely to survive than those not so prepared.

TASTE AVERSIONS Humans can develop classically conditioned taste aversions, even to their favorite foods. Ilene Bernstein (1978) gave one group of cancer patients Mapletoff ice cream an hour before they received nausea-provoking chemotherapy. A second group ate the same kind of ice cream on a day they did not receive chemotherapy. A third group got no ice cream. Five months later, the patients were asked to taste several ice cream flavors. Those who had never tasted Mapletoff and those who had not eaten it in association with chemotherapy chose it as their favorite. Those who had eaten Mapletoff before receiving chemotherapy found it very distasteful.

Evidence from several sources suggests other ways in which animals and people are innately prepared to learn associations between certain stimuli and certain responses. For example, people are much more likely to develop a conditioned fear of harmless dogs, snakes, and rats than of equally harmless doorknobs or stereos (Kleinknecht, 1991). And experiments with animals suggest that they are prone to learn the type of associations that are most common in or most relevant to their environment (Staddon & Ettinger, 1989). For example, birds of prey, so strongly dependent upon their vision in foraging for food, may develop taste aversions on the basis of visual stimuli. Coyotes and rats, who depend more on their sense of smell, tend to develop aversions related to odor.

Some Applications of Classical Conditioning

"In Review: Basic Processes of Classical Conditioning" summarizes the principles of classical conditioning. These principles have proven useful in fighting diseases, overcoming fears, controlling predators, and understanding drug effects and addictive processes, to name just a few examples.

Learned Immune Responses Research suggests that decreases in the body's *immune response*—the biological mechanisms that protect the body from infection—can be classically conditioned (Ader & Cohen, 1993; Markovif, Dimitrijevif & Jankovif, 1993). These results raise the possibility that *increases* in the immune response might also be conditioned. In one study, a particular sherbet flavor was paired with an injection of adrenaline, whose unconditioned effect is to increase the activity of the immune system's natural killer cells. Eventually this sherbet flavor alone elicited the immune response (Buske-Kirschbaum et al., 1994).

Someday doctors may treat disease by using stimuli associated with a drug's effects to enhance a person's immune response, so that less actual medication will be needed and side effects will be minimized. Researchers have already paired drug doses with an unusual odor in an effort to create a conditioned immune response that can be triggered between medication doses by the odor alone (Olness & Ader, 1992). Another possibility is to associate placebos with active drugs and then administer the placebos alone in the hope that they might trigger beneficial effects as a conditioned response (Turkkan, 1989).

Phobias *Phobias* are strong fears of objects or situations that either are not objectively dangerous—public speaking, for example—or are less dangerous than the phobic person's reaction suggests. Classical conditioning often plays a role in the development of

ie. tone - medication - healthy
⇒ tone - health.

IN REVIEW	Basic Processes of Classical Conditioning	
Process	**Description**	**Example**
Acquisition	A neutral stimulus and a UCS are paired. The neutral stimulus becomes a CS, eliciting a CR.	A child learns to fear (CR) the doctor's office (CS) by associating it with the reflexive emotional reaction (UCR) to a painful injection (UCS).
Stimulus generalization	A CR is elicited not only by the CS but also by stimuli similar to the CS.	A child fears most doctors' offices and places that smell like them.
Stimulus discrimination	Generalization is limited so that some stimuli similar to the CS do not elicit the CR.	A child learns that his mother's doctor's office is not associated with the UCS.
Extinction	The CS is presented alone, without the UCS. Eventually the CS no longer elicits the CR.	A child visits the doctor's office several times for a checkup, but does not receive a shot. Fear may eventually cease.

such fears; a child who is frightened by a large dog may learn a dog phobia that is so intense and generalized that it creates avoidance of *all* dogs. Dangerous situations can also produce classical conditioning of very long-lasting fears. Decades after their war experiences, some military veterans still respond to simulated battle sounds with large changes in heart rate, blood pressure, and other signs of emotional arousal (Edwards & Acker, 1972).

Classical conditioning has also been employed to treat phobias. Joseph Wolpe (1958) pioneered the development of this methodology. Using techniques first developed with laboratory animals, Wolpe showed that irrational fears could be relieved through *systematic desensitization,* a procedure that associates a new response, such as relaxation, with a feared stimulus. For example, to treat a thunderstorm phobia, a therapist might first teach the client to relax deeply and then associate that relaxation with gradually more intense sights and sounds of thunderstorms presented on videotape (Öst, 1978). Desensitization is discussed in more detail in Chapter 16, on treatment of psychological disorders.

Predator Control   The power of classically conditioned taste aversion has been put to work to help ranchers who are plagued by wolves and coyotes that kill and eat their sheep. To alleviate this problem without killing the predators, some ranchers have set out lithium-laced mutton for marauding wolves and coyotes to eat. The dizziness and severe nausea (UCR) caused by the lithium becomes associated with the smell and taste of mutton (CS), thus making sheep an undesirable meal for these predators and protecting the ranchers' livelihood (Garcia, Rusiniak & Brett, 1977; Gustavson et al., 1974).

LINKAGES: LEARNING AND CONSCIOUSNESS

People are constantly bombarded by stimuli in a changing world. If you tried to pay attention to every sight and sound, your information-processing system would be overloaded, and you would be unable to concentrate on anything. People appear to be genetically tuned to attend to and orient toward certain kinds of events, such as loud

PREDATOR CONTROL THROUGH CONDI-TIONING After learning to associate the taste of mutton with severe nausea created by lithium chloride, wolves and coyotes were placed in a pen with live sheep (mutton on the hoof—the **CS**). They started to attack, but after biting and smelling the sheep, they withdrew (the **CR**). When the doors of the pen were opened, the predators were chased away by the sheep! Today ranchers often lace a carcass with enough lithium chloride to make wolves and coyotes ill, thus "teaching" them not to kill sheep.

HABITUATION

LINKAGES   Can learning shape the effect of a drug on consciousness? (a link to Consciousness)

REASON FOR ADDICTION

sounds or pain. *Novel* stimuli are also very likely to attract attention. At the same time, people adapt, or become *habituated,* to events that are repeated often; in other words, their responsiveness to an unchanging stimulus decreases over time. For example, you will eventually cease to notice the loud ticking of a clock; in fact, you may become aware of the clock again only when it stops, because now something has changed.

Habituation is sometimes considered to be the simplest form of learning, and it has been observed even in the sea slug (Kandel, 1976). Habituation provides yet another example of how learning helps organisms adapt to their environments (Schwartz & Reisberg, 1991). And according to a theory proposed by Richard Solomon, it has a very direct connection to classical conditioning, as well as to the impact created by some of the drugs described in Chapter 6, on consciousness.

According to Solomon's (1980) *opponent-process theory,* habituation to repeated stimuli is the result of two processes in the organism that are triggered by those stimuli. The first is a relatively automatic, involuntary response, called the *A-Process,* which is essentially an unconditioned response. The second, or *B-Process,* is a conditioned response that follows and counteracts the A-Process. For example, an injection of adrenaline produces an increase in heart rate, the A-Process; the B-Process then decreases the heart rate somewhat. In other words, the B-Process is a conditioned response to the same stimulus that produced the unconditioned A-Process. As the UCS (injection) is repeated over time, the B-Process occurs more and more quickly and with greater intensity (see Figure 7.5). Thus, the net effect of the opposing A and B processes becomes smaller and smaller with repeated exposure to a stimulus; habituation results.

FIGURE 7.5

Solomon's Opponent-Process Theory

Solomon explains habituation to repeated stimuli as follows: The unconditioned response to an unconditioned stimulus (the A-Process) is followed by a small, but opposite, B-Process, which reduces the size of the unconditioned response. Over time, the B-Process occurs more quickly and with greater intensity, eventually resulting in a minimal net response.

CONDITIONING TRIALS

Early   **Middle**   **Late**

══ A-process

••••• B-process

━━ Net effect

Consider now what happens when someone first uses a drug such as heroin or crack cocaine. The unconditioned, pleasant reaction (the A-Process) is eventually countered or neutralized as the unpleasant B-Process becomes quicker and stronger. Thus progressively larger doses of the drug are required to obtain the same drug "high." According to Solomon, these opponent processes form the basis for the development of drug tolerance and addiction described in Chapter 6.

Solomon's analysis may also explain some accidental drug overdoses. If the learned B-Process becomes linked to environmental stimuli that are regularly present when the drug is taken, those stimuli may become conditioned stimuli that are capable of triggering the B-Process by themselves. Suppose that a person now takes a normal dose in a very different environment. The strength of the A-Process (the unconditioned drug effect) will still be the same; but without the environmental cues that normally help create the B-process, that counteracting process may be diminished. The net effect may be a stronger-than-usual drug reaction, possibly leading to the trauma of an overdose (Siegel et al., 1982; Turkkan, 1989).

INSTRUMENTAL AND OPERANT CONDITIONING: LEARNING THE CONSEQUENCES OF BEHAVIOR

Much of what people learn cannot be described in terms of classical conditioning. In classical conditioning, neutral and unconditioned stimuli are predictably paired, and the result is an association between the two. The association is evidenced by the conditioned response that occurs when the conditioned stimulus appears. Notice that both stimuli occur before or along with the conditioned response. But people also learn associations between responses and the stimuli that *follow* them—in other words, between behavior and its consequences. A child learns to say "Please" in order to get a piece of candy; a headache sufferer learns to take a pill in order to escape pain; a dog learns to "shake hands" in order to get a treat.

From the Puzzle Box to the Skinner Box

Much of the groundwork for research on the consequences of behavior was done by Edward L. Thorndike, an American psychologist. While Pavlov was exploring classical conditioning in animals, Thorndike studied their ability to think and reason. He would place an animal, usually a hungry cat, in a *puzzle box,* where it had to learn some response—say, stepping on a pedal—in order to unlock the door and get to some food (see Figure 7.6). The animal would solve the puzzle, but very slowly. It did not appear to understand, or suddenly gain *insight* into, the problem (Thorndike, 1898).

FIGURE 7.6

Thorndike's Puzzle Box

A sample "puzzle box," as used in Thorndike's research. His cats learned to open the door and reach food by pushing down on the pedal, but the learning came very gradually. Some cats actually took longer to get out of the box on one trial than on a previous trial.

EDWARD L. THORNDIKE (LEFT; 1874–1949) AND B.F. SKINNER (1904–1990) Thorndike and Skinner studied instrumental and operant conditioning, respectively. Though similar in most respects, these forms of conditioning differ in one way. In instrumental conditioning, the experimenter defines each opportunity for the subject to respond, and conditioning is usually measured by how long it takes for the response to appear. In operant conditioning, the subject can respond at any time; conditioning is measured by the *rate* of response. In this chapter, the term *operant conditioning* refers to both.

So, what were Thorndike's cats learning? Thorndike argued that any response (such as pacing or meowing) that does not produce a satisfying effect (opening the door) gradually becomes weaker, and any response (pressing the pedal) that does have a satisfying effect gradually becomes stronger. The cats' learning, said Thorndike, is governed by the **law of effect.** According to this law, if a response made in the presence of a particular stimulus is followed by satisfaction (such as a reward), that response is more likely to be made the next time the stimulus is encountered. Conversely, responses that produce discomfort are less likely to be performed again. Thorndike described this kind of learning as **instrumental conditioning** because responses are strengthened when they are instrumental in producing rewards (Thorndike, 1905).

About forty years after Thorndike published his work, another American psychologist, B. F. Skinner, extended and formalized many of Thorndike's ideas. Skinner (1938) emphasized that during instrumental conditioning an organism learns a response by *operating on* the environment, so he called the process of learning these responses **operant conditioning.** His primary aim was to analyze *how* behavior is changed by its consequences. To study operant conditioning, Skinner devised some new tools. One was a chamber known as the *Skinner box;* a version of which is shown in Figure 7.7.

Basic Components of Operant Conditioning

The tools Skinner devised allowed him and other researchers to arrange relationships between an arbitrary response and its consequences and then to analyze how those consequences affected behavior. They found that the basic phenomena of classical conditioning—for example, stimulus generalization and stimulus discrimination, extinction and spontaneous recovery—also occur in operant conditioning. In operant conditioning, however, the basic components are operants, reinforcers, and discriminative stimuli.

Operants and Reinforcers Skinner introduced the term *operant* or *operant response* to distinguish the responses in operant conditioning from those in classical conditioning. Recall that in classical conditioning the conditioned response does not affect whether or when the stimulus occurs. Dogs salivated when a buzzer sounded, but the salivation had no effect on the buzzer or on whether food was presented. In contrast,

FIGURE 7.7

A Skinner Box

In this Skinner box, the rat can press a bar to obtain food pellets from a tube.

an **operant** is a response that has some effect on the world; it is a response that *operates on* the environment. For example, when a child says, "Momma, I'm hungry" and is then fed, the child has made an operant response that influences when food will appear.

A **reinforcer** increases the probability that an operant behavior will occur again. There are two main types of reinforcers: positive and negative. **Positive reinforcers** are events that strengthen a response if they are experienced after that response occurs. They are roughly equivalent to rewards. The food given to a hungry pigeon after it pecks a key is a positive reinforcer; its presentation increases the pigeon's key pecking. For people, positive reinforcers can include food, smiles, money, and other desirable outcomes. Presentation of a positive reinforcer after a response is called *positive reinforcement.* **Negative reinforcers** are stimuli such as pain, threats, or a disapproving frown that strengthen a response if they are *removed* after the response occurs. For example, if the response of taking aspirin is followed by the removal of pain, aspirin taking is likely to occur when similar pain appears again. The process of strengthening behavior by following it with the removal of an aversive stimulus is called *negative reinforcement.* Note that whether it takes the form of presenting something pleasant or removing something aversive, reinforcement always *increases* the likelihood of the behavior that precedes it (see Figure 7.8).

Escape and Avoidance Conditioning   The effects of negative reinforcement can be studied through either escape conditioning or avoidance conditioning. **Escape conditioning** takes place when an organism learns to make a response in order to end an aversive stimulus, or negative reinforcer. Dogs learn to jump over the barrier in a shuttle box to escape shock (see Figure 7.9); parents often learn to give in to children's demands because doing so stops their whining. Now imagine that a signal—say, a buzzer or blinking light—occurs just a few seconds before the grid in one side of a shuttle box is electrified. If, at this signal, the animal jumps over the barrier, it can *avoid* the shock. Children sometimes avoid scolding by apologizing for misdeeds as soon as they see a parent's frown. When an animal or person responds to a signal in a way that avoids exposure to an aversive stimulus, **avoidance conditioning** has occurred.

These examples illustrate that avoidance conditioning often represents a marriage of classical and instrumental conditioning. Because it predicts the shock, the buzzer or blinking light becomes a conditioned stimulus that, through classical conditioning, elicits a conditioned fear response. Like the shock itself, conditioned fear is an unpleasant internal sensation. The animal then acquires an instrumental response—jumping the barrier—which is reinforced because it terminates the unpleasant fear stimulus.

Along with positive reinforcement, avoidance conditioning is one of the most important influences on everyday behavior. Most people go to work even when they would rather stay in bed, and they stop at red lights even when they are in a hurry. Each

FIGURE 7.8

Positive and Negative Reinforcement

Both positive and negative reinforcement *increase* the chances that a behavior will occur in the future. Behavior is strengthened through *positive reinforcement* when something pleasant or desirable occurs following the behavior. Behavior is strengthened through *negative reinforcement* when the behavior results in the removal or termination of something unpleasant.

POSITIVE REINFORCEMENT

| **Behavior** You put coins into a vending machine. | → | **Presentation of a pleasant or positive stimulus** You receive a cold can of soda. | → | **Frequency of behavior increases** You put coins in vending machines in the future. |

NEGATIVE REINFORCEMENT

| **Behavior** In the middle of a boring date, you say you have a headache. | → | **Removal of an unpleasant stimulus** The date ends early. | → | **Frequency of behavior increases** You use the same tactic on future boring dates. |

(A) (B) (C)

FIGURE 7.9

A Shuttle Box

A shuttle box has two compartments, usually separated by a barrier, and its floor is an electric grid. Shock can be administered through the grid to each compartment independently. In escape conditioning (A), the animal can get away from shock by jumping over the barrier when the shock occurs. In avoidance conditioning, a buzzer signals the onset of shock (B) and the animal can avoid the shock if it jumps as soon as the buzzer sounds (C).

of these behaviors reflects avoidance conditioning, because each behavior allows people to avoid a negative consequence, such as lost pay or a traffic ticket.

Avoidance is a very difficult habit to break, partly because avoidance responses are often reinforced by fear reduction (Solomon, Kamin & Wynne, 1953). Furthermore, avoidance responses prevent the opportunity to learn that the "rules" may have changed and that avoidance is no longer necessary. If you fear elevators and therefore avoid them, you will never discover that they are safe and comfortable. Avoidance conditioning may also prevent people from learning new, more desirable behaviors. For example, fear of doing something embarrassing may cause people with limited social skills to learn to shy away from social situations.

Discriminative Stimuli and Stimulus Control Even if you have been reinforced for telling jokes at parties, you are not likely to do so after everyone has left. Pigeons show similar wisdom. If they are reinforced for pecking a key when a red light is on but are not reinforced for pecking when a green light is on, they will eventually peck only when they see a red light. Their behavior demonstrates the effect of **discriminative stimuli,** which are stimuli that signal whether reinforcement is available if a certain response is made. When an organism learns to make a particular response in the presence of one stimulus but not another, *stimulus discrimination* has occurred (see Figure 7.10). Another way to say this is that the response is now under *stimulus control.* In general,

FIGURE 7.10

Stimulus Discrimination

In this experiment the rat could jump from a stand through any one of three doors, but it was reinforced only if it jumped through the door that differed from the other two. The rat learned to do so quite well: On this trial, it discriminated vertical from horizontal stripes.

stimulus discrimination allows people or animals to learn what is appropriate (reinforced) and inappropriate (not reinforced) in particular situations.

Stimulus generalization also occurs in operant conditioning; that is, organisms often perform a response in the presence of a stimulus that is similar, but not identical, to the one that previously signaled the availability of reinforcement. As in classical conditioning, the more similar the new stimulus is to the old, the more likely it is that the response will be performed. As an example, consider the student who got an A after engaging in lively dialogue with a friendly, informal instructor who encouraged discussion. The student will be more likely to repeat the same approach in future classes with other informal instructors than with those who are more aloof.

As in classical conditioning, stimulus discrimination and stimulus generalization often complement each other in operant conditioning. For example, Edward Wasserman (1995) trained pigeons to peck a key in different ways depending on whether they saw a picture of a car, a cat, a chair, or a flower. Later, the birds were shown pictures of *new* objects from these same four categories. About 65 percent of the time, they responded to the new examples as they had to the old ones. In other words, they not only discriminated among the four stimuli but, because of stimulus generalization, often responded appropriately to other examples of cars, cats, chairs, and flowers. Humans learn to place people and objects into even more finely detailed categories, such as "honest" or "dangerous." We discriminate one stimulus from another and then, through generalization, respond similarly to all those we perceive to be in a particular category. This process is closely related to the development of concepts (see Chapter 9), as well as to the development of prejudice and discrimination (see Chapter 17).

Forming and Strengthening Operant Behavior

Daily life is full of examples of operant conditioning. People go to movies, parties, classes, and jobs primarily because doing so brings reinforcement. What is the effect of the type or timing of the reinforcer? How are existing behaviors eliminated? How can new responses be established through operant conditioning?

Shaping   Imagine that you want to train your dog, Moxie, to sit and to "shake hands." The basic method using positive reinforcement is obvious: Every time Moxie sits and shakes hands, you give her a treat. But the problem is also obvious: Smart as Moxie is, she may never spontaneously make the desired response, so you will never be able to

LEARNING THROUGH SHAPING Shaping is used to help people learn new computer programs. In one case, correct procedures are first presented on the screen, then "happy faces" appear to reward the operator for coming closer and closer to the correct sequence of commands (Anger et al., 1994). Here, the computer says "You made it! Press enter for level 2."

SECONDARY REINFORCEMENT A touch, a smile, and a look of love are among the many social stimuli that can serve as positive reinforcers for humans.

give the reinforcer. Instead of your teaching and Moxie's learning, the two of you will just stare at each other.

The way around this problem is to shape Moxie's behavior. **Shaping** is accomplished by reinforcing *successive approximations*—that is, responses that come successively closer to the desired response. For example, you might first give Moxie a treat whenever she sits down. Then you might reinforce her only when she sits and partially lifts a paw. Next, you might reinforce more complete paw lifting. Eventually, you would require that Moxie perform the entire sit-lift-shake sequence before giving the treat. Shaping is an extremely powerful, widely used tool. Animal trainers have used it to teach chimpanzees to roller-skate, dolphins to jump through hoops, and pigeons to play Ping-Pong (Breland & Breland, 1966).

Secondary Reinforcement   Often, operant conditioning begins with the use of **primary reinforcers,** events or stimuli—such as food—that are inherently rewarding. But Moxie's training will be somewhat disrupted if she must stop and eat every time she makes a correct response. Furthermore, once she gets full, food will no longer act as an effective reinforcer. To avoid these problems, animal trainers and others in the teaching business capitalize on the principle of secondary reinforcement.

A **secondary reinforcer** is a previously neutral stimulus that, if paired with a stimulus that is already reinforcing, will itself take on reinforcing properties. In other words, secondary reinforcers are rewards that people or animals learn to like. For example, if you say "Good girl!" just before feeding Moxie, the words will become reinforcing after a few such pairings and can then be used alone to reinforce Moxie's behavior (especially if they are paired with food now and then). Does this remind you of classical conditioning? It should, because the primary reinforcer (food) is a UCS; if the sound of "Good girl!" predictably precedes and thus signals food, it becomes a CS. For this reason, secondary reinforcers are sometimes called *conditioned reinforcers.*

Secondary reinforcement greatly expands the power of operant conditioning (Schwartz & Reisberg, 1991). Money is the most obvious secondary reinforcer; some people will do anything for it (even though it tastes terrible!). Its reinforcing power lies in its association with the many rewards it can buy. Smiles and other forms of social approval (like the words "Good job!") are also important secondary reinforcers for human beings. However, what becomes a secondary reinforcer can vary a great deal from person to person and culture to culture. For example, tickets to a rock concert may be an effective secondary reinforcer for some teenagers, but not all. A ceremony honoring outstanding job performance might be highly reinforcing to most employees in individualist cultures, but it might be embarrassing for some from cultures where collectivist values emphasize group cooperation rather than personal distinction (Triandis, 1994). Still, when chosen carefully, secondary reinforcers can build or maintain behavior even when primary reinforcement is absent for long periods.

Delay and Size of Reinforcement   Much of human behavior is learned and maintained because it is regularly reinforced. But many people overeat, smoke, drink too much, or procrastinate, even though they know these behaviors are bad for them and even though they want to eliminate them. They just cannot seem to change; they seem to lack "self-control." If behavior is controlled by its consequences, why do people perform acts that are ultimately self-defeating?

Part of the answer lies in the timing of reinforcers. The good feelings (positive reinforcers) that follow, say, drinking too much are immediate; hangovers and other negative consequences are usually delayed. Recall that in classical conditioning, increasing the delay between the conditioned stimulus and the unconditioned stimulus usually weakens the conditioned response. Similarly, operant conditioning is stronger when there is little delay in receiving a reinforcer (Kalish, 1981). Thus, under some conditions, delaying a positive reinforcer for even a few seconds can decrease the effectiveness of positive reinforcement. (An advantage of praise or other secondary reinforcers is that they can easily be delivered immediately after a desired response occurs.)

The size of a reinforcer is also important. In general, conditioning proceeds faster when the reinforcer is large than when it is small.

Schedules of Reinforcement   So far, we have described reinforcement as if a reinforcer were delivered every time a particular response occurs. Sometimes it is, and this arrangement is called a **continuous reinforcement schedule.** Very often, however, reinforcement is administered only some of the time; the result is a **partial,** or **intermittent, reinforcement schedule.**

Most intermittent schedules can be classified according to (1) whether the delivery of reinforcers is determined by the number of responses made or by the time that has elapsed since the last reinforcer, and (2) whether the delivery schedule is fixed or variable. This way of classifying schedules produces four basic types of intermittent reinforcement.

1. **Fixed-ratio (FR) schedules** provide reinforcement following a fixed number of responses. Rats might receive food after every tenth bar press (FR 10) or after every twentieth one (FR 20); assembly workers might be paid for every ten lamps they produce.

2. **Variable-ratio (VR) schedules** also call for reinforcement after a given number of responses, but that number varies from one reinforcement to the next. On a VR 30 schedule, a rat might sometimes be reinforced after ten bar presses, sometimes after fifty bar presses, but an *average* of thirty responses would occur before reinforcement was given. Gambling also offers a variable-ratio schedule; a slot machine, for example, pays off only after a frustratingly unpredictable number of lever pulls, averaging perhaps one in twenty.

3. **Fixed-interval (FI) schedules** provide reinforcement for the first response that occurs after some fixed time has passed since the last reward, regardless of how many responses have been made during that interval. For example, on an FI 60 schedule, the first response after sixty seconds have passed will be rewarded. Some radio stations use fixed-interval schedules to discourage "professional contestants" by stating that listeners cannot win a prize more than once every thirty days.

4. **Variable-interval (VI) schedules** reinforce the first response after some period of time, but the amount of time varies. In a VI 60 schedule, for example, the first response to occur after an *average* of one minute is reinforced, but the actual time between reinforcements might vary from, say, 1 second to 120 seconds. Teachers use VI schedules when they give "points"—at unpredictably varying intervals—to children who are in their seats. A VI schedule has also been successfully used to encourage seat-belt use:

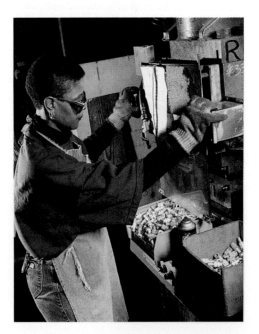

LINKAGES: REINFORCEMENT SCHEDULES ON THE JOB Workers at the Lincoln Electric Company, in Cleveland, Ohio, are paid for every piece of welding equipment they produce. This fixed ratio reinforcement schedule results in very high production rates and in annual incomes of up to $85,000. While most of the employees like the reward system, they are not necessarily satisfied with their jobs. This may be because, as described in Chapter 11, on motivation and emotion, job satisfaction is usually based on factors other than high pay.

During a ten-week test in Illinois, police stopped drivers at random times and awarded prizes to those who were buckled up (Mortimer et al., 1988).

Different schedules of reinforcement produce different patterns of responding, as Figure 7.11 shows (Skinner, 1961a). The figure illustrates two important points. First, both fixed- and variable-ratio schedules produce very high rates of behavior, because in both cases the frequency of reward depends directly on the rate of responding. Thus, manufacturers who want to maintain high production rates often use fixed-ratio schedules, paying factory workers on a *piecework* basis, according to the number of items they produce. Similarly, gamblers reinforced on a variable-ratio schedule for pulling the slot machine's handle tend to maintain a high rate of responding.

The second important aspect of Figure 7.11 relates to the "scallops" shown in the FI schedule. Under this schedule, it does not matter how many responses are made during the time between rewards. As a result, the rate of responding typically drops dramatically immediately after reinforcement and then increases as the time for another reward approaches. When teachers schedule quizzes on the same day each week, for example, most students will study just before each quiz and then almost cease studying immediately afterward. Behavior rewarded on variable-interval schedules looks quite different. The unpredictable timing of rewards typically generates slow but steady responding. Thus, if you know that a "pop quiz" might occur any day, your studying is likely to be relatively steady from day to day.

Schedules and Extinction   Just as breaking the link between a conditioned and unconditioned stimulus weakens a classically conditioned response, ending the relationship between an operant response and its consequences weakens that response. In other words, failure to reinforce a response *extinguishes* that response; the response occurs less often and eventually may disappear. If bar pressing no longer brings food, a rat stops pressing; if repeated phone calls to a friend bring nothing but ringing, you eventually stop phoning. As in classical conditioning, extinction in operant conditioning does not totally erase learned relationships. If a signaling stimulus reappears some

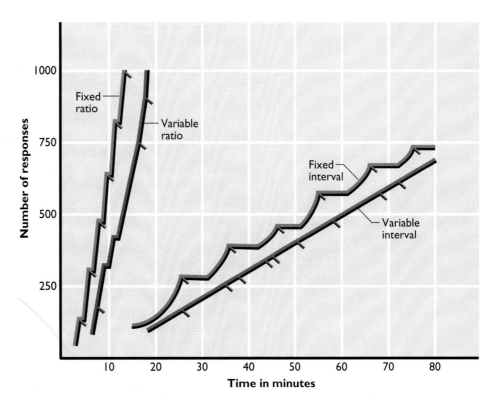

Source: Adapted from Skinner, 1961.

FIGURE 7.11

Schedules of Reinforcement

These curves illustrate the patterns of behavior typically seen under different reinforcement schedules. The steeper the curve, the faster the response rate; the thin diagonal lines crossing the curves show when reinforcement was given. In general, the rate of responding is higher under ratio schedules than under interval schedules.

**SUPERSTITION AND PARTIAL REINFORCE-
MENT** Partial reinforcement can
create superstitious athletic rituals,
such as a fixed sequence of actions
prior to swinging a golf club. If the
ritual has preceded success often
enough, failure to execute it may
upset the player and thus disrupt
performance.

time after an operant response has been extinguished, that response may recur (spontaneously recover) and, if again reinforced, it will be relearned even faster.

In general, behaviors learned under a partial reinforcement schedule are far more difficult to extinguish than those learned on a continuous reinforcement schedule. This phenomenon—called the **partial reinforcement extinction effect**—is easy to understand if you imagine yourself in a hotel lobby with a broken candy machine and a broken slot machine. If you deposit money in the broken candy machine, you will probably extinguish (stop putting money in) very quickly. Because the machine usually delivers its goodies on a continuous reinforcement schedule, it is easy to tell that it is not going to provide a reinforcer. But because slot machines are known to offer rewards on an intermittent and unpredictable schedule, you might put in coin after coin, unsure of whether the machine is broken or is simply not paying off at the moment.

Partial reinforcement also helps to explain why superstitious behavior is so resistant to extinction (Chance, 1988). Suppose you take a shower just before hearing that you passed an important exam. The shower did nothing to cause this outcome; the reward followed it through sheer luck. Still, for some people, this *accidental reinforcement* can function like a partial reinforcement schedule, strengthening actions that precede, and thus *appear* to cause, reward (Chance, 1988). Thus, someone who wins a lottery while wearing a particular shirt may begin wearing the "lucky shirt" more often. The laws of chance dictate that if you wear a "lucky shirt" often enough, a rewarding event will follow now and then, on a very sparse partial schedule.

[handwritten annotation: superstition = accidental reinforcement]

Why Reinforcers Work

What makes reinforcers reinforcing? For primary reinforcers, at least, the reason could be that they satisfy hunger, thirst, and other physiological needs basic to survival. This explanation is incomplete, however, because stimuli like saccharin, which have no nutritional value, can wield as much reinforcing power as sugar, which is nutritious. Other activities, like taking addictive drugs, are powerful reinforcers, despite their long-term threat to the health of the individual. Hence psychologists have sought other explanations for the mechanisms of reinforcement.

Some psychologists have argued that reinforcement is based, not on a stimulus itself, but on the opportunity to engage in an activity that involves the stimulus. According to David Premack (1965), for example, at any moment each person has a hierarchy of behavioral preferences, ranked from most to least desirable, like a kind of psychological Top 40. The higher on the hierarchy an activity is, the greater its power as a reinforcer, and any activity will serve as a reinforcer for any other activity that is less preferred at the moment. Thus, when parents allow their teenager to use the car after she mows the lawn, they are offering activities high on the teenager's preference hierarchy to reinforce performance of activities lower on the hierarchy.

Preference hierarchies differ from one person to the next and from one occasion to the next. To a hungry person, eating will reinforce almost any behavior. But once hunger is satisfied, eating drops so low on the preference hierarchy that it temporarily loses virtually all power as a reinforcer. Because money can be exchanged for whatever a person finds reinforcing at the moment, it is almost always a powerful reinforcer.

As a result of such preference shifts, the opportunity to engage in a normally less preferred activity can sometimes reinforce performance of a more preferred activity *if* the person is prevented from carrying out the less preferred action (Timberlake & Farmer-Dougan, 1991). For example, even if a child prefers studying over participating in gym class, the opportunity to participate in gym could reinforce studying, if the child is not allowed to engage in any gym activities for some time. When gym activity is held below its natural "baseline" level, its value as a reinforcer increases. Understanding activity preferences and the natural baseline distribution of activities over time can be very helpful in establishing effective reinforcers in "token economies" and other behavioral treatments (described in Chapter 16) for disruptive children or mentally disturbed adults.

The stimuli and activities known as reinforcers may work by exerting particular effects on the brain. This possibility was suggested when James Olds and Peter Milner (1954) discovered that mild electrical stimulation of certain areas of the hypothalamus of rats can be such a powerful reinforcer that a hungry rat will ignore food in a Skinner box, preferring to press for hours a lever that stimulates these "pleasure centers" of its brain (see also Olds, 1973). It is not yet clear whether physiological mechanisms underlie the power of all reinforcers, but evidence available thus far certainly suggests that these mechanisms are important components of the process. For example, as mentioned in Chapter 3, activation of dopamine systems is associated with the pleasure of many stimuli, including food, sex, and addictive drugs.

Punishment and Learning

Both positive and negative reinforcement *increase* the frequency of a response, either by presenting something pleasurable or by removing something unpleasant. In contrast to reinforcement, **punishment** involves the presentation of an aversive stimulus or the removal of a pleasant stimulus in order to *decrease* the frequency of the immediately preceding response. Shouting "No!" and swatting your dog when it begins chewing on the rug illustrates punishment that presents a negative stimulus following a response. Taking away a child's TV privileges because of rude behavior is a kind of punishment—sometimes called *penalty*—that removes a positive stimulus (see Figure 7.12).

Punishment and negative reinforcement are often confused, but they are quite different. Reinforcement of any sort always *strengthens* behavior; punishment *weakens* it. If shock is *turned off* when a rat presses a lever, that is negative reinforcement; it increases the probability that the rat will press the lever when shock occurs again. But if shock is *turned on* when the rat presses the lever, that is punishment; the rat will be less likely to press the lever again.

Although punishment can change behavior, it has several drawbacks. First, like extinction, it does not "erase" an undesirable habit; it merely suppresses it. Children often repeat punished acts when they think they can avoid detection. Second, punishment often produces unwanted side effects. For example, if you punish a child for swearing, the child may associate the punisher with the punishment and end up fearing you. Third, punishment is often ineffective, especially with animals or young children, unless it is given immediately after the response and each time the response is made. If a child gets into the cookie jar and enjoys a few cookies before being discovered and punished, the effect of punishment will be greatly reduced. If a child confesses to wrongdoing and is then punished, the punishment may discourage honesty rather than eliminate undesirable behavior. Fourth, physical punishment can become aggression, even abuse, especially when administered to a child in anger. Because children tend to imitate what they see, frequent punishment may lead children to behave aggres-

FIGURE 7.12

Two Kinds of Punishment

In one form of punishment, a behavior is followed by an aversive or unpleasant stimulus. In a second form of punishment, sometimes called penalty, a pleasant stimulus is *removed* following a behavior. In either case, punishment decreases the chances that the behavior will occur in the future.

PUNISHMENT I

| **Behavior** You touch a hot iron. | → | **Presentation of an unpleasant stimulus** Your hand is burned. | → | **Frequency of behavior decreases** You no longer touch hot irons. |

PUNISHMENT II (Penalty)

| **Behavior** You're careless with your ice cream cone. | → | **Removal of a pleasant stimulus** The ice cream falls on the ground. | → | **Frequency of behavior decreases** You're not as careless with the next cone. |

sively themselves. Finally, although punishment signals that inappropriate behavior occurred, by itself it does not specify correct alternatives. An "F" on a term paper says the assignment was poorly done, but the grade alone tells the student nothing about how to improve.

When used properly, however, punishment can work (see Figure 7.13). It is most effective when several guidelines are followed. First, to prevent development of a general fear of the punisher, he or she should specify why punishment is being given and that the behavior, not the person, is being punished. Second, without being abusive, punishment should be immediate and salient enough to eliminate the undesirable response. A half-hearted "Quit it" may actually reinforce a child's pranks, because almost any attention is reinforcing to some children. Finally, more appropriate responses should be identified and positively reinforced. As the frequency of appropriate behavior increases through reinforcement, the frequency of the undesirable response (and the need for further punishment) drops.

When these guidelines are not followed, the beneficial effects of punishment may be wiped out or only temporary (Hyman, 1995). As illustrated in the U.S. prison system, punishment alone does not usually lead to rehabilitation (Brennan & Mednick, 1994). In Illinois, for example, about 46 percent of the 21,808 prisoners released from prison during 1989 and 1990 behaved in ways that put them back in prison within three years (Illinois Department of Corrections, 1993). One man in Urbana, Illinois, recently received his fourth jail sentence in ten years for drunken driving.

Operant Conditioning of Human Behavior

The principles of operant conditioning were originally worked out with animals in the laboratory, but they are valuable for understanding human behavior in an endless variety of everyday situations. ("In Review: Reinforcement and Punishment" summarizes some key concepts of operant conditioning.) The unscientific but very effective use of rewards and punishments by parents, teachers, and peers is vital to helping children learn what is and is not appropriate behavior at the dinner table, in the classroom, at a birthday party. Indeed, people learn how to be "civilized" in their own particular culture partly through positive ("Good!") and negative ("Stop that!") responses from others. As described in Chapter 12, on human development, differing patterns of rewards and punishments for boys and girls also underlie the development of behaviors that fit culturally approved *gender roles*.

FIGURE 7.13

The Uses of Punishment

This child suffered from chronic ruminative disorder, a condition in which he regurgitated all food. At left, the boy was approximately one year old and had been vomiting for four months. At right is the same child thirteen days after punishment with electric shock had eliminated the vomiting response; his weight had increased 26 percent. He was physically and psychologically healthy when tested six months, one year, and two years later (Lang & Melamed, 1969).

Source: Lang & Melamed, 1969.

IN REVIEW	Reinforcement and Punishment	
Concept	**Description**	**Example or Comment**
Positive reinforcement	Increasing the frequency of behavior by following it with the presentation of a positive reinforcer—a pleasant, positive stimulus or experience.	Saying "Good job" after someone works hard to perform a task.
Negative reinforcement	Increasing the frequency of behavior by following it with the removal of a negative reinforcer—an unpleasant stimulus or experience.	Pressing the "mute" button on a TV remote control removes the sound of an obnoxious commercial.
Escape conditioning	A subject is conditioned to make a response that ends a negative reinforcer.	A little boy learns that crying will cut short the time that he must stay in his room.
Avoidance conditioning	A subject is conditioned to make a response that avoids a negative reinforcer.	You slow your car to the speed limit when you spot a police car, thus avoiding arrest and reducing the fear of arrest. Very resistant to extinction.
Punishment	Decreasing the frequency of behavior by either presenting an unpleasant stimulus or removing a pleasant one.	Swatting the dog after she steals food from the table. A number of cautions should be kept in mind before using punishment.

The scientific study of operant conditioning has led to numerous treatment programs for altering problematic behavior. Behavioral programs that combine the use of rewards for appropriate actions and extinction (or carefully administered punishment) for inappropriate behaviors have helped countless mental patients, mentally retarded individuals, autistic children, and hard-to-manage youngsters to develop the behavior patterns they need to live happier and more productive lives. Some of these procedures are discussed in Chapter 16, on treatment of psychological disorders. Many self-help books also incorporate principles of positive reinforcement, recommending self-reward following each small victory in people's efforts to lose weight, stop smoking, avoid procrastination, or reach other goals (Marx et al., 1992).

When people cannot do anything about the consequences of a behavior, discriminative stimuli may hold the key to changing the behavior. For example, people trying to quit smoking often find initial abstinence easier if they stay away from bars and other places that contain discriminative stimuli for smoking. Stimulus control can also help alleviate insomnia. Much more so than average, insomniacs tend to use their beds for nonsleeping activities such as watching television, writing letters, reading magazines, worrying, and so on. Soon the bedroom becomes a discriminative stimulus for so many activities that relaxation and sleep become less and less likely. But if, through the sleep restriction therapy mentioned in Chapter 6, insomniacs begin to use their beds only for sleeping, there is a good chance that they will sleep better (Morin et al., 1993).

COGNITIVE PROCESSES IN LEARNING

During the first half of the twentieth century, psychologists in North America tended to look at classical and operant conditioning through the lens of the behavioral approach that was dominant in psychology at the time. They saw two kinds of learning, each following different, but related, rules and each resulting from the automatic, unthinking formation or modification of associations between observable stimuli and observable responses. But they gave virtually no consideration to the role of mental activity that might accompany the learning process.

This strictly behavioral view of classical and operant conditioning is challenged by the cognitive approach, which, as described in Chapter 1, has become increasingly influential in recent decades. Cognitive psychologists see a common thread in these apparently different forms of learning. Both classical and operant conditioning, they argue, help animals and people to detect causality, to understand what causes what (Mackintosh, 1983; Schwartz & Robbins, 1995). By extension, both types of conditioning may result not only from automatic stimulus-response associations but also from the *mental processes* that organisms use to understand their environments and to interact with them adaptively.

Certainly there is evidence that cognitive processes—how people represent, store, and use information—play an important role in learning. This evidence includes research on learned helplessness, latent learning, cognitive maps, insight, and observational learning.

Learned Helplessness

Babies learn that crying attracts attention, children learn how to make the TV louder, and adults learn what it takes to succeed in the workplace. In short, people learn to expect that certain actions on their part predict certain consequences. If this learning is disrupted, problems may result. One such problem is **learned helplessness,** a tendency to give up any effort to control the environment (Seligman, 1975).

Learned helplessness was first demonstrated in animals. As described earlier, dogs placed in a shuttle box (see Figure 7.9) will normally learn to jump over a partition to escape a shock. However, if the dogs are first placed in a cage where they receive shocks they cannot escape, they do not even *try* to escape when the shock is turned on in the shuttle box (Seligman & Maier, 1967). It is as if the animals had learned that "shock happens, and there is nothing I can do about it."

Could lack of control over the environment lead to helplessness in humans as well? Donald Hiroto (1974) conducted an experiment to test the hypothesis that people would develop learned helplessness after either experiencing lack of control or simply being *told* that their control was limited.

The first independent variable manipulated in Hiroto's experiment was the ability or inability of male and female volunteer subjects to control a series of thirty randomly timed bursts of loud, obnoxious noise. Like dogs receiving inescapable shock, one-third of the ninety-six subjects had no way to stop the noise. A second group did have control; they could press a button to turn off the noise. A third group heard no noise at all.

After this preliminary phase, all subjects were exposed to eighteen more bursts of obnoxious noise, each preceded by a red warning light. During this second phase, *all* subjects could stop the noise by moving a lever to the left or right and, if they acted quickly enough, could even prevent it from starting. However, the subjects did not know which lever direction would be correct on any given trial.

Before these new trials began, the experimenter manipulated a second independent variable: *expectation* about control. For half the subjects, instructions emphasized personal control, noting that avoiding or escaping noise depended on *skill*. For the other half, control was downplayed; these subjects were told that, no matter how hard they tried, success would be a matter of *chance*. This was a *two-factor* experiment because the dependent variable—the degree to which subjects acted to control noise—could be affected by two independent variables: prior experience with noise (control, lack of control, or no noise) and expectation (skill or chance) about the ability to influence the noise. What were the results? On the average, subjects who had previously experienced lack of control now failed to control noise on almost four times as many trials (50 percent versus 13 percent) as did those who had earlier been in control. Further, regardless of whether subjects had experienced control before, those who expected control to depend on their skill exerted control on significantly more trials than did those who expected chance to govern the outcome.

These results support Hiroto's hypothesis that people, like animals, tend to make less effort to control their environment when prior experience leads them to expect those efforts to be in vain. Unlike animals, however, people can develop effort-reducing expectations either through personal experience with lack of control or through being told that they are powerless.

Hiroto's (1974) results appear to reflect a general phenomenon. When people's prior experience leads them to *believe* that nothing they can do will change their lives or control their destiny, they generally stop trying to improve their lot (Dweck & Licht, 1980; Peterson, Maier & Seligman, 1993). Instead, they tend to passively endure painful situations and, at the cognitive level, to attribute negative events to their own enduring and widespread shortcomings rather than to changeable external circumstances (Abramson, Metalsky & Alloy, 1989; Seligman, Klein & Miller, 1976). Learned helplessness may or may not be involved when battered women remain with abusive partners, but helplessness itself does appear to cause depression and other stress-related problems, as described in Chapters 13 and 15 (Abramson, Metalsky & Alloy, 1989; Metalsky et al., 1993). Indeed, one goal of the cognitive therapies for depression described in Chapter 16 is to help people deal successfully with negative events in the hope that doing so will re-establish their sense of control, alter their attributions, and lift their spirits.

Latent Learning and Cognitive Maps

The study of cognitive processes in learning goes back at least to the 1920s and Edward Tolman's research on maze learning in rats (see Figure 7.14). The rats' task was to find

FIGURE 7.14

Latent Learning

Notice that when rats in Group C did not receive food reinforcement, they continued to make many errors in locating the goal box of this maze. The day after first finding food there, however, they took almost no wrong turns! The reinforcement, argued Tolman, affected only the rats' performance; they must have learned the maze earlier, without reinforcement.

the goal box, where food awaited them. The rats typically took many wrong turns but over the course of many trials made successively fewer mistakes. The behavioral interpretation was that the rats learned a long chain of turning responses that were reinforced by the food. Tolman disagreed and offered evidence for a cognitive interpretation.

In one of Tolman's studies, three groups of rats were placed in the same maze once a day for several consecutive days (Tolman & Honzik, 1930). For Group A, food was placed in the goal box on each trial. These rats gradually improved their performance so that, by the end of the experiment, they made only one or two mistakes as they ran through the maze (see Figure 7.14). Group B also ran the maze once a day, but there was never any food in their goal box. These animals continued to make many errors throughout the experiment. Neither of these results is surprising, and each is consistent with a behavioral view of learning.

The third group of rats, Group C, was the critical one. For the first ten days, they received no reinforcement for running the maze and continued to make many mistakes. But on the eleventh day, food was placed in their goal box for the first time. Then a very surprising thing happened: On the day after receiving reinforcement, these rats made almost no mistakes. In fact, their performance was as good as that of the rats who had been reinforced every day. In other words, the single reinforcement trial on day 11 produced a dramatic change in their performance the next day.

Tolman argued that these results supported two conclusions. First, notice that the rats in Group C improved their performance the *first* time they ran the maze after being reinforced. The reinforcement on day 11 could not have significantly affected the rats' learning of the maze itself; it simply changed their subsequent performance. They must have learned the maze earlier. Therefore, the rats demonstrated **latent learning**—learning that is not evident when it first occurs. Second, because the rats' performance changed immediately after the first reinforcement trial, Tolman argued that the results he obtained could occur only if the rats had earlier developed a **cognitive map**—that is, a mental representation of the particular spatial arrangement of the maze.

Tolman concluded that cognitive maps develop naturally through experience, even in the absence of any overt response or reinforcement. Research on learning in the natural environment has supported these views. For example, we develop mental maps of shopping malls and city streets, even when we receive no direct reward for doing so (Tversky, 1991).

Thus, much as the Gestalt psychologists argued that the whole of a perception is different from the sum of its parts, cognitive views of learning hold that learning is more than the sum of reinforcement effects and stimulus-response associations. Just as perception may depend on the meaning attached to sensations, so, too, some forms of learning require higher mental processes and depend on how the learner attaches meaning to events.

Insight and Learning

Wolfgang Köhler was a Gestalt psychologist whose work on the cognitive aspects of learning happened almost by accident. A German, he was visiting the island of Tenerife when World War I broke out. The British confined Köhler to the island for the duration of the war, and he devoted his time to studying problem solving in a colony of chimpanzees (Köhler, 1924).

For example, Köhler would put a chimpanzee in a cage and place a piece of fruit so that it was visible but out of the animal's reach. He sometimes hung the fruit from a string too high to reach, or on the ground too far outside the cage to be retrieved. Many of the chimps overcame these obstacles easily. If the fruit was out of reach on the ground outside the cage, some chimps looked around the cage and, finding a long stick, used it to rake in the fruit. Surprised that the chimpanzees could solve these problems, Köhler tried more difficult tasks. Again, the chimps proved very adept, as Figure 7.15 illustrates.

In contrast to Thorndike, whose conclusions were drawn from puzzle box experiments, Köhler argued that animals' problem solving does not have to depend on automatic associations developing slowly through trial and error. He buttressed his claim with three observations. First, once a chimpanzee solved a particular problem, it would immediately do the same thing in a similar situation. In other words, it acted as if it understood the problem. Second, Köhler's chimpanzees rarely tried a solution that did not work. Third, they often reached a solution quite suddenly. When confronted with a piece of fruit hanging from a string, for example, a chimp might jump for it several

FIGURE 7.15

Insight

Here are three impressive examples of problem solving by chimpanzees. In (A) the animal fixed a fifteen-foot pole in the ground, climbed to the top, and dropped to the ground after grabbing the fruit. In (B) the chimp stacked up two boxes from different areas of the compound, climbed to the top, and used a pole to knock down the fruit. The chimp in (C) stacked three boxes and climbed them to reach the fruit.

(A)

(B)

(C)

Source: Köhler, 1976.

times. Then it would stop jumping, look up, and pace back and forth. Finally it would run over to a wooden crate, place it directly under the fruit, and climb on top of it to reach the fruit. Once, when there were no other objects in the room, a chimp went over to Köhler, dragged him by the arm until he stood beneath the fruit, and then started climbing up his back!

Köhler believed that the only explanation for these results was that the chimpanzees suddenly had **insight** into the problem as a whole, not just stimulus-response associations between its specific elements. According to some cognitive psychologists today, however, insight may not occur as suddenly as Köhler assumed. They suggest that insight results only after a "mental trial and error" process in which people (and some animals) envision a course of action, mentally simulate its results, compare it to the imagined outcome of other alternatives, and settle on the course of action most likely to aid complex problem-solving and decision-making (Klein, 1993). This process is described in more detail in Chapter 9.

Observational Learning: Learning by Imitation

Research on the role of cognitive processes in learning has been further stimulated by the finding that learning can occur not only by doing but also by observing what others do. Learning by watching others—called **observational learning,** or *social learning*—is efficient and adaptive. We don't have to find out for ourselves that a door is locked or an iron is hot if we have just seen someone else try the door or suffer a burn.

Children are particularly influenced by the adults and peers who act as *models* for appropriate behavior in various situations. In one classic experiment, Albert Bandura showed nursery school children a film starring an adult and a large, inflatable, bottom-heavy "Bobo" doll (Bandura, 1965). The adult in the film punched the Bobo doll in the nose, kicked it, threw objects at it, and hit its head with a hammer while saying things like "Sockeroo!" There were different endings to the film. Some children saw an ending in which the aggressive adult was called a "champion" by a second adult and rewarded with candy and soft drinks. Some saw the aggressor scolded and called a "bad person." Some saw a neutral ending in which there was neither reward nor punishment. After the film, each child was allowed to play alone with a Bobo doll. How the children played in this and similar studies led to some important conclusions about learning and about the role of cognitive factors in it.

LEARNING BY IMITATION **Much of our behavior is learned by imitating others, especially those who serve as role models.**

FIGURE 7.16

Observational Learning

After children have observed an aggressive model, they often reproduce many of the model's acts precisely, especially if the model's aggression was rewarded.

- Aggressive model rewarded
- Aggressive model punished
- Non-aggressive model
- No model

Source: Bandura, Ross & Ross, 1963.

Bandura found that children who saw the adult rewarded for aggression showed the most aggressive acts in play; they had received **vicarious conditioning,** a kind of observational learning in which one is influenced by seeing or hearing about the consequences of others' behavior. Those who had seen the adult punished for aggressive acts initially showed less aggression, but they still learned something. When later offered rewards for all the aggressive acts they could perform, these children displayed just as many as the children who had watched the rewarded adult. Observational learning can occur even when there are no vicarious consequences; many children in the neutral condition also imitated the model's aggression (see Figure 7.16).

Observational learning seems to be a powerful source of the socialization discussed in Chapter 12, on human development. Experiments show, for example, that children are more willing to help and share after seeing a demonstration of helping by a warm, powerful model—even after some months have elapsed (Bryan, 1975; Mussen & Eisenberg-Berg, 1977).

If observational learning is important, then surely television—and televised violence— must teach children a great deal. For one thing, it is estimated that the average child in the United States spends more time watching television than attending school (Liebert & Sprafkin, 1988; Nielsen Media, 1990). Much of what children see is violent; prime-time programs in the United States present an average of 5 violent acts per hour; some Saturday morning cartoons include more than 20 per hour (Gerbner et al., 1986; Radecki, 1990). As a result, the average child will have witnessed at least 8,000 murders and more than 100,000 other acts of televised violence *before graduating from elementary school* (Huston et al., 1992; Kunkel et al., 1996).

THINKING CRITICALLY

Does Watching Violence on Television Make People More Violent?

Psychologists have speculated that watching so much violence might be emotionally arousing, making viewers more likely to react violently to frustration (Huston & Wright, 1989). Televised violence might also provide models that viewers imitate, particularly if the violence is carried out by attractive, powerful models—the "good guys," for example (Bandura, 1983). Finally, prolonged viewing of violent TV programs may "desensitize" viewers, making them less emotionally moved when they see others suffer and, as a result, less disturbed about inflicting pain on others (Cline, Croft & Courrier, 1973).

What am I being asked to believe or accept?

Many have argued that, through one or more of these mechanisms, watching violence on television *causes* violent behavior in viewers (Eron, 1987; Hearold, 1986). Indeed, in 1993 a National Academy of Science report concluded that "overall, the vast majority of studies, whatever their methodology, showed that exposure to television violence resulted in increased aggressive behavior, both contemporaneously and over time" (Reiss & Roth, 1993, p. 371). An American Psychological Association Commission on Violence and Youth reached the same conclusion (American Psychological Association, 1993).

What evidence is available to support the assertion?

Three types of evidence back up the claim that watching violent television programs increases violent behavior. Some evidence comes from anecdotes and case studies. Children have poked each other's eyes out after watching the Three Stooges appear to do so on television (Associated Press, 1984). And adults have claimed that watching TV shows prompted them to commit murders or other violent acts matching those seen on the shows.

Second, many correlational studies have found a strong link between watching violent television programs and later acts of aggression and violence. One study tracked people from the age of eight (in 1960) until thirty (in 1982). Those who watched more television violence as children were significantly more likely to be convicted of violent crimes as adults. These same people were also more likely to rely on physical punishment of their own children, and their children tended to be much more aggressive than average. These results were found in the United States, Israel, Australia, Poland, and the Netherlands. A significant positive correlation between television violence and violent behavior was even observed in countries such as Finland, where the number of violent shows is very small (Centerwall, 1990; Eron, 1987).

Finally, as noted earlier, the results of numerous experiments support the view that TV violence increases aggression among viewers (American Psychological Association, 1993; Paik & Comstock, 1994; Reiss & Roth, 1993; Waite, Hillbrand & Foster, 1992; Wood, Wong & Chachere, 1991). In one study, groups of boys watched violent or nonviolent programs in a controlled setting and then played floor hockey (Josephson, 1987). Boys who had watched the violent shows were more likely than those who had watched nonviolent programs to behave aggressively on the hockey floor. This effect was greatest for those boys who had the most aggressive tendencies to begin with. More extensive experiments in which children are exposed for long periods to carefully controlled types of television programs also suggest that exposure to large amounts of violent activity on television results in aggressive behavior (Huesmann, Laperspetz & Eron, 1984; Parke et al., 1977). For example, compared with children who watched an equal number of nonviolent movies, children who were exposed to several violent movies became more aggressive in their interactions with other children (Leyens et al., 1975).

Are there alternative ways of interpreting the evidence?

Anecdotal reports and case studies are certainly open to different interpretations. If people face imprisonment or execution for their violent acts, how much credibility do you give to their claims that their actions were triggered by television programs? If anyone bothered to ask them, how many other people might say that the same programs made them *less* likely to be violent? Anecdotes alone do not provide a good basis for drawing solid scientific conclusions.

What about the correlational evidence? Recall from Chapter 2 that a correlation between two variables does not necessarily mean that one caused the other; both might be caused by a third factor. Why, for example, are certain people watching so much television violence in the first place? This question suggests two possible "third factors" that might account for the observed relationship between watching TV violence and acting aggressively.

For one thing, people who tend to be aggressive may prefer to watch more violent TV programs *and* behave aggressively toward others. Thus, personality may account for the observed correlations. Second, perhaps poverty, unemployment, or the effects of drugs and alcohol leave certain people both with more time to watch television *and* with frustration or other stressors that trigger aggressive behavior. One study tested this possibility by comparing the childhood television-viewing habits of forty-eight inmates imprisoned for violent crimes to those of forty-five noncriminals with similar socioeconomic backgrounds (Heath, Kruttschnitt & Ward, 1986). There was no significant difference between the groups' reported television watching as children, suggesting that early viewing habits did not create the difference in aggressiveness.

Finally, the results of controlled experiments on the effects of televised violence may lack generality (Freedman, 1988). Who is to say, for example, whether an increase in aggressive acts during a hockey game has any later bearing on a child's tendency to commit an act of violence?

What additional evidence would help to evaluate the alternatives?

By their nature, correlational studies of observed TV violence and violent behavior can never be conclusive because, as noted, a third, unidentified causal variable could always be responsible for the results. More important would be further evidence from controlled experiments in which equivalent groups of people are given different, long-term "doses" of TV violence and its effects on their subsequent behavior are observed. Such experiments could also explore the circumstances under which different people (for example, children versus adults) are affected by various forms of violence. However, studies like these create a potential ethical dilemma. If watching violent television programs does cause violent behavior, are psychologists justified in creating conditions that might lead some people to be more violent? If such violence occurred, would the researchers be partly responsible to the victims and to society? If some subjects commit violent acts, should the researchers continue the experiment to establish a pattern, or should they terminate these subjects' participation? Difficulty in answering questions like these is partly responsible for the prevalence of short-term experiments and correlational research in this area and for some of the remaining uncertainty about the effects of television violence.

It would also be important to better understand how observed violence relates to other causes of aggressive behavior, some of which are discussed in Chapter 18.

What conclusions are most reasonable?

The preponderance of evidence collected so far makes it reasonable to conclude that watching TV violence may be one cause of violent behavior. But any cause-effect relationship between watching TV violence and acting violently is not an inevitable one, and there are many circumstances in which the effect does not occur (Freedman, 1992; Widom, 1989). Parents, peers, and other environmental influences, along with personality factors, may dampen or amplify the effect of watching televised violence. Indeed, not every viewer cognitively interprets violence in the same way, and not every viewer is equally vulnerable (Wood, Wong & Chachere, 1991). Those most vulnerable may be those who are most aggressive or violence-prone in the first place, a trait that could well have been acquired by observing the behavior of parents or peers.

Still, the fact that violence on television *can* have a causal impact on violent behavior is reason for serious concern and continues to influence public debate about what should, and should not, be aired on television.

Neural Networks

The cognitive approach emphasizes that learning involves more than simple associations between conditioned stimuli and reflexes or between responses and their consequences, but are we to conclude that such associations are unimportant? No. Associations play an important role even in the mental processes that allow us to understand which events predict which other events. As a result of experience, some things remind us of other things, which remind us of still others, and so on.

How are associations actually stored in the brain? No one yet knows for sure, but the process probably involves a *network* of neural connections like those described in network models of feature recognition (Hintzman, 1991). These associative networks can be very complex. Consider the word *dog*. As shown in Figure 7.17, each person's experience builds many associations to this word, and the strength of each association will reflect the frequency with which "dog" has been mentally linked to the other concepts in that person's life.

Using what they know about the laws of learning and about the way neurons communicate and alter their synaptic connections, psychologists have been trying to discover the principles governing how these associations are established. We discussed some of these efforts in Chapter 5 in terms of *neural networks* and *parallel distributed processing* models of how perception takes place. A key aspect of such models is the idea of *distributed memory* or *distributed knowledge* (see Chapter 8, on memory). These models suggest, for example, that the knowledge of "dog" does not lie in a single location, or *node,* within the brain. Instead, knowledge is distributed throughout the network of associations that connect the letters *D, O,* and *G,* along with other "doglike" experiences. In addition, as shown in Figure 7.17, each of the interconnected nodes that makes up your knowledge of "dog" is also connected to many other nodes. Thus, the letter *D* will be connected to "Daisy," "Danger," and a host of other things.

Neural network models of learning focus on how these connections are laid down as a function of experience (Hanson & Burr, 1990). For example, suppose you are learning a new word in a foreign language. Each time you read the word and associate it with its English equivalent, you strengthen the neural connections between the sight of the letters forming that word and all of the nodes activated when its English equivalent is brought to mind. Neural network or *connectionist* models of learning predict how much the strength of each linkage grows (in terms of the likelihood of neural communication between the two connected nodes) each time the two words are experienced together.

The details of various theories about how these connections grow are very complex (see Schwartz & Reisberg, 1991; Hanson & Burr, 1990), but a theme common to many is that the weaker the connection between two items, the greater the *increase* in con-

FIGURE 7.17

An Associative Network

Here is an example of a network of associations to the concept of "dog." Network theorists suggest that the connections shown here represent patterns of neural connections in the brain.

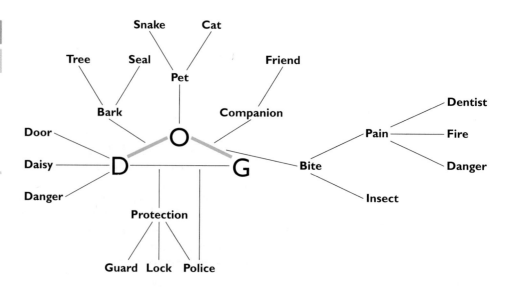

nection strength when they are experienced together. Thus, in a simple classical conditioning experiment, the connections between the nodes characterizing the UCS and those characterizing the CS will show the greatest increase in strength during the first few learning trials. Notice that this prediction nicely matches the typical learning curve shown in Figure 7.3 (Rescorla & Wagner, 1972).

Few neural network models today can handle the learning of complex tasks, nor can they easily account for how people adapt when the "rules of the game" are suddenly changed and old habits must be unlearned and replaced (Hintzman, 1991). Nevertheless, a better understanding of what we mean by associations may very well lie in future research on neural network models (Tryon, 1995).

USING RESEARCH ON LEARNING TO HELP PEOPLE LEARN

Teaching and training—explicit efforts to assist learners in mastering a specific skill or body of material—are major aspects of socialization in virtually every culture. The study of how people learn thus has important implications for improved teaching in our schools (Glaser & Bassok, 1989; Tharinger et al., 1996) and for helping people develop skills ranging from typing to tennis.

Classrooms Across Cultures

For centuries, education in Western cultures was guided by the principle of *formal discipline* (Halpern, 1989). Proponents of this principle argued that the mind has certain elemental abilities that are strengthened through practice. Accordingly, they believed that wrestling with difficult concepts enhances mental abilities, just as weight lifting increases physical strength. Formal discipline curricula were built around Latin, literature, mathematics, and other demanding courses that could improve students' mental functioning whether or not students would ever use the *specific* information they learned.

Edward Thorndike (1914), of puzzle box fame, was among the first to challenge the value of formal discipline. Thorndike saw education as a "transfer of training" problem. He claimed that what is learned in the classroom is valuable only to the degree that it can be transferred to, and used in, the student's life. Thorndike proposed an *identical elements* theory, which argues that material taught in school should have clear generalizability, or relevance, to the settings in which students will later find themselves.

Educational psychologists are still debating the degree to which school curricula should be based on formal discipline or identical elements. Controlled laboratory studies on the consequences of each are difficult to perform, and even research using the quasi-experimental approach outlined in Chapter 2 is inconclusive (Detterman, 1993). At present, the identical elements approach is dominant in U.S. educational systems, largely because it arises from laboratory data on transfer of training and makes intuitive sense to many teachers, parents, and students.

At the same time, many people believe that America's schools are not doing a very good job (Cannon-Bowers et al., 1991; Chronicle of Higher Education, 1992). The average performance of U.S. students on tests of reading, math, and other basic academic skills has tended to fall short of that of youngsters in other countries, especially Asian countries (U.S. Department of Commerce, 1992; Stigler, 1992). In one comparison study, Harold Stevenson (1992) followed a sample of pupils in Taiwan, Japan, and the United States from first grade, in 1980, to eleventh grade in 1991. In the first grade, the Asian students scored no higher than their U.S. peers on tests of mathematical aptitude, nor did they enjoy math more. And there were only small differences in mathematical skills between U.S. and Asian first-graders. However, by the fifth grade the U.S. students had fallen far behind. Corresponding differences were seen in reading skills.

The most important potential causes of these differences were found in the classroom itself. In a typical U.S. classroom session, teachers talked to students as a group;

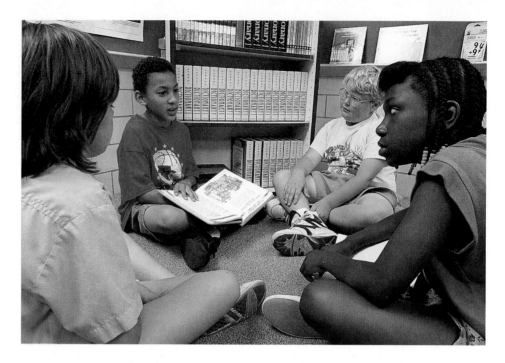

RECIPROCAL TEACHING Ann Brown and her colleagues (1992) have demonstrated the success of *reciprocal teaching,* in which children take turns actively teaching each other, a technique that closely parallels the cooperative arrangements characteristic of Japanese early education.

then students worked at their desks independently. Reinforcement or other feedback about performance on their work was usually delayed until the next day or, often, not provided at all. In contrast, the typical Japanese classroom placed greater emphasis on cooperative work between students. Teachers provided more immediate feedback on a one-to-one basis. And there was an emphasis on creating teams of students with varying abilities, a situation in which faster learners help teach slower ones. The Japanese children also practiced more: They spent more days in school during the year and on average spent more time doing homework. Interestingly, they were also given longer recesses than U.S. students and had more opportunities to get away from the classroom during a typical school day.

Although the significance of these cultural differences in learning and teaching is not yet clear, the educational community in the United States is paying attention to them. Indeed, psychologists and educators are considering how principles of learning can be applied to improve education (Tharinger et al., 1996). For example, one study concluded that the most successful educational techniques apply basic principles of operant conditioning, offering positive reinforcement for correct performance and immediate corrective feedback following mistakes (Walberg, 1987).

Teaching Machines Can machines help provide such feedback? For decades, psychologists have been working on "teaching machines" that offer automatic, but individualized, programs of instruction and rewards for progress (Holland, 1960). The first such machine—developed in 1925 by Sidney Pressey (1926)—did little more than present multiple-choice questions in a window area on a rotating drum device. It was not until after B. F. Skinner's machine appeared in 1954 that automated teaching and programmed instruction gained popularity in U.S. schools (Skinner, 1958). The window area of his device presented course material, with some words left blank. Students read the material, filled in the blanks, then discovered if their responses were correct. Skinner's idea was to use immediate reinforcement to shape correct responses to gradually more difficult tasks while minimizing frustrating errors. Today, computerized teaching machines use the same principle, but they also feature an interactive capability that allows student and computer to "talk" to one another. Using artificial intelligence systems of the type described in Chapter 9, these new machines can constantly adjust the level of instruction to meet the needs of each student (Anderson, 1995).

Active Learning

The importance of cognitive processes in learning is apparent in instructional methods that emphasize *active learning* (Bonwell & Eison, 1991). These methods take many forms, including, for example, small-group problem-solving tasks, discussion of "one-minute essays" written in class, use of "thumbs up" or "thumbs down" to indicate agreement or disagreement with the instructor's assertions, and multiple-choice questions that give students feedback about their understanding of the previous fifteen minutes of lecture. There is little doubt that, for many students, the inclusion of active learning experiences makes classes more interesting and enjoyable (Mehta, 1995). Active learning methods also help students to go beyond memorizing isolated facts by encouraging them to think more deeply about new information, consider how it relates to what they already know, and apply it in new situations.

The elaborate mental processing associated with active learning makes new information not only more personally meaningful but also, as described in Chapter 8, easier to remember. Indeed, active learning strategies have been found to be superior to passive teaching methods in a number of experiments with children and adults (Meyers & Jones, 1993). Consider this simple study of questioning methods in a fifth-grade science class. On some days, the teacher called on only those students whose hands were raised; the rest listened passively. On other days, *all* students were required to answer *every* question by holding up a card on which they had written their response. Scores on next-day quizzes and bi-weekly tests showed that students remembered more of the material covered on the active learning days than on the "passive" days (Gardner, Heward & Grossi, 1994). Similarly, in two consecutive medical school classes taught by the same instructor, scores on the final exam were significantly higher when students learned mainly through small-group discussions and case studies than mainly through lectures (Chu, 1994). Among adults being taught to use a new computer program, active learning through "hands-on" practice was more effective than passively watching a demonstration video (Kerr & Payne, 1994). Finally, high school and college students who passively listened to a physics lecture received significantly lower scores on a test of lecture content than did those who participated in a virtual reality lab that allowed them to actively "interact" with the physical forces covered in the lecture (Brelsford, 1993). Results such as these have fueled the popularity of active learning methods, but rigorous experimental research is still needed to compare their short- and long-term effects with those of more traditional methods in the teaching of different kinds of material.

Skill Learning

The complex action sequences, or *skills,* that people learn to perform in everyday life—tying a shoe, opening doors, operating a computer, shooting a basketball, driving a car—develop through direct and vicarious learning processes involving imitation, instructions, reinforcement, and, of course, lots of practice. Some skills, like those of a basketball player or violinist, demand exceptional perceptual-motor coordination. Others, like those involved in scientific thinking, have a large cognitive component, requiring rapid understanding. In either case, the learning of skills usually involves practice and feedback.

Practice—the repeated performance of a skill—is the most critical component of skill learning. For perceptual-motor skills, both physical and mental practice are beneficial (Druckman & Bjork, 1994). To be most effective, practice should continue past the point of correct performance until the skill can be performed automatically, with little or no attention. For many cognitive skills, what counts most seems to be practice in retrieving relevant information from memory. Trying to recall and write down facts that you have read, for example, is a more effective learning tool than simply reading them a second time—as active learning research would predict.

Large amounts of guidance may produce very good performance during practice, but too much of it may impair later performance (Wickens, 1992). Coaching students about correct responses in math, for example, may impair their ability later to retrieve

LEARNING FROM MISTAKES   Coaches often give intense feedback on performance to prevent the learner from making mistakes. But making mistakes—and learning to correct them—can be a key aspect of skill learning. If the learner comes to rely on the "crutch" of feedback, skill development may be impaired.

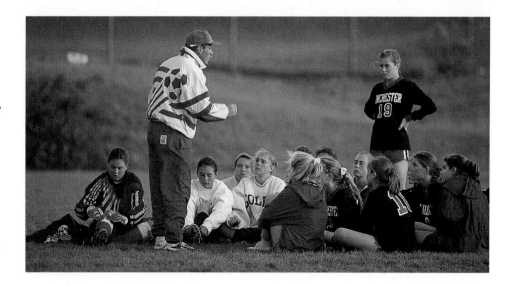

the correct response from memory on their own. Independent practice at retrieving previously learned responses or information requires more effort, but it is critical for skill development (Ericsson & Charness, 1994; Ericsson, Krampe & Tesch-Römer, 1993). Indeed, there is little or no evidence to support "sleep learning" or similar schemes designed to make learning effortless (Druckman & Bjork, 1994; Phelps & Exum, 1992). In short, "no pain, no gain."

So the most effective practice is carried out by learners who make independent choices and actions, but what if those choices are wrong? Suppose that a grade schooler starts "flailing" while practicing multiplication tables, coming up with essentially random answers. Clearly, in this case it is necessary to provide *feedback* about the correctness of the response. Our discussion of operant conditioning emphasized the importance for learning of prompt feedback in the form of reinforcement or punishment. But certain forms of feedback may not aid skill learning (Schmidt & Bjork, 1992). If given too soon after an action occurs or while it is still taking place, feedback may divert the learner's attention from understanding how that action was achieved and what it felt like to perform it. Similarly, if detailed feedback occurs for virtually everything the learner does, it can have the same negative effects as too much guidance during practice.

FUTURE DIRECTIONS

In more than a hundred years of intense research, psychologists have discovered many important laws of learning, but they want to know more. For example, researchers are exploring the similarities and differences between the most automatic, stimulus-bound—often subconscious—forms of learning and the learning that involves interpretation, reasoning, insight, and other cognitive processes.

Research will continue on the role of classical conditioning in a wide range of phenomena, including activation of the body's immune system and internal pain-control mechanisms. Indeed, as researchers recognize both the expanded role of classical conditioning in human behavior and the importance of cognitive processes in other animals, the principles of human and animal learning will draw closer to each other. This linkage of human and animal learning will be encouraged by the continued development of neural network models of learning, because the associations at the heart of these models are criti-

cal in both classical conditioning and cognitive learning. The development of computer-based artificial neural networks that can accurately imitate all forms of learning is a very exciting direction for future research. Recognition of the importance of neural networks might finally end the debate between behaviorists and cognitive psychologists over the nature of learning (Tryon, 1995). Other work will focus on the role that brain chemical processes play in both the consolidation of learning and the operation of reinforcers (Weisskopf & Nicoll, 1995).

Psychologists, educators, and trainers will continue to apply learning principles from the laboratory in an effort to more effectively teach academic information, improve employees' skills, and enhance athletic performance (Bonwell & Eison, 1991; Petrie & Diehl, 1995; Tharinger et al., 1996). Active learning methods are likely to be prominent in these efforts. Teaching will be aided by computers that provide instruction through artificial intelligence (Anderson, 1995) and virtual reality (Stansfield, 1994; see also Chapter 5). As in the physics-lab study mentioned earlier, virtual environments in which students can practice skills and "interact" with course materials may offer ideal active learning opportunities. Indeed, virtual reality systems are already being used to help train surgeons and prepare astronauts for spacewalks on Shuttle missions (Durlach & Mavor, 1995; Testa, 1994).

Unfortunately, virtual reality entertainment systems may also allow people to observe and "participate" in virtual violence that is more compelling than anything now available on television (Sheridan, 1993). Psychologists will undoubtedly explore the effects of such experiences on aggressiveness. They will also assist in the creation of training programs designed to sensitize children to the effects of violence in the real world and maybe even inoculate them against the potentially negative influences of televised or virtual entertainment (Vooijs & van der Voort, 1993).

To learn more about the field of learning, consider taking a course or two in the area. Some learning courses include laboratory sections that allow active learning about the principles of human and animal learning.

VIRTUAL SURGERY Using a virtual reality system called "Surgery in 3–D," this medical student at the University of North Carolina can learn and practice eye surgery techniques before working with real patients.

SUMMARY AND KEY TERMS

Individuals adapt to changes in the environment through the process of *learning*, which is the modification through experience of pre-existing behavior and understanding.

■ CLASSICAL CONDITIONING: LEARNING SIGNALS AND ASSOCIATIONS

Pavlov's Discovery

One form of learning is *classical conditioning*. It occurs when a *conditioned stimulus*, or *CS* (such as a tone), is repeatedly paired with an *unconditioned stimulus*, or *UCS* (such as meat powder on a dog's tongue), which naturally brings about an *unconditioned response*, or *UCR* (such as salivation). Eventually the conditioned stimulus will elicit a response, known as the *conditioned response*, or *CR*, even when the unconditioned stimulus is not presented.

Conditioned Responses Over Time: Extinction and Spontaneous Recovery

In general, the strength of a conditioned response grows as CS-UCS pairings continue. If the UCS is no longer paired with the CS, the conditioned response eventually disappears; this is *extinction*. After extinction, the conditioned response often reappears if the CS is presented after some time; this is *spontaneous recovery*. In addition, if the conditioned and unconditioned stimuli are paired once or twice after extinction, *reconditioning* occurs; that is, the conditioned response reverts to its original strength.

Stimulus Generalization and Discrimination

Because of *stimulus generalization*, conditioned responses occur to stimuli that are similar but not identical to conditioned stimuli. Generalization is limited by *stimulus discrimination*, which prompts conditioned responses to some stimuli but not to others.

The Signaling of Significant Events

Classical conditioning involves learning that the CS is an event that predicts the occurrence of another event, the UCS. The conditioned response is not just an automatic reflex but a means through which

animals and people develop mental models of the relation between events. Classical conditioning works best when the conditioned stimulus precedes the unconditioned stimulus, an arrangement known as forward conditioning. In general, a conditioned response develops best if the interval between the CS and UCS is no more than about one second. Conditioning is also more likely when the CS reliably signals the UCS. In general, the strength of a conditioned response and the speed of conditioning increase as the intensity of the UCS—and the strength or salience of the CS—increase. The particular CS likely to be linked to a subsequent UCS depends in part on which stimulus was being attended to when the UCS occurred. *Second-order conditioning* occurs when a CS becomes powerful enough to make CSs out of stimuli associated with it. Some stimuli are easier to associate than others; organisms seem to be biologically prepared to learn certain associations, as exemplified by taste aversions.

Some Applications of Classical Conditioning

Research suggests that changes in the body's immune response can be classically conditioned. Classical conditioning also plays a role in the development and treatment of phobias and in the humane control of predators in the wild.

■ LINKAGES: LEARNING AND CONSCIOUSNESS

People adapt, or become habituated, to events that are repeated often. According to Solomon's opponent-process theory, habituation is the result of a relatively automatic, involuntary A-Process—essentially an unconditioned response—and a conditioned B-Process that follows and counteracts the A-Process. This theory may help explain drug tolerance and some cases of drug overdose.

■ INSTRUMENTAL AND OPERANT CONDITIONING: LEARNING THE CONSEQUENCES OF BEHAVIOR

Learning occurs not only through associating stimuli but also through associating behavior with its consequences.

From the Puzzle Box to the Skinner Box

The *law of effect*, postulated by Edward Thorndike, holds that any response that produces satisfaction becomes more likely to occur again and any response that produces discomfort becomes less likely. He called this type of learning *instrumental conditioning*. Skinner called the process *operant conditioning*. In operant conditioning the organism is free to respond at any time, and conditioning is measured by the rate of responding. In most respects, instrumental and operant conditioning are alike.

Basic Components of Operant Conditioning

An *operant* is a response that has some effect on the world. A *reinforcer* increases the probability that the operant preceding it will occur again; in other words, reinforcers strengthen behavior. There are two types of reinforcers: *Positive reinforcers,* which strengthen a response if they are presented after that response occurs, and *negative reinforcers,* which strengthen a response if they are removed after it occurs. Both escape conditioning and avoidance conditioning are the result of negative reinforcement. *Escape conditioning* results when behavior terminates a negative reinforcer. *Avoidance conditioning* results when behavior avoids a negative reinforcer; it reflects both classical and operant conditioning. Behaviors learned through avoidance conditioning are very resistant to extinction. *Discriminative stimuli* indicate whether reinforcement is available for a particular behavior.

Forming and Strengthening Operant Behavior

Complex responses can be learned through *shaping*, which involves reinforcing successive approximations of the desired response. *Primary reinforcers* are inherently rewarding; *secondary reinforcers* are rewards that people or animals learn to like because of their association with primary reinforcers. In general, operant conditioning proceeds more quickly when the delay in receiving reinforcement is short rather than long, and when the reinforcer is large rather than small. Reinforcement may be delivered on a *continuous reinforcement schedule* or on one of four basic types of *partial*, or *intermittent*, *reinforcement schedules: fixed ratio (FR), variable ratio (VR), fixed interval (FI),* and *variable interval (VI)*. Ratio schedules lead to a rapid rate of responding. Behavior learned through partial reinforcement, particularly through variable schedules, is very resistant to extinction; this phenomenon is called the *partial reinforcement extinction effect*. Partial reinforcement is involved in superstitious behavior, which results when a response is coincidentally followed by a reinforcer.

Why Reinforcers Work

Psychologists are not certain what makes reinforcers rewarding, but activity preference hierarchies and activity in the brain's pleasure centers are two possibilities.

Punishment and Learning

Punishment decreases the frequency of a behavior by following it either with an unpleasant stimulus or with the removal of a pleasant one. Punishment modifies behavior but has several drawbacks. It only suppresses behavior; fear of punishment may generalize to the person doing the punishing; it is ineffective when delayed; it can be physically harmful and may teach aggressiveness; and it teaches only what not to do, not what should be done to obtain reinforcement.

Operant Conditioning of Human Behavior

The principles of operant conditioning have been used in many spheres of life, from the teaching of everyday social skills to treatment of overeating and sleep disorders to classroom education.

■ COGNITIVE PROCESSES IN LEARNING

Cognitive processes—how people represent, store, and use information—play an important role in learning.

Learned Helplessness

Learned helplessness appears to result when people believe that their behavior has no effect on the world.

Latent Learning and Cognitive Maps

Both animals and humans display *latent learning*. They also form *cognitive maps* of their environments, even in the absence of any reinforcement for doing so.

Insight and Learning

Experiments on *insight* also suggest that cognitive processes play an important role in learning, even by animals.

Observational Learning: Learning by Imitation

The process of learning by watching others is called *observational learning*, or social learning. Some observational learning occurs through *vicarious conditioning*, in which one is influenced by seeing or hearing about the consequences of others' behavior. Observational learning is more likely to occur when the person observed is rewarded for the observed behavior. Observational learning is a powerful source of socialization.

Neural Networks

According to neural network models, the associations so vital to learning are stored as a network of connections in the brain. These models emphasize that specific knowledge is distributed throughout an associative network of neural connections.

■ USING RESEARCH ON LEARNING TO HELP PEOPLE LEARN

Research on how people learn has implications for improved teaching and for the development of a wide range of skills.

Classrooms Across Cultures

The principle of generalizability suggests that school curricula should contain material that students will find useful outside the classroom. The degree to which other learning principles, such as immediate reinforcement, are used in teaching varies considerably from culture to culture.

Active Learning

The importance of cognitive processes in learning is seen in active learning methods designed to encourage people to think deeply about and apply new information instead of just memorizing isolated facts.

Skill Learning

Observational learning, practice, and corrective feedback play important roles in the learning of skills.

MEMORY

CHAPTER 8

LINKAGES

TO

MEMORY

BIOLOGICAL ASPECTS
OF PSYCHOLOGY

**Where are memories
stored?** *(ans. on p. 257)*

HUMAN DEVELOPMENT

**Why does memory improve
during childhood?**
(ans. on p. 397)

PERCEPTION

**How accurate is eyewitness
testimony?** *(ans. on p. 255)*

S everal years ago an air-traffic controller at Los Angeles International Airport cleared a USAir flight to land on runway 24L. A couple of minutes later, the USAir pilot radioed the control tower that he was on approach for runway 24L, but the controller did not reply because she was preoccupied by a confusing exchange with another pilot. After finishing that conversation, the controller told a SkyWest commuter pilot to taxi onto runway 24L for takeoff, completely forgetting about the USAir flight that was about to land on the same runway. The USAir jet hit the commuter plane, killing thirty-four people. The controller's forgetting was so complete that she assumed the fireball from the crash was an exploding bomb. How could the controller's memory have failed her at such a crucial time?

Memory is full of paradoxes. It is common, for example, for people to remember the name of their first-grade teacher but not the name of someone they met just a minute ago. And consider Rajan Mahadevan. He once set a world's record by reciting from memory the first 31,811 places of *pi* (the ratio of the circumference of a circle to its diameter), but on repeated visits to the psychology building at the University of Minnesota, he had trouble recalling the location of the nearest restroom (Biederman et al., 1992). Like perception, memory is selective. While people retain a great deal of information, they also lose a great deal (Bjork & Vanhuele, 1992).

As the Linkages diagram suggests, memory is intimately tied to many other aspects of psychology. Without memory, you would not know how to shut off your alarm clock, take a shower, get dressed, or recognize objects. You would be unable to communicate with other people because you would not remember what words mean, or even what you had just said. You would be unaware of your own likes and dislikes, and you would have no idea of who you were in any meaningful sense (Kihlstrom, 1993; Vorauer & Ross, 1993). In this chapter we describe what is known about both memory and forgetting.

THE NATURE OF MEMORY

Mathematician John Griffith estimated that, in an average lifetime, a person will have stored roughly five hundred times as much information as can be found in all the volumes of the *Encyclopedia Britannica* (Hunt, 1982). The impressive capacity of human memory depends on the operation of a complex mental system.

228

Basic Memory Processes

We know a psychologist who sometimes drives to work and sometimes walks. On one occasion, he drove, forgot that he had driven, and walked home. When he failed to find his car in its normal spot the next morning, he reported the car stolen. The police soon called to say that "some college kids" had probably stolen the car because it was found on campus (next to the psychology building!). What went wrong? There are several possibilities, because memory depends on three basic processes—encoding, storage, and retrieval (see Figure 8.1).

First, information must be put into memory, a step that requires **encoding.** Just as incoming sensory information must be coded so that it can be communicated to the brain, information to be remembered must be put in a form that the memory system can accept and use. In the memory system, sensory information is put into various *memory codes,* which are mental representations of physical stimuli. For example, **acoustic codes** represent information as sequences of sounds. **Visual codes** represent stimuli as pictures. **Semantic codes** represent an experience by its general meaning. Thus, if you see a billboard that reads "Huey's Going Out of Business Sale," you might encode the sound of the words as if they had been spoken (acoustic coding), the image of the letters as they were arranged on the sign (visual coding), or the fact that you saw an ad for Huey's (semantic coding). The type of coding used can influence what is remembered. For example, semantic coding might allow you to remember that a car was parked in your neighbors' driveway just before their house was robbed. If there was little or no other coding, however, you might not be able to remember the make, model, or color of the car.

The second basic memory process is **storage,** which refers to the maintenance of information over time, often over a very long time. When you find it possible to use a pogo stick or to recall a vacation from many years ago, you are depending on the storage capacity of your memory.

The third process, **retrieval,** occurs when you find information stored in memory and bring it into consciousness. Retrieving stored information such as your address or telephone number is usually so fast and effortless it seems automatic. Only when you try to retrieve other kinds of information—such as the answer to a quiz question that you know but cannot quite recall—do you become aware of the searching process. Retrieval processes include both recall and recognition. To *recall* information, as on an essay test, you have to retrieve it from memory without much help. *Recognition* is aided by clues, such as the alternatives given in a multiple-choice test item. Accordingly, recognition tends to be easier than recall.

Types of Memory

In which hand does the Statue of Liberty hold her torch? When was the last time you spent cash for something? What part of speech is used to modify a noun? Your attempt to answer the first question is likely to elicit a visual image; in order to answer the second, you must recall a particular event in your life; and the third question requires general knowledge that is unlikely to be tied to a specific event. Some theorists suggest that

FIGURE 8.1

Basic Memory Processes

Remembering something requires, first, that the item be encoded—put in a form that can be placed in memory. It must then be stored and, finally, retrieved, or recovered. If any of these processes fails, forgetting will occur.

Encoding Code and put into memory	Storage Maintain in memory	Retrieval Recover from memory
Types of memory codes ■ Acoustic ■ Visual ■ Semantic	Types of long- term memories ■ Episodic ■ Procedural ■ Semantic	Types of retrieval ■ Recall ■ Recognition

DRAWING ON MEMORIES   The human memory system allows people to encode, store, and retrieve a lifetime of experiences. Without it, you would have no sense of who you are.

LINKAGES: LEARNING BY DOING   Procedural memories involve skills that can usually be learned only through repetition. This is why parents not only tell children how to tie a shoe but also show them the steps and then let them practice. Factors that enhance skill learning are described in Chapter 7.

answering each of these questions requires a different type of memory (Brewer & Pani, 1984). How many types of memory are there? No one is sure, but most research suggests that there are at least three basic types. Each type of memory is named for the kind of information it handles: episodic, semantic, and procedural (Reed, 1992).

Any memory of a specific event that happened while you were present is an **episodic memory**—such as what you had for dinner yesterday, what you did last summer, or where you were last Friday night. **Semantic memory** contains generalized knowledge of the world that does not involve memory of a specific event. For example, you can answer a question like "Are wrenches pets or tools?" without remembering any specific episode in which you learned that wrenches are tools. As a general rule, people convey episodic memories by saying, "I remember when . . . ," whereas they convey semantic memories by saying, "I know that . . ." (Tulving, 1982). **Procedural memory,** which involves the *skill learning* discussed in Chapter 7, provides the memory for how to do things—how to ride a bike, read a map, or tie a shoelace, for example. Often, a procedural memory consists of a complicated sequence of movements that cannot be described adequately in words. For example, a gymnast might find it impossible to describe the exact motions in a particular routine.

Many activities require all three types of memory. Consider the game of tennis. Knowing the official rules or how many sets are needed to win a match involves semantic memory. Remembering which side served last requires episodic memory. Knowing how to lob or volley involves procedural memory.

Explicit and Implicit Memory

For many years, psychologists interested in memory focused most of their research on **explicit memory,** the processes through which people deliberately try to remember something (Masson & MacLeod, 1992). When you try to remember where you went on your last vacation or tell someone where you were born, you are using explicit memory. In contrast, **implicit memory** is the unintentional recollection and influence of prior experiences (Nelson, Schreiber & McEvoy, 1992). For example, while watching a movie about a long car trip, you might begin to feel anxious because you subconsciously recall the time you had engine trouble on such a trip. Implicit memory operates automatically and without conscious effort.

It is not surprising that experience affects how people behave. What is surprising is that they are often unaware that their actions have been influenced by previous events.

Because some influential events cannot be recalled even when people try to do so, implicit memory has been said to involve "retention without remembering" (Roediger, 1990). We mention some examples of this phenomenon in Chapters 5 and 6 in our discussions of subliminal perception and subconscious information processing.

In Canada, Endel Tulving and his colleagues undertook a series of experiments to map the differences between explicit and implicit memory (Tulving, Schacter & Stark, 1982). He knew he could measure explicit memory by giving a recognition test in which subjects simply said which words on a list they remembered seeing on a previous list. The problem was to find a way to measure implicit memory. How did Tulving solve this problem?

FOCUS ON RESEARCH METHODS

Measuring Explicit Versus Implicit Memory

First, he asked the participants in his experiment to study a long list of words (the "study list"). An hour later, they took a recognition test of explicit memory—saying which words on a new list had been on the original study list. Then, to test their implicit memory, Tulving asked the participants to perform a "fragment completion" task (Warrington & Weiskrantz, 1970). In this task, they were shown a word fragment such as *d-l--iu-* and asked to complete the word *(delirium)*. On the basis of priming studies such as those described in Chapter 6, Tulving assumed that memory from a previous exposure to the correct word would improve the subjects' ability to complete the fragment, even if they were unable to consciously recall having seen the word before. A week later, all participants took a second test of their explicit and implicit memory of the study list. As before, some of the words on this second test's list had been on the study list, but none had been used in the first set of memory tests.

The independent variable in this experiment, then, was the amount of time that elapsed since the participants read the study list (one hour versus one week), and the dependent variable was performance on each of the two types of memory tests. As shown in Figure 8.2, explicit memory for the study list decreased dramatically over time, but implicit memory was virtually unchanged. Results from several other experiments also show that the passage of time affects one type of memory but not the other (Komatsu & Naito, 1992; Mitchell, 1991). For example, it appears that the aging process has fewer negative effects on implicit memory than on explicit memory (Light, 1991).

The work of Tulving and others supports the idea of a *dissociation*, or independence, between explicit and implicit memory, suggesting that the two may operate on different principles (Gabrieli et al., 1995). Indeed, some researchers believe that explicit and implicit memory may involve the activity of distinct neural systems in the brain (Squire, 1987; Tulving & Schacter, 1990). Psychologists are now studying the role of implicit memory (and dissociations between explicit and implicit memory) in such important psychological phenomena as amnesia (Schacter, Church & Treadwell, 1994; Tulving, 1993), depression (Elliott & Greene, 1992), problem solving (Jacoby, Marriott & Collins, 1990), stereotyping (Smith, 1990), the development of self-concept in childhood (Nelson, 1993), and even the power of ads to associate brand names with good feelings (Duke & Carlson, 1993).

FIGURE 8.2

Measures of Explicit and Implicit Memory

This experiment showed that the passage of time greatly affected people's recognition (explicit memory) of a word list but left fragment completion (implicit memory) essentially intact. Results such as these indicate that explicit and implicit memory may be fundamentally different memory systems.

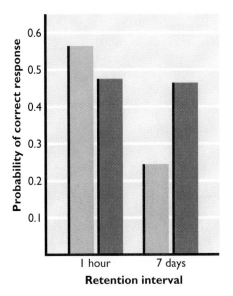

▓ Recognition (explicit)

█ Fragment completion (implicit)

Source: Tulving, Schacter & Stark, 1982.

Models of Memory

People remember some information far better and longer than other information. For example, suppose your friends throw a surprise party for you. Upon entering the room, you might barely notice, and later fail to recall, the flash from a camera. And you might forget in a few seconds the name of a person you met at the party. But if you live to be a hundred, you will never forget where the party took place or how surprised and pleased you were. Why do some stimuli leave no more than a fleeting impression and others remain in memory forever? In the following sections we examine four theoretical models of memory, each of which provides an explanation for this phenomenon.

Levels of Processing   The **levels-of-processing model** suggests that the most important determinant of memory is how extensively information is encoded or processed when it is first received. Consider situations in which people try to memorize something by mentally *rehearsing* it. There appear to be two basic types of mental rehearsal: maintenance and elaborative. **Maintenance rehearsal** involves simply repeating an item over and over. This method can be effective for remembering information for a short time. If you need to look up a phone number, walk across the room, and then dial the number, maintenance rehearsal would work just fine. But what if you need to remember something for hours or months or years? Far more effective in these cases is **elaborative rehearsal,** which involves thinking about how new material relates to information already stored in memory. For example, instead of trying to remember a new person's name by simply repeating it to yourself, try thinking about how the name is related to something you already know. If you are introduced to a man named Jim Crews, you might think, "He is as tall as my Uncle Jim, who always wears a crew cut."

Study after study has shown that memory is enhanced when people use elaborative rather than maintenance rehearsal (Anderson, 1990). According to the levels-of-processing model, this enhancement occurs because of the degree or "depth" to which

Drawing by Roz Chast; © 1995. The New Yorker Magazine. Inc.

incoming information is mentally processed during elaborative rehearsal. The more you think about new information, organize it, and relate it to existing knowledge, the "deeper" the processing, and the better your memory of it becomes.

Even when people are not trying to memorize information, their level of processing affects their memory. In one series of studies, for example, people were shown a long list of words but not asked to memorize them. Instead, some of the people were asked to indicate whether each word was printed in capital or small letters, a task that requires very shallow processing (the words do not even have to be read). After performing the task, these people showed very poor memory for the words. Other people were asked whether each word rhymed with some other word, a task requiring a slightly deeper level of processing; these people showed better memory for the words. Finally, some people were asked to say whether each word described their own behavior, a task that required a much deeper level of processing. This group showed the best memory for the words (Bellezza, 1993).

The most important conclusion to be drawn from levels-of-processing research is that memory is much more strongly determined by internal factors, such as how people think about information and whether they relate it to existing knowledge, than by external factors, such as how the information is displayed (Craik & Lockhart, 1972).

Transfer-Appropriate Processing The levels-of-processing model has inspired important lines of experimentation, but level of processing is not the only determinant of memory (Baddeley, 1992). Consider an experiment in which people were shown a long list of words and asked to answer one of two questions about each word (Morris, Bransford & Franks, 1977). The questions were designed so that the subject would use either a semantic (meaning) code or a rhyming code (a version of acoustic coding). Thus, if the word was *house,* they would be asked either if "*house* is a type of building" or if "*house* rhymes with *mouse.*" Later, the subjects were asked to pick from a list those words they had been shown before.

Figure 8.3 shows the results. The subjects did much better at recognizing the words for which they had used a semantic code rather than a rhyming code. But when asked to pick out words that *rhymed* with the ones they had seen (for example, *grouse,* which rhymes with *house*), the subjects did much better at identifying words that rhymed with words on which they had used a rhyming code rather than a semantic code. Results like these inspired the concept of **transfer-appropriate processing,** which suggests that the critical determinant of memory is how the encoding process matches up with what is ultimately retrieved.

In another test of transfer-appropriate processing, half the students in a class were told that an exam would be multiple-choice, while the other half expected a series of essay questions. Only some of the students got the type of exam they expected, however. These students did much better on the exam than those who took an unexpected type of exam. Apparently, in studying for the exam the two groups used encoding strategies that were most appropriate to the type of exam they expected; those who tried to retrieve the information in a way that did not match their encoding method had greater difficulty (d'Ydewalle & Rosselle, 1978). Results like these indicate that how well the encoding method transfers to the retrieval setting is just as important as the depth of processing.

Parallel Distributed Processing Over the last thirty years, virtually all approaches to memory have conceptualized it as a system in which individual pieces of information are put in and taken out (Roediger, 1990). Today, some theorists are pursuing an approach based on **parallel distributed processing** (or **PDP**) models of memory. These models suggest that new experiences don't just provide new facts that are later retrieved individually; they also change people's overall knowledge base, altering in a more general way their understanding of the world and how it operates. For example, if you compare your knowledge of college life today with what it was when you first arrived, chances are it has changed day by day in a way that is much more general than any single new fact you learned.

FIGURE 8.3

The Match Between Encoding and Retrieval

People who were asked to recognize words seen earlier did better if they had encoded the words on the basis of their meaning (semantic coding) rather than on the basis of what they rhymed with. But if asked to identify words that *rhymed* with those seen before, they did better on those that had been encoded using a rhyming code. These results support the transfer-appropriate model of memory.

Semantic recognition test

Rhyming recognition test

FIGURE 8.4

The Three Stages of Memory

This traditional information-processing model analyzes the memory system into three stages.

Because our understanding of neural network processing is still very limited, PDP memory theorists begin by asking how neural networks *might* provide a functional memory system (Anderson, 1990). We describe the essential features of neural networks in Chapters 5 and 7, on perception and learning. In the case of memory, each unit of knowledge is ultimately connected to every other unit. The connections between units become stronger as they are experienced together more frequently. From this perspective, "knowledge" is distributed across a dense network of associations that allows people to quickly and efficiently draw inferences and generalizations. Just seeing the word *sofa*, for example, allows us to immediately gain access to knowledge about what a sofa looks like, what it is used for, where it tends to be located, who might buy one, and the like. PDP models of memory can account for this phenomenon very effectively.

Information Processing   Historically, the most influential and comprehensive theories of memory have been based on a general information-processing model (Roediger, 1990). The **information-processing model** originally suggested that in order for information to become firmly embedded in memory, it must pass through three stages of mental processing: sensory memory, short-term memory, and long-term memory (Atkinson & Shiffrin, 1968; see also Figure 8.4).

In *sensory memory,* information from the senses—sights or sounds, for example—is held in *sensory registers* for a very brief period of time, often less than one second. Information in the sensory registers may be attended to, analyzed, and encoded as a meaningful pattern; this is the process of *perception* discussed in Chapter 5. If the information in sensory memory is perceived, it can enter *short-term memory.* If nothing further is done, the information will disappear in about eighteen seconds. But if the information in short-term memory is further processed, it may be encoded into *long-term memory,* where it may remain indefinitely.

The act of reading illustrates all three stages of memory processing. As you read any of these sentences, for example, light energy reflected from the page is converted to neural activity and registered in sensory memory. If you pay attention to these stimuli, your perception of the patterns of light can be held in short-term memory. This stage of memory holds the early parts of the sentence so that they can be integrated and understood as you read the rest of the sentence. As you read, you are constantly recognizing words by matching your perceptions of them with the patterns and meanings

FIGURE 8.5

The Role of Memory in Comprehension

Read the passage shown here, then turn away and try to recall as much of it as possible. Then read the footnote on page 236 and reread the passage. The second reading probably made a lot more sense and was much easier to remember because knowing the title of the passage allowed you to retrieve from long-term memory your knowledge about the topic.

The procedure is actually quite simple. First, you arrange items into different groups. Of course, one pile may be sufficient, depending on how much there is to do. If you have to go somewhere else due to lack of facilities that is the next step; otherwise, you are pretty well set. It is important not to overdo things. That is, it is better to do too few things at once than too many. In the short run, this may not seem important, but complications can easily arise. A mistake can be expensive as well. At first, the whole procedure will seem complicated. Soon, however, it will become just another facet of life. It is difficult to foresee any end to the necessity for this task in the immediate future, but then, one never can tell. After the procedure is completed, one arranges the materials into different groups again. Then they can be put into their appropriate places. Eventually they will be used once more, and the whole cycle will then have to be repeated. However, that is part of life.

Source: Bransford & Johnson, 1972.

IN REVIEW	Models of Memory
Model	**Assumptions**
Levels of processing	The more deeply material is processed, the better the memory of it.
Transfer-appropriate processing	Retrieval is improved when we try to recall material in a way that matches how the material was encoded.
Parallel distributed processing (PDP)	New experiences add to and alter our overall knowledge base; they are not separate, unconnected facts. PDP networks allow us to draw inferences and make generalizations about the world.
Information processing	Information is processed in three stages: sensory, short-term, and long-term memory.

you have stored in long-term memory. Thus, all three stages are necessary for you to understand a sentence.

Contemporary versions of the information-processing model emphasize the constant interactions among sensory, short-term, and long-term memory (Massaro & Cowan, 1993). For example, sensory memory can be thought of as that part of one's knowledge base (or long-term memory) that is momentarily activated by information sent to the brain via the sensory nerves. And short-term memory can be thought of as that part of one's knowledge base that is the focus of attention at any given moment. Like perception, memory is a very active process, and what is already in long-term memory influences how new information is encoded (Cowan, 1988). To better understand this interaction, try the exercise in Figure 8.5. (Also see "In Review: Models of Memory" for a summary of the four models we have discussed.)

ACQUIRING NEW MEMORIES

Sensory, short-term, and long-term memory are each thought to provide a different type of storage system.

Sensory Memory

In order to recognize incoming stimuli, the brain must analyze and compare them to what is already stored in long-term memory. Although this process is very quick, it still takes time. The major function of **sensory memory** is to hold information long enough for it to be processed further. This maintenance is the job of the **sensory registers**, whose storage capability retains an almost complete representation of a sensory stimulus (Best, 1992). There is a separate register for each of the five senses, and every register is capable of storing a relatively large amount of stimulus information.

Memories held in the sensory registers are fleeting, but they last long enough for stimulus identification to begin (Ellis & Hunt, 1989). As you read a sentence, for example, you identify and interpret the first few words. At the same time, subsequent words are being scanned, and these are maintained in your visual sensory register until you can process them as well.

In many ways, sensory memory brings coherence and continuity to the world. To appreciate this fact, turn your head slowly from left to right. Although your eyes may seem to be moving smoothly, like a movie camera scanning a scene, this is not what happens. Your eyes fixate at one point for about one-fourth of a second and then rapidly jump to a new position. The sensation of smoothness occurs because the scene is held in sensory memory until your eyes fixate again. Similarly, when you listen to someone speak, the auditory sensory register allows you to experience a smooth flow of information.

The fact that sensory memories quickly fade if they are not processed further is an adaptive characteristic of the memory system (Martindale, 1991). One simply cannot deal with all of the sights, sounds, odors, tastes, and tactile sensations that impinge on the sense organs at any given moment. As mentioned in Chapter 5, **selective attention** focuses mental resources on only part of the stimulus field, thus controlling what information is processed further. Indeed, it is through perception that the elusive impressions of sensory memory are captured and transferred to short-term memory.

Short-Term, or Working, Memory

The sensory registers allow your memory system to develop a representation of a stimulus, but they do not allow the more thorough representation and analysis needed if the information is going to be used in some way. These functions are accomplished by **short-term memory (STM),** the part of our memory system that stores limited amounts of information for up to about eighteen seconds. When you check *TV Guide* for the channel number of a show and then switch to that channel, you are using short-term memory.

Once viewed mainly as a temporary storehouse for information, short-term memory is now recognized as a more complex operation that serves a number of purposes. Accordingly, many researchers refer to STM as **working memory** because it enables people to do much of their mental work, from dialing a phone number to solving a complex math problem (Baddeley, 1992). Suppose, for example, you are buying something for 83 cents. You go through your change and pick out two quarters, two dimes, two nickels, and three pennies. To do this you must remember the price, retrieve the rules of addition from long-term memory, *and* keep a running count of how much change you have so far. Alternatively, try to recall how many windows there are on the front of the house or apartment where you grew up. In attempting to answer this question, you probably formed a mental image of the building, which required one kind of working-memory process, and then, while maintaining that image in your mind, you "worked" on it by counting the windows.

Clearly, then, more is involved in short-term memory than just storing information. In fact, some researchers view STM as one part of a more elaborate working-memory system whose components function together on a semi-independent basis (Baddeley & Hitch, 1974).

Encoding in STM The encoding of information in short-term memory is much more elaborative and varied than that in the sensory registers (Brandimonte, Hitch & Bishop, 1992). Often, acoustic coding seems to dominate. One piece of evidence for this assertion comes from an analysis of the mistakes people make when encoding information in short-term memory. These mistakes tend to be *acoustically related,* which means that they involve the substitution of similar sounds. For example, Robert Conrad (1964) showed people strings of letters and asked them to repeat the letters immediately. Their mistakes tended to involve replacing the correct letter—say, *C*—with another that sounded like it, such as *D, P,* or *T.* These mistakes occurred even though the letters were presented visually, without any sound.

Studies in several cultures have also shown that items are more difficult to remember if they are acoustically related rather than acoustically distinct. For example, native English speakers perform much more poorly when they must remember a string of letters like *ECVTGB* (which all have similar sounds) rather than one like *KRLDQS* (which have distinct sounds). Similar results have been found in Chinese, which is written using characters that correspond roughly to English syllables. When Chinese students are shown a series of characters and then asked to write them from memory, they get

Note: The title of the passage on page 234 is "Washing Clothes."

twice as many correct when the characters all have different sounds than when they all have the same sound (Zhang & Simon, 1985).

Notice, however, that the fact that the Chinese students remembered any of the acoustically identical characters suggests that they used some visual coding. Visual as well as acoustical codes are used in short-term memory. However, information that is coded visually tends to fade much more quickly (Cornoldi, DeBeni & Baldi, 1989).

Information in short-term memory may also be coded kinesthetically, in terms of physical movements. In one study, for example, congenitally deaf subjects were shown lists of words, which they were asked to immediately write down from memory (Shand, 1982). When these subjects made errors, they wrote words that are expressed through similar *hand movements* in American Sign Language, rather than words that *sounded* similar to the correct words. Apparently, these individuals had encoded the words on the basis of the movements they would use when signing them.

Storage Capacity of STM   You can easily determine the capacity of short-term memory by conducting the simple experiment shown in Figure 8.6 (Howard, 1983). The maximum number of items you can recall perfectly after one presentation is called your **immediate memory span.** If your memory span is like most people's, you can repeat about six or seven items from the test in this figure. The interesting thing is that you should come up with about the same number whether you estimate your immediate memory span with digits, letters, words, or virtually any type of unit (Hayes, 1952; Pollack, 1953). When George Miller (1956) noticed that studies of a wide variety of tasks showed the same limit on the ability to process information, he pointed out that the limit seems to be a "magic number" of seven plus or minus two. This is the capacity of short-term memory, at least as normally tested under laboratory conditions. It is generally considered to be somewhat less in more naturalistic settings (Martindale, 1991). In addition, the "magic number" refers not to a certain number of discrete elements but to the number of meaningful *groupings* of information, called **chunks.**

To see the difference between discrete elements and chunks, read the following letters to a friend, pausing at each dash: *FB-ITW-AC-IAI-BMB-MW.* The chances are very

FIGURE 8.6

Capacity of Short-Term Memory

Here is a test of your immediate, or short-term, memory span. Ask someone to read to you the numbers in the top row at the rate of about one per second; then try to repeat them back in the same order. Then try the next row, and the one after that, until you make a mistake. Your immediate memory span is the maximum number of items you can repeat back perfectly.

9 2 5	G M N
8 6 4 2	S L R R
3 7 6 5 4	V O E P G
6 2 7 4 1 8	X W D X Q O
0 4 0 1 4 7 3	E P H H J A E
1 9 2 2 3 5 3 0	Z D O F W D S V
4 8 6 8 5 4 3 3 2	D T Y N R H E H Q
2 5 3 1 9 7 1 7 6 8	K H W D A G R O F Z
8 5 1 2 9 6 1 9 4 5 0	U D F F W H D Q D G E
9 1 8 5 4 6 9 4 2 9 3 7	Q M R H X Z D P R R E H

CAT BOAT RUG
RUN BEACH PLANT LIGHT
SUIT WATCH CUT STAIRS CAR
JUNK LONE GAME CALL WOOD HEART
FRAME PATCH CROSS DRUG DESK HORSE LAW
CLOTHES CHOOSE GIFT DRIVE BOOK TREE HAIR THIS
DRESS CLERK FILM BASE SPEND SERVE BOOK LOW TIME
STONE ALL NAIL DOOR HOPE EARL FEEL BUY COPE GRAPE
AGE SOFT FALL STORE PUT TRUE SMALL FREE CHECK MAIL LEAF
LOG DAY TIME CHESS LAKE CUT BIRD SHEET YOUR SEE STREET WHEEL

Source: Howard, 1983.

good that your friend will not be able to repeat this string of letters perfectly. Why? There are fifteen letters, a total that exceeds most people's immediate memory span. But if you read the letters so that they are grouped as *FBI-TWA-CIA-IBM-BMW,* your friend will probably repeat the string easily (Bower, 1975). Although the same fifteen letters are involved, they will be processed as only five meaningful chunks of information.

The Power of Chunking   Chunks of information can become very complex. If someone read to you, "The boy in the red shirt kicked his mother in the shin," you could probably repeat the sentence very easily. Yet it contains twelve words and forty-three letters. How can you repeat the sentence so effortlessly? The answer is that people can build bigger and bigger chunks of information (Ericsson & Staszewski, 1989). In this case, you might represent "the boy in the red shirt" as one chunk of information rather than as six words or nineteen letters. Similarly, "kicked his mother" and "in the shin" represent separate chunks of information.

Learning to use bigger and bigger chunks of information can enhance short-term memory. Children's memories improve in part because they gradually become able to hold as many as seven chunks in memory, but also because they become better able to group information into chunks (Servan-Schreiber & Anderson, 1990). Adults, too, can greatly increase the capacity of their short-term memory by more appropriate chunking (Waldrop, 1987); one man increased his immediate memory span to approximately one hundred items (Chase & Ericsson, 1981). In short, although the capacity of short-term memory is more or less constant—five to nine chunks of meaningful information—the size of those chunks can vary tremendously.

Duration of STM   Imagine what life would be like if you kept remembering every phone number you ever dialed or every conversation you ever heard. This does not happen because most people usually forget information in short-term memory quickly unless they continue repeating it to themselves (through maintenance rehearsal). You may have experienced this adaptive, though sometimes inconvenient, phenomenon if you have ever been interrupted while repeating to yourself a new phone number you were about to dial, and then couldn't recall the number.

How long does unrehearsed information remain in short-term memory? To answer this question, John Brown (1958) and Lloyd and Margaret Peterson (1959) devised the **Brown-Peterson procedure,** which is a method for preventing rehearsal. A person is presented with a group of three letters, such as *GRB,* and then counts backward by threes from some number until a signal is given. Counting prevents the person from rehearsing the letters. At the signal, the person stops counting and tries to recall the letters. By varying the number of seconds that the person counts backward, the experi-

CHUNKING IN ACTION   Those who provide instantaneous translation during international negotiations must store long, often complicated segments of speech in short-term memory while searching long-term memory for the equivalent second-language expressions. The task is made easier by chunking the speaker's words into phrases and sentences.

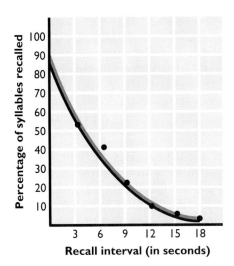

Source: Data from Peterson & Peterson, 1959.

FIGURE 8.7

Forgetting in Short-Term Memory

This graph shows the percentage of nonsense syllables recalled after various intervals during which rehearsal was prevented. Notice that virtually complete forgetting occurred after a delay of eighteen seconds.

menter can determine how much forgetting takes place over a certain amount of time. As you can see in Figure 8.7, information in short-term memory is forgotten gradually but rapidly: After eighteen seconds, subjects can remember almost nothing. Evidence from these and other experiments suggests that *unrehearsed* information can be maintained in short-term memory for no more than about eighteen seconds.

Long-Term Memory

Short-term, or working, memory holds information so briefly that it is not what people usually have in mind when they talk about memory. Usually, they are thinking about **long-term memory (LTM),** whose encoding and storage processes we now consider.

Encoding in LTM   Some information is encoded into long-term memory automatically, without any conscious attempt to memorize it (Ellis, 1991). However, encoding information into long-term memory is often the result of a relatively deep level of conscious processing, which usually involves some degree of *semantic coding*. In other words, encoding in long-term memory often ignores details and instead encodes the general, underlying meaning of the information.

The dominance of semantic coding in long-term memory was demonstrated in a classic study by Jacqueline Sachs (1967). First, people listened to tape-recorded passages. Then Sachs gave them sentences and asked whether each exact sentence had been in the taped passage. People did very well when they were tested immediately (using mainly short-term memory). However, after only twenty-seven seconds, at which point the information had to be retrieved from long-term memory, they could not determine which of two sentences they had heard if both sentences expressed the same meaning. For example, they could not determine whether they had heard "He sent a letter about it to Galileo, the great Italian scientist" or "A letter about it was sent to Galileo, the great Italian scientist." In short, they remembered the general meaning of what they had heard, but not the exact wording.

Counterfeiters depend on the fact that people encode the general meaning of visual stimuli rather than specific details. For example, look at Figure 8.8 and find the correct drawing of a U.S. penny (Nickerson & Adams, 1979). Most people from the United States are unsuccessful at this task, just as people from Great Britain do poorly at recognizing their country's coins (Jones, 1990).

FIGURE 8.8

Encoding into Long-Term Memory

Which is the correct image of a U.S. penny? (See the footnote on p. 240 for the answer.)

Source: Nickerson & Adams, 1979.

Long-term memory normally involves semantic coding, but people can also use visual coding to process images into long-term memory. In one study, people viewed 2,500 pictures. Although it took sixteen hours just to present the stimuli, the subjects later correctly recognized more than 90 percent of the pictures tested (Standing, Conezio & Haber, 1970). One reason pictures are remembered so well is that these stimuli may be represented in terms of both a visual code and a semantic code. *Dual coding theory* suggests that information is remembered better when it is represented in both codes rather than in only one (Paivio, 1986).

Storage Capacity of LTM   Whereas the capacity of short-term memory is limited, the capacity of long-term memory is extremely large; most theorists believe it is literally unlimited (Medin & Ross, 1992). It is impossible to prove this, but there are no cases of people being unable to learn something new because they had too much information stored in long-term memory. We do know for sure that people store vast quantities of information in long-term memory, and that they often remember it remarkably well for long periods of time. For example, people are amazingly accurate at recognizing the faces of their high school classmates after having not seen them for over twenty-five years (Bruck, Cavanagh & Ceci, 1991), and they do surprisingly well on tests of a foreign language or high school algebra fifty years after having formally studied these subjects (Bahrick, 1992; Bahrick & Hall, 1991).

Distinguishing Between Short-Term and Long-Term Memory

Some psychologists believe that there is no need to distinguish between short-term and long-term memory: What people call short-term, or working, memory is simply that part of memory that they happen to be thinking about at any particular time, whereas long-term memory is the part of memory that they are not thinking about at any given moment. However, other psychologists argue that short-term and long-term memory are qualitatively different, that they obey different laws (Cowan, 1988). Determining whether short-term and long-term memory are qualitatively distinct has become one of the most important topics in memory research. Evidence that information is transferred from short-term memory to a distinct storage system comes from experiments on recall and from the consequences of brain damage.

Experiments on Recall   To conduct your own recall experiment, look at the following list of words for thirty seconds, then look away and write down as many of the

A PHOTOGRAPHIC MEMORY Franco Magnani had been away from his hometown in Italy for more than 30 years, but he could still paint it from memory (see comparison photo; Sacks, 1992). People like Mr. Magnani display *eidetic imagery,* commonly called *photographic memory;* they have automatic, detailed, and vivid images of virtually everything they have ever seen. About 5 percent of all school-age children have eidetic imagery, but almost no adults have it (Haber, 1979; Merritt, 1979).

Drawing A shows the correct penny image in Figure 8.8.

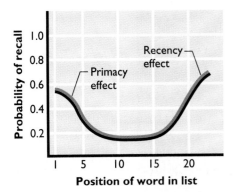

FIGURE 8.9

A Serial-Position Curve

The probability of recalling an item is plotted here as a function of its serial position in a list of items. Generally, the first several items and the last several items are most likely to be recalled.

words as you can, in any order: *bed, rest, quilt, dream, sheet, mattress, pillow, night, snore, pajamas.* Which words you recall depends in part on their *serial position*—that is, on where the words were in the list, as Figure 8.9 shows. This figure is a *serial-position curve,* which shows the chances of recalling words appearing in each position in a list. For the first two or three words in a list, recall tends to be very good, a characteristic that is called the **primacy effect.** The probability of recall decreases for words in the middle of the list and then rises dramatically for the last few words. The ease of recalling words near the end of a list is called the **recency effect.**

It has been suggested that the primacy effect reflects rehearsal that puts early words into *long-term memory,* and that the recency effect occurs because the last few words are still in *short-term memory* when we try to recall the list. If short- and long-term memory are indeed distinct, then we should be able to manipulate one without affecting the other. Murray Glanzer and Anita Cunitz (1966) tried to do just that. First, they gave a list of words to two groups of people. One group recalled the list immediately, but the second group performed a mental arithmetic task for thirty seconds before trying to recall the list. As Figure 8.10(A) shows, the subjects in both groups experienced a primacy effect, but no recency effect occurred among those in the second group. Doing arithmetic before recalling the list apparently displaced the last several words from short-term memory, making them no more likely to be recalled than those in the middle of the list. Second, Glanzer and Cunitz (1966) presented new lists at the rate of one word every 3 seconds, every 6 seconds, or every 9 seconds. As illustrated in Figure 8.10(B), a recency effect occurred among the subjects in all three groups, but those who heard the quickest presentations showed the smallest primacy effect—apparently because they did not have enough rehearsal time to place early words into long-term memory (Koppenaal & Glanzer, 1990).

Results of Brain Damage Evidence that information is transferred from short-term memory to another, distinct system also comes from observations of how certain brain injuries affect memory (Martinez, Schulteis & Weinberger, 1991). For example, damage to the hippocampus, which is part of the limbic system described in Chapter 3, often results in **anterograde amnesia,** a loss of memory for any event occurring after the injury.

A striking example is H.M., whose case was described in Figure 6.2 in the chapter on consciousness (Milner, 1966). Part of H.M.'s hippocampus had been removed in order to end severe epileptic seizures. Afterward, both his long-term and short-term memory appeared normal, but he had a severe problem. The operation had been performed when he was twenty-seven years old. Two years later, he still believed that he was twenty-seven. When his family moved into a new house, H.M. could not remember the

FIGURE 8.10

Separating Short-Term from Long-Term Memory

Part (A) shows that performing an arithmetic task before trying to recall a list destroys the recency effect but does not alter the primacy effect. Part (B) shows that presenting words at a faster rate reduces the primacy effect but does not change the recency effect.

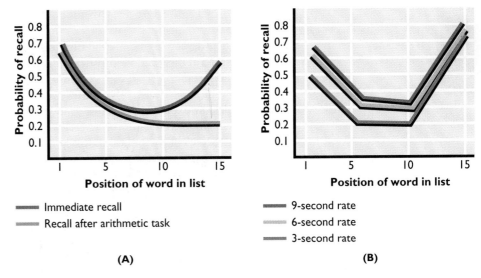

Source: Part A: data from Glanzer & Cunitz, 1966; part B: data from Koppenaal & Glanzer, 1990.

A CASE OF RETROGRADE AMNESIA   At right is Alabama businesswoman Patsy Cannon prior to a 1986 car crash that left her with retrograde amnesia so severe that she had to relearn virtually all that she had known about everything and everybody. She did not even recognize her own daughter: "It could have been any child off the street," she said. At left is Patsy as she looks today, working as an advocate for people with brain injuries (National Geographic, June 1995, p. 33).

new address or even how to get there. When he was told that his uncle had died, he grieved in a normal way. But soon thereafter, he began to ask why his uncle had not visited him. Each time he was told of his uncle's death, H.M. became just as upset as when he was first told. In short, the surgery had apparently destroyed the mechanism that transfers information from short-term to long-term memory.

Another condition, **retrograde amnesia,** involves a loss of memory for events *prior* to some critical injury. Often, a person with this condition is unable to remember anything that took place in the months, or even years, before the injury. In most cases, the memories return gradually. The most distant events are recalled first, and the person gradually regains memory for events leading up to the injury. Recovery is seldom complete, however, and the person may never remember the last few seconds before the injury. For example, one man received a severe blow to the head after being thrown from his motorcycle. After regaining consciousness, he claimed that he was eleven years old. Over the next three months, he gradually recalled more and more of his life. He remembered when he was twelve, thirteen, and so on—right up until the time he was riding his motorcycle the day of the accident. But he was never able to remember what happened just before the accident (Baddeley, 1982). Those final events must have been encoded into short-term memory, but apparently they were never transferred into long-term memory.

The damage to memory in these cases is consistent with the view that short-term and long-term memory are distinct systems; the problems are tied to an inability to transfer information from one system to the other. Psychologists do not yet know exactly how, physiologically, this transfer occurs. One view is that some physiological trace that codes the experience must be gradually transformed and stabilized, or *consolidated,* if the memory is to endure (Verfaellis & Cermak, 1991).

It seems likely that this consolidation depends primarily on the movement of electrochemical impulses within clusters of neurons in the brain (Berman, 1991). Events that suppress neural activity in the brain—physical blows to the head, anesthetics, carbon monoxide and other types of poisoning—all disrupt the transfer of information from short-term to long-term memory. Similarly, transfer of information from short-term to long-term memory is often disrupted by strong but random sets of electrical impulses, as in the electroshock treatments described in Chapter 16, on the treatment of psychological disorders. The information being transferred from short-term to long-term memory seems to be particularly vulnerable to destruction during the first minute or so (Donegan & Thompson, 1991).

RETRIEVING MEMORIES

Have you ever been unable to recall the name of an old rock band or movie star, only to think of it the next day? Remembering something requires not only that it be appropriately coded and stored but also that you have the ability to bring it into consciousness—in other words, to *retrieve* it.

Retrieval Cues and Encoding Specificity

Stimuli that help people retrieve information from long-term memory are called **retrieval cues.** They allow people to recall things that were once forgotten and help them to recognize information stored in memory. In general, recognition tasks are easier than recall tasks because they contain more retrieval cues. As noted earlier, it is usually easier to recognize the correct alternative on a multiple-choice exam than to recall material on an essay test.

Which cues are most effective at aiding retrieval depends on the degree to which they tap into information that was encoded at the time of learning (Tulving, 1979; Tulving & Thomson, 1973). This rule, known as the **encoding specificity principle,** is consistent with the transfer-appropriate model of memory. Because long-term memories are often encoded semantically, cues that evoke the meaning of the stored information tend to work best. For example, imagine you have learned a long list of sentences, one of which is either (1) "The man lifted the piano" or (2) "The man tuned the piano." Having the cue "something heavy" during a recall test would probably help you remember the first sentence, because you probably encoded something about the weight of a piano, but "something heavy" would probably not help you recall the second sentence. Similarly, the cue "makes nice sounds" would be likely to help you recall the second sentence, but not the first (Barclay et al., 1974).

Context and State Dependence

In general, people remember more when their efforts at recall take place in the same environment in which they learned, because they tend to encode features of the environment where the learning occurred (Richardson-Klavehn & Bjork, 1988). These features may later act as retrieval cues. In one experiment, people studied a series of pictures while in the presence of a particular odor. Later, they reviewed a larger set of photos and tried to identify the ones they had seen earlier. Half of these people were tested in the presence of the original odor and half in the presence of a different odor. Those who smelled the same odor during learning and testing did significantly better on the recognition task than those who were tested in the presence of a different odor. The matching odor served as a powerful retrieval cue (Cann & Ross, 1989).

When memory can be helped or hindered by similarities in environmental context, it is termed **context-dependent.** One study found that students remember better when tested in the classroom in which they learned the material than when tested in a different classroom (Smith, Glenberg & Bjork, 1978). This context-dependency effect is not always strong (Saufley, Otaka & Bavaresco, 1985; Smith, Vela & Williamson, 1988), but some students do find it helpful to study for a test in the classroom where the test will be given.

Like the external environment, the internal psychological environment can be encoded when people learn and thus can act as a retrieval cue. When a person's internal state can aid or impede retrieval, memory is called **state-dependent.** For example, if people learn new material while under the influence of marijuana, they tend to recall it better if they are also tested under the influence of marijuana (Eich et al., 1975). Similar effects have been found with alcohol (Overton, 1984), other drugs (Eich, 1989), and mood states. College students remember more positive incidents from their diaries or from their earlier life when they are in a positive mood at the time of recall (Bower, 1981; Ehrlichman & Halpern, 1988). More negative events tend to be recalled when people are in a negative mood (Lewinsohn & Rosenbaum, 1987). These *mood congruency effects* are strongest when people try to recall personally meaningful episodes, because these events were most likely to be colored by their own mood (Eich &

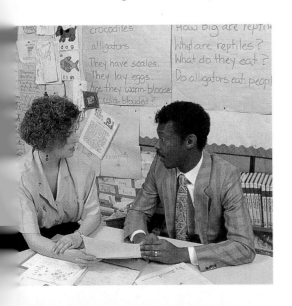

CONTEXT DEPENDENT MEMORIES
Some parents find that being in their child's schoolroom for a teacher conference provides context cues that bring back memories of their own grade school days.

IN REVIEW	Factors Affecting Retrieval from Long-Term Memory
Process	**Effect on Memory**
Encoding specificity	Retrieval cues are effective only to the extent that they tap into information that was originally encoded.
Context dependence	Retrieval is most successful when it occurs in the same environment in which the information was originally learned.
State dependence	Retrieval is most successful when people are in the same psychological state as when they originally learned the information.

Metcalfe, 1989). People who experience dramatic mood swings (such as those associated with bipolar disorder, discussed in Chapter 15) tend to show very strong state-dependent memory effects.

Retrieval from Semantic Memory

All of the retrieval situations we have discussed so far are relevant to *episodic memory* ("In Review: Factors Affecting Retrieval from Long-Term Memory" summarizes this material). Obviously, *semantic memory,* which stores general knowledge about the world, is also important in everyday functioning. Researchers studying semantic memory typically ask subjects general-knowledge questions such as (1) Are fish minerals? (2) Is a beagle a dog? (3) Do birds fly? and (4) Does a car have legs? As you might imagine, most people virtually always respond correctly to such questions. By measuring the amount of time people take to answer the questions, however, psychologists gain important clues about how semantic memory is organized and how information is retrieved.

Semantic Networks   One of the most influential theories of semantic memory suggests that concepts are represented in a dense network of associations (Collins & Loftus, 1975). Figure 8.11 presents a fragment of what a *semantic memory network* might look like. In general, semantic network theories suggest that information is retrieved from memory through **spreading activation** (Medin & Ross, 1992). That is, whenever you think about some concept, it is activated in the network, and spreading activation (in the form of neural energy) begins to travel down all the paths related to it. For example, if a person is asked to say whether "A robin is a bird" is true or false, the concepts of both robin and bird will become activated and the spreading activation from each will intersect in the middle of the path.

Some associations within the network are stronger than others. Differing strengths are depicted by the varying thickness of the lines in Figure 8.11; spreading activation travels more quickly along thick paths than along thin ones. For example, most people probably have a stronger association between "bat" and "can fly" or "has wings" than "is a mammal." Accordingly, most people respond more quickly to "Can a bat fly?" than to "Is a bat a mammal?"

Because of the tight organization of semantic networks and the speed at which activation spreads through the network, people gain access to an enormous body of knowledge about the world quickly and effortlessly. They retrieve not only facts that they have learned directly but also knowledge that allows them to infer or to compute other facts about the world (Medin & Ross, 1992). For example, imagine answering the following two questions: (1) Is a robin a bird? and (2) Is a robin a living thing? You can probably answer the first question "directly" because you probably learned this fact at some point in your life. However, you may never have consciously thought about the second ques-

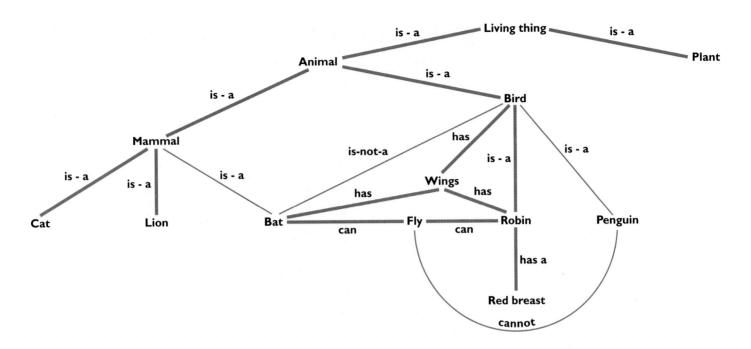

Semantic Networks

This drawing represents just a small part of a network of semantic associations. These networks allow people to retrieve specific pieces of previously learned information and to make new inferences about concepts.

tion, so answering it requires some inference. Figure 8.11 illustrates the path to that inference. Because you know that a robin is a bird, a bird is an animal, and animals are living things, you infer that a robin must be a living thing. As you might expect, however, it takes slightly longer to answer the second question than the first.

Retrieving Incomplete Knowledge Figure 8.11 also shows that concepts are represented in semantic memory as unique collections of features or attributes (concepts are discussed in more detail in Chapter 9, on thought and language). Often, people can retrieve some features but not enough to identify a whole concept. Thus, you might know that there is an animal that has wings, can fly, but is not a bird, and yet be unable to retrieve its name (Connor, Balota & Neely, 1992). In such cases you are said to be retrieving *incomplete knowledge*.

A very common example of incomplete knowledge is the *tip-of-the-tongue phenomenon*. In a typical experiment on this phenomenon, dictionary definitions of words are read to people and they are asked to name each word (Brown & McNeill, 1966). If they cannot recall a defined word, they are asked whether they can recall any feature of it, such as its first letter or how many syllables it has. People are surprisingly good at this task, indicating that they are able to retrieve at least some knowledge of the word (Brennen et al., 1990). Most people experience the tip-of-the-tongue phenomenon about once a week (Brown, 1991).

Another example of retrieving incomplete knowledge is the *feeling-of-knowing experience*, which is often studied by asking people trivia questions (Reder & Ritter, 1992). When they cannot answer a question, they are asked to estimate the probability that they could recognize the correct answer if they were given several options. Again, people are remarkably good at this task (Costermans, Lories & Ansay, 1992); even though they cannot recall the answer, people can retrieve enough knowledge to determine whether the answer is actually stored in memory.

Constructing Memories

The generalized knowledge about the world that each person has stored constantly affects memory (Harris, Sardarpoor-Bascom & Meyer, 1989). People use their existing knowledge to organize new information as they receive it and to fill in gaps in the information they encode and retrieve. In this way, memories are constructed.

To study this process, which is sometimes called *constructive memory*, Rebecca Sulin and D. James Dooling (1974) asked research participants to read a long passage about a dictator. In one case, the dictator was a fictitious character named Gerald Martin; in

A CONSTRUCTED MEMORY Through constructive memory processes, subjects who waited in this office "remembered" having seen books in it, even though none were present (Brewer & Treyens, 1981). Let a friend examine this photo for a minute or so (cover the caption), then close the book and ask whether each of the following items appeared in the office: chair, wastebasket, bottle, typewriter, coffee pot, and book. If your friend reports having seen a wastebasket or book, you will have demonstrated constructive memory.

another, Adolph Hitler. Later, the participants were asked if the passage contained the statement "He hated the Jews particularly and so persecuted them." This statement was not in the passage, but those who had been told that they were reading about Hitler "remembered" the statement more often than subjects who had read about Gerald Martin. This result indicates that generalized knowledge about Hitler affected their memory of the passage.

Another example of constructive memory comes from an experiment in which undergraduates waited for several minutes in the office of a graduate student (Brewer & Treyens, 1981). When later asked to recall everything that was in the office, most of the students mistakenly "remembered" that books were present, even though there were none. Apparently, the general knowledge that graduate students read many books influenced the subjects' memory of what was in the room.

Relating Semantic and Episodic Memory: PDP Models Parallel distributed processing models offer one way of explaining how semantic and episodic information become integrated in constructive memories. As noted earlier, PDP models suggest that newly learned facts alter our general knowledge of what the world is like. Figure 8.12 shows a simple PDP network model of just a tiny part of someone's knowledge of the world (Martindale, 1991). At its center lie the intersections of several learned associations between specific facts, each of which is represented by an arrow. Thus, the network "knows" that Joe is a male European-American professor who likes Brie cheese and drives a Subaru. It also "knows" that Claudia is a female African-American professor who drives a Maserati. Notice that the network has never learned what type of cheese she prefers.

Suppose Figure 8.12 represents your memory and that you now think about Claudia. Because of the connections in the network, the facts that she is a female African-American professor who drives a Maserati would be activated; you would automatically remember these facts about Claudia. However, "likes Brie cheese" would also be activated because it is linked to other professors in the network. If the level of activation for Brie cheese is low, then the proposition that Claudia likes Brie cheese might be considered a hypothesis or an educated guess. But suppose *every other* professor you knew liked Brie. In that case, the connection between professors and "likes Brie cheese" would

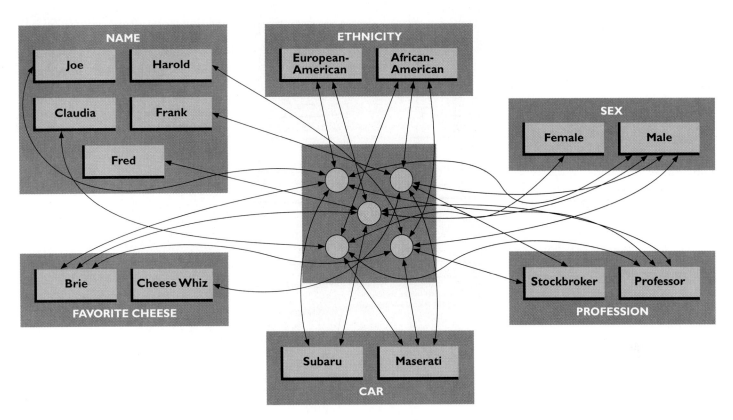

Source: Adapted from Martindale, 1991.

FIGURE 8.12

A PDP Network Model

This simple parallel distributed processing network model represents with arrows what someone knows about how five aspects of the world (depicted as circles) are related. More complex versions of such network models are capable of accounting not only for what people know but also for the inferences and generalizations they tend to make.

be strong, and the conclusion that Claudia likes Brie cheese would be held so confidently that it would take overwhelming evidence for you to change your mind (Rumelhart et al., 1986).

PDP networks also produce *spontaneous generalizations.* If your friend told you she just bought a new car, you would know without asking that—like all other cars you have experienced—it has four wheels. However, spontaneous generalizations can create significant errors if the network is based on limited or biased experience with a class of objects. For example, if the network in Figure 8.12 were asked what European-American males are like, it would think that all of them drive Japanese cars. Similarly, it would think that all African-American men are stockbrokers who drive expensive cars.

Ironically, researchers are encouraged by this prejudicial aspect of PDP networks because it is an accurate reflection of human thought and memory. As described in Chapter 17, on social cognition, virtually all people make spontaneous generalizations about males, females, European-Americans, African-Americans, and many other categories (Martindale, 1991). One difference between the prejudiced and unprejudiced groups is that relatively unprejudiced people tend to recognize that they are making the generalizations and consciously try to ignore or counteract them (Devine et al., 1991; Fazio et al., 1995).

Schemas   PDP models also help us understand constructive memory by explaining the operation of the schemas that guide it. As described in Chapters 9 and 12, **schemas** are mental representations of categories of objects, events, and people. For example, most Americans have a schema for *baseball game,* so that simply hearing these words is likely to activate whole clusters of information in long-term memory, including the rules of the game, images of players, bats, balls, a green field, summer days, and, perhaps, hot dogs and stadiums. The generalized knowledge contained in schemas provides a basis for making inferences about incoming information during the encoding stage. So if you hear that a baseball player was injured, your schema about baseball might prompt you to encode the incident as game related, even though the cause was

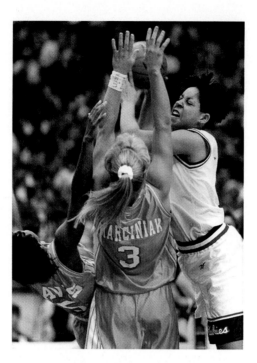

PDP MODELS AND CONSTRUCTIVE MEMORY If you hear that "our basketball team won last night," your associative network, and thus your schema, about basketball might prompt you to encode, and later retrieve, the "fact" that the players were men. Such spontaneous, though often incorrect, generalizations associated with **PDP** models of memory help account for constructive memory.

not mentioned. As a result, you are likely to recall the injury as having occurred during a game (see Figure 8.13 for another example).

There are several types of schemas (Searleman & Herrmann, 1994). Some take the form of *scripts,* which contain knowledge of how common events, such as baseball games, unfold. A *person schema* contains knowledge and beliefs about the people that you know (Fiske & Taylor, 1984). A person schema tells you, for example, how your boss would react in certain situations, such as being asked for a raise. Your *self schema* consists of your knowledge and beliefs about your own traits, abilities, goals, and other characteristics. We describe these and other schemas in more detail in Chapter 17.

As in the case of the students who falsely remembered books in a graduate student's office, people's schemas lead them to adjust their memories of events in accordance with what their prior experiences and cultural values tell them *probably* happened, or *should* have happened. The role of culture-specific schemas in constructive memory was demonstrated decades ago when Frederick Bartlett (1932) asked British university students to listen to a story about American Indian culture called "The War of the Ghosts," in which spirit warriors take a young man with them into battle. When asked to retell the story from memory, the students tended to remember aspects that were in

FIGURE 8.13

The Effect of Schemas on Recall

In one study, people were shown figures like these, along with labels designed to activate certain schemas (Carmichael, Hogan & Walter, 1932). For example, when showing the top figure, the experimenter said either "This resembles eyeglasses" or "This resembles a dumbbell." When these people were asked to reproduce the figures from memory, their drawings tended to resemble the items mentioned by the experimenter. In other words, their memory had been altered by the labels.

Figure shown to subjects	Group 1		Group 2	
	Label given	Figure drawn by subjects	Label given	Figure drawn by subjects
○—○	Eyeglasses	○○	Dumbbell	○—○
⋈	Hourglass	⋈	Table	⋈
7	Seven	7	Four	4
⊳—	Gun	⟼	Broom	⨰

accord with the schemas of their own culture, and to forget aspects reflecting American Indian schemas. One student, for example, retold the basics of the story, but left out the rather important fact that the warriors were ghosts!

EXPLORING MEMORY PROCESSES
Research by cognitive psychologist Elizabeth Loftus has demonstrated mechanisms through which false memories can be created. Her work has helped to focus scientific scrutiny on reports of recovered memories, especially those arising from contact with therapists who assume that most people have repressed memories of abuse.

In 1989, Eileen Franklin-Lipsker told police in California that, upon looking into her young daughter's eyes one day, she suddenly had a vivid memory of seeing her father kill her childhood friend more than twenty years earlier. Her father, George Franklin, Sr., was sent to prison for murder on the basis of her testimony about this memory (Loftus & Ketcham, 1994).

THINKING CRITICALLY

Can Traumatic Memories Be Repressed, Then Recovered?

What am I being asked to believe or accept?

The prosecution in the Franklin case successfully argued that Eileen had recovered a *repressed memory.* Similar arguments in more recent cases have resulted in the imprisonment of a number of parents whose now-adult children claim to have recovered childhood memories of physical or sexual abuse. The juries in these trials accepted the assertion that all memory of shocking events can be pushed into an inaccessible corner of the mind where, for decades, subconscious processes keep it out of awareness, yet potentially subject to recall (Kihlstrom, 1995; Loftus, 1993).

What evidence is available to support the assertion?

Proponents of the repressed memory argument point to several lines of evidence to support their claims. First, as described in the chapter on consciousness, a substantial amount of mental activity occurs outside of awareness (Kihlstrom, 1987). Second, research on implicit memory shows that information of which we are unaware can still influence our behavior (Schacter, Chiu, & Ochsner, 1993). Third, as noted earlier, retrieval cues can help people recall memories that had previously been inaccessible to conscious awareness (Landsdale & Laming, 1995). Fourth, research on *motivated forgetting* suggests that people may be more likely to forget unpleasant rather than pleasant events (Erdelyi, 1985). In one study, a psychologist kept a detailed record of his daily life over a six-year period. When he later tried to recall these experiences, he remembered more than half of the positive events but only one-third of the negative ones (Waagenaar, 1986). In another study, 129 adult women were asked routine questions about their medical histories. Hospital records indicated that all of these women had been victims of sexual abuse in childhood, but 12 percent of them said they had no memory of ever being abused (Williams, 1993). Finally, there is the confidence with which people report recovered memories; they say they are just too vivid to be anything but real.

Are there alternative ways of interpreting the evidence?

Those who are skeptical about repressed memories do not deny the operation of subconscious memory and retrieval processes (Greenwald, 1992). They also recognize that, sadly, child abuse and other traumas are all too common. But these facts do not eliminate the possibility that any given "recovered" memory may actually be a distorted, or constructed, memory (Loftus & Ketcham, 1994). As already noted, our recall of past events is affected by what happened at the time, what we knew beforehand, and everything we experience since. The people who "remembered" nonexistent books in a graduate student's office constructed that memory based on what prior knowledge led them to *assume* was there.

Research shows that *false memories*—distortions of actual events and the recall of events that didn't actually happen—can be just as vivid as accurate ones, and people can be just as confident in them (Brainerd, Reyna & Brandse, 1995; Roediger &

McDermott, 1995). In one case study, for example, a teenager named Chris was given descriptions of four incidents from his childhood and asked to write about each of them every day for five days (Loftus & Pickrell, in press). One of these incidents—being lost in a shopping mall at age five—never really happened. Yet Chris not only eventually "remembered" this event but added many details about the mall and the stranger whose hand he was supposedly found holding. He also rated this (false) memory as being more vivid than two of the other three (real) incidents. The same pattern of results has appeared in more formal experiments on the planting of emotion-laden false memories (Hyman, Husband & Billings, in press; Loftus & Pickrell, in press).

Why would anyone remember a trauma that did not actually occur? Elizabeth Loftus (1993) suggests that, for one thing, popular books such as *The Courage to Heal* (Bass & Davis, 1988) and *Secret Survivors* (Blume, 1990) have planted in many minds the idea that anyone who experiences guilt, depression, low self-esteem, overemotionality, or any of a long list of other problems is harboring repressed memories of abuse. This message, says Loftus, tends to be reinforced and extended by therapists who specialize in using guided imagination, hypnosis, and other methods to "help" clients to recover repressed memories (Polusny & Follette, 1996; Poole et al., 1995). In so doing, these therapists may influence people to construct false memories (Olio, 1994). As one client described her therapy, "I was rapidly losing the ability to differentiate between my imagination and my real memory" (Loftus & Ketcham, 1994, p. 25). To such therapists, a client's failure to recover memories of abuse, or refusal to accept their existence, is evidence of "denial" of the truth.

The possibility that recovered memories might actually be false memories has led to dismissed charges or not-guilty verdicts for defendants in some repressed memory cases, and to the release of previously convicted defendants in others (George Franklin's conviction has been overturned, but he may face retrial). It has also led to lawsuits. In 1994, California winery executive Gary Ramona received $500,000 in damages from two therapists who had "helped" his daughter recall alleged sexual abuse at his hands. Another recent suit led to a $2.5 million judgment against a Minnesota therapist whose client realized that her "recovered" memories of childhood abuse were false. Concern over the potential damage resulting from false memories has prompted the establishment of the False Memory Syndrome Foundation, a support group for families affected by abuse accusations stemming from allegedly repressed memories.

What additional evidence would help to evaluate the alternatives?

Evaluating reports of recovered memories would be aided by more information about how common it is for people to repress traumatic memories. So far, we know that intense emotional experiences usually produce memories that are vivid and long-lasting (Strongman & Kemp, 1991). Some are called *flashbulb memories* because they preserve particular experiences in great detail (Brown & Kulik, 1977; Heuer & Reisberg, 1990). Indeed, many people who live through trauma are *unable* to forget it (as described in Chapter 13, upsetting memories are often associated with posttraumatic stress disorder). In the medical survey study mentioned earlier, for example, 88 percent of the abuse victims did recall their trauma; some others might have preferred not to report their memory. More studies like this one—which track the fate of memories in known abuse cases—would not only help estimate the prevalence of repression but might also offer clues as to the kinds of people and events most likely to be associated with it.

It would also be valuable to know more about the processes through which repression might occur—such as a mechanism that specifically pushes traumatic memories out of awareness, then keeps them at a subconscious level for long periods. Cognitive psychologists have not found evidence of such a mechanism, however (Holmes, 1990; Loftus, 1993).

Discriminating recovered memories from constructed ones will certainly be aided by more research on the mechanisms and circumstances that lead people to develop false memories (Hyman, Husband & Billings, in press; Kihlstrom, 1995; Loftus & Pickrell, in press). The results of that research will be helpful to the judges and juries who must decide the fate of defendants in criminal cases stemming from recovered memories. It will also help therapists identify and avoid assessment and treatment methods that might inadvertently influence clients' memories. And it will remind everyone of the importance of seeking corroborating evidence for the validity of recovered memories.

What conclusions are most reasonable?

There is little doubt that people sometimes forget unpleasant events, and that memories of those events are sometimes recalled later. There is also strong evidence that our memories can be distorted in various ways; the very act of trying to recall an event can enhance the sense of having experienced it, whether it actually happened or not (Loftus, 1993; Roediger & McDermott, 1995).

Given these two streams of evidence, it is not reasonable to draw a conclusion about the validity of recovered memory reports in general. Perhaps the wisest course is to recognize that no such report should be uncritically accepted or uncritically rejected. We must evaluate each report in light of all the evidence available to support *or* undermine it, while keeping in mind that constructive memory processes *might* have influenced it. This careful, scientific approach is vital if we are to deal fairly and humanely with those who report recovered memories as well with those who face accusations arising from them.

FORGETTING

The frustrations of forgetting—where you left your keys, the answer to a test question, an anniversary—are apparent to most people nearly every day (Neisser, 1991). In this section we look more closely at the nature of forgetting, and at some of the mechanisms that are responsible for it.

The Course of Forgetting

Hermann Ebbinghaus, a German psychologist, began the systematic study of memory and forgetting about a hundred years ago. He used only himself as a subject. And to time his experiments, he used a metronome, a mechanical device that makes a sound at constant intervals. His aim was to study memory in its "pure" form, uncontaminated by emotional reactions and other pre-existing associations between new material and what was already in memory. To eliminate such associations, Ebbinghaus created the *nonsense syllable,* a meaningless set of two consonants and a vowel, such as *POF, XEM,* and *QAL.* He read aloud, to the beat of the metronome, a list of nonsense syllables. Then he tried to recall the syllables.

To measure forgetting, Ebbinghaus devised the **method of savings,** which involves computing the difference between the number of repetitions needed to learn a list of items and the number of repetitions needed to relearn it after some time has elapsed. This difference is called the *savings.* If it took Ebbinghaus ten trials to learn a list and ten more trials to relearn it, there would be no savings, and forgetting would have been complete. If it took him ten trials to learn the list and only five trials to relearn it, there would be a savings of 50 percent.

As you can see in Figure 8.14, Ebbinghaus found that savings declines (and forgetting increases) as time passes. However, the most dramatic drop in what people retain in long-term memory occurs during the first nine hours, especially in the first hour. After this initial decline, the rate of forgetting slows down considerably. In Ebbinghaus's study, some savings existed even thirty-one days after the original learning.

Ebbinghaus's research had some important limitations, but it produced two lasting discoveries. One is the shape of the forgetting curve depicted in Figure 8.14. Psychologists have subsequently substituted words, sentences, and even stories for nonsense syllables. In virtually all cases the forgetting curve shows the same strong initial drop in memory, followed by a much more moderate decrease over time (Slamecka &

DURABLE MEMORIES This woman has not used a pogo stick since she was ten. Her memory of how to do it is not entirely gone, however, so she will show some "savings": It will take her less time to relearn the skill than it took to learn it initially.

FIGURE 8.14

Ebbinghaus's Curve of Forgetting

Ebbinghaus found that most forgetting occurs during the first nine hours after learning, especially during the first hour.

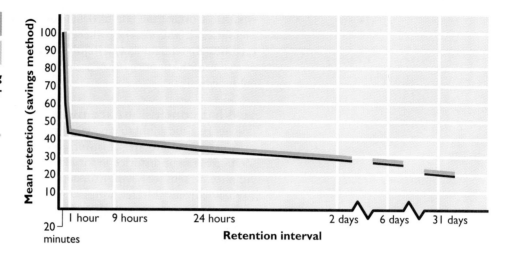

McElree, 1983). Of course, people remember sensible stories better than nonsense syllables, but the *shape* of the curve is the same no matter what type of material is involved (Davis & Moore, 1935). Even the forgetting of daily events from one's life tends to follow Ebbinghaus's forgetting function (Thomson, 1982).

The second of Ebbinghaus's important discoveries is just how long-lasting "savings" in long-term memory can be. Psychologists now know from the method of savings that information about everything from algebra to bike riding is often retained for decades (Medin & Ross, 1992). Thus, you may forget something you have learned if you do not use the information, but it is very easy to relearn the material if the need arises, indicating that the forgetting was not complete (MacLeod, 1988).

The Roles of Decay and Interference

Nothing we have said so far explains *why* forgetting occurs. In principle, either of two processes can be responsible (Reed, 1992). One process is **decay,** the gradual disappearance of the mental representation of a stimulus, much as letters on a piece of steel are eaten away by rust and become less distinct over time. Forgetting might also occur because of **interference,** a process through which either the storage or retrieval of information is impaired by the presence of other information. Interference might occur either because one piece of information actually *displaces* other information, pushing it out of memory, or because one piece of information makes storing or recalling other information more difficult.

In the case of short-term memory, we noted that if an item is not rehearsed or thought about, memory of it decreases consistently over the course of eighteen seconds or so. Thus decay appears to play a prominent role in forgetting information in short-term memory. But interference through displacement also produces forgetting from short-term memory. Like a workbench, short-term memory can hold only a limited number of items; when additional items are added, the old ones tend to "fall off" and are no longer available (Klatzky, 1980). Displacement is one reason why the phone number you just looked up is likely to drop out of short-term memory if you read another number before dialing. Rehearsal prevents displacement by continually re-entering the same information into short-term memory.

Analyzing the cause of forgetting from long-term memory is more complicated. In long-term memory there can be **retroactive interference,** in which learning of new information can interfere with recall of older information, or **proactive interference,** in which old information interferes with learning or remembering new information. For example, retroactive interference would help explain why studying French vocabulary this term might make it more difficult to remember the Spanish words you learned last term. And because of proactive interference, the French words you are learning now might make it harder to learn German next term. Figure 8.15 outlines the types of experiments used to study the influence of each form of interference in long-term memory.

Suppose a person learns something and then, when tested on it after various intervals, remembers less and less as the delay becomes longer. Is this forgetting due to decay or to interference? It is not easy to tell, because longer delays produce both more decay and more retroactive interference as the subject is exposed to further information while waiting. To separate the effects of decay from those of interference, Karl Dallenbach sought to create situations in which time passed but there was no accompanying interference. Evidence of forgetting in such a situation would suggest that decay, not interference, was operating.

The subjects in one experiment were, of all things, cockroaches (Minimi & Dallenbach, 1946). Cockroaches normally avoid light, but the researchers conditioned them to avoid a dark area of their cage by shocking them there. After learning to stay in the light, some of the roaches were returned to their normal laboratory environment. Others were placed individually in small cotton-lined boxes, in which they could

FIGURE 8.15

Procedures for Studying Interference

To recall the two types of interference, remember that the prefixes— *pro* and *retro*—indicate directions in time. In *proactive* interference, previously learned material interferes with *future* learning; *retroactive* interference occurs when new information interferes with the recall of *past* learning.

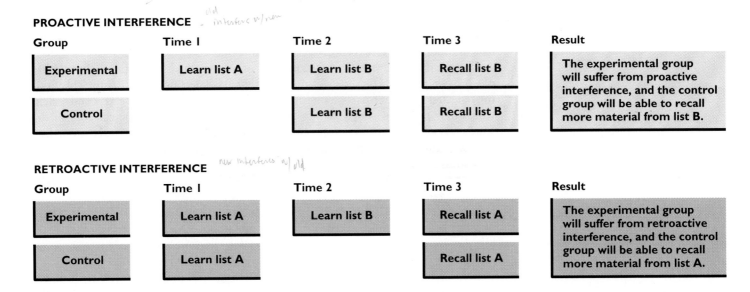

PROACTIVE INTERFERENCE

Group	Time 1	Time 2	Time 3	Result
Experimental	Learn list A	Learn list B	Recall list B	The experimental group will suffer from proactive interference, and the control group will be able to recall more material from list B.
Control		Learn list B	Recall list B	

RETROACTIVE INTERFERENCE

Group	Time 1	Time 2	Time 3	Result
Experimental	Learn list A	Learn list B	Recall list A	The experimental group will suffer from retroactive interference, and the control group will be able to recall more material from list A.
Control	Learn list A		Recall list A	

Interference and Forgetting

Forgetting is more rapid if (A) cock-roaches or (B) college students engage in normal activity after learning than if they spend the time asleep. These results suggest that interference is more important than decay in forgetting information in long-term memory.

Source: Minimi & Dallenbach, 1946.

LINKAGES   Do forgotten memories remain in the subconscious? (a link to Consciousness)

breathe but not move. The researchers reasoned that the second group would not experience the interference associated with normal physical activity. Later, all the cockroaches were again taught to avoid the dark area. Figure 8.16(A) shows their savings score. As the delay in reconditioning lengthened, the difference between the groups grew. Savings declined only slightly for the immobilized cockroaches but dropped dramatically for those that had been normally active. These results strongly supported the notion that forgetting, at least in this situation, was due to interference, not to decay.

So much for cockroaches; what about humans? In another of Dallenbach's studies, college students learned a list of nonsense syllables and then either continued with their waking routine or were sheltered from interference by going to sleep. While the delay (and thus the potential for decay) was held constant for both groups, the greater interference associated with being awake produced much more forgetting, as Figure 8.16(B) shows (Jenkins & Dallenbach, 1924).

Results like these suggest that although it is possible that decay sometimes occurs, interference is the major cause of forgetting from long-term memory. But does interference push the forgotten information out of memory, or does it merely hinder the ability to retrieve it? To find out, Endel Tulving and Joseph Psotka (1971) presented people with different numbers of word lists. Each list contained words from six semantic categories, such as types of buildings (*hut, cottage, tent, hotel*) or earth formations (*cliff, river, hill, volcano*). Some people learned a list and then recalled as many of the words as possible. Other groups learned the first list and then learned different numbers of other lists before trying to recall the first one.

The results were dramatic. As the number of intervening lists increased, the number of words that people could recall from the original list declined consistently. This finding reflected strong retroactive interference. Then the researchers gave a second test, in which they provided people with a retrieval cue by telling them the category of the words (such as types of buildings) to be recalled. Now the number of intervening lists had almost no effect on the number of words recalled from the original list, as Figure 8.17 shows. These results indicate that the words were still represented in long-term memory; they had not been pushed out, but the subjects had been unable to recall them without appropriate retrieval cues. In other words, the original forgetting was due to a failure in retrieval. Thus, putting more and more information in long-term memory may be like placing more and more marbles into a shoebox. Though none of the marbles disappears, it becomes increasingly difficult to find the specific one you are looking for.

Some theorists have concluded that all forgetting from long-term memory is due to some form of retrieval failure (Ratcliff & McKoon, 1989). Does this mean that every-

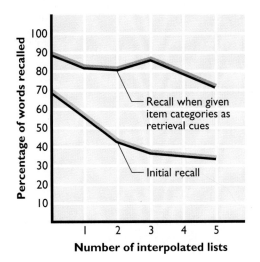

FIGURE 8.17

Retrieval Failures and Forgetting

On the initial test in Tulving and Psotka's experiment, people's ability to recall a list of items was strongly affected by the number of other lists they learned before being tested on the first one. When item-category (retrieval) cues were provided on a second test, however, retroactive interference from the intervening lists almost disappeared.

Recall when given item categories as retrieval cues

Initial recall

Number of interpolated lists

Percentage of words recalled

Source: Tulving & Psotka, 1971.

thing in long-term memory remains there until death, even if people cannot always, or ever, recall it? Some theorists say yes, but others point out that the possibility of displacement cannot be dismissed entirely. No one yet knows for sure.

LINKAGES: MEMORY AND PERCEPTION IN THE COURTROOM

How accurate is eyewitness testimony?

As described in Chapter 5, in order for incoming information to be encoded into memory, it must first be perceived. Perception, in turn, is influenced by a combination of the stimulus features we find "out there" in the world and what we already know, expect, or want—that is, by both bottom-up and top-down processing. The relationship between memory and perception, especially the impact of top-down processing on memory, is made dramatically evident in the courtroom.

Consider, for example, the accuracy of eyewitness memory and how it can be affected by extraneous information (Loftus, 1993a). The most compelling evidence a lawyer can provide is that of an eyewitness, but eyewitnesses make many mistakes (Loftus & Ketcham, 1991). During a federal arson trial in Chicago, for example, a witness was asked if she could identify the man she saw running from a burning building. "That's the guy," she said, looking toward a corner of the courtroom. The judge asked her to single out the man—whereupon she walked over and pointed at an assistant defense attorney (Gottesman, 1992).

Eyewitnesses can remember only what they perceived, and they can perceive only what they attended to (Backman & Nilsson, 1991). The witnesses' task is to report as accurately as possible what they saw or heard; but no matter how hard they try to be accurate, there are limits to how faithful their reports can be (Kassin, Rigby & Castillo, 1991). Further, new information, including the form of a lawyer's question, can alter a witness's memory (Loftus, 1979). Experiments show that when witnesses are asked "How fast was the blue car going when it slammed into the truck?" they are likely to recall a higher speed than when asked "How fast was the blue car going when it hit the truck?" (Loftus & Palmer, 1974; see also Figure 8.18). There is also evidence that an object mentioned after the fact is often mistakenly remembered as having been there in the first place (Dodson & Reisberg, 1991). For example, if a lawyer says that a screwdriver was lying on the ground (when it was not), witnesses often recall with great certainty having seen it (Ryan & Geiselman, 1991). Some theorists have speculated that mentioning an object creates retroactive interference, making the original memory more difficult to retrieve (Tversky & Tuchin, 1989). However, there is now considerable evidence that, when objects are subsequently mentioned, they are integrated into the

FIGURE 8.18

The Impact of Leading Questions on Eyewitness Memory

After seeing a filmed traffic accident, people were asked "About how fast were the cars going when they (smashed, hit, or contacted) each other?" As shown here, the witnesses' responses were influenced by the verb used in the question; "smashed" was associated with the highest average speed estimates. A week later, people who heard the "smashed" question remembered the accident as being more violent than did people in the other two groups (Loftus & Palmer, 1974).

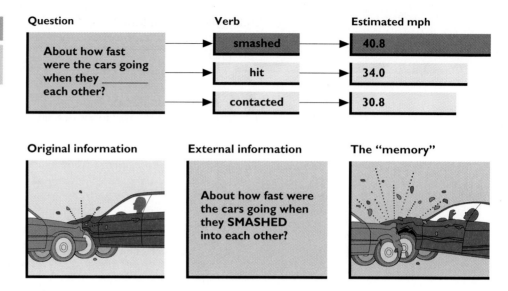

old memory representation and subsequently are not distinguished from what was originally seen (Loftus, 1992).

For jurors, the credibility of a witness often depends as much (or even more) on *how* the witness presents evidence as on the content or relevance of that evidence (Leippe, Manion & Romanczyk, 1992). Many jurors are impressed, for example, when a witness can recall a large number of details. Extremely detailed testimony from prosecution witnesses is especially likely to lead to guilty verdicts, even when the details reported are irrelevant (Bell & Loftus, 1989). Apparently, when a witness gives very detailed testimony, jurors infer that the witness paid especially close attention or has a particularly accurate memory. At first glance, these inferences might seem reasonable. However, as discussed in the chapter on perception, the ability to divide attention is limited. As a result, a witness might focus attention on the crime and the criminal or on the surrounding details, but probably not on both. Hence, witnesses who accurately remember unimportant details of a crime scene may not accurately recall the criminal's facial features or other identifying characteristics (Backman & Nilsson, 1991).

Even witnesses' confidence about their testimony is not always a reliable guide to their credibility. In several experiments, investigators have staged crimes for subjects who then report details of the crime and rate how confident they are about them. While witnesses' confidence tends to make jurors believe them (Leippe, Manion & Romanczyk, 1992), witness confidence ratings are frequently much higher than the accuracy of their reports (Sporer et al., 1995).

Many safeguards are built into the U.S. judicial system to minimize the chances that an innocent person will be falsely convicted. Nevertheless, experimental evidence suggests that the system is far from perfect and might be improved by changes that take into account research on perception, attention, and memory. That research may eventually lead to a court system that provides added protection of the rights and welfare of all citizens.

BIOLOGICAL BASES OF MEMORY

While most psychologists study memory by focusing on conscious and subconscious mental processes, some also consider the physical, electrical, and chemical changes that take place in the brain when people encode, store, and retrieve information.

Biochemical Mechanisms

Recall from Chapter 3 that communication between brain cells takes place at the synapses between axons and dendrites and that the communication depends on chemicals, called neurotransmitters, released at the synapses. There is evidence that new memories are associated with at least two kinds of changes in synapses.

First, new synapses may be formed, as discussed in the Linkages section of Chapter 3. In animals that have been exposed to a complicated environment or required to learn a new motor task, neurons in certain parts of the brain develop more synapses, thus increasing communication both to and from other neurons (Black & Greenough, 1991; Crutcher, 1991). It is likely that these new synapses are involved in the storage of new memories.

Second, when a memory is stored, communication at existing synapses may be improved. The enhancement of existing synapses has been most clearly demonstrated in brain tissue studied in a laboratory dish or in living marine snails. By studying individual synapses as a new memory is formed, researchers discovered that simultaneously activating two inputs to a synapse makes it easier for a signal from a single input to cross the synapse later (Goelet et al., 1986). Changing the pattern of electrical stimulation can also weaken synaptic connections (Malenka, 1995).

Forming new synapses and strengthening existing ones require proteins, so blocking the synthesis of new proteins blocks the formation of long-term memories (Mathies, 1989). As described in the behavioral genetics appendix, proteins are synthesized in accordance with instructions from genes in the form of DNA sequences. Scientists are now studying the role of specific proteins in the formation of memories by altering the DNA sequences for those proteins in the genes of mouse embryos, then looking at the animals' memory capacity when these mutated mice mature. Some specific proteins have already been shown to affect learning ability by strengthening existing synaptic connections (Silva et al., 1992; Grant et al., 1992), while others do so by aiding formation of new ones (Mayford et al., 1992; Qian et al., 1993). Existing synapses can also be strengthened or weakened by chemical modifications of proteins (O'Dell & Kandel, 1994).

In the hippocampus (see Figure 8.19), these changes appear to occur at synapses that use glutamate as a neurotransmitter. One type of glutamate receptor is initially activated only if the postsynaptic neuron is being stimulated by input from more than one neuron (Cotman, Monaghan & Ganong, 1988). After these multiple stimulations are repeated a number of times, this type of glutamate receptor appears to become sensitized so that input from just one neuron is sufficient to produce a response. Such a change in sensitivity could account for the development of conditioned responses, for example (see Chapter 7, on learning).

Acetylcholine also plays a prominent role in memory. The memory problems of Alzheimer's patients appear to be related to a deficiency in neurons that use acetylcholine and send fibers to the hippocampus and the cortex (Donegan & Thompson, 1991). Drugs that interfere with acetylcholine neurotransmission impair memory, and drugs or dietary supplements that increase the amount of acetylcholine in the brain sometimes improve memory in aging experimental animals and humans (Bartus et al., 1982). However, as mentioned in relation to "smart drugs" in Chapter 3, increasing acetylcholine levels is by no means certain to improve memory, partly because acetylcholine is also used as a neurotransmitter outside the brain—namely, at neuromuscular junctions and in the autonomic nervous system. Thus, it is difficult to selectively enhance acetylcholine activity at the synapses used in memory. One way of doing so in the future might be to implant in the brain some cells that have been genetically modified to produce acetylcholine. When this procedure was performed recently on brain-damaged animals, it improved their memory (Winkler et al., 1995).

Brain Structures

LINKAGES Where are memories stored? (a link to Biological Aspects of Psychology)

Where in the human brain do memory-related mechanisms occur? Do synapses develop and grow stronger only in special regions that store memories, or are memories distributed throughout the brain? It appears that memory involves both specialized regions for memory formation and widespread areas for storage (Zola-Morgan & Squire, 1990; McCarthy, 1995).

In the formation of new memories, several brain regions are vital (see Figure 8.19), including the hippocampus and nearby parts of the cortex and the thalamus (Squire, 1992). Damage to these areas results in anterograde amnesia (the inability to form new memories), as we described in the case of H.M., who had damage in the hippocampus and surrounding areas.

Interestingly, although such patients cannot form new episodic memories following hippocampal damage, they can use their *procedural* memory. For example, H.M. was presented with a complicated puzzle on which mistakes are common and performance gradually improves with practice. Over several days his performance steadily improved, just as it does with normal people, and eventually became virtually perfect. But each time he tried the puzzle, he insisted that he had never seen it before (Cohen & Corkin, 1981; see also Figure 6.2 in the chapter on consciousness). Other researchers have also found intact procedural memories in patients who have anterograde amnesia for any new episodic material (Tulving, Hayman & Macdonald, 1991; Squire & McKee, 1992). These patients are also able to keep information temporarily in working memory, which depends on the activity of dopamine neurons in the prefrontal cortex (Williams & Goldman-Rakic, 1995). Thus, while the hippocampus is crucial in the formation of new episodic memories, procedural memory and working memory appear to be governed by other regions of the brain (Squire, 1992).

It is also clear that the hippocampus does not provide permanent long-term storage for memories. (If it did, H.M. would not have retained memories from the years before part of his hippocampus had been removed.) The hippocampus and thalamus send nerve fibers to the cerebral cortex, and it is in the cortex that memories are probably stored (Squire & Zola-Morgan, 1991). As described in Chapters 3 and 4, messages from different senses are represented in different regions of the cortex; specific aspects of an experience are probably stored near these regions. For example, memory for sounds is disrupted by damage to the auditory association cortex (Colombo et al., 1990). A memory, however, involves more than one sensory system. Even in the simple case of a rat remembering a maze, the experience of the maze involves vision, olfaction, specific movements, and the like. Thus, memories are both localized and distributed; certain brain areas store specific aspects of each remembered event, but many brain systems are involved in experiencing a whole event (Squire, 1986).

The more scientists learn about the physiology of memory, the more they see that no single explanation will account for all types of memory. No single brain structure or neurotransmitter is exclusively involved in memory formation or storage.

FIGURE 8.19

Some Brain Structures Involved in Memory

Combined neural activity in many parts of the brain allows us to encode, store, and retrieve memories. The complexity of the biological bases of these processes is underscored by research showing that different aspects of a memory—such as the sights and sounds of some event—are stored in different parts of the cerebral cortex.

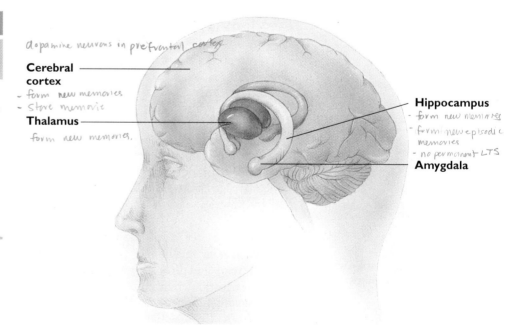

IMPROVING YOUR MEMORY

Even though some basic questions about what memory is and how it works resist final answers, psychologists know a great deal about how people can improve their memories (Bellezza, 1981).

Mnemonics

People with normal memory skills (Harris & Morris, 1984) as well as brain-damaged individuals (Wilson, 1987) can benefit from **mnemonics,** which are strategies for placing information into an organized context in order to remember it. For example, to remember the names of the Great Lakes, you might use the acronym HOMES (for Huron, Ontario, Michigan, Erie, and Superior). Verbal organization is the basis for many mnemonics. You can link items by weaving them into a story or a sentence or a rhyme. To help customers remember where they have parked their cars, some large garages have replaced section designations such as "A1" or "G8" with labels such as color names or months. Customers can then tie the location of their cars to information already in long-term memory—for example, "I parked in the month of my mother's birthday."

One simple but powerful mnemonic is called the *method of loci* (pronounced "low-sigh"), or the method of places. To use this method, first think about a set of familiar locations—your home, for example. You might imagine walking through the front door, around all four corners of the living room, and through each of the other rooms. Next, imagine each item to be remembered in one of these locations. Whenever you want to remember a list, use the same locations, in the same order. Vivid images of interactions or relationships seem to be particularly effective (Kline & Groninger, 1991). For example, tomatoes smashed against the front door or bananas hanging from the bedroom ceiling might be helpful in recalling these items on a grocery list.

All mnemonic systems require that you have a well-learned body of knowledge (such as locations) that can be used to provide a *context* for organizing incoming information (Hilton, 1986). The success of these strategies demonstrates again the importance of relating new information to knowledge already stored in memory.

Guidelines for More Effective Studying

When you want to remember more complex material, such as a textbook chapter, the same principles apply (Palmisano & Herrmann, 1991). Indeed, you can facilitate your memory for text material by first creating an outline or other overall context for learning, rather than by just reading and re-reading (Glover et al., 1990). Repetition may seem effective, because maintenance rehearsal keeps material in short-term memory; but for retaining information over long periods, maintenance rehearsal alone tends to be ineffective, no matter how much time you spend on it (Bjorklund & Green, 1992). In short, "work smarter, not harder."

In addition, spend your time wisely. *Distributed practice* is much more effective than *massed practice* for learning new information. If you are going to spend ten hours studying for a test, you will be much better off studying for ten one-hour blocks (separated by periods of sleep and other activity) than "cramming" for one ten-hour block. By scheduling more study sessions, you will stay fresh and tend to think about the material from a new perspective each session. This method will help you elaborate the material and remember it.

Reading a Textbook   More specific advice for remembering textbook material comes from a study that examined how successful and unsuccessful college students approach their reading (Whimbey, 1976). Unsuccessful students tend to read the material straight through; they do not slow down when they reach a difficult section; and they keep going even when they do not understand what they are reading. In contrast, successful college students monitor their understanding, reread difficult sections, and periodically stop to review what they have learned. In short, effective learners engage in a very deep level of

IN REVIEW	Improving Your Memory
Domain	**Helpful Techniques**
Lists of items	Use mnemonics.
	Look for meaningful acronyms.
	Try the method of loci.
Textbook material	Follow the SQ3R system.
	Allocate your time to allow for distributed practice.
	Read actively, not passively.
Lectures	Take notes, but record only the main points.
	Think about the overall organization of the material.
	Review your notes as soon after the lecture as possible in order to fill in missing points.
Studying for exams	Write a detailed outline of your lecture notes rather than passively reading them.

processing. They are active learners, thinking of each new fact in relation to other material, and they develop a context in which many new facts can be organized effectively.

Research on memory suggests two specific guidelines for reading a textbook. First, make sure that you understand what you are reading before moving on (Herrmann & Searleman, 1992). Second, use the *SQ3R method* (Thomas & Robinson, 1972), which is one of the most successful strategies for remembering textbook material (Anderson, 1990). SQ3R stands for five activities to engage in when you read a chapter: survey, question, read, recite, review. These activities are designed to increase the depth to which you process the information you read.

1. *Survey* Take a few minutes to skim the chapter. Look at the section headings and any boldfaced or italicized terms. Obtain a general idea of what material will be discussed, the way it is organized, and how its topics relate to one another and to what you already know. Some people find it useful to survey the entire chapter once and then survey each major section in a little more detail before reading it.

2. *Question* Before reading each section, ask yourself what content will be covered and what information should be extracted from it.

3. *Read* Read the text, but think about the material as you read. Are the questions you raised earlier being answered? Do you see the connections between the topics?

4. *Recite* At the end of each section, recite the major points. Resist the temptation to be passive and say, "Oh, I remember that." Be active. Put the ideas into your own words by reciting them aloud.

5. *Review* Finally, at the end of the chapter, review all the material. You should see connections not only within a section but also among the sections. The objective is to see how the material is organized. Once you grasp the organization, the individual facts will be far easier to remember.

By following these procedures you will learn and remember the material better and you will also save yourself considerable time.

Lecture Notes Effective note-taking is an acquired skill. Research on memory suggests some simple strategies for taking and using notes effectively.

Realize first that, in note-taking, more is not necessarily better. Taking detailed notes of everything requires that you pay close attention to unimportant as well as important content, leaving little time for thinking about the material. Note-takers who concentrate on expressing the major ideas in relatively few words remember more than those who try to catch every detail (Howe, 1970). In short, the best way to take notes is to think about what is being said, draw connections with other material in the lecture, and then summarize the major points clearly and concisely.

Once you have a set of lecture notes, review them as soon as possible after the lecture so that you can fill in missing details. (As noted earlier, most forgetting from long-term memory occurs within the first few hours after learning.) When the time comes for serious study, use your notes as if they were a chapter in a textbook. Write a detailed outline. Think about how various points are related. Once you have organized the material, the details will make more sense and will be much easier to remember. ("In Review: Improving Your Memory" summarizes tips for studying.)

FUTURE DIRECTIONS

Our understanding of memory has advanced considerably since Ebbinghaus began experimental investigations of it over a hundred years ago. During the rest of the 1990s, particularly spirited debates will center on exactly how many types of memory there are (Cowan, Wood & Borne, 1994; Neath, 1993), whether there are distinct biological structures devoted to each (Awh et al., 1996; Squire, 1992), the degree to which biological research into the chemical and anatomical substrates of memory can be integrated with the development of parallel distributed processing (PDP) models (Martindale, 1991), and the degree to which implicit memory processes affect consciousness (Nelson, Schreiber & McEvoy, 1992; Woike, 1995).

Researchers will also be studying the enormously elaborate autobiographical records that each individual retains over a lifetime. How people develop a representation of themselves in memory (Klein & Loftus, 1993a), how they relate this knowledge to memories of their early childhood (Nelson, 1993), and how they use knowledge about themselves as guides to choosing a mate or deciding on other actions (Vorauer & Ross, 1993)

are all questions being vigorously pursued. The increased interest in repressed memory will be reflected in the intensive study of false memories (Loftus & Pickrell, in press) and the role of suggestibility in memory processes (Ceci & Bruck, 1993; Zaragoza & Lane, 1994).

Expect the results of this and other research to challenge many traditional assumptions about such phenomena as clinical amnesia. Theorists will be examining case studies of amnesia to better understand how specific events become dissociated from more general knowledge of who we are, what we like, how we are motivated, and so on (Gabrieli et al., 1995; Klein & Loftus, 1993b; Schneider, Roediger & Khan, 1993; Tulving, 1993).

There are, of course, many other as yet unanswered questions. Courses on learning and memory provide an excellent starting place for learning more about the latest research, as well as for studying the basic principles of memory in more detail. Other relevant courses include cognitive psychology, social cognition, and experimental psychology.

SUMMARY AND KEY TERMS

■ THE NATURE OF MEMORY

Human memory depends on a complex mental system.

Basic Memory Processes

There are three basic memory processes. *Encoding* transforms stimulus information into some type of mental representation. Encoding can be *acoustic* (by sound), *visual* (by appearance), or *semantic* (by meaning). *Storage* maintains information in the memory system over time. *Retrieval* is the process of gaining access to previously stored information.

Types of Memory

Most psychologists agree that there are at least three types of memory. *Episodic memory* contains information about specific events in a person's life. *Semantic memory* contains generalized knowledge about the world. *Procedural memory* contains information about how to do various things.

Explicit and Implicit Memory

Most research on memory has concerned *explicit memory,* the processes through which people try to remember something. Recently, psychologists have also begun to examine *implicit memory,* which refers to the unintentional recollection and influence of prior experiences.

Models of Memory

Four theoretical models of memory have guided most research. According to the *levels-of-processing* model, the most important determinant of memory is how extensively information is encoded or processed when it is first received. In general, *elaborative rehearsal* is more effective than *maintenance rehearsal* in learning new information because it represents a deeper level of processing. According to the *transfer-appropriate processing* model, the critical determinant of memory is not how deeply information is encoded but whether the encoding process produces memory codes that are later accessed at the time of retrieval. *Parallel distributed processing* (or *PDP*) models of memory suggest that new experiences not only provide specific information but also become part of, and alter, a whole network of associations. The *information-processing* model suggests that, in order for information to become firmly embedded in memory, it must pass through three stages of processing: sensory memory, short-term memory, and long-term memory.

■ ACQUIRING NEW MEMORIES

Sensory Memory
Sensory memory maintains incoming stimulus information in the *sensory registers* for a very brief time. *Selective attention,* which focuses mental resources on only part of the stimulus field, controls what information in the sensory registers is actually perceived and transferred to short-term memory.

Short-Term, or Working, Memory
Short-term memory (STM), which is also known as *working memory,* has two major functions: It constructs and updates an internal model of the environment, and it provides a system in which people can store, organize, and integrate facts and thereby solve problems and make decisions. Various memory codes can be used in short-term memory, but acoustic codes seem to be preferred in most verbal tasks. Studies of the *immediate memory span* indicate that the capacity of short-term memory is approximately seven *chunks,* or meaningful groupings of information. Studies using the *Brown-Peterson procedure* show that information in short-term memory is usually forgotten within about eighteen seconds if it is not rehearsed.

Long-Term Memory
Long-term memory (LTM) normally involves semantic coding, which means that people tend to encode the general meaning of information, not specific details, into long-term memory. The capacity of long-term memory to store new information is extremely large, perhaps unlimited.

Distinguishing Between Short-Term and Long-Term Memory
According to the levels-of-processing model, there is no need to distinguish between short-term and long-term memory. Still, some evidence suggests that these systems may be distinct. For example, although serial-position curves show both a *primacy effect* and a *recency effect,* either effect can be eliminated without affecting the other. Further, clinical cases of *anterograde* and *retrograde amnesia* suggest that information is transferred from short-term to long-term memory.

■ RETRIEVING MEMORIES

Retrieval Cues and Encoding Specificity
Retrieval cues help people remember things that they would otherwise not be able to recall. The effectiveness of retrieval cues follows the *encoding specificity principle:* Cues help retrieval only if they match some feature of the information that was originally encoded.

Context and State Dependence
All else being equal, memory may be better when one attempts to retrieve information in the same environment in which it was learned; this is called *context-dependent* memory. When a person's internal state can aid or impede retrieval, memory is said to be *state-dependent.*

Retrieval from Semantic Memory
Researchers usually study retrieval from semantic memory by examining how long it takes people to answer world knowledge questions. It appears that ideas are represented as associations in a dense semantic memory network, and that the retrieval of information occurs by a process of *spreading activation.* Each concept in the network is represented as a unique collection of features or attributes. The tip-of-the-tongue phenomenon and the feeling-of-knowing experience represent the retrieval of incomplete knowledge.

Constructing Memories
In the process of constructive memory, people use their existing knowledge to fill in gaps in the information they encode and retrieve. PDP models provide one explanation of how people make spontaneous generalizations about the world. They also explain the *schemas* that shape the memories people construct.

■ FORGETTING

The Course of Forgetting
Hermann Ebbinghaus's research on long-term memory and forgetting introduced the *method of savings.* He found that most forgetting from long-term memory occurs during the first several hours after learning and that savings can be extremely long lasting.

The Roles of Decay and Interference
Decay and *interference* are two mechanisms of forgetting. While there is evidence of both decay and interference in short-term memory, it appears that most forgetting from long-term memory is due to either *retroactive interference* or *proactive interference.*

■ LINKAGES: MEMORY AND PERCEPTION IN THE COURTROOM

Eyewitnesses can remember only what they perceive, and they can perceive only what they attend to. As a result, eyewitness testimony is often much less accurate than witnesses, and jurors, think it is.

■ BIOLOGICAL BASES OF MEMORY

Biochemical Mechanisms
Research has shown that memory can result as new synapses are formed in the brain, and as communication at existing synapses is improved. Several neurotransmitters appear to be involved in the strengthening that occurs at synapses.

Brain Structures
The hippocampus and thalamus are among the brain regions known to play a role in the formation of memories. These structures send nerve fibers to the cerebral cortex, and it is there that memories are probably stored. Any single memory involves information from more than one sensory system, and messages from the different senses are represented in different regions of the cortex. Thus, memories appear to be both localized and distributed.

■ IMPROVING YOUR MEMORY

Mnemonics
Mnemonics are devices that are used to remember things better. One of the simplest but most powerful mnemonics is the method of loci. It is useful because it provides a context for organizing material more effectively.

Guidelines for More Effective Studying
The key to remembering textbook material is to read actively rather than passively. One of the most effective ways to do this is to follow the SQ3R method: survey, question, read, recite, and review. Similarly, to take lecture notes or to study them effectively, organize the points into a meaningful framework and think about how each main point relates to the others.

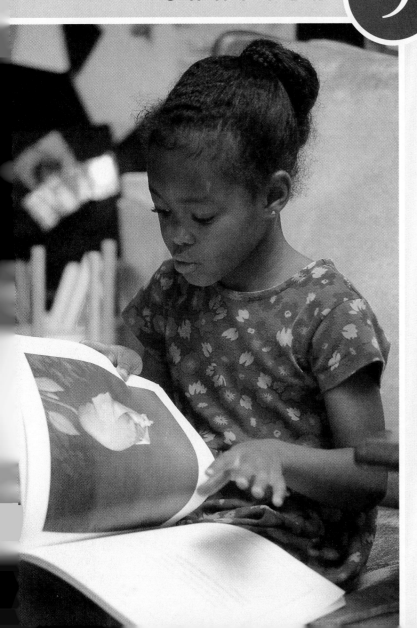

THOUGHT AND LANGUAGE

CHAPTER 9

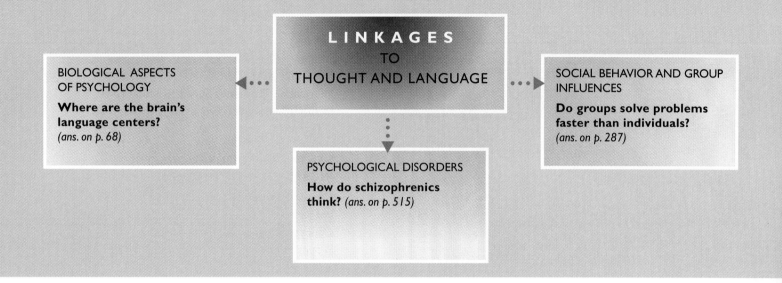

LINKAGES
TO
THOUGHT AND LANGUAGE

BIOLOGICAL ASPECTS
OF PSYCHOLOGY

**Where are the brain's
language centers?**
(ans. on p. 68)

SOCIAL BEHAVIOR AND GROUP
INFLUENCES

**Do groups solve problems
faster than individuals?**
(ans. on p. 287)

PSYCHOLOGICAL DISORDERS

**How do schizophrenics
think?** *(ans. on p. 515)*

D r. Joyce Wallace, a New York City internist, was having trouble figuring out what was the matter with a forty-three-year old patient, "Laura McBride." Laura reported pains in her stomach and abdomen, aching muscles, irritability, occasional dizzy spells, and fatigue (Rouéché, 1986). The doctor's initial hypothesis was iron-deficiency anemia, a condition in which the level of oxygen-carrying hemoglobin in the blood is too low. There was some evidence to support that hypothesis. A physical examination revealed that Laura's spleen was somewhat enlarged, and blood tests showed low hemoglobin and high production of red blood cells, suggesting that her body was attempting to compensate for the loss of hemoglobin. However, other tests revealed normal iron levels. Perhaps she was losing blood through internal bleeding, but a stool test ruled that out. Had Laura been vomiting blood? She said no. Blood in the urine? No. Abnormally heavy menstrual flow? No. During the next week, as Dr. Wallace puzzled over the problem, Laura's condition worsened. She reported more intense pain, cramps, shortness of breath, and severe loss of energy. Her blood was becoming less and less capable of sustaining her, but if it was not being lost, what was happening to it? Finally, the doctor looked at a smear of Laura's blood on a microscope slide. What she saw indicated that some poison was destroying the red blood cells. What could it be? Laura spent most of her time at home, but her teenage daughters, who lived with her, were perfectly healthy. Wallace asked herself, "What does Laura do that the girls do not?" She repairs and restores paintings. Paint. Lead! She might be suffering from lead poisoning! When the next blood test showed a lead level seven times higher than normal, Dr. Wallace knew she was right at last.

To solve this medical mystery, Dr. Wallace relied on her ability to think, solve problems, and make judgments and decisions. She used these higher mental processes to weigh the pros and cons of various hypotheses and to reach decisions about what tests to order and how to interpret them. She also consulted with the patient and other physicians using that remarkable human ability known as language.

This story provides just one example of the thinking, problem solving, decision making, and linguistic communication that occur in human beings all the time. How good are human judgments and decisions? What factors influence them? How are thoughts transformed into language? Psychologists have been studying these questions for many years. In this chapter, we introduce some of their findings and highlight the importance of their research (see the Linkages diagram). We first examine a general framework for understanding human cognition and then look at specific cognitive processes.

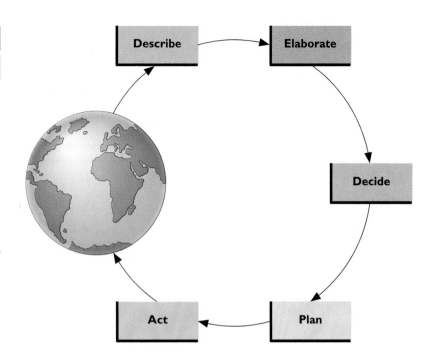

FIGURE 9.1

The Circle of Thought

The circle of thought begins as our sensory systems take in information from the world around us. Our perceptual system describes and elaborates this information, which is represented in the brain in ways that allow us to make decisions, formulate plans, and carry out actions. As our actions change our world, we receive new information—and the circle of thought begins again.

LINKAGES: "AUTOMATIC" THINKING
The sensory, perceptual, decision-making, and response-planning components that make up the circle of thought often occur so rapidly that we may be unaware of anything other than incoming information and our quick response to it. This is especially likely in skilled computer game players because, as described in Chapter 5, on perception, well-practiced tasks can be performed automatically.

BASIC FUNCTIONS OF THOUGHT

To begin our exploration of human thinking, we consider its five core functions, which are to *describe, elaborate, decide, plan,* and *guide action*. These functions can be seen as forming a circle of thought (see Figure 9.1).

The Circle of Thought

Consider how the circle of thought operated in Dr. Wallace's case. It began when she received the information about Laura's symptoms that allowed her to *describe* the problem. Next, Dr. Wallace *elaborated* on this information by using her knowledge and experience to consider what disorders might cause such symptoms. Then she made a *decision* to investigate a possible cause, such as anemia. To implement this decision, she formulated a *plan*—to order a blood test—and then *acted* on that plan. But the circle of thought did not stop there. Information from the blood test provided new descriptive information, which Dr. Wallace elaborated further to reach another decision, create a new plan, and guide her next action.

Usually, the circle of thought spins so quickly and its processes are so complex that the task of slowing it down for careful analysis might seem like trying to nail Jell-O to a tree. Some psychologists have approached this task by studying human thought processes as if they were components in a computer-like information-processing system. An **information-processing system** receives information, represents the information with symbols, and then manipulates those representations. According to this information-processing model, then, **thinking** is defined as the manipulation of mental representations. Figure 9.2 shows how an information-processing model might view the sequence of events that form each cycle in the circle of thought. Notice that, according to this model, information from the world is somewhat transformed as it passes through each stage of processing (Wickens, 1992).

In the first stage, information about the world reaches the brain by way of the sensory receptors described in Chapter 4. This stage does not require attention. In the second stage, the information must be perceived and recognized, using the attentional and perceptual processes detailed in Chapter 5. It is also during this stage that the information is consciously elaborated, using short-term, or working, memory processes that allow us to think about it in relation to knowledge stored in long-term memory. Once the information has been elaborated in this way, we must decide what to do with it. This third stage—decision making—also demands attention. The decision may simply be to

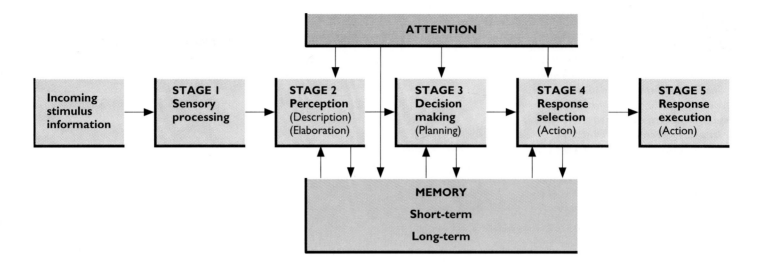

An Information-Processing Model

According to the information-processing model, each stage in the circle of thought takes a certain amount of time. Some stages depend heavily on both short-term and long-term memory and require some attention—that limited supply of mental energy required for information processing to be carried out efficiently.

store the information in memory, as described in Chapter 8. If, however, a decision is made to take some action, a response must be planned in the third stage, then carried out through a coordinated pattern of responses—the action itself—in the fourth and fifth stages. As suggested in Figure 9.1, this action usually affects the environment, providing new information that, in turn, is "fed back" to the system for processing in the ongoing circle of thought.

Information-Processing Speed: Reaction Time

The information-processing model developed in part from research on precisely the kind of high-speed thinking that seems so impossible to study. For example, imagine you are driving a little too fast and approach a green traffic light that suddenly turns yellow. You must immediately decide whether to apply the brakes or floor the accelerator. Here is a situation in which time is of the essence; in a second or less, the stimulus must be described and elaborated, a decision made, a plan created, and an action executed.

If thinking does involve distinct processes, as the circle of thought implies, then each of these processes must take some time. Indeed, psychologists began the laboratory investigation of thinking by exploring **mental chronometry,** which involves the timing of mental events (Posner, 1978). Specifically, they examined **reaction time,** the time elapsing between the presentation of a stimulus and the appearance of an overt response. Reaction time, they reasoned, would give us an idea of how long it takes for all the processes shown in Figure 9.2 to occur. A typical reaction-time experiment recreates the traffic light situation mentioned earlier: A person is asked to say a certain word or to push a certain button as rapidly as possible after a stimulus appears. Even in such simple situations, several factors influence reaction times (Wickens, 1992).

One important factor is the *complexity* of the decision. The larger the number of possible actions that might be carried out in response to a set of stimuli, the longer the reaction time. The tennis player who knows that her opponent usually serves to the same spot on the court will have a simple decision to make when the serve is completed and will react rapidly. In contrast, when she faces an opponent whose serve is less predictable, her reaction will be slower because a more complex decision about which way to move is now required.

Reaction time is also influenced by *stimulus-response compatibility*. If the spatial relationship between a set of stimuli and possible responses is a natural or compatible one, reaction time will be fast. If not, reaction time will be slower. Figure 9.3 illustrates compatible and incompatible relationships. Incompatible stimulus-response relationships are major culprits in causing errors in the use of all kinds of equipment (Norman, 1988; Proctor & Van Zandt, 1994).

Expectancy, too, affects reaction time. As noted in Chapter 5, expected stimuli are perceived more quickly and with greater accuracy than those that are surprising.

Stimulus-Response Compatibility

Imagine standing in front of an unfamiliar stove when a pan starts to boil over. Your reaction time in turning down the heat will depend in part on the stove's design. The response you make will be quicker on stove (A), because each knob is next to the burner it controls; there is compatibility between the source of the stimulus and the location of the response. Stove (B) shows less compatibility; here, which knob you should turn is not as obvious, so your reaction time will be slower.

(A) A COMPATIBLE RELATIONSHIP   **(B) AN INCOMPATIBLE RELATIONSHIP**

Expectancy has the same effect on response time: People respond faster to stimuli that they anticipate and more slowly to those that surprise them. Similarly, responses that people expect to make—such as hitting the brakes for a red light—occur more quickly than unexpected ones, such as warding off a purse-snatcher.

Finally, in any reaction-time task there is a *speed-accuracy tradeoff*. If you try to respond quickly, errors increase; if you try for an error-free performance, reaction time increases (Wickelgren, 1977). Sprinters who try too hard to anticipate the starting gun may have especially quick starts but may also have especially frequent false starts that disqualify them.

Picturing Information Processing: Evoked Brain Potentials

Research on reaction time has helped establish the time required for information processing to occur; it has also revealed how the entire sequence can be speeded or slowed. But reaction times alone cannot provide a detailed picture of what goes on between the presentation of a stimulus and the execution of a response. They do not tell us, for example, how long the perception stage lasts, or whether we respond more quickly to an expected stimulus because we perceive it faster or because we make a decision about it faster. Reaction-time measures have been used in many ingenious efforts to make inferences about such things (Coles, 1989; Posner, 1978); but to analyze mental events more directly, psychologists have turned to other methods, such as the analysis of evoked brain potentials.

The **evoked brain potential** is a small, temporary change in voltage on an electroencephalogram (EEG) that occurs in response to specific events (Rugg & Coles, 1995). Figure 9.4 shows an example. Each peak reflects the firing of large groups of neurons, within different regions of the brain, at different times during the information-processing sequence. Thus, the pattern of the peaks provides information that is more precise than overall reaction time. For example, a large positive peak, called P300, occurs 300–500 milliseconds after a stimulus is presented. The exact timing of P300 is sensitive to factors that alter the speed of perceptual processes, such as the difficulty of detecting a stimulus. But the timing of the P300 is not affected by factors that just alter the speed of response selection and execution, such as changes in stimulus-response compatibility (McCarthy & Donchin, 1979; Rugg & Coles, 1995). Hence, the timing of a subject's P300 may provide an index of the duration of the first two stages shown in Figure 9.2.

Evoked Brain Potentials

Shown here is the average EEG tracing produced from several trials on which a subject's name was presented. Evoked potentials are averaged in this way so as to eliminate random variations in the EEG tracings. The result is the appearance of a negative peak (N100) followed by a large positive peak (P300); by tradition, positive peaks are plotted as decreases while negative ones appear as increases on the tracings.

MENTAL REPRESENTATIONS: THE INGREDIENTS OF THOUGHT

Just as measuring, stirring, and baking are only part of the story of cookie-making, describing and timing the *processes* of thinking tell only part of the story behind the circle of thought. To understand thinking more fully, we also need to know what it is that these processes manipulate. Consistent with the information-processing model, most psychologists usually describe the ingredients of thought as *information*. But this is like saying that you make cookies with "stuff." What specific forms can information take in our minds? In other words, how do we mentally represent information?

Researchers in cognitive psychology have found that information can be mentally represented in at least four forms: (1) cognitive maps, (2) images, (3) concept schemas and event scripts, and (4) propositions. In the following sections we consider these ingredients of thought and how people manipulate them as they think.

Cognitive Maps

It is midnight. You are home alone when, suddenly, the power fails. Even though you can't see a thing, you are still able to find a flashlight or candle, not only because memory tells you where it is but because you carry with you a **cognitive map**—a mental representation of familiar parts of your world (Smythe et al., 1995). In this case, your cognitive map delineates the floor plan, furniture placements, door locations, and other physical features of your home. You would not have this mental map in an unfamiliar house; there, you would have to walk slowly, arms outstretched, to avoid wrong turns and painful collisions. In the chapter on learning we describe how experience shapes cognitive maps that, in turn, help animals navigate mazes and people navigate shopping malls.

What kind of experience do we need in order to create a cognitive map? Looking at our environment is obviously helpful, but research with blind people shows that visual experience is not necessary. For example, Barbara Landau (1986) gave a map with raised features to a young girl who had been blind from birth. The girl had never before touched such a map, but she was immediately able to understand what it was and to use it as effectively as sighted children of her age to plan routes through a room and locate toys. It appears that having the experience of moving through space is enough to allow us to represent information in the form of cognitive maps (Landau, 1986; Millar, 1994).

Useful as they are, cognitive maps are not accurate copies of the environment; they include systematic distortions. One distortion results from *rectangular bias*, a tendency to impose a rectangular north-south-east-west grid on the environment (Wickens, 1992). For example, when asked to draw a map of Paris, most Parisians straighten out the bends of the Seine River in an effort to make it conform more closely to an east-west flow (Milgram & Jodelet, 1976). The rectangular bias also distorts the sense of relative locations. If you were asked where Reno, Nevada, is with respect to San Diego, California, you would probably say northeast (Stevens & Coupe, 1978). After all, Nevada is east of California, and Reno is north of San Diego. But because southern California "bends" to the east, Reno is in fact northwest of San Diego.

Images

Think about how your best friend would look in a clown suit. Did you conjure up a mental picture? Often, thinking is based on the manipulation of **images,** which are mental representations of visual information. Research suggests that the manipulations performed on images of objects are very similar to those that would be performed on the objects themselves (Kosslyn, 1994).

For example, Steven Kosslyn (1976) asked people to form a mental image of an object such as a cat and then asked questions about it, such as "Does it have a head?" and "Does it have claws?" The smaller the detail in question, the longer people took to answer the question, as if they were mentally zooming in on the detail necessary to answer the question. The finer the detail required by the question, the greater the zoom and the longer the response time. Similarly, Keith Holyoak (1977) asked people to say which of two familiar objects was larger. When the objects were similar in size—a Popsicle and a pack of cards, for example—people took longer to answer than when they were of very different sizes—a Popsicle and a pickup truck, say. Apparently, when the objects are about the same size, we must summon an image of each, then carefully compare them—much as we would if the objects were actually present.

Concept Schemas and Event Scripts

As mental representations of our physical world, cognitive maps and images are important ingredients of thought, but understanding that world requires still other ingredients. For one thing, we need ways of thinking about the world that encode the *meaning* of things.

Think about anything—dogs, happiness, sex, movies, fame, pizza—and you are manipulating concepts, one of the most basic ingredients of thought. **Concepts** are categories of objects, events, or ideas with common properties. Concepts may be concrete and visual, such as the concepts "round" or "red," but they may also be abstract, such as the concepts "truth" and "justice." To "have a concept" is to recognize the properties, relationships, or *features* that are shared by and define members of the category, and to ignore those that are not. For example, the concept "bird" includes such properties as having feathers, laying eggs, and being able to fly.

Concepts are vital to thought because they allow you to relate each object or event you encounter to a category that is already known. Concepts make logical thought possible. If you have the concepts "whale" and "bird," you can decide whether a whale is a bird without having either creature in the room with you.

Types of Concepts   Some concepts—called **artificial concepts**—can be clearly defined by a set of rules or properties such that each member of the concept has all of the defining properties and no nonmember does. For example, the concept "square" can be defined as "a shape with four equal sides and four right-angle corners." Any object that does not have all of these features simply is not a square. To study concept learning in the laboratory, psychologists often use artificial concepts because the members of the concept can be neatly defined (Trabasso & Bower, 1968).

In contrast, try to define the concept "home" or "game." These are examples of **natural concepts,** concepts that have no fixed set of *defining* features but instead share a set of *characteristic* features. Members of a natural concept need not possess all of the characteristic features. One characteristic feature of the natural concept "bird," for example, is the ability to fly; but an ostrich is a bird even though it cannot fly, because it possesses enough other characteristic features of "bird" (feathers, wings, and the like). Having just one bird property is not enough; snakes lay eggs and bats can fly, but neither are birds. It is usually a *combination* of properties that defines a concept. Outside the laboratory, most of the concepts people use are natural rather than artificial. These natural

A NATURAL CONCEPT Both a space shuttle and a hot air balloon are examples of the natural concept "aircraft," but most people would probably think of the space shuttle, with its wings, as the better example. A prototype of the concept is probably an airplane.

concepts include both relatively stable "object" categories, such as "bird" or "house," and temporary goal-related categories, such as "things to put in a suitcase," that help people make plans (Barsalou, 1991, 1993).

The boundaries of a natural concept are fuzzy, and some members of the concept are better examples of the concept than others because they share more characteristic features of the concept (Rosch, 1975). A robin, a chicken, an ostrich, and a penguin are all birds. But a robin is a better example than the other three, because a robin can fly and is closer to the size and proportion of what most people, through experience, think of as a typical bird. A member of a natural concept that possesses all or most of its characteristic features is called a **prototype,** or is said to be prototypical. Thus, the robin is a prototypical bird. As described in relation to network models of memory in Chapter 8, the more prototypical a member of a concept is, the more quickly people can decide if it is an example of the concept. Thus people can decide more rapidly that "a robin is a bird" than that "a penguin is a bird."

Representing Concepts Concepts tend to be mentally represented as **schemas,** which, as described in Chapter 8, are generalizations we develop about categories of objects, events, and people. For example, our schema about birds probably includes a robin-like prototype, along with everything else we know about how birds look and act, where they live, and so on. Thus, schemas help us to understand birds as well as, say, what cars are, how baseball is played, and how police officers usually dress. As shown in the chapter on memory, schemas also generate *expectations* about objects, events, and people—that cars have four wheels, that baseball is played in the summer, that police officers help people, and so on.

As also noted in the chapter on memory, schemas about familiar sequences of events or activities are called **scripts** (Schank & Abelson, 1977). For example, your script of the events that typically occur when you enter a restaurant tells you what you should and should not do in that situation. You also tend to interpret new information and events in line with your scripts. You assume that the person who greets you in a restaurant is an employee, not a mugger. Events that violate scripts may be misinterpreted or even ignored. Thus, you might step over a heart-attack victim on the sidewalk because your script for walking down a city street tells you that someone lying on the sidewalk is drunk, not sick. Indeed, scripts are involved in the top-down processing (discussed in Chapter 5) that prompts people to recognize and react to expected events more quickly and correctly than to unexpected ones. If a bank customer pulls a gun and demands money, the script-violating aspect of the event—though attention getting—may slow observers' perception of the situation and interfere with decisions about a course of action.

Propositions

Often, as when a person is deciding which of two imagined objects is larger, thinking involves relating one concept to another. We tend to mentally represent relationships between and among concepts as **propositions,** the smallest units of knowledge that can stand as a separate assertion. These ingredients of thought tend to take the form of spoken or unspoken sentences. They may be true or false. Some propositions, such as "dogs chase cats," describe the relationship between concepts; others, such as "birds have wings," describe the relationship between a concept and its properties.

Mental Models Often, clusters of propositions are represented as **mental models,** which contain our understanding of how things (usually physical things) work. These models then guide our interaction with such things (Norman, 1988). For example, to understand the sequence of commands necessary to edit, save, and retrieve a computer file, you might use a mental model that consists of propositions such as "Each file must have its own name," "Pressing the F10 key stores the file in a place on the disk," and the like. When our mental models are incorrect, we are more likely to make mistakes (see Figure 9.5). Thus, people who hold an incorrect mental model of how physical illness is cured might stop taking medication when their symptoms begin to disappear, yet

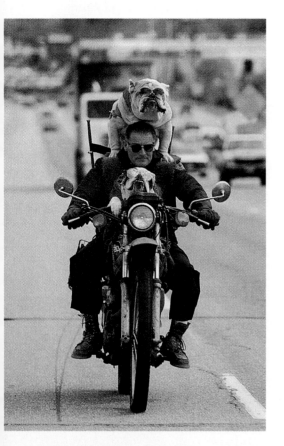

VIOLATING A SCHEMA Schemas, or learned generalizations about objects, events, and people, result in expectations about the world. People tend to be surprised when schema-based expectations are not met, as in the case of motorcycle-riding dogs or three-wheeled automobiles.

IN REVIEW	Ingredients of Thought	
Ingredient	**Description**	**How it is used**
Cognitive maps	Mental representations of familiar locations	Cognitive maps help us describe the world, plan routes, and reach destinations.
Images	Visual mental representations of physical objects, events, and scenes	Images can be manipulated—rotated, expanded, and examined—to help us think about spatial problems like those involved in navigation.
Concept schemas and event scripts	Generalizations about concepts formed by experience; mental representations of a typical sequence of activity, usually involving people's behavior	Concept schemas represent a large set of specific examples and create expectations; scripts may be used to interpret what will happen or is happening in familiar situations—a component of top-down processing.
Propositions	Smallest unit of knowledge that can stand as a separate assertion	Propositions are usually evaluated as to truth or falsity.
Mental models	Clusters of propositions that represent our understanding of how things work	Mental models guide our interactions with things; they may be correct or biased.

FIGURE 9.5

Applying a Mental Model

Try to imagine the path that the marble will follow when it leaves the curved tube. In one study, most people drew the incorrect (curved) path indicated by the dotted line, rather than the correct (straight) path indicated by the dashed line (McClosky, 1983). Their error was based on a faulty mental model of the behavior of physical objects.

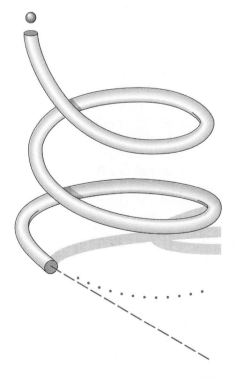

well before the bacteria causing those symptoms have been eliminated (Medin & Ross, 1992).

THINKING STRATEGIES

As already noted, our thinking capacity derives in large measure from our ability to manipulate mental representations—the ingredients of thought—much as a baker manipulates the ingredients of cookies (see "In Review: Ingredients of Thought" for a summary of these representations). But while the baker's food processor combines and transforms flour, sugar, milk, and chocolate into a delicious treat, our far more complex information-processing system combines, transforms, and elaborates mental representations in ways that allow us to engage in reasoning, problem-solving, and decision making. We begin our discussion of these strategies by considering **reasoning,** the process through which people generate and evaluate arguments, and reach conclusions about them.

Formal Reasoning

Astronomers tell us that the temperature at the core of the sun is about 27 million degrees Fahrenheit. How do they know this? As it is not possible to place a temperature probe inside the sun, the assertion is necessarily based on astronomers' *inferences* from other facts they know about the sun and about physical objects in general. For example, telescopic observations of the sun's volume and mass allowed astronomers to calculate its density, using the formula Density = Mass ÷ Volume. Such observations also enabled them to measure the energy output from a small region of the sun and—using what geometry told them about the surface area of spheres—to extrapolate that value to the sun as a whole. Further calculations yielded an estimate of how hot a body would have to be to generate that much energy. In short, the astronomers' highly educated guess about the sun's core temperature was based on **formal,** or **logical, reasoning**— the process of following a set of rigorous procedures for reaching valid, or correct, conclusions. Some of these procedures included the application of specific mathematical formulas to existing data in order to generate new data. Such formulas, in turn, are examples of **algorithms**—systematic methods that always reach a correct result.

The astronomers also followed the rules of **logic,** a set of mental procedures that provide a more general algorithm, or formula, for drawing valid conclusions about the world. For example, each step in the astronomers' thinking took the form of "if-then" propositions: *If* we know how much energy comes from one part of the sun's surface, and *if* we know how big the whole surface is, *then* we can calculate the total energy output. You use the same logical reasoning processes when you conclude, for example, that *if* your friend Jovan is two years older than you are, *then* his twin brother Jermaine will be two years older, too.

The rules of logic, which are traceable to the Greek philosopher Aristotle, have evolved into a system that allows valid, or correct, conclusions to be drawn from a set of statements—known as *premises.* Consider, for example, what conclusion can be drawn from these premises:

Premise 1: *People who study hard do well in this course.*
Premise 2: *You have studied hard.*

According to the rules of logic, it would be valid to conclude that you will do well in this course. Logical arguments containing two or more premises and a conclusion are known as **syllogisms.** Notice that the conclusion in a syllogism goes beyond what the premises actually say. The conclusion is an *inference* based on the premises and on the rules of logic. In this case, the logical rule was that if something is true of all members of a category and "A" is in that category, then that something will also be true of "A."

USING ALGORITHMS Scientists in many fields use algorithms to perform calculations and draw conclusions about everything from the behavior of subatomic particles and wind-blown skyscrapers to weather systems and solar flares.

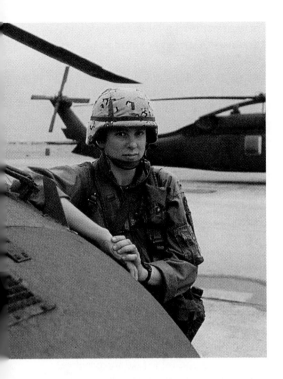

PITFALLS IN LOGICAL REASONING "No woman can be a combat pilot; this person is a woman, therefore, she should not be in combat." The *logic* of this syllogism is correct, but because the first premise is wrong, U.S. legislators and military policy-makers who base decisions on this logic alone will reach erroneous conclusions about women and combat. Indeed, the distinguished performance of women in dangerous close-support missions during the Gulf War and other more recent operations has led to an expansion of their role in combat.

Most of us try to use logical reasoning to reach valid conclusions and avoid erroneous ones (Rips, 1994), but we have to watch out for two pitfalls: incorrect premises and violations of the rules of logic. For example:

Premise 1: *All psychologists are brilliant.*
Premise 2: *The authors of this book are psychologists.*
Conclusion: *The authors of this book are brilliant.*

Do you agree? The conclusion follows logically from the premises, but, because the first premise is false, we cannot determine whether or not the conclusion is true. Now consider this syllogism:

Premise 1: *All gun owners are people.*
Premise 2: *All criminals are people.*
Conclusion: *All gun owners are criminals.*

Here, the premises are correct, but the logic is faulty. If "all A's are B" and "all C's are B," it does *not* follow that "all A's are C." In other words, even conclusions based on correct premises can be false if they do not follow the rules of logic.

Psychologists have discovered that both kinds of pitfalls lead people to make errors in logical reasoning, which is one reason why misleading advertisements or speeches can still attract sales and votes (Solso, 1991). Psychologists have identified several specific sources of these errors.

1. *Bias about conclusions.* What do you think of this syllogism? *The United States is a free country. In a free country all people have equal opportunity. Therefore, in the United States all people have equal opportunity.* People who agree with this conclusion often do so not because they have carefully considered the premises but because they hold a *prior belief* about the conclusion (McGuire, 1968). The same tendency often frustrates district attorneys prosecuting a celebrity, a member of the clergy, or a harmless-looking senior citizen. Jurors may remain unpersuaded by logically sound arguments based on true premises simply because the logical conclusion (that a nice elderly woman poisoned her sister) is at odds with their schemas about such people and with their scripts about how the world operates. In other words, the conclusions that people reach are often based on both logical and wishful thinking (Evans, Barsten & Pollard, 1983).

2. *The conversion effect.* People often assume that premises are symmetrical—that if A implies B, then B implies A. This is wrong, of course: Being a Democrat implies you are a person, but it does not follow that being a person implies you are a Democrat.

3. *Limits on working memory.* Evaluating syllogisms, particularly long ones, requires you to hold a lot of material in short-term, or working, memory while mentally manipulating it. This task is particularly difficult if elements in a syllogism involve negatives, as in "No dogs are nonanimals." If the amount of material to be manipulated exceeds the capacity of working memory, logical errors can easily result.

Cultural Differences in Formal Reasoning   Most of the time, logic and experience support the same conclusion. If they don't, the ideal option in most Western cultures is to rely on formal logic. But this ideal is not universal. In some cultures, direct experience is sometimes considered a surer guide than abstract logic.

As an example, consider the following syllogism-based question: *Ivan and Boris always eat together; Boris is eating; therefore, what is Ivan doing?* Most students in the United States would answer "eating," but in one study, a majority of Russian students said something like "I don't know. I wasn't there" (Solso, 1987). That answer is not incorrect; it is simply based on a qualitatively different line of reasoning, which argues that direct observation is the best, and perhaps only, way to establish the truth.

Alfred Bloom (1981) found that Chinese residents of Hong Kong showed a similar culturally based tendency to organize thought around known facts. His subjects had a difficult time responding to questions such as "If the Hong Kong government were to pass a law requiring people to make weekly reports of their activities, how would you react?" Bloom's research indicated that the Chinese language does not allow easy expression of *counterfactual arguments,* which are arguments that consider hypothetical propositions that are not currently true. Such arguments are rarely found in Chinese newspapers.

These results do not mean that Russians are illogical or that the Chinese are incapable of counterfactual thinking (Au, 1983, 1992; Liu, 1985); they suggest instead that people's thinking in certain situations is shaped by both formal logic-based schooling and the culture in which that schooling takes place.

Informal Reasoning

The use of algorithms and logic to discover new facts and draw inferences is only one kind of reasoning. A second kind—called *informal reasoning*—comes into play in situations where we are trying to assess the *credibility* of a conclusion based on the evidence available to support it. Psychologists use this kind of reasoning when they design experiments and other research methods whose results will provide evidence for (or against) their theories; jurors use informal reasoning when weighing evidence for the guilt or innocence of a defendant.

Formal reasoning is guided by algorithms, but there are no foolproof methods for informal reasoning. Consider, for example, how many white swans you would have to see before concluding that all swans are white. Fifty? A hundred? A million? A strictly formal, algorithmic approach would require that you observe every swan in existence to be sure they are all white, but such a task would be impossible. A more practical approach is to base your conclusion on the number of obervations that some mental rule of thumb leads you to *believe* is "enough." In other words, you would take a mental "shortcut" to reach a conclusion that is probably, but not necessarily, correct. Such mental shortcuts are called **heuristics.**

Suppose you are about to leave home but cannot find your watch. Applying an algorithm would mean searching in every possible location, room by room, until the watch is found. But you can reach the same outcome more quickly by using a heuristic—that is, by searching only where your experience suggests you might have left the watch. In short, heuristics are often valuable in guiding judgments about which events are probable or which hypotheses are likely to be true. Indeed, they are easy to use and frequently work well.

LINKAGES: REASONING AND CRITICAL THINKING   Informal reasoning about the quality of evidence available to support an assertion or hypothesis is an important part of critical thinking, as described in Chapter 2. Critical thinking incorporates formal reasoning, too, because we must decide whether certain conclusions can logically be drawn from even well-established evidence. The Thinking Critically sections in this book illustrate how both formal and informal reasoning can help people think about a variety of important and controversial topics.

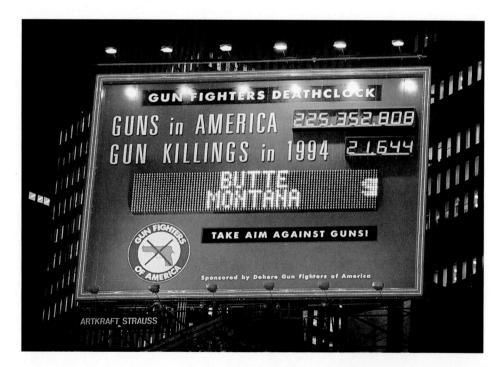

However, heuristics can also bias cognitive processes and cause errors. For example, if your rule of thumb is to vote for all political candidates in a particular party instead of researching the views of each individual, you might end up voting for someone with whom you strongly disagree on some issues. Amos Tversky and Daniel Kahneman have described three potentially problematic heuristics that people seem to use intuitively in making judgments (Tversky & Kahneman, 1974; Kahneman, Slovic & Tversky, 1982).

1. *The anchoring heuristic*   People use the **anchoring heuristic** when they estimate the probability of an event, not by starting from scratch but by adjusting an earlier estimate. This strategy sounds reasonable, but the starting value biases the final estimate. Once people have fixed a starting point, their adjustments of the initial judgment tend to be insufficient. It is as if they drop a mental anchor at one hypothesis or estimate and then are reluctant to move very far from that original judgment. Thus, if you thought that the probability of being mugged in New York is 90 percent and then found evidence that the figure is closer to 1 percent, you might reduce your estimate only to 80 percent. The anchoring heuristic presents a challenge for defense attorneys because, once affected by the prosecution's evidence (which is presented first), jurors' belief in a defendant's guilt may be difficult to alter (Hogarth & Einhorn, 1992). Similarly, as described in Chapter 17, first impressions of people are not easily shifted by later evidence.

2. *The representativeness heuristic*   Using the **representativeness heuristic,** people base conclusions about whether an example belongs in a certain class on how similar it is to other items in that class. For example, suppose you encounter a man who is tidy, small in stature, wears glasses, speaks quietly, and is somewhat shy. If asked whether this person is likely to be a librarian or a farmer, what would you say? Tversky and Kahneman (1974) found that most of their subjects chose *librarian*. But the chances are that this answer would be wrong because of differences in the *base rates* at which the two occupations occur. True, the description is more similar to the prototypical librarian than to the prototypical farmer, but because there are many more farmers in the world than librarians, there are probably more farmers than librarians who match this description. Therefore, a man matching this description is more likely to be a farmer than a librarian. In fact, almost any set of physical features is more likely to belong to a farmer than to a librarian.

Another study found that if a patient has symptoms that are similar to a common disease but are even more representative of a very rare one, physicians are likely to diagnose the rare disease (Christenssen-Szalanski & Bushyhead, 1981). In terms of base rates alone, it is more likely that the patient has the common disease, but the physicians used the representativeness heuristic in reaching a diagnosis. When using this heuristic, people ignore the overall probabilities and focus instead on what is representative or typical of the available evidence.

3. *The availability heuristic*   Even when people use probability information to help them judge group membership or to assess a hypothesis, they may employ a third heuristic that can bias their thinking. The **availability heuristic** involves judging the probability that an event may occur or that a hypothesis may be true by how easily the hypothesis or examples of the event can be brought to mind (Levi & Pryor, 1987). Thus, people tend to choose the hypothesis or alternative that is most mentally "available," much as you might choose which sweater to wear on the basis of which is on top in the drawer.

Like other heuristics, this shortcut tends to work well. After all, what people remember most easily *are* frequent events or hypotheses. However, the availability heuristic can lead to biased judgments, especially when mental availability and actual frequency fail to correspond. For example, television news reports showing the grisly aftermath of gang shootings and airline crashes may make these relatively rare events so memorable that people avoid certain cities or refuse to fly because they overestimate the frequency of crime or the probability of a crash (Slovic, 1984).

These three heuristics represent only a few of the many strategies that people use intuitively, and they describe only some of the biases and limitations evident in human reasoning (Hogarth & Einhorn, 1992). Other biases and limitations will become clear in the following sections as we consider two important goals of thinking: problem solving and decision making.

PROBLEM SOLVING

If where you are is not where you want to be, and when the path to getting there is not obvious, you have a *problem.* The circle of thought suggests that the most efficient approach to problem solving would be to first diagnose the problem in the elaboration stage, then formulate a plan for solving it, then execute the plan, and, finally, evaluate the results to determine whether the problem remains (Bransford & Stein, 1993). But people's problem-solving skills are not always so systematic, which is one reason why medical tests are sometimes given unnecessarily, diseases are sometimes misdiagnosed, and auto parts are sometimes replaced when there is nothing wrong with them.

Strategies for Problem Solving

When you are trying to get from a starting point to some goal, the best path may not necessarily be a straight line. In fact, obstacles may dictate going in the opposite direction. So it is with problem solving. Sometimes, the best strategy is not to take mental steps aimed straight at your goal. Psychologists have identified several strategies that work better for certain problems.

When a problem is so complicated that all of its elements cannot be held in working memory at once, you can use a strategy called *decomposition* to divide it into smaller, more manageable subproblems. Thus, instead of being overwhelmed by the big problem of writing a major term paper, you can begin by writing just an outline. Next, you can select the library materials most relevant to each successive section of the outline. Then you can write summaries of those materials, then a rough draft of an introduction, and so on.

A second strategy is to *work backward.* Many problems are like a tree. The trunk is the information you are given; the solution is a twig on one of the limbs. If you work forward by taking the "givens" of the problem and trying to find the solution, it will be easy to branch off in the wrong direction. A more efficient approach may be to start at the twig end and work backward (Best, 1995). Consider, for example, the problem of planning a climb to the summit of Mount Everest (Bonington, 1976). The best strategy is to figure out, first, what equipment and supplies are needed at the highest camp on the night before the summit attempt, then how many people are needed to stock that camp the day before, then how many people are needed to supply those who must stock the camp, and so on until the logistics of the entire expedition are established.

Third, try finding *analogies.* Many problems are similar to others you have encountered before. A supervisor may find, for example, that a seemingly hopeless impasse between co-workers may be resolved by the same compromise that worked during a recent family squabble. To take advantage of analogies, the problem solver must first recognize the similarities between current and previous problems, and then recall the

LINKAGES   Simply knowing about problem-solving strategies, such as decomposition, is not enough. As described in Chapter 11, on motivation and emotion, people must perceive the effort involved to be worth the rewards it is likely to bring.

solution that worked before. Surprisingly, most people are not very good at drawing analogies from one problem to another (Medin & Ross, 1992). They tend to concentrate on the surface features that make problems appear different.

Finally, in the case of an especially difficult problem, a helpful strategy is to allow it to "incubate" by laying it aside for a while. A solution that once seemed out of reach may suddenly appear after a person engages in unrelated mental activity for a while (Silviera, 1971). Indeed, the benefits of incubation probably arise from forgetting incorrect ideas that may have been blocking the path to a correct solution (Best, 1995).

FOCUS ON RESEARCH METHODS

Using Case Studies to Explore Problem-Solving Strategies

The problem-solving strategies just listed were identified mainly by laboratory studies in which psychologists observed volunteers wrestling with, and perhaps "thinking aloud" about, various kinds of problems. We do not yet know, though, how well, or how fully, the strategies seen in these studies reflect the problem-solving methods that people use outside the laboratory. To learn more about the relationship between artificial and "real-world" problem solving, some psychologists have turned to alternative research methods. Among the most promising is the development of *case studies,* using laboratory notes and other archival evidence, in order to reconstruct the problem-solving strategies associated with major inventions and discoveries (Simon, 1977; Weber, 1992).

As noted in Chapter 2, case studies have been used in many areas of psychology. However, as a source of evidence, they are vulnerable to two important problems: the striking-feature syndrome and causal uncertainty. The *striking-feature syndrome* occurs when an unusual feature in a case chosen for study is given too much weight. Consider the case of a woman who died of a brain tumor not long ago. Her grieving husband focused on a striking feature in her recent life—frequent use of a cellular telephone—and constructed a mental model in which the phone's high-frequency magnetic field was responsible for his wife's illness. The phone manufacturer's defense in the resulting lawsuit was based on *causal uncertainty;* the tumor could have been caused by the phone or by something else. As noted in Chapter 2, evidence from a single case study is not adequate to establish cause-effect relationships. Indeed, the company presented data showing that cellular telephone users have a *lower* incidence of brain cancer than the general population and, further, that the risk of brain cancer is not positively correlated with the amount of time spent using a cellular phone (Sandler, 1993). On the basis of this more extensive correlational evidence, the judge dismissed the lawsuit.

The limitations of single case studies have prompted the use of *comparative case studies* in the exploration of real-world problem-solving strategies. Here, the researcher collects a large number of cases, then looks for common features that suggest the operation of a particular mental strategy. For example, Gary Bradshaw (1993a, 1993b) used comparative case studies to identify the problem-solving strategies that led to the invention of the airplane. His database included turn-of-the-century records from 49 individuals or teams working on what they hoped would be a heavier-than-air flying machine. Of the 135 designs developed, only that of the Wright brothers was successful. In fact, the Wrights took only four years to develop the airplane, whereas others labored without success for decades.

How did the Wright brothers solve the problem of heavier-than-air flight? It took more than just good luck. Focusing on the Wright's case alone, Bradshaw found that several factors might have contributed to their success: (1) As bachelors, they had a lot of spare time to work on their designs; (2) as owners of a bicycle shop, they were familiar with lightweight but sturdy structures; (3) as brothers, they had a rapport that helped them work together; and (4) as mechanics, they were good with their hands. Were any of these striking features causally related to their ultimate success?

The Wright Brothers' Wind Tunnel

The Wright brothers built this wind tunnel to test the in-flight performance of various wing shapes and propellors. Decomposition of the problem of flight into smaller subproblems was probably the key to the Wrights' success.

Perhaps, but Bradshaw's use of comparative case studies revealed that everyone else working on the problem of flight shared one or more of these features with the Wright brothers. For example, as an engineer, Octave Chanute was good with his hands and familiar with sturdy, lightweight structures: The first bridge across the Missouri River was built on the basis of his expertise. In addition, two other pairs of brothers had worked to invent the airplane.

In other words, the comparative case study method showed that the most striking features of the Wrights' case were probably incidental to their success. It also revealed a feature unique to the Wright brothers' approach: They, alone, devoted large amounts of time and energy to testing more than a dozen aircraft *components* before field-testing complete machines (see Figure 9.6). This feature was important because even the best designs of the day flew for only a matter of seconds, far too briefly to reveal what was working and what was not. As a result, inventors were left to guess about what to fix, often ending up with an "improved" model that was worse than the previous one. The Wrights' testing program, by contrast, gave them the information they needed to develop an efficient propeller, improve the shape of wings for maximum lift, and refine other vital components of their aircraft.

In short, the comparative case study method suggests that decomposition, a problem-solving strategy often seen in the laboratory, is a potentially important aspect of major inventions and discoveries beyond the laboratory.

Obstacles to Problem Solving

The failure of the Wright brothers' competitors to use decomposition is just one example of the obstacles that face problem solvers every day. Difficulties frequently occur at the start, during the diagnosis stage, when a person forms and then tests hypotheses about a problem. In the following sections we describe four obstacles to efficient problem solving.

Multiple Hypotheses   Often, people begin to solve a problem with only a vague notion of which hypotheses to test. For example, there may be a dozen reasons why a car will not start. Which of these hypotheses should be tested, and in what order?

FIGURE 9.7

The Luchins Jar Problem

The problem is to obtain the number of quarts of liquid shown in the first column by filling jars with the capacities shown in the next three columns. Each line represents a different problem. In dealing with such problems, people often fall prey to mental sets that prevent them from using the most efficient solution.

QUANTITY	JAR A	JAR B	JAR C
1. 21 quarts	8	35	3
2. 10 quarts	6	18	1
3. 19 quarts	5	32	4
4. 21 quarts	20	57	8
5. 18 quarts	8	40	7
6. 6 quarts	7	17	2
7. 15 quarts	12	33	3

Problem: Measure out the above quantities by using jars with the stated capacities (in quarts).

People seem to have a difficult time entertaining more than two or three hypotheses at a time (Mehle, 1982). The limited capacity of working memory, discussed in Chapter 8, may be part of the reason. As a result, the correct hypothesis is often neglected. Which hypothesis a person considers may depend on the availability heuristic. In other words, the particular hypothesis considered may be the one that most easily comes to mind, not the one most likely to be correct (Tversky & Kahneman, 1974). Thus, the auto mechanic troubleshooting your car might diagnose the problem as the same as one encountered the day before, simply because that hypothesis is most easily remembered.

Mental Sets   Sometimes people are so blinded by one hypothesis or strategy that they continue to apply it even when better alternatives should be obvious (a clear case of the anchoring heuristic at work). An example devised by Abraham Luchins (1942) is shown in Figure 9.7. The object of each problem in the figure is to use three jars with specified capacities to obtain a certain amount of liquid. For example, in the first problem you are to obtain 21 quarts by using three jars that have capacities of 8, 35, and 3 quarts, respectively. The solution is to fill Jar B to its capacity, 35 quarts, and then use its contents to fill Jar A to its capacity of 8 quarts, leaving 27 quarts in Jar B. Then pour liquid from Jar B to fill Jar C to its capacity twice, leaving 21 quarts in Jar B $[27 - (2 \times 3) = 21]$. In other words, the general solution is $B - A - 2C$. Now solve the remaining problems.

If you went through the problems in Figure 9.7, you found that a similar solution worked each time. But what happened with problem 7? If you are like most people, you did not notice that it has a simpler solution (namely, $A + C$). Instead, you succumbed to a **mental set,** the tendency for old patterns of problem solving to persist (Sweller & Gee, 1978). In the Luchins jar problem, the mental set consists of a tendency to stick with a strategy or solution that worked in the past. Figures 9.8 and 9.10 show that a mental set may also restrict your perception of the problem itself.

Yet another restriction on problem solving may come from experience with objects. Once people become accustomed to using an object for one type of function, they may be blinded to other ways of using it. Thus, experience may produce **functional fixedness,** a tendency to use familiar objects in familiar, rather than creative ways. Figure 9.9 illustrates an example. An incubation strategy often helps to break mental sets.

The Confirmation Bias   Anyone who has had a series of medical tests knows that diagnosis is not a one-shot decision. Instead, physicians choose an initial hypothesis on the basis of observed symptoms and then order tests or evaluate additional symptoms to confirm or refute that hypothesis. This process may be distorted by the *confirmation bias:* Humans have a strong bias to confirm rather than to refute the hypothesis they have chosen, even in the face of strong evidence against the hypothesis. In other words,

FIGURE 9.8

The Nine-Dot Problem

The problem is to draw no more than four straight lines that run through all nine dots on the page without lifting your pencil from the paper. Figure 9.10 shows two ways of going beyond constraints to solve this problem.

FIGURE 9.9

An Example of Functional Fixedness

How would you fasten together two strings that are hanging from the ceiling but are out of reach of each other? Several tools are available, yet most people do not think of attaching, say, the pliers to one string and swinging it like a pendulum until it can be reached while holding the other string. This solution is not obvious because we tend to fixate on the function of pliers as a tool rather than as a weight. People are more likely to solve this problem if the tools are scattered around the room. When the pliers are in a tool box, their function as a tool is emphasized, and functional fixedness becomes nearly impossible to break.

FIGURE 9.10

Two Creative Solutions to the Nine-Dot Problem

Many people find puzzles like this difficult because their mental sets create artificial constraints on the range of solutions. In this case, the mental sets involve the tendency to draw within the frame of the dots and to draw through the middle of each dot. As shown here, however, there are other possibilities.

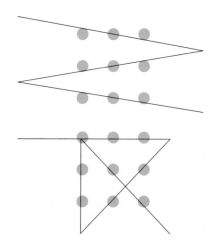

people are quite willing to perceive and accept data that support their hypothesis—that a defendant is guilty, for example—but they tend to ignore information that is inconsistent with it (Ditto & Lopez, 1992; Levin, Kao & Wasserman, 1991). Thus, the confirmation bias may be seen as a form of the anchoring heuristic, in that it involves reluctance to abandon an initial hypothesis.

Ignoring Negative Evidence   Often, what does *not* happen can be as important as what does. For example, when troubleshooting a car, you may be led by a failed headlight to hypothesize that the battery is low. But if this were the case, other battery-powered equipment should also have failed. The absence of symptoms can provide important evidence for or against a hypothesis. Compared with symptoms that are *present,* however, symptoms or events that do not occur are less likely to be noticed and observed (Hunt & Rouse, 1981). People have a difficult time using the absence of symptoms to help eliminate hypotheses from consideration (Ashcraft, 1989).

Building Problem-Solving Skills

Psychologists have reasoned that it should be possible to train people not to fall prey to the biases that impair problem solving, and attempts to do so have produced some modest benefits. For example, in one study, cautioning people against their tendency to anchor on a hypothesis reduced the magnitude of the confirmation bias and increased their openness to alternative evidence (Lopes, 1982).

How do experts avoid obstacles to problem solving? What do they bring to a situation that a novice does not? Knowledge based on experience is particularly important (Mayer, 1992). Experts frequently proceed by looking for analogies between current and past problems. Compared to novices, they are better able to relate new information and new experiences to past experiences and existing knowledge (Anderson, 1995; Bedard & Chi, 1992). Accordingly, experts can use existing knowledge to organize new information into chunks, as described in the chapter on memory. By chunking many elements of a problem into a smaller number of units, experts apparently can visualize problems more clearly and efficiently than novices.

Experts can use their experience as a guide because they tend to perceive the similarity between new and old problems more deeply than novices (Chi, Feltovitch & Glaser, 1981; Hardimann, Dufresne & Mestre, 1989). Specifically, experts see the similarity of underlying principles, while novices perceive similarity only in superficial features. As a result, experts can more quickly and easily apply these principles to solve the new problem. In one study, expert physicists and novice physics students sorted physics problems into groups (Chi, Feltovitch & Glaser, 1981). The novices grouped together problems that looked similar (such as those involving blocks lying on an inclined plane), while the experts grouped together problems that could be solved by the same principle (such as Newton's second law of motion).

Experience also gives experts a broader perspective on the problem domain, allowing them to perceive the whole problem "tree" so that they can work forward without error, thus avoiding the slower "working backward" strategy more suited to the novice (Medin & Ross, 1992). Finally, successful problem solvers can explain each step in the solution, and can maintain awareness of precisely what is and is not understood along the way (Medin & Ross, 1992).

Although experts are often better problem solvers than novices, expertise also carries a danger: Using past experience can lead to the traps of functional fixedness and mental sets. As a Zen proverb says, "In the mind of the beginner there are many possibilities; in the mind of the expert, few." The top-down, knowledge-driven processes described in the chapter on perception can bias you toward seeing what you expect or want to see and prevent you from seeing a problem in new ways. Indeed, the confirmation bias sometimes prevents experts from appreciating that a proposed solution is incorrect (Fischoff & Slovic, 1980). Several studies have shown that, although experts may be more confident in their solutions (Payne, Bettman & Johnson, 1992), they are not always more accurate than novices in such areas as medical diagnosis, accounting, and pilot judgment (Bedard, 1989; Wickens et al., 1992).

In short, there is a fine line between using past experience and being trapped by it. Experience alone does not ensure excellence at problem solving, and practice may not make perfect (see Table 9.1).

Problem Solving by Computer

In view of all the weaknesses of human problem solving, some people hope that computers can take over some aspects of human thinking. (For a summary of our discussion of human problem solving, see "In Review: Solving Problems.") Scientists in the field of **artificial intelligence,** or **AI,** are developing computer systems that imitate the

TABLE 9.1
Some Expert Opinions

Experts typically have a large store of knowledge about their realm of expertise, but even confidently stated opinions based on this knowledge can turn out to be incorrect, as these examples from Christopher Cerf's *The Experts Speak* (1984) clearly show.

On the possibility of painless surgery through anesthesia:
"'Knife' and 'pain' are two words in surgery that must forever be associated.... To this compulsory combination we shall have to adjust ourselves." (Dr. Alfred Velpeau, professor of surgery, Paris Faculty of Medicine, 1839)

On the hazards of cigarette smoking:
"If excessive smoking actually plays a role in the production of lung cancer, it seems to be a minor one." (Dr. W. C. Heuper, National Cancer Institute, 1954)

On the stock market (one week before the disastrous 1929 crash that wiped out over $50 billion in investments):
"Stocks have reached what looks like a permanently high plateau." (Irving Fisher, professor of economics, Yale University, 1929)

On the prospects of war with Japan (three years before the December 1941 Japanese attack on Pearl Harbor):
"A Japanese attack on Pearl Harbor is a strategic impossibility." (Major George F. Eliot, military science writer, 1938)

On the value of personal computers:
"There is no reason for any individual to have a computer in their home." (Ken Olson, president, Digital Equipment Corporation, 1977)

On the concept of the airplane:
"Heavier-than-air flying machines are impossible." (Lord Kelvin, mathematician, physicist, and president of the British Royal Society, 1895)

IN REVIEW	Solving Problems	
Steps	**Pitfalls**	**Remedies**
Define the problem	Inexperience: the tendency to see each problem as unique.	Gain experience and practice in seeing the similarity between present problems and previous problems.
Form hypotheses about solutions	Availability heuristic: the tendency to recall the hypothesis or solution that is most available to memory.	Force yourself to entertain different hypotheses.
	Anchoring heuristic, or mental set: the tendency to anchor on the first solution or hypothesis and not adjust your beliefs in light of new evidence or failures of the current approach.	Break the mental set, stop, and try a fresh approach.
Test hypotheses	The tendency to ignore negative evidence.	In evaluating a hypothesis, consider the things you should see (but don't) if the hypothesis were true.
	Confirmation bias: the tendency to seek only evidence that confirms your hypothesis.	Look for disconfirming evidence that, if found, would show your hypothesis to be false.

products of human perception and thought. For example, some computers can now beat all but the best chess masters (Kopec, Newborn & Valvo, 1992). Indeed, there is good evidence that, for problems such as those involved in medical diagnosis, computers using fairly simple formulas can perform just as well as humans, if not better (Dawes, Faust & Meehl, 1989; Bradshaw & Shaw, 1992). Actually, a human-computer combination seems to work best, with humans establishing the presence and nature of the patient's symptoms and the computer *combining* this information to identify the most likely diagnosis. This conclusion also applies to the diagnosis of psychological problems (Nietzel, Bernstein & Milich, 1994). Scientists in AI have adopted two somewhat different approaches: symbolic reasoning and neural networks.

Symbolic Reasoning and Computer Logic   Early efforts at developing artificial intelligence focused on computers' enormous capabilities for logical reasoning and symbol manipulation and on their abilities to follow general problem-solving strategies, such as working backward (Newell & Simon, 1972). This logic-based approach has been reasonably successful at addressing many problems through the development of expert systems. **Expert systems** are computer programs that solve problems in relatively restricted areas, like diagnosing infectious diseases, forecasting solar flares, or evaluating bank loan applications (Bradshaw & Shaw, 1992; Shortcliffe, 1983).

Valuable as it is, the logic-based approach to AI has important limitations. Expert systems, for example, are successful only in very narrowly defined fields. In spite of efforts to develop general problem-solving computers (Newell & Simon, 1972), the ability demonstrated in one domain (such as disease diagnosis) does not easily transfer to a different domain (locating mineral deposits, say).

Even within a domain, computers show limited ability. There are no ways of putting into computer code all aspects of the reasoning of human experts. Sometimes, the experts can only say, "I know it when I see it, but I can't put it into words" (Dreyfus & Dreyfus, 1988). And making connections among remote knowledge domains is far beyond the grasp of current systems, partly because the builders of the systems seldom know ahead of time which other areas of knowledge might lead to insight. Thus, they can't tell computers where to look for new ideas or how to use them. Yet drawing analogies and noting similarities across domains are important to expert problem solving. In the case that opened this chapter, it was knowledge about Laura McBride's occupation, which on the surface had nothing to do with her body chemistry, that led to Dr. Wallace's insightful diagnosis.

Finally, AI systems based on logical symbolic manipulations depend on "if-then" rules, and it is often very difficult to tell a computer how to recognize the "if" condition in the real world (Dreyfus & Dreyfus, 1988). Consider just one example: "If it's a clock, then set it." Humans can recognize all kinds of clocks because they have the natural concept of "clock," but computers are very poor at this task. As discussed earlier, forming natural concepts requires putting into the same category many examples that may have very different physical features—from a bedside digital alarm to Big Ben.

Neural Network Models Realizing that a large amount of intelligent diagnosis and problem solving depends on recognition and classification of current conditions and ill-defined patterns, many workers in the AI field have moved toward the *connectionist* or *neural network* approach discussed in earlier chapters (Anderson, 1995; Hinton, 1992). This approach is very effective for modeling many aspects of perceptual recognition. Neural network approaches to AI have greatly improved computer abilities in areas such as understanding speech and reading print (Churchland & Sejnowski, 1992) and forecasting solar flares (Bradshaw & Shaw, 1992).

Current computer models of neural networks still fall well short of the capacities of the human perceptual system, however (Hofstadter, 1995). For example, they are incredibly slow to learn how to classify visual patterns, and unlike humans, they don't show sudden insights when a key common feature is identified.

A DISASTROUS DECISION The decision to launch the space shuttle *Challenger* in 38-degree weather exemplifies a risky decision apparently flawed by biases in the decision makers' processing of information about the pros and cons of the options (Vaughan, 1996). All seven astronauts aboard were killed in the ensuing explosion.

DECISION MAKING

Dr. Wallace's patient, Laura McBride, faced a simple decision: Risk death by doing nothing or protect herself from lead poisoning. Most decisions are not so easy. Patients must decide whether to undergo a dangerous operation; a young adult must choose a career; a corporate executive must decide whether to shut down a factory. Unlike the high-speed decisions discussed earlier, these decisions require considerable time, planning, and mental effort.

Even carefully considered decisions sometimes lead to undesirable outcomes, however, because the world is uncertain. Decisions made when the outcome is uncertain are called *risky decisions* or *decisions under uncertainty.* Chance aside, psychologists have discovered many reasons why human decisions may lead to unsatisfactory outcomes, and we describe some of them here.

Evaluating Options

Suppose that you must choose between (1) an academic major that fascinates you but is unlikely to lead to a good job, or (2) a major that is less interesting but virtually guarantees a high-paying career. The fact that each option has positive and negative features, or *attributes,* greatly complicates decision making. Deciding which car to buy, which college to attend, or even how to spend the evening are all examples of *multiattribute decision making* (Edwards, 1987). Often these decisions are further complicated by difficulties in comparing the attributes and in estimating the probabilities of various outcomes.

Comparing Attributes   Multiattribute decisions can be difficult in part because the limited storage capacity of working memory does not permit people to easily keep in mind and compare all of the attributes of all of the options (Bettman, Johnson & Payne, 1990; Fischoff, Slovic & Lichtenstein, 1977). Instead, people tend to focus on the one attribute that is most important to them (Tversky, 1972). If, for instance, finishing a degree quickly is most important to you, then you might choose courses based mainly on curricular requirements, without giving much consideration to the reputations of the professors. (Listing the pros and cons of each option offers a helpful way of keeping them all in mind as you contemplate decisions.)

Furthermore, the attributes of the options involved in most important decisions cannot be measured in dollars or other relatively objective terms. Instead, people are forced to compare "apples and oranges." Psychologists use the term **utility** to describe the subjective, personal value of each attribute. In deciding on a major, for example, you would have to think about the positive and negative utilities of each attribute—such as the job prospects and intellectual stimulation—of each major. Then you must somehow weigh and combine these utilities. Will the positive utility of enjoying your courses be higher than the negative utility of risking unemployment?

Estimating Probabilities   Uncertainty adds other difficulties to the decision-making process: To make a good decision, you should take into account not only the attributes of the options but also the probabilities and risks of their possible outcomes. The economy could change by the time you graduate, closing many of today's job opportunities in one of the majors you are considering and perhaps opening opportunities in the other.

In studying risky decision making, psychologists begin by assuming that the best decision is the one that maximizes **expected value,** or the total amount of benefit you could expect to receive if the decision were repeated on several occasions. Suppose someone asks you to enter a raffle. You know that it costs $2 to enter and that the probability of winning the $100 prize is one in ten (.10). Should you enter? The expected value of entering is computed by multiplying the probability of gain (.10) by the size of the gain ($100); this is the average benefit you would receive if you entered the raffle many times. Next, from this product you would subtract the probability of loss, which is 1.0 (the entry fee is a certain loss), multiplied by the amount of the loss ($2). That is,

$(.10 \times \$100) - (1.0 \times \$2) = \$8$. Since this eight-dollar expected value is greater than the expected value of not entering (which is zero), you should enter. However, if the odds of winning the raffle were one in a hundred (.01), then the expected value of entering would be $(.01 \times \$100) - (1.0 \times \$2) = -\$1$. In this case, since the expected value is negative, you should not enter the raffle.

Biases and Flaws in Decision Making

In fact, people do not always behave so as to maximize expected values (Curim & Sarin, 1992), and it is important to consider some of the reasons why.

Gains, Losses, and Probabilities   For one thing, positive utilities are not mirror images of negative utilities. Instead, people generally feel worse about losing a certain amount than they feel good about gaining the same amount (Edwards, Lindman & Phillips, 1965), a phenomenon known as *loss aversion* (Tversky & Kahneman, 1991). Thus, they may be willing to expend more effort to try collecting a $100 debt than to try winning a $100 prize.

It also appears that the utility of a specific gain depends not on the absolute increase in value but on what the starting point was. Suppose you can take some action to receive a coupon for a free dinner worth $10. Does this gain have the same utility as having an extra $10 added to your paycheck? The dollar amount is the same, but people tend to behave as if the difference in utility between $0 and $10 is much greater than the difference between, say, $300 and $310. Thus, they may refuse to drive across town after work to earn a $10 bonus but would gladly make the same trip to pick up a $10 coupon. This tendency calls to mind Weber's law of psychophysics, discussed in Chapter 5, on perception. How much a difference in value means to you depends on how much you already have (Edwards, Lindman & Phillips, 1965); the more you have, the less it means.

Biases in the perception of probability are also a source of less than optimal decisions. Two such biases are especially interesting. The first is the tendency to overestimate rare probabilities—and to underestimate very frequent ones (Kahneman & Tversky, 1984). This bias helps explain not only why people buy insurance but also why they gamble and enter lotteries, even though the odds are against them and the decision to do so has a negative expected value. According to the formula for expected value, buying a $1 lottery ticket—when the probability of winning $4,000,000 is one in ten million—yields an expected value of −60 cents. But because people overestimate the

A HIGHLY UNLIKELY OUTCOME   By focusing public attention on the very few people who win big lottery prizes, state lottery agencies take advantage of the general human tendency to overestimate the probability of rare events. Lottery ads never show the millions of people whose tickets turn out to be worthless.

probability of winning, they believe there is a positive expected value. The tendency to overestimate the likelihood of unlikely events is amplified by the availability heuristic: Vivid memories of rare gambling successes and the publicity given to lottery winners help people recall gains rather than losses when deciding about future gambles (Waagenaar, 1989). This same tendency can also be amplified by mood. People in a good mood tend to overestimate the probability that good things will happen to them, while those in a bad mood tend to exaggerate the likelihood of being mugged, losing a wallet, or other negative events (Wright & Bower, 1992).

Another bias relating to probability is called the *gambler's fallacy:* People believe that events in a random process will correct themselves. This belief is false. For example, if you flip a coin and it comes up heads ten times in a row, the chance that it will come up heads on the eleventh try is still 50 percent. Some gamblers, however, will continue feeding a slot machine that hasn't paid off much for hours, assuming it is "due." This assumption may be partly responsible for the resistance to extinction of intermittently reinforced behaviors, as described in Chapter 7.

Yet another factor underlying flaws in human decision making is the tendency for people to be unrealistically confident in the accuracy of their predictions. Baruch Fischoff and Donald MacGregor (1982) used an ingenious approach to study this bias. They asked people whether they believed that a certain event would occur—for example, that a certain sports team would win—and how confident they were about this prediction. After the events in question, the accuracy of the forecasts was computed and compared with the confidence assigned to the predictions. Sure enough, people's confidence in their predictions was consistently greater than their accuracy. This overconfidence operates even when people make predictions concerning the accuracy of their own memory (Fischoff, 1980; Plous, 1993).

Overconfidence about knowledge and judgments appears in many cultures, and in some more than others. In one study, students in China and the United States were asked to say how confident they were about their answers to general knowledge questions (Wright & Phillips, 1980). Both groups were overconfident, but the Chinese students were especially so. A study comparing Chinese, Japanese, and American students found the same result (Yates et al., 1989). Cultural differences in overconfidence may stem partly from culturally based differences in how people think about their own judgments. For example, realistic evaluations of judgment accuracy require thinking of reasons why you might be wrong as well as reasons why you might be right. Cultural traditions that strongly discourage Chinese students from challenging what they are told by teachers may also make them less likely than Americans to question what they tell themselves, and thus more likely to be overconfident. Indeed, compared to American and Japanese students, Chinese students were able to list the fewest arguments *against* their own judgments (Yates, Lee & Shinotsuka, 1992).

The moral of the story is to be wary when people in any culture express confidence that a forecast or decision is correct. They will be wrong more often than they think.

How Biased Are We?   Though the previous discussion suggests that human decision making is flawed, psychologists are divided on the extent of the biases involved (Payne, Bettman & Johnson, 1992; Cohen, 1993). While nearly everyone has made decisions they later regret, many human decisions are intended not to maximize expected value but to satisfy some other criterion, such as minimizing expected loss or producing acceptable outcomes with a minimum expenditure of time or mental effort (Bettman, Johnson & Payne, 1990). For example, it makes no sense to perform time-consuming mental gymnastics aimed at deciding what to wear each day.

It is also true that the "goodness" or "badness" of many decisions is difficult to assess, because so many of them depend on personal values (utilities), and these vary from person to person and from culture to culture. As suggested by our discussion of cultural factors in Chapter 1, people in individualist cultures may tend to assign high utilities to attributes that promote personal goals, whereas those in collectivist cultures might place greater value on attributes that bring group harmony and the approval of family and friends (Feather, Volkmer & McKee, 1992).

Finally, some decisions—especially those made by skilled professionals in naturalistic situations—turn out to be quite good, even though these people do not always weigh and compare all possible options. For example, professional firefighters report that they rarely engage in a conscious comparison of various approaches when deciding how best to fight a fire (Klein et al., 1993). Instead, they simply compare the current situation with other fires they have encountered before, retrieving from long-term memory the best methods for dealing with such situations, and taking action to implement those methods.

LINKAGES: GROUP PROCESSES IN PROBLEM SOLVING AND DECISION MAKING

Do groups solve problems faster than individuals?

Whether they involve fighting a fire, balancing a budget, trying a defendant, or choosing a vacation spot, problem solving and decision making are often done in groups. The processes that influence an individual's problem solving and decision making continue to operate when the individual is in a group, but group interactions also shape the outcome.

Typically, group discussions follow a consistent pattern (Hastie, Penrod & Pennington, 1984). First, various options are proposed and debated until the group sees that no one has strong objections to one option; that option becomes the minimally acceptable solution. From then on, the group criticizes any other proposal and argues more and more strongly for the first minimally acceptable solution, which is likely to become the group's decision (Hoffman & Maier, 1979). Thus the order in which options are considered can determine the outcome.

In many cases, group discussion results in more extreme decisions than people would make if they were alone. For example, if you hold conservative, or liberal, political opinions, associating with people who share those opinions is likely to result in your becoming more conservative, or more liberal (Pascarella & Terenzini, 1991). This tendency toward extreme decisions is called **group polarization** (Kaplan, 1987). Two mechanisms apparently underlie group polarization. First, most arguments presented during the discussion favor the view of the majority, and most criticisms are directed at the minority view. Thus, it seems rational to those favoring the majority view to adopt an even stronger version of it (Stasser, 1991). Second, as a group begins to agree that a particular decision is desirable, members may try to associate themselves with it, perhaps by advocating a more extreme version (Kaplan & Miller, 1987).

Are people better at problem solving and decision making when they work in groups than when on their own? This is one of the questions about human thought studied by researchers in social psychology. In a typical experiment, a group of people is asked to solve a problem like the one in Figure 9.8 or to make a decision about the guilt or innocence of a hypothetical defendant. Each person is asked to reach an individual answer and then to join with the others to try to reach a consensus. Such research indicates that, in most instances, groups will outperform individuals. However, when people work as part of a group, they are less productive than when working alone (Baron et al., 1992; Levine & Moreland, 1995). In other words, groups tend to be more effective than individuals, but they also tend to be less efficient.

Other research (e.g., Laughlin, Vanderstoep & Hollingshead, 1991) suggests that three factors are responsible for the overall superiority of group versus individual performance. In a group, it is more likely that (1) someone will identify the correct hypothesis from those that were plausible; (2) incorrect hypotheses will be rejected by someone; and (3) the information-processing load will be shared, so that relevant information lost from one person's working memory might be available in another's.

Having more group members appears to increase the quality of group performance, but only up to a point. That is, juries of twelve seem to do better at reaching just verdicts than juries of six, but there would probably be little advantage to creating juries of, say, twenty-four (Davis, 1992). Group members who are confident or have high status are most likely to influence the group's deliberations (Driskell & Salas, 1991; Levine

GROUPS WORKING AT A DISTANCE The quality of group problem solving and decision making will become even more important in future years as people increasingly use electronic mail and teleconferencing to work together from a distance. It is not yet clear how "electronic groups" compare to their face-to-face counterparts. Some evidence suggests that group communication via e-mail tends to be more explicit and outspoken (a pattern dubbed "flaming"), and that group solutions tend to be riskier and less conventional (Kiesler & Sproull, 1992).

& Moreland, 1990), but whether these people will help or hurt the group's output depends on whether they express good ideas (Hinsz, 1990). Ironically, there is little evidence that members with the greatest competence (as opposed to status) always contribute more to group deliberations (Hastie, 1986). Finally, the longer a group works together, the closer group performance comes to the level of its most competent member. This is because longer work periods improve group communication and give the group more opportunities to recognize and be influenced by its most competent members (Foushee & Helmreich, 1988; Laughlin, Vanderstoep & Hollingshead, 1991).

LANGUAGE

Language is the primary means through which we communicate our thoughts to others. We use language not only to share our immediate thoughts and ideas but also to pass on cultural information and traditions from one generation to the next. In this section, we describe the elements that make up a language, the ways that people use language to communicate, and the means by which language is learned.

The Elements of Language

A **language** has two basic elements: symbols, such as words, and a set of rules, called **grammar,** for combining those symbols. These two components allow human language to be at once rule-bound and creative. Knowing approximately 50,000 to 100,000 words (the vocabulary of the typical college student), humans can create and understand an infinite number of sentences. All of the sentences ever articulated are created from just a few dozen categories of sounds. The power of language comes from the way these rather unimpressive raw materials are organized according to rules. This organization occurs at several levels.

From Sounds to Sentences   Organization occurs first at the level of sounds. A **phoneme** is the smallest unit of sound that affects the meaning of speech. Changing a phoneme changes the meaning of a spoken word, much as changing a letter in a printed word changes its meaning. *Tea* has a meaning different from *sea,* and *sight* is different from *sigh.*

Each spoken language consists of roughly thirty to fifty phonemes. English has twenty-six letters, but it has about forty phonemes. The *a* in *cat* and the *a* in *cake,* for example, are different English phonemes. Many of the letter sounds are phonemes (including *ell, aitch,* and *em*), but so are the sounds *th* and *sh.* Sounds that are considered one phoneme in English are different phonemes in other languages, and sounds that are different phonemes in English may be just one phoneme in another language. In Spanish, for example, *s* and *z* are considered the same phoneme.

Although changing a phoneme affects meaning, phonemes themselves are not meaningful. They are combined to form a higher level of organization: morphemes. A **morpheme** is the smallest unit of language that has meaning. Word stems like *dog* and *run* are morphemes, but so are prefixes like *un-* and suffixes like *-ed,* because they have meaning even though they cannot stand alone.

Words are made up of one or more morphemes. Words, in turn, are combined to form phrases and sentences according to a set of grammatical rules called **syntax.** For example, according to English syntax, a subject and a verb must be combined in a sentence, adjectives typically appear before the noun that they modify, and so forth. Compare the following sentences:

Fatal accidents deter careful drivers.
Snows sudden floods melting cause.

The first sentence makes sense, but the second sentence violates English syntax. If the words were reordered, however, they would produce the perfectly acceptable sentence "Melting snows cause sudden floods."

Even if you use English phonemes combined in proper ways to form morphemes strung together according to the laws of English syntax, you may not end up with an acceptable English sentence. Consider the sentence "Rapid bouquets deter sudden neighbors." It somehow sounds right, but it is nonsense. Why? It has syntax, but it ignores the set of rules, called **semantics,** that govern the meaning of words and sentences. For example, because of its meaning, the noun *bouquets* cannot be modified by the word *rapid.*

Surface Structure and Deep Structure   So far, we have discussed elements of language that are apparent in the sentences people produce. These elements were the focus of study for linguists for many decades. Then, in 1957, Noam Chomsky started a revolution in the study of language. He argued that if linguists studied only the language that people produce, they would never uncover the principles that account for all the sentences that people create. They could not explain, for example, how the sentence "This is my old friend" has more than one meaning. Nor could they account for the close relationship between the meanings of such sentences as "Don't give up just because things look bad" and "It ain't over 'til it's over."

To take these aspects of language into account, Chomsky proposed a more abstract level of analysis. Behind the word strings that people produce, called **surface structures,** there is, he said, a **deep structure,** an abstract representation of the relationships expressed in a sentence. For example, as Figure 9.11 illustrates, the surface structure "The shooting of the psychologist was terrible" may represent either of two deep structures: (1) that the psychologist had terrible aim, or (2) that it was terrible that someone shot the psychologist.

Chomsky also developed rules for transforming deep structures into surface structures and for relating sentences to one another. Since he proposed his first analysis of

FIGURE 9.11

Surface Structure and Deep Structure

The listener on the right has interpreted the speaker's message in a way that differs from the speaker's intended deep structure. Obviously, identical surface structures can correspond to distinctly different deep structures.

deep and surface structures, he and others have offered many revisions of those ideas. For our purposes, what is important about Chomsky's ideas is that they encouraged psychologists to analyze not just verbal behavior and grammatical rules but also mental representations.

Understanding Speech

When you listen to someone speak, your sensory, perceptual, and cognitive systems reconstruct the sounds into a representation of the speaker's idea: You develop an internal description of the ideas intended by the speaker. How? Like the perception of visual images discussed in Chapter 5, perception of speech depends not just on bottom-up processing of stimuli but also on top-down processing that uses knowledge, experience, and expectations to construct a mental representation of what is said. This construction occurs at several levels.

Perceiving Words and Sentences   When you listen to someone speak, you perceive the phonemes within a word as a continuous string, and you perceive a distinct pause between each word. However, as Figure 9.12 demonstrates, the pauses often actually occur *within* the words, not between them. You perceive breaks between the words because of the *top-down processing* discussed in Chapter 5. You know what the word should sound like, you recognize the sounds when they occur, and you perceive them as separate units, even if the physical stimuli are not separated (Miller & Eimas, 1995).

Similarly, when words are strung together as sentences, knowledge about both sentence structure and the world at large shapes the way they are processed. For example, people can remember the string "a haky deeb reciled the dison togently um flutests pav" more easily than the shorter string "Hak deem um flut recile pav togert disen," because the first is organized in a sentence-like structure (Epstein, 1961). In other words, people use their vast store of knowledge about grammatical structure, the meaning of words, and the world itself in order to process and understand language.

Using Context and Scripts   Suppose you have programmed a computer with all the rules and knowledge discussed so far—with rules for combining spoken phonemes and written letters into words, rules of syntax, a dictionary of the meanings of words, and an encyclopedia of knowledge of the world. Now you ask your computer to make sense of the following conversation:

A: You goin' to the gym today to work out?

B: Well I *am* flabby, but only if I can hook a ride with Jim. It's a long way.

A: I'm afraid I heard his transmission's conked out, and it's at the shop.

B: Oh [pause], then I guess it won't work out.

FIGURE 9.12

A Speech Spectrograph

This *speech spectrograph* indicates what speech looks like as someone says the phrase "Speech we may see." The vertical axis shows the frequencies of the speech sounds; the horizontal axis shows the passage of time. You would hear this phrase as four distinct words. Notice, however, that pauses actually occur not between the words themselves but between the "p" and "ee" in "speech" and again between "ee" and "ch" in the same word.

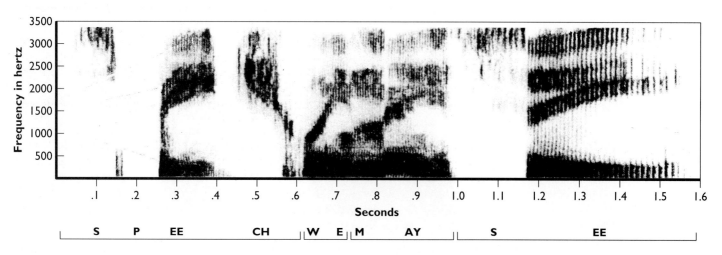

Source: Lachman, Lachman & Butterfield, 1979.

LINKAGES: PERCEIVING SPOKEN LANGUAGE Top-down perceptual processes, described in Chapter 5, help explain why speech in a language you do not understand sounds like a continuous stream being spoken faster than speech in your own language. You do not know where each unfamiliar word starts and stops, so, without perceived gaps, the speech sounds run together at what seems to be a faster-than-normal rate.

The computer would be at a loss. For one thing, certain ambiguous terms have different meanings in different sentences (for example, *work out* in lines 1 and 4; *gym* versus *Jim* in lines 1 and 2). Because you understand the gist of the conversation, you understand the meaning of words or phrases like *hook, I'm afraid,* and *conked out,* and you know that the transmission is part of Jim's car, not a part of Jim. But these are things that the computer could not easily understand.

Difficulties in programming a computer to understand conversations arise first because the use of language relies on the *context* in which words are spoken or written. As noted in Chapter 5, people use context to interpret and impose meaning on stimuli—including language. A statement like "Wow, are you smart!" can be interpreted as "I think you're an idiot," depending on the context (and perhaps the tone of voice).

Individuals' educational and cultural background also forms part of the context that shapes their understanding of a communication. That background may determine how a listener interprets ambiguous stimuli (Schank & Abelson, 1977). For example, what do you think is going on in this story?

Every Saturday night, four good friends get together. When Jerry, Mike, and Pat arrived, Karen was sitting in her living room writing some notes. She quickly gathered the cards and stood up to greet her friends at the door. They followed her into the living room but as usual they couldn't agree on exactly what to play. Jerry eventually took a stand and set things up. Finally, they began to play. Karen's recorder filled the room with soft and pleasant music. Early in the evening, Mike noticed Pat's hand and the many diamonds. As the night progressed the tempo of play increased. Finally, a lull in the activities occurred. Taking advantage of this, Jerry pondered the arrangement in front of him. Mike interrupted Jerry's reverie and said, "Let's hear the score." They listened carefully and commented on their performance. When the comments were all heard, exhausted but happy, Karen's friends went home. (Anderson et al., 1977)

Researchers found that music majors tended to interpret this passage as describing a musical rehearsal; other students typically read it as the description of a card game (Anderson et al., 1977). The two groups used different scripts as a framework for interpreting ambiguous words like *stand* and *diamonds.* Building scripts into a computer's memory to resolve ambiguities is one of the greatest challenges in developing artificial-intelligence systems for speech recognition.

Conventions and Nonverbal Cues Social *conventions,* commonly accepted practices and usage, also govern conversation. Though the words alone do not say so, "Will you join me in a cup of coffee?" conveys to most people an invitation to drink coffee, not to climb into a giant cup. Similarly, someone who asks, "Do you know what time it is?" is not expecting a yes or no answer.

People are often also guided to an understanding of conversations by nonverbal cues. The frown, the enthusiastic nod, the bored yawn—all signal differences in understanding or interest that have an important bearing on the exchange of information. Thus it is not surprising that face-to-face conversations are more efficient than those in which speakers cannot see each other—a fact that should be considered when groups or teams must try to solve problems in separate locations, whether by telephone, electronic mail, or other means (Chapanis et al., 1977).

Learning to Speak: Stages of Language Development

LINKAGES **How do we learn to speak?** (a link to Human Development)

Once people have learned to speak, they use the many rules of language naturally and automatically to generate correct sentences and to reject incorrect ones, even though most people would have a difficult time stating the rules. For example, in an instant you know that the words "Bei mir bist du schön" are not English and that the string of words "Quickly peaches sheep deserve" is not an acceptable sentence. Children the world over learn language with impressive speed and regularity. Developmental psychologists have painstakingly described the steps in this process.

From Babblings to Words **Babblings** are the first sounds infants make that resemble speech. These alternating consonant and vowel sounds ("bababa," "mamimamima," "dadada") begin at about four months of age. Although meaningless to the baby, they are a delight to parents. During much of the first year, infants of all nationalities make the same babbling sounds. At about nine months, however, babies who hear only English start to lose their German gutturals and French nasals. Their babbling becomes more complex and begins to sound like "sentences" in their native language. Beginning at this time, too, infants begin to shorten some of their vocalizations to "da," "duh," and "ma." These sounds seem very much like language. Babies use them in specific contexts and with obvious purpose (Dore, 1978). Accompanied by appropriate gestures, they may be used to express joy ("oohwow") or anger ("uh-uh-uh"), to get something that is out of reach ("engh-engh"), or to point out something interesting ("dah!").

Ten- to twelve-month-olds can understand a few words—certainly more words than they can say (Huttenlocher, 1974). Proper names and object words are among the first words they understand. Often the first word they understand is a pet's name.

GETTING READY TO TALK Long before they utter their first words, babies are getting ready to talk. Experiments in Patricia Kuhl's laboratory show that even six-month-olds tend to look longer at faces whose lip movements match the sounds of spoken words. This tendency reflects babies' abilities to focus on, recognize, and discriminate the sounds of speech, especially in their native language. These abilities are crucial to the development of language.

Proper names and object words—words like *mama, daddy, cookie, doggy,* and *car*—are also among the first words children are likely to say when, at around twelve to eighteen months of age, they begin to talk. Nouns for simple object categories *(dog, flower)* are acquired before more general nouns *(animal, plant)* or more specific names *(collie, rose)* (Rosch et al., 1976).

Of course, these early words do not sound exactly like adult language. Babies usually reduce them to a shorter, easier form, like "duh" for *duck* or "mih" for *milk.* Children make themselves understood, however, by using gestures, intonations, facial expressions, and interminable repetitions. If they have a word for an object, they may "overextend" it to cover more ground. Thus, they might use *dog* for cats, bears, and horses; they might use *fly* for all insects and perhaps for other small things like raisins and M&Ms (Clark & Clark, 1977). Children make these "errors" because their vocabularies are limited, not because they fail to notice the difference between dogs and cats or because they want to eat a fly (Fremgen & Fay, 1980; Rescorla, 1981).

Until they can say the conventional words for objects, children overextend the words they have, use all-purpose sounds (like "dat" or "dis"), and coin new words (like *pepping* for "shaking the pepper shaker"). During this period, children build up their vocabularies one word at a time. They also use their limited vocabulary one word at a time; they cannot yet put words together into sentences. This **one-word stage** of speech lasts for about six months.

First Sentences   By eighteen to twenty-four months of age, children usually have a vocabulary of some fifty words. Then their language undergoes a rapid acceleration: They may learn several new words a day and begin to put words together (Gleitman & Landau, 1994). At first, children's sentences consist of two-word pairs. These two-word utterances are **telegraphic.** Brief and to the point, they leave out any word that is not absolutely essential. If she wants her mother to give her a book, the twenty-month-old might first say, "Give book," then, "Mommy give," and, if that does not work, "Mommy book." The child also uses rising intonation to indicate a question ("Go out?") and word stress to indicate location ("Play *park*") or new information ("*Big* car").

Three-word sentences come next in the development of language. They are still telegraphic, but more nearly complete: "Mommy give book." The child can now speak in sentences that have the usual subject-verb-object form of adult sentences. Other words and word endings begin appearing, too, such as the suffix *-ing,* the prepositions *in* and *on,* the plural *-s,* and irregular past tenses ("It broke," "I ate") (Brown, 1973; Dale, 1976). Children learn to use the suffix *-ed* for the past tense ("I walked"), and then they often overapply the rule to irregular verbs that they previously used correctly, saying, for example, "It breaked" or "It broked" or "I eated."

Children also expand their sentences with adjectives, although, at first, they do not always get the antonyms straight. For example, they are likely to use both *less* and *more* to mean "more" or *tall* and *short* to mean "tall" (Donaldson & Balfour, 1968).

Complex Sentences   By age three or so, children begin to use auxiliary verbs ("Adam is going") and to ask questions using *wh-* words, such as *what, where, who,* and *why.* They begin to put together clauses to form complex sentences ("Here's the ball I was looking for"). Until they are about five years old, however, children join events in the order in which they occur ("We went to the zoo and had ice cream") and understand sentences better if they follow this order (Kavanaugh & Jirkovsky, 1982). By age five, children have acquired most of the syntax of their native language.

How Is Language Acquired?

Despite all that has been learned about the steps children follow in learning language, mystery and debate still surround the question of just how they learn it. Obviously, children pick up the specific content of language from the speech they hear around them; English children learn English, French children learn French. As parents and children share meals, playtime, and conversations, children learn that words refer to objects and actions and what the labels for them are. One study illustrated the influence of mothers' language input on their toddlers' vocabularies by comparing the language development of U.S. and Japanese children (Tamis-LeMonda et al., 1992). Mothers in the United States were more likely than Japanese mothers to label and describe objects for their toddlers; their children, in turn, were more likely than Japanese children to understand and say these object words. But how do children learn syntax?

Conditioning, Imitation, and Rules   Our discussion of conditioning in Chapter 7 suggests one possibility: Perhaps children learn syntax because their parents reinforce them for using it. In fact, however, parents usually are more concerned about *what* is said than about its form (Hirsch-Pasek, Treiman & Schneiderman, 1984). When the little boy with chocolate crumbs on his face says, "I not eat cookie," the mother is more likely to respond, "Yes, you did eat it" than to ask the child to say, "I did not eat the cookie" and then reinforce him for grammatical correctness. Observations suggest, then, that operant conditioning cannot fully explain the learning of syntax.

Learning through modeling, or imitation, appears to be more influential. Children learn syntax most rapidly when adults offer simple revisions of their sentences, implicitly correcting their syntax, and then continue with the topic they are discussing. For example,

> *Child:* Mommy fix.
>
> *Mother:* Okay, Mommy will fix the truck.
>
> *Child:* It breaked.
>
> *Mother:* Yes, it broke.
>
> *Child:* Truck broke.
>
> *Mother:* Let's see if we can fix it.

But if children learn syntax by imitation, why would they overgeneralize rules, such as the rule for making the past tense? Why, for example, do children who at one time said "I went" later say "I goed"? Adults never use this form of speech. Its sudden appearance indicates that the child either has mastered the rule of adding *-ed* or has generalized from similar-sounding words (such as "mowed" or "rowed"). In short, neither conditioning nor imitation seems entirely adequate to explain how children learn language. Children must still analyze for themselves the underlying patterns in the welter of language examples they hear around them (Bloom, 1995).

Biological Bases for Language Acquisition   The ease with which children everywhere discover these patterns and learn language encourages some to argue that humans are "prewired," or biologically programmed, to learn language. This biological preparedness is reflected in the unique speech-generating properties of the human mouth and throat (Aitchison, 1983), as well as in brain regions discussed in Chapter 3, such as Broca's area and Wernicke's area (see Figure 3.17 on page 67).

Chomsky (1957) suggested that human beings are born with a *language acquisition device—LAD* for short—that allows youngsters to gather ideas about the rules of language, without being aware of doing so. They then use these ideas to understand and construct their native language. This hypothesis is supported by the observation that children make up words like "goed," which shows that they understand language rules (in this case, the rule for forming past tense). It is also supported by the fact that there is some similarity in the syntax of all languages. Furthermore, children who are born deaf and never exposed to language make up gestural systems that have several properties of natural spoken language; for example, these systems place subjects before verbs and include agent-action-object sequences, such as "June saw Bob" (Goldin-Meadow & Feldman, 1977).

According to Elizabeth Bates (1993), however, one need not assume a special LAD to understand language acquisition. She suggests that the development of children's language is a reflection of their development of other cognitive skills (see Chapter 12). Thus, for example, children learn short words before long words because limitations in short-term memory and other cognitive abilities lead them to learn easy things before harder ones.

LEARNING A SECOND LANGUAGE The notion of a critical period for language acquisition is supported by the fact that, after the age of thirteen or fourteen, people learn a second language more slowly (Johnson & Newport, 1989) and virtually never learn to speak it without an accent (Lenneberg, 1967).

Regardless of whether language learning is guided by a specific language acquisition device or by more general cognitive skills, there appears to be a limited window of opportunity—or *critical period*—for language learning. The idea of such a critical period is supported by cases in which certain unfortunate children spent their early years in isolation from human contact and the sound of adult language. Even after years of therapy and language training, these individuals were not able to combine ideas into sentences. Such cases suggest that, in order to acquire complex features of language, a person must be exposed to speech before a certain age.

Bilingualism   Does trying to learn two languages at once, even before the critical period is over, impair the learning of either? Research suggests just the opposite. Although their early language utterances may be confused or delayed, children who are raised in a bilingual environment before the end of the critical period seem to show enhanced performance in each language (Hakuta & Garcia, 1989). There is also some evidence that *balanced bilinguals,* those who have roughly equal mastery of two languages, are superior to other children in cognitive flexibility, concept formation, and creativity (Padilla et al., 1991). It is as if each language offers a slightly different perspective on thinking, and this dual perspective makes the brain more flexible.

The apparent benefits of bilingualism have important implications for U.S. school systems, where children from non–English-speaking homes often receive instruction in their native language while taking classes in English. Although lack of control over school environments makes it difficult to perform true experiments on the effects of this practice, available evidence suggests that these bilingual programs facilitate educational achievement (Cavaliere, 1996; Padilla et al., 1991). The evidence also suggests that rapid immersion in an English-only program may do considerable educational harm to children who enter school with no English-language background (Crawford, 1989).

Some say that the ability of humans to learn and use language sets them apart from all other creatures. Yet animals do use symbols to communicate. Bees dance in a way that indicates the direction and distance of sources of

THINKING CRITICALLY

Can Nonhumans Use Language?

nectar; the grunts and gestures of chimpanzees signify various attitudes and emotions. These forms of communication do not necessarily have the grammatical characteristics of language, however. Are any animals other than humans capable of learning language?

What am I being asked to believe or accept?

Over the last forty years, several researchers have asserted that nonhumans *can* master language. Chimpanzees and gorillas have been the most popular subjects, because at maturity they are estimated to have the intelligence of two- or three-year-old children, who are usually well on their way to learning language. Dolphins, too, have been studied because they have a complex communication system and exceptionally large brains relative to their body size (Jerison, 1973). It would seem that if these animals are unable to learn language, their general intelligence cannot be blamed. Instead, failure would be attributed to the absence of a genetic makeup that permits language learning.

What evidence is available to support the assertion?

The question of whether nonhuman mammals can learn to use language is not a simple one, for at least two reasons. First, language is more than just communication, but defining just when animals are exhibiting that "something more" is a source of debate (Bradshaw, 1993c). What seems to set human language apart from the gestures, grunts, chirps, whistles, or cries of other animals is grammar—a formal set of rules for combining words. Using the rules of grammar, people can take a relatively small number of words and create with them an almost infinite number of unique sentences. Also, because of their muscular structures, nonhuman mammals will never be able to "speak" in the same way that humans do (Crelin, 1987). To test these animals' ability `to learn language, investigators therefore must devise novel ways for them to communicate.

David and Ann Premack taught their chimp, Sarah, to communicate by placing different-shaped chips, symbolizing words, on a magnetic board (Premack, 1971). Lana, a chimpanzee studied by Duane Rumbaugh (1977), learned to communicate by pressing keys on a specially designed computer. American Sign Language (ASL), the language of the deaf that is based on hand gestures, has been used by Beatrice and Allen Gardner with the chimp Washoe, by Herbert Terrace with a chimp named Nim Chimsky (after Noam Chomsky), and by Penny Patterson with a gorilla named Koko.

ANIMAL LANGUAGE?   Several chimpanzees and gorillas have been taught to use American Sign Language (ASL). Here, Nim signs "play" upon seeing the teacher sign "out." Are these animals' remarkable accomplishments with ASL equivalent to human language acquisition?

Kanzi, a bonobo or pygmy chimp studied by Sue Savage-Rumbaugh (1990; Savage-Rumbaugh et al., 1993), learned to recognize spoken words and communicated through a combination of gesturing and pressing word-symbol keys on a computer that would "speak" them. Kanzi was a special case: He learned to communicate by listening and watching as his mother, Matata, was being taught, then used what he had learned to interact with her trainers (Savage-Rumbaugh et al., 1986).

Studies of all six animals suggested that they could spontaneously use combinations of words to refer to things that were not present. Washoe, Lana, Sarah, Nim, Kanzi, and Koko all mastered from 130 to 500 words. Their vocabulary included names for concrete objects, such as *apple* or *me;* verbs, such as *tickle* and *eat;* adjectives, such as *happy* and *big;* and adverbs, such as *again*. The animals combined the words in sentences, expressing wishes like "You tickle me" or "If Sarah good, then apple." Sometimes the sentences referred to things in the past. When an investigator called attention to a wound that Kanzi had received, the animal produced the sentence "Matata hurt," referring to the fact that his mother had recently given him a disciplinary bite (Savage-Rumbaugh, 1990). Finally, all these animals seemed to enjoy their communication tools and used them spontaneously to interact with their caretakers and with other animals.

Most of the investigators mentioned here have argued that their animals mastered a crude grammar (Patterson, 1978; Premack, 1971; Greenfield & Savage-Rumbaugh, 1990). For example, if Washoe wanted to be tickled, she would gesture, "You tickle Washoe." But if she wanted to do the tickling, she would gesture, "Washoe tickle you." The correct placement of object and subject in these sentences suggested that Washoe was following a set of rules for word combination—in other words, a grammar (Gardner & Gardner, 1978). Louis Herman and his colleagues documented similar syntactic sensitivity in dolphins, who rarely confused subject-verb order in following instructions given by human hand signals (Herman, Richards & Wolz, 1984). Furthermore, Savage-Rumbaugh observed several hundred instances in which Kanzi understood sentences he had never heard before. Once, for example, while his back was turned to the speaker, Kanzi heard the sentence "Jeanie hid the pine needles in her shirt." He turned around, approached Jeanie, and searched her shirt to find the pine needles. His actions would seem to indicate that he understood this new sentence the first time he heard it.

Are there alternative ways of interpreting the evidence?

Many of the early conclusions about primate language learning were challenged by Herbert Terrace and his colleagues in their investigation of Nim (Terrace et al., 1979). Terrace noticed many subtle characteristics of Nim's communications that seemed quite different from a child's use of language, and he argued that animals in other studies demonstrated these same characteristics.

First, he said, their sentences were always very short. Nim could combine two or three gestures but never used strings that conveyed more sophisticated messages. Thus, the ape was never able to say anything equivalent to a three-year-old child's "I want to go to Wendy's for a hamburger, OK?" Second, Terrace questioned whether the animals' use of language demonstrated the spontaneity, creativity, and expanding complexity characteristic of children's language. Many of the animals' sentences were requests for food, tickling, baths, pets, and other pleasurable objects and experiences. Is such behavior qualitatively different from the behavior of the family dog, who learns to sit up and beg for table scraps? Other researchers also concluded that chimps are not naturally predisposed to associate seen objects with heard words, as human infants are (Savage-Rumbaugh et al., 1983). Finally, Terrace questioned whether experimenter bias influenced the reports of the chimps' communications. Consciously or not, experimenters who hope to conclude that chimps learn language might tend to ignore strings that violate grammatical order or to reinterpret ambiguous strings so that they make grammatical sense. If Nim sees someone holding a banana and signs, "Nim banana," the experimenter might assume the word order is correct and means "Nim wants the banana" rather than, for example, "That banana belongs to Nim," in which case the word order would be wrong.

What additional evidence would help to evaluate the alternatives?

Studies of animals' ability to learn language are expensive and take many years. Accordingly, the amount of evidence in the area is small—just a handful of studies, each based mainly on a single subject. Obviously, more data are needed from more subjects exposed to a common methodology.

It is important, as well, to study the extent to which limits on the length of the primate's spontaneous sentences result from limits on working memory (Savage-Rumbaugh, 1990). If memory is indeed the main limiting factor, then the failure to produce progressively longer sentences does not necessarily reflect an inability to master language.

Research on how primates might spontaneously acquire language by listening and imitating, as Kanzi did, as well as naturalistic observations of communications among primates in their natural habitat, would also help scientists better understand their capacity to communicate (Sevcik & Savage-Rumbaugh, 1994).

What conclusions are most reasonable?

Psychologists are still not in full agreement about whether our sophisticated mammalian cousins can learn language. Two things are clear, however. First, whatever the chimp, gorilla, and dolphin have learned is a much more primitive and limited form of communication than that learned by children. Second, their level of communication does not do justice to their overall intelligence; these animals are smarter than their "language" production suggests. Thus, the evidence to date favors the view that humans have language abilities that are unique, but that under the right circumstances, and with the right tools, other animals can master many language-like skills.

Knowledge, Language, and Culture

The language that people speak forms part of their knowledge of the world, and that knowledge, as noted in Chapter 5, guides perceptions. This relationship raises the question of whether differences among the languages of the world create differences in how people perceive and think about the world. As noted in Chapter 12, for example, differences in the names for numbers in Korean and English may be partly responsible for differences between Korean and American children's mental arithmetic skills (Fusan & Kwon, 1992b).

Benjamin Whorf claimed that language directly influences perception (Whorf, 1956). He noted, for example, that Inuit Eskimos have several different words for *snow* and proposed that this feature of their language should lead to a greater perceptual ability to discriminate among varieties of snow. When the discrimination abilities of Inuits and other people are compared, there are indeed significant differences. Are these differences in perception the *result* of differences in language?

One of the most interesting tests of Whorf's ideas was conducted by Eleanor Rosch (1975). She compared the perception of colors by Americans with that by members of the Dani tribe of New Guinea. In the language of the Dani, there are only two color names, one for dark, "cold" colors and one for lighter, "warm" ones. In contrast, English speakers have names for a vast number of different hues. Of these, it is possible to identify eleven *focal* colors; these are prototypes, the particular wavelengths of light that are the best examples of the eleven major color categories (red, yellow, green, blue, black, gray, white, purple, orange, pink, and brown). Thus, fire-engine red is the focal color for red. Rosch reasoned that, if Whorf's views were correct, then English speakers, who have verbal labels for focal colors, should recognize them better than nonfocal colors, but that for the Dani, the focal-nonfocal distinction should make no difference. In fact, however, Rosch found that both the Dani and the English-speaking Americans perceived focal colors more efficiently than nonfocal ones (Heider, 1972).

LANGUAGE AND PERCEPTION The Inuit language has several names for various kinds of snow. Inuits are also far better than native English speakers at perceiving differing varieties of snow. Does this mean that language shapes perception or that environmental conditions and culturally based learning shape attention, perception, and the words used to describe important stimuli and events?

Thus, the fact that Inuit people have verbal labels for differences among snow textures that, say, Texans don't even perceive suggests a *correlation* between language and perception in various cultures. But it appears doubtful that language *causes* these differences in perception, as Whorf suggested. It seems far more likely that, beneath the differences in both language and perception, there is a third variable: frequency of use and the need for certain objects. Inuits, for example, live in a snowy world. Their lives depend on making fine discriminations about the snow—between the snow bridge that is solid and the one that will collapse, for example. Hence, they learn to discriminate differences that are unimportant to people in warmer climates, and they attach names to those differences.

FUTURE DIRECTIONS

As some of the simpler, more easily observed phenomena associated with cognition yield their secrets, the challenge grows to understand the most complex aspects of mental activity. To study such complex phenomena, researchers are beginning to supplement laboratory research with field studies (Hancock et al., 1995; Sarter & Woods, 1995). These new approaches have revealed a complex interplay between human thought processes and the environment within which they occur, defining a new research domain called *situated cognition* (Hutchins, 1995; Lintern, 1995). Cognition is increasingly becoming understood not as an abstract set of mechanisms and processes but as a rich system well-tuned to coordinate with the natural world (Hancock et al., 1995; Smythe et al., 1995). (This trend corresponds to the ecological approach to intelligence, which, as described in the next chapter, highlights the role of the environment in shaping intellectual abilities [Sternberg & Wagner, 1994; Sternberg et al., 1995]). Similarly, research on naturalistic decision making will continue to expand our understanding of how people make decisions in such "real-world" arenas as medicine, fire-fighting, and air-traffic control (Klein & Crandall, 1995).

As our understanding of human thinking improves, so do the opportunities for applying that knowledge. The information-processing approach will continue to promote a better understanding of the sources of human errors in problem solving and decision making, and of ways to prevent such errors (Bagnon, 1994; Senders & Moray, 1991). In particular, researchers in the field of *cognitive engineering*, a discipline within engineering psychology, are applying knowledge about how people think to the design and display of complex systems related to aviation, industry, and computers (Rasmussen, Pejtersen & Goodstein, 1995). They are asking, for example, how computer menus or electronic databases should be organized to be most compatible with users' mental models of programs and data (Allen, 1991; Seidler & Wickens, 1992).

The study of artificial intelligence will also continue to expand. Although some researchers remain skeptical that computers will ever be able to match human mental abilities (Hofstadter, 1995), others are optimistic that AI systems can be programmed to effectively learn and thus acquire broader competence and skill (Nilsson, 1995). Work aimed at achieving this goal will continue to help psychologists learn more about the human mind and to guide other scientists in the design of computer-based expert systems.

In short, cognitive psychology is rapidly becoming one of the most exciting areas in psychology. To learn more about the research explosion taking place in the areas of thought, problem solving, decision making, and language, consider taking courses in experimental psychology, cognitive psychology (sometimes called *higher processes* or *thinking*), psycholinguistics, or engineering psychology (sometimes called *human factors*).

SUMMARY AND KEY TERMS

■ BASIC FUNCTIONS OF THOUGHT

The five core functions of thought are to describe, elaborate, decide, plan, and guide action.

The Circle of Thought
Many psychologists think of the components of the circle of thought as constituting an *information-processing system* that receives, represents, transforms, and acts on incoming stimuli. *Thinking,* then, is defined as the manipulation of mental representations by this system.

Information-Processing Speed: Reaction Time
Mental chronometry involves the timing of mental events. The time elapsing between the presentation of a stimulus and an overt response is the *reaction time.* Among the factors affecting reaction times are the complexity of the choice of a response, stimulus-response compatibility, expectancy, and the tradeoff between speed and accuracy.

Picturing Information Processing: Evoked Brain Potentials
Using methods such as the EEG, psychologists can also measure mental events as reflected in *evoked brain potentials.*

■ MENTAL REPRESENTATIONS: THE INGREDIENTS OF THOUGHT

Mental representations take the form of cognitive maps, images, concept schemas and event scripts, and propositions.

Cognitive Maps
Cognitive maps are mental representations of familiar parts of one's world. In contrast to paper maps, the information in cognitive maps is imprecise and subject to systematic distortion.

Images
Mental *images* may also be manipulated when people think. Images can be mentally inspected, expanded, and rotated. They contain details about what objects look like, how their component parts are arranged, and what textures they have.

Concept Schemas and Event Scripts
Concepts are categories of objects, events, or ideas with common properties. They may be natural or artificial. *Artificial concepts* are precisely defined by the presence or absence of certain features. *Natural concepts* are fuzzy; no fixed set of defining properties determines membership in a natural concept. A member of a natural concept that displays all or most of its characteristic features is called a *prototype. Schemas* serve as generalized mental representations of concepts and also generate expectations about them. *Scripts* are schemas of familiar patterns or sequences, usually involving human activities; they help people to think about those activities and to interpret new events.

Propositions
The raw material of thought may also take the form of *propositions,* which are assertions that state how different concepts are related or how a concept is related to its properties. Propositions can be true or false. *Mental models* are clusters of propositions describing people's understanding (whether accurate or inaccurate) of physical objects or processes.

■ THINKING STRATEGIES

By combining and transforming mental representations, our information-processing system makes it possible for us to reason, solve problems, and make decisions. *Reasoning* is the process through which people generate and evaluate arguments, and reach conclusions about them.

Formal Reasoning
Formal, or *logical, reasoning* seeks valid conclusions through the application of rigorous procedures. These procedures include formulas, or *algorithms,* which are guaranteed to reach correct results, and the rules of logic, which are useful in evaluating sets of premises and conclusions called *syllogisms.* To reach a sound conclusion, people should consider both the empirical truth or falsity of the premises and the *logic* of the argument itself. People are prone to logical errors; their belief in a conclusion is often affected by the extent to which the conclusion is consistent with their attitudes as well as by other factors, including cultural background.

Informal Reasoning
People use informal reasoning to assess the credibility of a conclusion based on the evidence for it. Errors in informal reasoning often stem from the use of *heuristics,* mental shortcuts or rules of thumb. Three important heuristics are the *anchoring heuristic* (estimating the probability of an event by adjusting a starting value), the *representativeness heuristic* (categorizing an event by how representative it is of a category of events), and the *availability heuristic* (estimating probability by how available an event is in memory).

■ PROBLEM SOLVING

Steps in problem solving include diagnosing the problem, then planning, executing, and evaluating a solution.

Strategies for Problem Solving
Especially when solutions are not obvious, problem solving can be aided by the use of strategies such as decomposition, working backward, finding analogies, and allowing for incubation.

Obstacles to Problem Solving
Many of the difficulties that people experience in solving problems arise when they are dealing with hypotheses. People do not easily entertain multiple hypotheses. Because of *mental sets* they may persevere in applying one hypothesis even when it is unsuccessful and, through *functional fixedness,* may tend to miss opportunities to use familiar objects in unusual ways. People are reluctant to revise or change hypotheses on the basis of new data. People may also fail to use the absence of symptoms as evidence in solving problems.

Building Problem-Solving Skills

Experts are superior to novices in problem solving because of their knowledge and experience. They can draw on knowledge of similar problems, visualize related components of a problem as a single chunk, and perceive relations among problems in terms of underlying principles rather than surface features. Thus, extensive knowledge is the main component of expertise; yet expertise itself can prevent the expert from seeing problems in new ways.

Problem Solving by Computer

Some specific problems can be solved by computer programs known as *expert systems.* These systems are one application of *artificial intelligence (AI).* There are two approaches to AI. One focuses on programming computers to imitate the logical manipulation of symbols that occurs in human thought; the other (involving connectionist, or neural network, models) attempts to imitate the connections among neurons in the human brain. Current problem-solving computer systems deal successfully only with specific domains. They cannot draw insight from different areas.

■ DECISION MAKING

Evaluating Options

Decisions are sometimes difficult because there are too many alternatives and too many attributes of each alternative to consider at one time. Furthermore, decisions often involve comparisons of *utility,* not of simple objective value. Decision making is also complicated by the fact that the world is unpredictable, which makes decisions risky. People should act in ways that maximize the *expected value* of their decisions.

Biases and Flaws in Decision Making

People often fail to maximize expected value in their decisions because losses are perceived differently from gains of equal size and because they tend to overestimate the probability of rare events, underestimate the probability of very frequent events, and feel overconfident in the accuracy of their forecasts. The gambler's fallacy leads people to believe that outcomes in a random process are affected by previous outcomes. People make decisions aimed at goals other than maximizing expected value; these goals may be determined by personal and cultural factors.

■ LINKAGES: GROUP PROCESSES IN PROBLEM SOLVING AND DECISION MAKING

Group decisions tend to show *group polarization,* the selection of more conservative or radical outcomes than would have been chosen by the average group member. Group performance at problem solving and decision making tends to be more effective, but less efficient, than that of a person working alone. Group performance rises toward that of the most competent member as group size increases (up to a point), if high-status members of the group, who exert the greatest influence, are also the most competent, and as groups work together for longer periods.

■ LANGUAGE

The Elements of Language

Language consists of *words* or word symbols and rules for their combination—a *grammar.* Spoken words are made up of *phonemes,* which are combined to make *morphemes.* Combinations of words must have both *syntax* (grammar) and *semantics* (meaning). Behind the word strings, or *surface structures,* is an underlying representation, or *deep structure,* that expresses the relationship among the ideas in a sentence. Ambiguous sentences occur when one surface structure reflects two or more deep structures.

Understanding Speech

When people listen to speech, the perceptual system allows them to perceive gaps between words, even when these gaps are not physically present. Syntax and semantics also help people understand spoken messages. To understand language generally and conversations in particular, people use their knowledge of the context and of the world. This knowledge is often described through scripts. In addition, communication in conversations is guided by conventions and aided by nonverbal cues.

Learning to Speak: Stages of Language Development

Children develop grammar according to an orderly pattern. *Babblings* and the *one-word stage* of speech come first, then *telegraphic* two-word sentences. Next come three-word sentences and certain grammatical forms that appear in a somewhat predictable order. Once children learn certain regular verb forms and plural endings, they may overgeneralize rules. Children acquire most of the syntax of their native language by the time they are five years old.

How Is Language Acquired?

Conditioning and imitation both play a role in a child's acquisition of language, but neither can provide a complete explanation of how children acquire syntax. Humans may be biologically programmed to learn language. In any event, it appears that language must be learned during a certain critical period if normal language is to occur. The critical-period notion is supported by research on second-language acquisition.

Knowledge, Language, and Culture

Although language has been thought to shape perceptions, it is more likely that environmental conditions and demands shape one's attention to and knowledge of the world and that language evolves to describe in more detail those aspects of the world that are especially important in one's culture.

MENTAL ABILITIES

BIOLOGICAL ASPECTS
OF PSYCHOLOGY

**Which parts of the brain
control which mental
abilities?** *(ans. on p. 70)*

THOUGHT AND LANGUAGE

**Are smarter people always
better problem solvers?**
(ans. on p. 325)

MEMORY

**Is mental retardation mainly
a matter of poor memory?**
(ans. on p. 329)

C onsider the following sketches that describe four college seniors and some of their varying abilities and interests. Do any of these descriptions remind you of anyone you know? Do any of them sound like you?

When Jack got into trouble at his urban grade school, he was always able to talk his way out of it. His "street smarts" were not reflected in his grades, however. He had great difficulty reading and was a terrible speller. When tests in middle school revealed that Jack had dyslexia, a learning disability, he was placed in a special reading program. In high school, Jack worked very hard to compensate for his disability, and he graduated with a grade-point average (GPA) of 3.78, but his SAT score was only 860 of a possible 1600. He attended a regional state college, where, under the Americans with Disabilities Act, he was granted extra time to complete exams. He held a half-time job throughout all four years, and his GPA was 2.95. After taking the Graduate Records Examination Jack applied to masters programs in special education. He also applied for a job at a local youth center, where the administrators glanced at his application and gave him a ten-minute interview.

Deneace grew up in the suburbs and earned straight A's in a public grade school. She attended a private high school, where she placed in the top fifth of her class and played the violin as a hobby. Her SAT score was 1340, but because her school does not give letter grades, she had no grade-point average to include in college applications. Instead, she submitted her teachers' written evaluations and a portfolio containing samples of her papers, class projects, and other work. Deneace was accepted at several prestigious liberal arts colleges, but not at major universities. She is enrolled in a pre-med program and has just completed her senior research project. With a GPA of 3.60, Deneace is hoping to be accepted by a medical school.

Ruthie grew up in a city apartment, has a wide range of interests, loves physical activities, has many friends, and can talk to anybody about almost anything. Her grades, however, have been only fair, averaging 2.60 in high school. She played four sports, though, and was captain of the state champion volleyball team. She scored only 18 out of a possible 36 on the ACT college entrance exam, but received an athletic scholarship at a large university. She majored in sociology, minored in sports therapy, and would now like to become a rehabilitation counselor. Focusing on just one sport has helped her achieve a 3.25 grade-point average. She applied to graduate schools but has also looked into a job as a city recreation director, for which she had to complete a state employment exam and a full afternoon of interviews.

George comes from a farming region and showed an early interest in computers. As a child, he was quiet and had few friends. In high school, despite straight A's in math, art, and shop classes, George's grade-point average was only 2.55, placing him in the bottom half of his class. He didn't get along with other students and spent his free time "hacking" on his computer. Everyone was surprised when he scored 1320 on the SAT. George was accepted at an agriculture and engineering college, where he majored in math and computer science. His grades suffered initially as he began to spend time with people who shared his interests, but his average is now 3.33. He expresses his artistic talent by writing computer animation software. He has applied to graduate programs in fields relating to artificial intelligence and human factors engineering, and he also took a computer programming test for a software company.

Before reading further, take a minute to rank these four people on **mental ability**—the capacity to reason, remember, understand, solve problems, and make decisions. Who came out on top? Now ask a friend to do the same and see if your rankings match. They may not, because each of the students excels in different ways.

In Western cultures, mental ability is often thought of in terms of intelligence. Deneace might score highest on general intelligence tests, which emphasize remembering, reasoning, and verbal and mathematical abilities. But would standard tests reflect Ruthie's social skills, Jack's "street smarts," or George's artistic ability? And should they? If you were hiring an employee or evaluating a student, what characteristics would you want a test to measure? For that matter, can two people's test scores be compared without consideration of their social and academic background?

These are among the questions addressed in this chapter as we consider how and why individuals demonstrate differences in mental abilities. The answers matter in part because, as the examples show, measurements of mental abilities often determine who goes into which kinds of classes, schools, and jobs. These measurements are also important tools for diagnosis and research (see the Linkages diagram).

After presenting the background of intelligence testing, we will examine some underlying qualities that tests of any kind must possess. Next, we will evaluate the adequacy of IQ tests in particular. We will then look at some of the ways in which psychologists study the concept of intelligence. Finally, we will expand our view to consider other aspects of mental abilities.

TESTING FOR INTELLIGENCE

Usually, it helps to begin the study of a concept by defining it, but defining intelligence has proved to be a difficult task. Psychologists do not agree on a single definition. Is intelligence the ability to think abstractly, or perhaps the ability to deal effectively with the environment? Robert Sternberg's (1985) working definition—which is accepted by many psychologists—describes **intelligence** in terms of three characteristics: the possession of knowledge, the ability to efficiently use knowledge to reason about the world, and the ability to employ that reasoning adaptively in different environments. IQ tests measure some, but not all, of these aspects of intelligence.

A Brief History of IQ Tests

In 1904 the French government appointed psychologist Alfred Binet to a commission charged with identifying, studying, and providing special educational programs for children who were not doing well in school. As part of his work on the commission, Binet developed a set, or *battery,* of intellectual test items that provided the model for today's intelligence tests. In creating his test, Binet assumed that intelligence is involved in many reasoning, thinking, and problem-solving activities. Therefore, he looked for tasks that would highlight differences in children's ability to reason, judge, and solve problems (Binet & Simon, 1905). His test included tasks such as unwrapping a piece of candy, repeating numbers or sentences from memory, and identifying familiar objects (Frank, 1976). Binet also assumed that children's abilities increase with age. To select the items for his test, Binet tried them out on children of various ages and then categorized the items according to the age at which the typical child could respond correctly. For example, a "six-year-old item" was one that a substantial majority of six-year-olds could answer. Binet's test was thus a set of *age-graded* items. It measured a child's "mental level"—now called *mental age*—by determining the age level of the most advanced items a child could consistently answer correctly. Children whose mental age equaled their actual or *chronological age* were considered to be of "regular" intelligence (Reisman, 1976).

About a decade after Binet published his test, Lewis Terman at Stanford University developed an English version known as the **Stanford-Binet** (Terman, 1916). Table 10.1 gives examples of the kinds of items included on the test. Terman added items to measure the intelligence of adults and, applying an idea suggested by William Stern, revised the method of scoring. Mental age was divided by chronological age, and the quotient was multiplied by 100; the result was called the *intelligence quotient,* or *IQ.* Thus, a child whose mental age and chronological age were equal would have an IQ of 100, which is considered "average" intelligence. A ten-year-old who scored at the mental age of twelve would have an IQ of $12/10 \times 100 = 120$. From this method of scoring came the term

TABLE 10.1	Age	Task
The Stanford-Binet	2	Place geometric shapes into corresponding openings; identify body parts; stack blocks; identify common objects.
Here are samples of the type of items included on the original Stanford-Binet test. As in Binet's earlier test, an age level was assigned to each item.	4	Name objects from memory; complete analogies (e.g., fire is hot; ice is _____); identify objects of similar shape; answer simple questions (e.g., "Why do we have schools?").
	6	Define simple words; explain differences (e.g., between a fish and a horse); identify missing parts of a picture; count out objects.
	8	Answer questions about a simple story; identify absurdities (e.g., in statements like "John had to walk on crutches because he hurt his arm"); explain similarities and differences among objects; tell how to handle certain situations (e.g., finding a stray puppy).
	10	Define more difficult words; give explanations (e.g., about why people should be quiet in a library); list as many words as possible; repeat 6-digit numbers.
	12	Identify more difficult verbal and pictured absurdities; repeat 5-digit numbers in reverse order; define abstract words (e.g., *sorrow);* fill in a missing word in a sentence.
	14	Solve reasoning problems; identify relationships among points of the compass; find similarities in apparently opposite concepts (e.g., *high* and *low);* predict the number of holes that will appear when folded paper is cut and then opened.
	Adult	Supply several missing words for incomplete sentences; repeat 6-digit numbers in reverse order; create a sentence using several unrelated words (e.g., *forest, businesslike,* and *dismayed);* describe similarities between concepts (e.g., *teaching* and *business).*

Source: Nietzel & Bernstein, 1987.

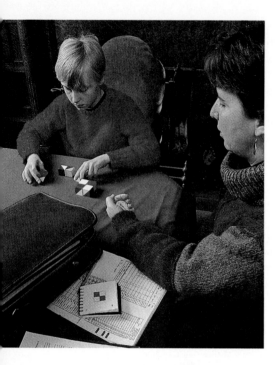

TAKING THE WECHSLER TEST Comparison of verbal and performance scores on the Wechsler test can be useful. For example, a high performance score and a low verbal score could mean that a child has a language deficiency that prevents the verbal scale from accurately measuring the child's mental abilities.

IQ test, a name that is widely used for any test designed to measure intelligence on an objective, standardized scale.

The scoring method used with the Stanford-Binet allowed testers to rank people on IQ. This goal was important to Terman and others who popularized the test in the United States because, unlike Binet—who suggested that intelligence improves with practice—they saw intelligence as a fixed and inherited entity. They believed that different individuals are favored with varying amounts of this thing called intelligence and that IQ tests could pinpoint who did and who did not have a suitable amount of intelligence. These beliefs led to some unfortunate consequences as enthusiasm for testing outpaced understanding of what was being tested.

Even before Terman developed the Stanford-Binet, psychologist Henry Goddard had translated Binet's test for use in studying mentally retarded children. When, in 1910, the U.S. government asked Goddard to help identify mentally defective immigrants, he took his English version of the French items from Binet's test and had them translated orally into the immigrants' languages. Today it is painfully obvious that this test was not a fair measure of intelligence, but Goddard (1917) concluded from its results that 83 percent of Jews, 80 percent of Hungarians, 87 percent of Russians, and 79 percent of Italians immigrating to America were "feeble-minded"! Ultimately, Goddard came to doubt the accuracy of his own conclusions and withdrew them in 1928 (Gregory, 1992).

The government also used mental tests to identify army recruits of low mental ability and to assign appropriate jobs to new soldiers. When the United States entered World War I, a team of psychologists developed the first group-administered tests for these purposes. The Army Alpha test, for recruits who could read English, assessed abilities such as arithmetic, analogies, and general knowledge. The Army Beta test was for those who could not read or did not speak English; it measured ability using nonverbal tasks, such as visualizing three-dimensional objects and solving mazes. The men who took either version were under stress in crowded rooms where instructions were not always audible or, for non-English speakers, understandable. Forty-seven percent of those tested showed a mental age of thirteen or lower (Yerkes, 1921). From these results C. C. Brigham (1923) incorrectly concluded that (1) from 1890 to 1915 the mental age of immigrants to America had declined and (2) the main source of this decline was the increase in immigration from Southern and Eastern Europe. Like Goddard, however, Brigham (1930) later repudiated his statements and noted that the Army tests were not very good measures of intelligence (Gould, 1983).

New tests developed by David Wechsler (1939, 1949) were designed to correct some of the weaknesses of their predecessors. Like the Alpha and Beta, Wechsler's tests were made up of several subtests, but they improved on those earlier tests in three key ways. First, both the verbal and nonverbal subtests were completed by all test takers. Second, answers depended less on familiarity with a particular culture. And third, the Wechsler tests allowed the tester to score each subtest separately and thus to develop a profile describing an individual's performance on several mental abilities.

IQ Tests Today

Modern editions of the Wechsler scales and the Stanford-Binet are the most widely used individually administered intelligence tests in schools today.

The Wechsler Adult Intelligence Scale includes eleven subtests. Six require verbal skills and make up the **verbal scale** of the test. These include such items as remembering a series of digits, solving arithmetic problems, defining vocabulary words, and understanding and answering questions (for example, "What did Shakespeare do?"). The remaining five subtests have little or no verbal content and make up the **performance scale.** They include tasks that require understanding the relations of objects in space and manipulation of materials—tasks such as assembling blocks, solving mazes, and completing pictures. Figure 10.1 gives examples of items from one section of the performance scale of the latest version of the Wechsler test for children. With Wechsler tests, one can compute a verbal IQ, performance IQ, and overall IQ.

Sample Items from the Performance Section of the Wechsler Intelligence Scale for Children (WISC-III)

Items like these tap aspects of intelligence but require little or no verbal ability.

PICTURE COMPLETION
What part is missing from this picture?

PICTURE ARRANGEMENT
These pictures tell a story, but they are in the wrong order. Put them in the right order so that they tell a story.

BLOCK DESIGN

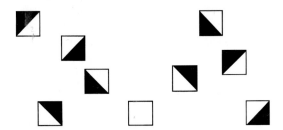

Put the blocks together to make this picture.

Source: Simulated items similar to those in the Wechsler Intelligence Scales for Adults and Children. Copyright © 1949, 1955, 1974, 1981, 1991 by the Psychological Corporation. Reproduced by permission. All rights reserved.

Like the Wechsler scales, the latest edition of the Stanford-Binet also uses subtests. It provides scores on verbal reasoning (e.g., "What is similar about an orange, apple, and grape?"), quantitative reasoning (e.g., math problems), abstract/visual reasoning (e.g., explaining why one should wear a coat in winter), and working memory (e.g., repeating a string of numbers in reverse order), along with a composite IQ (Thorndike, Hagan & Sattler, 1986).

IQ scores are no longer calculated by dividing mental age by chronological age. If you take an IQ test today, the points you earn for each correct subtest or age-level answer are summed. Then the summed score is compared to the scores earned by other people. The average score obtained by people at each age level is *assigned* the IQ value of 100. Other scores are assigned IQ values that reflect how far each score deviates from that average (see Figure 10.2). If you do better on the test than the average person in your age group, you will receive an IQ score above 100; how far above depends on how much better than average you do. Similarly, a person scoring below the age-group average will have an IQ below 100. This procedure may sound arbitrary, but it is based on a well-documented assumption about many characteristics: Most people's scores fall in the middle of the range of possible scores, creating a bell-shaped curve known as the *normal distribution* shown in Figure 10.2. (The statistics appendix provides a fuller explanation of the normal distribution and how IQ tests are scored.) As a result of this scoring method, your **intelligence quotient,** or **IQ score,** reflects your *relative* standing within a population of your age.

FIGURE 10.2

The Normal Distribution of IQ Scores in a Population

This bell-shaped curve represents the normal distribution of IQ scores in the population. Half of those tested score below 100 (the average performance of any given age group) and half above 100; about two-thirds of the IQ scores of an age group fall between 84 and 116; about one-sixth fall below 84 and one-sixth fall above 116.

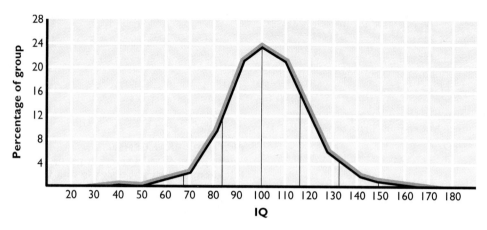

Note: Curve represents distribution of IQ scores in the standardized group for the 1937 version of the Stanford-Binet.

LINKAGES   How do you know if a personality test, or any other kind of test, is any good? (a link to Personality)

MEASURING THE QUALITY OF TESTS

As already noted, no particular IQ test can accurately measure all aspects of what various people think of as intelligence. So what does your IQ score say about you? Can it predict your performance in school or on the job? Is it a fair summary of your mental abilities? To scientifically answer questions like these, we have to measure the quality of the tests that yield IQ scores, using the same criteria that apply to tests of personality, language skill, driving, or anything else. We review these criteria in this section; then, in the next section, we use the same criteria to evaluate IQ tests.

Any **test** is a systematic procedure for observing behavior in a standard situation and describing it with the help of a numerical scale or a system of categories (Cronbach, 1970). A test has three major advantages over interviews and other means of evaluation. First, the administration, scoring, and interpretation of the test are *standardized;* that is, the conditions are as similar as possible for everyone who takes the test. Standardization helps ensure that no matter who gives and scores the test, the results will be the same; incidental factors—such as variations in the way a question is phrased—are less likely to affect test scores. Insofar as the biases of those giving the test do not influence the results, a test is said to be *objective.*

Second, tests summarize the test taker's performance in *quantifiable* terms known as scores. This characteristic allows testers to calculate **norms,** which are descriptions of the frequency of particular scores. Norms tell us, for example, what percentage of high school students obtained each possible score on a college entrance exam and whether a particular IQ score or entrance-exam score is above or below the average score. Third, tests are *economical* and *efficient.* Once a test has been developed, it can often be given to many people in less time and for less money than would be expended through other ways of obtaining information.

The two most important characteristics for determining the value of a test are reliability and validity.

Reliability

If you stepped on a scale, checked your weight, stepped off, stepped back on, and found that your weight had increased by twenty pounds, you would be wise to try a different scale. A good scale, like a good test, must have **reliability;** in other words, the results must be repeatable or stable. The test must measure the same thing in the same way every time it is used. If a person receives a very high score on a reasoning test the first time it is given but gets a very low score when the test is repeated, the test is probably unreliable. The higher the reliability of a test, the less susceptible its scores are to being affected by temperature, hunger, or other irrelevant changes in the environment or the test taker.

To estimate reliability, researchers often obtain two sets of scores on the same test from the same people and compute the *correlation coefficient* between the scores (see Chapter 2 and the statistics appendix). When the correlation is high and positive (usually above +.80 or so), the test is considered reliable. Sometimes, researchers also report the actual amount by which the same people's responses diverged from one another. The two sets of scores can be obtained in several ways. The most obvious method is to give the same test to the same people on two occasions. This method is called *test-retest reliability*. Of course, the test-retest method assumes that what is being measured does not change between the two testings. If you practiced typing between tests of typing skill, your second score would be higher than the first, but not because the test is unreliable.

The test-retest method of determining reliability has another limitation: Exposure to the first test can cause some people's second score to improve, thus making the test look unreliable. Other methods of calculating reliability prevent this problem. One method uses an *alternate form* of the test at the second testing, although great care must be taken to ensure that the second test is truly comparable to the first. And in the *split-half* method, a correlation coefficient is calculated between a person's scores on two comparable halves of the test (Cronbach, 1951). In practice, most researchers employ all these methods to check the reliability of their tests.

Validity

A test may be reliable and still not be valid. The **validity** of a test is the degree to which it measures what it is supposed to measure (Anastasi, 1976). No test has "high" or "low" validity in an absolute sense; *validity depends on how a test is being used*. Thus, measuring how long someone can keep a bare hand immersed in ice water might be a valid test of pain tolerance, but not of intelligence. In other words, the same test can be valid for one purpose but invalid for another.

Most measures of validity are correlation coefficients between test scores and something else. What that "something else" is depends on what the test is supposed to measure. For example, you might want to correlate people's scores on a creativity test with judgments about the quality of their artistic creations; if the correlation is high, the test has high validity as a measure of creativity. Similarly, a correlation between SAT scores and first-year college grades provides a measure of the SAT's validity for predicting success in college.

A test's validity can be studied in three main ways. The first approach is to analyze *content validity*, the degree to which the test's content is related to what the test is supposed to measure. If an instructor spends only five minutes out of twenty lectures discussing the mating behavior of the tree frog and then devotes half of the midterm exam to this topic, that exam would be low on content validity for measuring students' learning in the course. Similarly, a test that measures only math skills would not have acceptable content validity as an intelligence test. A content-valid test includes items relating to the entire area of interest, not just a narrow slice of it (Lawshe, 1975).

Another way of assessing validity is to look at *construct validity*, the extent to which scores on a test are in accordance with one's theory about what is being tested. For example, if your theory of intelligence says that people get smarter as they get older, then older people should have higher scores on the intelligence test you are evaluating. If they don't—if a positive correlation is not found between test scores and age—then the test has low construct validity with regard to this particular theory of intelligence.

A third approach is to measure *criterion validity*, the extent to which test scores correlate with another direct and independent measure of what the test is supposed to assess. This independent measure is called the *criterion*. Thus a test of eye-hand coordination would have high criterion validity for hiring laboratory technicians if its scores are highly correlated with skill at lab tasks. Why give a test if there is an independent criterion we can measure? The reasons often relate to convenience and cost. It would be silly to hire all technician applicants, then fire those who are unskilled, if a ten-minute test can identify the best candidates. When the goal is to predict future behavior, the criterion is some measure of later performance; in such cases, criterion validity is called *predictive validity.*

Again, consider the SAT, whose purpose is to help predict which college applicants will succeed if admitted. As suggested earlier, one can measure the SAT's predictive validity by determining the correlation between SAT scores and a criterion—namely, the grade-point average (GPA) of first-year college students. It turns out that when mathematical and verbal SAT scores are combined, their correlation with first-year GPA is about +.42 (Donlon, 1984). This figure is reasonably high, but not as high as it might be. The test's predictive validity is limited partly by the fact that colleges usually admit only students with high SAT scores. Because these students are then assigned grades from A to E in a more or less normal distribution, some of them will have low GPAs even though they have high SATs. Thus, although SAT scores are generally helpful during the admissions process, it is difficult to predict a particular student's grades on the basis of SAT scores alone.

Criteria for assessing the reliability and validity of tests are incorporated into the testing standards published by the American Psychological Association (1985). These standards are designed to maintain quality in educational and psychological testing by providing guidelines for the administration, interpretation, and application of tests in such areas as therapy, education, employment, certification or licensure, and program evaluation.

EVALUATING IQ TESTS

The meaning of IQ scores must be interpreted with caution, taking into account not only the reliability and validity of the tests from which they come but also a number of sociocultural factors that might influence the scores.

The Reliability and Validity of IQ Tests

The reliability and validity of IQ tests are generally evaluated on the basis of the stability, or consistency, of IQ scores and the accuracy of these scores in making predictions about people.

How Reliable Are IQ Tests? IQ scores obtained before the age of seven typically do not correlate very highly with scores on IQ tests given later, for two key reasons: (1) Test items used with very young children are different from those used with older children, and (2), as discussed in Chapter 12, cognitive abilities change rapidly in the early years. During the school years, however, IQ scores tend to remain stable (Anastasi, 1988). The less time that elapses between the two testings and the older the individuals are when first tested, the higher the test-retest correlations tend to be. For teenagers and adults, the reliability of IQ tests is high; split-half reliability correlations are generally above +.90.

Of course, a person's score may vary from one time to another if testing conditions, degree of motivation or anxiety, or other factors change. But overall, modern IQ tests usually provide exceptionally consistent results—especially compared to most other kinds of mental tests.

How Valid Are IQ Tests? Scores on various IQ tests correlate well with each other, but this does not necessarily mean they are measuring "intelligence." Because there is no independent criterion of intelligence—recall that psychologists do not fully agree on its definition—it is impossible to determine whether IQ tests are valid measures of intelligence. In short, we can assess their validity only for specific purposes.

IQ tests appear to be most valid for assessing aspects of intelligence that are related to schoolwork, such as abstract reasoning and verbal comprehension. Their predictive validity—as measured by correlating IQ scores with high school grades—is reasonably good, about +.50 (Cronbach, 1970).

In addition, there is evidence that employees who score high on tests of verbal and mathematical reasoning tend to perform better on the job than those who earned lower scores (Barrett & Depinet, 1991). The predictive validity of IQ scores is especially good in relation to success in managerial and other complex jobs (Hunter, 1986). IQ scores also appear to be highly correlated with performance on "real-life" tasks such as reading medicine labels and using the telephone book (Barrett & Depinet, 1991). Later, we describe one study that kept track of people for sixty years and found that children with high IQs tended to be well above average in terms of academic, and financial success in adulthood (Terman & Oden, 1947; Oden, 1968).

So, by the standard measures for judging psychological tests, IQ tests have good reliability and reasonably good predictive validity for certain criteria, such as success in school. As noted earlier, however, an IQ score is not an infallible measure of how "smart" people are. Because IQ tests do not measure the full array of mental abilities, a particular test score tells only part of the story, and even that part may be distorted. Many factors other than mental ability—including response to the tester—can influence test performance. Children might not do as well if they are suspicious of strangers, for example (Jones, 1989). And older adults who worry about making mistakes in unfamiliar situations may fail to even try answering some questions, thus artificially lowering their IQ scores (Zelinski, Schaie & Gribben, 1977).

How Fair Are IQ Tests?   Our review of the history of intelligence testing in the United States suggests that early IQ tests were biased against people who were unfamiliar with English or with the vocabulary and experiences associated mainly with middle-class culture at the time. For example, consider the question "Which is most similar to a xylophone? (*violin, tuba, drum, marimba, piano*)." No matter how intelligent children are, if they have never had a chance to see an orchestra or to learn about these instruments, they may miss the question. Test designers today try to avoid obviously biased questions (American Psychological Association, 1985; Educational Testing Service, 1987). Furthermore, because IQ tests now include more than one scale, areas that are most influenced by culture, such as vocabulary, can be assessed separately from dimensions that are less vulnerable to cultural bias.

The solutions to many of the technical problems in IQ *tests,* however, have not resolved the controversy over the fairness or unfairness of IQ *testing.* The debate continues partly because the results of IQ tests can have important social consequences (Messick, 1982, 1989). Recall that IQ tests were initially developed to identify and assist children with special educational needs. Yet today, such children may find themselves in special classes that not only isolate them from other students but also carry negative

IQ AND JOB PERFORMANCE   IQ scores are reasonably good at predicting the ability to learn job-relevant information and to deal with unpredictable, changing aspects of the work environment (Hunter, 1986)—characteristics that are needed for success in complex jobs.

social labels. Obviously, the social consequences of IQ testing can be evaluated separately from the quality of the tests themselves (Maguire, Hattie & Haig, 1994); but those consequences cannot be ignored, especially if they tend to affect some groups more than others.

Despite attempts to eliminate cultural bias from IQ tests, there are differences in the mean scores of various ethnic and cultural groups in the United States (Humphreys, 1988; Wainer, 1988; Chan & Lynn, 1989; Vincent, 1991; Taylor & Richards, 1991; Lynn, 1991; Geary, Fan & Bow-Thomas, 1992; Herrnstein & Murray, 1994). Asian-Americans typically score highest, followed, in order, by European-Americans, Hispanic-Americans, and African-Americans.

THINKING CRITICALLY

Are IQ Tests Unfairly Biased Against Certain Groups?

What am I being asked to believe or accept?

Some critics of IQ tests argue that a disproportionately large number of people in some ethnic minority groups score low on IQ tests for reasons that are unrelated to intelligence, job potential, or other criteria that the tests are supposed to predict (Helms, 1992). They say that using IQ tests to make decisions about people causes members of some ethnic minority groups to be unfairly deprived of equal opportunities.

What evidence is available to support the assertion?

Research reveals several possible sources of bias in IQ tests. First, whatever the content of a test, noncognitive factors such as motivation and trust influence performance on IQ tests and may put certain groups at a disadvantage. Children from some minority groups may be less likely than other children to be motivated to perform well on standardized tests and less likely to trust the adult tester (Bradley-Johnson, Graham & Johnson, 1986; Jones, 1989). Consequently, differences in IQ scores may reflect motivational differences among various groups, as described in the chapter on learning.

Second, many test items are still drawn from the vocabulary and experiences of the dominant middle-class culture in the United States. As a result, these tests often measure *achievement* in acquiring knowledge valued by that culture. Not all cultures value the same things, however (Serpell, 1994). A study of Cree Indians in northern Canada revealed that words and phrases synonymous with *competent* included *good sense of direction;* at the *incompetent* end of the scale was the phrase *lives like a white person* (Berry & Bennett, 1992). Thus, a European-American might not perform well on a Cree intelligence test based on these criteria (see Figure 10.3 for another example). "Culture-fair" tests that reduce, if not eliminate, dependence on knowledge of a specific culture do indeed produce smaller differences between majority and minority groups than more traditional measures. (See Figure 10.4.)

Third, IQ tests may reward those who *interpret* questions as expected by the test designer. Conventional IQ tests have clearly defined "right" and "wrong" answers. Yet a person may interpret test questions in a manner that is "intelligent" or "correct" but that produces a "wrong" answer. The fact that you don't give the answer that the test designer was looking for does not mean that you can't. When Liberian rice farmers were asked to sort objects, they tended to put a knife in the same group as vegetables. This was the clever way to do it, they said, because the knife is used to cut vegetables. When asked to sort the objects as a "stupid" person would, they grouped the cutting tools together, the vegetables together, and so on, much as most North Americans would (Ciborowski, cited in Segall et al., 1990).

1. **Black draught:**
   (a) winter's cold wind
   (b) laxative
   (c) black soldier
   (d) dark beer

2. **Clean:**
   (a) just out of the bathtub
   (b) very well dressed
   (c) very religious
   (d) has a great deal

3. **Crib:**
   (a) an apartment
   (b) a game
   (c) a job
   (d) hot stuff

4. **Do rag:**
   (a) the hair
   (b) the shoes
   (c) washing
   (d) tablecloth

5. **Four corners:**
   (a) rapping
   (b) singing
   (c) the streets
   (d) dancing

6. **Who wrote the Negro National Anthem?**
   (a) Langston Hughes
   (b) Paul Lawrence Dunbar
   (c) James Weldon Johnson
   (d) Frederick Douglass

Answers:
1. (b) 2. (b) 3. (a)
4. (a) 5. (d) 6. (c)

FIGURE 10.3

Sample Items from the Black Intelligence Test of Cultural Homogeneity

Shown here are some items from a test on which success depends heavily on familiarity with words, terms, and expressions from African-American culture. Robert L. Williams of the Black Studies Program at Washington University constructed this test in the 1970s to show that poor performance on a culture-specific test is probably due more to unfamiliarity with the culture represented than to lack of mental ability. How well did you do?

Source: Williams, 1972.

Are there alternative ways of interpreting the evidence?

The evidence might be interpreted as showing that although IQ tests do not provide an unbiased measure of mental ability in general, they *do* provide a fair test of whether a person is likely to succeed in school or on the job. In short, they may be biased—but not in a way that discriminates *unfairly* among groups. Perhaps familiarity with the culture reflected in IQ tests is just as important for success at school or work in that culture as it is for success on the tests themselves. After all, the ranking among groups on measures of academic achievement is similar to the ranking for mean IQ scores (Sue & Okazaki, 1990). According to this view, it doesn't matter very much if IQ tests measure culture-related achievement as long as they are useful in predicting whatever criterion is of interest. In fact, "culture-fair" tests do not predict academic achievement as well as conventional IQ tests do (Aiken, 1987; Humphreys, 1988).

What additional evidence would help to evaluate the alternatives?

Evaluation of whether tests differentiate fairly or unfairly depends on whether the sources of test-score differences are relevant to predicting performance in the environment for which the test is intended. To take an extreme example, perhaps mean score differences between ethnic groups result entirely from certain test items that have nothing to do with how well the test as a whole predicts academic success. It is important to conduct research on this possibility.

FIGURE 10.4

Culture-Fair Tests

The task on this item from the Learning Potential Assessment Device (LPAD) is to outline the square and two triangles embedded in patterns of dots, using each dot only once.

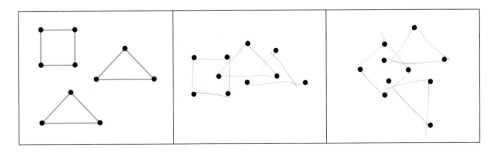

Source: Feuerstein, 1979.

Alternative tests must also be explored, particularly those that include assessment of problem-solving skills and other abilities not measured by most IQ tests (e.g., Sternberg et al., 1995). If new tests prove to be less biased than traditional tests but have equal or better predictive validity, many of the issues discussed in this section will have been resolved.

What conclusions are most reasonable?

The effort to reduce unfair cultural biases in tests is well-founded, but "culture-fair" tests will be of little benefit if they fail to predict success as well as conventional tests do. Whether one considers this circumstance good or bad, fair or unfair, it is important for people to have information and skills that are valued by the culture that establishes criteria for educational and occupational achievement. As long as this is the case, tests designed to predict success in such areas are reasonable insofar as they measure a person's skills and access to the information valued by that culture.

Stopping at that conclusion, however, would mean freezing the status quo, whereby members of certain groups are denied many educational and economic benefits. As discussed later, if attention were to be focused on altering the conditions that result in poverty, poor schools, and inadequate nutrition and health care, many of the reasons for concern about test bias might be eliminated.

IQ Scores as a Measure of Innate Ability

It is one thing to know that IQ tests predict academic or job success; it is something else to know what to make of particular test scores. How should teachers react if they are told that certain students have low IQ scores? If you receive a high IQ score, can you credit your parents' genes?

Years of research have led psychologists to conclude that both hereditary and environmental factors interact to influence mental abilities. For example, by asking many questions, bright children help generate an enriching environment for themselves; thus, innate abilities allow people to take better advantage of their environment (Scarr & Carter-Saltzman, 1982). In addition, if their own biologically influenced intelligence allows bright parents to give their children an environment favorable to the development of intelligence, their children are favored by both heredity and environment.

Psychologists have explored the influence of genetics on individual differences in IQ scores by comparing the strength of the correlation between the scores of people who have differing degrees of similarity in their genetic makeup and environment. For example, they have examined the IQ scores of identical twins—pairs with exactly the same genetic makeup—who were separated when very young and reared in different environments. They have also examined the scores of identical twins raised together. (You may want to review the Linkages section of Chapter 2, as well as the behavioral genetics appendix, for more on the quasi-experimental designs typically used to analyze hereditary and environmental influences.)

These studies find, first, that hereditary factors are strongly related to IQ scores. When identical twins who were separated at birth and adopted by different families are tested many years later, the correlation between their scores is usually high and positive, at least +.60 (Bouchard et al., 1990). If one twin receives a high IQ score, the other probably will too; if one is low, the other is likely to be low as well. However, studies of IQ correlations also highlight the importance of the environment (Capron & Duyme, 1989). Consider any two people—twins, siblings, or unrelated children—brought together in a foster home. No matter what the degree of genetic similarity in these pairs, the correlation between their IQ scores is higher if they share the same home than if they are raised in different environments, as Figure 10.5 shows (Scarr & Carter-Saltzman, 1982).

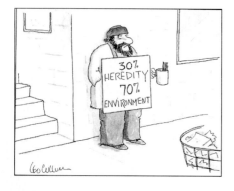

FIGURE 10.5

Correlations of IQ Scores

The correlation between pairs increases as heredity or environmental similarity increases.

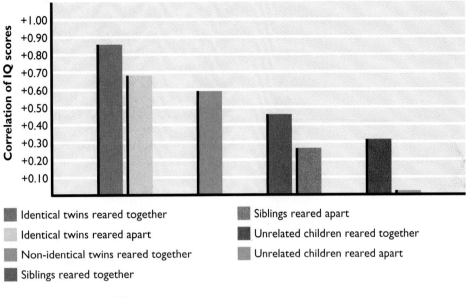

- Identical twins reared together
- Identical twins reared apart
- Non-identical twins reared together
- Siblings reared together
- Siblings reared apart
- Unrelated children reared together
- Unrelated children reared apart

Source: Bouchard et al., 1981.

The role of environmental influences is also seen in the results of studies that compare children's IQ scores before and after environmental changes such as adoption. Generally, studies of children from relatively impoverished backgrounds who were adopted into homes with more enriching intellectual environments—environments with interesting materials and experiences, as well as a supportive, responsive adult—find modest increases in the children's IQ scores (Weinberg, Scarr & Waldman, 1992).

A study of French children who were adopted soon after birth demonstrates the importance of both genetic and environmental influences. When these children were tested after years of living in their adopted homes, those whose biological parents were from higher socioeconomic groups (where superior IQs are most common) had higher IQ scores than those whose biological parents came from low socioeconomic groups, regardless of the socioeconomic status of the adopted homes (Capron & Duyme, 1989). These findings suggest that a genetic component of the children's mental abilities continued to exert an influence in the adopted environment. At the same time, the IQ scores of children from low socioeconomic backgrounds who were exposed to academically enriched environments through adoption rose by twelve to fifteen points (Capron & Duyme, 1989). Another study found that the IQ scores of adopted children were an average of fourteen points higher than those of siblings who remained with the biological parents in a poorer, less enriching environment (Schiff et al., 1978).

Some researchers have concluded that the influence of heredity and environment on mental abilities appears to be about equal; others see a somewhat larger role for heredity (Herrnstein & Murray, 1994; Loehlin, 1989; Plomin, 1990b). Still, it must be emphasized that such estimates of heritability—of the relative contributions of heredity and environment—apply only to groups, not to individuals. Thus, it would be inaccurate to say that 50 percent of *your* IQ score is inherited and 50 percent learned. It is far more accurate to say that about half of the *variability* in the IQ scores of a group of people can be attributed to hereditary influences, and about half can be attributed to environmental influences.

Here is yet another example of nature and nurture working together to shape behavior and mental processes. Further, their relative contributions can change over time. Environmental influences, for example, seem to be greater at younger ages (Plomin, 1990b) and tend to diminish over the years. Thus, IQ differences in a group of children will probably be affected more by parental help with preschool reading than by, say, the courses available in junior high school.

Group Differences in IQ Scores

Much of the controversy about differences in IQ scores is not over differences among individuals but over differences in the mean scores of groups such as poor people and rich people or Caucasian people and Asian people. Recently, this controversy centered on a book called *The Bell Curve,* in which Richard Herrnstein and Charles Murray (1994) reviewed research on IQ differences across ethnic and socioeconomic groups in North America. The authors concluded that defining intelligence in terms of abilities needed in school—and measuring it with IQ tests—has created a social class system in which members of a "cognitive elite" are likely to succeed while more and more intellectual "have-nots" will drop out of school to face unemployment, poverty, and dependence on welfare to support themselves and their children. Moreover, the book recommended that job training, birth control, and other social programs designed to reduce poverty and welfare costs should target people with the lowest IQs. A substantial majority of testing experts agreed with the authors' basic findings, though not necessarily with their recommendations. Public debate—which focused on what many saw as a negative evaluation of the intelligence and potential of African-Americans—revealed some common misunderstandings about the nature, extent, and meaning of group differences in IQ. To correctly interpret these differences and analyze their sources, we must avoid some pitfalls.

First, group scores are just that; they do not describe individuals. Although the *mean* IQ score of Asian-Americans is higher than the *mean* score of European-Americans, there will still be large numbers of European-Americans who score well above the Asian-American mean and large numbers of Asian-Americans who score below the European-American mean (see Figure 10.6).

Second, inherited characteristics are not necessarily fixed, and environmentally determined features are not necessarily changeable. A favorable environment may improve a child's performance, even if the inherited influences on that child's IQ are negative (Humphreys, 1984).

Socioeconomic Differences   Upper-class communities in the United States have shown mean IQ scores seventeen points higher than those of lower-class communities with the same ethnic makeup (Cleary et al., 1975; Jordan, Huttenlocher & Levine, 1992; Oakland & Glutting, 1990; Vane, 1972). IQ score differences associated with socioeconomic status also occur in other countries (Fergusson, Lloyd & Horwood, 1991; Murthy & Panda, 1987). Why should there be a relationship between IQ scores and family income?

Three factors seem to account for the correlation. First, parents' jobs and status depend on characteristics related to their own intelligence, and this intelligence is partly

FIGURE 10.6

A Representation of Ethnic Group Differences in IQ Scores

The average IQ score of Asian-Americans is about four to six points higher than the average of European-Americans, who average twelve to fifteen points higher than African-Americans and Hispanic-Americans. Notice, however, that the variation within these groups is much greater than between them.

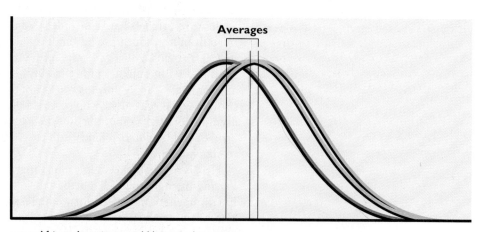

— African-Americans and Hispanic-Americans
— European-Americans
— Asian-Americans

determined by a genetic component that in turn contributes to the child's IQ score. Second, the parents' income affects the child's environment in ways that can increase or decrease the child's IQ score (Cronbach, 1975; MacKenzie, 1984). Third, motivational differences may play a role. Upper- and middle-income families demonstrate greater motivation to succeed and excel in academic endeavors (Atkinson & Raynor, 1974). Perhaps these families instill in their children greater motivation to succeed on IQ tests. As a result, children from middle- and upper-class families exert more effort and therefore obtain higher scores (Bradley-Johnson, Graham & Johnson, 1986; Zigler & Seitz, 1982).

Ethnic Differences   Some have argued that the mean differences in IQ among various ethnic groups in the United States are due mostly to heredity. Note, however, that the existence of hereditary differences among individuals *within* groups does not indicate whether differences *between* groups result from similar genetic causes (Lewontin, 1976). As shown in Figure 10.6, variation within ethnic groups is much greater than variation between those groups (Zuckerman, 1990).

There are large differences among the environments in which the average African-American, Hispanic-American, and European-American child grows up. To take only the most blatant evidence, the latest figures available show 28.2 percent of African-American families and 28.7 percent of Hispanic-American families living below the poverty level compared to 7.9 percent of European-American families (U.S. Bureau of the Census, 1991). Among children under age sixteen, the figures show 11.3 percent of European-Americans, 32.7 percent of African-Americans, and 36.6 percent of Hispanic-Americans living below the poverty line. Compared with European-Americans, African-Americans are more likely to have parents with poor educational backgrounds, as well as inferior nutrition, health care, and schools. All of these conditions are likely to pull down scores on IQ tests.

Evidence for the influence of environmental factors on the average black-white IQ difference comes from adoption studies. One such study involved African-American children from disadvantaged homes who were adopted by middle- to upper-class European-American families in the first years of their lives (Scarr & Weinberg, 1976). When measured a few years later, the mean IQ score of these children was 110. Using the scores of nonadopted children from similar backgrounds as a comparison suggests that adoption raised the children's IQ scores at least ten points. A ten-year follow-up study of these youngsters showed that their average IQ scores were still higher than the

HELPING WITH HOMEWORK   There are differences in the average IQ scores of European-Americans and African-Americans, but those who attribute these differences primarily to hereditary factors are ignoring a number of environmental, social, and other nongenetic factors that are important in creating, and are now narrowing, this IQ gap.

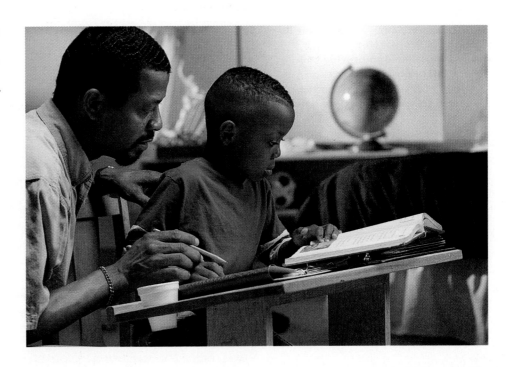

average scores of African-American children raised in disadvantaged homes (Weinberg, Scarr & Waldman, 1992).

As discussed in the chapters on human development and learning, cultural factors may also contribute to differences between the mean scores of various ethnic groups. For example, those means may partly reflect differences in motivation based on how much value is placed on academic achievement. In one study of 15,000 African-American, Asian-American, Hispanic-American, and European-American high school students, parental and peer influences related to achievement tended to vary with ethnic group (Steinberg, Dornbusch & Brown, 1992). The Asian-American students received strong support for academic pursuits from both their parents and their peers. European-American students whose parents expected high academic achievement tended to associate with peers who also encouraged achievement, and they tended to do better academically than African-American and Hispanic-American students. The parents of the African-American students in the study supported academic achievement, but because their peers did not, the students' performance may have suffered. The performance of the Hispanic-American students may have suffered from the fact that, in this study at least, they were more likely than the others to have authoritarian parents, whose emphasis on obedience (see Chapter 12) may have created conflicts with the schools' emphasis on independent learning.

In short, there appear to be important nongenetic factors working to decrease the mean scores of African-American and Hispanic-American children. Indeed, the recently narrowing gap between African-American and European-American children on tests of intelligence and mathematical aptitude may be related to improved environmental conditions for many African-American children (College Board, 1994; Vincent, 1991). Whatever heredity might be contributing to the performance of children, it may be possible for them to improve greatly, given the right conditions.

Conditions That Can Raise IQ Scores

A number of environmental conditions can help or deter cognitive development (see Chapter 12). For example, lack of caring attention or of normal intellectual stimulation can inhibit a child's mental growth. Low test scores have been linked with poverty, chaos and noise in the home, poor schools, and inadequate nutrition and health care (Humphreys & Davey, 1988; Wachs & Gruen, 1982; Weinberg, 1989). Efforts to improve

PROJECT HEAD START   **This teacher is working in Project Head Start, a program designed to provide children from impoverished backgrounds with the preparation they will need to succeed in grade school.**

LINKAGES Can the environment make children smarter? (a link to Human Development)

these conditions are part of a movement known as community psychology, which is discussed in Chapter 16.

Can the effects of bad environments be reversed? Not always, but efforts to intervene in the lives of children and enrich their environments have had some success. Conditions for improving children's performance include rewards for progress, encouragement of effort, and creation of expectations for success.

The best-known attempt to enrich children's environments in the United States is Project Head Start, a set of programs established by the federal government in the 1960s to help preschoolers from lower-income backgrounds. In some of these programs, teachers visit the home and work with the child and parents on cognitive skills. In others, the children attend classes in nursery schools. Some programs emphasize health and nutrition and, in recent years, family mental health and social skills as well (Murray, 1995). Head Start has brought measurable benefits to children's health as well as improvements in their academic and intellectual skills (Zigler & Seitz, 1982; Lee, Brooks-Gunn & Schnur, 1988). Closely related to Project Head Start are intervention programs for infants at risk because of low birth weight, low socioeconomic status, or low parental IQ scores. Such programs appear to enhance IQ scores by as much as nine points by the age of three; the effects appear especially strong for the infants of mothers with a high school education or less (Brooks-Gunn et al., 1992; Infant Health and Development Program, 1990; Ramey et al., 1992; Wasik et al., 1990).

In general, the most consistently effective programs for poor preschoolers provide a moderate degree of structure. They offer an orderly physical setting, a predictable schedule, high-quality educational materials, and teachers who try to provide regular opportunities for learning (Zigler & Seitz, 1982). Surprisingly, a review of 193 preschool programs found no difference in effectiveness between those in which parents did or did not play a role (White, Taylor & Moss, 1992).

Do the gains achieved by preschool enrichment programs last? Though program developers sometimes claim long-term benefits (Schweinhart & Weikart, 1991), such claims are disputed (Spitz, 1991). Various findings from more than 1,000 such programs are often contradictory, but the effect on IQ scores typically diminishes after a year or two (Woodhead, 1988). A study evaluating two of the better preschool programs concluded that they are at best only temporarily effective (Locurto, 1991a). One consistent, though very small, effect is that children who have taken part in enrichment programs are less likely to be held back in school or to need special-education programs (Palmer & Anderson, 1979; Locurto, 1991b). The fading of effects is probably due to reduced motivation, not loss of mental ability (Zigler & Seitz, 1982). Children may lose motivation when they leave a special preschool program and enter the substandard schools that often serve poor children.

Fading effects were also seen in programs such as the Abecedarian Project (Ramey, 1992), which identified children at risk for mental retardation while they were still in the womb, then offered five years of intense interventions to improve their chances of success once they entered school. At age twelve, these children scored significantly higher on IQ tests than at-risk children who were not in the program, but the size of the difference steadily declined over the next several years (Ramey, 1995).

Martin Woodhead (1988) has concluded that the primary benefits of early-enrichment programs probably lie in their effect on children's attitudes toward school. Especially in borderline cases, favorable attitudes toward school may help reduce the chances that children will be held back a grade or placed in special-education classes. Children who avoid these experiences may retain positive attitudes about school and enter a cycle in which gains due to early enrichment are maintained and amplified on a long-term basis (Woodhead, 1988; Zigler & Styfco, 1994).

IQ Scores in the Classroom

Obviously, IQ scores are neither a crystal ball into some predestined future nor a measure of some fixed quantity, but they can subtly affect how people are treated and how they behave. For example, Robert Rosenthal and Lenore Jacobson (1968) found that labels create *expectancies* that can become self-fulfilling prophecies. Teachers in their

IN REVIEW	Influences on IQ Scores	
Source of Effect	**Description**	**Examples of Evidence for Effect**
Genetics	Genes appear to play a significant role in IQ test performance.	The IQ scores of siblings who share no common environment are positively correlated. There is a greater correlation between scores of identical twins than between those of non-identical twins.
Environment	Environmental conditions interact with genetic inheritance. Nutrition, medical care, sensory and intellectual stimulation, interpersonal relations, and influences on motivation are all significant features of the environment.	IQ scores have risen among children who are adopted into homes that offer a stimulating, enriching environment. Correlations between IQs of twins reared together are higher than for those reared apart.

study were told that a test could indicate which grade-school students were about to enter a "blooming" period of rapid academic growth, and they were given the names of students who had supposedly scored high on the test. In fact, the experimenters *randomly* selected the "bloomers." But during the next year, the IQ scores of two-thirds of the bloomers dramatically increased, while only one-quarter of the children in the control group showed the same increase. Apparently, the teachers' expectancies about the children influenced them in ways that showed up on IQ tests.

Some attempts to replicate Rosenthal and Jacobson's findings have failed (Elashoff, 1979); others have disclosed that the effect of teacher expectancies, though statistically significant, is relatively small (Jussim, 1989; Snow, 1995). Still, there is little doubt that IQ-based teacher expectancies can have an effect on students (Rosenthal, 1994). To find out how, Alan Chaiken and his colleagues (1974) videotaped teacher-child interactions in a classroom in which teachers had been informed (falsely) that certain pupils were particularly bright. They found that the teachers tended to favor the supposedly "brighter" students—smiling at them more often than at other students, making more eye contact, and reacting more positively to their comments. Children receiving such extra social reinforcement not only get more intense teaching but are also more likely to enjoy school, to have their mistakes corrected, and to continue trying to improve. More recent research found that teachers provide a wider range of classroom activities for students for whom they have higher expectations, suggesting another way in which expectancies might influence IQ scores (Blatchford et al., 1989).

Indeed, these results suggest that the "rich get richer": Those perceived to be blessed with high mental abilities are given better opportunities to improve those abilities. Is there also a "poor get poorer" effect? In fact, there is evidence that teachers tend to be less patient, less encouraging, and less likely to try teaching as much material to students whom they do not consider bright (Cooper, 1979; Luce & Hoge, 1978; Trujillo, 1986). In Chapter 12, we describe how differential expectations about the academic potential of boys and girls can contribute to gender differences in performance and achievement motivation.

Whenever people try to "summarize" other people with a label, a test score, or a profile, they run the risk of oversimplifying reality and making errors. ("In Review: Influences on IQ Scores" lists the factors that can shape IQ scores.) But intelligence tests can also *prevent* errors. Boredom or lack of motivation at school can make a child appear mentally slow, even retarded. An IQ test conducted under the right circumstances is likely to reveal the child's potential. The test can prevent the mistake of moving a bright child to a class for the mentally handicapped. And, as Alfred Binet had hoped, IQ tests have been enormously helpful in identifying children who need special educational attention.

Furthermore, the alternatives to IQ tests may not be very attractive. Should teachers' judgments, analyses of students' work portfolios, or other subjective—and thus potentially biased—assessment methods replace testing? (Weinberg, 1989). This idea has recently gained popularity. Before reforms are undertaken, however, the new assessment methods must be carefully evaluated against objective mental abilities tests, which, despite their limitations, minimize the likelihood of assigning children to remedial work they don't need, or to advanced work they can't yet handle.

UNDERSTANDING INTELLIGENCE

Throughout this chapter we have noted that different researchers, and different cultures, define intelligence in different ways, meaning that IQ scores tell only part of the story of intelligence. It is an important part, though, so IQ tests will continue to be used as psychologists work to deepen their understanding of the elusive concept called intelligence. In this section, we consider several of the main approaches these researchers have taken.

The Psychometric Approach

Standard IQ tests reflect the **psychometric approach,** which analyzes people's responses to questions and tasks in order to describe the structure of intelligence. Researchers taking this approach ask whether intelligence is one general trait or a label for a bundle of more specific abilities. The answer matters, because if intelligence is a single "thing," an employer might assume that someone with a low IQ could not do any mental task well. But if intelligence is composed of many independent abilities, a poor showing in one area—say, spatial abilities—would not rule out good performance in understanding information or solving word problems.

At the turn of the century, statistician Charles Spearman made a suggestion that began the modern debate about the nature of intelligence. Spearman noted that scores on almost all tests of mental abilities were positively correlated (Spearman, 1904, 1927). That is, people who did well on one test also tended to do well on all of the others. Spearman concluded that these correlations were created by general mental ability, which he called **g,** for general intelligence, and a group of special intelligences, which he collectively referred to as **s.** The *s*-factors, he said, are the specific information and skills needed for particular tasks.

Spearman argued that people's scores on a particular test depend on both *g* and *s*'s. Further examination of test scores, however, revealed correlations that could not be explained by either *g* or *s* and were called *group factors*. Although Spearman modified his theory to accommodate these factors, he continued to assert that *g* represented a measure of mental force, or intellectual power (Gould, 1983).

In 1938, L. L. Thurstone published a paper criticizing Spearman's mathematical methods. Using a statistical technique called **factor analysis,** he analyzed the correlations among IQ tests to identify the underlying factors, or abilities, being measured by those tests. Thurstone's analyses did not reveal a single, dominating *g*-factor; instead, he found seven relatively independent *primary mental abilities*, which he labeled as numerical ability, reasoning, verbal fluency, spatial visualization, perceptual ability, memory, and verbal comprehension. Thurstone did not deny that *g* exists, but he argued that it was not as important as primary mental abilities in describing a particular person. Similarly, Spearman did not deny the existence of special abilities, but he maintained that *g* tells us most of what we need to know about a person's mental ability.

LINKAGES: BRAINPOWER AND INTELLI-GENCE Applying the information-processing model introduced in Chapter 9 to intelligence might suggest that those with the most rapid information-processors (the "fastest" brains) would do best on mental ability tests, including those required for college entrance. Research suggests, however, that this is true only to an extent and that there is more to intelligent behavior than sheer processing speed.

Raymond B. Cattell (1963) agreed with Spearman, but his own factor analyses suggested that there are two kinds of *g*, which he labeled fluid and crystallized. **Fluid intelligence,** he said, is the basic power of reasoning and problem solving. It allows us to evaluate the syllogisms described in Chapter 9, to think critically about assertions made in TV commercials, and to understand relationships between concepts (such as "Houses are bigger than people."). **Crystallized intelligence,** in contrast, involves specific knowledge gained as a result of applying fluid intelligence. It produces, for example, a good vocabulary and familiarity with the multiplication tables.

Who is right? After decades of research and debate, most psychologists today agree that there *is* a positive correlation between several tests of mental ability, a correlation that is due to a factor known as *g* (Carroll, 1991). However, the brain probably does not "contain" some unified "thing" corresponding to what people call intelligence; *g* is more likely a collection of subskills and mental abilities—such as reasoning ability, test-taking skill, reading ability, and so forth (Humphreys, 1984)—many of which are needed to succeed on any test of intelligence.

The Information-Processing Approach

The **information-processing approach** analyzes the *process* of intelligent behavior, not test answers and other *products* of intelligence (Hunt, 1983; Sternberg, 1982, 1986b; Vernon, 1987a; Sternberg & Gastel, 1989; Naglieri et al., 1991). This approach asks: What mental operations are necessary to answer the questions on an IQ test or to perform other intellectual tasks? What aspects of this performance depend on past learning, and what aspects depend on attention, working memory, and processing speed? In other words, the information-processing approach relates the basic mental processes discussed in the chapters on perception, memory, and thought to the concept of intelligence. Are there individual differences in these processes that correlate with measures of intelligence? More specifically, are measures of intelligence related to differences in the attention available for basic mental processes or in the speed of these processes?

The notion that intelligence may be related to attention builds on the results of research by Earl Hunt and others (Ackerman, 1994; Eysenck, 1987; Hunt, 1980). As discussed in the chapter on perception, attention represents a pool of resources or mental energy. When people perform difficult tasks or perform more than one task at a time, they must call on greater amounts of these resources. Does intelligent behavior depend on the amount of attention that can be mobilized? Early research by Hunt (1980) suggested that it does, that people with greater intellectual ability have more attentional resources available. There is also evidence for a positive correlation between IQ scores and performance on tasks requiring attention, such as mentally tallying the frequency of words in the "animal" category while reading a list of varied terms aloud (Stankov, 1989).

Another possible link between differences in information processing and differences in intelligence relates to processing speed. Perhaps intelligent people have "faster brains" than other people—perhaps they carry out basic mental processes more quickly. When a task is complex, having a "fast brain" might decrease the chance that information will disappear from memory before it can be used (Jensen, 1993; Vernon, 1987b; Larson & Saccuzzo, 1989). A "fast brain" might also allow people to do a better job of mastering material in everyday life and therefore to build up a good knowledge base (Vernon, 1983; Miller & Vernon, 1992). Hans Eysenck (1986) has even proposed that intelligence can be defined as the error-free transmission of information through the brain. Indeed, there have been recent attempts to measure various aspects of intelligence by looking at electrical activity in particular parts of the brain (Deary & Caryl, 1993; Eysenck, 1994).

These hypotheses sound reasonable, but research suggests that only about 25 percent of the variation seen in people's performance on general mental abilities tests can be accounted for by differences in their information-processing abilities (such as speed of access to long-term memory or the capacity of working memory) (Lohman, 1989; Baker, Vernon & Ho, 1991; Miller & Vernon, 1992). Are there other aspects of information processing that are correlated more strongly with performance on mental ability tests? And how is information processing related to aspects of intelligence—such as the ability to generate several possible solutions to a problem—that may not be measured by IQ tests? Robert Sternberg has integrated information-processing research into a broad theory of intelligence that addresses questions like these.

The Triarchical Theory of Intelligence

Sternberg's theory aims to explain a range of behavior that goes beyond what is measured by typical IQ tests. According to Sternberg (1988a), most theories of intelligence are incomplete, because a complete theory must deal with three aspects of intelligence: its internal components, the relation of these components to experience, and its external effects. Sternberg deals with each of these in his *triarchical theory* of intelligence.

The internal aspect of intelligence, says Sternberg, consists of the processes involved in thinking. There are three sets of these internal processes, or *components:* performance components, knowledge-acquisition components, and metacomponents. *Performance components* are such processes as perceiving stimuli, holding information in working memory, and calculating sums and differences. *Knowledge-acquisition components* involve the selective application of the processes used in gaining and storing new information. *Metacomponents* control the performance and knowledge-acquisition components; they are involved in organizing and setting up a problem. Metacomponents determine the problem-solving strategies people use—how they decide on the nature of a problem and know what performance components to use, how they determine what needs to be known before trying to solve a problem, and how they evaluate a proposed solution.

The second aspect of intelligence, says Sternberg, involves the relationship between the internal world of the components and the external world; it amounts to the ability to profit from experience by altering how the components are applied. According to Sternberg, intelligence involves being able to deal with novelty and to make some processes automatic. For example, the process of converting menu prices from, say, Swiss francs into American dollars becomes automatic for more intelligent tourists, enabling them to devote more time to other novel aspects of the situation (such as how much to tip).

Finally, in everyday life intelligence is manifested by adapting to or shaping environments. This aspect of intelligence might be thought of as "street smarts," as shown by Jack, one of the students described at the beginning of this chapter. Intelligent people can use performance components, knowledge-acquisition components, and metacomponents to achieve goals. Thus, intelligent behavior varies with the context. The kinds of knowledge and metacomponents that are appropriate for solving a physics problem in the laboratory are not the same as those needed for explaining your way out of an embarrassing situation, settling a family dispute, or getting the best price on a car.

Because it is so broad, many parts of Sternberg's theory are difficult to test. Determining exactly how to measure "street smarts," for example, is a challenge that is now being addressed by researchers (e.g., Sternberg et al., 1995). Nevertheless, Sternberg's theory is important because it extends the concept of intelligence into areas that most psychologists traditionally did not examine and emphasizes what intelligence means in everyday life.

Multiple Intelligences

Many people whose IQ scores are only average have exceptional ability in specific areas. Even some mentally retarded people show incredible ability in narrowly defined skills (Treffert, 1988). One child whose IQ score was 50 could correctly state the day of the week for any date between 1880 and 1950 (Scheerer, Rothmann & Goldstein, 1945). He could also play melodies on the piano by ear and sing Italian operatic pieces he had heard, although he had no understanding of what he was doing. In addition, he could spell—forward or backward—any word spoken to him and could memorize long speeches.

If only measuring the multifaceted concept of intelligence were this easy! To measure specific intelligences not tapped by standard IQ tests, Howard Gardner suggests options such as collecting samples of children's writing, assessing their ability to appreciate or produce music, and obtaining teacher reports of strength and weakness in athletic and social skills.

GROVER WASHINGTON, JR.   According to Gardner's theory of multiple intelligences, skilled musicians and athletes display forms of intelligence not assessed by standard intelligence tests.

Cases of remarkable ability in specific areas constitute part of the evidence cited by Howard Gardner in support of his theory of *multiple intelligences* (Gardner, 1983). To study intelligence, Gardner focused on how people learn and use symbol systems such as language, mathematics, and music. He asked: Do these systems all require the same abilities and processes, the same "intelligence"? To find out, Gardner looked not just at test scores and information-processing experiments but also at the ways in which children develop, at the exceptional abilities of child prodigies and remarkable adults, at biological research, and at the values and traditions of various cultures.

According to Gardner, all people possess a number of intellectual potentials, or "intelligences," each of which involves a set of skills that allows them to solve problems. Biology provides raw capacities unique to each of these intelligences; cultures provide symbolic systems such as language to mobilize the raw capacities. Although the intelligences normally interact, they can function with some independence, and individuals may develop certain intelligences further than others. The specific intelligences that Gardner proposes are (1) linguistic intelligence; (2) logical-mathematical intelligence; (3) spatial intelligence; (4) musical intelligence; (5) body-kinesthetic intelligence, which is demonstrated by the skills of dancers, athletes, and surgeons; and (6) personal intelligence, which refers to knowledge and understanding of oneself and of one's relations to others. Gardner notes that conventional IQ tests sample only the first three of these intelligences, mainly because these are the forms of intelligence most valued in school. But conventional IQ tests, he claims, fail to do justice to the diversity of intelligences.

Gardner's critics argue that including athletic or musical skill as part of intelligence dilutes the validity and usefulness of the concept, especially as it is applied in school and in many kinds of jobs. Nevertheless, Gardner and his colleagues (Kornhaber, Krechevsky & Gardner, 1990) are working on new ways of assessing "multiple intelligences." The value of Gardner's theory of intelligence will be decided by further research. Whatever the outcome, the theory highlights aspects of mental ability that are not measured by traditional IQ tests but that may be important in certain kinds of human activity. ("In Review: Analyzing Mental Abilities" summarizes Gardner's theory, along with the other views of intelligence we have discussed.)

The Ecological Approach

As psychologists become more attuned to the effects of cultural factors on human behavior and mental processes, the *ecological approach* to intelligence—emphasizing the role of the environment in shaping intelligence—may become more prominent. This approach views intelligence as mental activity that allows people to select, shape, and adapt to those aspects of the environment most relevant to their lives (Krechevsky

IN REVIEW	Analyzing Mental Abilities	
Approach	**Method**	**Key Findings or Propositions**
Psychometric	Define the structure of intelligence by examining factor analyses of the correlations between scores on tests of mental abilities.	Performance on many tests of mental abilities is highly correlated, but this correlation, represented by g, reflects a bundle of abilities, not just one trait.
Information processing	Understand intelligence by examining the mental operations involved in intelligent behavior.	The speed of basic processes and the amount of attentional resources available make significant contributions to performance on IQ tests.
Sternberg's triarchical theory	Understand intelligence by examining the information processing involved in thinking, changes with experience, and effects in different environments.	Thinking involves three components. High intelligence is shown in the effective organization of these components, in altering their use to deal with novel or familiar problems, and in adapting problem-solving strategies to different environments.
Gardner's theory of multiple intelligences	Understand intelligence by examining test scores, information processing, biological and developmental research, the skills valued by different cultures, and exceptional people.	Biology provides the capacity for six distinct "intelligences" valued by society: linguistic, logical-mathematical, spatial, musical, body-kinesthetic, and personal.

& Gardner, 1994; Sternberg, 1985). In other words, the ecological approach suggests that, as mentioned earlier, intelligence is not the same in all environments. Thus, rather than working on the improvement of tests designed to measure elements of intelligence that are universally shared, the ecological approach would recognize that what is "intelligent" in one situation isn't necessarily the same as what is "intelligent" in another. It will not be easy, however, to construct tests capable of measuring intelligence in a way that takes into account the environment in which a person operates.

LINKAGES: MENTAL ABILITIES AND THINKING

Are smarter people always better problem solvers?

In everyday usage, people's definition of "intelligence" surely includes some of the abilities described in Chapter 9, on thought and language—specifically, the abilities to think logically, solve problems efficiently, and make rational decisions. However, the relationship between IQ scores and the capacity for intelligent thinking is not necessarily strong or consistent. Part of the reason is that people who are good at solving problems depend on the mental abilities that IQ tests measure but *also* on knowledge and processes that such tests ignore (Ree & Earles, 1992; Sternberg, 1993).

COGNITIVE COMPLEXITY The outcome of a horse race depends on track conditions, temperature, the horses' training, the skill of the jockeys, and a multitude of other factors. People who can keep in mind and mentally combine numerous interacting factors tend to be especially successful at dealing with complicated situations, whether they involve betting, business decisions, or scientific research.

For example, a study of thirty avid racetrack bettors in Delaware revealed that some were clearly better bettors than others (Ceci & Liker, 1986). The good bettors, or "experts," predicted very accurately the final handicap that each horse was assigned at race time, a skill closely related to the ability to predict the winner. But the expert and nonexpert bettors did not differ significantly in their IQ scores; both groups had a mean IQ of around 100, and at least one expert bettor had an IQ of only 82!

The fact that IQ is a less than perfect predictor of problem-solving ability should not be surprising when you consider that IQ tests are designed to measure mental ability apart from knowledge about any particular domain. As discussed in Chapter 9, however, it is precisely that knowledge about an area—along with the ability to generate many possible solutions—that helps people solve problems in the area in question. Effective problem solving also requires the ability to avoid the obstacles to problem solving described in Chapter 9, such as mental sets and functional fixedness. Further, studies suggest that cognitive complexity and the ability to devise good strategies predict problem-solving ability; yet neither are measured by IQ tests.

Cognitive complexity involves flexibility of thought and the ability to anticipate events and alter a course of action based on unexpected happenings. Most important, cognitively complex people can think *multidimensionally;* in other words, they can interpret the consequences of their actions in a variety of ways and appreciate several aspects of a problem. In the study of Delaware bettors, experts and nonexperts reached their predictions in different ways. The experts used a more cognitively complex mental model. That is, in making their predictions, they considered more variables and considered more interactions among variables than did the nonexperts.

Siegfried Streufert (1986) measured cognitive complexity by asking business executives to play a game in which they managed a fictitious company. Streufert rated the executives high on cognitive complexity if they simultaneously considered several factors and thought through the many implications of a decision. Two findings were especially significant. First, cognitive complexity does not appear to be closely related to IQ scores. Second, cognitive complexity is *domain specific.* People who are cognitively complex in one domain, such as business decision making, may not show cognitive complexity at home or in other settings. Thus, for instance, an executive who considers all sides of a business problem may show no appreciation of a child's point of view in a family dispute.

Other studies have highlighted the importance of *strategies* in distinguishing good from bad problem solvers. In Chapter 9, we discussed an example in which expert physicists used more sophisticated problem-solving methods than did inexperienced students (Chi, Feltovitch & Glaser, 1981). The same results appeared in a study comparing problem solvers within a college physics class (Hardimann, Dufresne & Mestre, 1989). Poor problem solvers judged the similarity between physics problems in terms of surface features, such as whether the problems involved inclined planes; good problem solvers judged similarity in terms of underlying principles, such as whether problems could be solved using the same physical law. The differences were not related to underlying mathematical ability as measured by an IQ test.

DIVERSITY IN MENTAL ABILITIES

Though psychologists still don't agree on the details of what intelligence is, the study of IQ tests and intelligent behavior has yielded many insights into human mental abilities, and has highlighted the diversity of those abilities. In this section we briefly examine some of that diversity.

Creativity

In every area of human endeavor, there are people who demonstrate **creativity;** in other words, they can produce novel but effective solutions to challenges. Corporate executives and homemakers, scientists and artists, all may be more or less creative. Yet, like intelligence, creativity is difficult to define (Hausman, 1984). Does creativity include

CREATIVITY AND INTELLIGENCE
Creative people may share certain personality traits, but being creative says relatively little about one's IQ.

innovation based on previous ideas, or must it be utterly new? And must it be new to the world—as in Picasso's paintings—or only new to the creator—as when a child "makes up" the word *waterbird* without ever hearing it before? As with intelligence, psychologists have defined creativity not as a "thing" that people have or don't have but, rather, as mental activity that can be inferred from performance on creativity tests.

To measure creativity, some psychologists have generated tests of **divergent thinking,** the ability to think along many paths to generate many solutions to a problem (Guilford & Hoepfner, 1971). The Consequences Test is an example. It contains items such as "Imagine all of the things that might possibly happen if all national and local laws were suddenly abolished" (Guilford, 1959). Divergent thinking tests are scored by counting the number of *different* but plausible responses that a person can list for each item or by assessing the extent to which a person's answers are different from those given by most test takers.

Of course, the ability to come up with different answers or different ways of looking at a situation does not guarantee that anything creative will be produced. Some believe that creative behavior requires divergent thinking that is *appropriate* for a given situation or problem. To be productive rather than bizarre, a creative person must be firmly anchored to reality, understand society's needs, and learn from the experience and knowledge of others (Sternberg & Lubert, 1992). Therisa Amabile has identified three kinds of cognitive and personality characteristics necessary for creativity (Amabile, 1989; Amabile, Hennessey & Grossman, 1986).

1. Expertise in the field of endeavor, which is directly tied to what a person has learned. For example, a painter or composer must know the paints, techniques, or instruments available.

2. A set of creative skills, including persistence at problem solving, capacity for divergent thinking, ability to break problem-solving habits (mental sets), and willingness to take risks. Amabile believes that training can influence many of these skills (some of which are closely linked to the strategies for problem solving discussed in Chapter 9).

3. The motivation to pursue creative production for internal reasons, such as satisfaction, rather than for external reasons, such as prize money.

In fact, Amabile and her colleagues found that external rewards can deter creativity. They asked groups of children or adults to create artistic products such as collages or stories. Some were simply asked to work on the project. Others were informed that their project would be judged for its creativity and excellence and that rewards would be given or winners announced. Experts, who had no idea which products were created by which group, judged those from the "reward" group to be significantly less creative.

Is creativity inherited? To some extent, perhaps; but there is evidence that the environment influences creative behavior at least as much as it influences intelligence. For example, the correlation between the creativity scores of identical twins reared apart is lower than that between their IQ scores (Nichols, 1978).

Does creativity require a high IQ score? Correlations between people's scores on IQ tests and on tests of creativity are only modest, between +.10 and +.30 (Barron & Harrington, 1981; Rushton, 1990). This result is not surprising, because creativity as psychologists measure it requires divergent thinking, and traditional IQ tests test **convergent thinking**—the ability to apply logic and knowledge in order to narrow down the number of possible solutions to a problem. Thus, the questions on traditional IQ tests have only one or a small number of acceptable answers. The low correlation between IQ and creativity does not mean that the two are completely unrelated, however.

Unusual Mental Ability

Psychologists' understanding of mental abilities has been advanced by studying people whose mental abilities are unusual—the gifted, the mentally retarded, and those with learning disabilities.

Giftedness   Do all those with unusually high IQs become famous and successful in their chosen fields? Do their remarkable abilities mark them for social maladjustment? One of the best-known studies of the intellectually gifted was conducted by Louis Terman and his colleagues (Terman & Oden, 1947, 1959; Oden, 1968; Sears, 1977). This study began in 1921 with the identification of more than 1,500 children whose IQ scores were very high—most higher than 135 by age ten. Periodic interviews and tests over the next sixty years revealed that few if any became truly creative geniuses—such as world-famous inventors, authors, artists, or composers—but only 11 failed to graduate from high school, and more than two-thirds graduated from college. Ninety-seven earned Ph.Ds; 92, law degrees; and 57, medical degrees. In 1955 their median family income was well above the national average (Terman & Oden, 1959). In general, they were physically and mentally healthier than the nongifted and appear to have led happier, or at least more fortunate, lives (see the Focus on Research Methods section of Chapter 13). Thus, as mentioned earlier, high IQ scores tend to predict success in life, but an extremely high IQ does not guarantee special distinction. Indeed, research by Veronica Dark and Camilla Benbow (1993) suggests that gifted children are not fundamentally different kinds of people; they just have "more" of the same basic mental abilities seen in all children.

Mental Retardation   People whose IQ is less than about 70 *and* who fail to display the skill at daily living, communication, and other tasks that is expected of those their age have traditionally been described as mentally retarded, although they are now often referred to as "developmentally disabled" or "mentally challenged." People within this very broad category differ greatly in their mental abilities, and in their ability to function independently in daily life. Table 10.2 shows a classification that divides the range of low IQ scores into categories that reflect these differences.

Some cases of mental retardation have a clearly identifiable cause. The best-known example is *Down syndrome,* which is caused by an extra chromosome. Children with Down syndrome typically have IQ scores in the 40 to 55 range. Intelligence may also be limited by environmental conditions or traumas such as meningitis or encephalitis contracted during infancy, birth traumas resulting from an oversupply or undersupply of oxygen, and excessive use of drugs or alcohol by the mother during pregnancy.

In most cases, however, no genetic or environmental cause of retardation is directly observed. These are usually cases of mild retardation and are known as **familial retardation** for two reasons: Most people in this group (1) come from families of lower socioeconomic status, and (2) are more likely than those suffering from a genetic defect to have a relative who is also retarded (Plomin, 1989). These facts have led psychologists

TABLE 10.2		
Categories of Mental Retardation These categories are approximate. Especially at the upper end of the scale, many retarded persons can be taught to handle tasks well beyond what their IQ score might suggest. Furthermore, IQ is not the only diagnostic criterion for retardation. Many people with IQs lower than 70 can function adequately in their everyday environment and hence would not be classified as mentally retarded.		
Level of Retardation	**IQ Scores**	**Characteristics**
Mild	50–70	A majority of all the mentally retarded. Usually show no physical symptoms of abnormality. Individuals with higher IQs can marry, maintain a family, and work in unskilled jobs. Abstract reasoning is difficult for those with the lower IQs of this category. Capable of some academic learning to a sixth-grade level.
Moderate	35–49	Often lack physical coordination. Can be trained to take care of themselves and to acquire some reading and writing skills. Abilities of a 4- to 7-year-old. Capable of living outside an institution with their families.
Severe	20–34	Only a few can benefit from any schooling. Can communicate vocally after extensive training. Most require constant supervision.
Profound	Below 20	Mental age less than 3. Very limited communication. Require constant supervision. Can learn to walk, utter a few simple phrases, and feed themselves.

to conclude that familial retardation results from a complex interaction between heredity and environment.

Exactly *how* are the cognitive skills of mentally retarded people deficient? They are just as proficient as others at recognizing simple stimuli, and their rate of forgetting information from working memory is no more rapid (Belmont & Butterfield, 1971). But mildly retarded people do differ from other people in three important ways (Campione, Brown & Ferrara, 1982):

1. They perform certain mental operations more slowly, such as retrieving information from long-term memory. When asked to repeat something they have learned, they are not as quick as a person of normal intelligence.

LINKAGES   Is mental retardation mainly a matter of poor memory? (a link to Memory)

UNDERSTANDING MENTAL RETARDATION As the limitations and the potential of mentally retarded individuals are better understood, their opportunities and their role in society will continue to expand. The young retarded woman in the center of this picture is a successful, and obviously popular, teacher's assistant.

2. They simply know fewer facts about the world. It is likely that this deficiency is a consequence of a third problem.

3. They are not very good at using particular mental *strategies* that may be important in learning and problem solving. For example, they do not spontaneously rehearse material that must be held in working memory.

What are the reasons for these deficiencies in using strategies? The differences between normal and retarded children in some ways resemble the differences between older and younger children discussed in Chapter 12. Both younger children and retarded children show deficiencies in *metamemory*—the knowledge of how their memory works. More generally, retarded children are deficient in **metacognition:** the knowledge of what strategies to apply, when to apply them, and how to deploy them in new situations so that new specific knowledge can be gained and different problems mastered (Ferretti & Butterfield, 1989).

It is their deficiencies in metacognition that most limit the intellectual performance of the mildly retarded. If retarded children are simply taught a strategy, they are not likely to use it again on their own or to transfer the strategy to a different task. Because of this characteristic, it is important to teach retarded children to evaluate the appropriateness of strategies (Wong, 1986) and to monitor the success of their strategies. Finally, like other children, retarded children should be shown that effort, combined with effective strategies, pays off (Borkowski, Weyhing & Turner, 1986).

Despite such difficulties, the intellectual abilities of mentally retarded people can be raised. For example, one program emphasized positive parent-child communications and began when the children were as young as thirty months old. It helped children with Down syndrome to master reading skills at a second-grade level, providing the foundation for further achievement (Rynders & Horrobin, 1980; Turkington, 1987).

Designing effective programs for retarded children is complicated by the fact that the way people learn depends not just on cognitive skills but also on social and emotional factors. Much debate has focused on *mainstreaming,* the policy of teaching handicapped children, including those who are retarded, in regular classrooms with those who are not handicapped. Is mainstreaming good for retarded children? A number of studies of the cognitive and social skills of students who have been mainstreamed and those who were separated show few significant differences overall, though it appears that students at higher ability levels may gain more from being mainstreamed than their less mentally able peers (Cole et al., 1991).

Learning Disabilities　　People who show a significant discrepancy between their measured intelligence and their academic performance are said to have a *learning disability.* Learning disabilities are often seen in people with average or above-average IQ. For example, the problems with reading, writing, and math that Leonardo da Vinci and Thomas Edison had as children might have reflected such a disability; they certainly did not reflect low IQ! Many adults with learning disabilities find ways to compensate for their problems.

There are several kinds of learning disabilities (Myers & Hammill, 1990). People with *dyslexia* find it difficult to understand the meaning of what they read because the letters may appear distorted or jumbled; they may also have difficulty in sounding out and identifying written words. *Dysphasia* is difficulty with understanding spoken words or with recalling the words one needs for effective speech. *Dysgraphia*—problems with writing—appears as an inability to form letters, or as the omission or reordering of words and parts of words in one's writing. The least common learning disability, *dyscalculia,* is a difficulty with arithmetic that reflects not poor mathematical ability but, rather, an impairment in the understanding of quantity and/or in the comprehension of basic arithmetic principles and operations, such as addition and subtraction.

The National Joint Committee on Learning Disabilities (1994) suggests that these disorders are caused by dysfunctions in the brain, but specific neurological problems have not yet been found. Accordingly, most researchers describe learning disabilities in terms of dysfunctional information processing (Shaw et al., 1995). Diagnosis of a learning disability includes several steps, the first of which is to look for significant weak-

DIAGNOSING LEARNING DISABILITIES
Poor study skills, lack of motivation, and even the need for eyeglasses are among the many factors other than learning disabilities that can create a discrepancy between IQ scores and academic achievement. Accordingly, accurately diagnosing learning disability is not an easy task.

nesses in a person's listening, speaking, reading, writing, reasoning, or arithmetic skills (Brinckerhoff, Shaw & McGuire, 1993). The level of each of these abilities is compared to that predicted by the person's IQ score. Tests for brain damage are also given. To help rule out alternative explanations of poor academic performance, the person's hearing, vision, and other sensory systems are tested and factors such as poverty, family conflicts, and inadequate instruction are reviewed. Finally, alternative diagnoses such as attention deficit disorder (see Chapter 15) are eliminated.

FOCUS ON RESEARCH METHODS

Using Quasi-Experiments to Track Mental Abilities Over the Life Span

Various mental abilities change with time, but tracking them is not simple. Findings about age-related changes depend to some extent on the methods that are used to observe them. None of the methods include true experiments, because psychologists cannot randomly assign people to be a certain age and then give them mental tests. Instead, changes in mental abilities are explored through various quasi-experimental designs.

One of these, the *cross-sectional study,* compares data collected simultaneously from people of different ages. However, cross-sectional studies contain a major confounding variable: Because older people were born in a different year than younger ones, they may have had very different educational, cultural, nutritional, and medical experiences. This confounding variable is referred to as a *cohort effect.* Suppose two cohorts, or age-groups, are given a test of their ability to imagine the rotation of an object in space. The cohort born around 1940 might not do as well as the one born around 1970, but the difference may be due less to declining spatial ability in the older people than to the younger group's greater experience with video games and other spatial tasks. In short, it may be differences in experience, and not just age, that account for differences in ability among older and younger people in a cross-sectional study.

Changes associated with age can also be examined through *longitudinal studies,* in which a group of people are repeatedly tested as they grow older. But longitudinal designs contain their own inherent confounds. For one thing, fewer and fewer members of an age cohort can be tested over time as death, physical disability, relocation, and lack of interest reduce the sample size. Researchers call this problem the *mortality effect.* Further, those remaining are likely to be the healthiest in the group and may also have retained better mental powers than the dropouts (Botwinick, 1977). Hence, longitudinal studies may *underestimate* the degree to which abilities decline with age. Another confound can come from the *history effect.* In this situation, some event—such as a reduction in health care benefits for senior citizens—may have an effect on mental ability test scores that might be mistakenly attributed to age. Finally, longitudinal studies may be confounded by *testing effects,* meaning that participants may improve overtime because of what they learn during repeated testing procedures. People who become "testwise" in this way might even remember answers from one testing session to the next.

As part of the Seattle Longitudinal Study of cognitive aging, K. Warner Schaie (1993) devised the *cross-sequential with resampling design,* which measures the impact of the confounds we have discussed and thus allows corrections to be made for them. In 1956, Schaie randomly sampled 5,000 people from the membership of a health maintenance organization, and invited some of them to volunteer for the study. These volunteers, who ranged in age from twenty to eighty, were given a battery of intelligence tests designed to measure Thurstone's Primary Mental Abilities (PMA). The cross-sectional comparisons allowed by this first step were, of course, confounded by cohort effects. To control for those effects, the researchers retested the same participants seven years later, in 1963. Thus, the study combined cross-sectional and longitudinal methods. In this way, the size of the *difference* in PMA scores between, say, the twenty-year-olds and twenty-seven-year-olds tested in 1956 could be compared to the size of the *change* in PMA scores for these same people as they aged from twenty to twenty-seven and from twenty-seven to thirty-four. If the size of the longitudinal change was found to be about the same as the size of the cross-sectional difference, the latter could probably be attributed to aging, not to the era in which the participants were born.

What about the effect of confounds on the longitudinal changes themselves? To measure the impact of testing effects, the researchers randomly drew a new set of subjects from the pool of 5000. These people were of the same age range as the original sample, but they had not yet been tested. If the people from that original sample did better on their second PMA testing than the people of the same age who took the PMA for the first time, a testing effect would be suggested. (In this case, the size of the advantage would indicate the size of the testing effect.) To control for history effects, the researchers examined the scores of people who were the same age in different years. For example, they compared people who were thirty in 1956 to those who were thirty in 1963, people who were forty in 1956 to those who were forty in 1963, and so on. If PMA scores stayed the same for people at a given *age* no matter what *year* they were tested in, it is unlikely that events specific to certain years would have influenced test results. The researchers have tested participants six times between 1956 and 1991; on each occasion they retested some previous participants and tested others for the first time.

The results of the Seattle Longitudinal Study, and other more limited cross-sectional and longitudinal studies, suggest a reasonably consistent conclusion: Unless people are impaired by Alzheimer's disease or other brain disorders, their mental abilities usually remain about the same from early adulthood until about sixty to seventy years of age. Some components of intelligence, but not others, then begin to fail.

Crystallized intelligence, which depends on retrieving information and facts about the world from long-term memory, may continue to grow well into old age. *Fluid intelligence,* which involves rapid and flexible manipulations of ideas and symbols, remains stable during adulthood and then declines in later life (Hayslip & Sterns, 1979; Horn, 1978, 1982; Schaie, 1989). Among those over sixty-five or seventy, problems in several areas of information processing may impair problem-solving ability (Sullivan & Stankov, 1990). How and where does this decline show up?

1. *Working memory* The ability to hold and organize material in working memory declines beyond age fifty or sixty, particularly when attention must be redirected (Parkin & Walter, 1991).

2. *Processing speed* There is a general slowing of all mental processes (Lima, Hale & Myerson, 1991; Salthouse, Babcock & Shaw, 1991). Research has not yet isolated whether this slowing is due to reduced storage capacity, impaired processing efficiency, problems in coordinating simultaneous activities, or some combination of these factors (Salthouse, 1990; Babcock & Salthouse, 1990). For many tasks, this slowing does not create obstacles. But if a problem requires manipulating material in working memory, quick processing of information is critical (Rabbitt, 1977). To multiply two two-

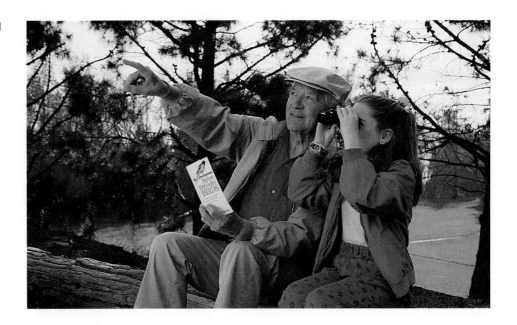

THE VOICE OF EXPERIENCE Even in old age, most people's crystallized intelligence remains intact. Their extensive storehouse of knowledge and experience makes older people a valuable resource for the young.

digit numbers mentally, for example, you must combine the subsums before they are forgotten.

3. *Organization* Older people seem to be less likely to solve problems by adopting specific strategies, or mental shortcuts (Young, 1966, 1971; Charness, 1987). For example, to locate a wiring problem, you might perform a test that narrows down the regions where the problem might be. The tests carried out by older people tend to be more random and haphazard (Young, 1966, 1971). This result may occur partly because many older people are out of practice at solving such problems.

4. *Flexibility* Older people tend to be less flexible in problem solving than their younger counterparts. They are less likely to consider alternative solutions (Salthouse & Prill, 1987), and they require more information before making a tentative decision (Rabbitt, 1977). Laboratory studies suggest that older people are also more likely than younger ones to choose conservative, risk-free options (Botwinick, 1966).

5. *Control of attention* The ability to direct or control attention declines with age (Kramer, Larish & Strayer, 1995; Wiegersma & Meertse, 1990). When required to switch their attention from one task to another, older subjects typically perform less well than younger subjects.

To summarize: Research shows that many kinds of mental abilities change in different ways throughout life. In general, there is a gradual, continual accumulation of knowledge about the world, some systematic changes in the limits of mental processes, and qualitative changes in the way those processes are carried out.

FUTURE DIRECTIONS

The study and testing of mental abilities will continue to generate interest and spark controversy among researchers and in society at large, partly because they have such far-reaching implications for education; for decisions as to who is hired, fired, graduated, or promoted; and for governmental policies for the disadvantaged (American Psychological Association, 1995). For example, local school boards will continue to struggle with questions about what testing procedures most adequately measure the effects of various teaching methods on students' abilities (Educational Testing Service, 1995).

In particular, IQ testing will continue to draw fire. People have already gone to court in an effort to halt the use of IQ tests as a guide for placing children in special-education classes (*Larry P.* v. *Riles,* 1975), or for hiring (*Griggs* v. *Duke Power Company,* 1971). Indeed, as noted in the Thinking Critically section, the concern is that using IQ tests to make decisions about people causes members of some ethnic minority groups to be unfairly deprived of equal opportunities. Accordingly, the Civil Rights Act of 1991 prohibits the use of IQ tests for hiring decisions if they result in bias against minority groups.

Ironically, the same law also prohibits employers from adding points to the scores of disadvantaged groups in order to correct for bias (Brown, 1994). Often, the emotional debates that rage around these issues are more reflective of people's personal biases and political agendas than of the results of scientific research. Yet as that research continues, some solid conclusions about intelligence and mental ability are emerging (Neisser et al., 1996).

First, it is becoming clearer that different definitions of intelligence are needed to serve different purposes. Second, most psychologists agree that the brain does not contain some unified "thing" corresponding to intelligence and that the correlation between tests of mental ability, labeled g, is likely to reflect a bundle of abilities. Third, most psychologists agree that the mental abilities of a particular individual result from a complex interaction between heredity and environment. A task force formed by the American Psychological Association to consider the issue of intelligence recently concluded that more research is needed on all these points, and that reports of that research should be evaluated in an atmosphere of scientific objectivity (American Psychological Association, 1995).

Where is the field moving? There will be increasing effort to understand the information-processing operations that underlie intelligent behavior and how they are related to traditional measures of intelligence (Sternberg, 1994). Further, we may see measures of intelligence that include processing speed, working-memory capacity, and the like (West, Crook & Barron, 1992). Computerized testing, linked with research in cognitive psychology, may lead to more accurate estimates of ability than paper-and-pencil testing (Embretson, 1992). And research in cognitive psychology can be expected to lead to more measures of mental ability that directly assess the cognitive mechanisms identified by that research (Kaufman & Harrison, 1991). Many tests will likely go beyond traditional formats in an effort to measure divergent thinking (Sternberg et al., 1995).

It has been shown that scores on traditional intelligence tests such as the Stanford-Binet correlate with biological measures of brain functioning, including PET scans, nerve conduction velocity, reaction time, and glucose metabolism rate (Haier et al., 1993; Vernon, 1993). Investigations into these "neural substrates of intelligence" are likely to become an important aspect of research on mental abilities in the next few decades.

There will also be increased interest in the ecological approach to mental abilities, with its focus on investigating the impact of environmental and cultural factors on various aspects of cognitive functioning, from IQ test performance to creativity (Azar, 1995). This approach is likely to be applied not only to studies of subcultural differences within countries but also to studies of differences that appear from culture to culture.

If you want to learn more about mental abilities, consider taking a course in tests and measurement, sometimes called psychometrics. Many courses in cognitive psychology also address the nature of individual differences in intelligent behavior. Advanced courses in behavioral genetics should also be of interest.

SUMMARY AND KEY TERMS

Mental ability refers to the capacity to perform the higher mental processes of reasoning, remembering, understanding, problem solving, and decision making.

■ TESTING FOR INTELLIGENCE

Psychologists have not reached a consensus on how best to define *intelligence*. Working definitions describe intelligence in terms of reasoning, problem solving, and dealing with the environment.

A Brief History of IQ Tests

Binet's pioneering test of intelligence included questions that required reasoning and problem solving of varying levels of difficulty, graded by age. Terman developed a revision of Binet's test that became known as the *Stanford-Binet;* it included items designed to assess the intelligence of adults as well as that of children and became the model for *IQ tests.* Early IQ tests in the United States required not just mental ability but also knowledge of U.S. culture. Wechsler's tests remedied some of the deficiencies of the earlier IQ tests. Made up of subtests, some of which have little verbal content, these tests allowed testers to generate scores for different aspects of mental ability.

IQ Tests Today

In schools the Stanford-Binet and Wechsler tests are the most popular individually administered intelligence tests. Both include subtests and provide scores for parts of the test as well as an overall score. For example, Wechsler subtests that depend heavily on vocabulary are combined into a *verbal scale;* the rest are combined into a *performance scale.* Currently, a person's *intelligence quotient,* or *IQ score,* reflects how far that person's performance on the test deviates from the average performance by people in his or her age group. An average performance is assigned an IQ of 100.

■ MEASURING THE QUALITY OF TESTS

Tests have three key advantages over other techniques of evaluation. They are standardized, so that the performances of different people can be compared; they produce scores that can be compared with *norms;* and they are economical and efficient.

Reliability

A good test must be *reliable,* which means that the results for each person are consistent, or stable. Reliability can be measured by test-retest, alternate-form, and split-half methods.

Validity

A test is said to be *valid* if it measures what it is supposed to measure. A test's validity for a particular purpose can be evaluated by measuring content validity, construct validity, or criterion validity; the last entails measurement of the correlation between the test score and some criterion. If the criterion is a measure of the performance that the test is supposed to predict, criterion validity is called predictive validity.

■ EVALUATING IQ TESTS

The Reliability and Validity of IQ Tests

IQ tests are reasonably reliable, and they do a good job of predicting academic success. However, IQ tests assess only some of the abilities that might be considered aspects of intelligence, and they may favor those most familiar with middle-class culture. Nonetheless, this familiarity is important for academic and occupational success.

IQ Scores as a Measure of Innate Ability

Both heredity and the environment influence IQ scores, and their effects interact. The influence of heredity is shown by the high correlation between IQ scores of identical twins raised in separate households and by the similarity in the IQ scores of children adopted at birth and their biological parents. The influence of the environment is revealed by the higher correlation of IQ between siblings who share the same environment than by those who do not and by the effects of environmental changes such as adoption.

Group Differences in IQ Scores

Different socioeconomic and ethnic groups have different mean IQ scores. These differences appear to be due to numerous factors, including differences in motivation, family support, educational opportunity, and other environmental conditions.

Conditions That Can Raise IQ Scores

An enriched environment sometimes raises IQ scores. Initial large gains in cognitive performance that result from interventions like Project Head Start may decline over time, but the programs may improve children's attitude toward school.

IQ Scores in the Classroom

Like any label, an IQ score can generate expectations that affect both how other people respond to a person and how that person behaves. Children labeled with low IQ scores may be offered fewer or lower-quality educational opportunities. On the other hand, IQ scores may help educators to identify a student's strengths and weaknesses and to offer the curriculum that will best serve that student.

■ UNDERSTANDING INTELLIGENCE

The Psychometric Approach

The *psychometric approach* attempts to analyze the structure of intelligence by examining correlations between tests of mental ability. Because scores on almost all tests of mental abilities are positively correlated, Spearman concluded that such tests measure a general factor of mental ability, called *s*, as well as more specific factors called *s*. As a result of *factor analysis,* other researchers have concluded that intelligence is not a single general ability but a collection of abilities and subskills needed to succeed on any test of intelligence. Cattell distinguished between *fluid intelligence,* the basic power of reasoning and problem solving, and *crystallized intelligence,* the specific knowledge gained as a result of applying fluid intelligence.

The Information-Processing Approach

The *information-processing approach* to intelligence focuses on the process of intelligent behavior. Only small positive correlations have been found between IQ scores and measures of the flexibility and capacity of attention, and between IQ scores and measures of the speed of information processing.

The Triarchical Theory of Intelligence

According to Sternberg, intelligent thinking involves performance components, knowledge-acquisition components, and metacomponents. Sternberg's triarchical theory also holds that intelligence depends on the ability to profit from experience and to deal with the environment.

Multiple Intelligences

Gardner's approach to intelligence suggests that biology equips us with the capacities for several intelligences that can function with some independence—specifically, linguistic, logical-mathematical, spatial, musical, body-kinesthetic, and personal intelligences.

The Ecological Approach

The ecological approach to intelligence highlights the role of the environment in shaping intellectual abilities that are functional for those in that environment. These abilities may differ somewhat from one culture to another.

■ LINKAGES: MENTAL ABILITIES AND THINKING

Because they attempt to measure ability independent of knowledge in a domain, IQ tests are not good predictors of problem-solving ability. Effective problem solving requires cognitive complexity and knowledge about the domain associated with the problem.

■ DIVERSITY IN MENTAL ABILITIES

Creativity

Tests of *divergent thinking* are used to measure differences in *creativity.* In contrast, IQ tests require *convergent thinking.* Although creativity and IQ scores are not highly correlated, creative behavior requires a certain amount of intelligence, along with expertise in a creative field, skills at problem solving and divergent thinking, and motivation to pursue a creative endeavor for its own sake.

Unusual Mental Ability

Knowledge about mental abilities has been expanded by research on giftedness, mental retardation, and learning disabilities. People with very high IQ scores tend to be successful in life, but are not necessarily geniuses. People are considered retarded if their IQ score is below about 70 and if their communication and daily living skills are less than expected of people their age. In *familial retardation,* no genetic or environmental causes are evident. Compared to those of normal intelligence, retarded people process information more slowly, know fewer facts, and are deficient at *metacognition*—that is, at knowing and using strategies. Mentally retarded people can be taught strategies, but they must also be taught how and when to use those strategies. People who show a significant discrepancy between their measured intelligence and their academic performance may have a learning disability. Learning disabilities can take several forms and must be carefully diagnosed.

Studies of changes in mental abilities over time reveal that crystallized intelligence increases well into old age, while fluid intelligence remains stable in adulthood, then declines in later life. Older people have reduced memory capacity, slower processing speed, greater difficulty in organizing strategies, less flexibility in problem solving, and reduced control of attention.

MOTIVATION AND EMOTION

CHAPTER **11**

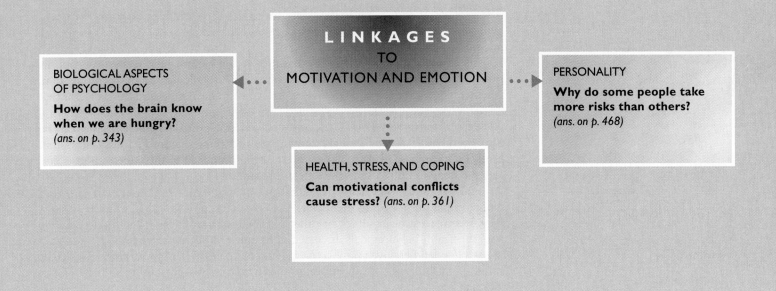

BIOLOGICAL ASPECTS OF PSYCHOLOGY

How does the brain know when we are hungry?
(ans. on p. 343)

LINKAGES
TO
MOTIVATION AND EMOTION

PERSONALITY

Why do some people take more risks than others?
(ans. on p. 468)

HEALTH, STRESS, AND COPING

Can motivational conflicts cause stress? *(ans. on p. 361)*

I n January 1994, despite temperatures reaching thirty degrees below zero, Brian Carr caught 155 fish, enough to win an annual ice-fishing contest in upstate New York. His first-place finish netted him the grand prize of eight dollars (Shepherd, 1994). Why would Mr. Carr and his competitors go fishing in such harsh conditions for such an apparently small reward? Why, for that matter, do any of us do what we do? Why do we help others or ignore them, overeat or diet, haunt art museums or sleazy bars, attend college or drop out of high school?

These are questions about **motivation,** the factors that influence the initiation, direction, intensity, and persistence of behavior (Evans, 1989). Psychologists who study motivation ask questions such as: What prompts a person to start looking for food, to register for dancing lessons, or to act in any other particular way? What determines whether the person chooses to go mountain climbing or to stay home and read? What makes some people go all out to reach a goal while others exert only half-hearted efforts and quit at the first obstacle?

Like the study of *how* people behave and think, the puzzle of *why* they do so involves questions related to many areas of psychology (see the Linkages diagram). Part of the motivation for behavior is to feel certain emotions, such as the joy of scaling a lofty peak or of becoming a parent. Motivation also affects emotion, as when hunger makes you more likely to become angry if people annoy you. In short, motivation and emotion are closely intertwined. In this chapter we review concepts of motivation and consider research on selected examples of motivated behavior. We also examine the features of emotions and consider their value to humans.

CONCEPTS AND THEORIES OF MOTIVATION

The concept of motivation helps psychologists to accomplish what Albert Einstein once called the whole purpose of science: to discover unity in diversity. Suppose that a man works two jobs, refuses party invitations, wears old clothes, drives a beat-up car, eats food others leave behind at lunch, never gives to charity, and keeps his furnace set at sixty degrees all winter. Why does he do these things? One could propose a separate explanation for each of these behaviors: Perhaps he likes to work hard, hates parties, fears new clothes and new cars, enjoys other people's leftovers, has no concern for the poor, and likes cold air. Alternatively, one could suggest a **motive,** a reason or purpose that provides a single explanation for this man's diverse and apparently unrelated behaviors. That unifying motive might be the man's desire to save as much money as possible.

This example illustrates the fact that motivation cannot be directly observed; its presence is inferred from what we *can* observe. Psychologists think of motivation, whether it be hunger or thirst or love or greed, as an *intervening variable*—a factor that helps to explain the relationships between environmental stimuli and behavioral responses. The three different responses shown in Figure 11.1, for example, can be understood as guided by a single unifying motive: thirst. Figure 11.1 also shows that motivation can help explain why different stimuli can lead to the same response, and why the same stimulus can evoke different responses.

Similarly, motivation helps explain why behavior varies over time. For example, many people cannot bring themselves to lose weight, quit smoking, or exercise until they experience a heart attack or other serious health problem. Then, in accordance with the health-belief models discussed in Chapter 13, these people may be motivated to eat a low-fat diet, give up tobacco, and exercise regularly. In other words, particular stimuli—including ice cream, cigarettes, and health clubs—elicit different responses at different times.

Sources of Motivation

The number of possible motives for human behavior seems endless. People are motivated to satisfy a need for food and water, of course, but they have many other needs as well. Some people seek the pleasures of creativity while many others are motivated by money or praise or power. And as social creatures, people are also influenced by motives to form emotional attachments to others, to become parents, and to join groups.

These and many other sources of human motivation fall into four general categories. First, human behavior is motivated by basic *biological factors,* particularly the need for food, water, sex, and temperature regulation (Tinbergen, 1989). *Emotional factors* are a second source of motivation (Izard, 1993). Panic, fear, anger, love, and hatred can be crucial to behavior ranging from selfless giving to brutal murder. Third, *cognitive factors* can motivate human behavior (Weiner, 1993). People often behave in a certain way because of their perceptions of the world, their beliefs about what they can do, and their anticipations of how others will respond. Fourth, motivation may stem from *social factors,* from reactions to parents, teachers, siblings, friends, television, and other sociocultural forces. The combined influence of such social factors in motivation has a profound effect on almost all human behavior (Baumeister & Leary, 1995).

How do these sources of motivation act on behavior? Does one type dominate? Psychologists have included these factors in various theories of human motivation. No

(handwritten margin note)
① biological
② emotional
③ cognitive
④ social.

Motives as Intervening Variables

Motives can act as explanatory links between apparently unrelated stimuli and responses. In this example, seeing thirst as the common motive provides an explanation of why each stimulus elicits the responses shown.

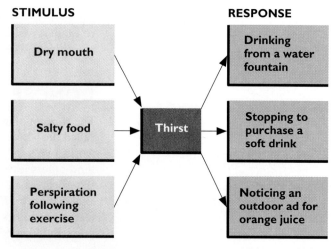

one theory gives a complete explanation of all aspects of motivation, but each of the four most prominent—instinct theory, drive reduction theory, arousal theory, and incentive theory—helps tell part of the story.

Instinct Theory and Its Descendants

Early in this century **instinct theory** was favored by many psychologists. **Instincts** are automatic, involuntary, and unlearned behavior patterns consistently "released" by particular stimuli (Tinbergen, 1989). For example, the male three-spined stickleback fish attacks aggressively when it sees the red underbelly of another male. Such behaviors are often called *fixed-action patterns* because they are unlearned, genetically coded responses to specific "releaser" stimuli.

William McDougall (1908) argued that human behavior, too, is motivated by instincts. He began by listing eighteen human instincts, including self-assertion, reproduction, pugnacity, and gregariousness. Within a few years, McDougall and other theorists had named more than 10,000 instincts, prompting one critic to suggest that his colleagues had "an instinct to produce instincts" (Bernard, 1924). Instincts had become meaningless labels that described behavior without explaining it. Saying that someone gambles because of a gambling instinct, golfs because of a golfing instinct, and works because of a work instinct explains nothing.

Despite the shortcomings of early instinct theories, psychologists have continued to explore the possibility that at least some aspects of human motivation are innate. Their interest has been stimulated partly by research showing that a number of human behaviors are present at birth. Among these are sucking and other reflexes (described in Chapter 12), as well as certain facial expressions such as smiling (described later in this chapter). There is also the fact that people do not have to learn to be hungry or thirsty or to want to stay warm, and—as discussed in the chapter on learning—that they appear to be biologically prepared to fear snakes and other potentially dangerous stimuli. Psychologists who take the evolutionary approach described in Chapter 1 suggest that all such behaviors have evolved because they are adaptive for promoting the survival of the human species. These theorists argue that many other aspects of human behavior, including helping, aggression, and mate selection, are also motivated by inborn factors—specifically, by the desire to pass on our own genes to the next generation.

INSTINCTIVE BEHAVIOR The male greater frigate bird displays his red throat as part of a mating ritual. This behavior is instinctive; it does not have to be learned.

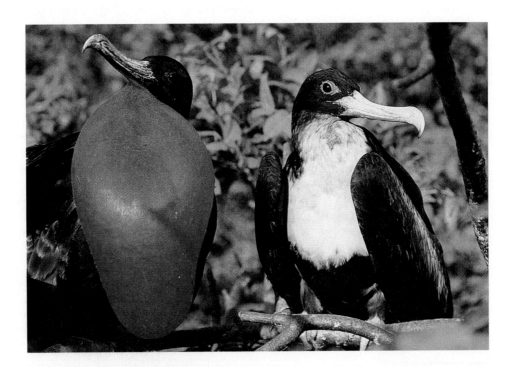

Evolution and Mate Selection   The evolutionary approach suggests, for example, that our choice of a marriage partner has a biological basis; love and marriage are seen as the result of inborn desires to create and nurture offspring so that our genes will survive in our children. According to this view, limits on the number of offspring women can produce make them more psychologically invested than men in the survival and development of their children (Townsend, Kline & Wasserman, 1995). The evolutionary approach further suggests that, in selecting an opposite-sex mate, females are likely to focus on a male's *resource acquisition capacity* (as signified by maturity, ambition, and earning power), while males are likely to place great emphasis on a female's *reproductive capacity* (as signified by youth, attractiveness, and good health).

These controversial speculations have received some support. For example, according to a survey of over 10,000 men and women in thirty-three countries on six continents and five isolated islands, males generally preferred youth and good health in prospective female mates, and females generally preferred males who were mature and wealthy (Buss, 1994a, 1994b). Critics argue that such preferences could stem from cultural traditions, not genetic programming. Indeed, among the Zulu of South Africa, where women are expected to build houses, carry water, and perform other physically demanding tasks, men tend to value maturity and ambition in a mate more than women do (Buss, 1989). The fact that women have been systematically denied economic and political power in many cultures may also account for their tendency to rely on the security and economic power provided by men (Derry, 1996; Silverstein, 1996). Still, evolutionary theories of human motivation are attracting increased research attention (Buss, 1995a, 1995b).

Drive Reduction Theory

Like instinct theory, drive reduction theory emphasizes biological factors, but it is based on the concept of homeostasis. **Homeostasis** is the tendency for organisms to keep physiological systems at a steady level, or *equilibrium,* by constantly making adjustments in response to change. We described a version of this concept in Chapter 3 when we discussed feedback loops that keep hormones at desirable levels.

According to **drive reduction theory,** an imbalance in homeostasis creates a **need**—a biological requirement for well-being. The brain responds to such needs, in the service of homeostasis, by creating a psychological state called **drive**—a feeling of arousal that prompts an organism to take action, restore the balance, and, as a result, reduce the drive (Hull, 1943). For example, if you have had no water for some time, the chemical balance of your body fluids is disturbed, creating a biological need for water. One consequence of this need is a drive—thirst—that motivates you to find and drink water. After you drink, the need for water is met, so the drive to drink is reduced. In other words, drives push people to satisfy needs, thus reducing drives and the arousal they create (see Figure 11.2).

Drive reduction theory recognizes the influence of learning on motivation by distinguishing between primary and secondary drives. **Primary drives** stem from biological needs, such as the need for food or water. (Food, water, and other things that satisfy primary drives are called *primary reinforcers;* see Chapter 7, on learning.) As already noted, people do not have to learn either these basic biological needs or the primary drives to satisfy them (Hull, 1951). However, we do learn other drives, called **secondary drives.** Once acquired, a secondary drive motivates us to act *as if* we have an unmet basic need. For example, as people learn to associate having money with the satisfaction of primary drives for food, shelter, and so on, having money may become a secondary drive. Having too little money thus motivates many behaviors—from hard work to thievery—to obtain more funds.

By recognizing secondary as well as primary drives, drive reduction theory can account for a wider range of behaviors than instinct theory. But humans and animals often go to extreme lengths to do things that do not obviously reduce *any* drive. Consider curiosity. Animals frequently explore and manipulate their surroundings, even though such activities do not lead to drive reduction. When new objects appear in the environment, most animals sniff, touch, and manipulate them in countless ways.

FIGURE 11.2

Drive Reduction Theory and Homeostasis

Homeostatic mechanisms, such as the regulation of body temperature or food and water intake, are often compared to thermostats. If the temperature in a house drops below the thermostat setting, the furnace comes on and brings the temperature up to that preset level, achieving homeostasis. When the temperature reaches the preset point, the furnace shuts off.

Unbalanced equilibrium → Need (biological disturbance) → Drive (psychological state that provides motivation to satisfy need)

Equilibrium restored ← Behavior that satisfies need and reduces drive ←

Rats will carefully explore every inch of a maze they have never seen, but the time they spend investigating a second maze depends on how similar it is to the first (Montgomery, 1953). Animals also exert great effort simply to enter a new environment, especially if it is complex and full of novel objects (Loewenstein, 1994). Monkeys are even willing to "pay" for a chance to satisfy their curiosity (Bolles, 1975), as Figure 11.3 shows. People are no less curious. Most cannot resist checking out anything new or unusual. They go to the new mall, read the newspaper, and travel the world just to see what there is to see.

Arousal Theory

People also go out of their way to ride roller coasters, sky dive, eat chili peppers, and do countless other things that, like curiosity-motivated behaviors, do not reduce any known drive (Deci, 1980; Rozin & Shenker, 1989). Quite the opposite. These behaviors *increase* people's levels of activation, or arousal. The realization that people sometimes try to reduce arousal and sometimes try to increase it has led theorists to argue that motivation is tied to the regulation of arousal.

Most of these theorists think of **arousal** as a general level of activation reflected in the state of several physiological systems (Brehm & Self, 1989). Thus, one's level of arousal can be measured by the brain's electrical activity, by heart action, or by muscle

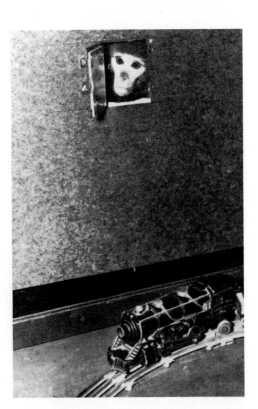

FIGURE 11.3

Curiosity

This monkey learned to perform a complicated task simply for the opportunity to look at a moving electric train.

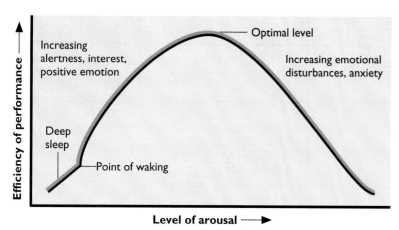

(A) GENERAL RELATIONSHIP BETWEEN PERFORMANCE AND AROUSAL LEVEL

(B) RELATIONSHIP BETWEEN PERFORMANCE AND AROUSAL LEVEL ON DIFFICULT VS. EASY TASKS

Source: Hebb, 1955.

FIGURE 11.4   The Arousal-Performance Relationship

Notice in part (A) that performance is poorest when arousal is very low *or* very high and best when arousal is at some intermediate level. When you are either nearly asleep or overly excited, for example, it may be difficult to think clearly or to be physically coordinated. In general, optimal performance comes at a lower level of arousal on difficult or complex tasks and at a higher level of arousal on easy tasks, as shown in part (B). Thus, even a relatively small amount of overarousal can cause students to perform far below their potential on difficult tests (Sarason, 1984). Because animal research early in this century by Robert Yerkes and his colleagues provided supportive evidence, this arousal-performance relationship is sometimes referred to as the Yerkes-Dodson law even though Yerkes never actually discussed performance as a function of arousal (Teigen, 1994).

LINKAGES: OPTIMAL AROUSAL AND PERSONALITY   People who enjoy high levels of arousal are likely to smoke, drink alcohol, engage in frequent sexual activity, listen to loud music, eat spicy foods, and do things that are novel and risky (Farley, 1986; Zuckerman, 1979). Those with lower optimal arousal tend to behave in ways that bring less intense stimulation and to take fewer risks. Most of the differences in optimal arousal have a strong biological basis and, as discussed in **Chapter 14**, may help shape broader differences in personality, such as introversion-extraversion.

tension (Deschaumes et al., 1991). Normally, arousal is lowest during deep, quiet sleep (stages 3 and 4) and highest during panic or great excitement. Many factors increase arousal, including hunger, thirst, intense stimuli, unexpected events, and stimulant drugs.

People perform best, and may feel best, when arousal is moderate (Teigen, 1994). Figure 11.4 illustrates the general relationship between arousal and performance. Overarousal can be harmful to performance. For example, it has been estimated that, in battle, 75 to 85 percent of soldiers sometimes become so overaroused that they do not fire their weapons (Marshall, 1947). Overarousal can also disrupt activity ranging from intellectual tasks (Ford, Wright & Haythornthwaite, 1985) to athletic competition (Davis & Harvey, 1992; Wright et al., 1995).

Arousal theories of motivation suggest that people are motivated to behave in ways that keep them at their own *optimal level* of arousal (Hebb, 1955; Fiske & Maddi, 1961). This optimal level is higher for some people than for others (Zuckerman, 1984). Generally, however, people try to increase arousal when it is too low and decrease it when it is too high. They seek excitement when bored and relaxation when overaroused. After classes and studying, for example, you may want to see an exciting movie. But if your day was spent playing baseball, fiercely debating a political issue, and helping a friend move, an evening of quiet relaxation may seem ideal.

Incentive Theory

Instinct, drive, and arousal theories of motivation all focus on internal processes that prompt people to behave in certain ways. By contrast, **incentive theory** emphasizes the role of environmental stimuli that can motivate behavior by pulling people toward them or pushing people away from them. According to this view, people act to obtain positive incentives and avoid negative incentives. Differences in behavior from one per-

IN REVIEW	Theories of Motivation
Theory	**Main Points**
Instinct	Innate biological instincts guide behavior.
Drive reduction	Behavior is guided by biological needs and learned ways of reducing drives arising from those needs.
Arousal	People seek to maintain an optimal level of physiological arousal, which differs from person to person. Maximum performance occurs at optimal arousal levels.
Incentive	Behavior is guided by the lure of rewards and the threat of punishment. Cognitive factors influence expectations of the value of various rewards and the likelihood of attaining them.

son to another, or from one situation to another, can be traced to the incentives available and the value a person places on them at the time. So if you *expect* a behavior (such as buying a lottery ticket) to lead to a valued outcome (winning money), you will want to engage in that behavior. The value of an incentive is influenced by biological as well as cognitive factors. For example, food is a more motivating incentive when you are hungry than when you are satiated (Balleine & Dickinson, 1994).

The theoretical approaches we have outlined are complementary (see "In Review: Theories of Motivation"). Each emphasizes different sources of motivation, and each has helped to guide research into motivated behaviors such as eating, sex, and work, which we consider in the sections that follow.

HUNGER AND EATING

Hunger is deceptively simple; you get hungry when you do not eat. Much as a car needs gas, you need fuel from food. Is there a bodily mechanism that, like a car's gas gauge, signals the need for fuel? What causes hunger? What determines which foods you eat, and how do you know when to stop? The answers to these questions involve not only interactions between the brain and the rest of the body but also learning and social factors (Rozin, 1996).

Biological Signals for Hunger and Satiety

A variety of mechanisms underlie **hunger,** the general state of wanting to eat, and **satiety,** (pronounced "se-tye´-a-tee"), the general state of no longer wanting to eat.

Signals from the Stomach   The stomach would seem to be a logical source of signals for hunger and satiety. After all, people say they feel "hunger pangs" from an "empty" stomach, and they complain of a "full stomach" after overeating. True, the stomach does contract during hunger pangs, and increased pressure within the stomach can reduce appetite (Cannon & Washburn, 1912; Houpt, 1994). But people who have lost their stomachs due to illness still get hungry when they do not eat and still eat normal amounts of food (Janowitz, 1967). Normal eating even occurs in rats whose stomachs are temporarily blocked from emptying into the digestive tract (Seeley, Kaplan & Grill, 1995). Thus, stomach cues can affect eating, but they do not always control it. Indeed, such cues appear to operate mainly when you are very hungry or very full.

Signals from the Blood   More precise signals about the body's fuel level and nutrient needs are sent to the brain from the blood. The brain's ability to "read" blood-borne signals about the body's nutritional needs was shown years ago when researchers deprived rats of food for a long period, then injected some of them with blood from rats that had just eaten. When offered food, the injected rats ate little or nothing (Davis et al., 1969);

LINKAGES   **How does the brain know when we are hungry?** (a link to Biological Aspects of Psychology) something in the injected blood of the well-fed animals apparently signaled the hungry rats' brains that there was no need to eat. What sent that satiety signal? Subsequent research showed that the brain constantly monitors both the level of food nutrients absorbed into the bloodstream from the stomach and the level of hormones released into the blood in response to those nutrients.

The nutrients that the brain monitors include *glucose* (the main form of sugar used by body cells), *fatty acids* (from fat), and *amino acids* (from protein). When the level of blood glucose drops, eating increases sharply (Mogenson, 1976). When large doses of glucose are injected into the blood of a food-deprived animal, it refuses to eat.

The hormones that the brain monitors include cholecystokinin (CCK), insulin, and leptin (a recently discovered substance that is sometimes called the "Ob protein"). During a meal, *cholecystokinin* is released as a neurotransmitter in the brain and as a hormone in the gut (Crawley & Corwin, 1994). Animals stop eating when CCK is injected into their brains (Parrott, 1994), and even well-fed animals start to eat after receiving drugs that block the brain's CCK receptors (Brenner & Ritter, 1995). At high levels, CCK causes nausea, which may explain the feelings that often accompany overeating.

When glucose levels rise, the pancreas releases *insulin,* a hormone that most body cells need in order to use the glucose they receive. Insulin may enhance the brain's satiety response to CCK. In one study, animals receiving CCK preceded by insulin infusions into the brain ate less food and gained less weight than animals getting either CCK or insulin alone (Riedy et al., 1995). Insulin itself may also provide a satiety signal; rats injected with insulin eat less than rats injected with a plain saline solution (Vanderweele, 1994).

Leptin also appears to provide a satiety signal. In addition, it may hold the key to the regulation of body fat. Normally, fat cells have active "Ob genes," which produce leptin for release into the blood. Animals with defective Ob genes make no leptin, and are obese. When leptin injections are given to Ob-defective animals, to other obese animals, or even to animals of normal weight, rapid loss of weight and body fat occurs, with no effect on muscle or other body tissues (Pelleymounter et al., 1995; Halaas et al., 1995; Campfield et al., 1995). Apparently, leptin sends its satiety signals directly to the hypothalamus, where special receptors for it have recently been discovered (Tartaglia et al., 1996). The hypothalamus also has receptors for satiety signals from a compound called glucagon-like peptide-1, or GLP-1 (Turton et al., 1996). Leptin and GLP-1 may someday be important in the treatment of obesity.

Hunger and the Brain

Many parts of the brain contribute to the control of hunger and eating, but research has focused on three regions of the hypothalamus that may play primary roles in detecting and reacting to the blood's signals about the need to eat (see Figure 11.5). These regions include the ventromedial nucleus, the lateral hypothalamus, and the paraventricular nucleus.

Activity in fibers passing through the *ventromedial nucleus* appears to tell an animal there is no need to eat. Thus, if a rat's ventromedial nucleus is electrically or chemically *stimulated,* the animal will stop eating (Kent et al., 1994). However, if the ventromedial nucleus is *destroyed,* the animal will eat ravenously, increasing its weight up to three-fold. Then the rat eats enough food to maintain this higher weight (Teitelbaum, 1961). Thus, the ventromedial nucleus seems to act as a "stop-eating" center.

In contrast, the *lateral hypothalamus* seems to act as a "start-eating" center. When fibers in the lateral hypothalamus are electrically or chemically *stimulated,* rats begin to eat vast quantities, even if they have just had a large meal (Stanley et al., 1993). When the lateral hypothalamus is *destroyed,* however, rats stop eating almost entirely. Most eventually resume eating, but they eat only small amounts of their most-liked foods and maintain a much-reduced weight (Keesey & Powley, 1975).

One theory maintains that these two hypothalamic regions interact so as to maintain a *set point* of body weight, food intake, or related metabolic signals—much as a

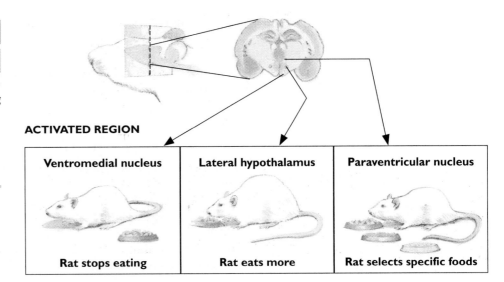

FIGURE 11.5

The Hypothalamus and Hunger

Studies of the hypothalamus have concentrated on stimulating or destroying fibers that pass through the ventromedial nucleus, the lateral hypothalamus, and the paraventricular nucleus. Here are some of the results of this research.

ACTIVATED REGION

Ventromedial nucleus	Lateral hypothalamus	Paraventricular nucleus
Rat stops eating	Rat eats more	Rat selects specific foods

home thermostat switches the furnace on and off in order to maintain a chosen temperature setting (Powley & Keesey, 1970; Cabanac & Morrissette, 1992). According to this theory, normal animals eat until their set point is reached, then stop eating until desirable intake falls below the set point. Destruction or activation of the lateral or ventromedial hypothalamus may alter the set point. For example, perhaps animals with a damaged ventromedial nucleus eat more and stay obese because their set points have been raised. Similarly, damage to the lateral hypothalamus may lower the set point, causing less eating and maintenance of a lower weight.

Research on the *paraventricular nucleus (PVN)* suggests, however, that the brain's control of eating involves more complexity than just the interaction of "stop-eating" and "start-eating" centers (Winn, 1995). For example, hungers for different types of food seem to be related to the action of different neurotransmitters on PVN neurons (Leibowitz, Xuereb & Kim, 1992; Lee, Schiffman & Pappas, 1994). Thus, for instance, *neuropeptide Y* stimulates carbohydrate eating (Jhanwar et al., 1993), *serotonin* acts to reduce carbohydrate consumption (Blundell, 1991), *galanin* motivates eating of high-fat food (Krykouli et al., 1990), and *enterostatin* reduces fat consumption (Shargill et al., 1991).

In short, several brain regions help to regulate hunger and eating. And although eating is controlled by processes that suggest the existence of a set point, that set point appears variable enough to be overridden by other factors.

Flavor, Cultural Learning, and Food Selection

One factor that can override a set point is the flavor of food. (As noted in the chapter on sensation, flavor results from the interaction of taste and odor cues.) Consider the following experiment, in which some animals were offered just one type of food while others were offered foods of several different flavors. The group getting the varied menu ate nearly four times more than the one-food group. As each new food appeared, the animals began to eat voraciously, regardless of how much they had already eaten (LeMagnen, 1971; Peck, 1978). Humans behave similarly. All things being equal, people eat more food during a multicourse meal than when only one food is served. Apparently, the flavor of a food becomes less enjoyable as more of it is eaten (Swithers & Hall, 1994). In one study, for example, people rated how much they liked four kinds of food; then they ate one of the foods and rated all four again. The food they had just eaten now got a lower rating, while liking increased for all the rest (Johnson & Vickers, 1993).

Another factor that can override blood-borne signals about satiety is *appetite,* the motivation to seek food's pleasures. For example, the appearance and aroma of certain foods come to elicit conditioned physiological responses—such as secretion of saliva, gastric juices, and insulin—in anticipation of eating those foods. (The process is based

A FAT RAT After surgical destruction of its ventromedial nucleus, this rat ate enough to triple its body weight. Such animals become picky eaters, choosing only foods that taste good and ignoring all others (Miller, Bailey & Stevenson, 1930; Teitelbaum, 1957).

on the principles of classical conditioning described in Chapter 7.) These responses then augment appetite. Thus, merely seeing a pizza on television may suddenly prompt you to order one, and if you see a delicious-looking cookie, you do not have to be hungry to start eating it. In other words, people eat not only to satisfy nutritional needs but also to experience enjoyment.

The choices people make about *which* foods to eat are governed by many factors, ranging from biological needs to culturally based learning. Consider food *cravings* (Hill & Heaton-Brown, 1994). The most common example, chocolate craving, can be intense enough to cause depression and anxiety when chocolate is not available (Macdiarmid & Hetherington, 1995). Apparently, "chocoholics" crave the flavor of chocolate, not the nutrients and other chemicals it contains. The results of one study showed that candies that tasted like chocolate but lacked its pharmacological components satisfied people's chocolate cravings; tasteless pills containing all the chemicals found in chocolate did not (Michener & Rozin, 1994).

A different mechanism appears to be responsible for *specific hungers,* or desires for particular foods at particular times. These hungers appear to reflect the biological need for the nutrients contained in certain foods. In one study, rats were allowed to eat from a bowl of carbohydrate-rich but protein-free food and also from a bowl of protein-rich but carbohydrate-free food. These animals learned to eat from both bowls in amounts that yielded a proper balance of carbohydrates and protein (Miller & Teates, 1985). In another study, rats were given three bowls of tasty, protein-free food and one bowl of bad-tasting food that was rich in protein. Again, the rats learned to eat enough of the unpalatable food to get a proper supply of dietary protein (Galef & Wright, 1995).

These results are remarkable in part because food nutrients such as carbohydrates, fats, and proteins have no inherent taste or odor. How, then, can they guide food choices that maintain nutritional balance? As with appetite, learning principles are probably involved. It may be that volatile odorants in foods come to be associated with the nutritional value of their fat and protein content. Evidence for this kind of learning comes from experiments in which rats received infusions of liquid directly into their stomachs. Some of these infusions consisted of plain water; others included nutritious cornstarch. Each kind of infusion was paired with the presence of a different taste—either sour or bitter—in the animals' normal supply of drinking water. After all the infusions were completed, both sour water and bitter water were made available. When the animals became hungry, they showed a strong preference for the water whose taste had been associated with the cornstarch infusions (Drucker, Ackroff & Sclafani, 1994). Related research shows that children come to prefer flavors that have been associated with high-fat ingredients (Johnson, McPhee & Birch, 1991).

The role of learning in food selection is also seen in the social rules and cultural traditions that influence eating. Munching popcorn at movies and hot dogs at ball games are common examples from North American culture of how certain social situations can stimulate appetite for particular items. Similarly, how much you eat may depend on what others do. Courtesy or custom might prompt you to select foods you might otherwise have avoided. Generally, the mere presence of others, even strangers, tends to increase consumption: Most people consume 60 to 75 percent more food when they are with others than when eating alone (Redd & de Castro, 1992; Clendenen, Herman & Polivy, 1995).

Eating and food selection are central to the way people function within their cultures. Celebrations, holidays, vacations, and even daily family interactions often revolve around food and what some call a *food culture* (Rozin, 1983). As any world traveler knows, there are wide cultural and subcultural variations in food selection. For example, chewing coca leaves is popular in the Bolivian highlands but illegal in the United States (Burchard, 1992). In China, people in urban areas eat a high-cholesterol diet rich in animal meat whereas those in rural areas eat so little meat as to be cholesterol deficient (Tian et al., 1995). And the insects known as palm weevils, a popular food for people in Papua New Guinea (Paoletti, 1995), are regarded by many Westerners as disgusting (Springer & Belk, 1994). In short, eating serves functions beyond nutrition—functions that help to remind us of who we are and with whom we identify.

BON APPETIT! The definition of "delicacy" differs from culture to culture. At this elegant restaurant in Mexico, diners pay to feast on baby alligators, insects, and other dishes that some people from other cultures would not eat even if the restaurant paid *them.*

Eating Disorders

Problems in the processes regulating hunger and eating may cause an *eating disorder.* The most common and dangerous examples are obesity, anorexia nervosa, and bulimia nervosa.

Obesity   About one-third of people in the United States weigh more than health guidelines say they should (Kuczmarski et al., 1994). **Obesity** is a state of severe overweight —often by as much as one hundred pounds—that threatens health by contributing to diabetes, high blood pressure, and increased risk of heart attack (Pi-Sunyer, 1994).

Why do obese people gain so much weight? The body maintains a given weight through a combination of food intake and energy output (Keesey & Powley, 1986). Obese people get more energy from food than their body *metabolizes,* or "burns up;" the excess energy, measured in calories, is stored as fat. Metabolism declines during sleep and rises with physical activity. Since women tend to have a lower metabolic rate than men, even when equally active, they tend to gain weight more easily than do men with similar diets (Ferraro et al., 1992).

Most obese people have normal resting metabolic rates and are as active as lean people (Meijer et al., 1992). However, obese people tend to be finicky eaters, eating above-average amounts of high-calorie, tasty foods but below-average amounts of less tasty foods (Peck, 1978; Kauffman, Herman & Polivy, 1995). And when trying to restrict eating, some obese people greatly underestimate how much they have eaten (Lichtman et al., 1992; Lowe, Kopyt & Buchwald, 1996).

The fact that most obese people are fat because they eat more of certain foods does not mean that they are "morally lax." For one thing, discovery of the "Ob genes" mentioned earlier suggests that people may be genetically predisposed to manage fat in different ways. Similarly, both genetic influences and the nature of childhood nutrition can raise a person's set point for body weight and create larger and more numerous fat cells (Grilo & Pogue-Geile, 1991; Keesey, 1980). Such factors may increase obese people's tendency to accumulate fat and also make them feel more hunger than lean people, even when they maintain similiar habits of diet and exercise.

Psychological explanations for obesity often focus on maladaptive reactions to stress. Many people tend to eat more when under stress, a reaction that may be especially extreme among those who become obese (Friedman & Brownell, 1995). However, obese people are no more likely than normal-weight people to display mental disorders (Stunkard & Wadden, 1992).

① women generally have lower metabolic rates

YOUNG COUCH POTATOES Inactivity during childhood is thought to contribute to weight gain, and television watching is a major cause of inactivity among overweight children (Dietz, 1991). Recent studies show that metabolic rates during television watching are even lower than during rest, and that the reduction while watching television may be even greater in obese children compared to those of normal weight (Klesges, Shelton & Klesges, 1993).

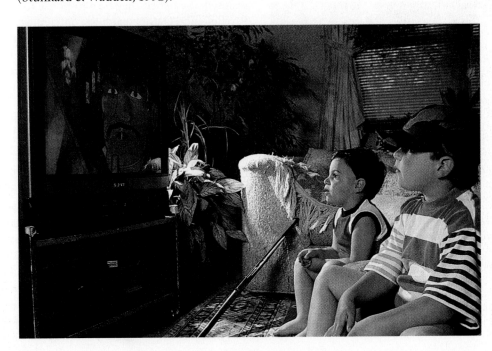

Losing weight and keeping it off for at least five years is extremely difficult for many people, especially those who are obese (NIH, 1992). Part of the problem may be due to metabolic changes that accompany weight loss. When food intake is reduced, the process of homeostasis leads to a drop in metabolic rate, thus saving energy and curbing weight loss (Leibel, Rosenbaum & Hirsch, 1995). This response makes evolutionary sense; conservation of energy during famine, for example, is adaptive for survival. But when obese people try to lose weight, their metabolic rate drops *below* normal. As a result, they can gain weight even while eating amounts that would maintain constant weight in others.

These facts suggest that attempts to lose a great deal of weight quickly will be met with compensatory changes in one's set point (Brownell & Rodin, 1994). Indeed, animal studies show that losing and then regaining large amounts of weight, so-called cycling, actually leads to a gradual rise in average weight (Archambault et al., 1989). Moreover, people whose body weight "cycles" tend to experience more depression and stress-related symptoms than do people whose average weight is similar but does not fluctuate (Foreyt et al., 1995).

To achieve the kind of gradual weight loss that is more likely to last, obese people are advised to increase regular exercise because it burns calories without slowing metabolism (Tremblay & Bueman, 1995). Indeed, in the long run, regular aerobic exercise *raises* the metabolic rate (McCarty, 1995). The most effective weight-loss programs include components designed to reduce food intake, change eating habits and attitudes toward food, and increase energy expenditure through exercise (Kirschenbaum & Fitzgibbons, 1995).

Anorexia Nervosa   At the opposite extreme of eating disorders is **anorexia nervosa,** which is characterized by self-starvation and severe weight loss. Anorexics often feel strong hunger yet refuse to eat. Some are obsessed with food and its preparation but eat almost nothing. Anorexic self-starvation causes serious, often irreversible, physical damage. Between 4 and 30 percent of anorexics actually starve themselves to death (Bryant & Lask, 1995). About 95 percent of people who suffer from anorexia are female. The prevalence of anorexia appears to be on the increase; it now affects about 1 percent of young women in the United States and is a growing problem in many other industrialized nations as well (American Psychiatric Association, 1994; Berry, Fried & Edlestein, 1995; Gillberg et al., 1995).

The causes of anorexia are not yet clear. Anorexics do have abnormally low levels of certain neurotransmitters; but because these levels return to normal when weight is restored, the deficit may be a response to starvation, not its cause (Kaye et al., 1988). Psychological factors that may contribute to the problem include a self-punishing, perfectionistic personality and a culturally reinforced obsession with thinness and attractiveness (Bastiani et al., 1995; Tiller et al., 1995). Anorexics appear to develop a fear of being fat, which they take to dangerous extremes (de Castro & Goldstein, 1995). Many anorexics continue to view themselves as too fat or misshapen even as they are wasting away (Heilbrun & Witt, 1990).

Drugs, hospitalization, and psychotherapy are all used to treat anorexia. In most cases, some combination of treatment and the passage of time brings recovery and maintenance of normal weight (Advokat & Kutlesic, 1995).

Bulimia Nervosa   Like anorexia, bulimia nervosa involves intense fear of being fat, but the person may be thin, normal in weight, or even overweight (Mitchell et al., 1990). **Bulimia nervosa** involves eating huge amounts of food (say, several boxes of cookies, a half-gallon of ice cream, and a bucket of fried chicken) and then getting rid of the food through self-induced vomiting or strong laxatives (Neims et al., 1995). These "binge-purge" episodes may occur as often as twice a day (Weltzin et al., 1995).

Like anorexics, bulimics are usually female; estimates of the frequency of anorexia and bulimia range from 1 to 10 percent of adolescent and college-age women (Haller, 1992). Their eating problems usually begin in their teens, with an obsession over being slender. However, bulimia and anorexia are separate disorders (Pryor, 1995). For one thing, most bulimics see their eating habits as problematic, while most anorexics do

AN ANOREXIA FATALITY   This photo of Christy Henrich, a former member of the U.S. Olympic gymnastics team, was taken in 1993, eleven months before she died of anorexia-related complications. At the time of her death, Christy was twenty-two years old, stood four feet, ten inches tall, and weighed sixty pounds.

IN REVIEW	Major Factors Controlling Hunger and Eating	
	Stimulate Eating	**Inhibit Eating**
Biological factors	Stomach contractions are associated with subjective feelings of hunger; taste becomes less enjoyable as more of a particular food is consumed, and thus varied tastes increase eating; the lateral area of the hypothalamus may be a start-eating center sensitive to reductions in blood sugar.	The ventromedial nucleus of the hypothalamus may be a stop-eating center that monitors blood; satiety signals come from hormones such as CCK, insulin, and leptin.
Nonbiological factors	Sights and smells of particular foods elicit eating because of prior associations; family customs and social occasions often include norms for eating in particular ways; stress is often associated with eating more.	Values in contemporary U.S. society encourage thinness, and thus can inhibit eating.

not. In addition, bulimia nervosa is usually not life-threatening (Hall et al., 1989; Schlesier-Stroop, 1984). There *are* consequences, however, including dehydration, nutritional problems, and intestinal damage. Many bulimics develop dental problems from the acids associated with vomiting. Frequent vomiting, and the insertion of objects to cause it, can also cause damage to the throat. More generally, preoccupation with eating and avoiding weight gain prevents many bulimics from working productively (Herzog, 1982).

Bulimia nervosa appears to be caused by a combination of factors, including culturally encouraged overconcern with thinness and attractiveness, depression and other emotional problems, and as-yet-undetermined biological problems that might include defective satiety mechanisms (Brewerton et al., 1995; Geliebter, 1995; Smith, Marcus & Eldredge, 1994). Treatments for bulimia typically include individual or group therapy and, sometimes, antidepressant drugs; these help the vast majority of bulimic people to eat more normally (Whitbread & McGown, 1994).

(For a summary of the processes involved in hunger and eating, see "In Review: Major Factors Controlling Hunger and Eating.")

SEXUAL BEHAVIOR

Unlike food, sex is not necessary for individual survival. A strong desire for reproduction does help ensure the survival of a species, however (Keeling & Roger, 1995). The various factors shaping sexual motivation and behavior differ in strength across species, but they often include a combination of the individual's physiology, learned behavior, and the physical and social environment. For example, one species of desert bird requires adequate sex hormones, a suitable mate, and a particular environment before it begins sexual behavior. As long as the dry season lasts, it shows no interest in sex, but within ten minutes of the first rainfall the birds vigorously copulate.

Rainfall is obviously much less influential as a sexual trigger for humans; indeed, people show a staggering diversity of *sexual scripts,* or patterns of behavior that lead to sex. One survey of college-age men and women identified 122 specific acts and 34 different tactics used for promoting sexual encounters (Greer & Buss, 1994). What happens next? The matter is exceedingly difficult to address scientifically, because most people are reluctant to allow researchers to observe their sexual behavior; many are reluctant even to respond to specific questions about their sexual practices. Yet having valid information about the nature of human sexual behavior is a vital first step for psychologists and other scientists who study topics such as individual differences in sexuality, sources of sexual orientation, types of sexual dysfunctions, and pathways through which HIV and other sexually transmitted diseases (STDs) reach new victims. This information also has important implications for helping people understand themselves ("Is my sexual behavior common?"), alleviating sexual problems, and preventing the spread of STDs (Kelly & Kalichman, 1995).

The most extensive studies of sexual behavior in the United States are contained in reports by Alfred Kinsey during the late 1940s and early 1950s (Kinsey, Pomeroy & Martin, 1948; Kinsey et al., 1953) and in a 1966 book, *Human Sexual Response,* by William Masters

FOCUS ON RESEARCH METHODS

A Survey of Human Sexual Behavior

and Virginia Johnson. In the Kinsey studies, volunteers were asked about their sexual practices; Masters and Johnson actually measured physiological response patterns as volunteers received natural or artificial sexual stimulation in a laboratory. Together, these pioneering studies broke new ground in the exploration of human sexuality, but critics have argued that the people who volunteered for such studies probably do not constitute a representative sample of humankind. Accordingly, the results—and any conclusions drawn from them—may not apply to people in general (see Chapter 2). Generalizability aside, the Kinsey data are now so old that they may not reflect sexual practices today. Unfortunately, the results of more recent surveys, such as reader polls in *Cosmopolitan* and other magazines (Davis & Smith, 1990), are also flawed by the use of nonrepresentative samples.

The shortcomings of previous work in this area recently led a team of researchers at the University of Chicago to conduct the "National Health and Social Life Survey," the first extensive survey of sexual behavior since Kinsey (Laumann et al., 1994). This survey is remarkable in that it included important design features that had been neglected in most other surveys of sexual behavior. First, the study did not depend on volunteers. Instead, the researchers sought out a particular sample of 3,432 people, ranging in age from eighteen to fifty-nine. Second, careful construction of the sample made it reflective of the sociocultural diversity of the U.S. population in terms of gender, ethnicity, socioeconomic status, geographical location, and the like. Third, unlike previous mail-in surveys, the Chicago survey was based on interviews. This face-to-face approach made it easier to ensure that the participants understood each question and provided them an opportunity to explain their responses. Fourth, to encourage candor, the researchers allowed participants to answer some of the survey's questions anonymously, by placing written responses in a sealed envelope. These techniques have been hailed as "light-years ahead" of previous methods (Gorner, 1994).

The results of the Chicago survey are striking, partly because they challenge some of the popular-culture and mass media images of sexuality in the United States. For one thing, the survey found that people in the United States have sex less often and with fewer people than many had speculated. For most, sex occurs about once a week in monogamous relationships; about a third of the participants reported having sex only a few times or not at all in the past year. In contrast to certain celebrities' splashy tales of dozens, even hundreds, of sexual partners per *year,* the average male survey participant had only six sexual partners in his entire life; the average female respondent reported a lifetime total of two. Further, the survey data suggested that people in committed, monogamous relationships had the most frequent and the most satisfying sex. And although a wide variety of specific sexual practices were reported, the overwhelming majority of heterosexual couples said they tend to engage mainly in penis-vagina intercourse.

In short, the Chicago survey suggests that people in the United States may be more sexually conservative than one might think on the basis of magazine reader polls and the testimony of guests on daytime talk shows. Still, many questions remain. For example, the Chicago survey did not ask about some of the more controversial aspects of sexuality—the effects of pornography, the nature and prevalence of pedophilia (sexual attraction to children), and the role in sexual activity of sexual fetishes such as shoes or other apparel. Had the researchers asked about such topics, their results might have painted a less conservative picture. Further, because the Chicago survey focused on a carefully drawn sample of people in the United States, its results tell us little or nothing about the sexual practices, traditions, and values of people in the rest of the world.

Even the best survey methods—like the best of all other research methods—usually yield results that raise as many questions as they answer.

There are some questions about human sexual behavior that a survey cannot easily or accurately explore: When do people become interested in sex, and why? How do they choose to express these desires, and why? What determines their sexual likes and dislikes? How do learning and sociocultural factors modify the biological forces that seem to provide the raw material of human sexual motivation?

The Biology of Sex

Some aspects of the sexual behavior observed in Masters and Johnson's laboratory may not have reflected exactly what goes on when people have sex in more familiar surroundings. Still, those observations led to important findings about the **sexual response cycle,** the pattern of physiological arousal during and after sexual activity (see Figure 11.6).

People's motivation to engage in sexual activity has biological roots in **sex hormones.** The female sex hormones are **estrogens** and **progestins;** the main ones are *estradiol* and *progesterone.* The male hormones are **androgens;** the principal example is

FIGURE 11.6

The Sexual Response Cycle

Masters and Johnson (1966) found that men show one primary pattern of sexual response, depicted in part (A); and that women display at least three different patterns from time to time (labeled A, B, and C in part B). In both men and women, the first, or *excitement,* phase begins with sexually stimulating input from the environment or from one's own thoughts. Continued stimulation leads to intensified excitement in the second, or *plateau,* phase. If stimulation continues, the person reaches the third, or *orgasmic,* stage, which, though it lasts only a few seconds, provides an intensely pleasurable release of physical and psychological tension. The *resolution* phase follows, during which the person returns to a state of relaxation. At this point, men enter a *refractory period* during which they are temporarily insensitive to sexual stimulation. Women are capable of immediately repeating the cycle if stimulation continues.

(A) CYCLE IN MEN

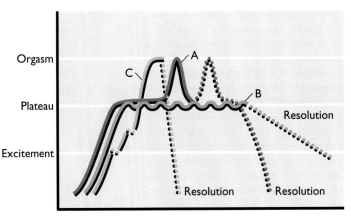

(B) CYCLE IN WOMEN

Source: Adapted from Masters & Johnson, 1966.

testosterone. Each sex hormone flows in the blood of *both* sexes, but males have relatively more androgens and women have relatively more estrogens and progestins. Figure 11.7 shows how feedback systems control the secretion of these hormones. Sex hormones have both organizational and activational effects. The *organizational effects* are permanent changes in the brain that alter the way a person thereafter responds to hormones. The *activational effects* are temporary behavioral changes that last only during the time a hormone level remains elevated.

The organizational effects of hormones occur around the time of birth, when certain brain areas are sculpted into a "male-like" or "female-like" pattern. These areas are thus described as *sexually dimorphic.* In rodents, for example, a sexually dimorphic area of the hypothalamus appears to underlie specific sexual behaviors. When these areas are destroyed in male gerbils, the animals can no longer copulate; yet damage to other nearby brain regions does not affect sexual behavior (Yahr & Jacobsen, 1994). Sexually dimorphic areas also exist in the human hypothalamus and other parts of the brain (Breedlove, 1994). For example, a hypothalamic area called BSTc is generally smaller in women than in men. Its possible role in some aspects of human sexuality was suggested by a recent study of *transsexual* men—genetic males who feel like women and who may request sex-change surgery in order to "be" female. The BSTc in these men was smaller than in other men; in fact, it was about the size usually seen in women (Zhou et al., 1995).

Rising levels of sex hormones during puberty have activational effects, resulting in increased sexual desire and interest in sexual behavior. Generally, estrogens stimulate females' sexual interest (Burleson, Gregory & Trevarthen, 1995). Androgens raise males' sexual interest (Davidson, Camargo & Smith, 1979), but they may also do so in females (Sherwin & Gelfand, 1987). The activational effects of hormones are evidenced, in part, by the reduced sexual motivation and behavior seen in people whose hormone-secret-

FIGURE 11.7

The Regulation of Sex Hormones

The secretion of sex hormones is controlled by feedback loops involving the hypothalamus, the pituitary gland, and the ovaries or testes. In males, high levels of testosterone reduce activity in the hypothalamus, which lowers secretion of luteinizing hormone (LH), which causes less testosterone to be secreted. This feedback system tends to keep the secretion of testosterone reasonably constant. In females, the feedback loops are more complex. High levels of estrogen increase hypothalamic activity, causing more LH to be secreted, which causes more estrogen to be secreted. At some point, the secretion of LH increases very rapidly, and a surge of hormone is released. This increased LH not only prompts the release of more estrogen but also causes the ovary to release an egg. Androgens fluctuate across the menstrual cycle just as estrogens and progestins do, and their levels peak around ovulation.

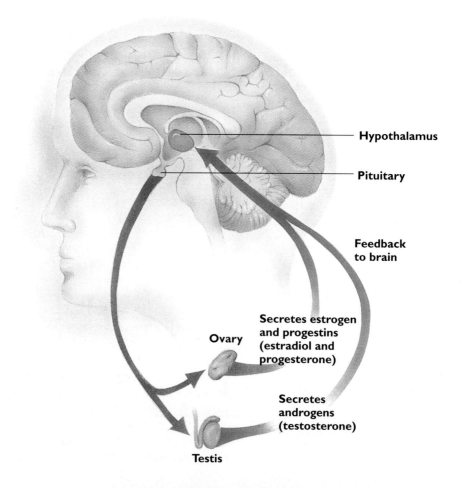

Hypothalamus

Pituitary

Feedback to brain

Secretes estrogen and progestins (estradiol and progesterone)

Ovary

Secretes androgens (testosterone)

Testis

ing ovaries or testes have been removed for medical reasons (Sherwin, Gelfand & Brender, 1985). Injections of hormones help restore these people's sexual interest and activity (Sherwin, Gelfand & Brender, 1985).

Generally, hormones affect sexual *desire,* not the physical *ability* to have sex (Wallen & Lovejoy, 1993). This fact may explain why castration does not prevent sex crimes in male offenders. Men with low testosterone levels due to medical problems or castration show less sexual desire, but they still have erections in response to erotic stimuli (Kwan et al., 1983). Thus a sex offender treated with androgen antagonists or castration would be less likely to *seek out* sex, but he would still respond as before to his favorite sexual stimuli (Wallen & Lovejoy, 1993).

Social and Cultural Factors in Sexuality

In humans, sexuality is profoundly shaped by a lifetime of learning and thinking that modifies the biological "raw materials" provided by hormones. For example, children learn some of their sexual attitudes and behaviors as part of the development of gender roles, as described in Chapter 12. The specific attitudes and behaviors learned depend partly on the nature of gender roles in their culture. One survey of the sexual experiences of more than 1,500 heterosexual college students in the United States, Japan, and Russia found numerous cross-cultural differences in the ways that men and women behave in sexual situations (Sprecher et al., 1994). As just one notable example, consider the finding that more women than men in the United States said they had consented to sex when they did not really want it; in both Russia and Japan, men and women were about equally likely to have had this experience.

Sexual behavior is also shaped by other sociocultural forces. In the United States, for example, concern over transmission of the AIDS virus during sex has prompted mass media campaigns and school-based educational programs to encourage sexual abstinence prior to marriage or "safe sex" using condoms. These efforts seem to be shaping young people's sexual attitudes and practices. At the beginning of one sex education program, only 36 percent of 1,800 students in grades seven through ten thought premarital sex was a bad idea and only 35 percent saw many benefits in premarital abstinence from sex. By the end of the semester-long program, these figures had risen to 66 percent and 58 percent, respectively (Eisenman, 1994). Another survey of 1,100 adolescents and young adults in the United States found that, prior to 1985, first-time heterosexual intercourse seldom included use of a condom or other contraceptive. With growing AIDS awareness since 1985, however, condom use had become very common in first-time heterosexual intercourse (Leigh, Schafer & Temple, 1995).

Sexual Orientation

Human sexual activity is most often **heterosexual,** involving members of the opposite sex. When sexual behavior is directed toward a member of one's own sex, it is called **homosexual.** People who engage in sexual activities with partners of both sexes are described as **bisexual.** Whether you engage in sexual activities with members of your own sex, the opposite sex, or both is one part of your *sexual orientation.*

In many cultures, heterosexuality has long been regarded as a moral norm, and homosexuality seen as a disease, a mental disorder, or even a crime (Hooker, 1993). Attempts to alter the sexual orientation of homosexuals—using psychotherapy, brain surgery, or electric shock—were usually ineffective (Haldeman, 1994). In 1973 the American Psychiatric Association dropped homosexuality from the *Diagnostic and Statistical Manual of Mental Disorders,* thus ending its official status as a form of psychopathology.

Nevertheless, many people still view homosexuality as repugnant and immoral. Because homosexuals and bisexuals are often the victims of discrimination and even hate crimes, many are reluctant to let their sexual orientation be known (Herek & Berrill, 1992; Rothblum, 1994). It is difficult, therefore, to obtain an accurate picture of the mix of heterosexual, homosexual, and bisexual orientations in a population. In the Chicago sex survey mentioned earlier, 1.4 percent of women and 2.8 percent of men

A COMMITTED RELATIONSHIP
Behavioral genetics research employing the twin study approach suggests that homosexuality might be genetically influenced. Richard Pillard, an author of one study of this issue, had personal reasons for suspecting this might be the case. He is gay, as is his brother and sister. He suspects that his father was gay, and one of his three daughters is bisexual (Burr, 1993).

identified themselves as exclusively homosexual (Laumann et al., 1994). However, the Chicago survey's face-to-face interviews did not allow respondents to give anonymous answers to questions about sexual orientation. Some researchers suggest that if anonymous responses to those questions had been permitted, the prevalence figures for homosexual and bisexual orientations would have been higher (Bullough, 1995). In fact, studies that have allowed anonymous responding estimate the percentage of homosexual people in the United States and elsewhere at between 6 and 20 percent (Fay et al., 1989; Rogers & Turner, 1991; Sell, Wells & Wypij, 1995).

The question of where sexual orientation comes from is a topic of intense debate in scientific circles, on talk shows, and in everyday conversation.

THINKING CRITICALLY

Do Genes Determine Sexual Orientation?

What am I being asked to believe or accept?

One point of view suggests that genes dictate sexual orientation. According to this view, we do not learn a sexual orientation but, rather, are born with it.

What evidence is available to support the assertion?

Implanting certain genetic material into male fruit flies causes them to approach male instead of female flies for sex (Ferveur, Stortkuhl & Stocker, 1995). A growing body of evidence from research in behavioral genetics (see Chapter 2) suggests that genes might influence sexual orientation in humans as well (Pillard & Bailey, 1995). One study examined pairs of monozygotic male twins (whose genes are identical), nonidentical twin pairs (whose genes are no more alike than those of any brothers), and pairs of adopted brothers (who are genetically unrelated). To participate in this study, at least one brother in each pair had to be homosexual. As it turned out, the other brother was also homosexual or bisexual in 52 percent of the identical-twin pairs, but in only 22 percent of the nonidentical pairs and in just 11 percent of the adoptive pairs (Bailey & Pillard, 1991). Similar findings have been reported for male identical twins raised apart; in such cases, a shared sexual orientation cannot be attributed to the effects of a shared environment (Whitam et al., 1993). The few available studies of female sexual orientation have yielded similar results (Bailey & Benishay, 1993).

Other evidence for the role of biological factors in sexual orientation comes from research on the impact of sex hormones. In adults, differences in the level of these hormones is not generally associated with differences in sexual orientation. However, hormonal differences during prenatal development might be involved in the shaping of sexual orientation. For example, women who had been exposed to high levels of androgens during their fetal development are much more likely to become lesbians than their sisters who were not similarly exposed (Money, Schwartz & Lewis, 1984; Meyer et al., 1995). In animals, such hormonal influences alter the structure of the hypothalamus, a brain region known to underlie some aspects of sexual functioning (Swaab & Hofman, 1995). In humans, hormones may likewise be responsible for anatomical differences in the hypothalamus that are seen not only in males versus females but in homosexual versus heterosexual men as well (Swaab & Hofman, 1990; LeVay, 1991). The anterior commissure, an area near the hypothalamus, also appears to differ in people with differing sexual orientations (Allen & Gorski, 1992; Gladue, 1994).

Finally, a biological basis for sexual orientation is suggested by the relatively weak effects of the environment on sexual orientation. For example, the sexual orientation of children's caregivers has little or no effect on those children's own orientation. Several studies have shown that children adopted by homosexual parents are no more or less likely to display a homosexual orientation than are children raised by heterosexual parents (Bailey et al., 1995; Gottman, 1989; Tasker & Golombok, 1995). Also, during the time that homosexuality was officially considered an illness, no successful treatment or other environmental "cure" was ever found (Haldeman, 1994).

Are there alternative ways of interpreting the evidence?

Correlations between genetics and sexual orientation are, like all correlational data, open to alternative interpretations. As described in Chapter 2, a correlation describes the strength and direction of the relationship between two variables, but it does not guarantee that one variable is actually influencing the other. Consider again the data showing that brothers who shared the most genes were also most likely to share a homosexual orientation. It is possible that what they shared was not a gene for homosexuality but, rather, a set of genes that influenced their activity level, emotionality, aggressiveness, or other general aspects of temperament or personality (see Chapters 12 and 14). It could have been these characteristics, and other people's reactions to them, that increased the likelihood of a particular sexual orientation. In other words, sexual orientation could arise as a *reaction* to the way people respond to a genetically determined, but nonsexual, aspect of personality. The influence of prenatal hormone levels could also influence sexual orientation by shaping aggressiveness or other nonsexual aspects of behavior.

It is also important to look at behavioral genetics evidence for what it can tell us about the role of *environmental* factors in sexual orientation. When we read a study showing that, 52 percent of the time, both members of identical twin pairs have a homosexual or bisexual orientation, it is easy to ignore the fact that the orientation of the twin pair members was *different* in nearly half the cases. Viewed in this way, the results suggest that genes do not tell the entire story of sexual orientation.

In other words, even if sexual orientation has a biological base, it is probably not determined by unlearned, genetic forces alone. As described in Chapter 3, the bodies we inherit are quite responsive to environmental input; the behaviors we engage in and the environmental experiences we have often result in physical changes in the brain and elsewhere (Wang et al., 1995). For example, physical changes occur in the brain's synapses as we form new memories (see Chapter 8). Thus, differences in the brains of people with differing sexual orientations could be the effect, not the cause, of their behavior or experiences.

[handwritten margin note: children of gay parents — don't become gay as well.]

[handwritten margin note: only looking at 52% that are and NOT the 48% that isn't.]

What additional evidence would help to evaluate the alternatives?

Much more evidence is needed regarding the extent to which genetic characteristics directly determine *any* sexual orientation, as well as the extent to which genetics shape physical and psychological characteristics that lead to the social construction of various sexual orientations. In studying this issue, researchers need to learn more not only about the genetic characteristics of people with different sexual orientations but also about their mental and behavioral styles. Are there personality characteristics associated with different sexual orientations? If so, do those characteristics have a strong genetic component? To what extent are heterosexuals, bisexuals, and homosexuals similar—and to what extent are they different—in terms of cognitive styles, biases, coping skills, developmental histories, and the like?

The more we learn about sexual orientation generally, the easier it will be to interpret data relating to its origins; but even defining sexual orientation is not simple. Alfred Kinsey and his colleagues (1948) viewed sexual orientation as occurring along a continuum rather than falling into a few discrete categories. Should a man who identifies himself as gay be considered bisexual because he occasionally has heterosexual daydreams? What sexual orientation label would be appropriate for a forty-year-old woman who experienced a few lesbian encounters in her teens but has engaged in exclusively heterosexual sex since then? Progress in understanding the origins of sexual orientation would be enhanced by a generally accepted system for describing and defining what is meant by sexual orientation.

or perimental.

What conclusions are most reasonable?

Given the antagonism and physical danger often faced by people with nonheterosexual orientations (Van de Ven, 1994), it seems unlikely that a homosexual or bisexual identity is entirely a matter of choice. Indeed, much of the evidence reviewed suggests that our sexual orientation chooses *us,* rather than the other way around. Given this evidence, a reasonable hypothesis is that genetic factors, probably operating via prenatal hormones, create differences in the brains of people with different sexual orientations. Even if this hypothesis is correct, however, the manner in which a person expresses a genetically influenced sexual orientation will be profoundly shaped by what that person learns through social and cultural experiences (Bancroft, 1994). In short, sexual orientation most likely results from the complex interplay of both genetic and nongenetic mechanisms—both nature and nurture. Extremists who characterize sexual orientation as either all "in the genes" or entirely a matter of choice are probably wrong.

Sexual Dysfunctions

The same biological, social, and psychological factors that shape human sexual behavior can also result in **sexual dysfunctions,** problems in a person's desire for or ability to have satisfying sexual activity. Fortunately, most of these problems respond to psychotherapy, drugs, or both (de Silva, 1994). For men, a common problem is *erectile disorder* (once called impotence), a persistent inability to have or maintain an erection adequate for sex. Physical causes—such as fatigue, diabetes, hypertension, and alcohol or other drugs—account for some cases, but psychological causes such as anxiety are also common (Everaerd & Laan, 1994). As its name implies, *premature ejaculation* is a recurring tendency to ejaculate during sex sooner than the man or his partner desires. Most men experience episodes of at least one of these problems at some point in their lives, but such episodes are considered dysfunctions only if they become a distressing obstacle to sexual functioning (American Psychiatric Association, 1994).

For women, the most common sexual dysfunction is *arousal disorder* (once called frigidity), which involves infrequent, or absent orgasms. Arousal disorder can stem from inadequate genital stimulation or insufficient vaginal lubrication (Mansfield, Voda & Koch, 1995), but it is most often tied to psychological factors such as guilt, self-consciousness, or low self-esteem (Davidson & Moore, 1994). Problems in reaching orgasm are also associated with difficulties in the emotional qualities of the romantic relationship (Kaplan, 1979).

ACHIEVEMENT MOTIVATION

This sentence was written at 6 A.M. on a beautiful Sunday in June. Why would someone get up that early to work on a weekend? Why do people take their work seriously and try to do the best that they can? People work hard partly due to *extrinsic motivation,* a desire for external rewards such as money. But work and other human behaviors also reflect *intrinsic motivation,* a desire to attain internal satisfaction.

The next time you visit someone's home or office, look at the mementos displayed there. You may see framed diplomas and awards, trophies and ribbons, pictures of memorable personal events, and photos of children and grandchildren. These badges of achievement affirm that a person has accomplished tasks that merit approval or establish worth. Much of human behavior is motivated by a desire for approval, admiration, and achievement—in short, for *esteem*—from others and from themselves. In this section, we examine two of the most common avenues to esteem: achievement in general and a job in particular.

Need for Achievement

Many athletes who hold world records still train intensely; many people who have built multimillion-dollar businesses still work fourteen-hour days. What motivates such people?

A possible answer is a motive called **need achievement** (Murray, 1938). People with a high need for achievement seek to master tasks—be they sports, business ventures, intellectual puzzles, or artistic creations—and feel intense satisfaction from doing so. They exert strenuous efforts in striving for excellence, enjoy themselves in the process, and take great pride in achieving at a high level.

Individual Differences   How do people with strong achievement motivation differ from others? To find out, researchers gave children a test to measure their need for achievement (Figure 11.8 shows a test for adults) and then asked them to play a ring-toss game. Children scoring low on the need-achievement test usually stood so close to or so far away from the ring-toss target that they either could not fail or could not succeed. In contrast, children scoring high on the need-achievement test stood at a moderate distance from the target, making the game challenging but not impossible (McClelland, 1958).

These and other experiments suggest that people with high achievement needs tend to set challenging—but realistic—goals. They actively seek success, take risks as needed, and are intensely satisfied with success. But if they feel they have tried their best, people with high achievement motivation are not too upset by failure. Those with low achievement motivation also like to succeed, but instead of joy, success tends to bring them relief at having avoided failure (Atkinson & Birch, 1978).

People with strong achievement motivation tend to be preoccupied with their performance and level of ability (Harackiewicz & Elliot, 1993). They select tasks with clear outcomes, and they prefer feedback from a harsh but competent critic rather than from one who is friendlier but less competent (Klich & Feldman, 1992). They like to struggle with a problem rather than get help, they can wait for delayed rewards, and they make careful plans for the future (Raynor, 1970). In contrast, people who are less motivated to achieve are less likely to seek or enjoy feedback, and they tend to quit in response to failure (Weiner, 1980).

Development of Achievement Motivation   Achievement motivation tends to be learned in early childhood, especially from parents. For example, in one study young boys were given a very hard task at which they were sure to fail. Fathers whose sons scored low on achievement motivation tests often became annoyed as they watched

Source: Murray, 1971.

"Maybe they didn't try hard enough."

high scoring tests of achievement motivation

their boys, discouraged them from continuing, and interfered or even completed the task themselves (Rosen & D'Andrade, 1959). A different pattern of behavior emerged among parents of children who scored high on tests of achievement motivation. Such parents tended to (1) encourage the child to try difficult tasks, especially new ones; (2) give praise and other rewards for success; (3) encourage the child to find ways to succeed rather than merely complaining about failure; and (4) prompt the child to go on to the next, more difficult challenge (McClelland, 1985).

Cultural influences also affect achievement motivation. For example, subtle messages about a culture's view of the importance of achievement often appear in the books children read and the stories they hear. Does the story's main character work hard and overcome obstacles (creating expectations of a payoff for persistence) or loaf and then win the lottery (suggesting that rewards come randomly regardless of effort)? If the main character succeeds, is this outcome the result of personal initiative (typical of an individualist culture) or of ties to a cooperative and supportive group (typical of a collectivist culture)? Such themes appear to act as blueprints for reaching the goals one should aspire to. Not surprisingly, then, ideas about achievement motivation differ from culture to culture. In one study, for example, individuals from Saudi Arabia and from the United States were asked to comment on short stories describing people succeeding at various tasks. Saudis tended to see the people in the stories as having succeeded because of the help they got from others, while Americans tended to attribute success to the internal characteristics of each story's main character (Zahrani & Kaplowitz, 1993; for another example, see the Focus on Research Methods section of Chapter 17).

Achievement motivation can be increased even among people whose cultural training had not fostered it in childhood (McClelland, 1985). In one study, high school and college students with low achievement motivation were helped to develop fantasies about their own success. They imagined setting goals that were difficult but not impossible. Then they imagined themselves concentrating on breaking a complex problem into small, manageable steps. They fantasized about working hard, failing but not being discouraged, continuing to work, and finally feeling elated at success. Afterward, the students' grades and academic success improved, suggesting an increase in their achievement motivation (McClelland, 1985).

Gender Differences in Achievement Motivation

The behavior of women with high achievement motivation varies more than that of men with equally high achievement motivation. In particular, these women do not always set challenging goals, and they do not always persist when faced with failure

(Dweck, 1986). In fact, some withdraw from and even avoid situations in which their achievement could be evaluated.

Gender differences in achievement motivation emerge early in life, perhaps because of differences in the ways that boys and girls learn to think of themselves and their performance (Burns & Seligman, 1989). Females are more likely than males to attribute failure on school-related tasks to lack of ability, and they tend to begin doing so at an early age (Dweck & Gilliard, 1975). Many persist in seeing themselves as incompetent even when grades and other objective evidence show that they excel (Licht & Dweck, 1984).

Girls' readiness to deprecate their own abilities in school may stem in part from the performance feedback they receive from their grade-school teachers. Observational studies show that both boys and girls are often told what they did wrong and what they should do instead. But boys are more likely than girls to also be told that they are not concentrating or are being careless. Thus, boys learn to see failure as due to lack of effort or some other situational factor. In contrast, the feedback that girls hear leads them to attribute failure to lack of ability (Dweck et al., 1978). Support for this view comes from a study in which researchers arranged for girls with high achievement motivation to receive the type of criticism normally directed toward boys. The girls' behavior became more like that of boys with high achievement motivation: They adopted challenging goals, worked hard, and persisted in the face of failure (Dweck, 1986).

In some cultures, gender-role stereotypes discourage achievement motivation in women. These stereotypes may portray the pursuit of excellence and mastery as "unfeminine" and threatening to men. As a result, some women in these cultures may hide successes or act in ways that undermine their chances of success—a pattern called *fear of success* (Horner, 1970; Santucci, Terzian & Kayson, 1989). Others may find satisfaction in the instrinsic rewards of a job well done, yet limit their achievements by avoiding competition with men for power (Offerman & Beil, 1992). In addition, teachers and parents may communicate gender-role stereotypes about achievement, including ideas about "appropriate" areas of achievement for boys and girls. For example, if boys are expected to be better at math and girls to be better at reading, boys may receive more help and encouragement in math than girls do (Leinhardt, Seewald & Engel, 1979). Such differential assistance may be one reason why, by the time they enter high school, girls don't do as well as boys in math (Hyde, Fennema & Lamon, 1990). Sadly, some of the same gender-based treatments appear even among university professors in their dealings with students—and other professors (Hall & Sandler, 1982; Wiley & Crittenden, 1992).

Achievement and Success in the Workplace

In the workplace, there is usually less concern with employees' general level of need achievement than with their motivation to work hard during business hours. Indeed, employers tend to set up jobs in accordance with their ideas about how intrinsic and extrinsic motivation combine to shape employees' performance (Riggio, 1989). Those who see workers as lazy, untrustworthy, ambitionless creatures tend to offer highly structured, heavily supervised jobs that give employees little say in deciding what to do or how to do it. Such employers assume that workers are motivated mainly by extrinsic rewards—money, in particular. They are thus often surprised when, in spite of good pay and benefits, employees express dissatisfaction with their jobs and show little motivation to work hard (Amabile et al., 1994; Rosen, 1991).

If good pay and benefits alone do not bring job satisfaction and the desire to excel on the job, what does? Research suggests that low worker motivation in Western cultures comes largely from the feeling of having little or no control over the work environment (Deci, Connell & Ryan, 1987; Rosen, 1991). Compared with those in rigidly structured jobs, workers tend to be more satisfied and productive if they are (1) encouraged to participate in decisions about how work should be done; (2) given problems to solve, without being told how to solve them; (3) taught more than one skill; (4) given individual responsibility; and (5) given public recognition, not just money, for good performance.

PROMOTING TEAMWORK Companies in the United States have followed Japanese examples in redesigning jobs to enhance responsibility and flexibility. The goal is to increase both employee productivity and job satisfaction by having employees work in teams that are responsible for solving production problems and making decisions about how best to do the job. Team members are publically recognized for outstanding work and part of their pay depends on the quality (not just number) of their products and on the profitability of the whole company.

Allowing people to set and achieve clear goals is one way to increase both job performance and job satisfaction (Abramis, 1994; Schneider, 1985). Goals that most effectively maintain work motivation have three features (Katzell & Thompson, 1990). First, they are personally meaningful. When a memo from a faceless administrator tells employees that their goal should be to increase production, they tend to feel put upon and not particularly motivated to meet the goal. Second, effective goals are specific and concrete. The goal of "doing better" is usually not a strong motivator. A specific target, such as increasing sales by 10 percent, is a far more motivating goal. It is there for all to see, and whether the goal has been reached is easily determined. Finally, goals are most effective if management supports the workers' own goal-setting, offers special rewards for reaching goals, and gives encouragement after failure.

specific goals →

In short, motivating jobs offer personal challenges, independence, and both intrinsic and extrinsic rewards. They provide enough satisfaction for people to feel excitement and pleasure in working hard. For employers, meanwhile, the rewards are more productivity, less absenteeism, and lower turnover (Ilgen & Klein, 1989).

RELATIONS AND CONFLICTS AMONG MOTIVES

Suppose you need to study for a test, want to return a friend's phone call, and are also very hungry. Any of these motives might guide your behavior in the next five minutes. What determines which one will?

Maslow's Hierarchy

Abraham Maslow (1970) suggested that human behavior is influenced by a hierarchy of five classes of needs, or motives (see Figure 11.9). Needs at the lowest level of the hierarchy, he said, must be at least partially satisfied before people can be motivated by higher-level goals. From the bottom to the top of Maslow's hierarchy these five motives are as follows:

1. *Biological,* such as food, water, oxygen, activity, and sleep.

2. *Safety,* such as being cared for as a child and having a secure income as an adult.

3. *Belongingness* and *love,* such as being part of various social groups and participating in affectionate sexual and nonsexual relationships.

4. *Esteem,* being respected as a useful, honorable individual.

5. *Self-actualization,* which means becoming all that one is capable of. People motivated by this need explore and enhance relationships with others, follow interests for

FIGURE 11.9

Maslow's Hierarchy of Motives

Abraham Maslow saw motives as organized in a hierarchy in which motives at lower levels take precedence over those at higher levels. According to this view, self-actualization is the essence of mental health; but Maslow recognized that only rare individuals, such as Mother Teresa or Dr. Martin Luther King, Jr., approach full self-actualization.

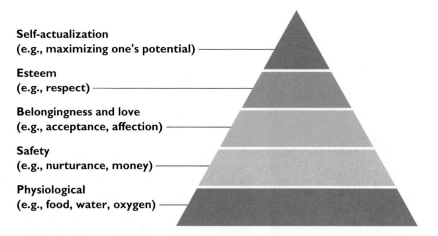

Self-actualization
(e.g., maximizing one's potential)

Esteem
(e.g., respect)

Belongingness and love
(e.g., acceptance, affection)

Safety
(e.g., nurturance, money)

Physiological
(e.g., food, water, oxygen)

Source: Adapted from Maslow, 1943.

intrinsic pleasure rather than status or esteem, and are concerned with issues affecting all people, not just themselves.

In general, research suggests that motives lower in Maslow's hierarchy do take precedence over those higher in the hierarchy (Baumeister & Leary, 1995; Ebersole & De Vore, 1995). But Maslow's system has been criticized as too simplistic (Neher, 1991). People do not always act according to his hierarchy; even when lower-level needs are unmet, some people continue to be motivated by higher-level needs. The motivation of people deeply involved in political and moral causes, for example, seems to defy Maslow's hierarchy; in 1981, Bobby Sand and eight others starved themselves to death protesting British rule in Northern Ireland. Nevertheless, Maslow's classification is useful for thinking about the relationships among human motives.

LINKAGES: CONFLICTING MOTIVES AND STRESS

Can motivational conflicts cause stress?

Maslow's hierarchy suggests that differing motives can sometimes conflict. What is the result? Imagine that, while alone and bored on a Saturday night, you think about going to a convenience store for a snack. What are your motives? Hunger might prompt you to go out, as might the prospect of the increased arousal and decreased boredom that a shopping trip will provide. Even sexual motivation might be involved, as you consider the chances of meeting someone exciting in the snack-food aisle. But safety-related motives may give you pause—What if you get mugged? Even an esteem motive might come into play, leading you to avoid being seen alone on a Saturday night.

These are just a few motives that may shape a trivial decision. When the decision is important, the number and strength of motivational pushes and pulls is often greater, creating more internal conflict and acting as a source of stress. Four basic types of motivational conflict have been identified (Miller, 1959):

1. *Approach-approach conflicts*   When a person must choose only one of two desirable activities—say, going to a movie or to a play—an *approach-approach conflict* exists. As the importance of the choice increases, so does the difficulty of making it.

2. *Avoidance-avoidance conflicts*   An *avoidance-avoidance conflict* arises when a person must select one of two undesirable alternatives. Someone forced either to sell the family farm or to declare bankruptcy faces an avoidance-avoidance conflict. Such conflicts are very difficult to resolve and often create intense emotions.

3. *Approach-avoidance conflicts*   If someone you can't stand has tickets to your favorite group's sold-out concert and invites you to come along, what would you do? When a single event or activity has both attractive and unattractive features, an *approach-avoidance conflict* is created. Conflicts of this type are also difficult to resolve and often result in long periods of indecision.

4. *Multiple approach-avoidance conflicts*   Suppose you must choose between two jobs. One offers a high salary with a well-known company, but requires long hours and relocation to a miserable climate. The other boasts good advancement opportunities, fringe benefits, and a better climate, but offers low pay and an unpredictable work schedule. This is an example of a *multiple approach-avoidance conflict,* in which two or more alternatives each have both positive and negative features. Such conflicts are difficult to resolve partly because, as discussed in the decision-making section of Chapter 9, the attributes of each option are often difficult to compare. For example, how many dollars a year does it take to compensate you for living in a bad climate?

Each of these conflicts may create stress, a topic described at length in Chapter 13. Most people in the midst of motivational conflicts are tense, irritable, and particularly vulnerable to physical and psychological problems. These reactions are especially likely when the correct choices are not obvious, when varying motives have approximately equal strength, and when a choice can have serious consequences (as in decisions to marry, to divorce, or to approve disconnection of a relative's life-support system). Resolution of such conflicts may take time or may be made impulsively and thoughtlessly, if only to end the discomfort of uncertainty. Even after a conflict is resolved, stress responses may continue in the form of anxiety about the wisdom of the decision or guilt over bad choices. These and other consequences of conflicting motives can even lead to depression or other serious disorders.

Opponent Processes, Motivation, and Emotion

Sometimes, people are motivated to engage in behaviors that produce effects that may be in opposition to one another. People who ride roller coasters, for example, often say that the experience gives rise to fear, but also to thrilling excitement. How do they decide whether or not to ride the coaster again? One answer lies in the changing value of incentives and the regulation of arousal described in Richard Solomon's *opponent-process theory*, which is discussed in the Linkages section of Chapter 7, on learning (Solomon & Corbit, 1974). As noted there, opponent-process theory is based on two assumptions. The first is that any reaction to a stimulus is automatically followed by an opposite reaction, called the opponent process. For example, being startled by a sudden sound is typically followed by relaxation and relief. Second, after repeated exposure to the same stimulus, the initial reaction weakens, and the opponent process becomes quicker and stronger.

Research on opponent-process theory has revealed a predictable pattern of emotional changes that helps explain some people's motivation to repeatedly engage in arousing but fearsome activities, such as skydiving, bungee-jumping, or roller-coaster riding. Prior to the first several episodes, people usually experience stark terror, followed by intense relief. With more experience, however, the terror becomes mild anxiety, and what had been relief grows to a euphoria that can appear *during* the activity (Solomon, 1980). As a result, says Solomon, some people's motivation to pursue such activities can become a virtual addiction.

The emotions associated with motivational conflicts and with the operation of opponent processes provide just two examples of the intimate links between human motivation and emotion. Motivation can intensify emotion, as when a normally timid person's hunger results in an angry protest over a late pizza delivery. But emotions can also create motivation. Happiness, for example, is an emotion that people want to feel, so they engage in whatever behaviors—studying, artwork, beachcombing—they think will achieve it. Similarly, as an emotion that most people want to avoid, anxiety prompts many behaviors, from leaving the scene of an accident to avoiding poisonous snakes. In the next section of this chapter, we take a closer look at emotions.

THE NATURE OF EMOTION

Everyone seems to agree that joy, sorrow, anger, fear, love, and hate are emotions, but it is hard to identify the shared features that make these experiences emotions rather than, say, thoughts or impulses. In fact, some cultures see emotion and thought as the same thing. The Chewong of Malaysia, for example, consider the liver the seat of both what we call thoughts and feelings (Russell, 1991).

Defining Characteristics

Most psychologists in Western cultures tend to see emotions as organized psychological and physiological reactions to changes in our relationship to the world. These reactions are partly subjective experiences and partly objectively measurable patterns of behavior and physiological arousal. The subjective experience of emotion has several characteristics:

1. Emotion is usually *transitory*; it tends to have a relatively clear beginning and end, and a relatively short duration. Moods, by contrast, tend to last longer.

2. Emotional experience has *valence,* which means it is either positive or negative.

WINNERS AND LOSERS Emotional experiences depend in part on our interpretation of situations and how those situations relate to our goals. The stimulus for these drastically different emotional reactions was the same—namely, the announcement of the winners of a cheerleading contest. Each woman's emotional experience following this stimulus depended on whether she perceived the situation as making her a winner or a loser.

3. Emotional experience is elicited partly by a *cognitive appraisal* of how a situation relates to your goals. The same event can elicit very different emotions depending on the way you interpret what the event means. An exam score of 75 percent may excite you if your previous score had been 50 percent, but it may upset you if you had never before scored below 90 percent.

4. Emotional experience *alters thought processes,* often by directing attention toward some things and away from others. The anguish of parents whose child is killed by a drunken driver, for example, may prompt them to alter their perception of the importance of drunk-driving laws.

5. Emotional experience *elicits an action tendency,* a motivation to behave in certain ways. The grieving parents' anger, for example, may motivate them to harm the driver or to work for stronger penalties for drunk driving.

6. Emotional experiences are *passions* that happen to you, usually without willful intent. You exert some control over emotions inasmuch as they depend partly on how you interpret situations. If you interpret an emotion as fear, for example, your experience of fear may be amplified as a result. Still, you cannot decide to experience joy or sorrow; instead, you "fall in love" or are "overcome by grief." Emotional experiences, much like personality traits, have a different relation to the self than conscious cognitions.

The subjective aspects of emotions are, therefore, experiences both *triggered by* the thinking self and felt as *happening to* the self. They reveal an individual as both agent and object, both I and me, both the controller of thoughts and the recipient of passions. The extent to which we are "victims" of our passions versus rational designers of our emotions is a central dilemma of human existence, as much a subject of literature as of psychology.

Objective aspects of emotion include learned and innate *expressive displays* and *physiological responses.* Expressive displays—a smile, a frown—communicate feelings to others. Physiological responses—changes in heart rate, for example—provide biological adjustments needed to perform the action tendencies generated by emotional experience. If you throw a temper tantrum at the object of your anger, for example, your heart must deliver additional oxygen and fuel to your muscles.

In summary, an **emotion** is a transitory, valenced experience that is felt with some intensity as happening to the self, generated in part by a cognitive appraisal of situations, and accompanied by both learned and innate physical responses. Through emotion, people communicate their internal states and intentions to others, but emotion also functions to direct and energize a person's own thoughts and actions. Emotion often disrupts thought and behavior, but it also triggers and guides cognitions and organizes, motivates, and sustains behavior and social relations.

The Biology of Emotion

The role of biology in emotion is seen in mechanisms of the central nervous system and the autonomic nervous system. In the *central nervous system,* specific brain areas are involved in the generation of emotions as well as in our experience of those emotions. The *autonomic nervous system* gives rise to many of the physiological changes associated with emotional arousal.

Brain Mechanisms Although many questions remain, researchers have described three basic features of the brain's control of emotion. First, it appears that activity in the *limbic system,* especially in the *amygdala,* is central to various aspects of emotion (Young et al., 1995; Lang, 1995; LeDoux, 1995; see also Figure 11.10). Evidence for this assertion comes partly from animal research in which the functioning of the amygdala was disrupted by a drug injected directly into it. After receiving the injection, the animals were unable to associate an unconditioned *emotional* response—fear—with a stimulus that had been repeatedly paired with electric shock. The injection did not disrupt *all* learning, however; the animals could still learn to associate a nonemotional unconditioned response—such as salivation—with a sound that had been repeatedly

FIGURE 11.10

Brain Regions Involved in Emotion

Incoming sensory information alerts the brain to an emotion-evoking situation. Most of the information goes through the thalamus; the cingulate cortex and hippocampus are involved in the interpretation of this sensory input. Output from these areas goes to the amygdala and hypothalamus, which control the autonomic nervous system via brainstem connections. There are also connections from the thalamus directly to the amygdala. The locus coeruleus is an area of the brainstem that causes both widespread arousal of cortical areas and changes in autonomic activity.

Frontal cortex
Basal ganglia
Thalamus
Hypothalamus
Pituitary

Cingulate cortex
Hippocampus
Amygdala
Sensory input
Locus coeruleus
Spinal cord

Activation of autonomic nervous system

paired with food (Davis et al., 1993). In people, too, disruptions in the amygdala appear to contribute to the emotional problems associated with certain kinds of brain damage or with psychological disorders such as schizophrenia (Aggleton, 1993). For example, victims of a disease that destroys only the amygdala are unable to judge other people's emotional state by looking at their facial expressions (Adolphs et al., 1994).

A second aspect of the brain's involvement in emotion is seen in its control over emotional and nonemotional facial expressions (Rinn, 1984). Take a moment to look in a mirror and put on your best fake smile. The voluntary facial movements you just made, like all voluntary movements, are controlled by the *pyramidal motor system*, a brain system that includes the motor cortex (see Figure 3.18 in Chapter 3). However, a smile that expresses genuine happiness is involuntary. That kind of smile, like the other facial movements associated with emotions, is governed by the *extrapyramidal motor system*, which depends on subcortical areas. Brain damage can disrupt either system (see Figures 11.11 and 11.12). Thus, people with pyramidal motor system damage show

FIGURE 11.11

Control of Voluntary and Emotional Facial Movements

This man has a tumor in his motor cortex that prevents him from voluntarily moving the muscles on the left side of his face. In the photograph at left he is trying to smile in response to a command from the examiner. He cannot smile on command, but he *can* smile with happiness, as the photograph at right shows, because the movements associated with genuine emotion are controlled by the extrapyramidal motor system.

normal facial expressions during genuine emotion, but cannot fake a smile. In contrast, people with damage to the extrapyramidal system can pose facial expressions at will, but remain straight-faced even when feeling genuine joy or profound sadness (Hopf, Muller & Hopf, 1992).

A third aspect of the brain's role in emotion is revealed by research on the differing contributions of its two cerebral hemispheres to the perception, experience, and expression of emotion. For example, after suffering damage to the right, but not the left, hemisphere, people no longer laugh at jokes—even though they can still understand the jokes' words, the logic (or illogic) underlying them, and the punch lines (Critchley, 1991). Further, when people are asked to name the emotions shown in slides of facial expressions, blood flow increases in the right hemisphere more than in the left hemisphere (Gur, Skolnic & Gur, 1994). People are also faster and more accurate at this emotion-naming task when the facial expressions are presented to the right hemisphere than when they are presented to the left (Hahdahl, Iversen & Jonsen, 1993). Finally, compared with normal people, depressed people display greater electrical activity in the right frontal cortex (Schaffer, Davidson & Saron, 1983) and perform more poorly on tasks that depend especially on the right hemisphere (Banich et al., 1992; Heller, Etienne & Miller, 1995).

Yet there is some debate about the relationship between hemispheric differences and emotion. Research has demonstrated that the right hemisphere is activated during many displays of emotion (Heller, 1993), including negative emotion. But some investigators argue that the *experiencing* of positive emotion depends on the left frontal cortex. For example, EEG recordings show that smiling during an experience of genuine

FIGURE 11.12

Separation of Emotional Experience from Emotional Expression

This woman has a neurological disease (amyotrophic lateral sclerosis) that causes involuntary nonemotional laughing. She reported that the laughter was painful and that she was struggling to suppress it.

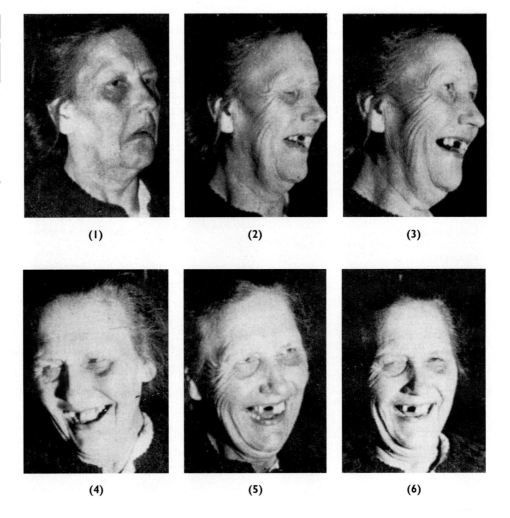

(1)   (2)   (3)

(4)   (5)   (6)

right hemisphere = emotion
left hemisphere = Action (express emotion)

positive emotion correlates with greater left frontal activity (Davidson et al., 1990). Generally, however, most other aspects of emotion—the *experiencing* of negative emotion, the *perception* of any emotion exhibited in faces or other stimuli, and the facial *expression* of any emotion—depend on the right hemisphere more than on the left.

If the right hemisphere is relatively dominant in emotion, which side of the face would you expect to be somewhat more involved in expressing emotion? If you said the left side, you are correct because, as described in Chapter 3, movements of each side of the body are controlled by the opposite side of the brain (Sackeim, Gur & Saucy, 1978).

Mechanisms of the Autonomic Nervous System   The autonomic nervous system (ANS) is involved in many of the physiological changes that accompany emotions (Vernet et al., 1995). If your hands get cold and clammy when you are nervous, it is because the ANS has increased perspiration and decreased the blood flow in your hands.

As described in Chapter 3, the ANS carries information between the brain and most organs of the body—the heart and blood vessels, the digestive system, and so on. Each of these organs has its own ongoing activity, but ANS input *modulates* this activity, increasing or decreasing it. By modulating the activity of organs, the ANS coordinates their functioning to meet the body's general needs and to prepare it for change (Porges, Doussard & Maita, 1995). If you are aroused to take action—to run to catch a bus, say—you need more glucose to fuel your muscles. The ANS frees needed energy by stimulating secretion of glucose-generating hormones and promoting blood flow to the muscles.

Figure 11.13 shows that the autonomic nervous system is organized into two divisions: the sympathetic nervous system and the parasympathetic nervous system.

FIGURE 11.13

The Autonomic Nervous System

Emotional responses involve activation of the autonomic nervous system, which includes sympathetic and parasympathetic subsystems. Which of the bodily responses depicted do you associate with emotional experiences?

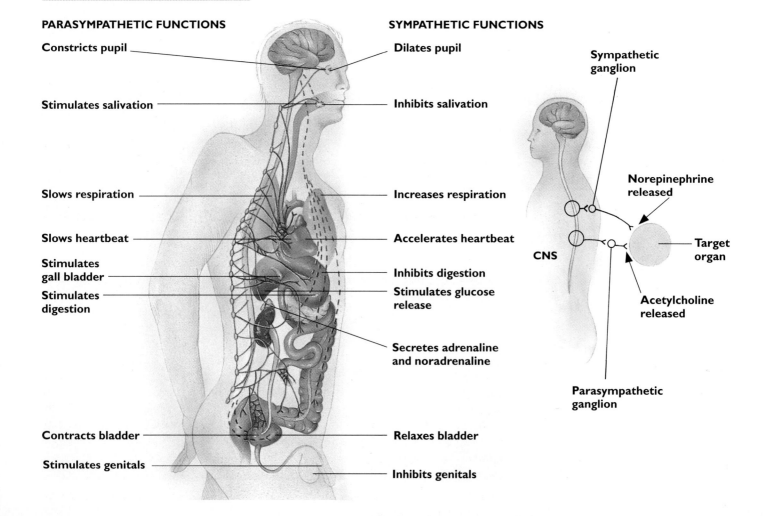

PARASYMPATHETIC FUNCTIONS

Constricts pupil

Stimulates salivation

Slows respiration

Slows heartbeat

Stimulates gall bladder

Stimulates digestion

Contracts bladder

Stimulates genitals

SYMPATHETIC FUNCTIONS

Dilates pupil

Inhibits salivation

Increases respiration

Accelerates heartbeat

Inhibits digestion

Stimulates glucose release

Secretes adrenaline and noradrenaline

Relaxes bladder

Inhibits genitals

Sympathetic ganglion

Norepinephrine released

CNS

Target organ

Acetylcholine released

Parasympathetic ganglion

Emotions can activate either of these divisions, both of which send axon fibers to each organ in the body. Generally, the sympathetic and parasympathetic fibers have opposite effects on these so-called target organs. Axons from the **parasympathetic system** release acetylcholine onto target organs, leading to activity related to the protection, nourishment, and growth of the body. For example, parasympathetic activity increases digestion by stimulating movement of the intestinal system, so that more nutrients are taken from food. Axons from the **sympathetic system** release norepinephrine onto target organs, helping to prepare the body for vigorous activity. When one part of the sympathetic system is stimulated, other parts are activated "in sympathy" with it (Gellhorn & Loofbourrow, 1963). For example, as described in Chapter 13, input from sympathetic neurons to the *adrenal medulla* causes that gland to dump norepinephrine and epinephrine into the bloodstream, thereby activating all sympathetic target organs (see Figure 13.3). The result is the **fight-or-flight syndrome,** a pattern of increased heart rate and blood pressure, rapid or irregular breathing, dilated pupils, perspiration, dry mouth, increased blood sugar, piloerection ("goose bumps"), and other changes that help prepare the body to combat or run from a threat.

The ANS is not directly connected to brain areas involved in consciousness, so sensory input about organ activity reaches the brain at a nonconscious level. Thus, you may hear your stomach grumble, but you can't actually feel it secrete acids. Similarly, you cannot consciously experience the brain mechanisms that alter the activity of your autonomic nervous system. This is why most people cannot exert direct, conscious control over blood pressure or other aspects of ANS activity. However, you can do things that have indirect effects on the ANS. For example, to arouse autonomic innervation of your sex organs, you might imagine an erotic situation. To raise your blood pressure, you might hold your breath or strain your muscles. And to lower your blood pressure, you might try the *biofeedback* methods described in Chapter 13.

THEORIES OF EMOTION

Are the physiological responses associated with emotion sufficient to produce an emotional experience, or are these responses simply by-products of an emotional experience that is created when we cognitively interpret events? In other words, is emotion in the heart, in the head, or both? Questions about the roles played by physiological and cognitive activity in the experience of emotion have been the focus of research for over a century—and have generated several important theories of emotion.

James's Theory

Suppose while walking in the woods you come upon a ferocious bear. Scared to death, you run for dear life. Do you run because you are afraid, or are you afraid because you run? The example and the question come from William James, who offered one of the first formal accounts of how physiological responses relate to emotional experience. James argued that you are afraid *because* you run. Your running and other physiological responses, he said, follow directly from your perception of the bear. Without some form of these responses, you would feel no fear because, said James, recognition of physiological responses *is* fear.

Presented in this simplified way, James's theory may sound preposterous. It defies common sense, which says that it would be silly to run from something unless you already fear it. James concluded otherwise after examining his own mental processes. He decided that once all physiological responses are stripped away, nothing remains of the experience of an emotion (James, 1890); hence emotion, he reasoned, is simply the result of experiencing a particular set of physiological responses. Because a similar view was offered by Carle Lange, a Danish physician, James's view is sometimes called the *James-Lange theory* of emotion.

Observing Peripheral Responses Figure 11.14 outlines the components of emotional experience, including those emphasized by James. First, a perception affects the cerebral cortex, said James;

1. **Sensation/perception**
   (It's a bear!)

2. **Cognitive interpretation**
   (That bear can kill me!)

3. **Activation of CNS
   and peripheral
   nervous system**

5. **Perception of
   peripheral responses**

4. **Peripheral responses**
   (e.g., increase in
   heart rate; change in
   facial expression)

6. **Cognitive
   interpretation of
   peripheral responses**

FIGURE 11.14

Components of Emotion

Emotion is associated with activity in the brain and spinal cord as well as with peripheral responses. Emotion theorists have argued about which of these components are essential for emotion. William James emphasized #5, the perception of peripheral responses, such as changes in heart rate, while Stanley Schachter emphasized #6, the cognitive interpretation and labeling of those peripheral responses. Walter Cannon believed that #3 was sufficient, that emotion could occur wholly in the central nervous system.

then quick as a flash, reflex currents pass down through their pre-ordained channels, alter the condition of muscle, skin, and viscus; and these alterations, perceived, like the original object, in as many portions of the cortex, combine with it in consciousness and transform it from an object-simply-apprehended into an object-emotionally-felt. (James, 1890, p. 759)

In other words, the brain interprets a situation and automatically directs a particular set of peripheral physiological changes—a palpitating heart, sinking stomach, facial grimace, perspiration, and certain patterns of blood flow. We are not conscious of the process, said James, until we become aware of these bodily changes; at that point, we experience an emotion. Thus, James's theory holds that reflexive peripheral responses precede the subjective experience of emotion, and that each particular emotion is created by a particular pattern of physiological responses.

Notice that, according to James's view, there is no emotional experience generated by activity in the brain alone, no special "emotion center" in the brain where the firing of neurons creates a direct experience of emotion. If this theory is accurate, it might account for the difficulty we sometimes have in knowing our true feelings: We must figure out what emotions we feel by perceiving subtle differences in specific physiological response patterns.

Evaluating James's Theory   In the English language there are more than 500 labels for emotions (Averill, 1980). Does a distinctly different pattern of physiological activity precede each of these emotions? According to James's theory, for example, fear would follow from one pattern of bodily responses, and anger would follow from a different pattern.

Research shows that certain emotional states are indeed associated with different patterns of autonomic changes. For example, blood flow to the hands and feet increases in association with anger and declines in association with fear (Levenson, Ekman &

Friesen, 1990). Thus, fear involves "cold feet"; anger does not. A pattern of activity associated with disgust includes increased muscle activity, but no change in heart rate. Even when people mentally "relive" different kinds of emotional experiences, they show different patterns of autonomic activity (Ekman, Levenson & Friesen, 1983). Note, too, that emotion-specific patterns of physiological activity have been found in widely different cultures (Levenson et al., 1992).

Furthermore, different patterns of autonomic activity are closely tied to specific emotional facial expressions, and vice versa (Ekman, 1993). When research subjects were told to make certain facial movements, various facial configurations led to autonomic changes resembling those normally accompanying emotion (Ekman, Levenson & Friesen, 1983; see also Figures 11.15 and 11.16). The patterns of autonomic activity produced by expressions of fear, anger, disgust, sadness, and happiness could be distinguished from each other. Also, almost all subjects reported feeling the emotion associated with the expression they had created, even though they could not see their own expressions and did not realize that a specific emotion was being portrayed. The emotion created by posed facial expressions can be significant enough to affect social judgments. In one study, participants who were asked to smile tended to form more positive impressions of other people than did those who received no special instructions (Ohira & Kurono, 1993).

Mimicking the face of another person may elicit in you the same feelings that person is having, including autonomic responses, and may thus create empathy. Indeed, people do best at describing another person's emotions when their own physiological responses match those of the other person (Levenson & Ruef, 1992). Edgar Allan Poe noted this relationship between facial expressions and feelings more than a hundred years ago:

When I wish to find out how wise or how stupid or how good or how wicked is anyone, or what are his thoughts at the moment, I fashion the expression of my face, as accurately as

FIGURE 11.15

Patterns of Physiological Change Associated with Different Emotions

In this experiment, movements of the face characteristic of different emotions produced different patterns of change in (A) heart rate; (B) peripheral blood flow, as measured by finger temperature; (C) skin conductance; and (D) muscle activity (Levenson, Ekman & Friesen, 1990). For example, making an angry face caused heart rate and finger temperature to rise, whereas making a fearful face raised heart rate but lowered finger temperature.

Source: Levenson, Ekman & Friesen, 1990.

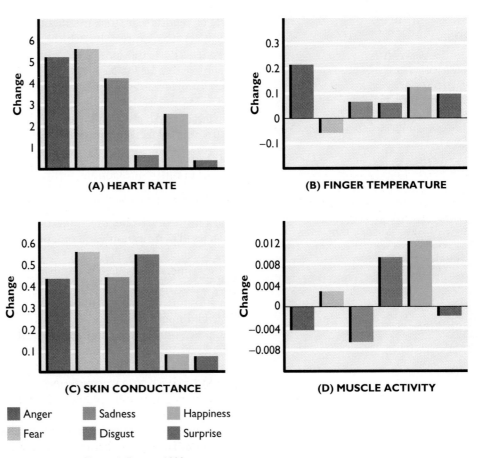

Source: Levenson, Ekman & Friesen, 1990.

FIGURE 11.16

Voluntary Facial Movements and Emotional Autonomic Responses

This man was instructed to (A) "raise your brows and pull them together"; (B) "raise your upper eyelids"; and (C) "also stretch your lips horizontally, back toward your ears." Carrying out these instructions produced changes in heart rate characteristic of fear *and* the experience of fear.

possible, in accordance with the expression of his, and then wait to see what thoughts or sentiments arise in my mind or heart, as if to match or correspond with the expression. (Quoted in Levenson, Ekman & Friesen, 1990)

James's theory implies that the experience of emotion would be blocked if a person were unable to detect physiological changes occurring in the body's periphery. For example, spinal cord injuries that reduce feedback from peripheral responses should reduce the intensity of emotional experiences. This was the result reported in a study performed during the 1960s (Hohmann, 1966); but at that time, many people with spinal injuries were being told to passively accept disability, perhaps leading them to withdraw from emotional situations (Chwalisz, Diener & Gallagher, 1988). More recent studies have shown that when people with spinal injuries actively pursue their life goals, they experience a full range of emotions, including as much happiness as noninjured people (Chwalisz, Diener & Gallagher, 1988; Bermond et al., 1991). These people reported that their emotional experiences are just as intense as before their injuries, even though they notice less intense physiological changes associated with their emotions.

Such reports seem to contradict James's theory, but spinal cord injuries do not usually affect facial expressions, which James included among the bodily responses that are experienced as emotions. Thus, some researchers have proposed a variant of James's theory, the *facial feedback hypothesis*, which maintains that involuntary facial movements provide sufficient peripheral information to drive emotional experience (Ekman & Davidson, 1993). This hypothesis predicts that feeling yourself smile should make you feel happy. It also helps to explain the results mentioned earlier suggesting that voluntarily posed facial expressions create the emotions normally associated with them.

Lie Detection   James's view that different patterns of physiological activity are associated with different emotions forms the basis for the lie detection industry. If people experience anxiety or guilt when they lie, specific patterns of physiological activity accompanying these emotions should be detectable on instruments, called *polygraphs,* that record heart rate, breathing rate, skin conductance (which is affected by slight changes in perspiration), and other autonomic responses.

To identify the perpetrator of a crime, a polygraph tester may ask questions specific to the crime, such as "Did you stab anyone on July 3, 1996?" Responses to such *relevant questions* are then compared to responses to *control questions,* such as "Have you ever tried to hurt someone?" Innocent people might have tried to hurt someone at some time and might feel guilty when asked, but they should have no reason to feel guilty about what they did on July 3, 1996. Thus, an innocent person should have a stronger emotional response to control questions than to relevant questions (Honts, 1994; Rosenfeld, 1995).

Most people do have emotional responses when they lie, but statistics about the accuracy of polygraphs are difficult to obtain. Estimates vary widely, from those suggesting that polygraphs detect 90 percent of guilty, lying individuals (Raskin, 1986) to those suggesting that polygraphs mislabel as many as 40 percent of truthful, innocent persons as guilty liars (Ben-Shakhar & Furedy, 1990). Obviously, the results of a poly-

SEARCHING FOR TRUTH Polygraph tests are not infallible, but they tend to be most effective when the person being tested believes in them. In a small town where the police could not afford a polygraph, one suspect confessed his crime when a "lie detector" consisting of a kitchen colander was placed over his head and attached by wires to a copy machine (Shepard, Kohut & Sweet, 1989).

graph test are not determined entirely by whether a person is telling the truth. What people think about the act of lying, and about the value of the test, can also influence the accuracy of its results. For example, people who consider lying to be acceptable—and who do not believe in the power of polygraphs—are unlikely to display emotion-linked physiological responses while lying during the test. However, an innocent person who believes in such tests and who thinks that "everything always goes wrong" might show a large fear response when asked about a crime, thus wrongly suggesting guilt.

Polygraphs can catch some liars, but most researchers agree that a guilty person can "fool" a polygraph lie detector. Thus, the American Psychological Association has expressed "great reservations about the use of polygraph tests to detect deception" (Abeles, 1985). Other lie-detecting devices are now under development. One of these measures the brain waves emitted during certain cognitive operations (Bashore & Rapp, 1992). Such devices may someday prove more accurate than polygraph tests because they do not depend on a link between deception and emotional responses.

Schachter's Theory

Contemporary theorists such as Stanley Schachter have expanded on James's views of emotion as the experience of physiological arousal. In Schachter's view, feedback about physiological changes may not vary enough to create all the subtle shadings of human emotional experiences. Instead, says Schachter, emotions emerge from a *combination* of feedback from peripheral responses and our cognitive interpretation of what caused those responses (Schachter & Singer, 1962; Sinclair et al., 1994). According to Schachter, cognitive interpretation comes into play twice: once when you perceive the situation that leads to bodily responses and again when you identify feedback from those responses as a particular emotion (see Figure 11.14).

Labeling Arousal Schachter and his colleague, Jerome Singer, offered the *Schachter-Singer theory* of emotion. This theory agrees with James's that the first step in emotion is perception of a situation, followed by bodily responses. However, whereas James saw emotion as solely based on feedback about specific physiological responses, Schachter viewed the brain as capable of *interpreting* this feedback in many ways. The same physiological responses, therefore, might be given many different labels, depending on one's interpretation. In short, Schachter argued that the core of emotion is the cognitive act of *labeling* an originally undifferentiated pattern of physiological arousal (Schachter & Singer, 1962).

LINKAGES: LABELING AROUSAL
Schachter's theory of emotion predicts that these people will attribute their physiological arousal to the game they are watching and will label their emotion "excitement." Further, as described in Chapter 13, the emotions they experience will also depend partly on their cognitive interpretation of the outcome (Lazarus & Folkman, 1984). Those who see their team's defeat as a disaster will experience more negative emotions than those who think of it as a challenge to improve.

The labeling of arousal depends on an **attribution,** the process of identifying the cause of some event. People may attribute their physiological arousal to different emotions depending on the information available about the situation. For example, if you are watching the final seconds of a close ball game, you might attribute your racing heart, rapid breathing, and perspiration to excitement; but you might attribute the *same* physiological reactions to anxiety if you are waiting for a big exam to begin. Thus, the emotion you experience upon seeing a bear in the woods might be fear, excitement, astonishment, or surprise, depending on how you label your bodily reactions.

afraid vs. worried
nervous vs. wired

Evaluating Schachter's Theory   Schachter's refinement of James's theory predicts that emotional experience will be less intense if arousal is attributed to a *nonemotional* cause. So if you notice your heart pounding before an exam but say to yourself, "Sure my heart's pounding—I just drank five cups of coffee!" then you should feel "wired" from caffeine rather than afraid or worried. This prediction has received some support (Schachter & Singer, 1962; Sinclair et al., 1994).

Schachter's theory also predicts that if arousal is artificially induced—by drugs, for example—emotion will be *created* if there is a situation to which the drug-induced arousal can reasonably be attributed. This prediction received some support in Schachter's early work (Schachter & Singer, 1962), but other investigators have been unable to replicate his results (Leventhal & Tomarken, 1986; Marshall & Zimbardo, 1979; Maslach, 1979).

Transfer of Excitation   There is evidence, however, that physiological arousal from nonemotional sources can *intensify* emotional experience (Zillmann, 1984). For example, people who have been aroused by physical exercise become more angry when provoked, or experience more intense sexual feelings when in the company of an attractive person, than do people who have been less physically active (White, Fishbein & Rutstein, 1981).

When arousal from one experience carries over to an independent situation, it is called **transferred excitation** (Reisenzein, 1983). This transfer is most likely to occur when the overt signs of physiological arousal have subsided but the sympathetic nervous system is still active. In one study, people were emotionally "primed" by reading words that were cheerful, neutral, or depressing. Next, they either engaged in physical exercise or sat quietly and then rated their mood, either immediately or after a short delay. Those who had not exercised, or who rated themselves *immediately* after exercise, reported being in no particular mood. However, the mood of those whose reports came several minutes after exercising tended to be positive, neutral, or negative, depending on which priming words they had read earlier. Apparently, the people in this latter group were still somewhat aroused; but because the delay had been long enough to keep them from attributing their lingering arousal to exercise, they instead used the emotional tone of the word list as a guide to labeling their mood (Sinclair et al., 1994).

Arousal created by one emotion can also transfer to intensify another. For example, arousal from fear, like arousal from exercise, can enhance sexual feelings. One study of this transfer took place in British Columbia over a deep river gorge. The gorge could be crossed either by a precarious swinging bridge or by a safe wooden structure. A female researcher asked men who had just crossed each bridge to fill out a questionnaire that included a measure of sexual imagery. The men who met the woman after crossing the dangerous bridge had much higher sexual imagery scores than the men who had crossed the safe bridge. Furthermore, they were more likely to rate her as attractive (Dutton & Aron, 1974). When the person giving out the questionnaire was a male, however, the type of bridge crossed had no impact on sexual imagery. To test the possibility that the men who crossed the dangerous bridge were simply more adventurous in both bridge crossing and sexual encounters, the researchers repeated the study, but with one change. This time, the woman approached the men farther down the trail, long after arousal from the bridge crossing had subsided. Now, the apparently adventurous men were no more likely than others to rate the woman as attractive. Apparently, it was indeed transfer of excitation, not just adventurousness, that produced the original result.

Cannon's Theory

The theories we have considered so far assume that the experience of emotion depends on facial movements and other bodily responses outside the brain. However, Walter Cannon believed that emotion can result from brain activity alone (Cannon, 1927/1987). He argued that you feel fear at the sight of a wild bear even before you take a step because emotional experience starts in the brain—specifically, in the thalamus, the brain structure that relays information from most sense organs to the cortex.

According to Cannon's theory of emotion (called the *Cannon-Bard theory*, in recognition of Philip Bard's contribution), sensory information about emotional situations first reaches the thalamus, which sends signals *simultaneously* to the autonomic nervous system and to the cerebral cortex, where the emotion becomes conscious. So when you see a bear, the brain receives sensory information about it, interprets that information as a bear, and *directly* creates the experience of fear while *at the same time* sending messages to the heart, lungs, and legs to initiate a rapid departure. According to Cannon's theory, there is a direct, central nervous system experience of emotion, with or without feedback about peripheral responses (see Figure 11.14).

Updating Cannon's Theory Subsequent research indicates that the thalamus is not the "seat" of emotion, as Cannon had suggested. Still, through its connections to the amygdala (see Figure 11.10), the thalamus does participate in some aspects of emotional processing (Lang, 1995; LeDoux, 1995). For example, animal studies show that the emotion of fear is generated by thalamic connections to the amygdala (LeDoux, 1995). The implication is that strong emotions can sometimes bypass the cortex without requiring conscious thought to activate them—thus possibly explaining why people find it so difficult to overcome an intense fear, or phobia, even though they may consciously know the fear is irrational.

An updated version of Cannon's theory suggests that specific brain areas produce the feelings of pleasure or pain associated with emotion. This idea arose from studies showing that electrical stimulation of certain parts of the brain is rewarding. The researchers found that rats kept returning to the place in their cage where they received stimulation through electrodes in their brains. When these animals were allowed to control delivery of the stimulation by pressing a bar, they pressed it until they were physically exhausted, ignoring even food and water (Olds & Milner, 1954). The brain areas in

IN REVIEW	Theories of Emotion	
Theory	**Source of Emotions**	**Evidence for Theory**
James-Lange	The CNS generates specific physical responses; observation of the physical responses constitutes emotion.	Different emotions are associated with different physical responses.
Schachter-Singer	The CNS generates non-specific physical responses; interpretation of the physical responses in light of the situation constitutes emotions.	Excitation generated by physical activity can transfer to increase emotional intensity.
Cannon-Bard	Parts of the CNS directly generate emotions; peripheral physiological responses are not necessary.	People with spinal cord damage experience a full range of emotions without feedback from peripheral responses.

which stimulation is experienced as especially pleasurable include the dopamine systems, which, as described in Chapter 6, are activated by drugs of abuse (Segal & Bloom, 1976; Wise, 1988). In contrast, stimulation of other brain regions is so unpleasant that animals work hard to avoid it.

Presumably, part of the direct central experience of emotions involves areas of the brain whose activity is experienced as either reinforcing or aversive. The areas of the brain activated by the kind of events that elicit emotion in humans have widespread connections throughout the brain. Thus, the central nervous system experience of emotion is probably widely distributed, not narrowly localized in any one emotion "center" (Derryberry & Tucker, 1992).

Some brain areas may form a kind of "autonomic nervous system" within the brain (Hartman et al., 1986). Just as the ANS modulates the activity of organs that can function without its input, some neurotransmitter systems modulate the activity of other brain cells. Cells in the locus coeruleus play this "autonomic" role, releasing norepinephrine and modulating the activity of other brain cells, as well as sending signals to the autonomic nervous system in the periphery (Olpe, Steinmann & Jones, 1985). An "autonomic nervous system" in the brain could be the equivalent of what Walter Cannon envisioned: a central mechanism that arouses the brain *and* activates emotional facial expressions and autonomic visceral responses (Levenson, Ekman & Friesen, 1990).

Indeed, there is increasing evidence for the main thrust of Cannon's theory: that emotion occurs through the activation of specific parts of the central nervous system. However, different parts of the central nervous system may be activated for different emotions and for different aspects of the total emotional experience.

Conclusions   "In Review: Theories of Emotion" summarizes key elements of the three theories we have discussed. It appears that both peripheral autonomic responses (including facial responses) and the cognitive interpretation of those responses add to emotional experience. In addition, the brain itself can apparently generate emotional experience, independent of physiological arousal. So emotion is probably both in the heart and in the head (including the face). The most basic emotions probably occur directly within the brain, while the many shades of discernible emotions probably arise from attributions, including evaluations of physiological responses. No theory has completely resolved the issue of which, if any, component of emotion is primary.

However, the theories we have discussed have helped psychologists better understand how these components interact to produce emotional experience.

COMMUNICATING EMOTION

Imagine a woman watching television. You can see her face, but not what she sees on the screen. She might be engaged in complex thought, perhaps comparing her investments with those of the experts on "Wall Street Week." Or she might be thinking of nothing at all as she loses herself in a rerun of "Gilligan's Island." In other words, your observation is not likely to tell you much about what she is thinking. If the television program creates an emotional experience, however, you will be able to make a reasonably accurate guess about which emotion she feels (Patrick, Craig & Prkachin, 1986). So far, we have described emotion from the inside, as people experience their own emotions. In this section, we examine the social organization of emotion—how people communicate emotions to each other.

Humans communicate emotions partly through tone of voice and body posture or movement, but mainly through facial movements and expressions. The human face can create thousands of different expressions (Izard, 1971), and people are good at detecting them. Observers can discern very small facial movements—a twitch of the mouth can carry a lot of information. Are emotional facial expressions innate, or are they learned? And how are they used in communicating emotion?

Innate Expressions of Emotion

Charles Darwin observed that some facial expressions seem to be universal (Darwin 1872/1965). He proposed that these expressions are genetically determined, passed on biologically from one generation to the next. The facial expressions seen today, said Darwin, are those that have been most effective at telling others something about how a person is feeling. If someone is scowling with teeth clenched, for example, you will probably assume that he or she is angry, and you will be unlikely to choose that particular moment to ask for a loan.

Infants provide one source of evidence for the innateness of some facial expressions. Newborns do not need to be taught to grimace in pain or to smile in pleasure or to blink when startled (Balaban, 1995). Even blind infants, who cannot imitate adults' expressions, show the same emotional expressions as do sighted infants (Goodenough, 1932).

A second line of evidence for innate facial expressions comes from studies showing that, for the most basic emotions, people in all cultures show similar facial responses to similar emotional stimuli (Izard, 1994). Participants in these studies look at photographs of people's faces and then try to name the emotion each person is feeling. The

THE UNIVERSAL SMILE The innate origin of some emotional expressions is supported by the fact that the facial movement pattern we call a smile is related to happiness, pleasure, and other positive emotions in human cultures throughout the world.

Elements of Ceremonial Facial
Masks That Convey Threat

**Certain geometrical elements are
common to threatening masks in
many cultures. When people in various
cultures were asked which member of
each of these pairs was more threatening, they consistently chose those,
shown here on the left, containing triangular and diagonal elements.
"Scary" Halloween pumpkins tend to
have such elements as well.**

pattern of facial movements we call a smile, for example, is universally related to positive emotions. Sadness is almost always accompanied by slackened muscle tone and a
"long" face. Likewise, in almost all cultures, people contort their faces in a similar way
when shown something they find disgusting. And a furrowed brow is frequently associated with frustration or unpleasantness (Ekman, 1994).

Anger is also linked with a facial expression recognized by almost all cultures. One
study examined artwork—particularly ceremonial masks—of various Western and
non-Western cultures (Aronoff, Barclay & Stevenson, 1988). The angry, threatening
masks of all eighteen cultures contained similar elements, such as triangular eyes and
diagonal lines on the cheeks. In particular, angular and diagonal elements carry the
impression of threat (see Figure 11.17).

Social and Cultural Influences on Emotional Expression

While some basic emotional expressions are innate, many others are neither innate nor
universal (Ekman, 1993). Even innate expressions are flexible and modifiable, changing
as necessary in the social contexts within which they occur (Fernández-Dols & Ruiz-
Belda, 1995; Fridlund, 1994). For example, facial expressions become more intense and
change more frequently while people are imagining social scenes as opposed to solitary
scenes (Fridlund et al., 1990). Similarly, facial expressions in response to odors tend to
be more intense when others are watching than when people are alone (Jancke &
Kaufmann, 1994).

Further, although a core of emotional responses is recognized by all cultures, there is
a certain degree of cultural variation in recognizing some emotions (Russell, 1995). In
one study, for example, Japanese and North American people agreed about which facial
expressions signaled happiness, surprise, and sadness, but they frequently disagreed
about which faces showed anger, disgust, and fear (Matsumoto & Ekman, 1989).
Members of preliterate cultures such as the Fore of New Guinea agree even less with
people in Western cultures on the labeling of facial expressions (Russell, 1994). In addition, there are variations in the ways that cultures interpret emotions expressed by tone
of voice (Mesquita & Frijda, 1992). An example is provided by a study showing that
Taiwanese subjects were best at recognizing a sad tone of voice whereas Dutch subjects
were best at recognizing happy tones (Van Bezooijen, Otto & Heenan, 1983).

People learn how to express certain emotions in particular ways, as specified by cultural rules. Suppose you say, "I just bought a new car," and all your friends stick their
tongues out at you. In North America, this may mean that they are envious or resentful. But in some regions of China, such a display expresses surprise.

Even smiles can vary as people learn to use them to communicate certain feelings.
Paul Ekman and his colleagues categorized seventeen types of smiles, including "false
smiles," which fake enjoyment, and "masking smiles," which hide unhappiness. They
called the smile that occurs with real happiness the *Duchenne smile,* after the French
researcher who first noticed a difference between spontaneous, happy smiles and posed
smiles. A genuine, Duchenne smile includes contractions of the muscles around the
eyes (creating a distinctive wrinkling of the skin in these areas) as well as of the muscles
that raise the lips and cheeks. Few people can successfuly contract the muscles around
the eyes during a posed smile, so this feature can be used to distinguish "lying smiles"
from genuine ones (Ekman, Friesen & O'Sullivan, 1988; Frank, Ekman, & Friesen,
1993). In one study, the Duchenne smile was highly correlated with reports of positive
emotions experienced while people watched a movie, as well as with a pattern of brain
waves known to be associated with positive emotions. These relationships did not
appear for other types of smiles (Ekman, Davidson & Friesen, 1990).

Learning About Emotions   The effects of learning are seen in a child's growing reper-
toire of emotional expressions. Although infants begin with an innate set of emotional
responses, they soon learn to imitate facial expressions and use them for more and more
emotions. In time, these expressions become more precise and personalized, so that a
particular expression conveys a clear emotional message to anyone who knows that
person well.

If facial expressions become too idiosyncratic, however, no one will know what the expressions mean, and they will fail to elicit responses from others. Operant shaping, described in the chapter on learning, probably helps keep emotional expressions within certain limits. If you could not see other people's facial expressions or observe their responses to yours, you might show fewer, or less intense, facial signs of emotion. Indeed, as congenitally blind people grow older, their facial expressions tend to become less animated (Izard, 1977).

As children grow, they learn an *emotion culture*—rules that govern what emotions are appropriate in what circumstances and what emotional expressions are allowed. These rules can vary from culture to culture. For example, the people of Ifaluk, a tiny Pacific island, condemn expressions of happiness as disruptive to carrying out one's duties (Lutz, 1987). Similarly, when viewing a distressing movie with a group of peers, Japanese students exhibited much more control over their facial expressions than North American students. When they watched the film while alone, however, the Japanese students' faces showed the same emotional expressions as those of the North American students (Ekman, Friesen & Ellsworth, 1972).

Emotion cultures can change over time. In the United States, for example, there has been a shift from relative unconcern with anger in the last century to stricter suppression of the expression of anger in this century (Stearns & Stearns, 1986). Changes in emotion culture can also be dictated by situational factors. Medical students, for example, must learn new rules about expressing emotions during contact with human bodies. As one student described the process:

How do I set aside 25 years of living, experience which made close contact with someone's body a sensual event? Maybe it's attraction, maybe disgust. But it isn't supposed to be part of what I feel when I touch a patient. I feel some of those things, and I want to learn not to. (Quoted in Smith & Kleinman, 1989)

Relearning the rules of emotion is part of an unofficial curriculum at medical school; by observing doctors, students learn how to modify and control these feelings (Smith & Kleinman, 1989).

Emotion cultures shape how people describe and categorize feelings, resulting in both similarities and differences across cultures (Russell, 1991). At least five of the seven basic emotions listed in an ancient Chinese book called the *Li Chi*—joy, anger, sadness, fear, love, disliking, and liking—are considered primary emotions by most Western theorists. Yet while English has over 500 emotion-related words, some emotion words in other languages have no English meaning. The Czech word *litost* apparently has no English word equivalent: "It designates a feeling as infinite as an open accordion, a feeling that is the synthesis of many others: grief, sympathy, remorse, and an indefinable longing. . . . *Litost* is a state of torment caused by a sudden insight into one's own miserable self" (quoted in Russell, 1991). The Japanese word *ijirashii* also has no English analog; it describes the feeling of seeing a praiseworthy person overcoming an obstacle (Russell, 1991).

Similarly, other cultures have no equivalent for some English emotion words. Many cultures do not see anger and sadness as different, for example. The Ilongot, a Philippine head-hunting group, have only one word, *liget,* for both anger and grief (Russell, 1991). Tahitians have different words for forty-six types of anger, but no word for sadness and, apparently, no concept of it. One Westerner described a Tahitian man as sad over separation from his wife and child, but the man himself felt *pe´a pe´a*—a generic word for feeling ill, troubled, or fatigued—and did not attribute it to the separation.

Social Referencing　Facial expressions, tone of voice, body postures, and gestures not only communicate information about the emotion someone is experiencing; they can also influence others' behavior, especially the behavior of people who are not sure what to do. A novice chess player, for instance, might reach out to move the queen, catch sight of a spectator's grimace, and infer that another move would be better. The process of letting another person's emotional state guide our own behavior is called **social referencing** (Campos, 1980).

The visual-cliff studies described in the chapter on perception have been used to create an uncertain situation for infants. To reach its mother, an infant in these experiments must cross the visual cliff (see Figure 5.27). If the apparent dropoff is very small or very large, there is no ambiguity, and a one-year-old knows to crawl across in the first case and to stay put in the second case. However, if the apparent dropoff is shallow enough to create uncertainty (say, two feet), the infant relies on its mother's facial expressions to decide what to do. In one study, mothers were asked to make either a fearful or a joyful face. When the mothers made a fearful face, no infant crossed the glass floor. But when they posed a joyful face, most infants crossed (Sorce et al., 1981). Here is yet another example of the adaptive value of sending, and receiving, emotional communications.

FUTURE DIRECTIONS

Psychological research has revealed much about motivation and emotion, but, as always, there is more to learn. In particular, further studies are likely to be directed to such areas as dieting, body weight regulation, and eating disorders. Even now, scientists are beginning to clarify the genetic mechanisms, biochemical signals, and specific brain areas involved in the body's ability to regulate and maintain body fat (Azar, 1994; Stanley & Gillard, 1994). Their work may one day lead to a way of helping people permanently lose—or lower the level of—excess body fat. In fact, the U.S. Food and Drug Administration recently approved a diet drug called *dexfenfluramine* that acts on the neurotransmitter serotonin (Associated Press, 1995). Placebo-controlled, double-blind studies show that dexfenfluramine causes significant weight loss (Blundell & Halford, 1995; Holdaway et al., 1995).

Other research will focus on developmental factors that might explain why some people, at or near puberty, become so preoccupied with their body image and body weight as to predispose themselves to eating disorders (de Castro & Goldstein, 1995). Psychologists will also continue to explore the emotional and physical consequences of weight-loss diets and their implications for psychological as well as physical health (Brownell & Rodin, 1994; Friedman & Brownell, 1995).

Research on the nature and origins of sexual behavior will intensify. The threat of HIV and other sexually transmitted diseases will prompt continued study of the prevalence of various sexual practices, with a focus on how the riskiest of them might be made less likely. Further, growing recognition of sexual orientation as an important sociocultural variable will lead more researchers to study its effects in such areas as eating disorders, sexual practices, mate selection, parenting, achievement motivation, and methods of coping with stress (Savin-Williams, 1994).

Research on emotion will continue to explore the question of which aspects of emotional experience and expression are innate and universal and which are learned and culture-specific. This work will become increasingly important as more people from different cultures communicate with one another—in person and through computers—in emotionally charged situations (Bower, 1994).

Other researchers will work to improve the traditional polygraph approach to lie detection (Bashore & Rapp, 1992). One method now being studied takes advantage of the fact that, when people view an unfamiliar person or scene, their eye movements tend to differ from those elicited by more familiar stimuli. By tracking these movements, scientists may one day be able to determine whether people shown a crime scene, for example, are telling the truth about ever having seen it before (Althoff, Maciukenas & Cohen, 1993; Cohen et al., 1996).

If you wish to study the topics discussed in this chapter in more detail, consider taking a course in motivation and emotion. Most courses in biological psychology also deal with the physiological and anatomical bases of motivation and emotion. A course in health psychology or stress and coping may offer valuable coverage of the negative effects of emotional overarousal, and courses in human sexuality deal extensively with the motivational and emotional aspects of sexual behavior. Finally, consider courses in personality or industrial-organizational psychology as sources of more information on achievement motivation in general and workplace behavior in particular.

SUMMARY AND KEY TERMS

Motivation refers to factors that influence the initiation, direction, intensity, and persistence of behavior. Emotion and motivation are often linked: Motivation can influence emotion, and people are often motivated to seek certain emotions.

■ CONCEPTS AND THEORIES OF MOTIVATION

Focusing on a *motive* often reveals a single theme within apparently diverse behaviors. Motivation is said to be an intervening variable, a way of linking various stimuli to the behaviors that follow them.

Sources of Motivation

The many sources of motivation fall into four categories: biological factors, emotional factors, cognitive factors, and social factors.

Instinct Theory and Its Descendants

An early argument held that motivation follows from *instincts*, automatic, involuntary, and unlearned behavior patterns consistently "released" by particular stimuli. Modern versions of *instinct theory* are seen in evolutionary accounts of helping, aggression, mate selection, and other aspects of social behavior.

Drive Reduction Theory

Drive reduction theory is based on *homeostasis,* a tendency to maintain equilibrium in a physical or behavioral process. When disruption of equilibrium creates a *need* of some kind, people are motivated to reduce the resulting *drive* by behaving in some way that satisfies the need and restores balance. *Primary drives* are unlearned; *secondary drives* are learned.

Arousal Theory

According to *arousal theories* of motivation, people are motivated to behave in ways that maintain a level of *arousal* that is optimal for their functioning.

Incentive Theory

Incentive theory highlights behaviors that are motivated by attaining desired stimuli (positive incentives) and avoiding undesirable ones (negative incentives).

■ HUNGER AND EATING

Hunger and eating are controlled by a complex mix of learning, culture, and biology.

Biological Signals for Hunger and Satiety

The desire to eat *(hunger)* or to stop eating *(satiety)* depends on signals from the stomach and from blood-borne substances such as glucose, fatty acids, amino acids, cholecystokinin (CCK), insulin, and leptin.

Hunger and the Brain

Activity in the ventromedial nucleus of the hypothalamus results in satiety, while activity in the lateral hypothalamus results in hunger. Neurons in the paraventricular nucleus appear to influence hungers for specific types of foods. These brain areas might be acting in concert to maintain a set point of body weight.

Flavor, Cultural Learning, and Food Selection

Eating may also be influenced by the flavor of food and by appetite for the pleasure of food. Food selection is influenced by biological needs (specific hungers) for certain nutrients, as well as by food cravings, social contexts, and cultural traditions.

Eating Disorders

Obesity has been linked to overconsumption of certain kinds of foods, to low energy metabolism, and to genetic factors. People suffering from *anorexia nervosa* starve themselves to avoid becoming fat. Those who suffer from *bulimia nervosa* engage in binge eating, followed by purging through self-induced vomiting or laxatives.

■ SEXUAL BEHAVIOR

Sexual motivation and behavior result from a rich interplay of biology and culture.

The Biology of Sex

Sexual stimulation generally produces a stereotyped *sexual response cycle,* a pattern of physiological arousal during and after sexual activity. *Sex hormones,* which include male hormones *(androgens)* and female hormones *(estrogens* and *progestins),* occur in different relative amounts in both sexes. They can have organizational effects, such as physical differences in the brain, and activational effects, such as increased desire for sex.

Social and Cultural Factors in Sexuality

Gender-role learning, educational experiences, media influences, and family dynamics are examples of cultural factors that can bring about variations in sexual attitudes and behaviors.

Sexual Orientation

Sexual orientation—*heterosexual, homosexual,* or *bisexual*—is increasingly viewed as a sociocultural variable that affects many other aspects of behavior and mental processes. Though undoubtedly shaped by a lifetime of learning, it appears to have strong biological roots.

Sexual Dysfunctions

Common male *sexual dysfunctions* include erectile disorder and premature ejaculation. Females may experience such problems as arousal disorder.

■ ACHIEVEMENT MOTIVATION

People gain esteem from achievement in many areas, including the workplace.

Need for Achievement

The motive to succeed is called *need achievement.* Individuals with high achievement motivation strive for excellence, persist despite failures, and set challenging but realistic goals.

Gender Differences in Achievement Motivation

Gender differences in achievement motivation often appear at a young age, apparently due to early learning experiences.

Achievement and Success in the Workplace

Workers are most satisfied when they are working toward their own goals and get concrete feedback. Jobs that offer clear and specific goals, a variety of tasks, individual responsibility, and other intrinsic rewards are the most motivating.

■ RELATIONS AND CONFLICTS AMONG MOTIVES

People's behavior reflects many motives, some of which may be in conflict.

Maslow's Hierarchy

Maslow proposed a hierarchy of five classes of human motives, from meeting basic biological needs to attaining self-actualization. Motives at the lowest levels, according to Maslow, must be at least partially satisfied before people can be motivated by higher-level goals.

■ LINKAGES: CONFLICTING MOTIVES AND STRESS

Four basic types of motivational conflict have been identified: approach-approach, avoidance-avoidance, approach-avoidance, and multiple approach-avoidance conflicts. Such conflicts act as stressors, and people caught in them often experience physical and psychological problems.

Opponent Processes, Motivation, and Emotion

Motivated behavior sometimes gives rise to opponent emotional processes, such as the fear and excitement associated with a roller-coaster ride. Opponent-process theory illustrates the close link between motivation and emotion.

■ THE NATURE OF EMOTION

Defining Characteristics

An *emotion* is a transitory, valenced experience that is felt with some intensity as happening to the self, is generated in part by a cognitive appraisal of a situation, and is accompanied by both learned and reflexive physical responses.

The Biology of Emotion
Several brain mechanisms are involved in emotion. The amygdala, in the limbic system, is deeply involved in emotional arousal. The expression of emotion through involuntary facial movement is controlled by the extrapyramidal motor system. Voluntary facial movements are controlled by the pyramidal motor system. The brain's right and left hemispheres play somewhat different roles in emotional expression. In addition to specific brain mechanisms, both the *sympathetic* and the *parasympathetic* divisions of the autonomic nervous system are involved in physiological changes that accompany emotional activation. The *fight-or-flight syndrome,* for example, follows from activation of the sympathetic system.

■ THEORIES OF EMOTION

James's Theory
William James's theory of emotion holds that physiological responses are the primary source of emotion and that self-observation of these responses constitutes emotional experience. James's theory is supported by evidence that, at least for several basic emotions, physiological responses are distinguishable enough for emotions to be generated in this way. Distinct facial expressions are linked to particular patterns of physiological change. Studies of people with spinal cord damage do not support an important role in emotion for autonomic activity in parts of the body beyond the face.

Schachter's Theory
Schachter's refinement of James's theory of emotion suggests that physiological responses are primary sources of emotion but that cognitive interpretations of the eliciting situation are required to label the emotion, a process that depends on *attribution*. Attributing arousal from one situation to stimuli in another situation can produce *transferred excitation,* intensifying the emotion experienced in the second situation.

Cannon's Theory
Cannon's theory of emotion proposes that emotional experience occurs independent of peripheral physiological responses and that there is a direct experience of emotion based on activity of the central nervous system. Updated versions of this theory suggest that various parts of the central nervous system may be involved in different emotions and different aspects of emotional experience. Some pathways in the brain, such as that from the thalamus to the amygdala, allow strong emotions to occur before conscious thought can take place. Specific parts of the brain appear to be responsible for the feelings of pleasure or pain in emotion. One updated version of Cannon's theory suggests that emotion depends on pathways in the brain, including those from the locus coeruleus, that constitute a kind of "autonomic nervous system" within the brain, modulating the activity of other areas of the brain.

■ COMMUNICATING EMOTION

In humans, voice tones, bodily movements, and, mainly, facial movement and expressions are involved in communicating emotions.

Innate Expressions of Emotion
Darwin suggested that certain facial expressions of emotion are innate and universal and that these expressions evolved because they effectively communicate one creature's emotional condition to other creatures. Some facial expressions of basic emotions do appear to be innate. Even blind infants smile when happy and frown when experiencing discomfort. And certain facial movements are universally associated with certain emotions.

Social and Cultural Influences on Emotional Expression
Many emotional expressions are learned, and even innate expressions are modified by learning and social contexts. As children grow, they learn an emotion culture, the rules of emotional expression appropriate to their culture. Accordingly, the same emotion may be communicated by different facial expressions in different cultures. Especially in ambiguous situations, other people's emotional expressions may serve as a guide about what to do or what not to do, a phenomenon called *social referencing*.

HUMAN DEVELOPMENT

CHAPTER 12

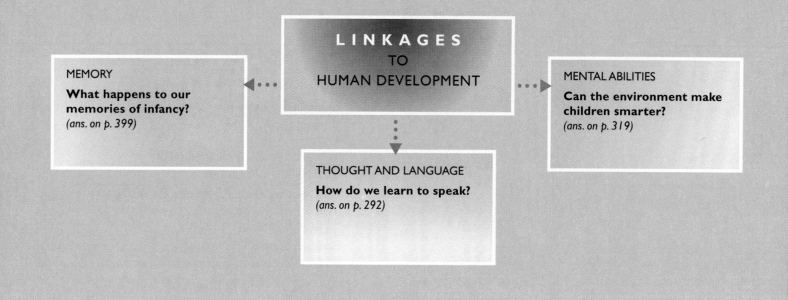

LINKAGES
TO
HUMAN DEVELOPMENT

MEMORY

What happens to our memories of infancy?
(ans. on p. 399)

MENTAL ABILITIES

Can the environment make children smarter?
(ans. on p. 319)

THOUGHT AND LANGUAGE

How do we learn to speak?
(ans. on p. 292)

F or several years in the late 1700s, people living in the Caune Woods of Aveyron, France, reported sighting a wild boy running naked with the animals. Supposedly, he had been lost or abandoned by his parents at a very early age and had grown up with animals. Eventually, when this Wild Boy of Aveyron was about eleven, hunters captured him, and he was sent to Paris.

The scientists in Paris expected to observe what philosopher Jean-Jacques Rousseau had called the "noble savage." After all, here was a human being who had grown up uncontaminated by the evils of society. But what the scientists found was a dirty, frightened creature who trotted like a wild animal and would eat garbage. He spent most of his time silently rocking but would snarl and attack anyone who tried to touch him. Although the scientists worked with the boy for more than ten years, he never learned to speak. He was never able to live unguarded among other people.

Could today's psychologists have "cured" this Wild Boy? Probably not. In recent times, children have been rescued after being confined for years in closets and other environments that cut them off from human contact (Rymer, 1993). Invariably, these children find it extremely difficult to interact with others. Often they are unable to learn language beyond the most rudimentary utterances.

These cases highlight the importance of early contacts with other people for normal human development. They underscore the need to know as much as possible about early development and what can help or hinder it. And they bear on a central issue in developmental psychology—the *nature-nurture* question introduced in Chapter 2 and discussed in subsequent chapters on perception and mental abilities. Specifically, to what extent is development a product of what we arrive with at birth—our inherited, biological nature—and to what extent is it a product of what the world provides—the nurture of the environment?

Developmental psychology addresses this question as it documents the course and causes of developmental changes over a person's life span. It is the study of the origins of and changes in the psychological processes described in virtually every other chapter in this book (see the Linkages diagram). To be considered *developmental,* the changes must be age-related, systematic, sequential, and long-lasting. Development does not include changes that are brief or reversible, such as those resulting from illness, accidents, or drugs. Nor does it include fluctuations in mood or behavior that are related to the time of day or the season of the year. Developmental psychologists study when certain kinds of behavior first appear, how they change with age, and whether the changes are sudden or gradual. They explore how development in one area, such as thinking, is related to development in another area, such as social behavior. They want to know whether everyone develops abilities at the same rate and, if not, whether slow starters ever catch up.

In this chapter, you will read about how a person develops from a fertilized egg into a mature adult and how adults, too, change as they get older. You will read about the milestones of growth in sensation, thinking, emotion, social behavior, and other important aspects of behavior and mental processes. Throughout, you will find evidence relating to the roles of nature and nurture.

EXPLORING HUMAN DEVELOPMENT

Arguments about the nature-nurture question can be traced back to philosophers' statements centuries ago. In essays published in the 1690s, the British empiricist philosopher John Locke argued for the dominance of nurture, suggesting that what happens during childhood has a profound and permanent effect on the individual. As mentioned in Chapter 1, empiricists saw the newborn as a blank slate, or *tabula rasa*. Adults write on that slate, said Locke, as they teach children about the world and how to behave in it. Some seventy years later, French philosopher Jean-Jacques Rousseau made the opposite argument; he claimed that children are capable of discovering how the world operates and how they should behave without instruction from adults. Accordingly, he advocated the idea that children should be allowed to grow as nature dictates, with little guidance or pressure from parents.

The first American psychologist to follow up on Rousseau's view was Arnold Gesell. In the early 1900s Gesell made many observations of children of all ages. He demonstrated that motor skills, such as standing and walking, picking up a cube, and throwing a ball, develop in a fixed sequence of stages in all children, as Figure 12.1 illustrates. The order of the stages and the age at which they develop, he suggested, are determined by nature and relatively unaffected by nurture. Only under extreme conditions such as famine, war, or poverty, he claimed, are children thrown off their biologically programmed timetable. This type of natural growth or change, which unfolds in a fixed sequence relatively independent of the environment, he called **maturation;** it clearly reflects the influence of nature on development.

STIMULATING ENVIRONMENTS An environment full of new and interesting stimuli provides the ideal circumstances for the fullest development of a child's inherited intellectual potential.

FIGURE 12.1

Motor Development

The left end of each bar indicates the age at which 25 percent of the infants tested were able to perform the behavior; 50 percent of the babies were performing the behavior at the age indicated by the vertical line in the bars; the right end indicates the age at which 90 percent could do so (Frankenberg & Dodds, 1967). Although different infants, especially in different cultures, achieve milestones of motor development at slightly different ages, all infants—regardless of their ethnicity, social class, or temperament—achieve them in the same order.

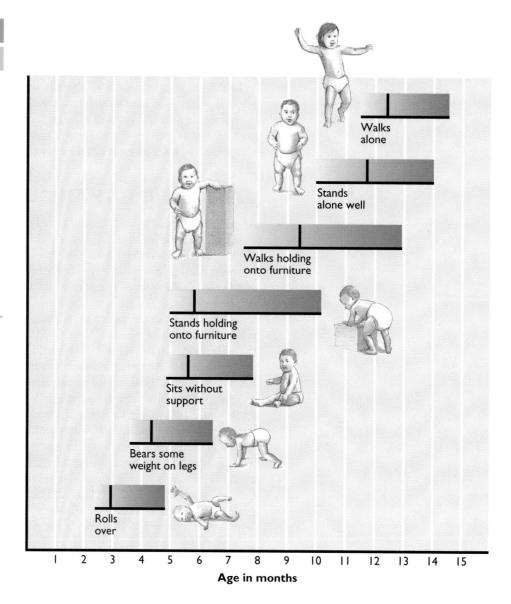

Walks alone

Stands alone well

Walks holding onto furniture

Stands holding onto furniture

Sits without support

Bears some weight on legs

Rolls over

| 1 | 2 | 3 | 4 | 5 | 6 | 7 | 8 | 9 | 10 | 11 | 12 | 13 | 14 | 15 |

Age in months

The environment, not nature, is the key to development in the view of a second American psychologist, John B. Watson. As described in Chapter 1, Watson was the founder of the behaviorist approach to psychology. Early in this century he began conducting experiments with children. From these experiments Watson inferred that children learn everything, from skills to fears.

It was Swiss psychologist Jean Piaget who first suggested that nature and nurture work together, and that their influences are inseparable and interactive. Through a series of books published from the 1920s until his death in 1980, Piaget's ideas influenced the field of developmental psychology more than those of any other person before or since (Beilin, 1992). Most developmental psychologists now accept the idea that both nature and nurture contribute to development. They use the family, twin, and adoption study methods described in Chapter 2 to analyze how—and how strongly—genes and the environment influence specific aspects of development.

These studies have demonstrated that nature and nurture contribute jointly to development in two ways. First, nature and nurture operate together to make all people *alike* as human beings. For example, we all achieve milestones of motor development in the same order and at roughly the same rate as a result of the nature of maturation supported by the nurture of basic care, nutrition, and exercise. Second, nature and nurture also both operate to make each person *unique*. The nature of inherited genes and the nurture of widely different family and cultural environments produce differences among individuals in such dimensions as athletic abilities, intelligence, speech patterns, and personality.

Just how much nature and nurture contribute varies from one characteristic to another. Nature shapes some characteristics, such as physical size and appearance, so strongly that only extreme environmental conditions can affect them. It takes a substantial difference in diet, for instance, to make a difference of even a few inches in a person's ultimate height. Indeed, variation in height has been estimated to be about 95 percent genetic (Azar, 1995). Nature affects other characteristics, such as motor skills, slightly less strongly. During early childhood, motor skills are only modestly affected by experience; nurture—in the form of soccer games and piano lessons, say—plays a larger role in children's motor abilities after the children have acquired basic motor skills. Other characteristics, such as intelligence and social skills, may be more easily affected by the environment from the very beginning.

Although the relative contributions of nature and nurture are different for specific aspects of development, their influences on *all* human characteristics are inextricably intertwined. This is so, for one thing, because heredity and environment are *correlated*. Parents with high intelligence provide their children with genes for intelligent behavior *and* typically provide them with stimulating environments. Parents with special athletic skills are likely to pass on genes that facilitate their children's athletic skill *and* are likely to play sports with them.

Heredity and environment are not only correlated but also mutually influential: Just as the environment encourages or discourages the expression of an individual's inherited characteristics, those inherited characteristics to some extent determine the individual's environment. For example, a stimulating environment—toys, books, lessons—encourages children's mental development and increases the chances that their full inherited intellectual potential will be reached. At the same time, more intelligent children seek out more stimulating environments, ask more questions, and evoke more attention from adults; their innate abilities influence and help them take advantage of their environments.

Today, leading developmental psychologists agree that development is the result of interacting forces arising from the person *and* the environment (Bronfenbrenner & Ceci, 1994; Plomin et al., 1994; Scarr, 1993). Heredity creates not fixed traits but predispositions, which interact with the immediate environment—family and teachers, books and computers—to produce developmental outcomes.

BEGINNINGS

Nowhere are the complementary contributions of heredity and environment clearer than during the eventful nine months before birth, when a single fertilized egg becomes a functioning newborn infant.

Prenatal Development

The process of development begins when a sperm from the father-to-be fertilizes the ovum of the mother-to-be and forms a brand-new cell called a *zygote*. This new cell carries a genetic heritage from both mother and father (see the behavioral genetics appendix).

Stages of Development   The zygote divides into many more cells and by the end of the second week has formed an **embryo.** During the *embryonic stage* of development, which extends until two months after fertilization, the heart, nervous system, stomach, esophagus, and ovaries or testes form. By two months, the embryo looks decidedly human, with eyes, ears, nose, jaw, mouth, and lips. The tiny arms have elbows, hands, and stubby fingers; the legs have knees, ankles, and toes.

The period remaining until birth is called the *fetal stage* of prenatal development. During this stage, the various organs grow and function more efficiently. By the end of the third month, the **fetus** can kick, make a fist, turn its head, open its mouth, swallow, and frown. In the sixth month, the eyelids, which have been sealed, open. The fetus now has a well-developed grasp and abundant taste buds, and can breathe regularly for as long as twenty-four hours at a time.

By the end of the seventh month, the organ systems, though immature, are all functional. In the eighth and ninth months, the fetus becomes sensitive to a variety of outside sounds and responds to light and touch. One study showed, for example, that newborns prefer to listen to recordings in the language—Spanish or English— spoken by their parents (Moon, Cooper & Fifer, 1993). Clearly, infants in the womb can hear—and remember—what is going on outside.

Prenatal Risks   During prenatal development, the *placenta* transmits nutrients from the mother and carries away wastes from the infant. The placenta lets in beneficial materials such as nutrients and screens out many potentially harmful substances, including most bacteria. This screening is imperfect, however; gases, viruses, nicotine, alcohol, and other drugs can pass through. Severe damage can occur if the baby's mother takes certain drugs, is exposed to certain toxic substances, or has certain illnesses while organs are forming during the embryonic stage. A baby whose mother has rubella (German measles) during the third or fourth week after conception, for example, has a 50 percent chance of being blind, deaf, or mentally retarded or of having a heart malformation. If the mother has rubella later in the pregnancy, after the eyes, ears, brain, and heart have formed, the likelihood that the baby will have one of these defects drops substantially.

Harmful external substances such as drugs or radiation that invade the womb and result in birth defects are called **teratogens** (pronounced "ta-rat´-a-jens"). Teratogens are especially damaging in the embryonic stage because it is a **critical period** in prenatal development, a time during which certain kinds of growth must occur if development is to proceed normally. If the heart, eyes, ears, hands, and feet do not appear during the embryonic stage, they cannot form later on, and if they form incorrectly, the defects will be permanent. During the fetal stage, the environment provided by the mother affects the baby's size, behavior, intelligence, and health, rather than the formation of organs and limbs.

The mother's health and age, her nutrition before and during pregnancy, the emotional and physical stresses she undergoes, and the nicotine, alcohol, and other drugs she consumes—all of these factors can affect the development of the embryo or fetus. Of special concern today are the effects of alcohol and cocaine on prenatal develop-

A COCAINE BABY   One in ten babies in the United States is exposed to illegal drugs while still in the womb. "Cocaine babies," sometimes called "crack babies," are born with numerous physical defects as the result of their mothers' drug use during pregnancy. To make matters worse, these mothers are likely to respond negatively to their infants because, for example, these babies often turn their heads away when the mother tries to play. This unfortunate reaction can impair the mother–child relationship and lead to a vicious cycle of child abuse in already fragile families.

ment. Babies born to women who abuse alcohol have a 44 percent chance of suffering from **fetal alcohol syndrome,** a pattern of defects that includes mental retardation and malformations of the face. Fetal alcohol syndrome is linked to heavy drinking, but even moderate drinking—a glass or two of wine a day—can harm infants' intellectual functioning (Streissguth et al., 1989). Mothers addicted to drugs like cocaine also put their infants at risk. They pass on their addiction to the fetus, and their babies are born premature, underweight, tense, and fussy (Jeremy & Hans, 1985). Constantly in motion, disorganized, and highly sensitive to stimuli, many of these babies are brain damaged and will have serious problems learning and concentrating (Hutchinson, 1991; Revkin, 1989). Their kidneys, genitals, or other organs may be malformed because the mother's use of cocaine leads to a loss of blood to the developing organs. A little drug for the mother is a lot for the fetus, who does not yet have the enzymes necessary to break it down.

The likelihood that potentially harmful conditions and substances will affect a particular infant depends on a combination of the infant's inherited strengths or weaknesses, the stage of prenatal development during which the infant is exposed to a teratogen, and the intensity of the teratogen. Malformation or deficiency is most likely when negative effects of nature and nurture combine, as when a genetically susceptible infant receives a strong dose of a damaging substance during a critical period of prenatal development.

Despite these vulnerabilities, mental or physical problems resulting from all harmful factors affect fewer than 10 percent of the babies born in the United States. Mechanisms built into the human organism maintain normal development under all but the most adverse conditions. The vast majority of fetuses arrive at the end of their nine-month gestation averaging a healthy seven pounds and ready to continue a normal course of development in the world.

The Newborn

Determining what newborns can see, hear, and do is one of the most frustrating—and fascinating—research challenges in developmental psychology, because young infants are extremely difficult subjects. About 70 percent of the time, newborns are asleep. When they are not sleeping, they are drowsy, crying, awake and active, or awake and inactive. It is only when they are in this last state, which occurs infrequently in segments only a few minutes long, that researchers can assess the infants' abilities.

To do so, psychologists show the infants objects or pictures and watch where they look and for how long. They film the infants' eye movements and record changes in their heart rates, sucking rates, brain waves, movements, and skin conductance (a measure of perspiration associated with emotion) when objects are shown or sounds are made. From studies using all these techniques, researchers have gleaned a fair picture of infants' sensory and motor abilities.

Vision and Other Senses   At birth, infants' vision is limited by immaturities in both the eye and the brain. Their eyes do not yet have a fovea—the area of retina on which images are focused. Their eye movements are slow and jerky. Pathways in the nervous system connecting the eyes to the brain are still inefficient, as is the processing of visual information within the brain. A very rough estimate is that the newborn has 20:600 eyesight; that is, an object 20 feet away looks as clear as it would if it were viewed from 600 feet away by an adult with normal vision. Although they cannot see small objects on the other side of the room, and although their vision is blurry, infants can see large objects close up—the distance at which most interaction with caregivers takes place. Infants look longest at what they can see best: Patterns with the largest visible elements, the most movement, the clearest contours, and the greatest amount of contrast (Banks & Salapatek, 1983).

Newborns do more than passively take in sensations; they actively use their senses to explore the world around them. At first they can attend to sights and sounds for only short periods, but gradually their attention span lengthens and their exploration becomes more systematic. In the first two months, they focus only on the edges of

One month   **Two months**   **Three months**   **Adult**

LINKAGES: A BABY'S-EYE VIEW OF THE WORLD   These photographs simulate what mother looks like to her infant at one, two, and three months of age. Although their vision is blurry, infants particularly seem to enjoy looking at faces. As mentioned in Chapter 5, their eyes will follow a moving face-like drawing (Johnson et al., 1991), and by one month of age they will stare at a human face longer than at other figures (Olson & Sherman, 1983).

objects, but by two months of age, they scan whole objects (Banks & Salapatek, 1983). Then, when they see an object, they get all the information they can from it before going on to something new (Hunter & Ames, 1988).

At two or three days of age, the newborn can hear soft voices and can notice the difference between tones about one note apart on the musical scale (Aslin, Pisoni & Jusczyk, 1983). But their hearing is not as acute as that of adults until well into childhood. Apparently this condition is not merely a hearing problem; it also reflects an inability to *listen* selectively to some sounds over others (Bargones & Werner, 1994). As infants grow, they develop sensory capacities *and* the skill to use them.

Although infants are not yet able to listen selectively, their hearing is particularly attuned to sounds that are in the range of speech. When they hear speech, babies open their eyes wider and look for the speaker. By four months of age, they can discriminate differences among almost all of the more than fifty phonetic contrasts in adult language (Kuhl, 1987; Werker & Desjardins, 1995). Judging from where infants look or how fast they suck in order to hear recordings of different voices, researchers have concluded that infants also prefer certain kinds of speech. They like rising tones spoken by women or children (Sullivan & Horowitz, 1983). They also like speech that is high-pitched, exaggerated, and expressive. In other words, they like to hear the *baby talk* used by most adults in all cultures when they talk to babies (Fernald, 1990; Glenn & Cunningham, 1983).

Newborns also like certain smells and tastes better than others. When they are given something sweet to drink, they suck longer and slower, pause for shorter periods, and smile and lick their lips (Ganchrow, Steiner & Daher, 1983). Within a few days after birth, breast-fed babies prefer the odor of their own mother's milk to that of another mother (Russell, 1976).

Reflexes and Motor Skills   In the first few weeks and months after birth, babies demonstrate involuntary, unlearned reactions called **reflexes.** These are swift, automatic movements that occur in response to external stimuli. Figure 12.2 illustrates the *grasping reflex;* more than twenty other reflexes have been observed in newborn infants. For example, in the *rooting reflex* the infant turns its mouth toward a finger or nipple that touches its cheek. In the *sucking reflex* the newborn sucks on anything that touches its lips. Many of these behaviors evolved because they were important for infants' survival. The absence of reflexes in the newborn signals problems in brain development. So does failure of reflexes to disappear as brain development during the first three or four months allows the infant to control muscles voluntarily.

Voluntary control permits the development of motor skills that allow infants to roll over, sit up, crawl, stand, and walk. Until a few years ago, most developmental psychologists accepted Gesell's view that, barring extreme environmental conditions, these motor abilities occur spontaneously as the central nervous system and muscles mature. Recent research clearly demonstrates, however, that maturation does not tell the whole story even in normal environments (Thelen, 1992, 1995).

Psychologists have discovered, for example, that motor development depends on infants' active experimentation. In one study, researchers observed six infants as they learned to crawl on their hands and knees (Freedland & Bertenthal, 1994). Once they had developed sufficient muscle strength to support their abdomens, the infants tried various crawling techniques—moving backward, moving one limb at a time, using the arms only, and so on. It was only after a week or two of trial and error that all six infants arrived at the same method: Moving diagonal limbs (right arm and left leg, left arm and right leg) together. This pattern turned out to be the most efficient way of getting around quickly without tipping over. Such observations suggest that the brain does not contain a "crawling generator" that programs exactly how and when infants will crawl. Instead, as maturation increases infants' strength, they try out motor patterns and select the ones that work best.

In short, milestones of motor development result from a combination of maturation and experience, not from the inexorable unfolding of a plan that is genetically inscribed in the brain. And, as always, nature and nurture influence one another. The brain controls developing behavior, but, as described in Chapter 3, its own development is affected by experience—including efforts at building motor skills.

INFANCY AND CHILDHOOD: COGNITIVE DEVELOPMENT

How does a crawling infant become a competent creature who can read a book, write a poem, and argue logically for going to computer camp? What leads to the dramatic shifts in thinking, knowing, and remembering that occur between early infancy and later childhood? Researchers studying *cognitive development* seek to answer these questions.

The Development of Knowledge: Piaget's Theory

Foremost among these researchers was Jean Piaget, who dedicated his life to a search for the origins of intelligence and the factors that lead to changes in knowledge over the life span. Piaget was the first to chart the fascinating journey from the simple reflexes of the newborn to the complex understandings of the adolescent. Although his theory turned out to be incomplete, and in some respects incorrect, his agenda for research in cognitive development is still being pursued.

Intensive observations of infants (including his own) and extensive interviews with children led Piaget to propose that cognitive development proceeds in a series of distinct stages, or periods, which are outlined in Table 12.1. He believed that all children's thinking goes through the same stages, in the same order, without skipping—building on previous stages, then moving progressively to higher ones. Thus, according to Piaget, the thinking of infants is different from the thinking of children, and the thinking of children is different from that of adolescents. Children are not just miniature adults, he inferred, and they are not dumber than adults; they just think in completely different ways at different stages of development. Entering each stage involves a *qualitative* change from whatever preceded it, as when a caterpillar is transformed into a butterfly.

Building Blocks of Development   To explain how infants and children move to ever-higher stages of understanding and knowledge, Piaget introduced the concept of **schemas** as the basic units of knowledge, the building blocks of intellectual development. As noted in previous chapters, schemas are the mental images or generalizations that form as people experience the world. Schemas, in other words, organize past experiences and provide a framework for understanding future experiences.

At first, infants form simple schemas. For example, a sucking schema consolidates their experiences of sucking into images of what objects can be sucked on—bottles, fingers, pacifiers—and what kinds of sucking can be done—soft and slow, speedy and vigorous. Later, children form more complex schemas, such as a schema for tying a knot or making a bed. Still later, adolescents form schemas about what it is to be in love.

Two complementary processes guide this development: assimilation and accommodation. In **assimilation,** infants and children take in information about new objects by trying out existing schemas and finding schemas that the new objects will fit. They

TABLE 12.1	Period	Activities and Achievements
Piaget's Periods of Cognitive Development According to Piaget, a predictable set of features characterizes each period of children's cognitive development. Note that the ages associated with the stages are approximate; Piaget realized that some children move through the stages slightly faster or slower than others.	**Sensorimotor** Birth–2 years	Infants discover aspects of the world through their sensory impressions, motor activities, and coordination of the two. They learn to differentiate themselves from the external world. They learn that objects exist even when they are not visible and that they are independent of the infant's own actions. They gain some appreciation of cause and effect.
	Preoperational 2–4 years 4–7 years	Children cannot yet manipulate and transform information in logical ways, but they now can think in images and symbols. They become able to represent something with something else, acquire language, and play games of pretend. Intelligence at this stage is said to be intuitive, because children cannot make general, logical statements.
	Concrete operational 7–11 years	Children can understand logical principles that apply to concrete external objects. They can appreciate that certain properties of an object remain the same, despite changes in appearance, and sort objects into categories. They can appreciate the perspective of another viewer. They can think about two concepts, such as longer and wider, at the same time.
	Formal operational Over 11 years	Only adolescents and adults can think logically about abstractions, can speculate, and can consider what might or what ought to be. They can work in probabilities and possibilities. They can imagine other worlds, especially ideal ones. They can reason about purely verbal or logical statements. They can relate any element or statement to any other, manipulate variables in a scientific experiment, and deal with proportions and analogies. They reflect on their own activity of thinking.

assimilate the new object into their existing schemas. A baby boy is given a new toy. He examines it, sucks on it, waves it, throws it—and discovers that this toy, like his familiar rattle, is suckable, wavable, and throwable. A toddler encounters a large dog. How she assimilates this new experience depends on her existing schema of dogs. If she has had positive experiences with a family pet she will have a positive schema and, expecting the dog to behave like her pet, she will greet it enthusiastically. Thus, past experiences affect what and how children think about new ones.

Sometimes, like Cinderella's sisters squeezing their oversized feet into the glass slipper, people distort information about a new object to make it fit their existing schemas. When squeezing won't work, though, people are forced to change, or accommodate, their schemas to the new objects. In **accommodation,** the person tries out familiar schemas on a new object, finds that the schemas cannot be made to fit the object, and changes the schema so that it will fit (see Figure 12.3). The baby boy is given a cup. He examines it, sucks on it, waves it, and throws it. He discovers that to suck on it, he can put only the edge in his mouth; to wave it, he must hold onto the handle; and throwing it will not work at all, because Mother removes the cup from his playpen. Similarly, the toddler will refine her "doggie" schema when she meets a snarling stray and discovers that her original schema does not extend to all dogs.

Sensorimotor Development   Piaget (1952) called the first stage of cognitive development the **sensorimotor period** because, he claimed, the infant's mental activity is confined to sensory functions, like seeing and hearing, and to motor skills, like grasping

FIGURE 12.3

Accommodation

Because the bars of the playpen are in the way, this child discovers that her schema for grasping and pulling objects toward her will not work. Thus she adjusts, or accommodates, her schema in order to achieve her goal.

and sucking. The infant's early schemas involve simple sensory and motor functions such as these. As motor skills develop and voluntary actions replace reflexes, babies elaborate these simple schemas into complex ones such as waving and shaking and, later, inserting and building.

According to Piaget, during the sensorimotor stage of cognitive development, infants can form schemas only of objects and actions that are present, things they can see or hear or touch. They cannot think about absent objects because they cannot act on them; thinking, for infants, is doing. They do not lie in the crib thinking about Mother or teddy. What is distinctive about the sensorimotor stage is that infants are not yet able to form schemas that are *mental representations* of objects and actions.

The sensorimotor period in Piaget's theory ends when infants *can* form mental representations and thus think about objects and actions even while the objects are not visible or the actions are not occurring. This is a remarkable milestone, according to Piaget. It frees the child from the here-and-now of the sensory environment and allows for the development of thought. One sign that children have reached this milestone appears as the ability to find a hidden object. This behavior was of particular interest to Piaget because, for him, it reflected infants' knowledge that they do not have to look at, touch, or suck an object to know that it exists; it exists even when out of sight. Piaget called this knowledge **object permanence.**

Before they acquire a knowledge of object permanence, infants do not search for objects that are placed out of sight. According to Piaget, out of sight is literally out of mind. The first evidence that object permanence is developing, he said, appears when infants are four to eight months old. At this age, for the first time, they can recognize a familiar object even if part of it is hidden—they know it's the bottle even if they can see only the nipple peeking out from under the blanket. Infants now have some primitive mental representation of objects. If an object is completely hidden, however, they will not search for it.

Several months later, infants will search briefly for a hidden object, but their search is haphazard and ineffective. Not until they are eighteen to twenty-four months old, said Piaget, do infants appear able to picture and follow events in their minds. They look for the object in places other than where they saw it last, sometimes in completely new places. According to Piaget, their concept of the object as permanent is now fully developed; they have a mental representation of the object that is completely separate from their immediate perception of it.

WHAT DO BABIES KNOW? **A baby in Karen Wynn's laboratory stares intently at the unexpected disappearance of one of three dolls. By observing how long infants of various ages look at events like this, researchers can make inferences about what babies know about numbers and other aspects of their world.**

New Views of Infants   In the years since Piaget developed his theory, other researchers have discovered that infants know a lot more, and know it sooner, than Piaget ever thought they did. It's not that infants are smarter now; rather, psychologists have found smarter ways to measure what is going on in infants' minds. Modern advances allow them to use infrared photography to record infants' eye movements, time-lapse photography to detect subtle hand movements, special equipment to measure and analyze infants' sucking rates, and computer technology that Piaget could not have imagined.

Using these methods, researchers have found that infants are not just sensing and moving in the sensorimotor period; they are already thinking as well. They are not just experiencing isolated sights and sounds but putting them together. For example, when infants are shown two different videotapes at the same time, while the sound track for only one of them comes from a speaker in the middle, they tend to look at the video that goes with the sound track—at a toy bouncing in synch with a tapping sound, at a pair of cymbals accompanied by clanging, at Dad's face when his voice is on the audio, even at an angry face when an angry voice is heard (Soken & Pick, 1992; Walker-Andrews et al., 1991).

As young as five months of age, infants can perform simple addition and subtraction. If you show them two dolls one at a time, hide the dolls behind a screen, and then remove the screen to reveal three dolls, they will stare in amazement (Wynn, 1992, 1995). These data suggest that infants have some basic knowledge of "numerosity"; they can recognize changes in a group of up to three or four objects (Starkey, 1992). Infants can remember, too. As young as two to three months of age, they can recall a particular mobile that was hung over their crib a few days before (Rovee-Collier, 1993; see Figure 12.4).

Although Piaget's methods were not sensitive enough to reveal it, young babies even seem to have a sense of object permanence. Piaget had required infants to demonstrate object permanence through rather grand movements, such as removing a cover that had been placed over an object. However, when experimenters simply turn off the lights, infants as young as five months of age have been shown to reach for now-unseen objects in the dark (Bower & Wishart, 1972; Clifton et al., 1991). Today, researchers recognize that finding a hidden object under a cover requires several abilities: mentally

FIGURE 12.4

Infant Memory

Infants as young as two or three months of age can remember a mobile that they had previously learned to move by kicking a foot, which was tied to the mobile by a ribbon. Even a month later, the babies indicate their recognition by kicking vigorously when they see above them this particular mobile as opposed to another one.

representing the hidden object, figuring out where it might be, and pulling off the cover. Piaget's tests did not allow for the possibility that infants *know* a hidden object still exists but do not have adequate strategies for finding it.

While developmental psychologists now generally agree that infants develop some mental representations earlier than Piaget had suggested, they disagree about whether this knowledge is "programmed" in infants (Spelke et al., 1992), quickly develops through interactions with the outside world (Baillargeon, 1995), or is constructed through the recombination of old schemas into new ones (Fischer & Bidell, 1993).

FOCUS ON RESEARCH METHODS

Experiments on Developing Minds

Renee Baillargeon (1987, 1992, 1994a, b) has employed a particularly creative experimental method to probe the depths of infants' knowledge about objects—including their understanding of object permanence. Baillargeon (pronounced "by-r-john") shows infants pairs of events, one of which is physically possible and the other, physically impossible. She then determines the infants' interest in each kind of event by measuring the amount of time they spend looking at it. Their tendency to look longer at new things provides an indication of which events have violated what the babies know about the world. Using these basic methods, Baillargeon has demonstrated that very young infants possess many of the same fundamental beliefs about objects that adults do. They are aware, for example, that objects continue to exist when masked by other objects and that one object cannot move though the space occupied by another.

In one series of studies, Baillargeon explored infants' knowledge of gravity—their knowledge that unsupported objects fall. The independent variable in these studies was the amount of physical support applied to the objects; the dependent variable was the length of time the infants looked at the objects. While being held in their mothers' laps, the infants viewed a bright-red gloved hand pushing a box from left to right along the top of a platform. On some trials, they saw physically possible events, as when the hand pushed the box until its edge reached the end of the platform; see event (A) in Figure 12.5. On others, they saw impossible events, as when the hand pushed the box until only the end of its bottom surface rested on the platform or until the box was beyond the platform; see events (B) and (C) in the figure. On still other trials, the gloved hand held on to the box while pushing it beyond the edge of the platform, as shown in event (D). Trials continued until the infants had seen at least four pairs of possible and impossible events in alternating order.

Baillargeon found that three-month-old infants looked longest at impossible event (C), when the box was entirely off the platform. However, they were not particularly interested in either event (D), when the box was held by the gloved hand, or event (A), when the box was still on the platform. These results suggest that the three-month-olds knew something about physical support: They expected the box to fall if it was entirely off the platform and acted surprised when it did not. But they would not yet know that a box should fall if its center of gravity was unsupported, as in event (B). At six-and-a-half months old, however, infants stared intently at event (B). By that age, they apparently knew about centers of gravity—that most of the box must be on the platform or it would fall. One-year-olds showed even greater knowledge of physics; they were able to understand that the *shape* of the box in event (B) could determine whether or not it should fall off the platform.

Baillargeon has proposed that infants' increasing knowledge *about* objects is the result of their experience *with* objects. She points out that very young infants have countless opportunities to learn that objects fall when released in midair; even with their blurry vision, they see people dropping potatoes in pots, toys in baskets, and shoes

(A)   (B)

(C)   (D)

Source: Baillargeon, 1992.

FIGURE 12.5

Events Demonstrating Infants'
Knowledge of Physics

**Infants look longer at things that
interest them—that is, at new things
rather than things they have seen
before and find boring. In her research
on the development of knowledge,
Renee Baillargeon (1995) has found
that physically impossible events (B)
and (C)—made possible by an experimenter reaching through a hidden
door to support a moving box—
attract the most attention from
infants. These results suggest that
humans understand some basic laws
of physics quite early in life.**

on floors. But they are much less likely to see people placing objects in such a way that
they extend far beyond the edges of surfaces; in other words, observation has not yet
taught them that less than fully supported objects will fall. By six-and-a-half months,
however, infants can discover this principle of physics for themselves as they sit up and
manipulate objects, often piling them on top of each other and watching them tumble.
By twelve months, having used blocks and other toys to build innumerable towers and
houses, infants have learned even more about gravity and about balancing differently
shaped objects.

Baillargeon's view seems logical, but how do we know that infants' understanding of
physics doesn't reflect the gradual emergence of innate knowledge? To explore the mix
of nature and nurture in object knowledge, Baillargeon could have correlated the age at
which infants develop knowledge about gravity with measures of how much time they
spend playing with blocks. High correlations would suggest the importance of experience, but they cannot confirm that more experience *causes* greater knowledge.
Baillargeon could also have conducted quasi-experiments, looking for naturally occurring situations in which—because of physical handicaps, for example—certain babies
have little or no hands-on experience with objects. If, compared to normal infants,
these babies showed impaired or delayed knowledge about gravity, lack of experience
could be responsible. But the difference could also be due to defective inherited knowledge, lack of parental involvement, or many other uncontrolled random variables.

Seeking greater control over the research situation, Baillargeon chose to conduct her
own experiments. After obtaining parents' permission, she randomly assigned infants,
ranging in age from three to six-and-a-half-months old, to receive either normal or
extra object-experience (the independent variable) and observed the effect on the
infants' understanding of gravity (the dependent variable). Preliminary results show
that, after only a few demonstrations in which unsupported objects fell off platforms,
infants in the extra object-experience group are surprised when an unsupported object
does not fall. It is still too early to say for sure whether Baillargeon's hypothesis about
the importance of experience in developing knowledge is correct, but the next time you
see an infant stacking blocks and watching them fall, consider the possibility that you
are watching a little scientist testing hypotheses about the workings of the universe.

Preoperational Development   According to Piaget, the sensorimotor stage of development is followed by the **preoperational period.** During the first half of this period, he observed, children begin to understand, create, and use *symbols* to represent things that are not present; they draw, pretend, and talk. (How children learn to talk is described in Chapter 9.)

The ability to use and understand symbols opens up vast new domains for two- to four-year-olds. At two, for the first time, children are able to play "pretend," perhaps using a finger to stand for a horse. They can watch a television show one day and, on the next, imitate what they saw. Before this age, Piaget observed, children can imitate what they are seeing at the moment, but not what they saw earlier. At the age of three or four, children can symbolize intricate roles and events, as they play house, doctor, or Power Rangers. They can appreciate the symbolic function of a miniature model. In one study, for example, three-year-olds shown a scale-model room in which a miniature dog was hidden behind a miniature sofa could then find an actual stuffed dog in a real room (DeLoache, 1987).

During the second half of the preoperational stage, according to Piaget, four- to seven-year-olds begin to make intuitive guesses about the world. However, Piaget observed that they cannot distinguish between the seen and the unseen, between the physical and the mental. Thus, in interviews with Piaget, children in this age range claimed that dreams are real and take place outside of themselves as "pictures on the window," "a circus in the room," or "something from the sky."

Children's thinking at this stage is so dominated by what they can see and touch for themselves, Piaget said, that they also do not realize that something is the same if its appearance is changed. In one study, for example, preoperational children thought that a cat wearing a dog mask was actually a dog, because that's what it looked like (DeVries, 1969). In short, they do not yet have what Piaget called **conservation,** the ability to recognize that important properties of a substance—including its volume, weight, and species—remain constant despite changes in its shape.

In a test of conservation, Piaget showed children water from two equal-sized glasses being poured into a tall, thin glass and a short, wide one and then asked them if one glass contained more water than the other. Children at the preoperational stage of development guessed that one glass (usually the taller one) contained more. They were dominated by the evidence of their eyes. If the glass looked bigger, then it contained

During the second half of the preoperational period, according to Piaget, children believe that inanimate objects are alive and have intentions, feelings, and consciousness. The clouds go slowly because they have no paws or legs. Flowers grow because they want to. Empty cars feel lonely.

©1993 Bil Keane, Inc.
Dist. by Cowles Synd., Inc.

"I think the moon likes us. It keeps on followin' us."

more. Children at this stage did not understand the logic of *reversibility* (you just poured the water from one container to another, so you can pour it back and it will still be the same amount) or *complementarity* (one glass is taller but also narrower; the other is shorter but also wider). Rather, they focused on only one dimension at a time—the most salient one—and made their best intuitive guess. Indeed, Piaget named this stage "*pre*operational" because children at this stage do not yet understand logical mental *operations* such as reversibility and complementarity.

Concrete Operational Thought   Sometime around the age of six or seven, Piaget observed, children do develop the ability to conserve number and amount. When they do so, they enter what Piaget called the stage of **concrete operations.** Now, he said, they can count, measure, add, and subtract; their thinking is no longer dominated by the appearance of things. They can use simple logic and perform simple mental manipulations and mental operations on things. They can sort objects into classes (such as tools, fruit, and vehicles) or series (such as largest to smallest) by systematic searching and ordering.

Still, concrete operational children can perform their logical operations only on real, concrete objects—sticks and glasses, tools and fruit—not on abstract concepts like justice and freedom. They can reason only about what is, not about what is possible. The ability to think logically about abstract ideas comes in the next stage of cognitive development. This *formal operational period* occurs during adolescence, which we discuss later in the chapter.

Modifying Piaget's Theory

Piaget's observations and demonstrations of children's cognitive development are vivid and fascinating. He was right in pointing out that there are significant shifts with age in children's thinking and that thinking becomes more systematic, consistent, and integrated as children get older. His descriptions of assimilation and accommodation as mechanisms by which development occurs remain one of the strong, if untestable, contributions of his theory. And his idea that children are active explorers and constructors of knowledge, not passive recipients of input from the environment, has been absorbed into our contemporary ways of thinking about childhood. Piaget also inspired other psychologists to test his findings and theory with experiments of their own. On the basis of these experiments it appears that Piaget's theory needs some modification.

What needs to be modified most is Piaget's notion of developmental stages. Several studies have shown that changes from one stage to the next are less consistent and global than Piaget suggested. For example, three-year-olds *can* sometimes make the distinction between physical and mental phenomena; they know the characteristics of real dogs versus pretend dogs (Wooley & Wellman, 1993). Children of this age know what thinking is, even though they can't yet tell when someone is doing it—because it doesn't look like anything is happening (Flavell, Green & Flavell, 1995). And they can do conservation tasks if they are allowed to count the number of objects or have been trained to focus on relevant dimensions such as number, height, and width (Gelman & Baillargeon, 1983).

Taken together, these studies suggest that children's knowledge and mental strategies develop at different ages in different areas, and in "pockets" rather than at global levels of understanding (Sternberg, 1989). Knowledge in particular areas is demonstrated sooner in children who are given specific experience in those areas or who are faced with very simple questions and tasks. Thus, children's reasoning depends not only on their general level of development but also on how easy the task is, how familiar they are with the objects involved, how well they understand the language being used, and what experiences they have had in similar situations. Recent research has also shown that the level of a child's thinking varies from day to day and may even shift when the child solves the same problem twice in the same day. Most five-year-olds, for example, have several different ways of thinking about conservation problems—or time telling, or addition, or block building, or map drawing. About a third of the time, they change mental strategies when trying to solve the same problem twice in a single session or on two successive days. Further, they are just as likely to switch from a more advanced strategy to a simpler one than the other way around (Siegler, 1994).

In summary, psychologists today are now beginning to think of cognitive development in terms of rising and falling "waves," not fixed stages—in terms of changing frequencies in children's use of different ways of thinking, not sudden, permanent shifts from one way of thinking to another (Siegler, 1994, 1995). They suggest that children systematically try out many different solutions to problems and gradually come to select the best of them.

Information Processing During Childhood

An alternative to Piaget's theory of cognitive development is based on the **information-processing** approach described in Chapters 8 and 9. This approach to development describes cognitive activities in terms of how people take in information, use it, and remember it. Developmental psychologists taking this approach focus on gradual quantitative changes in children's mental capacities, rather than on qualitative advances or stages of development.

Research by these psychologists demonstrates that, as children get older, their information-processing skills gradually get better. Older children have longer attention spans. They take in information and shift their attention from one task to another more rapidly (Manis, Keating & Morrison, 1980). They are also more efficient in processing information once it is received (Case, 1985). For instance, they code information into fewer dimensions and divide tasks into steps that can be processed one after another (Halford et al., 1994).

There are also marked improvements in children's memory storage capacity. Preschoolers can keep only two or three pieces of information in mind at the same time; older children can remember more (Morrison, Holmes & Haith, 1974). Their memory capacities get larger every year, though only up to a point. As noted in Chapter 8, even most adults can hold only about seven pieces of information in mind at any one time.

We don't yet know the whole story of what causes these increases in children's attention, information processing, and memory capacities. A full explanation will undoubtedly include both nature—specifically, maturation of the brain (Case, 1992; Robin & Holyoak, 1995)—and nurture, including increased familiarity with the information to be processed and memorized. Researchers have observed that the cognitive abilities of children improve dramatically when they are dealing with familiar rather than unfamiliar material. In one experiment, Mayan children in Mexico lagged behind their age-mates in the United States on standard memory tests of pictures and nouns, but they

LINKAGES Why does memory improve during childhood? (a link to Memory)

THE GROWTH OF MEMORY CAPACITY Memory abilities depend to some extent on the familiarity of the items to be remembered. For example, children who are chess experts have much better memories for the placement of chess pieces than non-expert adults—even though adults usually perform better than children on most other memory tests (Chi, 1978).

IN REVIEW	Milestones of Cognitive Development in Infancy and Childhood	
Age*	**Achievement**	**Description**
3–4 months	Maturation of senses	Immaturities that limit the newborn's vision and hearing are overcome.
	Voluntary movement	Reflexes disappear, and infants begin to gain voluntary control over their movements.
12–18 months	Mental representation	Infants can form images of objects and actions in their minds.
	Object permanence	Infants understand that objects exist even when out of sight.
18–24 months	Symbolic thought	Young children use symbols to represent things that are not present in their pretend play, drawing, and talk.
4 years	Intuitive thought	Children reason about events, real and imagined, by guessing rather than by engaging in logical analysis.
6–7 years	Concrete operations	Children can apply simple logical operations to real objects. For example, they recognize that important properties of a substance, such as number or amount, remain constant despite changes in shape or position.
	Conservation	
7–8 years	Information processing	Children can remember about seven pieces of information; they begin to learn strategies for memorization.

*These ages are approximate; they indicate the order in which children first reach these milestones of cognitive development rather than the exact ages.

did a lot better when researchers gave them a more familiar task, such as recalling miniature objects in a model of a Mayan village (Rogoff & Waddell, 1982).

Better memorization strategies—another aspect of nurture—may also help account for the improvement in children's memories. To a great extent, children learn these strategies in school. They learn how to memorize and how to study. They learn to repeat information over and over to help fix it in memory, to place information into categories, and, as discussed in Chapter 8, to use memory aids like "*i* before *e* except after *c*" to help them remember. They also learn what situations call for deliberate memorization and what factors, such as the length of a list, affect memory.

After about age seven, schoolchildren are also better at remembering more complex and abstract information, such as the gist of what several people have said during a conversation. Their memories are more accurate, extensive, and well organized. The knowledge they have accumulated allows them to draw more inferences and to integrate new information into a more complete network of facts, a more complete mental filing system. (See "In Review: Milestones of Cognitive Development in Infancy and Childhood.")

LINKAGES: DEVELOPMENT AND MEMORY

What happens to our memories of infancy?

The ability to remember facts and figures, pictures and objects, improves as we get older and more expert at processing information. But take a minute right now and try to recall anything that happened to you when you were, say, one year old. Most people can accurately recall a few autobiographical memories from age five or six but remember virtually nothing from before the age of three (Pillemer & White, 1989; Usher & Neisser, 1993).

Psychologists have not yet found a fully satisfactory explanation for this "infantile amnesia." Some have suggested that young children lack the memory encoding and storage processes described in Chapter 8, yet children of two or three can clearly recall experiences that happened weeks or even months earlier (Bauer, 1996; Fivush, Gray & Fromhoff, 1987; Peterson, 1995). Freud claimed that the defense mechanism of repression keeps us from recalling emotionally troubling memories (see Chapter 14), but most childhood memories are not emotionally troubling. Why should we repress virtually all of them? Still other psychologists suggest that infantile amnesia occurs because very young children lack a sense of self. Since they don't even recognize themselves in the mirror, they may not have a framework for organizing memories about what happens to them (Howe, 1995). However, this explanation would hold for only the first two years or so, because, after that, children do recognize themselves.

Another possibility is that early memories, though "present," are implicit rather than explicit. As described in Chapter 8, implicit memories form automatically and can affect our emotions and behavior even when we do not consciously recall them. Toddlers' implicit memories were demonstrated in one study in which two-and-a-half-year-olds apparently remembered a strange, pitch-dark room where they had participated in an experiment two years earlier (Perris, Myers & Clifton, 1990). Unlike children who had never been in the room, these children were unafraid and reached for noisy objects in the dark, just as they had learned to do at the previous session. Note, however, that children's implicit memories of their early years, like their explicit memories, are quite limited. For example, Nora Newcombe and Nathan Fox (1994) showed photographs of young children to a group of ten-year-old subjects. Some of the photos were of preschool classmates whom the subjects had not seen since they were five years old. They explicitly recalled 21 percent of their former classmates, and their skin conductance (an index of emotion) indicated that they had implicit memories of an additional 5 percent. Yet these subjects had *no* memory of 74 percent of their preschool pals, as compared to adults in another study who correctly identified 90 percent of photographs of high-school classmates they had not seen for thirty years (Bahrick, Bahrick & Wittlinger, 1975).

Other explanations of infantile amnesia suggest that our early memories are lost because we do not yet have the language skills to talk about, and thus solidify, those memories (Fivush, Haden & Adam, 1995; Nelson, 1993). Still others say that early memories are stored, but, because the schemas we used in early childhood to mentally represent them have changed, we no longer possess the retrieval cues necessary to recall them. A related possibility is that early experiences tend to be fused into *generalized event representations,* such as "going to Grandma's" or "playing at the beach," so that it becomes difficult to remember any specific event. Research on hypotheses such as these may someday unravel the mystery of infantile amnesia.

Culture and Cognitive Development

Whereas Piaget focused on the physical world of objects in explaining development, Russian psychologist Lev Vygotsky (1934/1962) focused on the social world of people. He viewed the human mind as a product of cultural history. The child's mind, said Vygotsky, grows through interaction with other minds. Indeed, cases like the Wild Boy of Aveyron show that, without society, children's minds do not develop much beyond those of animals. Vygotsky proposed that it is through interaction with parents, teachers, and other representatives of their culture that children acquire the ideas of that culture.

Researchers in the West have pursued Vygotsky's ideas by studying the effects of the social world on children's development. For example, Katherine Nelson (1986) has studied how participation in social routines affects children's developing knowledge of the world. In North American culture, such routines include shopping, eating at McDonald's, going to birthday parties, and attending religious services. In another culture they might include helping to make pottery, going hunting, and weaving baskets. Quite early, children develop mental representations, called *scripts,* for these activities (as described in Chapter 9). By the time they are three, children can describe routine activities quite accurately. Scripts, in turn, affect children's knowledge and understanding of cognitive tasks. Thus, for example, middle-class children can understand conservation problems earlier than inner-city children if the problems are presented, as Piaget's were, like miniature science experiments. But the performance of inner-city children is improved when the task is presented via a script that is more familiar to them, such as one involving what a "slick trickster" would do to fool someone (White & Glick, 1978, described by Nelson, 1986).

Children's cognitive abilities are influenced by the very language of their culture. Korean and Chinese children, for instance, show exceptional ability at adding and subtracting large numbers (Fuson & Kwon, 1992b; Miller et al., 1995). As third-graders, they can do in their heads three-digit problems—such as 702 minus 125—that their peers in the United States labor over or fail to solve. The difference seems traceable in part to the clear and explicit way that Asian languages label numbers from eleven to nineteen. In English, the meaning of the words *eleven* and *twelve,* for instance, is not as clear as *ten-one* and *ten-two.* Moreover, Asians use the metric system of measurement and the abacus—both of which are structured around the number ten. Korean math textbooks emphasize this tens structure by presenting the ones digits in red, the tens in blue, and the hundreds in green. Above all, for children in Asian cultures, educational achievement, especially in mathematics, is emphatically encouraged and conscientiously taught in school (Stevenson, Azuma & Hakuta, 1986; Stigler, 1992). Children's cognitive development is thus affected in ways large and small by the culture in which they are enmeshed.

Although *primary abilities* such as talking, comprehension of basic navigational principles, and simple arithmetic are learned by all children in all cultures as they play with objects and interact with people, *secondary abilities* such as reading, writing, formal geometry, and complex algebra develop only in those cultures where they are deliberately taught (Geary, 1995).

Individual Variations in Cognitive Development

Even within a single culture, some children are mentally precocious while others lag behind their peers. Why? As already suggested, heredity is an important factor (Plomin, 1989). Genes do not fix a child's cognitive development, but they do set some general limits on it. And within those limits, experience plays a role. To explore how significant that role is, psychologists have studied the cognitive development of children in many different rearing environments.

Cognitive development is profoundly delayed if children are raised in environments where they are deprived of the everyday sights, sounds, and feelings provided by conversation and loving interaction with family members, by pictures and books, even by television and radio. Children subjected to such severe deprivation show marked impairment in intellectual development by the time they are two or three years old (Rymer, 1993). Cognitive development may also be impaired by less extreme conditions of deprivation, including the neglect, malnourishment, noise, and chaos that occur in some homes (Sigman, 1995; Wachs, 1992). Sadly, about 22 percent of U.S. children are growing up in poverty (U.S. Bureau of the Census, 1992). An extensive study of such children found that they scored nine points lower on IQ tests by the time they were five years old than did children in families whose incomes were twice the poverty level—even after the researchers had controlled for all other family variables, such as family structure and parents' education (Duncan, Brooks-Gunn & Klebanov, 1994).

THE TRAGIC CASE OF GENIE When "Genie" was discovered at age fourteen, she weighed only fifty-nine pounds and could not hop, skip, or climb. The only words she could utter were "stopit" and "nomore." Investigators discovered that she had spent her life confined to a small bedroom, harnessed to a potty seat during the day and caged in a crib at night. She had not been permitted to hear or make many sounds. Although scientists and therapists worked intensively with Genie in the years after her discovery, like the Wild Boy of Aveyron, she never learned to speak in complete sentences.

In families above the poverty line, too, children's cognitive development is related to their surroundings and experiences. Parents can often make the difference between a child's getting A's or getting C's. To help children achieve those A's, adults can expose them, from the early years, to a variety of interesting materials and experiences—though not so many that the child is overwhelmed (Clarke-Stewart, 1988a). Children's cognitive development is also promoted when parents read and talk to them, encourage and help them to explore, and actively teach them (Gottfried, 1984)—in short, when they provide both support and challenge for their children's talents (Wong & Csikszentmihalyi, 1992). While no substitute for adult attention, electronic games also provide opportunities for school-age children to hone spatial skills that can help improve their performance in math and science (Subrahmanyam & Greenfield, 1994; Greenfield et al., 1994).

To improve the cognitive skills of children who do not get these kinds of stimulation, developmental psychologists have provided some children with extra lessons, materials, and educational contact with sensitive adults. In the United States, the most comprehensive effort to provide this kind of help has been through Head Start, a preschool program for poor children (see Chapter 10). Numerous smaller, more intensive programs have also been carried out. In a variety of such programs, children's cognitive abilities have been enhanced (Ramey & Ramey, 1992), demonstrating that the environment can directly affect cognitive development.

As a group, Asian-American students are prominent among those in the United States who have generally not needed educational support programs. Even first-generation Asian immigrants get better grades on average than their European-, African-, or Hispanic-American classmates (Steinberg, Dornbusch & Brown, 1992). Why? All these groups are learning in the same schools, so the performance difference cannot be due to the Asian numbering system, the abacus, or the more intense instructional methods mentioned earlier. Asian-American students' superior achievements are more likely due to better work habits rooted in their families' cultural traditions. One study of more than 4,000 students in the United States, Japan, and China, for example, found that Asian parents had the highest expectations for their children's achievement (Crystal et al., 1994). Parents of Asian-American students also appear to provide more help with homework and more after-school lessons than do other parents (Fuson & Kwon, 1992b). Compared to other groups, Asian-American students also receive more encouragement and help with their homework from older siblings (Caplan, Whitemore & Choy, 1989).

ENCOURAGING ACADEMIC ACHIEVEMENT
Asian-American children tend to do better in school than European-American children partly because Asian-American children's families tend to provide especially strong support for academic achievement.

INFANCY AND CHILDHOOD: SOCIAL AND EMOTIONAL DEVELOPMENT

Life for the child is more than learning about objects, doing math problems, and getting good grades. From the first months onward, infants are attracted by people—and most of them are immensely attractive creatures themselves, with their tiny bodies, large eyes, chubby cheeks, rosebud mouths, and soft gurgles. These qualities exert a powerful pull on people around them, especially parents and other caregivers.

Mutual attraction begins immediately. During the first hour or so after birth, babies are usually awake. During this time, researchers have observed, if they are with their mother, they gaze at her face while she gazes back and gives gentle touches (Klaus & Kennell, 1976). This is the first opportunity for the mother to display her *bond* to her infant—an emotional tie that begins even before the baby is born. Psychologists once believed that this immediate postbirth contact was critical—that the mother-infant bond would never be strong if the opportunity for early interaction was missed. Research has revealed, however, that such interaction is a luxury, not a requirement for a close relationship (Myers, 1987). With or without early contact, mothers *and* fathers, whether biological or adoptive, gradually form close attachments to their infants by interacting with them day after day.

From an early age, infants are sensitive to the people around them. They prefer to look at children and at attractive faces (Bigelow et al., 1990; Langlois et al., 1991), and they respond to facial expressions. They gaze at beaming faces, and smile at toothy grins (Malatesta & Izard, 1984; Oster, 1981). In one study, researchers tested the ability of three-month-olds to respond to emotional cues from their mothers (Cohn & Tronick, 1983). Some mothers acted normally, whereas others were asked to act depressed. Babies of the "depressed" mothers spent more time protesting, reacting warily, looking away, or giving only fleeting smiles.

Infants also communicate their feelings to their parents, not only by crying and screaming but also more subtly. They signal when they want to interact by looking and smiling; they indicate that they do not want to interact by turning away and sucking their thumbs (Tronick, 1989). If caregivers do not respond to their infants' emotional signals, babies will not learn that their behavior has consequences, and their development will be hindered (Lewis & Goldberg, 1969). In families where infants are generally healthy and adults are attentive and responsive, where infants are part of a mutual

being there to first have contact doesn't mean close bond.

FORMING A BOND Mutual eye contact, exaggerated facial expressions, and shared baby talk are an important part of the early social interactions that promote an enduring bond of attachment between parent and child.

communication system in which caregivers aid their attempts to achieve a goal, emotional development has a strong foundation and the children thrive.

Individual Temperament

From the moment infants are born, they differ from one another in the emotions they express. Some infants are happy, active, and vigorous; they splash, thrash, and wriggle. Others lie still most of the time. Some infants approach new objects with enthusiasm; others turn away or fuss. Some infants whimper; others kick, scream, and wail. Characteristics like these make up the infant's temperament. **Temperament** refers to the infant's individual style and frequency of expressing needs and emotions; it is constitutional, biological, and genetically based. In other words, it reflects a contribution by nature to the beginning of an individual's personality.

In some of the earliest research on infant temperament, Alexander Thomas and Stella Chess (1977) found three main temperament patterns. *Easy babies,* the most common kind, get hungry and sleepy at predictable times, react to new situations cheerfully, and seldom fuss. *Difficult babies* are irregular and irritable. Those in the third group, *slow-to-warm-up babies,* react warily to new situations but eventually come to enjoy them.

Traces of early temperamental characteristics weave their way throughout childhood (McNeil & Persson-Blennow, 1988). Easy infants usually stay easy, and difficult infants often remain difficult (Guerin & Gottfried, 1986; Riese, 1986). Timid toddlers tend to become shy preschoolers, restrained and inhibited eight-year-olds, and somewhat anxious teenagers (Kagan, et al., 1994; Schwartz, Kagan & Snidman, 1995). However, in temperament as in cognitive development, nature interacts with nurture. Many events take place between infancy and adulthood to shift the individual's development in one direction or another.

One possibly influential factor suggested by Thomas and Chess is the match between the infant's temperament and the parents' expectations, desires, and personal styles. When parents believe they are responsible for the infant's behavior, an easy child might reassure them. If parents are looking for signs of assertiveness, a difficult child might prove welcome.

If parent and infant are in tune, chances increase that temperamental qualities will be stable. Consider, for example, the temperament patterns of Chinese-American and European-American children (Kagan et al., 1994; Smith & Freedman, 1983). At birth, Chinese-American infants are calmer, less changeable, less perturbable, and more easily consoled when upset than European-American infants, suggesting that there may be an inherited predisposition toward self-control among the Chinese. This tendency is then powerfully reinforced by the Chinese culture. Compared with European-American parents, Chinese parents are less likely to reward and stimulate babbling and smiling, and more likely to maintain close control of their young children. The children, in turn, are more dependent on their mothers and less likely to play by themselves; they are less vocal, noisy, and active than European-American children.

These temperamental differences between children in different ethnic groups illustrate the combined contributions of nature and nurture. Many other illustrations are available in the cross-cultural literature. Mayan infants, for example, are relatively inactive from birth. The Zinacantecos, a Mayan group in southern Mexico, reinforce this innate predisposition toward restrained motor activity by swaddling their infants and by nursing at the slightest sign of movement (Greenfield & Childs, 1991). This combination of genetic predisposition and cultural reinforcement is culturally adaptive: Quiet infants do not kick off their covers at night, which is important in the cold highlands where they live; inactive infants are able to spend long periods on their mother's back as she works at the loom; infants who do not begin to walk until they can understand some language do not wander into the open fire at the center of the house. This adaptive interplay of innate and cultural factors in the development of temperament operates in all cultures.

The Infant Grows Attached

During the first year of life, as infants and caregivers respond to one another, the infant begins to form an **attachment**—a deep, affectionate, close, and enduring relationship—to these important figures. John Bowlby (1951, 1973), a British psychoanalyst, drew attention to the importance of attachment after he observed the dire effects of separation from parents on children who had been orphaned in World War II. These children's depression and other emotional scars led Bowlby to develop a theory about the importance of developing a strong attachment to one's primary caregivers, a tie that normally keeps infants close to their caregivers and, therefore, safe. Soon after Bowlby first described his theory, researchers in the United States began to investigate how such attachments are formed and what happens when they are not formed, or when they are broken by loss or separation. Perhaps the most dramatic of these studies was conducted with monkeys by Harry Harlow.

Motherless Monkeys   Harlow (1959) separated newborn monkeys from their mothers and reared them in cages containing two artificial mothers. One "mother" was made of wire with a rubber nipple from which the infant could get milk (see Figure 12.6); it provided food but no physical comfort. The other artificial mother had no nipple but was made of soft, comfortable terrycloth. If attachments form entirely because caregivers provide food, the infants would be expected to prefer the wire mother. In fact, they spent most of their time with the terrycloth mother. And when they were frightened by a mechanical robot, the infants immediately ran to their terrycloth mother and clung to it. Harlow concluded that the monkeys were motivated by the need for contact comfort. The terrycloth mother provided feelings of softness and cuddling, which were things the infants needed when their safety was in jeopardy.

Harlow also investigated what happens when attachments do not form. He isolated some monkeys from all social contact from birth. After a year of this isolation, the monkeys showed dramatic disturbances. When visited by normally active, playful monkeys, they withdrew to a corner, huddling or rocking for hours. These monkeys' problems continued into adulthood. The males seldom got further than touching a potential sexual partner; the females quickly ran from any male who made a sexual advance. When some of the females were made pregnant through artificial insemination, their maternal behaviors were woefully inadequate. In most cases, these mothers ignored their

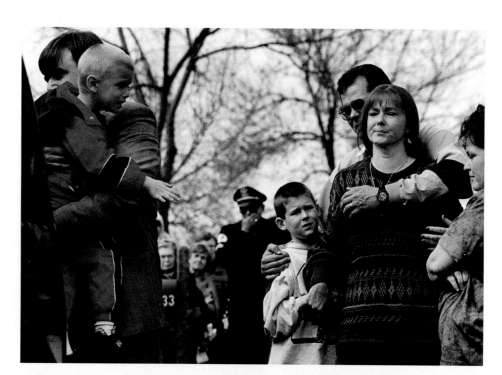

BREAKING A BOND   On April 30, 1995, after a four-year battle over his custody, "Baby Richard" was taken from the adoptive parents to whom he formed a strong emotional attachment, and turned over to his biological father. The tearful separation shown here, as Richard is carried away by his biological father, touched many hearts, and raised serious questions about the U.S. legal system, adoption laws, and apparent disregard for psychological research on attachment.

Wire and Terrycloth "Mothers"

Here are the two types of artificial mothers used in Harlow's research. Although baby monkeys received milk from the wire mother, they spent most of their time with the terrycloth version and would cling to it when frightened.

infants. When the infants began to send distress signals, the mothers physically abused and sometimes even killed them.

The degree to which this research might apply to humans is not entirely clear. Still, Harlow's work does demonstrate the effects of extreme deprivation, and one might expect that human babies would also suffer if their caregivers were unavailable or unresponsive.

Forming an Attachment   Researchers would never raise human babies like Harlow's monkeys, without social contact; but they have investigated the development of attachment in human babies as it occurs naturally under different conditions. In most cultures in which the attachment process has been studied, the mother is usually the first person to whom the baby forms an attachment. By the age of six or seven months, infants show signs of preferring the mother to anyone else—crawling after her, calling her, embracing her, clambering up into her lap, and protesting when she leaves (Ainsworth, 1973). Infants also develop attachments to their fathers, but usually a little later (Lamb, 1976).

Not only is father-infant interaction less frequent than mother-infant interaction, but most studies show that it has a somewhat different nature. Mothers tend to feed, bathe, dress, cuddle, and talk to their infants, whereas fathers are more likely to play with, jiggle, and toss them, especially sons (Clarke-Stewart, 1980; Lamb, 1977). Fathers are usually just as sensitive and responsive to their infant's expressions while things are going well; but when the baby gets bored or distressed, fathers may not do as well as mothers (Power & Parke, 1983).

Variations in Attachment   The amount of closeness and contact the infant seeks with either mother or father depends to some extent on the infant. Those who are ill or tired or slow to warm up may require more closeness. Closeness also depends to some extent on the parent. An infant whose parent has been absent, aloof, or unresponsive is likely to need more closeness than one whose parent is accessible and responsive.

Researchers have studied the differences in infants' attachments in a special situation that simulates the natural comings and goings of parents and infants—the so-called *Strange Situation* (Ainsworth et al., 1978). Mother and infant come to an unfamiliar playroom in a laboratory, where the infant interacts with the mother and an unfamiliar woman in brief episodes: The infant plays with the mother and stranger in the room,

CULTURAL DIFFERENCES IN PARENT-CHILD RELATIONS   In Japan, good mothers are expected to be completely devoted to the child, giving unconditional love and affection, and rarely separating from the infant (MiYake, Chen & Campos, 1985; White, 1987). In Japan, as in many other cultures, infants sleep with their parents. All these factors lead to extremely close mother-child attachments.

the mother and stranger leave the baby alone in the room, and the mother returns to the room.

Researchers have found that most infants in the United States display a *secure attachment* to the mother in the Strange Situation (Karen, 1994). Their urge to be close is balanced by their urge to explore the environment. In the unfamiliar room, the infant uses the mother as a home base, leaving her side to explore and play but returning to her periodically for comfort or contact. Securely attached children can tolerate the brief separation from their mother, but they are always happy to see her return and they are always receptive to her overtures of contact. These mother-child pairs, researchers have found, tend to have harmonious interactions from the earliest months (Isabella, Belsky & von Eye, 1989). The mothers themselves tend to be sensitive and responsive (Clarke-Stewart, 1988a).

Some infants, however, form an *anxious insecure attachment.* Their relationship may be (1) *avoidant*—they avoid or ignore the mother when she approaches or when she returns after the brief separation; (2) *ambivalent*—they are upset when their mother leaves, but when she returns they act angry and reject her efforts at contact, and when picked up they squirm to get down; or (3) *disorganized*—their behavior is inconsistent, disturbed, and disturbing; they may begin to cry again after the mother has returned and comforted them, or they may reach out for the mother while looking away from her.

Mothers who are rejecting, abusive, or neglectful are likely to have children with insecure attachments (Schneider-Rosen et al., 1985), but do these behaviors actually cause the problem? In the Netherlands, Dymphna van den Boom (1994) addressed this question by randomly assigning volunteer mothers of temperamentally difficult six-month-olds to either a no-treatment condition or a three-month parent-training program that taught them how to monitor, interpret, and properly respond to their infants' signals. Three times as many of the trained versus untrained mothers' infants showed secure attachments when observed at the age of one year.

The security of a child's attachment to parents has a number of far-reaching implications. Compared with insecurely attached children, those who are securely attached tend to be more socially and emotionally competent; more cooperative, enthusiastic, and persistent; better at solving problems; more compliant and controlled; and more popular and playful (Clarke-Stewart, 1988a; Elicker & Sroufe, 1992/3; Wartner et al., 1994). First-graders with secure attachments report less loneliness than do those with insecure ambivalent attachments (Berlin, Cassidy & Belsky, 1995). However, attachment is just one of many factors—including stressful events and family characteristics—that affect the course of a child's development.

Patterns of child care and attachment vary widely in different parts of the world. In northern Germany, for example, the proportion of infants who display avoidant behavior in the Strange Situation is much higher than in the United States (Grossmann et al.,

1985). In Japan, it is impossible for many mothers to leave their infants in the Strange Situation because the infants are so distressed by separation (Miyake, Chen & Campos, 1985). And in Israel, kibbutz babies who sleep in infant houses away from their parents are relatively likely to show insecure attachments (Sagi et al., 1994). Yet another pattern is seen among the Efe, a pygmy people. Efe infants spend almost all their time in contact with other people, but only about half of it is with their mothers (Tronick, Morelli & Ivey, 1992). As a consequence, their attachments are not as focused on a single maternal figure as are those of infants in other cultures.

With the mothers of half the infants in the United States working outside the home, concern has been expressed about how daily separations from their mothers affect infants. Some have argued that putting infants in day care, with a babysitter or in a day-care center, damages the quality of the mother-infant relationship and increases the babies' risk for psychological problems later on (Belsky, 1992; Leach, 1994; Karen, 1994).

THINKING CRITICALLY

Does Day Care Harm the Emotional Development of Infants?

What am I being asked to believe or accept?

The claim to be evaluated is that daily separations created by day care damage the formation of an attachment between the mother and infant and harm the infant's emotional development.

What evidence is available to support the assertion?

There is clear evidence that separation from the mother is painful for young children. Furthermore, if separation lasts a week or more, young children who have formed an attachment to their mother tend to protest, then become apathetic and mournful, and finally seem to lose interest in the missing mother (Robertson & Robertson, 1971). But day care does not involve such lasting separations, and research has shown that infants who are in day care do form attachments to their mothers. In fact, they prefer their mothers to their daytime caregivers (Clarke-Stewart & Fein, 1983).

Are these attachments as secure as the attachments formed by infants who are raised at home? Researchers have examined this question by comparing how infants react to brief separations from their mother in the Strange Situation. Combined data from about twenty observational studies reveal that infants in full-time day care are somewhat more likely to be classified as insecurely attached. About 36 percent of them are classified as insecure in this assessment of attachment; only 29 percent of the infants who were not in full-time day care were counted as insecure (Clarke-Stewart, 1989a; Lamb & Sternberg, 1990). These results appear to support the suggestion that day care harms infants' attachments to their mothers.

Are there alternative ways of interpreting the evidence?

Perhaps factors other than day care are at work, and the difference between infants in day care and those at home with their mothers is only apparent, not real. What could these other factors be?

One factor is the method that was used to assess attachment. Infants in these studies were judged insecure if they were relatively unperturbed by a brief separation from their mothers in an unfamiliar room with an unfamiliar woman. Maybe infants who experienced routine separations from their mothers when they were left in day care felt more comfortable in this situation and therefore sought out less closeness with their mothers. Maybe they were expressing their independence, not their insecurity. A second factor is the possible differences between the infants' mothers. Perhaps mothers who value independence in themselves and in their children are more likely to be working and to place their children in day care, whereas mothers who value closeness with their children are more likely to stay home. This self-selection could have led more infants of working mothers to be classified as insecure.

What additional evidence would help to evaluate the alternatives?

Finding a heightened rate of insecure attachment among the infants of working mothers does not, by itself, demonstrate that day care is harmful. To judge the effects of day care, we must consider other measures of emotional adjustment. If infants in day care showed consistent signs of impaired emotional relations in other situations (at home, say) and with other caregivers (for example, with the father), this evidence would support the argument that day care harms children's emotional development. Investigation of the behavior and attitudes of parents who use day care for their infants and those who do not would also be useful. If both groups of parents were comparable in every measurable way except for their use of day care, this too would support the argument. Finally, useful information might come from experimental research in which infants were randomly assigned to be in day care or to stay at home with Mother. But this kind of study has practical and ethical problems, and it is unlikely ever to be done.

What conclusions are most reasonable?

Psychologists cannot yet say whether day care, per se, is harmless or harmful. On the basis of available research (Clarke-Stewart, 1989a), the most reasonable conclusion at present is that there is an increased likelihood that infants in day care will ignore or avoid their mothers after a brief separation. Until we have figured out why, we should carefully study the development of infants in day care. Some day-care situations may be more harmful than others, and some infants may be more vulnerable than others to negative effects. For example, it seems likely that infants would be harmed if they were in unstable or low-quality day care, if they spent more than eight hours a day in the day-care setting, if they were temperamentally difficult, and if the parents were insensitive. To investigate these issues, the U.S. federal government has funded a study of infant care in ten sites around the country (NICHD Early Child Care Network, 1994). The psychological and physical development of more than 1,000 infants is being tracked from birth through the end of first grade and will be examined for the effects of experiences both in day care and at home.

Relationships with Parents and Peers

Erik Erikson (1968) saw the first year of life as the time when infants develop a feeling of basic trust (or mistrust) about the world. According to his psychodynamically oriented theory, an infant's first year represents the first of eight stages of lifelong psychosocial development (see Table 12.2). Each stage focuses on an issue or crisis that is especially important at that time of life. Erikson believed that the ways in which people resolve these issues shape their personalities and social relationships. Positive resolution of an issue provides the foundation for characteristics such as trust, autonomy, initiative, and industry. But if the crisis is not resolved positively, according to Erikson, the person will be psychologically troubled and cope less effectively with later crises. Thus, in Erikson's theory, forming basic feelings of trust during infancy is the bedrock for all future emotional development.

After children have formed strong emotional attachments to their parents, their next psychological task is to begin to develop a more autonomous relationship with them. In Erikson's theory, this task is reflected in the second stage (again, see Table 12.2). After developing a trusting relationship, children begin to exercise their wills, to develop some independence from their all-powerful parents, and to initiate activities on their own. According to Erikson, children who are not allowed to exercise their wills or ini-

	Age	Central Psychological Issue or Crisis
TABLE 12.2 Erikson's Stages of Psychosocial Development	First year	**Trust versus mistrust** Infants learn to trust that their needs will be met by the world, especially by the mother—or they learn to mistrust the world.
In each of Erikson's stages of development, a different psychological issue presents a new crisis for the person to resolve. The person focuses attention on the issue and by the end of the period has worked through the crisis and resolved it either positively, in the direction of healthy development, or negatively, hindering further psychological development.	Second year	**Autonomy versus shame and doubt** Children learn to exercise will, to make choices, and to control themselves—or they become uncertain and doubt that they can do things by themselves.
	Third to fifth year	**Initiative versus guilt** Children learn to initiate activities and enjoy their accomplishments, acquiring direction and purpose. Or, if they are not allowed initiative, they feel guilty for their attempts at independence.
	Sixth year through puberty	**Industry versus inferiority** Children develop a sense of industry and curiosity and are eager to learn—or they feel inferior and lose interest in the tasks before them.
	Adolescence	**Identity versus role confusion** Adolescents come to see themselves as unique and integrated persons with an ideology—or they become confused about what they want out of life.
	Early adulthood	**Intimacy versus isolation** Young people become able to commit themselves to another person—or they develop a sense of isolation and feel they have no one in the world but themselves.
	Middle age	**Generativity versus stagnation** Adults are willing to have and care for children and to devote themselves to their work and the common good—or they become self-centered and inactive.
	Old age	**Integrity versus despair** Older people enter a period of reflection, becoming assured that their lives have been meaningful and ready to face death with acceptance and dignity. Or they are in despair for their unaccomplished goals, failures, and ill-spent lives.

tiate their own activities will feel uncertain about doing things for themselves and guilty about seeking independence.

Socialization Styles **Socialization** is the process by which parents and others in authority channel children's impulses into socially accepted outlets and teach them the skills and rules needed to function in their society. Cultural values clearly shape this process. Parents in Hispanic cultures of Mexico, Puerto Rico, and Central America, for example, tend to be influenced by the collectivist tradition discussed in Chapter 1, in which family and community interests are emphasized over individual goals. Children in these cultures are expected to respect and obey their elders, and to do less of the questioning, negotiating, and arguing that is encouraged or allowed in many middle-class European-American families (Delgado-Gaitan, 1994; Greenfield, 1995). When parents from Hispanic cultures immigrate to the United States, their socialization goals may conflict with those of their children's European-American teachers (Raeff, Greenfield &

LINKAGES: PARENT-TRAINING PROGRAMS
Research in developmental psychology on the relationship between parents' socialization styles and children's behavior patterns has helped shape parent-training programs based on both the behavioral and the phenomenological approaches to personality described in Chapter 14. These programs are designed to teach parents authoritative methods that can avoid scenes like this.

Quiroz, 1995), and their own socialization efforts may become inconsistent (Harwood, Schulze & Wilson, 1995).

European-American parents tend to employ one of three distinct socialization patterns, as described by Diana Baumrind (1971). **Authoritarian parents** tend to be strict, punitive, and unsympathetic. They value obedience from children and try to shape their children's behavior to meet a set standard and to curb the children's wills. They do not encourage independence. They are detached and seldom praise their youngsters. In contrast, **permissive parents** give their children complete freedom and lax discipline. The third group, **authoritative parents,** fall between these two extremes. They reason with their children, encouraging give and take. They allow children increasing responsibility as they get older and better at making decisions. They are firm but understanding. They set limits but also encourage independence. Their demands are reasonable, rational, and consistent.

In her research with middle-class parents in Berkeley, California, Baumrind found these three socialization styles to be consistently related to young children's social and emotional development. Authoritarian parents had children who were unfriendly, distrustful, and withdrawn. The children of permissive parents were immature, dependent, and unhappy; they were likely to have tantrums or to ask for help when they encountered even slight difficulties. Children raised by authoritative parents were friendly, cooperative, self-reliant, and socially responsible. A follow-up study of the same children at age nine showed that the advantages of authoritative discipline were still present (Baumrind, 1986).

Other researchers following Baumrind's lead found authoritative socialization styles to be associated with additional positive outcomes, including better school achievement and better psychological adjustment to parental divorce (Hetherington & Clingempeel, 1992; Steinberg, Dornbusch & Brown, 1992; Steinberg et al., 1994). Socialization styles may also help mold children's moral behavior. Children who are given orders, threats, and punishments are more likely than others to cheat and less likely to experience guilt or to accept blame after doing something wrong (Hoffman, 1970).

The results of these studies of socialization are interesting, but they are limited in several ways. First, they are based on correlations, which, as discussed in Chapter 2, do not prove causation. Finding consistent correlations between parents' and children's behavior does not establish that parents are creating the differences seen in their children. Even evidence that differences between the children of authoritative and nonauthoritative parents tend to increase over time can only *suggest* that parents' socialization styles have a direct influence on children's behavior (Steinberg et al., 1994). In fact, parents' behavior may be shaped to some extent by the children, themselves, especially by their temperaments. A second limitation of socialization studies is that the correlations between socialization styles and children's behavior, though statistically significant, are not terribly strong. Expected outcomes do not always appear. For example, Baumrind (1971) found a small group of families in which, as with the permissive families, discipline was never observed, yet the children were thriving. Third, some developmental psychologists who take a cognitive approach suggest that it is not the parents' socialization practices *per se* that influence children but, rather, how the children perceive the discipline they receive—as stricter or more lenient than what an older sibling received, for example (Dunn & Plomin, 1990).

Finally, most socialization research has been done with European-American families in the United States. Therefore, the findings do not necessarily represent universal principles. As psychologists broaden their research to include families of diverse cultures and subcultures, they are discovering that the authoritative discipline so consistently linked with positive outcomes in European-American families may not be the ideal socialization style for *all* ethnic groups. It was not, for example, related to better school performance in African-American or Asian-American youngsters (Steinberg et al., 1992). One possible explanation is that different disciplinary styles have different meanings in different cultures. When Chinese-American parents use authoritarian discipline—which they do to a greater extent than European-American parents—their goal is usually to "train" *(chiao shun)* and "govern" *(guan)* children so that they will know what is expected of them (Chao, 1994). By contrast, European-American parents who use authoritarian discipline are more likely to do so to "break the child's will." Clearly, socialization—and its outcomes—must be evaluated in its cultural context.

Relationships with Peers   The saga of social development over the years of childhood is the story of an enlarging social world, which broadens to include brothers and sisters, playmates and classmates. Psychologists have observed that from a remarkably early age—as young as one year—children are interested in the behavior of other children, usually their siblings, and by the time they are a year-and-a-half old, they know how to hurt or comfort other children (Dunn, 1992).

Social skills, like cognitive skills, must be learned. Observations of two-year-old children in Western cultures show that the most they can do is to exchange—or fight over—toys (Mueller & Lucas, 1975). By the time these children are three, they can use toys as a means to an end, helping to elicit responses from peers; by age four, children begin to converse about the toys they are playing with. It is not until the end of the preschool period, however, that children are able to share toys and tasks cooperatively (Parten, 1932, 1971).

In the school years, peer interaction becomes more complex and structured as children play games with rules, play on teams, tutor each other, and cooperate—or compete—in achieving goals (Hartup, 1983). The school years are also the time when friends become important and friendships become long-lasting. In interviews with researchers, schoolchildren reveal that they now realize that feelings, not things, keep friends together (Selman, 1981). Friendships appear to be important for learning social skills such as cooperation and intimacy; they offer children a context for social and emotional growth. With friends, social activities are more intense, and children have more opportunities to resolve their conflicts than with mere acquaintances (Newcomb & Bagwell, 1995). Children who do not have friends usually experience problems in later life (Parker & Asher, 1987).

Social Skills and Understanding

The changes in peer interactions and relationships over the years of childhood can be traced in part to children's increasing social competence and understanding. Very young children do not have the social skills to engage in sustained, responsive interactions with other children. Parents can aid the development of these skills by initiating lots of pretend play and other positive social behaviors with their children (Kahen, Katz

CHILDREN'S FRIENDSHIPS Though relationships with peers may not always be cordial, they are often among the closest and most positive in a child's life. In North American cultures, children's friendships are almost always with children of the same sex. The reasons, presumably, are that children of the same sex share the same play interests and that children are attracted to others who are like themselves and want to avoid those who are different. Friends are more interactive than nonfriends; they smile and laugh together more, pay closer attention to equality in their conversations, and talk about mutual rather than their own idiosyncratic ends.

& Gottman, 1994), and by helping them to constructively express and deal with their emotions (Eisenberg, 1994).

Parents and other adults can also help children to detect and interpret emotional signals from others. Three- or four-year-old children can name typical facial expressions of happiness, sadness, anger, and fear (Camras, 1977). Girls are able to do this at younger ages than boys; their understanding of people's feelings is related to talking about feelings with their parents and having cooperative interactions with their siblings (Dunn et al., 1991). As they get older, children learn to recognize a wider range of emotions and to predict how a person will feel in emotion-provoking situations (Gnepp, 1983; Selman, 1980). These abilities are important because just as children's school performance depends on processing academic information, their social performance depends on processing information about other people. Knowing how to enter a play group or how to respond to teasing from a peer, for example, requires encoding what is happening and interpreting the other children's behavior (Dodge & Price, 1994). Children whose social skills allow them to understand another person's perspective, appreciate how that person might be feeling, and offer sympathy, cooperation, and help tend to be the most popular members of a peer group (Coie & Dodge, 1988; Dekovic & Gerris, 1994).

Gender Roles

LINKAGES   Do children perceive others as adults do? (a link to Social Cognition)

An important aspect of understanding other people is knowing about social roles. Toddlers pretend to perform imaginary acts such as bathing the baby or hosing the fire, but they are not aware that these acts are part of a social role. Later, they begin to understand that doctors wear white coats, ask to look at your tongue, and give injections; that parents buy things, make phone calls, and clean house. At age four, children understand how two or three roles fit together, and they can play family. By age six, they understand whole networks of roles, such as teacher, student, principal, and janitor, allowing them to play school (Watson, 1981).

Many of the roles children learn about are linked to being male or female. In all societies, some roles, like firefighter, have traditionally been male, whereas others, like nurse, have traditionally been female. These traditions are not nearly as strong in North American culture as they once were, but all cultures, North American included, do establish expectations about **gender roles,** which are general patterns of work, appearance, and behavior associated with being a man or a woman. Research by Deborah Best suggests that children learn gender-role expectations earliest in Muslim countries (where the roles are perhaps most extreme), but children in all twenty-five countries she studied eventually developed them (Best, 1992; Williams & Best, 1990). Gender roles persist because they are deeply rooted in both nature and nurture.

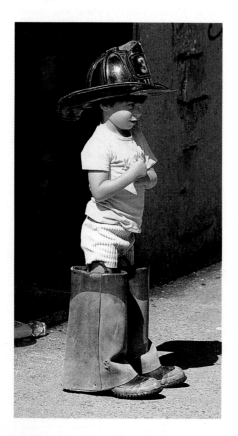

LEARNING GENDER ROLES   Socialization by parents and others typically encourages interests and activities traditionally associated with a child's own gender.

Small physical and behavioral differences between the sexes are evident early on and tend to increase over the years (Eagly, 1995; Feingold, 1988; Hyde, 1994; Jacklin, 1989; Linn & Peterson, 1985; Maccoby & Jacklin, 1974). For example, girls are less likely than boys to suffer from speech, learning, and behavior disorders, mental retardation, emotional problems, and sleep disorders. They tend to speak and write earlier and to be better at grammar and spelling. They are likely to be more nurturant and emotionally empathic; their play tends to be more orderly. At the same time, boys tend to be more skilled than girls at manipulating objects, constructing three-dimensional forms, and mentally manipulating complex figures and pictures. They are more physically active and aggressive and more inclined to hit obstacles or people; they play in larger groups and spaces, enjoying noisier, more strenuous physical games like soccer and football.

As described in Chapter 3, a biological contribution to these male-female differences is supported by studies of differences in anatomy, hormones, and brain organization and functioning (Begley, 1995; Hines & Green, 1991; Witelson, 1994). A biological basis of male-female differences is also supported by cross-cultural research showing consistency in gender patterns even in the face of differing socialization. In virtually every culture, for example, males are more violent than females. In one survey, there was not a single culture in which the number of women who killed women was

IN REVIEW	Social and Emotional Development During Infancy and Childhood		
Age	**Relationships with Parents**	**Relationships with Other Children**	**Social Understanding**
Birth–2 years	Infants form an attachment to the primary caregiver.	Play focuses on toys, not on other children.	Infants respond to emotional expressions of others.
2–4 years	Children become more autonomous and no longer need their parents' constant attention.	Toys are a way of eliciting responses from other children.	Young children can recognize emotions of others.
4–10 years	Parents actively socialize their children.	Children begin to cooperate, compete, play games, and form friendships with peers.	Children learn social rules, like politeness, and roles, like being a male or female; they learn to control their emotions.

LINKAGES   Who teaches boys to be men and girls to be women? (a link to Learning)

even one-tenth as great as the number of men who killed men; on average, men's homicides outnumbered women's by more than 30 to 1 (Daly & Wilson, 1988).

As always, however, it is difficult if not impossible to untangle biologically based gender differences from the socially created ones—to separate nature and nurture—because, from the moment they are born, boys and girls are treated differently. Adults usually play more gently and talk more to infants they believe to be girls than infants they believe to be boys (Culp, Cook & Housley, 1983). They often shower their daughters with dolls and doll clothes, their sons with trucks and tools (Rheingold & Cook, 1975). They tend to encourage boys to achieve, compete, and explore; to control their feelings, act independent, and assume personal responsibility. They more often encourage girls to be expressive, nurturant, reflective, dependent, domestic, obedient, and unselfish (Archer & Lloyd, 1985; Block, 1983; Hoffman, 1977; Shepherd-Look, 1982; Huston, Carpenter & Atwater, 1986). Thus parents, teachers, and television role models consciously or inadvertently pass on their ideas about "appropriate" behaviors for boys and girls.

Children also pick up notions of what is gender-appropriate behavior from their peers. Peer pressure exaggerates whatever differences may already exist. For example, boys tend to be better than girls at Nintendo and other computer or video games (Greenfield, 1994). This difference, however, stems in part from the fact that boys encourage and reward each other for skilled performance at these games more than girls do (Law, Pellegrino & Hunt, 1993). Children are more likely to play with other children of the same sex, and in gender-typical ways, on the playground than they are in private, at home, or in the classroom (Luria, 1992; Maccoby & Jacklin, 1987; Thorne, 1986). An analysis of 143 studies of sex differences in aggression showed that boys were significantly and consistently more aggressive than girls (especially in the preschool years), but especially so when they were being watched (Hyde, 1986). On the playground, at least, boys and girls form two different "cultures" (Maccoby, 1995).

In short, social training by both adults and peers tends to bolster and amplify any biological predispositions that distinguish boys and girls, thus creating gender roles that are the joint—and inextricably linked—products of nature and nurture. This and other elements of early development are summarized in "In Review: Social and Emotional Development During Infancy and Childhood."

The efforts of some parents to de-emphasize gender roles in their children's upbringing may be helping to reduce the magnitude of gender differences in areas such as verbal and quantitative skills (Halpern, 1992; Hyde, 1994). The evolutionary approach to psychology suggests, however, that other gender differences—such as males' greater ability to visualize the rotation of objects in space and females' greater ability to read facial expressions—are unlikely to change much. Proponents of this approach see such differences as deeply rooted reflections of gender-related hunting versus child-rearing duties that were adaptive eons ago for the survival of both sexes (Buss, 1995; Eagly, 1995).

ADOLESCENCE

The years of middle childhood usually pass smoothly, as children busy themselves with schoolwork, hobbies, friends, and clubs. But adolescence changes things drastically. All adolescents undergo significant changes in size, shape, and physical capacities. In Western cultures many adolescents also experience substantial changes in their social life, reasoning abilities, and views of themselves.

The Challenges of Change

The most visible sign to others that adolescence has begun is a sudden spurt in physical growth. This growth spurt peaks at about age twelve for girls and at about age fourteen for boys (see Figure 12.7; Tanner, 1978). Suddenly, adolescents find themselves in new bodies. At the end of the growth spurt, menstruation begins in females and live sperm are produced in males. This condition of being able for the first time to reproduce is called **puberty.**

In Western cultures, *early adolescence*—the period from age eleven to fourteen or so—is fraught with challenges. Sexual interest stirs, and there are opportunities to smoke, drink alcohol, and take other drugs. All of this can be very disorienting. Indeed, adolescents may experience bouts of depression and are vulnerable to other psychological problems as well (Kashani et al., 1989; see also Chapter 15).

Some of these problems appear as adolescents begin to face challenges to their *self-esteem,* their sense of being worthy, capable, and deserving of respect—especially if other stressors occur at the same time. Researchers have found that youths who experience more or stronger stressors—ranging from inadequate study space at home to parental divorce or unemployment—have more difficulty adapting to adolescence (DuBois et al., 1992).

Self-esteem is also related to physical maturity. In Western cultures, boys who go through puberty early tend to have higher status, to become leaders, and to be happy, poised, and relaxed. Those who reach puberty late are more likely to feel rejected, dependent, and dominated by others (Duke et al., 1982; Peterson, 1987). For girls, maturing early is likely to lead to embarrassment, sexual activity, and increased distance

At about ten-and-a-half-years of age, girls begin their growth spurt and by age twelve are taller than their male peers. When boys, at about twelve-and-a-half-years of age, begin their growth spurt, they usually grow faster and for a longer period of time than girls. Adolescents may grow as much as 5 inches a year. The development of sexual characteristics accompanies these changes in height. The ages at which these changes occur vary considerably across individuals, but their sequence is the same.

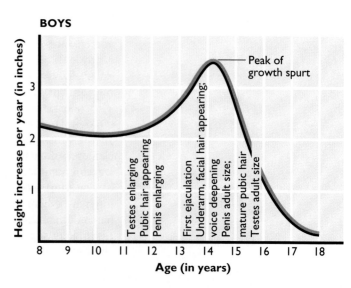

THE IMPACT OF TEENAGE PREGNANCY
A teenage pregnancy can wreak havoc for the baby as well as the parents. Teenage parents are less positive and stimulating with their children than older parents (Garcia-Coll, Oh & Hoffman, 1987) and are more likely to abuse them. The children of teenage parents, in turn, are likely to develop behavior problems and to do poorly in school (Furstenberg et al., 1989).

THIS IS CINDY.

CINDY IS 13 YEARS OLD.

WHICH MEANS SHE CAN'T DRINK.

SHE CAN'T DRIVE.

SHE CAN'T EVEN BUY CIGARETTES.

WHICH IS ALL THE BETTER FOR THE HEALTH AND SAFETY...

OF HER DAUGHTER.

MIKE SMITH

between the girls and their parents (Brooks-Gunn, 1988; Peterson, 1987). Differences between early and late maturers may persist into adulthood (Jones, 1957).

The changes and pressures of adolescence are often played out at home. Many teenagers become discontented with their parents' rules and values, leading to arguments over everything from taking out the garbage to who left the gallon of milk on top of the refrigerator. Serious conflicts may lead to serious problems, including running away, pregnancy, stealing, even suicide (Montemayor, 1983). In most families, however, the level of conflict is moderate (Steinberg, 1989, 1990). Especially in European-American families, adolescents whose parents retain an authoritative disciplinary style and maintain a balance between being too strict (authoritarian) and too lax (permissive) tend to remain well adjusted (Baumrind, 1991; Dornbusch et al., 1987).

In fact, although adolescence was once considered to be a period of inevitable storm and stress, contemporary research suggests that in Western cultures more than half of today's teens find early adolescence relatively trouble free; only about 15 percent of the adolescents studied experience serious turmoil (Peterson, 1987). Of those who do, sexuality is often involved. Surveys suggest that about half of North America's youth have had sexual intercourse by age sixteen; fifty years ago, the comparable figure was less than 10 percent (Brooks-Gunn & Furstenberg, 1989). The most dramatic increase has occurred among fifteen-year-old girls, of whom nearly one-third are now sexually active (Department of Health and Human Services, 1992). Teens who have sex differ from those who do not in a number of ways. They hold less conventional attitudes and values, and they are more likely to smoke, drink alcohol, and use other drugs. Their parents are less educated, exert less control over them, and are less likely to talk openly with them. A substantial number of sexually active girls were sexually abused as children (Musick, 1987).

Too often, sexual activity leads to declining school achievement and interest, sexually transmitted diseases, and, of course, unplanned and unwanted pregnancies. Teenagers have the highest rates of sexually transmitted diseases (such as gonorrhea, chlamydia, and pelvic inflammatory disease) of any age group. One-fifth of all AIDS cases start in adolescence. Nearly one-quarter of all teenage girls in the United States get pregnant before they reach age eighteen. More than 40 percent of U.S. adolescents who become pregnant elect to keep their babies and become single mothers. These girls are likely to end up with less education, poorer economic opportunities, and, usually, more children than they want or can afford to support (Furstenberg, Brooks-Gunn & Chase-Lansdale, 1989).

Identity and Development of the Self

In many Third World cultures today and in the United States during earlier times, the end of early adolescence, around the age of fourteen, marks the beginning of adulthood: of work, parenting, and grown-up responsibilities. In modern North America, the transition from childhood to adulthood often lasts well into the twenties. Adolescents spend a substantial amount of time being students or trainees. This lengthened adolescence has created special problems—among them, the matter of finding or forming an identity.

Forming a Personal and Ethnic Identity   Most adolescents have not previously thought about who they are. When preschool children are asked to describe themselves, they often mention a favorite or habitual activity: "I watch TV" or "I do the dishes" (Keller, Ford & Meacham, 1978). At eight or nine, children identify themselves by giving facts such as their sex, age, name, physical appearance, likes, and dislikes. They may still describe themselves in terms of what they do, but they now include how well they do it compared with other children (Secord & Peevers, 1974). Then, at about age eleven, children begin to describe themselves in terms of social relationships, personality traits, and general, stable psychological characteristics (Damon & Hart, 1982). These changes in the way children and adolescents describe themselves suggest changes in the way they think about themselves. As they become more self-conscious, they gradually develop a personal identity as unique individuals.

Adolescents may also describe themselves in terms of their ethnic or national identity. In the melting pot of the United States, some members of ethnic minorities may identify with their ethnic group—Chinese, Mexican, or Italian, for example—even more than with being Americans. Children are aware of ethnic cues such as skin color before they reach the age of three—minority-group children earlier than other children—and prefer to play with children from their own group (Hartrup, 1983; Milner, 1983). In high school, most students hang out with members of their own ethnic group; they tend not to know classmates in other ethnic groups well, seeing them more as members of those groups than as individuals (Steinberg, Dornbusch & Brown, 1992). These social processes solidify ethnic identity. A positive ethnic identity contributes to self-esteem; seeing their own group as superior makes people feel good about themselves (Turner, 1987). *Bicultural people,* who affirm both their ethnic and their national identities, also typically have a positive self-concept (Phinney, 1990). However, as described in Chapter 17, the same processes that foster ethnic identity can also sow the seeds of ethnic prejudice.

Facing the Identity Crisis   Identity formation is the central task of adolescence in Erik Erikson's theory of psychosocial development. According to Erikson (1968), events of late adolescence—graduating from high school, going to college, and forging new relationships—challenge the adolescent's self-concept, precipitating an **identity crisis** (see Table 12.2). In this crisis, the adolescent must develop an integrated self-image as a unique person by pulling together self-knowledge acquired during childhood. If infancy and childhood brought trust, autonomy, and initiative, according to Erikson, the adolescent will resolve the identity crisis positively, feeling self-confident and competent. If, however, infancy and childhood resulted in feelings of mistrust, shame, guilt, and inferiority, the adolescent will be confused about his or her identity and goals.

There is some limited empirical support for Erikson's ideas about the identity crisis in Western cultures. In late adolescence, young people do consider alternative identities (Waterman, 1982). They "try out" being rebellious, studious, or detached, as they attempt to resolve questions about sexuality, self-worth, industriousness, and independence. By the time they are twenty-one, about half of the adolescents studied have resolved the identity crisis in a way that is consistent with their self-image and the historical era in which they are living. They are ready to enter adulthood with self-confidence. Basically the same people who entered adolescence, they have more mature attitudes and behavior, more consistent goals and values, and a clearer idea of who they are (Adams & Jones, 1983; Savin-Williams & Demo, 1984). For those who fail to resolve identity issues—either because they avoided the identity crisis by accepting whatever identity their parents set for them or because they postponed dealing with the crisis and remain uncommitted and lacking in direction—there are often problems ahead.

Abstract Thought and Moral Reasoning

One reason that adolescents can develop a conscious identity is that at this age it is possible for the first time to think and reason about abstract concepts. For many young people in Western cultures, adolescence begins a stage of cognitive development that Piaget called the **formal operational period,** a stage marked by the ability to engage in hypothetical thinking, including the imagining of logical consequences. For example, adolescents who have reached the level of formal operations can consider various strategies for finding a part-time job and recognize that some methods are more likely to lead to success than others. They can form general concepts and understand the impact of the past on the present and the present on the future. They can question social institutions, think about the world as it might be and ought to be, and consider the ramifications of love, morality, work, politics, philosophy, and religion. They can think logically and systematically about symbols and propositions, regardless of whether the propositions are true. They can consider the possible consequences of there being no money in the world, for example.

Piaget explored adolescents' formal operational abilities by asking them to perform science experiments that involved formulating and systematically investigating hypotheses. Research indicates that only about half the people in Western cultures ever reach the formal operational level necessary to succeed in Piaget's experiments; those who have not had high school science and math are less likely to succeed (Keating, 1980; Neimark, 1982). In other cultures, too, people who have not gone to school are less likely to exhibit formal operations. Consider the following exchange in which a researcher tests the formal operations of an illiterate Kpelle farmer in a Liberian village (Scribner, 1977):

Researcher: All Kpelle men are rice farmers. Mr. Smith is not a rice farmer. Is he a Kpelle man?

Kpelle farmer: I don't know the man. I have not laid eyes on the man myself.

Kpelle villagers who had had formal schooling answered the question logically: "No, Mr. Smith is not a Kpelle man."

Even people who have been to school do not use a single mode of thinking in all situations. In adulthood, people are more likely to use formal operations for problems based on their own occupations; this is one reason that people whose logic is impeccable at work may still become victims of a home-repair or investment scam (Carraher, Schliemann & Carraher, 1988).

Kohlberg's Stages of Moral Reasoning   One domain in which adolescents can apply their advanced cognitive skills is morality. To examine how people think about morality, psychologists have asked them how they would resolve hypothetical moral dilemmas and why. Perhaps the most famous of these is the "Heinz dilemma," in which people must decide whether a man named Heinz should steal a rare and unaffordably expensive drug in order to save his wife from cancer.

Using moral dilemmas like this one, Lawrence Kohlberg found that the reasons given for moral choices change systematically and consistently with age (Kohlberg & Gilligan, 1971). Young children make moral judgments that are different from those of older children, adolescents, or adults. Kohlberg proposed that moral reasoning develops in six stages, which are summarized in Table 12.3. These stages, he said, are not tightly linked to a person's chronological age; there is a range of ages for reaching each stage, and not everyone reaches the highest level.

Stage 1 and Stage 2 moral judgments, which are most typical of children under the age of nine, tend to be selfish in nature. Kohlberg called this level of moral reasoning **preconventional** because reasoning at this level is not based on the conventions or rules

TABLE 12.3

Kohlberg's Stages of
Moral Development

Kohlberg's stages of moral reasoning describe differences in how people think about moral issues. Here are some examples of answers that people at different stages of development might give to the "Heinz dilemma" described in the text. Lest you think this dilemma unrealistic, a man was arrested in 1994 for robbing a bank in Jonesboro, Arkansas, after being turned down for a loan to pay for his wife's cancer treatments.

Stage	What Is Right?	Should Heinz Steal the Drug?
Preconventional		
1	Obeying and avoiding punishment from a superior authority	Heinz should not steal the drug because he will be jailed.
2	Making a fair exchange, a good deal	Heinz should steal the drug because his wife will repay him later.
Conventional		
3	Pleasing others and getting their approval	Heinz should steal the drug because he loves his wife and because she and the rest of the family will approve.
4	Doing your duty, following rules and social order	Heinz should steal the drug for his wife because he has a duty to care for her, or he should not steal the drug because stealing is illegal.
Post-conventional		
5	Respecting rules and laws, but recognizing that they may have limits	Heinz should steal the drug because life is more important than property.
6	Following universal ethical principles, such as justice, reciprocity, equality, and respect for human life and rights	Heinz should steal the drug because of the principle of preserving and respecting life.

that guide social interactions in society. People at this level of moral development are concerned with avoiding punishment or following rules when it is to their own advantage. At the **conventional** level of moral reasoning, Stages 3 and 4, people are concerned about other people; they think that morality consists of following rules and conventions such as duty to the family, to marriage vows, to the country. The moral reasoning of children from nine to nineteen is most often at this level. Stages 5 and 6 represent the highest level of moral reasoning, which Kohlberg called **postconventional** because it occurs after conventional reasoning. Moral judgments at this level are based on personal standards or on universal principles of justice, equality, and respect for human life, not on the dictates of authority figures or society. People who have reached this level view rules and laws as arbitrary but respect them because they protect human welfare. They believe that individual rights can sometimes supersede these laws if the laws become destructive. People do not usually reach this level until sometime after the end of adolescence. Stage 6 is seen only rarely in extraordinary individuals.

To test the validity of his stages of moral development, Kohlberg and his associates studied the moral reasoning of males in the United States as they developed from age ten to thirty-six (Colby et al., 1983; see Figure 12.8). The subjects proceeded through the stages in the order Kohlberg proposed. None of them skipped a stage; only rarely did any seem to move back a stage, although they moved through the stages at different rates and reached different levels. Other studies of Kohlberg's stages (e.g., Walker, 1989) generally support the sequence he proposed.

Limitations of Kohlberg's Stages   Have Kohlberg's findings been replicated across cultures? Forty-five studies in twenty-seven cultures from Alaska to Zambia showed

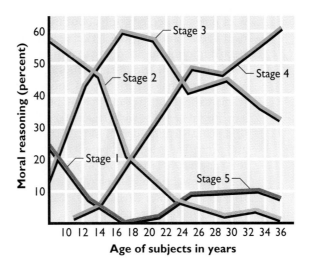

FIGURE 12.8
The Development of Moral Reasoning

The results of a longitudinal study by Colby et al. (1983) showed that, as adolescents, most of the male subjects reasoned at a Stage 3 level. Some of those tested never rose above Stage 2; only about 20 percent of the subjects tested as adults reached Stage 5; none reached Stage 6.

Source: Adapted from Colby et al., 1983.

that people do tend to make upward progress through Kohlberg's stages, without reversals (Snarey, 1987). Further, although Stages 5 and 6 did not always appear, Stages 1 through 4 did and thus appear universal. The reason may be that these lower levels of reasoning are more closely linked to cognitive development than is the highest level.

However, there are moral judgments made in other cultures that simply do not fit into Kohlberg's stages. Some people in collectivist cultures like Papua–New Guinea, Taiwan, and Israeli kibbutzim, for example, explained their answers to moral dilemmas by pointing to the importance of the community. People in India included in their moral reasoning the importance of acting in accordance with one's gender and caste and with maintaining personal purity (Shweder et al., 1994). As in other areas, culture plays a significant role in shaping moral judgments.

So does gender. Carol Gilligan (1982; Gilligan & Wiggins, 1987) has suggested that for North American females, the moral ideal is not the abstract, impersonal concept of justice that Kohlberg documented in males but, rather, the need to protect enduring relationships and fulfill human needs. Gilligan questioned Kohlberg's assumption that the highest level of morality is based on justice. When she asked people about moral conflicts, the majority of men focused on justice, but only half of the women did. The other half focused on caring. This difference between men and women has been found in some studies but not others (Miller & Bersoff, 1992; Rogers, 1987). One study found no difference between men and women in the "care ethic" they expressed; however, more women than men claimed that this ethic was related to their identity (Skoe & Diessner, 1994).

Taken together, the results of research in different countries and with both genders suggest that moral ideals are not absolute and universal. Moral development is apparently an adaptation to the moral world in which one finds oneself. Formal operational reasoning may be necessary for people to reach the highest level of moral reasoning, but this alone is not sufficient. To some extent, at the highest levels, moral reasoning is a product of culture and history.

Moral Reasoning and Moral Action   There is some evidence that moral reasoning can predict moral behavior. In one study, for example, juveniles who committed crimes ranging from burglary to murder tended to see obedience to laws mainly as a way of avoiding jail—a Stage 2 belief—while their nondelinquent peers, reasoning at Stage 3, believed that one should obey laws because they prevent chaos in society (Gregg, Gibbs & Basinger, 1994). But having high moral reasoning ability is no guarantee that a person will always act morally; other factors—such as the likelihood of being caught—also affect behavior (Krebs, 1967).

Children and adolescents can be encouraged to move to higher levels of moral reasoning through exposure to arguments at a higher stage, perhaps as they argue issues with one another. Hearing about moral reasoning that is one stage higher than their own or encountering a situation that requires more advanced reasoning seems to push people into moral reasoning at a higher level (Enright, Lapsley & Levy, 1983; Walker, 1982). But the development of moral behavior involves more than abstract knowledge. Vivid emotional experiences in solving real moral problems—like being asked by a friend to help with a plan to cheat, being asked to sell drugs, or getting pregnant—have a major influence as well (Haan, Aerts & Cooper, 1985). Children and adolescents need to see consistent models of moral reasoning and behavior in the actions of their parents and peers. They also need parents who promote moral behavior. Finally, situational factors may have a large effect on whether a person acts morally. For example, moral reasoning, as well as moral behavior, tends to be lower when people are out drinking with friends (Denton & Krebs, 1990). Not only do we sometimes fail to act at the highest level of which we are capable, we sometimes fail even to reason at this level.

ADULTHOOD

Development does not end with adolescence. Adults, too, go through transitions and experience physical, cognitive, and social changes. For our purposes, adulthood can be divided into three periods: *early adulthood* (ages twenty to forty), *middle adulthood* (ages forty to sixty-five), and *late adulthood* (age sixty-five on).

Physical Changes

In early adulthood, physical growth continues. Shoulder width, height, and chest size increase. People continue to develop their athletic abilities. By their mid-thirties nearly everyone shows some hearing impairment, but, for most people, the years of early adulthood are the prime of life.

In middle adulthood, one of the most common physical changes is the loss of sensory acuity (Fozard et al., 1977). People become less sensitive to light, less accurate at perceiving differences in distance, and slower and less acute at seeing details. Increased farsightedness is an inevitable change that begins around age forty.

Inside the body, bone mass is dwindling, the risk of heart disease is increasing, and fertility declines. Most people are well into late adulthood before their bodily functions are noticeably impaired. In late adulthood men shrink about an inch, and women about two inches, as their posture changes and cartilage disks between the spinal vertebra become thinner. Hardening of the arteries and a build-up of fat deposits on the artery walls may lead to heart disease. The digestive system slows down and becomes less efficient. Both digestive disorders and heart disease sometimes result from problems of diet—too little fluid, too little fiber—and inactivity. In addition, the brain shrinks during late adulthood. The few reflexes that remained after infancy (such as the knee-jerk reflex) weaken or disappear. The flow of blood to the brain slows. As in earlier years, many of these changes can be delayed or diminished by healthy diets and exercise.

Cognitive Changes

Despite the aging of the brain, cognition undergoes little change for the worse until late adulthood. Before that time, alert older people can think just as quickly as alert younger people. In fact, older adults may function as well as or better than younger adults in situations that tap their memories and learning skills. The experienced teacher may deal with an unruly child more skillfully than the novice, and the senior lawyer may understand the implications of a new law more quickly than the recent graduate. Their years of accumulating and organizing information can make older adults practiced, skillful, and wise.

Early and Middle Adulthood   In early and middle adulthood, until age sixty at least, important cognitive abilities improve. During this period, adults do better on tests of vocabulary, comprehension, and general knowledge, especially if they use these abilities

High above the hushed crowd, Rex tried to remain
focused. Still, he couldn't shake one nagging
thought: He was an old dog and this was a new trick.

© 1992 FarWorks, Inc./Dist. by Universal Press Syndicate

FIGURE 12.9

Mental Abilities Over the Life Span

**Mental abilities collectively known as
"fluid" intelligence—speed of information processing, accuracy, and basic
memory, for example—begin to
decline quite early in adult life.
Changes in these biologically based
aspects of thinking are usually not
marked until late adulthood, however.
"Crystallized" abilities learned over a
lifetime—such as reading, writing,
comprehension of language, and professional skills—do not diminish even
in old age (see Chapter 10).**

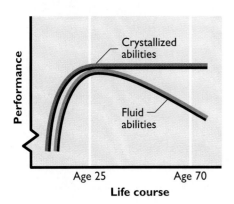

Source: Adapted from Baltes, 1994.

in their daily lives or engage in enriching activities such as travel or reading (Botwinick,
1977; Eichorn et al., 1981). Young and middle-aged adults learn new information and
new skills; they remember old information and hone old skills.

The nature of thought may also change during adulthood. Adult thought is often
more complex, adaptive, and relativistic than adolescent thought (Labouvie-Vief,
1992). Adults can understand, as adolescents cannot, the contradictions inherent in
thinking. They see both the possibilities and the problems in every course of action
(Riegel, 1975)—in deciding whether to start a new business or back a political candidate, whether to move to a new place or change jobs. Middle-aged adults are more
expert than adolescents or young adults at making rational decisions and at relating
logic and abstractions to actions, emotions, social issues, and personal relationships
(Tversky & Kahneman, 1981). As they appreciate these relationships, their thought
becomes more global, more concerned with broad moral and practical concerns
(Labouvie-Vief, 1982).

Late Adulthood   It is not until late in adulthood—after sixty-five or so—that some
intellectual abilities decline in some people (see Chapter 10). Generally, these are abilities that require rapid and flexible manipulation of ideas and symbols, active thinking
and reasoning, and sheer mental effort (Baltes, 1993; Craik, 1994; Schaie, 1993; see
Figure 12.9). Thus, older adults do just as well as younger ones at tasks they know
well— like naming familiar objects (Poon & Fozard, 1978). It is when they are asked to
perform an unfamiliar task or to solve a complex problem they have not seen before
that older adults are generally slower and less effective than younger ones (Craik &
Rabinowitz, 1984). When facing complex problems, older people apparently suffer
from having too much information to sift through; they have trouble considering,
choosing, and executing solutions (Arenberg, 1982). As people age, they grow less efficient at organizing the elements of a problem and at holding and manipulating more
than one idea at a time. They have difficulty doing tasks that require them to divide
their attention between two activities and are slower at shifting their attention back and
forth between two activities (Korteling, 1991; McDowd, Vercruyssen & Birrin, 1991). If
older adults have enough time, though, and can separate the two activities, they can
perform just as well as younger adults (Hawkins, Kramer & Capaldi, 1993). Barring
brain disorders such as Alzheimer's disease, the loss of intellectual abilities in older
adults is slow and need not cause severe problems.

The risk of cognitive decline in old age is significantly less for people who are healthy
and psychologically flexible, who have a high level of education, income, and occupation, and who live in an intellectually stimulating environment with mentally able
spouses or companions (Albert et al., 1995; Schaie, 1993; Shimamura et al., 1995).
Continued mental exercise—such as doing puzzles, painting, and talking to intelligent
friends—can help older adults think and remember effectively and creatively. How?
Research discussed in Chapter 3 suggests that there might be more neural connections
in the brains of people whose environments have offered lifelong intellectual stimulation. Perhaps these extra connections help compensate for pathways that are lost or
blocked in old age (Golden, 1994).

Longitudinal research on people tested since 1956 shows that scores on mental ability tests are declining less rapidly in old age now than they did before 1970 (Schaie,
1993). Even at age eighty-one, fewer than half of the subjects exhibited decrements in
mental abilities over the preceding seven years. Other research demonstrates that it
is never too late to work at preserving mental ability. Practice at memory and other
information-processing tasks, for example, can lead to some improvement in skills
impaired by old age and disuse (Schaie, 1993; Baltes, 1993). Several of the memory techniques described in Chapter 8 can help even victims of Alzheimer's disease to remember important information, such as when to take medication (Camp et al., 1995).

Social Changes

Adulthood is also a time when changes occur in social relationships and positions.
These changes do not come in neat, predictable stages but, instead, follow various

STAYING ACTIVE A lifetime of fitness through dancing or other forms of aerobic exercise has been associated with better maintenance of skills on a variety of mental tasks, including reaction time, reasoning, and divided attention (Offenbach, Chodzko-Zajko & Ringel, 1990; Clarkson-Smith & Hartley, 1989; Dustman et al., 1990; Hawkins, Kramer & Capaldi, 1993).

paths, depending on individual experiences—such as being abandoned by a spouse, getting fired from a job, going back to school, or remarrying (Schlossberg, 1987).

Early Adulthood   Men and women in Western cultures usually enter the adult world in their twenties. They decide on an occupation, or at least take a job, and often become preoccupied with their careers. They also become more concerned with issues of love (Vaillant, 1977; Whitbourne et al., 1992). Recall the sixth of Erikson's stages of psychosocial development noted in Table 12.2: "intimacy versus isolation." This intimacy may include sexual intimacy, friendship, or mutual intellectual stimulation. It may lead to marriage or some other form of committed relationship. All this comes at a time when, having separated from their parents, young adults may also be experiencing isolation and loneliness. They may view the future with a mixture of anticipation, fear, and insecurity (Levinson et al., 1978).

Just how willing and able people are to make intimate commitments may depend on their earlier attachment relationships. Researchers have discovered that young adults' views of intimate relationships parallel the patterns of infant attachment that we described earlier (Bartholomew & Horowitz, 1991; Howowitz, Rosenberg & Bartholomew, 1993). If their view reflects a secure attachment, they tend to feel valued and worthy of support and affection, develop closeness easily, and have relationships characterized by joy, trust, and commitment. If their view is ambivalent, they tend to be preoccupied with relationships and may feel misunderstood, underappreciated, and worried about being abandoned; their relationships are often negative, obsessive, jealous. People who express an avoidant attitude toward relationships tend to be aloof and cannot commit or trust; although they desire intimacy, they fear it or dismiss its importance. Researchers have videotaped young adult dating partners in slightly anxiety-provoking situations that somewhat resemble the Strange Situation used with infants (Simpson, Rholes & Nelligan, 1992). The tapes reveal that, as anxiety increases, people with a secure attachment style increase their requests for or offers of support to their partner whereas those with an avoidant view decrease support-seeking behaviors. In another study, avoidant individuals were found to engage in more one-night stands and less cuddling than did those whose attachment style was secure (Shaver, 1994).

In their thirties, adults tend to settle down and decide what is important in life (Levinson et al., 1978). According to Erikson, this is the time when people become concerned with producing something that will outlast them, usually through parenthood or job achievements. Erikson called this concern the crisis of **generativity** because peo-

BUILDING MONUMENTS Middle adulthood tends to be a time during which people become deeply committed to building personal monuments, either by raising children or through achievements outside the home. This parent seems to have accomplished both goals.

ple are focused on producing or generating something. If people do not resolve this crisis, he suggested, they stagnate.

For many North American adults, however, the greatest tension occurs between two types of generativity—parenthood versus achievement. Especially for women, the demands of children and career often pull in opposite directions. Devotion to a job may lead to guilt about depriving children of attention; too much emphasis on home life may impair productivity at work. This stressful balancing act can lead to anxiety, frustration, and conflicts at home and on the job. Most women, though, find satisfaction in work. They are more satisfied if they do work; they like the respect, the independence, the stimulation, and the companionship that working often provides (Crosby, 1991).

During young adulthood, the experience of becoming parents represents entry into a major new developmental phase that is accompanied by personal, social, and, often, occupational changes. For many couples, marital satisfaction declines (Belsky & Kelly, 1994; Cowen et al., 1985), and about half of all marriages crack under the strain. Young mothers experience particular dissatisfaction, especially if they resent the constraints an infant brings, if they see their career as important, if the infant is temperamentally difficult, and if their partner is not supportive. When the father does not do his share of caring for the baby, researchers have discovered, both mothers and fathers are dissatisfied (Levy-Shiff, 1994).

Relationship difficulties uncovered during the transition to parenthood not only threaten marriages but can interfere with child care (Belsky & Kelly, 1994; Erel & Burman, 1995). The quality of that care is also related to young parents' own attachment histories. New mothers whose attachment to their mother is secure are more responsive to their infants, and the infants, in turn, are more likely to develop secure attachments to them (Ainsworth & Eichberg, in press; Ward & Carlson, 1995; van IJzendoorn, 1995).

Middle Adulthood Sometime around age forty, people go through a **midlife transition.** They may reappraise and modify their lives and relationships; they may feel invigorated and liberated; they may feel upset and have a "midlife crisis" (Levinson et al., 1978; Vaillant, 1977).

No one knows how many people experience a crisis during the midlife transition. Researchers suspect that such people are in the minority (Beck, 1992). The contrast between youth and middle age may be especially upsetting for men who matured early in adolescence and were sociable and athletic rather than intellectual (Block, 1971). Women who chose a career over a family now hear the biological clock ticking out their last childbearing years. Women who have had children, however, become more independent and confident, oriented toward achievement and events outside the family (Helson & Moane, 1987). For both men and women, the emerging sexuality of teenage children, the emptiness of the nest as children leave home, or the declining health of a parent may precipitate a crisis. The transition is easier for those who can accept the idea that life may not turn out as planned—or whose life *has* turned out as planned. After the midlife transition, the middle years of adulthood are often a time of satisfaction and happiness.

Sometimes, though, these years are a time of divorce. Demographers predict that if divorce rates remain as they are, marriages today have a fifty-fifty chance of ending in divorce (Davis, 1983; Hetherington & Clingempeel, 1992). Divorce may free people from a bad relationship, but it is also likely to make them feel anxious, guilty, incompetent, depressed, and lonely; it may even lead to health problems and, ultimately, to earlier mortality (Brody, 1983; Cargan & Melko, 1982; Friedman et al., 1995). Furthermore, 70 percent of divorces in the United States involve couples with children (Furstenberg & Cherlin, 1991). When parents divorce, the effects on children may be even worse than those on the adults. The good news is that the negative effects are not inevitable and do not have to be permanent. By two or three years after the divorce, in most families, routines are back to normal, physical symptoms have disappeared, the intense psychological stress is over, and adults and children have improved self-esteem and are functioning competently (Furstenberg & Cherlin, 1991). Still, there may be

THE "SANDWICH" GENERATION People in the midlife transition may feel caught between the generations, pressured by the expenses of college on one side and retired parents on the other.

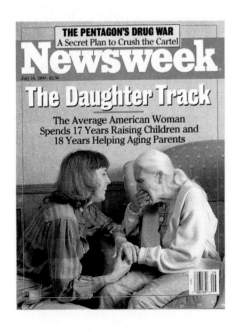

long-lasting effects. One longitudinal study found a shorter life expectancy for adults whose parents divorced (Friedman et al., 1995), but the divorces examined in this study occurred long ago, when divorce was rare. We do not know whether such effects exist today. Research on the effects of more recent divorces suggests that behavior problems may be delayed until the child whose parents had previously divorced reaches early adolescence (Amato & Keith, 1991; Hetherington & Clingempeel, 1992). One study found that many people who were in early adolescence when their parents divorced were still not able to form committed relationships ten years later (Wallerstein & Blakeslee, 1989). However, other research suggests that it is worse for children to experience continued conflict between their parents, married or not. Close to half the children exposed to marital violence exhibit psychopathology—a rate six times higher than that in the general population (Garber, 1992).

Late Adulthood   From sixty-five to seventy-five, most people think of themselves as middle-aged, not old (Neugarten, 1977). They are active and influential politically and socially; they often are physically vigorous. Men and women who have been employed usually retire from their jobs in this period. They adjust most easily to retirement if they view it as a choice (Neugarten, Havighurst & Tobin, 1968). Ratings of life satisfaction and self-esteem are on average as high in old age as during any other period of adulthood (Costa et al., 1987; Myers & Diener, 1995).

During late adulthood, people generally become more inward looking, cautious, and conforming (Neugarten, 1977; Reedy, 1983). They develop coping strategies that increasingly take into account the limits of their control—accepting what they cannot change, such as chronic health problems (Folkman et al., 1987; Brandtstadter & Renner, 1990). Many also become more *androgynous,* showing some of the characteristics of the other gender in addition to their own. Women become more assertive and men more nurturant, especially if they are grandparents (Fiske, 1980; Hyde & Phillis, 1979). Although they interact with others less frequently, older adults enjoy these interactions more, finding relationships more satisfying, supportive, and fulfilling than earlier in life (Carstensen, 1992). As they sense that time is running out, they value positive interactions and become selective about their social partners. The many changes associated

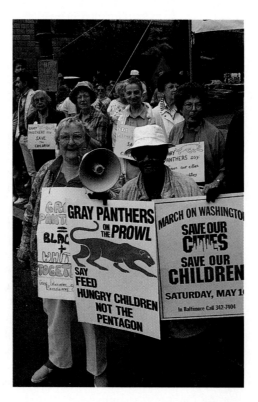

GRAY POWER   Even after seventy-five, many seniors continue leading active lives, sometimes as activists.

IN REVIEW	Milestones of Adolescence and Adulthood		
Age	**Physical Changes**	**Cognitive Changes**	**Social Events and Psychological Changes**
Early adolescence (11–15 years)	Puberty brings reproductive capacity and marked bodily changes.	Formal operations and principled moral reasoning become possible for the first time (this occurs only for some people).	Social and emotional changes result from growing sexual awareness, mood swings, physical changes, conflicts with parents.
Late adolescence (16–20 years)	Physical growth continues.	Formal operations and principled moral reasoning become more likely.	An identity crisis accompanies graduation from high school.
Early adulthood (20–39 years)	Physical growth continues; hearing impairment begins.	Increases continue in knowledge, problem-solving ability, and moral reasoning.	People choose a job and often a mate; they may become parents.
Middle adulthood (40–65 years)	Size and muscle mass decrease, fat increases, eyesight declines, reproductive capacity in women ends.	Thought becomes more complex, adaptive, and global.	Midlife transition may lead to change; for most, the middle years are satisfying.
Late adulthood (over 65 years)	Size decreases; organs become less efficient.	Reasoning, mathematical ability, comprehension, novel problem solving, and memory may decline.	Retirement requires adjustments; people look inward; awareness of death precipitates life review.

with adolescence and adulthood are summarized in "In Review: Milestones of Adolescence and Adulthood."

Death and Dying

With the onset of old age, people become aware that death is approaching. They watch as their friends disappear. They feel their health deteriorating, their strength waning, and their intellectual capabilities declining. A few years or a few months before death, people experience a sharp decline in mental functioning known as **terminal drop** (Berkowitz, 1965).

The awareness of impending death brings about the last psychological crisis, according to Erikson's theory, in which people evaluate their lives and accomplishments and affirm them as meaningful (leading to a feeling of integrity) or meaningless (leading to a feeling of despair). They tend to become more philosophical and reflective. They attempt to put their lives into perspective. They reminisce, resolve past conflicts, and integrate past events. They may also become more interested in the religious and spiritual side of life. This "life review" may trigger anxiety, regret, guilt, and despair, or it may allow people to face their own death and the deaths of friends and relatives with a feeling of peace and acceptance (Erikson, 1968; Lieberman & Tobin, 1983).

Older adults can be helped to feel better physically and psychologically if they continue to be socially active and useful. For example, old people who are given parties, plants, or pets are happier and more alert and do not die as soon as those who receive less attention (Kastenbaum, 1965; Rodin & Langer, 1977). Withdrawing care, control, and social contact from people who are sick is likely to make them sicker.

Even the actual confrontation with death does not have to bring despair and depression. People generally want to be told if they are dying (Hinton, 1967). When death finally is imminent, old people strive for a death with dignity, love, affection, physical contact, and no pain (Schulz, 1978). As they think about death, they are comforted by their religious faith, their achievements, and the love of their friends and family (Kastenbaum, Kastenbaum & Morris, 1989). Interestingly, very few take comfort from the thought that their children and grandchildren will survive and carry on their name and tradition.

FUTURE DIRECTIONS

The future of developmental psychology will probably involve further elaboration and more sophisticated analysis of both the biological underpinnings of development and the social contexts that influence it (Bronfenbrenner & Ceci, 1994). We can expect to see much more research exploring the significance of cultural differences in child rearing and how these differences affect children's knowledge, behavior, and attitudes. We can look forward to more studies documenting and assessing new worlds of childhood: The world of infant day care, the world of single mothers who are employed and highly educated, and, unfortunately, the world of homelessness. We can expect to see more research probing the limits—and limitations—of early education. How early should education start, and what should

it consist of? We can also expect to see more developmental research relating to social problems such as adolescent aggression, more evaluation of children's court testimony, and more experiments aimed at blunting the effects of Alzheimer's disease.

These new studies will extend our understanding of nature and nurture, cognitive abilities and social relationships, and other aspects of human development. If you wish to follow the progress of this research, consider taking courses in infancy, child development, adolescence, life-span development, language acquisition, cognitive development, and social development.

SUMMARY AND KEY TERMS

Developmental psychology is the study of the course and causes of systematic, sequential age-related changes in mental abilities, social relationships, emotions, and moral understanding over the life span.

■ EXPLORING HUMAN DEVELOPMENT

A central question in developmental psychology concerns the relative influences of nature and nurture, a theme that had its origins in the philosophies of Locke and Rousseau. In the twentieth century, Arnold Gesell stressed nature in his theory of development, proposing that development is *maturation*—the natural unfolding of abilities with age. John Watson took the opposite view, claiming that development is learning—shaped by the external environment. In his theory of cognitive development, Jean Piaget described how nature and nurture work together. According to Piaget, knowledge develops as children explore the environment while being guided by internal mental images. Today we accept as given the notion that both nature and nurture affect development and ask not whether but how and to what extent each contributes.

■ BEGINNINGS

Prenatal Development

Development begins with the union of an ovum and a sperm to form a zygote, which develops into an *embryo*. The embryonic stage is a *critical period* for development, a time when certain organs must develop properly or they never will. Development of organs at this stage is irrevocably affected by harmful *teratogens* like drugs and alcohol. After the embryo develops into a *fetus,* adverse conditions may harm the infant's size, behavior, intelligence, or health. Babies born to women who drink heavily have a strong chance of suffering from *fetal alcohol syndrome.*

The Newborn

Newborns have limited but effective senses of vision, hearing, taste, and smell. They exhibit many *reflexes:* swift, automatic responses to

external stimuli. Motor development proceeds as the nervous system matures, muscles grow, and the infant experiments with and selects the most efficient movement patterns.

■ INFANCY AND CHILDHOOD: COGNITIVE DEVELOPMENT

Cognitive development refers to the development of thinking, knowing, and remembering.

The Development of Knowledge: Piaget's Theory

According to Piaget, cognitive development occurs in a fixed sequence of stages, as *schemas* are modified through the complementary processes of *assimilation* (fitting new objects or events into existing schemas) and *accommodation* (changing schemas when new objects will not fit existing schemas). During the *sensorimotor period,* infants progress from using only simple senses and reflexes to forming mental representations of objects and actions. Thus, the child becomes capable of thinking about objects that are not immediately present. The ability to recognize that objects continue to exist even when they are hidden from view is what Piaget called *object permanence.* Recent research reveals that Piaget underestimated infants' mental abilities. During the *preoperational period,* children can use symbols, but they do not have the ability to think logically and rationally. Their understanding of the world is intuitive. When children develop the ability to think logically about concrete objects, they enter the period of *concrete operations.* At this time they can solve simple problems and have a knowledge of *conservation,* recognizing that, for example, the amount of a substance is not altered even when its shape changes.

Modifying Piaget's Theory

Developmental psychologists now believe that new levels of cognition are reached not in sharply marked stages of global understanding but more gradually, and in specific areas. Children's reasoning is affected by factors such as task difficulty and degree of familiarity with the objects and language involved.

Information Processing During Childhood

Psychologists who explain cognitive development in terms of *information processing* have documented age-related improvements in children's attention, their abilities to explore and focus on features of the environment, and their memories.

■ LINKAGES: DEVELOPMENT AND MEMORY

"Infantile amnesia" leaves us with virtually no memory of events from before the age of three. Several explanations have been suggested, but this phenomenon is not yet fully understood.

Culture and Cognitive Development

The specific content of cognitive development, including the development of scripts, depends on the cultural context in which children live.

Individual Variations in Cognitive Development

How fast children develop cognitive abilities depends to a certain extent on how stimulating and supportive their environments are. Children growing up in poverty are likely to have delayed or impaired cognitive abilities.

■ INFANCY AND CHILDHOOD: SOCIAL AND EMOTIONAL DEVELOPMENT

Infants and their caregivers, from the early months, respond to each other's emotional expressions.

Individual Temperament

Most infants can be classified as having easy, difficult, or slow-to-warm-up *temperaments*. Whether they retain these temperamental styles depends to some extent on their parents' expectations and demands.

The Infant Grows Attached

Over the first six or seven months of life, infants form a deep and abiding emotional *attachment* to their mother or other primary caregiver. This attachment may be secure or anxious-insecure, depending largely on whether the caregiver is responsive and loving, or rejecting.

Relationships with Parents and Peers

Parents teach their children the skills and rules needed in their culture using *socialization* styles described as *authoritarian, permissive,* or *authoritative.* Among European-American parents, those with an authoritative style tend to have more competent and cooperative children. Patterns of socialization depend upon the culture and conditions in which parents find themselves. Over the childhood years, interactions with peers are increasingly characterized by cooperation and competition. Children come to base their friendships on feelings, not things.

Social Skills and Understanding

Changes in children's relationships are in part related to their growing social competence. Children become increasingly able to interpret and understand social situations and emotional signals. They also learn social rules and roles, including those related to gender.

Gender Roles

Gender roles are based both on biological differences between the sexes and on implicit and explicit socialization by parents, teachers, and peers.

■ ADOLESCENCE

Adolescents undergo significant changes not only in size, shape, and physical capacity but also, typically, in their social lives, reasoning abilities, and views of themselves.

The Challenges of Change

Puberty brings about physical changes that lead to psychological changes. Early adolescence is a period of shaky self-esteem. It is also a time when conflict with parents as well as closeness and conformity to friends are likely to rise. Pregnancy is an acute problem during this period.

Identity and Development of the Self

Later adolescence focuses on finding an answer to the question: Who am I? Events like graduating from high school and going to college challenge the adolescent's self-concept, precipitating an *identity crisis.* To resolve this crisis the adolescent must develop an integrated self-image as a unique person, an image which often includes ethnic identity.

Abstract Thought and Moral Reasoning

For many people, adolescence begins a stage of cognitive development that Piaget called the *formal operational period.* Formal abstract reasoning now becomes more sophisticated, and moral reasoning may begin its progress through *preconventional, conventional,* and *postconventional* stages. Principled moral judgment—shaped by gender and culture—becomes possible for the first time. Such advanced understanding may be reflected in moral action.

■ ADULTHOOD

Physical, cognitive, and social changes occur throughout adulthood.

Physical Changes

Middle adulthood sees changes that include decreased acuity of the senses, increased risk of heart disease, and declining fertility. Nevertheless, most people do not experience major health problems until late adulthood.

Cognitive Changes

The cognitive changes that occur in early and middle adulthood are generally positive, including improvements in reasoning and problem-solving ability. In late adulthood, some intellectual abilities decline—especially those involved in tasks that are unfamiliar, complex, or difficult. Other abilities, such as recalling facts or making wise decisions, tend not to decline.

Social Changes

In their twenties, young adults make occupational choices and form intimate commitments. In their thirties, they settle down and decide what is important. They become concerned with *generativity,* with producing something that will outlast them. Sometime around age forty, adults experience a *midlife transition,* which may or may not be a crisis. The forties and fifties are often a time of satisfaction and, sometimes, of divorce. In their sixties, people contend with the issue of retirement. They generally become more inward looking, cautious, and conforming.

Death and Dying

In their seventies and eighties, people confront their own mortality. They may become more philosophical and reflective as they review their lives. A few years or months before death, they experience a sharp decline in mental functioning known as *terminal drop.* Still, they strive for a death with dignity, love, and no pain.

HEALTH, STRESS, AND COPING

CHAPTER

LINKAGES
TO
HEALTH, STRESS, AND COPING

BIOLOGICAL ASPECTS
OF PSYCHOLOGY

Can stress give you the flu?
(ans. on p. 445)

PSYCHOLOGICAL DISORDERS

**When do stress responses
become mental disorders?**
(ans. on p. 437)

SOCIAL BEHAVIOR AND GROUP
INFLUENCES

**How does stress affect group
decision making?** *(ans. on
p. 624)*

bout fifteen years ago, acquired immune deficiency syndrome (AIDS) was a rare and puzzling medical condition. Today, it threatens everyone and is one of the major causes of death in the United States (Belgrave & Randolph, 1993; Centers for Disease Control, 1996). As some researchers race against time to find a cure for AIDS and a vaccine against HIV, the virus that causes it, others work to take advantage of every factor that might prolong the lives of people infected with HIV or suffering with AIDS.

Expectations about survival may be one of those factors. Psychologist Geoffrey Reed and his associates asked seventy-four male AIDS patients about the extent to which they had accepted their situation and prepared themselves for the worst (Reed et al., 1994). While acknowledging the reality of a terminal illness has been considered by some to be a psychologically healthy adaptation (e.g., Kubler-Ross, 1975), Reed and his associates found that the men who had accepted their situation and prepared themselves for death died an average of nine months *earlier* than those who had neither accepted nor resigned themselves to their situation. This statistically significant difference is all the more impressive because it cannot be accounted for by differences among the patients in general health status, immune system functioning, psychological distress, or other factors that might have affected the time of death. Here is evidence that, compared to those who are "fighters," terminally ill patients who resign themselves to debilitation and death might actually hasten both.

Research like this has made psychologists and the medical community more aware of psychological factors that can affect health and illness. It also reflects the growth of **health psychology,** "a field within psychology devoted to understanding psychological influences on how people stay healthy, why they become ill, and how they respond when they do get ill" (Taylor, 1995, p. 4). As the Linkages diagram suggests, health psychologists use knowledge from many subfields of psychology to enhance understanding of the psychological and behavioral processes associated with health and illness (Matarazzo, 1984; Taylor, 1995). In this chapter we describe some of the ways in which health is related to psychological, social, and behavioral factors as well as what health psychologists are doing to understand these relationships and to apply their research to prevent illness and promote better health. We examine in particular how stress affects health, how psychological factors affect the processes underlying physical disorders, and what techniques are effective for coping with stress and for changing health-endangering behaviors.

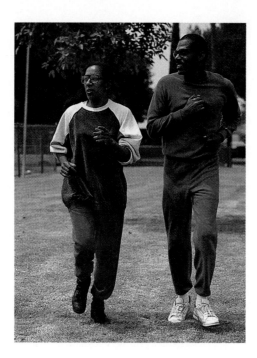

RUNNING FOR YOUR LIFE   Health psychologists have developed programs to help people increase exercise, stop smoking, eat healthier diets, and make other lifestyle changes that lower their risk of illness and death.

HEALTH PSYCHOLOGY

Although health psychology is a relatively new subfield, its underlying themes are ancient. For thousands of years, in many cultures around the world, people have believed that their mental state, their behavior, and their health are linked (Matarazzo, 1984). Today, there is scientific evidence for this belief (Taylor, 1995). We know, for example, that through their impact on psychological and physical processes, the stresses of life can influence physical health. Researchers have also associated anger, hostility, pessimism, depression, and hopelessness with the appearance of physical illnesses. Similarly, poor health has been linked to lack of exercise, inadequate diet, smoking, alcohol and drug abuse, and other behavioral factors.

Health psychology has become increasingly prominent in North America in part because of changing patterns of illness. Until the middle of the twentieth century, the major causes of illness and death in the United States and Canada were acute infectious diseases such as influenza, tuberculosis, and pneumonia. With these killers now tamed, chronic illness—such as coronary heart disease, cancer, and diabetes—have become the leading causes of disability and death. Compared with acute diseases, these chronic diseases develop more slowly and are more heavily influenced by psychological, lifestyle, and environmental factors (Taylor, 1995). As Table 13.1 shows, lifestyle choices such as whether to smoke affect the risk for the five leading causes of death in the United States. Further, the psychological and behavioral factors that contribute to these

TABLE 13.1		Alcohol	Smoking	Diet	Exercise	Stress
Lifestyle Behaviors That Affect the Leading Causes of Death in the United States	Heart disease	x	x	x	x	x
	Cancer	x	x	x		?
This table shows five of the leading causes of death in the United States today, along with behaviors that contribute to their development.	Accidents and injury	x	x			
	Stroke	x	x	x	?	?
	Lung disease		x			

Source: Adapted from USDHEW (1979); USDHHS (1990); Matarazzo (1984).

illnesses can be altered by psychological methods, including programs that promote nonsmoking and low-fat diets. Indeed, in 1990 the Secretary of the U.S. Department of Health and Human Services (USDHHS) stated that as many as 50 percent of deaths in the United States were due to potentially preventable lifestyle behaviors (USDHHS, 1990).

One goal of health psychology is to help people understand the role they can play in controlling their own health and longevity. For example, health psychologists have facilitated early detection of disease by educating people about signs of cancer, heart disease, and other serious illnesses and encouraging them to seek medical attention while life-saving treatment is still possible. Encouraging women to perform breast self-examinations and men to do testicular exams are just two examples of health psychology programs that can save thousands of lives each year (Taylor, 1995). Health psychologists have also studied why some people fail to follow the treatment regimes that are vital to the control of diseases such as diabetes, heart disease, and high blood pressure. Discovering these factors and devising procedures that encourage greater compliance could speed recovery, prevent unnecessary suffering, and save many lives. Health psychologists have also been instrumental in studying, and helping people understand, the role played by stress in physical health and illness.

UNDERSTANDING STRESS

You have probably heard that death and taxes are the only two things you can be sure of in life. If there is a third, it must surely be stress. Stress is basic to life—no matter how wealthy, powerful, attractive, or happy you might be. It comes in many forms—a difficult exam, an automobile accident, waiting in a long line, a day on which everything goes wrong. Mild stress can be stimulating, motivating, and sometimes desirable. But as it becomes more severe, stress can bring on physical, psychological, and behavioral problems.

Stress is the negative emotional and physiological process that occurs as individuals try to adjust to or deal with environmental circumstances that disrupt, or threaten to disrupt, their daily functioning (Lazarus & Folkman, 1984; Taylor, 1995). Thus stress involves a transaction between people and their environments. The environmental circumstances (such as exams or accidents) that cause people to make adjustments are called **stressors. Stress reactions** are the physical, psychological, and behavioral responses (such as nervousness, nausea, and fatigue) that people display in the face of stressors. It is important to understand stress because it contributes to psychological problems such as anxiety and depression, and adversely affects people's physical health.

Interestingly, some people are more strongly affected by stressors than other people, or may be more affected on one occasion or another. Why? The answer appears to lie in *mediating factors* that influence the transaction between people and their environments. Mediating factors include variables such as the extent to which people can predict and control their stressors, how they interpret the threat involved, the social support they get, and their stress-coping skills. These mediating factors dampen or amplify a stressor's impact. Thus, as shown in Figure 13.1, stress is not a specific event but a *process* in which the nature and intensity of stress responses depend to a large

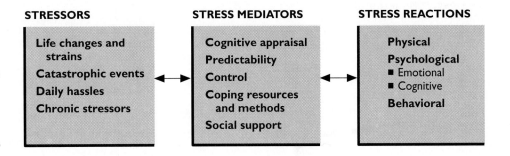

STRESSORS	STRESS MEDIATORS	STRESS REACTIONS
Life changes and strains	Cognitive appraisal	Physical
Catastrophic events	Predictability	Psychological
Daily hassles	Control	■ Emotional
Chronic stressors	Coping resources and methods	■ Cognitive
	Social support	Behavioral

degree on how stressors are mediated by factors such as the way people think about them and the skills and resources they have to cope with them.

Stressors

For humans, most stressors have both physical and psychological components. Students, for example, are challenged by psychological demands to do well in their courses, as well as by the physical fatigue that can result from the pressures of academics. Here, we focus on psychological stressors.

Psychological Stressors   Any event that forces people to accommodate or change can be a psychological stressor. Accordingly, even very pleasant events can be stressful (Brown & McGill, 1989). For example, the increased salary and status associated with a promotion may be desirable, but the upgrade usually brings new pressures as well. Similarly, people often feel exhausted after a vacation. Still, it is usually unpleasant circumstances that have the most adverse psychological and physical effects. These circumstances include catastrophic events, life changes and strains, chronic stressors, and daily hassles (DeLongis, Folkman & Lazarus, 1988; Gatchel, Baum & Krantz, 1989).

Catastrophic events are sudden, unexpected, potentially life-threatening experiences or traumas, such as physical or sexual assault, military combat, natural disasters, and accidents. *Life changes and strains* include divorce, illness in the family, difficulties at work, moving to a new place, and other circumstances that create demands to which people must adjust (Cohen & Williamson, 1991; Price, 1992; see Table 13.2). *Chronic stress*—stressors that continue over a long period of time—can involve anything from living near a noisy airport to being unable to earn a decent living because of adverse economic conditions or job discrimination (Evans, Hygge & Bullinger, 1995; McEwen & Stellar, 1993; Staples, 1996). *Daily hassles* include traffic jams, deadlines, and other irritations, pressures, and annoyances that might not be significant stressors by themselves but whose cumulative effects can be significant.

Measuring Stressors   Which stressors are most harmful? In order to study stress more precisely, psychologists have tried to measure the impact of particular stressors. In 1967, Thomas Holmes and Richard Rahe made a pioneering effort to find a standard way of measuring the stress in a person's life. Working on the assumption that all change, positive or negative, is stressful, they asked a large number of people to rate—in terms of *life-change units,* or *LCUs*—the amount of change and demand for adjustment represented by a list of events such as divorcing, being fired, retiring, losing a loved one, or becoming pregnant. (Getting married, the event against which raters were

---

TABLE 13.2

The Undergraduate
Stress Questionnaire

Here are some items from the Undergraduate Stress Questionnaire, which asks respondents to indicate whether various stressors have occurred during the past week (Crandall, Preisler & Aussprung, 1992).

Has this stressful event happened to you at any time during the last week? If it has, please check the space next to it. If it has not, please leave it blank.

____   1. Assignments in all classes due the same day

____   2. Having roommate conflicts

____   3. Lack of money

____   4. Trying to decide on major

____   5. Can't understand your professor

____   6. Stayed up late writing a paper

____   7. Sat through a boring class

____   8. Went into a test unprepared

____   9. Parents getting divorced

____   10. Incompetence at the registrar's office

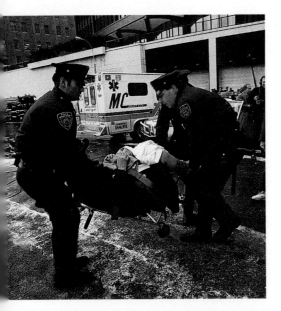

A BOMB AT THE WORLD TRADE CENTER Catastrophic events such as explosions, hurricanes, plane crashes, and other traumas can be psychologically devastating for victims, their families, and rescue workers. Health psychologists and other professionals provide on-the-spot counseling as well as follow-up sessions to help these people deal with the consequences of trauma.

told to compare all other stressors, was rated as slightly more stressful than losing one's job.) On the basis of these ratings, Holmes and Rahe created the Social Readjustment Rating Scale, or SRRS. People taking the SRRS receive a stress score equal to the sum of the LCUs for the events they have recently experienced.

Numerous studies show that people scoring high on the SRRS and other life-change scales are more likely to suffer physical illness, mental disorder, or other problems than those with lower scores (De Benedittis, Lornenzetti & Pieri, 1990; Dohrenwend & Dohrenwend, 1978; Monroe, Thase & Simons, 1992). Still, questions have been raised about whether measuring life change alone tells the whole stress story (Birnbaum & Sotoodeh, 1991). Accordingly, investigators have developed scales such as the Life Experiences Survey, or LES (Sarason, Johnson & Siegal, 1978), that go beyond the SRRS to measure not just what life events have occurred but also the respondents' *perception*—on a scale of −3 to +3—of how intensely positive or negative the events were. As you might expect, scales like the LES generally show that negative events have a stronger negative impact on health than positive events do (De Benedittis, Lornenzetti & Pieri, 1990).

The LES also gives respondents the opportunity to write in and rate any stressors they have experienced that are not on the printed list. This personalized approach is particularly valuable for capturing the differing impact and meaning that experiences may have for men compared to women and for individuals from various cultural or subcultural groups (Nicassio, 1985). Divorce, for example, may have very different meanings to people of different religious or cultural backgrounds. Similarly, members of certain ethnic groups are likely to experience stressors—such as prejudice and discrimination—that are not felt by other groups (Lopez & Takemoto-Chock, 1992).

Other researchers have developed questionnaires to assess daily hassles and uplifts (DeLongis, Folkman & Lazarus, 1988; Kanner et al., 1981). Some research suggests that daily hassles may also predict illness, perhaps even better than major negative life events (Garrett et al., 1991). However, research on this point is not yet clear, and much more information will be needed about the mediating influences shown in Figure 13.1 before accurate predictions about individuals can be made.

Stress Responses

Physical, psychological, and behavioral stress reactions often occur together, especially as stressors become more intense. Furthermore, one type of stress response can set off a stress response in another dimension. For example, a physical stress reaction—such as mild chest pains—may lead to the psychological stress response of worrying about a heart attack. Still, it is useful to analyze separately each category of stress responses.

Physical Stress Responses: The GAS   Anyone who has experienced a near accident or some other sudden, frightening event knows that the physical responses to stressors include rapid breathing, increased heartbeat, sweating, and, a little later, shakiness. These reactions are part of a general pattern, or *syndrome,* known as the fight-or-flight syndrome. As described in Chapters 3 and 11, this vital syndrome prepares the body to face or to flee an immediate threat. When the danger is past, fight-or-flight responses subside. However, when stressors are long-lasting, these responses are only the beginning of a sequence of reactions.

Careful observation of animals and humans led Hans Selye (pronounced "sell-yay") to suggest that the sequence of physical responses to stress occurs in a consistent pattern and is triggered by the effort to adapt to any stressor. Selye called this sequence the **general adaptation syndrome,** or **GAS** (Selye, 1956, 1976). The GAS has three stages, as Figure 13.2 shows.

The first stage is the *alarm reaction,* which involves some version of the fight-or-flight syndrome. In the face of a mild stressor such as a hot room, the reaction may simply involve changes in heart rate, respiration, and perspiration that help the body regulate its temperature. More severe stressors prompt more dramatic alarm reactions, rapidly mobilizing the body's adaptive energy, much as a burglar alarm alerts the police to take action (Selye, 1956).

FIGURE 13.2

The General Adaptation Syndrome

Hans Selye's research showed that physical reactions to stressors include an initial alarm reaction, followed by resistance and then exhaustion. During the alarm reaction, the body's resistance temporarily drops below normal as it absorbs a stressor's initial impact. Resistance increases, then levels off in the resistance stage, but ultimately declines if the exhaustion stage is reached.

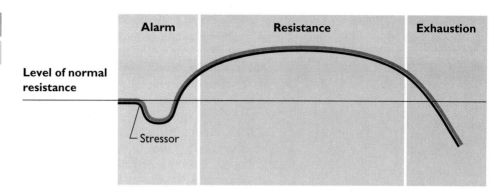

Source: Adapted from Selye, 1974.

How do alarm reactions occur? They are controlled by the sympathetic branch of the autonomic nervous system (ANS) through organs and glands that make up the *sympatho-adreno-medullary (SAM)* system. As shown on the right side of Figure 13.3, stressors trigger a process in which the brain's hypothalamus activates the sympathetic branch of the ANS, which stimulates the medulla (inner part) of the adrenal gland. The adrenal gland, in turn, secretes *catecholamines*—especially adrenaline and noradrenaline—which circulate in the bloodstream, activating various organs including the liver, the kidneys, the heart, and the lungs. The results are increased blood pressure, enhanced muscle tension, increased blood sugar, and other physical changes needed to cope with stressors. Even brief exposure to a stressor can produce major changes in these coordinated regulatory physiological mechanisms (Cacioppo et al., 1995).

If the stressor persists, the *resistance* stage of the GAS begins. Here, obvious signs of the initial alarm reaction diminish as the body settles in to resist the stressor on a long-term basis. The drain on adaptive energy is slower during the resistance stage than it was during the alarm reaction, but the body is working very hard as a second stress response pattern—involving the *hypothalamic-pituitary-adrenocortical (HPA)* system—comes into play. As shown on the left side of Figure 13.3, the hypothalamus activates the HPA system by stimulating the pituitary gland in the brain. The pituitary, in turn, secretes hormones such as adrenocorticotropic hormone (ACTH). Among other things, ACTH stimulates the adrenal gland's cortex (outer surface) to secrete *corticosteroids;* these hormones release the body's energy supplies and fight inflammation.

The overall effect of these stress systems is to generate emergency energy. The more stressors there are and the longer they last, the more resources the body must expend in an effort to resist them. This continued campaign of biochemical resistance is costly. It slowly but surely uses up the body's reserves of adaptive energy until the capacity to resist is gone. The body then enters the third GAS stage, known as *exhaustion.* In extreme cases, such as prolonged exposure to freezing temperatures, the result is death. More commonly, the exhaustion stage brings signs of physical wear and tear, especially in organ systems that were weak in the first place or heavily involved in the resistance process. For example, if adrenaline and cortisol, which help fight stressors during the resistance stage, remain at high levels for an extended time, they can damage the heart and blood vessels, suppress the functioning of the body's disease-fighting immune system, and thus promote illnesses ranging from heart disease, high blood pressure, and arthritis to colds and flu (Cohen & Williamson, 1991; Cohen et al., 1992; McEwen & Stellar, 1993). Selye referred to illnesses that are caused or worsened by stressors as **diseases of adaptation.**

Selye's model has been very influential, but it has also been criticized for underestimating the role of psychological factors in stress, such as a person's emotional state or the way a person thinks about stressors. These criticisms led to the development of *psychobiological models,* which emphasize the importance of psychological as well as biological variables in regulating and producing stress responses (Lazarus & Folkman, 1984). According to psychobiological models, psychological variables, such as whether

FIGURE 13.3

Organ Systems Involved in the GAS

Stressors produce a variety of physiological responses that begin in the brain and spread to organs throughout the body. For example, the pituitary gland triggers release of endogenous opiates, the body's natural painkillers. It also stimulates release of corticosteroids, which help resist stress but, as described later, also tend to suppress the immune system.

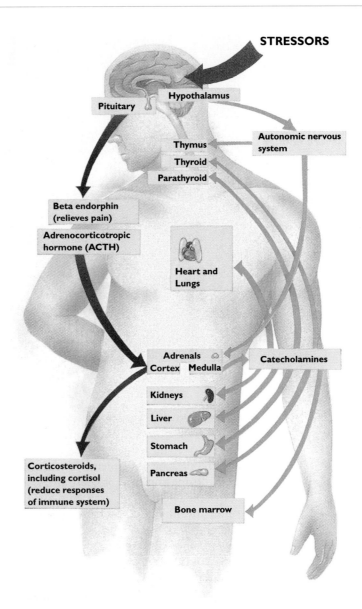

STRESSORS

Hypothalamus

Pituitary

Autonomic nervous system

Thymus

Thyroid

Parathyroid

Beta endorphin (relieves pain)

Adrenocorticotropic hormone (ACTH)

Heart and Lungs

Adrenals

Cortex Medulla

Catecholamines

Kidneys

Liver

Stomach

Pancreas

Corticosteroids, including cortisol (reduce responses of immune system)

Bone marrow

a person thinks of a stressor as being an uncontrollable threat or a controllable challenge, shape the impact of stressors. These models also note that psychological stressors can stimulate some of the same responses as physical danger (Cacioppo et al., 1995; Rozanski et al., 1988).

Emotional Stress Responses   The physical stress responses we have described are usually accompanied by emotional stress responses. If someone shows a gun and demands your money, you will no doubt experience the GAS alarm reaction, but you will also feel some strong emotion, probably fear, maybe anger. In fact, when people describe stress, they are more likely to say, "I was angry and frustrated!" than "My heart rate increased and my blood pressure went up." In other words, they are likely to mention changes in how they feel.

In most cases, emotional stress reactions subside soon after the stressors are gone. However, if stressors continue for a long time or occur in a tight sequence, emotional stress reactions may persist. When people do not have a chance to recover their emotional equilibrium, they commonly report feeling tense, irritable, short-tempered, or anxious more and more of the time.

Cognitive Stress Responses   Reductions in the ability to concentrate, to think clearly, or to remember accurately are typical cognitive stress responses. These problems appear partly because of *ruminative thinking,* the recurring intrusion of thoughts about

How we commonly describe ourselves when "stressed"

AGONY IN BOSNIA Even severe emotional stress responses usually ease eventually, but people plagued by numerous stressful events in quick succession may experience increasingly intense feelings of fatigue, depression, and helplessness. These reactions can become severe enough to be diagnosed as major depressive disorder, generalized anxiety disorder, or other stress-related mental disorders discussed in Chapter 15.

stressful events (Lyubomirsky & Nolen-Hoeksma, 1995). Ruminative thoughts about problems in a romantic relationship, for example, can seriously interfere with studying for a test. A related phenomenon is *catastrophizing,* which means dwelling on and overemphasizing the potential consequences of negative events (Sarason et al., 1986). Thus, during examinations, test-anxious college students are likely to say to themselves, "I'm falling behind" or "Everyone else is doing better than I am." As catastrophizing or ruminative thinking impairs cognitive functioning, a person may experience anxiety and other emotional arousal that adds to the total stress response and further hampers performance (Darke, 1988).

Overarousal created by stressors also tends to narrow the scope of attention, making it harder to scan the full range of possible solutions to complex problems (Darke, 1988; Keinan, Friedland & Ben-Porath, 1987). In addition, stress-narrowed attention may increase the problem-solving errors described in Chapter 9, on thought and language. Thus, people under stress are more likely to cling to *mental sets,* which are well learned but not always efficient, approaches to problems. Stress can also intensify *functional fixedness,* the tendency to use objects for only one purpose. Victims of hotel fires, for example, sometimes die trapped in their rooms because, in the stress of the moment, it did not occur to them to use the telephone or a piece of furniture to break a window.

Stressors may also impair decision making. People who normally consider all aspects of a situation before making a decision may, under stress, act impulsively and some-

LINKAGES As described in Chapter 11 on motivation and emotion, moderate arousal can facilitate performance, but overarousal can interfere with it.

STRESS FOR $500, ALEX   The effects of stress on memory and thought are often displayed by participants on "Jeopardy!" and other game shows. Under the intense pressure of time, competition, and the scrutiny of millions of viewers, contestants sometimes miss questions that seem ridiculously easy to those calmly recalling the answers at home.

times foolishly (Keinan, Friedland & Ben-Porath, 1987). High-pressure salespeople try to take advantage of this phenomenon by creating artificially time-limited offers or by telling customers that others are waiting to buy the item they are considering (Cialdini, 1988).

Behavioral Stress Responses   Clues about people's physical and emotional stress reactions come from changes in how they look, act, or talk. Strained facial expressions, a shaky voice, tremors or spasms, and jumpiness are common behavioral stress responses. Posture can also convey information about stress, a fact observed by skilled interviewers.

Even more obvious behavioral stress responses appear as people attempt to escape or avoid stressors. Some people quit their jobs, drop out of school, turn to alcohol, or even attempt suicide. Unfortunately, as discussed in the chapter on learning, escape and avoidance tactics deprive people of the opportunity to learn more adaptive ways of coping with stressful environments, including college (Cooper et al., 1992). Aggression is another common behavioral response to stressors. All too often, this response is directed at members of one's own family (MacEwan & Barling, 1988; Polusny & Follette, 1995). In the months after Hurricane Andrew hit south Florida in 1992, for example, the rate of domestic-violence reports in the devastated area doubled. As discussed in Chapter 18, stressors are just one of many factors that underlie human aggression.

LINKAGES: STRESS AND PSYCHOLOGICAL DISORDERS

When do stress responses become mental disorders?

Physical, psychological, and behavioral stress responses sometimes appear together in patterns known as burnout and posttraumatic stress disorder. **Burnout** (also called gradual mental stress) is an increasingly intense pattern of physical, psychological, and behavioral dysfunction in response to a continuous flow of stressors or to chronic stress (McKnight & Glass, 1995; Sauter, Murphy & Hurrell, 1990). As burnout approaches, previously reliable workers or once-attentive spouses may become indifferent, disengaged, impulsive, or accident prone. They may miss work frequently, oversleep, perform their jobs poorly, abuse alcohol or other drugs, and become irritable, suspicious, withdrawn, depressed, and unwilling to talk about stress or anything else (Taylor, 1995). Burnout accounts for some 11 percent of occupational disease claims by U.S. workers (Sauter, Murphy & Hurrell, 1990).

A different pattern of severe stress reactions is illustrated by the case of Mary, a thirty-three-year-old nurse who was raped at knife-point by an intruder in her apartment (Spitzer et al., 1983). In the weeks following the attack, she became afraid of being alone and was preoccupied with the attack and with the fear that it might happen again.

LIFE HANGING IN THE BALANCE Symptoms of burnout and posttraumatic stress disorder often plague fire-fighters, police, emergency medical personnel, air traffic controllers, and others continuously exposed to time pressure, trauma, and other stressors (DeAngelis, 1995; Weiss, et al., 1995). When such symptoms affect those so vital to the safety of the community, burnout and PTSD become a serious problem for us all.

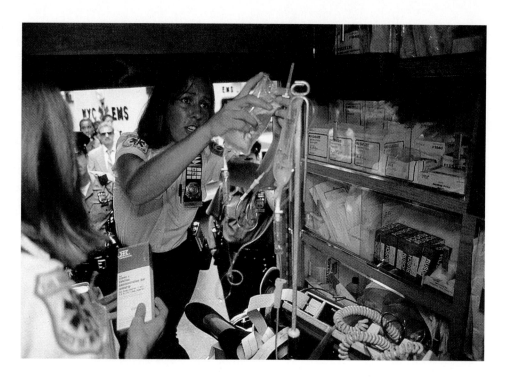

She had additional locks installed on her doors and windows but experienced difficulty concentrating and could not immediately return to work. She was repelled by the thought of sex.

Mary suffered from **posttraumatic stress disorder (PTSD),** a pattern of adverse reactions following a traumatic event. Among the characteristic reactions are anxiety, irritability, jumpiness, inability to concentrate or work productively, sexual dysfunction, and difficulty in getting along with others. People suffering from posttraumatic stress disorder also experience sleep disturbances, guilt, and intense startle responses to noise or other sudden stimuli. Posttraumatic stress disorder is most commonly associated with events such as war, assault, or rape, but researchers now believe that some PTSD symptoms can be triggered by any major stressor (Stuber et al., 1994). The most common feature of posttraumatic stress disorder is re-experiencing the trauma through nightmares or vivid memories. In rare cases, *flashbacks* occur in which the person behaves for minutes, hours, or days as if the trauma were occurring again.

Posttraumatic stress disorder may appear immediately following a trauma, or it may not occur until weeks, months, or even years later. The majority of those affected require professional help, although some seem to recover without it. For most, improvement takes time; for nearly all, the support of family and friends is vital to recovery (Solomon, Mikulincer & Avitzur, 1988).

As described in Chapter 15, stress has also been implicated in the development of a number of other psychological disorders, including depression and schizophrenia. The *diathesis-stress model* suggests that certain people are predisposed to these disorders, which they may or may not display depending on the frequency, nature, and intensity of the stressors they encounter.

Stress Mediators: Interactions Between People and Stressors

The interaction of particular people with particular stressors can be important in other ways, too. During the 1991 Persian Gulf War, for example, a number of United Nations soldiers were killed by "friendly fire" when pilots flying in close support of ground forces mistakenly identified them as the enemy. Many such tragic errors in decision making are probably a result of the stress of combat (Adler, 1993). But why does stress disrupt the performance of some individuals and not others? More generally, why is it that one individual survives, even thrives, under the same circumstances that lead another to break down, give up, and burn out? As mentioned earlier, a number of mediating factors help determine how much impact a given stressor will have (see Figure 13.1).

How Stressors Are Appraised   As discussed in Chapter 5, our perceptions of the world depend on which stimuli we attend to and how we interpret, or appraise, them. Similarly, as noted in Chapter 11, emotional reactions to events can depend on how people think of them. Any potential stressor, be it a hot elevator or a deskful of work, usually has more negative impact on those who perceive it as a threat than on those who see it as a challenge (Ganellen & Blaney, 1984; Rhodewalt & Zone, 1989).

Evidence for the effects of cognition on stress responses comes from both laboratory experiments and surveys. Figure 13.4 shows the results of a classic experiment that demonstrated these effects. In this case, the intensity of physiological arousal during a film depended on how the viewers were instructed to think about the film (Lazarus et al., 1965). Similarly, noise-related distress among people living near airports appears to have more to do with how they evaluate the airport (for example, as a nuisance or as a source of employment) than with how much noise they must endure (Tracor, Inc., 1971).

The influence of cognitive factors weakens somewhat as stressors become more extreme. For example, chronic-pain patients tend to show higher levels of physical activity if they feel a sense of control over their pain, but this effect does not hold for those whose pain is severe (Jensen & Karoly, 1991). Still, even the impact of natural disasters or major stressors such as divorce may be less severe for those who think of them as challenges to be overcome. In short, many stressful events are not inherently stressful; their impact depends partly on how people perceive them (Wiedenfeld et al., 1990). An important aspect of this appraisal is the degree to which the stressors are perceived to be predictable or controllable.

Predictability and Control   Knowing that a particular stressor *might* occur but being uncertain whether it will tends to increase the stressor's impact. For example, wives of American men missing in action in the Vietnam War showed poorer physical and emotional health than those who knew that their spouses had been killed in action or were being held as prisoners of war (Hunter, 1979).

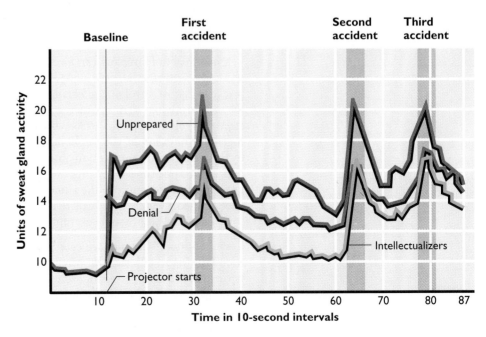

FIGURE 13.4

Cognition and Stress

Richard Lazarus gave differing instructions to three groups of students who were about to watch a stressful film showing bloody industrial accidents. There were clear differences in physiological arousal during the film, as measured by sweat-gland activity. The students who were instructed to remain detached from the bloody scenes (the intellectualizers) or to think of them as unreal (the denial group) were less upset than those in an unprepared control group. These results illustrate that people's cognitive appraisal of stressors can affect their responses to those stressors.

Source: Adapted from Lazarus et al., 1965.

In other words, predictable stressors tend to have less impact than those that are unpredictable (Lazarus & Folkman, 1984), especially when the stressors are intense and occur for relatively short periods (Abbott, Schoen & Badia, 1984). For example, rats given a reliable warning signal every time they are to receive a shock show less severe physiological responses and more normal eating and drinking habits than animals given no warnings (Weinberg & Levine, 1980). Among humans, men and women whose spouses had died suddenly displayed more immediate disbelief, anxiety, and depression than those who had weeks or months to prepare for the loss (Parkes & Weiss, 1983). This is not to say that predictability provides total protection against stressors. Laboratory research with animals has shown that predictable stressors, even if relatively mild, can be more damaging than unpredictable ones if they occur over long periods of time (Abbott, Schoen & Badia, 1984).

Perceptions of control can also mediate the effects of stressors. If people believe they can exert some control over them, stressors usually have less impact. For example, Albert Bandura and his colleagues found that, as snake phobic clients developed a sense of control through treatment, their physical stress responses—such as secretion of adrenaline, cortisol, and endogenous opiates—were reduced and their immune system functioning improved (Bandura et al., 1985, 1988; Wiedenfeld et al., 1990).

Simply believing that a stressor is controllable, even if it isn't, can reduce its impact (Thompson et al., 1993). In one study that examined the cause of panic disorder, clients inhaled a mixture of carbon dioxide and oxygen that typically causes such clients to have panic attacks (Sanderson, Rapee & Barlow, 1988). Half the clients were led to believe (falsely) that they could control the concentration of the mixture. Compared to those who believed they had no control, significantly fewer of the "in control" clients experienced full-blown panic attacks during the session, and their panic symptoms were fewer and less severe.

Conversely, people who feel they have no control over negative events appear especially prone to physical and psychological problems. They often experience feelings of helplessness and hopelessness that, in turn, may promote depression or other mental disorders (Taylor & Aspinwall, 1996). Similarly, studies have shown that breast cancer patients who harbor a sense of helplessness about their disease have a lower survival rate than those with a greater sense of control (Jensen, 1987; Rodin & Salovey, 1989).

Coping Resources and Coping Methods   People usually suffer fewer ill effects from a stressor if they have adequate coping resources and effective coping methods. *Coping resources* include, for example, the money and time to deal with stressful events. Thus, the physical and psychological responses to your car breaking down are likely to be more negative if you are broke and pressed for time than if you have money for repairs and the freedom to take a day off from work.

The impact of stressors can also be reduced by the application of effective coping methods (Sutker et al., 1995). Most of these methods can be categorized as either *problem-focused,* involving efforts to alter or eliminate a source of stress, or *emotion-focused,* involving attempts to regulate the negative emotional consequences of the stressor (Folkman et al., 1986a, b). These two forms of coping sometimes work together. For example, you might deal with the problem of noise from a nearby airport by forming a community action group to push for tougher noise abatement regulations and, at the same time, calm your anger when noise occurs by mentally focusing on the group's efforts to improve the situation. Susan Folkman and Richard Lazarus (1988) have devised a widely used scale to assess the specific ways that people cope with stressors; Table 13.3 shows some examples from their scale.

Social Support   If you have ever benefited from the comforting presence of a good friend during troubled times, you have experienced the value of social support in tempering the impact of stressful events. Social support consists of resources provided by other persons; the friends and social contacts on whom you can depend for support constitute your **social support network** (Cohen & Syme, 1985; Schwarzer & Leppin, 1991). The support may take many forms, from eliminating the stressor (as when a friend helps you fix your car) to buffering its impact with companionship, ideas for

TABLE 13.3	Coping Skills	Example
Ways of Coping	**Problem-focused coping**	
Coping is defined as one's cognitive and behavioral efforts to manage specific demands that are appraised as taxing one's resources (Folkman et al., 1986a). This table illustrates two major approaches to coping.	Confronting	"I stood my ground and fought for what I wanted."
	Seeking social support	"I talked to someone to find out more about the situation."
	Planful problem solving	"I made a plan of action and I followed it."
	Emotion-focused coping	
	Self-controlling	"I tried to keep my feelings to myself."
	Distancing	"I didn't let it get to me; I tried not to think about it too much."
	Positive reappraisal	"I changed my mind about myself."
	Accepting responsibility	"I realized I brought the problem on myself."
	Escape/avoidance (wishful thinking)	"I wished that the situation would go away or somehow be over with."

Source: Adapted from Folkman et al., 1986a; Taylor, 1995.

coping, or reassurance that one is cared about and valued and that everything will be all right (Rook, 1987; Sarason & Sarason, 1985).

The stress-reducing effects of social support have been documented for a wide range of stressors including cancer (Baron et al., 1990), crowding (Lepore, Evans & Schneider, 1991), military combat (Bartone et al., 1992), natural disasters (Kaniasty & Norris, 1993), and AIDS (Hays, Turner & Coates, 1992). These effects were well illustrated in a pair of studies involving undergraduate and graduate students (Goplerud, 1980; Lepore, 1995a). Compared with those who were part of a supportive network, students with the least adequate social support suffered more emotional distress and were more vulnerable to upper respiratory infections during times of high academic stress. Indeed, one team of researchers concluded that having inadequate social support is as dangerous as smoking cigarettes because it nearly doubles a person's risk of dying from disease, suicide, or other causes (House, Landis & Umberson, 1988). Conversely, having

YOU'VE GOT A FRIEND   Even when social support cannot eliminate stressors, it can help people, such as these breast cancer survivors, to feel less anxious, more optimistic, more capable of control, and more willing to try new ways of dealing with stressors.

strong social support can reduce the likelihood of illness, improve recovery from existing illness, and promote healthier behaviors (Broman, 1993; Wickrama, Conger & Lorenz, 1995).

However, the relationship between social support and the impact of stressors is not a simple one. First, just as the quality of social support may influence people's ability to cope with stress, the reverse may also be true: People's ability to cope may determine the quality of social support they receive (Billings & Moos, 1981; Dunkel-Schetter, Folkman & Lazarus, 1987). For example, people who complain endlessly about stressors but never try to do anything about them may discourage social support, while those with an optimistic, action-oriented approach may attract reliable support.

Second, social support refers not only to relationships with others but also to the cognitive recognition that others care and will help (Pierce, Sarason & Sarason, 1991; Lakey & Cassady, 1990). Some relationships in what appears to be a dense social network can be stormy and fragile, resulting in interpersonal conflicts that can have an adverse effect on health (Malarkey et al., 1994).

Finally, having too much support or the wrong kind of support can be as bad as not having enough. People whose friends and family are overprotective may actually put *less* energy into coping efforts. For example, such overprotection might lengthen the time it takes for a worker to return to work after an accident or illness (Garrity, 1973; Wortman, 1984). Similarly, people living in crowded conditions might initially perceive the situation as providing lots of social support, but these conditions may eventually become an added source of stress (Lepore, Evans & Schneider, 1991). Thus, the efforts of a social support network can sometimes become annoying, disruptive, or interfering, thereby increasing stress and intensifying psychological problems (Broman, 1993).

Stress and Personality   Some of the stress-mediating factors we have discussed reflect individual differences in cognitive habits—how people think about stressors and the world in general. Some cognitive habits, such as those characteristic of "disease-resistant" personalities, appear to help insulate people from the ill effects of stress; others, such as those associated with "disease-prone" personalities, may leave people especially vulnerable to those effects (Werner, 1995; Sutker et al., 1995).

For example, stress-related health problems tend to be more common among people who persist at mentally evading perceived stressors; who perceive them as long-term, catastrophic threats that they brought on themselves; and who are pessimistic

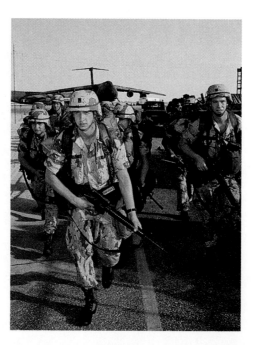

THE IMPACT OF STRESS MEDIATORS   Of the nearly 3 percent of U.S. soldiers who developed posttraumatic stress disorder during and after the 1991 Persian Gulf war, most were individuals who had the greatest exposure to combat, the least stress-resistant personalities, and the lowest levels of social support from other soldiers (Bartone et al., 1992).

about their ability to overcome negative situations (e.g., Bandura, 1989; Miller, Brody & Summerton, 1988; Peterson, Seligman & Vaillant, 1988; Scheier & Carver, 1987).

One component of the disease-resistant personality seems to be *dispositional optimism,* the belief or expectation that things will work out positively (Scheier & Carver 1987; Scheier, Carver & Bridges, 1994). Optimistic students, for example, experience fewer physical symptoms at the end of the academic term (Aspinwall & Taylor, 1992). Optimistic coronary bypass surgery patients have been shown to heal faster than pessimists (Scheier et al., 1989) and to perceive their quality of life following coronary surgery to be higher than that of those with less optimistic outlooks (Fitzgerald et al., 1993). And among HIV-positive men, dispositional optimism has been associated with lower psychological distress, fewer worries, and lower perceived risk of acquiring full-blown AIDS (Taylor et al., 1992). These effects appear due in part to optimists' tendency to use challenge-oriented, problem-focused coping strategies that attack stressors directly, in contrast to pessimists' tendency to use emotion-focused coping such as denial and avoidance (Taylor, 1995). Indeed, another study of HIV-positive men showed that active coping strategies are associated with improved functioning of the immune system (Goodkin et al., 1992).

People who tend to think of stressors as temporary and who do not constantly blame themselves for the onset of stressors appear to be harmed less by them. This cognitive stance can be quite adaptive, especially when combined with a challenge orientation. Its benefits can also be seen, however, among many devout people whose religious beliefs prompt them to think of poverty, disease, and other objective stressors, not as challenges to be overcome, but as temporary conditions to be endured until their suffering is rewarded (McIntosh, Silver & Wortman, 1993).

FOCUS ON RESEARCH METHODS

Mining Longitudinal Research for Insights into Personality and Health

Are there factors in addition to optimism that might be important in surviving the effects of life's stressors? A creative reanalysis of some major longitudinal research on the correlates of intelligence suggests that there are.

The research was referred to as the Terman Life Cycle Study because it was begun by Lewis Terman, author of the Stanford-Binet Intelligence Test. As described in Chapter 10, the study was originally designed to document the long-term development of 1,528 gifted California children (856 boys and 672 girls)—nicknamed the "Termites" (Terman & Odem, 1947). But Howard Friedman and his colleagues have recently found ways of using data from this study to explore the relationship between personality and health (Friedman et al., 1995a, 1995b).

Starting in 1921, and every five to ten years thereafter, Terman's research team gathered information about the Termites' personality traits, social relationships, stressors, health habits, and many other variables. The data were collected through questionnaires and interviews with the Termites themselves, as well as with their teachers, parents, and other family members. When, by the early 1990s, about half of the Termites had died, Friedman realized that the Terman Life Cycle Study was really a quasi-experiment in health psychology. As in most quasi-experiments (described in Chapter 2), the independent variable—in this case, personality characteristics—was not actually manipulated (the Termites had obviously not been randomly assigned different personalities by the researchers), but the various personality traits identified in these people could still be related to a dependent variable—namely, how long they lived.

Accordingly, Friedman gathered the death certificates of the Termites, noted the dates and causes of death, and then looked for associations between personality and longevity. One of the most important predictors of long life was conscientiousness, or social dependability. Termites who, in childhood, had been seen as truthful, prudent,

IN REVIEW	Stress Responses and Stress Mediators
Category	**Examples**
Responses	
Physical	Fight-or-flight syndrome (increased heart rate, respiration, and muscle tension, sweating, pupillary dilation); release of adrenaline and other chemicals. Eventual breakdown of organ systems involved in prolonged resistance to stressors.
Psychological	Anger, anxiety, depression, and other emotional states; inability to concentrate or think logically; catastrophic thinking.
Behavioral	Aggression and escape/avoidance tactics (including suicide attempts).
Mediators	
Appraisal	Thinking of a difficult new job as a challenge will create less discomfort than focusing on the threat of failure.
Predictability	A tornado that strikes without warning may have a more devastating emotional impact than a long-predicted hurricane.
Control	Repairing a disabled spacecraft may be less stressful for the astronauts doing the work than for their loved ones on Earth, who can do nothing to help.
Coping resources and methods	Having no effective way to relax after a hard day may prolong tension and other stress responses.
Social support	Having no one to talk to about a rape or other trauma may amplify the negative impact of the experience.

reliable, hard-working, and free from vanity tended to live longer than those whose parents and teachers had identified them as impulsive and lacking in self-control.

Friedman also mined the Terman Life Cycle Study for what it suggested about the relationship between health and social support. He compared the life spans of Termites who came from broken homes or who had been in unstable marriages with those who grew up in stable homes and who had stable marriages. He found that people who had experienced parental divorce during childhood or who themselves had unstable marriages died an average of four years earlier than those whose close social relationships had been less stressful.

Did differences in personality traits and social support actually *cause* some Termites to live longer than others? Friedman's research is based mainly on correlational analyses of a quasi-experiment, so it is difficult to draw conclusions about causality in the relationships observed. Still, Friedman and his colleagues searched the Terman data for clues to mechanisms through which personality and other factors *might* have exerted a causal influence on longevity. For example, they evaluated the hypothesis that conscientious, dependable Termites who lived socially stable lives might have followed healthier lifestyles than their impulsive and socially stressed age-mates. Indeed, people in the latter group did tend to eat less healthy diets and were more likely to smoke, drink to excess, or use drugs; but health behaviors alone did not fully account for their shorter average life spans. Another possible explanation is that conscientiousness and stability in social relationships instills a general attitude of caution that goes beyond eating right and avoiding substance abuse. Friedman found some support for this idea in the Terman data—Termites who were impulsive or low on conscientiousness were somewhat more likely to die from accidents or violence than those who were less impulsive.

Although the Terman Life Cycle Study cannot provide final answers about the relationship between personality and health, it has generated some important clues and a number of intriguing hypotheses to be evaluated in future research with more representative samples of subjects. Further, Friedman's decision to reanalyze a set of data on psychosocial development as a way of exploring issues in health psychology stands as a fine example of how creative a researcher can be in pursuing answers to complex questions that are difficult or impossible to study via controlled experiments.

Our review of personality and other factors that can alter the impact of stressors should make it obvious that what is stressful for a given individual is not determined simply by predispositions, coping styles, or situations. (See "In Review: Stress Responses and Stress Mediators.") Even more important are interactions between the person and the situation, the mixture of each individual's coping resources and the specific characteristics of the situations encountered (Smith, 1993).

THE PHYSIOLOGY AND PSYCHOLOGY OF HEALTH AND ILLNESS

Several studies mentioned so far have suggested that stress shapes the development of physical illness by affecting cognitive, physiological, and behavioral processes. Those studies are part of a much larger body of research in health psychology that sheds light on the relationship between stress and illness as well as on the issue of how people can behave in ways that preserve their health. In this section, we focus more specifically on the ways in which stress can, directly or indirectly, lead to physical illnesses. One of the most important connections between stress and illness occurs through the immune system.

Stress, the Immune System, and Illness

LINKAGES Can stress give you the flu? (a link to Biological Aspects of Psychology)

The role of physiological stress responses in the body's ability to fight disease was demonstrated more than a century ago. On March 19, 1878, at a seminar before the Academie de Médécine de Paris, Louis Pasteur showed his distinguished audience three chickens. One healthy bird, the control chicken, had been raised normally. A second bird had been intentionally infected with bacteria but given no other treatment; it was also healthy. The third chicken Pasteur presented was dead. It had been infected with the same bacteria as the second bird, but it had also been physically stressed by being exposed to cold temperatures (Kelley, 1985); as a result, the bacteria killed it.

Research conducted since Pasteur's time has greatly expanded knowledge about how stressors affect the body's reaction to disease. **Psychoneuroimmunology** is the field that examines the interaction of psychological and physiological processes that affect the body's ability to defend itself against disease.

The Immune System and Illness   The body's first line of defense against invading substances and microorganisms is the **immune system,** which we briefly discussed in Chapter 3, on biological aspects of psychology. Components of the immune system kill or inactivate foreign or harmful substances in the body such as viruses, bacteria, and cancer cells. If the immune system is impaired—by stressors, for example—a person is left more vulnerable to colds, mononucleosis, and many other infectious diseases (Cohen & Herbert, 1996). Disabling of the immune system is the process by which the human immunodeficiency virus (HIV) leads to AIDS and leaves the HIV-infected person defenseless against other infections or cancers.

There are many facets to the human immune system. One important component is the action of immune system cells, especially white blood cells, called *leukocytes,* which are formed in the bone marrow and serve as the body's mobile defense units.

**THE FIRST LINE OF DEFENSE   A
patrolling immune system cell sends
out an extension known as a *pseudo-
pod* to engulf and destroy a bacterial
cell before alerting more defenders.
Psychological stressors can alter
immune system functions through a
number of mechanisms. For example, they can activate neural connections between the sympathetic
nervous system and organs of the
immune system through response
systems that have direct suppressant effects on immune function.
These suppressant effects are due
largely to the release of cortisol and
other corticosteroid hormones from
the adrenal cortex (see Figure 13.3).**

Leukocytes are called into action when foreign substances are detected. Among the varied types of leukocytes are *B-cells,* which mature in the bone marrow, and *T-cells,* which
mature in the thymus. Generally, T-cells kill other cells, and B-cells produce *antibodies,*
which are circulating proteins that bind to specific foreign toxins and initiate their inactivation. *Natural killer cells,* another type of leukocyte, destroy a wide variety of foreign
organisms, but they have particularly important anti-viral and anti-tumor functions.
Yet another type of immune system cell is the *macrophage.* Macrophages engulf foreign
cells and digest them in a process called *phagocytosis* ("eating cells"). These scaven-
gers are able to squeeze out of the bloodstream and enter organs where they destroy
foreign cells.

The activity of immune system cells can be either strengthened or inhibited by a
number of systems, including the endocrine system and the central and autonomic nervous systems. It is through these connections that stress-related psychological and emotional factors can affect the functioning of the immune system (see Figure 3.25). The
precise mechanisms by which the nervous system affects the immune system are not yet
fully understood. There is evidence, however, that the brain can influence the immune
system indirectly by altering the secretion of hormones that modify circulating T-cells
and B-cells and directly by making connections with the immune organs, such as the
thymus, where T-cells and B-cells are stored (Felten et al., 1991).

The Immune System and Stress   Researchers have shown convincingly that people
under stress are more likely than their less stressed counterparts to develop infectious
diseases and to experience reactivation of latent viruses responsible for oral herpes
(cold sores) or genital herpes (Cohen & Herbert, 1996). For example, Sheldon Cohen
and his colleagues in the United Kingdom (Cohen, Tyrrell & Smith, 1991) exposed 394
healthy adult volunteers either to one of five respiratory viruses or to a placebo. After
being quarantined, the subjects were asked about the number and severity of life
stresses they had experienced in the previous year. After controlling for factors such as
prior history of colds, exposure to other viruses, and health practices, the researchers
found that the more stress the subjects had experienced, the greater was the likelihood
that their exposure to a virus would result in colds and respiratory infections.

These findings are supported by other research showing more directly that a variety
of stressors lead to suppression of the immune system. For example, one group of
researchers compared the activity of natural killer cells in medical students one month
before final exams and on the first day of the exams; natural killer cell activity was significantly lower at the stressful time of the exams (Kiecolt-Glaser et al., 1984; Glaser
et al., 1987). Similarly, decrements in natural killer cell activity have been observed in
both men and women following the death of their spouses (Irwin et al., 1987), and a
variety of immune system impairments have been found in people suffering the effects
of separation, divorce, lack of social support, and loneliness (Kiecolt-Glaser & Glaser,
1992). Each of these stressors has been associated with depression, which is itself associated with reductions in immune system activity (Petitto et al., 1992).

The relationship between stress and the immune system is especially important in
persons who are HIV-positive but do not yet have AIDS. Because their immune systems
are already seriously compromised, further stress-related decrements could be life
threatening (Kiecolt-Glaser & Glaser, 1992). Research indicates that psychological
stressors are associated with the progression of HIV-related illnesses (e.g., Reed et al.,
1994; Herbert & Cohen, 1993). Unfortunately, people with HIV (and AIDS) face a particularly heavy load of immune-suppressing psychological stressors, including bereavement, unemployment, uncertainty about the future, and daily reminders of serious
illness. A lack of perceived control and resulting depression can further amplify their
stress responses.

Moderators of Immune Function   The effects of social support and other stress-
moderating factors can be seen in the activity of the immune system. For example,
immune system functioning among students who can get emotional assistance from
friends during stressful periods appears better than among those with less adequate
social support (Jemmott & Magloire, 1988).

James Pennebaker (1985, 1990) has suggested that social support may help prevent illness by providing the person under stress with an opportunity to express pent-up thoughts and emotions. Keeping important things to oneself, says Pennebaker, is itself a stressor (Pennebaker, Colder & Sharp, 1990). In the laboratory, for example, subjects who were asked to try to deceive an experimenter displayed elevated physiological arousal (Pennebaker & Chew, 1985; Waid & Orne, 1981). Further, the spouses of suicide or accidental-death victims who do not or cannot confide their feelings to others are most likely to develop physical illnesses during the year following the death (Pennebaker & O'Heeron, 1984). Disclosing, even anonymously, the stresses and traumas one has experienced is associated with enhanced immune functioning and decreased use of health services among students (Greenberg & Stone, 1992; Pennebaker, Kiecolt-Glaser & Glaser, 1988; Petrie et al., 1995). Future research in psychoneuroimmunology promises to reveal vital links in the complex chain of mental and physical events that determine whether people become ill or stay healthy.

Heart Disease and Behavior Patterns

A number of stress responses—especially anger and hostility—have been linked to coronary heart disease (CHD), especially in men (Friedman & Rosenman, 1959, 1974). Current research is focusing on a response pattern called *cynical hostility,* which is characterized by suspiciousness, resentment, frequent anger, antagonism, and distrust of others (Smith & Frohm, 1985; Williams & Barefoot, 1988).

The identification of cynical hostility as a risk factor for coronary heart disease and myocardial infarction, or MI (commonly known as heart attack), may be an important breakthrough in understanding a category of illness that remains the chief cause of death in the United States and most other Western nations. Further, the fact that cynical hostility often develops in childhood (Woodall & Matthews, 1993) would suggest a need for intervention programs capable of altering this interpersonal style in time to prevent its negative consequences for health. But is cynical hostility as dangerous as health psychologists suspect?

TAKE THAT! For a time, researchers believed that anyone who displayed the pattern of aggressiveness, competitiveness, and nonstop work known as "Type A" behavior was at elevated risk for heart disease. More recent research shows, however, that the danger lies not in these characteristics alone, but in cynical hostility, a pattern seen in some, but not all, Type A people.

What am I being asked to believe or accept?

Many researchers contend that individuals displaying cynical hostility are at increased risk for coronary heart disease and heart attack. This risk, they say, is independent of coexisting risk factors such as heredity, diet, smoking, and drinking.

THINKING CRITICALLY

Does Cynical Hostility Increase the Risk of Heart Disease?

What evidence is available to support the assertion?

The precise mechanism underlying the relationship between hostility and heart disease is not clear, but there are several possibilities (Helmers et al., 1995). The risk of CHD and MI may be elevated in cynically hostile people because these people tend to be unusually reactive to stressors, especially when challenged (Suls & Wan, 1993). There is evidence, for example, that under interpersonally challenging circumstances, people predisposed to hostile behavior display not only overt hostility but also unusually large increases in blood pressure, heart rate, and other aspects of sympatho-adreno-medullary (SAM) reactivity (Suls & Wan, 1993). More important, it takes hostile individuals longer than normal to get back to their resting levels of SAM functioning. Like a driver who damages a car by simultaneously flooring the accelerator and applying the brakes, these "hot reactors" may create excessive wear and tear on the arteries and the heart, as their increased heart rate pushes blood through constricted vessels. Increased sympathetic nervous system activation not only puts stress on the coronary arteries but also leads to surges of stress-related hormones from the adrenal glands: the catecholamines (adrenaline and noradrenaline) and cortisol (Lundberg et al., 1989; Williams et al., 1991; Suarez et al., 1991). High levels of these hormones, in turn, are associated with increases in fatty substances, such as blood cholesterol, that are deposited in arteries and contribute to atherosclerosis (hardening of the arteries) and CHD. Plasma lipids, such as cholesterol and triglycerides, do appear to be elevated in hostile people (Dujovne & Houston, 1991).

Hostility may affect CHD/MI risk less directly as well, through its impact on social support. There is some evidence that hostile people may derive fewer benefits from their social support network (Lepore, 1995b). Failure to make use of such support—and possible alienation of potential supporters in the process—may intensify the impact of stressful events on hostile people. The result may be increased anger, antagonism, and, ultimately, additional stress on the cardiovascular system (Smith, 1992; Suls & Wan, 1993).

Are there alternative ways of interpreting the evidence?

The studies cited in support of the relationship between hostility and CHD are not true experiments. Researchers cannot manipulate the independent variable by creating hostility in people, nor can they create experimental conditions in which groups of individuals who differ *only* in terms of hostility are compared on heart disease, the dependent variable. Accordingly, it is difficult to reach unambiguous conclusions about cause-effect relationships in this and many other areas of health psychology.

Some researchers suggest that higher CHD/MI rates among those high in hostility are due not to the impact of hostility on autonomic reactivity and hormone surges but, rather, to a third variable that causes the other two. Specifically, it may be that genetically determined autonomic reactivity increases the likelihood of both hostility and heart disease (Krantz et al., 1988).

Supporting this alternative interpretation is evidence that, during surgical stress under general anesthesia, hostile individuals show unusually strong autonomic reactivity (Krantz & Durel, 1983). Since these individuals are not conscious, it is more likely that oversensitivity to stressors, not hostile thoughts, are causing this exaggerated response. Other data suggest that there is a genetic contribution to the development of hostility (Smith et al., 1991). Thus, it is at least plausible that some individuals are biologically predisposed to exaggerated autonomic reactivity *and* to hostility, each of which is independent of the other.

What additional evidence would help to evaluate the alternatives?

Several lines of evidence could assist in evaluating these two interpretations of the relationship between hostility and CHD/MI. One approach would be to examine the relationships among hostility, CHD, and social and cultural factors (Thoreson & Powell, 1992). If the strength of the relationship between hostility and CHD varies across social or cultural groups, then the theory of biological determination would be less tenable.

John Barefoot and his colleagues (1991) examined part of this issue using a sample of 2,500 adults. They found that the hostility scores of African-Americans were much higher than those of European-Americans and that, among the African-Americans, hostility scores were highest for those in groups with low income and little education. The relationship between hostility and income was not present among European-Americans. Further, African-Americans have been found to react to stressors with greater blood pressure increases than those exhibited by European Americans (Durel et al., 1989). Of course, elevations in hostility and blood pressure reactivity do not necessarily translate directly into CHD. Overall, African-Americans do not differ much from European-Americans in terms of CHD death rates. Moreover, when income level is controlled for, African-American death rates from CHD are *lower* than those of European-Americans, despite higher hostility scores (USDHHS, 1990).

What conclusions are most reasonable?

Although there is some inconsistency among the relevant studies, most continue to find that hostile individuals have a greater risk of heart disease and heart attacks than their nonhostile counterparts (Smith, 1992). But the causal relationships are probably more complex than any current theory suggests; it appears that many factors underlie the relationship between hostility and CHD.

A more elaborate psychobiological model may be required—one that takes into account that (1) some individuals may be biologically predisposed to react to stress and challenge with hostility and increased cardiovascular activity, which in turn can contribute to heart disease; (2) hostile people amplify and perpetuate their stress through aggressive thoughts and actions, which in turn provoke others and elicit additional stressors; and (3) those high in hostility also tend to harm their health more than less hostile people by smoking, drinking, overeating, not exercising, and engaging in other high-risk behaviors (Houston & Vavac, 1991; Smith, 1992).

In addition, we must keep in mind that the relationship between CHD/MI and hostility may not be universal. There is some evidence that this relationship may hold for women as well as men, and for individuals in various ethnic and cultural groups (Koskenvuo et al., 1988; Sprafka et al., 1990; Weidner et al., 1987), but we do not know for sure (Landrine & Klonoff, 1992; Smith, 1992; Thoresen & Powell, 1992). Final conclusions must await further research that examines the impact of gender, culture, and ethnicity on the relationship between hostility and CHD/MI.

Risking Your Life: Health-Endangering Behaviors

As we have seen, many of today's major health problems are caused or amplified by preventable behaviors such as those listed in Table 13.1 (USDHHS, 1990).

Smoking   Smoking is the single most preventable risk factor for fatal illnesses in the United States (Kaplan et al., 1995). Indeed, cigarette smoking accounts for more deaths than do all other drugs, car accidents, suicides, homicides, and fires *combined* (Grunberg, 1992). Further, nonsmokers who inhale "secondhand" smoke face an elevated risk for lung cancer and other respiratory diseases (Bauman, Koch & Fisher, 1989; USDHHS, 1990), a fact that has fueled a militant nonsmokers' rights movement in North America.

Although smoking is on the decline in the United States overall—only about 26 percent of adults now smoke—the habit is actually increasing among adolescent women (Stacy et al., 1992; Centers for Disease Control, 1993). Poorer, less educated people are particularly likely to smoke. High smoking rates are also found among certain American Indian tribes in the northern plains, among Hispanic-American males, and among African-Americans generally. Conversely, some American Indian tribes in the Southwest and most Asian groups are less likely than other groups to smoke (Gritz & St. Jeor, 1992; USDHHS, 1990). In many other countries, especially those of the Third World, smoking is still the rule rather than the exception. Smoking is a difficult habit to break; long-term success following most smoking cessation programs available today is still only about 35 percent (Jason et al., 1995; Shiffman, 1993). Improving this success rate and preventing adolescents from taking up smoking remain among health psychology's greatest challenges.

Alcohol   Like tobacco, alcohol is a potentially addicting substance that can lead to major health problems. In addition to its association with most leading causes of death, including heart disease, stroke, cancer, and liver disease, alcohol abuse contributes to irreversible damage to brain tissue and to gastrointestinal illnesses, among many others. Both male and female alcohol abusers may experience disruption of their reproductive functions, such as early menopause in women and erectile disorder in men. And as noted in the chapter on human development, alcohol consumption by pregnant women is the most preventable cause of birth defects. The economic costs of alcohol

A DEADLY HABIT It has been estimated that, if people did not smoke cigarettes, 400,000 fewer U.S. citizens would die in the next twelve months and 25 percent of all cancer deaths and thousands of heart attacks would never occur (USDHHS, 1990).

abuse total $70 billion a year (USDHHS, 1990); about 15 percent of U.S. health care costs relate to this problem, which is discussed further in Chapter 15, on psychological disorders.

Unsafe Sex   The threat of AIDS is a fact of life. In just the past decade, over one-quarter of a million Americans have been diagnosed as having AIDS and as many as 2 million more have been infected with HIV. An estimated 75,000 of these people are adolescents (St. Lawrence, 1993). Currently, the majority of those affected in the United States are male, but the rate for females is doubling every year or two (Ickovics & Rodin, 1992).

Unsafe sex—especially sexual relations without the use of a condom—greatly increases the risk of contracting HIV; yet many adolescents and adults continue this dangerous practice (Catania et al., 1992; DeAngelis, 1995). Like smoking and many other health-threatening behaviors, unprotected sex is disproportionately common among low-income individuals, many of whom are members of ethnic minority groups (St. Lawrence, 1993). Among African-American men the risk of contracting AIDS is three times greater than for European-American men; the risk for African-American women is fifteen times higher than for European-American women (Nyamathi, Stein & Brecht, 1995).

As described in the next section, health psychologists are deeply involved in the fight against the spread of HIV and AIDS (Kiecolt-Glaser & Glaser, 1992; Kelly & Murphy, 1992).

PROMOTING HEALTHY BEHAVIOR

The process of reducing or eliminating behaviors that pose risks to health and of increasing healthy behavior patterns is called **health promotion** (Taylor, 1995). In their health promotion efforts, many health psychologists conduct and apply research on the cognitive factors associated with the development and alteration of health-related behaviors. The aim is to better understand the thought processes that lead people to engage in health-endangering behaviors and to tailor intervention programs that alter those thought processes, or at least take them into account (Klepp, Kelder & Perry, 1995).

Health Beliefs and Health Behaviors

The cognitive approach to health psychology is embodied in various *health-belief models,* among which one of the most influential was developed by Irwin Rosenstock (1974). This model has been extensively tested (e.g., Aspinwall et al., 1991) and is based on the assumption that people's decisions about health-related behaviors (such as smoking) are guided by four main factors:

1. A perception of *personal* threat or susceptibility to contracting a specific illness. (Do you believe that *you* will get lung cancer from smoking?)

2. A perception of the seriousness of the illness and the severity of the consequences of having it. (How serious do *you* think lung cancer is, and what will happen to *you* if you get it?)

3. The belief that a particular practice will reduce the threat. (Will *your* stopping smoking prevent *you* from getting lung cancer?)

4. The decisional balance between the perceived costs of enacting a health practice and the benefits expected from this practice. (Will the reduced chance of getting cancer in the future be worth the discomfort and loss of pleasure associated with not smoking?)

On the basis of this health-belief model, one would expect that the people most likely to quit smoking would be those who believe that they are susceptible to getting cancer from smoking, that cancer is serious and life-threatening, and that the benefits of preventing cancer clearly outweigh the difficulties associated with quitting.

Other belief factors not included in Rosenstock's model may be important as well. For example, people are unlikely to try to quit smoking unless they believe they can succeed. Thus, *self-efficacy*, the belief that one is able to perform some behavior (see Chapter 14, on personality), is an additional determinant of decisions about health behaviors (Bandura, 1986; Taylor, 1995).

Health-belief models have been useful in predicting a variety of health behaviors, including exercise (McAuley, 1992), safe-sex practices among gay men at risk for AIDS (Fisher, Fisher & Rye, 1995), adherence to medical regimes among diabetic adolescents (Bond, Aiken & Somerville, 1992), and the decision to undergo mammogram screening for breast cancer (Champion & Huster, 1995).

Changing Health Behaviors: Stages of Readiness

Knowing *who* is most likely to practice healthy behaviors is important, but health psychologists have also sought to understand *how* people change their health habits. According to James Prochaska and his colleagues, successful change involves five stages (Prochaska, DiClemente & Norcross, 1992):

1. *Precontemplation* The person does not perceive a health-related problem and has no intention of changing in the foreseeable future.

2. *Contemplation* The person is aware of a problem behavior that should be changed and is seriously thinking about changing it. People often get stuck here. Cigarette smokers, for example, have been known to spend years contemplating quitting.

3. *Preparation* The person has a strong intention to change, has specific plans to do so, and may already have taken preliminary steps, such as cutting down on smoking.

4. *Action* The person at this stage is engaging successfully in behavior change. Because relapse is so prevalent in health-related behaviors, people in this stage must remain successful for up to six months before they officially reach the next stage.

5. *Maintenance* The person uses skills learned along the way to continue the healthy behavior and to prevent relapse.

The path from precontemplation through maintenance is not a smooth one (Prochaska, 1994). Usually, people relapse and go through the stages again until they finally achieve stability in the healthy behavior they desire (see Figure 13.5). For example, smokers typically require three to four cycles through the stages and up to seven years before they finally reach the maintenance stage.

What factors contribute to movement from one stage to the next? Prochaska and his colleagues found that the factors facilitating progress at one stage may be different from those most important at another. However, *decisional balance*, the outcome of weighing the pros and cons of changing, is important for predicting progress at any stage (Prochaska et al., 1994). This finding applies to many health-related behaviors, including getting mammograms (Rakowski et al., 1992), participating in exercise programs (Courneya, 1995), consuming a diet high in fruit and vegetables (Laforge, Greene & Prochaska, 1994), and quitting smoking, among others (Prochaska & DiClemente, 1992).

Programs for Coping with Stress and Promoting Health

LINKAGES **How can people manage stress?** (a link to Treatment of Psychological Disorders)

Helping people to tip the decisional balance in favor of healthy change is but one strategy that health psychologists apply in an effort to improve people's coping skills and promote healthier lifestyles. Let's consider a few specific procedures and programs used in this wide-ranging effort.

FIGURE 13.5

Stages of Readiness to Change
Health Behaviors

Prochaska's theory that readiness to change health behaviors progresses through predictable stages has guided decisions by many health psychologists about whether to encourage a person to start a program for changing health behaviors. These decisions are also guided by an exploration of the person's history of progress through the stages, and by an understanding of the stage at which the person seems to be at the moment.

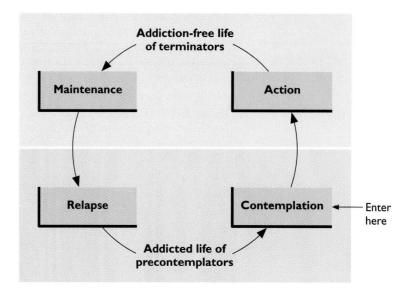

Source: Prochaska, DiClemente & Norcross, 1992.

Planning to Cope   Just as people with extra money in the bank have a better chance of weathering a financial crisis, those with effective coping skills may escape some of the more harmful effects of intense stress. Like family money, the ability to handle stress appears to come naturally to some people, but coping can also be learned.

The first step in learning to cope with stress is to make a systematic assessment of the degree to which stress is disrupting one's life. This assessment involves (1) identifying the specific events and situations, such as conflicts or life changes, that are operating as stressors; and (2) noting the effects of these stressors, such as headaches, lack of concentration, or excessive smoking or drinking.

Table 13.4 lists the other steps in a program to cope with stress. Notice that the second step is to select an appropriate goal. Should you try to eliminate stressors or to alter your response to them? Knowing the difference between changeable and unchangeable stressors is important. Stress-related problems appear especially prevalent among people who either exhaust themselves trying to change stressors that cannot be changed or miss opportunities to change stressors that can be changed (Folkman, 1984).

No single method of coping with stressors is universally successful. For example, denying the existence of an uncontrollable stressor may be fine in the short run but may lead to problems if no other coping method is used (Suls & Fletcher, 1985). Similarly, people who rely exclusively on an active problem-solving approach may handle controllable stressors well but find themselves nearly helpless in the face of uncontrollable

TABLE 13.4

Stages in Coping with Stress

Most successful programs for coping with stress move systematically through several stages and are aimed at removing stressors that can be changed and at tempering responses to stressors that remain (Silver & Wortman, 1980).

Stage	Task
1. Assessment	Identify the sources and effects of stress.
2. Goal setting	List the stressors and stress responses to be addressed. Designate which stressors are and are not changeable.
3. Planning	List the specific steps to be taken to cope with stress.
4. Action	Implement coping plans.
5. Evaluation	Determine the changes in stressors and stress responses that have occurred as a result of coping methods.
6. Adjustment	Alter coping methods to improve results, if necessary.

ones (Rodin & Salovey, 1989). Individuals most successful at stress management may be those who are best able to adjust their coping methods to the demands of changing situations and differing stressors (Carver, Scheier & Weintraub, 1989; Costa & McCrae, 1989; Folkman et al., 1986b).

Developing Coping Strategies   Like stress responses, strategies for coping with stress can be cognitive, emotional, behavioral, or physical. *Cognitive coping strategies* change how people interpret stimuli and events. They help people think more calmly, rationally, and constructively in the face of stress and may generate a more hopeful emotional state. For example, students with heavy course loads may experience anxiety, confusion, discouragement, lack of motivation, and the desire to run away from it all. Frightening, catastrophic thoughts about their tasks (for example, "What if I fail?") can amplify stress responses. Cognitive coping strategies replace catastrophic thinking with thoughts in which stressors are viewed as challenges rather than threats (Ellis & Bernard, 1985). This substitution process is often called **cognitive restructuring** (Lazarus, 1971; Meichenbaum, 1977; see Chapter 16). It can be done by practicing constructive thoughts such as "All I can do is the best I can." Cognitive coping does not eliminate stressors, but it can help people perceive them as less threatening and thus make them less disruptive.

Seeking and obtaining social support from others are effective *emotional coping strategies.* The perception that one has emotional support, and is cared for and valued by others, tends to be an effective buffer against the ill effects of many stressors (Taylor, 1995). With emotional support comes feedback from others, along with advice on how to approach stressors. Having enhanced emotional resources is associated with increased survival time in cancer patients (Anderson, 1992), improved immune function (Kiecolt-Glaser & Glaser, 1992), and more rapid recovery from illness (Taylor, 1995).

Behavioral coping strategies involve changing behavior in ways that minimize the impact of stressors. Time management is one example. You might keep track of your time for a week and start a time-management plan. The first step is to set out a schedule that shows how your time is now typically spent; then decide how to allocate your time in the future. A time-management plan can help control catastrophizing thoughts by providing reassurance that there is enough time for everything and a plan for handling it all.

Behavioral, emotional, and cognitive skills often interact closely. Discussing stressors and seeking feedback from others help you think more rationally and calmly, and make it easier to develop and use sensible plans for behavioral coping. When behavioral coping eliminates or minimizes stressors, people find it easier to think and feel better about themselves.

Physical coping strategies are aimed at directly altering one's physical responses before, during, or after stressors occur. The most common physical coping strategy is some form of drug use. Prescription medications are sometimes an appropriate coping aid, especially when stressors are severe and acute, such as the sudden death of one's child. But if people depend on prescriptions or other drugs, including alcohol, to help them face stressors, they often attribute any success to the drug, not to their own skill. Furthermore, the drug effects that blunt stress responses may also interfere with the ability to apply coping strategies. If the drug is abused, it can become a stressor itself. The resulting loss of perceived control over stressors may make those stressors even more threatening and disruptive.

Nonchemical methods of reducing physical stress reactions include progressive relaxation training, physical exercise, biofeedback training, and meditation, among others (Carrington, 1984; Dubbert, 1992; Tarler-Benlolo, 1978). Meditation is described in Chapter 6; here, we consider two other procedures.

In **biofeedback training,** special equipment records stress-related physiological activity, such as heart rate, blood pressure, and muscle tension, and then feeds this information to a person through a changing tone or meter reading. With practice, some

[handwritten margin note:] cause addiction = more stress.

DEALING WITH CHEMOTHERAPY Progressive relaxation training can be used to ease a variety of health-related problems. For example, one study found that this training resulted in significant reductions in anxiety, physiological arousal, and nausea following cancer chemotherapy (Burish & Jenkins, 1992).

people develop strategies that control these physiological processes and then use these strategies to reduce stress responses (Budzynski & Stoyva, 1984). Biofeedback has been useful in treating a variety of illnesses including asthma (Lehrer, Sargunaraj & Hochron, 1992) and tension headache (Blanchard, 1992b). Whether biofeedback alone can have significant and enduring effects on severe stress-related problems such as high blood pressure and migraine headache is less certain (Gatchel, Baum & Krantz, 1989; Holroyd et al., 1995).

Progressive relaxation training is one of the most popular physical methods for coping with stress. Edmund Jacobson developed the technique during the 1930s (Jacobson, 1938). Today, progressive relaxation is learned by tensing a group of muscles (such as the hand and arm) for a few seconds, then releasing the tension and focusing on the resulting feelings of relaxation. This procedure is repeated for each of sixteen muscle groups throughout the body (Bernstein & Borkovec, 1973). Once some skill at relaxation is developed, it can be used to calm down anywhere and anytime, often without lying down (Blanchard & Andrasik, 1985; Wolpe, 1982). ("In Review: Methods for Coping with Stress" summarizes our discussion of stress-coping methods.)

Preventing or Coping with AIDS The spread of AIDS has spurred efforts by health psychologists to help people change sexual behaviors that transmit the infection, as well as to minimize stress processes in those who have been infected with HIV (Bowen & Trotter, 1995; Goldman & Harlow, 1993; Kelly & Murphy, 1992).

Jeffrey Kelly and his colleagues, for example, have designed programs that reduce sex-related AIDS risks among gay men (Kelly & Murphy, 1992). The programs include role-playing as a way of teaching strategies to resist pressure for high-risk sex (such as unprotected sex with strangers). Compared to those in nonparticipating control groups, program participants displayed better knowledge about AIDS, greater skill at demanding safe sex, decreases in risky sexual behavior, and increased condom use during the sixteen months following the program. Similar programs have been developed to promote safe-sex practices among young African-American women (DiClemente & Wingood, 1995).

Michael Antoni and his colleagues (1991) have demonstrated significant stress reduction and enhanced immune function in a group of gay men awaiting the outcome of HIV tests. These changes were attributed to a five-week course in stress-coping strategies that included progressive relaxation training, cognitive restructuring, instruction in self-monitoring of stressors, and use of social support. The changes were especially significant because they were maintained even by men who learned that they were infected with HIV.

PREVENTING AIDS Adolescent-oriented **AIDS** prevention efforts focus on safe-sex media campaigns and studies of the cognitive and emotional factors that can enhance their effectiveness. Their impact is still being evaluated.

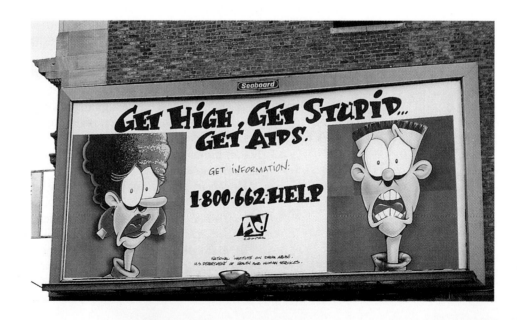

IN REVIEW	Methods for Coping with Stress
Type of Coping Method	**Examples**
Cognitive	Thinking of stressors as challenges rather than as threats; avoiding perfectionism.
Emotional	Seeking and obtaining social support; getting advice and feedback.
Behavioral	Implementing a time-management plan; where possible, making life changes to eliminate stressors.
Physical	Progressive relaxation training, exercise, biofeedback, meditation.

Health psychologists are also working on methods for lowering the risk for AIDS among adolescents (St. Lawrence et al., 1995). This is an important target group because many sexually active adolescents hold health beliefs that lead them to feel invulnerable to AIDS and thus cause them to greatly underestimate the risk of contracting the disease through unprotected sex (Abraham et al., 1992; Gladis et al., 1992; St. Lawrence, 1993).

FUTURE DIRECTIONS

Health psychology will likely become increasingly important in future health-promotion and disease-prevention efforts (Winett, 1995). The reason is that it works. The anti-smoking programs of recent decades, for example, have led to a steady decline in the overall percentage of smokers in the U.S. population. Although much more work needs to be done, we can expect decreased rates of lung cancer and other smoking-related diseases as a result of these health-promotion efforts (St. Lawrence et al., 1995).

Meanwhile, new research will be aimed at isolating more precisely the emotional and behavioral factors—such as cynical hostility—that may lead to coronary heart disease and at developing more effective measures for altering those factors. Also anticipated are new, culturally tailored health psychology programs for preventing the spread of HIV/AIDS (Kalichman et al., 1993). For example, a five-city, U.S. government–sponsored AIDS Community Intervention Demonstration Project is mobilizing the principles of learning, social psychology, and related concepts to teach and motivate intravenous drug users (and their partners), prostitutes, homeless children, and people in other high-risk groups to protect themselves from the disease (O'Reilly & Higgins, 1991; USDHHS, 1992; Wiebel, 1993).

In the foreseeable future we can expect to discover much more about the extent to which psychological processes affect changes in immunity and the degree to which people can alter these processes (Cohen & Herbert, 1996). In their efforts to understand stress and its impact, researchers are likely to focus on how people and situations reciprocally influence one another over time. Indeed, research on coping and social support is turning toward questions such as how particular coping styles attract or repel support and how expectation and perception buffer or amplify stressors (Matt & Dean, 1993).

Of continuing interest as well are questions about how coping skills develop and the degree to which they can be strengthened through formal training programs. Still other research may focus on adjusting environments to match individuals' coping styles. It has been suggested, for example, that hospitals should routinely assess patients' preferences for attending to or avoiding stressors and then adjust accordingly the information given to each patient about his or her illness or treatment (Ludwick-Rosenthal & Neufeld, 1993).

Future research will surely explore the extent to which findings in health psychology and stress generalize across cultural and subcultural groups (Lonner & Malpass, 1994). Given the likelihood that individuals from diverse cultural backgrounds conceptualize health, illness, and treatment in different ways (Beardsley, 1994; St. Lawrence et al., 1995), these individuals may also respond differently to stress-reduction or other health-promotion programs. Such cultural differences will be given increasing attention as new health psychology programs are developed for specific groups (Edwards, 1995).

For a more detailed look at health psychology, stress, and stress management, consider taking courses in health psychology, stress and coping, or other stress-related topics. Most courses in abnormal psychology and some in personality also examine the relationships among stress, health, mental disorder, and individual characteristics.

SUMMARY AND KEY TERMS

■ HEALTH PSYCHOLOGY

The development of *health psychology* was prompted by recognition of the link between stress and illness, as well as the role of behaviors such as smoking, in elevating the risk of illness. Researchers in this field seek to understand how psychological factors are related to physical disease and to help people behave in ways that prevent or minimize disease and promote health.

■ UNDERSTANDING STRESS

The term *stress* refers in part to *stressors,* which are events and situations to which people must adjust. The term is also used to refer to *stress reactions.* Most generally, however, stress is viewed as an ongoing, interactive process that takes place as people adjust to and cope with their environment.

Stressors

Stressors may be physical or psychological. Psychological stressors include catastrophic events, life changes and strains, chronic stress, and daily hassles. Stressors can be measured by tests like the SRRS and the LES, as well as by surveys of daily hassles, but scores on such tests provide only a partial picture of the stress in a given individual's life.

Stress Responses

Responses to stressors can be physical, psychological, and behavioral. These stress responses can occur alone or in combination, and the appearance of one can often stimulate that of others. (1) Physical stress responses include changes in heart rate, respiration, and many other processes that are part of a pattern known as the *general adaptation syndrome,* or *GAS.* The GAS has three stages: the alarm reaction, resistance, and exhaustion. The GAS helps people resist stress but, if present too long, can lead to depletion of immune system functions as well as to physical illnesses, which Selye called *diseases of adaptation.* (2) Psychological stress responses include emotional and cognitive reactions. Anxiety, anger, and depression are among the most common emotional stress reactions. Cognitive stress reactions include ruminative thinking, catastrophizing, and disruptions in the ability to think clearly, remember accurately, and solve problems efficiently. (3) Behavioral stress responses include specific changes in posture and coordination as well as facial expressions, tremors, or periods of jumpiness that reflect physical tension or emotional stress reactions. More global behavioral stress responses include irritability, absenteeism, and even suicide attempts.

■ LINKAGES: STRESS AND PSYCHOLOGICAL DISORDERS

Patterns of response to severe or long-lasting stressors can lead to *burnout* or psychological disorders, including *posttraumatic stress disorder.*

Stress Mediators: Interactions Between People and Stressors

The key to understanding stress appears to lie in observing the interaction of specific stressors with particular people. Stressors are likely to have greater impact if they are appraised as threats, or if they are unpredictable or uncontrollable. The people most likely to react strongly to a stressor are those whose coping resources, coping methods, and *social support networks* are inadequate.

■ THE PHYSIOLOGY AND PSYCHOLOGY OF HEALTH AND ILLNESS

Stress, the Immune System, and Illness

When a person is under stress, some of the hormones released from the adrenal gland, such as cortisol, reduce the effectiveness of the cells of the *immune system* (T-cells, B-cells, natural killer cells, macrophages) in combating foreign invaders such as viruses and cancer cells. *Psychoneuroimmunology* is the field that examines the interaction of psychological and physiological processes that affect the body's ability to defend itself against disease.

Heart Disease and Behavior Patterns

People who are cynically hostile are at greater risk for heart disease than other people. The heightened reactivity to stressors that these people experience may damage their cardiovascular system.

Risking Your Life: Health-Endangering Behaviors

Most of the major health problems in Western cultures are related to preventable behaviors such as smoking and drinking alcohol. Having unsafe sex is a major risk factor for contracting HIV.

■ PROMOTING HEALTHY BEHAVIOR

The process of altering or eliminating health-risky behaviors and fostering healthy behavior patterns is called *health promotion.*

Health Beliefs and Health Behaviors

People's health-related behaviors are partly guided by their beliefs about health risks and what they can do about them.

Changing Health Behaviors: Stages of Readiness

The process of changing health-related behaviors appears to involve several stages, including precontemplation, contemplation, preparation, action, and maintenance. Understanding which stage people are in, and helping them move through these stages, is an important task in health psychology.

Programs for Coping with Stress and Promoting Health

In order to cope with stress, people must recognize the stressors affecting them and develop a plan for coping with those stressors. Important coping skills include *cognitive restructuring,* acting to minimize the number or intensity of stressors, and using *biofeedback training, progressive relaxation training,* and other techniques for reducing physical stress reactions. These coping procedures are often part of health psychologists' disease-prevention and health-promotion efforts, which include developing and implementing programs aimed at reducing the spread of HIV and AIDS.

PERSONALITY

CHAPTER **14**

LINKAGES
TO
PERSONALITY

MENTAL ABILITIES

How do you know if a personality test, or any other kind of test, is any good? *(ans. on p. 308)*

TREATMENT OF PSYCHOLOGICAL DISORDERS

Can therapy change personality? *(ans. on p. 549)*

HUMAN DEVELOPMENT

Does culture determine personality? *(ans. on p. 478)*

It has been estimated that U.S. businesses lose more than $60 billion each year as a result of employee theft (Gatewood & Feild, 1994). Millions more are spent on security and surveillance designed to curb these losses, but it would be far better if companies could simply avoid hiring dishonest employees in the first place. Some firms have tried to screen out potential thieves by requiring prospective employees to take "lie detector" polygraph tests. As described in Chapter 11, however, these tests may not be reliable or valid; the federal government has banned their use in most kinds of employee selection.

Many employers have turned instead to paper-and-pencil "integrity" tests designed to identify job applicants who are likely to steal (Camara & Schneider, 1994). Some of these tests simply ask applicants if they have stolen from previous employers and if they might steal in the future. Such questions can screen out people who are honest about their stealing, but most applicants who steal will also lie to conceal previous crimes or criminal intentions. Accordingly, some companies now also give tests of applicants' general psychological characteristics and compare their scores to those of current or past employees. Applicants whose characteristics are most like the company's honest employees are hired; those who appear similar to dishonest employees are not.

Can employee honesty be predicted on the basis of such tests? To some extent, it can (Murphy, 1993). For example, scores on the *Reliability Scale*—which includes questions about impulse control and disruptive behavior during school years—are significantly correlated with a broad range of undesirable employee behaviors (Hogan & Hogan, 1992). But the correlation is less than perfect, so psychological tests leave room for errors in prediction; though better than polygraph tests, they still fail to detect dishonesty in some people and, worse, falsely identify some honest people as potential thieves. The best that companies can hope for is to find tests that will help reduce the *overall* likelihood of hiring dishonest people.

The use of psychological tests to find honest employees is really only a more formal version of the process that most of us employ when we meet someone new. We observe the person's behavior, form impressions, and draw conclusions about how that person will act at other times or under other circumstances. Like the employer, we are looking for clues to *personality*. Although there is no universally accepted definition, psychologists generally view **personality** as the unique pattern of enduring psychological and behavioral characteristics by which each person can be compared and contrasted with other people. Personality research, in turn, focuses on understanding the consistent patterns of cognition, emotion, and behavior that make people differ from and resemble one another. With such a large agenda, personality researchers must incorporate information from many other areas of psychology (see the Linkages diagram).

Indeed, personality has been said to lie at the crossroads of all psychological research (Mischel, 1993); it is the coalescence in a particular individual of all the psychological, behavioral, and biological processes discussed elsewhere in this book. To gain a comprehensive understanding of just one individual's personality, for example, one must know about developmental experiences (including cultural influences), genetic and other biological characteristics, perceptual and other information-processing habits and biases, typical patterns of emotional expression, and social skills. Psychologists also want to know about personality in general, such as how personality develops and changes across the life span, why some people are usually optimistic whereas others are usually pessimistic, and how consistent or inconsistent people's behavior tends to be from one situation to the next.

The specific questions psychologists ask about personality, and the approach they take to studying it, can vary considerably—depending in large measure on which of the theoretical approaches to psychology they prefer (see Figure 14.1). In this chapter we describe four theoretical approaches to the study of personality and some of the ways in which personality theory and research are being applied. We begin by presenting the psychodynamic approach, which was developed in the late nineteenth century by Sigmund Freud and subsequently modified by a number of those he influenced. Next, we describe the trait approach, which focuses on patterns of characteristic thoughts, feelings, and actions that form individual personalities. Then we describe the cognitive-behavioral approach, which explores the roles of learning and cognition in shaping human behavior and personality. Finally, we consider the phenomenological approach, with its emphasis on how each person's unique view of the world shapes personality. Our overview of these varying approaches is followed by a description of some of the tests that psychologists have developed to measure and compare people's personalities, along with some examples of how these instruments are being used in personality research and in other ways as well.

FIGURE 14.1

A Phrenological Map

Franz Gall, an eighteenth-century anatomist, took an anatomical approach to personality. He believed that each of thirty-five faculties was localized in a specific part of the brain and that bumps on the skull showed which ones were better developed. Gall's approach—called phrenology—could not withstand scientific evaluation, but it illustrates that all approaches to personality, even unsuccessful ones, include a personality theory, methods for assessing personality (Gall used examination of the skull), and procedures for evaluating the theory (Gall tried to relate bumps to behavior). Most approaches to personality also suggest methods for helping people change (see Chapter 16).

FOUNDER OF THE PSYCHODYNAMIC APPROACH Here, Sigmund Freud walks with his daughter, Anna, who eventually developed a revised version of her father's psychodynamic theories of personality and therapy.

FIGURE 14.2

Freud's Conception of the Personality Structure

According to Freud, some parts of the personality are conscious, while others are unconscious. Between these levels, Freud saw the preconscious—a region discussed in Chapter 6—as the location of memories and other material not usually in awareness but that can be brought into consciousness with little or no effort.

Conscious

Preconscious   EGO

Unconscious   SUPEREGO

                                      ID

Source: Adapted from Liebert & Spiegler, 1987.

THE PSYCHODYNAMIC APPROACH

Some people think they can understand personality by simply watching people behave. Someone with an "obnoxious personality," for example, shows it by acting obnoxiously. But is that all there is to personality? Not according to Sigmund Freud, who likened personality to an iceberg whose tip is clearly visible but whose bulk is hidden underwater.

As a physician during the 1890s, Freud specialized in treating "neurotic" disorders, such as blindness or paralysis for which there was no physical cause and which hypnosis could often remove. These cases led Freud to believe in *psychic determinism,* the idea that personality and behavior are determined more by psychological factors than by biological conditions or current events. He proposed, further, that people may not know why they feel, think, or act the way they do, because these activities are partly controlled by the *unconscious* portion of the personality—the part of which people are not normally aware. From these ideas Freud created the **psychodynamic approach** to personality, which holds that the interplay of various unconscious psychological processes determines thoughts, feelings, and behavior.

The Structure and Development of Personality

Freud believed that people are born with basic instincts or needs—not only for food, water, and air but also for sex and aggression. He believed that needs for love, knowledge, security, and the like are derived from these more fundamental desires. Each person faces the task of figuring out how to meet his or her needs in a world that often frustrates these efforts. According to Freud, personality develops out of each person's struggle with this task and is reflected in the ways he or she goes about satisfying a range of needs.

Id, Ego, and Superego As Figure 14.2 illustrates, Freud described the personality as having three major components: the id, the ego, and the superego.

Freud saw the **id** as the inborn, unconscious portion of the personality where instincts reside. The life instincts, which he called *Eros,* promote positive, constructive behavior and reflect a source of energy (sometimes called psychic energy) known as **libido.** Alternatively, he considered the death instincts, called *Thanatos,* to be responsible for human aggression and destructiveness (Schultz & Schultz, 1996). The id operates on the **pleasure principle,** seeking immediate satisfaction of both kinds of instincts, regardless of society's rules or the rights or feelings of others. The hungry person who snatches french fries from someone's table at McDonald's would be satisfying an Eros-driven id impulse.

As parents, teachers, and others place greater restrictions on the expression of id impulses, a second part of the personality—the ego (or "self")—evolves from the id. The **ego** is responsible for organizing ways to get what a person wants in the real world, as opposed to the fantasy world of the id. Operating on the **reality principle,** the ego makes compromises between the id's unreasoning demands for immediate satisfaction and the practical constraints of the real world.

As people gain experience with the rules and values of society, they tend to adopt them. This process of *internalizing* parental and societal values produces the third component of personality: the **superego,** which tells us what we should and should not do. The superego is just as relentless and unreasonable as the id in its demand to be obeyed.

Conflicts and Defenses Freud called the inner turmoil among personality components *intrapsychic* or *psychodynamic conflict,* and he believed that the number, nature, and outcome of these conflicts shape each individual's personality.

One of the most important functions of the ego is to prevent the anxiety or guilt that would arise if we became conscious of socially unacceptable id impulses or if we thought about behaving in violation of the superego's rules (Liebert & Spiegler, 1994). Sometimes, the ego motivates realistic actions, as when a person seeks help after experiencing impulses to abuse a child. However, it may also resort to **defense mechanisms,** which are unconscious tactics that either prevent threatening material from surfacing or disguise it when it does (see Table 14.1).

TABLE 14.1

Psychodynamic Defense Mechanisms

Defense mechanisms deflect anxiety or guilt in the short run, but they sap energy. Further, the use of such defenses to avoid dealing with the source of one's problems can be maladaptive in the long run.

Repression	Unconsciously pushing threatening memories, urges, or ideas from conscious awareness: A person may experience loss of memory for unpleasant events.
Rationalization	Attempts to make actions or mistakes seem reasonable: The reasons or excuses given (e.g., "I spank my children because it is good for them") have a rational ring to them, but they are not the real reasons for the behavior.
Projection	Unconsciously attributing one's own unacceptable thoughts or impulses to another person: Instead of recognizing that "I hate him," a person may feel that "He hates me."
Reaction formation	Defending against unacceptable impulses by acting opposite to them: Sexual interest in a married friend might appear as strong dislike instead.
Sublimation	Converting unacceptable impulses into socially acceptable actions, and perhaps symbolically expressing them: Sexual or aggressive desires may appear as artistic creativity or devotion to athletic excellence.
Displacement	Deflecting an impulse from its original target to a less threatening one: Anger at one's boss may be expressed through hostility toward a clerk, a family member, or even the dog.
Denial	Simply discounting the existence of threatening impulses: A person may vehemently deny ever having had even the slightest degree of physical attraction to a person of the same sex.
Compensation	Striving to make up for unconscious impulses or fears: A business executive's extreme competitiveness might be aimed at compensating for unconscious feelings of inferiority.

Stages in Personality Development   Freud proposed that personality develops during childhood in a series of **psychosexual stages.** Failure to resolve the problems and conflicts that arise at a given stage can leave a person *fixated*—that is, overly attached to or unconsciously preoccupied with the area of pleasure associated with that stage. Freud believed that the stage at which a person has fixated is revealed in adult personality characteristics.

In Freud's theory, a child's first year or so is called the **oral stage,** because the mouth—used by the infant to eat and explore—is the center of pleasure associated with this period. Freud said fixation at the oral stage can stem from early or late weaning and may produce adult characteristics ranging from overeating or alcoholism to the use of "biting" sarcasm or childlike dependence.

The **anal stage** occurs during the second year as the demand for toilet training shifts the focus of pleasure and conflict to the anal area. According to Freud, toilet training that is too harsh, or begins too early or too late, can lead to anal fixation. Adult characteristics associated with fixation at this stage range from being stingy and overconcerned with neatness (thus symbolically withholding feces) to being disorganized or impulsive (symbolically expelling feces at will).

Between the ages of three and five, according to Freud, the child's focus of pleasure shifts to the genital area. Because Freud emphasized male psychosexual development, he called this period the **phallic stage.** It is then, said Freud, that the boy experiences sexual desire for the mother and a desire to eliminate, even kill, the father, with whom the boy competes for the mother's affection. Freud named this constellation of impulses the **Oedipus complex,** because it echoes the plot of the Greek tragedy *Oedipus Rex.* The boy's fantasies create so much fear, however, that the ego represses the incestuous desires, and the boy seeks to identify with and be like his father. It is during this stage that the male's superego begins to develop.

According to Freud, the female child begins the phallic stage with a strong attachment to her mother; but upon realizing that boys have penises and girls don't, she allegedly develops *penis envy* and transfers her love to her father—a phenomenon Freud termed the **Electra complex.** To avoid her mother's disapproval, the girl identifies with and imitates her, thus forming the basis for her own superego.

Freud believed that unresolved conflicts from the phallic stage can lead to problems in adulthood, such as difficulties in dealing with authority figures or the inability to maintain a stable love relationship.

As the phallic stage draws to a close and its conflicts are dealt with by the ego, an interval of peace known as the **latency period** ensues. During adolescence, when sexual impulses reappear, the genitals again become the focus of pleasure. Thus begins what Freud called the **genital stage,** which lasts until death.

Variations on Freud's Personality Theory

Freud's ideas—especially those concerning the Oedipus and Electra complexes and the role of infantile sexuality—created instant controversy in public and professional circles. Even many of Freud's followers disagreed with him. Some of these dissenters have been called *neo-Freudian* theorists because they maintained many of the basic tenets of Freud's theory but developed their own ideas. Others are known as *ego psychologists* because their ideas focused more on the ego than on the id (A. Freud, 1946; Fraiberg, 1987; Loevinger, 1993).

Adler's Individual Psychology   The first major dissenter was Alfred Adler, who emphasized the role of social rather than sexual urges in personality development. Adler (1927) believed that it is not the id but, rather, an innate desire to overcome infantile feelings of helplessness that provides the impetus for the development of personality. Adler referred to this process as *striving for superiority,* by which he meant a drive for fulfillment as a person, not just a desire to best others. According to Adler, the ways in which each person tries to reach fulfillment constitute personality. Adler suggested that personality is directed not just by the unconscious but also by what he called guiding fictions: conscious ideas, goals, and beliefs that arise primarily from experiences within the family. For example, a child who is pampered and protected may believe that he or she is "special" and exempt from society's rules. The guiding fiction that "I'm special" is likely to lead to a selfish style of life in which personal fulfillment comes at the expense of others.

Jung's Analytic Psychology   Carl Jung (pronounced "yoong") was the next to split with Freud. Jung (1916) argued that libido was not just sexual instinct but a more general life force that includes an innate drive for creativity, for growth-oriented resolution of conflicts, and for the productive blending of basic impulses with real-world demands. Jung did not identify specific stages in personality development. He suggested instead that people develop, over time, differing degrees of *introversion* (a tendency to reflect on one's own experiences) or *extraversion* (a tendency to focus on the social world), along with differing tendencies to rely on specific psychological functions such as thinking versus feeling. The combination of these tendencies, said Jung (1933), creates personalities that display distinctive and predictable patterns of behavior.

Other Neo-Freudian Theorists   A number of other prominent neo-Freudians focused on how people's personalities are shaped by the people around them. Some, including Erik Erikson, Erich Fromm, and Henry Stack Sullivan, argued that once biological needs are met, the attempt to meet social needs (to feel protected, secure, and accepted, for example) is the primary influence on personality. The strategies people use to meet social needs, such as dominating other people or being dependent on them, thus become central aspects of the personality.

The first feminist personality theorist, Karen Horney (pronounced "horn-eye") challenged Freud's view that women's lack of a penis causes them to envy men and feel inferior to them. In fact, Horney (1937) argued that it is men who envy women: Realizing that they cannot bear children and may play only a small role in raising them, males see their lives as having less meaning or substance than women's. Horney called this condition "womb envy." She argued further that, when women feel inferior, it is

EARLY ATTACHMENT While Freud believed that personality problems involved conflicts among the structures of personality, object relations theorists believe that such problems arise from arrested personality development due to difficulties in early relationships and attachments.

because of the personal and political restrictions that men have placed upon them, not because of penis envy.

Contemporary Psychodynamic Theories

Today, some of the most influential psychodynamic approaches to personality focus on *object relations*—that is, on how people's perceptions of themselves and others influence their view of and reactions to the world (Westen, 1991, 1992). According to object relations theorists such as Melanie Klein (1975), Otto Kernberg (1976), Heinz Kohut (1984), and Margaret Mahler (1968), early relationships between infants and their love objects, usually the mother and other primary caregivers, are vitally important in the development of personality. These relationships, they say, shape a person's thoughts and feelings about social relationships later in life.

As described in Chapter 12, children ideally form a secure early bond to the mother or other caregiver, tolerate gradual separation from the object of attachment, and finally develop the ability to relate to others as an independent, secure individual (Ainsworth, 1989). Object relations theorists study how an infant's experience of a primary caregiver's protection, acceptance, and recognition influences the later development of his or her self-image, identity, security, social relationships, and other aspects of personality (Kirkpatrick & Davis, 1994; Mikulincer, 1995; van IJzendoorn, 1995). One study, for example, found a correlation between college students' early attachment styles and the quality of their current romantic relationships (Shaver & Brennan, 1992). Students whose attachments had been anxious or ambivalent tended to have shorter and less satisfying romances. Some object relations theorists believe that certain instances of child abuse may be related to abusive parents' perceptions of how their own parents treated them (van IJzendoorn, 1995).

Evaluation of the Psychodynamic Approach

Sigmund Freud developed the most comprehensive and influential personality theory ever proposed. His views influenced modern Western thinking about psychology, medicine, literature, religion, sociology, and anthropology. His ideas have also been applied in psychodynamic therapies aimed at helping people become aware of previously unconscious aspects of personality so that they can resolve old conflicts (see Chapter 16). In addition, Freud stimulated development of personality assessments, including the projective tests described later in this chapter. And, as described in Chapter 17, some of Freud's ideas have found a degree of support in research on cognitive processes, especially social cognition. There is substantial evidence, for example, that events and experiences that people are unable to recall can influence their thoughts and actions (Greenwald & Banaji, 1995). Other research, however, has revealed several weaknesses in Freud's psychodynamic theories.

criticism

For one thing, his theories are based almost entirely on case studies of a few individuals. As discussed in Chapter 2, conclusions drawn from case studies may not apply to people in general. Nor was Freud's sample representative of people in general. Most of his patients were upper-class Viennese women who not only had mental problems but were raised in a society in which discussion of sex was considered to be uncivilized. Moreover, Freud's thinking about personality and its development reflected Western European and North American values, which may or may not be helpful in understanding people in other cultures (Landrine & Klonoff, 1992). For example, the concepts of ego and self that are so central to Freud's personality theory (and the theories of his followers) are based on the self-oriented values of individualist cultures and thus may be less illustrative of personality development in the more collectivist cultures of, say, Asia and Africa (Matsumoto, 1994).

Freud's conclusions may have been distorted by other biases as well. Jeffrey Masson (1983) argued that Freud was afraid to accept his patients' accounts of sexual abuse by their parents because doing so would have brought him into conflict with those parents, many of whom had power and influence in Vienna. Instead, said Masson, Freud characterized the patients' reports as fantasies and wish fulfillment, not as memories of real events. Freudian scholars have largely rejected Masson's charges (Freudenberger, 1995), but they do acknowledge other possible problems. They note, for example, that Freud might have (unconsciously?) modified reports of what happened during therapy to better fit his theory (Esterson, 1993). He may also have asked leading questions that influenced patients to "recall" events from their childhood that never really happened (Powell & Boer, 1994). Today, there are similar concerns that some patients who recover allegedly repressed memories about childhood sexual abuse by parents may actually be reporting false memories implanted by their therapists (Ofshe & Watters, 1994; see also Chapter 8).

Freud's focus on male psychosexual development and his bias toward male anatomy as something to be envied by women have also caused both female and male feminists to reject some or all of his ideas. In the tradition of Karen Horney, some contemporary female neo-Freudians have proposed theories that focus specifically on the psychosexual development of women (Sayers, 1991).

Finally, as judged by contemporary standards, Freud's theory is not very scientific. His definitions of id, ego, unconscious conflict, and other concepts lack the precision required for scientific measurement and testing (Holzman, 1994). His belief that human beings are driven mainly by unconscious instinctual desires ignores evidence that much human behavior goes beyond instinct gratification. The conscious drive to attain personal, social, and spiritual goals is also an important determinant of behavior, as is learning from others.

Some of the weaknesses in Freudian theory have been addressed by those who have altered some of Freud's concepts and devoted more attention to social influences on personality. Attempts have also been made to increase precision and objectivity in the measurement of psychodynamic concepts (e.g., Barber & Crits-Christoph, 1993; Loevinger, 1993). Research on psychodynamic theory is indeed becoming more sophisticated and increasingly reflects interest in subjecting psychodynamic principles to empirical evaluation (Hardaway, 1990; Wallerstein, 1989). Still, the psychodynamic approach is better known for generating hypotheses about personality than for scientifically testing them. Accordingly, this approach to personality is less popular today than it was in past decades (Pervin, 1993; Mischel, 1993).

THE TRAIT APPROACH

If you were to describe the personality of someone you know, you would probably make a small number of descriptive statements. For example:

She is a truly caring person, a real extrovert. She is generous with her time, and she works very hard at everything she does. Yet, sometimes I think she also lacks self-confidence. She is submissive to other people's demands because she wants to be accepted by them.

In other words, most people describe others by referring to the kind of people they are ("extrovert") and to the thoughts, feelings, and actions that are most typical of them—to their most notable characteristics ("caring," "lacks confidence"), or to their needs ("wants to be accepted"). Together, these statements describe personality *traits*—the inclinations or tendencies that help to direct how a person usually thinks and behaves (Pervin, 1994).

The trait approach to personality makes three basic assumptions:

1. Personality traits are relatively stable and therefore predictable over time. Thus, a gentle person tends to stay that way day after day, year after year (McRae, 1993).

2. Personality traits are relatively stable across diverse situations, and they can explain why people act in predictable ways in many different settings. A person who is fiercely competitive at work will probably be competitive on the tennis court or at a party.

3. People differ with regard to how much of a particular personality trait they possess; no two people are exactly alike on all traits. The result is an endless variety of unique human personalities.

In short, the **trait approach** views personality as the combination of stable internal characteristics that people display consistently over time and across situations (Carver & Scheier, 1996).

Traits versus Types   Theories about differences in personality characteristics go back at least as far as Hippocrates, a physician of ancient Greece. He suggested that a certain temperament, or basic behavioral tendency, is associated with each of four bodily fluids, or humors: blood, phlegm, black bile, and yellow bile. Personality, said Hippocrates, depends on how much of each humor a person has. His terms for the four humor-driven personalities—sanguine (optimistic), phlegmatic, (slow, lethargic), melancholic (sad, depressive), and choleric (angry, irritable)—still survive today.

Notice that Hippocrates described personality *types,* not traits. A *type* is a discrete category; when people are "typed," they belong to one class or another—such as male or female. Type theories of personality thus try to place people in one category or another. There have been other type theories since Hippocrates. Beginning in the 1940s, for example, an American physician and psychologist named William Sheldon promoted *physiognomy*—the study of the link between personality and physique. To test his theory, Sheldon correlated body measurements taken from nude and seminude photographs of thousands of college students with personality-related data such as career choice and success in life. His subjects included George Bush, Hillary Rodham Clinton, and Meryl Streep (Rosenbaum, 1995).

Physiognomy was abandoned by almost all psychologists when they discovered that the endless variety of human personalities cannot be compressed into a few types based on facial or bodily characteristics. Echoes of type theories can still be found, however. One example is the Myers-Briggs personality test, which is based on Jung's (1933) system of sixteen personality types. Although this test is quite popular among nonpsychologists, its validity has been questioned by many personality researchers (Aiken, 1993).

Prominent Trait Theories

Rather than looking for discrete personality types, trait theorists measure the relative strength of many personality characteristics appearing in each individual (see Figure 14.3).

Allport's Trait Theory   Gordon Allport (1961) spent thirty years searching for the traits that combine to form the normal personality. When he listed the nearly 18,000 dictionary terms that can be used to describe human behavior (Block, 1995; Allport & Odbert, 1936), he noticed that many of these terms referred to the same thing ("hostile," "nasty," and "mean" all convey a similar meaning). To better understand this clustering, think of a close relative and quickly jot down the personality traits that describe him or her. If you are like most people, you were able to capture your relative's personality using only about seven trait labels. Allport believed that the set of labels chosen to describe a particular person reflects that person's *central traits,* those that are usually apparent to others and comprise characteristics that organize and control behavior in many different situations. Central traits are roughly equivalent to the descriptive terms used in letters of recommendation ("reliable" or "distractable," for example) that are meant to convey what can be expected from a person most of the time (Schultz & Schultz, 1996). Allport also believed that people possess *secondary traits,* those that are more specific to certain situations and control far less behavior. "Dislikes crowds" is an example of a secondary trait.

Allport's research helped to lay the foundation for modern research on personality traits. However, his focus on the uniqueness of each individual personality made it difficult to draw conclusions about the structure of human personality in general.

Cattell's Factor-Analytic Approach   Whereas Allport relied on logic and reasoning to identify important personality traits, Raymond Cattell used statistical analysis. He first asked people to rate themselves and other people on many of the trait-descriptive terms identified by Allport. Then, using a technique called *factor analysis,* he calculated the degree to which various personality traits correlate with each other (Goldberg, 1993).

Two Personality Profiles

From the trait perspective, personality is like a fabric of many different-colored threads, some bright, some dull, some thick, some thin, which are never woven together in exactly the same combination twice. Here are trait profiles for Rodney, an inner-city social worker, and James, a sales clerk in a department store. Compared to James, Rodney is about equally industrious, more generous, and less nervous, extraverted, and aggressive.

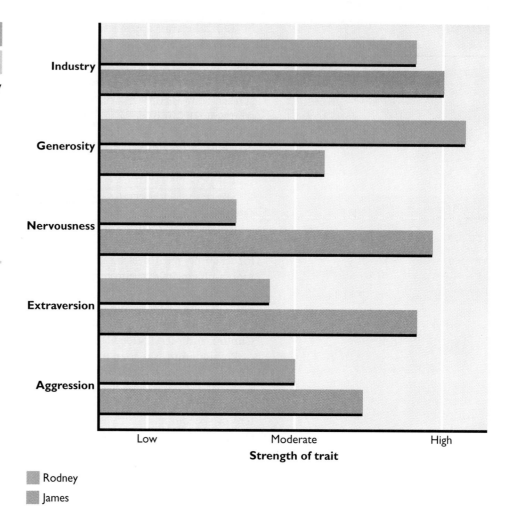

Rodney

James

Factor analysis can reveal, for example, whether someone who is optimistic is also likely to be happy, friendly, and hopeful. Cattell believed that certain traits would tend to cluster together because they reflect a basic dimension, or factor, of personality on which all people can be compared. Cattell eventually identified sixteen such factors, including shy versus bold, trusting versus suspicious, and relaxed versus tense. Cattell believed that these *common traits* are found in everyone, and he measured their strength through a test called the Sixteen Personality Factor Questionnaire, or 16PF.

Eysenck's Biological Trait Theory   British psychologist Hans Eysenck (pronounced "eye-sink") has used factor analysis to study the structure of both normal and disordered personalities. From his research, he has concluded that personality can be described in terms of three basic factors or dimensions (Eysenck, 1990a, 1990b):

1. *Psychoticism*—People high on psychoticism show such attributes as cruelty, hostility, coldness, oddness, and rejection of social customs. Those low on psychoticism do not show these attributes.

2. *Introversion-extraversion*—Extraverts are sociable and outgoing, enjoy parties and other social activities, take risks, and love excitement and change. Introverts tend to be quiet, thoughtful, and reserved, enjoying solitary pursuits and avoiding excitement and social involvement.

3. *Emotionality-stability*—At one extreme of emotionality-stability are people who exhibit such characteristics as moodiness, restlessness, worry, anxiety, and other negative emotions. People at the opposite end of this dimension are calm, even-tempered, relaxed, and emotionally stable. (This dimension is also often called *neuroticism*.)

EXTRAVERSION IN ACTION   This street entertainer enjoys showing off his skills while bantering with the audience. He would probably score high on extraversion if he were to take the Eysenck Personality Inventory.

Eysenck believes that personality traits are determined mainly in terms of where a person falls along these three dimensions, especially introversion-extraversion and emotionality-stability. He has presented data to show that scores on tests measuring these dimensions—such as the Eysenck Personality Inventory—can predict people's key characteristics, including specific behavior disorders (see Figure 14.4). Criminals, for example, are likely to be in the "choleric" quadrant and tend to display restless, aggressive, and impulsive behavior. People with anxiety disorders tend to be in the "melancholic" quadrant.

FIGURE 14.4

Eysenck's Major Personality Dimensions

According to Eysenck, varying degrees of emotionality-stability and introversion-extraversion combine to produce predictable trait patterns. For example, an introverted but stable person is likely to be controlled and reliable, whereas an introverted but emotional person is likely to be rigid and anxious. Note that the traits appearing in the quadrants created by crossing these two personality dimensions correspond roughly to Hippocrates' four temperaments.

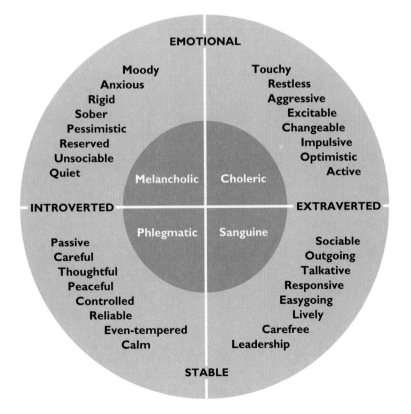

Source: Eysenck & Rachman, 1965.

LINKAGES   Why do some people take more risks than others? (a link to Motivation and Emotion)

Eysenck argues that variation in personality characteristics can be traced to inherited differences in the brain. These biological differences, he says, explain why some people are more physiologically aroused than others. For example, people who inherit a nervous system with a chronically low level of arousal will be relatively insensitive to the effects of rewards and punishments, and therefore will not readily develop conditioned responses, including conditioned fears. Without such fears, says Eysenck, they will not easily learn to play by the rules. Further, having a low arousal level may lead such people to look constantly for excitement and change in order to increase their arousal; in short, they will be extraverted. In contrast, Eysenck's theory predicts that people with sensitive, "overaroused" nervous systems are likely to be strongly affected by rewards and punishments, to readily develop conditioned responses such as fears and oversensitivities, and to avoid excessive stimulation—in other words, to be introverted.

The "Big-Five" Model of Personality

Building on the work of Allport, Cattell, and Eysenck, contemporary researchers continue to refine the core dimensions of personality. Factor analyses by researchers such as Paul Costa and Robert McCrae (1992) have led many trait theorists to believe that personality is organized around five basic factors (McCrae & Costa, in press; Goldberg & Saucier, 1995). The components of this so-called **big-five** or **five-factor model** of personality are Openness, Conscientiousness, Extraversion, Agreeableness, and Neuroticism (see Table 14.2).

The importance of the "big five" is underscored by the fact that different investigators find these factors (or a set very similar to them) when they factor-analyze data from numerous sources, including personality inventories, peer ratings of personality characteristics, and checklists of descriptive adjectives (Costa & McCrae, 1995; Goldberg, 1992; 1993; McCrae & John, 1992). These factors emerged even from subjects' ratings of how well drawings of people in social and solitary situations described the subjects' own personalities (Paunonen et al., 1992). The fact that some version of the "big-five" factors reliably appears in many countries and cultures—including Canada, Germany, Finland, India, the Philippines, Poland, China, and Japan (Church & Katigbak, 1989; Narayanan, Menon & Levine, 1995; Paunonen et al., 1992; Yang & Bond, 1990)—provides further evidence that they may represent basic components of human personality.

Where do the "big-five" factors or other personality traits come from? Do they arise, as Eysenck suggests, from our genes? One study described a pair of twins who had been separated at five weeks of age and did not meet again for thirty-nine years. Both men

THINKING CRITICALLY

Are Personality Traits Inherited?

drove Chevrolets, chain-smoked the same brand of cigarettes, had divorced a woman named Linda, were remarried to a woman named Betty, had sons named James Allan, had dogs named Toy, enjoyed similar hobbies, and had served as sheriff's deputies (Tellegen et al., 1988).

What am I being asked to believe or accept?

Cases like this have helped focus the attention of behavioral geneticists on the possibility that some core aspects of personality might be partly inherited (Bergeman et al., 1993; Heath et al., 1992; Waller et al., 1990).

What evidence is available to support the assertion?

The evidence and the arguments regarding this assertion are much like those presented in Chapter 10, where we discuss the origins of differences in mental abilities. Anecdotes about children who seem to "have" their parents' or grandparents' bad tem-

	Dimension	Defining Descriptors
TABLE 14.2	Openness to experience	Artistic, curious, imaginative, insightful, original, wide interests, unusual thought processes, intellectual interests
Descriptors of the Big-Five Personality Dimensions	Conscientiousness	Efficient, organized, planful, reliable, thorough, dependable, ethical, productive
Here is a list of the adjectives that define the big-five personality factors. You can more easily remember the names of these factors by noting that their first letters spell the word *ocean*.	Extraversion	Active, assertive, energetic, outgoing, talkative, gesturally expressive, and gregarious
	Agreeableness	Appreciative, forgiving, generous, kind, trusting, noncritical, warm, compassionate, considerate, straightforward
	Neuroticism	Anxious, self-pitying, tense, emotionally unstable, impulsive, vulnerable, touchy, worrying

Source: Adapted from McCrae & John, 1992.

per, generosity, or shyness are often presented in support of the heritability of personality. Indeed, resemblances in personality among family members do provide one important source of evidence. Several studies have found moderate but significant correlations between children's personality test scores and those of their parents and siblings (Davis, Luce & Kraus, 1994; McCartney, Harris & Bernieri, 1990.)

Stronger evidence comes from studies conducted around the world comparing identical twins raised together, identical twins raised apart, nonidentical twins raised together, and nonidentical twins raised apart (e.g., Saudino et al., 1995; Tellegen et al., 1988; Waller & Shaver, 1994). Identical twins (who have exactly the same genes) tend to be more alike in personality than nonidentical twins (whose genes are no more similar than those of other siblings), regardless of whether they are raised apart or together. Further, research consistently shows that identical twins are more alike than nonidentical twins in general temperament, such as how active, sociable, anxious, and emotional they are (Buss, 1995; Saudino et al., 1995). On the basis of such twin studies, behavioral geneticists have concluded that at least 30 percent and perhaps as much as 60 percent of the variability in adult personality traits is due to genetic factors (Carey & DiLalla, 1994; Waller & Shaver, 1994).

Are there alternative ways of interpreting the evidence?

Family resemblances in personality could reflect inheritance or social influence. An obvious alternative interpretation of this evidence might be that family similarities come not from common genes but from a common environment, especially from the modeling that parents and siblings provide. Children learn many rules, skills, and behaviors by watching those around them; perhaps they learn their personalities as well. And the fact that nontwin siblings are less alike than twins may well result from what is called *nonshared environments* (Plomin, 1994). A child's place in the family birth order, differences in the way parents treat each of their children, and accidents and illnesses that alter a particular child's life or health are examples of nonshared factors that can have a differential impact on each individual. Compared to twins, especially identical twins, nontwins tend to be affected by more nonshared environmental factors.

What additional evidence would help to evaluate the alternatives?

One way to evaluate the degree to which personality is inherited would be to study people in infancy, before the environment has had a chance to exert its influence. If the environment were entirely responsible for personality, newborn infants should be essentially alike. However, as discussed in Chapter 12, newborns do show differences in temperament—varying markedly in amount of activity, sensitivity to the environment, tendency to cry, and interest in new stimuli (Buss, 1995). These differences suggest biological and perhaps genetic influences.

**THE TRAIT APPROACH IN THE COURT-
ROOM**   The trait approach to personality is highlighted in the
courtroom, where defense attorneys
try to show that their clients are not
the type of people who would commit certain acts and where lawyers
on both sides seek to disqualify
jurors who display traits suggesting
that they might be unsympathetic to
their case. Here, Marcia Clark, prosecuting attorney in the O. J. Simpson
case, questions Kato Kaelin, a friend
of Mr. Simpson.

To evaluate the relative contributions of nature and nurture beyond infancy, psychologists have examined characteristics of adopted children. The influence of heredity in personality is supported if adopted children are more like their biological than
their adoptive parents. If they are more like their adoptive family, a strong role for environmental factors in personality would be suggested. In actuality, adopted children's
personalities tend to resemble the personalities of their biological parents and siblings
more than those of the families in which they are raised (Carey & DiLalla, 1994; Eaves,
Eysenck & Martin, 1989; Loehlin, 1992).

Nevertheless, further research is needed to determine more clearly what aspects of
the environment are most important in shaping personality. Thus far, most investigators conclude that elements of the shared environment—factors such as socioeconomic
status that equally affect all children in the same family—appear to have little influence
on personality variation. As noted above, however, nonshared environmental influences appear to be very important in personality development (Hoffman, 1991;
Plomin, 1994). The exact impact on personality development of nonshared environmental factors that may be different for twins and nontwin siblings has not yet been
fully or systematically examined. Additional research on the role of nonshared factors
in personality development and the ways in which these factors might differentially
affect twin and nontwin siblings' development is obviously vital.

What conclusions are most reasonable?

Even those researchers, such as Robert Plomin, who support genetic theories of personality caution that we should not replace "simple-minded environmentalism" with
the equally incorrect view that personality is almost completely biologically determined
(Plomin, Chipuer & Loehlin, 1990). As with mental abilities, it is pointless to talk about
heredity *versus* environment as causes of personality because nature and nurture always
intertwine to exert joint and simultaneous influences. With this caution in mind, we
would be well advised to draw rather tentative conclusions about the sources of personality.

The evidence available so far suggests that genetic influences do appear to contribute
significantly to the differences between people in many personality traits. However,
understanding the nature and implications of such a statement is important. First, there
is no evidence of a specific gene for any specific personality trait. The genetic contribution to personality most likely comes in the form of physical characteristics and general
predispositions toward certain temperaments, as measured by levels of activity, emotionality, and sociability (Buss, 1995; Kagan & Snidman, 1991). These physical characteristics and temperaments then interact with environmental factors such as family
experiences to produce specific features of personality. Thus, children who inherit a

frail body and/or high emotionality might play less with other children, withdraw from social interactions and, thus, fail to learn important social skills (Eisenberg, Fabes & Murphy, 1995). These experiences and tendencies, in turn, might foster the self-consciousness and shyness seen in introverted personalities.

Note, however, that genetic predispositions toward particular personality characteristics may or may not appear in behavior, depending on whether the environment supports or suppresses them. Changes in genetically predisposed traits are not only possible, they may actually be quite common as children develop (Kagan & Snidman, 1991). Even the personalities of identical twins become less similar over time as they are exposed to differing environmental experiences (McCartney, Harris & Bernieri, 1990). It appears that rather than inheriting specific traits, people inherit raw materials out of which personality is shaped by the world.

Evaluation of the Trait Approach

The trait approach, especially the big-five model, has gained such wide acceptance that it tends to dominate contemporary research in personality. Yet there are several problems and weaknesses associated with this approach.

For one thing, trait theories seem better at describing people than at understanding them. It is easy to say, for example, that Michelle is nasty to others because she has a strong hostility trait; but other factors, such as the way people treat her, could also be responsible. In short, trait theories say a lot about *how* people behave, but they don't always explain *why* (Funder, 1993; Pervin, 1993). Trait theories also don't say much about how traits are related to the thoughts and feelings that precede, accompany, and follow behavior. Do introverts and extraverts *decide* to act as they do, can they behave otherwise, and how do they feel about their actions and experiences? (Mischel, 1993). Some personality psychologists are currently trying to link their research with that of cognitive psychologists in an effort to better understand how thoughts and emotions influence, and are influenced by, personality traits (Cantor & Harlow, 1994; Klinger, 1995).

The trait approach has also been faulted for offering a short list of traits of varying strengths providing, at best, a static and superficial description of personality that fails to capture how traits combine to form a complex and dynamic individual (Epstein, 1994; Pervin, 1994). Even if the big-five model of personality is correct and universal, its factors are not all-powerful; situations, too, affect behavior. Thus, people high in extraversion are not always gregarious; whether they behave sociably depends, in part, on where they are and who else may be present. The importance of these person-situation interactions is emphasized by the cognitive-behavioral approach to personality, to which we now turn.

THE COGNITIVE-BEHAVIORAL APPROACH

According to the psychodynamic and trait approaches, personality consists of inner dynamics or traits that guide thinking and behavior. In contrast, those taking a **cognitive-behavioral approach** view personality mainly as the array of behaviors that people acquire through learning and display in particular situations. Some aspects of this approach reflect a traditional behavioral assumption—namely, that all behavior is learned through classical and operant conditioning. However, we shall see that the cognitive-behavioral approach expands that original scope by emphasizing (1) the role of *learned patterns of thought* in guiding our actions and (2) the fact that much of personality is learned in *social situations* through interaction with and observation of other people, including family members (Mischel, 1993; Rotter, 1990). Accordingly, the cognitive-behavioral approach is sometimes called the *social-learning* approach; it views personality as the sum total of the behaviors and cognitive habits that develop as people learn through experience in the social world.

"You know, we're just not reaching that guy."

LINKAGES   As noted in Chapter 13, being "internal" and optimistic are aspects of the so-called stress-resistant, or hardy, personality (Kobasa, 1982).

Roots of the Cognitive-Behavioral Approach

Elements of the cognitive-behavioral approach can be traced back to John B. Watson. As noted in Chapter 1, Watson (1924) used research on classical conditioning to support his claim that all human behavior, from mental disorder to scientific skill, is determined by learning. B. F. Skinner widened the behavioral approach by emphasizing the importance of operant conditioning in learning. Through what he called **functional analysis,** Skinner sought to understand behavior in terms of its function in obtaining rewards or avoiding punishment. For example, if observation of a schoolboy's aggressive behavior reveals that it occurs mainly when a teacher is present to break up fights, it may be that the aggression is being rewarded by teacher attention. Rather than describing personality traits, then, functional analysis summarizes what people find rewarding or punishing, what they are capable of, and what skills they lack.

Once the hallmark of the behavioral approach to personality, classical and operant conditioning principles are still considered vitally important in the development of behavior. However, much as Freud's followers challenged some of his original ideas, many proponents of the behavioral approach became dissatisfied with what they saw as its overly narrow focus on observable behaviors and its lack of attention to the role of thoughts in guiding behavior. The cognitive-behavioral approach to personality resulted from their efforts over the last two decades to address these perceived deficiencies.

Proponents of this very popular approach to personality seek to assess and understand how learned patterns of thought contribute to behavior and how behavior and its consequences alter cognitive activity as well as future actions. In dealing with the aggressive schoolboy, for example, cognitive behaviorists would want to know not only what he has learned to do under particular circumstances (and how he learned it) but also what he thinks about himself, his teachers, his behavior—and his expectations about each.

Prominent Cognitive-Behavioral Theories

Among the most influential cognitive-behavioral or social-learning theories are those of Julian Rotter, Albert Bandura, and Walter Mischel.

Rotter's Expectancy Theory   Rotter (1982) argued that learning creates cognitive expectancies that guide behavior. Specifically, he suggested that a person's decision to engage in a behavior is determined by (1) what the person expects to happen following

LINKAGES: EXPECTING INCENTIVES   As noted in Chapter 11, incentive theories of motivation emphasize the role of paychecks and external goals in explaining a wide range of behavior, from physical labor to diligent studying. Incentives also lie at the heart of Rotter's cognitive-behavioral theory of personality.

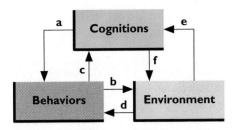

FIGURE 14.5

Reciprocal Determinism

Bandura's model of reciprocal determinism suggests that hostile thinking can lead to hostile behavior (line a), which in turn can intensify hostile thoughts (line c). At the same time, hostile behavior is likely to offend others and create an environment of anger (line b), which calls forth even more negative thoughts and actions (lines d and e). These negative thoughts then alter perceptions, making the environment seem more threatening (line f).

the behavior, and (2) the value the person places on the outcome. For example, people spend a lot of money on clothes to be worn at a job interview because (1) past learning leads them to expect that doing so will help get them the job, and (2) they place a high value on having the job. To Rotter, then, behavior is determined not only by the rewarding consequences Skinner emphasized but also by a cognitive *expectation* that a particular behavior will obtain that reward (Phares, 1991).

Rotter also suggested that people learn general ways of thinking about the world, especially about how life's rewards and punishments are controlled. Some people *(internals)* are likely to expect events to be controlled by their own efforts. That is, what they achieve and the reinforcements they obtain are seen as due to efforts they make themselves. Others *(externals)* tend to expect events to be determined by external forces over which they have no control. When externals succeed, they are likely to believe that the success was due to chance or luck.

Differences in generalized expectancies tend to correlate with differences in behavior (Rotter, 1990). For example, internals tend to get better grades and to score higher on standardized academic tests than externals (Schultz & Schultz, 1996). Internals are also more likely than externals to work at staying healthy; they are less likely to smoke, and more likely to exercise and to wear seat belts. If they are hospitalized, internals are more cooperative patients than externals, and are released sooner (Phares, 1991; Strickland, 1989).

Bandura and Reciprocal Determinism   In his social-learning theory, Albert Bandura has emphasized the complex and constant interaction among patterns of thought, the environment, and behavior. He points out that whether people learn through direct experience with rewards and punishments or through the observational learning processes described in Chapter 7, their behavior tends to affect their environment, which in turn may affect cognitions, which then may affect behavior, and so on. In short, according to Bandura (1986), personality is shaped by what he called *reciprocal determinism* (see Figure 14.5).

One cognitive element in this web of influence is especially important in Bandura's view: **self-efficacy,** which is the learned expectation of success, the belief that you can successfully perform a behavior regardless of past failures or current obstacles. Bandura says that overt behavior is largely controlled by individuals' expectations of their ability to perform. The higher a person's self-efficacy regarding a particular situation, the greater will be the actual accomplishments in that situation. Thus, going to a job interview with the belief that you have the skills necessary to be hired may help you get the job or, at least, help blunt the impact of rejection.

According to Bandura, self-efficacy interacts with expectancies about the outcome of behavior in general, and the result of this interplay helps to shape a person's psychological well-being (Bandura, 1986). Figure 14.6 shows how different interactions among these cognitions may produce different emotions and behaviors. If, for example, a person has little self-efficacy and also expects that nothing anyone does has much

FIGURE 14.6

Self-Efficacy and Psychological Well-Being

According to Bandura, if people with high self-efficacy perceive the environment as unresponsive to their best efforts, they may become resentful and socially active. If they perceive the environment as responsive to their efforts, they are more likely to be both active and self-assured.

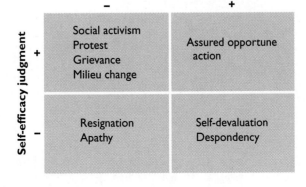

Source: Bandura, 1982a.

effect on the world, apathy may result. But if a person with low self-efficacy believes that other people are enjoying the benefits of their efforts, the result may be self-disparagement and depression.

Mischel's Person-Situation Theory Cognitive-behavioral theorists believe that learned beliefs or expectancies characterize each individual and make that individual different from other people. Social-learning theorist Walter Mischel (1993) calls these cognitive characteristics *person variables;* he believes that they outline the dimensions along which individuals differ.

The most important person variables, according to Mischel, are (1) competencies (the thoughts and actions the person can perform); (2) perceptions (how the person perceives the environment); (3) expectations (what the person expects to follow from various behaviors and what the person believes he or she is capable of doing—again, a matter of self-efficacy); (4) subjective values (the person's ideals and goals); and (5) self-regulation and plans (the person's standards for self-reward and plans for reaching goals).

Mischel distinguishes between person variables and personality traits, noting that traits may not be helpful in predicting behavior because people often behave differently in different situations. To predict how a person might behave, he says, we also need to know about the situation in which the behavior will occur. Mischel's views sparked a "person-situation" debate between cognitive-behavioral and trait theorists about whether personality traits or situational factors were more influential in guiding behavior. This debate produced no clear winners, but it has helped to clarify the interaction of personal and situational variables under various conditions (see Hogan, 1992; Kenrick & Funder, 1988). Many of the conclusions that have emerged are consistent with Bandura's concept of reciprocal determinism:

1. Traits influence behavior only in relevant situations. The trait of anxiousness, for example, may be predictive of anxiety, but only in situations where the person feels threatened.

THE IMPACT OF SITUATIONS Like the rest of us, pro-basketball star Hakeem Olajuwon tends to behave differently in different situations. Mischel's theory of personality underscores the importance of such person-situation interactions in determining behavior.

2. Traits can lead to behaviors that alter situations that, in turn, promote other behaviors. Thus, a hostile child can elicit aggression in others and, in turn, precipitate a fight.

3. People choose to be in situations that are in accord with their traits. Introverts, for instance, are more likely to choose quiet environments, while extraverts tend to seek out livelier, more social circumstances.

4. Traits are more influential in some situations than in others. In ambiguous or *game vs.* unconstrained situations—a picnic, for example—people's behavior may be predicted *funeral.* from their personality traits (extraverts will probably play games and socialize while introverts watch). However, in socially constrained situations such as a funeral, personality traits will not differentiate one person from another; all are likely to be quiet and somber.

Today, cognitive-behavioral and social-learning theorists devote much of their research to examining how person variables develop, how they are related to stress and health, and how they interact with situational variables to affect behavior.

Evaluation of the Cognitive-Behavioral Approach

The traditional behavioral perspective on personality holds many attractions. It offers an objective, experimentally oriented approach that operationally defines its concepts, relies on empirical data for its basic principles, and bases its applications on the results of empirical research (Mischel, 1993; Pervin, 1994). Evolution of the cognitive-behavioral approach has expanded the applications of learning principles to such socially important areas as aggression, the effects of mass media on children, and the development of self-regulatory processes that enhance personal control over behavior. The popularity of the cognitive-behavioral approach also stems from the ease with which its principles can be translated into treatment procedures for many types of psychological disorders (Goldfried & Davison, 1994; see Chapter 16).

Still, cognitive-behavioral approaches have not escaped criticism. Theories that emphasize classical and operant conditioning are accused of reducing human beings to a set of learned responses derived solely from relationships with the environment. This view, critics say, is too narrow, minimizes the importance of subjective experience, fails to consider unconscious processes, neglects the contribution of emotion to personality, and tends to exclude genetic, physiological, and other influences not based on learning. Cognitive-behavioral theories have addressed some of these objections through their emphasis on expectancies, self-efficacy, and person variables, but they are criticized by some for not going far enough in that direction (Carver & Scheier, 1996). For many, a far more palatable alternative is provided by the phenomenological approach to personality.

THE PHENOMENOLOGICAL APPROACH

Suppose you and a friend meet someone new at a party. Comparing notes later, you discover a major discrepancy in your reactions. You thought the new person was entertaining and warm and showed a genuine interest in others. Your friend saw the same person as a "phony" who merely pretended to be interested. How can two people draw such opposite conclusions from the same conversation? Perhaps it was not the same conversation. Just as each person sees something different in a cloud formation, each of you perceived a different reality, a different conversation, and a different person.

This interpretation reflects the **phenomenological approach** to personality, which maintains that the way people perceive and interpret the world forms their personalities and guides their behavior. Proponents of this view emphasize the fact that, as noted in the chapter on perception, each individual perceives reality somewhat differently, and these differences—rather than instincts, traits, or learning experiences—are central to understanding human personality. From this perspective, no one can understand

LINKAGES: WHAT IS REALITY? **Everyone present probably has somewhat differing perceptions about what actually happened during the play that precipitated this argument. The disagreement illustrates the phenomenological notion that each person's perceptions of the world shape personality and guide behavior. As described in Chapter 5, those perceptions are often influenced by top-down processing; in this case, expectations and motivation stemming from differing team loyalties are likely to influence reality—and reactions—for each side's players, coaches, and fans.**

another person without somehow perceiving the world through that person's eyes. All behavior, even if it looks bizarre, is meaningful to the person displaying it. Unlike theories that emphasize the instincts and learning processes that humans and lower animals seem to have in common, the phenomenological approach focuses on mental qualities that set humans apart: self-awareness, creativity, planning, decision making, and responsibility. For this reason, the phenomenological approach is also called the *humanistic* view of personality.

This approach to personality has many roots. The idea that each person perceives a different reality reflects the views of existential philosophers such as Kierkegaard and Sartre. That people actively shape their "reality" stems in part from the Gestalt psychologists whose work is described in Chapter 5. We can also hear echoes of Adler and other psychodynamic theorists who emphasized the positive aspects of human nature and the importance of the ego in personality development.

According to the phenomenological approach, the primary human motivator is an innate drive toward growth that prompts people to fulfill their unique and natural potential. Like the planted seed that naturally becomes a flower, people are inclined toward goodness, creativity, love, and joy.

Prominent Phenomenological Theories

By far, the most prominent phenomenological theories of personality are those of Carl Rogers and Abraham Maslow.

Rogers' Self Theory   The name of Carl Rogers is almost synonymous with the phenomenological approach (Rogers, 1942, 1951, 1961, 1970, 1980). Rogers assumed that each person responds as an organized whole to reality as he or she perceives it. He emphasized **self-actualization,** which he described as an innate tendency toward growth that motivates all human behavior. To Rogers, personality is the expression of each individual's self-actualizing tendency as it unfolds in that individual's uniquely perceived reality.

Central to Rogers' theory is the *self,* the part of experience that a person identifies as "I" or "me." According to Rogers, those who accurately experience the self—with all its preferences, abilities, fantasies, shortcomings, and desires—are on the road to self-actualization. The progress of those whose experiences of the self become distorted, however, is likely to be slowed or stopped.

Very early in life, children learn to need other people's approval or, as Rogers called it, *positive regard.* As a result, evaluations by parents, teachers, and others begin to affect children's self-evaluations. When evaluations by others concur with a child's own evaluation, the child's genuine reaction matches, or is *congruent* with, self-experience. The child not only feels the other's positive regard but also evaluates the self as "good" for having earned approval. The result is a clearly identified and positively evaluated experience of the self. This self-experience becomes part of the **self-concept,** which is the way one thinks of oneself. Unfortunately, things may not always go so smoothly. If a pleasurable self-experience is evaluated negatively by others, a child must either do without their positive regard or re-evaluate the experience. Thus, a little boy who is teased by his parents because he enjoys playing with dolls might adopt a distorted self-experience ("I don't like dolls" or "Feeling good is bad").

In other words, personality is shaped partly by self-actualizing tendencies and partly by others' evaluations. In this way, people come to like what they are "supposed" to like and to behave as they are "supposed" to behave. Although this process is adaptive, allowing people to get along in society, it often requires that they stifle the self-actualizing tendency and distort experience. Rogers argued that psychological discomfort, anxiety, or mental disorder can result when the feelings people experience or express are *incongruent* with their true feelings.

Incongruence is likely, said Rogers, when parents and teachers lead a child to believe that his or her worth as a person depends on displaying the "right" attitudes, behaviors, and values. These **conditions of worth** are created whenever *people* are evaluated instead of their behavior. For example, parents who find their toddler smearing Jell-O

SEEKING SELF-ACTUALIZATION
According to Rogers, conditions of worth can make it harder for children to become aware of and accept aspects of themselves that conflict with their parents' values. Progress toward self-actualization may be enhanced by associating with those whose positive regard is not conditional on displaying any particular pattern of behavior.

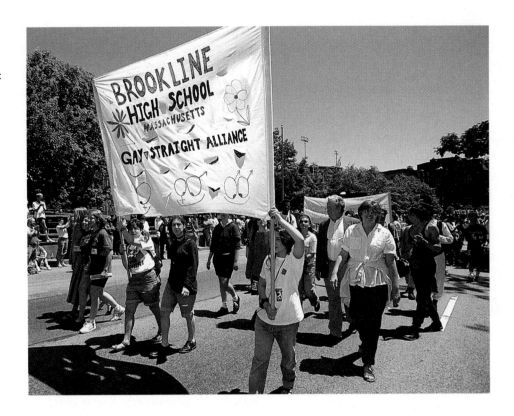

on the kitchen floor are unlikely to say, "I love you, but I do not approve of this particular behavior." They are more likely to shout, "Bad boy!" or "Bad girl!" thus suggesting that the child is lovable and worthwhile only when well behaved. As a result, the child's self-experience is not "I like smearing Jell-O but Mom and Dad don't approve" but, instead, "Playing with Jell-O is bad, and I am bad if I like it, so I don't like it," or "I like it, so I must be bad." The child may eventually display very neat and tidy behaviors that do not reflect the real self but, rather, are part of the ideal self dictated by the parents.

Like Freud's concept of superego, conditions of worth are first set up by external pressure but eventually become part of the person's belief system. Thus, to Rogers, rewards and punishments are important in personality development not just because they shape behavior but also because they can so easily create distorted self-perceptions and incongruence.

Maslow's Humanistic Psychology Like Rogers, Abraham Maslow (1954, 1962, 1971) saw personality as the expression of a basic human tendency toward growth and self-actualization. Maslow believed that self-actualization is not just a human capacity but a human need; as shown in Figure 11.9, he described it as the highest in a hierarchy of needs. Yet, said Maslow, people are often distracted from seeking self-actualization because of needs that are lower on the hierarchy.

Maslow saw most people as controlled by a **deficiency orientation,** a preoccupation with perceived needs for material things. Ultimately, he said, deficiency-oriented people come to perceive life as a meaningless exercise in disappointment and boredom, and they may begin to behave in problematic ways. For example, in an attempt to satisfy the need for love and belongingness, people may focus on what love can give them (security), not on what they can give to another. This deficiency orientation may lead a person to be jealous of a partner and to focus on what is missing; as a result, the person will never truly experience either love or security.

In contrast, people with a **growth orientation** do not focus on what is missing but draw satisfaction from what they have, what they are, and what they can do. This orientation opens the door to what Maslow called *peak experiences,* in which people feel joy, even ecstasy, in the mere fact of being alive, being human, and knowing that they are utilizing their fullest potential.

THE JOYS OF A GROWTH ORIENTATION
Maslow's humanistic theory of personality says the key to personal growth and fulfillment lies in focusing on the skills and experiences that we have, not on the material possessions we do not have.

IN REVIEW	Major Approaches to Personality	
Approach	Basic Assumptions About Behavior	Typical Research Methods
Psychodynamic	Determined by largely unconscious intrapsychic conflicts	Case studies
Trait	Determined by traits or needs	Analysis of tests for basic personality dimensions
Cognitive-behavioral	Determined by learning, cognitive factors, and specific situations	Analysis of interactions between people and situations
Phenomenological	Determined by unique perception of reality	Studies of relationships between perceptions and behavior

Evaluation of the Phenomenological Approach

The phenomenological approach to personality coincides with the way many people view themselves. It gives a central role to each person's immediate experience and emphasizes the uniqueness of each individual. The best-known application of the phenomenological approach is the client-centered therapy of Carl Rogers, which is discussed in Chapter 16. The phenomenological approach has also inspired short-term group experiences, such as sensitivity training and encounter groups, designed to help people to become more aware of themselves and the way they relate to others, and techniques to teach parents how to avoid creating conditions of worth while maximizing their children's potential (Gordon, 1970).

Yet to its critics, the phenomenological view is naive, romantic, and unrealistic. Are people all as inherently good and "growthful" as this approach suggests? Phenomenologists have also been faulted for underplaying the importance of inherited characteristics, learning, situational influences, and unconscious motivation in shaping personality. The idea that everyone is directed only by an innate growth potential is viewed by critics as an oversimplification. So, too, is the assumption that all human problems stem from blocked self-actualization. Like the trait approach, phenomenological theories seem to do a better job of describing personality than explaining it. And like many of the concepts in psychodynamic theories, phenomenological concepts seem too vague to be tested empirically. Thus, most of those who use empirical research to learn about personality do not favor the phenomenological approach.

Finally, the phenomenologists' tendency to define healthy people as independent and autonomous individuals may reflect culture-specific ideas about mental health that may not apply outside of North America and other Western cultures (Enns, 1994). As described in the next section, the foundations of phenomenological self theories may be in direct conflict with the values of non-Western, collectivist cultures. ("In Review: Major Approaches to Personality" summarizes key features of the phenomenological approach, along with those of the other approaches we have described.)

LINKAGES: PERSONALITY, CULTURE, AND HUMAN DEVELOPMENT

Does culture determine personality?

In many Western cultures, it is common to hear people encourage others to "stand up for yourself" or to "blow your own horn" in order to "get what you have coming to you." In middle-class North America, for example, the values of achievement and personal distinction are taught to children, particularly male children, very early in life (Josephs, Markus & Tafarodi, 1992; Smith & Bond, 1993). North American children are encouraged to feel special, to want self-esteem, and to feel good about themselves. Those who learn and display these values tend to receive praise and encouragement for doing so.

As a result of such cultural training, many people in North America and Europe develop personalities that are largely based on a sense of high self-worth. In a study by Hazel Markus and Shinobu Kitayama (1991), for example, 70 percent of a sample of U.S. students believed they were superior to their peers and 60 percent believed they were in the top 10 percent on a wide variety of personal attributes! This tendency toward self-enhancement is evident as early as age four.

Indeed, a sense of independence, uniqueness, and self-esteem is seen by many Western personality theorists as fundamental to mental health. As noted in Chapter 12, for example, Erik Erikson included the appearance of personal identity and self-esteem as part of normal psychosocial development. Middle-class Americans who fail to value and strive for independence, self-promotion, and unique personal achievement may be seen as displaying a personality disorder, some form of depression, or other psychological problems.

Do these ideas reflect universal truths about personality development or, rather, the influence of the cultures that generated them? It is certainly clear that people in many non-Western cultures develop personal orientations very different from those of North Americans and Europeans (Markus & Kitayama, 1995). In China and Japan, for example, an independent, unique self is not emphasized. In fact, children there are encouraged to develop and maintain harmonious relations with others and *not* to stand out from the crowd, lest they diminish someone else. In Japanese, the word for "different" *(tigau)* also means "wrong" (Kitayama & Markus, 1992). Japanese children are taught to be self-effacing, to diminish the value of personal contributions. As young as two-and-a-half, they are taught the joy and value of group work (Kitayama & Markus, 1992).

In contrast to the *independent* self-system common in Western cultures, this more collectivist orientation promotes an *interdependent* self-system through which people see themselves as a fraction of a whole, as an entity that has little or no meaningful definition without reference to the group. These cultural differences may produce differences in how people view their personal accomplishments. Kitayama and his colleagues found that, in Japan, positive moods or feelings, such as calmness or elation, were strongly associated with positive *inter*personal connections. However, there was no

WORKING FOR GROUP GOALS In Asian cultures where collectivist values prevail, a strong sense of personal self-worth tends to be seen as a less important characteristic of personality than it is in more individualist cultures. In other words, the features of "normal" personality development vary from culture to culture.

relationship between positive feelings and *personal* accomplishments; personal achievements were actually associated with generally negative emotions. For U.S. students, the results were the opposite: Positive feelings were most associated with personal achievement (Kitayama & Markus, 1992). In a study of more than 13,000 college students in thirty-one countries, Edward and Marissa Diener (1995) also found higher correlations between self-esteem and life satisfaction in individualist, self-oriented cultures than in collectivist, group-oriented cultures.

Given that cultural factors shape notions about ideal personality development, it is important to evaluate various approaches to personality in terms of how well they apply to cultures other than the one in which they were developed (Enns, 1994). Their applicability to males and females must be considered as well. Even within North American cultures, for example, there are gender differences in the development of self-esteem. Females tend to display an interdependent self-system, achieving their sense of self and self-esteem from attachments to others. By contrast, males' self-esteem tends to develop in relation to personal achievement, in a manner more in keeping with an independent self-system (Josephs, Markus & Tafarodi, 1992). Cross-gender and cross-cultural differences in the nature and determinants of a sense of self underscore the pervasive effects of gender and culture on the development of many aspects of human personality.

D o many aspects of personality remain relatively constant over long periods of time, as most trait theorists believe? (McCrae & Costa, 1994; Woodall & Matthews, 1993). To study this question, psychologists have conducted longitudinal studies, in which the same

FOCUS ON RESEARCH METHODS

Longitudinal Studies of Personality

people are studied at several different points in their lives. Some studies of basic personality traits such as sociability, agreeableness, neuroticism, conscientiousness, and openness have indeed found that these traits remain quite stable during adulthood (Costa, 1992; Costa & McCrae, 1988; McCrae & Costa, 1994). But are the stable traits we see in adults the same ones they displayed as children?

Rather impressive evidence for continuity from childhood to adulthood in some personality traits, at least, comes from a longitudinal study of a randomly selected group of 102 males and 112 females born in Berkeley, California, in 1928 and 1929. Using naturalistic observations, school records, and personal interviews, Avashalom Caspi and his colleagues measured various aspects of these people's personalities through 1971, at which time 87 men and 95 women were still alive and participating in the study (Caspi, Bem & Elder, 1989; Eichorn, 1981).

The first measurements, taken when the participants were eight, nine, and ten years old, consisted of their mothers' ratings of their personality characteristics—especially ill-temperedness. For example, the mothers provided information on the severity and frequency of their tantrums. Recognizing the fact that different mothers might have different personal definitions of "severe" or "mild" tantrums, the researchers asked them to use a 5-point rating scale that contained specific behavioral descriptions. A rating of 1, for example, was given to "anger reactions practically nonexistent," while the high end of the scale was labeled with such phrases as "biting, kicking, and throwing things" and "swearing, screaming, and shouting." A separate 5-point tantrum frequency scale contained labels ranging from a low of "less than once a month" to a high of "several times a day." The tantrum severity and frequency ratings were averaged to create an overall measure of tantrum intensity. Because each mother's ratings were quite consistent, or reliable, across the three measurement years, the data for each child could be combined into an overall measure of childhood ill-temperedness. Specifically, a child with an average score of 3 or above was classified as "ill-tempered."

As the participants passed through junior and senior high school, they were repeatedly interviewed by researchers who also recorded information about their behavior in class. Four clinical psychologists independently reviewed these materials and judged how well standard descriptions of an ill-tempered individual fit each participant. The psychologists' ratings, too, were quite consistent, both with one another and with the mothers' earlier ratings. Finally, when the participants were in their thirties, and then in their forties, interviews were conducted with them as well as with their spouses, children, and friends. These interviews included detailed questions about the participants' professional and personal lives. To reduce bias in the way the questions were asked or might be answered, the psychologists refrained from giving either the interviewers or the respondents any information about the childhood ratings.

Using statistical techniques that included correlations and tests of the significance of differences between means, Caspi and his colleagues (1989) found that childhood ill-temperedness was reflected in adult behavior and functioning, even when the effects of potentially confounding variables—such as IQ and educational status—had been statistically controlled. Men who were ill-tempered as children tended to have lower-status jobs and were more likely to lose their jobs than non-ill-tempered men. Of those who had served in the army, the ill-tempered men held significantly lower ranks. More than twice as many ill-tempered men as non-ill-tempered men had been divorced. As for the women in this study, the impact of their childhood personalities was not reflected in occupational status because most of them, having grown up in the 1930s and 1940s, did not work outside the home. Compared to their more even-tempered age-mates, however, ill-tempered women tended to marry men who held lower-status occupations and, like their male counterparts, were more than twice as likely to be divorced. If they stayed married, ill-tempered women experienced significantly more marital conflict than non-ill-tempered women. And as rated by their family members, ill-tempered women were seen as less adequate and more ill-tempered than other women in the study. Thus, although not every ill-tempered child became an ill-tempered adult, substantial continuity from childhood to adulthood was observed in this aspect of personality.

What factors lie behind this continuity? The explanation offered by Caspi and his colleagues (1989) draws heavily on cognitive-behavioral theories, particularly on Bandura's notion of reciprocal determinism. These researchers believe that long-term consistencies in behavior result from the mutual influence that personality traits and environmental events have on one another. They propose, for example, that people tend to put themselves in situations that reinforce their personality characteristics. Thus, ill-tempered people might choose to spend time with people who accept and even encourage rude or impolite behavior. When such behavior brings negative reactions, the world seems that much more unpleasant and ill-tempered people become even grouchier. So just as sociability toward others can bring about mutual reward, ill-tempered behavior can create a "vicious circle" of unpleasantness. Caspi and his colleagues see the results of their longitudinal study as evidence that this process can endure over a lifetime.

ASSESSING PERSONALITY

Suppose you are an industrial/organizational psychologist whose job it is to ensure that only honest, cooperative, and hard-working employees are hired by your company. How would you know which candidates have these characteristics? There are three basic methods of assessing and describing personality: observations, interviews, and tests. The data gathered through these methods are used not only in personnel selection but also in the diagnosis of psychological disorders, in making predictions about a convict's or mental patient's dangerousness, and in other risky decision situations (Borum & Grisso, 1995; Matarazzo, 1992).

As noted in Chapter 2, *observational* methods allow direct assessment of many aspects of behavior, including how often, how effectively, and how consistently various actions occur. *Interviews* provide a way to gather information about personality from the person's own point of view. They can be open-ended and tailored to the intellectual level, emotional state, and special needs of the person being assessed. Interviews can also be *structured,* aimed at gathering information about specific topics without spending much time on other issues. Structured interviews are routinely used in personality research because they elicit the same information from each person.

Personality tests offer a way of gathering information that is more standardized and economical than either observations or interviews. To be useful, however, a personality test must be reliable and valid. As described in Chapter 10, *reliability* refers to how stable or consistent the results of a test are; *validity* reflects the degree to which a test measures what it is intended to measure. The many personality tests available today are traditionally classified as either *objective* or *projective.*

Objective Tests

An **objective test** is a paper-and-pencil form containing questions ("Have you ever worried about your family without good reason?"), statements ("I think about sex more than most people"), or concepts ("My ideal self"). Responses to objective personality tests are sometimes called *self-reports.* Because of their standardized, written format, objective personality tests can be administered to many people at the same time. Usually, these tests can be scored like the multiple-choice tests used in many classrooms. And, just as in the classroom, results from a large number of people can be compared mathematically. For example, before interpreting your apparently high score on an objective test of anxiety, a psychologist would compare the score with *norms,* or average scores from others of your age and gender. Only if you were well above these averages would you be considered unusually anxious.

Some objective tests focus on one personality trait, such as optimism (Scheier et al., 1989). Others measure a small group of related traits, such as empathy and social responsibility (Penner et al., 1995). Still other objective tests measure the strength of a wider variety of traits to reveal general psychological functioning or signs of psychological disorders.

LINKAGES   Can personality tests be used to diagnose mental disorders? (a link to Psychological Disorders)

The most commonly used objective test for diagnosing psychological disorders is the *Minnesota Multiphasic Personality Inventory,* better known as the *MMPI* (Dahlstrom, 1992). This 566-item true-false test was originally developed during the 1930s at the University of Minnesota by Starke Hathaway and J. C. McKinley. It has subsequently been revised and updated in the MMPI-2 (National Computer Systems, 1992).

The MMPI is organized into ten *clinical scales.* These are groups of items that, in earlier research, had elicited a characteristic pattern of responses only from people who displayed particular psychological disorders or personality characteristics (see Figure 14.7). The MMPI and MMPI-2 also contain four *validity scales,* which are item groups designed to detect whether respondents distorted their answers, misunderstood the items, or were uncooperative. For example, someone who responds "true" to items such as "I never get angry" may not be giving honest answers to the test as a whole.

Interpreting the MMPI is largely a matter of comparing respondents' profiles—such as those shown in Figure 14.7—to the profiles of persons already known to display certain personality characteristics. Respondents are generally presumed to share characteristics with the group whose profile theirs most closely resembles. So while a very high score on one scale, such as depression, might indicate a problem in the dimension measured by that scale, MMPI interpretation usually focuses on the overall *pattern* in the clinical scales—particularly on the combination of two or three scales on which a person has unusually high scores.

There is considerable evidence for the reliability and validity of MMPI clinical scales, but even the latest editions of the test are far from perfect measurement tools (Helmes & Reddon, 1993; Humphrey & Dahlstrom, 1995). The validity of MMPI interpretations may be particularly suspect when—because of cultural factors—the perceptions, val-

FIGURE 14.7

The MMPI: Clinical Scales and Sample Profiles

A score of **50** on the clinical scales is average. Scores at or above **65** mean that the person's responses on that scale are more extreme than at least 95 percent of the normal population. The red line represents the profile of Kenneth Bianchi, the infamous "Hillside Strangler" who murdered thirteen women in the late 1970s. His profile would be interpreted as characteristic of a shallow person with poor self-control and little personal insight who is sexually preoccupied and unable to reveal himself to others. The profile in green comes from a more normal man, but it is characteristic of someone who is self-centered, passive, unwilling to accept personal responsibility for his behavior, and, when under stress, complains of numerous vague physical symptoms.

The clinical scales abbreviated in the figure are as follows:

1. Hypochondriasis (Hs) (Concern with bodily functions and symptoms)

2. Depression (D) (Pessimism, hopelessness, slowed thinking)

3. Hysteria (Hy) (Use of physical or mental symptoms to avoid problems)

4. Psychopathic deviate (Pd) (Disregard for social customs, emotional shallowness)

5. Masculinity/femininity (Mf) (Interests associated with a particular gender)

6. Paranoia (Pa) (Delusions, suspiciousness)

7. Psychasthenia (Pt) (Worry, guilt, anxiety)

8. Schizophrenia (Sc) (Bizarre thoughts and perceptions)

9. Hypomania (Ma) (Overactivity, excitement, impulsiveness)

10. Social introversion (Si) (Shy, insecure)

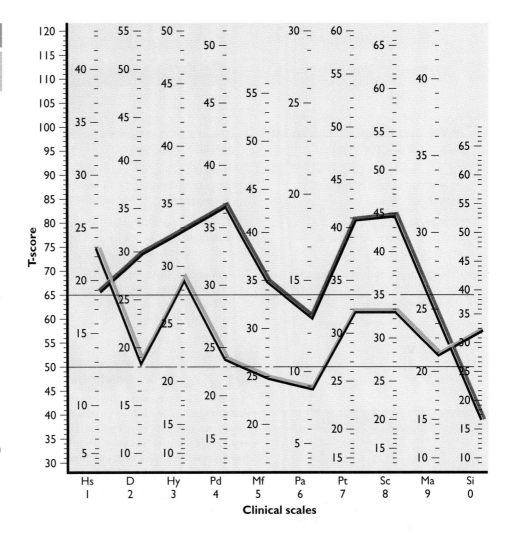

ues, and experiences of the respondent are very different from those of the test developers and the people to whom the respondent's results will be compared. Thus, a profile that looks typical of people with a certain disorder might reflect the culture-specific way the respondent interpreted the test items, not a mental problem (Dana, 1988; Greene, 1991).

Even though the MMPI-2 uses comparison norms that represent a more culturally diverse population than did those of the original MMPI, psychologists must remain cautious when interpreting profiles of people who identify with minority subcultures. One reason is that the responses people give on objective personality tests can be influenced by general cultural differences as well as by individual personality traits. For example, Chuansheng Chen and his colleagues (1995) found that when respondents were asked to rate their personal attributes, those from individualist countries such as Canada and the United States tended to select extreme alternatives ("very important" or "much below average"), while those from collectivist countries such as China and Japan tended to select more moderate alternatives ("somewhat important" or "average").

There are a number of objective tests designed to measure personality variables in normal populations, especially the "big-five" personality traits described earlier. One increasingly popular example is the *Neuroticism Extraversion Openness Personality Inventory, Revised* or *NEO-PI-R* (Costa & McCrae, 1992). Table 14.3 shows how the test's results are presented. One innovative feature of the NEO-PI-R is its "private" and "public" versions. The first asks for the respondent's self-assessment; the second asks a person who knows the respondent to rate her or him on various dimensions.

Compared with the responses of other people, your responses suggest that you can be described as:

☐ Sensitive, emotional, and prone to experience feelings that are upsetting.

☐ Extraverted, outgoing, active, and high-spirited. You prefer to be around people most of the time.

☐ Open to new experiences. You have broad interests and are very imaginative.

☐ Compassionate, good-natured, and eager to cooperate and avoid conflict.

☒ Conscientious and well-organized. You have high standards and always strive to achieve your goals.

☒ Generally calm and able to deal with stress, but you sometimes experience feelings of guilt, anger, or sadness.

☐ Moderate in activity and enthusiasm, You enjoy the company of others, but you also value privacy.

☐ Practical but willing to consider new ways of doing things. You seek a balance between the old and the new.

☒ Generally warm, trusting, and agreeable, but you can sometimes be stubborn and competitive.

☐ Dependable and moderately well-organized. You generally have clear goals but are able to set your work aside.

☐ Secure, hardy, and generally relaxed even under stressful conditions.

☒ Introverted, reserved, and serious. You prefer to be alone or with a few close friends.

☒ Down-to-earth, practical, traditional, and pretty much set in your ways.

☐ Hardheaded, skeptical, proud, and competitive. You tend to express your anger directly.

☐ Easygoing, not very well-organized, and sometimes careless. You prefer not to make plans.

TABLE 14.3   Sample Summary of Results from the NEO-PI-R Personality Inventory

The NEO-PI-R assesses the big-five personality dimensions. In this example of the results that a respondent might receive, the five factors scored are, from the top row to the bottom row, neuroticism, extraversion, openness, agreeableness, and conscientiousness. Because people with different NEO profiles tend to have different disorders, this test has also been used to aid in the diagnosis of personality disorders (Trull & Sher, 1994).

NEOAC

FIGURE 14.8

Interpretations of a Draw-a-Person Test

These drawings came from an eighteen-year-old male who had been caught stealing a television set. A psychologist interpreted the muscular figure as the young man's attempt to boast of masculine prowess, but saw the muscles' "puffy softness" as suggesting feelings of inadequacy. The drawing of the babylike figure was seen to reveal vulnerability, dependency, and a need for affection. Appealing as these interpretations may be, research does not generally support the value of projective tests in personality assessment (see Smith & Dumont, 1995).

Source: Hammer, 1968.

Personality descriptions derived from the two versions are often quite similar, but discrepancies may indicate problems. For example, if a person's self-ratings are substantially different from those of a spouse, marital problems may be indicated; in addition, the nature of the discrepancies could suggest a focus for marital therapy.

Projective Tests

Unlike objective tests, **projective tests** contain relatively unstructured stimuli, such as inkblots, which can be perceived in many ways. Proponents of projective tests tend to take a psychodynamic approach to personality. They believe that people's responses to the tests' ambiguous stimuli are guided by unconscious needs, motives, fantasies, conflicts, thoughts, and other hidden aspects of personality. Some projective tests (also called projective techniques) ask people to draw items such as a house, a person, or a tree (see Figure 14.8), to fill in the missing parts of incomplete pictures or sentences, or to say what they associate with a particular word.

One projective test, called the *Thematic Apperception Test,* or *TAT,* is described in Chapter 11 as a measure of need for achievement (see Figure 11.8). It is also used to assess the other needs that its developers, Henry Murray and Christina Morgan, saw as the basis of personality. Another well-known projective test, the *Rorschach Inkblot Test,* asks people to say what they see in a series of inkblots (see Figure 14.9).

In comparison to objective-test results, responses to projective tests are much more difficult to translate into numerical scores. In an effort to reduce the subjectivity involved in projective-test interpretation, some psychologists have developed more structured—and thus potentially more reliable—scoring systems for instruments like the Rorschach (Erdberg, 1990; Exner, 1993). Proponents claim that projective tests make it difficult for respondents to detect what is being measured and what the "best"

IN REVIEW	Personality Tests		
Type of Test	**Characteristics**	**Advantages**	**Disadvantages**
Objective	Paper-and-pencil format; quantitatively scored	Efficiency, standardization	Subject to deliberate distortion
Projective	Unstructured stimuli create maximum freedom of response; scoring is subjective, though some objective methods exist	"Correct" answers not obvious; designed to tap unconscious impulses; flexible use	Reliability and validity lower than those of objective tests

answers would be. They argue, therefore, that these tests can measure aggressive and sexual impulses and other personality features that people might otherwise be able to hide. The ambiguous stimuli in projective tests may also capture how people respond to the uncertainty that they confront in daily life. In addition, proponents point to specific instances—as in studies assessing achievement motivation via the TAT—where projectives show acceptable reliability and validity (Spangler, 1992). Accordingly, projective tests continue to be used by many clinical psychologists (Chan & Lee, 1995; Watkins et al., 1995).

Overall, however, projective personality tests are less reliable and valid than objective tests (Aiken, 1993; Rogers, 1995). Indeed, because of their generally low predictive validity, they often add little beyond what might be inferred from other information. One study showed, for example, that even untrained observers are able to make relatively accurate judgments about an individual's personality characteristics simply by watching a sample of his or her behavior on videotape (Funder & Colvin, in press).

("In Review: Personality Tests" summarizes the characteristics of objective and projective tests, along with some of their advantages and disadvantages.)

FIGURE 14.9

The Rorschach Inkblot Test

The Rorschach test consists of ten patterns, some in color, others in black and white. The subject is asked to tell what the blot might be and then to explain why. This pattern is similar to those in the Rorschach test. What do you see? Most scoring methods pay attention to (1) what part of the blot the person responds to; (2) what features (such as details or color) appear to determine each response; (3) the content of responses (for example, animals, maps, body parts); and (4) the popularity or commonness of the subject's responses.

Personality Tests and Employee Selection

How good are objective personality tests at selecting people for jobs? One study evaluated the validity of the MMPI as a predictor of job performance among law enforcement officers in small towns in Vermont (Bartol, 1991). The researchers had access to the MMPI profiles of 600 officers hired over a twelve-year period. They compared the profiles of those who did well in their jobs with those who were fired or forced to resign due to problems such as excessive use of force, inappropriate use of firearms, or poor performance in crisis situations. Had scores on certain MMPI scales been used to guide the initial hiring decisions, only a small fraction of the ultimately unacceptable candidates would have been hired, thus avoiding the majority of costly hiring mistakes. Several researchers have also found significant relationships between scores on one or more of the big-five personality dimensions and job success (Barrick & Mount, 1991; Tett, Jackson & Rothstein, 1991). Finally, a review of studies involving over 300,000 people showed that objective personality tests are of value in helping businesses reduce thefts and other disruptive employee behaviors (Ones, Viswesvaran & Schmidt, 1993).

Still, personality tests are far from perfect predictors of behavior—and, as noted earlier, they can lead to incorrect predictions. Sometimes, situational factors rather than person variables are responsible for people's actions. Further, some employees see personality tests as an invasion of their privacy. They worry also that test results in their personnel files might later be misinterpreted and hurt their chances for promotion or for employment by other companies. Lawsuits have resulted in a ban on the use of personality tests in the selection of U.S. federal employees. Concerns about privacy and other issues surrounding personality testing has also led the American Psychological Association to publish ethical standards relating to procedures for the development, dissemination, and use of all psychological tests (American Psychological Association, 1974, 1981, 1992b). The goal is not only to improve the reliability and validity of tests but also to ensure that their results are properly used and do not infringe on individuals' rights.

FUTURE DIRECTIONS

The many approaches to understanding personality are different in some respects. But they are also similar to one another. For one thing, they all recognize that personality development begins in childhood and that much of personality develops through experience. In addition, they all focus on the fundamental struggles each person faces in adapting to the world. Finally, because thoughts affect (and are affected by) behaviors and emotions, all of the current approaches deal with cognitive processes in personality.

Continued progress toward a fuller understanding of human personality will be aided by a growing tendency to integrate the scientifically validated aspects of each of these approaches, as well as by additional research on the many ways in which cultural factors affect personality development. This research will focus on differences not only among geographically separate cultures (North American, African, and Asian, for example) but also among people who are born and raised in diverse subcultures within a single country. By looking at similarities as well as differences, this research will help clarify whether or not personality dimensions such as the "big five" are culture-general (that is, universal), culture-specific, or somewhere in between (Almagor, Tellegen & Waller, 1995; Benet & Waller, 1995; Smith & Bond, 1994).

The genetic and biochemical bases of personality dimensions will also receive increased attention (Hershberger, Plomin & Pedersen, 1995; Zuckerman, 1995). Researchers will work to understand which traits or temperaments are inborn, how stable they are, and how they are altered and shaped by developmental and cultural experiences. New research will also examine personality from an evolutionary perspective, focusing on the adaptive nature of personality traits and the ways in which they have served to maintain the human species (Buss, 1995).

Objective personality assessment may become more sophisticated as it begins to rely less exclusively on self-report measures and to incorporate peer observations as well (Funder, Kolar & Blackman, 1995; Funder & Sneed, 1993). Ideally, these new testing approaches will minimize the problems of subjective bias that can cloud interpretations of some self-report personality measures.

Consistent with the current emphasis on cognitive factors in all aspects of psychology, personality research will continue to focus on such variables as how different people perceive and process information about themselves and their environment, what attributions they make about themselves and other people's behavior and personality, and how their emotions and thoughts interact to influence their attitudes and behavior.

If you want to learn more about personality and the latest research in the area, consider taking a course in personality psychology and perhaps a laboratory in personality research methods.

SUMMARY AND KEY TERMS

Personality refers to the unique pattern of psychological and behavioral characteristics by which each person can be compared and contrasted with other people. The four main theoretical approaches to personality are the psychodynamic, trait, cognitive-behavioral, and phenomenological approaches. 2PTC

■ THE PSYCHODYNAMIC APPROACH

The *psychodynamic approach,* first proposed by Freud, assumes that personality arises out of conflicts between basic needs and the demands of the real world. Most of these conflicts occur at an unconscious level.

The Structure and Development of Personality

Freud believed that personality has three components—the *id,* which has a reservoir of *libido* and operates according to the *pleasure principle;* the *ego,* which operates according to the *reality principle;* and the *superego,* which internalizes society's rules and values. The ego uses *defense mechanisms* to prevent unconscious conflicts among these components from becoming conscious and causing anxiety. Freud proposed that the focus of conflict changes as the child passes through the *psychosexual stages* of development he called the *oral stage,* the *anal stage,* the *phallic stage* (during which the *Oedipus* or *Electra complex* occurs), the *latency period,* and the *genital stage.*

Variations on Freud's Personality Theory

Many of Freud's early followers developed new theories that differed from his. Among these theorists were Adler, Jung, and Horney. These and other theorists tended to downplay the role of instincts and the unconscious, emphasizing instead the importance of conscious processes, ego functions, and social and cultural factors. Horney also challenged the male-oriented nature of Freud's original theory.

Contemporary Psychodynamic Theories

Current psychodynamic theories derive from neo-Freudians' emphasis on family and social relationships. According to object relations theorists, personality development depends mainly on the nature of early interactions between an individual and his or her caregivers (objects).

Evaluation of the Psychodynamic Approach

The psychodynamic approach is reflected in many forms of psychotherapy. In spite of recent attempts to measure psychodynamic concepts more precisely and objectively, critics still fault the approach for its lack of a scientific base and for its view of human behavior as driven by unmeasurable forces.

■ THE TRAIT APPROACH

The *trait approach* assumes that personality is made up of stable internal characteristics that appear at varying strengths in different people and guide their behavior.

Prominent Trait Theories

Allport believed that personality is created by a small set of central traits in each individual. Cattell and Eysenck have used factor analysis to identify common traits or core dimensions of personality. Eysenck believes that biological factors are responsible for these core dimensions.

The "Big-Five" Model of Personality

Recently, researchers have used factor analysis to identify five basic dimensions of personality, collectively referred to as the *big-five* or *five-factor model.* These dimensions, which have been found in many different cultures, may arise partly from inherited differences in temperament that provide the raw materials out of which experience molds each personality.

Evaluation of the Trait Approach

The trait approach has been criticized for being better at describing personality than at explaining it, for failing to consider mechanisms that motivate behavior, and for underemphasizing the role of situational factors. Nevertheless, the trait approach—particularly the big-five model—currently dominates the field.

■ THE COGNITIVE-BEHAVIORAL APPROACH

The *cognitive-behavioral approach* assumes that personality is a label that summarizes the unique patterns of thinking and behavior that a person learns in the social world.

Roots of the Cognitive-Behavioral Approach

With roots in research on classical and instrumental conditioning (including Skinner's *functional analysis* of behavior), the cognitive-behavioral approach has expanded on traditional behavioral approaches by emphasizing the role of cognitive factors, such as observational learning, in personality development.

Prominent Cognitive-Behavioral Theories

Julian Rotter's theory focuses on cognitive expectancies that guide behavior, especially general beliefs about whether rewards occur because of personal efforts (internal control) or chance (external control). Albert Bandura believes that personality develops largely through cognitively mediated learning, including observational learning. He sees personality as reciprocally determined by interactions among cognition, environmental stimuli, and behavior. *Self-efficacy*—the belief in one's ability to accomplish a given task—is an important determinant of behavior. Walter Mischel emphasizes the importance of situations—and their interactions with person variables—in determining behavior. According to Mischel, we must look at both person and situational variables in order to understand human consistencies and inconsistencies.

Evaluation of the Cognitive-Behavioral Approach

The cognitive-behavioral approach has led to new forms of psychological treatment and many other applications. Critics of the approach, however, consider even its latest versions to be too mechanistic and incapable of capturing what most psychologists mean by personality, including beliefs, intentions, and values.

■ THE PHENOMENOLOGICAL APPROACH

The *phenomenological approach,* also called the humanistic approach, is based on the assumption that personality is determined by the unique ways in which each individual views the world. These perceptions form a personal version of reality and guide behavior as the individual strives to reach his or her fullest human potential.

Prominent Phenomenological Theories

Carl Rogers believed that personality development is driven by an innate tendency toward *self-actualization,* but also that one's *self-concept* is shaped by social evaluations. He proposed that when people are free from the effects of *conditions of worth,* they will be psychologically healthy. Abraham Maslow saw self-actualization as the highest in a hierarchy of needs. Personality development is healthiest, he said, when people have a *growth orientation* rather than a *deficiency orientation.*

Evaluation of the Phenomenological Approach

Applications of the phenomenological approach include certain forms of psychotherapy and group experiences designed to enhance personal growth. Although it has a large following, the phenomenological approach is faulted for being too idealistic, for failing to explain personality development, for being vague and unscientific, and for underplaying cultural differences in "ideal" personalities.

■ LINKAGES: PERSONALITY, CULTURE, AND HUMAN DEVELOPMENT

Many people in the individualist cultures of North America and Europe are taught to believe in the importance of self-worth and personal distinction. This independent self-system contrasts with the interdependent self-system often fostered in collectivist cultures, where the self is defined mainly in relation to family or other groups. Contrasting definitions of the self in different cultures, and among males versus females, tend to exert differing influences on the development of personality.

■ ASSESSING PERSONALITY

Personality is usually assessed through some combination of observations, interviews, and tests. To be useful, personality assessments must be both reliable and valid.

Objective Tests

Objective tests usually present written items; their scores can be compared to group norms. The MMPI and the NEO-PI-R are examples of objective tests.

Projective Tests

Based on psychodynamic theories, *projective tests* present ambiguous stimuli in an attempt to tap unconscious personality characteristics. Two popular projective tests are the TAT and the Rorschach Inkblot Test. In general, projective tests are less reliable and valid than objective personality tests.

Personality Tests and Employee Selection

Objective personality tests are often used to identify the people best suited for certain occupations. Although such tests can be helpful in this regard, those who use them must be aware of the tests' limitations and take care not to violate the rights of test respondents.

PSYCHOLOGICAL DISORDERS

CHAPTER **15**

LINKAGES
TO
PSYCHOLOGICAL DISORDERS

BIOLOGICAL ASPECTS OF PSYCHOLOGY

Are some psychological disorders inherited? *(ans. on p. 512)*

PERSONALITY

Can personality tests be used to diagnose mental disorders? *(ans. on p. 482)*

LEARNING

Can we learn to become "abnormal"? *(ans. on p. 504)*

During his freshman year at college, Mark began to worry about news stories describing the deadly diseases resulting from hanta virus, "flesh-eating" strep bacteria, and HIV. He took a blood test for HIV, the virus that causes AIDS, and was relieved when it showed no infection. But then he wondered if he might have contracted HIV after the test. Library research and a call to the Centers for Disease Control AIDS hotline revealed that HIV antibodies may not appear until six months after infection. He took another blood test, also negative, but he still worried when he learned that the AIDS virus can live outside of the human body for anywhere from ten minutes to several hours or even days; no one knows for sure. He also read that no one can explain why hanta virus appears in new places or why some rare forms of bacteria cause deadly lesions.

Given all this uncertainty, Mark concluded that HIV, hanta virus, and "flesh-eating" strep bacteria can live indefinitely outside of the body and could therefore be anywhere and everywhere. He decided that the only safe course was not just sexual abstinence but absolute cleanliness. Mark began to scrub himself whenever he touched door knobs, money, walls, floors—anything. People with HIV or other deadly viruses or bacteria, he thought, could have touched these things, or they might have bled on the street and he might have tracked their infected blood into his car and house and bathroom. Eventually he felt the need to scrub everything around him up to forty times in each direction; it took him several exhausting hours simply to shower and dress. He washed himself and the shower knobs before touching them and, once in the shower, felt that he had to wash his body in cycles of thirteen strokes. If his feet touched the bare floor, he had to wash them again before putting on his underwear to ensure that his feet would not contaminate the fabric. He was sure his hands, rubbed raw from constant washing, were especially susceptible to infection so he wore gloves at all times except in the summer, when he wrapped his fingers in flesh-colored bandages. The process of protecting himself from infection was wearing him out and severely restricting his activities; he could not go anywhere without first considering the risk of infection.

Mark's case provides an example of someone who suffers from a psychological disorder, also called a mental disorder, or psychopathology. **Psychopathology** involves patterns of thought, emotion, and behavior that are maladaptive, disruptive, or uncom-

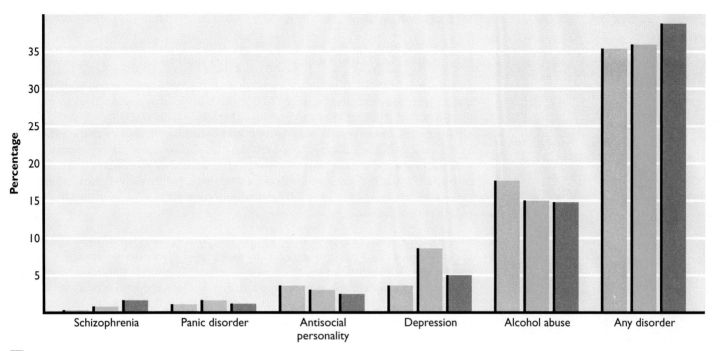

Hispanic-American

White non-Hispanic-American

African-American

Source: Data from Karno et al., 1987, and Robins et al., 1984.

FIGURE 15.1

Lifetime Prevalence of Mental Disorders

Surveys of 18,000 adults in five U.S. cities revealed that nearly one-third experienced some form of mental disorder at some time in their lives. Here are the prevalence data for several mental disorders among Hispanics, non-Hispanic whites, and African-Americans. Note that the size of the differences between these groups varies across disorders, but that all such differences are relatively small and none are statistically significant.

fortable either for the person affected or for others. Psychopathology is thus a social as well as a personal matter, and it has attracted the attention of psychologists in many subfields (see the Linkages diagram).

The number of people who display some form of psychological disorder is staggering. Surveys reveal that, in the United States alone, as many as 29.5 percent of the adult population have shown mild to severe mental disorder within the last year, and that as many as 48 percent have experienced a disorder at some point in their lives (Kessler et al., 1994; Robins et al., 1984). More than 22 percent of U.S. children display significant mental disorder in any given year (Costello et al., 1988). These overall rates of mental disorder are found, with only minor variations, in all segments of U.S. society (see Figure 15.1), including males and females in all ethnic groups (Burnham et al., 1987; Canino et al., 1987; Peterson et al., 1993). Psychological disorders are enormously costly in terms of human suffering and wasted potential, economic burden and lost resources. They can also cost lives.

In this chapter we describe major categories of psychological disorders, discuss some of their possible causes, and examine issues surrounding the nature of psychopathology.

UNDERSTANDING PSYCHOLOGICAL DISORDERS: SOME BASIC ISSUES

A woman's husband dies, and in her grief she stays in bed all day, weeping, refusing to eat, at times holding "conversations" with him. In India, a Hindu holy man on a pilgrimage rolls along the ground for more than 1,000 miles of deserts, mountains, and monsoons until he reaches the sacred place he seeks. Seven percent of U.S. adults surveyed say they have seen a UFO (Roper Organization, 1992). These and countless other examples raise the question of where to draw the line between normality and abnormality, between eccentricity and mental disorder (Kanner, 1995). We begin our exploration of psychopathology by considering some factors that determine what is considered normal and abnormal in various cultures today.

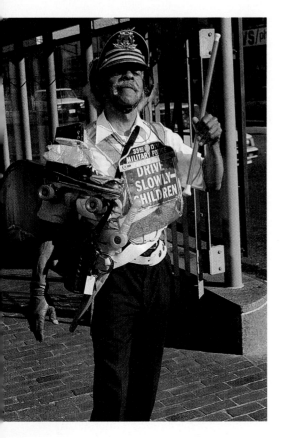

IS THIS MAN ABNORMAL? Whether this unusual individual will be labeled "abnormal" and perhaps given treatment for psychological disorder depends on a number of factors, including how abnormality is defined by the culture in which he lives and by those who are most directly affected by his behavior.

· age
· gender
· religion

What Is Abnormal?

There are several criteria for judging whether people's thinking, emotions, or behavior are abnormal. Each criterion has value, but also some flaws.

Infrequency   If we define normality as what most people do, an obvious criterion for abnormality is *statistical infrequency,* that which is atypical or rare. By this criterion, the few people who believe that space aliens are stealing their thoughts would be judged abnormal; the many people who worry about becoming victims of crime would not. Statistical infrequency alone is a poor criterion for abnormality, however, because some characteristics that appear only rarely—creative genius, extraordinary language skills, or world-class athletic ability, for example—may be highly valued. Further, equating rarity with abnormality can result in the oppression of nonconformists who express minority views in a society.

Personal Suffering   Another criterion for abnormality is *personal suffering.* Indeed, the experience of distress is the criterion that people often use in deciding that their psychological problems are severe enough to require treatment. But personal suffering alone is an inadequate criterion for abnormality, because it does not take into account the fact that some disordered behavior—such as the sexual abuse of children—can cause distress to others while leaving the perpetrator relatively unscathed.

Norm Violation   Concern for other people's suffering suggests that we could define abnormality in terms of whether someone violates social norms—the cultural rules that tell us how we should and should not behave in various situations, especially in relation to others (see Chapter 18). According to this *norm violation* criterion, when people behave in ways that are bizarre, unusual, or disturbing enough to violate social norms, they are described as abnormal. Like the other criteria, however, norm violation alone is an inadequate measure of abnormality. For one thing, some norm violations are better characterized as eccentric or illegal than as abnormal (Weeks & Weeks, 1995). People who bathe infrequently or who stand too close during conversation violate social norms, but are they abnormal or merely annoying? Further, whose norms are we talking about? Social norms vary across cultures, subcultures, and historical eras, so the behaviors that qualify as abnormal in one part of the world might be perfectly acceptable elsewhere.

Behavior in Context: A Practical Approach   Because no single criterion is entirely adequate for identifying abnormality, mental health practitioners and researchers tend to adopt a *practical approach* that combines aspects of all the criteria we've discussed. They consider the <u>content</u> of behavior—that is, what the person does; the sociocultural <u>context</u> in which the person's behavior occurs; and the <u>consequences</u> of the behavior for that person, and for others. This practical approach pays special attention to whether a person's thoughts, behavior, or emotions cause **impaired functioning**—that is, difficulty in fulfilling appropriate and expected social roles.

What is "appropriate" and "expected" depends on age, gender, and culture, as well as on the particular situation and historical era in which people find themselves. Thus, for example, the very short attention span considered normal in a two-year-old would be described as inappropriate and problematic in an adult. There are gender-specific norms as well. In the United States, it is more appropriate for women than for men to display emotion. Kisses, tears of happiness, and long embraces are common when women greet each other after a long absence; men tend to simply shake hands or, at most, hug briefly. Given cultural differences, hearing a dead relative's voice calling from the afterlife would be considered more acceptable in certain American Indian tribes than among, say, the families of suburban Toronto. Situational factors are important, too. Falling to the floor and "speaking in tongues" is considered appropriate, even desirable, during the worship services of certain religious groups, but the same behavior would be considered inappropriate, and a sign of disorder, in a college classroom. Finally, judgments about behavior are shaped by changes in social trends and cultural values. For example, the American Psychiatric Association once listed homosexuality as

SITUATIONAL FACTORS IN DEFINING ABNORMALITY In most Western cultures, being nude in private or in designated public places is not considered abnormal. But it is not tolerated in other situations, such as on a college campus. When this University of California-Berkeley student—shown here on his way to a court appearance—attended classes nude to protest "social repression," complaints from other students led to his dismissal.

a mental disorder but dropped this category from its *Diagnostic and Statistical Manual of Mental Disorders* in 1973. In taking this step, it was responding to changing views of homosexuality that were prompted in part by the political and educational efforts of gay and lesbian rights groups.

In summary, it is difficult, and probably impossible, to define a specific set of behaviors that everyone, everywhere, will agree constitutes abnormality. Instead, the practical approach sees abnormality as including those patterns of thought, behavior, and emotional reaction that impair people's functioning, make them uncomfortable, and/or disrupt the lives of others (Wakefield, 1992).

Explaining Psychological Disorders

Since the dawn of civilization, people throughout the world have tried to understand the causes of psychological disorder. They have focused on four main explanations: supernatural influences, biological factors, psychological processes, and sociocultural context.

Supernatural Influences According to the **supernatural** or **demonological model**, abnormal behavior is the result of possession by gods, demons, or other spirits. At various points in history, many cultures in Europe, Asia, the Middle East, and Africa have viewed disordered people either as innocent victims of malicious forces or as social deviants whose misdeeds have brought supernatural punishment. In medieval Europe, for example, a great deal of abnormal behavior was tolerated and even encouraged if it was attributed to devotion to God. Thus, whipping oneself for having sinned was generally viewed as godly (Kroll, 1973). Later in the Middle Ages, heresy (disbelief in established religious doctrine) and other unusual behaviors were viewed as the work of the devil and his witches. For several centuries in Europe and its colonies, hundreds of "witches"—mostly women—were burned at the stake and exorcisms were performed to rid people of controlling demons. Supernatural causes of abnormality are not emphasized in Western cultures today, but many other cultures around the world—as well as certain ethnic and religious subcultures in North America—employ supernatural (especially demonological) explanations of some psychological disorders.

Biological Factors A second major explanatory approach sees mental disorder as caused by *biological factors,* usually some kind of physical illness or imbalance in bodily processes. One of the earliest proponents of this **medical model** was the ancient

AN EXORCISM Though no longer dominant in Western cultures, supernatural explanations of mental disorder, and supernaturally oriented cures, such as the exorcism being performed by this Buddhist monk in Thailand, remain influential in many other cultures and subcultures.

VISITING BEDLAM As the medical model gained prominence in Western cultures after the Middle Ages, specialized hospitals for the insane were established throughout Europe. As shown in Hogarth's portrayal of "Bedlam" (the local name for London's St. Mary's of Bethleham hospital), most of these eighteenth-century *asylums* were little more than prisons where the public could buy tickets to gawk at the patients.

Greek physician Hippocrates. Psychological disorders, he said, resulted from imbalances among four *humors,* or bodily fluids (blood, phlegm, black bile, and yellow bile). Depression, according to Hippocrates, resulted from an excess of black bile (melancholia). Similarly, in ancient Chinese cultures, psychological disorders were seen as resulting from an imbalance of *yin* and *yang,* the dual forces of the universe flowing in the physical body.

The medical model gave rise to the concept of abnormality as *mental illness*—and, indeed, even though the specifics of the presumed illness are often vague, most people in Western cultures today still tend to seek medical doctors and hospitals for the diagnosis and treatment of psychological disorders. The medical model is now more properly called the **neurobiological model** because it explains psychological disorders in terms of particular disturbances in the anatomy and chemistry of the brain and in other biological processes. The neurobiological model dominates modern research on the causes—and treatments—of psychological disorders. Neuroscientists and others who investigate these disorders approach them as they would approach any physical illness, seeing problematic symptoms stemming from an underlying illness that can be diagnosed, treated, and cured.

The enduring influence of the medical model is based largely on the fact that some forms of abnormality have indeed been traced to biological causes (Spitzer et al., 1992). *Dementia,* for example, is characterized by a loss of intellectual functions, including disturbances in memory, personality, and cognitive abilities. The most frequent causes of dementia are progressive deterioration of the brain as a result of aging or long-term alcohol abuse; acute diseases and disorders such as encephalitis, brain tumors, or head injury; and drug intoxication. Alzheimer's disease is a severe form of dementia seen mostly in the elderly. Research in neuroscience and behavioral genetics has also implicated biological factors in a number of other psychological disorders to be described later, including schizophrenia, bipolar disorder, some forms of anxiety disorder, and autism and attention deficit disorder in children.

Psychological Processes A third explanatory approach views mental disorders as arising from *inner turmoil* or other psychological processes. The roots of this **psycho-**

logical model can be seen in ancient Greek literature and drama dealing with *psyche,* or mind—especially with the struggles of the mind to resolve inner conflicts, or with the effects of childhood experiences on adult behavior. These ideas gained far greater prominence in the late 1800s when Sigmund Freud, a Viennese physician, formally challenged the assumption that psychological disorders had only physical causes. Freud's explanations of these disorders came as part of a more general *psychodynamic* approach to personality, described in Chapter 14. Freud viewed psychological disorders as the result of unresolved, mostly unconscious clashes between instinctual desires of the id and the demands of the environment and society. These conflicts, he said, begin early in childhood. Contemporary versions of the psychodynamic model—such as *object relations* theory—focus less on instinctual urges and more on the role of attachment and other early interpersonal relationships (Fonagy et al., 1996).

LINKAGES Are psychological disorders learned behaviors? (a link to Learning)

Psychological explanations for mental disorders have also come from other theories of personality discussed in Chapter 14. *Cognitive-behavioral* theorists, for example, see most psychological disorders as the result of past learning and current situations. Just as people learn to avoid hot grills after being burned, say these theorists, bad experiences in school or a dental office can "teach" people to fear such places. Cognitive-behaviorists also emphasize the effects of expectancies and other mental processes. Depression, for example, is seen as stemming not only from negative events, such as losing a job, but also from learned patterns of thoughts about these events, such as "I never do anything right."

According to the humanistic, or *phenomenological,* approach to personality, behavior disorders appear when self-actualization is blocked, usually by a failure to be aware of and to express true feelings. When this happens, one's perceptions of reality become distorted. The greater the distortion, the more serious the psychological disorder. Phenomenologists assume that abnormal behavior, no matter how unusual or seemingly irrational, is a reasonable reaction to the world, as the person perceives it.

LINKAGES How do societies define what is abnormal? (a link to Social Behavior and Group Influences)

Sociocultural Context   Neither psychological nor neurobiological explanations *alone* can explain all forms of abnormality because, for one thing, many disorders have both biological *and* psychological causes. And even together, these explanations focus mainly on processes *within* the individual. As the name implies, **sociocultural explanations** of mental disorder emphasize the social and cultural factors that constitute the *context* through which abnormal behavior has been shaped and within which it must be viewed. As mentioned earlier, the sociocultural context of behavior includes such factors as gender and age, physical and social situations, cultural values and expectations, and historical eras. These factors influence not only what is and isn't labeled abnormal but also who displays what kind of disorder.

Consider gender, for instance. The view held in many cultures that excessive alcohol consumption is less appropriate for women than for men is a sociocultural factor that may set the stage for higher rates of alcohol abuse in men than in women (Helzer et al., 1990). Similarly, the greater tolerance in most cultures for open expression of emotional distress among women, but not men, may contribute to the higher rates of depression seen in women compared to men (Nolen-Hoeksma, 1990).

Sociocultural factors also influence the *form* that abnormality takes. For example, disorders such as schizophrenia and depression are *culture-general*—appearing virtually everywhere in the world—but their specific symptoms tend to differ depending on the disordered person's cultural background. In Western cultures, where emotional and physical components of disorder are generally viewed separately, symptoms of depression tend to revolve around despair and other signs of emotional distress (Kleinman, 1991). But in China and certain other Asian cultures where emotional and physical experiences tend to be viewed as one, a depressed person is as likely to report stomach or back pain as to complain of sadness (Brislin, 1993).

There are also *culture-specific* forms of disorder. For instance, Puerto Rican and Dominican Hispanic women sometimes experience *ataques de nervios,* a unique way of reacting to stress that includes heart palpitations, shaking, shouting, nervousness, depression, and, on occasion, fainting or seizure-like episodes (Liebowitz et al., 1994).

Another example can be found in Southeast Asia, Southern China, and Malaysia, where one encounters a condition called *Koro*. Victims of this condition, who are usually male, fear that their penis will shrivel, retract into the body, and cause death (in females, the fear relates to shriveling of the breasts). *Koro* appears only in cultures holding the specific supernatural beliefs that explain it, but epidemics of *Koro* are often triggered by economic hard times (Tseng et al., 1992).

In short, as sociocultural factors create differing social roles, stressors, opportunities, and experiences for people who differ in age, gender, and cultural traditions, they help shape the disorders and symptoms to which certain categories of people are prone. Any attempt to fully explain psychological disorders must take these sociocultural factors into account.

Diathesis-Stress as an Integrative Approach   More generally, research suggests that most psychological disorders arise from a varying combination of sources, including biological imbalances, genetically inherited characteristics, brain damage, enduring psychological traits, socioculturally mediated learning experiences, and stressful life events. All these causes of disorder are taken into account by the **diathesis-stress model,** which suggests that a person's inherited characteristics, biological processes, and early learning experiences may create a predisposition (or *diathesis*) for a psychological disorder, but that whether or not the disorder appears depends on the stressors the person encounters (National Advisory Mental Health Council, 1996).

For example, a person may have inherited a tendency toward dysregulation of a neurotransmitter associated with depression or may have learned depressing patterns of thinking, but these predispositions may be expressed as a depressive disorder only during a financial crisis or some other particularly stressful situation. If such circumstances do not often occur, or if the person has skills adequate for coping with them, depressive symptoms may never appear, or may be quite mild. You will encounter the diathesis-stress model in discussions of the causes of a number of psychological disorders described in this chapter. Table 15.1 provides an example of how this approach, and the other explanatory approaches we have described, might view and treat a particular case of psychopathology.

CLASSIFYING PSYCHOLOGICAL DISORDERS

In spite of differing definitions of abnormality within and across cultures, there does seem to be a set of behavior patterns that roughly defines the range of most abnormality in most cultures. It has long been the goal of those who study abnormal behavior to establish a system of classifying such patterns in order to understand and deal with them.

In 1952 the American Psychiatric Association published the first edition of what has become the "official" North American diagnostic classification system, the *Diagnostic and Statistical Manual of Mental Disorders (DSM)*. Each subsequent edition of the DSM has included more categories. The latest edition, DSM-IV, contains more than three hundred specific diagnostic labels. Mental health professionals outside North America diagnose mental disorders using the classification system that appears as Chapter V ("Mental and Behavioural Disorders") of the World Health Organization's *International Classification of Diseases,* now in its tenth edition (ICD-10). To facilitate international communication about—and cross-cultural research on—psychopathology, DSM-IV was designed to be compatible with ICD-10. Some inconsistencies still exist between the two systems, however (Frances, Pincus & Widiger, 1996).

A Classification System: DSM-IV

DSM-IV describes the abnormal patterns of thinking, emotion, and behavior that define various mental disorders. For each disorder, DSM-IV provides specific criteria outlining the conditions that must be present before a person is given that diagnostic label. A diagnostician using DSM-IV can evaluate a person on five dimensions, or *axes,*

Here are examples of how various
approaches to disorder might
account for and treat the problems
experienced by José, a fifty-five-year-
old electronics technician. A healthy
and vigorous father of two adult
children, he was recently forced to
take medical leave because of a
series of sudden, uncontrollable
panic attacks in which he experienced dizziness, heart palpitations,
sweating, and fear of impending
death. The attacks also kept him
from his favorite pastime, scuba div-
ing, but he has been able to maintain
a part-time computer business out
of his home. (Panic disorder is discussed in more detail later in this
chapter; the outcome of the case is
described in the next chapter.)

mppc b

Explanatory Approach	Possible Cause	Possible Treatment
Medical/neurobiological	Organic disorder (brain tumor?); endocrine (e.g., thyroid) disorder	Drugs, surgery
Psychodynamic	Unconscious conflicts and desires; instinctual impulses breaking through ego defenses into consciousness, causing panic.	Psychotherapy to gain insight into unconscious
Cognitive-behavioral	Bodily stress symptoms interpreted as signs of serious illness or impending death. Receives reward in the form of relief from work stress and opportunity to work at home.	Develop cognitive coping techniques such as relaxation and noncatastrophic thinking
Phenomenological	Failure to recognize genuine feelings about work and his place in life. Fear of expressing himself.	Therapy to put him in touch with feelings about life and work
Diathesis-stress	Biologically predisposed to be overly responsive to stressors. Stress of work and extra activity exceeds capacity to cope and triggers panic as stress response.	Learn to monitor stress level, learn new stress-coping techniques, and change lifesyle as needed

which together provide a broad picture of the person's problems and their context. As
shown in Table 15.2, major mental disorders, such as schizophrenia or major depressive
disorder, would be recorded on Axis I, while personality disorders and mental retardation would be noted on Axis II. Any medical conditions that might be important in
understanding the person's mental or behavioral problems would be listed on Axis III.
On Axis IV the diagnostician would note any psychosocial and environmental problems (such as loss of a loved one, physical or sexual abuse, discrimination, unemployment, poverty, homelessness, or inadequate health care) that are important for
understanding the person's psychological problems. Finally, a rating (from 100 down
to 1) of the person's current level of psychological, social, and occupational functioning would appear on Axis V. Here is a sample of a complete DSM-IV diagnosis.

Axis I Major depressive disorder, single episode; alcohol abuse.

Axis II Dependent personality disorder.

Axis III Alcoholic cirrhosis of the liver.

Axis IV Problems with primary support group (death of spouse).

Axis V Global assessment of functioning = 50.

Because they are too vague for diagnosis, the time-honored terms *neurosis* and *psychosis* are no longer major categories in the DSM; however, mental health professionals
still sometimes use them as a shorthand description of certain clients. Neurosis refers
to conditions in which some form of anxiety is the major characteristic. Psychosis refers
to conditions involving more extreme problems that leave patients "out of touch with

TABLE 15.2	The Diagnostic and Statistical Manual (DSM) of the American Psychiatric Association

Axis I of the fourth edition (DSM-IV) lists the major categories of mental disorders. Personality disorders and mental retardation are listed on Axis II.

Axis I (Clinical Syndromes)

1. *Disorders usually first diagnosed in infancy, childhood, or adolescence*   Problems such as hyperactivity, childhood fears, abnormal aggressiveness or other notable misconduct, frequent bedwetting or soiling, and other problems in normal social and behavioral development. Autistic disorder (severe impairment in social and behavioral development), as well as other problems in the development of skill in reading, speaking, mathematics, or English.

2. *Delirium, dementia, amnestic, and other cognitive disorders*   Problems caused by physical deterioration of the brain due to aging, disease, drugs or other chemicals, or other possible unknown causes. These problems can appear as an inability to "think straight" (delirium) or as loss of memory and other intellectual functions (dementia).

3. *Substance-related disorders*   Psychological, behavioral, physical, social, or legal problems caused by dependence on or abuse of a variety of chemical substances, including alcohol, heroin, cocaine, amphetamines, hallucinogens, marijuana, and tobacco.

4. *Schizophrenia and other psychotic disorders*   Severe conditions characterized by abnormalities in thinking, perception, emotion, movement, and motivation that greatly interfere with daily functioning. Problems involving false beliefs (delusions) about such things as being loved by some high-status person, having inflated worth or power, or being persecuted, spied on, cheated on, followed, harassed, or kept from reaching important goals.

5. *Mood disorders* (also called *affective disorders*)   Severe disturbances of mood, especially depression, overexcitement (mania), or alternating episodes of each extreme (as in bipolar disorder).

6. *Anxiety disorders*   Specific fears (phobias), panic attacks, generalized feelings of dread, rituals of thought and action (obsessive-compulsive behavior) aimed at controlling anxiety, and problems caused by traumatic events, such as rape or military combat (see Chapter 13 for more on posttraumatic stress disorder).

7. *Somatoform disorders*   Physical symptoms, such as paralysis and blindness, that have no physical cause. Unusual preoccupation with physical health or with nonexistent or elusive physical problems (hypochondriasis, somatization disorder, pain disorder).

8. *Factitious disorders*   False mental disorders, which are intentionally produced to satisfy some psychological need.

9. *Dissociative disorders*   Psychologically caused problems of consciousness and self-identification, e.g., loss of memory (amnesia) or the development of more than one identity (multiple personality).

10. *Sexual and gender identity disorders*   Problems of (a) finding sexual arousal through unusual objects or situations (like baby shoes or exposing oneself), (b) unsatisfactory sexual activity (sexual dysfunction; see Chapter 11), or (c) identifying with the opposite gender.

11. *Eating disorders*   Problems associated with eating too little (anorexia nervosa) or binge eating followed by self-induced vomiting (bulimia nervosa). (See Chapter 11.)

12. *Sleep disorders*   Severe problems involving the sleep-wake cycle, especially an inability to sleep well at night or to stay awake during the day. (See Chapter 6.)

13. *Impulse control disorders*   Compulsive gambling, stealing, or fire setting.

14. *Adjustment disorders*   Failure to adjust to or deal well with such stressors as divorce, financial problems, family discord, or other unhappy life events.

Axis II (Personality Disorders and Mental Retardation)

1. *Personality disorders*   Diagnostic labels given to individuals who may or may not receive an Axis I diagnosis but who show lifelong behavior patterns that are unsatisfactory to them or that disturb other people. The problematic features of their personality may involve unusual suspiciousness, unusual ways of thinking, self-centeredness, shyness, overdependency, excessive concern with neatness and detail, or overemotionality, among others.

2. *Mental retardation*   As described in Chapter 10, the label of mental retardation is applied to individuals whose measured IQ is less than about 70 *and* who fail to display the skill at daily living, communication, and other tasks expected of those their age.

reality" or unable to function on a daily basis. The disorders once gathered under these headings now appear in various Axis I categories in DSM-IV.

Purposes and Problems of Diagnosis

A major goal in diagnosing psychological disorders is to determine the nature of clients' problems so that the characteristics of these problems and the courses they take can be predicted, then treated by administration of the most appropriate methods. Diagnoses are also important for research on the causes of mental disorders. If researchers can accurately and reliably classify patients into groups with similar disorders, they will have a better chance of spotting commonalities in genetic features, biological abnormalities, and environmental experiences that might differentiate people in one disorder group from those in other groups, thereby providing clues to the origins of various problems.

How good is the diagnostic system? *Interrater reliability,* the degree to which different diagnosticians give the same person the same diagnostic label, has improved considerably for many diagnoses since about 1980, when, in DSM-III, broad, vague symptom descriptions were replaced with specific criteria for assigning each diagnosis. Some studies indicate interrater agreement as high as 83 percent on schizophrenia and mood disorders; agreement on many other Axis I categories is also considered high (Corty, Lehman & Myers, 1993; Foa & Kozak, 1995; Lahey et al., 1994; Yutzy et al., 1995). Still other categories—such as the Axis II personality disorders—remain more difficult to diagnose reliably.

Do diagnostic labels give accurate information about people? This *validity* question is difficult to answer because it is hard to find a fully acceptable standard for accuracy: Should a diagnosis be compared to the judgments of experts? Or should its predictions be tested against the course of the patient's disorder? Still, there is evidence to support the validity of some DSM criteria (Drake & Vaillant, 1985; Robins & Helzer, 1986). And validity is likely to improve further as diagnostic labels are refined in future editions of DSM to reflect what researchers are learning about the characteristics, causes, courses, and treatments of various disorders.

The diagnostic system is far from perfect, however. First, people's problems often do not fit neatly into a single category. Second, the same symptoms may appear as part of more than one disorder. Third, diagnostic judgments are to some extent subjective, raising the possibility that personal bias might creep into the labeling system. All of these factors can lead to misdiagnosis in some cases. Psychiatrist Thomas Szasz (pronounced "zaws") and other critics of the medical model also argue that labeling *people* instead of describing problems is dehumanizing because it ignores features that make each person's case unique. Calling people schizophrenics or alcoholics, he says, actually encourages the behaviors associated with these labels and undermines the confidence of clients (and therapists) about the chances of improvement (Szasz, 1987).

Indeed, no shorthand label can specify each person's problems or predict exactly how that person will behave in the future. All that can be reasonably expected of a diagnostic system is that it allows informative, general descriptions of the types of problems displayed by people who have been placed in different categories.

Some researchers and clinicians suggest that bias among diagnosticians contributes to problems with the reliability and validity of diagnostic labels. Like other people, diagnosticians hold expectations about certain groups of people, and such cognitive biases could color their judgments about how to label the behavior displayed by members of these groups.

THINKING CRITICALLY

Is Psychological Diagnosis Biased?

What am I being asked to believe or accept?

It has been alleged that a woman will be given a different, probably more severe, diagnosis than a man who presents similar symptoms, and that simply because they are members of a particular ethnic group, some people are diagnosed as suffering certain disorders more often than those in other groups. Gender is indeed an important variable—some disorders occur more often in men, others more often in women—but significant gender bias in diagnosis has not been found even though it has been studied intensely (Matlin, 1993; Mowbray, Herman & Hazel, 1992). Here, we focus on ethnicity as a possible biasing factor. It is of special interest because there is evidence that ethnicity, like social class and gender, is an important variable in the development of mental illness. Thus the argument to be considered here is that clinicians in the United States base their diagnoses partly on the ethnic group to which their clients belong and, more specifically, that there is bias in diagnosing African-Americans.

What evidence is available to support the assertion?

Several facts suggest the possibility of ethnic bias in psychological diagnosis. For example, African-Americans receive the diagnosis of schizophrenia more frequently than European-Americans do (Manderscheid & Barrett, 1987). Further, relative to their presence in the general population, African-Americans are overrepresented in public mental hospitals, where the most serious forms of disorder are seen, and underrepresented in private hospitals and outpatient clinics, where less severe problems are treated (Lindsey & Paul, 1989; Snowden & Cheung, 1990).

Are there alternative ways of interpreting the evidence?

Differences between ethnic groups in diagnosis or treatment do not automatically point to bias based on ethnicity. Perhaps real differences in psychological functioning are associated with different ethnic groups. For example, if, on the average, African-Americans are exposed to more poverty, violence, or other major stressors, they could be more vulnerable to more serious forms of mental disorder. And poverty, not diagnostic bias, could be responsible for the fact that African-Americans seek help more often at less expensive public hospitals rather than at more expensive private ones.

What additional evidence would help to evaluate the alternatives?

Do African-Americans actually display more signs of mental disorder, or do diagnosticians just perceive them as more disordered? One way of approaching this question would be to conduct experiments in which diagnosticians assign labels to clients on the basis of case histories, test scores, and the like. Unknown to the diagnosticians, the cases would be selected so that pairs of clients show about the same objective amount of disorder, but one member of the pair is identified as European-American, the other as African-American. Bias among the clinicians would be suggested if the African-American member of each pair more often received a diagnosis—or a more severe diagnosis. Unfortunately, studies like this are difficult to conduct in clinical settings.

A strategy that has been used with real clinical populations is to perform statistical analyses to identify the factors that influence clinicians' diagnostic judgments following extensive interviews with patients. If, after controlling for the type and severity of symptoms, a researcher discovers that African-Americans are still diagnosed with a certain disorder more often than European-Americans, evidence for bias would be rather strong. Studies conducted in hospital settings with African-American and European-American patients show that African-Americans are indeed more frequently diagnosed as schizophrenic (Pavkov, Lewis & Lyons, 1989). In contrast, a large-scale study of mental disorder found that when people were interviewed and diagnosed in their own homes, the diagnosis of schizophrenia was given only slightly more often to African-Americans than to European-Americans (Snowden & Cheung, 1990; Robins et al., 1984). In other words, there is little evidence that schizophrenia is more common among African-Americans in the community, but they appear more likely to receive this diagnosis when entering a hospital. Thus the presence of ethnic bias is suggested, at least in some diagnoses.

What conclusions are most reasonable?

Just as DSM-IV is imperfect, so are those who use it. Bias does not necessarily reflect deliberate discrimination, however; it may be unintentional. Chapters 9 and 17, on thinking and social cognition respectively, describe how cognitive biases and stereotypes shape human thought in matters large and small. No matter how precisely researchers specify the ideal criteria for assigning diagnostic labels, those biases and stereotypes still threaten the objectivity of the diagnostic process.

Minimizing diagnostic bias requires a better understanding of it. Steven Lopez (1989) emphasizes the need to recognize and understand the limitations in information processing that affect clinicians, while Hope Landrine (1991) stresses the need for understanding the sociocultural bases of our concepts of normality and abnormality. Research on memory, problem solving, decision making, social attributions, and other aspects of culture and cognition may indeed turn out to be key ingredients in reducing bias in the diagnosis of psychological disorders.

We do not have the space to cover all the DSM-IV categories, so we will sample several of the most prevalent, socially significant, or unusual examples. As you read, try not to catch "medical student's disease." Just as medical students often think they have the symptoms of every illness they read about, some psychology students worry that their behavior (or that of a relative or friend) signals a mental disorder. Remember that everyone has problems sometimes. Before deciding that you or someone you know needs psychological help, see if the nature and frequency of the behavior qualify it as abnormal according to the criteria of the practical approach.

ANXIETY DISORDERS

If you have ever been tense before an exam, a date, or a job interview, you have a good idea of what anxiety feels like. Increased heart rate, sweating, rapid breathing, a dry mouth, and a sense of dread are common components of anxiety. Brief episodes of moderate anxiety are a normal part of life for most people. For others, anxiety is so intense, long standing, or disruptive that it is called an **anxiety disorder.**

Types of Anxiety Disorders

We discuss four types of anxiety disorders: phobia, generalized anxiety disorder, panic disorder, and obsessive-compulsive disorder. Another type, called posttraumatic stress disorder, is described in Chapter 13, on health, stress, and coping. Together, these are the most common psychological disorders in the United States.

Phobia An intense, irrational fear of an object or situation that is not likely to be dangerous is called a **phobia.** The phobic person usually realizes that the fear makes no sense, but the discomfort and consequent avoidance of the object or event may greatly interfere with daily life. Thousands of phobias have been described (see Table 15.3).

DSM-IV classifies phobias into specific, social, and agoraphobia subtypes. **Specific phobias** involve fear and avoidance of heights, blood, animals, automobile or air travel, and other specific stimuli and situations. They are the most prevalent of the anxiety disorders, affecting 7 to 10 percent of U.S. adults and children (Kessler et al., 1994; Robins et al., 1984). Here is an example.

Mr. L. was a fifty-year-old office worker who became terrified whenever he had to drive over a bridge. For years, he avoided bridges by taking roundabout ways to and from work, and he refused to be a passenger in anyone else's car, lest they use a bridge. Even this very

As their name implies, specific phobias usually focus on specific objects or situations. They can sometimes be unusual enough to be grist for the humor mill, but the discomfort and dysfunction caused by any severe phobia are no laughing matter.

Luposlipaphobia: The fear of being pursued by timber wolves around a kitchen table while wearing socks on a newly waxed floor.

TABLE 15.3			
Common Phobias			

Phobia is the Greek word for morbid fear, after the lesser Greek god, Phobos. Phobias are usually named using the Greek word for the feared object or situation, followed by the suffix *phobia*.

Name	Feared Stimulus	Name	Feared Stimulus
Acrophobia	Heights	Aerophobia	Flying
Claustrophobia	Enclosed places	Entomophobia	Insects
Hematophobia	Blood	Gamophobia	Marriage
Gephyrophobia	Crossing a bridge	Ophdophobia	Snakes
Kenophobia	Empty rooms	Xenophobia	Strangers
Cynophobia	Dogs	Melissophobia	Bees

inconvenient adjustment failed when Mr. L. was transferred to a position requiring frequent automobile trips, many of which were over bridges. He refused the transfer and was fired.

Social phobias involve anxiety about being negatively evaluated by others or acting in a way that is embarrassing or humiliating. The anxiety is so intense and persistent that the person's normal functioning is impaired. Common social phobias are fear of public speaking, "stage fright," fear of eating in front of others, and fear of using public rest rooms. *Generalized social phobia* is a more severe and perhaps distinct form of social phobia in which fear occurs in virtually all social situations (Mannuzza et al., 1995).

Agoraphobia is a strong fear of being separated from a safe place like home or from a safe person, such as a spouse or close friend, or of being trapped in a place from which escape might be difficult or where help may be unavailable. Attempts to leave home lead to intense anxiety, so severe agoraphobics seldom even try to go out alone. Theaters, shopping malls, public transportation, and other potentially crowded places are particularly avoided because the person fears becoming helpless and incapacitated by some calamity, including an attack of intense anxiety or panic.

Like other phobias in Western cultures, agoraphobia is more often reported by women, many of whom are totally homebound by the time they seek help. Note, however, that in India, where homebound women are considered less unusual than in the United States, the people labeled agoraphobic tend to be male (Raguram & Bhide, 1985). Although agoraphobia occurs less frequently than specific phobias (affecting

CULTURE-SPECIFIC PHOBIA Sociocultural factors can alter the form of social phobias. In Japan, for example, where cultural training emphasizes group-oriented values and goals, a common social phobia is *Tai-jin Kyofu Sho,* fear of embarrassing those around you (Kleinknecht et al., 1994).

about 2.5 percent of the U.S. population), it is the phobia that most often leads people to seek treatment, mainly because it so severely disrupts everyday life (Barlow, 1988).

Generalized Anxiety Disorder   Excessive and long-lasting anxiety that is not focused on any particular object or situation marks **generalized anxiety disorder.** Because the problem occurs in virtually all situations and because the person cannot pinpoint its source, this type of anxiety is sometimes called *free-floating anxiety.* For weeks at a time, the person feels anxious and worried, sure that some disaster is imminent. The person becomes jumpy and irritable; sound sleep is impossible. Fatigue, inability to concentrate, and physiological signs of anxiety are also common (Borkovec & Inz, 1990). Generalized anxiety disorder affects about 5 percent of the U.S. population at some point in their lives (Kessler et al., 1994). It is more common in women, often accompanying other problems such as depression or substance abuse (Wittchen et al., 1994).

Panic Disorder   For some people, anxiety takes the form of **panic disorder.** Like the man described in Table 15.1, people suffering from panic disorder experience recurrent terrifying *panic attacks* that often come without warning or obvious cause and are marked by intense heart palpitations, pressure or pain in the chest, dizziness or unsteadiness, sweating, and a feeling of faintness; often, victims believe they are having a heart attack. They may worry constantly about suffering future panic episodes and thus curtail activities to avoid possible embarrassment. In fact, it is often the fear of experiencing panic attacks that leads to agoraphobia (Barlow, 1988); the person begins to fear and avoid places where help won't be available should panic recur. Panic disorder may become chronic, with periods of improvement followed by recurrence (Ehlers, 1995). As many as 30 percent of the U.S. population have experienced at least one panic attack within the past year, though in most cases this does not lead to full-blown panic disorder (Ehlers, 1995). Here is a case that did.

Geri, a thirty-two-year-old nurse, had her first panic attack while driving on a freeway. Afterward, she would not drive on freeways. Her next attack occurred while with a patient and a doctor in a small examining room. A sense of impending doom flooded over her and she burst out of the office and into the parking lot, where she felt immediate relief. From then on, fear of another attack made it impossible for her to tolerate any close quarters, including crowded shopping malls. She eventually quit her job because of terror of the examining rooms.

Obsessive-Compulsive Disorder   Anxiety is also the root of **obsessive-compulsive disorder (OCD).** As with Mark, whose case opened this chapter, people displaying obsessive-compulsive disorder are plagued by persistent, upsetting, and unwanted thoughts—called *obsessions*—that often revolve around the possibility of infection, contamination, or doing harm to oneself or others. These obsessive thoughts may then motivate repetitive behaviors—called *compulsions*—that the person believes will prevent infection, aggressive acts, or other events associated with the obsessions (Foa & Kozak, 1995). Mark engaged in incessant, ritualized cleaning to protect himself from infection; other common compulsions include rituals such as checking locks, repeating words, images, or numbers, counting things, or arranging objects "just so." Obsessions and compulsions are much more intense than the familiar experience of having a repetitive thought or tune "in the back of your mind" or rechecking that a door is locked. In OCD, the obsessions and compulsions are intense, disturbing, and often bizarre intrusions that can severely impair daily activities (DSM-IV defines compulsions as occupying more than one hour a day). Many of those who display OCD recognize the irrationality of their thoughts and actions, but still experience severe agitation and anxiety if they try to interrupt their obsessions or give up their compulsive behaviors.

Causes of Anxiety Disorders

As with all the forms of psychopathology we will consider, the exact causes of anxiety disorders are a matter of debate. All theoretical approaches offer explanations. Research suggests that biological factors, distortions in thinking, and learning are particularly important (Stemberger et al., 1995; Rachman, 1989).

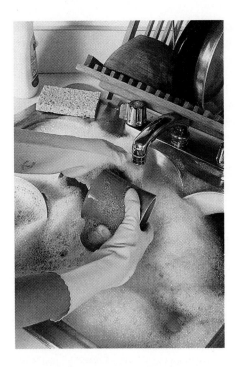

LINKAGES: A CLEANING COMPULSION Obsessive-compulsive disorder is diagnosed when a culturally expected degree of cleanliness evolves into an obsessive preoccupation with germs and a life-disrupting compulsion to clean things. Though learning and stress appear to play the major role in shaping and triggering this and other anxiety disorders, biological factors, including genetically inherited characteristics and deficiencies in certain neurotransmitters (see Chapter 3), may result in an oversensitive nervous system and a predisposition toward anxiety.

Biological Factors   Their genes may predispose some people to anxiety disorders. Research indicates, for example, that if one identical twin has an anxiety disorder, his or her co-twin is more likely also to have an anxiety disorder than is the case in nonidentical twin pairs (Torgersen, 1983). Most anxiety disorders, such as panic disorder, obsessive-compulsive disorder, and generalized social phobia appear to run in families (Kendler et al., 1995; Pauls et al., 1995; Wittchen et al., 1994). Perhaps, then, anxiety disorders develop out of a physiological predisposition to react with anxiety to a wide range of situations, a predisposition which results, in part, from inheriting an autonomic system that is oversensitive to stress (e.g., Barlow, 1988).

The predisposition to anxiety disorders may be based on abnormalities in neurotransmitter systems. Excessive activity of norepinephrine in certain parts of the brain has been linked with panic disorder, and excessive serotonin has been associated with obsessive-compulsive disorder (Gorman et al., 1989; Lickey & Gordon, 1991). In addition, there is evidence that anxiety-generating neural impulses may run unchecked when the neurotransmitter GABA is prevented from exerting its normal inhibitory influence in certain neural pathways (Friedman, Clark & Gershon, 1992; Zorumski & Isenberg, 1991).

Something may also be physically wrong in people with panic disorder. Unlike other people, many of these individuals have a panic episode after receiving an injection of lactate or caffeine, inhaling carbon dioxide, or taking yohimbine (a drug that blocks one type of norepinephrine receptor) (Papp et al., 1993). Because these substances all stimulate brainstem areas that control the autonomic nervous system, one hypothesis is that panic-disorder patients have hypersensitive brainstem mechanisms and are therefore especially prone to fear responses (Gorman et al., 1989).

While biological predispositions may set the stage for anxiety disorders, most researchers agree that environmental stressors and psychological factors, including cognitive processes and learning, bring about most anxiety disorders (Barlow, 1988; Ley, 1994).

Cognitive Factors   Persons suffering from an anxiety disorder may exaggerate the dangers in their environment, thereby creating an unrealistic expectation that bad events are going to happen (Mogg et al., 1993; Tomarken, Mineka & Cook, 1989). In addition, they tend to underestimate their own capacity for dealing with threatening events, resulting in anxiety and desperation when feared events do occur (Beck & Emery, 1985; Telch et al., 1989).

As an example, consider the development of a panic attack. Whereas the appearance of unexplained symptoms of physical arousal may set the stage for a panic attack, the person's cognitive interpretation of those symptoms can determine whether or not the attack actually develops. In one study of panic attacks induced by breathing air rich in carbon dioxide, some subjects were told that they could control the amount of carbon dioxide they were inhaling by turning a dial on a control panel. Others were told they could not control it. In fact, the dial had no effect for either group, but subjects who experienced the illusion of control were far less likely to have a full-blown panic attack (Rapee et al., 1992). In another study, panic disorder patients who inhaled carbon dioxide in the presence of a person they associated with safety were significantly less fearful than patients whose "safe person" was not present (Carter et al., 1995). Results like these suggest the existence of a role for cognitive factors in panic disorder.

LINKAGES: PSYCHOLOGICAL DISORDERS AND LEARNING

Can we learn to become abnormal?

Upsetting thoughts—about money or illness, for example—are often difficult to dismiss, especially when people are under stress or feel incapable of dealing effectively with the problems they are worried about. As the thoughts become more persistent, they engender increased anxiety. If an action such as cleaning temporarily relieves the anxiety, that action may be strengthened through the process of negative reinforcement dis-

I FEEL YOUR PAIN   As her baby receives an injection, this mother shows the pain she feels, too. Many phobias, including those of needles, blood, and medically related situations are acquired vicariously. Fear developed through observational learning can be as strong as through direct experience (Kleinknecht 1991), though direct conditioning is the more common pathway to phobia (Öst, 1992).

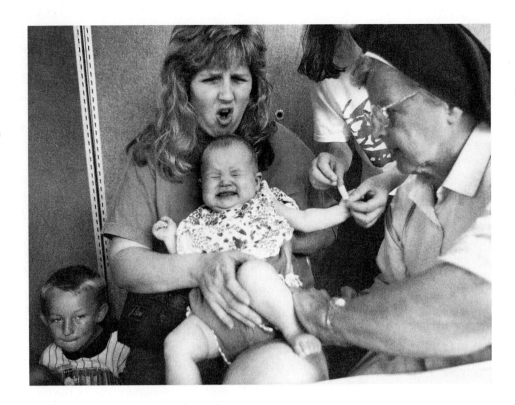

cussed in Chapter 7. But such actions do nothing to eliminate the obsessive thoughts and so become compulsive, endlessly repeated rituals that keep the person trapped in a vicious circle of anxiety (Barlow, 1988). Thus, according to the cognitive-behavioral approach, obsessive-compulsive disorder might be a pattern that is sparked by distressing thoughts and maintained by operant conditioning.

Phobias may also be explained in part by the principles of classical conditioning described in Chapter 7. The object of the phobia becomes an aversive conditioned stimulus through association with a traumatic event that acts as an unconditioned stimulus (Öst, 1992). Fear of dogs, for example, may result from a dog attack. Observing or hearing about other people's bad experiences can produce the same result; most people who fear flying have never been in a plane crash. Once the fear is learned, avoidance of the feared object prevents the person from finding out that there is no need to be afraid. This cycle of avoidance helps explain why many fears do not simply extinguish, or disappear, on their own.

Why are phobias about snakes and spiders so common even though people are seldom harmed by them? And why are there so few cases of electrical-outlet phobia when people are frequently shocked by them? As discussed in the chapter on learning, the answer may be that people are *biologically prepared* to learn associations between certain stimuli and certain responses. These stimuli and responses, then, would be especially easy to link through conditioning (Hamm, Vaitl & Lang, 1989). Specifically, people may be biologically prepared to learn to fear and to avoid stimuli that had the potential to harm their evolutionary ancestors (Seligman, 1971; Staddon & Ettinger, 1989).

Some laboratory evidence supports the notion that people are biologically prepared to learn certain phobias. A group of Swedish psychologists attempted to classically condition people to fear certain stimuli by associating the stimuli with electric shocks (Öhman, Dimberg & Öst, 1985; Öhman, Erixon & Lofberg, 1975). The subjects developed approximately equal conditioned anxiety reactions to slides of houses, human faces, and snakes. Later, however, when they were tested without shock, the reaction to snakes remained long after the houses and faces had failed to elicit a fear response. A series of investigations with animals has also supported preparedness theory (Cook & Mineka, 1990). If a monkey sees another monkey behaving fearfully in the presence of

BIOLOGICAL PREPAREDNESS Having a predisposition to learn fear of snakes and other potentially dangerous stimuli makes evolutionary sense. Animals (and humans) who rapidly learn a fear response to objects or situations that they see frightening their parents or peers are more likely to survive to pass on their genes to the next generation.

a live or toy snake, it quickly develops a strong and persistent fear of snakes. However, if the snake is entwined in flowers, the observer monkeys come to fear only the snake, not the flowers (Cook & Mineka, 1987). Thus the fear conditioning was selective, focusing only on potentially dangerous creatures such as snakes or crocodiles (Zinbarg & Mineka, 1991), not on harmless stimuli. Data like these suggest that anxiety disorders probably arise through the combined effects of genetic predispositions and learning.

SOMATOFORM DISORDERS

Sometimes people show symptoms of a *somatic*, or physical, disorder, even though there is no physical cause. Because these are psychological problems that take somatic form, such conditions are called **somatoform disorders.** The classic example is **conversion disorder,** a condition in which a person appears to be, but is not, blind, deaf, paralyzed, or insensitive to pain in various parts of the body. (An earlier term for this disorder was *hysteria*.) Conversion disorders are rare, accounting for only about 2 percent of diagnoses. Although they can occur at any point in life, they usually appear in adolescence or early adulthood.

Conversion disorders differ from true physical disabilities in several ways. First, they tend to appear when a person is under severe stress. Second, they often help reduce that stress by enabling the person to avoid unpleasant situations. Third, the person may show remarkably little concern about what is apparently a rather serious problem. Finally, the symptoms may be organically impossible or improbable, as Figure 15.2 illustrates. One university student, for example, experienced visual impairment that began each Sunday evening and became total blindness by Monday morning. Her vision would begin to return on Friday evenings and was fully restored in time for weekend football games and other social activities. She expressed no undue concern over her condition (Holmes, 1991).

Can people with a conversion disorder see and hear, even though they act as though they cannot? Experiments show that they can (Grosz & Zimmerman, 1970), but this does not necessarily mean that they are malingering, or lying. Research described in Chapter 6, on consciousness, suggests that people can use sensory input even when they are not consciously aware of doing so (Schacter, Chiu & Ochsner, 1993). Rather than destroying visual or auditory ability, the conversion process may prevent the person from being aware of information that the brain is still processing.

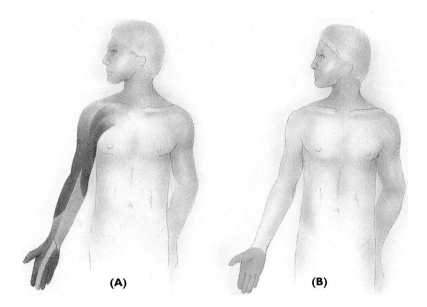

FIGURE 15.2

Glove Anesthesia

In this conversion disorder, lack of feeling stops abruptly at the wrist (B). But as shown in (A) the nerves of the hand and arm blend, so if they were actually impaired, part of the arm would also lose sensitivity. Other neurologically impossible symptoms of conversion disorder include sleepwalking at night on legs that are "paralyzed" during the day.

(A)   (B)

Another form of somatoform disorder is **hypochondriasis,** a strong, unjustified fear that one has, or might get, cancer, heart disease, AIDS, or other serious physical problems. The fear prompts frequent visits to physicians and reports of numerous symptoms. Their preoccupation with illness often leads hypochondriacs to become "experts" on their most feared diseases. In a related condition called **somatization disorder,** individuals make dramatic but often vague reports about a multitude of physical problems rather than any specific illness. **Pain disorder** is marked by complaints of severe, often constant pain (typically in the neck, chest, or back) with no physical cause.

Traditional explanations of somatoform disorders focus on the origins of conversion disorder. Freud believed that it results when anxiety related to unconscious conflict is converted into physical symptoms. (This belief is the source of the term *conversion.*) In explaining somatoform disorders, behavioral as well as psychodynamic theorists point out that these disorders can produce benefits by relieving sufferers of unpleasant responsibilities. Or perhaps some youngsters who endured stressful childhoods learned that illness is associated with nurturance (e.g., Barsky et al., 1994). Sociocultural factors may also shape some somatoform disorders. In many Asian, Latin American, and African cultures, people commonly channel psychological or interpersonal conflicts into headaches and other physical symptoms, whereas in North America such conflicts are more likely to result in anxiety or depression (Brislin, 1993). Genetic factors do not seem to be important in somatoform disorders.

DISSOCIATIVE DISORDERS

A sudden and usually temporary disruption in a person's memory, consciousness, or identity characterizes **dissociative disorders.** Temporary dissociative states are familiar to most people, as when, for example, after many hours of highway driving they suddenly realize they have little or no recollection of what happened during the last half-hour. Dissociative disorders are more intense and long lasting, as in the case of John, a thirty-year-old computer manufacturing executive. John was a meek person who was dependent on his wife for companionship and support. It came as a jolt when she announced that she was leaving him to live with his younger brother. John did not go to work the next day. In fact, nothing was heard from him for two weeks. Then he was arrested for public drunkenness and assault in a city more than three hundred miles from his home. The police discovered that during those two weeks John lived under another name at a cheap hotel and worked selling tickets at a pornographic movie theater. When he was interviewed, John did not know his real name or his home address, could not explain how he reached his present location, and could not remember much about the previous two weeks.

John's case illustrates the dissociative disorder known as **dissociative fugue,** which is characterized by a sudden loss of personal memory and the adoption of a new identity in a new locale. Another dissociative disorder, **dissociative amnesia,** also involves sudden memory loss. As in fugue, all personal identifying information may be forgotten, but the person does not leave home or create a new identity. These rare conditions usually last only hours or days, but they tend to attract intense publicity because they are so perplexing.

The most famous dissociative disorder is **dissociative identity disorder (DID),** formerly known—and still commonly called—*multiple personality disorder (MPD)*. DID is a condition in which a person has more than one identity, each of which speaks, acts, and writes in a very different way. Each personality seems to have its own memories, wishes, and (often conflicting) impulses. Here is a case example:

A 42-year-old woman was brought to a psychiatrist by her husband, who complained that during arguments about money or other matters, she would suddenly either change into uncharacteristically flamboyant clothes and go to a nearby bar to flirt with strangers, or curl up on the floor and talk as if she were a young child. An interview conducted under hypnosis revealed that during these times she experienced being "Frieda," the girlfriend of a Russian soldier who had been sexually molested in her native Poland after World War II. Once hypnosis was terminated, she had no memory of "Frieda." (Spitzer et al., 1989)

How do dissociative disorders develop? Psychodynamic theorists see massive repression of unwanted impulses or memories as the basis for creating a "new person" who acts out otherwise unacceptable impulses or recalls otherwise unbearable memories. Behavioral theorists focus on the fact that everyone is capable of behaving in different ways depending on circumstances (for example, boisterous in a bar, quiet in a museum) and that, in rare cases, this variation can become so extreme that a person feels and is perceived by others as a "different person." Further, an individual may be rewarded for a sudden memory loss or unusual behavior by escaping stressful situations, responsibilities, or punishment for misdeeds.

Evaluating these hypotheses has been difficult in part because of the rarity of dissociative disorders. Recently, however, DID has been diagnosed more frequently, either because clinicians are looking for it more carefully or because the conditions leading to it are more prevalent. One study in Canada speculated that between 5 and 10 percent

A FAMOUS CASE OF DISSOCIATIVE IDENTITY DISORDER   Chris Sizemore's dissociative identity disorder inspired the book and movie *The Three Faces of Eve*. Dramatizations of such cases, including that of *Sybil,* show that shifts among personalities are sudden, dramatic, and often stress-related. Ms. Sizemore, an artist, no longer displays her former disorder.

IN REVIEW	Anxiety, Somatoform, and Dissociative Disorders	
Disorder	**Subtypes**	**Major Symptoms**
Anxiety disorders	Phobias	Intense, irrational fear of objectively non-dangerous situations or things, leading to disruptions of behavior.
	Generalized anxiety disorder	Excessive anxiety not focused on a specific situation or object; free-floating anxiety.
	Panic disorder	Repeated attacks of intense fear involving physical symptoms such as faintness, dizziness, and nausea.
	Obsessive-compulsive disorder	Persistent ideas or worries accompanied by ritualistic behaviors performed to neutralize the anxiety-driven thoughts.
Somatoform disorders	Conversion disorder	A loss of physical ability (e.g., sight, hearing) that is related to psychological factors.
	Hypochondriasis	Preoccupation with or belief that one has serious illness in the absence of any physical evidence.
	Pain disorder	Preoccupation with pain in the absence of physical reasons for the pain.
Dissociative disorders	Amnesia/fugue	Sudden, unexpected loss of memory, which may result in relocation and the assumption of a new identity.
	Dissociative identity disorder (multiple personality disorder)	Appearance within same person of two or more distinct personalities, each with a unique way of thinking and behaving.

of the adult population may suffer from some form of dissociative disorder (Ross, Joshi & Currie, 1990). Research available so far suggests three conclusions. First, many people displaying multiple personality disorder have experienced events they would like to forget or avoid. The majority (some clinicians believe all) have suffered severe, unavoidable, persistent abuse in childhood (Ross et al., 1991). Second, most of these people appear to be skilled at self-hypnosis, through which they can induce a trance-like state. Third, most found that they could escape the trauma of abuse at least temporarily by creating "new personalities" to deal with stress (Ross et al., 1990, 1991). However, not all abused children display DID, and it has been suggested that some cases of DID may be triggered by media stories or even suggestions made to clients by their therapists. From this sociocultural perspective, the increased incidence of DID may reflect its status as a socially approved method of expressing distress (Spanos, 1994). Research on the existence and effects of repressed memories—discussed in Chapter 8, on memory—is sure to have an impact on our understanding of, and the controversy over, the causes of dissociative identity disorder. ("In Review: Anxiety, Somatoform, and Dissociative Disorders" presents a summary of our discussion of these topics.)

MOOD DISORDERS

Everyone's mood, or *affect*, tends to rise and fall from time to time. However, when people experience extremes of mood—wild elation or deep depression—for long periods, when they shift from one extreme to another, and especially when their moods are not consistent with the events around them, they are said to show a **mood disorder** (also known as *affective disorder*). We will describe two main types: depressive disorders and bipolar disorders.

Depressive Disorders

Depression can range from occasional, normal "down" periods to episodes severe enough to require hospitalization. A person suffering **major depressive disorder** feels sad and overwhelmed for weeks or months, typically losing interest in activities and relationships and taking pleasure in nothing (Coryell et al., 1993). Exaggerated feelings of inadequacy, worthlessness, hopelessness, or guilt are common. Despite one's best efforts, everything, from conversation to bathing, is an unbearable, exhausting effort. Changes in eating habits resulting in weight loss or, sometimes, weight gain often accompany major depressive disorder, as does sleep disturbance or, less often, excessive sleeping. Problems in working, concentrating, making decisions, and thinking clearly are also common. In extreme cases, depressed people may express false beliefs, or **delusions**—worrying, for example, that the government is planning to punish them. Major depressive disorder may come on suddenly or gradually. It may consist of a single episode or, more commonly, repeated depressive periods. Here is one case example:

Mr. J. was a fifty-one-year-old industrial engineer. . . . Since the death of his wife five years earlier, he had been suffering from continuing episodes of depression marked by extreme social withdrawal and occasional thoughts of suicide. . . . He drank, and when thoroughly intoxicated would plead to his deceased wife for forgiveness. He lost all capacity for joy. . . . Once a gourmet, he now had no interest in food and good wine . . . and could barely manage to engage in small talk. As might be expected, his work record deteriorated markedly. Appointments were missed and projects haphazardly started and left unfinished. (From Davison & Neale, 1990, p. 221)

Many cases of depression do not become this extreme. A less severe pattern of depression is called **dysthymic disorder,** in which the person shows the sad mood, lack of interest, and loss of pleasure associated with major depression, but less intensely and for a longer period. (The duration must be at least two years to qualify as dysthymic disorder.) Mental and behavioral disruption are also less severe; most people exhibiting dysthymic disorder do not require hospitalization.

Major depressive disorder occurs sometime in the lives of up to 20 percent of the North American or European population; at any given time, about 5 percent of these people are affected (Blazer et al., 1994; Smith & Weissman, 1992). Anyone can become depressed, but major depressive disorder is most likely to appear during the late teenage and early adult years (Burke et al., 1990); there is also evidence that rates of depression are increasing among young people (Cross-National Collaborative Group, 1992). Worldwide, women are two to three times more likely than men to experience depression (Nolen-Hoeksma, 1990).

Suicide and Depression   Suicide is associated with a variety of psychological disorders, but it is most closely tied to depression; some form of depression has been implicated in 40 to 60 percent of suicides (Clark & Fawcett, 1992; Fowler, Rich & Young, 1986). Indeed, suicidal thoughts are a symptom of depressive disorders. Hopelessness about the future—another depressive symptom—and a desire to seek instant escape from problems are also related to suicide attempts (Beck et al., 1990).

Suicide rates differ considerably depending on sociocultural variables such as age, gender, and ethnicity. The rate is as high as 25 per 100,000 individuals in some northern European countries and Japan, for example, and as low as 6 per 100,000 in countries with stronger religious prohibitions against suicide, such as Greece, Italy, Ireland, and the Middle East. In the United States, where the overall rate is about 12 per 100,000, suicides are most common among people sixty-five and older (Centers for Disease Control, 1996). However, since 1950 suicide among adolescents—especially fifteen- to nineteen-year-olds—has quadrupled; it is now the third leading cause of death among

A SUICIDE ATTEMPT **Between 240,000 and 600,000 people in the United States and Canada attempt suicide each year; over 30,000 succeed (McIntosh, 1991). Worldwide, the annual death toll from suicide is 120,000. Suicide is the second leading cause of death among college students; about ten thousand try to kill themselves each year, and about one thousand succeed. This rate is much higher than for 18 to 24-year-olds in general, but much lower than for the elderly (McIntosh, 1992).**

adolescents (Berman & Jobes, 1991; Garland & Zigler, 1993). Women attempt suicide three times as often as men, but men are twice as likely to actually kill themselves (Rockett & Smith, 1989; U.S. Bureau of the Census, 1987). It has been suggested that male attempters are more intent on dying and thus tend to choose more lethal means, while the tendency of females to choose less lethal methods reflects an effort to communicate the urgency of their problems or the intensity of their emotional distress.

Suicide rates also differ across ethnic groups in the United States. For example, although there is wide variation from tribe to tribe, the overall rate for American Indians is 13.6 per 100,000, compared to 12.9 for European-Americans, 9.1 for Asian-Americans, 7.5 for Hispanic-Americans, and 5.7 for African-Americans (Garland & Zigler, 1993; Howard-Pitney et al., 1992; McIntosh, 1992). The suicide rate among adolescent European-American males has stabilized since 1986, but it has continued to increase among African-American male teens (Shaffer, Gould & Hicks, 1994).

Predicting exactly who will commit suicide is very difficult. For one thing, suicidal thoughts are quite common—54 percent of one sample of college students reported having such thoughts (Meehan et al., 1992). Still, the results of hundreds of research studies provide some predictive guidelines. In the United States, at least, suicide is most likely among European-American males, especially those over forty-five, single or divorced, and living alone. The risk of suicide is also heightened among people who have made a specific plan and given away possessions (Clark et al., 1989). A previous suicide attempt may not always be a good predictor of eventual suicide, because such attempts may have been help-seeking gestures, not failed efforts to die. In fact, although about 10 percent of unsuccessful attempters try again and succeed, most people who commit suicide had made no prior attempts (Clark & Fawcett, 1992).

One myth about suicide is that people who talk about it will never try it. On the contrary, those who say they are thinking of suicide are much *more* likely to try suicide than people from the general population. In fact, according to Edwin Shneidman (1987), 80 percent of suicides are preceded by some kind of warning, whether direct ("I think I'm going to kill myself") or vague ("Sometimes I wonder if life is worth living"). Although not everyone who threatens suicide follows through, if you suspect that someone you know is thinking about suicide, encourage the person to contact a mental health professional or a crisis hotline. If the danger is imminent, make the contact yourself and ask for advice about how to respond.

Bipolar Disorder

The alternating appearance of two emotional extremes, or poles, characterizes **bipolar disorder.** We have already described one emotional pole: depression. The other is **mania,** which is a very agitated, usually elated, emotional state. People in a manic state tend to be utterly optimistic, boundlessly energetic, certain of having extraordinary powers and abilities, and bursting with all sorts of ideas. They become irritated with anyone who tries to reason with them or "slow them down." During manic episodes the person may make impulsive and unwise decisions, including spending their life savings on foolish schemes.

In bipolar disorder, manic episodes may alternate with periods of deep depression (sometimes, periods of relatively normal mood separate these extremes). This pattern has also been called *manic depression.* Compared with major depressive disorder, bipolar disorder is rare; it occurs in only about 1 percent of adults, and it affects men and women about equally. Slightly more common is a pattern of less extreme mood swings known as **cyclothymic disorder,** the bipolar equivalent of dysthymia. Like major depressive disorder, bipolar disorder is extremely disruptive to a person's ability to work or maintain social relationships (Goldberg, Harrow & Grossman, 1995).

Causes of Mood Disorders

Research on the causes of mood disorders has focused on biological as well as psychological factors.

LINKAGES   Are some psychological disorders inherited? (a link to Biological Aspects of Psychology)

Biological Factors   The role of genetics in mood disorders is suggested by twin studies and family studies showing that these disorders, especially bipolar disorder, tend to run in families. For example, if one twin displays bipolar disorder, the likelihood that the other one will, too, is much higher in genetically identical, rather than nonidentical, pairs (Allen, 1976; Egeland et al., 1987). Family studies also show that those who are closely related to people with bipolar disorder are more likely than others to develop the disorder themselves (Gershon, 1990; Winokur et al., 1995). Major depressive disorder is also more likely to occur in both members of identical, compared to nonidentical, twins (Nurnberger, 1993), but the difference is smaller than in bipolar disorder (Kendler et al., 1995). Researchers continue to look for the specific genes that might be involved in the transmission of elevated risk for mood disorders (Egeland et al., 1987; Suinn, 1995).

Other potential biological causes of mood disorders include imbalances in the brain's neurotransmitters, malfunctioning of the endocrine system, and disruption of biological rhythms. Neurotransmitters such as norepinephrine, serotonin, and dopamine were implicated decades ago when scientists discovered that drugs capable of altering these substances also relieved mood disorders. Early research suggested that depression was triggered by too little of these neurotransmitters while unusually high levels caused mania (Garver & Davis, 1979; Schildkraut, 1965), but the causal situation now appears more complex than that. More recent research suggests that mood disorders may result not just from abnormal levels of certain neurotransmitters but from a *dysregulation* of entire neurotransmitter systems, including changes in the sensitivity of the neuronal receptors at which these chemicals have their effects in the brain. The precise nature of this dysregulation is not yet fully understood (Delgado et al., 1994; Gold, Goodwin & Chrousos, 1988).

Mood disorders have also been related to malfunctions of the endocrine system, especially the hypothalamic-pituitary-adrenocortical system mentioned in Chapter 13 as being involved in the body's responses to stress. For example, research shows that as many as 70 percent of depressed people secrete abnormally high levels of the stress hormone *cortisol* (Lickey & Gordon, 1991; Poland et al., 1987). In addition, abnormal reactions to a synthetic hormone that normally temporarily suppresses the secretion of cortisol have been shown to predict a particularly severe form of depression (Ribeiro et al., 1993).

The cyclical pattern seen in bipolar disorder and in recurring episodes of major depressive disorder suggests that mood disorders may be related to disturbances in the

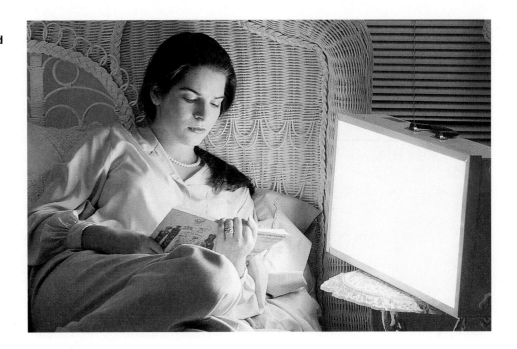

TREATING SAD Seasonal affective disorder (SAD) can often be relieved by exposure to full spectrum light for as little as a couple of hours a day (Blehar & Rosenthal, 1989).

body's biological clock, which is described in Chapter 6 (Goodwin & Jamison, 1990). This possibility seems especially likely to apply to the 15 percent of depressed people who experience a pattern known as *seasonal affective disorder*. During months of shorter daylight, these people slip into severe depression, accompanied by irritability and excessive sleeping (Blehar & Rosenthal, 1989). Their depression tends to lift as daylight hours increase (Faedda et al., 1993). Disruption of biological rhythms in mood disorder is also suggested by the fact that many depressed people tend to have trouble sleeping; some may feel as they do partly because, during the day, their biological clocks are telling them it is the middle of the night. Resetting biological rhythms through methods such as sleep deprivation has relieved depression in some cases (Kuhs & Tolle, 1991). Evidence for disrupted biological rhythms in mood disorders indirectly supports neurotransmitter theories of causation inasmuch as the disruptions may be traceable to abnormalities in norepinephrine, serotonin, dopamine, and other neurotransmitters that regulate the body's internal clock (Wehr et al., 1983).

Psychological Factors Traditional psychodynamic theory proposes that depression stems from unconscious processes associated with the loss of a loved one. According to Freud, in addition to experiencing grief we feel anger over being abandoned, and some of that anger is directed inward, resulting in self-hatred and other symptoms of depression. Although this theory is no longer a dominant one, modern psychological theories of mood disorders continue to emphasize the importance of people's reactions to loss and other negative events.

A variety of cognitive-behavioral theories are particularly influential. One of the earliest is based on the research on *learned helplessness* described in Chapter 7. Just as animals become inactive and appear depressed when they have no control over negative events, humans may experience depression as a result of feeling incapable of controlling their lives, especially the stressors besetting them (Klein & Seligman, 1976). But most of us have limited control; why aren't we all depressed? The ways in which people learn to *think* about events in their lives may hold the cognitive key. For example, Aaron Beck's (1967, 1976) cognitive theory of depression suggests that depressed people develop mental habits of (1) blaming themselves when things go wrong, (2) focusing on and exaggerating the dark side of events, and (3) jumping to overly generalized, pessimistic conclusions. Such cognitive habits, says Beck, are errors that lead to depressing thoughts and other symptoms of depression. There is ample evidence that depressed people do think about significant negative events in ways that are likely to increase or prolong their depression (Gotlib & Hammen, 1992).

Cognitive-behaviorists suggest that these negative ways of thinking may be acquired through maladaptive experiences in childhood. Children whose early relationships with parents or other primary caregivers were characterized by deprivation or abuse may be especially likely to develop depression in later life (Gotlib & Hammen, 1992; Hammen, 1991). As suggested by the object relations theorists discussed in Chapter 14, close, protective, predictable, and responsive early relationships may be necessary in order for children to form healthy views of themselves, positive expectations about others, and a sense of control over the environment (Bowlby, 1980; Suomi, 1991).

Some researchers have found that severe, long-lasting depression is especially likely among people who attribute lack of control or other problems they experience to a permanent, generalized lack of personal competence rather than to a temporary lapse or external cause (Abramson, Seligman & Teasdale, 1978; Seligman et al., 1988). Thus, *attributional style* may be another important cognitive factor in depression. People may be prone to depression when they blame negative events on themselves and believe they will always be incapable of doing better. One version of attributional theory even postulates *hopelessness* as a subtype of depression (Abramson, Metalsky & Alloy, 1989; Metalsky et al., 1993; Rose et al., 1994).

Depressed people do hold more negative beliefs about themselves and their lives than other people, but the exact significance of these beliefs is not yet clear (Gara et al., 1993; Haaga, Dyck & Ernst, 1991). For one thing, pessimistic beliefs may be a symptom of depression rather than its cause. Also, research indicates that the negative beliefs held by depressed persons are often an accurate reflection of these people's unfortunate life situations (Snyder & Higgins, 1988; Taylor & Brown, 1988). In any case, the cognitive-behavioral perspective suggests that whether depression continues, or worsens, depends in part on how people respond once they start to feel depressed. Those who ruminate about negative events, about why they occur, and even about feeling depressed are likely to feel more and more depressed. According to Susan Nolen-Hoeksma (1990), this *ruminative style* is especially characteristic of women and may help explain gender differences in the frequency of depression. When men start to feel sad, she says, they tend to use a *distracting style,* engaging in activity that helps bring them out of their depressed mood (Nolen-Hoeksma, 1990; Nolen-Hoeksma, Morrow & Fredrickson, 1993).

Notice that cognitive-behavioral explanations of depression are consistent with the diathesis-stress model of disorder. These explanations suggest that certain cognitive styles constitute a predisposition (or diathesis) that makes a person vulnerable to depression (Peterson & Seligman, 1984), the occurrence of which is made more likely by stressors. Indeed, most episodes of major depressive disorder are preceded by the onset of major stressors, such as the loss of a loved one. As suggested in Chapter 13, the depressing effects of these stressors are likely to be magnified by lack of social support, inadequate coping skills, and the presence of other stressful conditions such as poverty (Brown & Harris, 1978).

Given the number and complexity of biological, psychological, and situational factors potentially involved in causing mood disorders, the diathesis-stress model appears to be an especially appropriate guide to future research. One recent study based on this model looked at the role of genetics and stressful events in shaping mood disorders in a large group of female twin pairs. Both factors were associated with major depression; the women at highest genetic risk were the most likely to become depressed following a significant stressor (Kendler et al., 1995). In the final analysis, it may turn out that each subtype of mood disorder is caused by a unique combination of factors. The challenge for researchers is to identify these subtypes and map out their causal ingredients.

SCHIZOPHRENIA

Here is part of a letter that arrived in the mail a while ago:

Dear Sirs:
Pertaining to our continuing failure to prosecute violations of minor's rights to sovereign equality which are occurring in gestations being compromised by the ingestation of con-

trolled substances, . . . the skewing of androgyny which continues in female juveniles even after separation from their mother's has occurred, and as a means of promulflagitating my paying Governor Hickel of Alaska for my employees to have personal services endorsements and controlled substance endorsements, . . . the Iraqi oil being released by the United Nations being identified as Kurdistanian oil, and the July, 1991 issue of the Siberian Review spells President Eltsin's name without a letter y.

The disorganization and bizarre content of this letter suggests that its writer suffers from **schizophrenia,** a pattern of severely disturbed thinking, emotion, perception, and behavior that seriously impairs the ability to communicate and relate to others and disrupts most other aspects of daily functioning. Schizophrenia is one of the most severe and disabling of all mental disorders. Its core symptoms are seen virtually everywhere in the world, occurring in about 1 percent of the population (Gottesman, 1991). In the United States, it appears about equally in various ethnic groups, but, like most disorders, it tends to be diagnosed more frequently in economically disadvantaged populations. Schizophrenia is seen about equally in men and women, although some studies have suggested that, in women, it may appear later in life, be less severe, and respond better to treatment (Castle & Murray, 1993; Syzmanski et al., 1995).

Schizophrenia tends to develop in adolescence or early adulthood. The onset is gradual in some people and more rapid in others. About 40 percent of schizophrenics improve with treatment and are able to function reasonably well; the rest show continuous or intermittent symptoms that permanently impair their functioning (Breier et al., 1991; Hegarty et al., 1994). It has been estimated that 10 to 13 percent of homeless individuals suffer from schizophrenia (Fischer & Breakey, 1991).

One of the best predictors of the course of schizophrenia is *premorbid adjustment,* the level of functioning a person had achieved before schizophrenic symptoms first appeared. Improvement is more likely in those who had attained higher levels of education and occupation, and who had established supportive relationships with family and friends (Watt & Saiz, 1991). For as yet unknown reasons, schizophrenic individuals in developing countries have been found to function relatively better than those in the industrialized world (Eaton, 1991).

Symptoms of Schizophrenia

Schizophrenics display problems in both how they think and what they think. The nineteenth-century psychiatrist Eugen Bleuler coined the word *schizophrenia,* or "split mind," to refer to the peculiarities of schizophrenic thinking. Contrary to popular belief, *schizophrenia* does *not* mean "split personality," as in dissociative identity disorder (multiple personality), but refers instead to a splitting of normally integrated mental processes, such as thoughts and feelings. Thus, for instance, some schizophrenics may giggle while claiming to feel sad.

Schizophrenic thought and language are often disorganized. *Neologisms* ("new words" that have meaning only to the person speaking them) are common; "promulflagitating" in the letter above is one example. That letter also illustrates *loose associations,* the tendency for one thought to be logically unconnected, or only superficially related, to the next. Sometimes the associations are based on double meanings or on the way words sound *(clang associations).* For example, "My true family name is Abel or A Bell. We descended from the clan of Abel, who originated the bell of rights, which we now call the bill of rights." In the most severe cases, thought becomes just a jumble of words known as *word salad.* For example, "Upon the advisability of held keeping, environment of the seabeach gathering, to the forest stream, reinstatement to be placed, poling the paddleboat, of the swamp morass, to the forest compensation of the dunce" (Lehman, 1967, p. 627).

The *content* of schizophrenic thinking is also disturbed. Often it includes a bewildering assortment of delusions, especially delusions of persecution. Some patients say that space aliens are trying to steal their thoughts; they may interpret everything from TV commercials to casual hand gestures as part of the plot. Delusions that common events are somehow related to oneself are called *ideas of reference.* Delusions of grandeur may also be present; one young man was convinced that the president of the United

LINKAGES How do schizophrenics think? (a link to Thought and Language)

States was trying to contact him for advice. Other types of delusions include *thought broadcasting,* in which patients believe that their thoughts can be heard by others; *thought blocking* or *withdrawal,* the belief that someone is either preventing thoughts or "stealing" them as they appear; and *thought insertion,* the belief that other people's thoughts are appearing in one's own mind. Some schizophrenics believe that, as with puppets, their behavior is controlled by others.

Schizophrenics often report that they cannot focus their attention. They may feel overwhelmed as they try to attend to everything at once. Various perceptual disorders may also appear. The person may feel detached from the real world and see other people as flat cutouts. The body may feel like a machine, or parts of it may seem to be dead or rotting. **Hallucinations,** or false perceptions, are common, often emerging as voices. These voices may sound like an overheard conversation, or they may urge the person to do or not to do things; sometimes they comment on or narrate the person's actions. Hallucinations can also involve nonexistent sights, smells, tastes, and touches (see Figure 15.3). Emotional expression is often muted—a pattern called *flat affect.* But when schizophrenics do display emotion, it is often exaggerated or inappropriate; for example, they may cry for no apparent reason or fly into a rage in response to a simple question.

Some schizophrenics are very agitated, ceaselessly moving their limbs, making facial grimaces, or pacing the floor in highly ritualistic sequences. Others become so withdrawn that they move very little. Lack of motivation and poor social skills, deteriorating personal hygiene, and an inability to function day to day are other common characteristics of schizophrenia.

Disorganized thoughts, delusions, and hallucinations are sometimes called *positive symptoms* of schizophrenia because they appear as undesirable *additions* to a person's mental life (Andreasen et al., 1995). Conversely, the absence of pleasure and motivation,

FIGURE 15.3

PET Scan Showing Areas of the Brain Activated During Hallucinations

This 23-year-old schizophrenic patient said he saw rolling, disembodied heads which spoke to him and gave him instructions. PET scans revealed heightened activity in visual and auditory (language) association cortex, rather than the primary cortex regions for these senses. Posterior cingulate cortex (part of the limbic system) is also activated, and is known to be affected by drugs which produce hallucinations (Silbersweig, 1995).

CATATONIC STUPOR The symptoms of schizophrenia often occur in characteristic patterns. This woman displays the inactivity and odd-posturing associated with catatonic schizophrenia.

lack of emotional reactivity, social withdrawal, reduced speech, and other deficits seen in schizophrenia are sometimes called *negative symptoms* because they appear to *subtract* elements from normal mental life (Nicholson & Neufeld, 1993).

Types of Schizophrenia

DSM-IV lists five major subtypes of schizophrenia: paranoid, disorganized, catatonic, undifferentiated, and residual.

About 40 percent of all schizophrenics appear in the **paranoid schizophrenia** subtype. Its most prominent features are delusions of persecution or grandeur accompanied by anxiety, anger, argumentativeness, or jealousy. Sometimes these feelings lead to violence. Compared with the other subtypes, paranoid schizophrenia tends to appear later in life, typically after the age of twenty-five or thirty; the onset is often sudden; and there is much less obvious impairment (Fenton & McGlashan, 1991). In most cases, the person is able to complete an education, hold a job, and even have a family before problems become severe. Here is a description of one case with a particularly late onset:

Mr. S. was first admitted to the hospital at the age of forty-eight. Some weeks earlier, he had taken to sealing the cracks under doors and in window sashes with empty toothpaste tubes to "keep out radio waves" that were being directed at him by agents of "the Tsar Nicholas." He lost his job around this time because of similar behavior at work, but he attributed his dismissal to the machinations of enemies and unnamed fellow workers. On the hospital ward he was condescending to the other patients, demanding many privileges for himself and giving lengthy accounts of the importance attached to him by both the Russians and the White House. He spent many hours perusing newspapers to see if his movements were reported there. (Summarized from Maher, 1966, p. 308)

The main features of **disorganized schizophrenia** are unrelated delusions and hallucinations. Speech may be incoherent. Strange facial grimaces and ritualistic movements are common. Affect is flat, although there may be inappropriate laughter or giggling. Personal hygiene is neglected, and the person may lose bowel and bladder control. Only about 5 percent of schizophrenics fall into this category; many of them are found among the urban homeless.

The most significant characteristic of **catatonic schizophrenia** is disordered movement, which alternates between total immobility, or stupor, and wild excitement. Especially during stupor, the person may not speak, ignoring all attempts at communication, and either becomes rigid or shows a "waxy flexibility," which allows the person to be "posed" in virtually any posture. This subtype is also rare, occurring in only about 8 percent of all cases (McGlashan & Fenton, 1991).

Undifferentiated schizophrenia is marked by patterns of disordered behavior, thought, and emotion that cannot be placed easily in any of the other subtypes. About 40 percent of diagnosed schizophrenics fall into this category (Fenton & McGlashan, 1991). Finally, **residual schizophrenia** refers to persons who have had a prior episode of schizophrenia but currently are not displaying delusions, hallucinations, or other symptoms.

Researchers have also made other useful distinctions among various forms of schizophrenia. One of these is the positive-negative symptom dimension described earlier (Nicholson & Neufeld, 1993). Many patients exhibit both positive and negative symptoms, but when negative symptoms predominate, schizophrenia generally has a more severe course, including long-term disability and relative lack of response to treatment (e.g., Fenton & McGlashan, 1994). Some researchers believe that forms of schizophrenia dominated by positive versus negative symptoms may stem from different causes.

Causes of Schizophrenia

The search for the causes of schizophrenia has been more intense than for any other psychological disorder. The findings so far confirm one thing for certain: No single cause can adequately account for all forms of schizophrenia.

Biological Factors   Research in behavioral genetics shows that schizophrenia runs in families (Gottesman, 1991). One longitudinal family study found, for instance, that 16 percent of the children of schizophrenic mothers—compared to 2 percent of those of nonschizophrenic mothers—developed schizophrenia themselves over a twenty-five-year period (Parnas et al., 1993). Even if they are adopted by nonschizophrenic families, the children of schizophrenic parents are ten times more likely to develop schizophrenia than adopted children whose biological parents are not schizophrenic (Kety et al., 1994). Still, it is unlikely that a single gene transmits schizophrenia (Kendler & Diehl, 1993). Among identical-twin pairs in which one member displays schizophrenia, 40 percent of the other member will, too; but 60 percent will not (McGue, 1992). It is more likely that some people inherit a genetic *predisposition,* or diathesis, for schizophrenia (DiLalla & Gottesman, 1995; Tyrka et al., 1995).

The search for more specific causes of schizophrenia focuses on a number of abnormalities in brain structure, functioning, and chemistry that tend to appear in schizophrenics. For example, numerous MRI and other brain imaging studies have shown that, compared to nonschizophrenics, many schizophrenics have less tissue in thalamic regions, prefrontal cortex, and some subcortical areas (Andreasen et al., 1994; Breier et al., 1992; Buchsbaum et al., 1992). As shown in Figure 15.4, shrinkage of such tissue leads to corresponding enlargement in the brain's fluid-filled spaces, called *ventricles.* The brain areas in which anatomical abnormalities have been found are active in emotional expression, thinking, and information processing—functions that are disordered in schizophrenia. Enlarged ventricles and reduced prefrontal cortex are more often found in schizophrenics whose symptoms are predominantly negative; schizophrenics with mainly positive symptoms tend to have fairly normal-looking brains (Andreasen et al., 1990).

Hundreds of studies of brain functioning in schizophrenics provide general support for the idea that the impairment of their information-processing and other cognitive abilities is consistent with structural damage (Clementz, McDowell & Zisook, 1994). Thus, schizophrenics whose symptoms are predominantly negative are especially likely to display cognitive deficits associated with the frontal-cortex problems often seen in these patients (Buchanan et al., 1994). This research provides important clues, but we still do not know the extent to which, or exactly how, specific structural abnormalities are related to specific forms of schizophrenia. For one thing, not all schizophrenic patients show brain abnormalities, and some normal people do.

Researchers are also investigating the possibility that abnormalities in brain chemistry—especially in neurotransmitter systems that use dopamine—play a role in causing or intensifying schizophrenic symptoms. Because drugs that block the brain's

FIGURE 15.4

Brain Abnormalities in Schizophrenia

Here is a magnetic resonance imaging (MRI) comparison of the brains of identical twins. The schizophrenic twin (on the right) has greatly enlarged ventricles (see arrows) and correspondingly less brain tissue, including that in the hippocampal area, a region involved in memory and emotion. The same results appeared in fourteen other identical-twin pairs; by contrast, no significant differences appeared between members of a seven-pair control group of normal identical twins (Suddath et al., 1990). These results support the idea that brain abnormalities are associated with schizophrenia and, because identical twins have the same genes, that such abnormalities may stem from non-genetic factors.

dopamine receptors often reduce schizophrenics' hallucinations, disordered thinking, and other positive symptoms, some investigators speculate that schizophrenia results from excess dopamine. As we have seen in connection with neurochemical theories of mood disorders, however, the relationship between dopamine and schizophrenia is a complex one. For one thing, excess dopamine is not always associated with schizophrenia. Alternatively, schizophrenia might be related to *dysregulation* of dopamine mechanisms in several interconnected regions of the brain (Breier et al., 1993; Davis, Kahn, Ko & Davidson, 1991). Some research suggests, for example, that excessive activity in dopamine systems may be related to the appearance of hallucinations, delusions, and other positive symptoms of schizophrenia that are treatable with dopamine-blocking drugs. In addition, abnormally low dopamine system activity, especially in prefrontal brain areas, has been associated with negative symptoms such as withdrawal (Cohen & Servan-Schreiber, 1992; Davis et al., 1991).

Some researchers are integrating genetic and environmental explanations of schizophrenia by looking for *neurodevelopmental abnormalities.* Perhaps, they say, some forms of schizophrenia arise from disruptions in brain development during the period from gestation through childhood, when the brain is growing and its various functions are maturing. Studies have shown, for instance, that prenatal exposure to viral infections or other physical traumas are associated with increased risk for developing schizophrenia (Mednick et al., 1988; Takei et al., 1994). Similarly, children whose birth weight was low or who experienced oxygen deprivation during birth are more likely to have the brain abnormalities described earlier; these abnormalities are *especially* likely in children of schizophrenic parents (Cannon et al., 1993). Thus, it may be that the expression of a genetically transmitted predisposition for brain abnormality is enhanced by environmental stressors such as maternal drug use during pregnancy, complications during birth, and childhood malnutrition. Indeed, neurodevelopmental factors may help explain why children of schizophrenic parents tend to show the kinds of subtle cognitive and intellectual abnormalities associated with brain abnormalities (Cannon et al., 1994; Fish et al., 1992; Marcus et al., 1993; Neumann et al., 1995).

Psychological Factors   Psychodynamic theorists have suggested that schizophrenic symptoms represent regression to early childhood—an extreme reaction to anxiety about expressing or becoming aware of unacceptable unconscious impulses (Freud, 1924). Other theorists have attributed schizophrenia to unclear or conflicted communication in the family or to learned, maladaptive efforts at coping with anxiety (Bateson et al., 1956; Fromm-Reichmann, 1948; Mednick, 1958; Ullmann & Krasner, 1975).

None of these hypotheses has received strong research support. Indeed, psychological factors alone are no longer considered to be the primary causes of schizophrenia. Contemporary research does suggest, however, that psychological processes, including unfortunate learning experiences and stressful family communication patterns, can contribute to the appearance of schizophrenia and influence its course. For example, schizophrenic individuals who live with relatives who are critical, unsupportive, or emotionally overinvolved are especially likely to relapse following improvement (Leff & Vaughan, 1981; Kavanagh, 1992). Family members' negative attitudes may be a source of stress that actually increases the chances that disruptive or odd behaviors will persist or worsen (Rosenfarb et al., 1995; Weisman et al., 1993).

The Vulnerability Model: An Integrative View   The causal theories we have discussed are all consistent with the diathesis-stress model, which assumes that stress may activate a person's predisposition for disorder (Fowles, 1992). ("In Review: Schizophrenia" summarizes these causal theories as well as the symptoms and subtypes of schizophrenia.) The diathesis-stress perspective is embodied in the *vulnerability model* of schizophrenia (Cornblatt & Erlenmeyer-Kimling, 1985; Zubin & Spring, 1977). The vulnerability model suggests that (1) vulnerability to schizophrenia is mainly biological; (2) different people have differing degrees of vulnerability; (3) vulnerability is influenced partly by genetics and partly by neurodevelopmental abnormalities associated with prenatal risk factors, birth complications, and other problems (Barr, Mednick & Munk-Jorgensen, 1990; Susser & Lin, 1992); and (4) psychological components, such

IN REVIEW	Schizophrenia
Aspect	**Key Features**
Common Symptoms	
Disorders of thought	Disturbed *content,* including delusions; and disorganization, including loose associations, neologisms, and word salad.
Disorders of perception	Hallucinations or false perceptions; poorly focused attention.
Disorders of emotion	Flat affect; or inappropriate tears, laughter, or anger.
Subtypes	
Paranoid	Delusions most prominent; later onset than other subtypes.
Disorganized	Unrelated delusions and hallucinations most prominent; flat affect; incoherence and disorganized behavior.
Catatonic	Disorders of movement most prominent, including stupor, bizarre postures, and excitement.
Undifferentiated	Schizophrenic symptoms that do not fit any of the other subtypes.
Possible Causes	
Biological	Genetics; abnormalities in brain structure; abnormalities in dopamine systems; neurodevelopmental problems.
Psychological	Learned maladaptive behavior; disturbed patterns of family communication.

The Vulnerability Model of Schizophrenia

According to this model, a person can cross the threshold into schizophrenia through many combinations of predisposition and stress. A strong predisposition for schizophrenia and little environmental stress (point D), a weak predisposition and a lot of stress (point C), or any other sufficiently potent combination can lead to disorder.

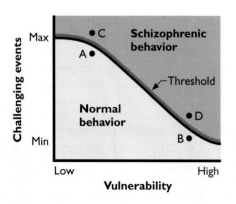

Source: Zubin & Spring, 1977.

as exposure to poor parenting or inadequate coping skills, may play a role in determining whether schizophrenia actually appears, but also may influence the course of the disorder. Many different blendings of vulnerability and stress can lead to schizophrenia, as Figure 15.5 illustrates. Persons whose genetic characteristics or prenatal experiences leave them vulnerable to develop schizophrenia may be especially likely to do so if they are later exposed to learning experiences or family conflicts and other stressors that elicit and maintain schizophrenic patterns of thought and action. Those same experiences and stressors would not be expected to lead to schizophrenia in people who are less vulnerable to developing the disorder. Clearly, then, schizophrenia is a highly complex disorder (probably more than one disorder) whose origins appear to lie in numerous biological and psychological domains, some of which are yet to be discovered (Heinrichs, 1993).

PERSONALITY DISORDERS

Personality disorders are long-standing, inflexible ways of behaving that are not so much severe mental disorders as styles of life. These disorders affect all areas of functioning and, from childhood or adolescence, create problems for those who display them and for others (Millon, 1981). Some psychologists view personality disorders as interpersonal strategies or as the expression of extreme, rigid, and maladaptive personality traits (Widiger & Kelso, 1983).

The ten personality disorders found on Axis II of DSM-IV can be thought of in terms of clusters that share certain features. Here, we describe just a few of these disorders. The *odd-eccentric* cluster includes paranoid, schizoid, and schizotypal personality

A DANGEROUS CASE OF ANTISOCIAL PERSONALITY DISORDER Serial killings by Ted Bundy, pictured here shortly before his execution, and the violent crime sprees documented in films such as *In Cold Blood* and *Natural Born Killers,* represent the antisocial personality at its worst.

disorders. People diagnosed as having **schizotypal personality disorder,** for example, display some of the peculiarities seen in schizophrenia but are not disturbed enough to be labeled as schizophrenic. Rather than hallucinating, these people may report "illusions" of people or objects. They may also exhibit "magical thinking," including odd superstitions or beliefs (such as that salt under the mattress will prevent insomnia). The *anxious-fearful* cluster includes the dependent, obsessive-compulsive, and avoidant personality disorders. The **avoidant personality disorder,** for example, is akin to social phobia in the sense that persons with this disorder tend to be "loners" with a longstanding pattern of avoiding social situations and of being particularly sensitive to criticism or rejection by others. They want to be with others but are too inhibited. Finally, the *dramatic-erratic* cluster includes the borderline, histrionic, narcissistic, and antisocial personality disorders. The main characteristics of **narcissistic personality disorder** are an exaggerated sense of self-importance, extreme sensitivity to criticism, constant need for attention, and a tendency to arrogantly overestimate personal abilities and achievements. Persons with this disorder feel entitled to special treatment by others but are markedly lacking in empathy.

From the perspective of public welfare and safety, the most serious and most widely studied personality disorder is **antisocial personality disorder.** It is marked by a longterm pattern of irresponsible, impulsive, unscrupulous, even criminal behavior, beginning in childhood or early adolescence. In the nineteenth century, the pattern was called *moral insanity,* because such persons appear to have no morals or common decency; later, people in this category were called *psychopaths* or *sociopaths.* The current "antisocial personality" label more accurately portrays them as troublesome, but not "insane" by the legal standards we will discuss shortly. About 3 percent of men and about 1 percent of women in the United States fall into this diagnostic category.

At their least troublesome, these people are a nuisance. They are often charming, intelligent, glib talkers who borrow money and fail to return it; they are arrogant and self-centered manipulators who "con" people into doing things for them, usually by lying and taking advantage of the decency and trust of others. A hallmark of those displaying antisocial personality is a lack of anxiety, remorse, or guilt, whether they have wrecked a borrowed car or killed an innocent person (Hare, 1991; Hare, Hart & Harpur, 1991). No method has yet been found for permanently altering the behavior of these people (American Psychiatric Association, 1989); fortunately, they tend to become less active and dangerous after the age of forty (American Psychiatric Association, 1994).

There are numerous theories about the causes of antisocial personality. Some research suggests a genetic predisposition, possibly in the form of chronic underarousal of both the autonomic and central nervous systems (Cadoret et al., 1985; Patrick, Cuthbert & Lang, 1994; Raine, Venables & Williams, 1990). This underarousal may render people less sensitive to punishment than is normally the case (Eysenck, 1964; Newman & Kosson, 1986). From psychological and social perspectives, broken homes, rejection by parents, poor discipline, lack of good parental models, lack of attachment to early caregivers, impulsivity, conflict-filled childhoods, and poverty have all been suggested as factors contributing to failure to acquire adaptive patterns of conformity to social standards (Lahey et al., 1995; Raine, Brennan & Mednick, 1994; Tremblay et al., 1994).

One of the most prominent environmental factors associated with the more violent forms of antisocial personality disorder is the experience of abuse in childhood. However, most of the studies in which a relationship has been found between childhood abuse and antisocial personality disorder are based on potentially biased retrospective reports (Monane, Leichter & Lewis, 1984; Rosenbaum & Bennett, 1986). People with antisocial personalities—especially those with criminal records—are likely to fabricate stories of

FOCUS ON RESEARCH METHODS

Searching for Links Between Child Abuse and Antisocial Personality Disorder

abuse in order to shift some blame for their behavior onto others. Even if these reports were accurate, however, most of these studies lacked a control group of non-antisocial people from similar backgrounds. Because of this design flaw, it is virtually impossible to separate the effects of reported child abuse from the effects of poverty or other factors that might also have contributed to the development of antisocial personality disorder.

Cathy Widom (1989) wanted to test the hypothesis that abuse can cause antisocial personality disorder. To correct some of the flaws in earlier studies, she used a *prospective* quasi-experimental design, first finding cases of childhood abuse, then looking for the effects of that abuse on adult behavior. Widom began by identifying 416 adults whose backgrounds included official records of their having been physically or sexually abused before the age of eleven. She then explored the story of these people's lives, as conveyed in police and school records as well as in a two-hour diagnostic interview. To reduce experimenter bias and distorted reporting, Widom ensured that the interviewers remained "blind" to the purpose of the study and that the respondents were told only that the study's purpose was simply to talk to people who had grown up in a midwestern metropolitan area of the United States in the late 1960s and early 1970s. Widom also selected a comparison group of 283 people who had no history of abuse, but who were similar to the abused sample in terms of age, gender, ethnicity, hospital of birth, schools attended, and area of residence. The goal was to obtain a nonabused control group that had been exposed to approximately the same environmental risk factors and socioeconomic conditions as the abused children.

First, Widom (1989) tested the hypothesis that exposure to abuse in childhood is associated with criminality and/or violence in later life. She found that 26 percent of the abused youngsters went on to commit juvenile crimes, 29 percent were arrested as adults, and 11 percent committed violent crimes. These percentages were significantly higher than the figures for the nonabused group. The correlations between criminality and abuse were higher for males than for females, and higher for African-Americans than for European-Americans. And, overall, victims of physical abuse were more likely to commit violent crimes as adults than were victims of sexual abuse.

Next, Widom tested the hypothesis that childhood abuse is associated with the development of antisocial personality disorder as defined in DSM (Luntz & Widom, 1994). Indeed, the abused group exhibited a significantly higher rate of antisocial personality disorder (13.5 percent) than did the comparison group (7.1 percent). The apparent role of abuse in antisocial personality disorder was particularly pronounced in men, and it remained strong even when other causal factors—such as age, ethnicity, criminal activity, and socioeconomic status—were held constant in the statistical analyses. Interestingly, one other factor—failure to graduate from high school—was also strongly associated with the appearance of antisocial personality disorder, whether or not childhood abuse had occurred.

In short, Widom's research supported earlier studies in finding an *association* between childhood abuse and criminality, violence, and antisocial personality disorder. Further, while her quasi-experiment did not permit a firm conclusion that abuse alone *causes* antisocial personality disorder, the data from its prospective rather than retrospective design added strength to the argument that abuse may be an important causal factor. The results suggest that there are probably other causes as well. For one thing, abuse is often part of a larger constellation of experiences such as exposure to deviant models, social rejection, poor supervision, and the like. Additional research will be needed to discover whether antisocial personality disorder stems from abuse itself, from one of the factors accompanying it, or from some other specific combination of known and still-unknown risk factors. For example, Widom's study suggests that one or more of the factors leading teenagers to drop out (or be thrown out) of high school might be an independent cause of antisocial personality disorder.

Widom's study also confirms that, whatever the other consequences of abuse, violence, criminal behavior, or antisocial personality disorder are seen in only a minority of abused children. Thus, her results raise the question of whether certain genetic characteristics or environmental experiences serve to protect children from at least some of the devastating effects of abuse. Indeed, an understanding of what these protective elements are might go a long way toward the development of programs for the prevention of antisocial personality disorder.

Finally, Widom's work offers yet another reason—as if more reasons were needed—as to why it is so important to prevent the physical and sexual abuse of children. The long-term consequences of such abuse can be tragic not only for its immediate victims but also for those victimized by the violence, criminal actions, and antisocial behavior perpetrated by some abused children as they grow up (Malinosky-Rummell & Hansen, 1993).

A SAMPLING OF OTHER PSYCHOLOGICAL DISORDERS

The disorders described so far represent some of the most prevalent and socially disruptive psychological problems encountered in cultures around the world. Several others are mentioned in other chapters. In Chapter 6, for example, we discuss insomnia, night terrors, and other sleep disorders; mental retardation is covered in Chapter 10; sexual dysfunctions are mentioned in Chapter 11; and posttraumatic stress disorder is described in Chapter 13. Here, we consider two other significant psychological problems: substance-related disorders and some disorders of childhood.

Substance-Related Disorders

When people use psychoactive drugs for months or years in ways that harm themselves or others, they exhibit what DSM-IV calls **substance-related disorders.** These disorders have created major political, economic, social, and health problems worldwide. The substances involved most often are alcohol and other depressants, such as barbiturates; opiates, such as heroin; stimulants, such as cocaine or amphetamines; and psychedelics, such as LSD.

As mentioned in Chapter 6, one effect of using some substances (including alcohol, heroin, and amphetamines) is **addiction,** a physical need for the substance. DSM-IV calls addiction *physiological substance dependence.* Usually, addiction is evident when the person begins to need more and more of a substance to achieve the desired state; this is called *building a tolerance.* When addicted people stop using the substance, they experience painful, often terrifying and potentially dangerous *withdrawal symptoms* as the body tries to readjust to a substance-free state. Even when use of a drug does not create physical addiction, some people may overuse, or *abuse,* it because it gives them temporary self-confidence, enjoyment, or relief from tension. DSM-IV defines *substance abuse* as a pattern of use that causes serious social, legal, or interpersonal problems. Thus, people can become *psychologically* dependent on psychoactive drugs without becoming physically addicted to them. We described these drugs and their impact on consciousness in Chapter 6; now we focus on the causes and broader consequences of their use.

Alcohol Use Disorders More than 13 percent of American adults—in excess of 20 million people—display *alcohol dependence or abuse,* a pattern of continuous or intermittent drinking that may lead to addiction and almost always causes severe social, physical, and other problems (Canino et al., 1987). Males exceed females in this category by a ratio of about 6 to 1, although the problem is on the rise among women and among teenagers of both genders. Prolonged overuse of alcohol can result in life-threatening liver damage, reduced cognitive abilities, vitamin deficiencies that can lead to an irreversible brain disorder called *Korsakoff's psychosis* (severe memory loss), and a host of other physical ailments. Alcohol dependence or abuse, commonly referred to as **alcoholism,** has been implicated in half of all the traffic fatalities, homicides, and suicides that occur each year; alcoholism also figures prominently in rape and child abuse

LINKAGES: ALCOHOL ABUSE   It is esti-mated that 43 percent of U. S. adults have an alcoholic in their families (NIDA, 1991). Children growing up in families in which one or both parents abuse alcohol are at increased risk for developing a host of mental disorders including substance-related disorders (Sher et al., 1991). As described in Chapter 12, children of mothers who abused alcohol during pregnancy may be born with fetal alcohol syndrome.

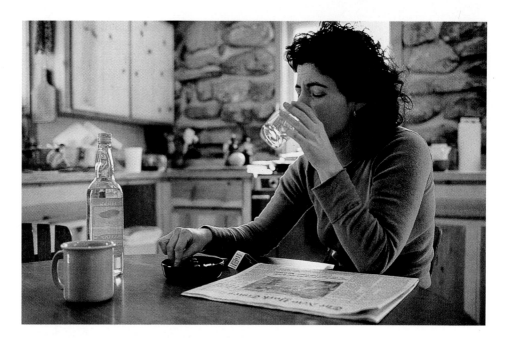

(ADAMHA, 1987; USDHHS, 1990), as well as in elevated rates of hospitalization and absenteeism from work (Julien, 1992).

The psychodynamic approach suggests that dependence on alcohol, or on other psychoactive drugs, results from dependency needs that were never satisfied in infancy (Shedler & Block, 1990). Research shows, however, that many other personality traits are also correlated with alcoholism, so the role of inordinate dependency, let alone its causal impact, has not been established. Alternatively, one behavioral theory suggests that people learn to use alcohol because it helps them cope with stressors. But use can become abuse, often addiction, if drinking is a person's main coping strategy (Walters, 1992; see also Table 15.4). The stress-reduction theory of alcoholism has been supported by studies indicating that alcohol can reduce animals' learned fear of a particular location and that animals in a stressful conflict situation will choose to drink alcohol if it is available (Conger, 1951; Freed, 1971). The stress-reducing effects of alcohol have also been shown in humans (Sher & Levenson, 1982), but not consistently (Steele & Josephs, 1988).

TABLE 15.4	Social Drinkers	Alcoholics
Social Drinking Versus Alcoholism **Social drinking differs markedly from alcoholism, but it is all too easy for people to drift from social to alcoholic drinking patterns. Alcoholism can include heavy drinking on a daily basis, on weekends only, or in isolated binges lasting weeks or months.**	Sip drinks.	Gulp drinks.
	Usually drink in moderation and can control the amount consumed.	Drink increasing quantities (develop tolerance). Sometimes drink until blacking out. May not recall events that occur while drinking.
	Usually drink to enhance the pleasure of social situations.	Drink for the chemical effect, often to relieve tension or face problems; often drink alone, including in the morning to reduce hangover or to face the day.
	Do not usually think about or talk about drinking in nondrinking situations.	Become preoccupied with getting next drink, often sneaking drinks during working hours or at home.
	Do not experience physical, social, or occupational problems caused by drinking.	Suffer physical disorders, damaged social relationships, and impaired capacity to work because of drinking.

The importance of learning is further suggested by evidence that alcoholism is more common among ethnic and cultural groups (such as the Irish and English) in which frequent drinking tends to be socially reinforced than among groups (such as Jews, Italians, and Chinese) in which all but moderate drinking tends to be discouraged (Frankel & Whitehead, 1981). Moreover, differing expressions of social support for drinking can result in differing consumption patterns within a cultural group. For example, one study found significantly more drinking among Japanese men living in Japan (where social norms for males' drinking are most permissive) compared to those living in Hawaii or California, where excessive drinking is less strongly supported (Kitano et al., 1992). Learning would also help explain why the prevalence of alcoholism is higher than average among people working as bartenders and cocktail servers, and in other jobs where alcohol is available and drinking is socially reinforced, even expected (Fillmore & Caetano, 1980). (Of course, it is also possible that attraction to alcohol led some of these people into such jobs in the first place.)

Learning, then, appears to be implicated in excessive drinking, but heredity may also play a role, especially among males (Azar, 1995). For example, the sons of alcoholics are more likely than others to become alcoholic themselves; and if the sons are identical twins, both are at increased risk for alcoholism, even when raised apart (Cloninger, 1987; McGue, Pickens & Svikis, 1992). The role of genetics appears to be greatest among males who begin their alcoholic drinking pattern at an early age and display other conduct problems as teenagers (McGue, Pickens & Svikis, 1992). For females, and for males whose problem drinking appears later in life, the evidence for genetic causes is much less compelling. In such cases, it may be that any genetic predisposition is too weak to result in alcoholism except when amplified by social and cultural family influences that promote drinking (McGue, Pickens & Svikis, 1992). Indeed, reanalysis of the evidence suggests that the genetic component of alcoholism may not be as strong overall as once believed (Gelernter, Goldman & Risch, 1993); just what might be inherited, or which genes are involved, is certainly not clear. One possible factor, however, is an abnormality in neurotransmitter activity or in the metabolism of alcohol (Devor, 1994; Kranzler & Anton, 1994). Sons of alcoholics do tend to be less sensitive than other males to the effects of alcohol—a factor that may contribute to greater consumption (Pollack, 1992)—but it is unclear whether this reduced sensitivity reflects a biological predisposition.

Heroin and Cocaine Dependence   Like alcoholics, heroin and cocaine addicts suffer many serious health problems, as a result both of the drug itself and of the poor eating and health habits it engenders. The risk of death from an overdose, contaminated drugs, or AIDS (contracted through blood in shared needles), as well as from suicide, is also always present. Drug dependence tends to be more prevalent among males, especially young males (Warner et al., 1995).

Continued use or overdoses of cocaine can cause problems ranging from nausea and hyperactivity to paranoid thinking, sudden depressive "crashes," and even death. An estimated 1 million Americans have become dependent on cocaine, and millions more use it on occasion (National Institute on Drug Abuse, 1991). The widespread availability of crack, a powerful and relatively cheap form of cocaine, has made it one of the most dangerous and addicting drugs in existence. Pregnant women who use cocaine are much more likely than nonusers to lose their babies through spontaneous abortions, placental detachments, early fetal death, or stillbirths. The more than 50,000 "crack babies" born each year to cocaine-using mothers are at risk for numerous physical and mental birth defects (Julien, 1992).

Although addiction to substances like heroin is largely understood to be a biological process brought about by the physical effects of the drugs, explaining why people first use them is more complicated. The causes of initial drug abuse are even less well established than the reasons for alcohol abuse. One line of theorizing suggests that there might be a genetic tendency toward behavioral dysregulation or compulsions that predisposes some people to abuse many kinds of drugs, including alcohol (Smith et al., 1992; Holden, 1991). One recent behavioral genetics study supported this idea when it found a link between alcoholism in biological parents and drug abuse in adopted-away sons (Caderet et al., 1995). The same study also found a link between antisocial personality traits in biological parents and antisocial acts—including drug abuse—in the sons they had put up for adoption.

Psychological factors, such as the need to reduce stress, emulation of drug-using peers, thrill seeking, and social maladjustment, have all been proposed as initial causes of substance abuse. Research has still not yet established why drugs become a problem for some people and not for others, but, again, it is likely that some predisposition sets the stage on which specific psychological processes and stressors play out their roles.

Psychological Disorders of Childhood

The physical, cognitive, emotional, and social changes seen in childhood—and the stress associated with them—can create or worsen psychological disorders in children. Stress can do the same in adults, but childhood disorders are not just miniature versions of adult psychopathology. Because children's development is still incomplete and because their capacity to cope with stress is limited in important ways, children are often vulnerable to special types of disorders. Two broad categories encompass the majority of childhood behavior problems: externalizing disorders and internalizing disorders (Achenbach, 1991; Quay, 1979).

The *externalizing,* or *undercontrolled,* category includes behaviors that are aversive to people in the child's environment. Lack of control shows up as *conduct disorders* in 4 to 10 percent of children, mostly boys (Martin & Hoffman, 1990). Conduct disorders are characterized by a relatively stable pattern of aggression, disobedience, destructiveness, and other obnoxious behaviors (Lahey et al., 1995). Often these behaviors involve criminal activity. A genetic predisposition toward conduct disorders is suggested by the fact that many such children have parents who display antisocial personality disorder. However, environmental and parenting factors also shape these children's antisocial behavior (Lahey et al., 1995; Patterson, DeBaryshe & Ramsey, 1989).

Another kind of externalizing problem, also seen primarily in boys, is *attention-deficit hyperactivity disorder (ADHD).* This label is given to children who are impulsive and unable to concentrate on an activity as well as other children their age can (Schachar & Logan, 1990). Many of these children are *hyperactive;* they have great difficulty sitting still or otherwise controlling their physical activity. Their impulsiveness and lack of self-control contribute to an astonishing ability to annoy and exhaust those around them and to create numerous problems, especially at school (Henker & Whalen, 1989). Genetic predisposition, the occurrence of brain damage, dietary problems, poisoning from lead or other household substances, and ineffective parenting have all been proposed as possible causes of hyperactivity, but the role played by each of these factors is still uncertain (Hauser et al., 1993; Marshall, 1989). Also uncertain is exactly what constitutes hyperactivity. Cultural standards about acceptable activity levels in children vary, so a "hyperactive" child in one culture might be considered merely "active" in another. Indeed, when mental health professionals from four cultures used the same rating scales to judge the presence and severity of hyperactivity in a videotaped sample of children's behavior, the Chinese and Indonesians rated the children as significantly more hyperactive than did their U.S. and Japanese colleagues (Mann et al., 1992). Such findings remind us again that sociocultural factors can be important determinants of what is acceptable, and hence what is abnormal, in various parts of the world.

The second broad category of child behavior problems involves *internalizing,* or *overcontrol.* Children in this category experience internal distress, especially depression and anxiety, and may be socially withdrawn. Children displaying *separation anxiety disorder,* for example, constantly worry that they will be lost, kidnapped, or injured or that some harm may come to a parent (usually the mother). The child clings desperately to the parent and becomes upset or sick at the prospect of any separation. Refusal to go to school (sometimes called "school phobia") is often the result.

A few childhood disorders do not fall in either the externalizing or internalizing category. An example is *autistic disorder,* a severe and puzzling condition, usually identified within the first thirty months of life, in which babies show no sign of attachment to their caregivers, or anyone else. Autistic babies do not smile, laugh, or make eye contact. They will not tolerate being held and cuddled; they seem unable to enter the social realm. As years go by, they ignore others and instead rock themselves repetitively or play endlessly, it seems, with ashtrays, keys, or other inanimate objects. Language development is seriously disrupted in these children. Half never learn to speak at all. Autistic disorder occurs in fewer than five children per ten thousand births; but, with few exceptions, it leads to a life of marginal adjustment, often within an institution.

Possible biological roots of autistic disorder include genetic factors (Bailey, 1993) or neurodevelopmental abnormalities affecting language and communication (Minshew, Payton & Sclabassi, 1986; Ornitz, 1989). The specific causes of autistic disorder remain unknown, but modern researchers have rejected the once-popular hypothesis that its profound problems are caused by cold and unresponsive parents.

Disorders of childhood differ from adult disorders not only because the patterns of behavior are distinct but also because their early onset renders childhood disorders especially capable of disrupting development. To take one example, children whose avoidance of school causes spotty attendance may not only fall behind academically but also fail to form the relationships with other children that promote normal social development. Some children never make up for this deficit. They may drop out of school and risk a life of poverty, crime, and violence. Moreover, children are dependent on others to obtain help for their psychological problems, and all too often those problems may go unrecognized or untreated. For some, the long-term result may be adult forms of mental disorder.

MENTAL ILLNESS AND THE LAW

Cheryl was barely twenty when she married Glen, a graduate student in biology. They moved into a large apartment complex near the university and within three years had two sons. Cheryl's friends had always been impressed by the attention and affection she showered on her boys; she seemed to be the ideal mother. She and Glen had serious marital problems, however, and she felt trapped and unhappy. One day Glen came home to find that Cheryl had stabbed both children to death. At her murder trial, she was found not guilty by reason of insanity and was placed in a state mental institution.

This verdict reflected U.S. laws and rules that protect people with severe psychological disorders when they are accused of crimes. Similar laws and rules are in effect in many other countries as well. The protection takes two forms.

First, under certain conditions, people designated as mentally ill may be protected from prosecution. If, at the time of their trial, individuals accused of a crime are unable to understand the proceedings and charges against them or to assist in their own defense, they are declared to be *mentally incompetent to stand trial*. In such cases, the defendant is sent to a mental institution until he or she becomes mentally competent. If still not competent after a court-specified period, two years in most cases, the defendant may be ruled permanently ineligible for trial and either committed in civil court to a mental institution or released. This is a rare outcome, however, because competency to stand trial requires only minimal mental abilities. If drugs can produce even temporary mental competence, the defendant will usually go to trial.

Second, the mentally ill may be protected from punishment. In most U.S. states, defendants may be judged *not guilty by reason of insanity* if, at the time of the crime, mental illness prevented them from (1) understanding what they were doing, (2) knowing that what they were doing was wrong, or (3) resisting the impulse to do wrong. The first two of these criteria—understanding the nature or wrongfulness of an act—are "cognitive" criteria known as the *M'Naughton rule*. This rule stems from an 1843 English case in which a man named Daniel M'Naughton, upon hearing "instructions from God," tried to kill Prime Minister Robert Peel; he was found not guilty by reason of insanity and put into a mental institution for life. The third criterion is known as the *irresistible impulse test.* All three criteria are combined in a rule proposed by the American Law Institute (ALI) in 1962 and now followed in many U.S. states:

A person is not responsible for criminal conduct if at the time of such conduct as a result of mental disease or defect he lacks substantial capacity either to appreciate the criminality (wrongfulness) of his conduct or to conform his conduct to the requirements of law. (ALI, 1962, p. 66)

In 1984, after John Hinckley was found not guilty by reason of insanity under the ALI rule for his attempted assassination of President Ronald Reagan, the U.S. Congress passed the Insanity Defense Reform Act that eliminated the lack-of-control criterion from the definition of insanity in federal cases. Such laws highlight the fact that *insanity* is a legal term, not a psychiatric diagnosis—it does not appear in DSM-IV. Thus, the responsibility falls on judges and juries to weigh evidence and testimony and decide whether or not a defendant should be held responsible for criminal acts. Defendants who are judged not guilty by reason of insanity and who still display a psychological disorder are usually required to receive treatment, typically through commitment to a hospital, until judged to be cured or no longer dangerous.

Insanity rules have been faulted on several grounds. Some critics argue that everyone, even those who meet legal criteria for insanity, should be held responsible for their actions and punished for their crimes. Others point out significant problems in the implementation of insanity rules. For example, different experts often give conflicting, highly technical testimony about a defendant's sanity at the time of the crime. (One expert said Cheryl was sane; another concluded she was insane.) The jury is left in the almost impossible position of deciding which expert to believe. Furthermore, in rare cases, defendants found not guilty by reason of insanity may spend more time in a mental hospital than they would have spent in prison had they simply been convicted. In short, well-intentioned laws can produce a miscarriage of justice.

What can be done about these problems? Three U.S. states have abolished the insanity defense. Three other, less extreme reforms have also been attempted. First, several states now permit a verdict of *guilty but mentally ill.* Defendants found guilty but mentally ill still serve a sentence but are supposed to receive treatment while in a prison or special institution. Critics object that this verdict is a compromise that ensures neither proper treatment nor proper verdicts since mentally ill prisoners should receive treatment anyway. Second, as already noted, federal courts no longer use the irresistible-impulse criterion in defining insanity. Third, the federal courts and some states now require defendants to prove that they were insane at the time of the crime, rather than requiring the prosecution to prove that the defendants were sane.

Clearly, communities are still seeking the right balance between protecting the rights of individuals and protecting society. Although certain high-profile cases might suggest otherwise, the insanity plea is raised in fewer than 1 percent of criminal cases in the United States—usually when the defendant displays very severe psychological disorder (McGreevy, Steadman & Callahan, 1991)—and this plea is successful only a tiny fraction of the time. Evidently, some of the same sociocultural values that shape people's views about what constitutes abnormality also influence their judgments about the extent to which abnormality relieves people of criminal responsibility for their actions.

FUTURE DIRECTIONS

Several recent themes in the study of abnormal behavior suggest the direction of future developments. One theme is the increasing emphasis on biological factors in psychological disorders. Computer-based imaging techniques are making it possible to study even the most obscure or minute regions and functions of the brain, while molecular biological methods are clarifying the actions of cells and the location and operation of genes. These methods have already identified the location of a gene for early-onset Alzheimer's disease (e.g., Levy-Lahad et al., 1995). Biological studies will also help us learn more about genetic and brain dysfunctions associated with mood disorders, anxiety disorders, schizophrenia, and several childhood disorders.

The focus will not be entirely biological, however. Adopting a diathesis-stress approach, researchers will examine how a variety of interacting biological, psychological, environmental, and sociocultural factors may or may not produce abnormality, depending on how these factors are combined (Suinn, 1995). Even now, for example, researchers who study depression are trying to identify not only which specific cognitive patterns are associated with depression (Metalsky et al., 1993) but also how these patterns are related to other personality characteristics (Colvin, Block & Funder, 1995) and how the patterns interact with negative life events and genetic predispositions (Kendler et al., 1995).

Another new direction is suggested by the kinds of behavioral problems that psychologists study. For example, increasing emphasis will be placed on the unique problems experienced by women (Weissman & Olfson, 1995), ethnic minorities (Brown et al., 1995), and lesbians and gay men (Rothblum, 1994). Children and youth, too, will continue to be a major focus of future research on psychological disorders. New research on the epidemiology of children's disorders (Jensen et al., 1995), on the origins of their problems (Lahey et al., 1995), and on interventions to prevent the development of problems is already under way (Tremblay et al, 1995). Also anticipated is a sharper focus on the family—and the extent to which it contributes to the development of healthy, or disordered, children (Cicchetti & Cohen, 1995).

SUMMARY AND KEY TERMS

Psychopathology involves patterns of thinking, feeling, and behaving that are maladaptive, disruptive, or distressing either for the person affected or for others.

■ UNDERSTANDING PSYCHOLOGICAL DISORDERS: SOME BASIC ISSUES

The definition of abnormality is largely determined by social and cultural factors.

What Is Abnormal?
The criteria for judging abnormality include statistical infrequency (a comparison to what most people do), personal suffering, and norm violations. Each of these criteria is flawed to some extent. The practical approach, which considers the content, context, and consequences of behavior, emphasizes the question of whether people show *impaired functioning* in fulfilling the roles appropriate for particular people in particular settings, cultures, and historical eras.

Explaining Psychological Disorders
Abnormal behavior has been attributed, at one time or another, to the action of gods or the devil (the *supernatural* or *demonological model*), to physical disorders (the *medical* or *neurobiological model*), or to various psychological processes (the *psychological model*) such as inner turmoil, learning, or blocked self-actualization. The medical model, which suggests that all mental disorder results from physical illness, is very influential in most Western cultures, but some form of the supernatural model is employed in some Western subcultures and many non-Western cultures. *Sociocultural* factors help define abnormality and influence the form that disorders take in different parts of the world. No single model can adequately explain all psychological disorders. However, the *diathesis-stress model* takes all of them into account by highlighting inherited biological predispositions or psychological characteristics that interact with stressors to produce disorder.

Finally, the future promises new research on improving the reliability and validity of diagnoses of psychological disorders (Mannuzza et al., 1995). We may even see new ways of defining, categorizing, and diagnosing disorders (Livesley et al., 1994; Widiger & Costa, 1994; Widiger et al., 1996). Even today the criteria for calling someone "crazy" differ from one culture or subculture to the next. Accordingly, mental health professionals are expanding the practical approach to consider the content and consequences of behavior within its sociocultural context. Future years are likely to see a continued trend, begun with DSM-IV, toward basing diagnoses not only on what a person does but also on what values and traditions the behavior reflects, where and when it occurs, and who, if anyone, suffers (Lilienfeld & Marino, 1995). Ideally, DSM's continuing evolution toward ever more specific criteria for assessing disorders, based on research, should leave less room for bias based on ethnicity, gender, and other sociocultural variables. Moreover, further clarification of the effects of such variables will help us understand their contribution to the experience and expression, as well as the causes, of disorder.

We have offered only a glimpse of the problems, issues, and theories that characterize the study of psychological disorders. For more detailed coverage, enroll in a course in abnormal psychology.

■ CLASSIFYING PSYCHOLOGICAL DISORDERS

There seems to be a set of behavior patterns that roughly defines abnormality in most cultures.

A Classification System: DSM-IV
The dominant system for classifying abnormal behavior in North America is the Diagnostic and Statistical Manual (DSM-IV) of the American Psychiatric Association. It includes more than three hundred specific categories of mental disorder that can be described using five dimensions, or axes.

Purposes and Problems of Diagnosis
Diagnosis helps to identify the features, causes, and most effective methods of treating various psychological disorders. Research on the reliability and validity of DSM-IV shows that it is a useful, but not perfect, classification system.

■ ANXIETY DISORDERS

Long-standing and disruptive patterns of anxiety characterize *anxiety disorders.*

Types of Anxiety Disorders
The most prevalent type of anxiety disorder are the *phobias,* which include *specific phobia, social phobia,* and *agoraphobia.* Other anxiety disorders are *generalized anxiety disorder,* which involves nonspecific anxiety; *panic disorder,* which brings unpredictable attacks of intense anxiety; and *obsessive-compulsive disorder,* in which uncontrollable repetitive thoughts and ritualistic actions occur.

Causes of Anxiety Disorders
The most influential explanations of anxiety disorders suggest that they may develop as a result of a combination of biological predisposition for strong anxiety reactions and the impact of fear-enhancing thought patterns and learned anxiety responses.

■ LINKAGES: PSYCHOLOGICAL DISORDERS AND LEARNING

Many anxiety disorders appear to develop in accordance with the principles of classical and operant conditioning, as well as with those of observational learning. People may be biologically prepared to learn fear of certain objects and situations.

■ SOMATOFORM DISORDERS

Somatoform disorders include *conversion disorder,* which involves physical problems that have no apparent physical cause; *hypochondriasis,* an unjustified concern over being or becoming ill; *somatization disorder,* in which the person complains of numerous, unconfirmed physical complaints; and *pain disorder,* in which pain is felt in the absence of a physical cause.

■ DISSOCIATIVE DISORDERS

Dissociative disorders involve such rare conditions as *dissociative fugue, dissociative amnesia,* and *dissociative identity disorder* (multiple personality disorder), in which a person suffers sudden memory loss or develops two or more identities. Still controversial is the question of whether abuse in childhood is a causal factor in dissociative identity disorder.

■ MOOD DISORDERS

Mood disorders, also known as affective disorders, are quite common and involve extreme moods that may be inconsistent with events.

Depressive Disorders

Major depressive disorder is marked by feelings of inadequacy, worthlessness, and guilt; in extreme cases, *delusions* may also occur. Also seen is *dysthymic disorder,* which includes similar but less severe symptoms persisting for a long period. Suicide is often related to these disorders.

Bipolar Disorder

Alternating periods of depression and *mania* characterize *bipolar disorder,* which is also known as manic depression. *Cyclothymic disorder,* an alternating pattern of less extreme mood swings, is more common.

Causes of Mood Disorders

Mood disorders have been attributed to biological causes such as genetic inheritance, disruptions in neurotransmitter and endocrine systems, and irregularities in biological rhythms. Self-directed anger, loss of significant sources of reward, and maladaptive patterns of thinking are among the psychological causes proposed. A predisposition toward some of these disorders may be inherited, although their appearance may be determined by a diathesis-stress process.

■ SCHIZOPHRENIA

Symptoms of Schizophrenia

Schizophrenia is perhaps the most severe and puzzling disorder of all. Among its symptoms are problems in thinking, perception (often including *hallucinations*), attention, emotion, movement, motivation, and daily functioning. "Positive" symptoms of schizophrenia include the presence of such features as hallucinations or disordered speech; "negative symptoms" can include behavioral withdrawal, immobility, and the absence of affect.

Types of Schizophrenia

Five subtypes of schizophrenia have been identified, including *paranoid, disorganized, catatonic, undifferentiated,* and *residual.*

Causes of Schizophrenia

Genetic factors, neurotransmitter problems, abnormalities in brain structure and functioning, and neurodevelopmental abnormalities are biological factors implicated in schizophrenia. Psychological explanations have pointed to regression, unfortunate learning experiences, and disturbed family interactions. The diathesis-stress approach, often described in terms of the vulnerability model, remains a promising framework for research into the multiple causes of schizophrenia.

■ PERSONALITY DISORDERS

Personality disorders are long-term patterns of maladaptive behavior that, while not always associated with personal discomfort, may be disturbing to others. Examples include *schizotypal, avoidant, narcissistic,* and *antisocial personality disorders.*

■ A SAMPLING OF OTHER PSYCHOLOGICAL DISORDERS

Substance-Related Disorders

Substance-related disorders involving alcohol and other drugs affect millions of people. *Addiction* to and psychological dependence on these substances contribute to disastrous personal and social problems, including physical illnesses, accidents, and crime. Genetic factors may create a predisposition for *alcoholism,* but learning, cultural traditions, and other nonbiological processes are also important. For addiction to heroin and cocaine, stress reduction, imitation, thrill seeking, and social maladjustment have been proposed as important factors, along with genetics; but the exact causes of initial use of these drugs are unknown.

Psychological Disorders of Childhood

Childhood disorders can be categorized as externalizing conditions, such as conduct disorders or attention deficit hyperactivity disorder, and as internalizing disorders, in which children show overcontrol, experiencing internal distress as in separation anxiety disorder. The most severe childhood disorder is autistic disorder, in which the child shows no concern for or attachment to others.

■ MENTAL ILLNESS AND THE LAW

Current rules protect people accused of crimes from prosecution or punishment if they are mentally incompetent at the time of their trial or if they were legally insane at the time of their crime. Difficulty in establishing the mental state of defendants and other knotty problems have created dissatisfaction with those rules and prompted a number of reforms, including the "guilty but mentally ill" verdict.

TREATMENT OF PSYCHOLOGICAL DISORDERS

CHAPTER 16

LINKAGES
TO
TREATMENT OF
PSYCHOLOGICAL DISORDERS

BIOLOGICAL ASPECTS
OF PSYCHOLOGY

**How do therapeutic drugs
work?** *(ans. on p. 563)*

HEALTH, STRESS, AND COPING

**How can people manage
stress?** *(ans. on p. 451)*

LEARNING

**Can people learn their way
out of a disorder?** *(ans. on
p. 541)*

In the last chapter, we described José, a fifty-five-year-old electronics technician who had to take medical leave from his job after experiencing panic
attacks (see Table 15.1). After four months of diagnostic testing turned up
no physical problems, José's physician suggested that he see a psychologist.
José resisted at first, saying that his condition was not "just in his head," but he eventually began psychological treatment. Within a few months, his panic attacks had ceased,
and José was back to all his old activities. After the psychologist helped him to recon-
sider his workload, José decided to retire from his job in order to pursue more satisfying work at his home-based computer business.

José's case is by no means unique. During any given year in the United States alone,
nearly 15 percent of the population is receiving some form of treatment for a psychological disorder (Regier et al., 1993). In this chapter, we describe a variety of these treatments, most of which are based on the theories of stress and coping, personality, and
psychological disorder reviewed in Chapters 13, 14, and 15. By spelling out proposed
explanations for what can go wrong in the development of personality and behavior,
and the role of stress in both, those theories provide important guidelines for treatment
(see the Linkages diagram).

After first examining some features seen in all forms of treatment, we discuss some
of the methods that have been derived from the psychodynamic, phenomenological,
and behavioral approaches to treatment. These approaches all rely on **psychotherapy,**
the treatment of psychological disorders through psychological methods, such as talking about problems and exploring new ways of thinking and acting. We then consider
biological approaches to treatment, which depend mainly on drugs and other physical
therapies. Although we discuss different approaches in separate sections, keep in mind
that the majority of mental health professionals see themselves as *eclectic therapists;* in
other words, they might lean toward one treatment approach, but, in working with particular clients or particular problems, they borrow methods from other types of therapy as well (Jensen, Bergin & Greaves, 1990). Further, many clients receive psychoactive
drugs during the course of psychological treatment (Lickey & Gordon, 1991).

BASIC FEATURES OF TREATMENT

All treatments for psychological disorders share certain basic features—not only with
one another but also with efforts to help the physically ill (Frank, 1973, 1978). These

MEDIEVAL TREATMENT METHODS The methods used to treat psychological disorders are related to the presumed cause of those disorders. In medieval times, when demons were widely blamed for abnormal behavior, magical-religious practitioners tried to make the victim's body inhospitable to evil spirits. Here, many such spirits are shown departing when an afflicted person's head is placed in an oven.

common features include a *client* or patient, a *therapist* or helper who is accepted as capable of helping the client, and a special relationship between the client and therapist. In addition, all forms of treatment are based on some *theory* about the causes of the client's problems. The theories may presume causes ranging from magic spells to infections and everything in between (Frank, 1973). From theories flow *procedures* for dealing with the client's problems. Thus, traditional healers combat supernatural forces with ceremonies and prayers, medical doctors treat chemical imbalances with drugs, and psychologists focus on altering psychological processes through psychotherapy.

People receiving psychotherapy can be classified into two general categories. *Inpatients* are treated in a hospital or other residential institution; in public hospitals, many are older adult males from lower social class backgrounds. Inpatients are hospitalized because their impairments are severe enough to constitute a threat to their own well-being or the safety of others. Depending on their level of functioning, inpatients may stay in the hospital for a few days or up to several years. Their treatment almost always includes psychoactive drugs. *Outpatients* receive psychotherapy while living in the community; they tend to be younger than the average inpatient, more often female than male, and often come from the middle or upper classes.

Those who provide psychological treatment are also a diverse group. **Psychiatrists** are medical doctors who complete specialty training in the treatment of mental disorders. Like other physicians, they are authorized to prescribe drugs for the relief of psychological problems. **Psychologists** who do psychotherapy have usually completed a doctoral degree in clinical or counseling psychology, often followed by additional specialized training. Psychologists are not authorized to prescribe drugs, although there is continuing debate over a controversial proposal to extend prescription privileges to clinical psychologists who have been specially trained for this function (Bell, Digman & McKenna, 1995; Hays & Heiby, 1996; Martin, 1995; Moyer, 1995). *Clinical social workers, marriage and family therapists,* and *licensed professional counselors* typically hold a masters' degree from a graduate program in their respective professions and provide treatment in a variety of settings including hospitals, clinics, and private practice. *Psychiatric nurses, substance abuse counselors,* and a host of paraprofessional providers, including some clergy, also provide various forms of therapy, often as part of a hospital or outpatient treatment team. (People using vague titles, such as "psychotherapist," may or may not have appropriate training in psychotherapy, so it is important to ask about their background before entering into treatment with them.)

GROUP THERAPY FOR BATTERED WOMEN
Some psychotherapy consists of
one-to-one sessions in an office setting, but no single image can capture
all its many formats. Therapy is also
conducted with couples, families,
and groups in hospitals, community
health centers, and facilities for former mental hospital residents.
Treatment is also provided in prisons, military bases, drug and alcoholism treatment centers, and other
places.

The general goal of treatment providers is to help troubled people change their
thinking, feelings, and behavior in ways that relieve discomfort, promote happiness,
and improve functioning as parents, students, workers, and the like. To reach this goal,
some therapists try to help clients gain insight into the hidden causes of problems, others seek to promote growth through more genuine self-expression, and still others help
clients learn and practice new ways of thinking and acting. The particular methods
employed in each case depend on the problems, preferences, and financial circumstances of the client, the time available for treatment, and the therapist's theoretical
leanings and methodological preferences. There are hundreds of specific psychotherapy
methods (Corsini & Wedding, 1995), most of which fall into one of three general categories: psychodynamic, phenomenological, and behavioral.

PSYCHODYNAMIC PSYCHOTHERAPY

The field of formal psychotherapy began in the late nineteenth century when Sigmund
Freud established the psychodynamic approach to personality and disorder described
in Chapters 14 and 15. Central to his approach, and to modern revisions of it, is the
assumption that personality and behavior reflect the efforts of the ego to referee conflicts, usually unconscious, among various components of the personality. Freud's
method of treatment, **psychoanalysis,** is aimed at understanding these unconscious
conflicts and how they affect the client. His one-to-one method of studying and treating people, his systematic search for relationships between an individual's life history
and current problems, his emphasis on thoughts and emotions in treatment, and his
focus on the client-therapist relationship are reflected in almost all forms of psychotherapy. We will describe Freud's original methods first, then consider some more
recently developed treatments that are rooted in his psychodynamic approach.

Classical Psychoanalysis

Classical psychoanalysis developed mainly out of Freud's medical practice. He was puzzled by patients who suffered from "hysterical" ailments—blindness, paralysis, or other
symptoms that had no physical cause. (As mentioned in Chapter 15, these are now
called conversion disorders in DSM-IV.) Freud tried to cure these patients with hypnotic suggestions, but he found them to be only partially and temporarily successful.
Later, Freud and his colleague Joseph Breuer asked hypnotized patients to recall events
that might have caused their symptoms. Eventually, Freud stopped using hypnosis and
merely had the patient lie on a couch and report whatever thoughts, memories, or
images came to mind (a process Freud called *free association*).

FREUD'S CONSULTING ROOM During psychoanalytic sessions, Freud's patients lay on this couch while he sat in the chair behind them. According to Freud, human actions are determined by a combination of conscious intentions and unconscious influences. Even apparently trivial or accidental behavior may hold important messages from the unconscious. Thus, forgetting a dream or the time of a therapy appointment might reflect a client's unconscious resistance to treatment. Even accidents may be meaningful. The waiter who spills hot soup on an elderly male customer might be seen as acting out unconscious aggressive impulses against a father figure.

The results of this "talking cure" were surprising. Freud and Breuer were struck by how many patients reported childhood memories of sexual abuse, usually by a parent or other close relative. Either child abuse was rampant in Vienna at the time or his patients' reports were distorted by psychological factors. Freud ultimately concluded that his patients' memories of childhood seduction probably reflected childhood fantasies (a conclusion that has come under attack, as discussed in the chapter on personality). This reasoning focused classical psychoanalysis on the exploration of unconscious impulses and fantasies. His patients' hysterical symptoms, Freud concluded, developed out of conflicts about those impulses and fantasies.

Classical psychoanalytic treatment aims to help clients gain insight into their problems by recognizing unconscious thoughts and emotions, and then to discover, or work through, the many ways in which those unconscious elements affect everyday life. The treatment may require as many as three to five sessions per week, usually over several years. Generally, the psychoanalyst aims to maintain a compassionate neutrality during treatment as the client slowly develops insight into how past conflicts determine current problems.

To gain glimpses into the unconscious, Freud considered not only his patients' free associations but also their dreams, their everyday behaviors, and their relationship with him. He believed that, hidden beneath the obvious or *manifest content* of dreams, there is *latent content* that reflects the wishes, impulses, and fantasies that the dreamer's defense mechanisms keep out of consciousness during waking hours. Accordingly, Freud devoted considerable time to interpreting the unconscious meaning of dreams. He also looked for meaning in "Freudian slips" of the tongue (such as saying "beast" instead of "best") and other seemingly insignificant behaviors. Similarly, tenderness, fear, dependency, hostility, and other aspects of the client's behavior in therapy sessions were viewed by Freud as part of an unconscious transference to the therapist of feelings and conflicts experienced in childhood in relation to parents and other significant people. Analysis of this *transference*, this "new edition" of the client's childhood conflicts and current problems, became another important psychoanalytic method; Freud believed that focusing on the transference allows clients to see how old conflicts haunt their lives and to resolve these problems from the past.

Contemporary Variations on Psychoanalysis

Though classical psychoanalysis is still practiced (Fonagy & Moran, 1990), it is not as prevalent as it was several decades ago (Jensen, Bergin & Greaves, 1990). The decline is due to such factors as disenchantment with Freud's instinct-based personality theory,

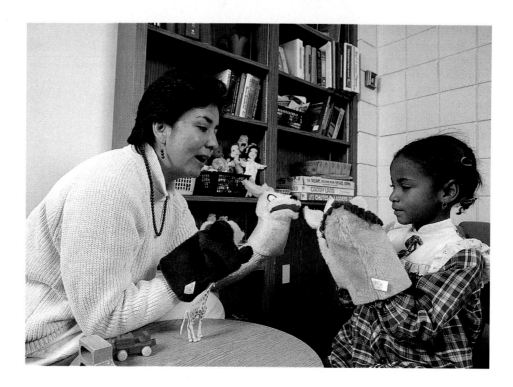

A PLAY THERAPY SESSION Contemporary variants of psychoanalytic treatment include fantasy play and other techniques that make the approach more useful with children. A child's behavior and comments while playing with puppets representing family members, for example, allows a form of free association that the therapist hopes will reveal important unconscious material (such as fear of abandonment).

the high cost of classical psychoanalysis in both time and money, its limited usefulness with children, and the availability of many alternative forms of treatment, including variations on classical psychoanalysis.

Many of the variations were developed by the neo-Freudian theorists discussed in Chapter 14. As noted there, these theorists tended to give less emphasis than Freud did to the past and to biologically based drives stemming from the id and unconscious. They also tended to stress the client's current problems and how the power of the ego can be harnessed to solve them. Treatment variations based on these neo-Freudian theories include *ego analysis* (Hartmann, 1958; Klein, 1960), *interpersonal therapy* (Sullivan, 1954), and *individual analysis* (Adler, 1963). Some versions have been designed for use with children (Klein, 1960; A. Freud, 1946). A particularly popular contemporary psychodynamic approach is known as *object relations therapy* (Bacal & Newman, 1990; Kohut, 1983).

Object relations analysts believe that personality, and the conflicts among its components, derive from the need for supportive human relationships. The mother-child relationship—and the attachment patterns described in Chapter 12, on development—form the prototype for these relationships (Kohut, 1971). (The term *object* refers to anything, from symbols to people, that can have emotional significance for a person.) The powerful need for human contact takes center stage in object relations therapy, since most of the difficulties that bring clients to treatment involve their relationships with others.

Psychodynamically oriented psychotherapists who adopt an object relations perspective take a much more active role than classical analysts do. The object relations therapist works to develop a nurturing relationship with the client, providing a "second chance" for the client to receive the support that might have been absent in infancy and to counteract some of the consequences of maladaptive early attachment patterns (e.g., Lieberman & Pawl, 1988). For example, the therapist takes pains to demonstrate that the client will not be abandoned.

Other variations on psychoanalysis retain more of Freud's ideas but alter the format of treatment so that it is less intense, less expensive, and appropriate for a broader range of clients. For example, *psychoanalytically oriented psychotherapy* (Alexander, 1963) and *time-limited dynamic psychotherapy* use basic psychoanalytic methods, but more flexibly (Davanloo, 1978; Sifneos, 1979; Strupp, 1989). The therapist may be more active than a classical psychoanalyst in directing the client's attention to evidence of particular conflicts. The goal of treatment may range from giving psychological support to achieving basic changes in personality, and therapy may be completed in fewer than thirty sessions.

Some version of transference analysis is seen in virtually all variations on classical psychoanalysis. In a short-term psychodynamic treatment called *supportive-expressive therapy*, for example, the therapist looks for a "core conflict" that appears repeatedly across a variety of relationships, including the therapy relationship (Luborsky, 1984). Consider this excerpt from the treatment of a depressed twenty-two-year-old college student who had been physically abused by his father in childhood:

Client: I feel mad at myself for not standing up to my roommate.

Therapist: What happened?

Client: I was talking to a friend and my roommate interrupted me. He wanted to use my car. I said, "Excuse me, but I am having a conversation." Instead of backing off he continued to interrupt me in a rude manner. I just couldn't stand up to him and when he left, my friend asked me why I just didn't "tell him to go to hell." But I just gave in, and later I started to have all these fantasies.

Therapist: Fantasies?

Client: Yes, things like, I imagined things like punching him in the mouth. Telling him to drop dead. Then I just kind of felt stupid, like I was overreacting and making a big deal out of nothing. I felt really stupid. I started getting down on myself again.

The supportive-expressive therapist might see in this client a core conflict between the desire to stand up for himself and the tendency to criticize himself for having that desire. The therapist would watch for this core conflict to appear in the therapy relationship—perhaps in the form of tentative assertiveness tempered by fear of having done wrong—then help the client see the links among his fear of asserting himself, his fantasies of getting even, and his childhood abuse experiences. This interpretation is part of the transference analysis. At the same time, the therapist would support the client's attempts to be more assertive with authority figures without having violent fantasies.

Variants on classical analysis focus not only on the client's feelings toward the therapist but also on the therapist's feelings toward the client—that is, on *countertransference*. For example, if transference leads a client to treat the therapist as a mother, the therapist might, because of countertransference, unintentionally begin treating the client as her child. Therapists must be alert to countertransference and its effects on their clinical objectivity. Ideally, the development and analysis of this emotionally intimate two-way relationship serves as a stepping stone for the client to develop healthier, more satisfying relationships with others.

With their focus on interpersonal relationships rather than instincts, their emphasis on clients' potential for self-directed problem solving, and their reassurance and emotional supportiveness, contemporary variants on classical psychoanalysis have helped the psychodynamic approach to retain its influence among mental health professionals (Cashdan, 1988; Jensen, Bergin & Greaves, 1990).

PHENOMENOLOGICAL PSYCHOTHERAPY

While some therapists who were trained in classical psychoanalysis sought to revise Freud's approach, others developed radical new therapies based on a phenomenological approach to personality. As discussed in Chapters 14 and 15, *phenomenologists,* also called *humanistic psychologists,* emphasize the subjective interpretations that people place on events. Phenomenologists view people as capable of consciously controlling their own actions and taking responsibility for their decisions. Many phenomenological therapists believe that human behavior is motivated not by sexual or aggressive instincts but by an innate drive toward growth that is guided from moment to moment by the way people interpret the world. Disordered behavior reflects a blockage of natural growth, brought on by distorted perceptions or lack of awareness about feelings. Thus, phenomenological therapists operate on the following assumptions:

1. Treatment is a human encounter between equals, not a cure given by an expert. It is a way to help clients restart their natural growth and to feel and behave as they really are.

2. Clients will improve on their own, given the right conditions. These ideal conditions promote clients' awareness, acceptance, and expression of their feelings and perceptions. Thus, as in psychodynamic approaches, therapy promotes insight. Phenomenological therapy, however, seeks insight into current feelings and perceptions, not into unconscious childhood conflicts.

3. Ideal conditions in therapy can best be established through a relationship in which clients feel totally accepted and supported as human beings, no matter how problematic or undesirable their *behavior* may be. It is the client's experience of this relationship that brings beneficial changes. (As noted earlier, this assumption is also important in object relations therapy.)

4. Clients must remain responsible for choosing how they will think and behave.

Of the many phenomenological treatments in use today, the most influential are those of Carl Rogers and Frederick S. Perls.

Client-Centered Therapy

Carl Rogers was trained in psychodynamic methods during the 1930s, but he soon began to question their value. He especially disliked being a detached, expert observer who "figured out" the client. He became convinced that a less formal approach would be more effective for the client and more comfortable for the therapist. Accordingly, Rogers developed *nondirective therapy,* which depends on the client's own drive toward growth or self-actualization. Rogers allowed his clients to decide what to talk about and when, without direction, judgment, or interpretation by the therapist. This approach, now called **client-centered—**or **person-centered—therapy,** relies on the creation of a relationship that reflects three intertwined therapist attitudes: unconditional positive regard, empathy, and congruence.

A CLIENT-CENTERED THERAPY GROUP
Carl Rogers (shown here in shirt-sleeves) believed that, as successful treatment progresses, clients become more self-confident, more aware of their feelings, more accepting of themselves, more comfortable and genuine with other people, more reliant on self-evaluation than on the judgments of others, and more effective and relaxed.

Unconditional Positive Regard   The attitude Rogers called **unconditional positive regard** consists of nothing more or less than treating the client as a valued person, no matter what. This attitude is communicated through the therapist's willingness to listen, without interrupting, and to accept what is said without evaluating it. The therapist need not *approve* of everything the client says, just accept it as reflecting a part of the person who said it. Because they trust clients to solve their own problems, Rogerian therapists rarely give advice. Doing so, said Rogers, would carry the subtle message that clients are incompetent, making them less confident and more dependent on help.

Empathy   Rogerian therapists try to appreciate how the world looks from the client's point of view. This involves far more than saying "I know what you mean." The client-centered therapist tries to replace an *external frame of reference*—looking at the client from the outside—with an *internal frame of reference* characterized by **empathy,** which involves an emotional understanding of what the client might be thinking and feeling. Client-centered therapists convey empathy by showing that they are actively listening to the client. Like other skillful interviewers, they make eye contact with the client, nod in recognition as the client speaks, and give other signs of careful attention. They also use **reflection,** a paraphrased summary of the client's words and especially the feelings and meanings that appear to accompany them; reflection confirms the communication, shows the therapist's interest, and helps the client to perceive thoughts and feelings. Here is an example:

Client: This has been such a bad day. I've felt ready to cry any minute and I'm not even sure what's wrong!

Therapist: You really do feel so bad. The tears just seem to well up inside, and it must be a little scary to not even know why you feel this way.

Notice that by paraphrasing what the client said, the therapist reflected back not only the obvious feelings of sadness but also the fear in the client's voice. Most clients respond to empathic reflection by elaborating on their feelings. In this example, the client went on to say, "It *is* scary, because I don't like to feel in the dark about myself. I have always prided myself on being in control."

By communicating the desire to listen and understand, the therapist can bring important material into the open without asking disruptive questions. Empathic listening tends to be so effective in promoting self-understanding and awareness that it is used across a wide range of therapies (Greenberg, Rice & Elliot, 1993). Even outside of therapy, people who are thought of as easy to talk to tend to be "good listeners" who reflect back the important messages they hear from others.

Congruence   Sometimes called *genuineness,* **congruence** refers to a consistency between the way the therapist feels and acts toward the client. When the therapist's unconditional positive regard and empathy are genuine, then the client is able to see that relationships can be built on openness and honesty. Ideally, this experience will help the client become more congruent in other relationships. Here is an excerpt that illustrates the therapeutic attitudes just described.

Client: . . . I cannot be the kind of person I want to be. I guess maybe I haven't the guts or the strength to kill myself and if someone else would relieve me of the responsibility or I would be in an accident I, I . . . just don't want to live.

Therapist: At the present time things look so bad that you can't see much point in living. [Note the use of empathic reflection and the absence of any criticism.]

Client: Yes. I wish I'd never started this therapy. I was happy when I was living in my dream world. There I could be the kind of person I wanted to be. But now there is such a wide, wide gap between my ideal and what I am. . . . [Notice how the client responds to reflection by giving more information.]

Therapist: It's really a tough struggle digging into this like you are and at times the shelter of your dream world looks more attractive and comfortable. [Reflection]

NONVERBAL CUES IN GESTALT THERAPY
Gestalt therapists pay particular attention to clients' "body language," especially when it conflicts with what they are saying. If this client had just said that she is looking forward to starting her new job, the therapist would probably challenge that statement in an effort to make the client more aware of her ambivalence.

Client: My dream world or suicide. . . . So I don't see why I should waste your time—coming in twice a week—I'm not worth it—What do you think?

Therapist: It's up to you. . . . It isn't wasting my time. I'd be glad to see you whenever you come but it's how you feel about it. . . . [Note the congruence in stating an honest desire to see the client and the unconditional positive regard in trusting her capacity and responsibility for choice.]

Client: You're not going to suggest that I come in oftener? You're not alarmed and think I ought to come in every day until I get out of this?

Therapist: I believe you are able to make your own decision. I'll see you whenever you want to come. [Positive regard]

Client: (*Note of awe in her voice*) I don't believe you are alarmed about—I see—I may be afraid of myself but you aren't afraid for me. [Here the client experiences the therapist's confidence in her. She did not kill herself, by the way.] (Rogers, 1951, p. 49)

Gestalt Therapy

Another form of phenomenological treatment was developed by Frederick S. (Fritz) Perls, a European psychoanalyst who was greatly influenced by Gestalt psychology. As noted in the chapter on perception, Gestalt psychologists emphasized the idea that people actively organize their view of the world. Perls believed that (1) people create their own versions of reality and (2) people's natural psychological growth continues only as long as they perceive, remain aware of, and act on their true feelings. Growth stops and symptoms appear, said Perls, when people are not aware of all aspects of themselves (Perls, Hefferline & Goodman, 1951).

Like client-centered therapy, **Gestalt therapy** seeks to create conditions in which clients can become more unified, self-aware, and self-accepting, and thus ready to grow again. However, Gestalt therapists use more direct and dramatic methods than do Rogerians. Often working in group settings, Gestalt therapists prod clients to become aware of feelings and impulses that they have disowned and to discard feelings, ideas, and values that are not really their own. For example, the therapist or other group members might point out incongruities between what clients say and how they behave. Gestalt therapists may also ask clients to engage in imaginary dialogues with other people, with parts of their own personalities, and even with objects. Like a shy person who can be socially outgoing only while in a Halloween costume, clients often find that these dialogues help to get them in touch with, and express, their feelings (Paivio & Greenberg, 1995).

BEHAVIOR THERAPY

The psychodynamic and phenomenological approaches assume that if clients gain insight or self-awareness about underlying problems, the symptoms created by those problems will disappear. Behavior therapists emphasize a different kind of insight or self-awareness: They try to help clients view psychological problems as learned behaviors that can be changed without first searching for hidden meanings or underlying processes.

For example, suppose you have a panic attack every time you leave home and find relief only when you return. Making excuses when friends invite you out temporarily eases your anxiety but does nothing to solve the problem. Could you reduce your fear without looking for its "meaning"? Behavior therapy would offer just such an alternative by first helping you to understand the learning principles that maintain your fear and then helping you to learn new responses in feared situations.

This approach is the logical outcome of the assumptions of the behavioral approach to psychology. As described in Chapters 1, 14, and 15, behaviorists see learning as the basis of normal personality, and of most behavior disorders. According to this perspective, disordered behavior and thinking are samples of the maladaptive thoughts and actions that the client has learned. Fear of leaving home (agoraphobia), for example, is seen by behaviorists as developing through classically conditioned associations between panic attacks and situations outside the home. The problem is maintained in part through operant conditioning; staying home, and making excuses for doing so, is rewarded by reduced anxiety. Therapists who adopt a behavioral approach argue that if past learning experiences can produce problems, systematic new learning experiences can help alleviate them. Even if the learning that led to phobias and other problems began in childhood, behaviorists focus on solving today's problems through new experiences based on the principles of learning discussed in Chapter 7.

Behavioral approaches to treatment have their roots in the work of Watson, Pavlov, and others who studied the learned nature of fear in the 1920s, as well as in B. F. Skinner's research on the impact of reward and punishment on behavior. In the late 1950s and early 1960s, researchers began using classical and operant conditioning principles to alter disordered human behavior (Kazdin, 1978). By 1970, behavioral treatment had become a popular alternative to psychodynamic and phenomenological methods. Some of the most notable features of behavioral treatment include:

1. Developing a good therapist-client relationship. As in other therapies, this relationship enhances clients' confidence that change is possible and makes it easier for them to speak freely and to cooperate in the treatment.

2. Careful listing of the behaviors and thoughts to be changed. This assessment and the establishment of specific goals sometimes replace the formal diagnosis used in certain other approaches. Thus, instead of treating "depression" or "schizophrenia," behavior therapists work to change the specific thoughts, behaviors, and emotional reactions that cause people to receive these labels.

3. A therapist who acts as a kind of teacher/assistant by providing learning-based treatments, giving "homework" assignments, and helping the client make specific plans for dealing with problems.

4. Continuous monitoring and evaluation of treatment along with constant adjustments to any procedures that do not seem to be effective.

Behavioral treatment can take many forms. By tradition, those that rely mainly on *classical conditioning* principles are usually referred to as **behavior therapy.** Those that focus on *operant conditioning* methods are usually called **behavior modification.** And behavioral treatment that focuses on changing thinking patterns as well as overt behaviors is called **cognitive-behavior therapy.**

Techniques for Modifying Behavior

LINKAGES Can people learn their way out of a disorder? (a link to Learning)

Some of the most important and commonly used behavioral treatment techniques are systematic desensitization, modeling, positive reinforcement, extinction, aversive conditioning, and punishment.

Systematic Desensitization   A behavioral treatment often used to help clients deal with phobias and other forms of irrational anxiety was developed by Joseph Wolpe (1958). Called **systematic desensitization,** it is a method for reducing intense anxiety in which the client visualizes a graduated series of anxiety-provoking stimuli while maintaining a state of relaxation. Wolpe believed that this process so weakens the learned association between anxiety and the feared object that the fear disappears.

Wolpe first arranged for clients to do something incompatible with being afraid. Since it is hard to be tense and deeply relaxed at the same time, Wolpe used a technique called *progressive relaxation training* (described in Chapter 13) to prevent anxiety. Next the client relaxes while imagining an item from a *desensitization hierarchy,* a sequence of increasingly fear-provoking situations (see Table 16.1). The client works through the hierarchy gradually, imagining a more difficult scene only after being able to tolerate the previous one without distress. Once clients can calmly imagine being in feared situations, they are better able to deal with them. Desensitization may be especially effective if the client can work on a hierarchy in real life (Chambliss, 1990), but this *in vivo*

TABLE 16.1

A Sample Desensitization Hierarchy

Desensitization hierarchies are lists of increasingly fear-provoking stimuli that the client visualizes while using relaxation to remain calm. Here are some items from a hierarchy that was used to reduce a client's fear of flying.

1. You are reading a newspaper and notice an ad for an airline.
2. You are watching a television program that shows a group of people boarding a plane.
3. Your boss tells you that you need to take a business trip by air.
4. You are in your bedroom packing your suitcase for your trip.

    ·
    ·
    ·

12. Your plane begins to move as you hear the flight attendant say, "Be sure your seat belt is securely fastened."
13. You look at the runway as the plane is readied for takeoff.
14. You look out the window as the plane rolls down the runway.
15. You look out the window as the plane leaves the ground.

FIGURE 16.1

Participant Modeling

In the first convincing demonstration of the benefits of participant modeling, it was compared to systematic desensitization, symbolic modeling (watching filmed models), and no treatment (control). Notice that, compared to no treatment, all three methods helped snake-phobic clients approach live snakes, but participant modeling was clearly the best; 92 percent of the subjects in that group were virtually free of any fear. The value of participant modeling has been repeatedly confirmed (e.g., Öst, Salkovskis & Hellström, 1991).

- Live modeling with participation
- Symbolic modeling
- Systematic desensitization
- Control

Source: Data from Bandura, Blanchard & Ritter, 1969.

exposure is not always easy to arrange or control, especially when the fear involves commercial air travel or freeway driving, for example. Recently, however, virtual reality technology has made it possible for clients to "experience" extremely vivid, and gradually more intense, versions of feared situations without actually being in those situations. In one study, for example, clients with acrophobia (fear of heights) stood on a platform surrounded by a railing while wearing a head-mounted visual display. The images presented on the display gave the impression of standing on bridges that were seven to eighty meters above water, on outdoor balconies at increasing heights, or in a glass elevator as it rose forty-nine floors (Rothbaum et al., 1995).

Exactly why systematic desensitization works is not clear. Most clinicians believe that change occurs either through classical conditioning of a new, calmer response to the fear-provoking stimulus or through extinction, as the object or situation that had been a conditioned fear stimulus repeatedly occurs without being paired with pain or any other unconditioned stimulus (Rachman, 1990).

Modeling   Therapists often teach clients desirable behaviors by demonstrating those behaviors. In **modeling,** the client watches other people perform desired behaviors, thus vicariously learning skills without going through a lengthy shaping process. In fear treatment, modeling can teach the client how to respond fearlessly while vicariously extinguishing conditioned fear responses. For example, one therapist showed a twenty-four-year-old student with a severe spider phobia how to kill spiders with a fly swatter and had her practice this skill at home with rubber spiders (MacDonald & Bernstein, 1974). The combination of live modeling with gradual practice is called *participant modeling;* it is one of the most powerful treatments for fear (see Figure 16.1).

Modeling is also a major part of **assertiveness and social skills training,** which teaches clients how to interact with people more comfortably and effectively. The goals of social skills training range from helping college students with social phobias make conversation on dates to rebuilding mental patients' ability to interact normally with people outside the hospital (Wallace et al., 1992; Wong et al., 1993). In assertiveness training, the therapist helps clients learn to be more direct and expressive in social situations. Note that *assertiveness* does not mean aggressiveness; it means clearly and directly expressing both positive and negative feelings and standing up for one's rights while respecting the rights of others (Alberti & Emmons, 1986). Assertiveness training is often done in groups and involves both modeling and role playing of specific situations. In one program, group assertiveness training helped wheelchair-bound adults more comfortably handle the socially awkward situations in which they sometimes find themselves (Gleuckauf & Quittner, 1992).

Positive Reinforcement   Behavior therapists also use systematic **positive reinforcement** to alter problematic behaviors and to teach new skills in cases ranging from childhood tantrums and juvenile delinquency to schizophrenia and self-starvation.

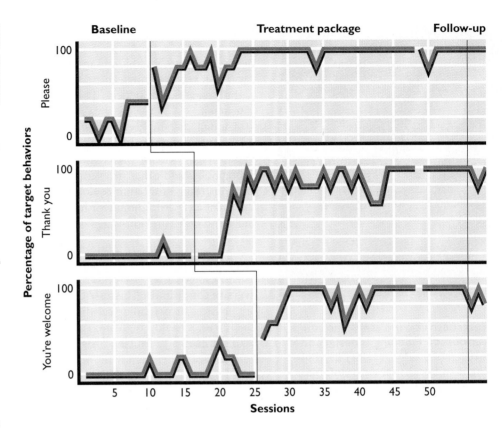

FIGURE 16.2

A Positive Reinforcement Program for an Autistic Child

During each pretreatment baseline period, the child rarely said "please," "thank you," or "you're welcome," but these statements began to occur spontaneously once they were reinforced. The causal role of reinforcement in producing these changes is supported by the fact that each response remained low until it was specifically reinforced.

Source: Matson et al., 1990.

EXTINCTION VIA "TIME OUT" When undesirable behavior cannot be ignored or is being rewarded (as when a child gets laughs by teasing a classmate), the client may be placed in a boring place for a few minutes. This "time out" from positive reinforcement discourages the undesirable behavior by interrupting the reward process that had been maintaining it.

Employing the operant conditioning principles described in Chapter 7, they set up contingencies, or rules, that specify the behaviors to be strengthened through reinforcement. In one study, autistic children, who, as described in Chapter 15, use very little language, were given grapes, popcorn, or other items they liked for saying "please," "thank you," and "you're welcome" while exchanging crayons and blocks with a therapist. The therapist initially modeled the behavior by saying the appropriate words. The children almost immediately began to utter the phrases spontaneously. The effects generalized to situations involving other toys, and, as indicated in Figure 16.2, the new skills were still evident six months later (Matson et al., 1990).

For severely retarded or disturbed clients in institutions, behavior therapists sometimes establish a **token economy,** a system of reinforcing desirable behaviors with poker chips or other tokens that are later exchanged for snacks, access to television, or other desired rewards (Ayllon & Azrin, 1968; Kazdin, 1982). The goal is to shape behavior patterns that will persist outside the institution (Morisse et al., 1996).

Extinction   Just as reinforcement can be used to make desirable behaviors more likely, other behavioral techniques can make undesirable behaviors less likely. In operant conditioning, **extinction** is the process of removing the reinforcers that normally follow a particular response. If you have ever given up telephoning someone whose line is busy, you know how extinction works: When a behavior does not "pay off," people usually stop it. Extinction changes behavior rather slowly, but it has been a popular way of treating children and retarded or seriously disturbed adults because it provides a gentle way to eliminate undesirable behaviors.

Another application of extinction is **flooding,** a procedure that keeps people in a feared but harmless situation, depriving them of their normally rewarding escape pattern. (Flooding and related methods based on the extinction of classically conditioned fear responses are also called *exposure techniques.*) When someone is kept in contact with a fear-eliciting conditioned stimulus (CS), without experiencing a severe unconditioned stimulus (UCS), the fear-eliciting power of the CS eventually diminishes and

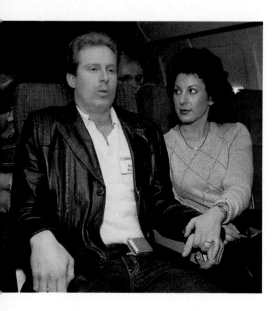

LINKAGES: TREATING FEAR THROUGH FLOODING Flooding is designed to extinguish severe anxiety by allowing it to occur without reinforcement. By the end of his airplane flight, this fearful client was much less anxious than he had been at the beginning. Like other behavioral treatments, flooding stems from the behavioral approach to personality described in Chapter 14. That approach suggests that disordered behavior, like normal behavior, is learned and can thus be "unlearned."

the fear response extinguishes. In one study, clients who feared needles were given continuous *in vivo* exposure to needles, including mild finger pricks, harmless subcutaneous injections, and blood samplings (Öst, Hellström & Kåver, 1992). After a single, two-hour session, nineteen of twenty clients were able to have their blood drawn without significant anxiety. These effects were maintained at a one-year follow-up assessment.

Though often highly effective, flooding is equivalent to immediately exposing a fearful client to the most distressing item on a desensitization hierarchy. Accordingly, some therapists and clients prefer more gradual exposure methods, especially for treating agoraphobia and other problems in which a client's fear is not focused on a specific stimulus (Foa, Rothbaum & Kozak, 1989). In such cases, exposure involves escorting the client away from home for increasing periods, eventually venturing into shopping malls and other previously avoided places (Kleinknecht, 1991).

Aversive Conditioning　　Many unwanted behaviors are so habitual and temporarily rewarding that they must be made less attractive if the client is to have any chance of learning alternatives. Methods for lessening the appeal of certain stimuli are known as **aversive conditioning,** because they employ classical conditioning principles to associate physical or psychological discomfort with behaviors, thoughts, or situations the client wishes to stop or avoid. For example, alcoholics might be allowed to drink after taking a nausea-producing drug, so that the taste and smell of alcohol are associated with nausea rather than with the usual pleasurable feelings (Cannon & Baker, 1981).

A form of aversive conditioning called *covert sensitization* is, in a sense, the opposite of systematic desensitization. The client first thinks of the inappropriately attractive stimulus or situation and is then exposed to tape-recorded depictions of frightening or disgusting stimuli. For example, covert sensitization was used to treat a man who had been repeatedly arrested for making obscene phone calls. While imagining making an obscene call, the client heard vivid descriptions of his greatest fears: snakes, vomiting, and choking. Finally, he imagined his mother walking in on him during a call. After a month of treatment he was no longer sexually aroused by thoughts of making obscene calls, and he had made none even two years later (Moergen, Merkel & Brown, 1990).

Because aversive conditioning is unpleasant and uncomfortable, and its effects often temporary, many therapists avoid this method or use it only long enough to allow the client to learn alternative behaviors.

Punishment　　Sometimes the only way to eliminate a dangerous or disruptive behavior is to punish it with an unpleasant but not harmful stimulus, such as a shouted "No!" or a mild electric shock. Unlike aversive conditioning, in which the unpleasant stimulus occurs along with the behavior to be eliminated (a classical conditioning approach), **punishment** is an operant conditioning technique; it presents the unpleasant stimulus *after* the undesirable response occurs. (Though technically distinct, the two methods may overlap.) As discussed in the chapter on learning, most therapists prefer using punishment mainly as a last resort, such as when a client's life is in danger or all other methods have failed. Just such a case is illustrated in Figure 7.13 on page 210.

Cognitive-Behavior Therapy

Psychodynamic and phenomenological therapists have long recognized that problematic thought patterns may lead to depression, anger, or anxiety. Behavior therapists have also attacked these problems, using methods known collectively as cognitive-behavior therapy. In simplest terms, *cognitive-behavior therapy* helps clients change the way they think as well as the way they behave. For example, some clients already know *how* to be assertive in social situations but need to identify the habitual thoughts (such as "I shouldn't draw attention to myself") that get in the way of self-expression. Once these cognitive obstacles are brought to light, the therapist encourages the client to try new ways of thinking. The therapist may also help clients learn to say things to themselves that promote desirable behavior and prevent a relapse into undesirable behavior (Marlatt & Gordon, 1985).

ALBERT ELLIS **The rational emotive therapy (RET) developed by Ellis focuses on altering the self-defeating thoughts that he believes underlie client's problems. Ellis says, for example, that you do not get upset because you fail a test but because you believe failure is a disaster that indicates you are no good. Many of Ellis's ideas have been incorporated into various forms of cognitive-behavior therapy.**

Rational Emotive Therapy and Cognitive Restructuring   One prominent form of cognitive behavior therapy is **rational-emotive therapy (RET)**. Developed by Albert Ellis (1962, 1973, 1993), RET is based on the principle that anxiety, guilt, depression, and other psychological problems are caused by how people think about events. RET aims first at identifying self-defeating thoughts such as "I must be loved or approved by everyone" or "I must be perfectly competent, adequate, and achieving to be worthwhile." After the client learns to recognize thoughts like these and see how they cause problems, the therapist uses modeling, encouragement, and logic to help the client replace these thoughts with more realistic and beneficial ones. Here is part of an RET session with a thirty-nine-year-old woman who suffered from panic attacks. She has just said that it would be "terrible" if she had an attack in a restaurant and that people "should be able to handle themselves!"

Therapist: . . . The reality is that . . . "shoulds" and "musts" are the rules that other people hand down to us, and we grow up accepting them as if they are the absolute truth, which they most assuredly aren't.

Client: You mean it is perfectly okay to, you know, pass out in a restaurant?

Therapist: Sure!

Client: But . . . I know I wouldn't like it to happen.

Therapist: I can certainly understand that. It would be unpleasant, awkward, inconvenient. But it is illogical to think that it would be terrible, or . . . that it somehow bears on your worth as a person.

Client: What do you mean?

Therapist: Well, suppose one of your friends calls you up and invites you back to that restaurant. If you start telling yourself, "I might panic and pass out and people might make fun of me and that would be terrible," . . . you might find you are dreading going to the restaurant, and you probably won't enjoy the meal very much.

Client: Well, that is what usually happens.

Therapist: But it doesn't have to be that way. . . . The way you feel, your reaction . . . depends on what you choose to believe or think, or say to yourself. . . . (Masters et al., 1987)

Cognitive-behavior therapists use many techniques related to RET to help clients learn to think in more adaptive ways, thus allowing them to practice new behaviors that irrational thoughts once prevented. Behavioral techniques aimed at replacing upsetting thoughts with alternative thinking patterns were originally described as *cognitive restructuring* (Lazarus, 1971). They help clients to plan calming thoughts to use during exams, tense discussions, and other anxiety-provoking situations. These thoughts might take the form of "OK, stay calm, you can handle this if you just focus on the task and don't worry about being perfect" (Meichenbaum, 1977). Sometimes, the methods are expanded into *stress inoculation training,* in which clients imagine being in a stressful situation, then practice newly learned cognitive skills to remain calm (Meichenbaum, 1985).

Beck's Cognitive Therapy   Especially in cases of depression or anxiety disorders, behavior therapists often use Aaron Beck's **cognitive therapy,** which entails another type of cognitive restructuring (Beck, 1976, 1993; Beck et al., 1992). As described in Chapter 15, Beck bases his approach on the idea that negative cognitive patterns are maintained by errors in logic and erroneous beliefs such as "I can't do anything right," or (if something is accomplished) by value-minimizing thoughts such as "Anyone could do that." These thoughts and beliefs, in turn, lead to low self-esteem, depression, and anxiety.

Cognitive therapy is an organized problem-solving approach in which the therapist helps clients notice how certain negative thoughts precede anxiety and depression. Then, much as in the five-step critical thinking system illustrated throughout this book, these thoughts and beliefs are considered as hypotheses to be tested rather than as asser-tions to be uncritically accepted. Accordingly, therapist and client take the role of "investigators" and develop ways to test beliefs such as "I can never do anything right." For example, they might agree on tasks that the client will attempt as "homework"—such as completing an overdue household project or meeting a new neighbor. Success at accomplishing these tasks provides concrete evidence to challenge the erroneous beliefs that are viewed as underlying anxiety and depression, thus helping to alleviate these problems (Beck et al., 1979, 1992).

As mentioned in Chapter 15, however, depressed peoples' specific thoughts may not be in error; depression may be associated with a general cognitive style in which people attribute negative events to their own general and enduring incompetence rather than, say, to bad luck or a temporary lack of effort (Peterson & Seligman, 1984). Accordingly, cognitive-behavior therapists also help depressed clients develop more optimistic ways of thinking and reduce their tendency to blame themselves for negative outcomes (Jacobson & Hollon, 1996; Taylor, 1989).

GROUP, FAMILY, AND COUPLES THERAPY

Psychotherapy is often conducted in individual interviews, but it can also be done with groups of clients or with family units.

Group therapy refers to the simultaneous treatment of several clients under the guidance of a therapist who tries to facilitate helpful interactions among group mem-bers. Psychodynamic, phenomenological, and behavioral treatment can all be adapted for use in groups. Many groups are organized around one type of problem (such as alcoholism) or one type of client (such as adolescents). In most cases, six to twelve clients meet with their therapist at least once a week for about two hours. All group members agree to hold confidential everything that occurs within group sessions.

Group therapy offers features not found in individual treatment (Fuhriman & Burlingame, 1995; Yalom, 1995). First, group therapy allows the therapist to observe clients interacting with one another. Second, clients often feel less alone as they listen to others and recognize that many people struggle with difficulties at least as severe as their own. This recognition tends to raise each client's expectations for improvement, a factor important in all forms of treatment. Third, group members can bolster one

A MEETING OF OVEREATERS ANONYMOUS
The self-help movement is part of a rapidly growing network of inexpen-sive mental health and anti-addic-tion services offered by volunteer helpers, including friends and rela-tives of troubled people. The ser-vices provided by these nonpro-fessional groups have come to com-prise some 21 percent of the total mental health and anti-addiction services offered in the United States (Regier, et al., 1993). While some welcome this trend, many profes-sionals doubt the effectiveness of these groups.

another's self-confidence and self-acceptance as they come to trust and value one another and develop group cohesiveness. Fourth, clients learn from one another. They share ideas for solving problems and give one another honest feedback about how each member "comes across." Fifth, perhaps through mutual modeling, the group experience makes clients more willing to share their feelings and more sensitive to other people's needs, motives, and messages. Finally, group therapy allows clients to try out new skills in a supportive environment.

Some of the advantages of group therapy are also put to use in *self-help,* or *mutual help, organizations.* Self-help groups are made up of people who share some problematic experience—ranging from drug addiction, childhood sexual abuse, or cancer to overeating, compulsive gambling, or schizophrenia—and who meet to help one another (Zimmerman et al., 1991). The worldwide self-help movement has grown dramatically during the last two decades (Gidron, Chesler & Chesney, 1991), partly because many troubled people would rather seek help from friends, teachers, or other "unofficial" helpers before turning to mental health practitioners, and partly because some people have been dissatisfied with professional treatment. Often following the lead of groups like Alcoholics Anonymous (AA), dozens of self-help organizations operate through hundreds of thousands of local chapters, enrolling 10 to 15 million participants in the United States and about half a million in Canada (Gottlieb & Peters, 1991; Jacobs & Goodman, 1989; Powell, 1990). Lack of reliable data makes it difficult to assess the value of many self-help groups, but available information suggests that active members may obtain some moderate improvement in their lives (Nietzel, Guthrie & Susman, 1990). Some therapists view these groups as compatible with the therapies they offer and urge clients to participate in self-help groups as part of their treatment. This is especially true for clients with problems such as eating disorders, alcoholism, and other substance abuse disorders.

As its name implies, **family therapy** involves treatment of two or more individuals from the same "family system," one of whom—often a troubled adolescent or child—is the initially identified client. The term *family system* highlights the idea that the problems displayed by one family member often reflect problems in the entire family's functioning (Nugent, 1994). Ultimately, then, the family becomes the client, and treatment involves as many members as possible. Indeed, the goal of family therapy is not just to alleviate the identified client's problems but to create harmony and balance within the family by helping each member understand family interaction patterns and the problems they create (Goldenberg & Goldenberg, 1995). As with group therapy, the family format gives the therapist an excellent view of how the initially identified client interacts with others, thus providing a forum for discussion of important issues.

Family therapy has been adapted to fit many theoretical approaches (Goldenberg & Goldenberg, 1995). For example, therapists who emphasize object relations theory point out that if parents have not worked out conflicts with their own parents, these conflicts will surface in relation to their spouses and children. Accordingly, family therapy sessions might focus on the parents' problems with their own parents and, when possible, include members of the older generation (Framo, 1982; Nugent, 1994). A related approach, called *structural family therapy,* concentrates on family communication patterns (Minuchin & Fishman, 1981). It focuses on changing the rigid patterns and rituals that create alliances (such as mother and child against father), which perpetuate conflict and prevent the communication of love, support, or even anger. Structural family therapists argue that when dysfunctional communication patterns are eliminated, problematic behaviors decrease because they are no longer necessary for survival in the family system. The well-known family therapist Virginia Satir (1982) draws on phenomenological theory. She believes that family members' symptoms result from blocked emotional growth and that removing these blocks frees people to take advantage of innate resources. Her version of family therapy aims not only to improve communication patterns but also to promote self-esteem (Nugent, 1994). Behavior therapists use family therapy sessions as meetings at which family members can discuss and agree on behavioral "contracts." Often based on operant conditioning principles, these contracts establish rules and reinforcement contingencies that help parents

A COUPLES THERAPY SESSION   Here, a therapist (in beard and red shirt) works with a group of several couples. Discussion in such sessions typically focuses on identifying and improving the miscommunication, or lack of communication, that is interfering with the couples' happiness and intimacy.

encourage their children's desirable behaviors (and discourage undesirable ones) and help spouses become more supportive of one another (Tiedemann & Johnston, 1992).

As in family therapy, therapists of many theoretical persuasions offer **couples therapy** in which communication between partners is the most important focus of treatment (Cordova & Jacobson, 1993; Epstein et al., 1993). Often, the sessions revolve around learning to abide by certain "rules for talking," such as those listed in Table 16.2.

EVALUATING PSYCHOTHERAPY

LINKAGES   Is it possible to do experiments on psychotherapy? (a link to Research in Psychology)

Psychotherapy has been available for a hundred years, and people are still asking if it works. The question persists because although most psychotherapists and their clients attest to psychotherapy's effectiveness (*Consumer Reports*, 1995), confirming that effectiveness through experimental research has proved to be challenging and controversial (Dawes, 1992, 1994; Seligman, 1995).

The value of psychotherapy was first widely questioned in 1952 when British psychologist Hans Eysenck reviewed studies in which thousands of clients had received either traditional psychodynamic therapy, various other therapies, or no treatment. To the surprise and dismay of many therapists, Eysenck (1952) found that the percentage

TABLE 16.2

Some "Rules for Talking" in Couples Therapy

Many forms of couples therapy help partners improve communication through rules such as these.

1. Always begin with something positive when stating a problem.
2. Use specific behaviors rather than derogatory labels or overgeneralizations to describe what is bothersome about the other person.
3. Make connections between those specific behaviors and feelings that arise in response to them (e.g., "It makes me sad when you . . .").
4. Admit your own role in the development of the problem.
5. Be brief; don't lecture or harangue.
6. Maintain a focus on the present or the future; don't review all previous examples of the problem or ask "why" questions such as "Why do you always . . . ?"
7. Talk about observable events; don't make inferences about them (e.g., say "I get angry when you interrupt me" rather than "Stop trying to make me feel stupid").
8. Paraphrase what your partner has said, and check out your own perceptions of what was said before responding. (Note that this suggestion is based on the same principle as Rogers' empathic listening.)

of clients who improved following any kind of psychotherapy was actually lower than that for people who received no treatment. Eysenck (1961, 1966) later supported his conclusions with additional evidence.

Critics argued that Eysenck was wrong (Bergin, 1971; de Charms, Levy & Wertheimer, 1954; Lambert, 1976; Luborsky, 1954, 1972). They claimed that he ignored studies supporting the value of psychotherapy and misinterpreted his data. They pointed out, for example, that untreated clients may have been less disturbed than those in treatment; that untreated clients may have received informal treatment from their medical doctors; and that physicians who judged untreated clients' progress might have used more lenient criteria than the psychotherapists who rated their own clients. Indeed, other reviewers' subsequent "box score" counts of successes and failures suggested that psychotherapy tends to be *more* helpful than no treatment (Bergin, 1971; Meltzhoff & Kornreich, 1970).

Debate over Eysenck's findings—and the contradictory reports that followed them—highlighted several reasons why it is so difficult to definitively answer the apparently simple question "Does psychotherapy work?" Above all, there is the problem of how to measure improvement in psychotherapy. Should such assessment depend on psychological tests, behavioral observations, interviews, or a combination of all three? For that matter, what *kinds* of tests should be used, where should clients be observed (and by whom), and should equal weight be given to interviews with clients, friends, relatives, therapists, and teachers? The fact that all these measures tend to correlate only moderately with one another makes it that much harder for researchers to compare or combine the results of different studies and, hence, to draw conclusions about the overall effectiveness of treatment (Lambert & Hill, 1994).

The question of effectiveness is further complicated by the broad range of clients, therapists, and treatments involved in the psychotherapy enterprise. Clients differ not only in terms of their problems but also in terms of their motivation to solve them. Therapists differ in skill, experience, and personality—and, as we have seen, their treatment procedures can vary widely. To the extent that a client's improvement is influenced by all these factors, results from an evaluative study of one treatment may not apply to other clients and therapists (Kazdin, 1994).

LINKAGES Can therapy change personality? (a link to Personality)

While some researchers continue to study the outcome of psychotherapy in independent experiments, others work on summarizing and comparing the results of those experiments in ways designed to improve upon the "box score" approach. Their goal is to find a way to look at the "big picture" so that objective conclusions can be drawn about the general effectiveness of all kinds of psychotherapy with all kinds of clients and all kinds of disorders. Mary Smith, Gene Glass, and Thomas Miller (1980) pioneered this approach by applying the statistical technique known as *meta-analysis* to the outcome of 475 controlled experiments that included almost 25,000 clients and a wide assortment of psychotherapy methods.

FOCUS ON RESEARCH METHODS

Meta-Analysis of Experiments on Psychotherapy

Through meta-analysis, Smith and her colleagues computed the average difference in improvement between treated and untreated clients in each experiment. These average differences, called *effect sizes,* were obtained for a variety of dependent variables, including clients' reports of improvement, therapists' ratings of client improvement, and the degree of improvement observed by clients' friends and families. Some effect sizes reflected improvement measured immediately after treatment, while others were based on measures taken several months later. The researchers averaged all the effect sizes from a given experiment in order to determine how much the average treated client in that experiment improved in comparison to the average untreated person.

FIGURE 16.3

A Meta-Analysis of Experiments
on Psychotherapy

These curves show the results of one large-scale meta-analysis of the effects of psychotherapy. Notice that, on average, people who received therapy were better off than 80 percent of those who did not.

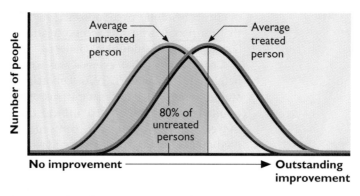

Source: Data from Smith, Glass & Miller, 1980.

Then, by averaging the effect sizes for all 475 experiments, they were able to make an overall comparison of the amount of improvement seen in people who did and did not receive treatment.

This meta-analytic procedure showed that the average person who received treatment was better off than 80 percent of the untreated control subjects (see Figure 16.3). Other, more recent meta-analyses have reached similar conclusions about the benefits of psychotherapy (Anderson & Lambert, 1995; Lipsey & Wilson, 1993; Scoggin & McElreath, 1994; Kirsch, Montgomery & Sapirstein, 1995; Lambert, Weber & Sykes, 1993; Weisz et al., 1995). In other words, meta-analyses have yielded results that are consistently more optimistic than Eysenck's. Specifically, most reviews suggest that therapy is often more helpful than placebos or no treatment at all (Lambert & Bergin, 1994).

The benefits of therapy tend to be long lasting (Nicholson & Berman, 1983) and statistically significant—that is, greater than would be expected by chance—but they are not necessarily clinically significant. To be *clinically significant,* therapeutic changes must be not only measurable but also substantial enough to make important differences in the person's life, as Figure 16.4 illustrates. For example, a reduction in treated clients' anxiety test scores might be *statistically* significant; but if those clients do not feel and act noticeably less anxious in daily life, the change is probably not *clinically* significant. In recent years, the need to demonstrate the clinical significance of treatment effects has become clearer than ever as increasingly cost-conscious clients—and their health insurance companies—decide whether, and how much, to pay for psychotherapy services (Dawes, 1992, 1994; Lambert & Hill, 1994; Seligman, 1995).

FIGURE 16.4

Clinical Significance

Evaluation of psychological treatment must consider the clinical, as well as statistical, significance of observed changes. Here, the shaded area shows the range of deviant behaviors per minute displayed at home by normal boys. The solid line shows the average rate of deviant behavior for a group of boys in an operant conditioning treatment for severe behavior problems. The improvement following reinforcement of appropriate behavior was not only statistically significant (compared to the pretreatment baseline) but also clinically significant, inasmuch as the once-deviant behavior came to resemble that of normal boys.

Source: Patterson, 1974.

Can therapy ever make people worse? A number of studies conducted since the 1950s suggest that "deterioration effects" sometimes do occur (Hadley & Strupp, 1976; Lambert & Bergin, 1994; Mays & Franks, 1985; Mohr, 1995). About 5 to 10 percent of all clients in all forms of therapy may experience a worsening of their original problems or the development of new ones, including a sense of failure, low self-esteem, or hopelessness over the inability to profit from therapy (Lambert, Shapiro & Bergin, 1986; Hadley & Strupp, 1976; Ogles, Lambert & Sawyer, 1995).

It is reassuring to know that therapy-related deterioration is rare—and that the *average* client receiving the *average* treatment improves. But most people considering treatment also want to know which form of psychotherapy is most likely to bring about clinically significant improvements in *their*

THINKING CRITICALLY

Is One Approach to Psychotherapy Better Than the Others?

problems. Although most therapists believe that their own brand of treatment is superior to others (e.g., Giles, 1990), the popularity of an eclectic approach suggests that most therapists also believe that no single approach to treatment is always the best one.

What am I being asked to believe or accept?

Indeed, some researchers argue that theories of behavior disorder and the specific treatment methods based on them are irrelevant to the success of psychotherapy: All approaches, they say, are equally effective. This has been called the "Dodo Bird Verdict," after the *Alice in Wonderland* creature who, when called upon to judge who had won a race, answered, "Everybody has won and all must have prizes" (Luborsky, Singer & Luborsky, 1975).

What evidence is available to support the assertion?

Some evidence does suggest that there are no significant differences in the overall effectiveness of the psychodynamic, phenomenological, and behavioral approaches to therapy. Studies comparing the effects of these treatment approaches in the same experiment have failed to show that one approach is notably superior to another (Cross, Sheehan & Kahn, 1982; Sloane et al., 1975; Snyder & Wills, 1989; Stiles, Shapiro & Elliott, 1986). Further, the meta-analyses described earlier showed that, on average, the three approaches are associated with about the same degree of success (Smith, Glass & Miller, 1980; Lambert & Bergin, 1994).

Are there alternative ways of interpreting the evidence?

It is possible, however, that the evidence for the Dodo Bird Verdict is based on methods that simply cannot detect genuine differences among treatments. For example, the averaging methods used in meta-analyses might obscure important differences in the effectiveness of particular treatments for particular problems (Eysenck, 1978; Wilson, 1985). It may also be that some specific techniques are more successful than others, but because "box score" reviews and meta-analyses usually group therapies by theoretical approach (psychodynamic, phenomenological, behavioral) rather than by specific procedures, the impact of those procedures may not be detected (Giles, 1990; Mahrer & Nadler, 1986; Marmar, 1990).

Further, differential effects of specific procedures might be obscured by the beneficial features shared by almost all forms of therapy—such as the support of the therapist, the hope and expectancy for improvement that therapy instills, the trust that develops between client and therapist, and the discovery of new perspectives on problem solving (Grencavage & Norcross, 1991). Thus, a therapist whose personal characteristics motivate a client to change might promote that change even if the formal methods used are mediocre (Lambert, 1989).

What additional evidence would help to evaluate the alternatives?

It is obviously important for psychologists to continue their research on factors that might explain similarities in the effects of different approaches to treatment. However, the Dodo Bird Verdict may actually be the right answer to the wrong question about psychotherapy. Instead of looking only for one "best" approach, researchers also need to explore what Gordon Paul called the "ultimate question" about psychotherapy: "What treatment, by whom, is most effective for this individual with that specific problem, under what set of circumstances?" (Paul, 1969a, p. 44).

What conclusions are most reasonable?

This analysis suggests caution in drawing conclusions about the relative value of different approaches to therapy. The question "Which approach is best?" has no simple answer. As described in the next section, troubled people or their relatives must carefully consider several factors highlighted by Paul's "ultimate question" when choosing a treatment approach and therapist most likely to be best for them.

Addressing the "Ultimate Question"

The combinations of treatment methods and therapist and client characteristics best suited to remedying particular psychological problems have not yet been mapped out, but there are a few trends. For example, when differences do show up in meta-analyses or comparative studies of adult psychotherapy, they tend to reveal a small to moderate advantage for behavioral and cognitive-behavioral methods, especially in the treatment of phobias and certain other anxiety disorders (Borkovec et al., 1991; Lambert & Bergin, 1994; Weisz et al., 1995). The same tends to be true for child and adolescent clients (Weiss & Weisz, 1995; Weisz et al., 1995; Epstein et al., 1994). ("In Review: Approaches to Psychological Treatment" summarizes key features of the main approaches to treatment.)

Further, the client-therapist relationship seems to play a major role in the success of all forms of treatment. Certain people seem to be particularly effective in forming productive human relationships. Even without formal training, these people can sometimes be as helpful as professional therapists because of personal qualities that are inspiring, healing, and soothing to others (Stein & Lambert, 1995). Their presence in self-help groups may well underlie some of the success of those groups and, among professionals, may help account for the success of many kinds of formal therapy.

Indeed, the choice of both treatment and therapist needs to be made with the "ultimate question" in mind. Careful consideration should be given to (1) what treatment approach, methods, and goals the client finds comfortable and appealing, (2) information about the potential therapist's "track record" of clinically significant success with a particular method for treating problems like those the client faces, and (3) the likelihood of forming a productive relationship with the therapist. This last consideration assumes special importance when client and therapist do not share similar cultural backgrounds.

Cultural Factors in Psychotherapy

Imagine that you have become very depressed after entering a different culture to pursue your education or occupation. One of your new friends refers you to a therapist who specializes in such problems. During your first session the therapist stares at you

IN REVIEW	Approaches to Psychological Treatment			
Dimension	**Classical Psychoanalytic**	**Contemporary Psychodynamic**	**Phenomenological**	**Behavioral**
Nature of the human being	Driven by sexual and aggressive urges	Driven by the need for human relationships	Has free will, choice, and capacity for self-actualization	A product of social learning and conditioning; behaves on the basis of past experience
Therapist's role	Neutral; helps client explore meaning of free associations and other material from the unconscious	Active; develops relationship with client as a model for other relationships	Facilitates client's growth; some therapists are active, some nondirective	Teacher/trainer who helps client replace undesirable thoughts and behaviors; active, action-oriented
Time frame	Emphasizes unresolved unconscious conflicts from the distant past	Understanding the past, but focusing on current relationships	Here and now; focuses on immediate experience	Current behavior and thoughts; may not need to know original causes in order to create change
Goals	Psychosexual maturity through insight; strengthening of ego functions	Correction of effects of failures of early attachment; development of satisfying intimate relationships	Expanded awareness, fulfillment of potential; self-acceptance	Changes in thinking and behaving in particular classes of situations; better self-management
Typical methods	Free association; dream analysis, analysis of transference	Analysis of transference and counter-transference	Reflection-oriented interviews designed to convey unconditional positive regard, empathy, congruence; exercises to promote self-awareness	Systematic desensitization, modeling, assertiveness and social skills training, positive reinforcement, aversive conditioning, punishment, extinction, cognitive restructuring

intently, touches your head for a moment, and says, "You have taken in a spirit from the river and it is trying to get out. I will help." The therapist then begins chanting softly and appears to go into a trance.

What would you think? Would you return for a second visit? If you are like most people in Western cultures, you might decide not to seek further help unless you could find someone with whom you shared certain beliefs and expectations about what is wrong with you and what should be done about it.

Though not always so extreme, a similar culture clash may occur in Western countries when clients bring to therapy a cultural or subcultural background or world view that is not shared by their therapist. This clash may be partly to blame for the underuse of, or withdrawal from, mental health services among recent immigrants as well as African-Americans, Asian-Americans, Hispanic-Americans, American Indians, and other minority populations (Price & McNeill, 1992; Spencer & Hemmer, 1993; Sue, Zane & Young, 1994). Often, the problem lies in mismatched goals. A therapist raised to believe that one should confront and overcome life's problems may encounter a client who believes that one should work at calmly accepting such problems (Sundberg & Sue, 1989). The result may be much like two people singing a duet using the same music but different lyrics.

MAKING A CONNECTION The formation of a productive therapeutic
relationship can be easier for clients
and therapists who share similar
sociocultural backgrounds.

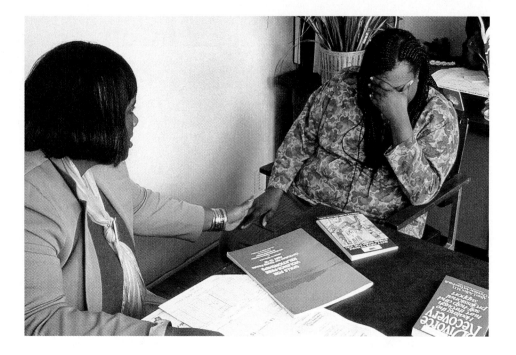

LINKAGES Should clients from
different cultural backgrounds
receive different kinds of treatment? (a link to Introducing
Psychology)

Major efforts are under way to ensure that cultural differences between clients and
therapists do not impede the delivery of treatment to anyone who wants or needs it
(Pederson, 1994). Virtually every mental health training program in North America is
seeking to recruit higher percentages of students from traditionally underserved
minority groups in order to make it easier to match clients with therapists from similar cultural backgrounds (e.g., Hammond & Yung, 1993).

Still, in most cases, minority clients are likely to encounter a therapist from a differing background, so researchers are also examining the value of matching therapeutic
techniques with clients' culturally based expectations and preferences (Hays, 1995; Sue,
1992; Tanaka-Matsumi & Higginbotham, 1994; Preciado 1994). For example, many
clients from collectivist cultures—where the emphasis is on subjugating personal
wishes to the expectations of family and friends—might expect to receive instructions
from a therapist about how to overcome problems. How would such clients respond to
a therapist whose client-centered treatment emphasizes such individualist goals as
being independent and taking responsibility for the direction of change? David Sue and
his students have investigated the hypothesis that the collectivist values of Asian cultures would lead Asians and Asian-Americans to prefer a directive, problem-solving
approach, such as behavior therapy, over nondirective, client-centered methods. Sue
(1992) found that a preference for directive treatment was highest among foreign-born
Asians compared to American-born Asians and European-Americans. However, there
are always individual differences; two clients from the same culture may react very differently to a treatment that group research suggests should be ideal for both of them. In
Sue's (1992) study, for example, more than a third of the foreign-born Asians preferred
the nondirective approach and 28 percent of the European-Americans preferred the
directive approach.

Today, psychotherapists are more sensitive than ever to the cultural values of particular groups and the nuances of intercultural communication (LaFromboise, 1992).
Indeed, some states now require psychologists to complete courses on the role of cultural factors in therapy before being licensed. This training helps clinicians appreciate,
for example, that it is considered impolite in some cultures to make eye contact with a
stranger and, hence, that clients from those cultures are not necessarily depressed, lacking in self-esteem, or inappropriately deferent just because they fix their eyes on the
floor during an interview (e.g., Ibrahim, 1991). Graduate students are getting similar
training—and practical experience—as part of their coursework in clinical or counseling psychology (Allison et al., 1994; Neville et al., 1996). Research with these students

PREPARING FOR THERAPY When cultural or subcultural differences suggest that clients are unfamiliar with the general rules and procedures of psychotherapy, special pre-treatment orientation programs may be offered. These programs provide a preview of what psychotherapy is, how it can help, and what the client is expected to do to make it work better (Prochaska & Norcross, 1994; Sue, Zane & Young, 1994).

suggests that the training increases their sensitivity to cultural factors in treatment but does not necessarily increase their competence in actually working with members of ethnic minorities (Pope-Davis et al., 1994, 1995; Quintana & Bernal, 1995). Nevertheless, by providing a cultural extension of Carl Rogers' concept of empathy, cultural sensitivity training helps therapists to appreciate the client's view of the world and thus to set goals that are in harmony with that view (Pederson, 1994; Yutrzenka, 1995). Minimizing the chances of cultural misunderstanding and miscommunication is one of the many obligations that therapists assume whenever they see a client.

Rules and Rights in the Therapeutic Relationship

Treatment can be an intensely emotional experience, and the relationship established with a therapist can profoundly affect a client's life. Professional ethics and common sense require the therapist to ensure that this relationship does not harm the client. For example, the American Psychological Association's *Ethical Principles for Psychologists and Code of Conduct* forbid a sexual relationship between therapist and client because of the severe harm it can cause the client (American Psychological Association, 1992b; Williams, 1992). These standards also require therapists, with a few exceptions, to keep everything a client says in therapy strictly confidential.

Confidentiality is one of the most important features of a successful therapeutic relationship because it allows the client to discuss unpleasant or embarrassing feelings, behaviors, or events without fear that the therapist might disclose this information to others. Professionals may consult with one another about a client, but each is required not to reveal information to outsiders (including members of the client's family) without the client's consent.

Professional rules about confidentiality are backed up in most states by laws recognizing that information revealed in therapy—like information given to a priest, a lawyer, or a physician—is privileged communication. This means that a therapist can refuse, even in court, to answer questions about a client or to provide personal notes or tape recordings from therapy sessions. The law may require a therapist to violate confidentiality only under special circumstances, including those in which (1) the client is so severely disturbed or suicidal that hospitalization is needed, (2) the client uses his or her mental condition and history of therapy as part of his or her defense in a civil or criminal trial, (3) the therapist must defend against the client's charge of malpractice, (4) the client reveals information about sexual or physical abuse of a child, and (5) the therapist believes the client may commit a violent act against a specific person.

RIGHTS OF THE MENTALLY ILL **Larry Hogue, a homeless crack cocaine addict, had been arrested or sent to mental hospitals more than thirty times in ten years for threatening people on the streets of New York City. However, laws protecting the rights of the mentally ill—and the fact that he had not committed any serious crimes—prevented him from being committed to a hospital against his will. Local authorities' frustration over his case highlights the difficulties inherent in balancing the rights of mental patients and those of the public.**

This last condition poses a dilemma. Suppose a client says, "Someday I'm going to kill that brother of mine!" Should the therapist consider this a serious threat and warn the brother? In most cases, the danger is not real, but there have been tragic exceptions. A famous example occurred in 1969. A graduate student receiving therapy at the University of California at Berkeley revealed his intention to kill Tatiana Tarasoff, a young woman whom he had dated the previous year but who later rejected him. The therapist took the threat seriously and consulted his supervisor and the campus police. It was decided that there was no real danger, so neither Tatiana nor her parents were warned. After terminating therapy, the client killed Ms. Tarasoff. Her parents sued the university, the campus police, and the therapist. The parents won their case, thus setting an important precedent. Several states now have laws that make a therapist liable for failing to take steps to protect those who are threatened with violence by the therapist's clients (Monahan, 1993).

Clients are also protected from being casually committed to mental hospitals. According to decisions by U.S. federal courts, people threatened with commitment can expect written notice; an opportunity to prepare a defense with the help of an attorney; a court hearing, with a jury if desired; and the right to take the Fifth Amendment to avoid self-incrimination. Furthermore, before people can be forcibly committed, the state must provide "clear and convincing" evidence that they are not only mentally ill but also gravely disabled or an "imminent danger" to themselves or others. Most states now require a periodic review of every committed person's records to determine whether he or she should be released. Clients have the right to receive treatment while hospitalized, but they also have the right to refuse certain forms of treatment and to be subjected to as little restriction of their freedom as possible.

Rules designed to protect hospitalized mental patients from abuse, neglect, coercion, and exploitation can also create some difficulties. For example, staff members at mental health facilities worry that they might be sued if they keep patients unnecessarily confined *or* if they release a patient who then harms someone. Thus the dilemma: to find a way to balance the legal rights of the patient against those of the public.

BIOLOGICAL TREATMENTS

Hippocrates, a physician of ancient Greece, was among the first to propose that psychological problems have physical causes. He prescribed rest, special diets, laxatives, and abstinence from alcohol or sex as treatments for psychological disorders. In the mental hospitals of Europe and America during the sixteenth through eighteenth centuries, treatment of psychological disorders was based in part on Hippocrates' formulations and consisted mainly of physical restraints, laxative purges, bleeding of "excess" blood, and induced vomiting. Cold baths, hunger, and other physical discomforts were also used in efforts to shock patients back to normality. Biological treatments for psychological problems have advanced considerably since then and, today, mainly involve

THE "CRIB" **This device, used in the nineteenth century to restrain unmanageable mental patients, was gentle compared with some of the methods endorsed in the late 1700s by Benjamin Rush. Known as the "father" of American psychiatry, Rush advocated curing patients by frightening or disorienting them—for example, by placing them in a coffinlike box which was then briefly immersed in water.**

the prescription of psychoactive drugs. Earlier in this century, however, the most common biological treatment methods were electroconvulsive therapy and psychosurgery.

Electroconvulsive Therapy

In the 1930s, a Hungarian physician named Von Meduna used a drug to induce convulsions in schizophrenics. He believed—incorrectly—that, since schizophrenia and epilepsy rarely occurred in the same person, epileptic-like seizures might combat schizophrenia. In 1938, Italian physicians Ugo Cerletti and Lucio Bini created seizures more easily by passing an electric current through schizophrenics' brains. During the next twenty years or so, this procedure, called **electroconvulsive therapy (ECT),** became a routine treatment for schizophrenia, depression, and, sometimes, mania. Upon awakening after an ECT session, the patient typically remembered nothing about the events just preceding the shock and experienced confusion. Although many patients improved, they often relapsed. ECT's benefits also had to be weighed against such side effects as varying degrees of memory loss, speech disorders, and, in some cases, death due to cardiac arrest (Lickey & Gordon, 1991).

Recent modifications in ECT procedures—such as applying shock to only one side of the brain, ensuring that patients have sufficient oxygen, and inducing profound muscle relaxation—have made modern ECT less hazardous (Abrams, 1993). When ECT is used in combination with other forms of treatment, its relapse rate is significantly diminished as well (Lickey & Gordon, 1991; Janicak et al., 1991; NIMH, 1985). About 100,000 people a year receive ECT in the United States; about twice that number in Great Britain (Fink, 1993; Julien, 1995; Squire, 1987). ECT is used primarily for patients whose depression is severe, who cannot tolerate or do not respond to antidepressant drugs, or who are at high risk for suicide (American Psychiatric Association, 1993). ECT is also occasionally used with manic patients (Julien, 1995; Mukherjee, Sackheim & Schnur, 1994). Contrary to Von Meduna's early claims, however, ECT is not an effective treatment for schizophrenia unless the patient is also severely depressed (American Psychiatric Association, 1993).

No one knows for sure how ECT works. It may be that it somehow improves neurotransmitter function and thereby alters mood (Julien, 1995; Kapur & Mann, 1993). Another view is that the neurotransmitters that help the brain recover from convulsions also reduce activity in areas of the brain associated with depression, thus relieving it

ELECTROCONVULSIVE THERAPY To make electroconvulsive therapy (ECT) safer, patients are now given an anesthetic to make them unconscious before the shock is delivered and a muscle relaxant to prevent bone fractures during convulsions. Also, the duration of the shock is now only about a half a second and, in contrast to the dozens of treatments administered decades ago, patients now receive only about six to twelve shocks, one approximately every two days (Abrams, 1993).

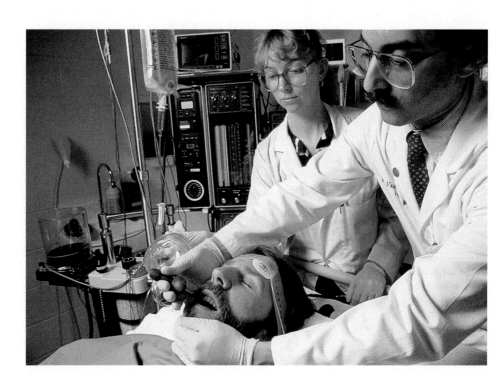

(Sackeim, 1985). Since shock affects many aspects of brain function, identifying the specific mechanisms underlying ECT's effects on depression is exceedingly difficult (Abrams, 1992; Julien, 1995).

Because of its dramatic and potentially dangerous nature, ECT remains a controversial method of treatment for serious depression. Critics want it outlawed; proponents perceive its benefits as outweighing its potential costs in most cases (Breggin, 1991; Lickey & Gordon, 1991; Small, Small & Milstein, 1986).

Psychosurgery

In 1937, Egas Moniz introduced a surgical technique called **prefrontal lobotomy** for the treatment of mental disorder. In this form of **psychosurgery,** small holes were drilled in the skull and a sharp instrument was inserted and moved from side to side to destroy brain tissue (Freeman & Watts, 1942). The theory was that emotional reactions become exaggerated in disturbed people by neural processes in the frontal lobes and that the lobotomy disrupts these processes. During the 1940s and 1950s, psychosurgery was almost routine in the treatment of schizophrenia, depression, anxiety, aggressiveness, and obsessive-compulsive disorder (Valenstein, 1980). Unfortunately, brain surgery is risky, sometimes fatal; its benefits are uncertain; and its side effects and complications, including epilepsy, are irreversible. Today, psychosurgery is performed only in rare cases where all else has failed, and it focuses on much smaller brain areas than those involved in lobotomies (Jenike et al., 1991; Sachdev, Hay & Cumming, 1992).

Psychoactive Drugs

The use of psychosurgery and ECT declined after the 1950s, not only because of their complications and general distastefulness but also because the advent of psychoactive drugs had begun to offer more effective treatment alternatives. In Chapters 3 and 6 we discussed how psychoactive drugs affect neurotransmitter systems and consciousness. Here, we describe how drugs are used to combat anxiety, depression, mania, and schizophrenia. Table 16.3 lists a few of these drugs, along with their uses, effects, and side effects.

Neuroleptics (Antipsychotics)   The early 1950s saw the introduction of a new group of drugs that revolutionized the treatment of severe mental disorder. Called **neuroleptics,** or **antipsychotics,** these drugs dramatically reduced the intensity of such psychotic symptoms as hallucinations, delusions, paranoid suspiciousness, disordered thinking, and incoherence in many mental patients, especially schizophrenics. As a result of taking these drugs, many mental patients became better able to care for themselves and more responsive to their environments. Thousands were able to leave their hospitals. For those who remained, straightjackets, padded cells, and other once-common restraints were rarely needed.

The most widely used antipsychotic drugs are the *phenothiazines,* of which the first, chlorpromazine (Thorazine), has been especially popular. Another neuroleptic called haloperidol (Haldol) is comparable to the phenothiazines in overall effectiveness, but it creates less sedation (Julien, 1995). Patients who do not respond to one of these neuroleptics may respond to the other. Between 60 and 70 percent of patients receiving these drugs show improvement, though fewer than 30 percent respond well enough to live entirely on their own.

These neuroleptics do have problematic side effects, the mildest of which include dry mouth, blurred vision, urinary retention, dizziness, and skin pigmentation problems. More serious side effects include symptoms similar to those of Parkinson's disease, such as muscle rigidity, restlessness, tremors, and slowed movement. Some of these side effects can be treated with medication; but the most serious, *tardive dyskinesia (TD),* is an irreversible disorder of the motor system that appears only after years of neuroleptic use. Affecting at least 25 percent of patients who take chlorpromazine or haloperidol, TD involves grotesque, uncontrollable, repetitive movements of the body, often including tic-like movements of the face and thrusting of the tongue. Sometimes the

> **LINKAGES**   How do drugs help people who suffer from schizophrenia? (a link to Biological Aspects of Psychology)

TABLE 16.3
A Sampling of Psychoactive Drugs Used for Treating Psychological Disorders

For Schizophrenia: Neuroleptics (Antipsychotics)

Chemical Name	Trade Name	Effects and Side Effects
Chlorpromazine	Thorazine	Reduces hallucinations, delusions, incoherence, jumbled thought processes
Haloperidol	Haldol	
		Causes movement-disorder side effects, including tardive dyskinesia
Clozapine	Clozaril	Reduces psychotic symptoms; causes no movement disorders, but raises risk of serious blood disease

For Mood Disorders: Antidepressants and Mood Elevators

Tricyclics		
Imipramine	Tofranil	Acts as antidepressant, but also has anti-panic action; causes sleepiness and other moderate side effects; potentially dangerous if taken with alcohol
Amitriptyline	Elavil, Amitid	
Other Antidepressants		
Fluoxetine	Prozac	Has antidepressant, anti-panic, and anti-obsessive action
Clomipramine	Anafranil	
Fluvoxamine	Luvox	
Other Drugs		
Lithium	Lithium carbonate	Calms mania; reduces mood swings of bipolar disorder; overdose harmful, potentially deadly

For Anxiety Disorders: Anxiolytics

Benzodiazepines		
Chlordiazepoxide	Librium	Acts as potent anxiolytic for generalized anxiety, panic, stress; extended use may cause physical dependence and withdrawal syndrome if abruptly discontinued
Diazepam	Valium	
Alprazolam	Xanax	Also has antidepressant effects; often used in agoraphobia (has high dependence potential)
Other Anti-anxiety Agents		
Buspirone	BuSpar	Has slow-acting anti-anxiety action; no known dependence problems

person's arms or legs flail unpredictably. Indeed, TD can be far worse than the mental disorder that led to treatment.

Clozapine (Clozaril) has effects like those of the phenothiazines, but it does not cause movement disorders. Though no more effective overall than the phenothiazines, clozapine has helped many patients who did not respond to the phenothiazines or haloperidol (Breier et al., 1994). Unfortunately, for about 2 percent of those who take it, clozapine greatly increases the risk of developing a fatal blood disease called *agranulo-cytosis,* which is marked by the loss of white blood cells and consequent susceptibility to infectious disease. Weekly blood tests are required to detect early signs of this disease, thus greatly increasing the cost of clozapine treatment (Lickey & Gordon, 1991).

Antidepressants   Soon after antipsychotic drugs appeared, they were joined by **antidepressants,** which, as their name suggests, are drugs designed to relieve symptoms of depression. About 60 to 70 percent of patients who take these drugs show improved mood, greater physical activity, increased appetite, and more deep (stage 4) sleep. Curiously, although these drugs have almost immediate effects on neurotransmitters (usually increasing serotonin or norepinephrine availability), their effects on depressive symptoms do not occur until a week or two after dosage begins; maximum effects take even longer. The mechanism underlying these drugs' effects is consistent with some theories about the biology of depression discussed in Chapter 15, but the time lag suggests that the effects occur through some sort of long-term compensatory process in the nervous system.

There are several classes of antidepressant drugs. The *monoamine oxidase inhibitors (MAO-I)* are effective in many cases of depression, and in some cases of panic disorder; but they can produce severe hypertension if mixed with foods containing tyramine, a substance found in aged cheeses, red wine, and chicken livers (Julien, 1995). Fortunately, a new class of MAO-I drugs is now available that does not carry this side effect risk (Julien, 1995).

Another popular class of antidepressant is the *tricyclic antidepressants (TCAs).* The TCAs have been prescribed more frequently than MAO-I drugs because they seem to work somewhat better. They also have fewer side effects, though some patients stop taking TCAs because of the sleepiness, dry mouth, dizziness, blurred vision, hypotension, constipation, and urinary retention they can cause. Further, taking TCAs and drinking alcohol can increase the effects of both, with potentially fatal results. Still, if side effects are controlled, TCAs can help many depressed patients and, like the MAO-I drugs, can also reduce the severity and frequency of panic attacks in some panic disorder patients.

A "second generation" of antidepressants affects serotonin rather than norepinephrine (Julien, 1995). The most prominent drug in this group is *fluoxetine* (Prozac). Introduced in 1986, fluoxetine has now been prescribed for more than 10 million people (Barondes, 1994), making it the most widely prescribed antidepressant in the United States. Its popularity is due to the fact that it is at least as effective as the TCAs (about 60 to 80 percent of depressed people who take it find significant relief) and in most cases has milder side effects. Fluoxetine and other serotonin-related drugs, such as clomipramine (Anafranil) and fluvoxamine (Luvox), are also effective in treating panic disorder and obsessive-compulsive disorder (Julien, 1995; Lickey & Gordon, 1991).

Lithium   Around 1970 the mineral salt *lithium* was found to calm manic patients and, if taken regularly, to prevent both the depression and the mania associated with bipolar disorder (Berger, 1978; Coppen, Metcalf & Wood, 1982). Administered as lithium carbonate—often in combination with two or three mood stabilizers or anticonvulsive agents—lithium is effective for about 80 percent of manic patients (Kahn, 1995). Without lithium, the typical bipolar patient has a manic episode about every fourteen months and a depressive episode about every seventeen months (Lickey & Gordon, 1991). With lithium, attacks of mania occur as rarely as every nine years. The lithium dosage, however, must be exact and carefully controlled; taking too much can cause vomiting, nausea, tremor, fatigue, slurred speech, and, with severe overdoses, coma or death. Further, lithium is not useful for treating a manic episode in progress because, like antidepressants, it takes a week or two of regular use before its effects are seen. So, as with the antidepressants, lithium's effects probably occur through some form of long-term adaptation as the nervous system adjusts to the presence of the drug.

Anxiolytics   During the 1950s, a new class of drugs called **tranquilizers** was shown to reduce mental and physical tension and the symptoms of anxiety. The first of these

IN REVIEW	Biological Treatments for Psychological Disorders		
Method	**Typical Disorders Treated**	**Possible Side Effects**	**Mechanism of Action**
Electroconvulsive therapy (ECT)	Severe depression	Temporary confusion, memory loss	Uncertain
Psychosurgery	Schizophrenia, severe depression, obsessive-compulsive disorder	Listlessness, overemotionality, epilepsy	Uncertain
Psychoactive drugs	Anxiety disorders, depression, obsessive-compulsive disorder, mania, schizophrenia	Variable, depending on drug used: movement disorders, physical dependence	Alteration of neurotransmitters in the brain

drugs, called meprobamate (Miltown or Equanil), acts somewhat like barbiturates (see Chapter 6), meaning that overdoses can cause sleep and even death. Because they do not pose this danger, the *benzodiazepines,* particularly chlordiazepoxide (Librium) and diazepam (Valium), became the worldwide drug treatment of choice for anxiety (Blackwell, 1973). Today, these and other anti-anxiety drugs, now called **anxiolytics,** continue to be the most widely prescribed and used of all legal drugs. They have an immediate calming effect on anxiety and are quite useful in treating the symptoms of generalized anxiety and posttraumatic stress disorder. One of the newest of the benzodiazepines, alprazolam (Xanax), has also become especially popular for the treatment of panic disorder and agoraphobia (Greenblatt, Harmatz & Shader, 1993; Lesser et al., 1992).

Benzodiazepines can have bothersome side effects such as sedation, lightheadedness, and impaired psychomotor and mental functioning. Combining these drugs with alcohol can have fatal consequences, and continued use of anxiolytics can lead to tolerance and physical dependence. After heavy or long-term use, attempts to stop taking these drugs, particularly if the change is abrupt, can result in severe withdrawal symptoms, including seizures and a return of anxiety more intense than the patient had initially experienced (Rickels et al., 1993).

An anxiolytic called buspirone (BuSpar) provides an alternative anxiety treatment that eliminates some of these problems, but it acts more slowly. As with the antidepressants, buspirone's effects do not occur for days or weeks after treatment begins; in fact, many patients stop taking it because they think it has no effect other than dizziness, headache, and nervousness (Lickey & Gordon, 1991). Yet buspirone can ultimately equal diazepam in reducing generalized anxiety (Feighner, Merideth & Hendrickson, 1982; Schnabel, 1987). Further, it does not seem to promote dependence, causes less cognitive and psychomotor impairment than the benzodiazepines, and does not interact negatively with alcohol.

Human Diversity and Drug Treatment   So far, we have talked about drug treatment effects in general ("In Review: Biological Treatments for Psychological Disorders" summarizes our discussion of drugs and other biological treatments), but there can be significant differences among members of various ethnic groups and between men and women in terms of the psychoactive drug dose necessary to produce clinical effects. For example, Keh-Ming Lin, director of the Center on the Psychobiology of Ethnicity at UCLA, has demonstrated that, compared to Asians, Caucasians need significantly higher doses of the benzodiazepines, haloperidol, lithium, and possibly the tricyclic antidepressants in order to obtain equally beneficial effects (Lin, Poland & Nakasaki, 1993; Silver, Poland & Lin, 1993). In addition, African-Americans may show a faster response to TCAs than European-Americans and respond to lower doses of lithium (Strickland et al., 1991). Whether Hispanics differ from other ethnic groups is not yet clear (Mendoza et al., 1991). Some of these ethnic differences are thought to be a function of genetically regulated differences in drug metabolism, while others may be due to dietary practices.

Gender differences in drug response are also being investigated. Some studies suggest that females may maintain higher levels of therapeutic psychoactive drugs in their blood, show better response to neuroleptics, but experience more adverse effects such as tardive dyskinesia (Yonkers et al., 1992). It is believed that hormonal and body-composition differences (such as the ratio of body fat to muscle), among other factors, may be the sources of gender differences in drug response (Dawkins & Potter, 1991; Yonkers et al., 1992). Continued research on these and other dimensions of human diversity will undoubtedly lead to more effective, and safer, drug treatments for psychological disorders.

Evaluating Psychoactive Drug Treatments

Despite the widespread success of psychoactive drugs in the treatment of psychological disorders, critics point out several problems with them.

First, even if a disorder has physical components, drugs may mask the problem without curing it. This masking effect is desirable in treating otherwise incurable physical conditions such as diabetes, but it may divert attention from potentially effective non-drug approaches to psychological problems. For example, anxiolytics may facilitate psychotherapy (Koenigsberg, 1994), but these drugs alone cannot teach people to cope with the source of their anxiety. Critics are concerned that psychiatrists, and especially general practitioners, rely too heavily on anxiolytics and other drugs to solve patients' psychological problems (Beardsley et al., 1988). For example, the antidepressant Prozac is being widely prescribed—overprescribed, critics say—for problems ranging from hypersensitivity to criticism and fear of rejection to low self-esteem and premenstrual syndrome (Barondes, 1994). Second, abuse of some drugs (such as the benzodiazepines) can result in physical or psychological dependence. Third, side effects present a problem. Some are merely annoying, such as the thirst and dry mouth produced by some antidepressants. Other side effects, like tardive dyskinesia, are far more serious. Although these side effects occur in a minority of patients, some are irreversible, and it is impossible to predict in advance who will develop them.

Still, research on psychoactive drugs holds the promise of creating better drugs, a fuller understanding of the origin and nature of some psychological disorders, and more informed prescription practices (Peuskens, 1995). For example, advances in research on individual variations in the structure of the genes that create different types of dopamine receptors may explain why some schizophrenics respond to phenothiazines that bind primarily to one type of dopamine receptor while others respond only to clozapine, which has a preference for another type of dopamine receptor (Van Tol et al., 1992). This research may guide the development of new drugs matched to specific receptors, so that the symptoms of schizophrenia can be alleviated without the risk of movement disorders posed by the phenothiazines or the potentially lethal side effects of clozapine. Similarly, research on anxiolytics promises to reveal information about the chemical aspects of anxiety.

Drugs and Psychotherapy

We have seen that both drugs and psychotherapy can be effective in treating psychological disorders. Is one better than the other? Can they be effectively combined? Considerable research is being conducted to address these questions.

So far, although the occasional study does show one approach or the other to be more effective, there is no clear consensus; overall, neither form of therapy is clearly superior for treating problems such as anxiety disorders and major depressive disorder (Antonuccio, Danton & DeNelsky, 1995). For example, one large-scale study on the treatment of depression found that, in general, two forms of psychotherapy (cognitive-behavior therapy and interpersonal therapy) were equally effective and that neither differed from treatment with imipramine, a tricyclic antidepressant drug (Elkins et al.,

1989). There was some indication that imipramine was more effective than psychotherapy in the most severe cases of depression, however. Similarly, a study on the treatment of panic disorder found no significant differences between groups receiving behavior therapy or the anxiolytic drug alprazolam (Xanax) (Klosko et al., 1990).

Most studies that have examined the joint use of drugs and psychotherapy have found surprisingly little overall advantage in their combination (Hollon, Shelton & Loosen, 1991; Elkins, 1994). At the same time, some evidence suggests that a combination of drugs and psychotherapy can be more effective than either treatment alone in treating certain disorders, including attention deficit hyperactivity disorder (ADHD) (Engeland, 1993), obsessive-compulsive disorder, alcoholism, stammering, compulsive sexual behavior, and panic (e.g., deBeurs et al., 1995; Coleman, 1992). This combined approach is especially valuable to clients who are initially too depressed or anxious to cooperate in psychotherapy (Kahn, 1995). Thus, it has been suggested that the most conservative strategy for treating anxiety and depression is to begin with some form of psychotherapy (which has no major negative side effects) and then to add or switch to drug treatment only if the psychotherapeutic approach is ineffective. Often, clients who do not respond to one method will be helped by the other.

LINKAGES: BIOLOGICAL ASPECTS OF PSYCHOLOGY AND THE TREATMENT OF PSYCHOLOGICAL DISORDERS

How do therapeutic drugs work?

As noted in Chapter 3, all sensing, perceiving, thinking, feeling, and behaving, whether normal or abnormal, is ultimately mediated by biological processes, especially those in the brain, and most especially those involving neurotransmitters. Alterations in the availability of these neurotransmitters, and thus in the activity of the neural circuits they influence, affect the ebb and flow of neural communication, the integration of information in the brain, and, ultimately, behavior and mental processes. Because different neurotransmitters are especially active in particular brain regions or circuits (see Figure 3.23 on p. 77), altering the functioning of particular neurotransmitter systems will have relatively specific psychological and behavioral effects.

Some of the drugs we have described for the treatment of psychological disorders were developed specifically to alter a neurotransmitter system that biological theories suggest might be involved in particular types of disorder; in other cases, causal theories evolved from (often accidental) findings that drugs known to affect certain neurotransmitters help patients who display some disorder.

Let's consider in a little more detail some of the ways in which therapeutic psychoactive drugs affect neurotransmitters. Recall from Chapter 3 that a given neuron can receive excitatory ("fire") or inhibitory ("don't fire") signals via neurotransmitters that facilitate or inhibit firing. Some therapeutic drugs amplify excitatory signals, while others increase inhibition. For example, the benzodiazepines (Valium, Xanax) exert their anti-anxiety effects by helping the inhibitory neurotransmitter GABA to bind to postsynaptic receptors and, thus, suppress neuronal firing. This enhanced inhibitory effect acts as a sort of braking system that slows the activity of GABA-sensitive neurons involved in the experience of anxiety. However, benzodiazepines also slow the action of all neural systems that use GABA, including those associated with motor activity and mental processing, which are spread throughout the brain. The result is the decreased psychomotor coordination and reduced clarity of thinking that appear as benzodiazepine side effects.

Other therapeutic drugs reduce postsynaptic activity by serving as *receptor antagonists* (see Figure 6.13 on page 180), acting to block the receptor site normally used by a particular neurotransmitter. Some neuroleptics, the phenothiazines and haloperidol, for example, exert their antipsychotic effects by blocking receptors for dopamine, a neurotransmitter that, as described in Chapter 3, is important for movement. Thus, these drugs compete with dopamine, blocking the firing of neurons that normally use it. The fact that dopamine blockage seems to normalize the jumbled thinking processes of many schizophrenics suggests that, as discussed in Chapter 15, schizophrenia may be partly due to excess dopamine activity. Unfortunately, reducing this activity can create severe disorders—such as tardive dyskinesia—in the movement systems that are also controlled by dopamine.

Another mechanism through which psychoactive drugs exert their therapeutic influence is increasing the amount of a neurotransmitter available at the receptors, thus maximizing its effects. This enhanced availability can be accomplished either by stimulating production of the neurotransmitter or, as is more common in therapeutic drugs, by keeping it in circulation in the synapse. Normally, after a neurotransmitter has been released, it flows back to the presynaptic terminal where it is stored for later use. If this *reuptake* process is blocked, the neurotransmitter remains in the synapse, ready to work. The tricyclic antidepressants, for example, operate by blocking the reuptake of norepinephrine. Fluoxetine, clomipramine, and other "second generation" antidepressants are called selective serotonin reuptake inhibitors, or SSRIs, because they block the reuptake of serotonin. Again, these effects are consistent with biological theories suggesting that some cases of depression are traceable to faulty norepinephrine or serotonin systems.

COMMUNITY PSYCHOLOGY: FROM TREATMENT TO PREVENTION

It has long been argued that even if psychologists knew exactly how to treat every psychological problem, there would never be enough mental health professionals to help everyone who needs it (Albee, 1968). This view fostered the rise of **community psychology,** a movement that aims both to treat troubled people in their home communities and to promote social and environmental changes that would minimize or prevent psychological disorders.

One aspect of community psychology, the *community mental health movement,* arose during the 1960s as an attempt to make treatment available to people in their own communities. Thanks to the availability of antipsychotic drugs, as well as to the concern that mental hospitals were little more than warehouses for patients, thousands of people were released from mental institutions. It was expected that they would receive low-cost mental health services in newly funded community mental health centers. This

COMMUNITY MENTAL HEALTH EFFORTS Professional and nonprofessional staff of community mental health centers provide traditional therapy and mental health education, along with walk-in facilities or "hotlines" for people who are suicidal or in crises related to rape or domestic violence. They also offer day treatment to former mental patients, many of whom are homeless.

deinstitutionalization process did spare patients the oppressive tedium of the hospital environment, but the mental health services available in the community never matched the need for them. As a result, former mental patients have swelled the ranks of the homeless who risk the dangers of life on city streets (Kelly et al., 1992; Freiberg, 1992).

Community psychology also attempts to prevent psychological disorders by addressing unemployment, poverty, overcrowded substandard housing, and other stressful social problems that may underlie some disorders (Albee, 1985). Less ambitious, but perhaps even more significant, are efforts to detect psychological problems in their earliest stages and keep them from becoming worse, as well as to minimize the long-term effects of psychological disorders and prevent their recurrence (e.g., Borduin et al., 1995; Dishion & Andrews, 1995; Gillham et al., 1995). Examples include suicide prevention (Garland & Zigler, 1993); programs that train teachers to identify early signs of child abuse; programs that help emotionally disturbed or mentally retarded individuals develop the skills necessary for semi-independent living (Wallace et al., 1992); and programs, including Project Head Start, that help preschoolers whose backgrounds hurt their chances of doing well in school and put them at risk for delinquency (Zigler, Taussig & Black, 1992; Tremblay et al., 1995).

FUTURE DIRECTIONS

Though still far from its ultimate goals, community psychology will continue to reach out to those in need and to pursue the ideal of preventing psychological disorders (Fish, 1996; Shore, 1992). There are indications that helping people learn how to control stress, to develop new competencies, and to help one another may make it possible to prevent or minimize the impact of certain social-psychological problems (e.g., Hall, 1995; Sullivan & Bradbury, 1996). As research illuminates more of the social and cultural causes and cures of psychological disorder, community psychology will become even more valuable.

The self-help movement is also likely to continue growing, and to expand to deal with new areas of human distress. Although the relationship between self-help groups and mental health professionals has been characterized by a certain amount of mutual suspicion and conflict (Humphreys, 1993), both approaches are likely to flourish, especially if professionals and nonprofessionals can reach a clearer understanding of what the other can contribute to the task of helping distressed people (Humphrey & Rappaport, 1994).

In formal psychotherapy, the trend toward eclecticism will likely continue as therapists of all theoretical preferences borrow techniques from one another. So will research on new forms of psychotherapy (Tolin et al., 1996). Researchers will also focus on finding ever-better ways of measuring treatment outcomes (Speer & Greenbaum, 1995) and of demonstrating the clinical, not just the statistical, significance of treatments (Lambert & Hill, 1994).

Future years will also see the discovery of new psychoactive drugs, perhaps drugs without serious side effects. Prescription practices will be guided by further research on differences in drug effects that are related to gender and ethnicity. Similarly, therapists' increased sensitivity to the importance of their clients' cultural backgrounds will make therapeutic services more palatable to, and more effective with, increasingly diverse populations (Chambless & Williams, 1995; Pederson, 1994). These improvements will come as part of continuing efforts to answer the "ultimate question" mentioned earlier: "What treatment, by whom, is most effective for this individual with that specific problem, under what set of circumstances?" (Paul, 1969a, p. 44).

Several courses can help you learn more about the treatment of psychological disorders. In particular, we suggest that you take courses in abnormal psychology, psychotherapy, counseling, behavior modification, psychopharmacology, and community psychology.

SUMMARY AND KEY TERMS

Psychotherapy for psychological disorders is usually based on psychodynamic, phenomenological, or behavioral theories of personality and behavior disorder. Most therapists combine features of these theories in an eclectic approach. The biological approach is reflected in the use of drugs and other physical treatment methods.

■ BASIC FEATURES OF TREATMENT

All forms of treatment include a client, a therapist, an underlying theory of behavior disorder, a set of treatment procedures suggested by the underlying theory, and a special relationship between the client and therapist, which may make it easier for improvement to occur. Therapy may be offered to inpatients and outpatients in many different settings by *psychologists, psychiatrists,* and other mental health professionals. The goal of treatment is to help people change their thinking, feelings, and behavior so that they will be happier and function better. This goal may be pursued by promoting insight into hidden causes of behavior problems, fostering personal growth through genuine self-expression, or helping clients learn new ways of thinking and acting.

■ PSYCHODYNAMIC PSYCHOTHERAPY

Psychodynamic psychotherapy began with Freud's *psychoanalysis* and seeks to help clients gain insight into unconscious conflicts and impulses and then to explore how those factors have created disorders.

Classical Psychoanalysis

Exploration of the unconscious is aided by the use of free association, dream interpretation, and analysis of transference.

Contemporary Variations on Psychoanalysis

Some variations on psychoanalysis focus less on the id, the unconscious, and the past and more on helping clients to harness the ego to solve problems in the present. Other forms retain most of Freud's principles but use a more flexible format. Object relations therapy, for example, examines the effects of early family relationships on current ones, and seeks to improve the latter.

■ PHENOMENOLOGICAL PSYCHOTHERAPY

Phenomenological psychotherapy helps clients to become more aware of discrepancies between their feelings and their behavior. According to the phenomenological approach, these discrepancies are at the root of behavior disorders and can be resolved by the client once they are brought to light in the context of a genuine, trusting relationship with the therapist.

Client-Centered Therapy

Therapists using Carl Rogers's *client-centered therapy*, also known as *person-centered therapy*, help mainly by adopting attitudes toward the client that express *unconditional positive regard, empathy*, and *congruence*. These attitudes create a nonjudgmental atmosphere that facilitates the client's honesty with the therapist, with himself or herself, and with others. One way of creating this atmosphere is through *reflection*.

Gestalt Therapy

Therapists employing the *Gestalt therapy* of Fritz Perls use more active techniques than Rogerian therapists, often confronting and challenging clients with evidence of defensiveness, game playing, and other efforts to escape self-exploration.

■ BEHAVIOR THERAPY

Behavior therapy, behavior modification, and *cognitive-behavior therapy* apply learning principles to eliminate undesirable patterns of thought and behavior and to strengthen more desirable alternatives.

Techniques for Modifying Behavior

Common behavioral treatments include *systematic desensitization, modeling*, and *assertiveness and social skills training*. More generally, behavior therapists use *positive reinforcement* (sometimes in a *token economy*), techniques based on *extinction* (such as *flooding*), *aversive conditioning*, and *punishment* to make desirable behaviors more likely or problematic behaviors less likely.

Cognitive-Behavior Therapy

Many behavior therapists also employ cognitive-behavior therapy to help clients alter the way they think as well as the way they behave. Among the specific cognitive-behavioral methods are *rational-emotive therapy (RET)*, cognitive restructuring, stress inoculation training, and *cognitive therapy*.

■ GROUP, FAMILY, AND COUPLES THERAPY

Therapists of all theoretical persuasions offer *group therapy, family therapy*, and *couples therapy*. These forms of treatment take advantage of relationships in the group, family, or couple to enhance the effects of treatment. The group format is also adopted in many self-help or mutual help organizations.

■ EVALUATING PSYCHOTHERAPY

There is little agreement about exactly how to measure improvement following psychotherapy and how best to ensure that observed improvement was actually due to the treatment itself and not to some other factor. One prominent method for outcome research is meta-analysis. Recent meta-analyses have found that clients who receive psychotherapy are better off than most clients who receive no treatment but that no single approach is uniformly better than all others for all clients and problems.

Addressing the "Ultimate Question"

Research is needed to discover the combinations of therapists, clients, and treatments ideally suited to treating particular psychological problems. Several factors, including personal preferences, must be considered when choosing a form of treatment and a therapist.

Cultural Factors in Psychotherapy

The effects of cultural differences in values and goals between therapist and client have attracted increasing attention. Efforts are under way to minimize the problems that these differences can create.

Rules and Rights in the Therapeutic Relationship

Whatever the specific form of treatment, the client's rights include the right to confidentiality and protection from unjustified confinement in a mental hospital.

■ BIOLOGICAL TREATMENTS

Biological treatment methods seek to relieve psychological disorders by physical rather than psychological means.

Electroconvulsive Therapy

Electroconvulsive therapy (ECT) involves passing an electric current through the patient's brain, usually in an effort to relieve severe depression.

Psychosurgery

Psychosurgery procedures once involved mainly *prefrontal lobotomy*; when used today, usually as a last resort, they focus on more limited areas of the brain.

Psychoactive Drugs

Today the most prominent form of biological treatment involves psychoactive drugs, including those with *antipsychotic (neuroleptic), antidepressant*, or *tranquilizing (anxiolytic)* effects. There appear to be significant differences among members of various ethnic groups, and between men and women, in the dosages of psychoactive drugs necessary to produce clinical effects.

Evaluating Psychoactive Drug Treatments

Psychoactive drugs have proven impressively effective in many cases, but critics point out a number of undesirable side effects associated with these drugs, the risks of abuse, and the dangers of overreliance on chemical approaches to human problems that might have other solutions.

Drugs and Psychotherapy

So far, neither psychotherapy nor drug treatment has been found clearly superior overall for treating problems such as anxiety or depression; however, a combination of the two may be more effective in treating certain disorders than either one alone.

■ LINKAGES: BIOLOGICAL ASPECTS OF PSYCHOLOGY AND THE TREATMENT OF PSYCHOLOGICAL DISORDERS

The biological basis for the effects of psychoactive drug treatment lies in the drugs' effects on neurotransmitter systems. These effects include enhancing or blocking the action of neurotransmitters.

■ COMMUNITY PSYCHOLOGY: FROM TREATMENT TO PREVENTION

Concern about the effectiveness of individual treatment and the realization that there will never be enough therapists to treat all who need help prompted the development of *community psychology*. Community mental health programs and efforts to prevent mental disorders are the two main elements of community psychology.

SOCIAL COGNITION

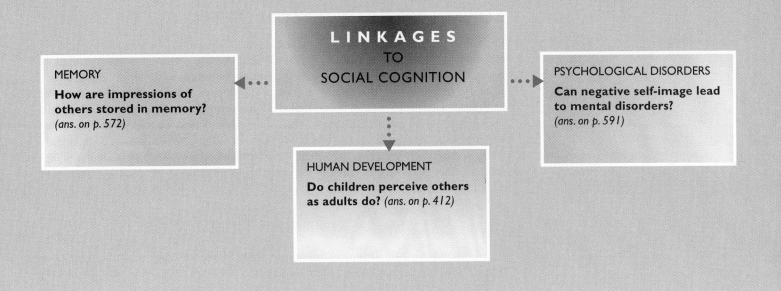

LINKAGES
TO
SOCIAL COGNITION

MEMORY

How are impressions of others stored in memory? *(ans. on p. 572)*

HUMAN DEVELOPMENT

Do children perceive others as adults do? *(ans. on p. 412)*

PSYCHOLOGICAL DISORDERS

Can negative self-image lead to mental disorders? *(ans. on p. 591)*

In the summer of 1995, Susan Smith went on trial in Union, South Carolina, for the murder of her two young sons. There was no doubt as to her guilt—she admitted rolling her car into a lake with the boys strapped into their car seats. As outlined in Chapter 15, the only legal question was whether she should be executed, imprisoned, or, if found not guilty by reason of insanity, committed to a mental institution or released. The jury heard about two Susan Smiths. The Susan portrayed by the prosecution was a cold, selfish, manipulative woman who cheated on her husband and killed her children because her boyfriend didn't like them. The Susan described by the defense was a devoted, loving mom who was suicidal with remorse and whose horrible crime reflected mental instability stemming from sexual abuse. In the end, the jury found Smith guilty and she was sentenced to life imprisonment.

Was the jurors' decision based on their discovery of the "real" Susan Smith, or was it influenced mainly by which attorney did a better job of altering their perceptions of her? You might ask the same question about any trial, because attorneys always try to influence juries to see the facts of a case in a way that favors their side. Like psychologists, they know that our perception of people as well as objects can be influenced by motivation, expectations, contexts, emotions, and other "top-down" factors described in Chapter 5. The mental processes associated with the ways in which people perceive and react to other individuals and groups is called **social cognition;** as the Linkages diagram suggests, it influences many aspects of behavior. Through social cognition, each of us constructs our own version of reality (Fiske, 1995; Smith & Mackie, 1995), including our view of what is true and what is false.

Understanding the ways in which social cognition affects jury verdicts is but one aspect of **social psychology,** the study of how people influence and are influenced by other people. In the next chapter, we describe how social influences produce group and interpersonal behaviors such as conformity, aggression, and cooperation. In this chapter, our coverage of social psychology focuses on social cognition, particularly on how perception, learning, memory, thinking, and emotion occur in relation to other people. We examine how people think about themselves and others, why they may like one person but dislike another, how they form and change attitudes, and why and how they use stereotypes to judge other people, sometimes in prejudiced ways.

SOCIAL CONSTRUCTION OF THE SELF

Each of us lives in both a personal and social world. You experience your thoughts and feelings as personal, but they are products of the social and cultural environment, influenced by others in important ways. In the chapters on human development and personality, we described how each individual develops within a cultural context. We explored how collectivist and individualist cultures emphasize different core values and encourage contrasting definitions of the self. In this section we look at the processes whereby other people in the culture in which we live affect two important components of the self: our **self-concept,** the beliefs we hold about who we are and what characteristics we have, and our **self-esteem,** the evaluations we make about how worthy we are as human beings.

Social Comparison

People spend a lot of time thinking about themselves, trying to evaluate their own perceptions, opinions, values, abilities, and so on. Decades ago, Leon Festinger (1954) noted that self-evaluation involves two distinct types of questions: those that can be answered by taking objective measurements and those that cannot. You can determine your height or weight by measuring it, but for other types of questions—about mental ability or athletic prowess, for example—there are no objective criteria. In these cases, according to Festinger's theory of **social comparison,** people evaluate themselves in relation to others. When you wonder how intelligent, interesting, or attractive you are, you use *social* rather than objective criteria (Butler, 1992; Wheeler & Miyake, 1992).

Who serves as your basis of comparison? Festinger said that people usually look to others who are similar to themselves. For example, if you are curious about how good a swimmer you are, you are likely to compare yourself to the people with whom you compete, not to Olympic champions. That is, you tend to choose swimmers at your own level of experience and ability (Major, Sciacchtinano & Crocker, 1993). The categories of people to which you see yourself as belonging and to which you habitually compare yourself are called **reference groups.**

The performance of people in a reference group can influence your self-esteem (Buunk, 1995). For example, if being a good swimmer is very important to you, knowing that someone in your reference group swims much faster than you can lower your self-esteem. To protect their self-esteem, people sometimes choose to compare themselves to those who are not as good, a strategy called *downward social comparison* (Wills, 1991). Alternatively, they might tell themselves that the superior performer is not really similar enough to be in their reference group, or even that the ability in question is not really that important to them (Baumeister, 1995; Tesser, 1988).

An unfavorable comparison of your own status with that of others can produce a phenomenon known as **relative deprivation**—the belief that, no matter how much you are getting in terms of recognition, status, money, or whatever, it is less than you deserve (Aronson, Wilson & Akert, 1994). Relative deprivation explains why an actor who receives $5 million to star in a film feels abused if a co-star is receiving $10 million. When the average person constantly identifies very wealthy people as a reference group, the resulting relative deprivation can create depression and anxiety (Taylor & Lobel, 1989). And when a large group experiences relative deprivation, political unrest may follow. The turmoil leading to great political upheavals, from the American Revolution to the overthrow of European communism, usually starts after the members of an oppressed group experience some improvement in their lives and begin to compare their circumstances with those in other groups (Aronson, Wilson & Akert, 1994). With this improvement comes elevated expectations about what they deserve.

Social Identity Theory

Stop reading for a moment and fill in the blank in the following sentence: "I am a(n) _____."

personal vs.
social identity

Some people complete the sentence using characteristics such as "hard worker," "good sport," or some other aspect of their *personal* identity. However, many others identify themselves using a word or phrase that reflects their nationality, gender, or religion. These responses reflect **social identity,** our beliefs about the groups to which we belong. Our social identity is thus part of our self-concept (Smith & Henry, 1996).

Our social, or group, identity permits us to feel part of a larger whole (Smith & Mackie, 1995). Its importance is seen in the pride that people feel when a member of their family graduates from college or when a local team wins a big game (Hogg & Hardie, 1991). In wars between national, ethnic, or religious groups, individuals sacrifice and sometimes die for the sake of their group identity. A group identity is also one reason people donate money to those in need, support friends in a crisis, and display other helping behaviors. As we shall see later, however, defining ourselves in terms of a group identity can foster an "us versus them" mentality that sets the stage for prejudice, discrimination, and intergroup conflict (Smith, 1993).

LINKAGES: SOCIAL COGNITION AND PSYCHOLOGICAL DISORDERS

Can negative self-image lead to mental disorders?

unified self-schema
vs.
differentiated.

Through social comparison and the formation of social identity, people develop mental representations of themselves. These mental representations, called **self-schemas,** not only shape how people think about themselves but also can alter their vulnerability to various forms of psychological disorder. Patricia Linville has found that people vary with respect to the complexity and differentiations of their self-schemas (Linville & Carlston, 1994). Some individuals have a *unified self-schema;* they think of themselves as having more or less the same characteristics or attributes in every situation (at home, at a party, and so on) and in every role (as student, friend, or romantic partner). In contrast, other individuals have *differentiated self-schemas;* they think of themselves as having different attributes in different roles or situations.

Variations in the way people think about themselves have a strong impact on their emotional experiences (Clark, 1994). For example, students with a unified self-schema are likely to have an especially strong emotional reaction to failing an exam because they would tend to interpret failure in this one area as implying incompetence in all areas (Niedenthal, Setterlund & Wherry, 1992). After failing, they are likely to lower their opinions of themselves not only as students but in a variety of other roles as well—as sons or daughters, for example. In contrast, people with a differentiated self-schema may think less of themselves as students, but failing an exam will have fewer implications for the way they think of themselves in their other social roles (Kihlstrom & Klein, 1994).

As described in Chapter 15, a tendency to see oneself as generally and permanently inadequate rather than as merely prone to specific or temporary weaknesses may form the cognitive basis for depression and other psychological disorders. In contrast, people with differentiated self-schemas seem better able to separate failure in one part of their life from their total worth as individuals. This ability may be part of the reason they typically become less depressed following the breakup of a romance than do people with undifferentiated self-schemas, and they may be less prone to stress-related illness (Linville, 1987; Smith & Cohen, 1993).

Self-schemas contain information not only about what people are like (the *actual self*) but also about how they want to be (the *ideal self*) and what their moral training says they should be (the *ought self*). For most people, thinking about the discrepancy between the actual self and the ideal self produces emotions such as sadness, disappointment, and dissatisfaction (Higgins, 1987). In more extreme cases, people may become so focused on such matters that they show symptoms of depression (Scott & O'Hara, 1993; Weary & Edwards, 1994). Discrepancies between the actual self and the ought self usually produce emotions such as guilt and fear of rejection; in some cases these emotions result in anxiety-related disorders (Higgins, 1989; Scott & O'Hara, 1993).

SOCIAL PERCEPTION

There is a story about a company president who was having lunch with a man being considered for an executive position. When the man salted his food without first tasting it, the president decided not to hire him. The reason, she explained, was that the company had no room for a person who acted before collecting all relevant information. The candidate lost his chance because of the president's **social perception,** the processes through which people interpret information about others, form impressions of them, and draw conclusions about the reasons for their behavior. In this section we will examine how and why social perception influences our thoughts, feelings, and actions.

The Role of Schemas

The perception of people follows many of the same laws that govern the perception of objects, including the Gestalt principles discussed in Chapter 5. Consider Figure 17.1. Consistent with Gestalt principles, most people would describe it as "a square with a notch in one side," not as eight straight lines (Woodworth & Schlosberg, 1954). The reason is that they interpret new information using the mental representations, or schemas, they already have about squares; in short, they interpret this diagram as a square with a slight modification.

Schemas about people, too, can have a significant influence on our perception of them. For one thing, schemas influence what we pay attention to and what we ignore. Characteristics or events that are consistent with our schema about another person usually get more attention than those that are inconsistent with that schema. Thus, we tend to process information about the other person more quickly if it confirms our beliefs about that person's gender or ethnic group, for example, than if it violates those beliefs (Devine, 1995). Second, schemas influence what we remember about others. In one study, if people thought a woman they saw in a videotape was a waitress, they recalled that she had a beer with dinner and owned a TV set; those who thought she was a librarian remembered that she was wearing glasses and liked classical music (Cohen, 1981). Finally, schemas affect our judgment about the behavior of others (Fiske, 1995). Thomas Hill and his colleagues (1989) found that subjects' ratings of male and female friends' sadness were influenced not only by the friends' actual behavior but also by the subjects' general schemas about how much sadness men versus women tend to experience.

In other words, through "top-down" processing, schemas about people influence—and sometimes bias—person perception in some of the same ways that schemas about objects affect object perception (see Chapter 5). And just as they help us read sentences whose words are missing letters, schemas also allow us to efficiently "fill in the blanks" about people. Accordingly, medical patients and airline passengers do not usually ask their doctors or pilots for credentials. Their schemas about these professionals lead to perceptions that the person who examines us or flies our plane is competent, confident, skilled, experienced, and serious. And, usually, these perceptions are correct. It is only when our expectations are violated that we realize that schemas can create errors in judgment about other people.

First Impressions

The schemas we have about people act as lenses that shape our first impression of them. That impression, in turn, influences both our subsequent perceptions of their behavior and our reactions to it. First impressions are formed quickly, usually change slowly, and typically have a long-lasting influence. No wonder first impressions are so important in the development of social relations (Smith & Mackie, 1995). How do people form impressions of other people? And why are they so resistant to change?

Forming Impressions   Think about your first impression of a close friend. It probably formed rapidly, because, as mentioned earlier, existing schemas create a tendency to

LINKAGES Do we sometimes perceive people as we perceive objects? (a link to Perception)

LINKAGES How are impressions of others stored in memory? (a link to Memory)

FIGURE 17.1

A Schema-Plus-Correction

People who see an object like this tend to use a pre-existing mental representation (their schema of a square) and then correct or modify it in some way (here, with a notch).

"You are fair, compassionate, and intelligent, but you are perceived as biased, callous, and dumb."

automatically infer a great deal about a person on the basis of limited information (Fiske, 1995). An ethnic name, for example, might have caused you to draw inferences about your friend's religion, food preferences, or temperament. Clothing or hairstyle might have led you to make assumptions about her political views or taste in music. These inferences and assumptions may or may not be accurate; how many turned out to be true in your friend's case?

One schema has a particularly strong influence on first impressions: We tend to assume that the people we meet hold attitudes and values similar to our own (Hoyle, 1993). So, all else being equal, we are predisposed to like other people. However, it does not take much negative information to change our minds. Why? Others can behave positively toward us because they are nice, because they like us, because they want to sell us insurance, or for many other reasons. Negative acts, however, suggest only that they are unfriendly or have other undesirable traits (Coovert & Reeder, 1990). Accordingly, negative information attracts more attention and carries more weight than positive information in shaping first impressions (Klein, 1991).

Lasting Impressions   Does your friend seem the same today as when you met? First impressions can change, but the process is usually very slow. One reason is that humans tend to be "cognitive misers" (Fiske, 1995). We like to maintain our existing beliefs about the world, often using our schemas to preserve a reality that fits our expectations. Holding onto existing impressions appears to be part of this effort. Thus, if your friend has recently said or done something that violates your expectations, your view of her probably did not change much, if at all. In fact, you may have acted to preserve your impression by thinking something like "She is not herself today." In short, impressions are slow to change because the meaning we give to new information about people is shaped by what we already know or believe about them (Ditto & Lopez, 1992).

Self-Fulfilling Prophecies   Another reason first impressions tend to be stable is that we often do things that cause others to confirm our impressions (Harris et al., 1992). Students whose teachers expect them to do poorly in mathematics may get the message, exert less effort, and perform below their ability level (Jussim & Eccles, 1992). Job interviewers' questions are often unintentionally slanted to elicit responses consistent with their first impression of an applicant (Phillips & Dipboye, 1989). And counselors can

VIOLATING A SCHEMA   This particular grandmother probably does not fulfill your schema—your mental representation—of how grandmothers are supposed to look and act. Schemas help us to categorize quickly and respond appropriately to the people we meet, but they can also create narrowmindedness and, as we shall see later, prejudice.

draw extraverted behavior from clients whom they believe to be extraverted, whether they are or not (Copeland & Snyder, in press). When, without our awareness, schemas cause us to subtly lead people to behave in line with our expectations, a **self-fulfilling prophecy** is at work.

In one experiment on self-fulfilling prophecies, men and women participated in "get acquainted" conversations over an intercom system. Before the conversations took place, the men were shown photographs and told, falsely, that they were pictures of their partners. Some saw a photograph of an obese woman, while others saw a picture of a woman of normal weight. In fact, the photographs bore no relationship to the women's actual appearance. Independent judges listened to tapes of the ensuing conversations (but saw neither participant) and rated the women's behavior and personality. The women whom the men thought were of normal weight were judged as more articulate, lively, interesting, exciting, and fun to be with. Apparently, when the men thought their partners were of normal weight, they were more friendly and engaging themselves, and this behavior, in turn, elicited more positive reactions from the women. In contrast, men who thought their partners were overweight behaved in ways that drew comparatively dull responses (Snyder & Haugen, 1994, 1995).

Self-fulfilling prophecies also help maintain judgments about groups. If you assume that members of a certain ethnic group are pushy or aggressive, for example, you might display defensiveness or even hostility toward them. Faced with this behavior, members of the group might become frustrated and angry. Their reactions fulfill your prophecy and perpetuate the impressions that created it (Ross & Jackson, 1991).

Explaining Behavior: Attribution

So far, we have examined how people form impressions about the characteristics of other people. But perceptions of others include another key element: explanations of behavior. People tend to form *implicit theories* about why people (including themselves) behave as they do and about what behavior to expect in the future (Gilbert, 1995). Psychologists use the term **attribution** to describe the process people go through to explain the causes of behavior (including their own).

As an example, suppose a classmate fails to return borrowed notes on time. You could attribute the behavior to many causes, from an unanticipated emergency to simple selfishness. Which of these alternatives you choose is important because it will help you to *understand* your classmate's behavior, *predict* what will happen if this person asks to borrow something in the future, and decide how to *control* the situation should it arise again. Similarly, whether a person attributes a spouse's nagging to stress-induced irritability or to lack of love can influence whether that person will work on the marriage or work to dissolve it (Clark, 1994).

People tend to attribute behavior in a particular situation to either primarily internal causes—characteristics of the person—or primarily external (situational) causes. For example, if you thought your classmate's failure to return notes was due to lack of consideration or laziness, you would be making an *internal attribution*. If you thought that the oversight was due to time pressure caused by an upcoming exam or a family crisis, you would be making an *external attribution*. Similarly, if you were to fail an exam, you could explain it by concluding that you're not very smart (internal attribution) or that your work schedule left you too little time to study (external attribution). The attribution that you make, in turn, might determine how much you study for the next exam or even whether you decide to stay in school.

Sources of Attributions   Harold Kelley (1973) proposed an influential theory of how people (whom Kelley called *observers*) make attributions about the actions of other people (whom Kelley called *actors*). To illustrate this theory, let's imagine that your father refuses to allow your friend, Ralph, to eat dinner at your house tonight. According to Kelly, understanding the reasons for your father's behavior requires information about three key variables: consensus, consistency, and distinctiveness (Kelley, 1973).

1. *Consensus* is the degree to which other people's behavior is similar to that of the actor—in this case, your father. If everyone you know avoids Ralph, your father's

LINKAGES: SELF-FULFILLING PROPHESIES IN THE CLASSROOM   As discussed in the chapter on mental abilities, first impressions of a student's potential can alter a teacher's behavior. If teachers inadvertently spend less time helping children who impressed them as "dull," those children may in fact not learn as much, thus fulfilling the teachers' expectations.

behavior has a high degree of consensus, and you would attribute his reaction to an external cause (probably something about Ralph). However, if everyone else treats Ralph well, your father's negative response would have low consensus. Accordingly, you would probably attribute it to something about your father, such as his being a grouch, or his personal dislike for Ralph.

2. *Consistency* is the degree to which the behavior occurs repeatedly in a particular situation. If your father has warmly invited Ralph to dinner several times in the past but rejects him this time, the consistency of his behavior is low. Low consistency suggests that your father's behavior is attributable to external causes, such as the fact that Ralph had just played three hours of basketball and did not shower afterward. Conversely, if his behavior toward Ralph is always hostile, it has high consistency. But is your father's consistent behavior attributable to a stable internal cause (his consistent grouchiness) or to a stable external cause (Ralph's consistent offensiveness)? This question is difficult to answer without information about distinctiveness.

3. *Distinctiveness* concerns the extent to which similar stimuli elicit the same behaviors from the actor. If your father is nasty to *all* your friends, his behavior toward Ralph has low distinctiveness. Behavior that is low in distinctiveness is usually attributable to internal causes, such as a grouchy personality. However, if dad gets along with everyone except Ralph, his behavior has high distinctiveness and your attribution about the cause of his behavior is likely to shift toward a cause other than your father's personality, such as how Ralph acts.

In summary, Kelley's theory suggests that internal attributions about an actor's behavior are most likely when there is low consensus, high consistency, and low distinctiveness. If you observe your boss insulting customers (a situation of low consensus, inasmuch as most people in business are polite to customers) every day (high consistency) no matter who the customers are (low distinctiveness), you would probably attribute this behavior to the boss's personality rather than to some external cause such as the weather or the customers' rudeness. On the other hand, if you saw the boss on just one day (low consistency) being rude (low consensus) to one particular customer (high distinctiveness), you would be more likely to attribute the incident to the customer's behavior or some other external factor. External attributions are often made in response to other information patterns as well, as Figure 17.2 illustrates.

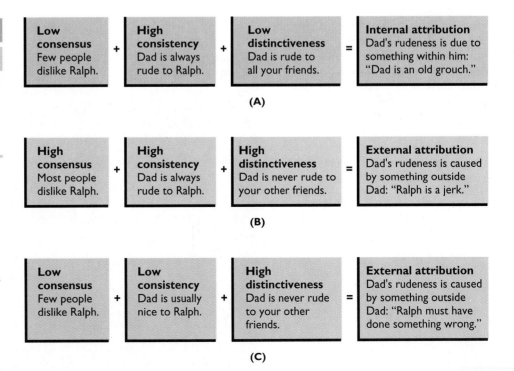

Most theories of causal attribution were developed by North American psychologists who implicitly assumed that the factors leading to internal or external attributions are the same all over the world. These theories predict, for example, that anyone, anywhere who sees a woman helping someone who had once helped her would attribute her actions to an obligation to return a favor (an external cause), not to her general helpfulness (an internal cause).

Are such attributional patterns indeed universal? To explore this question, Joan Miller and David Bersoff (1994) conducted a cross-cultural experiment in India and the United States. The experimenters asked sixty U.S.-born students at Yale University and sixty Hindu students from the University of Mysore in India to read a brief story about helping. Half the students were male, half were female, and they all read the story in their own language. The independent variable in the study was the kind of helping that occurred in the stories (reciprocal versus spontaneous). The dependent variable was the students' explanations for the helping that was portrayed.

Here is a modified version of one of the stories about reciprocal helping:

One day John noticed that a neighbor, Bill, was planting a new garden. John had plenty of free time so he helped Bill plant his garden. Several weeks later, Bill, the man whom John had helped previously, noticed that John was painting a fence in his yard. Bill had plenty of free time, so he offered to help John paint his fence.

In a similar story about spontaneous helping, a man offers to help his friend paint a fence, but the friend had not previously helped him. Half the stories were about males, half about females. After reading the stories, each participant was asked to rate how well each of several reasons explained the helper's actions. Giving a high rating to a reason such as "because he likes to help" would suggest an internal attribution; a high rating for "she owed her a favor" would suggest an external attribution. The students were also asked to say whether they thought the helper felt a moral responsibility to be helpful.

Taking cultural differences into account, the researchers hypothesized that the Americans would attribute repayment of a favor to external factors, whereas the Hindus in India would attribute it to internal factors (Miller, 1994; Miller & Bersoff, 1995). Results from both male and female students supported this hypothesis. The American students tended to rate "repaying a favor" (an external cause) as a much better expla-

WHY ARE THEY HELPING?   **Helping occurs all around the world, but research shows that people's explanations about why it happens can differ from culture to culture.**

nation of reciprocal helping than "liking to help" (an internal cause). Fewer than 2 percent of them thought that reciprocal helpers felt a moral responsibility to help. In contrast, the Indian students tended to believe that reciprocal helping occurred mainly because the helper liked to help; almost 80 percent also said that helpers who returned a favor felt a moral responsibility to do so. Compared to their own ratings of reciprocal helping, the American students saw spontaneous helping as much more attributable to the helper's enjoyment of helping. The Indian students thought that spontaneous helpers liked to help slightly *less* than reciprocal helpers.

Miller (1994) suggested that the differences in the two groups' responses reflected differences in their cultural experiences. She noted that Hindus in India have a "duty-based" moral system in which helping out of social obligation is just as moral as helping in the absence of prior favors. Further, they tend not even to distinguish between helping that is motivated by personal traits and helping that is motivated by social duty. In contrast, people from Euro-American cultures tend to believe that social obligations may force a person to help even if that person does not have a "helpful" personality.

The results of Miller and Bersoff's experiment highlight once again the danger of assuming that phenomena seen in Euro-American cultures generalize to all cultures. Cross-cultural differences in attribution and other aspects of social cognition may help to explain why people in different cultures sometimes have so much difficulty in understanding one another.

The Fundamental Attribution Error Whatever their background, most people are usually logical in their attempts to explain behavior (Trope, Cohen & Alfieri, 1991). However, they are also prone to *attributional biases* that can distort their view of behavior (Gilbert, 1995).

North American psychologists have paid special attention to the **fundamental attribution error,** a tendency to overattribute the behavior of others to internal factors (Gilbert & Malone, 1995). Imagine that you hear a student give an incorrect answer in class. You are liable to attribute this behavior to an internal cause and infer that the person is not very smart. In doing so, however, you would fail to take into account possible external factors (such as lack of study time).

The fundamental attribution error has some significant consequences. For one thing, it may generate overconfidence about impressions of other people. It also leads to underestimates of the extent to which another person's behavior is due to external causes, and thus how much the behavior of that person might vary across situations (Gilbert & Malone, 1995). In relation to personality, the fundamental attribution error helps explain why, despite the fact that situations often influence our behaviors more than traits, most people believe that traits are the major cause of behaviors.

A related form of cognitive bias is called the *ultimate attribution error,* whereby positive actions performed by people from a different ethnic or social group are attributed to external causes, such as expectation of payment, while their negative actions are attributed to internal causes, such as dishonesty (Pettigrew, 1979). People who commit this error see good deeds done by those in their *own* group as due to internal factors and bad deeds as stemming from external causes. Thus the ultimate attribution error fosters and maintains negative views of other groups and positive views of one's own group (Devine, 1995).

Like other aspects of social cognition, these attributional biases are not universal. Recent research suggests that people in collectivist cultures such as India, China, Japan, and Korea are less likely than those in the individualist cultures of North America and Europe to commit the fundamental attribution error or the ultimate attribution error (Morris & Peng, 1994; Rhee et al., 1995). And even within Euro-American cultures themselves, there are individual differences in people's vulnerability to these errors (Ross & Nisbett, 1991). According to one study, for example, people raised in the southern United States were more inclined than northerners to make external attributions (Sims & Baumann, 1972).

Other Attributional Biases   The inclination toward internal attributions is much less pronounced when people explain their own behavior. In fact, there tends to be an **actor-observer bias:** Whereas people often attribute *other* people's behavior to internal causes, they tend to attribute their *own* behavior to external factors, especially when the behavior is inappropriate or inadequate (Baumeister, 1995). For example, when you drive slowly, it is because you are looking for an address, not because you are a dim-witted loser, like that jerk who crawled along in front of you yesterday.

The actor-observer bias occurs mainly because people have different kinds of information about their own and others' behavior. When *you* are acting in a situation—giving a speech, perhaps—the stimuli that are most salient to you are likely to be external and situational, such as the temperature of the room and the size of the audience. You also have a lot of information about other external factors, such as the amount of time you had to prepare your talk or the upsetting conversation that occurred this morning. Whatever the outcome of your efforts, you can easily attribute it to one or all of these external causes. But when you observe someone else, the most salient stimulus in the situation is *that person*. You do not know what happened to the person last night or this morning, so you are likely to attribute whatever he or she does to stable, internal characteristics (Gilbert & Malone, 1995).

Of course, people do not always attribute their own behavior to external forces. In fact, the degree to which they do so depends on whether the outcome is positive or negative. One group of researchers assessed the attributions made by introductory psychology students about their performance on a midterm examination (Smith & Ellsworth, 1987). The students who did well perceived the test as being fair and attributed their performance to their ability. But the ones who performed poorly believed that the test was unfair, and they attributed their performance to a picky instructor. These students showed a **self-serving bias,** the tendency to take personal credit for success but to blame external causes for failure.

The Self-Protective Functions of Social Cognition

The self-serving bias occurs, in part, because people are motivated to maintain their self-esteem—and ignoring negative information is one way to do so. If you just failed an exam, it is painful to admit that it was fair. Other forms of social cognition, too, help people think about their failures and shortcomings in ways that protect their self-esteem (Aronson, Wilson & Akert, 1994).

Unrealistic optimism is one example. People tend to believe that positive events (such as financial success or having a gifted child) are more likely to happen to themselves than to others, and that negative events (such as being in an accident or having cancer) are more likely to happen to others than to themselves (Weinstein, 1989). Unrealistic optimism tends to persist even when there is evidence against it. For example, Shelley Taylor and her associates (1992) found that gay men who knew they were HIV-positive were *more* optimistic that they would not develop AIDS than were gay men who had tested negative for the virus.

Unrealistic optimism is fueled, in part, by another self-protective form of social cognition called *unique invulnerability*. For example, people tend to judge *other people's* unprotected sexual intercourse with multiple partners as creating a high risk for unwanted pregnancy and sexually transmitted diseases, but they believe that they themselves are at low risk and often fail to take precautions (Catania et al., 1992; Taylor et al., 1992).

The *self-handicapping strategy* protects self-esteem by providing a way for one's failures to be attributed to an external cause (Luginbuhl & Palmer, 1991). Thus, people may procrastinate, take drugs or alcohol, get too little sleep, or reduce their level of effort—actions that make subsequent poor performance attributable to external causes, not negative internal characteristics (Hirt, Deppe & Gordon, 1991; Tice, 1991). This strategy is used primarily when people have succeeded in the past but doubt whether they can continue to do so (Tice & Baumeister, 1990).

Self-protective cognitive biases can help us temporarily escape from something painful, but they also set the stage for a distorted view of reality and, in the long run,

IN REVIEW	Some Biases in Social Perception
Bias	**Description**
Importance of first impression	Ambiguous information is interpreted in line with a first impression, and the initial schema is recalled better and more vividly than any later correction to it. Actions based on this impression may elicit behavior that confirms it.
Fundamental attribution error	The tendency to attribute the behavior of others to internal factors.
Actor-observer bias	The tendency for actors to attribute their own behavior to external causes and for observers to attribute the behavior of others to internal factors.
Self-serving bias	The tendency to attribute one's successes to internal factors and one's failures to external factors.
Unrealistic optimism	The tendency to assume that positive events are more likely and negative events are less likely to occur to oneself than to others.

can create problems. ("In Review: Some Biases in Social Perception" summarizes the common cognitive biases discussed here.) Like the defense mechanisms described in Chapter 14, cognitive strategies such as unrealistic optimism may temporarily decrease anxiety and blunt the impact of stress, but these strategies may also keep people from taking the rational steps necessary for long-term protection. Because people believe they are "hardy," they may not quit smoking; because they believe they live in a secure building, they may not lock their doors (Gollwitzer & Kinney, 1989). Over the long term, these forms of self-deception may complicate the task of coping with negative events.

ATTITUDES

People's views about health or safety reflect their attitudes, an aspect of social cognition that social psychologists have studied longer and more intensely than any other. An **attitude** is the tendency to think, feel, or act positively or negatively toward objects in our environment (Eagly & Chaiken, 1993; Petty, 1995). Attitudes play an important role in guiding how we react to other people, what causes and politicians we support, which products we buy, and countless other daily decisions.

The Structure of Attitudes

Social psychologists have long viewed attitudes as having three components, as illustrated in Figure 17.3 (Eagly & Chaiken, 1993). The *cognitive* component is a set of beliefs about the attributes of the attitude object. The emotional, or *affective*, component includes feelings about the object, and the *behavioral* component pertains to the way people act toward the object. Ideally, these components would be in harmony, allowing us to predict people's behavior toward the homeless, for example, on the basis of the thoughts or feelings they express, and vice versa. This is often not the case, however (Kraus, 1995). Many people's charitable thoughts and sympathetic emotions regarding the homeless are never translated into actions aimed at helping them.

What determines whether people's behavior will be consistent with the cognitive and affective components of their attitudes? Several factors are important. For one thing, consistency is most likely when the behavior in question is in line with a *subjective norm*, our view of how important figures in our lives want us to act. Conflict between

FIGURE 17.3

Three Components of an Attitude

Different attitude components may or may not be consistent with one another. For example, people may deplore drunken driving (cognitive component) *and* be upset by its tragic consequences (affective component), yet not do anything to solve the problem. They may even get behind the wheel after having had one too many (behavioral component).

ATTITUDE TOWARD DRUNK DRIVING   **ASSESSMENT METHODS**

Cognitive component (belief)	Believes driving after drinking is dangerous	←	Paper-and-pencil tests (questionnaires)
Affective component (feeling)	Is upset by widespread drunk driving	←	Physiological indices (heart rate, GSR)
Behavioral component (action)	Participates in demonstrations against drunk driving	←	Directly observed behaviors

A REMINDER ABOUT POVERTY   Photographs like this one are among the cues used by fund-raising organizations to make positive attitudes toward needy people and other social causes more salient and accessible to viewers. As a result, people may be more likely to behave in accordance with their attitudes and make a donation.

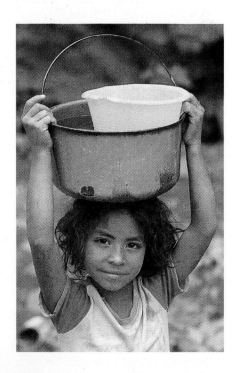

attitudes and subjective norms may cause people to behave in ways that are inconsistent with their attitudes (Eagly & Chaiken, 1993). Thus, for example, someone who believes that the rights of gays and lesbians should be protected might not campaign for this cause because doing so would upset family members or co-workers who are strongly against it. Second, attitude-consistent behavior is more likely when people have *perceived control,* the belief that they can actually perform such behavior (Madden, Ellen & Ajzen, 1992). You may hold a positive attitude about becoming an opera star, but if you don't believe it is possible, you are not likely to even try. Third, *direct experience* with the attitude object increases the likelihood of attitude-consistent behavior (Kraus, 1995). If your positive attitude toward caviar, say, is based on having actually tasted it, you are more likely to buy it than if your attitude stems solely from its image. Finally, people who *monitor,* or pay close attention to, the behavior of others in social situations are less likely to behave in accordance with their own attitudes (Kraus, 1995).

Another explanation of attitude-behavior consistency or discrepancy is derived from the cognitive theories of learning and memory described in Chapters 7 and 8. According to this view, attitudes reside in networks of cognitions—interconnected evaluations and beliefs about attitude objects—that are stored in our long-term memory (Ostrom, Skowronski & Nowack, 1994; see also Figure 8.12 on page 247). When you encounter an attitude object, the cognitions associated with it are activated. If these thoughts and feelings are well defined and come easily to mind, then our behavior is likely to be consistent with them; if not, there may be less consistency (Kraus, 1995; Neuberg, 1988). This notion of easy accessibility may help explain why, as just noted, attitude-behavior consistency is especially likely when attitudes are based on direct (rather than secondhand) experience with an attitude object. People are likely to have clearer, more accessible memories about objects they have personally encountered than about those they have only heard about.

Forming Attitudes

People are not born with specific attitudes toward specific objects, but their attitudes about new objects begin to appear in early childhood and continue to emerge throughout life. How do attitudes form?

The inherited predispositions of temperament described in Chapters 12 and 14 may have some indirect effects (Oskamp, 1991; Tesser, 1993), but the formation of new attitudes is influenced mainly by the learning principles discussed in Chapter 7. In childhood, modeling and other forms of social learning are especially important. Children learn not only the names of objects but also what they should believe and feel about them and how they should act toward them. For example, a parent's words may teach a child not only that snakes are reptiles but also that they should be feared and avoided. So as children learn concepts such as "reptile" or "work," they learn attitudes about those concepts, too (Olson & Zanna, 1993).

Classical and operant conditioning can also shape positive or negative attitudes (Krosnick et al., 1992). Advertisers associate enjoyable music or soothing colors with the products they are trying to sell (Pratkanis & Aronson, 1991; Aronson, Wilson & Akert, 1994), and parents, teachers, and peers reward children for stating particular views. The *mere-exposure effect* described in Chapter 6 is influential as well. All else being equal, attitudes toward an object will become more positive the more frequently people are exposed to it (Bornstein, 1992). Often, people come to like a song only after they have heard it several times; so guess why certain commercials and political ads are aired so often.

Changing Attitudes

The nearly $100 billion a year spent on advertising in the United States alone provides but one example of how people are constantly trying to change our attitudes. Stop for a moment and make a list of other examples, starting, perhaps, with the messages of groups concerned with abortion or recycling—and don't forget your friends who want you to do something that you think is a waste of time.

Two Routes to Attitude Change   Whether a persuasive message succeeds in changing attitudes depends primarily on three factors: ① the characteristics of the person communicating the message, ② the content of the message, and ③ the audience who receives it (Petty, 1995). The **elaboration likelihood model** of attitude change—illustrated in Figure 17.4—provides a framework for understanding when and how these factors affect attitude change. The model is based on the premise that persuasive messages can change people's attitudes through one of two main routes. The first is called the ① *peripheral route* because, when it is activated, we devote little attention to the central content of the persuasive message and tend to be affected instead by peripheral *persuasion cues,* such as the confidence, attractiveness, or other characteristics of the person delivering the message. Persuasion cues influence attitude change even though they say nothing about the logic or validity of the message content. Commercials in which movie stars or other attractive nonexperts endorse pain relievers are designed to operate via the peripheral route to attitude change. By contrast, when the ② *central route* to attitude change is activated, the content of the message becomes more important in determining attitude change than the characteristics of the communicator. A person following the central route uses logical steps—like those outlined in the Thinking Critically sections of this book—to rationally analyze the content of the persuasive message, including the validity of its claims, whether it leaves out pertinent information, alternative interpretations of evidence, and so on.

What determines which route people will follow? Personal involvement with message content is one important factor. The elaboration likelihood model proposes that the more personally involving a topic is, the more likely the central route will be activated (Petty, 1995; Petty, Priester & Wegener, 1994). Suppose, for example, that you hear someone advocating the abolition of student loans in Chile. This message might persuade you via the peripheral route if it comes from someone who looks attractive and sounds intelligent. However, you are more likely to follow the central route if the message proposes terminating student loans at *your* school. You might be persuaded, but

FIGURE 17.4

The Elaboration Likelihood Model of Attitude Change

The central route to attitude change begins with high elaboration, which includes careful processing and evaluation of a message's content. The peripheral route involves low elaboration and reliance on persuasion cues such as the attractiveness of the person making the argument (Cacioppo, Petty & Crites, 1993).

LOW INVOLVEMENT

HIGH INVOLVEMENT

Strong arguments

Weak arguments

Source: Data from Petty, Cacioppo & Goldman, 1981 and Petty, Cacioppo & Shumann, 1983.

FIGURE 17.5

Personal Involvement and Routes to Attitude Change

In the study represented here, students' reactions to messages advocating exit exams for seniors depended on whether they thought the policy would begin immediately (high involvement) or only after they had graduated (low involvement). In the low involvement condition, students followed a peripheral route to attitude change, agreeing with messages from highly credible communicators regardless of how logical they were. More involved students followed a central route, changing their minds only if the message contained a strong argument.

only if the logic of the message is irrefutable (see Figure 17.5). This is why celebrity endorsements tend to be most effective when the products being advertised are relatively unimportant to the audience.

"Cognitive busyness" is another factor affecting which attitude-change route is activated. If you are busy thinking about other things while a message is being delivered, you will be unable to pay much attention to its content—in which case activation of the peripheral route becomes more likely.

Audience personality characteristics are also related to attitude-change processes. For example, people with a strong *need for cognition* (Petty, 1995) like to engage in thoughtful mental activities and are therefore more likely to use the central route to attitude change. In contrast, people whose discomfort with uncertainty creates a *need for closure* are more likely to use the peripheral route (Cacioppo & Petty, 1982; Kruglanski, Webster & Klem, 1993).

Persuasive messages are not the only means of changing attitudes. Another approach is to get people to act in ways that are inconsistent with their current attitudes, in the hope that they will adjust those attitudes to match their behavior. Often, such adjustments do occur. Cognitive dissonance theory and self-perception theory each attempt to explain why.

Cognitive Dissonance Theory   Leon Festinger's (1957) classic **cognitive dissonance theory** holds that people want their thoughts, beliefs, and attitudes to be consistent with one another. When these various cognitions are inconsistent, or *dissonant,* people become anxious and are motivated to make them more consistent (Eliot & Devine, 1994). For example, someone who believes that "smoking is bad" but must also acknowledge that "I smoke" would be motivated to reduce the resulting dissonance. But it is often difficult to change behavior, so people usually reduce cognitive dissonance by changing inconsistent attitudes: Rather than quit smoking, the smoker might decide that smoking is not so bad.

In one of the first studies of cognitive dissonance, Festinger and his colleague Merrill Carlsmith (1959) asked people to turn pegs in a board, a very dull task. Later, some of these people were asked to persuade a person waiting to participate in the study that the task was "exciting and fun." Some were told that they would be paid $1 to tell this lie; others were promised $20. After they had talked to the waiting person, their attitudes toward the dull task were measured.

Figure 17.6 shows the surprising results. The people who were paid just $1 to lie liked the dull task more than those who were paid $20. Why? Festinger and Carlsmith (1959) argued that telling another person that a boring task is enjoyable will produce dissonance (between the thoughts "I think the task is boring" and "I am saying it is fun"). To reduce this dissonance, the people who were paid just $1 adopted more favorable attitudes toward the task, making their cognitions consistent: "I think the task is fun" and "I am saying it is fun." But if a person has adequate justification for the behavior, any dissonance that exists will be reduced simply by thinking about the justification. The participants who were paid $20 thought they had adequate justification for lying and so did not need to change their attitudes toward the task.

Hundreds of other experiments have supported the conclusion that people often reduce dissonance by changing their attitudes (Aronson, 1992; Aronson, Wilson & Akert, 1994). For example, Michael Lieppe and Donna Eisenstadt (1994) asked European-American college students to write essays in support of larger scholarships for African-American students—an idea that most of the essay-writers opposed. Some of the students were told that writing the essays was voluntary; for others, the essays were required. In accordance with cognitive dissonance theory, the students whose only justification for writing the essays was their own free choice developed more positive attitudes toward African-American students. The attitudes of the no-choice students did not change, presumably because they could justify their attitude-inconsistent behavior as having been demanded by the experimenter.

The power of cognitive dissonance to change attitudes may be greater in the individualist cultures of Europe and North America than in collectivist cultures such as

IN REVIEW	Forming and Changing Attitudes
Type of Influence	**Description**
Modeling and conditioning	Attitudes are usually formed through observation of how others behave and speak about an attitude object, as well as through classical and operant conditioning.
Elaboration likelihood model	People change attitudes through either a central or peripheral route, depending on factors such as personal involvement, "cognitive busyness," and personal preferences.
Cognitive dissonance and self-perception	Holding inconsistent cognitions can motivate attitude change, as can reviewing one's behavior in light of circumstances.

FIGURE 17.6

Cognitive Dissonance and Attitude Change

According to cognitive dissonance theory, people paid $20 to say a boring task was enjoyable had clear justification for lying and should experience little dissonance between what they said and what they felt about the task. Indeed, their attitude toward the task did not change much. However, subjects who received just $1 had little justification to lie and reduced their dissonance mainly by displaying a more positive attitude toward the task.

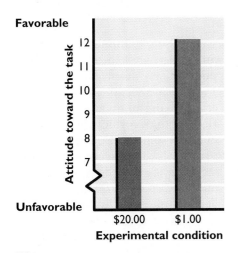

■ High justification (low dissonance)

■ Low justification (high dissonance)

Japan (Moghaddam, Taylor & Wright, 1993). Where group rather than individual values and goals are emphasized, behaving at odds with one's personal beliefs may create less discomfort—and less motivation for attitude change—because holding to those beliefs tends to be less important for self-esteem. One recent study, for example, showed that Canadian students were much more likely to experience cognitive dissonance than their Japanese counterparts (Heine & Lehman, 1995).

Self-Perception Theory Cognitive dissonance theory assumes that the inconsistencies among a person's thoughts produce tension that results in attitude change, but Daryl Bem (1967) suggested an alternative explanation that does not presuppose internal tension. According to Bem's **self-perception theory,** situations often arise in which people are not quite sure about their attitudes. When this happens, Bem says, people consider their own behavior under particular circumstances and then *infer* what their attitude must be. That is, a person says, "If I did that under those circumstances, my attitude must be this." This process requires no tension. Self-perception theory would suggest, for example, that in the essay-writing study mentioned earlier, students who wrote voluntarily changed their attitudes after saying to themselves, "I wouldn't have written this if I did not believe African-Americans deserve special help." Conversely, those forced to write the essay could say "I would never have written this on my own, so I still don't support the idea of special help for African-Americans."

Self-perception theory and cognitive dissonance theory often make the same predictions, and both may be correct to some extent. Self-perception theory seems to apply best when people have no prior attitude or, if they do, the attitude is weak and ill-defined, as in the case of never-tasted foods (Olson, 1992). But when attitudes are strong and clearly defined, and especially when internal consistency is important to one's self-esteem, dissonance theory appears to hold (Thibodeau & Aronson, 1992). ("In Review: Forming and Changing Attitudes" summarizes some of the major processes through which attitudes are formed and changed.)

PREJUDICE AND STEREOTYPES

All of the principles underlying impression formation, attribution, attraction, and attitudes come together in prejudice and stereotypes (Hamilton & Sherman, 1994). **Stereotypes** are the perceptions, beliefs, and expectations a person has about members of some group; they are schemas about entire groups of people (Mackie et al., in press). Usually, they involve the false assumption that all members of a group share the same characteristics. The characteristics that make up the stereotype may be positive, but usually they are negative. The most prevalent and powerful stereotypes focus on observable personal attributes, particularly ethnicity, gender, and age (Devine, 1995; Dovidio & Gaertner, 1986).

Stereotyping often leads to **prejudice,** which is a positive or negative attitude toward an individual based simply on his or her membership in some group (Fiske & Von Hend, 1992). *Prejudice* means literally "to prejudge." Many theorists believe that prejudice, like other attitudes, has cognitive, affective, and behavioral components. Stereotyped thinking is the cognitive component of prejudicial attitudes. The hatred, admiration, anger, and other feelings people have about stereotyped groups constitute the affective component. The behavioral component of prejudice involves **discrimination,** which is differential treatment of individuals who belong to different groups.

Theories of Prejudice

Not all prejudice and stereotyping occur for the same reason (Duckitt, 1994). We describe three explanatory theories, each of which has empirical support and accounts for some, but not all, instances of stereotyping and prejudice.

Motivational Theories   For some people, prejudice against certain groups enhances their sense of security and meets other needs described in Chapter 11. Research by T. W. Adorno and his colleagues suggests that prejudice may be especially likely among people whose parents used punishment or harsh words to instill the belief that they must defer to and obey all those with a higher status than themselves. This kind of upbringing was described in Chapter 12 as authoritarian parenting, which, according to these researchers, encourages the development of a cluster of traits called the *authoritarian personality* (Adorno et al., 1950; Stone, Lederer & Christie, 1993). People with an authoritarian personality view the world as a threatening place. One way they protect themselves from threat is to strongly identify with their own ethnic, cultural, or social group—their *in-group*—and to reject, dislike, and perhaps even punish anyone who is a member of other groups. Derogating these *out-group* members may help people with an authoritarian personality to feel safer and better about themselves. Some psychodynamic theorists even suggest that prejudice displaces onto out-groups the hostility that authoritarian personalities originally felt toward their punitive parents.

[handwritten margin note: parental cause — act out hostility really felt towards parents.]

A more recent motivational explanation of prejudice invokes the concept of social identity discussed earlier. Recall that, whether they have authoritarian parents or not, most people are motivated to identify with their in-group and tend to see it as better than other groups (Smith, 1993; Billig & Tajfel, 1973). As a result, members of an in-group often see all members of out-groups as less attractive and less socially appropriate than those of the in-group members and may thus treat them badly (Beike & Sherman, 1994; Hamilton & Sherman, 1994; Smith & Mackie, 1995). In other words, prejudice may result when people's motivation to enhance their self-esteem causes them to derogate other people.

Cognitive Theories   Stereotyping and prejudice may also result from the social-cognitive processes people use in dealing with the world. There are so many other people, so many situations in which one meets them, and so many possible behaviors they might perform that one cannot possibly attend to and remember them all. Therefore, people must use schemas and other cognitive shortcuts to organize and make sense out of their social world (Hamilton & Sherman, 1994). Often these cognitive processes provide accurate and useful summaries of other people, but sometimes they lead to inaccurate stereotypes. For example, one effective way to deal with social complexity is to group people into *social categories.* Rather than remembering every detail about everyone they have ever encountered, people tend to put other people into categories such as doctor, senior citizen, Republican, student, Italian, and the like (Rothbart & Lewis, 1994). To further simplify perception of these categories we tend to see their members as being quite similar to one another. Thus, members of an ethnic group may find it harder to distinguish among specific faces in other ethnic groups than in their own (Anthony, Cooper & Mullen, 1992). People also tend to assume that all members of a different group hold the same beliefs and values, and that those beliefs and values differ from their own (Rokeach & Mezei, 1966). Finally, as we saw in the chapter on perception, people's attention tends to be drawn to distinctive stimuli. Thus, noticeably rude behavior by even a few members of an easily identified ethnic group may lead other people to see an *illusory correlation* between rudeness and ethnicity (Hamilton & Sherman, 1994). As a result, they may incorrectly believe that *most* members of that group are rude. People may be especially likely to recall negative stereotypes when they are in a negative mood (Esses & Zanna, 1995).

Learning Theories   Some prejudice results from conflicts between members of different groups, but people also develop negative attitudes toward groups with whom they have had little or no contact. Like other attitudes, prejudice can be learned. Learning theories suggest that children acquire prejudices just by watching and listening to the words and deeds of parents, peers, and others (Karlins, Coffman & Walter, 1969). Movies and television may also portray ethnic or other groups in ways that teach stereotypes and prejudice (Liebert & Sprafkin, 1988). And, as mentioned earlier, children may be directly reinforced for expressing prejudice. In fact, small children often know about the supposed negative characteristics of many groups long before they ever meet people in those groups (Mackie et al, in press).

Reducing Prejudice

One clear implication of the cognitive and learning theories of prejudice and stereotyping is that members of one group are often ignorant or misinformed about the characteristics of people in other groups (Miller & Davidson-Podgorny, 1987). Before 1954, for example, most black and white schoolchildren in the United States knew very little about one another because they went to separate schools. Then the Supreme Court declared that segregated public schools should be prohibited. In addition to ruling segregation to be unconstitutional, the court provided a real-life test of the **contact hypothesis,** which states that stereotypes and prejudice toward a group will diminish as contact with the group increases.

Did the school desegregation process of the 1960s and 1970s confirm the contact hypothesis? In a few schools, integration was followed by a decrease in prejudice, but in most places either no change occurred or prejudice actually increased (Devine, 1995; Stephan, 1987). However, these results did not necessarily disprove the contact hypothesis. In-depth studies of schools where desegregation was successful suggested that contact alone was not enough—indeed, that integration reduced prejudice only when

FIGHTING ETHNIC PREJUDICE   Negative attitudes about members of ethnic groups are often based on negative personal experiences or the negative experiences and attitudes people hear about from others. Cooperative contact between equals can help promote mutual respect and reduce ethnic prejudice.

certain social conditions were created (Miller, Brewer & Edwards, 1985; Cook, 1985). First, members of the two groups had to be of roughly equal social and economic status. Second, school authorities had to promote cooperation and interdependence among the members of ethnic groups by having them work together on projects that required reliance on one another to reach success. Third, the contact between group members had to occur on a one-on-one basis; it was only when *individuals* got to know each other that the errors contained in stereotypes became apparent. Finally, the members of each group had to be seen as typical and not unusual in any significant way. When these four conditions were met, the children's attitudes toward one another became more positive.

Elliot Aronson (1995) describes a teaching strategy, called the *jigsaw technique,* that helps create these conditions. Children from several ethnic groups must work on a team to complete a task such as writing a report about a famous figure in history; each child is asked to provide the team with a separate piece of information about this figure, such as place of birth (Aronson, 1990). Studies show that children from various ethnic groups who take part in the jigsaw technique and other cooperative learning experiences show substantial reductions in prejudice toward other groups (e.g., Aronson, Wilson & Akert, 1994). The success reported in these studies has greatly increased the popularity of cooperative learning exercises in U.S. classrooms. Such exercises may not eliminate all aspects of ethnic prejudice in children, but they seem to be a step in the right direction.

Can friendly, cooperative, interdependent contact between adults reduce the more entrenched forms of prejudice? It may. When two equal-status adults work jointly toward a common goal, their mutual respect and liking tend to increase (Cook, 1984). Their successes lead to joint pride, and even mistakes or failures by a partner are often tolerated (Lanzetta & Englis, 1989). The challenge to be met in creating such cooperative experiences in the real world is that the participants must be of equal status—a challenge made more difficult, in the United States and elsewhere, by the sizable status differences that still exist between ethnic groups (Foster & Finchilescu, 1986).

In the final analysis, contact can provide only part of the solution to the problems of stereotyping, prejudice, and discrimination. To reduce ethnic prejudice, we must develop additional educational techniques that address the social cognitions and perceptions that lie at the core of bigotry and hatred toward people who are different from us (Monteith, Zuwerink & Devine, 1994).

There is little doubt that overt forms of ethnic prejudice have decreased dramatically in the United States over the last thirty to forty years. According to a survey in the 1950s, for example, less than half of European-American college students were willing to live in integrated neighborhoods; today, about 95 percent say they would be willing to do so. And three decades ago, fewer than 40 percent of European-Americans said they would vote for an African-American presidential candidate; over 95 percent now say they might do so (Dovidio et al., in press). Nevertheless, polls suggest that most African-Americans in the United States think that prejudice against them is still a very serious problem (*USA Today,* 1995).

THINKING CRITICALLY

Is Ethnic Prejudice Too Ingrained Ever to Be Eliminated?

What am I being asked to believe or accept?

Even people who see themselves as nonprejudiced, and who disavow ethnic stereotypes and discrimination, still hold negative stereotypes about ethnic out-groups and, in certain situations, will display prejudice and discrimination toward them (Devine, 1995; Monteith, Zuwerink & Devine, 1994). Some people claim, therefore, that negative attitudes toward ethnic out-groups are so deeply ingrained in all of us that ethnic prejudice can never be eliminated.

What evidence is available to support the assertion?

Evidence for this assertion focuses on prejudice against African-Americans by European-Americans and comes, first, from studies testing the theory of *aversive racism* (Gaertner & Dovidio, 1986). This theory holds that even though many European-Americans consider ethnic prejudice to be aversive, they will still sometimes display it—especially when they can do so without admitting, even to themselves, that they are prejudiced. In one study of aversive racism, a male experimenter telephoned male and female European-Americans who were known to believe in ethnic equality. The man claimed to be a stranded motorist who had misdialed while trying to call a service station for help. When told he had dialed the wrong number, the man replied that he was out of coins and asked the person he'd reached to call a service station for him. *If* people listened long enough to learn of the man's problem they were just as likely to contact the service station whether the caller "sounded" European-American or African-American. However, if the caller "sounded" African-American, these supposedly unprejudiced people were almost five times as likely to hang up even before the caller could ask for help (Gaertner & Dovidio, 1986). In a second study, female European-American college students were asked to help another female student who was doing poorly on some task. When the student's poor performance was described as being due to the task's difficulty, the students agreed to help, regardless of the other student's ethnicity. But if the problem was said to be due to lack of effort, help was offered much more often to European-Americans than to African-Americans (Frey & Gaertner, 1986; McPhail & Penner, 1995). Both studies suggest that even people who do not display prejudice in most situations may do so in others.

A second line of evidence for the entrenchment of prejudice comes from research showing that people can be unaware of their negative ethnic stereotypes. After classifying European-American volunteers as prejudiced or nonprejudiced on the basis of their stated attitudes toward African-Americans, Patricia Devine (1989) asked them to read a description of a man's behavior. The subjects received no direct information about the man's ethnicity, but in some cases they were exposed to a subliminal presentation of a term such as *black* or *Negro* just before seeing the description. In the chapter on consciousness, we noted that such "priming" can alter our reactions to stimuli without our awareness. Here, priming appeared to activate ethnic stereotypes even in people who had claimed not to have them; both prejudiced and nonprejudiced subjects rated the man as more hostile if they had first been primed by words associated with African-Americans. In other studies, the speed of response to a person's positive attributes was shown to increase after subjects were primed by stimuli associated with European-Americans but not by those associated with African-Americans. Indeed, only negative traits gave rise to quicker response times when the subjects were primed by terms such as *black* (Baker & Devine, 1988; Dovidio, Evans & Tyler, 1986). All of these findings suggest that, even among "nonprejudiced" people, racial stereotypes are so overlearned that they may be activated automatically and without awareness (Fazio et al., 1995).

Are there alternative ways of interpreting the evidence?

Obviously, the elimination of prejudice becomes a lot more difficult if people are truly unaware of their prejudice. But are they truly unaware? Perhaps subjects in subliminal priming studies are more conscious of their views than they like to admit, in which case their views may indeed be accessible to change.

What additional evidence would help to evaluate the alternatives?

One way to evaluate whether or not prejudice can be truly outside of awareness is to use a procedure developed by Larry Jacoby (1991) in which conscious and subconscious processes create opposite responses and thus can be measured separately. (The procedure involves measuring how frequently a person's stereotypes subtly influence his or her responses about a certain group while the person consciously tries to avoid being influenced.) Using Jacoby's procedure, several researchers have demonstrated that bias against women and the elderly can exist without conscious awareness (Banaji

LINKAGES Can subconscious processes alter our reaction to people? (a link to Consciousness)

& Greenwald, 1995; Hense, Penner & Nelson, in press). This procedure holds promise for learning more about the role of subconscious processes in prejudice against African-Americans.

What conclusions are most reasonable?

The evidence available so far presents a mixed picture regarding the possibility of eliminating ethnic prejudice. Clearly, people in the United States are not nearly as "color-blind" as we might hope, and ethnic prejudice may be so ingrained in some people as to be subconscious. Nonetheless, it makes sense to do everything possible to reduce prejudice in everyone; indeed, even if subconscious thoughts and feelings toward out-groups cannot be altered, our survival as a society demands that we continue fighting the many forms of stereotyping, prejudice, and discrimination of which people are aware.

INTERPERSONAL ATTRACTION

Research on prejudice helps illuminate some of the reasons for which people, from childhood on, may come to dislike or even hate other people. An equally fascinating aspect of social cognition is why people like, or love, other people. Folklore tells us that "opposites attract," but it also maintains that "birds of a feather flock together." Though valid to some degree, each of these statements needs to be qualified in important ways. We begin our coverage of interpersonal attraction by discussing the factors that lead to initial attraction; we then examine how liking sometimes develops into more intimate relationships.

Keys to Attraction

Whether you like someone or not depends partly on situational factors and partly on personal characteristics.

The Environment   One of the most important determinants of attraction is simple physical proximity (Clark & Pataki, 1995). As long as you do not initially dislike the person, your liking for him or her will increase with additional contact (Bornstein, 1992).

PROXIMITY AND LIKING   In general, the more often people make contact with someone, the more they tend to like that person. This is one reason why next-door neighbors are much more likely to become friends than people who live farther from one another. Chances are, most of your friends are people whom you met as neighbors, co-workers, or classmates.

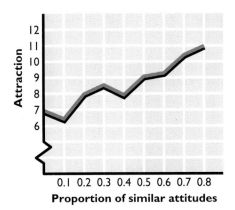

Source: Adapted from Byrne & Nelson, 1965.

FIGURE 17.7

Attitude Similarity and Attraction

This graph shows the results of a study in which people learned about another person's attitudes. Their liking of that person was strongly related to the proportion of his or her attitudes that were similar to their own.

This phenomenon is another example of the *mere-exposure effect* mentioned earlier. For example, Richard Moreland and Scott Beach (1992) varied the number of times that several experimental assistants (masquerading as students) attended a class. Even though none of the assistants spoke to anyone in the class, they were rated by the other students as more likable the more often they attended.

The circumstances under which people first meet also influence attraction. Thus, in accordance with the principles of learning discussed in Chapter 7, you are much more likely to be attracted to a stranger you meet in comfortable as opposed to uncomfortable physical conditions. Similarly, if you receive a reward in the presence of a stranger, the chances that you will like that stranger are increased, even if the stranger is not the one giving the reward (Clark & Pataki, 1995). In one study, for example, an experimenter judged one person's creativity while another person watched. Compared to those who received a negative evaluation, subjects who were evaluated positively tended to like the observer more (Griffitt & Guay, 1969). At least among strangers, then, liking can occur through associating someone with something pleasant.

Similarity   People also tend to like those whom they perceive as similar to themselves on variables such as age, religion, smoking or drinking habits, or being a "morning" or "evening" person. As shown in Figure 17.7, similarity in attitudes is an especially important influence on attraction. This relationship has been found among children, college students, adult workers, and senior citizens (Duck & Barnes, 1992).

Similarity in attitudes about mutual acquaintances is a particularly good predictor of liking because, in general, people prefer relationships that are *balanced*. Thus, as illustrated in Figure 17.8, if Meagan likes Abigail, the relationship is balanced as long as they agree on their evaluation of a third person, regardless of whether they like or dislike that third person. However, the relationship will be imbalanced if Meagan and Abigail disagree on their evaluation of a third person.

One reason for the correlation between attitude similarity and liking is that people who share attitudes tend to validate one another's view of the world (Swann, Stein-Seroussi & Giesler, 1992). But like many correlations, this one can also reflect *reciprocal causality;* in other words, attraction can be both a cause and a consequence of similarity (Brehm, 1992). Thus, for example, you might like someone because his attitudes are similar to yours, but it is also possible that, as a result of liking him, your attitudes will become more similar to his. Some people even change their perceptions of a liked person's attitudes so that they seem more similar to their own (Curtis & Miller, 1986).

Physical Attractiveness   Physical characteristics are another important factor in attraction, particularly during the initial stages of a relationship (Feingold, 1992). From preschool through adulthood, physical attractiveness is a key to popularity with members of both sexes (Aronson, Wilson & Akert, 1994; Dion, 1992). Consistent with the

FIGURE 17.8

Balanced and Imbalanced Relationships

Shown here are some common examples of balanced and imbalanced patterns of relationships among three people. The plus and minus signs refer to liking and disliking, respectively. Balanced relationships are comfortable and harmonious; imbalanced ones often bring conflict.

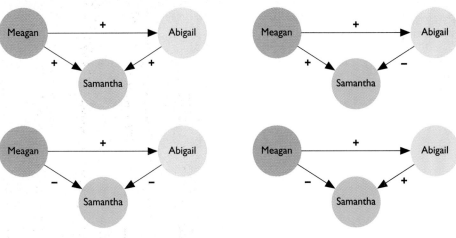

(A) BALANCED RELATIONSHIPS   **(B) IMBALANCED RELATIONSHIPS**

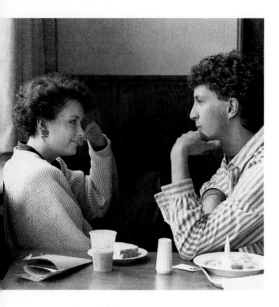

AN INTIMATE PAIR In intimate relationships, each person tends to be more concerned with providing love and support to their partner than with being rewarded for what they contribute (Clark & Mills, 1993).

matching hypothesis of interpersonal attraction, however, people tend to date, marry, or form other committed relationships with those who are similar in physical attractiveness (Brehm, 1992; Kalick, 1988; Kalick & Hamilton, 1986). One possible reason for this outcome: Although people tend to be most attracted to those with the greatest physical appeal, they also want to avoid rejection by such individuals. In short, it may be compromise, not preference, that leads people to pair off with those who are roughly equivalent to themselves in physical attractiveness (Carli, Ganley, & Pierce-Otay, 1991).

Intimate Relationships and Love

There is much about intimate relationships that psychologists do not—and may never—understand, but they are learning all the time. As mentioned in Chapter 11, proponents of evolutionary psychology suggest that men and women employ different strategies to ensure the survival of their genes, and that each gender looks for different attributes in a potential mate (Buss, 1994; Kenrick, 1994; Kenrick, et al., 1995; Singh, 1995; Sprecher, Sullivan & Hatfield, 1994). Some attributes are attractive to both genders, however, as shown in Table 17.1 (Buss, 1988).

Intimate Relationships Eventually, people who are attracted to each other usually become *interdependent,* which means that the thoughts, emotions, and behaviors of one person affect the thoughts, emotions, and behaviors of the other (Clark & Pataki, 1995). Interdependence occurs in large measure as the thoughts and values of one person become part of the self-concept of the other (Aron et al., 1991). It is thus one of the defining characteristics of intimate relationships.

When asked to name the key ingredients of a successful intimate relationship, people most often mention *affection* and *emotional expressiveness* (Helgeson, Shaver & Dyer, 1987). Signs of affection are important because if one person perceives the other to be uninterested, communication will deteriorate and the person will begin to withdraw (Sayers & Baucom, 1991). Emotional expressiveness is important not only because it enhances feelings of closeness and commitment, but also, as noted in Chapter 13, because the expression of strong emotions is comforting (Greenberg & Stone, 1992).

Other key components of intimate relationships appear to be the *result* of intimacy (Clark & Reis, 1988). One is *social support,* which refers in part to helping with the daily hassles of life and in part to psychological support, such as propping up a friend's confidence (McGuire, 1994). Intimacy also frequently brings *cohesiveness,* which refers to joint activities such as taking a vacation together, and *sexuality* (Clark, 1994).

Analyzing Love Affection, emotional expressiveness, social support, cohesiveness, sexuality—these characteristics of intimate relationships are likely to bring something

TABLE 17.1	Male Attributes	Female Attributes
Attributes Rated Most Attractive by Members of the Opposite Sex	1. Displayed a good sense of humor.	1. Displayed a good sense of humor.
Here, according to research by David Buss (1988), are the ten attributes that males and females found most attractive in one another.	2. Was sympathetic to her troubles.	2. Kept herself well-groomed.
	3. Showed good manners.	3. Was sympathetic to his troubles.
	4. Kept himself well-groomed.	4. Showed good manners.
	5. Made an effort to spend a lot of time with her.	5. Showered daily.
	6. Offered to help her.	6. Kept physically fit to create a healthy appearance.
	7. Showered daily.	7. Made up jokes to make men laugh.
	8. Kept physically fit to create a healthy appearance.	8. Made an effort to spend a lot of time with him.
	9. Exercised.	9. Wore stylish, fashionable clothes.
	10. Wore attractive outfits.	10. Offered to help him.

else to mind: love. Yet intimacy and love are not synonymous. Most theorists agree that there are several different types of love (Brehm, 1992). One widely accepted view distinguishes between passionate love and companionate love (Hatfield, 1988). *Passionate love* is intense, arousing, and marked by both strong physical attraction and deep emotional attachment. Sexual feelings are very strong and thoughts of the other intrude on a person's awareness frequently. *Companionate love* is less arousing but psychologically more intimate. It is marked by mutual concern for the welfare of the other (Hendrick & Hendrick, 1986).

Robert Sternberg (1988) has offered a more comprehensive analysis of love. According to his *triangular theory*, the three basic components of love are *passion, intimacy,* and *commitment.* Various combinations of these components result in quite different types of love, as illustrated in Figure 17.9. For example, Sternberg suggests that *romantic love* involves a high degree of passion and intimacy, yet lacks substantial commitment to the other person. *Companionate love* is marked by a great deal of intimacy and commitment but little passion. And *consummate love* is the most complete and satisfying. It is the most complete because it includes a high level of all three components. It is the most satisfying because the relationship is likely to fulfill many of the needs of each partner.

Cultural factors have a strong influence on the value that people place on love. In the United States, love is idealized in the popular media; 87 percent of Americans believe that love is crucial to a satisfying marriage. However, in the former Soviet Union, only 40 percent of the people say that they married for love; most did so because of loneliness, shared interests, or an unplanned pregnancy (Baron & Byrne, 1994). In collectivist cultures such as India and Japan, love is considered less important to a successful marriage than is the ability to resolve family conflicts (Matsumoto, 1994; Simmons, von Kolke & Shimizu, 1986).

FIGURE 17.9

A Triangular Theory of Love

According to Sternberg, different types of love result when the three basic components proposed in his triangular theory occur in different combinations.

Source: "Triangulating Love" in *The Psychology of Love* by R. J. Sternberg & M. L. Barnes, Copyright © 1988 by Yale University Press. Reprinted by permission.

HAPPY AND HEALTHY People in satisfying marriages and other long-term relationships tend to enjoy better physical and psychological health than those in unsatisfying relationships (Burman & Margolin, 1992).

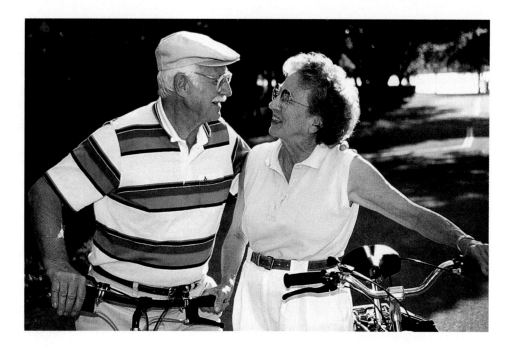

Strong and Weak Marriages In Western cultures, good communication appears to be very important to marital satisfaction. In fact, the mutual sharing of interests, beliefs, opinions, and the like is often more important than sex (Sternberg & Grajek, 1984). In general, women—but not men—tend to be more satisfied with their marriage when the partners talk a lot about the relationship (Acitelli, 1992). Partners in successful marriages also tend to share one another's view of themselves and each other, even if that view is a negative one (Swann, De La Ronde & Hixon, 1994).

The perception that a relationship is fair or equitable also enhances marital satisfaction (Clark, 1994). After the birth of a first child, for example, many wives find that they have much more work than they had anticipated. If their husbands do not share this work to the degree they expected, wives' marital satisfaction tends to decrease (Hackel & Ruble, 1992). One survey of over 60,000 people found that those who felt unfairly treated in their marriage were the most likely to have had an extramarital affair (Walster, Traupmann & Walster, 1978).

A related determinant of long-term marital satisfaction is how the couple deals with the conflict and anger that occur in virtually all marriages. In both happy and unhappy marriages, men tend to respond to their spouse's anger with anger of their own. But in happy marriages, the cycle of angry reactions is ultimately broken, usually by the wife, allowing the couple to deal with the problem at hand during moments of calm (Rusbult et al., 1991). In unhappy marriages, both the husband and wife trade increasingly angry and hurtful remarks until communication breaks down (Gottman & Levenson, 1992). When these episodes become frequent, attributional biases begin to appear. Distressed couples tend to attribute their spouse's negative behaviors to internal causes (such as lack of concern) and positive behaviors to such external causes as the proximity of a holiday (Fincham & Bradbury, 1993). Thus, even if one spouse tries to improve the marriage, these efforts may be dismissed by the other as insincere or unimportant.

FUTURE DIRECTIONS

Social cognition is an exciting aspect of social psychology. Each year new discoveries are reported, novel theories are proposed, and researchers examine the intricacies of social interaction at a finer level of detail (Karney & Bradbury, 1995; Wyer & Srull, 1994). There is little doubt that this trend will continue.

One issue that cuts across all of the areas discussed in this chapter is the degree to which social cognition occurs automatically, without conscious awareness. More and more research is showing that social thought is often spontaneous, automatic, and sometimes beyond conscious control (Bargh & Barndollar,

1995; Bargh et al., in press). Now that this fact has been established, its implications for complex and important social behaviors will receive increased attention. In addition to studying subconscious cognitive processes related to prejudice and discrimination (Devine, 1995; Dovidio et al., in press; Mackie et al., in press), social psychologists will conduct research on how both conscious and subconscious social cognitions affect interpersonal behavior (Azar, 1996). One topic sure to maintain researchers' attention concerns the conditions that improve or impair the accuracy of social perception. The results of their work are likely to have many applications, including in business and industry. For example, many industrial-organizational psychologists believe that social perception research will help companies improve the objectivity and fairness of the procedures they use to select and evaluate employees.

Future years will also see research that focuses more intensely on genetic and biological factors that affect, and are affected by, social cognition and social behavior (e.g., Crites et al., 1995). In particular, the evolutionary approach to social psychology is gaining increased acceptance among a large number of psychologists. One claim of the evolutionary psychologists that will certainly be a source of continued research and controversy is the extent to which gender differences in

social behavior have a genetic basis (see Eagly, 1995). Social psychologists will also be studying how social cognitions affect physical and mental health. For example, in line with research described in Chapter 15, Gifford Weary has demonstrated that depressed and nondepressed people differ significantly in terms of how they think about their own behavior and that of others (Weary & Edwards, in press).

Finally, social psychologists will be devoting attention to exploring cross-cultural differences in social cognition. They have already discovered that cultural factors can influence the processing of social information (e.g., Morris & Peng, 1994) and that attributional biases, cognitive dissonance, and other aspects of social cognition are more likely to appear in some cultures than in others. But these findings form just the tip of the iceberg. The more that becomes known about differences in the ways people from various cultures think about one another, the likelier it is that those people will someday be able to fully understand—and cooperate with—one another.

If you are interested in learning more about these and other exciting developments in social cognition, consider taking an introductory social psychology course. Many psychology departments also offer more advanced courses in this subfield, including courses on social cognition, attitudes, interpersonal processes, and prejudice.

SUMMARY AND KEY TERMS

Social cognition, the mental processes through which people perceive and react to others, is one aspect of *social psychology,* the study of how people influence and are influenced by other people. Through social cognition, each person creates a unique perception of reality.

■ SOCIAL CONSTRUCTION OF THE SELF

People's social and cultural environments affect their thoughts and feelings about themselves, including their *self-esteem* and their *self-concept.*

Social Comparison
When people have no objective criteria by which to judge themselves, they look to others as the basis for *social comparison.* Such comparison can affect self-evaluation, or self-esteem. Categories of people that are habitually used for social comparison are known as *reference groups.* Comparison to reference groups sometimes produces *relative deprivation,* which, in turn, can cause personal and social turmoil.

Social Identity Theory
A person's *social identity* is formed from beliefs about the groups to which the person belongs. Social identity affects the beliefs we hold about ourselves, our self-concept. Social identity permits people to feel part of a larger group, engendering loyalty and sacrifice from group members, but also potentially creating bias and discrimination toward people who are not members of the group.

■ LINKAGES: SOCIAL COGNITION AND PSYCHOLOGICAL DISORDERS

People's mental representations of themselves, their *self-schemas,* differ from person to person. People with unified self-schemas tend to think of themselves as more or less the same all the time, while people

with differentiated self-schemas tend to think of themselves as having different attributes in different roles or situations. People with unified self-schemas may also have more intense emotional reactions to unpleasant situations and be more prone to depression or anxiety.

■ SOCIAL PERCEPTION

Social perception concerns the processes by which people interpret information about others, form impressions of them, and draw conclusions about the reasons for their behavior.

The Role of Schemas
Schemas, the mental representations about people and social situations that we carry into social interactions, affect what we pay attention to, what we remember, and how we judge people and events.

First Impressions
First impressions are formed easily and quickly, in part because people apply existing schemas to their perceptions of others. First impressions change slowly because people are "cognitive misers"; once we form an impression about another person, we try to maintain it because doing so simplifies the world. Schemas, however, can create *self-fulfilling prophecies,* leading people to act in ways that bring out in others behavior that is consistent with first impressions.

Explaining Behavior: Attribution
Attribution is the process of explaining the causes of people's behavior, including one's own. Observers tend to attribute behavior to causes that are either internal or external to the actor. In general, they do this by looking at three aspects of the behavior: consensus, consistency, and distinctiveness. People from different cultures may sometimes reach different conclusions about the causes of an actor's behavior. Attributions are also affected by biases that systematically

distort one's view of behavior. The most common attributional biases are the *fundamental attribution error* (and its cousin, the ultimate attribution error), the *actor-observer bias,* and the *self-serving bias.* Personal and cultural factors can affect the extent to which people exhibit attributional biases.

The Self-Protective Functions of Social Cognition

People often protect themselves from admitting something threatening about themselves through unrealistic optimism, a feeling of unique invulnerability, and self-handicapping strategies.

■ ATTITUDES

An *attitude* is the tendency to respond positively or negatively to a particular object. Attitudes affect a wide range of behaviors.

The Structure of Attitudes

Some theorists believe that attitudes have three components: the cognitive (beliefs), affective (feelings), and behavioral (actions). However, it is often difficult to predict a specific behavior from a person's beliefs or feelings about an object. Cognitive theories propose that attitudes consist of evaluations of an object that are stored in memory. This approach suggests that the likelihood of attitude-behavior consistency depends on accessibility of evaluations in memory, subjective norms, perceived control over the behavior, prior direct experience with the attitude object, and how closely people monitor the behavior of others.

Forming Attitudes

Attitudes can be learned through modeling as well as through classical or operant conditioning. They are also subject to the mere-exposure effect: All else being equal, people develop greater liking for a new object the more often they are exposed to it.

Changing Attitudes

The effectiveness of persuasive messages in changing attitudes is influenced by the characteristics of the person who communicates it, by its content, and by the audience receiving it. The *elaboration likelihood model* suggests that attitude change can occur via either the peripheral or the central route, depending on a person's ability and motivation to carefully consider an argument. Accordingly, different messages will produce attitude change under different circumstances. Another approach is to change a person's behavior, in the hope that his or her attitude will be adjusted to match the behavior. *Cognitive dissonance theory* holds that inconsistency between cognitions about attitudes and cognitions about behavior creates discomfort that often results in tension-reducing attitude change. *Self-perception theory* holds that people sometimes look to their behavior for clues to what their attitudes are.

■ PREJUDICE AND STEREOTYPES

Stereotypes often lead to *prejudice* and *discrimination.*

Theories of Prejudice

Motivational theories of prejudice suggest that some people have a need to derogate and dislike others. This need may stem from an authoritarian personality, as well as from a strong social identity. In either case, feeling superior to members of out-groups helps these people to feel better about themselves. As a result, in-group members tend to discriminate against out-groups. Cognitive theories suggest that people categorize others into groups in order to reduce social complexity. And learning theories maintain that stereotypes, prejudice, and discriminatory behaviors can be learned from parents, peers, and the media.

Reducing Prejudice

The *contact hypothesis* proposes that intergroup contact can reduce prejudice and lead to more favorable attitudes toward the stereotyped group—but only if it occurs under specific conditions, such as equal status between groups.

■ INTERPERSONAL ATTRACTION

Keys to Attraction

Interpersonal attraction is a function of many variables. Physical proximity is important because it allows people to meet. And the situation in which they meet is important because positive or negative aspects of the situation tend to be associated with the other person. Characteristics of the other person are also important. Attraction tends to be greater when two people share similar attitudes and personal characteristics. Physical appearance plays a role in attraction; initially, attraction is strongest to those who are most physically attractive. But for long-term relationships, the *matching hypothesis* applies: People tend to choose others whose physical attractiveness is about the same as theirs.

Intimate Relationships and Love

A defining characteristic of intimate relationships is interdependence. The most important ingredients of such relationships are affection and emotional expressiveness, which in turn often lead to social support, cohesiveness, and sexuality. Sternberg's triangular theory suggests that love is a function of three components: passion, intimacy, and commitment. Varying combinations of these three components create qualitatively different types of love. Marital satisfaction depends on communication, the perception that the relationship is equitable, and the couple's ability to deal effectively with conflict and anger.

SOCIAL BEHAVIOR AND GROUP INFLUENCES

CHAPTER 18

LINKAGES

TO

SOCIAL BEHAVIOR AND GROUP INFLUENCES

BIOLOGICAL ASPECTS OF PSYCHOLOGY

Does human aggression have biological roots? *(ans. on p. 609)*

PSYCHOLOGICAL DISORDERS

How do societies define what is abnormal? *(ans. on p. 495)*

MOTIVATION AND EMOTION

Do people perform better or worse when others are watching? *(ans. on p. 598)*

Well-publicized suicides are often followed by a rash of other suicides, and the murder rate tends to increase after well-publicized homicides (Phillips, 1983; Phillips & Cartensen, 1986). Murders even increase following telecasts of major professional boxing matches! Do these correlations mean that media coverage of violence triggers similar violence? As described in Chapter 7, televised violence can play a causal role in aggressive behavior; but there are additional reasons to believe that when suicides and murders become media events, they stimulate people to imitate them. For one thing, many of the people who are murdered soon after a celebrated homicide bear some notable similarity to the victim (Cialdini, 1993). Further, in the days after a professional championship fight in which the loser is white, murders of young white men increase; if the loser is black, a rise in murders of young black men is seen (Miller et al., 1991).

Imitative or "copycat" violence illustrates the effects of *social influence,* the process whereby the words or actions of other people directly or indirectly influence a person's behavior. This influence occurs in many ways, some more obvious than others (see the Linkages diagram). In this chapter we discuss several different kinds of social influence, from unspoken social norms to commands for obedience, and we review some of the cooperative, competitive, and aggressive ways people tend to behave toward one another in groups and other social situations.

SOCIAL INFLUENCE

As illustrated by copycat violence, people can influence the way other people think, feel, and act, even without specifically trying to do so (Goodwin, 1992). The most pervasive yet subtle form of social influence is communicated through social norms.

Norms are learned, socially based rules that prescribe what people should or should not do in various situations (Levine & Moreland, 1995). They are transmitted by parents, teachers, clergy, peers, and other agents of culture. Although many cannot be verbalized, norms are so powerful that people often follow them automatically. At movie theatres in North America, for example, norms tell us that we should get in line to buy a ticket rather than crowd around the ticket window; they also lead us to expect that others will do the same. By informing people what is expected of them and others, norms make social situations less ambiguous and more comfortable.

LINKAGES: CLOTHING AND CULTURE
The social norms that guide how people dress and behave in various situations are part of the culturally determined socialization process described in Chapter 12, on human development. The process is the same worldwide—parents, teachers, peers, religious leaders, and others communicate their culture's social norms to children—but differences in those norms result in quite different behaviors from culture to culture.

FIGURE 18.1

Descriptive and Injunctive Norms

A descriptive norm communicated by the littering of a messy parking lot led many observers to litter too. A clean lot changed the descriptive norm, leading fewer observers to imitate a litterer; but an injunctive norm (communicated by the picking up of litter) was not altered significantly by the condition of the lot (Reno et al., 1993).

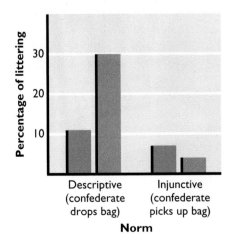

■ Clean environment

■ Littered environment

Source: Adapted from Reno, Cialdini & Kallgren, 1993.

Robert Cialdini and his associates (1990) have classified social norms as either descriptive or injunctive. *Descriptive norms* indicate how most other people act and thereby provide permission and a suggestion to do the same. *Injunctive norms* give more specific information about what others approve or disapprove, applying subtle pressure to behave accordingly. A study by Raymond Reno and his colleagues (Reno, Cialdini & Kallgren, 1993) illustrates the differing effects of these two types of norms. People were observed as they walked through a littered parking lot and saw a confederate of the experimenter either toss a paper bag on the ground or pick one up. As shown in Figure 18.1, seeing another person litter appeared to communicate the descriptive norm that "many people litter"; 30 percent of the people in this condition then littered the parking lot themselves. By contrast, seeing someone *pick up* litter appeared to communicate the injunctive norm that, even though many people litter, one should not do so. In this latter condition, fewer than 5 percent of the people littered.

One very powerful injunctive norm is *reciprocity,* the tendency to respond to others as they have acted toward you (Cialdini, 1993). When an investigator sent Christmas cards to strangers, most responded with a card of their own; some even added a personal note of good cheer (Kunz & Woolcott, 1976). But this norm and others are neither universal nor unchanging (Triandis, 1994). For example, people around the world differ greatly in terms of the physical distance they maintain between themselves and others while interacting. Indeed, people from South America usually stand much closer to one another than do people from North America. Thus, as suggested in Chapter 15, on psychological disorders, behavior considered normal and friendly in one culture may be seen as abnormal, even offensive, in another.

The social influence exerted by norms creates orderly social behavior. But social influence can also lead to a breakdown in order. For example, **deindividuation** is a psychological state in which a person becomes "submerged in the group" and loses the sense of individuality (Prentice-Dunn & Rogers, 1989). When people experience deindividuation, they undergo heightened emotional arousal and an intense feeling of cohesiveness with the group; they appear to become part of the "herd," and they may perform acts that they would not do otherwise. Deindividuation appears to be caused by two factors (Prentice-Dunn & Rogers, 1989). The first is the belief that one cannot be held personally accountable for one's actions. The second is a shifting of attention away from internal thoughts and standards and toward the external environment. Having members of the group sing in unison or wear unusual uniforms (such as Ku Klux Klan robes) fosters this shift of attention.

Deindividuation usually results in antisocial acts, and the emotional arousal that is generated makes such behavior difficult to stop (Prentice-Dunn & Rogers, 1989). Fans at rock concerts and athletic events have trampled one another to death in their frenzy to get the best seats; normally mild-mannered adults have thrown rocks or fire bombs at police during political protests. The greater the perceived anonymity, the more extreme the behavior. An analysis of newspaper accounts of lynchings in the United States over a fifty-year period showed that larger lynch mobs were more savage and vicious than smaller ones (Mullen, 1986). Similarly, college students whose heads were covered by hoods were more willing than unhooded students to shock an innocent victim (Zimbardo, 1970). Deindividuation provides an example of how, given the right circumstances, quite normal people can engage in destructive, even violent behavior.

LINKAGES: MOTIVATION AND THE PRESENCE OF OTHERS

Do people perform better or worse when others are watching?

In Chapter 11 we noted that social factors such as parental attitudes toward achievement often affect motivation. But a person's current motivational state is also affected by the mere presence of other people. To illustrate, consider what was probably the first experiment in social psychology, conducted by Norman Triplett in 1897.

Triplett noticed that bicyclists tended to race faster when a competitor was near than when all competitors were out of sight. Did seeing one another remind the riders of the need to go faster to win? To test this possibility, Triplett arranged for bicyclists to complete a twenty-five-mile course under three conditions: riding alone, in a race against the clock; riding with another cyclist, but not in competition; or competing directly with another rider. The cyclists went much faster when another rider was present than when they were simply racing against time. This was true even when they were not competing against the other person. Something about the presence of the other person, rather than competition, produced increased speed.

The term **social facilitation** describes circumstances in which the mere presence of other people can improve performance. This improvement does not always occur, however. The presence of other people sometimes hurts performance, a process known as **social impairment.** For decades these results seemed contradictory; then Robert

ELVIS STOJKO IN ACTION According to Robert Zajonc, the more familiar an athletic routine becomes, the more likely it is that the presence of a crowd will facilitate rather than impair the athlete's performance.

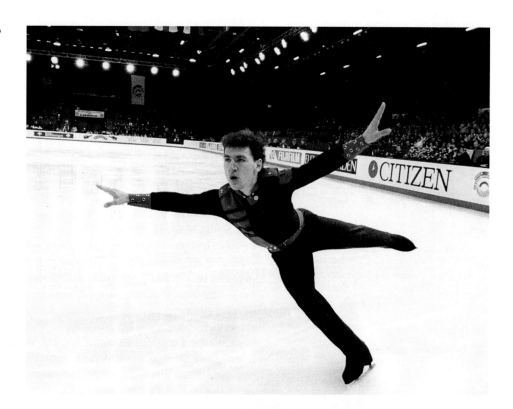

Zajonc (pronounced "zye-onze") suggested that both effects could be explained by one process: arousal.

The presence of other people, said Zajonc, increases a person's general level of arousal or motivation (Zajonc, 1965). Arousal increases the tendency to perform those behaviors that are most *dominant*—the ones you know best—and this tendency may either help or hinder performance. When you are performing an easy, familiar task such as riding a bike, increased arousal due to the presence of others should allow you to ride even faster than normal. But when a task is hard or unfamiliar, the most dominant responses may be incorrect and cause performance to suffer. Thus, the impact of other people on performance depends on whether the task is easy or difficult. This is true even when the "other person" is a machine that records one's errors at a task (Aiello & Kolb, 1995).

Why does the presence of others increase arousal? One reason is that being watched increases our sense of being evaluated, producing apprehension that in turn increases emotional arousal (Penner & Craiger, 1992). The presence of others may also distract us from the task at hand, or cause us to focus on only one part of it, thus impairing performance (Baron, Kerr & Miller, 1992).

What if a person is not merely in the presence of others but is working on a task with them? Research indicates that their impact changes slightly (Sanna, 1992). When a group performs a task, it is not always possible to identify each individual's contributions. In these situations, people often exert less effort than when performing alone, a phenomenon termed **social loafing** (Karau & Williams, 1993, 1995). Whether the task is pulling on a rope, clapping as loudly as possible, or trying to solve intellectual puzzles, people tend to work harder when performing alone than with others (Baron, Kerr & Miller, 1992; Geen, 1991). Steven Karau and Kipling Williams (1993) have proposed that social loafing occurs in groups for two reasons. First, because rewards may come whether or not one exerts maximum effort, and, second, because rewards will be divided among the members of the group. A review of experiments on social loafing shows that it occurs more often among men than women in Western cultures, and that it is much less likely among people of either gender in cultures such as China and Japan (Smith & Bond, 1994). These differences probably reflect the collectivist orientation which tends to be associated not only with women but also with people from Eastern cultures. This orientation emphasizes the importance of group performance and discourages social loafing.

In Western countries social loafing can be seen in groups of all sorts, from volunteer committees to search parties. Because social loafing can reduce productivity in business situations, it is important for managers to develop ways of evaluating the efforts of every individual in a work group, not just the overall output of a team (Ilgen & Klein, 1989; Shepperd, 1993).

CONFORMITY AND COMPLIANCE

Suppose you are with three friends. One says that Franklin Roosevelt was the greatest president in the history of the United States. You think that the greatest president was Abraham Lincoln, but before you can say anything, another friend agrees that it was Roosevelt, and then the other one does as well. What would you do? Disagree with all three? Maintain your opinion but keep quiet? Change your mind?

When people change their behavior or beliefs to match those of other members of a group, they are said to conform. **Conformity** occurs as a result of *unspoken* group pressure, real or imagined (Turner, 1991). You probably have experienced such group pressure when everyone around you stands to applaud a performance you thought was mediocre. You may conform by standing as well, though no one told you to do so; the group's behavior creates a silent but influential pressure to follow suit. **Compliance,** in contrast, occurs when people adjust their behavior because of a direct request, such as "Please pass the salt." When the last holdouts for conviction on a jury succumb to other jurors' browbeating, they have complied with overt social pressure.

MASS CONFORMITY These worshippers at Mecca exemplify the power of religion and other social forces to produce conformity to group norms.

FIGURE 18.2

Types of Stimulus Lines Used in Experiments by Asch

Subjects in Asch's experiments saw a new set of lines like these on each trial. Which line in (B) matches the one in (A)?

(A) STANDARD LINE

(B) TEST LINES

Source: Asch, 1955.

The Role of Norms

Conformity and compliance are usually generated by a group's spoken or unspoken norms. In a classic experiment, Muzafer Sherif (1937) managed to chart the formation of a group norm by taking advantage of a perceptual illusion, called the *autokinetic phenomenon,* whereby a stationary point of light in a completely dark room appears to move. Estimates of this movement tend to stay the same over time—if the observer is alone in the room. But when Sherif tested several people at once, asking each person to say aloud how far the light moved on repeated trials, their estimates tended to converge; they had established a group norm. Even more important, when the individuals from the group were later tested alone, they continued to be influenced by this norm.

In another classic experiment, Solomon Asch (1956) examined how people would respond when they faced a norm that already existed but was obviously wrong. The participants in this experiment saw a standard line like the one in Figure 18.2(A); then they saw a display like that in Figure 18.2(B). Their task was to pick out the line in the display that was the same length as the one they had initially been shown.

Each participant performed this task in a small group of people who posed as fellow participants, but who were actually confederates of the experimenter. There were two conditions. In the control condition, the real participant responded first. In the experimental condition, the participant did not respond until after the confederates did. The confederates chose the correct response on six trials, but on the other twelve trials they all gave the same, obviously incorrect response. Thus, on twelve trials, each participant was confronted with a "social reality" created by a group norm that conflicted with the physical reality created by what the person could clearly see. Only 5 percent of the participants in the control condition ever made a mistake on this easy perceptual task. However, among participants who heard the confederates' responses before giving their own, about 70 percent made at least one error by conforming to the group norm. A recent analysis of one hundred thirty-three studies conducted in seventeen countries reveals that conformity in Asch-type situations has declined somewhat in the United States since the 1950s, but that it still occurs; it is especially likely in collectivist cultures, where conformity to group norms is emphasized (Bond & Smith, 1996).

Why Do People Conform?

Why did so many people in Asch's experiment give incorrect responses when they were capable of near-perfect performance? One possibility, called *public conformity,* is that they gave an answer they did not believe simply because it was the socially desirable thing to do. Another possibility is called *private acceptance:* Perhaps the participants used the confederates' responses as legitimate evidence about reality, were convinced that their own perceptions were wrong, and actually changed their minds. Morton Deutsch and Harold Gerard (1955) reasoned that if conformity disappeared when people gave their responses without identifying themselves, then Asch's findings must reflect public conformity, not private acceptance. In fact, conformity does decrease when people respond anonymously instead of publicly, but it is not eliminated (Deutsch & Gerard, 1955). People sometimes publicly produce responses that they do not believe, but hearing other people's responses also influences their private beliefs (Moscovici, 1985).

Why do group norms wield such power? Research suggests three influential factors (Baron & Byrne, 1994). First, people are motivated to be correct, and norms provide information about what is right and wrong. This factor may help explain why some extremely disturbed or distressed people consider stories about suicide to be "social proof" that self-destruction is a reasonable way out of their problems (Cialdini, 1993). Second, people are motivated to be liked by other group members. Finally, norms guide the dispensation of social reward and punishment (Cialdini, 1995; Turner, 1991). From childhood on, people in many cultures learn that going along with group norms is good and earns rewards. (These positive outcomes presumably help compensate for not always saying or doing exactly what we please.) People also learn that breaking a norm may bring punishments ranging from scoldings for small transgressions to imprisonment for violation of norms that have been translated into laws.

When Do People Conform?

Clearly, people do not always conform to group influence. In the Asch studies, for example, nearly 30 percent of the participants did not go along with the confederates' obviously erroneous judgments. Countless experiments have probed the question of what combinations of people and circumstances do and do not lead to conformity.

Ambiguity of the Situation   Ambiguity is very important in determining how much conformity will occur. As the physical reality of a situation becomes less certain, people rely more and more on others' opinions and conformity to a group norm becomes increasingly likely (Aronson, Wilson & Akert, 1994).

You can demonstrate this aspect of conformity on any street corner. First, create an ambiguous situation by having several people look at the sky or the top of a building. When passers-by ask what is going on, be sure everyone excitedly reports seeing something interesting but fleeting—perhaps a faint light or a tiny, shiny object. If you are especially successful, conforming newcomers will begin persuading other passers-by that there is something fascinating to be seen.

Unanimity and Size of the Majority   If ambiguity contributes so much to conformity, why did so many of Asch's participants conform to a judgment that was unambiguously wrong? The answer has to do with the unanimity of the group's judgment and the number of people expressing it. Specifically, people experience great pressure to conform as long as the majority is unanimous. If even one other person in the group disagrees with the majority view, conformity drops greatly. For example, when Asch (1951) arranged for just one confederate to disagree with the others, fewer than 10 percent of the real participants conformed. Once unanimity is broken, it becomes much easier to disagree with the majority, even if the other nonconformist does not agree with the person's own view (Turner, 1991).

Conformity also depends on the size of the group. Asch (1955) demonstrated this phenomenon by varying the number of confederates in the group from one to fifteen. Conformity to incorrect norms grew as the number of people in the group increased. But most of the growth in conformity occurred as the size of the majority rose from one to about three or four members; further additions had little effect. Several years after Asch's research, Bibb Latané (pronounced "lat-a-nay") sought to explain this phenomenon via his *social impact theory.* This theory holds that a group's impact on an individual depends not only on group size but also on how important and close the group

REACHING A COMPROMISE The door-in-the-face strategy is the heart and soul of bargaining between political groups or labor and management. Each side usually asks for things that are more extreme than they really expect to get so that, by comparison, their later proposals will appear to be a compromise.

is to the person. According to Latané (1981), the impact of increasing the size of a majority depends on how big it was already. Thus, increasing a majority from, say, two to three will have much more impact than increasing it from, say, sixty to sixty-one. The reason is that the increase from sixty to sixty-one is psychologically much smaller than that from two to three; it attracts far less notice in relative terms. Does this explanation sound familiar? The principles underlying it are similar to those of Weber's Law, which, as described in Chapter 5, governs our perception of changes in brightness, weight, and other physical stimuli.

Gender Early research on conformity suggested that women conform more than men, but this gender difference stemmed mainly from the fact that the tasks used in those experiments were often more familiar to men than to women. And, indeed, people are especially likely to conform when they are faced with an unfamiliar situation (Levine & Moreland, 1995). No male-female differences in conformity have been found in subsequent research using materials that are equally familiar to both genders (Maupin & Fisher, 1989). Why do some people still perceive women as more conforming than men despite evidence to the contrary? Part of the answer may lie in their perception of the relative social status of males and females. Those who think of women as having lower social status than men in most social situations are likely to see females as easier to influence, even though men and women conform equally often (Eagly, 1987).

Inducing Compliance

In the experiments just described, the participants experienced psychological pressure to conform to the views or actions of others, even though no one specifically asked them to do so. In contrast, *compliance* involves changing what you say or do because of a direct request.

How is compliance brought about? Many people believe that the direct approach is always best: If you want something, ask for it. But salespeople, political strategists, social psychologists, and other experts have learned that often the best way to get something is to ask for something else. Three examples of this strategy are the foot-in-the-door technique, the door-in-the-face procedure, and the low-ball approach.

The *foot-in-the-door technique* consists of getting a person to agree to small requests and then working up to larger ones. In the original experiment on this strategy, homeowners were asked to do one of two things. Some were asked to allow a large, unattractive "Drive Carefully" sign to be placed on their front lawn. Approximately 17 percent of the people approached in this way complied with the request. In the foot-in-the-door condition, however, homeowners were first asked only to sign a petition supporting legislation aimed at reducing traffic accidents. Several weeks later, when a different person asked these same people to put the "Drive Carefully" sign on their lawn, 55 percent of them complied (Freedman & Fraser, 1966).

Why should the granting of small favors lead to larger ones? First, people are usually far more likely to comply with a request that costs little in time, money, effort, or inconvenience. Second, complying with a small request makes people think of themselves as being committed to the cause or issue (Cialdini, 1995). This occurs through the processes of self-perception and cognitive dissonance discussed in Chapter 17. In the study just described, participants who signed the petition might have thought "I must care enough about traffic safety to do something about it." Compliance with the higher-cost request (displaying the sign) was thus increased because it was consistent with these people's self-perceptions and past actions (Eisenberg et al., 1987).

The foot-in-the-door technique can be very effective. Steven Sherman (1980) created a 700 percent increase in the rate at which people actually volunteered to work for a charity simply by first getting them to say that, in a hypothetical situation, they would volunteer if asked. For some companies, the foot-in-the-door is a request that potential customers merely answer a few questions; the request to buy something comes later. Others offer a small gift, or "door-opener," as salespeople call it. Acceptance of the gift not only allows a foot in the door but may also invoke the reciprocity norm: Many people who get something free feel obligated to reciprocate by buying something (Cialdini, 1993).

The second approach, known as the *door-in-the-face procedure,* can also be effective in obtaining compliance (Cialdini, 1995; Reeves et al., 1991). This strategy begins with a request for a favor that is likely to be denied. The person making the request then concedes that asking for the initial favor was excessive and substitutes a lesser alternative—which was what he or she really wanted in the first place. Because the person appears willing to compromise, and because the new request seems modest in comparison to the first one, it is more likely to be granted than if it had been made at the outset.

The third technique, called the *low-ball approach,* is commonly used by car dealers and other businesses (Cialdini, 1993). The first step in this strategy is to obtain a person's oral commitment to do something, such as to purchase a car at a certain price. Once this commitment is made, the cost of fulfilling it is increased, often because of an "error" in computing the car's price. Why do buyers end up paying much more than originally planned for "low-balled" items? Apparently, once people commit themselves to do something, they feel obligated to follow through, especially when the person who obtains the initial commitment also makes the higher-cost request (Burger & Petty, 1981).

OBEDIENCE

Compliance involves a change in behavior in response to an explicit request. In the case of **obedience,** the behavior change comes in response to a *demand* from an authority figure (Kelman & Hamilton, 1989). In the 1960s Stanley Milgram developed a laboratory procedure to study obedience. In his first experiment he used newspaper ads to recruit forty male volunteers between the ages of twenty and fifty. Among the participants were professionals, white-collar businessmen, and unskilled workers (Milgram, 1963).

Imagine you are one of the people who answered the ad. When you arrive for the experiment, you join a fifty-year-old gentleman who has also volunteered and has been scheduled for the same session. The experimenter explains that the purpose of the experiment is to examine the effects of punishment on learning. One of you—the "teacher"—will help the learner remember a list of words by administering electric shock whenever he makes a mistake. Then the experimenter turns to you and asks you to draw one of two cards out of a hat. Your card says "TEACHER." You think to yourself that this must be your lucky day.

Now the learner is taken into another room and strapped into a chair, as shown in Figure 18.3. Electrodes are attached to his arms. You are shown a shock generator with thirty switches. The experimenter explains that the switch on the far left administers a mild, 15-volt shock and that each succeeding switch increases the shock by 15 volts; the one on the far right delivers 450 volts. The far left section of the shock generator is labeled "Slight shock." Looking across the panel, you see "Moderate shock," "Very strong shock," and, at the far right, "Danger—severe shock." The last two switches are ominously labeled "XXX." The experimenter explains that you, the teacher, will begin by reading a list of word pairs to the learner. Then you will go through the list again, presenting just one word of each pair; the learner should indicate which word went with it. After the first mistake, you are to throw the switch to deliver 15 volts of shock. Each time the learner makes another mistake, you are to increase the shock by 15 volts.

You begin, following the experimenter's instructions. But after the learner makes his fifth mistake and you throw the switch to give him 75 volts, you hear a loud moan. At 90 volts, the learner cries out in pain. At 150 volts, he screams and asks to be let out of the experiment. You look to the experimenter, who says, "Proceed with the next word."

In fact, no shock was delivered in Milgram's experiments. The "learner" was always an accomplice of the experimenter, and the moans and other signs of pain came from a prerecorded tape. But you do not know that. What would you do in this situation? Suppose you continue and eventually deliver 180 volts. The learner screams that he cannot stand the pain any longer and starts banging on the wall. The experimenter says, "You have no other choice; you must go on." Would you continue? Would you keep going even when the learner begged to be let out of the experiment and then fell silent?

FIGURE 18.4

Results of Milgram's Obedience Experiment

When Milgram asked a group of undergraduates and a group of psychiatrists how participants in his experiment would respond, they estimated that fewer than 2 percent would go all the way to 450 volts. In fact, 65 percent of the participants did so.

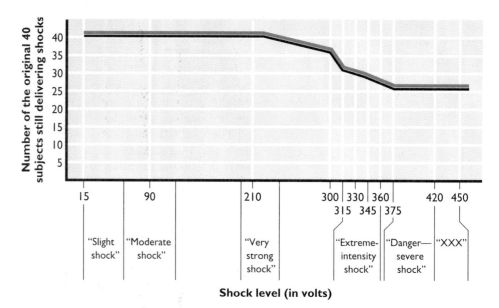

Source: Milgram, 1963.

Would you administer 450 volts of potentially deadly shock to a perfect stranger just because an experimenter demands that you do so?

Figure 18.4 shows that only five participants in Milgram's experiment stopped before 300 volts, and twenty-six out of forty (or 65 percent) went all the way to the 450-volt level. The decision to continue was difficult and stressful for the participants. Many protested repeatedly; but each time the experimenter told them to continue, they did so. Here is a partial transcript of what a typical participant said.

[After throwing the 180-volt switch]: *He can't stand it. I'm not going to kill that man in there. Do you hear him hollering? He's hollering. He can't stand it. What if something happens to him? I'm not going to get that man sick in there. He's hollering in there. Do you know what I mean? I mean, I refuse to take responsibility. He's getting hurt in there. . . . Too many left here. Geez, if he gets them wrong. There are too many of them left. I mean, who is going to take responsibility if anything happens to that gentleman?*

FOLLOWING GHASTLY ORDERS   **When authority figures issue orders, they tend to be obeyed—sometimes with tragic consequences. In recent years, for example, troops fighting in Bosnia have murdered and raped civilians in response to "ethnic cleansing" orders from their superiors.**

PROXIMITY AND OBEDIENCE Milgram's research suggested that the close proximity of an authority figure enhances obedience to authority (Rada & Rogers, 1973). This principle is employed in the military, where no one is ever far away from the authority of a higher-ranking person.

[After the experimenter accepts responsibility]: *All right. . . .*

[After administering 240 volts]: *Oh, no, you mean I've got to keep going up the scale? No sir, I'm not going to kill that man. I'm not going to give him 450 volts.*

[After the experimenter says, "The experiment requires that you go on"]: *I know it does, but that man is hollering in there, sir.*

This participant administered shock up to 450 volts (Milgram, 1974).

Factors Affecting Obedience

Milgram had not expected so many people to deliver such apparently intense shocks. Was there something about his procedure that produced this high level of obedience? To find out, Milgram and other researchers varied the original procedure in numerous ways. The overall level of obedience to an authority figure was usually quite high, but the degree of obedience was affected by several characteristics of the situation and procedure.

Prestige One possibility is that the experimenter's status as a Yale University professor helped produce high levels of obedience in Milgram's original experiment. To test the effects of status and prestige, Milgram rented an office in a run-down building in Bridgeport, Connecticut. He then placed a newspaper ad for research sponsored by a private firm; there was no mention of Yale. In all other ways, the experimental procedure was identical to the original.

Under these less prestigious circumstances, the level of obedience dropped, but not as much as Milgram expected; 48 percent of the participants continued to the maximum level of shock, compared with 65 percent in the original study. Milgram concluded that people were willing to do great harm to another even if the authority figure was not particularly reputable or distinguished.

Presence of Others Who Disobey To assess how the presence of other people might affect obedience, Milgram (1965) created a situation in which there were three teachers. Teacher 1 (a confederate of the experimenter) read the words to the learner. Teacher 2 (also a confederate) indicated whether or not the learner's response was correct. And Teacher 3 (the actual participant) was to deliver shock when mistakes were made. At 150 volts, when the learner began to complain that the shock was too painful, Teacher 1 refused to participate any longer and left the room. The experimenter asked him to

CIVIL DISOBEDIENCE In 1955, Rosa Parks was arrested and finger-printed in Montgomery, Alabama, after refusing an order to move to the "colored" section in the back of a segregated bus. Ms. Parks' coura-geous act of disobedience sparked the civil rights movement in the United States.

come back, but he refused. The experimenter then instructed Teachers 2 and 3 to continue by themselves. The experiment continued for several more trials. However, at 210 volts, Teacher 2 said that the learner was suffering too much and also refused to participate further. The experimenter then told Teacher 3 (the actual participant) to continue the procedure. In this case, only 10 percent of the participants (compared with 65 percent in the original study) continued to deliver shock all the way up to 450 volts. Thus, as research on conformity would suggest, the presence of others who disobey appears to be the most powerful factor reducing obedience.

Personality Characteristics   Were the participants in Milgram's original experiment heartless creatures who would have given strong shocks even if there had been no pressure on them to do so? Quite the opposite; most of them were nice people who were influenced by experimental situations to behave in apparently antisocial ways. In a later demonstration of the same phenomenon, college students playing the role of prison guards behaved with aggressive heartlessness toward other students who were playing the role of prisoners (Zimbardo, 1973).

   Still, not everyone is equally obedient to authority. For example, people high in *authoritarianism* (discussed in Chapter 17) are more likely than others to comply with an experimenter's request to shock the learner. The same tends to be true of people who have an external *locus of control* (Blass, 1991). As described in Chapter 14, such people believe that what happens to them is controlled by factors outside of themselves.

Evaluating Milgram's Studies

Not long ago, two protesters of U.S. foreign policy lay down in front of a train to prevent it from delivering its cargo of weapons. The train crew saw the men on the tracks, but, having been ordered not to stop, they did not even slow down. The train severed both legs of one protester, who forgave the crew because "they were following orders …" (Cialdini, 1993). Such incidents suggest that even though Milgram's studies were conducted more than thirty years ago, they are still relevant (Saks, 1992). Indeed, his results have been replicated in several Western countries, with female as well as male partici-

IN REVIEW	Types of Social Influence	
Type	**Definition**	**Key Findings**
Conformity	A change in behavior or beliefs to match those of others	In cases of ambiguity, people develop a group norm and then adhere to it.

Conformity occurs because people want to be right, because they want to be liked by others, and because conformity to group norms is usually reinforced.

Conformity usually increases with the ambiguity of the situation, as well as with the unanimity and psychological size of the majority. |
| Compliance | A change in behavior or beliefs because of a direct request | Compliance increases with the foot-in-the-door technique, which begins with a small request and works up to a larger one.

The door-in-the-face procedure can also be used. After making a large request that is denied, the person substitutes a less extreme alternative that was desired all along.

The low-ball approach also elicits compliance. An oral commitment for something is first obtained; then the person claims that only a higher-cost version of the original request will suffice. |
| Obedience | A change in behavior in response to an explicit demand, typically from an acknowledged authority figure | People may inflict great harm on others when an authority demands that they do so.

Even when people obey orders to harm another person, they often agonize over the decision.

People are most likely to disobey orders to harm someone else when they see another person disobey. |

pants (Smith & Bond, 1994). Other aspects of his work continue to be debated, however. (For a summary of Milgram's results, plus those of studies on conformity and compliance, see "In Review: Types of Social Influence.")

LINKAGES Is it ethical to deceive people in order to learn about their social behavior? (a link to Research in Psychology)

Ethical Questions Although the "learners" in Milgram's experiment suffered no discomfort, the participants did. Milgram (1963) observed participants "sweat, stutter, tremble, groan, bite their lips, and dig their fingernails into their flesh" (p. 375). Against the potential harm inflicted by Milgram's experiments stand the potential gains. For example, people who learn about Milgram's work often take his findings into account when deciding how to react in social situations (Sherman, 1980). But even if social value has come from Milgram's studies, the question remains: Was it ethical for Milgram to treat his participants as he did?

In the years before his death in 1984, Milgram defended his experiments (e.g., Milgram, 1977). He argued that his debriefing of the participants after the experiment prevented any lasting harm. For example, to demonstrate that their behavior was not unusual, Milgram told them that most people went all the way to the 450-volt level. He also explained that the learner did not experience any shock; indeed, the learner came in and chatted with each participant. On a later questionnaire, 84 percent of the participants said that they had learned something important about themselves and that the experience had been worthwhile. Thus, Milgram argued, the experience was actually a positive one. Still, today's committees charged with protecting human participants in research would be unlikely to approve Milgram's experiments, and less controversial ways to study obedience have now been developed (Sackoff & Weinstein, 1988).

Questions of Meaning Do Milgram's dramatic results mean that most people are putty in the hands of authority figures and that most of us would blindly follow inhumane orders from our leaders? Some critics have argued that Milgram's results cannot be interpreted in this way because his participants knew they were in an experiment and may simply have been playing the role of cooperative subjects (Orne & Holland, 1968). Most psychologists believe, however, that Milgram demonstrated a basic truth about human behavior—namely, that, under certain circumstances, human beings are capable of unspeakable acts of brutality toward other humans. Sadly, examples abound. One of the most horrifying aspects of Nazi atrocities against the Jews—and of more recent campaigns of genocide against ethnic groups in Eastern Europe and Africa—is that the perpetrators were not necessarily demented, sadistic fiends. Most of them were normal people who, because of the situation they faced, were influenced to behave in a demented and fiendish manner.

Worse, inhumanity can occur even without pressure for obedience. For example, a good deal of people's aggressiveness toward other people appears to come from within. In the next section, we consider human aggressiveness and some of the circumstances that influence its expression.

AGGRESSION

Aggression is an action intended to harm another person (Baron & Richardson, 1994). It is all too common. For example, almost half of the dating couples interviewed in one study said that one of them had been physically aggressive toward the other (O'Leary, Malone & Tyree, 1994). There is less aggression among married couples, but not much less. About one-third of married people in the United States display aggression toward each other that ranges from pushing, shoving, and slapping to beatings and the threatened or actual use of weapons (Pan, Neidig & O'Leary, 1994). Overall, more than 1.5 million violent crimes are committed each year in the United States, including more than 90,000 rapes and 20,000 murders (Saks, 1992). In many urban areas, murder is the leading cause of death among men under twenty-five (Huesmann & Miller, 1994). Surprisingly, people are about 3.5 times as likely to be murdered by a relative or acquaintance as by a stranger (*Newsweek,* 1994).

Why Are People Aggressive?

LINKAGES   What makes some people so aggressive? (a link to Introducing Psychology)

An early theory of human aggression was offered by Freud, who suggested it was partly due to *Thanatos,* the death instinct described in Chapter 14. He proposed that aggression is an instinctive biological urge that gradually builds up in everyone and must at some point be released. Sometimes, he said, release takes the form of physical or verbal abuse against others; at other times, the aggressive impulse is turned inward and leads to suicide or other self-damaging acts.

A slightly more complicated view is offered by evolutionary psychologists. As discussed in Chapters 1 and 11, these psychologists believe that human social behavior is related to our evolutionary heritage. From this perspective, aggression is thought to have helped prehistoric people compete for mates, thus ensuring survival of their genes in the next generation. Through the principles of natural selection, then, aggressive tendencies were passed on through successive generations. Some evolutionary psychologists believe that, even now, aggression sometimes occurs because it promotes the survival of the aggressor's genes (e.g., Wright, 1995).

Freudian and evolutionary theories seem too simplistic to fully account for human aggressiveness, however. For one thing, there are large differences in aggression from culture to culture. The murder rate in the Philippines, for example, is forty-six times higher than in China or Finland, and almost nine times higher in the United States than in those latter two countries (Triandis, 1994). These data suggest that, even if aggressive *impulses* are universal, the appearance of aggressive *behavior* reflects an interplay of nature and nurture (Lore & Schultz, 1993). No equation can predict when people will be aggressive, but years of research have revealed a number of important biological, learning, emotional, and environmental factors that combine in various ways to produce aggression in various situations.

LINKAGES **Does human aggression have biological roots?** (a link to Biological Aspects of Psychology)

FIGURE 18.5

Testosterone and Aggression

In the study illustrated here, the children of women who had taken testosterone during pregnancy to prevent miscarriage became more aggressive than the mothers' other children of the same sex who had not been exposed to testosterone during prenatal development. This effect held for both males and females.

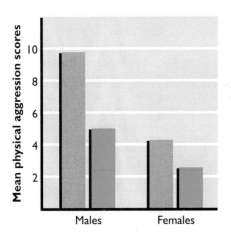

Subjects exposed to high doses of testosterone during prenatal development

Unexposed subjects

Source: Data from Reinisch, Ziemba-Davis & Sanders, 1991.

Genetic and Biological Mechanisms The evidence for hereditary influences on aggression is strong, especially in animals (Cairns, Gariepy & Hood, 1990). In one study, the most aggressive members of a large group of mice were interbred; then the most aggressive of their offspring were also interbred. After this procedure was followed for twenty-five generations, the resulting animals would immediately attack any mouse put in their cage. Continuous inbreeding of the least aggressive members of the original group produced animals that were so nonaggressive that they would refuse to fight even when attacked (Lagerspetz & Lagerspetz, 1983). Research on human twins reared together or apart suggests that there is a genetic component to aggression in people as well (Rushton et al., 1986; Tellegen et al., 1988). However, other research suggests that people do not necessarily inherit the tendency to be aggressive; instead, they may inherit certain temperaments, such as impulsiveness, that in turn make aggression more likely (Baron & Richardson, 1994; Mednick, Gabrielli & Hutchings, 1987).

Several parts of the brain influence aggression (Geen, 1990). One of these is the limbic system, which includes the amygdala, the hypothalamus, and related areas (see Figure 3.15). Damage to these structures may produce *defensive aggression,* which includes heightened aggressiveness to stimuli that are not usually threatening or a decrease in the responses that normally inhibit aggression (Coccaro, 1989; Eichelman, 1983). The prefrontal cortex may also be involved in aggression (see Figure 3.17). One study found that the prefrontal cortex metabolized glucose significantly more slowly in murderers than in nonmurderers (Raine et al., 1994).

Hormones also play an important role in aggression. One possibility is that aggression is related to one's level of *testosterone,* the masculine hormone that is present in both sexes (Dabbs, in press). Experiments have shown that aggressive behavior increases or decreases dramatically with the amount of testosterone in an animal's body (Frank, Glickman & Licht, 1991), and violent criminals have been found to have higher levels of testosterone than nonviolent ones (Dabbs et al., 1995). Among normal men, variations in testosterone show a small but statistically significant correlation with aggressiveness (Gray, Jackson & McKinley, 1991; Dabbs & Morris, 1990).

Testosterone may have its most significant and durable influence not so much through its day-to-day variations as through its impact on early brain development. One natural test of this hypothesis occurred when pregnant women were given testosterone in an attempt to prevent miscarriages. Accordingly, their children were exposed to high doses of testosterone during prenatal development. Figure 18.5 shows that these children grew up to be more aggressive than their same-sex siblings who were not exposed to testosterone during prenatal development (Reinisch, Ziemba-Davis & Sanders, 1991).

Drugs that affect the central nervous system can also affect the likelihood that a person will act aggressively. Even relatively small amounts of alcohol, for example, can substantially increase some people's aggressiveness (Bushman, 1993; LaPlace, Chermack & Taylor, 1994). One study demonstrated that when male alcoholics stopped drinking, the amount of violence directed toward their spouses decreased significantly (O'Farrell & Murphy, 1995). No one knows exactly why alcohol affects aggression, but recent research suggests that the drug may affect areas of the brain that normally inhibit aggressive responses (Lau, Pihl & Peterson, 1995).

Learning and Cultural Mechanisms Although biological factors may increase or decrease the likelihood of aggression, cross-cultural research makes it clear that learning also plays a role. Aggressive behavior is much more common in individualist than in collectivist cultures, for example (Oatley, 1993). Cultural differences in the expression of aggression appear to stem in part from differing cultural values. Thus, in contrast to many so-called advanced peoples, the Utku—an Inuit culture—view aggression in any form as a sign of social incompetence. In fact, the Utku word for "aggressive" also means "childish" (Oatley, 1993). The effects of culture on aggression can also be seen in the fact that the incidence of aggression in a given culture changes over time as cultural values change (Baron & Richardson, 1994).

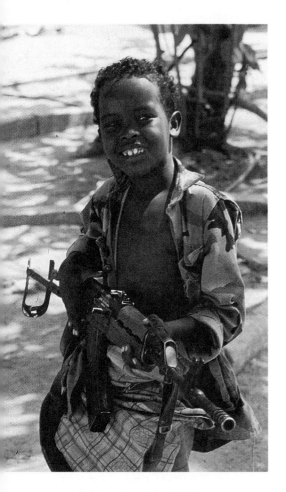

FOLLOWING ADULT EXAMPLES
Learning to express aggression is
especially easy for children in
Somalia and in other places where
aggressive acts are modeled daily.

In addition, people learn many aggressive responses by watching others (Geen, 1995). The most obvious examples are copycat crimes. More generally, children learn and perform many novel aggressive responses that they see modeled by others (Bandura, 1983). Bandura's "Bobo doll" experiments, which are described in the chapter on learning, provide impressive demonstrations of the power of observational learning. Its significance is highlighted by studies of the effects of televised violence, also discussed in Chapter 7. For example, the amount of violent content watched on television by eight-year-olds predicts aggressiveness in these children even ten years later (Huesmann & Miller, 1994). Fortunately, not everyone who sees aggression becomes aggressive; individual differences in temperament, the modeling of nonaggressive behaviors by parents, and other factors can temper the effects of violent television. Nevertheless, observational learning does play a significant role in the development and display of aggressive behavior (Huesmann & Miller, 1994).

Immediate reward or punishment can also alter the frequency of aggressive acts; people become more aggressive when rewarded for aggressiveness and less aggressive when punished for aggression (Geen, 1990). In short, a person's accumulated experiences—including culturally transmitted teachings—combine with daily rewards and punishments to influence whether, when, and how aggressive acts occur (Baron & Richardson, 1994).

When Are People Aggressive?

In general, people are more likely to be aggressive when they are both physiologically aroused and experiencing strong emotion such as anger (Lang, 1993). People tend either to lash out at those who make them angry or to displace their anger onto defenseless targets such as children or pets. However, aggression can also be made more likely by other forms of emotional arousal—especially *frustration,* a condition that occurs when obstacles block the fulfillment of goals.

Frustration and Aggression   Suppose that a friend interrupts your studying for an exam by coming over to borrow a book. If things have been going well that day and you are feeling confident about the exam, you are likely to be friendly and accommodating. But what if you are feeling frustrated because your friend's visit represents the fifth interruption in the last hour? Under these emotional circumstances, you may react aggressively, perhaps berating your startled visitor for not calling ahead (Eron, 1994).

Your aggressiveness in this situation conforms to the predictions of the **frustration-aggression hypothesis,** which was originally developed by John Dollard and his colleagues (Dollard et al., 1939). They proposed that frustration always results in aggression and, conversely, that aggression will not occur unless a person is frustrated. Research on this hypothesis showed that it was too simple and too general, however. For one thing, frustration sometimes produces depression and withdrawal, not aggression (Baron & Richardson, 1994; Seligman, 1991). In addition, not all aggression is preceded by frustration (Berkowitz, 1994). In many of the experiments described earlier, for example, participants were not frustrated, but they still made aggressive responses.

After many years of research, Leonard Berkowitz modified the frustration-aggression hypothesis in two ways. First, he suggested that frustration produces not aggression but a readiness to respond aggressively (Berkowitz, 1993). Once this readiness exists, "cues" in the environment that are associated with aggression will often lead a frustrated person to behave aggressively. The cues might be guns or knives, televised scenes of people arguing, and the like. Neither the frustration alone nor the cues alone are sufficient to set off aggression. When combined, however, they often do. Support for this aspect of Berkowitz's theory has been quite strong (Carlson, Marcus-Newhall & Miller, 1990).

Second, Berkowitz proposed that the more negative the emotion created by frustration, the stronger is the readiness to respond aggressively (Berkowitz, 1994). For example, unexpected failure at some task tends to create a more intense negative reaction than a failure that is expected. For this reason, aggression is more likely to occur fol-

CRITICISM

modification

lowing an unexpected failure than after an expected one. A number of experiments have supported this aspect of Berkowitz's theory as well (Finman & Berkowitz, 1989).

Generalized Arousal Imagine you have just jogged three miles. You are hot, sweaty, and out of breath, but you are not angry. Still, the physiological arousal caused by jogging may increase the probability that you will become aggressive if, say, a passer-by shouts an insult (Zillmann, 1988). Why? The answer lies in a phenomenon described in the chapter on motivation and emotion: Arousal from one experience may carry over to an independent situation, producing what is called *transferred excitation.* Thus, the physiological arousal caused by jogging may intensify your reaction to an insult (Geen, 1995).

By itself, however, generalized arousal does not lead to aggression. It is most likely to produce aggression when the situation contains some reason, opportunity, or target for aggression (Zillmann, 1988). In one study, for example, people engaged in two minutes of vigorous exercise. Then they had the opportunity to deliver electric shock to another person. The exercise increased the level of shock delivered only if the participants were first insulted (Zillmann, Katcher & Milavsky, 1972). Apparently, the arousal resulting from the exercise made aggression more likely; the insult "released" it. These findings are in keeping with the notion suggested by learning theorists (and by Berkowitz in his revision of the frustration-aggression hypothesis) that aggression occurs not merely as a function of internal impulses *or* particular situations but as a result of the interaction of individual characteristics and particular environmental circumstances.

In both men and women, sexual stimulation produces strong, generalized physiological arousal, especially in the sympathetic nervous system. If arousal in general can make a person more likely to be aggressive (given a reason,

THINKING CRITICALLY

Does Pornography Cause Aggression?

opportunity, or target), could stimuli that create sexual excitement be dangerous? In particular, does viewing pornographic material make people more likely to be aggressive? Over the years, numerous scholars concluded that there is no evidence for an overall relationship between any type of antisocial behavior and mere exposure to pornographic material (Donnerstein, 1984b). However, in 1986 the U.S. Attorney General's Commission on Pornography re-examined the question and concluded that pornography is dangerous.

What am I being asked to believe or accept?

Specifically, the commission proposed that there is a causal link between viewing erotic material and several forms of antisocial behavior, including sexually related crimes.

What evidence is available to support the assertion?

The commission cited several types of evidence in support of its conclusion. First, there was the testimony of men convicted of sexually related crimes. Rapists, for example, are unusually heavy consumers of pornography, and they often say that they were aroused by erotic material immediately before committing a rape (Silbert & Pines, 1984). Similarly, child molesters often view child pornography immediately before committing their crimes (Marshall, 1989).

In addition, the commission cited experimental evidence that men who are most aroused by aggressive themes in pornography are also the most potentially sexually aggressive. One study, for example, showed that men who said they could commit a rape became sexually aroused by scenes of rape and less aroused by scenes of mutually consenting sex; this was not true for men who said they could never commit a rape (Malamuth & Check, 1983).

Perhaps the most compelling evidence cited by the commission, however, came from transferred excitation studies. In a typical study of this type, people are told that a person in a separate room (actually a confederate of the experimenter) will be performing a learning task and that they are to administer an electric shock every time the person makes a mistake. The intensity of shock can be varied (none actually reaches the confederate), but participants are told that changing the intensity will not affect the speed of learning. So the shock intensity (and presumed pain) that they choose to administer is taken as an index of aggressive behavior. Some participants watch a sexually explicit film before beginning the learning trials. The arousal created by the film appears to transfer into aggression, especially when the arousal is experienced in a negative way. For example, after watching a film in which several men have sex with the same woman, the participants became aroused but tended to label the experience as somewhat unpleasant. In this condition, their aggressiveness during the learning experiment was greater than after watching no film at all (Donnerstein, 1984b).

Are there alternative ways of interpreting the evidence?

The commission's interpretation of evidence was criticized on several counts. First, critics argued that some of the evidence should be given little weight. In particular, how credible is the testimony of convicted sex offenders? It may reflect self-serving attempts to lay the blame for their crimes on pornography. These reports cannot establish that exposure to pornography causes aggression. Indeed, it may be that pornography partially *satisfies* sex offenders' aggressive impulses rather than creating them (Byrne & Kelley, 1989). Similarly, the fact that potential rapists are most aroused by rape-oriented material may show only that they prefer violence-oriented pornography, not that such materials created their impulse to rape.

What about the evidence from transferred excitation studies? To interpret these studies, you need to know that the pornography that led to increased aggression contained violence as well as sex; the sexual activity depicted was painful for or unwanted by the woman. Thus, the subsequent increase in aggression could have been due to the transfer of sexual arousal, the effects of observing violent behavior, or the effects of seeing sex combined with violence (Donnerstein, Slaby & Eron, 1995).

In fact, several careful experiments have found that highly arousing sexual themes, in and of themselves, do not produce aggression. When men in transferred excitation studies experience *pleasant* arousal by viewing a film depicting nudity or mutually consenting sexual activity, their subsequent aggression is actually less than when they viewed no film or a neutral film (Donnerstein, Linz & Penrod, 1987). In short, the transferred excitation studies might be interpreted as demonstrating not that sexually arousing material causes aggression but that portrayals of sexual violence influence aggressiveness.

What additional evidence would help to evaluate the alternatives?

Two types of evidence are needed to understand more clearly the effects of pornography on aggression. First, since pornography can include sexual acts, aggressive acts, or both, the effects of each of these components must be more carefully examined (Hall & Hirschman, 1991). Second, factors affecting males' reactions to pornography, particularly pornography that involves violence, must be more clearly understood (Malamuth et al., 1991). Work has already begun on each of these fronts.

Aggressive themes—whether specifically paired with sexual activity or not—do appear to increase subsequent aggression (Malamuth, Heavy & Linz, 1993). Research has focused on *aggressive pornography,* which contains sexual themes but also scenes of violence against women (Linz, Wilson & Donnerstein, 1992). In laboratory experiments, males often administer larger amounts of shock to females after viewing aggressive pornographic films as compared to neutral films. Yet there is no parallel increase in aggression against other males, indicating that the films create not a generalized increase in aggression but an increase in aggressiveness directed toward women (Zillmann & Weaver, 1989). Similarly, viewing aggressive pornography that depicts the *rape myth*—in which the victim of sexual violence appears to be aroused by the aggression—usually leads males to become less sympathetic toward the rape victim and more tolerant of aggressive acts toward women (Donnerstein & Linz, 1995). Sexually explicit films that do not contain violence have no effects on attitudes toward rape (Linz, Donnerstein & Penrod, 1987).

In one study, 35 percent of all college men reported having been exposed to aggressive pornography within the past twelve months (Demare, Briere & Lips, 1988), and the figure may be even higher in the general population. Are all these men equally likely to become rapists? The evidence available so far suggests that the answer is no. Whether aggressive pornography alters men's behavior and attitudes toward women depends to some extent on the men. For example, men who are inclined to be sexually aggressive in general (not just toward women) show much greater sexual arousal in response to rape scenes than do less sexually aggressive men (Hall, Shondrick & Hirschman, 1993). Further, the men who appear most prone to acting out the scenes of violence against women portrayed in aggressive pornography appear to be those who hold positive attitudes toward the domination of women and who feel anger toward women in general (Hall & Hirschman, 1994; Malamuth, 1988).

What conclusions are most reasonable?

The attorney general's commission appeared to ignore numerous studies showing that the relationship between sexual arousal and aggression is neither consistent nor simple (Baron & Richardson, 1994). Analysis of this relationship reveals the importance of distinguishing between pornography in general and aggressive pornography in particular. Overall, there is no reason to assume that sexual arousal created by nonaggressive pornography is associated with aggressive behavior. Indeed, for most people, sexual arousal and aggression remain quite separate.

Nevertheless, ample evidence suggests that aggressive pornography affects attitudes toward aggression, and that it may increase the likelihood of sexual violence in some viewers (Donnerstein, Slaby & Eron, 1995; Hall & Hirschman, 1994). Thus, there is reason for concern over the impact of sexual violence commonly seen on television and in films—especially "slasher" movies. Remarkably, such films are sometimes given less restrictive ratings ("R" or even "PG-13") than films that are nonviolent but erotic. It may be possible to blunt the impact of violent movies on viewers, but doing so will take time and money. In one study, Margaret Intons-Peterson and her colleagues (Intons-Peterson et al., 1989) gave men educational materials about rape and violence against women just before they saw a "slasher" film. Subsequent tests showed that, instead of becoming more accepting of violence toward women, as is usually the case following the viewing of such material, these men became more concerned about the victims of sexual violence and the dangers of rape. The film's usual effect *was* seen, however, in a control group of men who did not receive the educational materials.

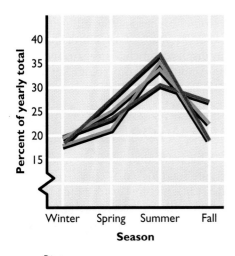

FIGURE 18.6

Effects of Temperature on Aggression

Studies of police reports reveal that rapes, assaults, family disturbances, and street riots are most likely to occur during the hottest days of the year.

— Riots
— Family disturbances
— Assault
— Rape

Source: Anderson, 1989.

Environmental Influences on Aggression   The link between physiological arousal and the likelihood of aggressive behavior points to the possibility that stressful environmental conditions can create enough arousal to make aggressive behavior more likely (Bell, 1992). This possibility is one of the research topics in **environmental psychology,** the study of the relationship between people's physical environment and their behavior (Bell et al., 1990). One aspect of the environment that clearly affects social behavior is the weather, especially temperature. High temperatures are a source of stress; as Figure 18.6 indicates, aggression and violence are most likely to occur during the hottest days of summer (Anderson, 1989; Baron & Richardson, 1994).

Air pollution and noise—usually defined as any unwanted sound (Bell et al., 1990)—are also sources of stress, and they can influence whether a person displays aggression (Holahan, 1986). For example, people tend to become more aggressive when breathing air that contains ethyl mercapton, a mildly unpleasant-smelling pollutant

CROWDING AND AGGRESSION Studies of prisons suggest that as crowding increases, so does aggression (Paulus, 1988). Accordingly, environmental psychologists are working with architects on the design of prisons that minimize the sense of crowding and may, ideally, help prevent some of the violence that endangers staff and prisoners.

common in urban areas (Rotton et al., 1979). A study conducted in Dayton, Ohio, found that the frequency of aggressive family disturbances increased along with the ozone level in the air (Rotton & Frey, 1985). And in laboratory studies, nonsmokers are more likely to become aggressive when breathing smoke-filled rather than clean air (Zillmann, Baron & Tamborini, 1981). Long-term exposure to toxins such as lead has also been associated with increased aggression (Needleman, 1996). Noise, too, tends to make people more likely to display aggression, especially if the noise is unpredictable and irregular (Geen & McCown, 1984).

Living arrangements also influence aggressiveness. Compared with the tenants of crowded apartment buildings, those in buildings with relatively few residents are less likely to behave aggressively (Bell et al., 1990). This difference appears to be due in part to how people feel when they are crowded. Crowding tends to create physiological arousal and to make people tense, uncomfortable, and more likely to report negative feelings (Epstein, Woolfolk & Lehrer, 1981). This arousal and tension can influence people to like one another less and to be more aggressive. One study of juvenile delinquents found that the number of behavior problems they displayed (including aggressiveness) was directly related to how crowded their living conditions had become (Ray et al., 1982).

ALTRUISM AND HELPING BEHAVIOR

Reginald Denny had the misfortune to be driving his truck through the center of the riots that broke out in Los Angeles in 1992. As his path was blocked by crowds, the camera aboard a local TV station's helicopter broadcast live pictures of four men pulling him out of the truck and beating him mercilessly. Among the viewers were two men and two women living in the riot area who, unlike thousands of their neighbors, left the safety of their homes to try to help Denny. Though threatened by Denny's attackers and the crowd, these four people got the severely injured trucker back into his vehicle and drove him to the hospital. Doctors there said that, had he arrived five minutes later, Reginald Denny would have died (Schroeder et al., 1995).

The actions of these individuals provide a dramatic example of another relatively common social behavior: people helping one another. **Helping behavior** is defined as any act that is intended to benefit another person. Helping can range from picking up dropped packages to donating a kidney. Closely related to helping is **altruism,** an unselfish concern for another's welfare (Batson, 1995, in press). In the following sections we examine some of the reasons for helping and altruism, along with some of the conditions under which people are most likely to help others.

Why Do People Help?

The tendency to help others begins early, although at first it is not spontaneous. In most cultures, very young children generally help others only when they are asked to do so or are offered a reward (Grusec, 1991). Still, Carolyn Zahn-Waxler and her associates (1992) found that almost half of the two-year-olds they observed acted helpfully toward a friend or family member. As they grow older, children use helping behavior to gain social approval, and their efforts at helping become more elaborate. The role of social influence in the development of helping is seen as children follow examples set by people around them; their helping behaviors are shaped by the norms established by their families and the broader culture (Grusec & Goodnow, 1994). In addition, children are praised and given other rewards for helpfulness, but scolded for selfishness. Eventually children come to believe that being helpful is good and that they are good when they are helpful. By the late teens, people often help others even when no one is watching and no one will know that they did so (Cialdini, Baumann & Kenrick, 1981). There are three major theories about why people help even when they cannot expect any external rewards for doing so.

Arousal: Cost-Reward Theory   The first of these—called the **arousal: cost-reward theory**—has been invoked to explain actions like those of the people who saved Reginald Denny (Piliavin et al., 1981). This theory proposes that people find the sight of a victim distressing and anxiety-provoking and that this experience motivates them to do something to reduce the unpleasant arousal. Indeed, several studies have shown that, all else being equal, the more physiologically aroused bystanders are, the more likely they are to help someone in an emergency (Dovidio et al., 1991; Schroeder et al., 1995). Before rushing to a victim's aid, however, the bystander will first evaluate two aspects of the situation: the costs associated with helping and the costs (to the bystander and the other person) of not helping. Whether or not the bystander actually helps depends on the outcome of this evaluation (Dovidio et al., 1991). If the costs of helping are low (as when helping someone pick up a dropped grocery bag) and the costs of not helping are high (as when the other person is physically unable to do this alone), the bystander will almost certainly help. However, if the costs of helping are high (as when helping to load a heavy air conditioner into a car) and the costs of not helping are low (because there are several others around who could help, for example), the bystander is unlikely to offer help.

It is more difficult for this theory to predict what the bystander will do when the cost of helping and the cost of not helping are *both* high. In that case, helping (or not helping) may depend on several situational factors and, sometimes, on the personality of the potential helper.

The *clarity of the need for help* has a major impact on whether others provide help (Dovidio et al., 1991). In one study, undergraduate students waiting alone in a campus building observed what appeared to be an accident involving a window washer. The man screamed as he and his ladder fell to the ground; then he began to clutch his ankle and groan in pain. All of the students looked out of the window to see what had happened, but only 29 percent of them did anything to help. Other students experienced the same situation, with one important difference: The man said he was hurt and needed help. In this case, more than 80 percent of the participants came to his aid (Yakimovich & Saltz, 1971). Apparently, this one additional *cue* eliminated any ambiguity in the situation and led the vast majority of people to offer their help.

The *presence of others* also has a strong influence on the tendency to help. Somewhat surprisingly, however, their presence tends to *inhibit* helping behavior. One of the most highly publicized examples of this phenomenon was the Kitty Genovese incident, which occurred on a New York City street in 1964. During a thirty-minute struggle, a

A YOUNG HELPER   Even before their second birthday, some children offer help to those who are hurt or crying by snuggling, patting, or offering food or even their own teddy bears.

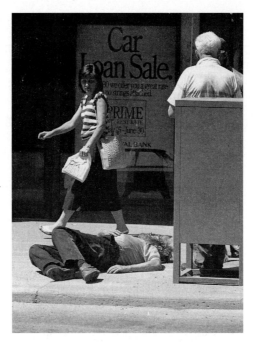

DIFFUSION OF RESPONSIBILITY Does the man on the sidewalk need help? This woman was probably not sure, and might have assumed that, if so, someone else will assist him. Research on factors affecting helping and altruism suggests that if you need help, especially if a number of others are present, it is important not only to clearly ask for help, but to tell a specific onlooker to take specific action (for example, "You, in the yellow shirt, please call an ambulance!").

man stabbed Ms. Genovese repeatedly, but none of the dozens of neighbors who witnessed the attack intervened or even called the police until it was too late to save her life. Public dismay and disbelief followed. Psychologists wondered whether something about the situation that night had deterred people from helping.

The numerous studies of helping behavior stimulated by this tragedy revealed the *bystander effect*, a phenomenon whereby, in general, the more people there are who witness an emergency, the *less* likely it is that any one of them will help (Schroeder et al., 1995). One explanation for the inhibiting effect of others is that each person thinks someone else will help the victim. This tendency to deny any personal responsibility for responding when others are present is known as **diffusion of responsibility** (Schroeder et al., 1995). The degree to which the presence of other people will inhibit helping may depend on who those other people are. When they are strangers, perhaps poor communication inhibits helping. People have difficulty speaking to strangers, particularly in an emergency, and without speaking, they have difficulty knowing what the others intend to do. According to such logic, if people are with friends rather than strangers, they should be less embarrassed, more willing to discuss the problem, and thus more likely to help.

In one experiment designed to test this idea, a female experimenter left a research participant in a waiting room, either alone, with a friend, with a stranger, or with a stranger who was a confederate of the experimenter (Latané & Rodin, 1969). The experimenter then stepped behind a curtain into an office. For nearly five minutes, she could be heard opening and closing the drawers of her desk, shuffling papers, and so on. Then there was a loud crash, and she screamed, "Oh, my god.... My foot, I ... I can't move it. Oh, my ankle.... I can't get this ... thing off me." Then the participant heard her groan and cry.

Would the participant go behind the curtain to help? Once again, people were most likely to help if they were alone. When one other person was present, participants were more likely both to communicate with one another and to offer help if they were friends than if they were strangers. When the stranger was the experimenter's confederate (who had been instructed not to help), very few participants offered to help. Other studies have confirmed that bystanders' tendency to help increases when they know each other (Rutkowski, Gruder & Romer, 1983).

Environmental factors can be important as well. Research conducted in several countries has revealed, for example, that people in urban areas are generally less helpful than those in rural areas (Hedge & Yousif, 1992; Steblay, 1987). Why? It is probably not the simple fact of living in a city but, rather, the stressors one finds there that tend to make some urban people less helpful. In Chapter 1 we mentioned a study showing that help-ing is less likely in a noisy environment (Mathews & Canon, 1975; see also Figure 1.2 on page 7). Another study of helping in thirty-six U.S. cities found population density (crowding) to be the environmental stressor that most consistently influenced helping (Levine et al., 1994). The higher the population per square mile, the less likely people were to help others. Two explanations have been suggested for this association between environmental stress and less helping. The first is that stressful environments create bad moods—and, generally speaking, people in a bad mood are relatively unlikely to help (Salovey, Mayer & Rosenhan, 1991). A second possibility is that noise, crowding, and other urban stressors create too much stimulation. To reduce this excessive stimu-lation, people may pay less attention to their surroundings, including individuals who need help.

Research suggests that the *personality of the helper* may sometimes be important in determining who will help; some people are just more likely to help than others. Consider, for example, the Christians who risked their lives to save Jews from the Nazi Holocaust. Samuel and Pearl Oliner (1988) interviewed over 200 of these rescuers and compared their personalities to those of people who had a chance to save Jews but did not do so. The rescuers were found to have more empathy (the ability to understand or experience another's emotional state) (Davis, 1994), more concern about others, a greater sense of responsibility for their own actions, and a greater sense of self-efficacy (confidence in the success of their efforts, as discussed in Chapter 14). Louis Penner and his associates (1995) found the same traits in college students who engage in other kinds of helping.

Empathy-Altruism Theory   The second major approach to helping is embodied in **empathy-altruism theory,** which maintains that people are more likely to engage in altruistic, or unselfish, helping—even when the cost of helping is high—*if* they feel empathy toward the person in need (Batson, 1991; Batson & Oleson, 1991). In one experiment illustrating this phenomenon, students watched what they thought was live footage of a woman in great distress as she received a series of painful electric shocks (Batson et al., 1983). (In actuality, they were viewing a videotape of an actress pretend-ing to be shocked.) When the students were asked about their emotional reactions to the woman's plight, some expressed great empathy for her, whereas others expressed very little empathy. The experimenter then asked the students if they would be willing to help the woman by taking her place for the remainder of the shock series. Half the participants were told they could leave immediately if they were not willing to be shocked; the other half were told that if they did not volunteer, they would still have to watch the woman getting the rest of her shocks. Figure 18.7 shows that, among the stu-dents who felt low empathy toward the woman and who could leave immediately, only 40 percent offered to help her. However, most of those who felt high empathy for the woman agreed to stay and take her shocks, whether they could have left immediately or not.

Were the helpers in this experiment being utterly, unselfishly altruistic, or was there a selfish component to their actions? Some studies suggest that people in such situa-tions may help because doing so makes them feel good about themselves or relieves their sadness over another person's plight (Cialdini et al., 1987; Smith, Keating & Stotland, 1989). Although the final verdict on this question is not yet in, the evidence appears to support Batson's contention that empathizing with another person can sometimes lead to unselfish helping (Dovidio, Allen & Schroeder, 1990).

Evolutionary Theory   The third approach to explaining helping is based on an evolu-tionary approach to social psychology, which views many human social behaviors as echoes of actions that contributed to the survival of our prehistoric ancestors (Buss, 1995). At first glance, it might not seem reasonable to apply evolutionary theory to helping and altruism, because helping others at the risk of our own well-being does not appear adaptive. If we die while trying to save others, it will be their genes, not ours, that will survive. Indeed, according to Darwin's concept of the "survival of the fittest," helpers—and their genes—should have disappeared long ago. Contemporary evolu-tionary theorists suggest, however, that Darwin's thinking about natural selection

FIGURE 18.7

The Effect of Empathy on Helping

In this study, most people who expressed high empathy for a victim tended to help her, even when they could have refused and immediately left the situation. Those who felt little empathy tended to help only if they would have had to stay and watch the victim suffer. The helpers themselves did not actually receive any shock.

Source: Data from Batson et al., 1983.

focused too much on the survival of the fittest *individuals* and not enough on the survival of their genes *in others.* Thus, survival of the fittest has been replaced by the concept of *inclusive fitness,* the survival of one's genes in future generations (Hamilton, 1964). Because we share genes with our relatives, helping or even dying for a cousin, a sibling, or, above all, our own child, potentially increases the likelihood that at least some of our genetic characteristics will be passed on to the next generation through the beneficiary's future reproduction (Buss, 1995; Knauft, 1989). Thus, *kin selection—*helping a relative to survive—may produce genetic benefits for the helper.

There is considerable evidence that kin selection occurs among birds, squirrels, and other animals. The more closely the animals are related, the more likely they are to risk their lives for one another. Studies in a wide variety of cultures show the same pattern of helping among humans (Essock-Vitale & McGuire, 1985). For example, people in the United States are three times as likely to donate a kidney to a relative as to a nonrelative (Borgida, Conner & Monteufel, 1992).

I n and of themselves, kidney donations do not confirm evolutionary theories of helping and altruism. The tendency to donate to relatives could also be due to the effects of empathy toward more familiar people, social pressure from family members, or other environmental factors. How can we explore the role of evolutionary forces in helping behavior while controlling for the effects of these confounding variables?

FOCUS ON RESEARCH METHODS

A Laboratory Analogue of Kin Selection

Eugene Burnstein, Christian Crandell, and Shinobu Kitayama (1994) reasoned that if the kin selection process really does occur, it should be possible to predict how people will behave in certain kinds of life-or-death situations. First, given the role of gene-sharing in kin selection, people should be more inclined to save the lives of relatives than those of nonrelatives. Second, because more genes are shared with close relatives, people should be more likely to save their lives than those of distant relatives. Third, the tendency to save even a close relative should be lessened if that relative is unlikely to produce offspring and thereby preserve the family gene pool.

The most direct way to test the accuracy of these predictions would be to put people's lives in danger and then observe which (if any) of their relatives try to save them. But an experiment of this nature would be unthinkable, so instead the researchers used a laboratory simulation, or *analogue,* of a life-or-death situation (Burnstein, Crandell & Kitayama, 1994). Specifically, they asked people to imagine such a situation and, then, to say how they would respond if the situation were real.

The participants in this analogue experiment were 110 men and 48 women enrolled at U.S. or Japanese universities. The first independent variable was the kind of helping situation described. On the basis of random assignment, some participants were asked to imagine several life-or-death situations in which there was time to save only one of three people who were asleep in separate rooms of a burning house. The remaining participants were asked to imagine several everyday situations in which they had time to help only one of three people who needed a small favor. The other independent variables were the characteristics of the people needing help in each situation—their age, sex, physical health, and genetic relatedness to the potential helper. The dependent variable was the participants' choice of which person they would help first.

In line with the first prediction of evolutionary theory, the participants were more than twice as likely to say they would save the life of a close relative than that of an unrelated friend. The second prediction was also supported: The more closely related the endangered people were to the potential helpers, the more likely they were to be saved. Is this the case simply because people tend to help closer relatives in any situation? Probably not; when the participants imagined everyday helping situations, they were only slightly more likely to do a favor for their siblings than for an aunt or uncle. Several different findings supported the third prediction—that even close relatives may not be

IN REVIEW	Helping Behavior

Possible Reasons Why People Help	When People Are Most Likely to Help
Helping reduces unpleasant arousal, especially when the cost of helping is low.	The need of the other person is recognized.
Helping is triggered by empathy with those in need.	The environment is not filled with stressors.
Our genetic heritage predisposes us to help.	Few others are present.
	The others present are friends or acquaintances of the potential helper.
	The potential helper has "helpful" traits.

FIGURE 18.8

Kin Selection and Helping

In this analogue experiment, students said they would be more likely to save the life of a healthy relative than that of a sick one, but more likely to do a favor for the sick relative. Results like these have been cited in support of the evolutionary approach to helping behavior (Burnstein, Crandell & Kitayama, 1994).

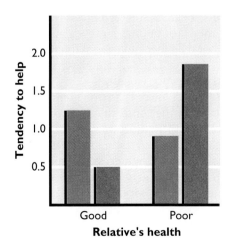

Source: Burnstein, Crandell & Kitayama, 1994.

saved if they are unlikely to produce offspring. For one thing, the participants were more willing to do a favor for a seventy-five-year-old relative than for a ten- or eighteen-year-old relative, but they were much more likely to save the lives of the younger relatives. Similarly, they were also more likely to do a favor for a sick relative than for a healthy one; but in a life-or-death situation, they chose to save the healthy relative more often than the sick one (see Figure 18.8). Finally, the participants were more likely to save the life of a female relative than that of a male relative *unless* she was past childbearing age. There were no substantial differences between the responses of students in the United States and those in Japan.

The results of this experiment are persuasive and, in many respects, consistent with the predictions of evolutionary theory. However, they must be interpreted with caution, and in light of the methods that were used to obtain them. Analogue studies give clues to behavior—and allow experimental control—in situations that approximate, but may not precisely duplicate, those outside the laboratory. They tend to be used when it would be unethical or impractical to expose people to "the real thing." The more closely the analogue approximates the natural situation, the more confident we can be that conclusions drawn about behavior observed in the laboratory will apply, or generalize, to the world beyond the laboratory.

In the analogue experiment we have described, one might question how closely the natural situation was approximated. For one thing, the participants predicted what their responses would be in hypothetical situations. Those responses might be different if the students were actually in the situations described. In addition, while the predictions obtained provide information about what people might do if they had to choose only one person to save, their choices tell only part of the story. For example, the fact that the students said they were more likely to save their closest relatives does not mean that they were unconcerned about the well-being of more distant relatives, or of unrelated people. As described earlier, people sometimes risk their lives for strangers. Thus, the analogue methodology in this study allowed the researchers to show that kin selection *may* play a role in human helping behavior. The evolutionary approach to social psychology would certainly have been undermined had the analogue results been inconsistent with it.

Moreover, even if evolutionary theory explains some general human tendencies to help, it cannot predict the behavior of specific individuals in specific situations (Hettema, 1993). Like all behavior, helping and altruism depend on the interplay of many genetic and environmental factors—including interactions between particular people and particular situations. (See "In Review: Helping Behavior" for a summary of the major reasons why people help and the conditions under which they are most likely to do so.)

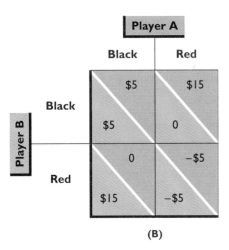

FIGURE 18.9

The Prisoner's Dilemma

In the prisoner's dilemma game, mutual cooperation benefits each person and mutual competition is harmful to both, but one party can exploit the cooperativeness of the other. These diagrams show the potential payoffs for prisoners—and game players.

COOPERATION, COMPETITION, AND CONFLICT

Helping is one of the many ways in which people cooperate in order to accomplish their goals, but people also compete with others for limited resources. For example, several law students might form a study group to help one another pass the bar exam. But the same students might then compete with one another for a single job opening at a prestigious law firm.

Cooperation is any type of behavior in which people work together to attain a goal. **Competition** exists whenever individuals try to attain a goal for themselves while denying that goal to others. When do people choose to cooperate, and when do they choose to compete?

The Prisoner's Dilemma

One technique used to study cooperation and competition—called the **prisoner's dilemma game**—is based on a scenario in which two people are separated immediately after being arrested for a serious crime (Schopler et al., 1991). The district attorney believes they are guilty but does not have the evidence to convict them. Each prisoner can either confess or not. If they both refuse to confess, each will be convicted of a minor offense and will be jailed for one year. If they both confess, the district attorney will recommend a ten-year sentence. However, if one prisoner remains silent and one confesses, the district attorney will allow the confessing prisoner to go free, while the other will serve the maximum fifteen-year sentence.

Each prisoner faces a dilemma. Figure 18.9(A) outlines the possible outcomes. Obviously, the strategy that will guarantee the best *mutual* outcome—short sentences for both prisoners—is cooperation: Both should remain silent. But the prisoner who remains silent runs the risk of receiving a very long sentence if the other prisoner confesses, and the prisoner who talks has the chance of gaining individually if the other prisoner does not talk. Thus, each prisoner has an incentive to compete for freedom by confessing. But if they *both* compete and confess, each will end up going to jail for longer than if nothing was said.

In the typical prisoner's dilemma experiment, two people sit at separate control panels. Each of them has a red button and a black button, one of which is to be pushed on each of many trials. If, on a given trial, both participants press their black buttons, each wins five dollars. If both press the red button, each loses five dollars. However, if player A presses the red button and player B presses the black button, A will win fifteen dollars and B will win nothing. Thus, pressing the black button is a cooperative response, allowing both players to gain; pressing the red button is a competitive response.

Figure 18.9(B) shows the possible outcomes for each trial. Over the course of the experiment, the combined winnings of the players are greatest if each presses the black button—that is, if they cooperate. By pressing the black button, however, one player becomes open to exploitation, because on any trial the other can take all the winnings and deny that person any gain by pressing the red button. Indeed, each player stands to benefit the most individually by pressing the red button occasionally.

What happens when people play this game? Overall, there is a strong tendency to respond competitively; people find it difficult to resist the competitive choice on any given trial (Komorita & Parks, 1995). This choice wins them more money on that trial, but in the long run they gain less than they would have gained through cooperation.

The prisoner's dilemma game parallels many real-life dilemmas. When competing companies establish advertising budgets or when competing nations plan military budgets, each side could save enormous sums by cutting back, but neither side is certain that the other will do the same. Fearing that the other side will spend enough to pull ahead, they continue to compete. This competitive cycle dominated political life for nearly fifty years of Cold War between the United States and the former Soviet Union.

If acting competitively leads to smaller rewards in the long run, why do people persist in competing? There seem to be two reasons (Komorita, 1984). First, winning more than an opponent seems to be rewarding in itself. In the prisoner's dilemma game, many people want to outscore an opponent even if the result is that they win less money

REASONS FOR COMPETING.

overall. Second, and more important, once several competitive responses are made, the competition seems to feed on itself (Insko et al., 1990). Each person becomes distrustful of the other, and cooperation becomes increasingly difficult. The more competitive one person acts, the more competitive the other becomes (McClintock & Liebrand, 1988).

Social Dilemmas

Psychologists also study conflict by observing behavior in **social dilemmas,** which are situations—usually occurring in large communities—in which an action that is most rewarding for each individual will, if adopted by all, become catastrophic for everyone. For instance, it might be in a factory owner's self-interest to dump toxic waste into a river; but if all factories do the same, the environment will eventually become uninhabitable for everyone. Similarly, each person is financially better off by refusing to donate to the public broadcasting system; but if everyone refuses to donate, no one will have access to its programs. Social dilemmas reflect inherent conflicts between the interests of the individual and those of the group and between short-term and long-term interests (Schroeder, 1995).

Fostering Cooperation

Communication can have an impact on people's tendency to act competitively (Kerr & Kaufman-Gilliland, 1994). Unfortunately, however, not all communication increases cooperation, just as not all contact between ethnic groups reduces prejudice. If the communication takes the form of a threat, people apparently interpret the threat itself as a competitive response and are likely to respond competitively (Kiesler, Sproull & Waters, in press). Furthermore, the communication must be relevant. In one prisoner's dilemma study, cooperation increased only when people spoke openly about the game and how they would be rewarded for various responses. Praising each other for past cooperation was most beneficial (Orbell, van de Kragt & Dawes, 1988).

People can also communicate implicitly, through the strategy they use. We have already noted that being competitive makes the other person less cooperative. In the prisoner's dilemma the most effective strategy for producing long-term cooperation is to use basic learning principles and play *tit-for-tat,* rewarding cooperative responses with cooperation and punishing exploitation by generating exploitative strategies of one's own. Cooperating after a cooperative response and competing after a competitive response produces a high degree of cooperation over time (Nowak, May & Sigmund, 1995). Apparently, the players learn that the only way to come out ahead is to cooperate. There is even evidence from computer simulation studies that societies whose members use cooperative strategies with each other are more likely to survive and prosper than are those whose members act competitively (Nowak, May & Sigmund, 1995).

Interpersonal Conflict

In both prisoner's dilemmas and social dilemmas, cooperation ultimately leads to the greatest payoff for everyone. But in situations called **zero-sum games,** one person can win only at the other's expense. In these situations, what one person gains is subtracted from the other person's resources; the sum of the gains and losses is zero. Election campaigns, lawsuits over a deceased relative's estate, and competition between children for a coveted toy are all examples of zero-sum games. These situations lead to **interpersonal conflict,** a process of social dispute in which one person believes that another stands in the way of something of value.

One might think that people from collectivist cultures—where cooperation is emphasized—would be less likely to compete in a prisoner's dilemma or to act selfishly in a social dilemma. This may be true in general, but conflict in such situations does appear in all cultures (Smith & Bond, 1994).

Causes of Conflict   There are four major causes of interpersonal conflict (Baron & Byrne, 1994). One is competition for scarce resources. If a business has only five offices with windows, for example, employees will compete for them. Some managers report

CHAIRMAN OF THE BOARD
~~THOMAS MEDVECKY~~
~~EDWARD SHANNON~~
~~THOMAS MEDVECKY~~
~~EDWARD SHANNON~~
THOMAS MEDVECKY

JOSEPH FARRS

"There's quite a power struggle going on."

Interpersonal conflict is a major problem in the workplace. It is not uncommon for employees who feel wronged to seek revenge against their employers. In extreme cases, fired employees have returned to murder those they blame for perceived injustices against them.

[handwritten annotation: MANAGE / NOT ELIMINATE CONFLICT]

spending as much as 20 percent of their time dealing with interpersonal conflicts based on such competition (Thomas & Schmidt, 1976).

2. A second major cause of interpersonal conflict is revenge. People reciprocate not only positive actions but also negative ones. Some people who feel exploited or deprived or otherwise aggrieved spend months, even years, plotting ways of getting back at those they hold responsible (Baron & Richardson, 1994).

3. Interpersonal conflict may also arise because people attribute unfriendly or selfish motives to others (Rubin, Pruitt & Kim, 1994). For example, if people who must share some resource, such as copy paper, attribute a shortage of that resource to each other's selfishness rather than to factors over which they have no control, such as an inadequate supply, conflict is likely to emerge (Samuelson & Messick, 1995). Sometimes these attributions are accurate, but often conflict results from the attributional errors discussed in Chapter 17—especially the fundamental attribution error. It is easy, for example, to attribute a co-worker's silence to an internal cause such as resentment toward you when it might actually reflect the person's preoccupation with a sick relative or some other external event.

4. Attributional errors are related to a final source of interpersonal conflict: faulty communication. A comment intended as a compliment is sometimes interpreted as a snide remark; constructive criticism is sometimes perceived as a personal attack. Such miscommunication may start a cycle of increasingly provocative actions, in which each person believes the other is being aggressive and unfair (Pruitt & Carnevale, 1993).

Managing Conflict   Interpersonal conflict can damage relationships between people and impair the effectiveness of organizations, but it can also lead to beneficial changes. Industrial-organizational psychologists have found that often it is much better to manage conflict effectively than to try to eliminate it. The most common way of managing organizational conflict is through *bargaining*. Each side—labor and management, for example—produces a series of offers and counteroffers until a solution that is acceptable to both emerges. At its best, bargaining can produce a win-win situation in which each side receives what is most important and gives up what is less important (Carnevale & Pruitt, 1992).

If bargaining fails, *third-party interventions* may be useful. Like a therapist working with a couple, an outside mediator can often help the two sides focus on important issues, defuse emotions, clarify positions and proposals, and make suggestions that allow each side to compromise without losing face (Pruitt & Carnevale, 1993).

Other techniques for managing conflict, especially conflict over resources, involve the introduction of *superordinate goals* or a *superordinate identity* (Williams, Jackson & Karau, 1995). For example, if people who are competing for scarce resources can be made to feel that they are all part of the same group and share the same goals, they will act less selfishly and manage the limited resources more efficiently.

In short, although interpersonal conflict can be very harmful if left unchecked, it can also be managed in a way that benefits the group. Much as psychotherapy can help people resolve personal conflict in a way that leads to growth, interpersonal conflict within an organization can be handled in a way that leads to innovations, increased loyalty and motivation, and other valuable changes.

GROUP PROCESSES

Although Western industrialized cultures tend to emphasize individuals over groups, the fact remains that most important governmental and business decisions in those cultures and elsewhere are made by groups, not individuals. Sometimes group decisions are effective; at other times they are disastrous. When Scott O'Grady, a U.S. fighter pilot, was shot down over Bosnia in 1995, a daring rescue was organized and carried out to perfection by a group of senior military personnel. But a few years earlier, in Somalia, other senior officers made decisions that turned the attempted rescue of trapped U.S. soldiers into a military debacle in which several rescuers lost their lives. In the chapter on thought and language we describe some of the factors—such as the size of a group, the status of its various members, and the order in which options are considered—that influence the nature and quality of group decisions. Here, we consider some of the social psychological processes that often occur in groups to alter the behavior of their members and the quality of their collective efforts.

Group Leadership

A good leader can help a group pursue its goals; a poor one can impede a group's functioning. What makes a good leader? Early research suggested that the personalities of good and bad leaders were about the same, but we now know that certain personality traits often distinguish effective from ineffective leaders. For example, using tests similar to those that measure the "big-five" traits described in Chapter 14, Robert Hogan and his colleagues (1994) found that effective leaders tend to score high on dominance, emotional stability, agreeableness, and conscientiousness. Other researchers have found that, in general, effective leaders are intelligent, success-oriented, and flexible (Levine & Moreland, 1995).

Having particular personality traits does not guarantee good leadership ability, however. People who are effective leaders in one situation may be ineffective in another (Yukl & Van Fleet, 1992). The reason is that effective leadership also depends on the characteristics of the group members, the task at hand, and, most important, the interaction between these factors and the leader's style.

Two main styles of leadership have been identified. **Task-oriented** leaders provide very close supervision, lead by giving directives, and generally discourage group discussion (Yukl & Van Fleet, 1992). Their style may not endear them to group members. In contrast, **person-oriented** leaders provide loose supervision, ask for group members' ideas, and are generally concerned with subordinates' feelings. They are usually well liked by the group, even when they must reprimand someone (Boyatzis, 1982).

Research on leadership effectiveness and gender provides one explanation as to why one leadership style is not invariably better than another. According to Alice Eagly and her associates, men and women in Western cultures tend to have different leadership styles (Eagly & Johnson, 1990; Eagly, Karau & Makhijani, 1995). Men tend to be more task-oriented; women, more person-oriented. One interpretation of these differences is that the gender-role learning processes described in Chapter 12 lead men and women to "specialize" in different leadership behaviors.

A SEASONED LEADER Corporate executives such as Katherine Graham, publisher of the *Washington Post,* bring impressive leadership skills to the running of their complex organizations. To help future leaders hone their skills, management training programs focus on the importance of leader-situation interactions; they also alert women and members of ethnic minorities to the unique pressures they are likely to face on the job (Morrison & Von Glinow, 1990).

Overall, men and women are equally capable leaders, but men tend to be more effective when success requires a more task-oriented leader and women are more effective when success requires a more person-oriented leader. In other words, people of each gender tend to be most effective when they are acting in a manner consistent with gender role traditions (Eagly, Karau & Makchijani, 1995; Eagly & Karau, 1991). This may be one reason some people do not like female leaders who act in a "masculine" manner or occupy leadership positions traditionally held by men (Eagly, Makhijani & Klonsky, 1992). In certain circumstances, such responses create bias against women leaders, particularly among male members of the groups they lead (Eagly, Makhijani & Klonsky, 1992).

Most contemporary theories of leadership are known as *contingency* theories (Schreisheim, Tepper & Tetrault, 1994), because they suggest that leadership effectiveness is contingent, or depends, on factors such as the leader's relations with group members and the nature of the group's task. They note, for example, that task-oriented leaders tend to be most effective when the group is working under time pressure, when the task is unstructured, and when circumstances make it unclear as to what needs to be done first and how the duties should be divided. People stranded in an elevator in a burning building, for example, need a task-oriented leader. Conversely, person-oriented leaders tend to be most effective when the task is structured and there are no severe time limitations (Chemers, 1987). These people would be particularly successful, for example, in managing an office in which the workers know their jobs well.

Groupthink

The emphasis on group decisions in most large organizations is based on the belief that a group of people working together will make better decisions than will individuals working alone. As noted in Chapter 9, this belief is generally correct; yet, under certain circumstances, groups have been known to make amazingly bad decisions (Levine & Moreland, 1995). Consider two examples. First, in the late 1930s, U.S. government leaders decided not to take special precautions to defend Pearl Harbor. The Japanese attack there on December 7, 1941 killed 2,500 people. Second, in 1986, NASA administrators ignored engineers' warnings about the effects of cold weather and decided to launch the space shuttle *Challenger*. The spacecraft exploded seventy-three seconds after liftoff,

THE DANGERS OF GROUPTHINK
Groupthink appeared to influence decisions by both sides during the 1993 standoff between federal agents and members of David Koresh's Branch Davidians near Waco, Texas. After fifty-one days, the agents saw no alternative but to batter holes in the compound and pump in tear gas; Koresh and his followers decided to set their compound afire. All but nine of nearly one hundred cult members died in the inferno, including twenty-five children.

LINKAGES   How does stress affect group decision making? (a link to Health, Stress, and Coping)

killing all aboard. After analyzing these and other disastrous governmental decisions, Irving Janis (1989) proposed that they can be attributed to a phenomenon called **groupthink.** Groupthink occurs, he said, when group members are unable to realistically evaluate the options available to them or to fully consider the potential negative consequences of a contemplated decision.

Groupthink is particularly likely when three conditions exist: (1) The group is isolated from outside influences (Turner et al., 1992); (2) the group is working under time pressure or other intense stressors (Worchel & Shackelford, 1991); and (3) the leader is not impartial. This last condition appeared to play a crucial role in President Kennedy's decision to support a disastrously unsuccessful invasion of Cuba by anti-Castro Cubans in 1961. Before the final decision was made, several advisers were told that Kennedy had made up his mind and that it was time to "close ranks with the president." This situation created enormous pressure for conformity (McCauley, 1989).

When these three conditions exist, groups tend to become very close-minded and to rationalize their decision as the only reasonable one. They dismiss other options and quickly suppress any dissenting voices. As a result, the group becomes more and more certain that its decision cannot possibly be wrong. Although some researchers have recently questioned the prevalence and dangers of groupthink (Aldag & Fuller, 1993), most researchers agree that it does occur, at least under conditions similar to those originally identified by Janis (Baron, Kerr & Miller, 1992). Some psychologists have worked on developing techniques to help groups avoid groupthink. One is to designate someone to play "devil's advocate," constantly challenging the group's emerging consensus and offering alternatives (Janis, 1985). Another is to encourage the expression of diverse opinions by making them anonymous. The group members might sit at separate computers and type out all the options that occur to them. Each option is displayed for all to see on an electronic mail system that protects the sender's identity; the group then discusses the options through e-mail without knowing who is saying what. Research on this procedure suggests that it is effective in stimulating logical debate and making people less inhibited about disagreeing with the group (O'Brien, 1991).

FUTURE DIRECTIONS

Research in social psychology has helped to illuminate group and social influence processes, and it will continue to do so. For example, we can expect to see increasing research on genetic and biological causes of social behavior. In addition, social psychologists will be paying more attention to the ways in which culture influences social behavior. One focus of their research is likely to be cross-cultural comparisons in areas such as social influence, aggression, helping and altruism, and the resolution of interpersonal conflict. Today, people from different cultures commonly experience clashes of values and expectations that lead to misunderstandings, especially during the initial stages of interaction (Triandis, Kurowski & Gelfand, 1993). With problems like these in mind, social psychologists will continue to look for ways to help culturally diverse groups perform more effectively.

Future programs designed to reduce the incidence of aggression will likely be based on the theories of aggression presented in this chapter and implemented in accordance with the principles of learning described in Chapter 7. Efforts will be made, for example, to head off aggression by teaching children less violent ways of dealing with interpersonal conflicts (Guerra et al., 1995). The American Psychological Association and other organizations are already supporting such programs (e.g., Eron, Gentry & Schlegel, 1995).

Increased interest in improving the efficiency of work groups is also likely (Levine & Moreland, 1995). This interest has been sparked, in part, by a recent trend among large companies toward organizing employees into self-directed work teams, which manage themselves with little or no outside supervision (Nygren & Levine, in press). Social psychological theory and research on group processes and leadership effectiveness will have much to contribute to the goal of maximizing the efficiency and effectiveness of these teams.

Finally, social psychologists will continue to apply their research on interpersonal and intergroup conflict in the service of preventing international conflicts and promoting world peace (Deutsch, 1993; Nelson & Christie, 1995; Sleek, 1996). As noted in the previous chapter, liking, cooperation, and mutual understanding are enhanced as people learn, through contact and other means, to perceive members of out-groups as more similar to themselves. Psychologists will be working on ways to foster this perception of similarity. In fact, psychologists from numerous countries have formed an organization called Psychologists for Social Responsibility. Its members are dedicated to studying issues such as group conflict as well as to providing workshops to find international solutions to the conflicts and social dilemmas that the people of the world must face and resolve together.

SUMMARY AND KEY TERMS

■ SOCIAL INFLUENCE

Norms establish the rules for what should and should not be done in a particular situation. Descriptive norms indicate what most other people do and create pressure to do the same. Injunctive norms provide specific information about what others approve or disapprove. *Deindividuation* is a psychological state in which people temporarily lose their individuality, their normal inhibitions are relaxed, and they may perform aggressive or illegal acts that they would not do otherwise.

■ LINKAGES: MOTIVATION AND THE PRESENCE OF OTHERS

A person's motivational state is affected by the presence of other people. By enhancing one's most likely behavior in a situation, other people sometimes create *social facilitation,* which improves performance, and sometimes create *social impairment,* which interferes with it. When people work in groups, they often exert less effort than when alone, a phenomenon termed *social loafing.*

■ CONFORMITY AND COMPLIANCE

When behavior or beliefs change as the result of unspoken or implicit group pressure, *conformity* has occurred; when the change is the result of a direct request, *compliance* has occurred.

The Role of Norms
People tend to follow the normative responses of others, and groups create norms when none already exist.

Why Do People Conform?
People sometimes exhibit public conformity without private acceptance; at other times, the responses of others have a genuine impact on private beliefs. People conform because they want to be right, because they want to be liked, and because they tend to be rewarded for doing so.

When Do People Conform?
People are most likely to conform when the situation is ambiguous, as well as when others in the group are in unanimous agreement. Up to a point, conformity usually increases as the number of people holding the majority view grows larger.

Inducing Compliance
Effective strategies for inducing compliance include the foot-in-the-door technique, the door-in-the-face procedure, and the low-ball approach.

■ OBEDIENCE

Obedience involves complying with an explicit demand, typically from an authority figure. Research by Stanley Milgram indicates that levels of obedience are high even when obeying an authority appears to result in pain and suffering for another person.

Factors Affecting Obedience
Obedience declines when the status of the authority figure declines, as well as when others are observed to disobey. Some people may be more likely to obey orders than others.

Evaluating Milgram's Studies
Because participants in these studies experienced considerable stress, the experiments have been questioned on ethical grounds. Never-

theless, Milgram's research showed that people do not have to be disordered to inflict pain on others.

■ AGGRESSION

Aggression is an act intended to harm another person.

Why Are People Aggressive?
Freud saw aggression as due partly to self-destructive instincts. More recent theories attribute aggressive tendencies to genetic factors, brain dysfunctions, and hormonal influences. Learning is also important; people learn to display aggression by watching others and by being rewarded for aggressive behavior. There are wide cultural differences in the incidence of aggression.

When Are People Aggressive?
A variety of emotional factors play a role in aggression. The *frustration-aggression hypothesis* suggests that frustration can lead to aggression, particularly if cues that invite or promote aggression are present. Arousal from sources unrelated to aggression, such as exercise, can also make aggressive responses more likely, especially if aggression is already a dominant response in that situation. Research in *environmental psychology* suggests that factors such as high temperature, air pollution, noise, and crowding increase the likelihood of aggressive behavior, particularly among people who are already angry.

■ ALTRUISM AND HELPING BEHAVIOR

Human behavior is also characterized by *helping behavior* and *altruism.*

Why Do People Help?
There are three major theories of why people help others. According to the *arousal: cost-reward theory,* people help in order to reduce the unpleasant arousal they experience when others are in distress. Their specific reaction to a suffering person depends on the costs associated with helping or not helping. Helping behavior is most likely when the need for help is clear, and when *diffusion of responsibility* is not created by the presence of other people. Environmental and personality factors also affect willingness to help. *Empathy-altruism theory* suggests that helping can be truly unselfish if the helper feels empathy for the person in need. Evolutionary theory suggests that humans have an innate tendency to help others, especially relatives, because doing so increases the likelihood that family genes will survive.

■ COOPERATION, COMPETITION, AND CONFLICT

Cooperation is behavior in which people work together to attain a goal; *competition* exists when individuals try to attain a goal while denying that goal to others.

The Prisoner's Dilemma
When given a choice between cooperation and competition, people often compete with one another. This is true even when, as in the *prisoner's dilemma game,* they receive fewer rewards for competing than for cooperating.

Social Dilemmas
In *social dilemmas,* selfish behavior that benefits individuals in the short run may spell disaster for the entire group in the long run.

Fostering Cooperation
Communication between competing parties can increase cooperation, especially if the communication is nonthreatening and relevant

to the situation. One of the most effective strategies for producing long-term cooperation in a prisoner's dilemma is playing tit-for-tat—that is, rewarding cooperative responses with cooperation and punishing exploitation by generating exploitative strategies of one's own.

Interpersonal Conflict

In *zero-sum games,* competition is inevitable because there can be only one winner. Such situations lead to *interpersonal conflict* in which one person believes that another stands in the way of something of value. Competition for scarce resources, revenge, attribution of another's behavior to unfriendly motives, and faulty communication are frequent sources of interpersonal conflict. Bargaining, third-party interventions, and reminders about broader goals and shared identity are helpful procedures for managing conflict. Many of the principles of conflict resolution between individuals apply to understanding and preventing conflicts between nations.

■ GROUP PROCESSES

Many of the world's most important decisions are made by groups.

Group Leadership

No single personality type or behavioral style always results in good leadership. *Task-oriented* leaders are most effective when the task is unstructured and the group is working under time pressure. *Person-oriented* leaders are most effective when the task is structured and there are no severe time limitations. Contingency theories of leadership effectiveness propose that success depends on the extent to which a leader's style fits the characteristics of the group and its tasks.

Groupthink

The pattern of thinking called *groupthink* is most likely to occur when a group is isolated from outside forces, when it lacks a truly impartial leader, and when its decisions are made under stress.

BEHAVIORAL GENETICS

THINK ABOUT SOME TRAIT on which you are well above or well below average. Perhaps it relates to your skill at sports, languages, or music, or maybe to your fearfulness, sociability, or other aspects of personality. Have you ever wondered what made you the way you are? If you are shy, for example, it is easy to think of possible environmental explanations. Perhaps you are shy because, as a child, you had few opportunities to meet new children or because you had embarrassing or unpleasant experiences when you did meet them. Maybe your parents are shy and thus served as the role models you imitated. Such environmental explanations are certainly reasonable, but it is also possible that you *inherited* a disposition toward shyness from your parents.

Issues such as this are addressed by researchers in the field of *behavioral genetics,* the study of how genes affect behavior (see Chapter 2). These researchers have developed methods to explore genetic as well as environmental origins of behavioral differences among people. The results of behavioral genetics research make it clear that heredity has a surprisingly strong influence, not just on shyness but on personality more generally (Chapter 14), on mental abilities (Chapter 10), on psychological disorders (Chapter 15), and on many other aspects of human behavior and mental processes. However, behavioral genetics is just as much the study of environment as of genetics. In the process of trying to disentangle genetic from environmental factors, researchers have made several important discoveries about the impact of the environment.

In this appendix, we discuss behavioral genetics in more detail than in Chapter 2. We begin with a review of the biochemical mechanisms underlying genetics and heredity. We then offer a brief history of genetic research in psychology, followed by a discussion of what research on genetic influences can, and cannot, tell us about the origins of human differences. Finally, we describe some findings from behavioral genetics research that illuminate several important aspects of human behavior and mental processes.

THE BIOLOGY OF GENETICS AND HEREDITY

What does it mean to say that someone has genetically inherited some physical feature or behavioral trait? The answer lies in **genetics,** the biology of inheritance. The story begins with the chemistry of the human body and with the chromosomes contained within each of its cells. Most human cells contain forty-six chromosomes, arranged in twenty-three matching pairs. These **chromosomes** are long, thin structures that are made up of thousands of genes. **Genes** are the biochemical units of heredity that govern the development of an individual by controlling the synthesis of protein. They are composed of **deoxyribonucleic acid (DNA)**—strands of sugar, phosphate, and nitrogen-containing molecules twisted around each other in a double spiral (see Figure 1). It is the particular order in which the nitrogen-containing molecules are arranged in the DNA that determines, through the production of *ribonucleic acid (RNA),* which protein each gene will produce. Protein molecules, in turn, form the physical structure of each cell and also direct the activity of the cell. Thus, as a function

The human body contains 100 trillion *cells.*

There is a *nucleus* inside each human cell (except red blood cells).

Each nucleus contains 46 *chromosomes,* arranged in 23 pairs.

One *chromosome* of every pair is from each parent.

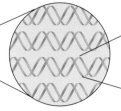

The chromosomes are filled with tightly coiled strands of *DNA.*

Genes are segments of DNA that contain instructions to make proteins — the building blocks of life.

FIGURE 1

Genetic Building Blocks

GENETIC DIVERSITY Diversity in genetic makeup gives rise to the infinite variability that serves as the basis for evolution through natural selection (see Chapter 1). Abnormalities in genetic makeup can lead to a wide range of problems, however. For example, children born with a trio instead of a pair of chromosome 21 develop the distinctive physical appearance and slowed intellectual growth known as Down syndrome (see Chapter 10).

of DNA, the genes contain a coded message that provides a blueprint for constructing every aspect of a physical human being, including eye color, height, blood type, inherited disorders, and the like—and all in less space than the period that ends this sentence.

New cells are constantly being produced by the division of existing cells. Most of the body's cells divide through a process called *mitosis,* in which the cell's chromosomes duplicate themselves, so that each new cell contains copies of the twenty-three pairs of chromosomes in the original.

A different kind of cell division occurs when a male's sperm cells and a female's egg cells (called *ova*) are formed. This process is called *meiosis.* In meiosis, the chromosome pairs are not copied. Instead, they are randomly split and rearranged, leaving each new sperm and egg cell with just *one* member of each chromosome pair, or twenty-three *single* chromosomes. No two of these special new cells are quite the same, and none contains an exact copy of the person who produced it. So, at conception, when a male's sperm cell penetrates, or *fertilizes,* the female's ovum, a truly new cell is formed. This fertilized cell, called a *zygote,* carries twenty-three pairs of chromosomes—half of each pair from the mother and half from the father. Thus, the zygote represents a unique heritage, a complete genetic code for a new person that combines randomly selected aspects from both parents. As described in the chapter on human development, the zygote divides first into copies of itself and then into the billions of specialized cells that form a new human being.

Whether or not genes express themselves in the individual who carries them depends on whether they are dominant or recessive. *Dominant* genes are outwardly expressed whenever they are present; *recessive* genes are expressed only when they are paired with a similar gene from the other parent. For example, phenylketonuria (PKU)—a disorder seen in about 1 in 10,000 newborns—is caused by a recessive gene. When inherited from *both* parents, this gene disrupts the body's ability to control phenylalanine, an amino acid in milk and other foods. As a result, this acid is converted into a toxic substance that can cause severe mental retardation. (Discovery of this genetic defect made it possible to prevent retardation in PKU children simply by making sure they did not consume foods high in phenylalanine.) PKU is an example of a single-gene disorder, but relatively few human characteristics are controlled by just one gene or even just one pair of genes. Most characteristics are **polygenic,** meaning that they are controlled by many genes. Even a person's eye color and height are affected by more than one pair of genes.

The genes contained in the forty-six chromosomes inherited from parents make up an individual's **genotype.** Because identical twins develop from one fertilized egg cell, they are described as *monozygotic;* they have exactly the same genotype. So, why don't all identical twins look exactly alike? Because they do not have the same **phenotype.** An individual's phenotype is the set of observable characteristics that result from the interaction of heredity and environment. Thus, in twins and nontwins alike, the way people actually look and act is influenced by the combination of genes they carry as well as by environmental factors—in other words, by both nature and nurture.

A BRIEF HISTORY OF GENETIC RESEARCH IN PSYCHOLOGY

The field now known as behavioral genetics began in the late 1800s with the work of Sir Francis Galton. A cousin of Charles Darwin, Galton was so impressed with Darwin's book on evolution that he decided to study heredity in the human species, especially as it related to human behavior. Galton suggested the family, twin, and adoption study designs that are the mainstays of human behavioral genetics research today (see Chapter 2). He even coined the phrase *nature-nurture* to refer to genetic and environmental influences. Galton's most famous behavioral genetics study was one in which he showed that genius runs in families. Unfortunately, Galton went too far in interpreting the evidence from this family study when he concluded that "nature prevails enormously over nurture" (Galton, 1883, p. 241). As noted in Chapter 2, family similarity can be due to environmental as well as hereditary factors. Still, Galton's work helped to stimulate psychologists' interest in the influence of genetics. The first twin and adoption studies were conducted in 1924. Both focused on IQ, and both suggested the existence of an important genetic contribution to intelligence.

However, research on the influence of genetics on behavior and mental processes was inhibited for a while because of two factors. The first was the impact of John B. Watson's behaviorism, which, as mentioned in Chapter 1, suggested that we are what we learn. In 1925, Watson insisted "that there is no such thing as an inheritance of capacity, talent, temperament, mental constitution and characteristics. These things again depend on training that goes on mainly in the cradle" (Watson, 1925, pp. 74–75). The second factor discouraging attention to human genetics was its association with the view proclaimed by Adolph Hitler and his Nazis that certain groups of people were "genetically inferior." This view led to the Holocaust during World War II, a campaign of genocide during which millions of Jews and other allegedly "inferior" people were killed.

Whereas genetic research on human behavior was reduced to a trickle during the 1930s and 1940s, research on animals led, in 1960, to the first behavioral genetics textbook (Fuller & Thompson, 1960) and to signs of increased interest in human genetics. In 1963 an influential article reviewed family, twin, and adoption findings and concluded that genetic influences are important in determining IQ (Erlenmeyer-Kimling & Jarvik, 1963). Around the same time, the first adoption study of schizophrenia pointed to a strong genetic contribution to that disorder (Heston, 1966).

In the early 1970s, however, interest in human behavioral genetics faded again, this time because of reactions to two publications. The first was a paper by Arthur Jensen suggesting that differences in average IQ between Blacks and Whites might be partly due to genetic factors (Jensen, 1969). The second was a book by Richard Herrnstein in which he argued that genetics might contribute to social class differences (Herrnstein, 1973). The furious public and scientific response to these publications—which included branding the authors as racists—inhibited genetic research in psychology, even though very few behavioral geneticists were studying ethnic or class differences. It was not until later in the 1970s, and into the 1980s, that major genetic studies were again conducted in psychology and psychiatry.

Today most psychologists recognize the role of both genetics and environment in behavior and mental processes, including the controversial area of mental abilities (Snyderman & Rothman, 1987). Indeed, in 1992 the American Psychological Association selected behavioral genetics as one of two themes best representing the past, present, and, especially, the future of psychological research (Plomin & McClearn, 1993). To some, though, the study of human behavioral genetics still carries a hint of racism and class elitism. Such concerns were recently resurrected by a book entitled *The Bell Curve*, which considers the role of genetics in ethnic differences in intelligence and the implications of intelligence for social class structure (Herrnstein & Murray, 1994; see also Chapter 10). It remains to be seen whether reaction to that book will alter the balanced perspective that recognizes the importance of nature as well as nurture in psychology.

THE FOCUS OF RESEARCH IN BEHAVIORAL GENETICS

Much of the controversy about behavioral genetics, and about nature and nurture in general, comes from misunderstandings about what behavioral genetics researchers study and, more specifically, what it means to say that genes influence behavior.

For one thing, behavioral genetics is the study of genetic and environmental factors responsible for *differences* between individuals or groups of individuals, not for the characteristics of a single individual. Consider height, for example. Identical twins are much more similar in height than are fraternal twins (who share no more genes than other siblings), and individuals who are genetically related but raised separately are just as similar in height as are relatives reared together. Further, genetically unrelated individuals reared together are no more similar in height than random pairs of individuals. Such data suggest, not surprisingly, that height is highly *heritable.* This means that much of the *variability* in height that we see among people—actually about 80 percent of it—can be explained by genetic differences among them rather than by environmental differences. (It does *not* mean that a person who is six feet tall grew four of those feet because of genes and the other two feet because of environment!) It also follows that if a person is, say, shorter than average, genetic reasons are probably the primary cause. We say "probably" because finding a genetic influence on height involves referring only to the origins of *average* individual differences in the population. Thus, while the *difference* in people's heights is attributable mainly to genetic factors, a *particular* person's height could be due solely to an early illness or other growth-stunting *environmental* factors.

To see how this logic applies to conclusions about psychological characteristics, suppose a researcher found that the heritability of a personality trait is 50 percent. This result would mean that approximately half of the *differences between people* on that trait is attributable to genetic factors. It would *not* mean that each person inherits half of the trait and gets the other half from environmental influences. As in our height example, behavioral geneticists want to know how much variability among people can be accounted for by genetic and environmental factors. The results of their research allow generalizations about the influence of nature and nurture on certain characteristics, but those generalizations do not necessarily apply to the origin of a particular person's characteristics.

Another misconception about genetic influences is that they are "hard-wired" and thus have inevitable effects. This is true in the case of single-gene disorders such as PKU, but more complex traits—intelligence, for example—are influenced by many genes as well as by many environmental factors. So genetic influence means just that—*influence* (Plomin, Owen & McGuffin, 1994). Genes can affect a trait without completely determining whether or not it will appear.

THE ROLE OF GENETIC FACTORS IN PSYCHOLOGY

It is no coincidence that the areas of psychology in which genes have been found to play an important role are areas that focus on individual differences—mental abilities, personality, and psychological disorders. Much less is known about individual differences in areas such as sensation, perception, consciousness, learning, memory, and motivation and emotion. Consequently, much less behavioral genetics research has been conducted on these variables. Nonetheless, enough is known about genetic factors to suggest that they probably influence every area of psychology to some extent. In the following sections, we consider behavioral genetics research results that tell a little more of the story about how genes can have an impact on behavior and mental processes.

Genetic Influences Over the Life Span

One particularly interesting finding about genetic influences on general mental ability is that they continue to increase throughout the life span (McGue et al., 1993; Plomin, 1986). That is, the proportion of individual differences (variance) in IQ scores that can be explained by genetic factors increases from 40 percent in childhood to 60 percent in adolescence and young adulthood and then to 80 percent later in life. This increase in the magnitude of genetic influence can be seen, for example, in the expanding difference between IQ correlations for identical twins and those for fraternal twins: Identical twins become more similar in IQ over the life span, whereas fraternal twins become less similar as the years go by. This finding is all the more interesting for overturning the common assumption that environmental influences become increasingly important as accidents, illnesses, and other experiences accumulate throughout life. We still do not have enough data available to permit firm conclusions about whether the magnitude of genetic influences on other traits changes during development.

How can it be that genetic influences become more important over time? One possible explanation is that, as discussed later, genetic predispositions lead people to select and even create environments that foster the continued development of their abilities.

Genes Affecting Multiple Traits

Behavioral genetics research has also revealed that genes affecting one trait can sometimes affect others as well. For example, it appears that the same genetic factors affecting anxiety also affect depression (Kendler et al., 1992). Thus, if we could identify specific genes responsible for genetic influences on anxiety, we would expect to find that the same genes were associated with the appearance of depression.

A similar finding has emerged for mental ability and scholastic achievement. Tests of scholastic achievement show almost as much genetic influence as do tests of mental ability. Moreover, tests of scholastic achievement correlate substantially with tests of mental ability. To what extent is a common set of genes responsible for this overlap? Research suggests that the answer is "almost entirely." It appears that the genes influencing performance on mental ability tests are the same ones that influence students' performance at school (Wadsworth, 1994).

Identifying Genes Related to Behavior

One of the most exciting new developments in behavioral genetics involves identifying the specific genes responsible for genetic influences in psychology (Plomin, 1995). For example, there are hundreds of rare, single-gene disorders that affect behavior. One of these is Huntington's disease, an ultimately fatal disorder that involves loss of motor control and progressive deterioration of the central nervous system. Huntington's disease emerges only in adulthood, beginning with personality changes, forgetfulness, and other behavioral problems. It is caused by a single dominant gene whose identification in 1983 made it possible to determine who will get this disease—even though the mechanism for the disorder is still not understood and prevention is not yet possible.

Researchers are also tracking down the numerous genes involved in the appearance of Alzheimer's disease. (As described in Chapter 3, Alzheimer's causes memory loss and increasing confusion in many older people.) One of these, a gene that contributes to the risk for late-onset Alzheimer's disease, was identified in 1993. This gene increases the risk for Alzheimer's disease about fivefold, but its presence is neither necessary nor sufficient for the disease to appear. That is, many people with Alzheimer's disease do not have the gene, and many people with the gene do not have the disease. Nonetheless, this gene is by far the strongest risk factor known for Alzheimer's disease, and its discovery marks the beginning of a new era in which specific genes—or regions of DNA near specific genes—will be identified as influencing disorders and psychological traits. Recent additional examples include reports of linkages between DNA and reading disability (Cardon et al., 1994), homosexuality (Hamer et al., 1993; Hu et al., 1995), and the personality trait of novelty-seeking (Benjamin et al., 1996; Ebstein et al., 1996). Studies of animals are able to take advantage of even more powerful genetic research techniques and have identified several genes associated, for example, with fearfulness (Flint et al., 1995). These continuing discoveries will help fill in the causal picture about a variety of characteristics and disorders that are influenced by many genes and many environmental factors.

BEHAVIORAL GENETICS AND ENVIRONMENTAL INFLUENCES

As suggested earlier, research on genetic influences in psychology has also provided some of the best evidence for the importance of environmental influences, because it has shown that genetics cannot explain everything about human behavior. Indeed, we must remember the crucial role of environmental influences—particularly at this point in history, when explanations for human behavior seem to increasingly favor nature over nurture.

For example, in the early 1960s it was thought that schizophrenia was caused mainly by environmental factors, especially by early interactions with parents. However, twin and adoption studies provided evidence of the importance of genetic factors in this disorder, and as a result many researchers are now trying to identify the specific genes responsible. Enthusiasm for genetic explanations of schizophrenia makes it easy to forget, however, that environmental factors can be at least as important as genes. As described in Chapter 15, for example, when one member of an identical-twin pair is schizophrenic, the chances are about 40 percent that the other member of the pair is also schizophrenic. This result surely provides evidence of a strong genetic contribution to schizophrenia, but it also suggests that schizophrenia appears in both identical twins *only* 40 percent of the time. Most of the time, the identical twin of a person with schizophrenia will *not* display the disorder. Such lack of concordance within pairs of identical twins can be due only to the operation of environmental factors.

Indeed, research generally suggests that genetic factors account for less than half of the variance among individuals for psychological characteristics such as personality and psychopathology. This means that at least half of the variance among individuals on these characteristics is due to environmental factors. These environmental—or, more properly, *nongenetic*—factors encompass everything other than genetic inheritance. They include such biological factors as prenatal events, nutrition, and illnesses, as well as more traditional environmental factors such as parenting, schooling, and peer influences.

Thus, one of the most important findings to emerge from behavioral genetics research has concerned not genetics but the environment. Such research also suggests that, for psychologists, the most important environmental influences are likely to be those that different family members do not share. Psychologists need to find out more about these nonshared factors and how they act to create differences in children—twins or not—who grow up in the same family.

So far, research on this topic has shown that children growing up in the same family actually experience quite different environments, especially in relation to their parents. Siblings perceive that their parents treat them very differently—and, indeed, observational studies back up such perceptions of differential treatment (Plomin, 1994a). Even events such as parental divorce, which would seem to be shared by all children in the family, appear to be experienced very differently by each child, depending especially upon age, personality, and the nature of the relationship with each parent (Plomin, 1994a).

Research is also beginning to focus on environmental influences beyond the family—such as relationships with teachers or friends—that are even more likely than home-related factors to vary among siblings. If you have a brother or sister, think about a psychological trait on which you and your sibling differ—confidence, for example. Why do you think you two are different on that trait? Perhaps one of you experienced a loss of self-confidence when faced by the demands of an impatient grade-school teacher or after being betrayed by a childhood friend. Did these differing experiences occur randomly and thus make you considerably more confident or less confident than your sibling? Or is it possible that differences in your genetic makeups helped bring about these different experiences? Unless you and your sibling are identical twins, you share only about 50 percent of your genes. Perhaps genetically influenced differences between the two of you—in emotionality or other aspects of temperament, for example—caused parents, peers, and others to respond to each of you differently. This brings us to the second major discovery about the environment to emerge from research on behavioral genetics: Environmental influences that appear to cause differences between siblings might themselves be caused by genetic differences between the siblings.

Indeed, in the past decade, most of the measures used by psychologists to assess environmental factors have been shown to be influenced by genetic factors (Plomin & Bergeman, 1991). These measures include, for example, adolescents' ratings of how their parents treated them, observations of parent-child interactions, and questionnaires about life events and social support. If measures such as these reflected only environmental factors, one would expect the scores of identical twins to be no more similar than those of fraternal twins. By the same token, one would expect no significant similarity in environmental-experience measures for genetically related individuals who were adopted into different families.

The results reported by behavioral geneticists do not fit these expectations (Braungart, Plomin & Fulker, 1992; Plomin, 1994b). For example, parents differ in terms of how responsive they are to their children, but these differences in responsiveness correlate with the children's mental ability—a trait that has a clear genetic component. Thus, as described in Chapters 10 and 12, parental responsiveness can influence cognitive development, and—as behavioral genetics research suggests—children's inherited mental abilities can alter the responsiveness of their parents. That is, parents tend to be more responsive to bright children who ask lots of questions and are interested in the answers.

Outside the family, too, genetic factors appear to play a role in generating environmental experiences. For example, research on the characteristics of children's peer groups shows that children tend to choose their friends—and to be chosen as friends—partly on the basis of genetically influenced traits, such as mental ability and temperament (Manke et al., 1995). Several studies also suggest that genetic factors can increase or decrease the likelihood of family conflicts and other social stressors (see Chapter 13) that threaten one's physical and psychological well-being (Pike et al., in press).

An important implication of genetic influences on environmental events is that measuring the impact of family relationships, peer influences, and other environmental factors on behavior and mental processes may be more difficult than psychologists thought. A measure that is aimed at assessing an environmental factor may nonetheless be affected by the genetic characteristics of the people being studied.

In human development, nature and nurture work together, as described in Chapter 12. Children select, modify, and create environments that are correlated with their genetic inclinations. As developmental psychologists have long argued, children are not formless blobs of clay passively molded by the environment. Rather, they are active participants in their experiences. The new findings we have described here suggest that genetics plays an important role in those experiences (Plomin, 1994b).

SUMMARY AND KEY TERMS

Behavioral genetics is the study of how genes affect behavior.

■ THE BIOLOGY OF GENETICS AND HEREDITY

Research on the ways in which nature and nurture interact to shape behavior and mental processes requires a knowledge of *genetics,* the biology of inheritance. The genetic code that transmits characteristics from one generation to the next is contained in the *DNA* that comprises the *genes* that make up *chromosomes. Dominant* genes are expressed whenever they are present; *recessive* genes are expressed only when inherited from both parents. Most human characteristics are controlled by more than one gene or gene pair; they are *polygenic.*

The genes in a person's forty-six chromosomes make up the *genotype;* the phenotype—how people actually look and act—is influenced by genes and the environment.

■ A BRIEF HISTORY OF GENETIC RESEARCH IN PSYCHOLOGY

Galton's work in the nineteenth century helped to stimulate psychologists' interest in the influence of genetics on behavior. The popularity of research in this area has waxed and waned over the years, but today most psychologists recognize the role of genetic as well as environmental influences on many aspects of behavior and mental processes.

■ THE FOCUS OF RESEARCH IN BEHAVIORAL GENETICS

Behavioral genetics research identifies the genetic and environmental factors responsible for *differences* between individuals, not for the characteristics of a particular person. Though genes can influence a trait, they may not completely determine whether that trait appears.

■ THE ROLE OF GENETIC FACTORS IN PSYCHOLOGY

Genetic factors probably influence to some extent every aspect of behavior and mental processes.

Genetic Influences Over the Lifespan

Genetic influences on general mental ability appear to increase over time, possibly because genetic predispositions lead people to select and even create environments that foster the continued development of abilities that are in line with those predispositions.

Genes Affecting Multiple Traits

Genes that affect one trait, such as anxiety, can sometimes also affect others, such as depression.

Identifying Genes Related to Behavior

Current research in behavioral genetics is identifying specific genes responsible for specific characteristics—especially rare, single-gene disorders, such as Huntington's disease.

■ BEHAVIORAL GENETICS AND ENVIRONMENTAL INFLUENCES

Research in behavioral genetics has actually provided evidence for the importance of environmental influences, too, because it shows that genetics alone cannot account for such characteristics as intelligence, personality, and mental disorders. Some of the most important environmental influences are likely to be those which members of the same family do not share. In short, neither nature nor nurture is conducting the performance of the other: They are playing a duet.

STATISTICS IN PSYCHOLOGICAL RESEARCH

UNDERSTANDING AND INTERPRETING THE results of psychological research depends on *statistical analyses,* which are methods for describing and drawing conclusions from data. Chapter 2 introduced some terms and concepts associated with *descriptive statistics*—the numbers that psychologists use to describe and present their data—and with *inferential statistics*—the mathematical procedures used to draw conclusions from data and to make inferences about what they mean. Here, we present more details about these statistical analyses that will help you to evaluate research results.

DESCRIBING DATA

To illustrate our discussion, consider a hypothetical experiment on the effects of incentives on performance. The experimenter presents a simple list of mathematics problems to two groups of subjects. Each group must solve the problems within a fixed time, but for each correct answer, the low-incentive group is paid ten cents, while the high-incentive group gets one dollar. The hypothesis to be tested is the **null hypothesis,** the assertion that the independent variable manipulated by the experimenter will have no effect on the dependent variable measured by the experimenter. In this case, the null hypothesis holds that the size of the incentive (the independent variable) will not affect performance on the mathematics task (the dependent variable).

Assume that the experimenter has obtained a random sample of subjects, assigned them randomly to the two groups, and done everything possible to avoid the confounds and other research problems discussed in Chapter 2. The experiment has been run, and the psychologist now has the data: a list of the number of correct answers given by each subject in each group. Now comes the first task of statistical analysis: describing the data in a way that makes them easy to understand.

The Frequency Histogram

The simplest way to describe the data is to draw up something like Table 1, in which all the numbers are simply listed. After examining the table, you might discern that the high-incentive group seems to have done better than the low-incentive group, but the difference is not immediately obvious. It might be even harder to see if more subjects had been involved and if the scores included three-digit numbers. A picture is worth a thousand words, so a more satisfactory way of presenting the same data is in a picture-like graphic known as a **frequency histogram** (see Figure 1).

Construction of a histogram is simple. First, divide the scale for measuring the dependent variable (in this case, the number of correct solutions) into a number of categories, or "bins." The bins in our example are 1–2, 3–4, 5–6, 7–8, and 9–10. Next, sort the raw data into the appropriate bin. (For example, the score of a subject who had 5 correct answers would go into the 5–6 bin, a score of 8 would go into the 7–8 bin, and so on.) Finally, for each bin, count the number of scores in that bin and draw a bar up to the height of that number on the vertical axis of a graph. The set of bars makes up the frequency histogram.

TABLE I		Low Incentive	High Incentive
A Simple Data Set		4	6
		6	4
Here are the test scores obtained by		2	10
thirteen subjects performing under		7	10
low-incentive conditions and		6	7
thirteen subjects performing under		8	10
high-incentive conditions.		3	6
		5	7
		2	5
		3	9
		5	9
		9	3
		5	8

Because we are interested in comparing the scores of two groups, there are separate histograms in Figure 1: one for the high-incentive group and one for the low-incentive group. Now the difference between groups that was difficult to see in Table 1 becomes clearly visible: more people in the high-incentive group obtained high scores than in the low-incentive group.

Histograms and other pictures of data are useful for visualizing and better understanding the "shape" of research data, but in order to analyze data statistically, the data making up these graphic presentations must be handled in other ways. For example, before we can tell whether two histograms are different statistically or just visually, the data they represent must be summarized using descriptive statistics.

Descriptive Statistics

The four basic categories of descriptive statistics (1) measure the number of observations made; (2) summarize the typical value of a set of data; (3) summarize the spread, or variability, in a set of data; and (4) express the correlation between two sets of data.

N   The easiest statistic to compute, abbreviated as N, simply describes the number of observations that make up the data set. In Table 1, for example, $N = 13$ for each group, or 26 for the entire data set. Simple as it is, N plays a very important role in more sophisticated statistical analyses.

Measures of Central Tendency   It is apparent in the histograms in Figure 1 that there is a difference in the pattern of scores between the two groups. But how much of a difference? What is the typical value, the *central tendency,* that represents each group's performance? As described in Chapter 2, there are three measures that capture this typical value: the mode, the median, and the mean. Recall that the *mode* is the value or score that occurs most frequently in the data set. The *median* is the halfway point in a set of data: half the scores fall above the median, half fall below it. The *mean* is the arithmetic average. To find the mean, add the values of all the scores and divide by the number of scores.

Measures of Variability   The variability, or spread, or dispersion of a set of data is often just as important as its central tendency. This variability can be quantified by measures known as the *range* and the *standard deviation.*

As described in Chapter 2, the range is simply the difference between the highest and the lowest value in a data set. For the data in Table 1, the range for the low-incentive group is $9 - 2 = 7$; for the high-incentive group, the range is $10 - 3 = 7$.

The standard deviation, or SD, measures the average difference between each score and the mean of the data set. To see how the standard deviation is calculated, consider

FIGURE I

Frequency Histograms

The height of each bar of a histogram represents the number of scores falling within each range of score values. The pattern formed by these bars gives a visual image of how research results are distributed.

(A) LOW INCENTIVE

(B) HIGH INCENTIVE

■ I–2   ■ 7–8
■ 3–4   ■ 9–10
■ 5–6

the data in Table 2. The first step is to compute the mean of the set—in this case, 20/5 = 4. Second, calculate the difference, or *deviation* (*D*), of each score from the mean by subtracting the mean from each score, as in column 2 of Table 2. Third, find the average of these deviations. However, if you calculated the average by finding the arithmetic mean, you would sum the deviations and find that the negative deviations exactly balance the positive ones, resulting in a mean difference of 0. Obviously there is more than zero variation around the mean in the data set. So, instead of employing the arithmetic mean, we compute the standard deviation by first squaring the deviations (which removes any negative values), summing these squared deviations, dividing by *N*, and then taking the square root of the result. These simple steps are outlined in more detail in Table 2.

The Normal Distribution   Now that we have described histograms and reviewed some descriptive statistics, we will re-examine how these methods of representing research data relate to some of the concepts discussed elsewhere in the book.

In most subareas in psychology, when researchers collect many measurements and plot their data in histograms, the pattern that results often resembles that shown for the low-incentive group in Figure 1. That is, the majority of scores tend to fall in the middle of the distribution, with fewer and fewer occurring as one moves toward the extremes. As more and more data are collected, and as smaller and smaller bins are used (perhaps containing only one value each), the histograms tend to smooth out, until they resemble the bell-shaped curve known as the **normal distribution,** or *normal curve,* which is shown in Figure 2(A). When a distribution of scores follows a truly normal curve, its mean, median, and mode all have the same value. Furthermore, if the curve is normal, we can use its standard deviation to describe how any particular score stands in relation to the rest of the distribution.

IQ scores provide an example. They are distributed in a normal curve, with a mean, median, and mode of 100 and an SD of 16 (see Figure 2(B)). In such a distribution, half of the population will have an IQ above 100, and half will be below 100. The shape of the true normal curve is such that 68 percent of the area under it lies within one standard deviation above and below the mean. In terms of IQ, this means that 68 percent of the population has an IQ somewhere between 84 (100 minus 16) and 116 (100 plus 16). Of the remaining 32 percent of the population, half falls more than 1 SD above the mean, and half falls more than 1 SD below the mean. Thus, 16 percent of the population has an IQ above 116, and 16 percent scores below 84.

The normal curve is also the basis for percentiles. A **percentile score** indicates the percentage of people or observations that fall below a given score in a normal distribution. In Figure 2(B), for example, the mean score (which is also the median) lies at a point below which 50 percent of the scores fall. Thus, the mean of a normal distribution is at the 50th percentile. What does this mean for IQ? If you score 1 SD above the

TABLE 2	Raw Data	Difference from Mean = D	D^2
Calculating the Standard Deviation	2	2 − 4 = − 2	4
	2	2 − 4 = − 2	4
The standard deviation of a set of scores reflects the average degree to which those scores differ from the mean of the set.	3	3 − 4 = − 1	1
	4	4 − 4 = 0	0
	9	9 − 4 = 5	25
	Mean = 20/5 = 4		$\Sigma D^2 = 34$

$$\text{Standard deviation} = \sqrt{\frac{\Sigma D^2}{N}} = \sqrt{\frac{34}{5}} = \sqrt{6.8} = 2.6$$

Note: Σ means "the sum of."

FIGURE 2

The Normal Distribution

Many kinds of research data approximate the symmetrical shape of the normal curve, in which most scores fall toward the center of the range.

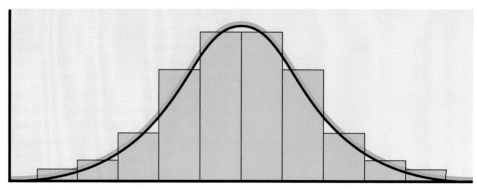

(A) NORMAL DISTRIBUTION, SHOWING THE SMOOTHED APPROXIMATION TO THE FREQUENCY HISTOGRAM

(B) THE NORMAL DISTRIBUTION OF IQ

mean, your score is at a point above which only 16 percent of the population falls. This means that 84 percent of the population (100 percent minus 16 percent) must be below that score; so this IQ score is at the 84th percentile. A score at 2 SDs above the mean is at the 97.5 percentile, because only 2.5 percent of the scores are above it in a normal distribution.

Scores may also be expressed in terms of their distance in standard deviations from the mean, producing what are called **standard scores.** A standard score of 1.5, for example, is 1.5 standard deviations from the mean.

Correlation   Histograms and measures of central tendency and variability describe certain characteristics of one dependent variable at a time. However, psychologists are often concerned with describing the *relationship* between two variables. Measures of correlation are often used for this purpose. We discussed the interpretation of the *correlation coefficient* in Chapter 2; here we describe how to calculate it.

Recall that correlations are based on the relationship between two numbers associated with each subject or observation. The numbers may represent, say, a person's height and weight or the IQ of a parent and child. Table 3 contains this kind of data for four subjects from our incentives study who took the test twice. (As you may recall from Chapter 11, the correlation between their scores would be a measure of *test-retest reliability.*) The formula for computing the Pearson product-moment correlation, or *r,* is as follows:

$$r = \frac{\Sigma(x - M_x)(y - M_y)}{\sqrt{\Sigma(x - M_x)^2 \, \Sigma(y - M_y)^2}}$$

where:

x = each score on variable 1 (in this case, test 1)
y = each score on variable 2 (in this case, test 2)
M_x = the mean of the scores on variable 1
M_y = the mean of the scores on variable 2

The main function of the denominator in this formula is to ensure that the coefficient ranges from +1.00 to −1.00, no matter how large or small the values of the variables being correlated. The "action element" of this formula is the numerator. It is the result of multiplying the amounts by which each of two observations (x and y) differ from the means of their respective distributions (M_x and M_y). Notice that, if the two variables "go together" (so that, if one is large, the other is also large, and if one is small, the other is also small), then either both will tend to be above the mean of their distribution or both will tend to be below the mean of their distribution. When this is the case, $x - M_x$ and $y - M_y$ will both be positive, or they will both be negative. In either case, their product will always be positive, and the correlation coefficient will also be positive. If, on the other hand, the two variables go opposite to one another, such that, when one is large, the other is small, one of them is likely to be smaller than the mean of its distribution, so that either $x - M_x$ or $y - M_y$ will have a negative sign, and the other will have a positive sign. Multiplying these differences together will always result in a product with a negative sign, and r will be negative as well.

Now compute the correlation coefficient for the data presented in Table 3. The first step (step a in the table) is to compute the mean (M) for each variable. M_x turns out to be 3 and M_y is 4. Next, calculate the numerator by finding the differences between each x and y value and its respective mean and by multiplying them (as in step b of Table 3). Notice that, in this example, the differences in each pair have like signs, so the correlation coefficient will be positive. The next step is to calculate the terms in the denominator; in this case, as shown in steps c and d in Table 3, they have values of 18 and 4. Finally, place all the terms in the formula and carry out the arithmetic (step e). The result in this case is an r of +.94, a high and positive correlation suggesting that performances on repeated tests are very closely related. A subject doing well the first time is very likely to do well again; a person doing poorly at first will probably do no better the second time.

INFERENTIAL STATISTICS

The descriptive statistics from the incentives experiment tell the experimenter that the performances of the high- and low-incentive groups differ. But there is some uncertainty. Is the difference large enough to be important? Does it represent a stable effect or a fluke? The researcher would like to have some *measure of confidence* that the difference between groups is genuine and reflects the effect of incentive on mental tasks in

TABLE 3	Subject	Test 1	Test 2	$(x - M_x)(y - M_y)^{(b)}$
Calculating the Correlation Coefficient	A	1	3	$(1-3)(3-4) = (-2)(-1) = +2$
	B	1	3	$(1-3)(3-4) = (-2)(-1) = +2$
Though it appears complex,	C	4	5	$(4-3)(5-4) = (1)(1)\quad = +1$
calculation of the correlation	D	6	5	$(6-3)(5-4) = (3)(1)\quad = +3$
coefficient is quite simple. The resulting r reflects the degree to which two sets of scores tend to be related, or to co-vary.		$^{(a)}M_x = 3$	$M_y = 4$	$\Sigma(x - M_x)(y - M_y)\quad = +8$

$^{(c)}\Sigma(x - M_x)^2 = 4 + 4 + 1 + 9 = 18$
$^{(d)}\Sigma(y - M_y)^2 = 1 + 1 + 1 + 1 = 4$

$$^{(e)}r = \frac{\Sigma(x - M_x)(y - M_y)}{\sqrt{\Sigma(x - M_x)^2 \Sigma(y - M_y)^2}} = \frac{8}{\sqrt{18 \times 4}} = \frac{8}{\sqrt{72}} = \frac{8}{8.48} = +.94$$

the real world, rather than the effect of the particular subjects used, the time of the year, or other random or uncontrolled factors. One way of determining confidence would be to run the experiment again with a new group of subjects. Confidence that incentives produced differences in performance would grow stronger if the same or a larger between-group difference occurs again. In reality, psychologists rarely have the opportunity to repeat, or *replicate*, their experiments in exactly the same way three or four times. But **inferential statistics** provide a measure of how likely it was that results came about by chance. They put a precise mathematical value on the confidence or probability that rerunning the same experiment would yield similar (or even stronger) results.

Differences Between Means: The t Test   One of the most important tools of inferential statistics is the *t* test. It allows the researcher to ask how likely it is that the difference between two means occurred by chance rather than as a function of the effect of the independent variable. When the *t* test or other inferential statistic says that the probability of chance effects is small enough (usually less than 5 percent), the results are said to be *statistically significant*. Conducting a *t* test of statistical significance requires the use of three descriptive statistics.

The first component of the *t* test is the size of the observed effect, the difference between the means. Recall that the mean is calculated by summing a group's scores and dividing by the number of scores. In the example shown in Table 1, the mean of the high-incentive group is 94/13, or 7.23, and the mean of the low-incentive group is 65/13, or 5. Thus, the difference between the means for the high- and low-incentive groups is 7.23 − 5 = 2.23.

Second, the standard deviation of scores in each group must be known. If the scores in a group are quite variable, the standard deviation will be large, indicating that chance may have played a large role in producing the results. The next replication of the study might generate a very different set of group scores. If the scores in a group are all very similar, however, the standard deviation will be small, which suggests that the same result would probably occur for that group if the study were repeated. Thus, the *difference* between groups is more likely to be significant when each group's standard deviation is small. If variability is high enough that the scores of two groups overlap (in Table 1, for example, some people in the low-incentive group actually did better on the math test than some in the high-incentive group), the mean difference, though large, may not be statistically significant.

Third, we need to take the sample size, *N*, into account. The larger the number of subjects or observations, the more likely it is that a given difference between means is significant. This is so because, with larger samples, random factors within a group—the unusual performance of a few people who were sleepy or anxious or hostile, for example—are more likely to be canceled out by the majority, who better represent people in general. The same effect of sample size can be seen in coin tossing. If you toss a quarter five times, you might not be too surprised if heads comes up 80 percent of the time. If you get 80 percent heads after one hundred tosses, however, you might begin to suspect that this is probably not due to chance alone and that some other effect, perhaps some bias in the coin, is significant in producing the results. (For the same reason, a relatively small correlation coefficient—between diet and grades, say—might be statistically significant if it was based on 50,000 students. As the number of subjects increases, it becomes less likely that the correlation reflects the influence of a few oddball cases.)

To summarize, as the differences between the means get larger, as *N* increases, and as standard deviations get smaller, *t* increases. This increase in *t* raises the researcher's confidence in the significance of the difference between means.

Now we will calculate the *t* statistic and show how it is interpreted. The formula for *t* is:

$$t = \frac{(M_1 - M_2)}{\sqrt{\frac{(N_1 - 1)S_1^2 + (N_2 - 1)S_2^2}{N_1 + N_2 - 2}\left(\frac{N_1 + N_2}{N_1 N_2}\right)}}$$

where:

M_1 = mean of group 1
M_2 = mean of group 2
N_1 = number of scores or observations for group 1
N_2 = number of scores or observations for group 2
S_1 = standard deviation of group 1 scores
S_2 = standard deviation of group 2 scores

Despite appearances, this formula is quite simple. In the numerator is the difference between the two group means; t will get larger as this difference gets larger. The denominator contains an estimate of the standard deviation of the *differences* between group means; in other words, it suggests how much the difference between group means would vary if the experiment were repeated many times. Since this estimate is in the denominator, the value of t will get smaller as the standard deviation of group differences gets larger. For the data in Table 1,

$$t = \frac{(M_1 - M_2)}{\sqrt{\dfrac{(N_1 - 1)S_1^{2} + (N_2 - 1)S_2^{2}}{N_1 + N_2 - 2}\left(\dfrac{N_1 + N_2}{N_1 N_2}\right)}}$$

$$= \frac{7.23 - 5}{\sqrt{\dfrac{(12)(5.09) + (12)(4.46)}{24}\left(\dfrac{26}{169}\right)}}$$

$$= \frac{2.23}{\sqrt{.735}} = 2.60 \text{ with 24 df}$$

To determine what a particular t means, we must use the value of N and a special statistical table called, appropriately enough, the t *table*. We have reproduced part of the t table in Table 4.

First, find the computed value of t in the row corresponding to the **degrees of freedom, or df,** associated with the experiment. In this case, degrees of freedom are simply $N_1 + N_2 - 2$ (or two less than the total sample size or number of scores). Since our experiment had 13 subjects per group, df = 13 + 13 − 2 = 24. In the row for 24 df in Table 4, you will find increasing values of t in each column. These columns correspond to decreasing p values, the probabilities that the difference between means occurred by chance. If an obtained t value is equal to or larger than one of the values in the t table (on the correct df line), then the difference between means that generated that t is said to be significant at the .10, .05, or .01 level of probability. Suppose, for example, that an obtained t (with 19 df) was 2.00. Looking along the 19 df row, you find that 2.00 is larger than the value in the .05 column. This allows you to say that the probability that

TABLE 4			
The t Table		*p Value*	
This table allows the researcher to determine whether an obtained t value is statistically significant. If the t value is larger than the one in the appropriate row in the .05 column, the difference between means that generated that t score is usually considered statistically significant.	**df**	**.10 (10%)**	**.05 (5%)**	**.01 (1%)**
	4	1.53	2.13	3.75
	9	1.38	1.83	2.82
	14	1.34	1.76	2.62
	19	1.33	1.73	2.54
	22	1.32	1.71	2.50
	24	1.32	1.71	2.49

the difference between means occurred by chance was no greater than .05, or 5 in 100. If the *t* had been less than the value in the .05 column, the probability of a chance result would have been greater than .05. As noted earlier, when an obtained *t* is not large enough to exceed *t* table values at the .05 level, at least, it is not usually considered statistically significant.

The *t* value from our experiment was 2.60, with 24 df. Because 2.60 is greater than all the values in the 24 df row, the difference between the high- and low-incentive groups would have occurred by chance less than 1 time in 100. In other words, the difference is statistically significant.

Beyond the t Test   Many experiments in psychology are considerably more complex than simple comparisons between two groups. They often involve three or more experimental and control groups. Some experiments also include more than one independent variable. For example, suppose we had been interested not only in the effect of incentive size on performance but also in the effect of problem difficulty. We might then create six groups whose subjects would perform easy, moderate, or difficult problems with low or high incentives.

In an experiment like this, the results might be due to the incentive, the problem difficulty, or the combined effects (known as the *interaction*) of the two. Analyzing the size and source of these effects is typically accomplished through procedures known as *analysis of variance.* The details of analysis of variance are beyond the scope of this book; for now, note that the statistical significance of each effect is influenced by differences between means, standard deviation, and sample size in much the same way as described for the *t* test.

For more detailed information about how analysis of variance and other inferential statistics are used to understand and interpret the results of psychological research, consider taking courses in research methods and statistical or quantitative methods.

Summary and Key Terms

Psychological research generates large quantities of data. Statistics are methods for describing and drawing conclusions from data.

■ DESCRIBING DATA

Researchers often test the *null hypothesis,* which is the assertion that the independent variable will have no effect on the dependent variable.

The Frequency Histogram
Graphic representations such as *frequency histograms* provide visual descriptions of data, making the data easier to understand.

Descriptive Statistics
Numbers that summarize a set of data are called descriptive statistics. The easiest statistic to compute is *N,* which gives the number of observations made. A set of scores can be described by two other types of descriptive statistics: a measure of central tendency, which describes the typical value of a set of data, and a measure of variability. Measures of central tendency include the mean, median, and mode; variability is typically measured by the range and by the standard deviation. Sets of data often follow a *normal distribution,* which means that most scores fall in the middle of the range, with fewer and fewer scores occurring as one moves toward the extremes. In a truly normal distribution the mean, median, and mode are identical. When a set of data shows a normal distribution, a data point can be cited in terms of a *percentile score,* which indicates the percentage of people or observations falling below a certain score, and in terms of *standard scores,* which indicate the distance, in standard deviations, that a score is located from the mean. Another type of descriptive statistic, a correlation coefficient, is used to measure the correlation between sets of scores.

■ INFERENTIAL STATISTICS

Researchers use inferential statistics to quantify the probability that conducting the same experiment again would yield similar results.

Differences Between Means: The t Test
One inferential statistic, the *t test,* assesses the likelihood that differences between two means occurred by chance or reflect the effect of an independent variable. Performing a *t* test requires using the difference between the means of two sets of data, the standard deviation of scores in each set, and the number of observations or subjects. Interpreting a *t* test requires that *degrees of freedom* also be taken into account. When the *t* test indicates that the experimental results had a low probability of occurring by chance, the results are said to be statistically significant.

Beyond the t Test
When more than two groups must be compared, researchers typically rely on analysis of variance in order to interpret the results of an experiment.

GLOSSARY

Absolute threshold The minimum amount of stimulus energy that can be detected 50 percent of the time. (See also *internal noise.*) (*p. 129*)

Acetylcholine A neurotransmitter used by neurons in the peripheral and central nervous systems in the control of functions ranging from muscle contraction and heart rate to digestion and memory. Alzheimer's disease is associated with the neurons that use acetylcholine. (*p. 77*)

Accessory structure A structure, such as the lens of the eye, that modifies a stimulus. In some sensory systems, this modification is the first step in sensation. (*p. 88*)

Accommodation (1) The ability of the lens to change its shape and bend light rays so that objects are in focus. (*p. 138*) (2) The process of modifying schemas as an infant tries out familiar schemas on objects that do not fit them. (*pp. 98, 390*)

Acoustic code A mental representation of information as a sequence of sounds. (*p. 229*)

Action potential An impulse that travels down an axon when the neuron becomes depolarized and sodium rushes into the cell. This kind of nerve communication is all or none: The cell either fires at full strength or does not fire at all. (*p. 50*)

Active sleep (also called *REM sleep*) A stage of sleep during which the EEG resembles that of someone who is active and awake; the heart rate, respiration, blood pressure, and other physiological patterns are also very much like those occurring during the day. At the same time, the sleeper begins rapid eye movements beneath closed lids, and muscle tone decreases to the point of paralysis. (*p. 171*)

Actor-observer bias The tendency to attribute other people's behavior to internal causes while attributing one's own behavior (especially errors and failures) to external causes. (*p. 578*)

Acuity Visual resolution or clarity, which is greatest in the fovea because of its large concentration of cones. (*p. 99*)

Adaptation The process through which responsiveness to an unchanging stimulus decreases over time. (*p. 88*)

Addiction Development of a physical need for a psychoactive drug. (*pp. 181, 523*)

Affective disorder See *mood disorder.*

Age regression A phenomenon displayed by some hypnotized people that involves recalling and re-enacting behaviors from childhood. (*p. 177*)

Aggression An act that is intended to cause harm or damage to another person. (*p. 608*)

Agonists Drugs that bind to a receptor and mimic the effects of the neurotransmitter that normally fits that receptor. (*p. 180*)

Agoraphobia A strong fear of being alone or away from the security of home. (*p. 502*)

AI See *artificial intelligence.*

Alcoholism A pattern of continuous or intermittent drinking that may lead to addiction and almost always causes severe social, physical, and other problems. (*p. 523*)

Algorithm A systematic procedure that cannot fail to produce a solution to a problem—but often not the most efficient way to produce a solution. (See also *heuristic.*) (*p. 272*)

Altered state of consciousness (also called *alternate state of consciousness*) A condition that exists when quantitative and qualitative changes in mental processes are extensive enough that the person or objective observers notice significant differences in psychological and behavioral functioning. (*p. 169*)

Altruism An unselfish concern with another's welfare. (*p. 615*)

Amplitude The difference between the peak and the baseline of a waveform. (*p. 90*)

Amygdala A structure in the forebrain that, among other things, associates features of stimuli from two sensory modalities, such as linking the shape and feel of objects in memory. (*p. 63*)

Analgesia The absence of the sensation of pain in the presence of a normally painful stimulus. The brain appears to use serotonin and endorphins to block painful stimuli. (*p. 119*)

Anal stage The second of Freud's psychosexual stages, usually occurring during the second year of life, in which the focus of pleasure and conflict shifts from the mouth to the anus. The demand for toilet training conflicts with the child's instinctual pleasure in having bowel movements at will. (*p. 461*)

Anchoring heuristic A shortcut in the thought process that involves adding new information to existing information to reach a judgment. (*p. 275*)

Androgens Masculine hormones that circulate in the bloodstream and regulate sexual motivation in both sexes. The principal androgen is testosterone, and relatively more androgens circulate in men than in women. (*p. 351*)

Anorexia nervosa An eating disorder characterized by self-starvation and dramatic weight loss. (*p. 348*)

ANS See *autonomic nervous system.*

Antagonists Drugs that bind to a receptor and prevent the normal neurotransmitter from binding. (*p. 181*)

Anterograde amnesia A loss of memory for any event that occurs after a brain injury. (See also *retrograde amnesia.*) (*p. 241*)

Antidepressant A drug that relieves depression. (*p. 560*)

Antipsychotic A drug that alleviates the symptoms of schizophrenia or other severe forms of psychological disorder. (*p. 558*)

Antisocial personality disorder A personality disorder involving a long-term, persistent pattern of impulsive, selfish, unscrupulous, even criminal behavior. (*p. 521*)

Anxiety disorder A condition in which intense feelings of apprehension are long-standing or disruptive. (See also *generalized anxiety disorder, panic disorder, phobia,* and *obsessive-compulsive disorder.*) (*p. 501*)

Anxiolytic A drug that reduces feelings of tension and anxiety. (See also *tranquilizer.*) (*p. 561*)

Arousal A general level of activation that is reflected in several physiological systems and can be measured by electrical activity in the brain, heart action, muscle tension, and the state of many other organ systems. (*p. 341*)

Arousal: cost-reward theory A theory that attributes helping behavior to people's efforts to reduce the unpleasant arousal they feel when confronted with a suffering victim. (*p. 615*)

Arousal theory A theory of motivation stating that people are motivated to behave in ways that maintain what is, for them, an optimal level of arousal. (*p. 342*)

Artificial concept A concept that can be clearly defined by a set of rules or properties, so that each member of the concept has all of the defining properties and no nonmember does. (See also *natural concept.*) (*p. 269*)

Artificial intelligence (AI) The field that studies how to program computers to imitate the products of human perception, understanding, and thought. (*p. 281*)

Assertiveness and social skills training A set of methods for teaching clients who are anxious or unproductive in social situations how to interact with others more comfortably and effectively. (*p. 542*)

Assimilation The process of taking in new information about objects by trying out existing schemas on objects that fit those schemas. (*p. 389*)

Association cortex Those parts of the cerebral cortex that receive information from more than one sense or combine sensory and motor information to perform such complex cognitive tasks as abstract thought or associating words with images. (*p. 68*)

Attachment A deep, affectionate, close, and enduring relationship with the single person with whom a baby has shared many experiences. (*p. 404*)

Attention The process of directing and focusing certain psychological resources, usually by voluntary control, to enhance information processing, performance, and mental experience. (*p. 151*)

Attitude A predisposition toward a particular cognitive, emotional, or behavioral reaction to an object, individual, group, situation, or action. (*p. 579*)

Attribution The process of explaining the causes of people's behavior, including one's own. (See also *attributional bias*.) (*pp. 372, 574*)

Auditory nerve The bundle of axons that carries stimuli from the hair cells of the cochlea to the brain to facilitate hearing. (*p. 93*)

Auditory scene analysis The perceptual process through which sounds are mentally represented and interpreted. (*p. 135*)

Authoritarian parent A firm, punitive, and unsympathetic parent who values obedience from the child and authority for himself or herself, does not encourage independence, is detached, and seldom praises the child. The result of this parenting style is often an unfriendly, distrustful, and withdrawn child. (*p. 410*)

Authoritative parent A parent who reasons with the child, encourages give and take, is firm but understanding, and gives the child more responsibility as he or she gets older. Children of this type of parent are usually friendly, cooperative, self-reliant, and socially responsible. (*p. 410*)

Autoimmune disorders Physical problems caused when cells of the body's immune system attack normal body cells as if they were foreign invaders. (*p. 82*)

Autonomic nervous system (ANS) A subsystem of the peripheral nervous system that carries messages between the central nervous system and the heart, lungs, and other organs and glands in the body. The ANS regulates the activity of these organs and glands to meet varying demands placed upon the body and also provides information to the brain about that activity. (*p. 57*)

Availability heuristic A shortcut in the thought process that involves judging the frequency or probability of an event or hypothesis by how easily the hypothesis or examples of the event can be brought to mind. Thus, people tend to choose the hypothesis or alternative that is most mentally available. (*p. 275*)

Aversive conditioning A method for reducing unwanted behaviors by using classical conditioning principles to create a negative response to some stimulus. (*p. 544*)

Avoidance conditioning A type of learning in which an organism responds to a signal in a way that avoids exposure to an aversive stimulus. (*p. 202*)

Avoidant personality disorder A personality disorder characterized by avoidance of social situations and extreme sensitivity to criticism or rejection by others. (*p. 521*)

Axon The fiber that carries signals from the body of a neuron out to where communication occurs with other neurons. Each neuron generally has only one axon leaving the cell body, but that one axon may have many branches. (*p. 50*)

Babblings Repetitions of syllables; the first sounds infants make that resemble speech. (*p. 292*)

Basilar membrane The floor of the fluid-filled duct that runs through the cochlea. Waves passing through the fluid in the duct move the basilar membrane, and this movement deforms hair cells that touch the membrane. (See also *cochlea*.) (*p. 93*)

Behavioral approach (also called *behavioral model*) Personality theories based on the assumption that human behavior is determined mainly by what a person has learned in life, especially by the rewards and punishments the person has experienced in interacting with other people. According to this approach, the consistency of people's learning histories, not an inner personality structure, produces characteristic behavior patterns. (*p. 13*)

Behavioral genetics The study of the effect of genes on behavior. (*p. 42*)

Behavior modification Treatments that use operant conditioning methods to change behavior by helping, often literally teaching, clients to act differently. (*p. 541*)

Behavior therapy Treatments that use classical conditioning principles to change behavior by helping, often literally teaching, clients to act differently. (*p. 541*)

Biased sample A group of research subjects selected from a population each of whose members did not have an equal chance of being chosen for study. (*p. 36*)

Big five The five traits found in many factor-analytic studies of personality that have been proposed as the basic components of human personality: neuroticism, extraversion, openness to experience, agreeableness, and conscientiousness. (*p. 468*)

Binocular disparity A depth cue based on the difference between the two retinal images. It exists because each eye receives a slightly different view of the world. This difference, which decreases with distance, is measured by the brain, which combines the two images to create the perception of a single image located at a particular distance. (*p. 138*)

Biofeedback training Training methods whereby people can monitor and attempt to control normally unconscious physiological processes such as blood pressure, skin conductance, and muscle tension. (*p. 453*)

Biological approach (also called *biological model*) A view in which behavior and behavior disorders are seen as the result of physical processes, especially those relating to the brain and to hormones and other chemicals. (*p. 12*)

Biological psychologist (also called *physiological psychologist*) A psychologist who analyzes the biological factors influencing behavior and mental processes. (*p. 16*)

Biological psychology (also called *physiological psychology*) The psychological specialty that researches the physical and chemical changes that cause and occur in response to behavior and mental processes. (*p. 47*)

Bipolar cells Cells through which a visual stimulus passes after going to the photoreceptor cells and before going to the ganglion cells. (*p. 100*)

Bipolar disorder A condition in which a person alternates between the two emotional extremes of depression and mania. (*p. 512*)

Bisexual People who engage in sexual activities with partners of both sexes. (*p. 353*)

Blind spot The point at which the axons from all of the ganglion cells converge and exit the eyeball. This exit point has no photoreceptors and is therefore insensitive to light. (*p. 106*)

Blood-brain barrier The aspect of the structure of blood vessels supplying the brain that allows only certain substances to leave the blood and interact with brain tissue. (*p. 186*)

Bottom-up processing Aspects of recognition that depend first on the information about the stimulus that comes up to the brain from the sensory receptors. (See also *top-down processing*.) (*p. 144*)

Brightness The overall intensity of all of the wavelengths that make up light. (*p. 102*)

Brown-Peterson procedure A method for determining how long unrehearsed information remains in short-term memory. It involves presenting a stimulus to individuals, preventing them from rehearsing it by having them perform a counting task, and then testing recall of the stimulus. (*p. 238*)

Bulimia nervosa An eating disorder that involves eating massive quantities of food and then eliminating the food by self-induced vomiting or strong laxatives. (*p. 348*)

Burnout A gradually intensifying pattern of physical, psychological, and behavioral dysfunctions in response to a continuous flow of stressors. *(p. 432)*

Case study A research method involving the intensive examination of some phenomenon in a particular individual, group, or situation. It is especially useful for studying complex or relatively rare phenomena. *(p. 31)*

Catatonic schizophrenia A type of schizophrenia characterized by a movement disorder in which the individual may alternate between total immobility or stupor (sometimes holding bizarre, uncomfortable poses for long periods) and wild excitement. *(p. 517)*

Central nervous system (CNS) The part of the nervous system encased in bone, including the brain and the spinal cord, whose primary function is to process information provided by the sensory systems and decide on an appropriate course of action for the motor system. *(p. 56)*

Cerebellum The part of the hindbrain whose function is to control finely coordinated movements and to store learned associations that involve movement, such as those movements required in dancing or athletics. *(p. 60)*

Cerebral cortex The outer surface of the cerebrum, consisting of two cerebral hemispheres. It is physically divided into four areas, called the frontal, parietal, occipital, and temporal lobes. It is divided functionally into the sensory cortex, the motor cortex, and the association cortex. *(p. 66)*

Cerebral hemisphere One-half, either right or left, of the round, almost spherical, outermost part of the cerebrum. *(p. 66)*

Cerebrum (also called *telencephalon*) The largest part of the forebrain; it is divided into the right and left cerebral hemispheres and contains the striatum and the limbic system. *(p. 63)*

Chromosome A long, thin structure in every biological cell that contains genetic information in the form of more than a thousand genes strung out like a chain. *(p. A-1)*

Chunk Stimuli that are perceived as one unit or a meaningful grouping of information. Most people can hold five to nine (seven plus or minus two) chunks of information in short-term memory. *(p. 237)*

Circadian rhythm A cycle, such as waking and sleeping, that repeats about once a day. *(p. 173)*

Classical conditioning A procedure in which a neutral stimulus is paired with a stimulus that elicits a reflex or other response until the neutral stimulus alone comes to elicit a similar response. *(p. 193)*

Client-centered therapy (also called *person-centered therapy*) A type of therapy in which the client decides what to talk about and when, without direction, judgment, or interpretation from the therapist. This type of treatment is characterized by three important and interrelated therapist attitudes: unconditional positive regard, empathy, and congruence. (See also *congruence, empathy,* and *unconditional positive regard.*) *(p. 538)*

Clinical psychologist A psychologist who seeks to assess, understand, and correct abnormal behavior. *(p. 17)*

Closure A Gestalt grouping principle stating that people tend to fill in missing contours to form a complete object. *(p. 134)*

CNS See *central nervous system.*

Cochlea A fluid-filled spiral structure in the ear in which auditory transduction occurs. *(p. 92)*

Coding Translation of the physical properties of a stimulus into a pattern of neural activity that specifically identifies those physical properties. *(p. 89)*

Cognitive approach A way of looking at human behavior that emphasizes research on how the brain takes in information, creates perceptions, forms and retrieves memories, processes information, and generates integrated patterns of action. *(p. 14)*

Cognitive-behavioral approach An approach to personality that views personality as a label summarizing the unique patterns of thinking and behavior that a person learns. *(p. 471)*

Cognitive-behavior therapy Treatment methods that help clients change the way they think as well as the way they behave. Cognitive obstacles are brought to light, and the therapist encourages the client to try new ways of thinking. *(p. 541)*

Cognitive dissonance theory A theory that proposes that uneasiness results when people's cognitions about themselves or the world are inconsistent with one another. Dissonance motivates people to take some action to make the cognitions consistent. *(p. 582)*

Cognitive map A mental representation, or picture, of the environment. *(pp. 214, 268)*

Cognitive psychologist A psychologist whose research focus is on analysis of the mental processes underlying judgment, decision making, problem solving, imagining, and other aspects of human thought or cognition. *(p. 16)*

Cognitive restructuring A therapy technique or process for coping with stress that involves replacing stress-provoking thoughts with more constructive thoughts in order to make stressors less threatening and disruptive. *(p. 453)*

Cognitive therapy An organized problem-solving approach in which the therapist actively collaborates with clients to help them notice how certain negative thoughts precede anxiety and depression. *(p. 545)*

Common fate A Gestalt grouping principle stating that objects moving in the same direction and at the same speed are perceived as belonging together. *(p. 135)*

Community psychologists Psychologists who work to obtain psychological services for people in need of help and to prevent psychological disorders by working for changes in social systems. *(p. 17)*

Community psychology A movement whose goal is to minimize or prevent psychological disorders through promoting changes in social systems and through community mental health programs designed to make treatment methods more accessible to the poor and others who are unserved or underserved by mental health professionals. *(p. 564)*

Common region A principle of perceptual organization in which elements located within some perimeter or other boundary tend to be grouped together. *(p. 135)*

Competition Any type of behavior in which individuals try to attain a goal for themselves while denying that goal to others. *(p. 620)*

Complementary colors Colors that result in gray when lights of those two colors are mixed. Complementary colors are roughly opposite each other on the color circle. *(p. 105)*

Compliance Adjusting one's behavior to match that of a group because of directly expressed social influence. *(p. 599)*

Computational view An approach to perception that focuses on how perception occurs; it tries to explain how computations by the nervous system translate raw sensory stimulation into an experience of reality. *(p. 127)*

Concept A class or category of objects, events, or ideas that have common properties. (See also *artificial concept* and *natural concept.*) *(p. 269)*

Concrete operations According to Piaget, the third stage of cognitive development, during which children can learn to count, measure, add, and subtract; their thinking is no longer dominated by visual appearances. *(p. 396)*

Conditioned response (CR) In classical conditioning, the response that the conditioned stimulus elicits. *(p. 193)*

Conditioned stimulus (CS) In classical conditioning, the originally neutral stimulus that, through pairing with the unconditioned stimulus, comes to elicit a conditioned response. *(p. 193)*

Conditions of worth According to Rogers, the feelings an individual experiences when the entire person, instead of a specific behavior, is evaluated. The person may feel that his or her worth as a person depends on displaying the right attitudes, behaviors, and values. *(p. 476)*

Cones Photoreceptors in the retina that use one of three varieties of iodopsin, a color-sensitive photopigment, to distinguish colors. (See also *rods.*) *(p. 99)*

Conformity   Changing one's behavior or beliefs to match those of other group members, generally as a result of real or imagined, though unspoken, group pressure. *(p. 599)*

Confounding variable   In an experiment, any factor that affects the dependent variable along with or instead of the independent variable. Confounding variables include random variables, the placebo effect, and experimenter bias. *(p. 34)*

Congruence   In client-centered therapy, a consistency between the way therapists feel and the way they act toward the client; therapists' unconditional positive regard and empathy must be real, not manufactured. *(p. 539)*

Conscious level   The level at which mental activities that people are aware of from moment to moment occur. (See also *preconscious level.*) *(p. 166)*

Consciousness   The awareness of external stimuli and our own mental activity. *(p. 161)*

Conservation   The ability to recognize that the important properties of a substance, such as number, volume, or weight, remain constant despite changes in shape, length, or position. *(p. 395)*

Constructionist view   A view of perception taken by those who argue that the perceptual system uses fragments of sensory information to construct an image of reality. (See also *ecological view.*) *(p. 127)*

Contact hypothesis   The idea that stereotypes and prejudice toward a group will diminish as contact with the group increases. *(p. 585)*

Context-dependent memory   Memories that can be helped or hindered by similarities or differences between the context in which they are learned and that in which they are recalled. *(p. 243)*

Continuity   A Gestalt grouping principle stating that sensations that appear to create a continuous form are perceived as belonging together. *(p. 134)*

Continuous reinforcement schedule   In operant conditioning, a pattern in which a reinforcer is delivered every time a particular response occurs. *(p. 206)*

Control group   In an experiment, the group that receives no treatment or provides some other base line against which to compare the performance or response of the experimental group. *(p. 34)*

Conventional moral reasoning   Reasoning that reflects a concern about other people as well as the belief that morality consists of following rules and conventions. *(p. 418)*

Convergence   (1) The receiving of information by one bipolar cell from many photoreceptors. Convergence allows bipolar cells to compare the amount of light on larger regions of the retina and increases the sensation of contrast. *(p. 100)* (2) A depth cue involving the rotation of the eyes to project the image of an object on each retina. The closer an object is, the more cross-eyed the viewer must become to achieve a focused image of it. *(p. 138)*

Convergent thinking   The ability to apply the rules of logic and what one knows about the world in order to narrow down the number of possible solutions to a problem or perform some other complex cognitive task. *(p. 328)*

Conversion disorder   A somatoform disorder in which a person appears to be, but actually is not, blind, deaf, paralyzed, insensitive to pain in various parts of the body, or even pregnant. (See also *somatoform disorder.*) *(p. 506)*

Cooperation   Any type of behavior in which several people work together to attain a goal. *(p. 620)*

Cornea   The curved, transparent, protective layer through which light rays enter the eye. *(p. 97)*

Corpus callosum   A massive bundle of fibers that connects the right and left cerebral hemispheres and allows them to communicate with each other. Severing the corpus callosum causes difficulty in performing tasks that require information from both hemispheres, such as recognizing and naming objects. *(p. 70)*

Correlation   In research, the degree to which one variable is related to another; the strength and direction of the relationship is measured by a correlation coefficient. Correlation does not guarantee causation. *(p. 39)*

Correlation coefficient   A statistic, *r*, that summarizes the strength and direction of a relationship between two variables. Correlation coefficients vary from 0.00 to 1.00. The plus or minus sign indicates the direction, positive or negative, of a relationship. An *r* of 1.00 or −1.00 indicates a perfect correlation, which means that if you know the value of one variable, you can predict with certainty the value of the other variable. *(p. 39)*

Counseling psychologist   See *clinical psychologist.*

Couples therapy   A form of therapy that focuses on improving communication between partners. *(p. 548)*

Creativity   The capacity to produce original solutions or novel compositions. *(p. 326)*

Critical period   An interval during which certain kinds of growth must occur if development is to proceed normally. *(p. 386)*

Critical thinking   The process of assessing claims and making judgments on the basis of well-supported evidence. *(p. 27)*

Crystallized intelligence   The specific knowledge gained as a result of applying fluid intelligence. It produces verbal comprehension and skill at manipulating numbers. (See also *fluid intelligence.*) *(p. 322)*

Culture   The accumulation of values, rules of behavior, forms of expression, religious beliefs, occupational choices, and the like, for a group of people who share a common language and environment. *(p. 21)*

Cyclothymic disorder   A more common bipolar disorder characterized by an alternating pattern of less extreme mood swings. *(p. 512)*

Dark adaptation   The increasing ability to see in the dark as time passes, due to the synthesis of more photopigments by the photoreceptors. *(p. 99)*

Data   Numbers that represent research findings and provide the basis for research conclusions. *(p. 37)*

Decay   The gradual disappearance of the mental representation of a stimulus. *(p. 252)*

Deep structure   An abstract representation of the relationships expressed in a sentence; the various underlying meanings of a given sentence. *(p. 289)*

Defense mechanism   A psychological response that helps protect a person from anxiety and the other negative emotions accompanying stress; it does little or nothing to eliminate the source of stress. *(p. 460)*

Deficiency orientation   According to Maslow, a preoccupation with meeting perceived needs for material things a person does not have that can lead to perceiving life as a meaningless exercise in disappointment and boredom. *(p. 477)*

Degrees of freedom   The total sample size or number of scores in a data set, less the number of experimental groups. *(p. A-15)*

Deindividuation   A hypothesized psychological state occurring in group members that results in loss of individuality and a tendency to do things not normally done when alone. *(p. 597)*

Delusion   A false belief, such as that experienced by people suffering from schizophrenia or extreme depression. *(p. 510)*

Demonological model   See *supernatural model.*

Dendrite   In a neuron, the fiber that receives signals from the axons of other neurons and carries that signal to the cell body. A neuron can have up to several hundred dendrites. *(p. 50)*

Deoxyribonucleic acid (DNA)   The molecular structure of a gene that provides the genetic code. Each DNA molecule consists of two strands of sugar, phosphate, and nitrogen-containing molecules twisted around each other in a double spiral. *(p. A-1)*

Dependent variable   In an experiment, the factor affected by the independent variable. *(p. 33)*

Depressant   A psychoactive drug that inhibits the functioning of the central nervous system. *(p. 182)*

Depth perception   Perception of distance, one of the most important factors underlying size and shape constancy. Depth perception allows us to experience the world in three-dimensional depth, not as a two-dimensional movie. *(p. 135)*

Descriptive statistics   Numbers that summarize a set of research data. *(p. A-9)*

Developmental psychologist   A psychologist who seeks to understand, describe, and explore how behavior and mental processes change over the course of a lifetime. *(p. 17)*

Developmental psychology   The psychological specialty that documents the course of people's social, emotional, moral, and intellectual development over the life span and explores how development in different domains fits together, is affected by experience, and relates to other areas of psychology. *(p. 382)*

Diathesis-stress model   An integrative approach to psychological disorders that recognizes that each person inherits certain physical predispositions that leave him or her vulnerable to problems that may or may not appear, depending on what kinds of situations that person confronts. People who must deal with particular stressors may or may not develop psychopathology, depending on their predisposition and ability to cope with those stressors. *(p. 496)*

Difference threshold   See *just-noticeable difference*.

Diffusion of responsibility   The process through which a person tends not to take personal responsibility for helping someone in trouble when others are present. *(p. 616)*

Discrimination   Differential treatment of various groups; the behavioral component of prejudice. (See also *prejudice*.) *(p. 584)*

Discriminative stimuli   Stimuli that signal whether reinforcement is available if a certain response is made. *(p. 203)*

Diseases of adaptation   Illnesses that are caused or promoted by stressors. *(p. 434)*

Disorganized schizophrenia   A rare type of schizophrenia characterized by a variety of jumbled and unrelated delusions and hallucinations. The person may display incoherent speech, strange facial grimaces, and meaningless ritual movements and may neglect personal hygiene and lose bowel and bladder control. *(p. 517)*

Dissociation theory   A theory that defines hypnosis as a condition in which people relax central control of mental processes and share some of that control with the hypnotist, who is allowed to determine what the person will experience and do. According to this theory, hypnosis is a socially agreed-upon opportunity to display one's ability to let mental functions become dissociated. (See also *role theory* and *state theory*.) *(p. 178)*

Dissociative amnesia   A psychological disorder marked by a sudden loss of memory, which results in the inability to recall one's own name, occupation, or other identifying information. *(p. 508)*

Dissociative disorder   A rare condition that involves a sudden and usually temporary disruption in a person's memory, consciousness, or identity. *(p. 507)*

Dissociative fugue   A sudden loss of memory and the assumption of a new identity in a new locale. *(p. 508)*

Dissociative identity disorder   (previously known as *multiple personality disorder*) The most famous and least commonly seen dissociative disorder, in which a person reports having more than one identity, and sometimes several, each of which speaks, acts, and writes in a very different way. *(p. 508)*

Divergent thinking   The ability to think along many alternative paths to generate many different solutions to a problem. *(p. 327)*

DNA   See *deoxyribonucleic acid*.

Dopamine   A neurotransmitter used in the parts of the brain—such as the substantia nigra and the striatum—that regulate movement. Dopamine is also involved in the the experience of pleasure. Malfunctioning dopamine systems are related to the appearance of movement disorders such as Parkinson's disease, as well as to schizophrenia. *(p. 78)*

Double-blind design   A research design in which neither the experimenter nor the subjects know who is in the experimental group and

who is in the control group. This design helps prevent experimenter bias (a confounding variable). *(p. 35)*

Dream   A story-like sequence of images, sensations, and perception that lasts anywhere from several seconds to many minutes and occurs mainly during REM sleep (though it may take place at other times). *(p. 176)*

Drive   In drive reduction theory, a psychological state of arousal, created by an imbalance in homeostasis that prompts an organism to take action to restore the balance and, in the process, reduce the drive. (See also *need, primary drive*, and *secondary drive*.) *(p. 340)*

Drive reduction theory   A theory of motivation stating that much motivation arises from constant imbalances in homeostasis. (See also *drive* and *homeostasis*.) *(p. 340)*

Dysthymic disorder   A pattern of depression in which the person shows the sad mood, lack of interest, and loss of pleasure associated with major depressive disorder, but to a lesser degree. (See also *major depressive disorder*.) *(p. 510)*

Ecological view   An approach to perception that states that humans and other species are so well adapted to their natural environment that many aspects of the world are perceived automatically and at the sensory level, without requiring higher-level analysis and inferences. (See also *constructionist view*.) *(p. 127)*

ECT   See *electroconvulsive therapy*.

Educational psychologists   Psychologists who study methods by which instructors teach and students learn, and who apply their results to improving such methods. *(p. 17)*

Ego   In psychodynamic theory, that part of the personality that makes compromises and mediates conflicts between and among the demands of the id, the superego, and the real world; the ego operates according to the reality principle. (See also *id* and *reality principle*.) *(p. 460)*

Elaboration likelihood model   A model of attitude change suggesting that people who have the motivation and ability to carefully evaluate an argument change their attitudes by considering the argument's content (the central route), while those with less motivation or ability tend to take a peripheral route and over-rely on various (often irrelevant) persuasion cues. *(p. 581)*

Elaborative rehearsal   A memorization method that involves thinking about how new information relates to information already stored in long-term memory. *(p. 232)*

Electra complex   A pattern proposed by Freud in which young girls develop an attachment to their fathers and compete with their mothers for their father's attention. *(p. 462)*

Electroconvulsive therapy (ECT)   A brief electric shock administered to the brain, usually to reduce profound depression that does not respond to drug treatments. *(p. 557)*

Embryo   The developing individual from the fourteenth day after fertilization until the third month after fertilization. *(p. 385)*

Emotion   A transitory, valenced experience that is felt as happening to the self, is generated, in part, by the cognitive appraisal of a situation, and is accompanied by both learned and reflexive physical responses. *(p. 363)*

Empathy   In client-centered therapy, the therapist's attempt to appreciate how the world looks from the client's point of view. Empathy requires an internal perspective, a focus on what the client might be thinking and feeling. *(p. 539)*

Empathy-altruism theory   A theory that suggests that people help others because of empathy with their needs. *(p. 617)*

Encoding   The process of putting information into a form that the memory system can accept and use; the process of constructing mental representations of physical stimuli. *(p. 229)*

Encoding specificity principle   A retrieval principle stating that the ability of a cue to aid retrieval effectively depends on the degree to which it taps into information that was encoded at the time of the original learning. *(p. 243)*

Endocrine system   Cells that form organs called glands and communicate with one another by secreting chemicals called hormones. *(p. 80)*

Endorphin   One of a class of neurotransmitters that can bind to the same receptors that opiates, such as morphine and heroin, bind to and that produces the same behavioral effects of pain relief, euphoria, and, in high doses, sleep. *(p. 79)*

Environmental psychologists   Psychologists who study the effects of the physical environment on behavior and mental processes. *(p. 18)*

Environmental psychology   The study of the effects of the general physical environment on people's behavior and mental processes. *(p. 613)*

Episodic memory   A person's recall of a specific event that happened while he or she was present. *(p. 230)*

Escape conditioning   A type of learning in which an organism learns to make a particular response in order to terminate an aversive stimulus. *(p. 202)*

Estrogens   Feminine hormones that circulate in the bloodstream of both men and women; relatively more estrogens circulate in women. One of the main estrogens is estradiol. (See also *progestins.*) *(p. 351)*

Ethologist   A scientist who studies animals in their natural environment to observe how environmental cues affect behavior. *(p. 12)*

Evoked brain potential   A small, temporary change in EEG voltage that is evoked by some stimulus. One such change is the P300, a positive swing in electrical voltage that occurs about 300 milliseconds after a stimulus. It can be used to determine if a stimulus distracts a person's attention from a given task. *(p. 267)*

Evolutionary approach   An approach to psychology that emphasizes the inherited, adaptive aspects of behavior and mental processes. *(p. 12)*

Excitatory postsynaptic potential (EPSP)   A postsynaptic potential that depolarizes the neuronal membrane, bringing the cell closer to threshold for firing an action potential. *(p. 54)*

Expected value   The total benefit to be expected if a decision, though not always correct, were repeated several times. *(p. 284)*

Experiment   A situation in which the researcher manipulates one variable and then observes the effect of that manipulation on another variable, while holding all other variables constant. *(p. 33)*

Experimental group   In an experiment, the group that receives the experimental treatment; its performance or response is compared with that of one or more control groups. *(p. 34)*

Experimental psychologist   A psychologist who conducts experiments aimed at understanding learning, memory, perception, and other basic behavioral and mental processes. *(p. 15)*

Experimenter bias   A confounding variable that occurs when an experimenter unintentionally encourages subjects to respond in a way that supports the hypothesis. *(p. 35)*

Expert system   A computer program that helps people solve problems in a fairly restricted, specific area, such as the diagnosis of diseases. *(p. 282)*

Explicit memory   The process through which people deliberately try to remember something. *(p. 230)*

Extinction   The gradual disappearance of a conditioned response or operant behavior due to elimination either of the association between conditioned and unconditioned stimuli or of rewards for certain behaviors. *(pp. 194, 543)*

Factor analysis   A statistical technique that involves computing correlations between large numbers of variables. Factor analysis is commonly used in the study of intelligence and intelligence tests. *(p. 321)*

Familial retardation   Cases of mild retardation for which no environmental or genetic cause can be found. Most of the people in this group come from families in the lower socioeconomic classes and are more likely than those suffering from a genetic defect to have a relative who is also retarded. *(p. 328)*

Family therapy   A type of treatment inspired by the psychodynamic theory that many psychological disorders are rooted in family conflicts. It involves two or more individuals from the same family, one of whose problems make him or her the initially identified client, although the family itself ultimately becomes the client. *(p. 547)*

Feature detector   A cell in the cortex that responds to a specific feature of an object. *(p. 109)*

Fetal alcohol syndrome   A pattern of defects found in babies born to alcoholic women that includes physical malformations of the face and mental retardation. *(p. 387)*

Fetus   The developing individual from the third month after conception until birth. *(p. 385)*

FI   See *fixed interval schedule.*

Fiber tract   Axons that travel together in bundles. They are also known as *pathways.* *(p. 58)*

Fight-or-flight syndrome   The physical reactions initiated by the sympathetic nervous system that prepare the body to fight or to run from a threatening situation. These reactions include increased heart rate and blood pressure, rapid or irregular breathing, dilated pupils, perspiration, dry mouth, increased blood sugar, decreased gastrointestinal motility, and other changes. (See also *adrenal gland* and *sympathetic nervous system.*) *(pp. 81, 367)*

Figure   That part of the visual field that has meaning, stands in front of the rest, and always seems to include the contours or borders that separate it from the relatively meaningless background. (See also *ground.*) *(p. 133)*

Five-factor model   See *big five.*

Fixed interval (FI) schedule   In operant conditioning, a type of partial reinforcement schedule that provides reinforcement for the first response that occurs after some fixed time has passed since the last reward. *(p. 206)*

Fixed ratio (FR) schedule   In operant conditioning, a type of partial reinforcement schedule that provides reinforcement following a fixed number of responses. *(p. 206)*

Flooding   A procedure for reducing anxiety that involves keeping a person in a feared, but harmless, situation. Once deprived of his or her normally rewarding escape pattern, the client has no reason for continued anxiety. *(p. 543)*

Fluid intelligence   The basic power of reasoning and problem solving. Fluid intelligence produces induction, deduction, reasoning, and understanding of relationships between different ideas. (See also *crystallized intelligence.*) *(p. 322)*

Forebrain   The most highly developed part of the brain; it is responsible for the most complex aspects of behavior and mental life. *(p. 62)*

Formal operational period   According to Piaget, the fourth stage in cognitive development, usually beginning around age eleven. It is characterized by the ability to engage in hypothetical thinking, including the imagining of logical consequences and the ability to think and reason about abstract concepts. *(p. 417)*

Formal reasoning   The process of following a set of rigorous procedures for reaching valid conclusions. *(p. 272)*

Fovea   A region in the center of the retina where cones are highly concentrated. *(p. 99)*

FR   See *fixed ratio schedule.*

Free-floating anxiety   See *generalized anxiety disorder.*

Frequency   The number of complete waveforms, or cycles, that pass by a given point in space every second. For sound waves, the unit of measure is called a hertz (Hz); one hertz is one cycle per second. *(p. 91)*

Frequency histogram   A graphic presentation of data that consists of a set of bars, each of which represents how frequently different values of variables occur in a data set. *(p. A-9)*

Frequency matching (also called *volley theory*)   A theory of hearing that explains how frequency is coded: The firing rate of a neuron matches the frequency of a sound wave. For example, one neuron might fire at every peak of a wave; so a 20-hertz sound could be coded by a neuron that fires twenty times per second. *(p. 95)*

Frustration-aggression hypothesis   A proposition that the existence of frustration always leads to some form of aggressive behavior. *(p. 610)*

Functional analysis   A method of understanding behavior (and thus the person) that involves analyzing exactly what responses occur under what conditions. This approach emphasizes the role of operant conditioning. (See also *operant conditioning*.) *(p. 472)*

Functional fixedness A tendency to think about familiar objects in familiar ways that may prevent using them in other, more creative ways. *(p. 279)*

Fundamental attribution error A bias toward overattributing the behavior of others to internal factors. *(p. 577)*

g A general intelligence factor that Charles Spearman postulated as accounting for positive correlations between people's scores on all sorts of mental ability tests. *(p. 321)*

GABA A neurotransmitter that inhibits the firing of neurons. Disruptions in GABA systems are related to the appearance of anxiety, epilepsy, and Huntington's disease, a disorder characterized by uncontrollable movements and loss of cognitive ability. *(p. 78)*

Ganglion cells The cells in the retina that generate action potentials. They are stimulated by bipolar cells; their axons extend out of the retina and travel to the brain. *(p. 101)*

GAS See *general adaptation syndrome.*

Gate control theory A theory of pain suggesting a functional gate in the spinal cord that either lets pain impulses travel upward to the brain or blocks their progress. *(p. 118)*

Gender role General patterns of work, appearance, and behavior that a society associates with being male or female. *(p. 412)*

Gene The biological instructions inherited from both parents and located on the chromosomes that provide the blueprint for physical development throughout the life span. (See also *deoxyribonucleic acid, genotype,* and *phenotype*.) *(p. A-1)*

General adaptation syndrome (GAS) A consistent and very general pattern of responses triggered by the effort to adapt to any stressor. The syndrome consists of three stages: alarm reaction, resistance, and exhaustion. *(p. 433)*

Generalized anxiety disorder A condition that involves relatively mild but long-lasting anxiety that is not focused on any particular object or situation. *(p. 503)*

Generativity The concern of adults in their thirties with producing or generating something. *(p. 422)*

Genetics The biology of inheritance. *(p. A-1)*

Genital stage The fifth and last of Freud's psychosexual stages, which begins during adolescence when the person begins to mature physically and sexual impulses begin to appear at the conscious level. The young person begins to seek out relationships through which sexual impulses can be gratified. This stage spans the rest of life. *(p. 462)*

Genotype The full set of genes, inherited from both parents, contained in twenty-three pairs of chromosomes. *(p. A-2)*

Gestalt psychologists A group of psychologists who suggested, among other things, that there are six principles or properties behind the grouping of stimuli that lead the human perceptual system to glue raw sensations together in particular ways, organizing stimuli into a world of shapes and patterns. (See also *closure, continuity, proximity, similarity,* and *simplicity*.) *(p. 134)*

Gestalt therapy A form of treatment based on the assumption that clients' problems arise when people behave in accordance with other people's expectations rather than on the basis of their own true feelings. Gestalt therapy seeks to create conditions in which clients can become more unified, more self-aware, and more self-accepting. *(p. 540)*

Glands Organs that secrete hormones into the bloodstream. *(p. 80)*

Glial cells Cells in the nervous system that hold neurons together and help them communicate with one another. *(p. 49)*

Glutamate A neurotransmitter that helps strengthen synaptic connections between neurons, thereby facilitating learning and memory. *(p. 79)*

Gradient A continuous change across the visual field. (See also *movement gradient* and *textural gradient*.) *(p. 136)*

Grammar A set of rules for combining the symbols, such as words, used in a given language. (See also *language*.) *(p. 288)*

Ground The meaningless, contourless part of the visual field; the background. (See also *figure*.) *(p. 133)*

Group polarization The tendency for groups to make decisions that are more extreme than the decision an individual group member would make. *(p. 287)*

Group therapy Psychotherapy involving five to ten individuals. Clients can be observed interacting with one another; they can feel relieved and less alone as they listen to others who have similar difficulties, which tends to raise each client's hope and expectations for improvement; and they can learn from one another. *(p. 546)*

Groupthink A pattern of thinking that, over time, renders group members unable to evaluate realistically the wisdom of various options and decisions. *(p. 625)*

Growth orientation According to Maslow, drawing satisfaction from what is available in life, rather than focusing on what is missing. *(p. 477)*

Gustation The sense that detects chemicals in solutions that come into contact with receptors inside the mouth; the sense of taste. *(p. 112)*

Health promotion The process of altering or eliminating behaviors that pose risks to health and at the same time fostering healthy behavior patterns. *(p. 450)*

Health psychologists Psychologists who study the effects of behavior and mental processes on health and illness, and vice versa. *(p. 18)*

Health psychology A field in which psychologists conduct and apply research aimed at promoting human health and preventing illness. *(p. 429)*

Height in the visual field A depth cue whereby more distant objects are higher in the visual field than those nearby. *(p. 135)*

Helping behavior Any act that is intended to benefit another person. *(p. 614)*

Heterosexual Sexual motivation that is focused on members of the opposite sex. *(p. 353)*

Heuristic A mental shortcut or rule of thumb. (See also *anchoring heuristic, availability heuristic,* and *representativeness heuristic*.) *(p. 274)*

Hindbrain An extension of the spinal cord contained inside the skull. Nuclei in the hindbrain, especially in the medulla, control blood pressure, heart rate, breathing, and other vital functions. *(p. 59)*

Hippocampus A structure in the forebrain associated with the formation of new memories. *(p. 63)*

Homeostasis The tendency for organisms to keep their physiological systems at a stable, steady level by constantly adjusting themselves in response to change. *(p. 340)*

Homosexual Sexual motivation that is focused on members of a person's own sex. *(p. 353)*

Hormone A chemical that is secreted by a gland into the bloodstream, which carries it throughout the body, enabling the gland to stimulate remote cells with which it has no direct connection. *(p. 80)*

Hue The essential color determined by the dominant wavelength of a light. Black, white, and gray are not considered hues because they have no predominant wavelength. *(p. 102)*

Humanistic approach An approach to psychology that views behavior as controlled by the decisions that people make about their lives based on their perceptions of the world. (See *phenomenological approach*.) *(p. 14)*

Hunger The general state of wanting to eat. *(p. 343)*

Hypnosis An altered state of consciousness brought on by special induction techniques and characterized by varying degrees of responsiveness to suggestions for changes in experience and behavior. *(pp. 28, 177)*

Hypnotic susceptibility The degree to which people respond to hypnotic suggestions. *(p. 177)*

Hypochondriasis A strong, unjustified fear of physical illness. *(p. 507)*

Hypothalamus A structure in the forebrain that regulates hunger, thirst, and sex drives; it has many connections to and from the autonomic nervous system and to other parts of the brain. *(p. 62)*

Hypothesis   In scientific research, a prediction stated as a specific, testable proposition about a phenomenon. *(p. 28)*

Id   In psychodynamic theory, a personality component containing a reservoir of unconscious psychic energy (sometimes called *libido*) that includes the basic instincts, desires, and impulses with which all people are born. The id operates according to the pleasure principle, seeking immediate satisfaction, regardless of society's rules or the rights or feelings of others. (See also *pleasure principle*.) *(p. 460)*

Identity crisis   A phase during which an adolescent attempts to develop an integrated image of himself or herself as a unique person by pulling together self-knowledge acquired during childhood. *(p. 416)*

Images   Mental representations of visual information. *(p. 268)*

Immediate memory span   The maximum number of items a person can recall perfectly after one presentation of the items, usually six or seven items. (See also *chunk*.) *(p. 237)*

Immune system   The body's first line of defense against invading substances and microorganisms. The immune system includes T-cells, which attack virally infected cells; B-cells, which form antibodies against foreign substances; and natural killer cells, which kill invaders like tumor cells and virally infected cells. *(pp. 81, 445)*

Impaired functioning   A criterion for abnormality involving difficulty in fulfilling appropriate and expected social roles. *(p. 492)*

Implicit memory   The unintentional recollection and influence of prior experiences. *(p. 230)*

Incentive theory   A theory of motivation stating that behavior is goal directed; actions are directed toward attaining desirable stimuli, called positive incentives, and toward avoiding unwanted stimuli, called negative incentives. *(p. 342)*

Independent variable   The variable manipulated by the researcher in an experiment. *(p. 33)*

Industrial-organizational psychologists   Psychologists who study the influence of social factors on human performance in the workplace. *(p. 16)*

Inferential statistics   A set of procedures that provides a measure of how likely it is that research results came about by chance. These procedures put a precise mathematical value on the confidence or probability that rerunning the same experiment would yield similar (or even stronger) results. *(pp. 40, A-14)*

Information processing   The process of taking in, remembering or forgetting, and using information. It is one model for understanding people's cognitive abilities. *(p. 397)*

Information-processing approach   An approach to the study of intelligence that focuses on mental operations, such as attention and memory, that underlie intelligent behavior. *(pp. 322, 397)*

Information-processing model   A model of memory in which information must pass through sensory memory, short-term memory, and long-term memory in order to become firmly embedded in memory. *(p. 234)*

Information-processing system   The procedures for receiving information, representing information with symbols, and manipulating those representations so that the brain can interpret and respond to the information. *(pp. 234, 265)*

Inhibitory postsynaptic potential (IPSP)   A postsynaptic potential that hyperpolarizes the neuronal membrane, taking the cell farther from the threshold for firing an action potential. *(p. 54)*

Insight   In problem solving, a sudden understanding about what is required to produce a desired effect. *(p. 216)*

Insomnia   The most common sleeping problem, in which a person feels tired during the day because of trouble falling asleep or staying asleep at night. *(p. 172)*

Instinct   An innate, automatic disposition toward responding in a particular way when confronted with a specific stimulus; instincts produce behavior over which an animal has no control. *(p. 339)*

Instinct theory   A view that explains human behavior as motivated by automatic, involuntary, and unlearned responses. *(p. 339)*

Instrumental conditioning   A process through which responses are learned that help produce some rewarding or desired effect. *(p. 201)*

Intelligence   Those attributes that center around reasoning skills, knowledge of one's culture, and the ability to arrive at innovative solutions to problems. *(p. 304)*

Intelligence quotient   An index of intelligence once calculated by dividing one's tested mental age by one's chronological age and multiplying by 100. Today, IQ is a number that reflects the degree to which a person's score on an intelligence test deviates from the average score of others in his or her age group. *(p. 307)*

Interference   The process through which either the storage or the retrieval of information is impaired by the presence of other information. (See also *proactive interference* and *retroactive interference*.) *(p. 253)*

Intermittent reinforcement schedule   See *partial reinforcement schedule*.

Internal noise   The spontaneous, random firing of nerve cells that occurs because the nervous system is always active. Variations in internal noise can cause absolute thresholds to vary. *(p. 129)*

Interneurons   Cells in the retina through which photoreceptor cells make connections to other types of cells in the retina. *(p. 100)*

Interpersonal conflict   A process of social dispute in which one person believes that another stands in the way of something of value. *(p. 621)*

Interposition   A depth cue whereby closer objects block one's view of things farther away. *(p. 135)*

Ions   Molecules that carry a positive or negative electrical charge. *(p. 50)*

IQ score   See *intelligence quotient*.

IQ test   A test designed to measure intelligence on an objective, standardized scale. *(p. 305)*

Iris   The part of the eye that gives it its color and adjusts the amount of light entering it by constricting to reduce the size of the pupil or relaxing to enlarge it. *(p. 97)*

Jet lag   A syndrome of fatigue, irritability, inattention, and sleeping problems caused by air travel across several time zones. *(p. 174)*

JND   See *just-noticeable difference*.

Just-noticeable difference (JND) (also called *difference threshold*)   The smallest detectable difference in stimulus energy. (See also *Weber's law*.) *(p. 131)*

Kinesthesia   The sense that tells you where the parts of your body are with respect to one another. *(p. 121)*

Language   Symbols and a set of rules for combining them that provides a vehicle for the mind's communication with itself and the most important means of communicating with others. *(p. 288)*

Latency period   The fourth of Freud's psychosexual stages, usually beginning during the fifth year of life, in which sexual impulses lie dormant and the child focuses attention on education and other matters. *(p. 462)*

Latent learning   Learning that is not demonstrated at the time it occurs. *(p. 214)*

Lateral geniculate nucleus (LGN)   A region of the thalamus in which the axons from most of the ganglion cells in the retina finally end and form synapses. *(p. 107)*

Lateral inhibition   The enhancement of the sensation of contrast that occurs when greater response to light in one photoreceptor cell suppresses the response of a neighboring cell. *(p. 100)*

Lateralization   The tendency for one cerebral hemisphere to excel at a particular function or skill compared to the other hemisphere. *(p. 71)*

Law of effect   A law stating that if a response made in the presence of a particular stimulus is followed by a reward, that same response is more likely to be made the next time the stimulus is encountered. Responses that are not rewarded are less likely to be performed again. *(p. 201)*

Learned helplessness   A phenomenon that occurs when an organism has or believes that it has no control over its environment. The typical result of this situation or belief is to stop trying to exert control. *(p. 212)*

Learning   The modification through experience of pre-existing behavior and understanding. *(p. 191)*

Lens The part of the eye directly behind the pupil. Like the lens in a camera, the lens of the eye is curved so that it bends light rays, focusing them on the retina, at the back of the eye. *(p. 97)*

Levels-of-processing model A view stating that differences in how well something is remembered reflect the degree or depth to which incoming information is mentally processed. How long the information stays in memory depends on how elaborate the mental processing and encoding becomes. *(p. 232)*

LGN See *lateral geniculate nucleus.*

Libido See *id.*

Light and shadow A feature of visual stimuli that contributes to depth perception. *(p. 136)*

Light intensity A physical dimension of light waves that refers to how much energy the light contains; it determines the brightness of light. (See also *light wavelength.*) *(p. 97)*

Light wavelength A physical dimension of light waves that refers to their length. At a given intensity, different light wavelengths produce sensations of different colors. (See also *light intensity.*) *(p. 97)*

Limbic system A set of brain structures that play important roles in regulating emotion and memory. The limbic system is a system because its components have major interconnections and influence related functions. *(p. 63)*

Linear perspective A depth cue whereby the closer together two converging lines are, the greater the perceived distance. *(p. 136)*

Locus coeruleus A small nucleus in the brainstem that contains most of the cell bodies of neurons that use norepinephrine in the brain. *(p. 60)*

Logic The mental procedures that yield a valid conclusion during the reasoning process. (See also *reasoning.*) *(p. 272)*

Logical reasoning See *formal reasoning.*

Long-term memory The stage of memory in which semantic encoding dominates, and for which the capacity to store new information is believed to be unlimited. *(p. 239)*

Looming A motion cue involving a rapid expansion in the size of an image so that it fills the available space on the retina. People tend to perceive a looming object as an approaching stimulus, not as an expanding object viewed at a constant distance. *(p. 138)*

Loudness A psychological dimension of sound determined by the amplitude of a sound wave; waves with greater amplitude produce sensations of louder sounds. Loudness is described in units called decibels. *(p. 92)*

Lucid dreaming The awareness that a dream is a dream while it is happening. This phenomenon is evidence that sleep does not involve a total loss of consciousness or mental functioning. *(p. 176)*

Magnetic resonance imaging (MRI) A highly advanced technique that detects naturally occurring magnetic fields surrounding atoms in brain tissue to create exceptionally clear pictures of the structures of the brain. *(p. 61)*

Maintenance rehearsal Repeating information over and over to keep it active in short-term memory. This method is ineffective for encoding information into long-term memory. (See also *elaborative rehearsal.*) *(p. 232)*

Major depressive disorder A condition in which a person feels sad and hopeless for weeks or months, often losing interest in all activities and taking pleasure in nothing. Weight loss and lack of sleep or, in some cases, overeating and excessive sleeping are frequent accompaniments, as are problems in concentrating, making decisions, and thinking clearly. *(p. 510)*

Mania An elated, very active emotional state. *(p. 512)*

Matching hypothesis A hypothesis that people are most likely to be attracted to others who are similar to themselves in physical attractiveness. *(p. 590)*

Maturation Natural growth or change, triggered by biological factors, that unfolds in a fixed sequence relatively independent of the environment. *(p. 383)*

Mean A measure of central tendency that is the arithmetic average of the scores in a set of data; the sum of the values of all the scores divided by the total number of scores. *(p. 39)*

Median A measure of central tendency that is the halfway point in a set of data: Half the scores fall above the median, half fall below it. *(p. 38)*

Medical model An approach that views mental disorder as caused by physical illness or an imbalance in bodily processes. (See also *neurobiological model.*) *(p. 493)*

Meditation A set of techniques designed to create an altered state of consciousness characterized by inner peace, calmness, and tranquility. *(p. 179)*

Medulla An area in the hindbrain that controls blood pressure, heart rate, breathing, and other vital functions through the use of reflexes and feedback systems. *(p. 59)*

Mental ability A capacity to perform the higher mental processes of reasoning, remembering, understanding, problem solving, and decision making. *(p. 304)*

Mental chronometry The timing of mental events that allows researchers to infer what stages exist during cognition. (See also *evoked potential* and *information-processing system.*) *(p. 266)*

Mental model A cluster of propositions that represents people's understanding of how things work and guides their interaction with those things. *(p. 270)*

Mental set The tendency for old patterns of problem solving to persist, even when they might not be the most efficient method for solving a given problem. *(p. 279)*

Metacognition The knowledge of what strategies to apply, when to apply them, and how to deploy them in new situations so that new specific knowledge can be gained and different problems mastered. *(p. 330)*

Method of savings A method for measuring forgetting by computing the difference between the number of repetitions needed to learn, say, a list of words and the number of repetitions needed to relearn it after some time has elapsed. *(p. 257)*

Midbrain A small structure that lies between the hindbrain and the forebrain. The midbrain relays information from the eyes, ears, and skin, and controls certain types of automatic behaviors in response to information received through those structures. *(p. 62)*

Midlife transition A point at around age forty when adults take stock of their lives, reappraise their priorities, and, sometimes, modify their lives and relationships. *(p. 423)*

Mnemonics Strategies for placing information in an organized context in order to remember it. Two powerful methods are the peg-word system and the method of loci. *(p. 259)*

Mode A measure of central tendency that is the value or score that occurs most frequently in a data set. *(p. 38)*

Modeling A method of therapy in which desirable behaviors are demonstrated as a way of teaching them to clients. *(p. 542)*

Mood disorder (also called *affective disorder*) A condition in which a person experiences extremes of mood for long periods, shifts from one mood extreme to another, and experiences moods that are inconsistent with the happy or sad events around them. *(p. 510)*

Morpheme The smallest unit of language that has meaning. (See also *phoneme.*) *(p. 288)*

Motivation The influences that account for the initiation, direction, intensity, and persistence of behavior. *(p. 337)*

Motive A reason or purpose for behavior. *(p. 337)*

Motor cortex The part of the cerebral cortex whose neurons control voluntary movements in specific parts of the body. Some neurons control movement of the hand; others stimulate movement of the foot, the knee, the head, and so on. *(p. 66)*

Motor systems The parts of the nervous system that influence muscles and other organs to respond to the environment in some way. *(p. 56)*

Movement gradient The graduated difference in the apparent movement of objects across the visual field. Faster relative movement across the visual field indicates closer distance. *(p. 136)*

Multiple personality disorder   See *dissociative identity disorder.*

Myelin   A fatty substance that wraps around some axons and increases the speed of action potentials. *(p. 51)*

Narcissistic personality disorder   A personality disorder characterized by an exaggerated sense of self-importance combined with self-doubt. *(p. 521)*

Narcolepsy   A daytime sleep disorder in which a person switches abruptly and without warning from an active, often emotional waking state into several minutes of REM sleep. In most cases the muscle paralysis associated with REM causes the person to collapse on the spot and to remain briefly immobilized even after awakening. *(p. 173)*

Natural concept   Concepts that have no fixed set of defining features but instead share a set of characteristic features. Members of a natural concept need not possess all of the characteristic features. *(p. 269)*

Naturalistic observation   The process of watching without interfering as a phenomenon occurs in the natural environment. *(p. 31)*

Need   In drive reduction theory, a biological requirement for well-being that is created by an imbalance in homeostasis. (See also *drive, primary drive,* and *secondary drive.*) *(p. 340)*

Need achievement   A motive influenced by the degree to which a person establishes specific goals, cares about meeting those goals, and experiences feelings of satisfaction by doing so; it is often measured by the Thematic Apperception Test. *(p. 357)*

Negative feedback system   An arrangement in which the output of a system is monitored, such that output above a certain level will terminate further output until activity returns to an acceptable level. *(p. 81)*

Negative reinforcer   An unpleasant stimulus, such as pain. The removal of a negative reinforcer following some response is likely to strengthen the probability of that response recurring. The process of strengthening behavior by following it with the removal of a negative reinforcer is called negative reinforcement. (See also *positive reinforcer.*) *(p. 202)*

Nervous system   A complex combination of cells whose primary function is to allow an organism to gain information about what is going on inside and outside the body and to respond appropriately. *(p. 48)*

Neurobiological model   A more contemporary name for the medical model of psychological disorder, which reflects a focus on disturbances in the anatomy and chemistry of the brain and other biological processes. *(p. 494)*

Neuroleptic   See *antipsychotic.*

Neuromodulators   Neurotransmitters that in some circumstances modify the response to other neurotransmitters at a synapse. *(p. 77)*

Neuron   The fundamental unit of the nervous system; a nerve cell. Neurons have the ability to communicate with one another. *(p. 49)*

Neurotransmitter   A chemical that assists in the transfer of signals from the axon of one neuron (presynaptic cell) across the synapse to the receptors on the dendrite of another neuron (postsynaptic cell). *(p. 52)*

Neurotransmitter system   A group of neurons that communicates by using the same neurotransmitter, such as acetylcholine or dopamine. *(p. 76)*

Nightmare   A frightening, sometimes recurring dream that takes place during REM sleep. *(p. 173)*

Night terrors   A rapid awakening from stage 4 sleep, often accompanied by a horrific dream that causes the dreamer to sit up staring, let out a bloodcurdling scream, and experience a state of intense fear that may last up to thirty minutes. This phenomenon is especially common in children, but milder versions occur among adults. *(p. 173)*

Nonconscious level   A segment of mental activity devoted to those processes that are totally inaccessible to conscious awareness, such as blood flowing through veins and arteries, the removal of impurities from the blood, and the measuring of blood sugar by the hypothalamus. *(p. 166)*

Noradrenaline   See *norepinephrine.*

Norepinephrine   (also called *noradrenaline*) A neurotransmitter involved in arousal, as well as in learning and mood regulation. *(p. 77)*

Norm   (1) A description of the frequency at which a particular score occurs, which allows scores to be compared statistically. *(p. 308)* (2) A learned, socially based rule that prescribes what people should or should not do in various situations. *(p. 596)*

Normal distribution   A dispersion of scores such that the mean, median, and mode all have the same value. When a distribution has this property, the standard deviation can be used to describe how any particular score stands in relation to the rest of the distribution. *(p. A-11)*

Nuclei   Collections of nerve cell bodies in the central nervous system. *(p. 58)*

Null hypothesis   The assertion that the independent variable manipulated by the experimenter will have no effect on the dependent variable measured by the experimenter. *(p. A-9)*

Obedience   A form of compliance in which people comply with a demand, rather than with a request, because they think they must or should do so; obedience can be thought of as submissive compliance. (See also *compliance.*) *(p. 603)*

Obesity   A condition in which a person is severely overweight, often by as much as one hundred pounds. *(p. 347)*

Objective test   A paper-and-pencil form containing clear, specific questions, statements, or concepts to which the respondent is asked to give yes-no, true-false, or multiple-choice answers. *(p. 482)*

Object permanence   The knowledge, resulting from an ability to form mental representations of objects, that objects exist even when they are not in view. *(p. 391)*

Observational learning   Learning how to perform new behaviors by watching the behavior of others. *(p. 216)*

Obsessive-compulsive disorder   An anxiety disorder in which a person becomes obsessed with certain thoughts or images or feels a compulsion to do certain things. If the person tries to interrupt obsessive thinking or compulsions, severe agitation and anxiety usually result. *(p. 503)*

Oedipus complex   According to psychodynamic theory, during the phallic stage a boy's id impulses involve sexual desire for the mother and the desire to eliminate, even kill, the father, who is competition for the mother's affection. The hostile impulses create a fear of retaliation so strong that the ego represses the incestuous desires. Then the boy identifies with the father and begins to learn male sex-role behaviors. (See also *phallic stage.*) *(p. 461)*

Olfaction   The sense that detects chemicals that are airborne, or volatile; the sense of smell. *(p. 112)*

Olfactory bulb   The brain structure that receives messages regarding olfaction, or the sense of smell. *(p. 113)*

One-word stage   A stage of language development during which children build their vocabularies one word at a time, tend to use one word at a time, and tend to overextend the use of a single word. *(p. 293)*

Operant   A response that has some effect on the world; it is a response that operates on the environment in some way. (See also *operant conditioning.*) *(p. 202)*

Operant conditioning   A virtual synonym for instrumental conditioning; a process studied by B. F. Skinner in which an organism learns to respond to the environment in a way that helps produce some desired effect. Skinner's primary aim was to analyze how behavior is changed by its consequences. *(p. 201)*

Operational definitions   Statements that define variables describing the exact operations or methods used in research. *(p. 29)*

Opiates   Psychoactive drugs, such as opium, morphine, or heroin, that have the ability to produce both sleep-inducing and pain-relieving effects. *(p. 186)*

Opponent-process theory   (1) A theory of color vision stating that the visual elements sensitive to color are grouped into three pairs: a red-green element, a blue-yellow element, and a black-white element. Each element signals one color or the other—red or green, for example—but never both. *(p. 104)*

Optic chiasm   Part of the bottom surface of the brain where half of the optic nerve fibers cross over to the opposite side of the brain; beyond the chiasm the fibers ascend into the brain itself. *(p. 107)*

Optic nerve   A bundle of fibers composed of axons from ganglion cells that carries visual information to the brain. *(p. 106)*

Oral stage The first of Freud's psychosexual stages, occurring during the first year of life, in which the mouth is the center of pleasure. *(p. 461)*

Otolith A small crystal in the fluid-filled vestibular sacs of the inner ear that, when shifted by gravity, stimulates nerve cells that inform the brain of the position of the head relative to the earth. *(p. 122)*

Pain disorder A somatoform disorder marked by complaints of severe, often constant, pain with no physical cause. *(p. 507)*

Panic disorder Anxiety in the form of terrifying panic attacks that come without warning or obvious cause. These attacks last for a few minutes and are marked by heart palpitations, pressure or pain in the chest, dizziness or unsteadiness, sweating, and faintness. They may be accompanied by feeling detached from one's body or feeling that people and events are not real. The person may think he or she is about to die or go crazy. *(p. 503)*

Papillae Structures that contain groups of taste receptors; the taste buds. *(p. 113)*

Parallel distributed processing (PDP) models An approach to understanding object recognition in which various elements of the object are thought to be simultaneously analyzed by a number of widely distributed but connected neural units in the brain. When applied to memory, these models suggest that new experiences don't just provide new facts that are later retrieved individually; they also change people's overall knowledge base, altering in a more general way their understanding of the world and how it operates. *(pp. 148, 233)*

Paranoid schizophrenia A type of schizophrenia characterized by delusions of persecution or grandeur accompanied by anxiety, anger, superiority, argumentativeness, or jealousy; these feelings sometimes lead to violence. *(p. 517)*

Parasympathetic system The subsystem of the autonomic nervous system that typically influences activity related to the protection, nourishment, and growth of the body. (See also *autonomic nervous system.*) *(p. 367)*

Partial reinforcement extinction effect A phenomenon in which behaviors learned under a partial reinforcement schedule are far more difficult to extinguish than those learned on a continuous reinforcement schedule. Individuals on a partial reinforcement schedule usually are not immediately aware that their behavior is no longer being reinforced; they are used to not being rewarded for every response. However, individuals on a continuous reinforcement schedule are accustomed to being reinforced for each response and are more sensitive to the lack of reward. *(p. 208)*

Partial reinforcement schedule (also called *intermittent reinforcement schedule*) In operant conditioning, a pattern of reinforcement in which a reinforcer is administered only some of the time after a particular response occurs. (See also *fixed interval schedule, fixed ratio schedule, variable interval schedule,* and *variable ratio schedule.*) *(p. 206)*

Pathway See *fiber tract.*

Percentile score The percentage of people or observations that fall below a given score in a normal distribution. *(p. A-11)*

Perception The process through which people take raw sensations from the environment and interpret them, using knowledge, experience, and understanding of the world, so that the sensations become meaningful experiences. *(p. 126)*

Perceptual constancy The perception of objects as constant in size, shape, color, and other properties despite changes in their retinal image. *(p. 139)*

Performance scale Five subtests in the Wechsler scales that include tasks that require spatial ability and the ability to manipulate materials; these subtests provide a performance IQ. (See also *verbal scale.*) *(p. 306)*

Peripheral nervous system All of the nervous system that is not housed in bone. It has two main subsystems: the somatic nervous system and the autonomic nervous system. *(p. 56)*

Permissive parent A parent who gives his or her child complete freedom and whose discipline is lax. Children of this type of parent are often immature, dependent, and unhappy, lack self-reliance and self-control, and seek parental help for even the slightest problems. *(p. 410)*

Personality The pattern of psychological and behavioral characteristics by which each person can be compared and contrasted with other people; the unique pattern of characteristics that emerges from the blending of inherited and acquired tendencies to make each person an identifiable individual. *(p. 458)*

Personality disorder Long-standing, inflexible ways of behaving that are not so much severe mental disorders as styles of life, which, from childhood or adolescence, create problems, usually for others. *(p. 520)*

Personality psychologist A psychologist who focuses on the unique characteristics that determine individuals' behavior. *(p. 16)*

Person-centered therapy See *client-centered therapy.*

Person-oriented leaders Leaders who provide loose supervision, ask for group members' ideas, and are generally concerned with subordinates' feelings; they are usually well liked by those they lead. *(p. 623)*

Phallic stage The third of Freud's psychosexual stages, lasting from approximately ages three to five, in which the focus of pleasure shifts to the genital area; the Oedipus complex occurs during this stage. (See also *Oedipus complex.*) *(p. 461)*

Phenomenological approach (also called *phenomenological model*) A view of personality based on the assumption that each personality is created out of each person's unique way of perceiving and interpreting the world. Proponents of this view believe that one's personal perception of reality shapes and controls behavior from moment to moment. *(p. 475)*

Phenotype How an individual looks and acts, which depends on how a person's inherited characteristics interact with the environment. *(p. A-2)*

Pheromones Chemicals that are released by one animal and detected by another, and then shape that second animal's behavior or physiology. Often, though not always, the pheromone is detected by the olfactory system. *(p. 113)*

Phobia An anxiety disorder that involves a strong, irrational fear of an object or situation that does not objectively justify such a reaction. The phobic individual usually realizes that the fear makes no sense but cannot keep it from interfering with daily life. *(p. 501)*

Phoneme The smallest unit of sound that affects the meaning of speech. (See also *morpheme.*) *(p. 288)*

Photopigment A chemical contained in photoreceptors that responds to light and assists in changing light into neural activity. *(p. 98)*

Photoreceptor A nerve cell in the retina that codes light energy into neural activity. (See also *rods* and *cones.*) *(p. 98)*

Physical dependence See *addiction.*

Physiological psychologist See *biological psychologist.*

Physiological psychology See *biological psychology.*

Pinna The crumpled, oddly shaped part of the outer ear that collects sound waves. *(p. 92)*

Pitch How high or low a tone sounds; the psychological dimension determined by the frequency of sound waves. High-frequency waves are sensed as sounds of high pitch. *(p. 92)*

Placebo A physical or psychological treatment that contains no active ingredient but produces an effect because the person receiving it believes it will. In an experiment, the placebo effect (a confounding variable) occurs when the subject responds to the belief that the independent variable will have an effect, rather than to the actual effect of the independent variable. *(p. 34)*

Place theory (also called *traveling wave theory*) A theory of hearing stating that hair cells at a particular place on the basilar membrane respond most to a particular frequency of sound. High-frequency sounds produce a wave that peaks soon after it starts down the basilar membrane. Lower-frequency sounds produce a wave that peaks farther along the basilar membrane. *(p. 94)*

Pleasure principle In psychodynamic theory, the operating principle of the id, which guides people toward whatever feels good. (See also *id.*) *(p. 460)*

Polygenic   Describing characteristics that are determined by more than one gene or pair of genes. *(p. A-2)*

Positive reinforcement   See *positive reinforcer.*

Positive reinforcer   A stimulus that strengthens a response if it follows that response. It is roughly equivalent to a reward. Presenting a positive reinforcer after a response is called positive reinforcement. (See also *negative reinforcer.*) *(pp. 202, 542)*

Positron emission tomography (PET scanning)   A technique that detects and creates a visual image of activity in various parts of the brain. *(p. 61)*

Postconventional moral reasoning   Reasoning that reflects moral judgments based on personal standards or universal principles of justice, equality, and respect for human life. *(p. 418)*

Posthypnotic amnesia   The inability of hypnotic subjects to recall what happened during hypnosis. For some, recall fails even when they are told what went on. *(p. 177)*

Posthypnotic suggestion   Instructions about experiences or behavior to take place after hypnosis has been terminated. *(p. 177)*

Postsynaptic potential   The change in the membrane potential of a neuron that has received stimulation from another neuron. *(p. 53)*

Posttraumatic stress disorder (PTSD)   A pattern of adverse and disruptive reactions following a traumatic event. One of its most common features is re-experiencing the original trauma through nightmares or vivid memories. *(p. 438)*

Preconscious level   A segment of mental activity devoted to sensations and everything else that is not currently conscious, but of which people can easily become conscious at will. The amount of material at this level far surpasses what is present at the conscious level at any given moment. (See also *conscious level, nonconscious level, subconscious level,* and *unconscious level.*) *(p. 167)*

Preconventional moral reasoning   Reasoning that is not based on the conventions or rules that guide social interactions in society. *(p. 417)*

Prefrontal lobotomy   A form of psychosurgery in which a sharp instrument is inserted into the brain and used to destroy brain tissue. *(p. 558)*

Prejudice   A positive or negative attitude toward an entire group of people. (See also *discrimination.*) *(p. 584)*

Preoperational period   According to Piaget, the second stage of cognitive development, during which children begin to understand, create, and use symbols to represent things that are not present. *(p. 395)*

Primacy effect   A characteristic of recall in which recall for the first two or three items in a list is particularly good. (See also *recency effect.*) *(p. 241)*

Primary cortex   The area of cerebral cortex that is first to receive information about a particular sense, such as vision or hearing. See also *primary auditory cortex* and *primary visual cortex.*) *(p. 90)*

Primary auditory cortex   The area in the temporal lobe of the cerebral cortex that is first to receive information about sounds. It is connected to areas of the brain involved in language perception and production. *(p. 95)*

Primary drive   A drive that arises from basic biological needs. (See also *drive, need,* and *secondary drive.*) *(p. 340)*

Primary reinforcer   Something that meets an organism's most basic needs, such as food, water, air, and moderate temperatures. A primary reinforcer does not depend on learning to exert its influence. (See also *secondary reinforcer.*) *(p. 205)*

Primary visual cortex   An area in the occipital lobe, at the back of the brain, to which neurons in the lateral geniculate nucleus relay visual input. *(p. 107)*

Prisoner's dilemma game   A research situation in which mutual cooperation guarantees the best mutual outcome; mixed cooperative and competitive responses by each person guarantee a favorable outcome for one person and an unfavorable outcome for the other; and mutual competition guarantees the worst mutual outcome. *(p. 620)*

Proactive interference   A cause of forgetting in which previously learned information, now residing in long-term memory, interferes with the ability to remember new information. (See also *retroactive interference.*) *(p. 253)*

Procedural memory (also called *skill memory*)   A type of memory that contains information about how to do things. *(p. 230)*

Progestins   Feminine hormones that circulate in the bloodstream of both men and women; relatively more progestins circulate in women. One of the main progestins is progesterone. (See also *estrogens.*) *(p. 351)*

Progressive relaxation training   A procedure for learning to relax that involves tensing a group of muscles for a few seconds, then releasing that tension and focusing attention on the resulting feelings of relaxation; the procedure is repeated at least once for each of sixteen muscle groups throughout the body. Progressive relaxation training is a popular physiological method for coping with stress and an important part of systematic desensitization, a method for treating phobias. *(p. 454)*

Projective test   Personality tests made up of relatively unstructured stimuli, such as inkblots, which can be perceived and responded to in many ways; particular responses are seen as reflecting the individual's needs, fantasies, conflicts, thought patterns, and other aspects of personality. *(p. 484)*

Proposition   The smallest unit of knowledge that can stand as a separate assertion, may be true or false, and may represent a relationship between a concept and a property of that concept or between two or more concepts. *(p. 270)*

Proprioceptive   The sensory systems that allow us to know about where we are and what each part of our body is doing. (See also *kinesthesia* and *vestibular sense.*) *(p. 121)*

Prototype   A member of a natural concept that possesses all or most of its characteristic features. *(p. 270)*

Proximity   A Gestalt grouping principle stating that the closer objects are to one another, the more likely they are to be perceived as belonging together. *(p. 134)*

Psychedelic   Psychoactive drugs, such as LSD, PCP, and marijuana, that alter consciousness by producing a temporary loss of contact with reality and changes in emotion, perception, and thought. *(p. 186)*

Psychiatrist   A medical doctor who has completed special training in the treatment of mental disorders. Psychiatrists can prescribe drugs. *(p. 533)*

Psychoactive drug   A chemical substance that acts on the brain to create some psychological effect. *(p. 180)*

Psychoanalysis   A method of psychotherapy that seeks to help clients gain insight by recognizing, understanding, and dealing with unconscious thoughts and emotions presumed to cause their problems and work through the many ways in which those unconscious causes appear in everyday behavior and social relationships. *(p. 534)*

Psychodynamic approach (also called *psychodynamic model*)   A view developed by Freud that emphasizes the interplay of unconscious mental processes in determining human thought, feelings, and behavior. *(p. 13)*

Psychological dependence   A condition in which a person continues drug use despite adverse effects, needs the drug for a sense of well-being, and becomes preoccupied with obtaining the drug if it becomes unavailable. *(p. 181)*

Psychological model   An approach that views mental disorder as arising from inner turmoil or other psychological processes. *(p. 494)*

Psychologist   In the realm of treatment, a therapist whose education includes completion of a master's or doctoral degree in clinical or counseling psychology, often followed by additional specialized training. Unlike psychiatrists, psychologists are not authorized to prescribe drugs. *(p. 533)*

Psychology   The science of behavior and mental processes. *(p. 3)*

Psychometric approach   A way of studying intelligence that emphasizes the analysis of the products of intelligence, especially scores on intelligence tests. *(p. 321)*

Psychoneuroimmunology The field that examines the interaction of psychological and physiological processes that affect the ability of the body to defend itself against disease. *(p. 445)*

Psychopathology Patterns of thinking and behaving that are maladaptive, disruptive, or uncomfortable for the person affected or for those with whom he or she comes in contact. *(p. 490)*

Psychopharmacology The study of psychoactive drugs and their effects. *(p. 180)*

Psychophysics An area of research that focuses on the relationship between the physical characteristics of environmental stimuli and the conscious psychological experience those stimuli produce. Psychophysical researchers seek to understand how people make contact with and become conscious of the world. *(p. 128)*

Psychosexual stage In psychodynamic theory, a period of personality development in which internal and external conflicts focus on particular issues. There are five stages during which pleasure is derived from different areas of the body. (See also *anal stage, genital stage, latency period, oral stage,* and *phallic stage.*) *(p. 461)*

Psychosurgery Procedures that destroy various regions of the brain in an effort to alleviate psychological disorders; this surgery is done infrequently and only as a last resort. *(p. 558)*

Psychotherapy The treatment of psychological disorders through psychological methods, such as analyzing problems, talking about possible solutions, and encouraging more adaptive ways of thinking and acting. *(p. 532)*

PTSD See *posttraumatic stress disorder.*

Puberty The condition of being able for the first time to reproduce; it occurs during adolescence and is characterized by fuller breasts and rounder curves in females and by broad shoulders and narrow hips in males. Facial, underarm, and pubic hair grows. Voices deepen, and acne may appear. *(p. 414)*

Punishment The presentation of an aversive stimulus or the removal of a pleasant stimulus; punishment decreases the frequency of the immediately preceding response. *(pp. 209, 544)*

Pupil An opening in the eye, just behind the cornea, through which light passes. (The pupil appears black because there is no light source inside the eyeball and very little light is reflected out of the eye.) *(p. 97)*

Quantitative psychologists Psychologists who develop statistical methods for evaluating and analyzing data from psychological research. *(p. 17)*

Quasi-experiments Research studies whose designs approximate the control of a true experiment (*quasi-* means resembling) but may not include manipulation of the independent variable, random assignment of subjects to groups, or other elements of experimental control. *(p. 35)*

Quiet sleep (also called *slow-wave sleep*) Sleep stages 1 through 4, which are accompanied by slow, deep breathing; a calm, regular heartbeat; and reduced blood pressure. *(p. 170)*

Random assignment The procedure by which random variables are evenly distributed in an experiment—specifically, through placement of subjects in experimental and control groups by means of a coin flip or some other random process. *(p. 34)*

Random sample A group of research subjects selected from a population each of whose members had an equal chance of being chosen for study. *(p. 36)*

Random variable In an experiment, a confounding variable in which an uncontrolled or uncontrollable factor affects the dependent variable along with or instead of the independent variable. Random variables can include factors such as differences in the subjects' backgrounds, personalities, and physical health, as well as differences in experimental conditions. *(p. 34)*

Range A measure of variability that is the difference between the highest and the lowest value in the data set. *(p. 39)*

Rational-emotive therapy (RET) A treatment that involves identifying self-defeating, problem-causing thoughts that clients have learned and using modeling, encouragement, and logic to help the client replace these maladaptive thought patterns with more realistic and beneficial ones. *(p. 545)*

Reaction time The elapsed time between the presentation of a stimulus and an overt response to it. *(p. 266)*

Reality principle According to psychodynamic theory, the operating principle of the ego that involves, for example, compromises between the unreasoning demands of the id to do whatever feels good and the demands of the real world to do what is acceptable. (See also *ego.*) *(p. 460)*

Reasoning The process by which people evaluate and generate arguments and reach conclusions. (See also *logic.*) *(p. 271)*

Recency effect A characteristic of recall in which recall is particularly good for the last few items on a list. (See also *primacy effect.*) *(p. 241)*

Receptive field The portion of the world that affects a given neuron. For example, in the auditory system, one neuron might respond only to sounds of a particular pitch; that pitch is its receptive field. *(p. 101)*

Receptor (1) A site on the surface of the postsynaptic cell that allows only one type of neurotransmitter to fit into it and thus trigger the chemical response that may lead to an action potential. *(p. 88)* (2) A cell that is specialized to detect certain types of energy and convert it into neural activity. This conversion process is called transduction. *(p. 88)*

Reconditioning The relearning of a conditioned response following extinction. Because reconditioning takes much less time than the original conditioning, some change in the organism must persist even after extinction. *(p. 194)*

Reduced clarity A depth cue whereby an object whose retinal image is unclear is perceived as being farther away. *(p. 136)*

Reference group A category of people to which people compare themselves. *(p. 570)*

Reflection Restating or paraphrasing what the client has said, which shows that the therapist is actively listening and helps make the client aware of the thoughts and feelings he or she is experiencing. *(p. 539)*

Reflexes Involuntary, unlearned reactions in the form of swift, automatic, and finely coordinated movements in response to external stimuli. Reflexes are organized completely within the spinal cord. *(pp. 58, 388)*

Refractory period A short rest period between action potentials; it is so short that a neuron can send action potentials down its axon at rates of up to one thousand per second. *(p. 51)*

Reinforcer A stimulus event that increases the probability that the response that immediately preceded it will occur again. (See also *positive reinforcer* and *negative reinforcer.*) *(p. 202)*

Relative deprivation The sense that a person is not doing as well as others in the same reference group. *(p. 570)*

Relative size A depth cue whereby larger objects are perceived as closer than smaller ones. *(p. 135)*

Reliability The degree to which a test can be repeated with the same results. Tests with high reliability yield scores that are less susceptible to insignificant or random changes in the test taker or the testing environment. *(p. 308)*

REM behavior disorder A sleep disorder in which a person fails to show the decreased muscle tone normally seen in REM sleep, thus allowing the sleeper to act out dreams, sometimes with dangerous results. *(p. 173)*

REM sleep See *active sleep.*

Representativeness heuristic A shortcut in the thought process that involves judging the probability that a hypothesis is true or that an example belongs to a certain class of items by first focusing on the similarities between the example and a larger class of events or items and then determining whether the particular example represents essential features of the larger class. *(p. 275)*

Residual schizophrenia The designation for persons who have displayed symptoms of schizophrenia in the past, but not in the present. *(p. 517)*

Response criterion   The internal rule a person uses to decide whether or not to report a stimulus; it reflects the person's motivation and expectations. (p. 129)

RET   See *rational-emotive therapy.*

Reticular formation   A network of nuclei and fibers threaded throughout the hindbrain and midbrain. This network alters the activity of the rest of the brain. (p. 59)

Retina   The surface at the back of the eye onto which the lens focuses light rays. (p. 97)

Retrieval   The process of recalling information stored in memory and bringing it into consciousness. (p. 229)

Retrieval cues   Stimuli that allow people to recall things that were once forgotten and help them to recognize information stored in memory. (p. 243)

Retroactive interference   A cause of forgetting in which new information placed in memory interferes with the ability to recall information already in memory. (p. 253)

Retrograde amnesia   A loss of memory for events prior to some critical brain injury. Often, a person will be unable to remember anything that occurred in the months, or even years, before the injury. In most cases, the memories return gradually, but recovery is seldom complete. (See also *anterograde amnesia.*) (p. 242)

Rods   Photoreceptors in the retina that allow sight even in dim light because their photopigment contains rhodopsin, a light-sensitive chemical. Rods cannot discriminate colors. (See also *cones.*) (p. 99)

Role theory   A theory that states that hypnotized subjects act in accordance with a special social role, which demands compliance. According to this theory, the procedures for inducing hypnosis provide a socially acceptable reason to follow the hypnotist's suggestions. (See also *dissociation theory* and *state theory.*) (p. 178)

s   A group of special abilities, or intelligences, that Charles Spearman saw as accompanying general intelligence (*g*). (p. 321)

Sampling   The process of selecting subjects who are members of the population that the researcher wishes to study. (p. 36)

Satiety   The condition of no longer wanting to eat. (p. 343)

Saturation   The purity of a color. A color is more pure, more saturated, if a single wavelength is relatively more intense—contains more energy—than other wavelengths. (p. 102)

Schema   A basic unit of knowledge; a generalization based on experience of the world. Schemas organize past experience and provide a framework for understanding future experience; a coherent, organized set of beliefs and expectations that can influence the perception of others and objects. (pp. 147, 247, 270, 389)

Schizophrenia   A pattern of severely disturbed thinking, emotion, perception, and behavior that constitutes one of the most serious and disabling of all mental disorders. (p. 515)

Schizotypal personality disorder   A pattern of emotional and behavior disorder that is similar to, but significantly less intense than, schizophrenia. (p. 521)

School psychologists   Psychologists who test IQs, diagnose students' academic problems, and set up programs to improve students' achievement. (p. 17)

Script   A mental representation of a familiar sequence of activity, usually involving people's behavior. (p. 270)

SD   See *standard deviation.*

Secondary drive   A stimulus that acquires the motivational properties of a primary drive through classical conditioning or other learning mechanisms. (See also *drive, need,* and *primary drive.*) (p. 340)

Secondary reinforcer   A reward that people or animals learn to like. Secondary reinforcers gain their reinforcing properties through association with primary reinforcers. (p. 205)

Second-order conditioning   A phenomenon in learning when a conditioned stimulus acts like a UCS, creating conditioned stimuli out of events associated with it. (p. 196)

Selective attention   The focusing of mental resources on only part of the stimulus field. (p. 236)

Self-actualization   According to Rogers, an innate tendency toward growth that motivates all people to seek the full realization of their highest potential. (p. 476)

Self-concept   The way one thinks of oneself. (p. 570)

Self-efficacy   According to Bandura, learned expectations about the probability of success in given situations; a person's expectation of success in a given situation may be enough to create that success and even to blunt the impact of minor failures. (p. 473)

Self-esteem   The evaluations people make about how worthy they themselves are as human beings. (p. 570)

Self-fulfilling prophecy   An impression-formation process in which an initial impression elicits behavior in another that confirms the impression. (p. 574)

Self-perception theory   A theory that holds that when people are unsure of their attitude in a situation, they consider their behavior in light of the circumstances and then infer what their attitude must have been. (p. 583)

Self-schemas   Mental representations that people form of themselves. (p. 571)

Self-serving bias   The cognitive tendency to attribute one's successes to internal characteristics while blaming one's failures on external causes. (p. 578)

Semantic code   A mental representation of an experience by its general meaning. (p. 229)

Semantic memory   A type of memory containing generalized knowledge of the world that does not involve memory of specific events. (p. 230)

Semantics   In language, the rules that govern the meaning of words and sentences. (See also *syntax.*) (p. 289)

Semicircular canal   An arc-shaped tube in the inner ear containing fluid that, when shifted by head movements, stimulates nerve cells that provide information to the brain about the rate and direction of those movements. (p. 122)

Sensation   A message from a sense, which comprises the raw information that affects many kinds of behavior and mental processes. (p. 87)

Sense   A system that translates data from outside the nervous system into neural activity, giving the nervous system, especially the brain, information about the world. (p. 87)

Sensitivity   The ability to detect a stimulus; sensitivity is influenced by neural noise, the intensity of the stimulus, and the capacity of the sensory system. (p. 129)

Sensorimotor period   The first in Piaget's stages of cognitive development, when the infant's mental activity is confined to sensory perception and motor skills. (p. 390)

Sensory cortex   The part of the cerebral cortex located in the parietal, occipital, and temporal lobes that receives stimulus information from the skin, eyes, and ears, respectively. (p. 66)

Sensory memory   A type of memory that is very primitive and very brief, but lasts long enough to connect one impression to the next, so that people experience a smooth flow of information. (See also *sensory register.*) (p. 235)

Sensory register   A memory system that holds incoming information long enough for it to be processed further. (See also *sensory memory.*) (p. 235)

Sensory systems   The parts of the nervous system that provide information about the environment; the senses. (p. 56)

Serotonin   A neurotransmitter used by cells in those parts of the brain involved in the regulation of sleep, mood, and eating. (p. 78)

Sex hormones   Chemicals in the blood of males and females that have both organizational and motivational effects on sexual behavior. (p. 351)

Sexual dysfunction   Problems with sex that involve sexual motivation, arousal, or orgasmic response. (p. 356)

Sexual response cycle The pattern of arousal during and after sexual activity. *(p. 351)*

Shaping In operant conditioning, a procedure that involves reinforcing responses that come successively closer to the desired response. *(p. 205)*

Short-term memory (also called *working memory*) A stage of memory in which information can last less than half a minute unless rehearsed. *(p. 236)*

Signal-detection theory A formal mathematical model of what determines a person's report that a near-threshold stimulus has or has not occurred. *(p. 129)*

Similarity A Gestalt grouping principle stating that similar elements are perceived to be part of a group. *(p. 134)*

Simplicity A Gestalt grouping principle stating that people tend to group stimulus features in a way that provides the simplest interpretation of the world. *(p. 134)*

Sleep apnea A sleep disorder in which people briefly but repeatedly stop breathing during the night. *(p. 173)*

Sleepwalking A phenomenon that starts primarily in non-REM sleep, especially in stage 4, and involves walking while one is asleep. It is most common during childhood. In the morning sleepwalkers usually have no memory of their travels. *(p. 173)*

Slow-wave sleep See *quiet sleep.*

Social cognition Mental processes associated with people's perceptions of and reactions to other people. *(p. 569)*

Social comparison Using other people as a basis of comparison for evaluating oneself. *(p. 570)*

Social dilemma A situation in which the short-term decisions of individuals become irrational in combination and create long-term, clearly predictable damage for a group. *(p. 621)*

Social facilitation A phenomenon in which the mere presence of other people improves a person's performance on a given task. *(p. 598)*

Social identity The beliefs we hold about the groups to which we belong. Social identity is part of the self-concept. *(p. 571)*

Social impairment A reduction in human performance due to the presence of other people. *(p. 598)*

Socialization The process by which parents, teachers, and others teach children the skills and social norms necessary to be well-functioning members of society. *(p. 409)*

Social loafing Exerting less effort when performing a group task (in which one's contribution cannot be identified) than when performing the same task alone. *(p. 599)*

Social perception The processes through which people interpret information about others, draw inferences about them, and develop mental representations of them. *(p. 572)*

Social phobia A strong, irrational fear relating to social situations. Common examples include fear of being negatively evaluated by others or publicly embarrassed by doing something impulsive, outrageous, or humiliating. *(p. 502)*

Social psychologist A psychologist who studies how people influence one another's behavior and attitudes, especially in groups. *(p. 16)*

Social psychology The psychological subfield that explores the effects of the social world on the behavior and mental processes of individuals, pairs, and groups. *(p. 569)*

Social referencing A phenomenon in which other people's facial expressions, tone of voice, and bodily gestures serve as guidelines for how to proceed in uncertain situations. *(p. 377)*

Social support network The friends and social contacts on whom one can depend for help and support. *(p. 440)*

Sociocultural explanation An approach to explaining mental disorder that emphasizes the role of such social and cultural factors as gender and age, physical situation, cultural values and expectations, and historical era. *(p. 495)*

Somatic nervous system The subsystem of the peripheral nervous system that transmits information from the senses to the central nervous system and carries signals from the CNS to the muscles that move the skeleton. *(p. 56)*

Somatic sense (also called *somatosensory system*) A sense that is spread throughout the body, not located in a specific organ. Somatic senses include touch, temperature, pain (the skin senses), and kinesthesia. *(p. 115)*

Somatization disorder A somatoform disorder in which the person has numerous physical complaints without verifiable physical illness. *(p. 507)*

Somatoform disorder A psychological problem in which a person shows the symptoms of some physical (somatic) disorder, even though there is no physical cause. (See also *conversion disorder.*) *(p. 506)*

Somatosensory system See *somatic sense.*

Sound A repetitive fluctuation in the pressure of a medium like air. *(p. 90)*

Spatial codes In the sensory systems, coding attributes of a stimulus in terms of the location of firing neurons relative to their neighbors. *(p. 89)*

Specific nerve energies A doctrine that states that stimulation of a particular sensory nerve provides codes for that one sense, no matter how the stimulation takes place. *(p. 89)*

Specific phobias Phobias that involve fear and avoidance of heights, blood, animals, and other specific stimuli and situations. *(p. 501)*

Spinal cord The part of the central nervous system contained within the spinal column that receives signals from peripheral senses (such as touch and pain) and relays them to the brain. It also conveys messages from the brain to the rest of the body. *(p. 58)*

Spontaneous recovery The reappearance of the conditioned response after extinction and without further pairings of the conditioned and unconditioned stimuli. *(p. 194)*

Sport psychologists Psychologists who explore the relationships between athletic performance and such psychological variables as motivation and emotion. *(p. 18)*

Spreading activation A principle that, in semantic network theories of memory, explains how information is retrieved. *(p. 244)*

Standard deviation (SD) A measure of variability that is the average difference between each score and the mean of the data set. *(p. 39)*

Standard score A value that indicates the distance, in standard deviations, between a given score and the mean of all the scores in a data set. *(p. A-12)*

Stanford-Binet A test for determining a person's intelligence quotient, or IQ. *(p. 305)*

State-dependent memory Memories that are aided or impeded by a person's internal state. *(p. 243)*

State of consciousness The characteristics of consciousness at any particular moment—for example, what reaches awareness, what levels of mental activity are most prominent, and how efficiently a person is functioning. *(p. 169)*

State theory A theory that proposes that hypnosis does indeed create an altered state of consciousness. (See also *dissociation theory* and *role theory.*) *(p. 178)*

Statistically significant In statistical analysis, a term used to describe the results of an experiment when the outcome of a statistical test indicates that the probability of those results occurring by chance is small (less than 5 percent). *(p. 40)*

Stereotype An impression or schema of an entire group of people that involves the false assumption that all members of the group share the same characteristics. *(p. 583)*

Stimulant A psychoactive drug that has the ability to increase behavioral and mental activity. Amphetamines and cocaine do so primarily by augmenting the action of the neurotransmitters dopamine and norepinephrine. *(p. 184)*

Stimulus discrimination A process through which individuals learn to differentiate among similar stimuli and respond appropriately to each one. (See also *stimulus generalization.*) *(p. 194)*

Stimulus generalization   A phenomenon in which a conditioned response is elicited by stimuli that are similar but not identical to the conditioned stimulus. The greater the similarity between a stimulus and the conditioned stimulus, the stronger the conditioned response will be. *(p. 194)*

Storage   The process of maintaining information in the memory system over time. *(p. 229)*

Stress   The process of adjusting to circumstances that disrupt, or threaten to disrupt, a person's equilibrium. *(p. 431)*

Stressor   An event or situation to which people must adjust. *(p. 431)*

Stress reaction   The physical, psychological, and behavioral responses people display in the face of stressors. *(p. 431)*

Striatum   A structure within the forebrain that is involved in the smooth initiation of movement. *(p. 62)*

Subconscious level   The term used to designate the mental level at which important but normally inaccessible mental processes take place. (See also *unconscious level.*) *(p. 167)*

Substance abuse   The self-administration of psychoactive drugs in ways that deviate from a culture's social norms. *(p. 181)*

Substance-related disorder   A problem that involves use of psychoactive drugs for months or years in ways that harm the user or others. *(p. 523)*

Substantia nigra   An area of the midbrain involved in the smooth initiation of movement. *(p. 62)*

Sudden infant death syndrome (SIDS)   A disorder in which a sleeping baby stops breathing but does not awaken and suffocates. *(p. 173)*

Superego   According to psychodynamic theory, the component of personality that tells people what they should and should not do. Its two subdivisions are the conscience, which dictates what behaviors are wrong, and the ego ideal, which sets perfectionistic standards for desirable behaviors. *(p. 460)*

Supernatural model   An explanation of abnormal behavior as the work of the devil or other supernatural forces. *(p. 493)*

Suprachiasmatic nuclei   Nuclei in the hypothalamus that generate biological rhythms. *(p. 62)*

Surface structure   The strings of words that people produce; the order in which words are arranged. *(p. 289)*

Survey   A research method that involves giving people questionnaires or special interviews designed to obtain descriptions of their attitudes, beliefs, opinions, and intentions. *(p. 32)*

Syllogism   In the reasoning process, an argument made up of two propositions, called premises, and a conclusion based on those premises. (See also *proposition.*) *(p. 272)*

Sympathetic system   The subsystem of the autonomic nervous system that usually prepares the organism for vigorous activity, including the fight-or-flight syndrome. (See also *autonomic nervous system* and *fight-or-flight syndrome.*) *(p. 367)*

Synapse   The tiny gap between neurons across which the neurons communicate. *(p. 50)*

Synaptic plasticity   The ability to create synapses and to change the strength of synapses. *(p. 72)*

Syntax   In language, the set of rules that govern the formation of phrases and sentences. (See also *semantics.*) *(p. 288)*

Systematic desensitization   A behavioral method for treating anxiety in which clients visualize a graduated series of anxiety-provoking stimuli while maintaining a state of relaxation. *(p. 541)*

Task-oriented leadership   A leadership style in which the leader provides close supervision, leads by giving directives, and generally discourages group discussion. *(p. 623)*

Telegraphic   Pertaining to utterances that are brief and to the point and that leave out any word not absolutely essential to the meaning the speaker wishes to convey; children's first sentences, consisting of two-word utterances. *(p. 293)*

Temperament   An individual's basic, natural disposition; the beginning of an individual's identity or personality, which is evident from infancy. *(p. 403)*

Temporal codes   In the sensory systems, coding attributes of a stimulus in terms of changes in the timing of neural firing. *(p. 89)*

Teratogen   A harmful substance, such as alcohol and other drugs, that can cause birth defects. *(p. 386)*

Terminal drop   A sharp decline in mental functioning that tends to occur in late adulthood, a few years or months before death. *(p. 425)*

Test   A systematic procedure for observing behavior in a standard situation and describing it with the help of a numerical scale or a category system. *(p. 308)*

Textural gradient   A graduated change in the texture, or grain, of the visual field, whereby changes in texture across the retinal image are perceived as changes in distance; objects with finer, less detailed textures are perceived as more distant. *(p. 136)*

Texture   A Gestalt grouping principle stating that when features of stimuli have the same texture (such as the orientation of certain elements) they tend to be grouped together. *(p. 134)*

Thalamus   A structure in the forebrain that relays signals from the eyes and other sense organs to higher levels in the brain and plays an important role in processing and making sense out of this information. *(p. 62)*

Theory   An integrated set of propositions that can be used to account for, predict, and even control certain phenomena. *(p. 29)*

Thinking   The manipulation of mental representations, performed in order to form new representations. *(p. 265)*

Timbre   The quality of sound that identifies it, so that, for example, a middle C played on the piano is clearly distinguishable from a middle C played on a trumpet. The timbre depends on the mixture of frequencies and amplitudes that make up the sound. *(p. 92)*

Token economy   A system for improving the behavior of severely disturbed or mentally retarded clients in institutions that involves rewarding desirable behaviors with tokens that can be exchanged for snacks, field trips, access to television, or other privileges. *(p. 543)*

Tolerance   A condition in which increasingly larger drug doses are needed to produce a given effect. *(p. 181)*

Top-down processing   Those aspects of recognition that are guided by higher-level cognitive processes and psychological factors like expectations. (See also *bottom-up processing.*) *(p. 144)*

Topographical representation   A map of each sense, contained in the primary cortex. Any two points that are next to each other in the stimulus will be represented next to each other in the brain. *(p. 90)*

Trait approach   A perspective on personality that views it as the combination of stable characteristics that people display over time and across situations. *(p. 465)*

Tranquilizer   A class of drugs used to reduce mental and physical tension and symptoms of anxiety. (See also *anxiolytic.*) *(p. 560)*

Transduction   The second step in sensation, which is the process of converting incoming energy into neural activity through receptors. *(p. 88)*

Transfer-appropriate processing   A model of memory that suggests that a critical determinant of memory is how the encoding process matches up with what is ultimately retrieved. *(p. 233)*

Transferred excitation   The process of carrying over arousal from one experience to an independent situation, which is especially likely to occur when the arousal pattern from the nonemotional source is similar to the pattern associated with a particular emotion. *(p. 372)*

Trichromatic theory   The theory postulated by Young and Helmholtz that there are three types of visual elements, each of which is most sensitive to different wavelengths, and that information from these three elements combines to produce the sensation of color. *(p. 104)*

Tympanic membrane   A tightly stretched membrane (also known as the eardrum) in the middle ear that generates vibrations that match the sound waves striking it. *(p. 92)*

Unconditional positive regard   In client-centered therapy, the therapist's attitude that expresses caring for and acceptance of the client as a valued person. *(p. 539)*

Unconditioned response (UCR) In classical conditioning, the automatic or unlearned reaction to a stimulus. (See also *conditioned response.*) (*p. 193*)

Unconditioned stimulus (UCS) In classical conditioning, the stimulus that elicits a response without conditioning. (See also *conditioned stimulus.*) (*p. 193*)

Unconscious level A segment of mental activity proposed by Freud that contains sexual, aggressive, and other impulses, as well as once-conscious but unacceptable thoughts and feelings of which an individual is completely unaware. (See also *conscious level, nonconscious level, preconscious level,* and *subconscious level.*) (*p. 167*)

Undifferentiated schizophrenia Patterns of disordered thought, behavior, and emotions that are characteristic of schizophrenia but that cannot easily be placed in any specific schizophrenic subtype. (*p. 517*)

Utility In rational decision making, any subjective measure of value. (*p. 284*)

Validity The degree to which a test measures what it is supposed to measure. (*p. 309*)

Variable interval (VI) schedule In operant conditioning, a type of partial reinforcement schedule that provides reinforcement for the first response after some varying period of time. For example, in a VI 60 schedule the first response to occur after an average of one minute would be reinforced, but the actual time between reinforcements could vary from, say, 1 second to 120 seconds. (*p. 206*)

Variable ratio (VR) schedule A type of partial reinforcement schedule that provides reinforcement after a varying number of responses. For example, on a VR 30 schedule, a rat might sometimes be reinforced after ten bar presses, sometimes after fifty bar presses, but an average of thirty responses would occur before reinforcement is given. (*p. 206*)

Variables Specific factors or characteristics that can take on different values in research. (*p. 29*)

Verbal scale Six subtests in the Wechsler scales that measure verbal skills as part of a measure of overall intelligence. (See also *performance scale.*) (*p. 306*)

Vestibular sacs Organs in the inner ear that connect the semicircular canals and the cochlea, and contribute to the body's sense of balance. (*p. 122*)

Vestibular sense The proprioceptive sense that provides information about the position of the body in space and about its general movements. It is often thought of as the sense of balance. (*p. 122*)

VI See *variable interval schedule.*

Vicarious conditioning Learning the relationship between a response and its consequences (either reinforcement or punishment) or the association between a conditioned stimulus and a conditioned response by watching others. (*p. 217*)

Visible light Electromagnetic radiation that has a wavelength from about 400 nanometers to about 750 nanometers. (A nanometer is one-billionth of a meter.) (*p. 97*)

Visual code A mental representation of stimuli as pictures. (*p. 229*)

Volley theory See *frequency matching.*

Vomeronasal organ A portion of the mammalian olfactory system that is sensitive to nonvolatile pheromones. (*p. 113*)

Wavelength The distance from one peak to the next in a waveform. (*p. 91*)

Weber's law A law stating that the smallest detectable difference in stimulus energy, the just-noticeable difference (JND), is a constant fraction, K, of the intensity of the stimulus, I. The constant varies for each sensory system and for different aspects of sensation within those systems. In algebraic terms, Weber's law is $JND = KI$. (See also *just-noticeable difference.*) (*p. 130*)

Withdrawal syndrome A complex of symptoms associated with the termination of administration of a habit-forming substance. (*p. 181*)

Word A unit of language composed of one or more morphemes. (See also *morpheme.*) (*p. 288*)

Working memory See *short-term memory.*

Zero-sum game A social situation in which one person's gains are subtracted from another person's resources, such that the sum of the gains and losses is zero. (*p. 621*)

REFERENCES

Abbott, B. B., Schoen, L. S., & Badia, P. (1984). Predictable and unpredictable shock: Behavioral measures of aversion and physiological measures of stress. *Psychological Bulletin, 96,* 45–71.

Abel, E. L. (1975). Cannabis: Effects on hunger and thirst. *Behavioral Biology, 15*(3), 255–281.

Abeles, N. (1985). Proceedings of the American Psychological Association, 1985. *American Psychologist, 41,* 633–663.

Abraham, C., Sheeran, P., Spears, R., & Abrams, D. (1992). Health beliefs and promotion of HIV-preventive intentions among teenages: A Scottish perspective. *Health Psychology, 11,* 363–370.

Abraham, H. D., & Wolf, E. (1988). Visual function in past users of LSD: Psychophysical findings. *Journal of Abnormal Psychology, 97,* 443–447.

Abramis, D. J. (1994). Work role ambiguity, job satisfaction, and job performance: Meta-analyses and review. *Psychological Reports, 75,* 1411–1433.

Abrams, R. (1992). *Electroconvulsive therapy.* New York: Oxford University Press.

Abrams, R. (1993). ECT technique: Electrode placement, stimulus type, and treatment frequency. In C. E. Coffey (Ed.), *The clinical science of electroconvulsive therapy.* Washington, DC: American Psychiatric Press.

Abramson, L. Y., Metalsky, G. I., & Alloy, L. B. (1989). Hopelessness depression: A theory-based subtype. *Psychological Review, 96,* 358–372.

Abramson, L. Y., Seligman, M. E. P., & Teasdale, J. D. (1978). Learned helplessness in humans: Critique and reformulation. *Journal of Abnormal Psychology, 87,* 49–74.

Achenbach, T. (1991). *Manual for the child behavior checklist: 4–18 and 1991 profile.* Burlington: University of Vermont Department of Psychiatry.

Acitelli, L. K. (1992). Gender differences in relationship awareness and marital satisfaction among young married couples. *Personality and Social Psychology Bulletin, 18,* 102–110.

Ackerman, P. L. (1994). Intelligence, attention, and learning: Maximal and typical performance. In D. K. Detterman (Ed.), *Current topics in human intelligence* (Vol. 4). Norwood, NJ: Ablex.

Adams, G. R., & Jones, R. M. (1983). Female adolescents' identity development: Age comparisons and perceived child-rearing experience. *Developmental Psychology, 19,* 249–256.

Adams, K. M., & Bieliauskas, L. A. (1994). On perhaps becoming what you had previously despised: Psychologists as prescribers of medication. *Journal of Clinical Psychology in Medical Settings, 1*(3), 189–197.

Adams, R., Maurer, D., & Davis, M. (1986). Newborns' discrimination of chromatic from achromatic stimuli. *Journal of Experimental Child Psychology, 41,* 267–281.

Ader, D. N., & Johnson, S. B. (1994). Sample description, reporting, and analysis of sex in psychological research: A look at APA and APA division journals in 1990. *American Psychologist, 49,* 216–218.

Ader, R., Felten, D., & Cohen, N. (1990). Interactions between the brain and the immune system. *Annual Review of Pharmacology and Toxicology, 30,* 561–602.

Ader, R., & Cohen, N. (1993). Psychoneuroimmunology: Conditioning and stress. *Annual Review of Psychology, 44,* 53–85.

Adler, A. (1927). *The practice and theory of individual psychology.* Paterson, NJ: Littlefield Adams. (Reprinted in 1963)

Adler, T. (1993, March). Bad mix: Combat stress, decisions. *APA Monitor,* p. 1.

Adolphs, R., Tranel, D., Damasio, H., & Damasio, A. (1994). Impaired recognition of emotion in facial expressions following bilateral damage to the human amygdala. *Nature, 372*(6507), 669–672.

Adorno, T. W., Frenkel-Brunswik, E., Levinson, D. J., & Sanford, R. N. (1950). *The authoritarian personality.* New York: Harper & Row.

Advokat, C., & Kutlesic, V. (1995). Pharmacotherapy of the eating disorders: A commentary. *Neuroscience and Biobehavioral Reviews, 19*(1), 59–66.

Aggleton, J. F. (1993). The contribution of the amygdala to normal and abnormal emotional states. *Trends in Neuroscience, 16*(8), 328–333.

Aiello, J. R., & Kolb, K. J. (1995). Electronic performance monitoring and social context: Impact on productivity and stress. *Journal of Applied Psychology, 80,* 339–353.

Aiken, L. R. (1987). *Assessment of intellectual functioning.* Boston, MA: Allyn & Bacon.

Aiken, L. R. (1993). *Psychological testing and assessment* (8th ed.). Boston, MA: Allyn & Bacon.

Ainsworth, M. D. S. (1973). The development of infant-mother attachment. In B. M. Caldwell & H. N. Ricciuti (Eds.), *Review of child development research: Vol. 3.* Chicago: University of Chicago Press.

Ainsworth, M. D. S. (1989). Attachments beyond infancy. *American Psychologist, 44,* 709–716.

Ainsworth, M. D. S., Blehar, M. D., Waters, E., & Wall, S. (1978). *Patterns of attachment: A psychological study of the Strange Situation.* Hillsdale, NJ: Lawrence Erlbaum Associates.

Ainsworth, M. D. S., & Eichberg, C. (in press). Effects on infant-mother attachment of mother's unresolved loss of an attachment figure or other traumatic experience. In P. Marris, J. Stevenson-Hinde, & C. Parkes (Eds.), *Attachment across the life cycle.* New York: Routledge.

Aitchison, J. (1983). *The articulate mammal: An introduction to psycholinguistics* (2nd ed.). New York: Universe.

Albee, G. (1968). Conceptual models and manpower requirements in psychology. *American Psychologist, 23,* 317–320.

Albee, G. (1985, February). The answer is prevention. *Psychology Today.*

Albert, M. S., Savage, C. R., Blazer, D., Jones, K., Berkman, L., & Seeman, T. (1995). Predictors of cognitive change in older persons: MacArthur studies of successful aging. *Psychology and Aging, 10,* 578–589.

Alberti, R. E., & Emmons, M. L. (1986). *Your perfect right: A guide to assertive living* (5th ed.). San Luis Obispo, CA: Impact Publishers.

Alcantara, A. A., Chaney, K. A., Pazdera, T. M., Woziwodzkia, P. K., & Greenough, W. T. (1993). CFOS expression in learning—Associated areas of rat cerebellum during initial acquisition of a motor learning task. *Behavioral and Neural Biology.*

Alcock, J. E. (1987). Parapsychology: Science of the anomalous or search for the soul? *Brain and Behavior Science, 10,* 553–643.

Alcock, J. E. (1995). The belief engine. *Skeptical Inquirer, 19,* 14–18.

Alcohol, Drug Abuse, and Mental Health Administration (ADAMHA). (1987). *Update: Facts from the sixth special report to Congress on alcohol and health.* Washington, DC: ADAMHA.

Aldag, R. J., & Fuller, S. R. (1993). Beyond fiasco: A reappraisal of the groupthink phenomenon and a new model of group decision processes. *Psychological Bulletin, 113,* 533–552.

Alderete, E., Eskenazi, B., & Sholtz, R. (1995). Effect of cigarette smoking and coffee drinking on time to conception. *Epidemiology, 6*(4), 403–408.

Alexander, F. M. (1963). *Fundamentals of psychoanalysis.* New York: W. W. Norton.

Allen, B. L. (1991). Cognitive research in information science: Implications for design. In M. Williams (Ed.), *Annual Review of Information Science and Technology, 26,* 3–37.

Allen, L. S., & Gorski, R. A. (1992). Sexual orientation and the size of the anterior commissure in the human brain. *Proceedings of the National Academy of Sciences of the United States of America, 89,* 7199–7202.

Allen, L. S., Hines, M., Shryne, J. E., & Gorski, R. A. (1989). Two sexually dimorphic cell groups in the human brain. *Journal of Neuroscience, 9,* 497–506.

Allen, M. G. (1976). Twin studies of affective illness. *Archives of General Psychiatry, 33,* 1476–1478.

Allison, K. W., Crawford, I., Echemendia, R., Robinson, L., & Knepp, D. (1994). Human diversity and professional competence. *American Psychologist, 49*(9), 792–796.

Allport, G. W. (1961). *Pattern and growth in personality.* New York: Holt, Rinehart & Winston.

Allport, G. W., & Odbert, H. S. (1936). Trait names: A psycholexical study. *Psychological Monographs, 47*(1, Whole No. 211).

Almagor, M., Tellegen, A., & Waller, N. G. (1995). The big-seven model: A cross cultural replication and further exploration of the basic dimensions of natural language trait descriptors. *Journal of Personality and Social Psychology, 69,* 300–307.

Alston, J. H. (1920). Spatial condition of the fusion of warmth and cold in heat. *American Journal of Psychology, 31,* 303–312.

Altarriba, J., & Santiago-Rivera, A. L. (1994). Current perspectives on using linguistic and cultural factors in counseling the Hispanic client. *Professional Psychology: Research and Practice, 25*(4), 388–397.

Althoff, R. R., Maciukenas, M., & Cohen, N. J. (1993). Indirect assessment of memory using eye movement monitoring. *Society for Neuroscience Abstracts, 19,* 439.

Alvarez, F. J., Delrio, M. C., & Prada, R. (1995). Drinking and driving in Spain. *Journal of Studies on Alcohol, 56*(4), 403–407.

Amabile, T. M. (1989). *Growing up creative.* New York: Random House.

Amabile, T. M., Hennessey, B. A., & Grossman, B. S. (1986). Social influences on creativity: The effects of contracted-for reward. *Journal of Personality & Social Psychology, 50,* 14–23.

Amabile, T. M., Hill, K. G., Hennessey, B. A., & Tighe, E. M. (1994). The Work Preference Inventory: Assessing intrinsic and extrinsic motivational orientations. *Journal of Personality and Social Psychology, 66*(5), 950–967.

Amato, P. R., & Keith, B. (1991). Parental divorce and the well-being of children: A meta-analysis. *Psychological Bulletin, 110,* 26–46.

Ambrosini, M. V., Langella, M., Gironi-Carnivale, U. A., & Giuditta, A. (1992). The sequential hypothesis of sleep function: III. The structure of postacquisition sleep in learning and nonlearning rats. *Physiology and Behavior, 51,* 217–226.

American Law Institute. (1962). *Model penal code: Proposed offical draft.* Philadelphia: Author.

American Psychiatric Association. (1989). *Treatments of psychiatric disorders.* Washington, DC: Author.

American Psychiatric Association (1993, April). Practice guide for major depressive disorder in adults. *American Journal of Psychiatry, 150* (Suppl.), 1–26.

American Psychiatric Association (1994). *Diagnostic and statistical manual of mental disorders* (4th ed.). Washington, DC: American Psychiatric Association.

American Psychological Association. (1974). *Standards for educational and psychological test and manuals.* Washington, DC: Author.

American Psychological Association. (1981). Ethical principles of psychologists. *American Psychologist, 36,* 633–638.

American Psychological Association. (1985). *Standards for Educational and Psychological Testing.* Washington, DC: Author.

American Psychological Association. (1992a, May). APA continues to refine its ethics code. *APA Monitor.*

American Psychological Association. (1992b). Ethical principles of psychologists and code of conduct. *American Psychologist, 47,* 1597–1611.

American Psychological Association (1993). *Violence and youth: Psychology's response.* Washington: DC: Author.

American Psychological Association (1995a). *Report of the task force on the changing gender composition of psychology.* Washington, DC: APA.

American Psychological Association (1995b). *Intelligence: Knowns and unknowns: Report.* Washington, D.C.: Author.

American Psychological Association (1995). Sex, race/ethnicity data available. *Trends in Education, 2,* 2–3.

Anastasi, A. (1976). *Psychological testing* (4th ed.). New York: Macmillan.

Anastasi, A. (1988). *Psychological testing* (6th ed.). New York: Macmillan.

Andersen, G. J. (1986). The perception of self motion: Psychological and computational approach. *Journal of Experimental Psychology: Perception and Human Performance, 11,* 122–132.

Anderson, C. A. (1989). Temperature and aggression: Ubiquitous effects of heat on occurrence of human violence. *Psychological Bulletin, 106,* 74–96.

Anderson, E. M., & Lambert, M. J. (1995). Short-term dynamically oriented psychotherapy: A review and meta-analysis. *Clinical Psychology Review, 9*(6), 503–514.

Anderson, J. A. (1995). *An introduction to neural networks.* Cambridge, MA: MIT Press.

Anderson, J. R. (1990). *The adaptive character of thought.* Hillsdale, NJ: Lawrence Erlbaum Associates.

Anderson, J. R. (1990). *Cognitive psychology and its implications* (3rd ed.). New York: W. H. Freeman.

Anderson, J. R. (1992). Problem solving and learning. *American Psychologist, 48,* 35–44.

Anderson, J. R. (1995). *Learning and memory: An integrated approach.* New York: John Wiley & Sons.

Anderson, J. R. (1995). *Cognitive psychology and its implications* (4th ed.). New York: W. H. Freeman.

Anderson, R. C., Reynolds, R. E., Schallert, D. L., & Goetz, E. T. (1977). Frameworks for comprehending discourse. *American Educational Research Journal, 14,* 367–382.

Anderson, S. K., & Kitchener, K. S. (1996). Nonromantic, nonsexual posttherapy relationships between psychologists and former clients: An exploratory study of critical incidents. *Professional Psychology: Research and Practice, 27,* 59–66.

Andreasen, N. C., Arndt, S., Swayze, V., II, Cizadlo, T., Flaum, M., O'Leary, D., Ehrhandt, J. C., & Yuh, W. T. C. (1994). Thalamic abnormalities in schizophrenia visualized through magnetic resonance image averaging. *Science, 266,* 294–298.

Andreasen, N. C., Arndt, S., Alliger, R., Miller, D., & Flaum, M. (1995). Symptoms of schizophrenia. *Archives of General Psychiatry, 52,* 341–351.

Andreasen, N. C., Swayze, V. W., Flaum, M., Yates, W. R., Arndt, S., & McChesney, C. (1990). Ventricular enlargement in schizophrenia evaluated with computed tomographic scanning: Effects of gender, age, and stage of illness. *Archives of General Psychiatry, 47,* 1008–1015.

Anger, W. K., Rohlman, D. S., & Sizemore, O. J. (1994). A comparison of instruction formats for administering a computerized behavioral test. *Behavior Research Methods, Instruments, and Computers, 26,* 209–212.

Anrep, G. V. (1920). Pitch discrimination in the dog. *Journal of Physiology, 53,* 367–385.

Anthony, T., Cooper, C., & Mullen, B. (1992). Cross-racial facial identification: Five studies of sex differences in facial prominence. *Personality and Social Psychology Bulletin, 18,* 296–301.

Antoni, M. H., Baggett, L., Ironson, G., LaPerriere, A., August, S., Klimas, N., Schneiderman, N., & Fletcher, M. A. (1991). Cognitive-behavioral stress management interventions buffer distress responses and immunologic changes following notification of HIV-1 seropositive. *Journal of Consulting and Clinical Psychology, 59,* 906–915.

Antonuccio, D. O., Danton, W. G., & DeNelsky, G. Y. (1995). Psychotherapy versus medication for depression: Challenging the conventional wisdom with data. *Professional Psychology: Research and Practice, 26,* 574–585.

Arbib, M. A., & Liaw, J. S. (1995). Sensorimotor transformations in the worlds of frogs and robots. *Artificial Intelligence, 72,* 53–79.

Archambault, C. M., Czyzewski, D., Cordua y Cruz, G. D., Foreyt, F. P., & Mariotto, M. J. (1989). Effects of weight cycling in female rats. *Physiology and Behavior, 46,* 417–421.

Archer, J. (1991). The influence of testosterone on human aggression. *British Journal of Psychiatry, 82,* 1–28.

Archer, J., & Lloyd, B. (1985). *Sex and gender.* Cambridge: Cambridge University Press.

Arenberg, D. (1982). Changes with age in problem solving. In F. I. M. Craik & S. Trehub (Eds.), *Aging and cognitive processes* (pp. 221–236). New York: Plenum.

Armitage, R. (1995). The distribution of EEG frequencies in REM and NREM sleep stages in healthy young adults. *Sleep, 18*(5), 334–341.

Aron, A., Aron, E. N., Tudor, M., & Nelson, G. (1991). Close relationships as including others in the self. *Journal of Personality and Social Psychology, 60,* 241–253.

Aronoff, J., Barclay, A. M., & Stevenson, L. A. (1988). The recognition of threatening stimuli. *Journal of Personality and Social Psychology, 54,* 647–655.

Aronson, E. (1990). Applying social psychology to desegregation and energy conservation. *Personality and Social Psychology Bulletin, 16,* 118–132.

Aronson, E. (1992). The return of the repressed: Dissonance theory makes a comeback. *Psychological Inquiry, 3,* 303–311.

Aronson, E. (1995). *The social animal* (7th ed.). New York: W. H. Freeman.

Aronson, E., Wilson, T. D., & Akert, R. M. (1994). *Social psychology: The heart and mind.* New York: HarperCollins.

Artiberry, M., Yonas, A., & Bensen, A. S. (1989). Self-produced locomotion and development of responsiveness to textural gradients. *Developmental Psychology, 25,* 976–982.

Asch, S. E. (1951). Effects of group pressure upon the modification and distortion of judgments. In H. Guetzkow (Ed.), *Groups, leadership, and men.* Pittsburgh: Carnegie Press.

Asch, S. E. (1955). Opinions and social pressure. *Scientific American, 193,* 31–35.

Asch, S. E. (1956). Studies of independence and conformity: A minority of one against a unanimous majority. *Psychological Monographs, 70,* 1–70.

Ashcraft, M. H. (1989). *Human memory and cognition.* Glenview, IL: Scott, Foresman.

Ashcraft, M. H. (1993). *Human memory and cognition* (2nd ed.). New York: HarperCollins.

Ashton, H. (1995). Protracted withdrawal from benzodiazepines: The post-withdrawal syndrome. *Psychiatric Annals, 25*(3), 174–179.

Aslin, R. N., Pisoni, D. B., & Jusczyk, P. W. (1983). Auditory development and speech perception in infancy. In P. H. Mussen (Ed.), *Handbook of child psychology: Vol. 2.* New York: Wiley.

Aspinwall, L., Kemeny, M., Taylor, S., Schneider, S., & Dudley, J. (1991). Psychosocial predictors of gay men's AIDS risk-reduction behavior. *Health Psychology, 10,* 432–444.

Aspinwall, L. G., & Taylor, S. E. (1992). Modeling cognition adaptation: A longitudinal investigation of the impact of individual differences and coping on college adjustment and performance. *Journal of Personality and Social Psychology, 63,* 989–1003.

Associated Press. (1984). *Man sets wife afire after watching TV movie.*

Associated Press. (1992, April 23). *Rape survey raises count.*

Associated Press (1995, November 17). "FDA approves obesity drug." *Daily Illini.*

Aston-Jones, G., Chiang, C., & Alexinsky, T. (1991b). Discharge of noradrenergic locus coeruleus neurons in behaving rats and monkeys suggests a role in vigilance. *Progress in Brain Research, 88,* 501–520.

Aston-Jones, G., Shipley, M. T., Chouvet, G., Ennis, M., van Bockstaele, E., Pieribone, V., Shiekhattar, R., Akaoka, H., Drolet, G., Astier, B., Charlety, P., Valentino, R. J., & Williams, J. T. (1991a). Afferent regulation of locus coeruleus neurons: Anatomy, physiology and pharmacology. *Progress in Brain Research, 88,* 47–75.

Atkinson, J. W., & Birch, D. (1978). *Introduction to motivation* (2nd ed.). New York: D. Van Nostrand.

Atkinson, J. W., & Raynor, J. O. (1974). *Personality, motivation, and achievement.* Washington, DC: Hemisphere.

Atkinson, R. C., & Shiffrin, R. M. (1968). Human memory: A proposed system and its control processes. In K. Spence (Ed.), *The psychology of learning and motivation: Vol. 2.* New York: Academic Press.

Au, T. K. (1983). Chinese and English counterfactuals: The Sapir-Whorf hypothesis revisited. *Cognition, 15,* 155–187.

Au, T. K. (1992). Counterfactual reasoning. In G. R. Semin & K. Fiedler (Eds.), *Language, interaction and social cognition.* London: Sage.

Averill, J. S. (1980). On the paucity of positive emotions. In K. R. Blankstein, P. Pliner, & J. Polivy (Eds.), *Advances in the study of communication and affect: Vol. 6. Assessment and modification of emotional behavior.* New York: Plenum.

Awh, E., Jonides, J., Smith, E. E., Schumacher, E. H., Koeppe, R. A., & Katz, S. (1996). Dissociation of storage and rehearsal in verbal working memory: Evidence from positron emission tomography. *Psychological Science, 7,* 25–31.

Ayllon, T., & Azrin, N. H. (1968). *The token economy: A motivational system for therapy and rehabilitation.* New York: Appleton-Century-Crofts.

Azar, B. (1994). Psychology weighs in on "Bell Curve" debate. *APA Monitor, 25*(12), 1–23.

Azar, B. (1994, November). Eating fat: Why does the brain say, "Ahhh"? *APA Monitor,* p. 20.

Azar, B. (1995, January). DNA-environment mix forms intellectual fate. *American Psychological Association Monitor,* p. 24.

Azar, B. (1995, May). Several genetic traits linked to alcoholism. *APA Monitor.*

Azar, B. (1995, August). Word choices reveal creative abilities. *APA Monitor.*

Azar, B. (1996, January). Healthy brain cells can do the work of damaged ones. *APA Monitor,* p. 19.

Azar, B. (1996, February). Influences from the mind's inner layers. *APA Monitor,* pp. 1, 25.

Azar, B. (1996, March). The VR pricetag: Nausea, dizziness and disorientation. *APA Monitor, 25.*

Babcock, R., & Salthouse, T. (1990). Effects of increased processing demands on age differences in working memory. *Psychology and Aging, 5,* 421–428.

Bacal, H. A., & Newman, K. M. (1990). *Theories of object relations: Bridges to self psychology.* New York: Columbia University Press.

Bach, S., & Klein, G. S. (1957). The effects of prolonged subliminal exposure of words. *American Psychologist, 12,* 397–398.

Backman, L., & Nilsson, L. (1991). Effects of divided attention on free and cued recall of verbal events and action events. *Bulletin of the Psychonomic Society, 29,* 51–54.

Baddeley, A. (1982). *Your memory: A user's guide.* New York: Macmillan.

Baddeley, A. (1992). Working memory. *Science, 255,* 556–559.

Baddeley, A., & Hitch, G. (1974). Working memory. In G. H. Bower (Ed.), *The psychology of learning and motivation* (Vol. 8, pp. 47–89). New York: Academic Press.

Bagnon, M. S. (1994). *Human error in medicine.* Hillsdale, NJ: Lawrence Erlbaum Associates.

Bahrick, H. P. (1992). Stabilized memory of unrehearsed knowledge. *Journal of Experimental Psychology: General, 121,* 112–113.

Bahrick, H. P., Bahrick, P. O., & Wittlinger, R. P. (1975). Fifty years of memory for names and faces: A cross-cultural approach. *Journal of Experimental Psychology: General, 104,* 54–75.

Bahrick, H. P., & Hall, L. K. (1991). Lifetime maintenance of high school mathematics content. *Journal of Experimental Psychology: General, 120,* 20–33.

Bailey, A. J. (1993). The biology of autism. *Psychological Medicine, 23,* 7–11.

Bailey, J. M., & Benishay, D. S. (1993). Familial aggregation of female sexual orientation. *American Journal of Psychiatry, 150,* 272–277.

Bailey, J. M., Bobrow, D., Wolfe, M., & Mikach, S. (1995). Sexual orientation of adult sons of gay fathers. *Developmental Psychology, 31*(1), 124–129.

Bailey, J. M., & Pillard, R. C. (1991). A genetic study of male sexual orientation. *Archives of General Psychiatry, 48,* 1089–1096.

Baillargeon, R. (1987). Object permanence in 3 1/2- and 4 1/2-month-old infants. *Developmental Psychology, 23,* 655–664.

Baillargeon, R. (1992). The object concept revisited: New directions in the investigation of infants' physical knowledge. In C. E. Granrud (Ed.), *Visual perception and cognition in infancy: Carnegie-Mellon Symposia on Cognition* (Vol. 23). Hillsdale, NJ: Lawrence Erlbaum Associates.

Baillargeon, R. (1992). A model of physical reasoning in infancy. In C. Rovee-Collier & L. P. Lipsett (Eds.), *Advances in infancy research.* Norwood, NJ: Ablex.

Baillargeon, R. (1993). The object concept revisited: New directions in the investigation of infants' physical knowledge. In C. E. Granrud (Ed.), *Carnegie Symposium on Cognition: Visual perception and cognition in infancy.* Hillsdale, NJ: Lawrence Erlbaum Associates.

Baillargeon, R. (1994a). How do infants learn about the physical world? *Current Directions in Psychological Science, 3,* 133–139.

Baillargeon, R. (1994b). Physical reasoning in young infants: Seeking explanations for impossible events. *British Journal of Development Psychology, 12,* 9–33.

Baillargeon, R. (1995). Physical reasoning in infancy. In M. S. Gazzaniga (Ed.), *The cognitive neurosciences* (pp. 181–204). Cambridge, MA: MIT Press.

Baker, L. T., Vernon, P. A., & Ho, H. (1991). The genetic correlation between intelligence and speed of information processing. *Behavior Genetics, 21,* 351–367.

Baker, S. M., & Devine, P. G. (1988, April). *Faces as primes for stereotype activation.* Paper presented at the 66th annual meeting of the Midwestern Psychological Association, Chicago.

Balaban, M. T. (1995). Affective influences on startle in five-month-old infants: Reactions to facial expressions of emotion. *Child Development, 66*(1), 28–36.

Balestreri, R., Fontana, L., & Astengo, F. (1987). A double-blind placebo-controlled evaluation of the safety and efficacy of vinpocetine in the treatment of patients with chronic vascular senile cerebral dysfunction. *Journal of the American Geriatric Society, 35,* 425–430.

Ball, S. G., Buchwald, A. M., & Waddell, M. T. (1995). Depression and generalized anxiety symptoms in panic disorder: Implications for comorbidity. *Journal of Nervous and Mental Disorders, 183*(5), 304–308.

Ballard, M. E., & Wiest, J. R. (1995, March). *Mortal Kombat: The effects of violent video technology on males' hostility and cardiovascular responding.* Paper presented at the biennial meeting of the Society for Research in Child Development, Indianapolis.

Balleine, B., & Dickinson, A. (1994). Role of cholecystokinin in the motivational control of instrumental action in rats. *Behavioral Neuroscience, 108*(3), 590–605.

Baltes, P. B. (1993). The aging mind: Potential and limits. *The Gerontologist, 33,* 580–594.

Baltes, P. B. (1994, August). *Life-span developmental psychology: On the overall landscape of human development.* Invited address presented at the annual meeting of the American Psychological Association, Los Angeles.

Bamford, C. R. (1993). Carbamazepine in REM sleep behavior disorder. *Sleep, 16*(1), 33–34.

Banaji, M. R., & Greenwald, A. J. (1995). Implicit stereotyping in judgments of fame. *Journal of Personality and Social Psychology, 68,* 181–198.

Bancroft, J. (1994). Homosexual orientation: The search for a biological basis. *British Journal of Psychiatry, 164,* 437–440.

Bandura, A. (1965). Influence of a model's reinforcement contingencies on the acquisition of imitative responses. *Journal of Personality and Social Psychology, 1,* 589–595.

Bandura, A. (1983). Psychological measurement of aggression. In R. G. Green and C. I. Donnerstein (Eds.), *Aggression: Theoretical and empirical reviews* (Vol. 1). New York: Academic Press.

Bandura, A. (1986). *Social foundations of thought and action: A social cognitive theory.* Englewood Cliffs, NJ: Prentice-Hall.

Bandura, A. (1989). Self-efficacy mechanism in physiological activation and health-promoting behavior. In J. Madden IV, S. Matthysse, & J. Barchas (Eds.), *Adaptation, learning, and affect.* New York: Raven Press.

Bandura, A., Blanchard, E. B., & Ritter, B. (1969). The relative efficacy of desensitization and modeling approaches for inducing behavioral, affective, and attitudinal changes. *Journal of Personality and Social Psychology, 13,* 173–199.

Bandura, A., Cioffi, D., Taylor, C. B., & Brouillard, M. E. (1988). Perceived self-efficacy in coping with cognitive stressors and opioid activation. *Journal of Personality and Social Psychology, 55,* 479–488.

Bandura, A., Ross, D., & Ross, S. A. (1963). Imitation of film-mediated aggressive models. *Journal of Abnormal and Social Psychology, 66,* 3–11.

Bandura, A., Taylor, C., Williams, S., Mefford, I., & Barchas, J. (1985). Catecholamine secretion as a function of perceived coping self-efficacy. *Journal of Personality and Social Psychology, 53,* 406–414.

Banich, M. T., & Shenker, J. I. (1994). Investigations of interhemispheric processing: Methodological considerations. *Neuropsychology, 8*(2), 263-277.

Banich, M. T., Stolar, N., Heller, W., & Goldman, R. B. (1992). A deficit in right-hemisphere performance after induction of a depressed mood. *Neuropsychiatry, Neuropsychology, and Behavioral Neurology, 5*(1), 20–27.

Banks, M. S., & Salapatek, P. (1983). Infant visual perception. In P. H. Mussen (Ed.), *Handbook of child psychology: Vol. 2. Infancy and developmental psychobiology.* New York: Wiley.

Banks, W. P., & Krajicek, D. (1991). Perception. *Annual Review of Psychology, 42,* 305–332.

Barbee, J. G. (1993). Memory, benzodiazepines, and anxiety: Integration of theoretical and clinical perspectives. *Journal of Clinical Psychiatry, 54*(10 supplement), 86–101.

Barber, J. P., Crits-Christoph, P., & Paul, C. C. (1993). Advances in measures of psychodynamic formulations. *Journal of Consulting and Clinical Psychology, 61,* 574–585.

Barclay, J. R., Bransford, J. D., Franks, J. J., McCarrell, N. S., & Nitsch, K. (1974). Comprehension and semantic flexibility. *Journal of Verbal Learning and Verbal Behavior, 13,* 471–481.

Barefoot, J., Dodge, K., Peterson, B., Dalhstrom, G., & Williams, R. (1991). The Cook-Medley Hostility Scale: Item content and ability to predict survival. *Psychosomatic Medicine, 51,* 46–57.

Barfield, W., & Furness, T. (Eds.). (1995). *Virtual environments and advanced interface design.* New York: Oxford University Press.

Bargh, J. A., & Barndollar, K. (1995). Automaticity in action: The unconscious as repository of chronic goals and motives. In P. M. Gollwitzer & J. A. Bargh (Eds.), *The psychology of action.* New York: Guilford.

Bargh, J. A., Chaiken, S., Raymond, P., & Hymes, C. (in press). The automatic evaluation effect: Unconditional automatic attitude activation with pronunciation task. *Journal of Experimental Social Psychology.*

Bargones, J. Y., & Werner, L. A. (1994). Adults listen selectively; infants do not. *Psychological Science, 5,* 170–174.

Barinaga, M. (1994, May 6). Neurons tap out a code that may help locate sounds. *Science, 264,* 775.

Barlow, D. (1988). *Anxiety and its disorders.* New York: Guilford.

Barlow, D. H., Rapee, R. M., & Brown, T. A. (1992). Behavioral treatment of generalized anxiety disorder. *Behavior Therapy, 23,* 551–570.

Baron, M., Risch, N., Hamburger, R., Mandel, B., Kushner, S., Newman, M., Drumer, D., & Belmaker, R. H. (1987). Genetic linkage between X-chromosome markers and bipolar affective illness. *Nature, 326,* 289–292.

Baron, R., Cutuona, C., Hicklin, D., Russell, D., & Lubaroff, D. (1990). Social support and immune function among spouses of cancer patients. *Journal of Personality and Social Psychology, 59,* 344–352.

Baron, R. A., & Byrne, D. (1994). *Social psychology: Understanding human interaction* (7th ed.). Boston: Allyn & Bacon.

Baron, R. A. , & Richardson, D. C. (1994). *Human aggression* (2nd ed.) New York: Plenum.

Baron, R. S., Kerr, N. L., & Miller, N. (1992). *Group process, group decision, group action.* Pacific Grove, CA: Brooks/Cole.

Baron-Cohen, S., Leslie, A. M., & Frith, U. (1985). Does the autistic child have a "theory of mind"? *Cognition, 21,* 36–47.

Barondes, S. H. (1994). Thinking about Prozac. *Science, 263,* 1102–1103.

Barr, C., Mednick, S., & Munk-Jorgensen, P. (1990). Exposure to influenza epidemics during gestations and adult schizophrenia: A 40-year study. *Archives of General Psychiatry, 47,* 869–874.

Barrett, G. V., & Depinet, R. L. (1991). A reconsideration of testing for competence rather than for intelligence. *American Psychologist, 46,* 1012–1024.

Barrick, M. R., & Mount, M. K. (1991). The Big Five personality dimensions and job performance: A meta-analysis. *Personnel Psychology, 44,* 1–26.

Barron, F., & Harrington, D. M. (1981). Creativity, intelligence, and personality. *Annual Review of Psychology, 52,* 439–476.

Barsalou, L. W. (1991). Deriving categories to achieve goals. In G. H. Bower (Ed.), *The psychology of learning and motivation.* New York: Academic Press.

Barsalou, L. W. (1993). Flexibility, structure, and linguistic vagary in concepts: Manifestations of a compositional system of perceptual symbols. In A. F. Collins, S. E. Gathercole, M. A. Conway, & P. E. Morris (Eds.), *Theories of memory.* Hove, Eng.: Erlbaum.

Barsky, A. J., Wool, C., Barnett, M. C., & Cleary, P. D. (1994). Histories of childhood trauma in adult hypochondriacal patients. *American Journal of Psychiatry, 151,* 397–401.

Bartholomew, K., & Horowitz, L. M. (1991). Attachment styles among young adults: A test of a four-category model. *Journal of Personality and Social Psychology, 61,* 226–244.

Bartlett, F. C. (1932). *Remembering: A study in experimental and social psychology.* New York: Macmillan.

Bartol, C. (1991). Predictive validation of the MMPI for small-town police officers who fail. *Professional Psychology: Research and Practice, 22,* 127–132.

Barton, S. (1994). Chaos, self-organization, and psychology. *American Psychologist, 49,* 5–14.

Bartone, P., Gifford, R., Wright, K., Marlowe, D., & Martin, J. (1992). *U.S. soldiers remain healthy under Gulf War stress.* Paper presented at the 4th annual convention of the American Psychological Society, San Diego.

Bartoshuk, L. M. (1990). Distinctions between taste and smell relevant to the role of experience. In E. D. Capaldi, E. D. & T. L. Powley (Eds.), *Taste, experience, and feeding.* Washington, DC: American Psychological Association.

Bartoshuk, L. M. (1991). Taste, smell, and pleasure. In R. C. Bollef (Ed.), *The hedonics of taste.* Hillsdale, NJ: Lawrence Erlbaum Associates.

Bartoshuk, L. M., & Wolfe, J. M. (1990). Conditioned taste aversion in humans: Are there olfactory versions? *Chemical Senses, 15,* 551.

Bartus, R. T., Dean, R. L., III, Beer, B., and Lippa, A. S. (1982). The cholinergic hypothesis of geriatric memory dysfunction. *Science, 217,* 408–417.

Bashore, T. R., & Rapp, P. E. (1992). Are there alternatives to traditional polygraph procedures? *Psychological Bulletin, 113*(1), 3–22.

Bass, E., & Davis, L. (1988). *The courage to heal: A guide for women survivors of child sexual abuse.* New York: Harper & Row.

Bastiani, A. M., Rao, R., Weltzin, T., & Kaye, W. H. (1995). Perfectionism in anorexia nervosa. *International Journal of Eating Disorders, 17*(2), 147–152.

Bates, E. (1993, March). *Nature, nurture, and language development.* Paper presented at the biennial meeting of the Society for Research in Child Development, New Orleans.

Bateson, G., Jackson, D. D., Haley, J., & Weakland, J. (1956). Toward a history of schizophrenia. *Behavioral Science, 1,* 251–264.

Batson, C. D. (1991). *The altruism question: Toward a social-psychological answer.* Hillsdale, NJ: Lawrence Erlbaum Associates.

Batson, C. D. (1995). Prosocial motivation: Why do we help others? In A. Tesser (Ed.), *Advanced social psychology* (pp. 333–382). New York: McGraw-Hill.

Batson, C. D. (in press). Altruism and helping. In G. Lindzey & D. Gilbert (Eds.), *Handbook of social psychology* (4th ed.). Hillsdale, NJ: Lawrence Erlbaum Associates.

Batson, C. D., & Oleson, K. C. (1991). Current status of empathy-altruism hypothesis. In M. Clark (Ed.), *Review of personality and social psychology: Vol. 12. Prosocial behavior* (pp. 62–85). Newbury Park, CA: Sage.

Batson, C. D., O'Quin, K., Fultz, J., Vanderplas, M., & Isen, A. (1983). Influence of self-reported distress and empathy on egoistic versus altruistic motivation to help. *Journal of Personality and Social Psychology, 45,* 706–718.

Battaglia, G., Yeh, S. Y., & De Souza, E. B. (1988). MDMA-induced neurotoxicity: Parameters of degeneration and recovery of brain serotonin neurons. *Pharmacology, Biochemistry and Behavior, 29,* 269–274.

Bauer, P. J. (1996). What do infants recall of their lives?: Memory for specific events by one- to two-year-olds. *American Psychologist, 51,* 29–41.

Bauman, K., Koch, G., & Fisher, L. (1989). Family cigarette smoking and test performance by adolescents. *Health Psychology, 8,* 97–106.

Bauman, W., & Melnyk, W. T. (1994). A controlled comparison of eye movements and finger tapping in the treatment of test anxiety. *Journal of Behaviour Therapy and Experimental Psychiatry, 25,* 29–33.

Baumeister, R. (1995). Self and identity: An introduction. In A. Tesser (Ed.), *Advanced social psychology* (pp. 51–98). New York: McGraw-Hill.

Baumeister, R. F. (1995). Disputing the effects of championship pressures and home audiences. *Journal of Personality and Social Psychology, 68,* 644–648.

Baumeister, R. F., & Leary, M. R. (1995). The need to belong: Desire for interpersonal attachments as a fundamental human motivation. *Psychological Bulletin, 117*(3), 497–529.

Baumrind, D. (1971). Current patterns of parental authority. *Developmental Psychology Monographs, 4*(1, part 2).

Baumrind, D. (1986). *Familial antecedents of social competence in middle childhood.* Unpublished monograph, Institute of Human Development, University of California, Berkeley.

Baumrind, D. (1989, April). *Sex-differentiated socialization effects in childhood and adolescence in divorced and intact families.* Paper presented at the meeting of the Society for Research in Child Development, Kansas City, MO.

Baumrind, D. (1991). Effective parenting during the early adolescent transition. In P. A. Cowan & E. M. Hetherington (Eds.), *Family transition* (pp. 111–163). Hillsdale, NJ: Lawrence Erlbaum Associates.

Baylis, G. C., & Driver, J. (1992). Visual parsing and response competition: The effect of grouping factors. *Perception and Psychophysics, 51,* 145–162.

Beardsley, L. M. (1994). Medical diagnosis and treatment across culture. In W. J.

Lonner and R. S. Malpass (Eds.), *Psychology and Culture*. New York: Allyn & Bacon.

Beardsley, R. S., Gardocki, G. J., Larson, D. B., & Hidalgo, J. (1988). Prescribing of psychotropic medication by primary-care physicians and psychiatrists. *Archives of General Psychiatry, 45,* 1117–1119.

Beauchamp, G. K., Katahira, K., Yamazaki, K., Mennella, J. A., Bard, J., & Boyse, E. A. (1995). Evidence suggesting that the odortypes of pregnant women are a compound of maternal and fetal odortypes. *Proceedings of the National Academy of Sciences of the United States of America, 92,* 2617–2621.

Beauchamp-Turner, D. L., & Levinson, D. M. (1992). Effects of meditation on stress, health, and affect. *Medical Psychotherapy: An International Journal, 5,* 123–131.

Beck, A. T. (1967). *Depression: Clinical, experimental and theoretical aspects.* New York: Harper & Row.

Beck, A. T. (1976). *Cognitive therapy and the emotional disorders.* New York: International Universities Press.

Beck, A. T. (1993). Cognitive therapy: Past, present, and future. *Journal of Consulting and Clinical Psychology, 61,* 194–198.

Beck, A. T., Brown, G., Berchick, R. J., Stewart, B. L., & Steer, R. A. (1990). Relationship between hopelessness and ultimate suicide: A replication with psychiatric outpatients. American Journal of Psychiatry, 147, 190–195.

Beck, A. T., & Emery, G. (1985). *Anxiety disorders and phobias: A cognitive perspective.* New York: Basic Books.

Beck, A. T., Rush, A. J., Shaw, B. F., & Emery, G. (1979). *Cognitive therapy of depression.* New York: Guilford.

Beck, A. T., Sokol, L., Clark, D., Berchick, R., & Wright, F. (1992). A crossover study of focused cognitive therapy for panic disorder. *American Journal of Psychiatry, 149,* 778–783.

Beck, M. (1992, December 7). The new middle age. *Newsweek,* pp. 50–56.

Bedard, J. (1989). Expertise in auditing: Myth or reality? *Accounting, Organizations and Society, 14,* 113–131.

Bedard, J., & Chi, M. T. H. (1992). Expertise. *Current Directions in Psychological Science, 1,* 135–139.

Begley, S. (1995, March 27). Gray matters. *Newsweek,* pp. 48–54.

Beike, D. R., & Sherman, S. J. (1994). Social inference: Inductions, deductions, and analogies. In R. S. Wyer & T. K. Srull (Eds.), *Handbook of social cognition* (2nd ed.). Hillsdale, NJ: Lawrence Erlbaum Associates.

Beilin, H. (1992). Piaget's enduring contribution to developmental psychology. *Developmental Psychology, 28,* 191–204.

Belgrave, F. Z., & Randolph, S. M. (Eds.). (1993). *Journal of Black Psychology: Special Issue on the Psychosocial Aspects of AIDS Prevention Among African-Americans, 19* (whole issue).

Bell, B. E., & Loftus, E. F. (1989). Trivial persuasion in the courtroom: The power of (a few) minor details. *Journal of Personality and Social Psychology, 56,* 669–679.

Bell, P. A. (1992). In defense of the negative affect escape model of heat and aggression. *Psychological Bulletin, 111,* 342–346.

Bell, P. A., Fisher, J. D., Baum, A., & Greene, T. (1990). *Environmental psychology* (3rd ed.). Forth Worth, TX: Holt, Rinehart & Winston.

Bell, P. F., Digman, R. H., Jr., & McKenna, J. P. (1995). Should psychologists obtain prescription privileges? A survey of family physicians. *Professional Psychology: Research and Practice, 26,* 371–376.

Bellezza, F. S. (1981). Mnemonic devices: Classification, characteristics, and criteria. *Review of Educational Research, 51,* 247–275.

Bellezza, F. S. (1993). Does "perplexing" describe the self-reference effect? Yes! In T. K. Srull & R. S. Wyer (Eds.), *The mental representation of trait and autobiographical knowledge about the self: Advances in social cognition: Vol. V.* Hillsdale, NJ: Lawrence Erlbaum Associates.

Belmont, J. M., & Butterfield, E. C. (1971). Learning strategies as determinants of memory deficiencies. *Cognitive Psychology, 2,* 411–420.

Belsky, J. (1992). Consequences of child care for children's development: A deconstructionist view. In A. Booth (Ed.), *Child care in the 1990s: Trends and consequences.* Hillsdale, NJ: Lawrence Erlbaum Associates.

Belsky, J., & Kelly, J. (1994). *The transition to parenthood.* New York: Dell.

Bem, D. J. (1967). Self-perception: An alternative interpretation of cognitive dissonance phenomena. *Psychological Review, 74,* 183–200.

Bem, D. J., & Honorton, C. (1994). Does psi exist? Replicable evidence for an anomalous process of information transfer. *Psychological Bulletin.*

Ben-Shakhar, G. & Furedy, J. J. (1990). *Theories and applications in the detection of deception: A psychophysiological and international perspective.* New York: Springer-Verlag.

Benca, R. M., Obermeyer, W. H., Thisted, R. A., & Gillin, J. C. (1992). Sleep and psychiatric disorders. A meta-analysis. *Archives of General Psychiatry, 49,* 651–658.

Benet, V. & Waller, N.G. (1995). The big seven factor model of personality description: Evidence for its cross-cultural generality in a Spanish sample. *Journal of Personality and Social Psychology, 69,* 701–718.

Benjamin, J., Li, L., Patterson, C., Greenberg, B. D., Murphy, D. L., & Hamer, D. H. (1996). Population and familial association between the D_4 dopamine receptor gene and measures of novelty seeking. *Nature Genetics, 12,* 81–84.

Benjamin, L. T., Jr. (1988). E. B. Titchener and structuralism. In L. T. Benjamin, Jr. (Ed.), *A history of psychology: Original sources and contemporary research.* New York: McGraw-Hill.

Bennet, W. M. (1994). Marijuana has no medicinal value. *Hospital Practice, 29*(4), 26–27.

Bennett, H. L., Giannini, J. A., & Davis, H. S. (1985). Nonverbal response to intra-operational conversation. *British Journal of Anaesthesia, 57,* 174–179.

Benson, H. (1975). *The relaxation response.* New York: Morrow.

Bergeman, C. S., Chipuer, R., Plomin, R., Pederson, N. L., Mclearn, J. R., Nesselroade, P. T., Costa, P. T., Jr., & McRae, R. R. (1993). *Journal of Personality, 61,* 159–180.

Berger, A., Henderson, M., Nadoolman, W., Duffy, V., Cooper, D., Saberski, L., & Bartoshuk, L. (1995). Oral capsaicin provides temporary relief for oral mucositis pain secondary to chemotherapy/radiation therapy. *Journal of Pain and Symptom Management, 10,* 243–248.

Berger, P. A. (1978). Medical treatment of mental illness. *Science, 200,* 974–981.

Bergin, A. E. (1971). The evaluation of therapeutic outcomes. In A. E. Bergin & S. L. Garfield (Eds.), *Handbook of psychotherapy and behavior change: An empirical analysis* (pp. 217–270). New York: Wiley.

Berkowitz, B. (1965). Changes in intellect with age: IV. Changes in achievement and survival in older people. *Journal of Genetic Psychology, 107,* 3–14.

Berkowitz, L. (1993). Toward a general theory of anger and emotional aggression. In R. S. Wyer & T. K. Srull (Eds.), *Toward a general theory of anger and emotional aggression: Advances in social cognition, Vol. VI.* Hillsdale, NJ: Lawrence Erlbaum Associates.

Berkowitz, L. (1994). Is something missing? Some observations prompted by the Cognitive-neoassociationist view of anger and emotional aggression. In L. R. Huesmann (Ed.), *Human aggression: Current perspectives* (pp. 35–60). New York: Plenum.

Berlin, L. J., Cassidy, J., & Belsky, J. (1995). Loneliness in young children and infant-mother attachment: A longitudinal study. *Merrill-Palmer Quarterly, 41,* 91–103.

Berman, A. L., & Jobes, D. A. (1991). *Adolescent suicide: Assessment and intervention.* Washington, DC: American Psychological Association.

Berman, R. F. (1991). Electrical brain stimulation used to study mechanisms and models of memory. In J. L. Martinez & R. P. Kesner (Eds.), *Learning and memory: A biological view* (2nd ed.). San Diego, CA: Academic Press.

Bermond, B., Fasotti, L., Nieuwenhuyse, B., & Schuerman, J. (1991). Spinal cord lesions, peripheral feedback and intensities of emotional feelings. *Cognition and Emotion, 5,* 201–220.

Bernard, L. L. (1924). *Instinct.* New York: Holt, Rinehart & Winston.

Bernstein, D. A. (1970). The modification of smoking behavior: A search for effective variables. *Behaviour Research and Therapy, 8,* 133–146.

Bernstein, D. A., & Borkovec, T. D. (1973). *Progressive relaxation training: A manual for the helping professions.* Champaign, IL: Research Press.

Bernstein, D. M., & Roberts, B. (1995). Assessing dreams through self-report questionnaires: Relation with past research and personality. *Dreaming: Journal of the Association for the Study of Dreams, 5,* 13–27.

Bernstein, I. L. (1978). Learned taste aversions in children receiving chemotherapy. *Science, 200,* 1302–1303.

Berry, E. M., Fried, S., & Edlestein, E. L. (1995). Abnormal oral sensory perception in patients with a history of anorexia nervosa and the relationship between physiological and psychological improvement in this disease. *Psychotherapy and Psychosomatics, 63*(1), 32–37.

Berry, J. W., & Bennett, J. A. (1992). Cree conceptions of cognitive competence. *International Journal of Psychology, 27,* 73–88.

Berry, J. W., Poortinga, Y. A., Segall, M. H., & Dasen, P. R. (1992). *Cross-cultural psychology: Research and applications.* New York: Cambridge University Press.

Bertenthal, B. I. (1993, March). *Emerging trends in perceptual development.* Master lecture presented at the biennial meeting of the Society for Research in Child Development, New Orleans.

Berthier, M. L. (1994). Foreign accent syndrome. *Neurology, 44,* 990–991.

Best, D. (1992, June). *Cross-cultural themes in developmental psychology.* Paper presented at workshop on cross-cultural aspects of psychology. Western Washington University, Bellingham.

Best, J. B. (1995). *Cognitive Psychology* (4th ed.). Minneapolis, MN: West Publishing Company.

Betancourt, H., & Lopez, S. R. (1993). The study of culture, ethnicity, and race in American psychology. *American Psychologist, 48,* 629–637.

Bettman, J. R., Johnson, E. J., & Payne, J. W. (1990). A componential analysis of cognitive effort in choice. *Organizational Behavior and Human Decision Processes, 45,* 111–139.

Bettman, J. R., Payne, J. W., & Staelin, R. (1986). Cognitive considerations in designing effective labels for presenting risk information. *Journal of Marketing and Public Policy, 5,* 1–28.

Bevan, S., & Geppetti, P. (1994). Protons: Small stimulants of capsaicin-sensitive sensory nerves. *Trends in Neuroscience, 17,* 509–512.

Biederman, I. (1987). Recognition by components. *Psychological Review, 94,* 115–147.

Biederman, I., Cooper, E. E., Fox, P. W., & Mahadevan, R. S. (1992). Unexceptional spatial memory in an exceptional memorist. *Journal of Experimental Psychology: Learning, Memory, and Cognition, 18,* 654–657.

Bigelow, A., MacLean, J., Wood, C., & Smith, J. (1990). Infants' responses to child and adult strangers: An investigation of height and facial configuration variables. *Infant Behavior and Development, 13,* 21–32.

Bigelow, J. (1887). *The complete works of Benjamin Franklin.* New York: Putnam Press.

Biklen, D. (1990). Communication unbound: Autism and praxis. *Harvard Educational Review, 60,* 291–314.

Billig, M., & Tajfel, H. (1973). Social categorization and similarity in intergroup behavior. *European Journal of Social Psychology, 3,* 27–52.

Billings, A. G., & Moos, R. H. (1981). The role of coping responses and social resources in attentuating the impact of stressful life events. *Journal of Behavioral Medicine, 4,* 139–157.

Binet, A., & Simon, T. (1905). Methodes nouvelles pour le diagnostic du niveau intellectuel des anormaux. *L'Annee Psychologique, 11,* 191–244.

Birnbaum, M. H., & Sotoodeh, Y. (1991). Measurement of stress: Scaling the magnitudes of life changes. *Psychological Science, 2,* 236–243.

Bjork, R. A., & Vanhuele, M. (1992). Retrieval inhibition and related adaptive peculiarities of human memory. *Advances in Consumer Research, 19,* 155–160.

Bjorklund, D. F., & Green, B. L. (1992). The adaptive nature of cognitive immaturity. *American Psychologist, 47,* 46–54.

Black, J. E., & Greenough, W. T. (1991). Developmental approaches to the memory process. In J. L. Martinez & R. P. Kesner (Eds.), *Learning and memory: A biological view* (2nd ed.). San Diego: Academic Press.

Blackwell, B. (1973). Psychotropic drugs in use today. *Journal of the American Medical Association, 225,* 1637–1641.

Blair, M. E., & Shimp, T. A. (1992). Consequences of an unpleasant experience with music: A second-order negative conditioning perspective. *Journal of Advertising, 21,* 35–43.

Blalock, J. E. (1994). The syntax of immune neuroendocrine communication. *Immunology Today, 15,* 504–511.

Blanchard, E. (1992a). Introduction to the special issue on behavioral medicine: An update for the 1990s. *Journal of Consulting and Clinical Psychology, 60,* 491–492.

Blanchard, E. (1992b). Psychological treatment of benign headache disorders. *Journal of Consulting and Clinical Psychology, 60,* 537–551.

Blanchard, E. B., & Andrasik, F. (1985). *Management of chronic headaches: A psychological approach.* New York: Pergamon Press.

Blanck, R., & Blanck, G. (1986). *Beyond ego psychology: Developmental object relations theory.* New York: Columbia University Press.

Blass, T. (1991). Understanding behavior in the Milgram obedience experiment: The role of personality, situations, and their interactions. *Journal of Personality and Social Psychology, 60,* 398–413.

Blatchford, P., Burke, J., Farquhar, C., & Plewis, I. (1989). Teacher expectations in infant school: Associations with attainment and progress, curriculum coverage and classroom interaction. *British Journal of Educational Psychology, 59,* 19–30.

Blazer, D. G., Kessler, R. C., McGonagle, K. A., & Swartz, M. S. (1994). The prevalence and distribution of major depression in a national community sample: The national comorbidity survey. *American Journal of Psychiatry, 151,* 979–986.

Blehar, M., & Rosenthal, N. (1989). Seasonal affective disorders and phototherapy. *Archives of General Psychiatry, 46,* 469–474.

Block, J. (1971). *Lives through time.* Berkeley: Bancroft Books.

Block, J. A. (1995). A contrarian view of the five-factor approach. *Psychological Bulletin, 117,* 187–215.

Block, J. H. (1983). Differential premises arising from differential socialization of the sexes: Some conjectures. *Child Development, 54,* 1335–1354.

Block, R. I., Farinpour, R., & Braverman, K. (1992). Acute effects of marijuana on cognition: Relationships to chronic effects and smoking techniques. *Pharmacology, Biochemistry and Behavior, 43*(3), 907–917.

Block, R. I., & Ghoneim, M. M. (1993). Effects of chronic marijuana use on human cognition. *Psychopharmacology, 110*(1–2), 219–228.

Bloom, A. H. (1981). *The linguistic shaping of thought: A study of the impact of language on thinking in China and the West.* Hillsdale, NJ: Lawrence Erlbaum Associates.

Bloom, L. (1995). *The transition from infancy to language: Acquiring the power of expression.* New York: Cambridge University Press.

Blumberg, M. S., & Lucas, D. E. (1994). Dual mechanisms of twitching during sleep in neonatal rats. *Behavioral Neuroscience, 108*(6), 1196–1202.

Blume, E. S. (1990). *Secret survivors: Uncovering incest and its aftereffects in women.* New York: Ballantine.

Blundell, J. E., & Halford, J. C. G. (1995). Pharmacological aspects of obesity treatment—Towards the 21st century. *International Journal of Obesity, 19,* 51–55.

Bogen, J. E. (1995). On the neurophysiology of consciousness: I. An overview. *Consciousness and Cognition, 4,* 52–62.

Bolles, R. C. (1975). *Theory of motivation* (2nd ed.). New York: Harper & Row.

Bond, G., Aiken, L., & Somerville, S. (1992). The Health Beliefs Model and adolescents with insulin-dependent diabetes mellitus. *Health Psychology, 11,* 190–198.

Bond, R., & Smith, P. B. (1996). Culture and conformity: A meta-analysis of studies using Asch's (1952b, 1956) line judgment task. *Psychological Bulletin, 119,* 111–137.

Bonica, J. J. (1992). Importance of the problem. In G. M. Aronoff (Ed.), *Evaluation and treatment of chronic pain.* Baltimore: Williams & Wilkins.

Bonington, C. (1976). *Everest the hard way.* New York: Random House.

Bonwell, C. C., & Eison, J. A. (1991). *Active learning: Creating excitement in the classroom.* Washington, DC: George Washington University.

Borduin, C. M., Mann, B. J., Cone, L. T., Henggeler, S. W., Fucci, B. R., Blaske, D. M., & Williams, R. A. (1995). Multisystemic treatment of serious juvenile offenders: Long-term prevention of criminality and violence. *Journal of Consulting and Clinical Psychology, 63,* 569–578.

Borgida, E., Conner, C., & Monteufel, L. (1992). Understanding living kidney donors: A behavioral decision-making perspective. In S. Spacapan & S. Oskamp (Eds.), *Helping and being helped* (pp. 183–212). Newbury Park, CA: Sage.

Boring, E. G. (1930). A new ambiguous figure. *American Journal of Psychology, 42,* 444–445.

Borkovec, T. D., & Costello, E. (1993). Efficacy of applied relaxation and cognitive-behavioral therapy in the treatment of generalized anxiety disorder. *Journal of Consulting and Clinical Psychology, 61,* 611–619.

Borkovec, T. D., Hopkins, M., Lyonfields, J., Lytle, R., Possa, S., Roemer, L., & Shadick, R. (1991, November). *Efficacy of nondirective therapy, applied relaxation, and combined cognitive behavioral therapy for generalized anxiety disorder.* Paper presented at the meeting of the Association for the Advancement of Behavior Therapy, New York.

Borkovec, T. D., & Inz, J. (1990). The nature of worry in generalized anxiety disorder: A predominance of thought activity. *Behaviour Research and Therapy, 28,* 153–158.

Borkovec, T. D., & Mathews, A. M. (1988). Treatment of nonphobic anxiety disorders: A comparison of nondirective, cognitive, and coping desensitization therapy. *Journal of Consulting and Clinical Psychology, 56,* 877–884.

Borkowski, J. G., Weyhing, R. S., & Turner, L. A. (1986). Attributional retraining and the teaching of strategies. *Exceptional Children, 53,* 130–137.

Bornstein, R. F. (1992). Subliminal mere exposure effects. In R. F. Bornstein & T. S. Pittman (Eds.), *Perception without awareness: Cognitive, clinical, and social perspectives* (pp. 191–210). New York: Guilford.

Borum, R. & Grisso, T. (1995). Psychological test use in criminal forensic evaluations. *Professional Psychology: Research and Practice. 26,* 465–473.

Botwinick, J. (1961). Husband and father-in-law: A reversible figure. *American Journal of Psychology, 74,* 312–313.

Botwinick, J. (1966). Cautiousness in advanced age. *Journal of Gerontology, 21,* 347–353.

Botwinick, J. (1977). Intellectual abilities. In J. E. Birren & K. W. Schaie (Eds.), *Handbook of the psychology of aging.* New York: Van Nostrand Reinhold.

Bouchard, T. J., Jr., Lykken, D. T., McGue, M., Segal, N. L., & Tellegen, A. (1990). Sources of human psychological differences: The Minnesota study of twins reared apart. *Science, 250,* 223–228.

Bouchard, T. J., & McGue, M. (1981). Familial studies of intelligence: A review. *Science, 212,* 1055–1059.

Bouchard, T. J., Segal, N. L., & Abraham, L. M. (1989). Job satisfaction: Environmental and genetic components. *Journal of Applied Psychology, 74,* 187–192.

Bowen, A. M., & Trotter, R. T., II (1995). HIV risk in intravenous drug users and crack cocaine smokers: Predicting stage of change for condom use. *Journal of Consulting and Clinical Psychology, 63,* 238–248.

Bower, G. H. (1975). Cognitive psychology: An introduction. In W. K. Estes (Ed.), *Handbook of learning and cognitive processes: Vol. 1.* Hillsdale, NJ: Lawrence Erlbaum Associates.

Bower, G. H. (1981). Mood and memory. *American Psychologist, 36,* 129–148.

Bower, G. H. (1994, September 9). *Emotion and social judgements.* Speech presented to the Capital Hill Seminar, sponsored by the Federation of Behavioral, Psychological, and Cognitive Sciences.

Bower, T. G. R., & Wishart, J. G. (1972). The effects of motor skill on object permanence. *Cognition, 1,* 165–172.

Bowers, K. S. (1992). Imagination and dissociation in hypnotic responding. *International Journal of Clinical and Experimental Hypnosis, 40,* 253–275.

Bowlby, J. (1951). *Maternal care and mental health.* World Health Organization Monograph 2. Geneva: World Health Organization.

Bowlby, J. (1973). *Attachment and loss: Vol. 2. Separation.* New York: Basic Books.

Bowlby, J. (1980). *Loss: Sadness and depression.* New York: Basic Books.

Boyatzis, R. E. (1982). *The competent manager.* New York: Wiley.

Bozarth, M. A., & Wise, R. A. (1984). Anatomically distinct opiate receptor fields mediate reward and physical dependence. *Science, 224,* 516–518.

Bradbury, T. N., Campbell, S. M., & Fincham, F. D. (1995). Longitudinal and behavioral analysis of masculinity and femininity in marriage. *Journal of Personality and Social Psychology, 68,* 328–341.

Bradley-Johnson, S., Graham, D. P., & Johnson, C. M. (1986). Token reinforcement on WISC-R performance for white, low-socioeconomic, upper and lower elementary-school-age students. *Journal of School Psychology, 24,* 73–79.

Bradshaw, G. L. (1993a). Why did the Wright brothers get there first? Part 1. *Chemtech, 23*(6), 8–13.

Bradshaw, G. L. (1993b). Why did the Wright brothers get there first? Part 2. *Chemtech, 23*(7), 16–22.

Bradshaw, G. L. (1993c). Beyond animal language. In H. L. Roitblat, L. M. Herman, & P. E. Nachtigall (Eds.), *Language and communication: Comparative perspectives.* Hillsdale, NJ: Lawrence Erlbaum Associates.

Bradshaw, G. L., & Shaw, D. (1992). Forecasting solar flares: Experts and artificial systems. *Organizational Behavior and Human Decision Performance, 53,* 135–157.

Brainerd, C. J., Reyna, V. F., & Brandse, E. (1995). Are children's false memories more persistent than their true memories? *Psychological Science, 6,* 359–364.

Brandimonte, M. A., Hitch, G. J., & Bishop, D. V. M. (1992). Influence of short-term memory codes on visual image processing: Evidence from image transformation tasks. *Journal of Experimental Psychology: Learning, Memory, and Cognition, 18,* 157–165.

Brandtstadter, J., & Renner, G. (1990). Tenacious goal pursuit and flexible goal adjustment: Explication and age-related analysis of assimilative and accommodative strategies of coping. *Psychology and Aging, 5,* 58–67.

Bransford, J. D., & Johnson, M. K. (1972). Contextual prerequisites for understanding: Some investigations of comprehension and recall. *Journal of Verbal Learning and Verbal Behavior, 11,* 717–726.

Bransford, J. D., & Stein, B. S. (1993). *The ideal problem solver* (2nd ed.). New York: W. H. Freeman.

Braungart, J. M., Plomin, R., & Fulker, D. W. (1992). Genetic mediation of the home environment during infancy: A sibling adoption study of the HOME. *Developmental Psychology, 28,* 1048–1055.

Braunstein, M. (1990). Structure from motion. In J. Elkind, S. Card, J. Hochberg, & B. Huey (Eds.), *Human performance models for computer-aided engineering.* Orlando, FL: Academic Press.

Breedlove, S. M. (1994). Sexual differentiation of the human nervous system. *Annual Review of Psychology, 45,* 389–418.

Breggin, P. (1991). *Toxic psychiatry.* New York: St. Martin's Press.

Bregman, A. S. (1990). *Auditory scene analysis.* Cambridge, MA: Bradford/MIT Press.

Brehm, J. W., & Self, E. A. (1989). The intensity of motivation. *Annual Review of Psychology, 40,* 109–131.

Brehm, S. (1992). *Intimate relationships.* New York: McGraw-Hill.

Breier, A., Buchanan, R. W., Elkashef, A., Munson, R. C., Kirkpatrick, B., & Gellad, F. (1992). Brain morphology and schizophrenia: A magnetic resonance imaging study of limbic, prefrontal cortex, and caudate structures. *Archives of General Psychiatry, 49,* 921–926.

Breier, A., Buchanan, R. W., Kirkpatrick, B., Davis, O. R., Irish, D., Summerfelt, A., & Carpenter, W. T. (1994). Effects of clozapine on positive and negative symptoms in outpatients with schizophrenia. *American Journal of Psychiatry, 151,* 20–26.

Breier, A., Davis, O. R., Buchanan, R. W., Moricle, L. A., & Munson, R. C. (1993). Effects of metabolic perturbation on plasma homovanillic acid in schizophrenia. *Archives of General Psychiatry, 50,* 541–550.

Breier, A., Schreiber, J. L., Dyer, J., & Pickar, D. (1991). National Institute of Mental Health longitudinal study of chronic schizophrenia: Prognosis and predictors of outcome. *Archives of General Psychiatry, 48,* 239–246.

Breland, K., & Breland, M. (1966). *Animal behavior.* New York: Macmillan.

Brelsford, J. W. (1993). Physics education in a virtual environment. In *Proceedings of the 37th Annual Meeting of the Human Factors and Ergonomics Society.* Santa Monica, CA: Human Factors.

Brennan, P. A., & Mednick, S. A. (1994). Learning theory approach to the deterrence of criminal recidivism. *Journal of Abnormal Psychology, 103,* 430–440.

Brennen, T., Baguley, T., Bright, J., & Bruce, V. (1990). Resolving semantically induced tip-of-the-tongue states for proper nouns. *Memory & Cognition, 18,* 339–347.

Brenner, L., & Ritter, R. C. (1995). Peptide cholecystokinin receptor antagonist increases food intake in rats. *Appetite, 24,* 1–9.

Breuer, J., & Freud, S. (1896). *Studies on hysteria.* New York: Avon. (Reprinted in 1966)

Brewer, M. (1993). Social identity, distinctiveness, and ingroup homogeneity. *Social Cognition, 11,* 150–164.

Brewer, W. F., & Pani, J. R. (1984). The structure of human memory. In G. H. Bower (Ed.), *The psychology of learning and motivation: Vol. 17.* New York: Academic Press.

Brewer, W. F., & Treyens, J. C. (1981). Role of schemata in memory for places. *Cognitive Psychology, 13,* 207–230.

Brewerton, T. D., Lydiard, R. B., Herzog, D. B., & Brotman, A. W. (1995). Comorbidity of Axis I psychiatric disorders in bulimia nervosa. *Journal of Clinical Psychiatry, 56*(2), 77–80.

Brewin, C. R., Andrews, B., & Gotlib, I. H. (1993). Psychopathology and early experience: A reappraisal of retrospective reports. *Psychological Bulletin, 113,* 82–98.

Brigham, C. C. (1923). *A study of American intelligence.* Princeton, NJ: Princeton University Press.

Brigham, C. C. (1930). Intelligence tests of immigrant groups. *Psychological Review, 37,* 158–165.

Brinckerhoff, L. C., Shaw, S. F., & McGuire, J. M. (1993). *Promoting postsecondary education for students with learning disabilities.* Austin, TX: Pro-ed.

Brislin, R., (1993). *Understanding culture's influence on behavior.* Fort Worth: Harcourt, Brace, Jovanovich.

Brock, J. W., Farooqui, S. M., Ross, K. D., & Payne, S. (1994). Stress-related behavior and central norepinephrine concentrations in the REM sleep-deprived rat. *Physiology and Behavior, 55*(6), 997–1003.

Brody, J. E. (1983, December 13). Divorce's stress exacts long-term health toll. *New York Times,* p. 17

Broman, C. L. (1993). Social relationships and health-related behavior. *Journal of Behavioral Medicine, 16,* 335–350.

Bronfenbrenner, U., & Ceci, S. J. (1994). Nature-nurture reconceptualized in developmental perspective: A bioecological model. *Psychological Review, 101.*

Brooks-Gunn, J. (1988). Antecedents and consequences of variations in girls' maturational timing. *Journal of Adolescent Health Care, 9*(5), 1–9.

Brooks-Gunn, J., & Furstenberg, F. F. (1989). Adolescent sexual behavior. *American Psychologist, 44,* 249–257.

Brooks-Gunn, J., Gross, R. T., Kraemer, H. C., Spiker, D., & Shapiro, S. (1992). Enhancing the cognitive outcomes of low birth weight, premature infants: For whom is the intervention most effective? *Pediatrics, 89,* 1209–1215.

Brown, A. L., Campione, J. C., Webber, L. S., & McGilly, K. (1992). Interactive learning environments: A new look at assessment and instruction. In B. Gifford & M. C. O'Connor (Eds.), *Changing assessments: Alternative views of aptitude, achievement, and instruction.* Boston: Kluever.

Brown, A. S. (1991). A review of the tip-of-the-tongue experience. *Psychological Bulletin, 109,* 204–233.

Brown, D., Ahmed, F., Gary, L., & Milburn, N. (1995). Major depression in a community sample of African-Americans. *American Journal of Psychiatry, 152,* 373–378.

Brown, D. C. (1994). Subgroup norming: Legitimate testing practice or reverse discrimination? *American Psychologist, 49*(11), 927–928.

Brown, G. M. (1994). Light, melatonin, and the sleep–wake cycle. *Journal of Psychiatry and Neuroscience, 19*(5), 345–353.

Brown, G. W., & Harris, T. (1978). *Social origins of depression.* London: Free Press.

Brown, J. (1958). Some tests of the decay theory of immediate memory. *Quarterly Journal of Experimental Psychology, 10,* 12–21.

Brown, J. D., & McGill, K. L. (1989). The cost of good fortune: When positive life events produce negative health consequences. *Journal of Personality and Social Psychology, 57,* 1103–1110.

Brown, J. D., Novick, N. J., Lord, K. A., & Richards, J. M. (1992). When Gulliver travels: Social context, psychological closeness, and self-appraisals. *Journal of Personality and Social Psychology, 62,* 717–727.

Brown, R. A. (1973). *First language.* Cambridge, MA: Harvard University Press.

Brown, R., & Kulik, J. (1977). Flashbulb memories. *Cognition, 5,* 73–99.

Brown, R., & McNeill, D. (1966). The "tip-of-the-tongue" phenomenon. *Journal of Verbal Learning and Verbal Behavior, 5,* 325–337.

Brownell, K. D., & Rodin, J. (1994). The dieting maelstrom: Is it possible and advisable to lose weight? *American Psychologist, 49*(9), 781–791.

Bruce, H. M. (1969). Pheromones and behavior in mice. *Acta Neurologica Belgica, 69,* 529–538.

Bruck, M., Cavanagh, P., & Ceci, S. J. (1991). Fortysomething: Recognizing faces at one's 25th reunion. *Memory & Cognition, 19,* 221–228.

Brunvald, J. H. (1989). *Curses! Broiled again! The hottest urban legends going.* New York: Norton.

Brunvald, J. H. (1995). Lights out! A faxlore phenomenon. *Skeptical Inquirer, 19,* 32–37.

Bruyer, R. (1991). Covert face recognition in prosopagnosia. *Brain and Cognition, 15,* 223–235.

Bryan, J. H. (1975). Children's cooperation and helping behaviors. In E. M. Hetherington (Ed.), *Review of child development research: Vol. 5.* Chicago: University of Chicago.

Bryant, R. A., & McConkey, K. M. (1989). Hypnotic blindness: A behavioral and experiential analysis. *Journal of Abnormal Psychology, 98,* 71–77.

Bryant, W. R., & Lask, B. (1995). Eating disorders: An overview. *Journal of Family Therapy, 17*(1), 13–30.

Buchanan, R. W., Strauss, M., Kirkpatrick, B., Holstein, C., Breier, A., & Carpenter, W. T., Jr., (1994). Neuropsychological impairments in deficit vs. nondeficit forms of schizophrenia. *Archives of General Psychiatry, 51,* 804–811.

Buchsbaum, M. S., Haier, R. J., Potkin, S. G., Nuehterlein, K., Bracha, H. S., Katz, M., Lohr, J., Wu, J., Lottenberg, S., Jerabek, P. A., Trenary, M., Tafalla, R., Reynolds, C., & Bunney, W. E. (1992). Frontostriatal disorder of cerebral metabolism in never-medicated schizophrenics. *Archives of General Psychiatry, 49,* 935–942.

Buck, L., & Axel, R. (1991). A novel multigene family may encode odorant receptors: A molecular basis for odor recognition. *Cell, 65,* 175–181.

Budzynski, T. H., & Stoyva, J. M. (1984). Biofeedback methods in the treatment of anxiety and stress. In R. L. Woolfolk & P. M. Lehrer (Eds.), *Principles and practice of stress management.* New York: Guilford.

Buie, J. (1989, January). Traditional analyses may be changing. *APA Monitor,* p. 18.

Bullough, V. L. (1995, August). Sex matters. *Scientific American,* pp. 105–106.

Buonocor, M. H., & Hecht, S. T. (1995). Functional magnetic resonance imaging depicts the brain in action. *Nature Medicine, 1,* 379–381.

Burchard, R. E. (1992). Coca chewing and diet. *Current Anthropology, 33*(1), 1–24.

Burger, J. M., & Petty, R. E. (1981). The low-ball compliance technique: Task or person commitment? *Journal of Personality and Social Psychology, 40,* 492–500.

Burish, T., & Jenkins, R. (1992). Effectiveness of biofeedback and relaxation training in reducing the side effects of cancer chemotherapy. *Health Psychology, 11,* 17–23.

Burke, K. C., Burke, J. K., Jr., Regier, D. A., & Rae, D. S. (1990). Age at onset of selected mental disorders in five community populations. *Archives of General Psychiatry, 47,* 511–518.

Burleson, M. H., Gregory, W. L., & Trevarthen, W. R. (1995). Heterosexual activity: Relationship with ovarian function. *Psychoneuroendocrinology, 20*(4), 405–421.

Burman, B., & Margolin, G. (1992). Analysis of the association between marital relationships and health problems: An interactional perspective. *Psychological Bulletin, 112,* 39–63.

Burnham, M., Hough, R., Escobar, J., Karno, M., Timbers, D., Telles, C., & Locke, B. (1987). Six-month prevalence of specific psychiatric disorders among Mexican Americans and non-Hispanic whites in Los Angeles. *Archives of General Psychiatry, 44,* 687–694.

Burns, M. O., & Seligman, M. E. P. (1989). Explanatory style across the life span: Evidence for stability over 52 years. *Journal of Personality and Social Psychology, 56,* 471–477.

Burnstein, E., Crandell, C., & Kitayama, S. (1994). Some Neo-Darwinian decision rules for altruism: Weighing cues for inclusive fitness as a function of the biological importance of the decision. *Journal of Personality and Social Psychology, 67,* 773–789.

Burr, C. (1993). Homosexuality and biology. *Atlantic Monthly, 271,* 47–65.

Bushman, B. J. (1993). Human aggression while under the influence of alcohol and other drugs: An integrative research review. *Current Directions in Psychological Science, 2,* 148–152.

Buske-Kirschbaum, A., Kirschbaum, C., Stierle, H., Jabaij, L., & Hellhammer, D.

(1994). Conditioned manipulation of natural killer (NK) cells in humans using a discriminative learning protocol. *Biological Psychology, 38,* 143–155.

Buske-Kirschbaum, A., Kirschbaum, C., Stierle, H., Lehnert, H., & Hellhammer, D. (1992). Conditioned increase of natural killer cell activity (NKCA) in humans. *Psychosomatic Medicine, 54,* 123–132.

Buss, A. H. (1989). Personality as traits. *American Psychologist, 44,* 1378–1388.

Buss, A. H. (1995). *Personality: Temperament, social behavior, and the self.* Boston: Allyn & Bacon.

Buss, D. M. (1988). The evolution of human intrasexual competition: Tactics of mate attraction. *Journal of Personality and Social Psychology, 54,* 616–628.

Buss, D. M. (1994). *The evolution of desire.* Philadelphia: Temple University Press.

Buss, D. M. (1994a). Individual differences in mating strategies. *Behavioral and Brain Sciences, 17*(3), 581–582.

Buss, D. M. (1994b). *The evolution of desire: Strategies of human mating.* New York: Basic Books.

Buss, D. M. (1995a). Evolutionary psychology: A new paradigm for psychological science. *Psychological Inquiry, 6,* 1–30.

Buss, D. M. (1995b). The future of evolutionary psychology. *Psychological Inquiry, 6,* 81–87.

Buss, D. M. (1995). Psychological sex differences: Origins through sexual selection. *American Psychologist, 50,* 164–168.

Buss, D. M., & Schmitt, D. P. (1993). Sexual strategies theory: An evolutionary perspective on human mating. *Psychological Review, 100,* 204–232.

Butler, R. (1992). What young people want to know when: Effects of mastery and ability goals on interest in different kinds of social comparisons. *Journal of Personality and Social Psychology, 62,* 934–943.

Buunk, B. (1995). Comparison direction and comparison dimension among disabled individuals: Toward a refined conceptualization of social comparison under stress. *Personality and Social Psychology Bulletin, 21,* 316–330.

Byrne, D., & Kelley, K. (1989). Basing legislative action on research data: Prejudice, prudence, and empirical limitations. In D. Zillmann & J. Bryant (Eds.), *Pornography: Research advances and policy considerations.* Hillsdale, NJ: Lawrence Erlbaum Associates.

Byrne, D., & Nelson, D. (1965). Attraction as a linear function of proportion of positive reinforcements. *Journal of Personality and Social Psychology, 1,* 659–663.

Cabanac, M., & Morrissette, J. (1992). Acute, but not chronic, exercise lowers the body weight set-point in male rats. *Physiology and Behavior, 52*(6), 1173–1177.

Cacioppo, J. T., Malarkey, W. B., Kiecolt-Glaser, J. K., Uchino, B. N., Sgoutas-Emch, S. A., Sheridan, J. F., Berntson, G. G., & Glaser, R. (1995). Heterogeneity in neuroendocrine and immune responses to brief psychological stressors as a function of autonomic cardiac activation. *Psychosomatic Medicine, 57,* 154–164.

Cacioppo, J. T., & Petty, R. E. (1982). The need for cognition. *Journal of Personality and Social Psychology, 42,* 116–131.

Cacioppo, J. T., Petty, R. E., & Crites, S. L. (1993). Attitude change. In V. S. Ramachandran (Ed.), *Encyclopedia of human behavior.* San Diego, CA: Academic Press.

Cadoret, R. J., O'Gorman, T., Troughton, E., & Heywood, E. (1985). Alcoholism and antisocial personality: Interrelationships, genetics and environmental factors. *Archives of General Psychiatry, 42,* 161–167.

Cadoret, R. J., Yates, W. R., Troughton, E., Woodworth, G., & Stewart, M. A. (1995). Adoption study demonstrating two genetic pathways to drug abuse. *Archives of General Psychiatry, 52,* 42–52.

Cairns, R. B., Gariepy, J., & Hood, K. E. (1990). Development, microevolution, and social behavior. *Psychological Review, 97,* 49–65.

Calvert, S. L., & Tan, S.-L. (1994). Impact of virtual reality on young adults' physiological arousal and aggressive thoughts: Interaction versus observation. *Journal of Applied Developmental Psychology, 15,* 125–139.

Camara, W., & Schneider, D. L. (1994). Integrity tests: Facts and unresolved issues. *American Psychologist, 49,* 112–119.

Camp, C. J., Foss, G. W., Stevens, A. B., Reichard, C. C., McKitrick, L. A., & O'Hanlon, A. M. (1993). Memory training in normal and demented elderly populations: The E-I-E-I-O Model. *Experimental Aging Research, 19,* 277–290.

Campbell, D. T., & Stanley, J. C. (1966). *Experimental and quasi-experimental designs for research.* Chicago: Rand McNally.

Campfield, L. A., Smith, F. J., Guisez, Y., Devos, R., & Burn, P. (1995). Recombinant mouse OB protein: Evidence for a peripheral signal linking adiposity and central neural networks. *Science, 269,* 546–549.

Campione, J. C., Brown, A. L., & Ferrara, R. A. (1982). Mental retardation and intelligence. In R. J. Sternberg (Ed.), *Handbook of human intelligence.* Cambridge: Cambridge University Press.

Campos, J., Langer, A., & Krowitz, A. (1970). Cardiac responses on the visual cliff in prelocomotor human infants. *Science, 170,* 196–197.

Campos, J. J. (1980). Human emotions: Their new importance and their role in social referencing. *Research and Clinical Center for Child Development, 1980–81 Annual Report,* 1–7.

Camras, L. A. (1977). Facial expressions used by children in a conflict situation. *Child Development, 48,* 1431–1435.

Canino, G., Bird, H., Shrout, P., Rubio-Stipec, M., Bravo, M., Martinez, R., Sesman, M., & Guevara, L. (1987). The prevalence of specific psychiatric disorders in Puerto Rico. *Archives of General Psychiatry, 44,* 727–735.

Cann, A., & Ross, D. A. (1989). Olfactory stimuli as context cues in human memory. *American Journal of Psychology, 102,* 91–102.

Cannon, D. S., & Baker, T. B. (1981). Emetic and electric shock alcohol aversion therapy: Assessment of conditioning. *Journal of Consulting and Clinical Psychology, 49,* 20–33.

Cannon, T. D., Mednick, S. A., Parnas, J., Schulsinger, F., Praestholm, J., & Vestergaard, A. (1993). Developmental brain abnormalities in the offspring of schizophrenic mothers. *Archives of General Psychiatry, 50,* 551–564.

Cannon, T. D., Zorrilla, L. E., Shtasel, D., Gur, R. E., Gur, R. C., Marco, E. J., Moberg, P., & Price, A. (1994). Neuropsychological functioning in siblings discordant for schizophrenia and healthy volunteers. *Archives of General Psychiatry, 51,* 651–661.

Cannon, W. B. (1987). The James-Lange theory of emotions: A critical examination and an alternative theory. Special issue: 100 years of the American Journal of Psychology. *American Journal of Psychology, 100*(3–4), 567–586.

Cannon, W. B., & Washburn, A. L. (1912). An explanation of hunger. *American Journal of Physiology, 29,* 444–454.

Cannon-Bowers, J. A., Tannenbaum, S. I., Salas, E., & Converse, S. A. (1991). Toward an integration of training theory and technique. *Human Factors, 33*(3), 281–292.

Cantor, N., & Harlow, R. E. (1994). Personality, strategic behavior and daily life problem-solving. *Current Directions in Psychological Science, 3,* 169–172.

Cao, Y., Vikingstad, E. M., Huttenlocher, P. R., Towle, V. L., & Levin, D. N. (1994). Functional magnetic resonance studies of the reorganization of the human head sensorimotor area after unilateral brain injury in the perinatal period. *Proceedings of the National Academy of Sciences of the United States of America, 91,* 9612–9616.

Caplan, N., Whitemore, J. K., & Choy, M. H. (1989). *The boat people and achievement in America: A study of family life, hard work, and cultural values.* Ann Arbor: University of Michigan Press.

Caporael, L. R., & Brewer, M. B. (1995). Hierarchical evolutionary theory: There is an alternative and it's not creationism. *Psychological Inquiry, 6,* 31–34.

Capron, C., & Duyme, M. (1989). Assessment of effects of socio-economic status on IQ in a full cross-fostering study. *Nature, 340,* 552–553.

Caramazza, A., & Hillis, A. E. (1991). Lexical organization of nouns and verbs in the brain. *Nature, 349,* 788–790.

Cardon, L. R., Smith, S. D., Fulker, D. W., Kimberling, W. J., Pennington, B. F., & DeFries, J. C. (1994). Quantitative trait locus for reading disability on chromosome 6. *Science, 266,* 276–279.

Cargan, L., & Melko, M. (1982). *Singles: Myths and realities.* Beverly Hills, CA: Sage.

Carli, L. L., Ganley, R., & Pierce-Otay, A. (1991). Similarity and satisfaction in romantic relationships. *Personality and Social Psychology Bulletin, 17,* 419–426.

Carlson, M., Marcus-Newhall, A., & Miller, N. (1990). Effects of situational aggression cues: A quantitative review. *Journal of Personality and Social Psychology, 58,* 622–633.

Carmichael, L. L., Hogan, H. P., & Walter, A. A. (1932). An experimental study of the effect of language on the reproduction of visually perceived form. *Journal of Experimental Psychology, 15,* 73–86.

Carnegie Corporation of New York (1994). Saving youth from violence. *Carnegie Quarterly, 34*(1).

Carnevale, P. J., & Pruitt, D. G. (1992). Negotiation and mediation. *Annual Review of Psychology, 43,* 531–582.

Carraher, T., Schliemann, A. D., & Carraher, D. W. (1988). Mathematical concepts in everyday life. In C. G. Saxe & M. Gearhart (Eds.), *Children's mathematics: Vol. 41. New directions for child development* (pp. 71–87). San Francisco: Jossey-Bass.

Carrington, P. (1984). Modern forms of meditation. In R. L. Woolfolk & P. M. Lehrer (Eds.), *Principles and practice of stress management.* New York: Guilford.

Carroll, J. B. (1991). No demonstration that *g* is not unitary. *Intelligence, 15,* 423–436.

Carroll, K. M., Rounsaville, B. J., & Nich, C. (1994). One-year follow-up of psychotherapy and pharmacotherapy for cocaine dependence: Delayed emergence of psychotherapy effects. *Archives of General Psychiatry, 51*(12), 989–997.

Carry, G., & DiLalla, D. L. (1994). Personality and psychopathology: Genetic perspectives. *Journal of Abnormal Psychology, 103,* 32–43.

Carstensen, L. L. (1992). Motivation for social contact across the life span: A theory of socioemotional selectivity. In R. Dienstbier & J. E. Jacobs (Eds.), *Developmental perspectives on motivation: Nebraska symposium on motivation* (pp. 209–254), Nebraska.

Carter, M. M., Hollon, S. D., Carson, R., & Shelton, R. C. (1995). Effects of a safe person on induced distress following a biological challenge in panic disorder with agoraphobia. *Journal of Abnormal Psychology, 104,* 156–163.

Cartwright, R. D. (1978). *A primer on sleep and dreaming.* Reading, MA: Addison-Wesley.

Cartwright, R. D. (1993). Who needs their dreams? The usefulness of dreams in psychotherapy. *Journal of the American Academy of Psychoanalysis, 21*(4), 539–547.

Cartwright, R. D., Lloyd, S., Knight, S., & Trenholme, I. (1984). Broken dreams: A study of the effects of divorce and depression on dream content. *Psychiatry, 47,* 251–259.

Carver, C. S., & Scheier, M. F. (1995). *Perspectives on personality.* (3rd ed.) Boston, MA: Allyn & Bacon.

Carver, C. S., Scheier, M. F., & Weintraub, J. K. (1989). Assessing coping strategies: A theoretically based approach. *Journal of Personality and Social Psychology, 56,* 267–283.

Casagrande, V. A. (1994). A third parallel visual pathway to primate area V1. *Trends in Neuroscience, 17,* 305–310.

Case, R. (1985). *Intellectual development: A systematic reinterpretation.* New York: Academic Press.

Case, R. (1992). The role of the frontal lobes in the regulation of cognitive development. *Brain and Cognition, 20,* 51–73.

Caseley-Rondi, G., Merikle, P. M., & Bowers, K. S. (1994). Unconscious cognition in the context of general anesthesia. *Consciousness and Cognition, 3,* 166–195.

Cashdan, S. (1988). *Object relations therapy: Using the relationship.* New York: W. W. Norton.

Caspi, A., Bem, D. J., & Elder, G. H., Jr. (1989). Continuities and consequences of interactional styles across the life course. *Journal of Personality, 57,* 375–406.

Castle, D. J., & Murray, R. M., (1993). The epidemiology of late-onset schizophrenia. *Schizophrenia Bulletin, 19,* 691–700.

Catania, J. A., Coates, T. J., Stall, R., Turner, H., Peterson, J., Hearst, N., Dolcini, M. M., Hudes, E., Gagnon, J., Wiley, J., & Groves, R. (1992). Prevalence of AIDS-related risk factors and condom use in the United States. *Science, 258,* 1101–1106.

Cattell, R. B. (1963). Theory of fluid and crystallized intelligence: A critical experiment. *Journal of Educational Psychology, 54,* 1–22.

Cavaliere, F. (1996, February). Bilingual schools face big political challenges. *APA Monitor,* p. 36.

Cechetto, D. F., & Saper, C. B. (1990). Role of the cerebral cortex in autonomic function. In A. D. Loewy & K. M. Spyer (Eds.), *Central regulation of autonomic functions.* New York: Oxford University Press.

Ceci, S. J., & Bruck, M. (1993). The suggestibility of the child witness. *Psychological Bulletin, 113,* 403–439.

Ceci, S. J., Huffman, M. L. C., Smith, E., & Loftus, E. F. (1994). Repeatedly thinking about non-events. *Consciousness and Cognition, 3,* 388–407.

Ceci, S. J., & Liker, J. K. (1986). A day at the races: A study of IQ, expertise and cognitive complexity. *Journal of Experimental Psychology: General, 115,* 255–266.

Centers for Disease Control (1993). *Morbidity, mortality weekly report, 42,* 230–233.

Centers for Disease Control. (1996). *Suicide in the United States: 1980–1992.* Atlanta, GA: Centers for Disease Control and Prevention.

Centers for Disease Control and Prevention (1996). Update: Mortality attributable to HIV infection among persons aged 25–44 years. *United States Morbidity and Mortality Weekly Report, 45,* 121–125.

Centerwall, L. (1990). Controlled TV viewing and suicide in countries: Young adult suicide and exposure to television. *Social Psychiatry and Social Epidemiology, 25,* 149–153.

Centerwell, B. S. (1989). Exposure to television as a cause of violence. In G. Comstock (Ed.), *Public communication and behavior* (Vol. 2). San Diego: Academic Press.

Cerf, C. (1984). *The experts speak.* New York: Pantheon.

Chaiken, A. L., Sigler, E., & Derlega, V. J. (1974). Nonverbal mediators of teacher expectancy effects. *Journal of Personality and Social Psychology, 30,* 144–149.

Chambliss, D. L. (1990). Spacing of exposure sessions in the treatment of agoraphobia and simple phobia. *Behavior Therapy, 21,* 217–229.

Chambliss, D. L., & Williams, K. E. (1995). A preliminary study of African-Americans with agoraphobia: Symptom severity and outcome of treatment with in vivo exposure. *Behavior Therapy, 26,* 501–515.

Champion, V., & Huster, G. (1995). Effect of interventions on stage of mammography adoption. *Journal of Behavioral Medicine, 18,* 159–188.

Chan, D. W., & Lee, H. B. (1995). Patterns of psychological test use in Hong Kong in 1993. *Professional Psychology: Research and Practice, 26,* 292–297.

Chan, J., & Lynn, R. (1989). The intelligence of six-year-olds in Hong Kong. *Journal of Biosocial Science, 21,* 461–464.

Chance, P. (1988, April). Knock wood. *Psychology Today.*

Chao, R. K. (1994). Beyond parental control and authoritarian parenting style: Understanding Chinese parenting through the cultural notion of training. *Child Development, 65,* 1111–1119.

Chapanis, A., Parrish, R., Ockman, R. B., & Weeks, G. D. (1977). Studies in interactive communications: II. *Human Factors, 19,* 101–126.

Charness, N. (1987). Component processes in bridge bidding and novel problem-solving tasks. *Canadian Journal of Psychology, 41,* 223–243.

Charney, D., Newman, J. H., & Palmquist, M. (1995). "I'm just no good at writing": Epistemological style and writing attitudes. *Written Communication, 12*(3), 298–329.

Chase, W. G., & Ericsson, K. A. (1981). Skilled memory. In J. R. Anderson (Ed.), *Cognitive skills and their acquisition.* Hillsdale, NJ: Lawrence Erlbaum Associates.

Chemers, M. M. (1987). Leadership processes: Intrapersonal, interpersonal, and societal influences. In C. Hendrick (Ed.), *Group processes.* Newbury Park, CA: Sage.

Chermack, S. T., & Taylor, S. P. (1995). Alcohol and human physical aggression: Pharmacological versus expectancy effects. *Journal of Studies on Alcohol, 56*(4), 449–456.

Chi, M. (1978). Knowledge structures and memory development. In R. S. Siegler (Ed.), *Children's thinking: What develops?* Hillsdale, NJ: Lawrence Erlbaum Associates.

Chi, M. T., Feltovitch, P. J., & Glaser, R. (1981). Representation of physics knowledge by novices and experts. *Cognitive Science, 5,* 121–152.

Chomsky, N. (1957). *Syntactic structures.* The Hague: Mouton.

Christensen, A., & Jacobson, N. S. (1994). Who (or what) can do psychotherapy: The status and challenge of nonprofessional therapies. *Psychological Science, 5*(1), 8–14.

Christensen, L. (1988). Deception in psychological research: When is its use justified? *Personality and Social Psychology Bulletin, 14,* 664–675.

Christenssen-Szalanski, J. J., & Bushyhead, J. B. (1981). Physicians' use of probabilistic information in a real clinical setting. *Journal of Experimental Psychology: Human Perception and Performance, 7,* 928–936.

Chronicle of Higher Education. (1992). *Almanac.* Washington, DC.

Chu, J. (1994). Active learning in epidemiology and biostatistics. *Teaching and Learning in Medicine, 6,* 191–193.

Chua, W., & Chediak, A. D. (1994). Obstructive sleep apnea: Treatment improves quality of life and may prevent death. *Postgraduate Medicine, 95*(2), 123.

Chuansheng, C., Shin-Ying, L., & Stevenson, H. W. (1995). Response style and cross-cultural comparisons of rating scales among East Asian and North American students. *Psychological Science, 6,* 170–175.

Chugani, H. T., & Phelps, M. E. (1986). Maturational changes in cerebral function in infants determined by 18FDG positron emission tomography. *Science, 231,* 840–843.

Church, A. T., & Katigbak, M. S. (1989). Internal, external, and self-report structure of personality in a non-Western culture: An investigation of cross-language and cross-cultural generalizability. *Journal of Personality and Social Psychology, 57,* 857–872.

Churchland, P. S., & Sejnowski, T. J. (1992). *The computational brain.* Cambridge, MA: MIT Press/Bradford Books.

Chwalisz, K., Diener, E., & Gallagher, D. (1988). Autonomic arousal feedback and emotional experience: Evidence from the spinal cord injured. *Journal of Personality and Social Psychology, 54,* 820–828.

Cialdini, R. B. (1988). *Influence: Science and practice.* Glenview, IL: Scott, Foresman.

Cialdini, R. B. (1993). *Influence: Science and practice* (3rd ed.). New York: HarperCollins.

Cialdini, R. B. (1995). Principles and techniques of social influence. In A. Tesser (Ed.), *Advanced social psychology* (pp. 257–282). New York: McGraw-Hill.

Cialdini, R. B., Baumann, D. J., & Kenrick, D. T. (1981). Insights from sadness: A three-step model of the development of altruism as hedonism. *Developmental Review, 1,* 207–223.

Cialdini, R. B., Reno, R. R., & Kallgren, C. A. (1990). A focus theory of normative conduct: Recycling the concept of norms to reduce littering in public places. *Journal of Personality and Social Psychology, 58,* 1015–1026.

Cialdini, R. B., Schaller, M., Houlihan, D., Arps, K., Fultz, J., & Beaman, A. L. (1987). Empathy-based helping: Is it selflessly or selfishly motivated? *Journal of Personality and Social Psychology, 52,* 749–758.

Cicchetti, D., & Cohen, D. (1995). *Development and psychopathology* (Vol. 2). New York: Wiley-Interscience.

Cicogna, P. (1994). Dreaming during sleep onset and awakening. *Perceptual and Motor Skills, 78*(3, Pt. 1), 1041–1042.

Clark, D. C., & Fawcett, J. (1992). Review of empirical risk factors for evaluation of the suicidal patient. In B. Bongar (Ed.), *Suicide: Guidelines for assessment, management, and treatment* (pp. 16–48). New York: Oxford University Press.

Clark, D. C., Gibbons, R. D., Fawcett, J., & Scheftner, W. A. (1989). What is the mechanism by which suicide attempts predispose to later suicide attempts? A mathematical model. *Journal of Abnormal Psychology, 98,* 42–49.

Clark, E. (1978). Strategies for communicating. *Child Development, 49,* 953–959.

Clark, H., & Clark, E. (1977). *Psychology and language: An introduction to psycholinguistics.* New York: Harcourt Brace Jovanovich.

Clark, L. F. (1994). Social cognition and health psychology. In R. S. Wyer & T. K. Srull (Eds.), *Handbook of social cognition* (2nd ed.). Hillsdale, NJ: Lawrence Erlbaum Associates.

Clark, M. (1994). Close relationships. In R. S. Wyer & T. K. Srull (Eds.), *Handbook of social cognition* (2nd ed.). Hillsdale, NJ: Lawrence Erlbaum Associates.

Clark, M. S., & Mills, J. (1993). The difference between communal and exchange relationships: What is and is not. *Personality and Social Psychology Bulletin, 19,* 677–683.

Clark, M. S., & Pataki, S. P. (1995). Interpersonal processes influencing attraction and relationships. In A. Tesser (Ed.), *Advanced social psychology* (pp. 283–332). New York: McGraw-Hill.

Clark, M. S., & Reis, H. T. (1988). Interpersonal processes in close relationships. *Annual Review of Psychology, 39,* 609–672.

Clarke-Stewart, K. A. (1980). The father's contribution to child development. In F. A. Pedersen (Ed.), *The father-infant relationship: Observational studies in a family context.* New York: Praeger Special Studies.

Clarke-Stewart, K. A. (1988). Parents' effects on children's development: A decade of progress? *Journal of Applied Developmental Psychology, 9,* 41–84.

Clarke-Stewart, K. A. (1989). Infant day care: Maligned or malignant? *American Psychologist, 44,* 266–273.

Clarke-Stewart, K. A., & Fein, G. G. (1983). Early childhood programs. In P. H. Mussen (Ed.), *Handbook of child psychology: Vol. 2. Infancy and developmental psychobiology.* New York: Wiley.

Claus, J. J., Ludwig, C., Mohr, E., Giuffra, M., Blin, J., & Chase, T. N. (1991). Nootropic drugs in Alzheimer's disease—Symptomatic treatment with pramiracetam. *Neurology, 41,* 570–574.

Clausen, J., Sersen, E., & Lidsky, A. (1974). Variability of sleep measures in normal subjects. *Psychophysiology, 11,* 509–516.

Cleary, T. A., Humphreys, L. G., Kendrick, S. A., & Wesman, A. (1975). Educational use of tests with disadvantaged students. *American Psychologist, 30,* 15–41.

Clementz, B. A., McDowell, J. E., & Zisook, S. (1994). Saccadic system functioning among schizophrenia patients and their first-degree biological relatives. *Journal of Abnormal Psychology, 103,* 277–287.

Clendenen, V. I., Herman, C. P., & Polivy, J. (1995). Social facilitation of eating among friends and strangers. *Appetite, 23,* 1–13.

Clifton, R. K., Rochat, P., Litovsky, R., & Perris, E. (1991). Object representation guides infants' reaching in the dark. *Journal of Experimental Psychology: Human Perception and Performance, 17,* 323–329.

Cline, V. B., Croft, R. G., & Courrier, S. (1973). Desensitization of children to television violence. *Journal of Personality and Social Psychology, 27,* 360–365.

Cloninger, C. (1987). Neurogenic adaptive mechanisms in alcoholism. *Science, 236,* 410–416.

Coccaro, E. F. (1989). Central serotonin and impulsive aggression. *British Journal of Psychiatry, 155,* 52–62.

Cocco, N., & Sharpe, L. (1993). An auditory variant of eye movement desensitization in a case of childhood posttraumatic stress disorder. *Journal of Behaviour Therapy and Experimental Psychiatry, 24,* 373–377.

Cofer, L. F., Grice, J., Palmer, D., Sethre-Hofstad, L., & Zimmermann, K. (1992, June 20–22). *Evidence for developmental continuity of individual differences in morningness-eveningness.* Paper presented at the annual meeting of the American Psychological Society, San Diego, CA.

Cohen, C. E. (1981). Person categories and social perception: Testing some boundaries of the processing effects of prior knowledge. *Journal of Personality and Social Psychology, 40,* 441–452.

Cohen, J. (1994). The earth is round (p<.05). *American Psychologist, 49,* 997–1003.

Cohen, J., & Servan-Schreiber, D. (1992). Context, cortex, and dopamine: A connectionist approach to behavior and biology in schizophrenia. *Psychological Review, 99,* 45–77.

Cohen, M. S. (1993). Three paradigms for viewing decision biases. In G. A. Klein, J. Orasanu, R. Calderwood, & C. E. Zasmbok (Eds.), *Decision making in action: Models and methods.* Norwood, NJ: Ablex.

Cohen, M., & Wenzel, E. (1995). The design of multidimensional sound interfaces. In W. Barfield & T. Furness (Eds.), *Virtual environments and advanced interface design.* New York: Oxford University Press.

Cohen, N. J., Althoff, R. R., Webb, J. M., McConkie, G. W., Holden, J. A., & Noll, E. L. (1996). Eye movement monitoring as an indirect measure of memory. Unpublished manuscript, University of Illinois.

Cohen, N. J., & Corkin, S. (1981). The amnesic patient H.M.: Learning and retention of a cognitive skill. *Neuroscience Abstracts, 7,* 235.

Cohen, S., & Herbert, T. B. (1996). Health psychology: Psychological factors and physical disease from the perspective of human psychoneuroimmunology. In J. Spence, D. Foss, & J. Darley (Eds.), *Annual review of psychology* (Vol. 42). El Camino, CA: Annual Review, Inc.

Cohen, S., Kaplan, J. R., Cunnick, J. E., Manuck, S. B., & Rabin, B. S. (1992). Chronic social stress, affiliation, and cellular immune response in nonhuman primates. *Psychological Science, 3,* 301–304.

Cohen, S., & Syme, S. L. (1985). Issues in the study and application of social support. In S. Cohen & S. L. Syme (Eds.), *Social support and health.* New York: Academic Press.

Cohen, S., Tyrrell, D., & Smith, A. (1991). Psychological stress and susceptibility to the common cold. *New England Journal of Medicine, 325,* 606–612.

Cohen, S., & Williamson, G. (1991). Stress and infectious disease. *Psychological Bulletin, 109,* 5–24.

Cohn, J. F., & Tronick, E. Z. (1983). Three-month-old infants' reaction to simulated maternal depression. *Child Development, 54,* 185–193.

Cohn, J. F., & Tronick, E. Z. (1989). Specificity of infants' response to mothers' affective behavior. *Journal of the American Academy of Child and Adolescent Psychiatry, 28,* 242–248.

Coie, J. D., & Dodge, K. A. (1988). Multiple sources of data on social behavior and social status in the school: A cross-age comparison. *Child Development, 59,* 815–829.

Coile, D. C., & Miller, N. E. (1984). How radical animal activists try to mislead humane people. *American Psychologist, 39,* 700–701.

Colby, A., Kohlberg, L., Gibbs, J., & Lieberman, M. (1983). A longitudinal study of moral judgment. *Monographs of the Society for Research in Child Development, 48*(1, Serial No. 200).

Cole, K. N., Mills, P. E., Dale, P. S., & Jenkins, J. R. (1991). Effects of preschool integration for children with disabilities. *Exceptional Children, 58,* 36–45.

Coleman, D. (1992). Why do I feel so tired? Too little, too late. *American Health, 11*(4), 43–46.

Coles, M. (1989). Modern mind-brain reading: Psychophysiology, physiology & cognition. *Psychophysiology, 26,* 251–269.

College Board (1994, August 25). *News from the college board.* Media release. New York: College Board Publications.

Collins, A. M., & Loftus, E. F. (1975). A spreading activation theory of semantic processing. *Psychological Review, 82,* 407–428.

Colombo, M., D'Amato, M. R., Rodman, H. R., & Gross, C. G. (1990). Auditory association cortex lesions impair auditory short-term memory in monkeys. *Science, 247,* 336–338.

Colvin, C. R., Block, J., & Funder, D. C. (1995). Overly positive self-evaluations and personality: Negative implications for mental health. *Journal of Personality and Social Psychology, 68,* 1152–1162.

Conger, J. J. (1951). The effects of alcohol on conflict behavior in the albino rat. *Quarterly Journal of Studies on Alcohol, 12,* 1–29.

Connor, L. T., Balota, D. A., & Neely, J. H. (1992). On the relation between feeling of knowing and lexical decision: Persistent subthreshold activation of topic familiarity? *Journal of Experimental Psychology: Learning, Memory, and Cognition, 18,* 544–554.

Conrad, R. (1964). Acoustic confusions in immediate memory. *British Journal of Psychology, 55,* 75–84.

Consumer Reports (1995, November). Mental health: Does therapy help? pp. 734–739.

Cook, R. G., Cavoto, K. K., & Cavoto, B. R. (1995). Same-different texture discrimination and concept learning by pigeons. *Journal of Experimental Psychology: Animal Behavior Processes, 21,* 253–260.

Cook, S. W. (1984). The 1954 social science statement and school desegregation: A reply to Gerard. *American Psychologist, 39,* 819–832.

Cook, S. W. (1985). Experimenting on social issues: The case of school desegregation. *American Psychologist, 40,* 452–460.

Cook, T., & Mineka, S. (1987). Second-order conditioning and overshadowing in the observational conditioning of fear in monkeys. *Behaviour Research and Therapy, 25,* 349–364.

Cook, T., & Mineka, S. (1990). Selective association in the observational conditioning of fear in rhesus monkeys. *Journal of Experimental Psychology: Animal Behavior Processes, 16,* 372–389.

Cooper, H. (1979). Pygmalion grows up: A model for teacher expectation communication and performance influence. *Review of Educational Research, 49,* 389–410.

Cooper, L. A., Schacter, D. L., Ballesteros, S., & Moore, C. (1992b). Priming and recognition of transformed three-dimensional objects: Effects of size and reflection. *Journal of Experimental Psychology: Learning, Memory, and Cognition, 18,* 43–57.

Cooper, M., Russell, M., Skinner, J., Frone, M., & Mudar, P. (1992a). Stress and alcohol use: Moderating effects of gender, coping and alcohol expectancies. *Journal of Abnormal Psychology, 101,* 139–152.

Cooper, R. M., & Zubek, J. P. (1958). Effects of enriched and restricted early environments on the learning ability of bright and dull rats. *Canadian Journal of Psychology, 12,* 159–164.

Coovert, M. D., & Reeder, G. D. (1990). Negativity effects in impression formation: The role of unit formation and schematic expectations. *Journal of Experimental Social Psychology, 26,* 49–62.

Copeland, J., & Snyder, M. (in press). When counselors confirm: A functional analysis. *Personality and Social Psychology Bulletin.*

Coppen, A., Metcalf, M., & Wood, K. (1982). Lithium. In E. S. Paykel (Ed.), *Handbook of affective disorders.* New York: Guilford.

Corbetta, M., Miezin, F. M., Dobmeyer, S., Shulman, G. L., & Petersen, S. E. (1991). Selective and divided attention during visual discriminations of shape, color, and speed: Functional anatomy by positron emission tomography. *Journal of Neuroscience, 11,* 2383–2402.

Cordova, J. V., & Jacobson, N. S. (1993). Couple distress. In D. H. Barlow (ed.), *Clinical handbook of psychological disorders: A step-by-step treatment manual* (2nd ed.). New York: Guilford.

Coren, S., Ward. L. M., & Enns, J. T. (1994). *Sensation and perception* (4th ed.). Fort Worth, TX: Harcourt Brace.

Corina, D. P., Vaid, J., & Bellugi, U. (1992). The linguistic basis of left hemisphere specialization. *Science, 255,* 1258–1260.

Cork, R. C., Kihlstrom, J. F., & Hameroff, S. R. (1992). Explicit and implicit memory dissociated by anesthetic technique. *Society for Neuroscience Abstracts, 22,* 523.

Cornblatt, B., & Erlenmeyer-Kimling, L. E. (1985). Global attentional deviance in children at risk for schizophrenia: Specificity and predictive validity. *Journal of Abnormal Psychology, 94,* 470–486.

Cornoldi, C., DeBeni, R., & Baldi, A. P. (1989). Generation and retrieval of general, specific, and autobiographical images representing concrete nouns. *Acta Psychologica, 72,* 25–39.

Corsini, R. J. (1995). *Current psychotherapies* (5th ed.). Itasca, IL: Peacock.

Corsini, R. J., & Wedding, D. (1995). *Current psychotherapies* (5th ed.). Itasca, IL: Peacock.

Corty, E., Lehman, A. F., & Myers, C. P. (1993). Influence of psychoactive substance use on the reliability of psychiatric diagnosis. *Journal of Consulting and Clinical Psychology, 61,* 165–170.

Corwin, J. T. (1992). Regeneration in the auditory system. *Experimental Neurology, 115,* 7–12.

Coryell, W., Scheftner, W., Keller, M., Endicott, J., Maser, J., & Klerman, G. (1993). The enduring consequences of mania and depression. *American Journal of Psychiatry, 150,* 720–727.

Cosmides, L., & Tooby, J. (1994). Beyond intuition and instinct blindness: Toward an evolutionarily rigorous cognitive science. *Cognition, 50,* 41–77.

Costa, P. T. (1992). *Set like plaster? Evidence for the stability of adult personality.* Paper presented at the American Psychological Association Convention, Washington, DC.

Costa, P. T., Jr., & McCrae, R. R. (1988). Personality in adulthood: A six-year longitudinal study of self-reports and spouse ratings on the NEO personality inventory. *Journal of Personality and Social Psychology, 54,* 853–863.

Costa, P. T., Jr., & McCrae, R. R. (1989). Personality, stress, and coping: Some lessons from a decade of research. In K. S. Markides & C. L. Cooper (Eds.), *Aging, stress, social support, and health.* New York: Wiley.

Costa, P. T., Jr., & McCrae, R. (1992). *Revised NEO Personality Inventory: NEO PI and NEO Five-Factor Inventory (NEO FFI: Professional Manual).* Odessa, FL: Psychological Assessment Resources, Inc.

Costa, P. T., Jr., & McCrae, R. R. (1995). Primary traits of Eysenck's P-E-N system: Three- and five-factor solutions. *Journal of Personality and Social Psychology, 69,* 308–317.

Costa, P. T., Jr., Zonderman, A. B., McCrae, R. R., Cornoni-Huntley, J., Locke, B. Z., & Barbano, H. E. (1987). Longitudinal analyses of psychological well-being in a national sample: Stability of mean levels. *Journal of Gerontology, 42,* 50–55.

Costello, E., Costello, A., Edelbrock, C., Burns, B., Dulcan, M., Brent, D., & Janiszewski, S. (1988). Psychiatric disorders in pediatric primary care. *Archives of General Psychiatry, 45,* 1107–1116.

Costermans, J., Lories, G., & Ansay, C. (1992). Confidence level and feeling of knowing in question answering: The weight of inferential processes. *Journal of Experimental Psychology: Learning, Memory, and Cognition, 18,* 142–150.

Cotman, C. W., Monaghan, D. T., & Ganong, A. H. (1988). Excitatory amino acid neurotransmission: NMDA receptors and Hebb-type synaptic plasticity. *Annual Review of Neuroscience 11,* 61–80.

Cottingham, J., Stoothoff, R., & Murdoch, D. (Trans.). (1985). *The philosophical writings of Descartes* (Vol. 1). New York: Cambridge University Press.

Courneya, K. S. (1995). Understanding readiness for regular physical activity in older individuals: An application of the theory of planned behavior. *Health Psychology, 14,* 80–87.

Cowan, C. P., Cowan, P. A., Heming, G., Garret, E., Coysh, W. S., Curtis-Boles, H., & Boles, A. J. (1985). Transition to parenthood: His, hers, and theirs. *Journal of Family Issues, 6,* 451–481.

Cowan, N. (1988). Evolving concepts of memory storage, selective attention, and their mutual constraints within the human information-processing system. *Psychological Bulletin, 104,* 163–191.

Cowan, N., Wood, N. L., & Borne, D. N. (1994). Reconfirmation of the short-term storage concept. *Psychological Science, 5,* 103–106.

Cowan, W. M. (1979). The development of the brain. *Scientific American, 241,* 112–133.

Crabbe, J. C., Belknap, J. K., & Buck, L. K. (1994). Genetic animal models of alcohol and drug abuse. *Science, 264,* 1715–1723.

Craig, A. D., & Bushnell, M. C. (1994). The thermal grill illusion: Unmasking the burn of cold pain. *Science, 265,* 252–254.

Craig, A. D., Bushnell, M. C., Zhang, E.-T., and Blomqvist, A. (1994). A thalamic nucleus specific for pain and temperature sensation. *Nature, 372,* 770–773.

Craik, F. I. M. (1994). Memory changes in normal aging. *Current Directions in Psychological Science, 3,* 155–158.

Craik, F. I. M., & Lockhart, R. S. (1972). Levels of processing: A framework for memory research. *Journal of Verbal Learning and Verbal Behavior, 11,* 671–684.

Craik, F. I. M., & Rabinowitz, J. C. (1984). Age differences in the acquisition and use of verbal information. In H. Bouma & D. G. Bouwhuis (Eds.), *Attention and performance: Vol. 10.* Hillsdale, NJ: Lawrence Erlbaum Associates.

Crandall, C. S., Preisler, J. J., & Aussprung, J. (1992). Measuring life event stress in the lives of college students: The Undergraduate Stress Questionnaire (USQ). *Journal of Behavioral Medicine, 15,* 627–662.

Crawford, H. J., Brown, A. M., & Moon, C. E. (1993). Sustained attentional and disattentional abilities: Differences between low and highly hypnotizable persons. *Journal of Abnormal Psychology, 102*(4), 534–543.

Crawford, J. (1989). *Bilingual education: History, politics, theory, and practice.* New York: Crane.

Crawford, M., & Marecek, J. (1989). Psychology reconstructs the female. *Psychology of Women Quarterly, 13,* 147–165.

Crawley, J. N., & Corwin, R. L. (1994). Biological actions of cholecystokinin. *Peptides, 15*(4), 731–755.

Crelin, E. S. (1987). *The human vocal tract: Anatomy, function, development, and evolution.* New York: Vantage Press.

Critchley, E. M. (1991). Speech and the right hemisphere. *Behavioural Neurology, 4*(3), 143–151.

Crites, S. L., Jr., Cacioppo, J. T., Gardner, W. L., & Berntson, G. G. (1995). Bioelectrical echoes from evaluative categorization: II. A late positive brain potential that varies as a function of attitude registration rather than attitude report. *Journal of Personality and Social Psychology, 68,* 997–1013.

Crits-Christoph, P., Baranackie, K., Kurcias, J. S., Beck, A. T., Carroll, K., Perry, K., Luborsky, L., McLellan, A. T., Woody, B. E., Thompson, L., Gallagher, D., & Zitrin, C. (1991). Meta-analysis of therapist effects in psychotherapy outcome studies. *Psychotherapy Research, 1,* 81–91.

Cronbach, L. J. (1951). Coefficient alpha and the internal structure of tests. *Psychometrica, 16,* 297–334.

Cronbach, L. J. (1970). *Essentials of psychological testing* (3rd ed.). New York: Harper & Row.

Cronbach, L. J. (1975). Five decades of public controversy over mental testing. *American Psychologist, 30,* 1–14.

Crosby, F. J. (1991). *Juggling: The unexpected advantages of balancing career and home for women and their families.* New York: Free Press.

Cross, D. G., Sheehan, O. W., & Kahn, J. A. (1982). Short- and long-term follow-up of clients receiving insight-oriented therapy and behavior therapy. *Journal of Consulting and Clinical Psychology, 50,* 103–112.

Cross-National Collaborative Group. (1992). The changing rate of major depression: Cross-national comparisons. *Journal of the American Medical Association, 268,* 3098–3105.

Crowe, R. R., Black, D. W., Wesner, R., Andreasen, N. C., Cookman, A., & Roby, J. (1991). Lack of linkage to chromosome 5q11-q13 markers in six schizophrenia pedigrees. *Archives of General Psychiatry, 48,* 357–361.

Crutcher, K. A. (1991). Anatomical correlates of neuronal plasticity. In J. L. Martinez & R. P. Kesner (Eds.), *Learning and memory: A biological view* (2nd ed.). San Diego: Academic Press.

Crystal, D. S., Chen, C., Fuligni, A. J., Stevenson, H. W., Hsu, C.-C., Ko, H.-J., Kitamura, S., & Kimura, S. (1994). Psychological maladjustment and academic achievement: A cross-cultural study of Japanese, Chinese, and American high school students. *Child Development, 65,* 738–153.

Culp, R. E., Cook, A. S., & Housley, P. C. (1983). A comparison of observed and reported adult-infant interactions: Effects of perceived sex. *Sex Roles, 9,* 475–479.

Cummings, E. M. (1994). Marital conflict and children's functioning. *Social Development, 3,* 16–36.

Cuomo, M. J., Dyment, P. G., & Gammino, V. M. (1994). Increasing use of "ecstacy" (MDMA) and other hallucinogens on a college campus. *Journal of American College Health, 42*(6), 271–274.

Curcio, C. A., Sloan, D. R., Jr., Packer, O., Hendrickson, A. E., & Kalina, R. E. (1987). Distribution of cones in human and monkey retina: Individual variability and radial asymmetry. *Science, 236,* 579–582.

Curim, I. S., & Sarin, R. K. (1992). Robustness of expected utility model in predicting individual choices. *Organizational Behavior and Human Decision Processes, 52,* 544–568.

Curtis, R. C., & Miller, K. (1986). Believing another likes or dislikes you: Behaviors making the beliefs come true. *Journal of Personality and Social Psychology, 51,* 284–290.

Curtiss, S. (1977). *Genie: A psycholinguistic study of a modern-day wild child.* New York: Academic Press.

D'Antonio, M. (1994, December 4). The trouble with boys. *Los Angeles Times Magazine,* pp. 16ff.

d'Ydewalle, G., & Rosselle, H. (1978). Text expectations in text learning. In M. M. Gruneberg, P. E. Morris, & R. N. Sykes (Eds.), *Practical aspects of memory.* Orlando, FL: Academic Press.

Dabbs, J. M., Carr, T. S., Frady, R. L., & Riad, J. K. (1995). Testosterone, crime, and misbehavior among 692 male prison inmates. *Personality and Individual Differences, 18,* 627–633.

Dabbs, J. M. (in press). *Testosterone: Power, passion, poison.* New York: Plenum.

Dabbs, J., & Morris, R. (1990). Testosterone, social class, and antisocial behavior in a sample of 4462 men. *Psychological Science, 1,* 209–211.

Dahlstrom, W. G. (1992). The growth in acceptance of the MMPI. *Professional Psychology: Research and Practice, 23,* 345–348.

Dale, P. S. (1976). *Language and the development of structure and function.* New York: Holt, Rinehart & Winston.

Daly, M., & Wilson, M. (1988). *Homicide.* New York: Aldine de Gruyter.

Damon, W., & Hart, D. (1982). The development of self-understanding from infancy through adolescence. *Child Development, 53,* 841–864.

Damos, D. (1992). *Multiple task performance.* London: Taylor & Francis.

Dana, R. H. (1988). Culturally diverse groups and MMPI interpretation. *Professional Psychology: Research and Practice, 19,* 490–495.

Dark, V. J., & Benbow, C. P. (1993). Cognitive differences among the gifted: A review and new data. In D. K. Detterman (Ed.), *Current topics in human intelligence* (Vol. 3). Norwood, NJ: Ablex.

Darke, S. (1988). Effects of anxiety on inferential reasoning task performance. *Journal of Personality and Social Psychology, 55,* 499–505.

Darwin, C. E. (1965). *The expression of emotions in man and animals.* Chicago: University of Chicago Press. (Original work published in 1872)

Dasgupta, A. M., Juza, D. M., White, G. M., & Maloney, J. F. (1995). Memory and hypnosis: A comparative analysis of guided memory, cognitive interviews, and hypnotic hypermnesia. *Imagination, Cognition, and Personality, 14*(2), 117–130.

Davanloo, J. (Ed.) (1978). *Basic principles and techniques in short-term dynamic psychotherapy.* New York: Spectrum.

Davidson, J. K., & Moore, N. B. (1994). Guilt and lack of orgasm during sexual intercourse: Myth versus reality in college women. *Journal of Sex Education and Therapy, 20*(3), 153–174.

Davidson, J. M., Camargo, C. A., & Smith, E. R. (1979). Effects of androgen on sexual behavior in hypogonadal men. *Journal of Clinical Endocrinological Metabolism, 48,* 955–958.

Davidson, R. J., Ekman, P., Saron, C., Senulis, J., & Friesen, W. V. (1990). Approach-withdrawal and cerebral asymmetry: Emotional expression and brain physiology: I. *Journal of Personality and Social Psychology, 58,* 330–341.

Davis, J. A., & Smith, T. W. (1990). *General social surveys, 1972–1990: Cumulative codebook.* Chicago: National Opinion Research Center.

Davis, J. D., Gallagher, R. J., Ladove, R. F., & Turansky, A. J. (1969). Inhibition of food intake by a humoral factor. *Journal of Comparative and Physiological Psychology, 67,* 407–414.

Davis, J. H. (1992). Some compelling intuitions about group consensus decisions, theoretical and empirical research, and interpersonal aggregation phenomena: Selected examples, 1950–1990. *Organizational Behavior and Human Decision Processes, 52,* 3–38.

Davis, K. (1983). The future of marriage. *Bulletin of the American Academy of Arts and Sciences, 36,* 33.

Davis, K. L., Kahn, R. S., Ko, G., & Davidson, M. (1991). Dopamine in schizophrenia: A review and reconceptualization. *American Journal of Psychiatry, 148,* 1474–1486.

Davis, M., Falls, W. A., Campeau, S., & Kim, M. (1993). Fear-potentiated startle: A neural and pharmacological analysis. *Behavioural Brain Research, 58*(1–2), 175–198.

Davis, M., Rainnie, D., & Cassell, M. (1994). Neurotransmission in the rat amygdala related to fear and anxiety. *Trends in Neuroscience, 17,* 208–214.

Davis, M. H. (1994). *Empathy: A social psychological approach.* Madison, WI: Brown & Benchmark.

Davis, M. H., & Harvey, J. C. (1992). Declines in major league batting performance as a function of game pressure: A drive theory analysis. *Journal of Applied Social Psychology, 22*(9), 714–735.

Davis, M. H., Luce, C., & Kraus, S. J. (1994). The heritability of characteristics associated with dispositional empathy. *Journal of Personality, 60,* 369–391.

Davis, R. A., & Moore, C. C. (1935). Methods of measuring retention. *Journal of General Psychology, 12,* 144–155.

Davison, G. C., & Neale, J. M. (1990). *Abnormal psychology* (5th ed.). New York: Wiley.

Dawes, R. (1992). *Psychology and psychotherapy: The myth of professional expertise.* New York: Free Press.

Dawes, R., Faust, D., & Meehl, P. E. (1989). Clinical versus actuarial judgment. *Science, 243,* 1668–1674.

Dawes, R. M., (1994). *House of cards: Psychology and psychotherapy built on myth.* New York: Free Press.

Dawkins, K., & Potter, W. (1991). Gender differences in pharmacokinetics and pharmacodynamics of psychotropics: Focus on women. *Psychopharmacology Bulletin, 27,* 417–426.

Dawson, D., Encel, N., & Lushington, K. (1995). Improving adaptation to simulated night shift: Timed exposure to bright light versus daytime melatonin administration. *Sleep, 18*(1), 11–21.

Dawson, T. M., & Dawson, V. L. (1995). Nitric oxide: Actions and pathological roles. *The Neuroscientist, 1,* 7–18.

Day, N. L., Richardson, G. A., Goldschmidt, L., Robles, N., Taylor, P. M., Stoffer, D. S., Cornelius, M. D., & Geva, D. (1994). Effect of prenatal marijuana exposure on the cognitive development of offspring at age three. *Neurotoxicology and Teratology, 16,* 169–175.

DeAngelis, T. (1995, February). Firefighters' PTSD at dangerous levels. *APA Monitor,* pp. 36–37.

DeAngelis, T. (1995, February). APA group tries to boost diversity of the profession. *APA Monitor,* p. 40.

DeAngelis, T. (1996, March). Women's contributions large: recognition isn't. *APA Monitor,* (pp. 12–13).

De Benedittis, G., Lornenzetti, A., & Pieri, A. (1990). The role of stressful life events in the onset of chronic primary headache. *Pain, 40,* 65–75.

deBeurs, E., van Balkom, A. J. L. M., Lange, A., Koele, P., & van Dyck, R. (1995). Treatment of panic disorder with agoraphobia: Comparison of fluvoxamine, placebo, and psychological panic management combined with exposure and of exposure in vivo alone. *American Journal of Psychiatry, 152*(5), 683–691.

de Castro, J. M., & Goldstein, S. J. (1995). Eating attitudes and behaviors pre- and postpubertal females: Clues to the etiology of eating disorders. *Physiology and Behavior, 58*(1), 15–23.

de Charms, R., Levy, J., & Wertheimer, M. (1954). A note on attempted evaluations of psychotherapy. *Journal of Clinical Psychology, 10,* 233–235.

de Jong, B. M., Shipp, S., Skidmore, B., Frankowiak, R. S. J., & Zeki, S. (1994). The cerebral activity related to the visual perception of forward motion in depth. *Brain, 117*(5), 1039–1035.

de Lacoste-Utamsing, C., & Holloway, R. L. (1982). Sexual dimorphism in the human corpus callosum. *Science, 216,* 1431–1432.

de Rios, M. D. (1992). Power and hallucinogenic states of consciousness among the Moche: An ancient Peruvian society. In C. A. Ward (Ed.) *Altered states of consciousness and mental health: A cross-cultural perspective.* Newberry Park, CA: Sage.

de Silva, P. (1994). Psychological treatment of sexual problems. *International Review of Psychiatry, 6*(2–3), 163–173.

Deary, I. J., & Caryl, P. G. (1993). Intelligence, EEG and evoked potentials. In P. A. Vernon (Ed.), *Biological approaches to the study of human intelligence.* Norwood, NJ: Ablex.

Deci, E. L. (1980). *The psychology of self-determination.* Lexington, MA: D. C. Heath.

Deci, E. L., Connell, J. P., & Ryan, M. (1987). *Self-determination in a work organization.* Unpublished manuscript, University of Rochester, Rochester, NY.

Dekovic, M., & Gerris, J. R. M. (1994). Developmental analysis of social, cognitive and behavior differences between popular and rejected children. *Journal of Applied Developmental Psychology, 15,* 367–386.

Delgado, P. L., Price, L. H., Miller, H. L., Salomon, R. M., Aghajanian, G. K., Heniger, G. R., & Charney, D. S. (1994). Serotonin and the neurobiology of depression. *Archives of General Psychiatry, 51,* 865–874.

Delgado-Gaitan, C. (1994). Socializing young children in Mexican-American families: An intergenerational perspective. In P. M. Greenfield & R. R. Cocking (Eds.), *Cross-cultural roots of minority child development* (pp. 41–54). Hillsdale, NJ: Lawrence Erlbaum Associates.

Delmolino, L. M., & Romanczyk, R. G. (1995). Facilitated communication: A critical review. *The Behavior Therapist, 18,* 27–30.

DeLoache, J. S. (1987). Rapid change in the symbolic functioning of very young children. *Science, 238,* 1556–1557.

DeLongis, A., Folkman, S., & Lazarus, R. S. (1988). The impact of daily stress on health and mood: Psychological and social resources as mediators. *Journal of Personality and Social Psychology, 54,* 486–495.

Demare, D., Briere, J., & Lips, H. M. (1988). Violent pornography and self-reported likelihood of sexual aggression. *Journal of Research in Personality, 22,* 140–153.

Dement, W. (1960). The effect of dream deprivation. *Science, 131,* 1705–1707.

Dement, W., Guilleminault, C., & Zarcone, V. (1975). The pathologies of sleep: A case series approach. In D. B. Tower (Ed.), *The Nervous System: Vol. 2. The Clinical Neurosciences* (pp. 501–518). New York: Raven Press.

Dement, W., & Kleitman, N. (1957). Cyclic variations in EEG during sleep and their relation to eye movements, body motility and dreaming. *Electroencephalography and Clinical Neurophysiology, 9,* 673–690.

Denmark, F., Russo, N. F., Frieze, I. H, & Sechzer, J. A. (1988). Guidelines for avoiding sexism in psychological research. *American Psychologist, 43,* 582–585.

Dennett, D. C. (1991). *Consciousness explained.* Boston: Little, Brown.

Dennett, D. C. (1993). Caveat emptor. *Consciousness and Cognition, 2,* 48-57.

Denton, G. (1980). The influence of visual pattern on perceived speed. *Perception, 9,* 393–402.

Denton, K., & Krebs, D. (1990). From the scene to the crime: The effect of alcohol and social context on moral judgment. *Journal of Personality and Social Psychology, 59,* 242–248.

Derogowski, J. B. (1989). Real space and represented space: Cross-cultural perspectives. *Behavior and Brain Sciences, 12,* 51–73.

DeRosier, M. E., Cillessen, A. H. N., Coie, J. D., & Dodge, K. A. (1994). Group social context and children's aggressive behavior. *Child Development, 65,* 1068–1079.

Derry, P. S. (1996). Buss and sexual selection: The issue of culture. *American Psychologist, 51,* 159–160.

Derryberry, D., & Tucker, D. M. (1992). Neural mechanisms of emotion. *Journal of Consulting and Clinical Psychology, 60,* 329–338.

Deschaumes, M. C., Dittmar, A., Sicard, G., & Vernet, M. E. (1991). Results from six autonomic nervous system responses confirm "autonomic response specificity" hypothesis. *Homeostasis in Health and Disease, 33*(5–6), 225–234.

Detterman, D. K. (1993). The case for the prosecution: Transfer as an epiphenomenon. In D. K. Detterman & R. J. Sternberg (Eds.), *Transfer on trial: Intelligence, cognition, and instruction.* Norwood, NJ: Ablex.

Deutsch, L. (1992, May 10). Bias, confusion, emotion led to verdict, responses show. *Champaign-Urbana News-Gazette.*

Deutsch, M. (1993). Educating for a peaceful world. *American Psychologist, 48,* 510–517.

Deutsch, M., & Gerard, H. B. (1955). A study of normative and informative social influences on individual judgments. *Journal of Abnormal and Social Psychology, 51,* 629–636.

Devine, P. G. (1989). Stereotypes and prejudice: Their automatic and controlled components. *Journal of Personality and Social Psychology, 56,* 5–18.

Devine, P. G. (1995). Prejudice and out-group perception. In A. Tesser (Ed.), *Advanced social psychology* (pp. 467–524). New York: McGraw-Hill.

Devine, P. G., Monteith, M. J., Zuwerink, J. R., & Elliot, A. J. (1991). Prejudice with and without compunction. *Journal of Personality and Social Psychology, 60,* 817–830.

Devor, E. J. (1994). A developmental–genetic model of alcoholism: Implications for genetic research. *Journal of Consulting and Clinical Psychology, 62,* 1108-1115.

DeVries, R. (1969). Constancy of generic identity in the years three to six. *Monographs of the Society for Research in Child Development, 34*(3, Serial No. 127).

DeWitt, L. A., & Samuel, A. G. (1990). The role of knowledge-based function in music perception. *Journal of Experimental Psychology: General, 119,* 123–144.

DiClemente, R. J., & Wingood, G. M. (1995). A randomized controlled trial of an HIV sexual risk-reduction intervention for young African-American women. *Journal of the American Medical Association, 274,* 1271–1276.

Diener, E., & Diener, M. (1995). Cross-cultural correlates of life satisfaction and self-esteem. *Journal of Personality and Social Psychology, 68,* 653–663.

Dietz, W. (1991). Physical activity and childhood obesity. *Nutrition, 7,* 295–296.

DiLalla, D. L., & Gottesman, I. I. (1995). Normal personality characteristics in identical twins discordant for schizophrenia. *Journal of Abnormal Psychology, 104,* 490–499.

Dimarzo, V., Fontana, A., Cadas, H., Schinelli, S., Cimino, G., Schwartz, J. C., & Piomelli, D. (1994). Formation and inactivation of endogenous cannabinoid anandamide in central neurons. *Nature, 372,* 686–691.

Dion, K. K. (1992). Stereotyping based on physical attractiveness. Issues and conceptual perspectives. In C. P. Herman, M. P. Zanna, & E. T. Higgins (Eds.), *The Ontario Symposium: Vol 3. Physical appearance, stigma, and social behavior* (pp. 209–239). Beverly Hills, CA: Sage.

Dionne, V. E., & Dubin, A. E. (1994). Transduction diversity in olfaction. *Journal of Experimental Biology, 194,* 1–21.

Dishion, T. J., & Andrews, D. W. (1995). Preventing escalation in problem behaviors with high-risk young adolescents: Immediate and 1-year outcomes. *Journal of Consulting and Clinical Psychology, 63,* 538–548.

Ditto, P. H., & Lopez, D. F. (1992). Motivated skepticism: Use of differential decision criteria for preferred and nonpreferred conclusions. *Journal of Personality and Social Psychology, 63,* 568–584.

Dixon, M., Brunet, A., & Lawrence, J.-R. (1990). Hynotizability and automaticity: Toward a parallel distributed processing model of hynotic responding. *Journal of Abnormal Psychology, 99,* 336–343.

Dodge, K. A., & Price, J. M. (1994). On the relation between social information processing and socially competent behavior in early school-aged children. *Child Development, 65,* 1385–1398.

Dodson, C., & Reisberg, D. (1991). Indirect testing of eyewitness memory: The (non)effect of misinformation. *Bulletin of the Psychonomic Society, 29,* 333–336.

Dohrenwend, B. S., & Dohrenwend, B. P. (1978). Some issues in research on stressful life events. *Journal of Nervous and Mental Disease, 166,* 7–15.

Doll, R., Peto, R., Wheatley, K., Gray, R., & Sutherland, I. (1994). Mortality in relation to smoking: 40 years of observations on male British doctors. *British Medical Journal, 309*(6959), 901–911.

Dollard, J., Doob, L., Miller, N., Mowrer, O. H., & Sears, R. R. (1939). *Frustration and aggression.* New Haven, CT: Yale University Press.

Donaldson, M., & Balfour, G. (1968). Less is more: A study of language comprehension in children. *British Journal of Psychology, 59,* 461–471.

Donegan, N. H., & Thompson, R. F. (1991). The search for the engram. In J. L. Martinez & R. P. Kesner (Eds.), *Learning and memory: A biological view* (2nd ed.). San Diego, CA: Academic Press.

Donlon, T. F. (Ed.). (1984). *College board technical handbook for the SAT.* New York: College Entrance Examination Board.

Donnerstein, E. (1984a). Aggression. In A. S. Kahn (Ed.), *Social psychology.* Dubuque, IA: William C. Brown.

Donnerstein, E. (1984b). Pornography: Its effects on violence against women. In N. M. Malamuth & E. Donnerstein (Eds.), *Pornography and sexual aggression.* New York: Academic Press.

Donnerstein, E., & Linz, D. (1995). The mass media: A role in injury causation and prevention. *Adolescent Medicine: State of the Art Reviews, 6,* 271–284.

Donnerstein, E., Linz, D., & Penrod, S. (1987). *The question of pornography: Research findings and policy implications.* New York: Free Press.

Donnerstein, E., Slaby, R. G., & Eron, L .D. (1995). The mass media and youth aggression. In L. Eron, J. Gentry, & P. Schlegel (Eds.), *Reason to hope: A psychoso-*

cial perspective on violence and youth (pp. 219–250). Washington, DC: American Psychological Association.

Dordain, G., & Deffond, D. (1994). Pyridoxine neuropathies: Review of the literature. *Therapie, 49*(4), 333–337.

Dore, J. (1978). Conditions for the acquisition of speech acts. In I. Markova (Ed.), *The social context of language.* New York: Wiley.

Dornbusch, S. M., Ritter, P. L., Leiderman, P. H., Roberts, D. F., & Fraleigh, M. J. (1987). The relation of parenting style to adolescent school performance. *Child Development, 58,* 1244–1257.

Dovidio, J. F., Allen, J., & Schroeder, D. A. (1990). The specificity of empathy-induced helping: Evidence for altruism. *Journal of Personality and Social Psychology, 59,* 249–260.

Dovidio, J. F., Brigham, J. C., Johnson, B. T., & Gaertner, S. L. (in press). Stereotyping, prejudice, and discrimination: Another look. In N. Macrae, M. Hewstone, & C. Stangor (Eds), *Foundations of stereotypes and stereotyping.* New York: Guilford.

Dovidio, J. F., Evans, N., & Tyler, R. B. (1986). Racial stereotypes: The contents of their cognitive representations. *Journal of Experimental Social Psychology, 22,* 22–37.

Dovidio, J. F., & Gaertner, S. L. (1986). Prejudice, discrimination, and racism: Historical trends and contemporary approaches. In J. F. Dovidio & S. L. Gaertner (Eds.), *Prejudice, discrimination, and racism* (pp. 1–34). Orlando, FL: Academic Press.

Dovidio, J. F., & Gaertner, S. L. (1991). Changes in the nature and expression of racial prejudice. In H. Knopke, J. Norrell, & R. Rogers (Eds.), *Opening doors: An appraisal of race relations in contemporary America* (pp. 201–241). Tuscaloosa: University of Alabama Press.

Dovidio, J. F., & Gaertner, S. L. (1993). Stereotypes and evaluative intergroup bias. In D. M. Mackie & D. L. Hamilton (Eds.), *Affect, cognition, and stereotyping: Interactive processes in group perception* (pp. 167–193). San Diego, CA: Academic Press.

Dovidio, J. F., Piliavin, J. A., Gaertner, S. L., Schroeder, D. A., & Clark, R. D., III (1991). The arousal: cost-reward model and the process of intervention: A review of the evidence. In M. Clark (Ed.), *Review of personality and social psychology: Vol. 12. Prosocial behavior* (pp. 86–118). Newbury Park, CA: Sage.

Downey, G., & Coyne, J. C. (1990). Children of depressed parents: An integrative review. *Psychological Bulletin, 108,* 50–76.

Dowson, D. I., Lewith, G. T., & Machin, D. (1985). The effects of acupuncture versus placebo in the treatment of headache. *Pain, 21,* 35–42.

Drake, R. E., & Vaillant, G. E. (1985). A validity study of Axis II of DSM-III. *American Journal of Psychiatry, 142,* 553–558.

Dreyfus, H. L., & Dreyfus, S. E. (1988). Making a mind versus modeling the brain: Intelligence back at a branchpoint. In S. R. Graubard (Ed.), *The artificial intelligence debate.* Cambridge, MA: MIT Press.

Driskell, J. E., & Salas, E. (1991). Group decision making under stress. *Journal of Applied Psychology, 76*(3), 473–478.

Drucker, D. B., Ackroff, K., Sclafani, A. (1994). Nutrient-conditioned flavor preference and acceptance in rats: Effects of deprivation state and nonreinforcement. *Physiology and Behavior, 56*(4), 701–707.

Drucker-Colin, R. R., & McGaugh, J. L. (Eds.). (1977). *Neurobiology of sleep and memory.* San Diego, CA: Academic Press.

Druckman, D., & Bjork, R. A. (1994). *Learning, remembering, believing: Enhancing human performance.* Washington, DC: National Academy Press.

Druckman, D., & Swets, J. A. (1988). *Enhancing human performance: Issues, theories, and techniques.* Washington, DC: National Academy Press.

Dubbert, P. (1992). Exercise in behavioral medicine. *Journal of Consulting and Clinical Psychology, 60,* 613–618.

DuBois, D. L., Felner, R. D., Brand, S., Adan, A. M., & Evans, E. G. (1992). A prospective study of life stress, social support, and adaptation in early adolescence. *Child Development, 63,* 542–557.

Duck, S., & Barnes, M. H. (1992). Disagreeing about agreement: Reconciling differences about similarity. *Communication Monographs, 59,* 199–208.

Duckitt, J. H. (1994). *The social psychology of prejudice.* Westport, CT: Praeger.

Dujovne, V., & Houston, B. (1991). Hostility-related variables and plasma lipid levels. *Journal of Behavioral Medicine, 14,* 555–564.

Duke, C. R., & Carlson, L. (1993). Applying implicit memory measures: Word fragment completion in advertising tests. *Journal of Consumer Psychology.*

Duke, P. M., Carlsmith, J. M., Jennings, D., Martin, J. A., Dornbusch, S. M., Gross, R. T., & Siegel-Gorelick, B. (1982). Educational correlates of early and late sexual maturation in adolescence. *Journal of Pediatrics, 100,* 633–637.

Duncan, G. J., Brooks-Gunn, J., & Klebanov, P. K. (1994). Economic deprivation and early childhood development. *Child Development, 65,* 296–318.

Dunkel-Schetter, C., Folkman, S., & Lazarus, R. S. (1987). Correlates of social support receipt. *Journal of Personality and Social Psychology, 53,* 71–80.

Dunn, A. J. (1989). Psychoneuroimmunology for the psychoneuroendocrinologist: A review of animal studies of nervous system-immune system interactions. *Psychoneuroendocrinology, 14,* 251–274.

Dunn, J. (1992). Siblings and development. *Current Directions in Psychological Science, 1*(1), 6–9.

Dunn, J., Brown, H., Slomkowski, C., Tesla, C., & Youngblade, L. (1991). Young children's understanding of other people's feelings and beliefs: Individual differences and their antecedents. *Child Development, 62,* 1352–1366.

Dunn, J. F., & Plomin, R. (1990). *Separate lives: Why siblings are so different.* New York: Basic Books.

Durel, L. A., Carver, C., Spitzer, S., Llabre, M. M., Weintraub, G. J., Saab, P. G., & Schneiderman, N. (1989). Association of blood pressure with self-report measures of anger and hostility among black and white men and women. *Health Psychology, 8,* 557–576.

Durlach, N. I., & Mavor, A. S. (Eds.).(1995). *Virtual reality: Scientific and technological challenges.* Washington, DC: National Academy Press.

Dusek, J. B., & Flaherty, J. F. (1981). The development of the self-concept during the adolescent years. *Monographs of the Society for Research in Child Development, 46*(4, Serial No. 191).

Dustman, R., Emmerson, R., Ruhling, R., Shearer, D., Steinhaus, L., Johnson, S., Bonekat, H., & Shigeoka, J. (1990). Age and fitness effects on EEG, ERPs, visual sensitivity, and cognition. *Neurobiology of Aging, 11,* 193–200.

Dutton, D. G., & Aron, A. P. (1974). Some evidence for heightened sexual attraction under conditions of high anxiety. *Journal of Personality and Social Psychology, 30,* 510–517.

Dweck, C. S. (1986). Motivational processes affecting learning. Special Issue: Psychological science and education. *American Psychologist, 1*(10), 1040–1048.

Dweck, C. S., Davidson, W., Nelson, S., & Enna, B. (1978). Sex differences in learned helplessness: II. The contingencies of evaluative feedback in the classroom, and III. An experimental analysis. *Developmental Psychology, 14,* 268–276.

Dweck, C. S., & Gilliard, D. (1975). Expectancy statements as determinants of reactions to failure: Sex differences in persistence and expectancy change. *Journal of Personality and Social Psychology, 32,* 1077–1084.

Dweck, C. S., & Licht, B. G. (1980). Learned helplessness and intellectual achievement. In M. E. P. Seligman & J. Garber (Eds.), *Human helplessness: Theory and application.* New York: Academic Press.

Dyck, M. J. (1993). A proposal for a conditioning model of eye movement desensitization treatment for posttraumatic stress disorder. *Journal of Behaviour Therapy and Experimental Psychiatry, 24,* 201–210.

Eagly, A. H. (1987). *Sex differences in social behavior: A social-role interpretation.* Hillsdale, NJ: Lawrence Erlbaum Associates.

Eagly, A. H. (1995). The science and politics of comparing women and men. *American Psychologist, 50,* 145–158.

Eagly, A. H., & Chaiken, S. (1993). *The psychology of attitudes.* Fort Worth, TX: Harcourt Brace Jovanovich.

Eagly, A. H., & Johnson, B. T. (1990). Gender and leadership style: A meta-analysis. *Psychological Bulletin, 108,* 233–256.

Eagly, A. H., & Karau, S. J. (1991). Gender and the emergence of leaders: A meta-analysis. *Journal of Personality and Social Psychology, 60,* 685–710.

Eagly, A. H., Karau, S. J., & Makhijani, M. G. (1995). Gender and the effectiveness of leaders: A meta-analysis. *Psychological Bulletin, 117,* 125–145.

Eagly, A. H., Makhijani, M. G., & Klonsky, B. G. (1992). Gender and evaluation of leaders: A meta-analysis. *Psychological Bulletin, 111,* 3–22.

Eaton, W. W. (1991). Update on the epidemiology of schizophrenia. *Epidemiological Review, 13,* 320–328.

Eaves, L. J., Eysenck, H., & Martin, N. G. (1989). *Genes, culture, and personality: An empirical approach.* San Diego, CA: Academic Press.

Ebersole, P., & De Vore, G. (1995). Self-actualization, diversity, and meaning in life. *Journal of Social Behavior and Personality, 10*(1), 37–51.

Eberts, R., & MacMillan, A. C. (1985). Misperception of small cars. In R. Eberts & C. Eberts (Eds.), *Trends in ergonomics/human factors III.* Amsterdam: Elsevier.

Ebstein, R. P., Novick, O., Umansky, R., Priol, B., Osher, Y., Blaine, D., Bennett, E. K., Nemanov, L., Katz, M., & Belmaker, R. H. (1996). Dopamine D_4 receptor (D4DR) exon III polymorphism associated with the human personality trait of novelty seeking. *Nature Genetics, 12,* 78–80.

Educational Testing Service (1987). *ETS sensitivity review process.* Princeton, NJ: ETS.

Educational Testing Service (1995). *Performance assessment.* Princeton, NJ: College Board.

Edwards, A. E., & Acker, L. E. (1972). A demonstration of the long-term retention of a conditioned GSR. *Psychosomatic Science, 26,* 27–28.

Edwards, R. (1995, July). Meeting tackles the toll of work stress. *APA Monitor,* p. 12.

Edwards, W. (1987). Decision making. In G. Salvendy (Ed.), *Handbook of human factors.* New York: Wiley.

Edwards, W., Lindman, H., & Phillips, L. D. (1965). Emerging technologies for making decisions. In T. M. Newcomb (Ed.), *New directions in psychology II.* New York: Holt, Rinehart & Winston.

Egeland, J. A., Gerhard, D. S., Pauls, D. L., Sussex, J. N., Kidd, K. K., Allen, C. R., Hostetter, A. M., & Housman, D. E. (1987). Bipolar affective disorders linked to DNA markers on chromosome 11. *Nature, 325,* 783–787.

Ehlers, A. (1995). A 1-year prospective study of panic attacks: Clinical course and factors associated with maintenance. *Journal of Abnormal Psychology, 104,* 164–172.

Ehrlichman, H., & Halpern, J. N. (1988). Affect and memory: Effects of pleasant and unpleasant odors on retrieval of happy and unhappy memories. *Journal of Personality and Social Psychology, 55,* 769–779.

Ehrman, R. N., Robbins, S. J., Childress, A. R., & O'Brien, C. P. (1992). Conditioned responses to cocaine-related stimuli in cocaine abuse patients. *Psychopharmacology, 107,* 523–529.

Eich, E. (1989). Theoretical issues in state dependent memory. In H. L. Roediger & F. I. M. Craik (Eds.), *Varieties of memory and consciousness.* Hillsdale, NJ: Lawrence Erlbaum Associates.

Eich, E., & Metcalfe, J. (1989). Mood dependent memory for internal versus external events. *Journal of Experimental Psychology: Learning, Memory, and Cognition, 15,* 443–455.

Eich, J. E., Weingartner, H., Stillman, R. C., & Gillin, J. C. (1975). State dependent accessibility of retrieval cues in the retention of a categorized list. *Journal of Verbal Learning and Verbal Behavior, 14,* 408–417.

Eichelman, B. (1983). The limbic system and aggression in humans. *Neuroscience and Bio-behavioral Reviews, 7,* 391–394.

Eichenbaum, H., Otto, T., & Cohen, N. J. (1994). Two functional components of the hippocampal memory system. *Behavior and Brain Sciences, 17*(3), 449–517.

Eichorn, D. (1981) Samples and procedures. In D. Eichorn, J. Clausen, N. Haan, M. P. Honzik, & P. Mussen (Eds.). *Present and past in middle life* (pp. 33–51). New York: Academic Press.

Eichorn, D. H., Clausen, J. A., Haan, N., Honzik, M. P., & Mussen, P. H. (1981). *Present and past in middle life.* New York: Academic Press.

Einhorn, H., & Hogarth, R. (1982). Prediction, diagnosis and causal thinking in forecasting. *Journal of Forecasting, 1,* 23–36.

Eisenberg, N. (1994, August). *Empathy and prosocial behavior.* Invited address presented at the annual meeting of the American Psychological Association, Los Angeles.

Eisenberg, N., Cialdini, R. B., McCreath, H., & Shell, R. (1987). Consistency-based compliance: When and why do children become vulnerable? *Journal of Personality and Social Psychology, 52,* 1174–1181.

Eisenberg, N., Fabes, R. A., & Murphy, B. C. (1995). Relations of shyness and low sociability to regulation and emotionality. *Journal of Personality and Social Psychology, 68,* 505–518.

Eisenman, R. (1994). Conservative sexual values: Effects of an abstinence program on student attitudes. *Journal of Sex Education and Therapy, 20*(2), 75–78.

Ekman, P. (1993). Facial expression and emotion. *American Psychologist, 48,* 384–392.

Ekman, P. (1994). Strong evidence for universals in facial expressions: A reply to Russell's mistaken critique. *Psychological Bulletin, 115*(2), 268–287.

Ekman, P., & Davidson, R. J. (1993). Voluntary smiling changes regional brain activity. *Psychological Science, 4*(5), 342–345.

Ekman, P., Davidson, R. J., & Friesen, W. V. (1990). The Duchenne smile: Emotional expression and brain physiology II. *Journal of Personality and Social Psychology, 58,* 342–353.

Ekman, P., & Friesen, W. V. (1986). A new pan-cultural facial expression of emotion. *Motivation and Emotion, 10,* 159–168.

Ekman, P., Friesen, W. V., & Ellsworth, P. (1972). *Emotion in the human face: Guidelines for research and a review of findings.* New York: Pergamon Press.

Ekman, P., Friesen, W. V., & O'Sullivan, M. (1988). Smiles when lying. *Journal of Personality and Social Psychology, 54,* 414–420.

Ekman, P., Levenson, R. W., & Friesen, W. V. (1983). Autonomic nervous system activity distinguishes among emotions. *Science, 221,* 1208–1210.

Elashoff, J. D. (1979). Box scores are for baseball. *Brain and Behavioral Sciences, 3,* 392.

Elicker, J., & Sroufe, L. A. (1992/3). Predicting peer competence and peer relationships in childhood from early parent-child relationships. In R. Parke & G. Ladd

(Eds.), *Family-peer relationships: Modes of linkage.* Hillsdale, NJ: Lawrence Erlbaum Associates.

Eliot, A. J., & Devine, P. G. (1994). On the motivational nature of dissonance: Dissonance as psychological discomfort. *Journal of Personality and Social Psychology, 67,* 382–394.

Elkins, I. (1994). The NIMH treatment of depression collaborative research program: Where we began and where we are. In A. E. Bergin & S. L. Garfield (Eds.), *Handbook of psychotherapy and behavior change.* New York: Wiley.

Elkins, I., Shea, T., Watkins, J., Imber, S., Sotsky, S., Collins, J., Glass, D., Pilkonis, P., Leber, W., Docherty, J., Fiester, S., & Perloff, M. (1989). National Institute of Mental Health treatment of depression collaborative research program. *Archives of General Psychiatry, 46,* 971–982.

Elliott, C. L., & Greene, R. L. (1992). Clinical depression and implicit memory. *Journal of Abnormal Psychology, 101,* 572–574.

Ellis, A. (1962). *Reason and emotion in psychotherapy.* New York: Lyle Stuart.

Ellis, A. (1973). Rational-emotive therapy. In R. Corsini (Ed.), *Current psychotherapies.* Itasca, IL: Peacock.

Ellis, A. (1993). Reflections on rational-emotive therapy. *Journal of Consulting and Clinical Psychology, 61,* 199–201.

Ellis, A. (1993). Changing rational-emotive therapy (RET) to rational-emotive behavior therapy (REBT). *The Behavior Therapist, 16*(10). 257–258.

Ellis, A., & Bernard, M. E. (1985). *Clinical applications of rational-emotive therapy.* New York: Plenum.

Ellis, H. C., & Hunt, R. R. (1989). *Fundamentals of human memory and cognition* (4th ed.). Dubuque, IA: William C. Brown.

Ellis, N. R. (1991). Automatic and effortful processes in memory for spatial location. *Bulletin of the Psychonomic Society, 29,* 28–30.

Embretson, S. E. (1992). Computerized adaptive testing: Its potential substantive contributions to psychological research and assessment. *Current Directions in Psychological Science, 1,* 129–131.

Engel, A. K., Konig, P., Kreiter, A. K., Schillen, T. B., & Singer, W. (1992). Temporal coding in the visual cortex: New vistas on integration in the nervous system. *Trends in Neuroscience, 15,* 218–226.

Engeland, H. V. (1993). Pharmacotherapy and behaviour therapy: Competition or cooperation? *Acta Paedopsychiatrica International Journal of Child and Adolescent Psychiatry, 56*(2), 123–127.

Engen, T. (1987). Remembering odors and their names. *American Scientist, 75,* 497–502.

Engen, T., Gilmore, M. M., & Mair, R. G. (1991). Odor memory. In T. V. Getchell et al. (Eds.), *Taste and smell in health and disease.* New York: Raven Press.

Enns, C. Z. (1994). On teaching about the cultural relativism of psychological constructs. *Teaching of Psychology, 21,* 205–211.

Enright, R. D., Lapsley, D. K., & Levy, V. M., Jr. (1983). Moral education strategies. In M. Pressley & J. R. Levin (Eds.), *Cognitive strategy research: Educational application.* New York: Springer-Verlag.

Epstein, L. H., Valoski, A., Wing., R. R., & McCurley, J. (1994). Ten-year outcomes of behavioral family-based treatment for childhood obesity. *Health Psychology, 13,* 373–383.

Epstein, N., Baucom, D. H., & Rankin, L. A. (1993). Treatment of marital conflict: A cognitive-behavioral approach. *Clinical Psychology Review, 13*(1), 45–57.

Epstein, S. (1994). Trait theory as personality theory: Can a part be as great as the whole? *Psychological Inquiry, 5,* 120–122.

Epstein, W. (1961). The influence of syntactical structure on learning. *American Journal of Psychology, 74,* 80–85.

Epstein, Y. M., Woolfolk, R. L., & Lehrer, P. M. (1981). Physiological, cognitive, and nonverbal responses to repeated experiences of crowding. *Journal of Applied Social Psychology, 11,* 1–13.

Erdberg, P. (1990). Rorschach assessment. In G. Goldstein & M. Hersen (Eds.), *Psychological Assessment* (2nd ed.). New York: Pergamon Press.

Erdelyi, M. H. (1985). *Psychoanalysis: Freud's cognitive psychology.* San Francisco: W. H. Freeman.

Erel, O., & Burman, B. (1995). Interrelatedness of marital relations and parent-child relations: A meta-analytic review. *Psychological Bulletin, 118,* 108–132.

Ericsson, K. A., & Charness, N. (1994). Expert performance: Its structure and acquisition. *American Psychologist, 49,* 725–747.

Ericsson, K. A., Krampe, R. T., & Tesch-Römer, C. (1993). The role of deliberate practice in the acquisition of expert performance. *Psychological Review, 100,* 363–406.

Ericsson, K. A., & Simon, H. A. (1994). *Protocol analysis: Verbal reports as data* (rev. ed.). Cambridge, MA: MIT Press.

Ericsson, K. A., & Staszewski, J. (1989). Skilled memory and expertise: Mechanisms of exceptional performance. In D. Klahr & K. Kotovsky (Eds.), *Complex informa-*

tion processing: The impact of Herbert A. Simon. Hillsdale, NJ: Lawrence Erlbaum Associates.

Erikson, E. H. (1968). *Identity: Youth and crisis.* New York: W. W. Norton.

Erlenmeyer-Kimling, L., & Jarvik, L. F. (1963). Genetics and intelligence: A review. *Science, 142,* 1477–1479.

Eron, L. (1994). Theories of aggression: From drives to cognitions. In L. R. Huesmann (Ed.), *Human aggression: Current perspectives* (pp. 3–12). New York: Plenum.

Eron, L., Gentry, J., & Schlegel, P. (1995). *Reason to hope: A psychosocial perspective on violence and youth.* Washington, DC: American Psychological Association.

Eron, L., & Huesmann, R. (1994, February). Televised violence and kids: A public health problem? *ISR Newsletter, 18*(1), 5–7 (University of Michigan).

Eron, L. D. (1987). The development of aggressive behavior from the perspective of a developing behaviorism. *American Psychologist, 42,* 435–442.

Eron, L. D. (1994). Children and violence. *Merrill-Palmer Quarterly, 40,* 290–291.

Erwin, T. D. (1983). The scale of intellectual development: Measuring Perry's scheme. *Journal of College Student Personnel, 24,* 6–12.

Esses, V. M., & Zanna, M. P. (1995). Mood and the expression of ethnic stereotypes. *Journal of Personality and Social Psychology, 69,* 1052–1068.

Essock-Vitale, S. M., & McGuire, M. T. (1985). Women's lives viewed from an evolutionary perspective: II. Patterns of helping. *Ethology and Sociobiology, 6,* 155–173.

Esterson, A. (1993). *Seductive mirage: An exploration of the work of Sigmund Freud.* Chicago: Open Court.

Evans, D. A., Funkenstein, H., Alber, M. S., Scherr, P. A., Cook, N. R., Chown, M. J., Hebert, L. E., Hennekens, C. H., & Taylor, J. O. (1989). Prevalence of Alzheimer's disease in a community population of older persons. *Journal of the American Medical Association, 262,* 2551–2556.

Evans, G. W., Hygge, S., & Bullinger, M. (1995). Chronic noise and psychological stress. *Psychological Science, 6,* 333–338.

Evans, J., Barsten, J., & Pollard, P. (1983). On the conflict between logic and belief in syllogistic reasoning. *Memory & Cognition, 11,* 295–306.

Evans, P. (1989). *Motivation and emotion.* New York: Routledge.

Everaerd, W., & Laan, E. (1994). Cognitive aspects of sexual functioning and dysfunctioning. *Sexual and Marital Therapy, 9,* 225–230.

Exner, J. E., (1993). *The Rorschach: A comprehensive system: Vol. 1. Basic Foundations* (3rd ed) New York: Wiley.

Eysenck, H. J. (1952). The effects of psychotherapy: An evaluation. *Journal of Consulting Psychology, 16,* 319–324.

Eysenck, H. J. (1961). The effects of psychotherapy. In H. J. Eysenck (Ed.), *Handbook of abnormal psychology.* New York: Basic Books.

Eysenck, H. J. (1964). *Crime and personality.* London: Routledge & Kegan Paul.

Eysenck, H. J. (1966). *The effects of psychotherapy.* New York: International Science Press.

Eysenck, H. J. (1978). An exercise in mega-silliness. *American Psychologist, 33,* 517.

Eysenck, H. J. (Ed.). (1982). *A model for intelligence.* Heidelberg: Springer-Verlag.

Eysenck, H. J. (1986). What is intelligence? In R. J. Sternberg and D. K. Detterman (Eds.), *What is intelligence? Contemporary viewpoints on its nature and definition.* Norwood, NJ: Ablex.

Eysenck, H. J. (1987). Speed of information processing, reaction time, and the theory of intelligence. In P. A. Vernon (Ed.), *Speed of information-processing and intelligence* (pp. 21–67). Norwood, NJ: Ablex.

Eysenck, H. J. (1990a). Genetic and environmental contributions to individual differences: The three major dimensions of personality. *Journal of Personality, 58,* 245–261.

Eysenck, H. J. (1990b). Biological dimensions of personality. In L. A. Pervin (Ed.), *Handbook of personality: Theory and research.* (pp. 244–276). New York: Guilford.

Eysenck, H. J. (1994). A biological theory of intelligence. In D. K. Detterman (Ed.), *Current topics in human intelligence* (Vol. 4). Norwood, NJ: Ablex.

Eysenck, H. J., & Rachman, S. (1965). *The causes and cures of neurosis: An introduction to modern behavior therapy based on learning theory and the principle of conditioning.* San Diego: Knapp.

Facchinetti, F., Centini, G., Parrini, D., Petroglia, F., D'Antona, N., Cosmi, E. V., & Genazzani, A. R. (1982). Opioid plasma levels during labor. *Gynecology & Obstetrics Investigations, 13,* 155–163.

Faden, A. I., Demediuk, P., Panter, S. S., & Vink, R. (1989). The role of excitatory amino acids and NMDA receptors in traumatic brain injury. *Science, 244,* 798–800.

Faedda, G., Tondo, L., Teicher, M., Baldessarini, R., Gelbard, H., & Floris, G. (1993). Seasonal mood disorders: Patterns of seasonal recurrence in mania and depression. *Archives of General Psychiatry, 50,* 17–23.

Fantz, R. L. (1964). Visual experience in infants: Decreased attention to familiar patterns relative to novel ones. *Science, 146,* 668–670.

Farah, M. J., Hammond, K. M., Levine, D. N., & Calvanio, R. (1988). Visual and spatial mental imagery: Dissociable systems of representation. *Cognitive Psychology, 20,* 439–462.

Faraone, S. V., Seidman, L. J., Kremen, W. S., Pepple, J. R., Lyons, M. J., & Tsuang, M. T. (1995). Neuropsychological functioning among the nonpsychotic relatives of schizophrenic patients: A diagnostic efficiency analysis. *Journal of Abnormal Psychology, 104,* 286–304.

Farley, F. (1986, May). The big T in personality. *Psychology Today.*

Farrera, V. P., Nealey, T. A., & Maunsell, J. H. R. (1992). Mixed parvocellular and magnocellular geniculate signals in visual area V4. *Nature, 358,* 756–758.

Faust, W. L. (1959). Group vs. individual problem-solving. *Journal of Abnormal and Social Psychology, 59,* 68–72.

Fay, R. E., Turner, C. F., Klassen, A. D., & Gagnon, J. H. (1989). Prevalence and patterns of same-gender sexual contact among men. *Science, 243,* 338–348.

Fazio, R. H., Jackson, J. R., Dunton, B. C., & Williams, C. J. (1995). Variability in autommatic activation as an unobtrusive measure of racial attitudes: A bona fide pipeline? *Journal of Personality and Social Psychology, 69,* 1013–1027.

Feather, N. T., Volkmer, R. E., & McKee, I. R. (1992). A comparative study of the value priorities of Australians, Australian Baha'is, and expatriate Iranian Baha'is. *Journal of Cross-Cultural Psychology, 23,* 95–106.

Feighner, J., Merideth, C., & Hendrickson, G. (1982). A double blind comparison of buspirone and diazepam in outpatients with generalized anxiety disorder. *Journal of Clinical Psychiatry, 43,* 103–107.

Feinberg, L., & Campbell, I. G. (1993). Total sleep deprivation in the rat transiently abolishes the delta amplitude response to darkness: Implications for the mechanism of the "negative delta rebound." *Journal of Neurophysiology, 70*(6), 2695–2699.

Feingold, A. (1988). Cognitive gender differences are disappearing. *American Psychologist, 43,* 95–103.

Feingold, A. (1992). Good-looking people are not what we think. *Psychological Bulletin, 111,* 304–341.

Felten, D. L., Cohen, N., Ader, R., Felten, S. Y., Carlson, S. L., & Roszman, T. L. (1991). Central neural circuits involved in neural-immune interactions. In R. Ader (Ed.), *Psychoneuroimmunology* (2nd ed.). New York: Academic Press.

Fenton, W., & McGlashan, T. (1991). Natural history of schizophrenia subtypes: I. Longitudinal study of paranoid, hebephrenic, and undifferentiated schizophrenia. *Archives of General Psychiatry, 48,* 969–977.

Fenton, W. S., & McGlashan, T. H. (1994). Antecedents, symptom, progression, and long-term outcome of the deficit syndrome in schizophrenia. *American Journal of Psychiatry, 151,* 351–356.

Fergusson, D. M., Lloyd, M., & Horwood, L. J. (1991). Family ethnicity, social background and scholastic achievement: An eleven-year longitudinal study. *New Zealand Journal of Educational Studies, 26,* 49–63.

Fernald, A. (1990, December). Cited by T. Adler, "Melody is the message" of infant-directed speech. *APA Monitor,* p. 9.

Fernández-Dols, J.-M. & Ruiz-Belda, M.-A. (1995). Are smiles a sign of happiness?: Gold medal winners at the Olympic Games. *Journal of Personality and Social Psychology, 69,* 1113–1119.

Ferraro, R., Lillioja, S., Fontvieille, A. M., Rising, R., Bogardus, C., & Ravussin, E. (1992). Lower sedentary metabolic rate in women compared with men. *Journal of Clinical Investigation, 90,* 780–784.

Ferretti, R. P., & Butterfield, E. C. (1989). Intelligence as a correlate of children's problem solving. *American Journal of Mental Retardation, 93,* 424–433.

Ferveur, J. F., Stortkuhl, K. F., & Stocker, R. F. (1995). Genetic feminization of brain structures and changed sexual orientation in male *Drosophila. Science, 267*(5199), 902–905.

Festinger, L. (1954). A theory of social comparison processes. *Human Relations, 7,* 117–140.

Festinger, L. (1957). *A theory of cognitive dissonance.* Evanston, IL: Row, Petersen.

Festinger, L., & Carlsmith, J. M. (1959). Cognitive consequences of forced compliance. *Journal of Abnormal and Social Psychology, 58,* 203–210.

Fillenbaum, S. (1974). Pragmatic normalization: Further results for some conjunctive and disjunctive sentences. *Journal of Experimental Psychology, 103,* 913–921.

Fillmore, K. M., & Caetano, R. (1980, May 22). *Epidemiology of occupational alcoholism.* Paper presented at the National Institute on Alcohol Abuse and Alcoholism's Workshop on Alcoholism in the Workplace, Reston, VA.

Fillmore, M. T., & Vogelsprott, M. (1995). Expectancies about alcohol-induced motor impairment predict individual differences in responses to alcohol and placebo. *Journal of Studies on Alcohol, 56,* 90–98.

Fincham, F. D., & Bradbury, T. N. (1993). Marital satisfaction, depression, and attributions: A longitudinal analysis. *Journal of Personality and Social Psychology, 64,* 442–452.

Finer, B. (1980). Hypnosis and anesthesia. In G. D. Burrows & L. Dennerstein (Eds.), *Handbook of hypnosis and psychosomatic medicine.* Amsterdam: Elsevier.

Fink, M. (1993). Who should get ECT? In C. E. Coffey (Ed.), *The clinical science of electroconvulsive therapy.* Washington, DC: American Psychiatric Press.

Finman, R., & Berkowitz, L. (1989). Some factors influencing the effects of depressed mood on anger and overt hostility toward another. *Journal of Research in Personality, 23,* 70–84.

Fischer, K., & Bidell, T. R. (1993, Fall). Beyond the stage debate: Keeping the constructor in constructivism. *Society for Research in Child Development Newsletter,* pp. 5ff.

Fischer, P. J., & Breakey, W. R. (1991). The epidemiology of alcohol, drug, and mental disorders among homeless persons. *American Psychologist, 46,* 1115–1128.

Fischoff, B. (1980). A little learning: Confidence in multicue judgment tasks. In R. Nickerson (Ed.), *Attention and performance VIII.* Hillsdale, NJ: Lawrence Erlbaum Associates.

Fischoff, B., & MacGregor, D. (1982). Subjective confidence in forecasts. *Journal of Forecasting, 1,* 155–172.

Fischoff, B., & Slovic, P. (1980). A little learning. . . . Confidence in multicue judgment tasks. In R. Nickerson (Ed.), *Attention and performance: VIII.* Hillsdale, NJ: Lawrence Erlbaum Associates.

Fischoff, B., Slovic, P., & Lichtenstein, S. (1977). Knowing with certainty: The appropriateness of extreme confidence. *Journal of Experimental Psychology: Human Perception and Performance, 3,* 552–564.

Fish, B., Marcus, J., Hans, S. L., Auerbach, J. G., & Perdue, S. (1992). Infants at risk for schizophrenia: Sequelae of a genetic neurointegrative defect: A review and replication analysis of Pandymaturation in the Jerusalem Infant Development Study. *Archives of General Psychiatry, 49,* 221–235.

Fish, J. (1996). Prevention, solution-focused therapy, and the illusion of mental disorders. *Applied and Preventive Psychology, 5,* 37–40.

Fisher, C. B., & Fyrberg, D. (1994). Participant partners: College students weigh the costs and benefits of deceptive research. *American Psychologist, 49,* 417–427.

Fisher, W. A., Fisher, J. D., & Rye, B. J. (1995). Understanding and promoting AIDS-preventive behavior: Insights from the theory of reasoned action. *Health Psychology, 14,* 255–264.

Fiske, A. D., & Taylor, S. E. (1984). *Social cognition.* Reading, MA: Addison-Wesley.

Fiske, D. W., & Maddi, S. R. (1961). *Functions of varied experience.* Homewood, IL: Dorsey Press.

Fiske, M. (1980). Tasks and crises of the second half of life: The interrelationship of commitment, coping, and adaptation. In J. E. Birren & R. B. Sloane (Eds.), *Handbook of mental health and aging.* Englewood Cliffs, NJ: Prentice-Hall.

Fiske, S. (1995). Social cognition. In A. Tesser (Ed.), *Advanced social psychology* (pp. 149–194). New York: McGraw-Hill.

Fiske, S. T., & Von Hend, H. M. (1992). Personality feedback and situational norms can control stereotyping processes. *Journal of Personality and Social Psychology, 62,* 577–596.

Fitzgerald, T. E., Tennen, H., Afflect, G. S., & Pransky, G. (1993). The relative importance of dispositional optimism and control appraisals in quality of life after coronary artery bypass surgery. *Journal of Behavioral Medicine. 16,* 25–43.

Fivush, R., Gray, J. T., & Fromhoff, F. A. (1987). Two-year-olds talk about the past. *Cognitive Development, 2,* 393–409.

Fivush, R., Haden, C., & Adam, S. (1995). Structure and coherence of preschoolers' personal narratives over time: Implications for childhood amnesia. *Journal of Experimental Child Psychology, 60,* 32–56.

Fivush, R., & Hammond, N. R. (1990). Autobiographical memory across the preschool years: Towards reconceptualizing childhood amnesia. In R. Fivush & J. A. Hudson (Eds.), *Knowing and remembering in young children* (pp. 223–248). New York: Cambridge University Press.

Flavell, J. H., Green, F. L., & Flavell, E. R. (1995). Young children's knowledge about thinking. *Monographs of the Society for Research in Child Development, 60*(1, Serial No. 243).

Flint, J., Corley, R., DeFries, J. C., Fulker, D. W., Gray, J. A., Miller, S., & Collins, A. C. (1995). A simple genetic basis for a complex psychological trait in laboratory mice. *Science, 269,* 321–327.

Foa, E. B., & Kozak, M. J. (1995). DSM-IV field trial: Obsessive-compulsive disorder. *American Journal of Psychiatry, 152,* 90–96.

Foa, E. B., Rothbaum, B. O., & Kozak, M. J. (1989). Behavioral treatments for anxiety and depression. In P. C. Kendall & D. Watson (Eds.), *Anxiety and depression: Distinctive and overlapping features* (pp. 413–454). San Diego, CA: Academic Press.

Foenander, G., & Burrows, G. D. (1980). Phenomena of hypnosis: 1. Age regression. In G. D. Burrows & L. Dennerstein (Eds.), *Handbook of hypnosis and psychosomatic medicine.* Amsterdam: Elsevier.

Foley, K. M., & Macaluso, C. (1992). Adjuvant analgesic drugs in cancer pain management. In G. M. Aronoff (Ed.), *Evaluation and treatment of chronic pain.* Baltimore: Williams & Wilkins.

Folk, C. L., Remington, R. W., & Wright, J. H. (1994). The structure of attentional control: Contingent attentional capture by apparent motion, abrupt onset, and color. *Journal of Experimental Psychology: Human Perception and Performance, 20,* 317–329.

Folkman, S. (1984). Personal control and stress and coping processes: A theoretical analysis. *Journal of Personality and Social Psychology, 46,* 839–852.

Folkman, S., & Lazarus, R. (1988). *Manual for the ways of coping questionnaire.* Palo Alto, CA: Consulting Psychologists Press.

Folkman, S., Lazarus, R., Dunkel-Shetteer, DeLongis, A., & Gruen, R. (1986b). Dynamics of a stressful encounter: Cognitive appraisal, coping, and encounter outcomes. *Journal of Personality and Social Psychology, 50,* 992–1003.

Folkman, S., Lazarus, R. S., Gruen, R. J., & DeLongis, A. (1986a). Appraisal, coping, health status, and psychological symptoms. *Journal of Personality and Social Psychology, 50,* 571–579.

Folkman, S., Lazarus, R. S., Pimley, S., & Novacek, J. (1987). Age differences in stress and coping processes. *Psychology and Aging, 2,* 171–184.

Fonagy, P., Leigh, T., Steele, M., Steele, H., Kennedy, R., & Mattoon, G. (1996). The relation of attachment status, psychiatric classification, and response to psychotherapy. *Journal of Consulting and Clinical Psychology, 64,* 22–31.

Fonagy, P., & Moran, S. (1990). Studies on the efficacy of child psychoanalysis. *Journal of Consulting and Clinical Psychology, 58,* 684–695.

Foote, S. L., Bloom, F. E., & Aston-Jones, G. (1983). Nucleus locus coeruleus: New evidence of anatomical and physiological specificity. *Physiology Review, 63,* 844–914.

Ford, C. E., Wright, R. A., & Haythornthwaite, J. (1985). Task performance and magnitude of goal valence. *Journal of Research in Personality, 19,* 253–260.

Ford, D. E., & Kamerow, D. B. (1989). Epidemiological study of sleep disturbances and psychiatric disorders: An opportunity for prevention? *Journal of the American Medical Association, 262,* 1479–1484.

Foreyt, J. P., Brunner, R. L., Goodrick, G. K., & Cutter, G. (1995). *International Journal of Eating Disorders, 17*(3), 263–275.

Forsyth, D. R. (1992). *An introduction to group dynamics.* Monterey, CA: Brooks/Cole.

Foster, D., & Finchilescu, G. (1986). Contact in a "non-contact" society: The case of South Africa. In M. Hewstone & R. Brown (Eds.), *Contact and conflict in intergroup encounters.* New York: Blackwell.

Foulke, E. (1991). Braille. In M. A. Heller & W. Shiff (Eds.), *The psychology of touch.* Hillsdale, NJ: Lawrence Erlbaum Associates.

Foushee, H. C., & Helmreich, R. L. (1988). Group interaction and flightcrew performance. In E. Wiener & D. Nagel (Eds.), *Human factors in aviation.* San Diego, CA: Academic Press.

Fowler, R. C., Rich, C. L., & Young, D. (1986). San Diego suicide study: Substance abuse in young cases. *Archives of General Psychiatry, 43,* 962–965.

Fowles, D. (1992). Schizophrenia: Diathesis-stress revisited. *Annual Review of Psychology, 43,* 303–336.

Fozard, J., Wolf, E., Bell, B., Farland, R., & Podolsky, S. (1977). Visual perception and communication. In J. Birren & K. Schaie (Eds.), *Handbook of the psychology of aging.* New York: Van Nostrand Reinhold.

Fraiberg, S. (1987). Pathological defenses in infancy. In L. Fraiberg (Ed.), *Selected writings of Selma Fraiberg.* Columbus: Ohio State University Press.

Framo, J. L. (1982). *Explorations in marital and family therapy.* New York: Springer-Verlag.

Frances, A. J., Pincus, H. A., & Widiger, T. A. (1996). DSM-IV and international communication in psychiatric diagnosis. In Y. Honda, M. Kastrup, & J. E. Mezzich (eds.) *Psychiatric diagnosis: A world perspective.* New York: Springer.

Frank, G. (1976). Measures of intelligence and critical thinking. In I. B. Weiner (Ed.), *Clinical methods in psychology.* New York: Wiley.

Frank, J. S. (1973). *Persuasion and healing* (rev. ed.). Baltimore: Johns Hopkins University Press.

Frank, J. S. (1978). *Psychotherapy and the human predicament.* New York: Schocken Books.

Frank, L. G., Glickman, S. E., & Licht, P. (1991). Fatal sibling aggression, precocial development, and androgens in neonatal spotted hyenas. *Science, 252,* 702–704.

Frank, M. G., Ekman, P., & Friesen, W. V. (1993). Behavioral markers and recognizability of the smile of enjoyment. *Journal of Personality and Social Psychology, 64*(1), 83–93.

Frankel, B. G., & Whitehead, P. C. (1981). *Drinking and damage: Theoretical advantages and implications for prevention* (Monograph 14). New Brunswick, NJ: Rutgers Center of Alcohol Studies.

Frankenberg, W. K., & Dodds, J. B. (1967). The Denver developmental screening test. *Journal of Pediatrics, 71,* 181–191.

Frankmann, S. P., & Green, B. G. (1987). Differential effects of cooling on the intensity of taste. *Annals of the New York Academy of Science, 510,* 300–303.

Freed, E. X. (1971). Anxiety and conflict: Role of drug-dependent learning in the rat. *Quarterly Journal of Studies on Alcohol, 32,* 13–29.

Freedland, R. L., & Bertenthal, B. I. (1994). Developmental changes in interlimb coordination: Transition to hands-and-knees crawling. *Psychological Science, 5,* 26–32.

Freedman, J. L. (1988). Television violence and aggression: What the evidence shows. In S. Oskamp (Ed.), *Television as a social issue.* Newbury Park, CA: Sage.

Freedman, J. L. (1992). Television violence and aggression: What psychologists should tell the public. In P. Suedfeld & P. E. Tetlock (Eds.), *Psychology and social policy.* New York: Hemisphere.

Freedman, J. L., & Fraser, S. C. (1966). Compliance without pressure: The foot-in-the-door technique. *Journal of Personality and Social Psychology, 4,* 195–202.

Freeman, W., & Watts, J. W. (1942). *Psychosurgery.* Springfield, IL: Charles C. Thomas.

Freiberg, P. (1992, August). Steps outlined to help homeless mentally ill. *APA Monitor,* p. 57.

Fremgen, A., & Fay, D. (1980). Overextensions in production and comprehension: A methodological clarification. *Journal of Child Language, 7,* 205–211.

Freud, A. (1946). *The ego and the mechanisms of defense.* New York: International Universities Press.

Freud, S. (1900). The interpretation of dreams. In J. Strachey (Ed.), *The standard edition of the complete psychological works of Sigmund Freud: Vol. 8.* London: Hogarth Press.

Freud, S. (1924). The loss of reality in neurosis and psychosis. *Collected papers, 2,* 277–282.

Freudenberger, H. J. (1995). A critique of the critic. *Contemporary Psychology, 40,* 482.

Frey, P. L., & Gaertner, S. L. (1986). Helping and the avoidance of inappropriate interracial behavior: A strategy that perpetuates a nonprejudiced self-image. *Journal of Personality and Social Psychology, 50,* 1083–1090.

Fride, E., & Mechoulam, R. (1993). Pharmacological activity of the cannabinoid receptor agonist, anandamide, a brain constituent. *European Journal of Pharmacology, 231,* 313–314.

Fridlund, A. (1994). *Human facial expression: an evolutionary view.* New York: Academic Press.

Fridlund, A., Sabini, J. P., Hedlund, L. E., Schaut, J. A., Shenker, J. I., & Knauer, M. J. (1990). Audience effects on solitary faces during imagery: Displaying to the people in your head. *Journal of Nonverbal Behavior, 14*(2), 113–137.

Fried, P. A., Watkinson, B., & Gray, R. (1992). A follow-up study of attentional behavior in 6-year-old children exposed prenatally to marijuana, cigarettes, and alcohol. *Neurotoxicity and Teratology, 14*(5), 299–311.

Friedman, E., Clark, D., & Gershon, S. (1992). Stress, anxiety, and depression: Review of biological, diagnostic, and nosologic issues. *Journal of Anxiety Disorders, 6,* 337–363.

Friedman, H. S., Tucker, J. S., Schwartz, J. E., Martin, L. R., Tomlinson-Keasey, C., Wingard, D. L., & Criqui, M. H. (1995a). Childhood conscientiousness and longevity: Health behaviors and cause of death. *Journal of Personality and Social Psychology, 68,* 696–703.

Friedman, H. S., Tucker, J. S., Schwartz, J. E., Tomlinson-Keasey, C., Martin, L. R., Wingard, D. L., & Criqui, M. H. (1995b). Psychosocial and behavioral predictors of longevity: The aging and death of the "Termites." *American Psychologist, 50,* 69–78.

Friedman, H. S., Tucker, J. S., Tomlinson-Keasey, C., Schwartz, J. E., Wingard, D. L., & Criqui, M. H. (1993). Does childhood personality predict longevity? *Journal of Personality and Social Psychology, 65,* 176–185.

Friedman, M., & Rosenman, R. H. (1959). Association of specific overt behavior patterns with blood and cardiovascular findings: Blood cholesterol level, blood clotting time, incidence of arcus senilis, and clinical coronary artery disease. *Journal of the American Medical Association, 169,* 1286–1296.

Friedman, M., & Rosenman, R. H. (1974). *Type A behavior and your heart.* New York: Knopf.

Friedman, M. A., & Brownell, K. D. (1995). Psychological correlates of obesity: Moving to the next research generation. *Psychological Bulletin, 117*(1), 3–20.

Fromm-Reichmann, F. (1948). Notes on the development of treatment of schizophrenia by psychoanalytic psychotherapy. *Psychiatry, 11,* 263–273.

Fuhriman, A. J., & Burlingame, G. M. (1995). *The handbook of group psychotherapy: An empirical and clinical synthesis.* New York: Wiley-Interscience.

Fuller, J. L., & Thompson, W. R. (1960). *Behavior genetics.* New York: Wiley.

Funder, D., & Sneed, C. D. (1993). Behavioral manifestations of personality: An ecological approach to judgmental accuracy. *Journal of Personality and Social Psychology, 64,* 479–490.

Funder, D. C. (1993). Explaining traits. *Psychological Inquiry, 5,* 125–127.

Funder, D. C., & Colvin, C. R. (in press). Congruence of self and others' judgments of personality. In R. Hogan & S. R. Briggs (Eds.), *Handbook of personality psychology.* San Diego, CA: Academic Press.

Funder, D. C., Kolar, D. C., & Blackman, M. C. (1995). Agreement among judges of personality: Interpersonal relations, similarity, and acquaintanceship. *Journal of Personality and Social Psychology, 69,* 656–672.

Furstenberg, F. F., Brooks-Gunn, J., & Chase-Lansdale, L. (1989). Teenaged pregnancy and childbearing. *American Psychologist, 44,* 313–320.

Furstenberg, F. F., Jr., and Cherlin, A. J. (1991). *Divided families: What happens to children when parents part.* Cambridge, MA: Harvard University Press.

Fuson, K. C., & Kwon, Y. (1992a). Effects on children's addition and subtraction of the system of number words and other cultural tools. In J. Bideaud & C. Meljac (Eds.), *Pathways to number.* Villeneueve d'asq, France: University de Lille.

Fuson, K. C., & Kwon, Y. (1992b). Korean children's understanding of multidigit addition and subtraction. *Child Development, 63,* 491–506.

Gabrieli, J. D. E., Fleischman, D. A., Keane, M. M., Reminger, S. L., & Morrell, F. (1995). Double dissociation between memory systems underlying explicit and implicit memory in the human brain. *Psychological Science, 6,* 76–82.

Gaertner, S. L., & Dovidio, J. F. (1986). The aversive form of racism. In J. F. Dovidio & S. L. Gaertner (Eds.), *Prejudice, discrimination, and racism* (pp. 61–89). Orlando, FL: Academic Press.

Galanter, E. (1962). Contemporary psychophysics. In R. Brown (ed.), *New directions in psychology* (Vol. 1). New York: Holt, Rinehart, Winston.

Galef, B. G., & Wright, T. J. (1995). Groups of naive rats learn to select nutritionally adequate foods faster than do isolated rats. *Animal Behaviour, 49*(2), 403–409.

Galton, F. (1883). *Inquiries into human faculty and its development.* London: Macmillan.

Games, D., Adams, D., Alessandrini, R., Barbour, R., Berthelette, P., Blackwell, C., Carr, T., Clemens, J., Donaldson, T., Gillespie, F., Guido, T., Hagopian, S., Johnsonwood, K., Khan, K., Lee, M., Leibowitz, P., Lieburg, I., Little, S., Masliah, E., McConlogue, L., Montoyazavala, M., Mucke, L., Paganini, L., Penniman, E., Power, M., Schenk, D., Seubert, P., Snyder, B., Soriano, F., Tan, H., Vitale, J., Wadsworth, S., Wolozin, B., & Zhao, J. (1995). Alzheimer-type neuropathology in transgenic mice overexpressing V717F beta-amylois precursor protein. *Nature, 73,* 523–527.

Ganchrow, J. R., Steiner, J. E., & Daher, M. (1983). Neonatal facial expressions in response to different qualities and intensities of gustatory stimuli. *Infant Behavior and Development, 6,* 189–200.

Ganellen, R. J., & Blaney, P. H. (1984). Hardiness and social support as moderators of the effects of life stress. *Journal of Personality and Social Psychology, 47,* 156–163.

Gara, M. A., Woolfolk, R. L., Cohen, B. D., Goldston, R. B., Allen, L. A., & Novalany, J. (1993). Perception of self and other in major depression. *Journal of Abnormal Psychology, 102,* 93–100.

Garber, R. J. (1992). Long-term effects of divorce on the self-esteem of young adults. *Journal of Divorce and Remarriage, 17,* 131–138.

Garcia-Coll, C. T., Oh, W., & Hoffman, J. The social ecology: Early parenting of Caucasian American mothers. *Child Development, 58,* 955–963.

Garcia, J., & Koelling, R. A. (1966). Relation of cue to consequences in avoidance learning. *Psychonomic Science, 4,* 123–124.

Garcia, J., Rusiniak, K. W., & Brett, L. P. (1977). Conditioning food-illness aversions in wild animals: Caveat Canonici. In H. Davis & H. M. B. Hurwitz (Eds.), *Operant-Pavlovian interactions.* Hillsdale, NJ: Lawrence Erlbaum Associates.

Gardner, H. (1983). *Frames of mind: The theory of multiple intelligences.* New York: Basic Books.

Gardner, R., Heward, W. L., & Grossi, T. A. (1994). Effects of response cards on student participation and academic achievement: A systematic replication with inner-city students during whole-class science instruction. *Journal of Applied Behavior Analysis, 27,* 63–71.

Gardner, R. A., & Gardner, B. T. (1978). Comparative psychology and language acquisition. *Annals of the New York Academy of Science, 309,* 37–76.

Garland, A. F., & Zigler, E. (1993). Adolescent suicide prevention: Current research and social policy implications. *American Psychologist, 48,* 169–182.

Garrett, V., Brantley, P., Jones, G., & McNight, G. (1991). The relation between daily stress and Crohn's Disease. *Journal of Behavioral Medicine, 14,* 187–196.

Garrity, T. F. (1973). Vocational adjustment after first myocardial infarction: Comparative assessment of several variables suggested in the literature. *Social Science and Medicine, 7,* 705–717.

Garry, M., & Loftus, E. (1994). Pseudomemories without hypnosis. *International Journal of Clinical and Experimental Hypnosis, 42*(4), 363–373.

Garver, D. L., & Davis, J. M. (1979). Biogenic amine hypotheses of affective disorders. *Life Sciences, 24,* 383–394.

Gatchel, R. J., Baum, A., & Krantz, D. S. (1989). *An introduction to health psychology* (2nd ed.). New York: Random House.

Gatewood, R. D., & Field, H. S. (1994). *Human resource selection* (3rd ed.). Ft. Worth, TX: Dryden Press.

Gaver, W. W. (1986). Auditory icons: Using sound in computer interfaces. *Human-Computer Interaction, 2,* 167–177.

Gazzaniga, M. S., Fendrich, R., & Wessinger, C. M. (1994). Blindsight reconsidered. *Current Directions in Psychological Science, 3*(3), 93–95.

Gazzaniga, M. S., & LeDoux, J. E. (1978). *The integrated mind.* New York: Plenum.

Geary, D. C. (1995). Reflections of evolution and culture in children's cognition: Implications for mathematical development and instruction. *American Psychologist, 50,* 24–37.

Geary, D. C., Fan, L., & Bow-Thomas, C. C. (1992). Numerical cognition: Loci of ability differences comparing children from China and the United States. *Psychological Sciences, 3,* 180–185.

Geen, R. G. (1990). *Human aggression.* Pacific Grove, CA: Brooks/Cole.

Geen, R. G. (1991). Social motivation. *Annual Review of Psychology, 42,* 377–399.

Geen, R. G. (1995). Human aggression. In A. Tesser (Ed.), *Advanced social psychology* (pp. 383–418). New York: McGraw-Hill.

Geen, R. G., & McCown, E. J. (1984). Effects of noise and attack on aggression and physiological arousal. *Motivation and Emotion, 8,* 231–241.

Gelernter, J., Goldman, D., & Risch, N. (1993). The A1 allele at the D$_2$ dopamine receptor gene and alcoholism: A reappraisal. *Journal of the American Medical Association, 269,* 1673–1677.

Geliebter, A. (1995). Gastric distension and capacity in normal, obese and bulimic women. *Appetite, 24,* 167.

Gellhorn, E., & Loofbourrow, G. N. (1963). *Emotions and emotional disorders.* New York: Harper & Row.

Gelman, R., & Baillargeon, R. (1983). A review of some Piagetian concepts. In P. H. Mussen (Ed.), *Handbook of child psychology* (Vol. 3). New York: Wiley.

Gentner, D., & Collins, A. (1981). Studies of inference from lack of knowledge. *Memory & Cognition, 9,* 434–443.

Gentner, D., & Stevens, A. L. (Eds.). (1983). *Mental models.* Hillsdale, NJ: Lawrence Erlbaum Associates.

George, J. M. (1991). State or trait: Effects of positive mood on prosocial behaviors at work. *Journal of Applied Psychology, 76,* 299–307.

Gerbner, G., Gross, L., Morgan, M., & Signorielli, N. (1986). Living with television: The dynamics of the cultivation process. In J. Bryant & D. Zillmann (Eds.), *Perspectives on media effects.* Hillsdale, NJ: Lawrence Erlbaum Associates.

Gerschman, J. A., Reade, P. C., & Burrows, G. D. (1980). Hypnosis and dentistry. In G. D. Burrows & L. Dennerstein (Eds.), *Handbook of hypnosis and psychosomatic medicine.* Amsterdam: Elsevier.

Gershon, E. S. (1990). Genetics. In F. K. Goodwin & K. R. Jamison (Eds.), *Manic-depressive illness* (pp. 373–399). New York: Oxford University Press.

Geschwind, N. (1979). Specializations of the human brain. *Scientific American, 241,* 180–199.

Gfeller, J. D. (1994). Hypnotizability enhancement: Clinical implications of empirical findings. *American Journal of Clinical Hypnosis, 37*(2), 107–116.

Gibson, E. J., & Walk, R. D. (1960). The visual cliff. *Scientific American, 202,* 64–71.

Gibson, J. J. (1979). *The ecological approach to visual perception.* Boston: Houghton Mifflin.

Gidron, B., Chesler, M. A., & Chesney, B. K. (1991). Cross-cultural perspectives on self-help groups: Comparisons between participants and nonparticipants in Israel and the United States. *American Journal of Community Psychology, 19,* 667–681.

Gilbert, C. D. (1992). Horizontal integration and cortical dynamics. *Neuron, 9,* 1–13.

Gilbert, D. T. (1995). Attribution and interpersonal perception. In A. Tesser (Ed.), *Advanced social psychology* (pp. 99–148). New York: McGraw-Hill.

Gilbert, D. T., & Malone, P. S. (1995). The correspondence bias. *Psychological Bulletin, 117,* 21–38.

Gilbert, R. M. (1984). Caffeine consumption. In G. A. Spiller (Ed.), *The methylxanthine beverages and foods: Chemistry, consumption, and health effects.* New York: Liss.

Giles, T. R. (1990). Bias against behavior therapy in outcome reviews: Who speaks for the patient? *The Behavior Therapist, 13,* 86–90.

Gillberg, I. C., Rastan, I. M., & Gillberg, C. (1995). Anorexia nervosa 6 years after onset: I. Personality disorders. *Comprehensive Psychiatry, 36*(1), 61–69.

Gillette, M. U. (1986). The suprachiasmatic nuclei: Circadian phase-shifts induced at the time of hypothalamic slice preparation are preserved in vitro. *Brain Research, 379,* 176–181.

Gillham, J. E., Reivich, K. J., Jaycocx, L. H., & Seligman, M. E. P. (1995). Prevention of depressive symptoms in schoolchildren. *Psychological Science, 6,* 343–351.

Gilligan, C. (1982). *In a different voice: Psychological theory and women's development.* Cambridge, MA: Harvard University Press.

Gilligan, C., & Wiggins, G. (1987). The origins of morality in early childhood relationships. In J. Kagan & S. Lamb (Eds.), *The emergence of morality.* Chicago: University of Chicago Press.

Gilman, A. G., Goodman, L. S., Rall, T. W., & Murad, F. (1985). *Goodman and Gilman's the pharmacological basis of therapeutics* (7th ed.). New York: Macmillan.

Givens, B. (1995). Low doses of ethanol impair spatial working memory and reduce hippocampal theta activity. *Alcoholism Clinical and Experimental Research, 19*(3), 763–767.

Gladis, M. M., Michela, J. L., Walter, H., & Vaughan, R. (1992). High school students' perceptions of AIDS risk: Realistic appraisal or motivated denial? *Health Psychology, 11,* 307–316.

Gladue, B. A. (1994). The biopsychology of sexual orientation. *Current Directions in Psychological Science, 3*(5), 150–154.

Glanzer, M., & Cunitz, A. (1966). Two storage mechanisms in free recall. *Journal of Verbal Learning and Verbal Behavior, 5,* 351–360.

Glaser, R., & Bassok, M. (1989). Learning theory and the study of instruction. *Annual Review of Psychology, 40,* 631–666.

Glaser, R., Rice, J., Sheridan, J., Fertel, R., Stout, J. C., Speicher, C., Pinsky, D., Kotur, M., Post, A., Beck, M., & Kiecolt-Glaser, J. (1987). Stress-related immune suppression: Health implications. *Brain, Behavior, and Immunity, 1,* 7–20.

Gleitman, L., & Landau, B. (1994). *The acquisition of the lexicon.* Cambridge, MA: MIT Press.

Glenn, S. M., & Cunningham, C. C. (1983). What do babies listen to most? A developmental study of auditory preferences in nonhandicapped infants and infants with Down's syndrome. *Developmental Psychology, 19,* 332–337.

Gleuckauf, R., & Quittner, A. (1992). Assertiveness training for disabled adults in wheelchairs: Self-report, role-play, and activity pattern outcomes. *Journal of Consulting and Clinical Psychology, 60,* 419–425.

Glicksohn, J. (1991). Altered sensory environments, altered states of consciousness, and altered-state cognition. *Journal of Mind and Behavior, 14*(1), 1–11.

Glover, J. A., Krug, D., Dietzer, M., George, B. W., & Hannon, M. (1990). "Advance" advance organizers. *Bulletin of the Psychonomic Society, 28,* 4–6.

Glowinski, J. (1981). In vivo release of transmitters in the cat basal ganglia. *Federation Proceedings, 40,* 135–141.

Gnepp, J. (1983). Children's social sensitivity: Inferring emotions from conflicting cues. *Developmental Psychology, 19,* 805–814.

Goddard, H. H. (1917). Mental tests and the immigrant. *Journal of Delinquency, 2,* 243–277.

Goelet, P., Castellucci, V. F., Schacher, S. & Kandel, E. R. (1986). The long and the short of long-term memory: A molecular framework. *Nature, 322,* 419–422.

Goetz, C. G., Stebbins, G. T., Klawans, H. L., Koller, W. C., Grossman, R. G., Bakay, R. A., & Penn, R. D. (1991). United Parkinson Foundation Neurotransplantation Registry on adrenal medullary transplants: Presurgical, and 1- and 2-year follow-up. *Neurology, 41,* 1719–1722.

Gold, M. S. (1994). The epidemiology, attitudes, and pharmacology of LSD use in the 1990s. *Psychiatric Annals, 24*(3), 124–126.

Gold, P. W., Goodwin, F. K., & Chrousos, G. P. (1988a). Clinical and biochemical manifestations of depression: Relation to the neurobiology of stress, Part I. *New England Journal of Medicine, 319,* 348–413.

Gold, P. W., Goodwin, F. K., & Chrousos, G. P. (1988b). Clinical and biochemical manifestations of depression: Relation to the neurobiology of stress, Part II. *New England Journal of Medicine, 319,* 413–420.

Goldberg, J. F., Harrow, M., & Grossman, L. S. (1995). Course and outcome in bipolar affective disorder: A longitudinal follow-up study. *American Journal of Psychiatry, 152,* 379–384.

Goldberg, L. R. (1992). The development of markers of the Big-Five factor structure. *Psychological Assessment, 4,* 26–42.

Goldberg, L. R. (1993). The structure of phenotypic personality traits. *American Psychologist, 48,* 26–34.

Goldberg, L. R., & Saucier, G. (1995). So what do you propose we use instead? A reply to Block. *Psychological Bulletin, 117,* 221–225.

Golden, D. (1994, July). Building a better brain. *Life,* pp. 62–70.

Goldenberg, I., & Goldenberg, H. (1995). Family therapy. In R. J. Corsini & D. Wedding (Eds.), *Current psychotherapies* (5th ed.). Itasca, IL: Peacock.

Goldfried, M. R., & Davison, G. C. (1994). *Clinical behavior therapy.* New York: Wiley Interscience.

Goldin-Meadow, S., & Feldman, H. (1977). The development of language-like communication without a language model. *Science, 197,* 401–403.

Goldman, A., & Greenberg, L. (1992). Comparison of integrated systemic and emotionally focused approaches to couples therapy. *Journal of Consulting and Clinical Psychology, 60*(6), 962–969.

Goldman, J. A., & Harlow, L. L. (1993). Self-perception variables that mediate AIDS-preventive behavior in college students. *Health Psychology, 12,* 489–498.

Goldman, M. S., Brown, S. A., Christiansen, B. A., & Smith, G. T. (1991). Alcoholism and memory: Broadening the scope of alcohol-expectancy research. *Psychological Bulletin, 110,* 137–146.

Goldman-Rakic, P. S. (1987). Development of cortical circuitry and cognitive function. *Child Development, 58,* 601–622.

Goldstein, B. (1989). *Sensation and perception* (3rd ed.), Belmont, CA: Wadsworth.

Goldstein, J. M., & Tsuang, M. T. (1990). Gender and schizophrenia: An introduction and synthesis of findings. *Schizophrenia Bulletin, 16,* 179–184.

Gollwitzer, P. M., & Kinney, R. F. (1989). Effects of deliberative and implemental mind-sets on illusion of control. *Journal of Personality and Social Psychology, 56,* 531–542.

Golomb, J., Kluger, A., De Leon, M. J., Ferris, S. H., Convit, A., Mittelman, M. S., Cohen, J., Rusinek, H., De Santi, S., & George, A. E. (1994). Hippocampal formation size in normal human aging: A correlate of delayed secondary memory performance. *Learning and Memory, 1,* 45–54.

Goodale, M. A., & Milner, A. D. (1992). Separate visual pathways for perception and action. *Trends in Neuroscience, 15,* 20–25.

Goodall, J. (1986). *The chimpanzees of Gombe: Patterns of behavior.* Cambridge, MA: Harvard University Press.

Goodenough, F. L. (1932). Expression of the emotions in a blind-deaf child. *Journal of Abnormal and Social Psychology, 27,* 328–333.

Goodkin, K., Blaney, N., Feaster, D., Fletcher, M. A., Baum, M., Mantero-Atienza, E., Klimas, N., Millon, C., Szapocznik, J., & Eisdorfer, C. (1992). Active coping style is associated with natural killer cell cytotoxicity in asymptomatic HIV-1 seropositive homosexual men. *Journal of Psychosomatic Research, 36,* 635–650.

Goodman-Gilman, A. G., Rall, T. W., Nies, A. S., & Taylor, P. (1990). *The pharmacological basis of therapeutics* (8th ed.). New York: Pergamon Press.

Goodwin, C. (1992). A conceptualization of motives to seek privacy for nondeviant consumption. *Journal of Consumer Psychology, 1,* 261–284.

Goodwin, F. K., & Jamison, K. R. (Eds.). (1990). *Manic-depressive illness.* New York: Oxford University Press.

Goplerud, E. N. (1980). Social support and stress during the first year of graduate school. *Professional Psychology, 11,* 283–290.

Gordon, T. (1970). *Parent effectiveness training: The no-lose program for raising responsible children.* New York: Wyden.

Gorman, J. M., Liebowitz, M. R., Fyer, A. J., & Stein, J. (1989). A neuroanatomical hypothesis for panic disorder. *American Journal of Psychiatry, 146,* 148–161.

Gorner, P. (1994, October 6). "Sex study shatters kinky assumptions." *Chicago Tribune,* pp. 1–2.

Gorvin, J. J., & Roberts, M. S. (1994). Lunar phases and psychiatric hospital admissions. *Psychological Reports, 73,* 1435–1440.

Gossop, M., Griffiths, P., Powis, B., & Strang, J. (1994). Cocaine: Patterns of use, route of administration, and severity of dependence. *British Journal of Psychiatry, 164*(5), 660–664.

Gotlib, I. H., & Hammen, C. L. (1992). *Psychological aspects of depression: Toward cognitive interpersonal integration.* Chichester, Eng: John Wiley & Sons.

Gottesman, A. (1992, July 19). Asking witness to point out suspect can court embarrassment. *Chicago Tribune,*.

Gottesman, I. I. (1991). *Schizophrenia genesis.* New York: W. H. Freeman.

Gottfried, A. W. (1984). *Home environment and early cognitive development.* Orlando, FL: Academic Press.

Gottlieb, B. H., & Peters, L. (1991). A national demographic portrait of mutual aid group participants in Canada. *American Journal of Community Psychology, 19,* 651–666.

Gottman, J. M., & Levenson, R. W. (1992). Marital processes predictive of later dissolution: Behavior, physiology, and health. *Journal of Personality and Social Psychology, 63,* 221–233.

Gottman, J. S. (1989). Children of gay and lesbian parents. *Marriage and Family Review, 14*(3–4), 177–196.

Gould, E., Cameron, H. A., & McEwen, B. S. (1994). Blockade of NMDA receptors increases cell death and birth in the developing rat dentate gyrus. *Journal of Comparative Neurology, 340,* 551–565.

Gould, S. J. (1983). *The mismeasure of man.* New York: W. W. Norton.

Graber, J. A., Brooks-Gunn, J., Paikoff, R. L., & Warren, M. P. (1994). Prediction of eating problems: An 8-year study of adolescent girls. *Developmental Psychology, 30,* 823–834.

Graham, S. (1992). "Most of the subjects were white and middle class." *American Psychologist, 47,* 629–639.

Grant, S. G. N., O'Dell, T. J., Karl, K. A., Stein, P. L., Soriano, P., & Kandel, E. R. (1992). Impaired long-term potentiation, spatial learning, and hippocampal development in FYN mutant mice. *Science, 258,* 1903–1910.

Gray, A., Jackson, D. N., & McKinley, J. B. (1991). The relation between dominance, anger, and hormones in normally aging men: Results from the Massachusetts male aging study. *Psychosomatic Medicine, 53,* 375–385.

Green, D. M., & Swets, J. A. (1966). *Signal detection theory and psychophysics.* New York: Wiley.

Green, E. J., Greenough, W. T., & Schlumpf, B. E. (1983). Effects of complex or isolated environments on cortical dendrites of middle-aged rats. *Brain Research, 264*(2), 233–240.

Green, J. P., & Lynn, S. J. (1995). Hypnosis, dissociation, and simultaneous task performance. *Journal of Personality and Social Psychology, 69,* 728–735.

Green, M. (1991). Visual search, visual strains, and visual architecture. *Perception and Psychophysics, 50,* 388–404.

Green, R. A., Cross, A. J., & Goodwin, G. M. (1995). Review of the pharmacology and clinical pharmacology of 3,4-methylenedioxymethamphetamine (MDMA or "ecstacy"). *Psychopharmacology, 119,* 247–260.

Greenberg, E., O'Neil, R., & Nagel, S. K. (1994). Linking workplace and homeplace: Relations between the nature of adults' work and their parenting behaviors. *Developmental Psychology, 30,* 990–1002.

Greenberg, L. S., Rice, L. N., Elliot, R. (1993). *Process-experiential therapy: Facilitating emotional change.* New York: Guilford.

Greenberg, M., & Stone, A. (1992). Emotional disclosure about trauma and its relation to health: Effects of previous disclosure and trauma severity. *Journal of Personality and Social Psychology, 63,* 75–84.

Greenblatt, D., Harmatz, J., & Shader, R. I. (1993). Plasma alprazolam concentrations: Relation to efficacy and side effects in the treatment of panic disorder. *Archives of General Psychiatry, 50,* 715–732.

Greene, R. (1991). *The MMPI-2/MMPI: An interpretive manual.* Needham Heights, MA: Allyn & Bacon.

Greenfield, P. M. (1994). Video games as cultural artifacts. *Journal of Applied Developmental Psychology, 15,* 3–12.

Greenfield, P. M. (1995, Winter). Culture, ethnicity, race, and development: Implications for teaching theory and research. *Society for Research in Child Development Newsletter,* pp. 3ff.

Greenfield, P. M., Camaioni, L., Ercolani, P., Weiss, L., Lauber, B. A., & Perucchini, P. (1994). Cognitive socialization by computer games in two cultures: Inductive discovery or mastery of an iconic code? *Journal of Applied Developmental Psychology, 15,* 59–86.

Greenfield, P. M., & Childs, C. P. (1991). Developmental continuity in biocultural context. In R. Cohen & A. W. Siegel (Eds.), *Context and development* (pp. 135–159). Hillsdale, NJ: Lawrence Erlbaum Associates.

Greenfield, P. M., & Savage-Rumbaugh, E. S. (1990). Grammatical combination in *pan paniscus*: Processes of learning and invention in the evolution of language development. In S. Parker & K. Gibson (Eds.), *Comparative developmental psychology of language and intelligence in primates.* New York: Cambridge University Press.

Greenough, W. T., Black, J. E., & Wallace, C. S. (1987). Experience and brain development. *Child Development, 58,* 539–559.

Greenwald, A. G. (1992). New look 3: Unconscious cognition reclaimed. *American Psychologist, 47,* 766–779.

Greenwald, A. G., & Banaji, M. R. (1995). Implicit social cognition: Attitudes, self-esteem, and stereotypes. *Psychological Review, 102,* 4–27.

Greenwald, A. G., Klinger, M. R., & Schuh, E. S. (1995). Activation by marginally perceptible ("subliminal") stimuli: Dissociation of unconscious from conscious cognition. *Journal of Experimental Psychology: General, 124*(1), 22–42.

Greenwald, A. G., & Spangenberg, E. R. (1991). Double-blind tests of subliminal self-help audiotapes. *Psychological Science, 2,* 119–122.

Greenwald, J. (1991, December 22). Smart as you wanna be. *Los Angeles Times Magazine.*

Greer, A. E., & Buss, D. M. (1994). Tactics for promoting sexual encounters. *Journal of Sex Research, 31*(3), 185–201.

Gregg, V., Gibbs, J. C., & Basinger, K. S. (1994). Patterns of developmental delay in moral judgment by male and female delinquents. *Merrill-Palmer Quarterly, 40,* 538–553.

Gregory, R. J. (1992). *Psychological Testing: History, Principles, and Applications.* Boston: Allyn & Bacon.

Gregory, R. L. (1968). Visual illusions. *Scientific American, 219,* 66–67.

Gregory, R. L. (1973). *Eye and brain* (2nd ed.). New York: McGraw Hill.

Grencavage, L., & Norcross, J. C. (1991). Where are the commonalities among the therapeutic common factors. *Professional Psychology: Research and Practice, 21,* 372–378.

Griffitt, W. B., & Guay, P. (1969). "Object" evaluation and conditioned affect. *Journal of Experimental Research in Personality, 4,* 1–8.

Grilo, C. M., Pogue-Geile, M. F. (1991). The nature of environmental influences on weight and obesity: A behavior genetic analysis. *Psychological Bulletin, 110,* 520–537.

Grinspoon, L., & Bakalar, J. B. (1995). Marijuana as medicine: A plea for reconsideration. *Journal of the American Medical Association, 273*(23), 1875–1876.

Gritz, E., & St. Jeor, S. (1992). Task Force 3: Implications with respect to intervention and prevention. *Health Psychology, 11*(suppl.), 17–25.

Grob, C., & Dobkin-de-Rios, M. (1992). Adolescent drug use in cross-cultural perspective. *Journal of Drug Issues, 22*(1) 121–138.

Grossberg, S. (1988). *Neural networks and natural intelligence.* Cambridge, MA: MIT Press.

Grossmann, K., Grossmann, K. E., Spangler, G., Suess, G., & Unzner, L. (1985). Maternal sensitivity and newborns' orientation responses as related to quality of attachment in Northern Germany. In I. Bretherton & E. Waters (Eds.), Growing points of attachment theory and research. *Monographs of the Society for Research in Child Development, 50*(1–2, Serial No. 209).

Grosz, H. I., & Zimmerman, J. (1970). A second detailed case study of functional blindness: Further demonstration of the contribution of objective psychological data. *Behavior Therapy, 1,* 115–123.

Grunberg, N. (1992). Cigarette smoking and body weight: A personal journey through a complex field. *Health Psychology, 11*(suppl.), 26–31.

Grunberg, N. E. (1994). Overview: Biological processes relevant to drugs of dependence. *Addiction, 89*(11), 1443–1446.

Grusec, J. E. (1991). Socialization of concern for others in the home. *Developmental Psychology, 27,* 338–342.

Grusec, J. E., & Goodnow, J. J. (1994). Impact of parental discipline methods on the child's internalization of values. *Developmental Psychology, 30,* 4–19.

Guarnaccia, P. J., Good, B. J., & Kleinman, A. (1990). A critical review of epidemiological studies of Puerto Rican mental health. *American Journal of Psychiatry, 147,* 1449–1456.

Guenther, F. H. (1994). A neural network model of speech acquisition and motor-equivalent speech production. *Biological Cybernetics, 72,* 43–53.

Guerin, D., & Gottfried, A. W. (1986). Infant temperament as a predictor of preschool behavior problems. *Infant Behavior and Development, 9,* 152. (Special issue: Abstracts of papers presented at the Fifth International Conference on Infant Studies.)

Guerra, N. G., Huesmann, L. R., Tolan, P. H., Van Acker, R., & Eron, L. D. (1995). Stressful events and individual beliefs as correlates of economic disadvantage and aggression among urban children. *Journal of Consulting and Clinical Psychology, 63,* 518–528.

Guevara, M. A., Lorenzo, I., Ramos, J., & Corsi–Cabrera, M. (1995). Inter- and intra-hemispheric EEG correlation during sleep and wakefulness. *Sleep, 18*(4), 257–265.

Guilford, J. P. (1956). The structure of intellect. *Psychological Bulletin, 53,* 267–293.

Guilford, J. P. (1959). The three faces of intellect. *American Psychologist,* pp. 469–479.

Guilford, J. P. (1959). Traits of creativity. In H. H. Anderson (Ed.), *Creativity and its cultivation.* New York: Harper & Row.

Guilford, J. P., & Hoepfner, R. (1971). *The analysis of intelligence.* New York: McGraw-Hill.

Guisinger, S., & Blatt, S. J. (1994). Individuality and relatedness: Evolution of a fundamental dialectic. *American Psychologist, 49,* 104–111.

Guntheroth, W. G., & Spiers, P. S. (1992). Sleeping prone and the risk of sudden infant death syndrome. *Journal of the American Medical Association, 267,* 2359–2362.

Gur, R. C., Mozley, L. H., Mozley, P. D., Resnick, S. M., Karp, J. S., Alavi, A., Arnold, S. E., & Gur, R. E. (1995). Sex differences in regional cerebral glucose metabolism during a resting state. *Science, 267,* 528–531.

Gur, R. C., Skolnic, B. E., & Gur, R. E. (1994). Effects of emotional discrimination tasks on cerebral blood flow: Regional activation and its relation to performance. *Brain and Cognition, 25*(2), 271–286.

Gurman, E. B. (1994). Debriefing for all concerned: Ethical treatment of human subjects. *Psychological Science, 5,* 139.

Guroff, G. (1980). *Molecular neurobiology.* New York: Marcel Dekker.

Gustavson, C. R., Garcia, J., Hawkins, W. G., & Rusiniak, K. W. (1974). Coyote predation control by aversive conditioning. *Science, 184,* 581–583.

Guthrie, R. V. (1976). *Even the rat was white: A historical view of psychology.* New York: Harper & Row.

Guyton, A. C. (1991). *Textbook of medical physiology* (8th ed.). Philadelphia: Saunders.

Ha, H., Tan, E. C., Fukunaga, H., & Aochi, O. (1981). Naloxone reversal of acupuncture analgesia in the monkey. *Experimental Neurology, 73,* 298–303.

Haaga, D., Dyck, M., & Ernst, D. (1991). Empirical status of the cognitive theory of depression. *Psychologial Bulletin, 110,* 215–236.

Haan, N., Aerts, E., & Cooper, B. A. B. (1985). *On moral grounds: The search for practical morality.* New York: New York University Press.

Haber, R. N. (1979). Twenty years of haunting eidetic imagery: Where's the ghost? *The Behavioral and Brain Sciences, 2,* 583–629.

Hackel, L. S., & Ruble, D. N. (1992). Changes in the marital relationship after the first baby is born: Predicting the impact of expectancy disconfirmation. *Journal of Personality and Social Psychology, 62,* 944–957.

Hadley, S. W., & Strupp, H. H. (1976). Contemporary views of negative effects in psychotherapy: An integrated account. *Archives of General Psychiatry, 33*(1), 1291–1302.

Hahdahl, K., Iversen, P. M., & Jonsen, B. H. (1993). Laterality for facial expressions: Does the sex of the subject interact with the sex of the stimulus face? *Cortex, 29*(2), 325–331.

Haier, R. J., Siegel, B. V. Jr., Crinella, F. M., & Buchsbaum, M. S. (1993). Biological and psychometric intelligence: Testing an animal model in humans with positron emission tomography. In D. K. Detterman (Ed.), *Current topics in human intelligence* (Vol. 3). Norwood, NJ: Ablex.

Hakuta, K., & Garcia, E. E. (1989). Bilingualism and education. *American Psychologist, 44,* 374–379.

Halaas, J. L., Gajiwala, K. S., Maffei, M., Cohen, S. L., Chait, B. T., Rabinowitz, D., Lallone, R. L., Burley, S. K., & Friedman, J. M. (1995). Weight-reducing effects of the plasma protein encoded by the *obese* gene. *Science, 269,* 543–546.

Haldeman, D. C. (1994). The practice and ethics of sexual orientation conversion therapy. *Journal of Consulting and Clinical Psychology, 62*(2), 221–227.

Halford, G. S., Maybery, M. R., O'Hare, A. W., & Grant, P. (1994). The development of memory and processing capacity. *Child Development, 65,* 1338–1356.

Hall, G. C. N. (1995). The preliminary development of theory-based community treatment of sexual offenders. *Professional Psychology: Research and Practice, 26,* 478–483.

Hall, G. C. N., & Hirschman, R. (1991). Toward a theory of sexual aggression: A quadripartite model. *Journal of Consulting and Clinical Psychology, 59,* 662–669.

Hall, G. C. N., & Hirschman, R. (1994). The relationship between men's sexual aggression inside and outside the laboratory. *Journal of Consulting and Clinical Psychology, 62,* 375–380.

Hall, G. C. N., Shondrick, D. D., & Hirschman, R. (1993). The role of sexual arousal in sexually aggressive behavior: A meta-analysis. *Journal of Consulting and Clinical Psychology, 61,* 1091–1095.

Hall, R. C., Hoffman, R. S., Beresford, T. P., Wooley, B., et al. (1989). Physical illness encountered in patients with eating disorders. *Psychosomatics, 30,* 174–191.

Hall, R. M., & Sandler, B. R. (1982). *The classroom climate: A chilly one for women?* Washington, DC: Association of American Colleges.

Haller, E. (1992). Eating disorders: A review and update. *Western Journal of Medicine, 157,* 658–662.

Halpern, D. F. (1989). *Thought and knowledge: An introduction to critical thinking* (2nd ed.). Hillsdale, NJ: Lawrence Erlbaum Associates.

Halpern, D. F. (1992). Sex differences in cognitive abilities (2nd ed.). Hillsdale, NJ: Lawrence Erlbaum Associates.

Hamer, D. H., Hu, S., Magnuson, V. L., Hu, N., & Pattatucci, A. M. L. (1993). A linkage between DNA markers on the X chromosome and male sexual orientation. *Science, 261,* 321–327.

Hamilton, D. L., & Sherman, J. (1994). Social stereotypes. In R. S. Wyer & T. K. Srull (Eds.), *Handbook of social cognition* (2nd ed.). Hillsdale, NJ: Lawrence Erlbaum Associates.

Hamilton, W. D. (1964). The evolution of social behavior: Parts I and II. *Journal of Theoretical Biology, 7,* 1–52.

Hamm, A. O., Vaitl, D., & Lang, P. J. (1989). Fear conditioning, meaning, and belongingness: A selective association analysis. *Journal of Abnormal Psychology, 98,* 395–406.

Hammen, C. (1991). *Depression runs in families: The social context of risk and resilience in children of depressed mothers.* New York: Springer-Verlag.

Hammer, E. (1968). Projective drawings. In A. I. Rabin (Ed.), *Projective techniques in personality assessment.* New York: Springer.

Hammond, W. R., & Yung, B. (1993). Minority student recruitment and retention practices among schools of professional psychology: A national survey and analysis. *Professional Psychology: Research and Practice, 24,* 3–12.

Hancock, P., Flach, J., Caird, J., & Vicente, K. (Eds.). (1995). *Local applications of the ecological approach to human-machine systems.* Hillsdale, NJ: Lawrence Erlbaum Associates.

Hansel, C. E. M. (1980). *ESP: A scientific evaluation.* New York: Scribner.

Hanson, S. J., & Burr, D. J. (1990). What connectionist models learn: Learning and representations in connectionist networks. *Behavioral and Brain Sciences, 13,* 471–518.

Harackiewicz, J. M. & Elliot, A. J. (1993). Achievement goals and intrinsic motivation. *Journal of Personality and Social Psychology, 65(5),* 904–915.

Hardaway, R. (1990). Subliminally activated symbiotic fantasies: Facts or artifacts. *Psychological Bulletin, 107,* 177–195.

Hardimann, P. T., Dufresne, R., & Mestre, J. (1989). The relation between problem categorization and problem solving among experts and novices. *Memory & Cognition, 17,* 627–638.

Hare, R. (1991). *The Hare Psychopathy Checklist—Revised.* Toronto: Multi-Health Systems.

Hare, R., Hart, S., & Harpur, T. (1991). Psychopathy and the DSM-IV criteria for antisocial personality disorder. *Journal of Abnormal Psychology, 100,* 391–398.

Harlow, H. F. (1959, June). Love in infant monkeys. *Scientific American,* 68–74.

Harper, R. C., Frysinger, J. D., Marks, J. X., & Zhang, R. B. (1988). Cardiorespiratory control during sleep. In P. J. Schwartz (Ed.), *The sudden infant death syndrome: Cardiac and respiratory mechanisms and interventions* (Annals of the New York Academy of Sciences, Vol. 533). New York: New York Academy of Sciences.

Harris, G. C., & Aston-Jones, G. (1995). Involvement of D2 dopamine receptors in the nucleus acumbens in opiate withdrawal syndrome. *Nature, 371,* 155–157.

Harris, J. E., & Morris, P. E. (Eds.) (1984). *Everyday memories, actions, and absent-mindedness.* New York: Academic Press.

Harris, M. J., Milich, R., Corbitt, E. M., Hoover, D. W., & Brady, M. (1992). Self-fulfilling effects of stigmatizing information on children's social interactions. *Journal of Personality and Social Psychology, 63,* 41–50.

Harris, R. J., Sardarpoor-Bascom, F., & Meyer, T. (1989). The role of cultural knowledge in distorting recall for stories. *Bulletin of the Psychonomic Society, 27,* 9–10.

Hart, J., Jr., Berndt, R. S., & Caramazza, A. (1985). Category-specific naming deficit following cerebral infarction. *Nature, 316,* 439–440.

Hartman, B. K., Cozzari, C., Berod, A., Kalmbach, S. J., & Faris, P. L. (1986). Central cholinergic innervation of the locus coeruleus. *Society for Neuroscience Abstracts, 12,* 770.

Hartman, E., Baekeland, F., & Zwilling, G. (1972). Psychological differences between long and short sleepers. *Archives of General Psychiatry, 26,* 463–468.

Hartmann, H. (1958). *Ego psychology and the problem of adaptation.* New York: International Universities Press.

Hartup, W. W. (1983). Peer relations. In P. H. Mussen (Ed.), *Handbook of child psychology: Vol. 4.* New York: Wiley.

Harwood, R. L., Schulze, P. A., & Wilson, S. P. (1995, March). *Cultural values and acculturation among lower-class Puerto Rican mothers living in the United States.* Poster presented at the biennial meeting of the Society for Research in Child Development, Indianapolis.

Haskell, I., & Wickens, C. D. (1993). Two- and three-dimensional displays for aviation. *International Journal of Aviation Psychology, 4.*

Hastie, R. (1986). Review essay: Experimental evidence on group accuracy. In B. Grofman & G. Owen (Eds.), *Information pooling and group decision making* (pp. 129–264). Greenwich, CT: JAI Press.

Hastie, R., Penrod, S. D., & Pennington, N. (1984). *Inside the jury.* Cambridge, MA: Harvard University Press.

Hatfield, E. (1988). Passionate and companionate love. In R. J. Sternberg & M. L. Barnes (Eds.), *The psychology of love.* New Haven: Yale University Press.

Hauser, P., Zametkin, A. J., Martinez, P., Vitiello, B., Matochik, J. A., Mixson, J., & Weinstraub, B. D. (1993). Attention deficit hyperactivity disorder in people with generalized resistance to thyroid hormone. *New England Journal of Medicine, 328,* 997–1001.

Hausman, C. R. (1984). *A discourse on novelty and creation.* Albany, NY: SUNY Press.

Hawkins, H. L., Kramer, A. R., & Capaldi, D. (1993). Aging, exercise, and attention. *Psychology and Aging, 7,* 643–653.

Hayes, C. (1951). *The ape in our house.* New York: Harper.

Hayes, J. R. (1985). Three problems in teaching general skills. In J. Segal, S. Chipman, & R. Glaser (Eds.), *Thinking and learning* (Vol. 2). Hillsdale, NJ: Lawrence Erlbaum Associates.

Hayes, J. R. M. (1952). *Memory span for several vocabularies as a function of vocabulary size.* Massachusetts Institute of Technology Acoustic Laboratory Progress Report. Cambridge: MIT Press.

Hays, P. A. (1995). Multicultural applications of cognitive-behavior therapy. *Professional Psychology: Research and Practice, 26,* 309–315.

Hays, R., Turner, H., & Coates, T. (1992). Social support, AIDS-related symptoms, and depression among gay men. *Journal of Consulting and Clinical Psychology, 60,* 463–469.

Hays, S. C., & Heiby, E. (1996). Psychology's drug problem: Do we need a fix or should we just say no? *American Psychologist, 51,* 198–206.

Hays, W. L. (1981). *Statistics* (3rd ed.). New York: Holt, Rinehart & Winston.

Hayslip, B., & Sterns, H. L. (1979). Age differences in relationships between crystallized and fluid intelligences and problem solving. *Journal of Gerontology, 14,* 404–414.

He, L. F. (1987). Involvement of endogenous opioid peptides in acupuncture analgesia. *Pain, 31,* 99–121.

Hearold, S. (1986). A synthesis of 1043 effects of television on social behavior. In G. Comstock (Ed.), *Public communication and behavior.* New York: Academic Press.

Heath, A., Neale, M., Kessler, R., Eaves, L., & Kendler, K. (1992). Evidence for genetic influences on personality from self-reports and informant ratings. *Journal of Personality and Social Psychology, 63,* 85–96.

Heath, L., Kruttschnitt, C., & Ward, D. (1986). Television and violent criminal behavior: Beyond the Bobo doll. *Violence and Victims, 1,* 177–190.

Hebb, D. O. (1955). Drives and the C.N.S. (conceptual nervous system). *Psychological Review, 62,* 243–254.

Hedge, A., & Yousif, Y. H. (1992). Effects of urban size, urgency, and cost of helping: A cross-cultural comparison between the United Kingdom and Saudi Arabia. *Journal of Cross-Cultural Psychology, 23,* 107–115.

Hedge, J. W., & Borman, W. C. (in press). In A. Howard (Ed.), *The changing nature of work.* San Francisco: Jossey-Bass.

Hegarty, J. D., Baldessarini, R. J., Tohen, M., Waternaux, C., & Oepen, G. (1994). One hundred years of schizophrenia: A meta-analysis of the outcome literature. *American Journal of Psychiatry, 151,* 1409–1416.

Heider, E. (1972). Universals of color naming and memory. *Journal of Experimental Psychology, 93,* 10–20.

Heilbrun, A. B., & Witt, N. (1990). Distorted body image as a risk factor in anorexia nervosa: Replication and clarification. *Psychological Reports, 66,* 407–416.

Heine, S. J., & Lehman, D. R. (1995). Culture, dissonance, and self-affirmation. Unpublished manuscript. University of British Columbia, Vancouver.

Heinrichs, R. W. (1993). Schizophrenia and the brain. *American Psychologist, 48,* 221–233.

Heise, G. A., & Miller, G. A. (1951). An experimental study of auditory patterns. *American Journal of Psychology, 64,* 68–77.

Helgeson, V. S., Shaver, P., & Dyer, M. (1987). Prototypes of intimacy and distance in same-sex and opposite-sex relationships. *Journal of Social and Personal Relationships, 4,* 195–233.

Heller, W. (1993). Neuropsychological mechanisms of individual differences in emotion, personality, and arousal. *Neuropsychology, 7*(4), 486–489.

Heller, W., Etienne, M. A., & Miller, G. A. (1995). Patterns of perceptual asymmetry in depression and anxiety: Implications for neuropsychological models of emotion and psychopathology. *Journal of Abnormal Psychology, 104*(2), 327–333.

Helmers, K. F., Krantz, D. S., Merz, C. N. B., Klein, J., Kop, W. J., Gottdiener, J. S., & Rozanski, A. (1995). Defensive hostility: Relationship to multiple markers of cardiac ischemia in patients with coronary disease. *Health Psychology, 14,* 202–209.

Helmes, E., & Reddon, J. R. (1993). A perspective on developments in assessing psychopathology: A critical review of the MMPI-2. *Psychological Bulletin, 113,* 453–471.

Helms, J. E. (1992). Why is there no study of cultural equivalence in standardized cognitive ability testing? *American Psychologist, 47,* 1083–1101.

Helson, R., & Moane, G. (1987). Personality change in women from college to midlife. *Journal of Personality and Social Psychology, 53,* 176–186.

Helzer, J. E., Canino, G. J., Yeh, E., Bland, R. C., Lee, C. K., Hwu, H., & Newman, S. (1990). Alcoholism—North America and Asia: A comparison of population surveys with the diagnostic interview schedule. *Archives of General Psychiatry, 47,* 313–319.

Henderson, C. E., Phillips, H. S., Pollock, R. A., Davies, A. M., Lemeulle, C., Armanini, M., Simpson, L. C., Moffet, B., Vandlen, R. A., Koliatsos, V. E., & Rosenthal, A. (1994). GDNF—A potent survival factor for motorneurons present in peripheral nerve and muscle. *Science, 266,* 1062–1064.

Hendrick, C., & Hendrick, S. (1986). A theory and method of love. *Journal of Personality and Social Psychology, 50,* 392–402.

Henker, B., & Whalen, C. K. (1989). Hyperactivity and attention deficits. *American Psychologist, 44,* 216–223.

Hense, R., Penner, L. A., & Nelson, D. L. (in press). Implicit memory for age stereotypes. *Social Cognition.*

Herbert, T. B., & Cohen, S. (1993). Depression and immunity: A meta-analytic review. *Psychological Bulletin, 113,* 472–486.

Herek, G. M., & Berrill, K. T. (eds.) (1992). *Hate crimes.* Beverly Hills: Sage.

Herman, J. L., & Schatzow (1987). Recovery and verification of memories of childhood and sexual trauma. *Psychoanalytic Psychology, 4,* 1–14.

Herman, L. M., Richards, D. G., & Wolz, J. P. (1984). Comprehension of sentences by bottlenosed dolphins. *Cognition, 16,* 129–219.

Herrmann, D. J., & Searleman, A. (1992). Memory improvement and memory theory in historical perspective. In D. Herrmann, H. Weingartner, A. Searlman, & C. McEvoy (Eds.), *Memory improvement: Implications for memory theory.* New York: Springer-Verlag.

Herrnstein, R. (1973). *I.Q. in the meritocracy.* Boston: Little, Brown.

Herrnstein, R. J., & Murray, C. (1994). *The bell curve: Intelligence and class structure in American Life.* New York: Free Press.

Hershberger, S. L., & D'Augelli, A. R. (1995). The impact of victimization on the mental health and suicidality of lesbian, gay, and bisexual youths. *Developmental Psychology, 31,* 65–74.

Hershberger, S. L., Plomin, R. & Pedersen, N. L. (1995). Traits and metatraits: Their reliability, stability, and shared genetic influence. *Journal of Personality and Social Psychology, 69,* 673–685.

Hershenon, M. (1989). *The moon illusion.* Hillsdale, NJ: Lawrence Erlbaum Associates.

Herzog, D. B. (1982). Bulimia: The secretive syndrome. *Psychosomatics, 22,* 481–487.

Herzog, D. B., Newman, K. L., & Warshaw, M. (1991). Body image dissatisfaction in homosexual and heterosexual males. *Journal of Nervous and Mental Disease, 179*(6), 356–359.

Hesse, J., Mogelvang, B., & Simonsen, H. (1994). Acupuncture versus metropolol in migraine prophylaxis: A randomized trial of trigger point inactivation. *Journal of Internal Medicine, 235,* 451–456.

Heston, L. L. (1966). Psychiatric disorders in foster home–reared children of schizophrenic mothers. *British Journal of Psychiatry, 112,* 819–825.

Hetherington, E. M., & Clingempeel, W. G. (1992). Coping with marital transitions. *Monographs of the Society for Research in Child Development, 57*(2–3, Serial No. 227).

Hettema, J. (1993). Adaptation: A biosocial approach to personality. In G. L. Van Heck, P. Bonaiuto, I. J. Deary, & W. Nowack (Eds.), *Personality psychology in Europe* (Vol. 4). Tilburg, Netherlands: University of Tilburg Press.

Heuer, F., & Reisberg, D. (1990). Vivid memories of emotional events: The accuracy of remembered minutiae. *Memory & Cognition, 18,* 496–506.

Higgins, E. T. (1987). Self-discrepancy: A theory relating self and affect. *Psychological Review, 94,* 319–340.

Higgins, E. T. (1989). Knowledge accessibility and activation: Subjectivity and suffering from unconscious sources. In J. S. Uleman & J. A. Bargh (Eds.), *Unintended thought.* New York: Guilford.

Hildebrand, J. G. (1995). Analysis of chemical signals by nervous systems. *Proceedings of the National Academy of Sciences of the United States of America, 92,* 67–74.

Hilgard, E. R. (1965). *Hypnotic susceptibility.* New York: Harcourt, Brace & World.

Hilgard, E. R. (1977). *Divided consciousness: Multiple controls in human thought and action.* New York: Wiley.

Hilgard, E. R. (1979). *Personality and hypnosis: A study of imaginative involvement.* Chicago: University of Chicago Press.

Hilgard, E. R. (1980). Consciousness in contemporary psychology. *Annual Review of Psychology, 31,* 1–26.

Hilgard, E. R. (1982). Hypnotic susceptibility and implications for measurement. *International Journal of Clinical and Experimental Hypnosis, 30,* 394–403.

Hilgard, E. R. (1992). Divided consciousness and dissociation. *Consciousness and Cognition, 1,* 16–31.

Hilgard, E. R., Morgan, A. H., & MacDonald, H. (1975). Pain and dissociation in the cold pressor test: A study of "hidden reports" through automatic key-pressing and automatic talking. *Journal of Abnormal Psychology, 84,* 280–289.

Hill, A. J., & Heaton-Brown, L. (1994). The experience of food craving: A prospective investigation in healthy women. *Journal of Psychosomatic Research, 38*(8), 801–814.

Hill, B. (1968). *Gates of horn and ivory.* New York: Taplinger.

Hill, C. E. (1990). Exploratory in-session process research in individual psychotherapy: A review. *Journal of Consulting and Clinical Psychology, 58,* 288–294.

Hill, D. L., & Mistretta, C. M. (1990). Developmental neurobiology of salt taste sensation. *Trends in Neuroscience, 13,* 188–195.

Hill, D. L., & Przekop, P. R., Jr. (1988). Influences of dietary sodium on functional taste receptor development: A sensitive period. *Science, 241,* 1826–1828.

Hill, T., Lewicki, P., Czyzewska, M., & Boss, A. (1989). Self-perpetuating biases in person perception. *Journal of Personality and Social Psychology, 57,* 373–386.

Hillman, D. C., Siffre, M., Milano, G., & Halberg, F. (1994). Free-running psychophysiologic circadians and three-month pattern in a woman isolated in a cave. *New Trends in Experimental and Clinical Psychiatry, 10*(3), 127–133.

Hilton, H. (1986). *The executive memory guide.* New York: Simon & Schuster.

Hines, M., & Green, R. (1991). Human hormonal and neural correlates of sex-typed behavior. *Review of Psychiatry, 10,* 536–555.

Hinsz, V. B. (1990). Cognitive and consensus processes in group recognition memory performance. *Journal of Personality and Social Psychology, 59,* 705–718.

Hinton, G. E. (1992, September). How neural networks learn for expense. *Scientific American, 267,* 145–151.

Hinton, J. (1967). *Dying.* Harmondsworth, UK: Penguin.

Hintzman, D. (1991). Human learning and memory. *Annual Review of Psychology,* 110–130.

Hiroto, D. S. (1974). Locus of control and learned helplessness. *Journal of Experimental Psychology, 102,* 187–193.

Hirschfeld, J. A. (1995). The "Back-to-Sleep" campaign against SIDS. *American Family Physician, 51,*(3), 611–612.

Hirsch-Pasek, K., Treiman, R., & Schneiderman, M. (1984). Brown and Hanlon revisited: Mothers' sensitivity to ungrammatical forms. *Journal of Child Language, 11,* 81–88.

Hirt, E. R., Deppe, R. K., & Gordon, L. J. (1991). Self-reported versus behavioral self-handicapping: Empirical evidence for a theoretical distinction. *Journal of Personality and Social Psychology, 61,* 981–991.

Hobson, J. A., & Stickgold, R. (1994). Dreaming: A neurocognitive approach. *Consciousness and Cognition, 3,* 1–15.

Hodgkinson, S., Sherrington, R., Gurling, H., Marchbanks, R., Redders, S., Mallet, J., McInnis, M., Petursson, H., & Brynjolfsson, J. (1987). Molecular genetic evidence for heterogeneity in manic depression. *Nature, 325,* 805–806.

Hoffer, B. J., & van Horne, C. (1995). Survival of dopaminergic neurons in fetal-tissue grafts. *New England Journal of Medicine, 332,* 1163–1164.

Hoffert, M. J. (1992). The neurophysiology of pain. In G. M. Aronoff (Ed.), *Evaluation and treatment of chronic pain.* Baltimore: Williams & Wilkins.

Hoffman, L. (1991). The influence of the family environment on personality: Accounting for sibling differences. *Psychological Bulletin, 110,* 187–203.

Hoffman, L. R. (Ed.). (1979). *The group problem solving process: Studies of a valence model.* New York: Praeger.

Hoffman, L. R., & Maier, N. R. F. (1979). Valence in the adoption of solutions by problem-solving groups: Concept, method, and results. In L. R. Hoffman (Ed.), *The group problem solving process: Studies of a valence model.* New York: Praeger.

Hoffman, M. L. (1970). Moral development. In P. H. Mussen (Ed.), *Carmichael's manual of child psychology: Vol. 2.* New York: Wiley.

Hoffman, M. L. (1977). Sex differences in empathy and related behaviors. *Psychological Bulletin, 84,* 712–722.

Hoffman, R. E., & McGlashan, T. H. (1993). Parallel distributed processing and the emergence of schizophrenic symptoms. *Schizophrenia Bulletin, 19,* 119–140.

Hofstadter, D. (1995). *Fluid concepts and creative analogies.* New York: Basic Books.

Hogan, R., Curphy, G. J., & Hogan, J. (1994). What we know about leadership: Effectiveness and personality. *American Psychologist, 49,* 493–504.

Hogan, R., & Hogan, J. (1992). *Hogan Personality Inventory Manual.* Tulsa, OK: Hogan Assessment Systems.

Hogan, R. J. (1992). Personality and personality measurement. In M. D. Dunnette & L. M. Hough (Eds.), *Handbook of Industrial/Organizational Psychology* (2nd ed., Vol 2, pp. 873–919). Palo Alto, CA: Consulting Psychologists Press.

Hogarth, R. M., & Einhorn, H. J. (1992). Order effects in belief updating: The belief adjustment model. *Cognitive Psychology, 24,* 1–55.

Hogg, M. A., & Hardie, E. A. (1991). Social attraction, personal attraction, and self-categorization: A field study. *Personality and Social Psychology Bulletin, 17,* 175–180.

Hohmann, G. W. (1966). Some effects of spinal cord lesions on experienced emotional feelings. *Psychophysiology, 3,* 143–156.

Holahan, C. J. (1986). Environmental psychology. *Annual Review of Psychology, 37,* 381–407.

Holdaway, I. M., Wallace, E., Westbrooke, L., & Gamble, G. (1995). Effect of dexfen-

fluramine on body weight, blood pressure, insulin resistance and serum cholesterol in obese individuals. *International Journal of Obesity, 19,* 749–751.

Holden, C. (1991). Probing the complex genetics of alcoholism. *Science, 251,* 163–164.

Holland, J. G. (1960). Teaching machines: An application of principles from the laboratory. *Journal of the Experimental Analysis of Behavior, 3,* 275–287.

Hollon, S., Shelton, R., & Loosen, P. (1991). Cognitive therapy and pharmacotherapy for depression. *Journal of Consulting and Clinical Psychology, 59,* 88–99.

Holman, B. R. (1994). Biological effects of central nervous system stimulants. *Addiction, 89*(11), 1435–1441.

Holmes, D. S. (1984). Meditation and somatic arousal reduction: A review of the experimental evidence. *American Psychologist, 39,* 1–10.

Holmes, D. S. (1990). The evidence for repression: An examination of sixty years of research. In J. Singer (Ed.), *Repression and dissociation: Implications for personality theory, psychopathology, and health.* Chicago: University of Chicago Press.

Holmes, D. S. (1991). *Abnormal psychology.* New York: HarperCollins.

Holroyd, K. A., France, J. L., Cordingley, G. E., Rokicki, L. A., Kvall, S. A., Lipchik, G. L., & McCool, H. R. (1995). Enhancing the effectiveness of relaxation-thermal biofeedback training with propranolol hydrochloride. *Journal of Consulting and Clinical Psychology, 63,* 327–330.

Holway, A. H., & Boring, E. G. (1941). Determinants of apparent visual size with distance variant. *American Journal of Psychology, 54,* 21–37.

Holyoak, K. J. (1977). The forms of analog size information in memory. *Cognitive Psychology, 9,* 31–51.

Holzman, P. S. (1994). Hilgard on psychoanalysis. *Psychological Science, 5,* 190–191.

Honorton, C., Berger, R. E., Varvoglis, M. P., Quant, M., Derr, P., Schechter, E. I., & Ferrari, D. C. (1990). Psi communication in the ganzfeld. *Journal of Parapsychology, 54,* 99–139.

Honorton, C., & Harper, S. (1974). Psi-mediated imagery and ideation in an experimental procedure for regulating perceptual input. *Journal of the American Society for Psychical Research, 68,* 156–168.

Honts, C. R. (1994). Psychophysical detection of deception. *Current Directions in Psychological Science, 3*(3), 77–82.

Hooker, E. (1993). Reflections of a 40-year exploration: A scientific view on homosexuality. *American Psychologist, 48,* 450–453.

Hopf, H. C., Muller, F. W., & Hopf, N. J. (1992). Localization of emotional and volitional facial paresis. *Neurology, 42*(10), 1918–1923.

Hoptman, M. J., & Davidson, R. J. (1994). How and why do the two cerebral hemispheres interact? *Psychological Bulletin, 116,* 195–219.

Horgan, J. (1994). Can science explain consciousness? *Scientific American, 271*(1), 88–94.

Horn, J. L. (1978). Human ability systems. In P. Baltes (Ed.), *Life-span Developmental Psychology* (Vol. 1). New York: Academic Press.

Horn, J. L. (1979). The rise and fall of human abilities. *Journal of Research and Development in Education, 12,* 59–78.

Horn, J. L. (1982). The theory of fluid and crystallized intelligence in relation to concepts of cognitive psychology and aging in adulthood. In F. I. M. Craik and S. Trehub (Eds.), *Aging and cognitive processes.* New York: Plenum.

Horner, M. S. (1970). Femininity and successful achievement: A basic inconsistency. In J. M. Bardwicks (Ed.), *Feminine personality and conflict.* Monterey, CA: Brooks/Cole.

Horney, K. (1937). *Neurotic personality of our times.* New York: W. W. Norton.

Horowitz, L. M., Rosenberg, S. E., & Bartholomew, K. (1993). Interpersonal problems, attachment styles, and outcome in brief dynamic psychotherapy. *Journal of Consulting and Clinical Psychology, 61,* 549–560.

Houpt, T. R. (1994). Gastric pressure in pigs during eating and drinking. *Physiology and Behavior, 56*(2), 311–317.

House, J. S., Umberson, D., & Landis, K. R. (1988). Structures and processes of social support. *Annual Review of Sociology, 14,* 293–318.

Houston, B., & Vavac, C. (1991). Cynical hostility: Developmental factors, psychosocial correlates and health behaviors. *Health Psychology, 10,* 9–17.

Howard, D. V. (1983). *Cognitive psychology.* New York: Macmillan.

Howard, K. E., Kopta, S. M., Krause, M. S., & Orlinsky, D. E. (1986). The dose-effect relationship in psychotherapy. *American Psychologist, 41,* 159–164.

Howard-Pitney, B., LaFramboise, T., Basil, M., September, B., & Johnson, M. (1992). Psychological and social indicators of suicide ideation and suicide attempts in Zuni adolescents. *Journal of Consulting and Clinical Psychology, 60,* 473–476.

Howe, M. J. A. (1970). Using students' notes to examine the role of the individual learner in acquiring meaningful subject matter. *Journal of Educational Research, 64,* 61–63.

Howe, M. L. (1995, March). *Differentiating cognitive and sociolinguistic factors in the decline of infantile amnesia.* Paper presented at the biennial meeting of the Society for Research in Child Development, Indianapolis.

Howe, M. L. (in press). What children's memories tell us about recalling our childhoods: A review of storage and retrieval processes in the development of long-term retention. *Psychonomic Bulletin and Review.*

Hoyle, R. H. (1993). Interpersonal attraction in the absence of explicit attitudinal information. *Social Cognition, 11,* 309–320.

Hoyle, R. H. (1994). Introduction to the special section: Structural equation modeling in clinical research. *Journal of Consulting and Clinical Psychology, 62,* 427–428.

Hser, Y., Anglin, D., & Powers, K. (1993). A 24-year follow-up of California narcotics addicts. *Archives of General Psychiatry, 50,* 577–584.

Hu, S., Patatucci, A. M. L., Patterson, C., Li, L., Fulker, D. W., Cherny, S. S., Kruglyak, L., & Hamer, D. H. (1995). Linkage between sexual orientation and chromosome Xq28 in males but not females. *Nature Genetics, 11,* 248–256.

Hubel, D. H., & Wiesel, T. N. (1962). Receptive fields, binocular interaction and functional architecture in the cat's visual cortex. *Journal of Physiology, 160,* 106–154.

Hubel, D. H., & Weisel, T. N. (1965). Receptive fields and functional architecture in two nonstriate visual areas (18 and 19) of the cat. *Journal of Neurophysiology, 28,* 229–289.

Hubel, D. H., & Wiesel, T. N. (1979). Brain mechanisms of vision. *Scientific American, 241,* 150–162.

Hudspeth, A. J. (1983). The hair cells of the inner ear. *Scientific American, 248,* 54–64.

Huesmann, L. R., Laperspetz, K., & Eron, L. D. (1984). Intervening variables in the TV violence-aggression relation: Evidence from two countries. *Developmental Psychology, 20,* 746–775.

Huesmann, L. R., & Miller, L. S. (1994). Long-term effects of repeated exposure to media violence in childhood. In L. R. Huesmann (Ed.), *Human aggression: Current perspectives* (pp. 153–186). New York: Plenum.

Hughes, J. R., Higgins, S. T., & Bickel, W. K. (1994). Nicotine withdrawal versus other drug withdrawal syndromes: Similarities and dissimilarities. *Addiction, 89*(11), 1461–1470.

Hull, C. L. (1943). *Principles of behavior.* New York: Appleton-Century-Crofts.

Hull, C. L. (1951). *Essentials of behavior.* New Haven, CT: Yale University Press.

Humphrey, D. H., & Dahlstrom, W. G. (1995). The impact of changing from the MMPI to the MMPI-2 on profile configurations. *Journal of Personality Assessment, 64,* 428–439.

Humphreys, K. (1993). Psychotherapy and the twelve-step approach for substance abusers: The limits of integration. *Psychotherapy, 30.*

Humphreys, K., & Rappaport, J. (1994). Researching self help/mutual help aid groups and organizations: Many roads, one journey. *Applied and Preventive Psychology, 3,* 217–231.

Humphreys, L. G. (1984). General intelligence. In C. R. Reynolds & R. T. Brown (Eds.), *Perspectives on bias in mental testing.* New York: Plenum.

Humphreys, L. G. (1988). Trends in levels of academic achievement of blacks and other minorities. *Intelligence, 12,* 231–260.

Humphreys, L. G., & Davey, T. C. (1988). Continuity in intellectual growth from 12 months to 9 years. *Intelligence, 12,* 183–197.

Hunt, C. B. (1980). Intelligence as an information processing concept. *British Journal of Psychology, 71,* 449–474.

Hunt, D. M., Dulai, K. S., Bowmaker, J. K., & Mollon, J. D. (1995). The chemistry of John Dalton's color blindness. *Science, 267,* 984–988.

Hunt, E. (1983). On the nature of intelligence. *Science, 219,* 141–146.

Hunt, M. (1982). *The universe within.* New York: Simon & Schuster.

Hunt, R., & Rouse, W. B. (1981). Problem solving skills of maintenance trainees in diagnosing faults in simulated power plants. *Human Factors, 23,* 317–328.

Hunter, E. J. (1979). *Combat casualties who remain at home.* Paper presented at Western Regional Conference of the Inter University Seminar, "Technology in Combat." Naval Postgraduate School, Monterey, CA.

Hunter, J. E. (1986). Cognitive ability, cognitive aptitudes, job knowledge, and job performance. *Journal of Vocational Behavior, 29,* 340–362.

Hunter, M. A., & Ames, E. W. (1988). A multifactor model of infants' preferences for novel and familiar stimuli. In C. Rovee-Collier & L. P. Lipsitt (Eds.), *Advances in infancy research: Vol. 5* (pp. 69–91). Norwood, NJ: Ablex.

Hurd, M. W., & Ralph, M. R. (1992). Suprachiasmatic nucleus transplants normalize entrainment in aged *tau* mutant hamsters. *Society for Neuroscience Abstracts, 22,* 1223.

Hurt, H., Brodsky, N. L., Betancourt, L., & Braitman, L. E. (1995). Cocaine-exposed children: Follow-up through 30 months. *Journal of Developmental and Behavioral Pediatrics, 16*(1), 29–35.

Huston, A. C., Carpenter, C. J., & Atwater, J. B. (1986). Gender, adult structuring of activities, and social behavior in middle childhood. *Child Development, 57,* 1200–1209.

Huston, A. C., Donnerstein, E., Fairchild, H., Feshbach, N. D., Katz, P. A., Murray, J. P., Rubinstein, E. A., Wilcox, B. L., & Zuckerman, D. (1992). *Big world, small screen: The role of television in American society.* Lincoln: University of Nebraska Press.

Huston, A. C., & Wright, J. C. (1989). The forms of television and the child viewer. In G. Comstock (Ed.), *Public communication and behavior* (Vol. 2). San Diego, CA: Academic Press.

Hutchins, E. (1995). *Cognition in the wild.* Cambridge, MA: MIT Press.

Hutchinson, J. (1991, Spring). What crack does to babies. *American Educator,* pp. 31–32.

Huttenlocher, J. (1974). The origins of language comprehension. In R. L. Solso (Ed.), *Theories in cognitive psychology.* Hillsdale, NJ: Lawrence Erlbaum Associates.

Huttenlocher, P. R. (1979). Synaptic density in human frontal cortex: Developmental changes and effects of aging. *Brain Research, 163,* 195–205.

Hyde, J. S. (1986). Gender differences in aggression. In J. S. Hyde & M. C. Linn (Eds.), *The psychology of gender: Advances through meta-analysis.* Baltimore: Johns Hopkins University Press.

Hyde, J. S. (1994). Can meta-analysis make feminist transformations in psychology? *Psychology of Women Quarterly, 18,* 451–462.

Hyde, J. S., Fennema, E., & Lamon, S. J. (1990). Gender differences in mathematics performance: A meta-analysis. *Psychological Bulletin, 107,* 139–155.

Hyde, J. S., & Phillis, D. E. (1979). Androgyny across the life span. *Developmental Psychology, 15,* 334–336.

Hyman, I. A. (1995). Corporal punishment, psychological maltreatment, violence, and punitiveness in America: Research, advocacy, and public policy. *Applied and Preventive Psychology, 4,* 113–130.

Hyman, I. E., Husband, T. H., & Billings, F. J. (in press). False memories of childhood experiences. *Applied Cognitive Psychology.*

Ibrahim, F. (1991). Contributions of cultural worldview to generic counseling and development. *Journal of Counseling and Development, 70,* 13–19.

Ickovics, J., & Rodin, J. (1992). Women and AIDS in the United States: Epidemiology, natural history, and mediating mechanisms. *Health Psychology, 11,* 1–16.

Ilgen, D. R., & Klein, H. J. (1989). Organizational behavior. *Annual Review of Psychology, 40,* 327–351.

Illinois Department of Corrections (1993). *Statistical presentation.* Springfield, IL.

Infant Health and Development Program. (1990). Enhancing the outcomes of low-birth-weight, premature infants. *Journal of the American Medical Association, 263,* 3035–3042.

Insko, C. A., Schopler, J., Hoyle, R. H., Dardis, G. J., & Graetz, K. A. (1990). Individual-group discontinuity as a function of fear and greed. *Journal of Personality and Social Psychology, 58,* 68–79.

Intons-Peterson, M. Roskos-Edoldson, B., Shirley, M., & Blut, D. (1989). Will educational materials reduce negative effects of exposure to sexual violence? *Journal of Social and Clinical Psychology, 8,* 256–275.

Irwin, M., Daniels, M., Smith, T., Bloom, E., & Weiner, H. (1987). *Brain, Behavior, and Immunity, 1,* 98–104.

Isabella, R. A., Belsky, J., & von Eye, A. (1989). Origins of infant-mother attachment: An examination of interactional synchrony during the infant's first year. *Developmental Psychology, 25,* 12–21.

Isenberg, D. J. (1986). Group polarization: A critical review and meta-analysis. *Journal of Personality and Social Psychology, 50,* 1141–1151.

Iwahashi, K., Matsuo, Y., Suwaki, H., Nakamura, K., & Ichikawa, Y. (1995). CYP2E1 and ALDH2 genotypes and alcohol dependence in Japanese. *Alcoholism Clinical and Experimental Research, 19*(3), 564–566.

Iwamura, Y., Iriki, A., & Tanaka, M. (1994). Bilateral hand representation in the postcentral somatosensory cortex. *Nature, 369,* 554–556.

Izard, C. (1993). Organizational and motivational functions of discrete emotions. In M. Lewis and J. M. Haviland (Eds.), *Handbook of emotions.* New York: Guilford.

Izard, C. E. (1971). *The face of emotion.* New York: Appleton-Century-Crofts, New York.

Izard, C. E. (1977). *Human emotions.* New York: Plenum.

Izard, C. E. (1994). Innate and universal facial expressions: Evidence from developmental and cross-cultural research. *Psychological Bulletin, 115*(2), 288–299.

Jacklin, C. N. (1989). Female and male: Issues of gender. *American Psychologist, 44,* 127–133.

Jacobs, M. K., & Goodman, G. (1989). Psychology and self-help groups: Predictions on a partnership. *American Psychologist, 44,* 536–545.

Jacobson, E. (1938). *Progressive relaxation.* Chicago: University of Chicago Press.

Jacobson, J. W., Mulick, J. A., & Schwartz, A. A. (1995). A history of facilitated communication. *American Psychologist, 50,* 750–765.

Jacobson, N. S., & Hollon, S. D. (1996). Cognitive-behavior therapy versus pharmacotherapy: Now that the jury's returned its verdict, it's time to present the rest of the evidence. *Journal of Consulting and Clinical Psychology, 64,* 74–80.

Jacoby, L. L. (1991). A process dissociation framework: Separating automatic from intentional uses of memory. *Journal of Memory and Language, 30,* 513–541.

Jacoby, L. L., Marriott, M. J., & Collins, J. G. (1990). The specifics of memory and cognition. In T. K. Srull & R. S. Wyer (Eds.), *Advances in social cognition: Vol. III. Content and process specificity in the effects of prior experiences.* Hillsdale, NJ: Lawrence Erlbaum Associates.

Jahn, R. (1982). The persistent paradox of ESP: An engineering perspective. *Proceedings of the IEEE, 70,* 136–170.

James, W. (1884). Some omissions of introspective psychology. *Mind, 9,* 1–26.

James, W. (1890). *Principles of psychology.* New York: Holt.

James, W. (1892). *Psychology: briefer course.* New York: Holt.

Jancke, L., & Kaufmann, N. (1994). Facial EMG responses to odors in solitude and with an audience. *Chemical Senses, 19*(2), 99–111.

Janicak, P., Sharma, R., Israni, T., Dowd, S., Altman, E., & Davis, J. (1991). Effects of unilateral-nondominant vs. bilateral ECT on memory and depression: A preliminary report. *Psychopharmacology Bulletin, 27,* 353–357.

Janis, I. L. (1989). *Crucial decisions: Leadership in policy making and crisis management.* New York: Free Press.

Janowiak, J. J., & Hackman, R. (1994). Meditation and college students' self-actualization and rated stress. *Psychological Reports, 75*(2), 1007-1010.

Janowitz, H. D. (1967). Role of gastrointestinal tract in the regulation of food intake. In C. F. Code (Ed.), *Handbook of physiology: Alimentary canal 1.* Washington, DC: American Physiological Society.

Jason, L. A., McMahon, S. D., Salina, D., Hedeker, D, Stockton, M., Dunson, K., & Kimball, P. (1995). Assessing a smoking cessation intervention involving groups, incentives, and self-help manuals. *Behavior Therapy, 26,* 393–408.

Jemmott, J. B., III, & Magloire, K. (1988). Academic stress, social support, and secretory immunoglobulin A. *Journal of Personality and Social Psychology, 55,* 803–810.

Jenike, M., Baer, L., Ballantine, T., Martuza, R., Tynes, S., Giriunas, I., Buttolph, L., & Cassem, N. (1991). Cingulotomy for refractory obsessive-compulsive disorder: A long-term follow-up of 33 patients. *Archives of General Psychiatry, 48,* 548–555.

Jenkins, J. G., & Dallenbach, K. M. (1924). Oblivescence during sleep and waking. *American Journal of Psychology, 35,* 605–612.

Jenner, P. (1995). The rationale for the use of dopamine agonists in Parkinson's disease. *Neurology, 45,* S6–S12.

Jensen, A. R. (1969). How much can we boost IQ and scholastic achievement? *Harvard Educational Review, 39,* 1–123.

Jensen, A. R. (1993). Why is reaction time correlated with psychometric *g? Current Directions in Psychological Science, 2,* 53–55.

Jensen, J. P., Bergin, A. E., & Greaves, D. W. (1990). The meaning of eclecticism: New survey and analysis of components. *Professional Psychology: Research and Practice, 21,* 124–130.

Jensen, M., & Karoly, P. (1991). Control beliefs, coping efforts, and adjustment to chronic pain. *Journal of Consulting and Clinical Psychology, 59,* 431–438.

Jensen, M. R. (1987). Psychological factors predicting the course of breast cancer. *Journal of Personality, 55,* 317–342.

Jensen, P., Roper, M., Fisher, P., Piacentini, J., Canino, G., Richters, J., Rubio-Stipec, M., Dulcan, M., Goodman, S., Davies, M., Rae, D., Shaffer, D., Bird, H., Lahey, B., & Schwab-Stone, M. (1995). Test-retest reliability of the Diagnostic Interview Schedule for Children (DISC 2.1). *Archives of General Psychiatry, 52,* 61–71.

Jensen-Campbell, L. A., Graziano, W. G., & West, S. G. (1995). Dominance, prosocial orientation, and female preferences: Do nice guys really finish last? *Journal of Personality and Social Psychology, 68,* 427–440.

Jeremy, R. J., & Hans, S. L. (1985) . Behavior of neonates exposed in utero to methadone as assessed on the Brazelton Scale. *Infant Behavior and Development, 8,* 323–336.

Jerison, H. J. (1973). *Evolution of the brain and intelligence.* New York: Academic Press.

Jhanwar, U. M., Beck, B., Jhanwar, Y. S., & Burlet, C. (1993). Neuropeptide Y projection from the arcuate nucleus to the parvocellular division of the paraventricular nucleus: Specific relation to the ingestion of carbohydrate. *Brain Research, 631*(1), 97–106.

John, O. P., & Donahue, E. M. (1994). *The big five inventory: Technical report of the 44-item version.* Berkeley, CA: Institute of Personality and Social Research, University of California.

Johnson, H. H., & Torcivia, J. M. (1967). Group and individual performance on a single-stage task as a function of distribution of individual performance. *Journal of Experimental Social Psychology, 3,* 266–273.

Johnson, J., & Vickers, Z. (1993). Effects of flavor and macronutrient composition of food servings on liking, hunger and subsequent intake. *Appetite, 21*(1), 25–39.

Johnson, J. S., & Newport, E. L. (1989). Critical period effects in second language learning. *Cognitive Psychology, 21,* 60–99.

Johnson, M. A., Dziurawiec, S., Ellis, H., & Morton, J. (1991). Newborns' preferential tracking of face-like stimuli and its subsequent decline. *Cognition, 4,* 1–19.

Johnson, S. L., McPhee, L., & Birch, L. L. (1991). Conditioned preferences: Young children prefer flavors associated with high dietary fat. *Physiology and Behavior, 50,* 1245–1251.

Johnson-Laird, P. N. (1983). *Mental models: Towards a cognitive science of language, inference, and consciousness.* Cambridge, MA: Harvard University Press.

Jones, B. E. (1991). Paradoxical sleep and its chemical/structural substrates in the brain. *Neuroscience, 40,* 637–656.

Jones, G. V. (1989). Back to Woodworth: Role of interlopers in the tip-of-the-tongue phenomenon. *Memory & Cognition, 17,* 69–76.

Jones, G. V. (1990). Misremembering a common object: When left is not right. *Memory & Cognition, 18,* 174–182.

Jones, L. V., & Appelbaum, M. I. (1989). Psychometric methods. *Annual Review of Psychology, 40,* 23–44.

Jones, M. C. (1957). The later careers of boys who were early or late maturing. *Child Development, 28,* 113–128.

Jonides, J., & Mack, R. (1984). On the cost and benefit of cost and benefit. *Psychological Bulletin, 96,* 29–44.

Jordan, N. C., Huttenlocher, J., & Levine, S. C. (1992). Differential calculation abilities in young children from middle- and low-income families. *Developmental Psychology, 28,* 644–653.

Josephs, R., Markus, R., & Tafarodi, R. (1992). Gender and self-esteem. *Journal of Personality and Social Psychology, 63,* 391–402.

Josephson, W. L. (1987). Television violence and children's aggression: Testing the priming, social script, and disinhibition predictions. *Journal of Personality and Social Psychology, 53,* 882–890.

Julien, R. M. (1992). *A primer of drug action* (6th ed.). New York: W. H. Freeman.

Julien, R. M. (1995). *A primer of drug action* (7th ed.). New York: W. H. Freeman.

Jung, C. G. (1916). *Analytical psychology.* New York: Moffat.

Jung, C. G. (1933). *Psychological types.* New York: Harcourt, Brace and World.

Jussim, L. (1989). Teacher expectations: Self-fulfilling prophecies, perceptual biases, and accuracy. *Journal of Personality and Social Psychology, 57,* 469–480.

Jussim, L., & Eccles, J. S. (1992). Teacher expectations II: Construction and reflection of student achievement. *Journal of Personality and Social Psychology, 63,* 947–961.

Kadera, S. W., Lambert, M. J., & Andrews, A. A. (1996). How much therapy is really enough? A session-by-session analysis of the psychotherapy dose-effect relationship. *Psychotherapy: Research and Practice.*

Kagan, J., Arcus, D., Snidman, N., Feng, W. Y., Hendler, J., & Greene, S. (1994). Reactivity in infants: A cross-national comparison. *Developmental Psychology, 30,* 342–345.

Kagan, J. R., Snidman, N., Arcus, D., & Resnick, J. S. (1994). *Galen's prophecy: Temperament in human nature.* New York: Basic Books.

Kagan, J., & Snidman, N. (1991). Temperamental factors in human development. *American Psychologist, 46,* 856–862.

Kahen, V., Katz, L. F., & Gottman, J. M. (1994). Linkages between parent-child interaction and conversations of friends. *Social Development, 3,* 238–254.

Kahn, A. S. (1984). *Social psychology.* Dubuque, IA: William C. Brown.

Kahn, D. A. (1995). New strategies in bipolar disorder: Part II. Treatment. *Journal of Practical Psychiatry and Behavioral Health, 3,* 148–157.

Kahneman, D., Slovic, P., & Tversky, A. (Eds.). (1982). *Judgment under uncertainty: Heuristics and biases.* New York: Cambridge University Press.

Kahneman, D., & Tversky, A. (1984). Choices, values, and frames. *American Psychologist, 29,* 341–356.

Kalaska, J. F., & Crammond, D. J. (1992). Cerebral cortical mechanisms of reaching movements. *Science, 255,* 1517–1523.

Kales, A., & Kales, J. (1973). Recent advances in the diagnosis and treatment of sleep disorders. In G. Usdin (Ed.), *Sleep research and clinical practice.* New York: Brunner/Mazel.

Kalichman, S. C., Kelly, J. A., Hunter, T. L., Murphy, D. A., & Tyler, R. (1993). Culturally tailored HIV-AIDS risk-reduction messages targeted to African-American urban women: Impact on risk sensitization and risk reduction. *Journal of Consulting and Clinical Psychology, 61,* 291–295.

Kalick, S. M. (1988). Physical attractiveness as a status cue. *Journal of Experimental Social Psychology, 24,* 469–489.

Kalick, S. M., & Hamilton, T. E. (1986). The matching hypothesis reexamined. *Journal of Personality and Social Psychology, 51,* 673–682.

Kalish, H. I. (1981). *From behavioral science to behavior modification.* New York: McGraw-Hill.

Kandel, E. (1976). *Cellular basis of behavior.* San Francisco: Freeman.

Kaniasty, K., & Norris, F. H. (1993). A test of the social support deterioration model in the context of natural disaster. *Journal of Personality and Social Psychology, 64,* 395–408.

Kanner, A. D., Coyne, J. C., Schaefer, C., & Lazarus, R. S. (1981). Comparison of two modes of stress measurement: Daily hassles and uplifts versus major life events. *Journal of Behavioral Medicine, 4,* 1–39.

Kanner, B. (1995). *Are you normal?* New York: St. Martin's Press.

Kaplan, H. S. (1979). *Disorders of sexual desire.* New York: Brunner/Mazel.

Kaplan, M. F. (1987). The influencing process in group decision making. In C. Hendrick (Ed.), *Group processes.* Newbury Park, CA: Sage.

Kaplan, M. F., & Miller, C. E. (1987). Group decision making and normative vs. informational influence: Effects of type of issue and assigned decision rule. *Journal of Personality and Social Psychology, 53,* 306–313.

Kaplan, R. M., Orleans, C. T., Perkins, K. A., & Pierce, J. P. (1995). Marshaling the evidence for greater regulation and control of tobacco products: A call for action. *Annals of Behavioral Medicine, 17,* 3–14.

Kapur, S., & Mann, J. J. (1993). Antidepressant action and the neurobiologic effects of ECT: Human studies. In C. E. Coffey (Ed.), *The clinical science of electroconvulsive therapy.* Washington, DC: American Psychiatric Press.

Karau, S. J., & Williams, K. D. (1993). Social loafing: A meta-analytic review and theoretical integration. *Journal of Personality and Social Psychology, 65,* 681–707.

Karau, S. J., & Williams, K. D. (1995). Social loafing: Research findings, implications, and future directions. *Current Directions in Psychological Science, 4,* 134–140.

Kardiner, A. (1977). *My analysis with Freud: Reminiscences.* New York: Norton.

Karen, R. (1994). *Becoming attached.* New York: Warner Books.

Karlins, M., Coffman, T. L., & Walter, G. (1969). On the fading of social stereotypes: Studies in three generations of college students. *Journal of Personality and Social Psychology, 13,* 1–16.

Karney, B. R., & Bradbury, T. N. (1995). The longitudinal course of marital quality and stability: A review of theory, method, and research. *Psychological Bulletin, 118,* 3–34.

Karni, A., Meyer, G., Adams, M., Turner, R., & Ungerleider, L. G. (1994). The acquisition and retention of a motor skill: A functional MRI study of long-term motor cortex plasticity. *Abstracts of the Society for Neuroscience, 20,* 1291.

Karni, A., Tanne, D., Rubenstein, B. S., Askenasy, J. J. M., & Sagi, D. (1994). Dependence on REM sleep of overnight improvement of a perceptual skill. *Science, 265,* 679–682.

Karno, M., Hough, R. L., Burnam, M., Escobar, J. I., Timbers, D. M., Santana, F., & Boyd, J. (1987). Lifetime prevalence of specific psychiatric disorders among Mexican Americans and non-Hispanic whites in Los Angeles. *Archives of General Psychiatry, 44,* 695–701.

Kashani, J. H., Orvaschel, H., Rosenberg, T. K., & Reid, J. C. (1989). Psychopathology in a community sample of children and adolescents: A developmental perspective. *Journal of the American Academy of Child and Adolescent Psychiatry, 28,* 701–706.

Kass, J. H. (1995). Vision without awareness. *Nature, 373,* 195.

Kassin, S. M., Rigby, S., & Castillo, S. R. (1991). The accuracy-confidence correlation in eyewitness testimony: Limits and extensions of the retrospective self-awareness effect. *Journal of Personality and Social Psychology, 61,* 698–707.

Kastenbaum, R. (1965). Wine and fellowship in aging: An exploratory action program. *Journal of Human Relations, 13,* 266–275.

Kastenbaum, R., Kastenbaum, B. K., & Morris, J. (1989). Strengths and preferences of the terminally ill: Data from the National Hospice Demonstration Study.

Kato, S., Wakasa, Y., & Yamagita, T. (1987). Relationship between minimum reinforcing doses and injection speed in cocaine and pentobarbital self-administration in crab-eating monkeys. *Pharmacology, Biochemistry, and Behavior, 28,* 407–410.

Katz, S. E., & Landis, C. (1935). Psychologic and physiologic phenomena during a prolonged vigil. *Archives of Neurology and Psychiatry, 34,* 307–317.

Katzell, R. A., & Thompson, D. E. (1990). Work motivation: Theory and practice. *American Psychologist, 45,* 144–153.

Kauffman, N. A., Herman, C. P., & Polivy, J. (1995). Hunger–induced finickiness in humans. *Appetite, 24,* 203–218.

Kaufman, A. S., & Harrison, P. L. (1991). Individual intellectual assessment. In E. E. Walker (Ed.), *Clinical psychology: Historical and research foundations.* New York: Plenum.

Kaufman, L., & Rock, I. (1962). The moon illusion. *Science, 136,* 953–961.

Kavanagh, D. J. (1992). Recent developments in expressed emotion in schizophrenia. *British Journal of Psychiatry, 160,* 601–620.

Kavanaugh, R. D., & Jirkovsky, A. M. (1982). Parental speech to young children: A longitudinal analysis. *Merrill-Palmer Quarterly, 28,* 297–311.

Kawachi, I., Colditz, G. A., & Stone, C. B. (1994). Does drinking coffee increase the risk of coronary heart disease? Results from a meta-analysis. *British Heart Journal, 72*(3), 269–275.

Kaye, W. H., Gwirtsman, H. E., George, D. T., & Jimerson, D. C. (1988). CSF 5-HIAA concentrations in anorexia nervosa: Reduced values in underweight subjects normalize after weight gain. *Biological Psychiatry, 23*(1), 102–105.

Kazdin, A. E. (1978). Evaluating the generality of findings in analogue therapy research. *Journal of Consulting and Clinical Psychology, 46,* 673–686.

Kazdin, A. E. (1982). The token economy: A decade later. *Journal of Applied Behavior Analysis, 15,* 431–445.

Kazdin, A. E. (1994). Methodology, design, and evaluation in psychotherapy research. In A. E. Bergin & S. L. Garfield (Eds.), *Handbook of psychotherapy and behavior change.* New York: Wiley.

Keating, D. P. (1980). Thinking processes in adolescence. In J. Adelson (Ed.), *Handbook of adolescent psychology.* New York: Wiley.

Keating, D. P. (1990). Adolescent thinking. In S. S. Feldman & G. R. Elliott (Eds.), *At the threshold: The developing adolescent* (pp. 4–89). Cambridge, MA: Harvard University Press.

Keeling, P. J., & Roger, A. J. (1995). The selfish pursuit of sex. *Nature, 375,* 283.

Keesey, R. E. (1980). A set-point analysis of the regulation of body weight. In A. J. Stunkard (Ed.), *Obesity.* Philadelphia: W. B. Saunders.

Keesey, R. E., & Powley, T. L. (1975). Hypothalamic regulation of body weight. *American Scientist, 63,* 558–565.

Keesey, R. E., & Powley, T. L. (1986). The regulation of body weight. *Annual Review of Psychology, 37,* 109–133.

Keinan, G., Friedland, N., & Ben-Porath, Y. (1987). Decision making under stress: Scanning of alternatives under physical threat. *Acta Psychologica, 64,* 219–228.

Keller, A., Ford, L. H., & Meacham, J. A. (1978). Dimensions of self-concept in preschool children. *Developmental Psychology, 14,* 483–489.

Kelley, K. W. (1985). Immunological consequences of changing environmental stimuli. In G. P. Moberg (Ed.), *Animal stress.* Bethesda, MD: American Physiological Society.

Kelly, D. H., & Burbeck, C. A. (1984). Critical problems in spatial vision (review). *Critical Reviews in Biomedical Engineering, 10,* 2, 125–177.

Kelley, H. H. (1973). The processes of causal attribution. *American Psychologist, 28,* 107–128.

Kelly, J., & Murphy, D. (1992). Psychological intervention with AIDS and HIV: Prevention and treatment. *Journal of Consulting and Clinical Psychology, 60,* 576–585.

Kelly, J., Murphy, D., Bahr, G., Brasfield, T., Davis, D., Hauth, A., Morgan, M., Stevenson, L., & Eilers, K. (1992). AIDS/HIV risk behavior among the chronically mentally ill. *American Journal of Psychiatry, 149,* 886–889.

Kelly, J. A., & Kalichman, S. C. (1995). Increased attention to human sexuality can improve HIV-AIDS prevention efforts: Key research issues and directions. *Journal of Consulting and Clinical Psychology, 63,* 907–918.

Kelly, T. H., Foltin, R. W., Emurian, C. S., & Fischman, M. W. (1990). Multidimensional behavioral effects of marijuana. *Progress in Neuro-Psychopharmacology and Biological Psychiatry, 14,* 885–902.

Kelman, H. C., & Hamilton, V. L. (1989). *Crimes of obedience.* New Haven, CT: Yale University Press.

Kempenaers, C., Bouillon, E., & Mendlewicz, J. (1994). A rhythmic movement disorder in REM sleep: A case report. *Sleep, 17*(3), 274–279.

Kendler, K., & Diehl, (1993). The genetics of schizophrenia: A current genetic-epidemiologic perspective. *Schizophrenia Bulletin, 19,* 87–112.

Kendler, K. S., Kessler, R. C., Walters, E. E., MacLean, C., Neale, M. C., Heath, A. C., & Eaves, L. J. (1995). Stressful life events, genetic liability, and onset of an episode of major depression in women. *American Journal of Psychiatry, 152,* 833–842.

Kendler, K. S., Neale, M. C., Kessler, R. C., Heath, A. C., & Eaves, L. J. (1992). Major depression and generalized anxiety disorder: Same genes, (partly) different environments? *Archives of General Psychiatry, 49,* 716–722.

Kenrick, D. T. (1994). Evolutionary social psychology: From sexual selection to social cognition. In M. Zanna (Ed.), *Advances in experimental social psychology* (Vol. 26, pp. 75–122). San Diego, CA: Academic Press.

Kenrick, D. T., & Funder, D. C. (1988). Profiting from controversy: Lessons from the person-situation debate. *American Psychologist, 43,* 23–34.

Kenrick, D. T., Keefe, R. C., Bryan, A., Barr, A., & Brown, S. (1995). Age preferences and mate choice among homosexuals and heterosexuals: A case for modular psychological mechanisms. *Journal of Personality and Social Psychology, 69,* 1166–1172.

Kenrick, D. T., Neuberg, S. L., Zierk, K., & Krones, J. (1994). Evolution and social cognition: Contrast effects as a function of sex, dominance, and physical attractiveness. *Personality and Social Psychology Bulletin, 20,* 210–217.

Kenrick, D. T., Sadalla, E. K., Groth, G., & Trost, M. R. (1990). Evolution, traits and the stages of human courtship: Qualifying the parental investment model. *Journal of Personality, 58,* 97–117.

Kent, S., Rodriguez, F., Kelley, K. W., & Dantzer, R. (1994). Reduction in food and water intake induced by microinjection of interleukin-1b in the ventromedial hypothalamus of the rat. *Physiology and Behavior, 56*(5), 1031–1036.

Kernberg, O. (1976). *Object relations theory and clinical psychoanalysis.* New York: Jason Aronsen.

Kerns, K. (1991). Data-link communication between controllers and pilots: A review and synthesis of the simulation literature. *International Journal of Aviation Psychology, 1,* 181–204.

Kerr, M. P., & Payne, S. J. (1994). Learning to use a spreadsheet by doing and by watching. *Interacting with Computers, 6,* 3–22.

Kerr, N. L., & Kaufman-Gilliland, C. M. (1994). Communication, commitment, and cooperation in social dilemmas. *Journal of Personality and Social Psychology, 66,* 513–529.

Kessler, R. C., McGonagle, K. A., Zhao, S., Nelson, C. B., Hughes, M., Eshleman, S., Wittchen, H. U., & Kendler, K. S. (1994). Lifetime and 12-month prevalence of DSM-III-R psychiatric disorders in the United States. *Archives of General Psychiatry, 51,* 8–19.

Kety, S. S., Wender, P. H., Jacobsen, B., Ingraham, L. J., Jansson, L., Faber, B., & Kinney, D. K. (1994). Mental illness in the biological and adoptive relatives of schizophrenic adoptees. *Archives of General Psychiatry, 51,* 442–455.

Kiecolt-Glaser, J. K., Garner, W., Speicher, C. E., Penn, G. M., Holliday, J., & Glaser, R. (1984). Psychosocial modifiers of immunocompetence in medical students. *Psychosomatic Medicine, 46,* 7–14.

Kiecolt-Glaser, J. K., & Glaser, R., (1992). Psychoneuroimmunology: Can psychological interventions modulate immunity? *Journal of Consulting and Clinical Psychology, 60,* 569–575.

Kiesler, S., & Sproull, L. (1992). Group decision making and communications technology. *Organizational Behavior and Human Decision Processes, 52,* 96–123.

Kiesler, S., Sproull, L., & Waters, K. (in press). A prisoner's dilemma experiment on cooperation with people and human-like computers. *Journal of Personality and Social Psychology.*

Kihlstrom, J. F. (1987). The cognitive unconscious. *Science, 237,* 1445–1452.

Kihlstrom, J. F. (1993). What does the self look like? In T. K. Srull & R. S. Wyer (Eds.), *The mental representation of trait and autobiographical knowledge about the self: Advances in social cognition: Vol. V.* Hillsdale, NJ: Lawrence Erlbaum Associates.

Kihlstrom, J. F. (1995). The trauma-memory argument. *Consciousness and Cognition, 4,* 63–67.

Kihlstrom, J. F., & Klein, S. B. (1994). The self as a knowledge structure. In R. S. Wyer & T. K. Srull (Eds.), *Handbook of social cognition* (2nd ed.). Hillsdale, NJ: Lawrence Erlbaum Associates.

Kim, J. J., & Fanselow, M. S. (1992). Modality-specific retrograde amnesia of fear. *Science, 256,* 675–677.

King, G. A., & Sorrentino, R. M. (1988). Uncertainty orientation and the relation between individual accessible constructs and person memory. *Social Cognition, 6,* 128–149.

King, P. M., & Kitchener, K. S. (1994). *Developing reflective judgment.* San Francisco: Jossey-Bass.

Kinnamon, S. C., & Cummings, T. A. (1992). Chemosensory transduction mechanisms in taste. *Annual Review of Physiology, 54,* 715–731.

Kinney, H. C., Korein, J., Panigrahy, A., Dikkes, P., & Goode, R. (1994). Neuropathological findings in the brain of Karen Ann Quinlan: The role of the thalamus in the persistent vegetative state. *New England Journal of Medicine, 330*(21), 1469–1475.

Kinnunen, T., Zamansky, H. S., & Block, M. L. (1994). Is the hypnotized subject lying? *Journal of Abnormal Psychology, 103*(2), 184–191.

Kinsey, A. C., Pomeroy, W. B., & Martin, C. E. (1948). *Sexual behavior in the human male.* Philadelphia: Saunders.

Kinsey, A. C., Pomeroy, W. B., Martin, C. E., & Gebhard, P. H. (1953). *Sexual behavior in the human female.* Philadelphia: Saunders.

Kirkpatrick, L. A., & Davis, K. E. (1994). Attachment style, gender, and relationship stability: A longitudinal analysis. *Journal of Personality and Social Psychology, 66,* 502–512.

Kirsch, I. (1994a). Defining hypnosis for the public. *Contemporary Hypnosis, 11*(3), 142–143.

Kirsch, I. (1994b). Clinical hypnosis as a nondeceptive placebo: Empirically derived techniques. *American Journal of Clinical Hypnosis, 37*(2), 95–106.

Kirsch, I., & Lynn, S. J. (1995). The altered state of hypnosis: Changes in theoretical landscape. *The American Psychologist, 50,* 846–858.

Kirsch, I., Montgomery, G., & Sapirstein, G. (1995). Hypnosis as an adjunct to cognitive-behavioral psychotherapy: A meta-analysis. *Journal of Consulting and Clinical Psychology, 63* (2), 214–220.

Kirschenbaum, D. S., & Fitzgibbons, M. L. (1995). *Behavior Therapy, 26*(1), 43–68.

Kishioka, S., Miyamoto, Y., Fukunaga, Y., Nishida, S., & Yamamoto, H. (1994). Effects of a mixture of peptidase inhibitors (Amastatin, Captopril and Phosphoramidon) on met enkephalin, beta-endorphin, dynorphin (1–13) and electroacupuncture-induced antinociception in rats. *Japanese Journal of Pharmacology, 1994, 66,* 337–345.

Kitano, H., Chi, I., Rhee, S., Law, C., & Lubben, J. (1992). Norms and alcohol consumption: Japanese in Japan, Hawaii, and California. *Journal of Studies on Alcohol, 53,* 33–39.

Kitayama, S., & Markus, H. R. (1992, May). *Construal of self as cultural frame: Implications for internationalizing psychology.* Paper presented to the Symposium on Internationalization and Higher Education, Ann Arbor.

Kitchener, K. S., & King, P. M. (1981). Reflective judgment: Concepts of justification and their relationship to age and education. *Journal of Applied Developmental Psychology, 2*(2), 89–116.

Klahr, D., Chase, W. G., & Lovelace, E. A. (1983). Structure and process in alphabetic retrieval. *Journal of Experimental Psychology: Learning, Memory, and Cognition, 9,* 462–477.

Klatzky, R. L. (1980). *Human memory: Structures and processes* (2nd ed.). San Francisco: W. H. Freeman.

Klaus, M. H., & Kennell, J. H. (1976). *Maternal infant bonding: The impact of early separation or loss on family development.* St. Louis: Mosby.

Klein, D. C., & Seligman, M. E. P. (1976). Reversal of performance deficits and perceptual deficits in learned helplessness and depression. *Journal of Abnormal Psychology, 85,* 11–26.

Klein, D. N. (1993). False suffocation alarms, spontaneous panics, and related conditions: An integrative hypothesis. *Archives of General Psychiatry, 50,* 306–316.

Klein, D. N., Riso, L. P., Donaldson, S. K., Schwartz, J. E., Anderson, R. L., Ouimette, P. C., Lizardi, H., & Aronson, T. A. (1995). Family study of early-onset dysthmyia. *Archives of General Psychiatry, 52,* 487–496.

Klein, G. (1993). *Naturalistic decision making: Implications for design.* Wright-Patterson Air Force Base, Crew System Ergonomics Information Analysis Center, Ohio.

Klein, G. A. (1989). Recognition-primed decisions. In W. B. Rouse (Ed.), *Advances in man-machine system research* (Vol. 5, pp. 47–92). Greenwich, CT: JAI Press.

Klein, G. A. (1993). A recognition-primed decision (RPD) model of rapid decision making. In G. A. Klein, J. Orasanu, R. Calderwood, & C. E. Zsambok (Eds.), *Decision making in action: Models and methods.* Norwood, NJ: Ablex.

Klein, G. A., & Crandall, B. W. (1995). The role of simulation in problem solving and decision making. In P. Hancock, J. Flach, J. Caird, & K. Vicente (Eds.), *Local applications of the ecological approach to human-machine systems.* Hillsdale, NJ: Lawrence Erlbaum Associates.

Klein, G. A., Orasanu, J., Calderwood, R., & Zsambok, C. E. (Eds.). (1993). *Decision making in action: Models and methods.* Norwood, NJ: Ablex.

Klein, J. G. (1991). Negativity effects in impression formation: A test in the political arena. *Personality and Social Psychology Bulletin, 17,* 412–418.

Klein, M. (1960). *The psychoanalysis of children.* New York: Grove Press.

Klein, M. (1975). *The writings of Melanie Klein: Vol. 3.* London: Hogarth Press.

Klein, S. B., & Loftus, J. (1993a). The mental representation of trait and autobiographical knowledge about the self. In T. K. Srull & R. S. Wyer (Eds.), *The mental representation of trait and autobiographical knowledge about the self: Advances in social cognition: Vol. V.* Hillsdale, NJ: Lawrence Erlbaum Associates.

Klein, S. B., & Loftus, J. (1993b). Some lingering self-doubts: Reply to commentaries. In T. K. Srull & R. S. Wyer (Eds.), *The mental representation of trait and autobiographical knowledge about the self: Advances in social cognition: Vol. V.* Hillsdale, NJ: Lawrence Erlbaum Associates.

Kleinknecht, R. A. (1991). *Mastering anxiety: The nature and treatment of anxious conditions.* New York: Plenum.

Kleinknecht, R. A. (1993). Rapid treatment of blood and injection phobias with eye movement desensitization. *Journal of Behaviour Therapy and Experimental Psychiatry, 24,* 211–217.

Kleinknecht, R. A., Dinnel, D. L., Tanouye-Wilson, S., & Lonner, W. (1994). Cultural variation in social anxiety and phobia: A study of *Taijin Kyofusho*. *The Behavior Therapist, 17,* 175–178.

Kleinman, A. (1991, April). *Culture and DSM-IV: Recommendations for the introduction and for the overall structure.* Paper presented at the National Institute of Mental Health–sponsored Conference on Culture and Diagnosis, Pittsburgh, PA.

Klepp, K.-I., Kelder, S. H., & Perry, C. L. (1995). Alcohol and marijuana use among adolescents: Long-term outcomes of the class of 1989 study. *Annals of Behavioral Medicine, 17,* 19–24.

Klesges, R. C., Shelton, M. L., & Klesges, L. M. (1993). Effects of television on metabolic rate: Potential implications for childhood obesity. *Pediatrics, 91,* 281–286.

Klich, N. R., & Feldman, D. C. (1992). The role of approcal and achievement needs in feedback-seeking behavior. *Journal of Managerial Issues, 4*(4), 554–570.

Kline, S., & Groninger, L. D. (1991). The imagery bizarreness effect as a function of sentence complexity and presentation time. *Bulletin of the Psychonomic Society, 29,* 25–27.

Klinger, E. (1995). Effects of motivation and emotion on thought flow and cognition: Assessment and findings. In P. E. Shrout & S. E. Fiske (Eds.), *Personality research, methods, and theory* (pp. 257–270). Hillsdale, NJ: Lawrence Erlbaum Associates.

Klinger, M. R., & Greenwald, A. G. (1995). Unconscious priming of association judgements. *Journal of Experimental Psychology: Learning, Memory, and Cognition, 21*(3), 569–581.

Klonoff-Cohen, H. S., & Edelstein, S. L. (1995). A case-control study of routine death scene sleep position in sudden infant death syndrome in Southern California. *Journal of the American Medical Association, 273*(10), 790–794.

Klosko, J. S., Barlow, D. H., Tassinari, R., & Cerny, J. A. (1990). A comparison of alprazolam and behavior therapy in treatment of panic disorder. *Journal of Consulting and Clinical Psychology, 58,* 77–84.

Knauft, B. M. (1989). Sociality versus self-interest in human evolution. *Behavioral and Brain Sciences, 12,* 712–713.

Knight, G. P., Virdin, L. M., & Roosa, M. (1994). Socialization and family correlates of mental health outcomes among Hispanic and Anglo American children: Consideration of cross-ethnic scalar equivalence. *Child Development, 65,* 212–224.

Knox, R. E., & Safford, R. K. (1976). Group caution at the racetrack. *Journal of Experimental Social Psychology, 12,* 317–324.

Kobasa, S. C. (1982). The hardy personality: Toward a social psychology of stress and health. In G. S. Sanders & J. Suls (Eds.), *Social psychology of health and illness.* Hillsdale, NJ: Lawrence Erlbaum Associates.

Koch, C., & Davis, J. L. (Eds.). (1994). *Large-scale neuronal theories of the brain.* Cambridge, MA: MIT Press.

Koelega, H. S. (1993). Stimulant drugs and vigilance performance: A review. *Psychopharmacology, 111*(1), 1–16.

Koenigsberg, H. W. (1994). The combination of psychotherapy and pharmacotherapy in the treatment of borderline patients. *Journal of Psychotherapy Practice and Research, 3*(2), 93–107.

Kohlberg, L. (1966). A cognitive-developmental analysis of children's sex role concepts and attitudes. In E. E. Maccoby (Ed.), *The development of sex differences.* Stanford, CA: Stanford University Press.

Kohlberg, L., & Gilligan, C. (1971). The adolescent as a philosopher: The discovery of the self in a postconventional world. *Daedalus, 100,* 1051–1086.

Köhler, W. (1924). *The mentality of apes.* New York: Harcourt Brace.

Köhler, W. (1925). *The mentality of apes.* New York: Harcourt, Brace.

Köhler, W. (1976). *The mentality of apes.* London: Routledge & Kegan Paul.

Kohut, H. (1971). *Analysis of the self.* New York: International Universities Press.

Kohut, H. (1983). Selected problems of self-psychological theory. In J. D. Lichtenberg & S. Kaplan (Eds.), *Reflections on self psychology* (pp. 387–416). Hillsdale, NJ: Lawrence Erlbaum Associates.

Kohut, H. (1984). Selected problems of self-psychological theory. In J. D. Lichtenberg & S. Kaplan (Eds.), *Reflections on self psychology* (pp. 387–416). Hillsdale, NJ: Lawrence Erlbaum Associates.

Komatsu, S.-I., & Naito, M. (1992). Repetition priming with Japanese Kana scripts in word-fragment completion. *Memory & Cognition, 20,* 160–170.

Komorita, S. S. (1984). Coalition bargaining. In L. Berkowitz (Ed.), *Advances in experimental social psychology: Vol. 18.* New York: Academic Press.

Komorita, S. S., & Parks, C. D. (1995). Interpersonal relations: Mixed-motive interaction. *Annual Review of Psychology, 46,* 183–207.

Konkol, R. J., Murphey, L. J., Ferriero, D. M., Dempsey, D. A., & Olsen, G. D. (1994). Cocaine metabolites in the neonate: Potential for toxicity. *Journal of Child Neurology, 9*(3), 242–248.

Koob, G. F., & Bloom, F. E. (1988). Cellular and molecular mechanisms of drug dependence. *Science, 242,* 715–723.

Kopec, D., Newborn, M., & Valvo, M. (1992). The 22nd Annual ACM International Computer Chess Championship. *Communications of the ACM, 35*(11), 100–110.

Koppenaal, L., & Glanzer, M. (1990). An examination of the continuous distractor task and the "long-term recency effect." *Memory & Cognition, 18,* 183–195.

Kordower, J. H., Freeman, T. B., Snow, B. J., Vingerhoets, F. J. G., Mufson, E. J., Sanberg, P. R., Hauser, R. A., Smith, D. A., Nauert, G. M., Perl, D. P., & Olanow, C. W. (1995). Neuropathological evidence of graft survival and striatal reinnervation after the transplantation of fetal mesencephalic tissue in a patient with Parkinson's disease. *The New England Journal of Medicine, 332,* 1118–1124.

Kornhaber, M., Krechevsky, M., & Gardner, H. (1990). Engaging intelligence. *Educational Psychologist, 25,* 177–199.

Korolenko, C., Minevich, V., & Segal, B. (1994). The politicization of alcohol in the USSR and its impact on the study and treatment of alcoholism. *International Journal of the Addictions, 29*(10), 1269–1285.

Korteling, J. (1991). Effects of skill integration and perceptual competition on age-related differences in dual-task performance. *Human Factors, 33,* 35–44.

Koskenvuo, M., Kaprio, J., Rose, R., Kesanieme, A., Sarna, S., Heikkila, K., & Langinvainio, H. (1988). Hostility as a risk factor for mortality and ischemic heart disease in men. *Psychosomatic Medicine, 50,* 330–340.

Koss, M. P., Goodman, L. A., Browne, A., Fitzgerald, L. F., Keita, G. P., & Russo, N. F. (1994). *No safe haven: Male violence against women at home, at work, and in the community.* Washington, DC: American Psychological Association.

Kosslyn, S. M. (1976). Can imagery be distinguished from other forms of internal representation? Evidence from studies of information retrieval times. *Memory & Cognition, 4,* 291–297.

Kosslyn, S. M. (1983). *Ghosts in the mind's machine.* New York: W. W. Norton.

Kosslyn, S. M. (1988). Aspects of a cognitive neuroscience of mental imagery. *Science, 240,* 1621–1626.

Kosslyn, S. M. (1994). *Image and brain: The resolution of the imagery debate.* Cambridge, MA: MIT Press.

Kosslyn, S. M., & Ochsner, K. N. (1994). In search of occipital activation during visual mental imagery. *Trends in Neuroscience, 17,* 290–292.

Kovacs, J. A., Baseler, M., Dewar, R. J., Vogel, S., Davey, R. T., Falloon, J., Polis, M. A., Walker, R. E., Stevens, R., Salzman, N. P., Metcalf, J. A., Masur, H., & Lane, H. C. (1995). Increases in CD4 T lymphocytes with intermittent courses of interleukin-2 in patients with human immunodeficiency virus infection: A preliminary study. *New England Journal of Medicine, 332*(9), 567–575.

Kraft, C. (1978). A psychophysical approach to air safety: Simulator studies of visual illusions in night approaches. In H. L. Pick, H. W. Leibowitz, J. E. Singer, A. Steinschneider, & H. W. Stevenson (Eds.), *Psychology: From research to practice.* New York: Plenum.

Kramer, A., Larish, J., & Strayer, D. (1995). Training for attentional control in dual task settings: A comparison of young and old adults. *Journal of Experimental Psychology: Applied, 2,* 50–76.

Krantz, D., Contrada, R., Hill, D., & Friedler, E. (1988). Environmental stress and biobehavioral antecedents of coronary heart disease. *Journal of Consulting and Clinical Psychology, 56,* 333–341.

Krantz, D., & Durel, L. (1983). Psychobiological substrates of the Type A behavior pattern. *Health Psychology, 2,* 393–411.

Kranzler, H. R., & Anton, R. F. (1994). Implications of recent neuropsychopharmacologic research for understanding the etiology and development of alcoholism. *Journal of Consulting and Clinical Psychology, 62,* 1116–1126.

Kraus, S. J. (1995). Attitudes and the prediction of behavior: A meta-analysis of the empirical literature. *Personality and Social Psychology Bulletin, 21,* 58–75.

Krauzlis, R. J., & Lisberger, S. G. (1991). Visual motion commands for pursuit eye movements in the cerebellum. *Science, 253,* 568–571.

Krebs, R. L. (1967). *Some relations between moral judgment, attention, and resistance to temptation.* Unpublished doctoral dissertation, University of Chicago, Chicago, IL.

Krechevsky, M., & Gardner, H. (1994). Multiple intelligences in multiple contexts. In D. K. Detterman (Ed.), *Current topics in human intelligence* (Vol. 4). Norwood, NJ: Ablex.

Krishnakumar, K., Sawhney, S., & Wai, R. (1994). Neuro-controllers for adaptive helicopter hover training. *IEEE Transactions on Systems, Man, and Cybernetics, 24,* 1142–1152.

Kroll, J. (1973). A reappraisal of psychiatry in the middle ages. *Archives of General Psychiatry, 26,* 276–283.

Krosnick, J. A., Betz, A. L., Jussim, L. J., & Lynn, A. R. (1992). Subliminal conditioning of attitudes. *Personality and Social Psychology Bulletin, 18,* 152–162.

Krosnick, J. A., Jussim, L. J., & Lynn, A. R. (1992). Subliminal conditioning of attitudes. *Personality and Social Psychology Bulletin, 18,* 152–162.

Kruglanski, A. W., Webster, D., & Klem, A. (1993). Motivated resistance and openness to persuasion in the presence and absence of prior information. *Journal of Personality and Social Psychology, 65,* 861–876.

Krykouli, S. E., Stanley, B. G., Seirafi, R. D., & Leibowitz, S. F (1990). Stimulation of feeding by galanin: Anatomical localization and behavioral specificity of this peptide's effects in the brain. *Peptides, 11*(5), 995–1001.

Kubler-Ross, E. (1975). *Death: The final stage of growth.* Englewood Cliffs, NJ: Prentice-Hall.

Kuczmanski, R. J., Flegal, K. M., Campbell, S. M., & Johnson, C. L. (1994). Increasing prevalence of overweight among U.S. adults: The National Health and Nutrition Examination Surveys, 1960 to 1991. *Journal of the American Medical Association, 272*(3), 205–211.

Kuffler, S. W., & Nicholls, J. G. (1976). *From neuron to brain: A cellular approach to the function of the nervous system.* Sunderland, MA: Sinauer Associates.

Kuhl, P. K. (1987). Perception of speech and sound in early infancy. In P. Salapatek & L. Cohen (Eds.), *Handbook of infant perception* (Vol. 2, pp. 275–382). Orlando, FL: Academic Press.

Kuhs, H., & Tolle, R. (1991). Sleep deprivation therapy. *Biological Psychiatry, 29,* 1129–1148.

Kunkel, D., Wilson, B. J., Linz, D., Potter, J., Donnerstein, E., Smith, S. L., Blumenthal, E., & Gray, T. (1996). *The national television violence study.* Studio City, CA: Mediascope.

Kunz, P. R., & Woolcott, M. (1976). Season's greetings: From my status to yours. *Social Science Research, 5,* 269–278.

Kwan, M., Greenleaf, W. J., Mann, J., Crapo, L., & Davidson, J. M. (1983). The nature of androgen action on male sexuality: A combined laboratory-self-report study on hypogonadal men. *Journal of Clinical Endocrinology and Metabolism, 57,* 557–562.

Kyriacou, C. P. (1994). Working round the clock with mouse 25. *Trends in Neuroscience, 17*(8), 313–314.

LaBerge, D. (1991). Thalamic and cortical mechanisms of attention suggested by recent positron emission tomographic experiments. *Journal of Cognitive Neuroscience, 2,* 358–372.

LaBerge, S. (1993). Lucid dreaming. In M. Carskadon (Ed.), *Encyclopedia of sleep and dreaming* (pp. 338–341). New York: Macmillan.

Labouvie-Vief, G. (1982). Discontinuities in development from childhood. In T. M. Field, A. Huston, H. C. Quay, L. Troll, & G. E. Finley (Eds.), *Review of human development.* New York: Wiley.

Labouvie-Vief, G. (1992). A new-Piagetian perspective on adult cognitive development. In R. J. Sternberg & C. A. Berg (Eds.), *Intellectual development.* New York: Cambridge University Press.

Lacayo, A. (1995). Neurologic and psychiatric complications of cocaine abuse. *Neuropsychiatry, Neuropsychology, and Behavioral Neurology, 8*(1), 53–60.

Lacayo, R. (1995, June 12). Violent reaction. *Time, 145*(24), 38–44.

Lachman, R., Lachman, J. L., & Butterfield, E. C. (1979). *Cognitive psychology and information processing.* Hillsdale, NJ: Lawrence Erlbaum Associates.

Ladd, E. C. (1994, July/August). The holocaust poll error: A modern cautionary tale. *The Public Perspective.*

Laforge, R. G., Greene, G. W., & Prochaska, J. O. (1994). Psychosocial factors influencing low fruit and vegetable consumption. *Journal of Behavioral Medicine, 17,* 361–388.

LaFromboise, T. D. (1992). An interpersonal analysis of affinity, clarification, and helpful responses with American Indians. *Professional Psychology: Research and Practice, 23,* 281–286.

Lagerspetz, K. M. J., & Lagerspetz, K. Y. H. (1983). Genes and aggression. In E. C. Simmel, M. E. Hahn, & J. K. Walters (Eds.), *Aggressive behavior: Genetic and neural approaches.* Hillsdale, NJ: Lawrence Erlbaum Associates.

Lahey, B., Applegate, B., Barkley, R., Garfinkel, B., McBurnett, K., Kerdyk, L., Greenhill, L., Hynd, G., Frick, P., Newcorn, J., Biederman, J., Ollendick, T., Hart, E., Perez, D., Waldman, I., & Shaffer, D. (1994). DSM-IV Field Trials for oppositional defiant disorder and conduct disorder in children and adolescents. *American Journal of Psychiatry, 151,* 1163–1171.

Lahey, B. B., Loeber, R., Hart, E. L., Frick, P. J., & Applegate, B. (1995). Four-year longitudinal study of conduct disorder in boys: Patterns and predictors of persistence. *Journal of Abnormal Psychology, 104,* 83–93.

Lakey, B., & Cassady, P. (1990). Cognitive processes in perceived social support. *Journal of Personality and Social Psychology, 59,* 337–343.

Lamb, M., & Sternberg, K. M. (1990). Do we really know how day care affects children? *Journal of Applied and Developmental Psychology, 11,* 351–379.

Lamb, M. E. (1976). Parent-infant interaction in 8-month-olds. *Child Psychiatry and Human Development, 7,* 56–63.

Lamb, M. E. (1977). Father-infant and mother-infant interaction in the first year of life. *Child Development, 48,* 167–181.

Lambert, M. J. (1976). Spontaneous remission in adult neurotic disorders: A revision and summary. *Psychological Bulletin, 83*(1), 107–119.

Lambert, M. J. (1989). The individual therapist's contribution to psychotherapy process and outcome. *Clinical Psychology Review, 9,* 469–486.

Lambert, M. J., & Bergin, A. E. (1994). The effectiveness of psychotherapy. In A. E. Bergin & S. L. Garfield (Eds.), *Handbook of psychotherapy and behavior change* (4th ed.). New York: Wiley.

Lambert, M. J., & Hill, C. E. (1994). Assessing psychotherapy outcomes and processes. In A. E. Bergin & S. L. Garfield (Eds.), *Handbook of psychotherapy and behavior change* (4th ed.). New York: Wiley.

Lambert, M. J., Shapiro, D. A., & Bergin, A. E. (1986). The effectiveness of psychotherapy. In S. L. Garfield & A. E. Bergin (Eds.), *Handbook of psychotherapy and behavior change* (3rd Ed.). New York: Wiley.

Lambert, M. J., Weber, F. D., & Sykes, J. D. (1993, April). *Psychotherapy versus placebo.* Poster presented at the annual meeting of the Western Psychological Association, Phoenix.

Land, M. F., & Fernald, R. D. (1992). The volution of eyes. *Annual Review of Neuroscience, 15,* 1–29.

Landau, B. (1986). Early map use as an unlearned ability. *Cognition, 22,* 201–223.

Landrine, H. (1991). Revising the framework of abnormal psychology. In P. Bronstein & K. Quina (Eds.), *Teaching a psychology of people.* Washington, DC: American Psychological Association.

Landrine, H., & Klonoff, E. (1992). Culture and health-related schemas: A review and proposal for interdisciplinary integration. *Health Psychology, 11,* 267–276.

Landsdale, M., & Laming, D. (1995). Evaluating the fragmentation hypothesis: The analysis of errors in cued recall. *Acta Psychologica, 88,* 33–77.

Lang, A. R., Goeckner, D. J., Adesso, V. J., & Marlatt, G. A. (1975). Effects of alcohol on aggression in male social drinkers. *Journal of Abnormal Psychology, 84,* 508–518.

Lang, P. J. (1993). The network model of emotion: Motivational connections. In R. S. Wyer & T. K. Srull (Eds.), *Toward a general theory of anger and emotional aggression: Advances in social cognition, Vol. VI.* Hillsdale, NJ: Lawrence Erlbaum Associates.

Lang, P. J. (1995). The emotion probe: Studies of motivation and attention. *American Psychologist, 50*(5), 372–385.

Lang, P. J., & Melamed, B. G. (1969). Avoidance conditioning therapy of an infant with chronic ruminative vomiting. *Journal of Abnormal Psychology, 74,* 1–8.

Langlois, J. H., Ritter, J. M., Roggman, L. A., & Vaughn, L. S. (1991). Facial diversity and infant preferences for attractive faces. *Developmental Psychology, 27,* 79–84.

Lanzetta, J. T., & Englis, B. G. (1989). Expectations of cooperation and competition and their effects on observers' vicarious emotional responses. *Journal of Personality and Social Psychology, 56,* 543–554.

LaPlace, A. C., Chermack, S. T., & Taylor, S. P. (1994). Effects of alcohol and drinking experiences on human physical aggression. *Personality and Social Psychology Bulletin, 20,* 431–438.

Larson, G. E., & Saccuzzo, D. P. (1989). Cognitive correlates of general intelligence: Toward a process theory of *g. Intelligence, 13,* 5–32.

Larson, R., & Lampman-Petraitis, C. (1989). Daily emotional states as reported by children and adolescents. *Child Development, 60,* 1250–1260.

Latané, B. (1981). The psychology of social impact. *American Psychologist, 36,* 343–356.

Latané, B., & Rodin, J. (1969). A lady in distress: Inhibiting effects of friends and strangers on bystander intervention. *Journal of Experimental Social Psychology, 5,* 189–202.

Lau, M. A., Pihl, R. O., & Peterson, J. B. (1995). Provocation, acute alcohol intoxication, cognitive performance, and aggression. *Journal of Abnormal Psychology, 104,* 150–155.

Laughlin, P. R., & Ellis, A. L. (1986). Demonstrability and social combination processes on mathematical intellective tasks. *Journal of Experimental Social Psychology, 22,* 177–189.

Laughlin, P. R., Vanderstoep, S. W., & Hollingshead, A. B. (1991). Collective versus individual induction: Recognition of truth, rejection of error, and collective information processing. *Journal of Personality and Social Psychology, 61*(1), 50–67.

Laumann, E. O., Gagnon, J. H., Michael, R. T., & Michaels, S. (1994). *The social organization of sexuality: Sexual practices in the United States.* Chicago: University of Chicago Press.

Law, D. J., Pellegrino, J. W., & Hunt, E. B. (1993). Comparing the tortoise and the hare: Gender differences and experience in dynamic spatial reasoning tasks. *Psychological Science, 4,* 35–40.

Lawford, B. R., Young, R. M., Rowell, J. A., Qualichefski, J., Fletcher, B. H., Syndulko, K., Ritchie, T., & Noble, E. P. (1995). Bromocriptine in the treatment of alcoholics with the D_2 dopamine receptor A_1 allele. *Nature Medicine, 1*(4), 337–341.

Lawless, H. T., & Engen, T. (1977). Associations to odors: Interference, memories and verbal learning. *Journal of Experimental Psychology, 3,* 52–59.

Lawry, J., Upitis, M. K., Anderson, A., Inkpen, K., Ndunda, M., Hsu, D., Leroux, S., & Sedighian, K. (1993). *Exploring common conceptions about boys and electronic games.* Unpublished manuscript, University of British Columbia, Vancouver, BC.

Lawshe, C. H. (1975). A quantitative approach to content validity. *Personnel Psychology, 28,* 563–575.

Lazarus, A. A. (1971). *Behavior therapy and beyond.* New York: McGraw-Hill.

Lazarus, R. S., & Folkman, S. (1984). *Stress, appraisal, and coping.* New York: Springer-Verlag.

Lazarus, R. S., Opton, E. M., Nomikos, M. S., & Rankin, M. O. (1965). The principle of short-circuiting of threat: Further evidence. *Journal of Personality, 33,* 622–635.

Leach, P. (1994). *Children first.* New York: Knopf.

Leary, M. R., Robertson, R. B., Barnes, B. D., & Miller, R. S. (1986). Self-presentations of small group leaders: Effects of role requirements and leadership orientation. *Journal of Personality and Social Psychology, 51,* 742–748.

LeDoux, J. E. (1995). Emotion: Clues from the brain. *Annual Review of Psychology, 46,* 209–235.

Lee, M. C., Schiffman, S. S., & Pappas, T. N. (1994). Role of neuropeptides in the regulation of feeding behavior: A review of cholecystokinin, bombesin, neuropeptide Y, and galanin. *Neuroscience and Biobehavioral Reviews, 18*(3), 313–323.

Lee, V. E., Brooks-Gunn, J., & Schnur, E. (1988). Does Head Start work? A 1-year follow-up comparison of disadvantaged children attending Head Start, no preschool, and other preschool programs. *Developmental Psychology, 24,* 210–222.

Leeper, R. (1935). A study of a neglected portion of the field of learning: The development of sensory organization. *Journal of Genetic Psychology, 46,* 41–75.

Leff, J., & Vaughan, C. (1981). The role of maintenance therapy and relatives' expressed emotion in relapse of schizophrenia: A two-year follow up. *British Journal of Psychiatry, 138,* 102–104.

Lehman, H. E. (1967). Schizophrenia: IV. Clinical features. In A. M. Freedman, H. I. Kaplan, & H. S. Kaplan (Eds.), *Comprehensive textbook of psychiatry.* Baltimore: Williams & Wilkins.

Lehrer, P. M., Sargunanaj, D., & Hochron, S. (1992). Psychological approaches to the treatment of asthma. *Journal of Consulting and Clinical Psychology, 60,* 639–643.

Leibel, R. L., Rosenbaum, M., & Hirsch, J. (1995). Changes in energy expenditure resulting from altered body weight. *New England Journal of Medicine, 332*(10), 621–628.

Leibowitz, H. W., Brislin, R., Perlmutter, L., & Hennessy, R. (1969). Ponzo perspective illusion as a manifestation of space perception. *Science, 166,* 1174–1176.

Leibowitz, S. F., Xuereb, M., & Kim, T. (1992). Blockade of natural and neuropeptide Y-induced carbohydrate feeding by a receptor antagonist PYX-2. *Neuroreport: An international journal for the rapid communication of research in neuroscience, 3*(11), 1023–1026.

Leigh, B. C., Schafer, J., & Temple, M. T. (1995). Alcohol use and contraception in first sexual experiences. *Journal of Behavorial Medicine. 18*(1), 81–95.

Leiner, H. C., Leiner, A. L., & Dow, R. S. (1993). Cognitive and language functions of the human cerebellum. *Trends in Neuroscience, 16,* 444–447.

Leinhardt, G., Seewald, A., & Engel, M. (1979). Learning what's taught: Sex differences in instruction. *Journal of Educational Psychology, 71,* 432–439.

Leippe, M. R., Manion, A. P., & Romanczyk, A. (1992). Eyewitness persuasion: How and how well do fact finders judge the accuracy of adults' and children's memory reports? *Journal of Personality and Social Psychology, 63,* 181–197.

LeMagnen, J. (1971). Advances in studies on the physiological control and regulation of food intake. In E. Stellar & J. M. Sprague (Eds.), *Progress in physiological psychology: Vol. 4.* New York: Academic Press.

Lenneberg, E. H. (1967). *Biological foundations of language.* New York: Wiley.

Lepore, S., Evans, G., & Schneider, M. (1991). Dynamic role of social support in the link between chronic stress and psychological distress. *Journal of Personality and Social Psychology, 61,* 899–909.

Lepore, S. J. (1995a). Measurement of chronic stressors. In S. Cohen, R. C. Kessler, & L. U. Gordon (Eds.), *Measuring stress: A guide for health and social scientists.* New York: Oxford University Press.

Lepore, S. J. (1995b). Cynicism, social support, and cardiovascular reactivity. *Health Psychology, 14,* 210–216.

Leslie, A. M. (1992). Pretense, autism, and the theory-of-mind module. *Current Directions in Psychological Science, 1,* 18–21.

Lesser, I., Lydiard, R. B., Antal, A., Rubin, R., Ballenger, J., & Dupont, R. (1992).

Alprazolam plasma concentrations and treatment response in panic disorder and agoraphobia. *American Journal of Psychiatry, 149,* 1556–1562.

Lett, J. (1992). The persistent popularity of the paranormal. *Skeptical Inquirer, 16,* 381–388.

Lettvin, J. Y., Maturana, H. R., McCulloch, W. S., & Pitts, W. H. (1959). What the frog's eye tells the frog's brain. *Proceedings of the Institute of Radio Engineers 47,* 1940–1951.

LeVay, S. (1991). A difference in hypothalamic structure between heterosexual and homosexual men. *Science, 253,* 1034–1037.

Levenson, R. W., Ekman, P., Heider, K., & Friesen, W. V. (1992). Emotion and autonomic nervous system activity in the Minangkabau of West Sumatra. *Journal of Personality and Social Psychology, 62*(6), 972–988.

Levenson, R. W., & Ruef, A. M. (1992). Empathy: A physiological substrate. *Journal of Personality and Social Psychology, 63,* 234–246.

Levenson, R. W., Ekman, P., & Friesen, W. V. (1990). Voluntary facial action generates emotion-specific autonomic nervous system activity. *Psychophysiology, 27*(4), 363–384.

Leventhal, H., & Tomarken, A. J. (1986). Emotion: Today's problems. *Annual Review of Psychology, 37,* 565–610.

Levi, A. S., & Pryor, J. B. (1987). Use of the availability heuristic in probability estimates of future events. *Organizational Behavior and Human Decision Processes, 40,* 219–234.

Levin, I. P., Kao, S. F., & Wasserman, E. A. (1991). *Biased information usage in contingency judgments.* Paper presented at the meeting of the Midwestern Psychological Association, Chicago.

Levin, S., Yurgelun-Todd, D., & Craft, S. (1989). Contributions of clinical neuropsychology to the study of schizophrenia. *Journal of Abnormal Psychology, 98,* 341–356.

Levine, J. M. & Moreland, R. (1990). Progress in small group research. *Annual Review of Psychology, 41,* 55–63.

Levine, J. M., & Moreland, R. L. (1995). Group processes. In A. Tesser (Ed.), *Advanced social psychology* (pp. 419–466). New York: McGraw-Hill.

Levine, M. W., & Schefner, J. M. (1981). *Fundamentals of sensation and perception.* Reading, MA: Addison-Wesley.

Levine, R. V., Martinez, T. M., Brase, G., & Sorenson, K. (1994). Helping in 36 U.S. cities. *Journal of Personality and Social Psychology, 67,* 69–82.

Levinson, D. J., Darrow, C. N., Klein, E. B., Levinson, M. H., & McKee, B. (1978). *The seasons of a man's life.* New York: Knopf.

Levinthal, C. F. (1996). *Drugs, behavior, and modern society.* Boston: Allyn & Bacon.

Levy-Lahad, E., Wijsman, E., Nemens, E., Anderson, L., Goddard, K., Weber, J., Bird, T., & Schellenberg, G. (1995). A familial Alzheimer's Disease locus on chromosome 1. *Science, 269,* 970–973.

Levy-Shiff, R. (1994). Individual and contextual correlates of marital change across the transition to parenthood. *Developmental Psychology, 30,* 591–601.

Lewicki, P. (1992). Nonconscious acquisition of information. *American Psychologist, 47,* 796–801.

Lewinsohn, P. M., & Rosenbaum, M. (1987). Recall of parental behavior by acute depressives, remitted depressives, and nondepressives. *Journal of Personality and Social Psychology, 52,* 611–619.

Lewis, M., & Goldberg, S. (1969). Perceptual-cognitive development in infancy: A generalized expectancy model as a function of the mother-infant interaction. *Merrill-Palmer Quarterly, 15,* 81–100.

Lewontin, R. (1976). Race and intelligence. In N. J. Block & G. Dworkin (Eds.), *The IQ controversy: Critical readings.* New York: Pantheon.

Ley, R. (1994). The "suffocation alarm" theory of panic attacks: A critical commentary. *Journal of Behavior Therapy and Experimental Psychiatry, 25,* 269–273.

Leyens, J. P., Camino, L., Parke, R. D., & Berkowitz, L. (1975). The effects of movie violence on aggression in a field setting as a function of group dominance and cohesion. *Journal of Personality and Social Psychology, 32,* 346–360.

Liben, L. S. (1991). Adults' performance on horizontality tasks: Conflicting frames of reference. *Developmental Psychology, 27*(2), 285–294.

Lichstein, K. L., & Riedel, B. W. (1994). Behavioral assessment and treatment of insomnia: A review with an emphasis on clinical application. *Behavior Therapy, 25,* 659–688.

Licht, B. G., & Dweck, C. S. (1984). Determinants of academic achievement: The interaction of children's achievement orientations with skill area. *Developmental Psychology, 20,* 628–636.

Lichtenstein E., & Penner, M. P. (1977). Long-term effects of rapid smoking treatment for dependent cigarette smokers. *Addictive Behaviors, 2,* 109–112.

Lichtman, A. H., Dimen, K. R., & Martin, B. R. (1995). Systemic or intrahippocampal cannabinoid administration impairs spatial memory in rats. *Psychopharmacology, 119,* 282–290.

Lichtman, S. W., Pisarska, K., Berman, E. R., Pestone, M., Dowling, H., Offenbacher, E., Weisel, H., Heshka, S., Matthews, D. E., & Heymsfield, S. B. (1992). Discrepancy between self-reported and actual caloric intake and exercise in obese subjects. *New England Journal of Medicine, 327,* 1893–1898.

Lickey, M., & Gordon, B. (1991). *Medicine and mental illness: The use of drugs in psychiatry.* San Francisco: W. H. Freeman.

Lieberman, A., & Pawl, J. (1988). Clinical applications of attachment theory. In J. Bellsky & T. Nezworski (Eds.), *Clinical applications of attachment.* Hillsdale, NJ: Lawrence Erlbaum Associates.

Lieberman, M. A., & Tobin, S. (1983). *The experience of old age.* New York: Basic Books.

Liebert, R., & Sprafkin, J. (1988). *The early window: Effects of television on children and youth* (3rd ed.). New York: Pergamon Press.

Liebert, R. M., & Spiegler, M. D. (1994). *Personality: Strategies and issues.* Pacific Grove, CA: Brooks/Cole.

Liebert, R. M., & Sprafkin, J. (1988). *The early window* (3rd ed.). New York: Pergamon.

Liebowitz, M. R., Salman, E., Jusino, C. M., Garfinkel, R., Street, L., Cardenas, D. L., Silvestre, J., Fyer, A. J., Carrasco, J. L., Davies, S., Guarnaccia, P., & Klein, D. F. (1994). Ataque de nervios and panic disorder. *American Journal of Psychiatry, 151,* 871–875.

Lieppe, M. R., & Eisenstadt, D. (1994). Generalization of dissonance reduction: Decreasing prejudice through induced compliance. *Journal of Personality and Social Psychology, 67,* 395–413.

Light, L. L. (1991). Memory and aging: Four hypotheses in search of data. *Annual Review of Psychology, 42,* 333–376.

Lilienfeld, S. O. (1996). EMDR treatment: Less than meets the eye. *Skeptical Inquirer, 20,* 25–31 (January/February).

Lilienfeld, S. O. & Marino, L. (1995). Mental disorder as a Roschian concept: A critique of Wakefield's "harmful dysfunction" analysis. *Journal of Abnormal Psychology, 104,* 411–420.

Lillywhite, A. R., Wilson, S. J., & Nutt, D. J. (1994). Successful treatment of night terrors and somnambulism with paroxetine. *British Journal of Psychiatry, 16,* 551–554.

Lima, S. D., Hale, S., & Myerson, J. (1991). How general is general slowing? Evidence from the lexical domain. *Psychology and Aging, 6,* 416–425.

Lin, K.-M., Poland, R., & Nakasaki, G. (1993). (Eds.). *Psychopharmacology and psychobiology of ethnicity.* Washington, DC: American Psychiatric Association Press.

Lindsey, K. P., & Paul, G. L. (1989). Involuntary commitments to public mental institutions: Issues involving the overrepresentation of blacks and assessment of relevant functioning. *Psychological Bulletin, 106,* 171–183.

Lindvall, O., Widner, H., Rehncrona, S., Brundin, P., Odin, P., Gustavii, B., Frackowiak, R., Leenders, K. L., Sawle, G., Rothwell, J. C., Bjorklund, A., & Marsden, C. D. (1992). Transplantation of fetal dopamine neurons in Parkinson's disease—One-year clinical and neurophysiological observations in 2 patients with putaminal implants. *Annals of Neurology, 31,* 155–165.

Linn, M. C., & Peterson, A. C. (1985). Emergence and characterization of sex differences in spatial ability: A meta-analysis. *Child Development, 56,* 1479–1498.

Lintern, G. (1991). An informational perspective on skill transfer in human-machine systems. *Human Factors, 33,* 251–266.

Lintern, G. (1995). Flight instruction: Challenges from situated cognition. *International Journal of Aviation Psychology, 5,* 327–350.

Linville, P. W. (1987). Self-complexity as a cognitive buffer against stress-related illness and depression. *Journal of Personality and Social Psychology, 52,* 663–676.

Linville, P. W., & Carlston, D. E. (1994). Social cognition of the self. In P. G. Devine, D. L. Hamilton, & T. M. Ostrom (Eds.), *Social cognition: Impact on social psychology* (pp. 144–195). San Diego, CA: Academic Press.

Linz, D., Donnerstein, E., & Penrod, S. (1987). The findings and recommendations of the Attorney General's Commission on Pornography: Do the psychological facts fit the political fury? *American Psychologist, 42,* 946–953.

Linz, D., Wilson, B. J., & Donnerstein, E. (1992). Sexual violence in the mass media: Legal solutions, warnings, and mitigation through education. *Journal of Social Issues, 48,* 145–172.

Lips, H. (1988). *Sex and gender.* Mountain View, CA: Mayfield.

Lipsey, M. W., & Wilson, D. B. (1993). The efficacy of psychological, educational, and behavioral treatment. *American Psychologist, 48*(12), 1181–1209.

Liu, L. G. (1985). Reasoning counterfactually in Chinese: Are there any obstacles? *Cognition, 21,* 239–270.

Livesley, W. J., Schroeder, M., Jackson, D., & Jang, K. (1994). Categorical distinctions in the study of personality disorder: Implications for classification. *Journal of Abnormal Psychology, 103,* 6–17.

Livingstone, M., & Hubel, D. (1988). Segregation of form, color, movement, and depth: Anatomy, physiology, and perception. *Science, 240,* 740–749.

Livingstone, M. S., & Hubel, D. H. (1987). Psychological evidence for separate channels for the perception of form, color, movement and depth. *Journal of Neuroscience, 7,* 3416–3468.

Locurto, C. (1991a). Beyond IQ in preschool programs? *Intelligence, 15,* 295–312.

Locurto, C. (1991b). Hands on the elephant: IQ, preschool programs, and the rhetoric of inoculation—a reply to commentaries. *Intelligence, 15,* 335–349.

Loeber, R. (1990). Development and risk factors of juvenile antisocial behavior and delinquency. *Clinical Psychology Review, 10,* 1–41.

Loehlin, J. C. (1989). Partitioning environmental and genetic contributions to behavioral development. *American Psychologist, 44,* 1285–1292.

Loehlin, J. C. (1992). *Genes and environment in personality development.* Newbury Park, CA: Sage.

Loehlin, J. C., Horn, J. M., & Willerman, L. (1990). Heredity, environment, and personality change: Evidence from the Texas Adoption Project. *Journal of Personality, 58,* 221–243.

Loevinger, J. (1993). Measurement of personality: True or false. *Psychological Inquiry, 4,* 1–17.

Loewenstein, G. (1994). The psychology of curiosity: A review and reinterpretation. *Psychological Bulletin, 116*(1), 75–98.

Loftus, E. F. (1979). *Eyewitness testimony.* Cambridge, MA: Harvard University Press.

Loftus, E. F. (1982). Memory and its distortions. *G. Stanley Hall Lectures,* 518–537.

Loftus, E. F. (1992). When a lie becomes memory's truth: Memory distortion after exposure to misinformation. *Psychological Science, 3,* 121–123.

Loftus, E. F. (1993). The reality of repressed memories. *American Psychologist, 48,* 518–537.

Loftus, E. F., Garry, M., & Feldman, J. (1994). Forgetting sexual trauma: What does it mean when 38% forget? *Journal of Consulting and Clinical Psychology, 62,* 1177–1181.

Loftus, E. F., & Ketcham, K. (1991). *Witness for the defense.* New York: St. Martin's Press.

Loftus, E. F., & Ketcham, K. (1994). *The myth of repressed memory: False memories and allegations of sexual abuse.* New York: St. Martin's Press.

Loftus, E. F., & Palmer, J. C. (1974). Reconstruction of automobile destruction: An example of the interaction between language and memory. *Journal of Verbal Learning and Verbal Behavior, 13,* 585–589.

Loftus, E. F., & Pickrell, J. E. (in press). The formation of false memories. *Psychiatric Annals.*

Loftus, E. F., Smith, K. D., Klinger, M. R., & Fiedler, J. (1993). Memory and mismemory for health events. In J. M. Tanur (Ed.), *Questions about questions: Inquiries into the cognitive psychology of surveys* (pp. 102–137). New York: Sage.

Logue, A. W. (1985). Conditioned food aversion in humans. *Annals of the New York Academy of Sciences, 104,* 331–340.

Lohman, D. A. (1989). Human intelligence: An introduction to advances in theory and research. *Review of Educational Research, 59,* 333–373.

Lohr, J. M., Kleinknecht, R. A., Tolin, D. F., & Barrett, R. H. (1995). The empirical status of the clinical application of eye movement desensitization and reprocessing. *Journal of Behaviour Therapy and Experimental Psychiatry, 26,* 285–302.

Lonner, W. J., & Malpass, R. S. (Eds.) (1994). *Psychology and culture.* Boston: Allyn & Bacon.

Lopes, L. L. (1982). *Procedural debiasing* (Tech. Rep. WHIPP 15). Madison: University of Wisconsin, Human Information Processing Program.

Lopez, M., & Takemoto-Chock, N. (1992, April). *Assessment of adolescent stressors: The adolescent Life Events Scale.* Paper presented at the meetings of the Western Psychological Association, Portland, OR.

Lopez, S. R. (1989). Patient variable biases in clinical judgment: Conceptual overview and methodological considerations. *Psychological Bulletin, 106,* 184–203.

Lore, R. K., & Schultz, L. A. (1993). Control of human aggression: A comparative perspective. *American Psychologist, 48,* 16–25.

Lowe, M. R., Kopyt, D., & Buchwald, J. (1996). Food intake underestimation: Its nature and potential impact on obesity treatment. *The Behavior Therapist, 19,* 17–20.

Luborsky, L. (1954). A note on Eysenck's article, "The effects of psychotherapy: An evaluation." *British Journal of Psychology, 45,* 129–131.

Luborsky, L. (1972). Another reply to Eysenck. *Psychological Bulletin, 78,* 406–408.

Luborsky, L. (1984). *Principles of psychoanalytic psychotherapy: A manual for supportive expressive treatment.* New York: Basic Books.

Luborsky, L., Singer, B., & Luborsky, L. (1975). Comparative studies of psychotherapies: Is it true that everyone has won and all must have prizes? *Archives of General Psychiatry, 32,* 995–1008.

Luce, S., & Hoge, R. (1978). Relations among teacher ratings, pupil-teacher interactions, and academic achievement: A test of teacher expectancy hypothesis. *American Educational Research Journal, 15,* 489–500.

Luchins, A. S. (1942). Mechanization in problem solving: The effect of Einstellung. *Psychological Monographs, 54*(6, Whole No. 248).

Ludwick-Rosenthal, R., & Neufeld, R. W. J. (1993). Preparation for undergoing an invasive medical procedure: Interacting effects of information and coping style. *Journal of Consulting and Clinical Psychology, 61,* 156–164.

Luginbuhl, J., & Palmer, R. (1991). Impression management aspects of self-handicapping: Positive and negative effects. *Personality and Social Psychology Bulletin, 17,* 655–662.

Lundberg, U., Hedman, M., Melin, B., & Frankenhaeuser, M. (1989). Type A behavior in healthy males and females as related to physiological reactivity and blood lipids. *Psychosomatic Medicine, 51,* 113–122.

Luntz, B. K., & Widom, C. S. (1994). Antisocial personality disorder in abused and neglected children grown up. *American Journal of Psychiatry, 151,* 670–674.

Luria, Z. (1992, February). *Gender differences in children's play patterns.* Paper presented at University of Southern California, Los Angeles.

Lutz, C. (1987). Goals, events and understanding in Ifaluk emotion theory. In N. Quinn & D. Holland (Eds.), *Cultural models in language and thought.* Cambridge, Eng.: Cambridge University Press.

Lykken, D. T., & Tellegen, A. (1993). Is human mating adventitious or the result of lawful choice? A twin study of mate selection. *Journal of Personality and Social Psychology, 65,* 56–68.

Lynn, R. (1991). Race differences in intelligence. *Mankind Quarterly, 31,* 255–297.

Lynn, S. J., & Rhue, J. W. (1986). The fantasy-prone person: Hypnosis, imagination, and creativity. *Journal of Personality and Social Psychology, 51,* 404–408.

Lyons, C. A., & Ghezzi, P. M. (1995). Wagering on a large scale: Relationships between public gambling and game manipulations in two state lotteries. *Journal of Applied Behavior Analysis, 28,* 127–137.

Lyubomirsky, S., & Nolen-Hoeksema, S. (1995). Effects of self-focused rumination on negative thinking and interpersonal problem solving. *Journal of Personality and Social Psychology, 69,* 176–190.

MacAndrew, C., & Edgerton, R. B. (1969). *Drunken comportment.* Chicago: Aldine.

Maccoby, E. (1995, March 6). *The separate "cultures" of boys and girls.* Colloquium presented to the School of Social Ecology, University of California, Irvine.

Maccoby, E. E., & Jacklin, C. N. (1974). *The psychology of sex differences.* Stanford, CA: Stanford University Press.

Maccoby, E. E., & Jacklin, C. N. (1987). Gender segregation in childhood. In H. W. Reese (Ed.), *Advances in child development and behavior* (Vol. 20). New York: Academic Press.

Macdiarmid, J. I., & Hetherington, M. M. (1995). Mood modulation by food: An exploration of affect and cravings in "chocolate addicts." *British Journal of Clinical Psychology, 34*(1), 129–138.

MacDonald, M., & Bernstein, D. A. (1974). Treatment of a spider phobia with in vivo and imaginal desensitization. *Journal of Behavior Therapy and Experimental Psychiatry, 5,* 47–52.

MacEwan, K. E., & Barling, J. (1988). Multiple stressors, violence in the family of origin, and marital aggression: A longitudinal investigation. *Journal of Family Violence, 3,* 73–87.

MacKenzie, B. (1984). Explaining race differences in IQ: The logic, the methodology, and the evidence. *American Psychologist, 39,* 1214–1233.

Mackie, D. M., Hamilton, D. L., Susskind, J., & Roselli, F. (in press). Social psychological foundations of stereotype formation. In N. Macrae, M. Hewstone, & C. Stangor (Eds.), *Foundations of stereotypes and stereotyping.* New York: Guilford.

Mackintosh, N. J. (1983). *Conditioning and associative learning.* New York: Oxford University Press.

MacLeod, C. M. (1988). Forgotten but not gone: Savings for pictures and words in long-term memory. *Journal of Experimental Psychology: Learning, Memory, and Cognition, 14,* 195–212.

Madden, T. J., Ellen, P. S., & Ajzen, I. (1992). A comparison of the theory of planned behavior and the theory of reasoned action. *Personality and Social Psychology Bulletin, 18,* 3–9.

Magee, J. C., & Johnston, D. (1995, April 14). Synaptic activation of voltage-gated channels in the dendrites of hippocampal pyramidal neurons. *Science, 268,* 301–304.

Maguire, T., Hattie, J., & Haig, B. (1994). Construct validity and achievement assessment. *Alberta Journal of Educational Research, 40*(2), 109–126.

Maher, B. A. (1966). *Principles of psychopathology: An experimental approach.* New York: McGraw-Hill.

Mahler, M. S. (1968). *On human symbiosis and the vicissitudes of individuation: Infantile psychosis.* New York: Basic Books.

Mahrer, A. R., & Nadler, W. P. (1986). Good moments in psychotherapy: A preliminary review, a list, and some promising research avenues. *Journal of Consulting and Clinical Psychology, 54,* 10–15.

Major, B., Sciacchtinano, A. M., & Crocker, J. (1993). In-group versus out-group comparisons and self-esteem. *Personality and Social Psychology Bulletin, 19,* 711–721.

Malamuth, N. M. (1988). Predicting laboratory aggression against female and male targets: Implications for sexual aggression. *Journal of Research in Personality, 22,* 474–495.

Malamuth, N. M., & Check, J. V. P. (1983). Sexual arousal to rape depictions: Individual differences. *Journal of Abnormal Psychology, 92,* 55–67.

Malamuth, N. M., Heavy, C., & Linz, D. (1993). Predicting men's antisocial behavior against women: The interaction model of sexual aggression. In N. G. Hall & R. Hirschman (Eds.), *Sexual aggression: Issues in etiology and assessment, treatment and policy* (pp. 63–97). New York: Hemisphere.

Malamuth, N. M., Sockloskie, R. J., Koss, M. P., & Tanaka, J. S. (1991). Characteristics of aggressors against women: Testing a model using a national sample of college students. *Journal of Consulting and Clinical Psychology, 59,* 670–681.

Malarkey, W. B., Kiecolt-Glaser, J. K., Pearl, D., & Glaser, R. (1994). Hostile behavior during marital conflict alters pituitary and adrenal hormones. *Psychosomatic Medicine, 56,* 41–51.

Malatesta, C. Z., & Izard, C. E. (1984). The ontogenesis of human social signals: From biological imperative to symbol utilization. In N. A. Fox & R. J. Davidson (Eds.), *The psychobiology of affective development* (pp. 161–206). Hillsdale NJ: Lawrence Erlbaum Associates.

Malenka, R. C. (1995). LTP and LTD: Dynamic and interactive processes of synaptic plasticity. *The Neuroscientist, 1,* 35–42.

Malinosky-Rummell, R., & Hansen, D. J. (1993). Long-term consequences of childhood physical abuse. *Psychological Bulletin, 114,* 68–79.

Manderscheid, R., & Barrett, S. (Eds.) (1987). *Mental health, United States, 1987* (National Institute of Mental Health, DHHS Pub. No. ADM 87–1518). Washington, DC: U.S. Government Printing Office.

Mangweth, B., Pope, H. G., & Hudson, J. I. (1995). Bulimia nervosa in two cultures: A comparison of Australian and American college students. *International Journal of Eating Disorders, 17*(4), 403–412.

Manis, F., Keating, D. P., & Morrison, F. J. (1980). Developmental differences in the allocation of processing capacity. *Journal of Experimental Child Psychology, 29,* 156–159.

Manke, B., McGuire, S., Reiss, D., Hetherington, E. M., & Plomin, R. (1995). Genetic contributions to children's extrafamilial social interactions: Teachers, best friends, and peers. *Social Development, 4,* 238–256.

Mann, K., Roschke, J., Nink, M., Aldenhoff, J., Beyer, J., Benkert, O., & Lehnert, H. (1992). Effects of corticotropin-releasing hormone administration in patients suffering from sleep apnea syndrome. *Society for Neuroscience Abstracts, 22,* 196.

Mannuzza, M., Schneider, F. R., Chapman, T. F., Liebowitz, M. R., Klein, D. F., & Fyer, A. J. (1995). Generalized social phobia. *Archives of General Psychiatry, 52,* 230–237.

Mansfield, P. K., Voda, A., & Koch, P. B. (1995). Predictors of sexual response changes in heterosexual midlife women. *Health Values, 19*(1), 10–20.

Marazziti, D., Rotondo, A., Martini, C., & Giannaccini, G. (1994). Changes in peripheral benzodiazepine receptors in patients with panic disorder and obsessive-compulsive disorder. *Neuropsychology, 29*(1), 8–11.

Marcus, J., Hans, S., Auerbach, J., & Auerbach, A. (1993). Children at risk for schizophrenia: The Jerusalem Infant Development Study. II. Neurobehavioral deficits at school age. *Archives of General Psychiatry, 50,* 797–809.

Marecek, J. (1995). Gender, politics, and psychology's way of knowing. *American Psychologist, 50,* 162–163.

Margolin, D. I. (1991). Cognitive neuropsychology: Resolving enigmas about Wernicke's aphasia and other higher cortical disorders. *Archives of Neurology, 48,* 751–765.

Margolis, D. (1994, January/February). Feed a cold, starve a fever, and 10 other medical myths you should not believe. *American Health.*

Marino, J., Gwynn, M. I., & Spanos, N. P. (1989). Cognitive mediators in the reduction of pain: The role of expectancy, strategy use, and self-presentation. *Journal of Abnormal Psychology, 98,* 256–262.

Maris, R. W. (1992). How are suicides different? In R. Maris, A. L. Berman, J. T. Maltsberger, & R. I. Yufit (Eds.), *Assessment and prediction of suicide.* New York: Guilford.

Markman, H. J., Renick, M. J., Floyd, F. J., Stanley, S. M., & Clements, M. (1993). Preventing marital distress through communication and conflict management training: A 4- and 5-year follow-up. *Journal of Consulting and Clinical Psychology, 61,* 70–77.

Markoviƒ, B. M., Dimitrijeviƒ, M., Jankoviƒ, B. D. (1993). Immunomodulation by conditioning: Recent developments. *International Journal of Neuroscience, 71,* 231–249.

Markus, H. R., & Kitayama, S. (1991). Culture and the self: Implications for cognition, emotion, and motivation. *Psychological Review, 98,* 224–253.

Markus, H. R., & Kitayama, S. (1994). A collective fear of the collective: Implications for selves and theories of selves. *Personality and Social Psychology Bulletin, 20,* 568–579.

Markus, H. R., & Kitayama, S. (1995). Cultural variation in the self-concept. In G. R. Goethals & J. Strauss (Eds.), *Multidisciplinary perspectives on the self.* New York: Springer-Verlag.

Marlatt, G. A., & Gordon, J. R. (1985). *Relapse prevention.* New York: Guilford.

Marmar, C. R. (1990). Psychotherapy process research: Progress, dilemmas, and future directions. *Journal of Consulting and Clinical Psychology, 58,* 265–272.

Marr, D. (1982). *Vision.* New York: W. H. Freeman.

Marshall, G. D., & Zimbardo, P. G. (1979). Affective consequences of inadequately explained arousal. *Journal of Personality and Social Psychology, 37,* 970–985.

Marshall, S. L. A. (1947). *Men against fire.* New York: Morrow.

Marshall, W. L. (1989). Pornography and sex offenders. In D. Zillmann & J. Bryant (Eds.), *Pornography: Research advances and policy considerations.* Hillsdale, NJ: Lawrence Erlbaum Associates.

Martin, B., & Hoffman, J. (1990). Conduct disorders. In M. Lewis & S. M. Miller (Eds.), *Handbook of developmental psychopathology.* New York: Plenum.

Martin, J. E., Silva, D., Newman, J. H., & Thayer, J. F. (1994). An investigation into the structure of epistemological style. *Personality and Individual Differences, 16*(4), 617–629.

Martin, S. (1995, September). APA to pursue prescription privileges. *APA Monitor,* p. 6.

Martindale, C. (1981). *Cognition and consciousness.* Homewood, IL: Dorsey Press.

Martindale, C. (1991). *Cognitive psychology: A neural-network approach.* Pacific Grove, CA: Brooks/Cole.

Martinez, J. L., Schulteis, G., & Weinberger, S. B. (1991). How to increase and decrease the strength of memory traces: The effects of drugs and hormones. In J. L. Martinez & R. P. Kesner (Eds.), *Learning and memory: A biological view* (2nd ed.). San Diego: Academic Press.

Marx, J. A., Zsuzsanna, K. G., Royalty, G. M., & Stern, T. E. (1992). Use of self-help books in psychotherapy. *Professional Psychology: Research and Practice, 23,* 300–305.

Marzuk, P. M., Tardiff, K., Leon, A. C., Hirsch, C. S., Stajic, M., Portera, L., Hartwell, N., & Iqbal, I. (1995). Fatal injuries after cocaine use as a leading cause of death among young adults in New York City. *New England Journal of Medicine, 332*(26), 1753–1757.

Masand, P., Popli, A. P., & Welburg, J. B. (1995). Sleepwalking. *American Family Physician, 51*(3), 649–653.

Maslach, C. (1979). Negative emotional biasing of unexplained arousal. *Journal of Personality and Social Psychology, 37,* 953–969.

Masling, J. M., & Bornstein, R. F. (1991). Perception without awareness and electrodermal responding: A strong test of subliminal psychodynamic activation effects. *Journal of Mind and Behavior, 12,* 33–47.

Maslow, A. H. (1943). A theory of human motivation. *Psychological Review, 50,* 370–396.

Maslow, A. H. (1954). *Motivation and personality.* New York: Harper.

Maslow, A. H. (1962). *Toward a psychology of being.* Princeton, NJ: Van Nostrand.

Maslow, A. H. (1970). *Motivation and personality* (2nd ed.). New York: Harper & Row.

Maslow, A. H. (1971). *The farther reaches of human nature.* New York: McGraw-Hill.

Mason, R. T., Fales, H. M., Jones, T. H., Pannell, L. K., Chinn, J. W., & Crews, D. (1989). Sex pheromones in snakes. *Science, 245,* 290–293.

Massaro, D. W., & Cowan, N. (1993). Information processing models: Microscopes of the mind. *Annual Review of Psychology, 44,* 383–425.

Masson, J. M. (1983). *Assault on the truth: Freud's suppression of the seduction theory.* New York: Farrar, Straus, & Giroux.

Masson, M. E. J., & MacLeod, C. M. (1992). Reenacting the route to interpretation: Enhanced perceptual identification without prior perception. *Journal of Experimental Psychology: General, 121,* 145–176.

Masters, J. C., Burish, T. G., Hollon, S. D., & Rimm, D. C. (1987). *Behavior therapy: Techniques and empirical findings* (3rd ed.). San Diego: Harcourt Brace Jovanovich.

Masters, W. H., & Johnson, V. E. (1966). *Human sexual response.* Boston: Little, Brown.

Matarazzo, J. (1984). Behavioral health: A 1990 challenge for the health sciences professions. In J. D. Matarazzo, S. M. Weiss, J. A. Herd, N. E. Miller, & S. E Weiss (Eds.), *Behavioral health: A handbook of health enhancement and disease prevention.* New York: Wiley.

Matarazzo, J. (1992). Psychological assessment versus psychological assessment: Validation from Binet to the school, to the clinic, to the courtroom. *American Psychologist, 45,* 999–1017.

Mathews, K. E., & Canon, L. K. (1975). Environmental noise level as a determinant of helping behavior. *Journal of Personality and Social Psychology, 32,* 571–577.

Mathies, H. (1989). Neurobiological aspects of learning and memory. *Annual Review of Psychology, 40,* 381–404.

Mathur, C. N., & Jain, P. (1992). A study of clitoral stimulation in the treatment of female sexual dysfunctions: 8th World Congress for Sexology. *Journal of Personality and Clinical Studies, 8*(1–2), 181–183.

Matlin, M. (1993). The psychology of women (2nd ed.). Fort Worth, TX: Harcourt Brace Jovanovich.

Matson, J., Sevin, J., Fridley, D., & Love, S. (1990). Increasing spontaneous language in autistic children. *Journal of Applied Behavior Analysis, 23,* 227–223.

Matsumoto, D. (1994). *People: Psychology from a cross-cultural perspective.* Pacific Grove, CA: Brooks/Cole.

Matsumoto, D., and Ekman, P. (1989). American-Japanese cultural differences in intensity ratings of facial expressions of emotion. *Motivation and Emotion, 13,* 143–157.

Matt, G. E., & Dean, A. (1993). Social support from friends and psychological distress among elderly persons: Moderator effects of age. *Journal of Health and Social Behavior, 34,* 187–200.

Matuszczyk, J. V., & Larsson, K. (1994). Experience modulates the influence of gonadal hormones on sexual orientation of male rats. *Physiology and Behavior, 55*(3), 527–533.

Maunder, R. (1995). Implications of mind-body theory for integration in psychiatry. *Psychiatry: Interpersonal and Biological Processes, 58*(1), 85–97.

Maupin, H. E., & Fisher, J. R. (1989). The effects of superior female performance and sex-role orientation in gender conformity. *Canadian Journal of Behavioral Science, 21,* 55–69.

Mayer, D. J., & Price, D. D. (1982). A physiological and psychological analysis of pain: A potential model of motivation. In D. W. Pfaff (Ed.), *The physiological mechanisms of motivation.* New York: Springer-Verlag.

Mayer, R. E. (1992). *Thinking, problem solving, and cognition* (2nd ed.). New York: W. H. Freeman.

Mayford, M., Barzilai, A., Keller, F., Schacher, S., & Kandel, E. R. (1992). Modulation of an ncam-related adhesion molecule with long-term synaptic plasticity in aplysia. *Science, 256,* 638–644.

Mays, D. T., & Franks, C. M. (1985). *Negative outcome in psychotherapy and what to do about it.* New York: Springer-Verlag.

Mazur, R. H. (1991). The future of synthetic sweeteners. In D. E. Walters et al. (Eds.), *Sweeteners, discovery, molecular design, and chemoreception.* Washington, DC: American Chemical Society.

McAuley, E. (1992). The role of efficacy cognitions in the prediction of exercise behavior in middle-aged adults. *Journal of Behavioral Medicine, 15,* 65–88.

McCarley, R. W. (1987). REM sleep generation: Intracellular studies of pontine reticular neurons. *Neuroscience, 22,* 387.

McCarthy, G. (1995). Functional neuroimaging of memory. *The Neuroscientist, 1,* 155–163.

McCarthy, G., & Donchin, E. (1979). Event-related potentials: Manifestations of cognitive activity. In F. Hoffmeister & C. Muller (Eds.), *Bayer symposium: VIII. Brain function in old age.* New York: Springer-Verlag.

McCartney, K., Harris, M., & Bernieri, F. (1990). Growing up and growing apart: A developmental meta-analysis of twin studies. *Psychological Bulletin, 107,* 226–237.

McCarty, M. F. (1995). Optimizing exercise for fat loss. *Medical Hypotheses, 44*(5), 325–330.

McCauley, C. (1989). The nature of social influence in groupthink: Compliance and internalization. *Journal of Personality and Social Psychology, 57,* 250–260.

McClelland, D. C. (1958). Risk-taking in children with high and low need for achievement. In J. W. Atkinson (Ed.), *Motives in fantasy, action, and society.* Princeton, NJ: Van Nostrand.

McClelland, D. C. (1985). *Human motivation.* Glenview, IL: Scott, Foresman.

McClelland, J. L. (1996). Integration of information: Reflections on the theme of *Attention and Performance XVI.* In T. Inui & J. L. McClelland (Eds.), *Attention and Performance XVI: Integration of information in perception and communication.* Cambridge, MA: MIT Press.

McClintock, C. G., & Liebrand, W. B. G. (1988). Role of interdependence structure, individual value orientation, and another's strategy in social decision making: A transformational analysis. *Journal of Personality and Social Psychology, 55,* 396–409.

McCloskey, D. I. (1978). Kinesthetic sensibility. *Physiological Reviews, 58,* 763.

McCloskey, M. (1983). Naive theories of motion. In D. Gentner & K. Stevens (Eds.), *Mental models.* Hillsdale, NJ: Lawrence Erlbaum Associates.

McCormick, D. A., & Thompson, R. F. (1984). Cerebellum essential involvement in the classically conditioned eyelid response. *Science, 223,* 296–299.

McCrae, R., & John, O. (1992). An introduction to the five-factor model and its applications. *Journal of Personality, 60,* 175–215.

McCrae, R. R., & Costa, P. T. (1940). The stability of personality: Observations and evaluations. *Current Directions in Psychological Science, 3,* 173–175

McDougall, W. (1904). The sensations excited by a single momentary stimulation of the eye. *British Journal of Psychology, 1,* 78–113.

McDowd, J., Vercruyssen, M., & Birren, J. (1991). Aging, divided attention, and dual-task performance. In D. Damos (Ed.), *Multiple Task Performance.* Bristol, PA: Taylor & Francis.

McEwen, B. S. (1991). Steroid-hormones are multifunctional messengers to the brain. *Trends in Endocrinology and Metabolism, 2,* 62–67.

McEwen, B. S., & Stellar, E. (1993). Stress and the individual: Mechanisms leading to disease. *Archives of Internal Medicine, 153,* 2093–2101.

McGarvey, R. (1989, February). Recording success. *USAIR Magazine,* pp. 94–102.

McGehee, D. S., Heath, M. J. S., Gelber, S., Devay, P., & Role, L. W. (1995). Nicotine enhancement of fast excitation synaptic transmissions in CNS by presynaptic receptors. *Science, 269,* 5231, 1692–1696.

McGlashan, T., & Fenton, W. (1991). Classical subtypes for schizophrenia: Literature reveiw for DSM-IV. *Schizophrenia Bulletin, 17,* 610–632.

McGlone, J. (1980). Sex differences in human brain asymmetry: A critical survey. *The Behavioral and Brain Sciences, 3,* 215–263.

McGreevy, M. A., Steadman, H. J., & Callahan, L. A. (1991). The negligible effects of California's 1982 reform of the insanity defense test. *American Journal of Psychiatry, 148,* 744–750.

McGreevy, M. W. (1991). Virtual reality and planetary exploration. *29th AAS Goddard Memorial Symposium.* Washington, DC.

McGue, M. (1992). When assessing twin concordance, use the probandwise not the pairwise rate. *Schizophrenia Bulletin, 18,* 171–176.

McGue, M., Bouchard, Jr., T. J., Iacono, W. G., & Lykken, D. T. (1993). Behavioral genetics of cognitive ability: A life-span perspective. In R. Plomin & G. E. McClearn (Eds.), *Nature, nurture and psychology* (pp. 59–76). Washington, DC: American Psychological Association.

McGue, M., Pickens, R., & Svikis, D. (1992). Sex and age effects on the inheritance of alcohol problems: A twin study. *Journal of Abnormal Psychology, 101,* 3–17.

McGuire, A. M. (1994). Helping behaviors in the natural environment: Dimensions and correlates of helping. *Personality and Social Psychology Bulletin, 20,* 45–56.

McGuire, W. J. (1968). Personality and susceptibility to social influence. In E. F. Borgatta & W. W. Lambert (Eds.), *Handbook of personality theory and research.* Chicago: Rand McNally.

McHugh, M., Koeske, R., & Frieze, I. (1986). Issues to consider in conducting nonsexist psychological research: A guide for researchers. *American Psychologist, 41,* 879–890.

McIntosh, D. N., Silver, R. C., & Wortman, C. B. (1993). Religion's role in adjustment to a negative life event: Coping with the loss of a child. *Journal of Personality and Social Psychology, 65,* 812–821.

McIntosh, J. L. (1991). Epidemiology of suicide in the U.S. In A. A. Leenaars (Ed.), *Life span perspectives on suicide.* New York: Plenum.

McIntosh, J. L. (1992). Suicide of the elderly. In B. Bonger (Ed.), *Suicide: Guidelines for assessment, management, and treatment.* New York: Oxford University Press.

McKenna, J. J., Thoman, E. B., Anders, T. F., Sadeh, A., Schechtman, V. L., & Glotzbach, S. F. (1993). Infant-parent co-sleeping in an evolutionary perspective: Implications for understanding infant sleep development and the sudden infant death syndrome. *Sleep, 16*(3), 263–282.

McKnight, J. D., & Glass, D. C. (1995). Perceptions of control, burnout, and depressive symptomatology: A replication and extension. *Journal of Consulting and Clinical Psychology, 63,* 490–494.

McNeal, E. T., &, Cimbolic, P. (1986). Antidepressants and biochemical theories of depression. *Psychological Bulletin, 99,* 361–374.

McNeely, B. L., & Meglino, B. M. (1994). The role of dispositional and situational antecedents in prosocial organizational behavior: An examination of the intended beneficiaries of prosocial behavior. *Journal of Applied Psychology, 79,* 836–844.

McNeil, J. E., & Warrington, E. K. (1993). Prosopagnosia: A face-specific disorder. *Quarterly Journal of Experimental Psychology: Human Experimental Psychology, 46A*(1), 1–10.

McNeil, T. F., & Persson-Blennow, I. (1988). Stability of temperament characteristics in childhood. *American Journal of Orthopsychiatry, 58,* 622–626.

McNemar, Q. (1942). *The revision of the Stanford-Binet Scale.* New York: Houghton Mifflin.

McPhail, T. L., & Penner, L. A. (1995, August). *Can similarity moderate the effects of aversive racism?* Paper presented at the 103rd annual meeting of the American Psychological Association, New York.

McRae, R. R. (1993). Moderated analyses of longitudinal personality stability. *Journal of Personality and Social Psychology, 65,* 577–585.

McRae, R. R., & Costa, P. T., Jr. (1994). The stability of personality: Observations and evaluations. *Current Directions in Psychological Science, 3,* 173–176.

McRae, R. R., & Costa, P. T., Jr. (in press). Toward a new generation of personality theories. Theoretical contexts for the five-factor model. In J. S. Wiggins (Ed.), *The five-factor model of personality: Theoretical perspectives.* New York: Guilford.

Medin, D. L., & Ross, B. H. (1992). *Cognitive psychology.* Fort Worth, TX: Harcourt Brace Jovanovich.

Mednick, S. A. (1958). A learning theory approach to research in schizophrenia. *Psychological Bulletin, 55,* 316–327.

Mednick, S. A. (1970). Breakdown in individuals at high-risk for schizophrenia: Possible predispositional perinatal factors. *Mental Hygiene, 54,* 50–63.

Mednick, S. A., Gabrielli, W. F., Jr., & Hutchings, B. (1987). Genetic factors in the etiology of criminal behavior. In S. A. Mednick, T. E., Moffitt, & S. A., Stack (Eds.), *The causes of crime: New biological approaches* (pp. 74–91). New York: Cambridge University Press.

Mednick, S. A., Machon, R. A., Huttunen, M. O., & Bonett, D. (1988). Adult schizophrenia following prenatal exposure to an influenza epidemic. *Archives of General Psychiatry, 45,* 189–192.

Meehan, P., Lamb, J., Saltzman, L., & O'Carroll, P. (1992). Attempted suicide among young adults: Progress toward a meaningful estimate of prevalence. *American Journal of Psychiatry, 149,* 41–44.

Mehle, T. (1982). Hypothesis generation in an automobile malfunction inference task. *Acta Psychologica, 52,* 87–116.

Mehta, S. I. (1995). A method for instant assessment and active learning. *Journal of Engineering Education, 84,* 295–298.

Meichenbaum, D. (1977). *Cognitive behavior modification: An integrative approach.* New York: Plenum.

Meichenbaum, D. (1985). *Stress-inoculation training.* New York: Pergamon Press.

Meijer, G. A., Westerterp, K. R., van Hulsel, A. M., & ten Hoor, F. (1992). Physical activity and energy expenditure in lean and obese adult human subjects. *European Journal of Applied Physiology and Occupational Physiology, 65,* 525–528.

Mello, N. K., Mendelson, J. H., Bree, M. P., & Lukas, S. E. (1989). Buprenorphine suppresses cocaine self-administration by rhesus monkeys. *Science, 245,* 859–862.

Meltzhoff, J., & Kornreich, M. (1970). *Research in psychotherapy.* New York: Atherton Press.

Melzack, R., & Wall, P. D. (1965). Pain mechanisms: A new theory. *Science, 150,* 971–979.

Mendoza, R., Smith, M., Poland, R., Lin, K-M., & Strickland, T. (1991). Ethnic psychopharmacology: The Hispanic and Native American perspective. *Psychopharmacology Bulletin, 27,* 449–461.

Menini, A., Picco, C., & Firestein, S. (1995, February 2). Quantal-like current fluctuations induced by odorants in olfactory receptor cells. *Nature, 373,* 435–437.

Merritt, J. O. (1979). None in a million: Results of mass screening for eidetic ability using objective tests published in newspapers and magazines. *The Behavioral and Brain Sciences, 2,* 612.

Mesquita, B., & Frijda, N. H. (1992). Cultural variations in emotions: A review. *Psychological Bulletin, 112,* 179–204.

Messick, S. (1982). Test validity and the ethics of assessment. *Diagnostica, 28*(1), 1–25.

Messick, S. (1989). Validity. In R. L. Linn (Ed.), *Educational measurement* (3rd ed., pp. 13–103). New York: Macmillan.

Metalsky, G. I., Joiner, T. E., Jr., Hardin, T. S., & Abramson, L. Y. (1993). Depressive reactions to failure in a naturalistic setting: A test of the hopelessness and self-esteem theories of depression. *Journal of Abnormal Psychology, 102,* 101–109.

Meyer, B. H. F. L., Ehrhardt, A. A., Rosen, L. R., & Gruen, R. S. (1995). Prenatal estrogens and the development of homosexual orientation. *Developmental Psychology, 31*(1), 12–21.

Meyer, D., Leventhal, H., & Gutmann, M. (1985). Common-sense models of illness: The example of hypertension. *Health Psychology, 4,* 115–135.

Meyer, R. G. (1975). A behavioral treatment of sleepwalking associated with test anxiety. *Journal of Behavior Therapy and Experimental Psychiatry, 6,* 167–168.

Meyers, C., & Jones, T. B. (1993). *Promoting active learning: Strategies for the college classroom.* San Francisco: Jossey-Bass.

Michener, W., & Rozin, P. (1994). Pharmacological versus sensory factors in the satiation of chocolate craving. *Physiology and Behavior, 56*(3), 419–422.

Middlebrooks, J. C., Clock, A. E., Xu, L., & Green, D. M. (1994, May 6). A panoramic code for sound location by cortical neurons. *Science, 264,* 842–844.

Mignard, M., & Malpeli, J. G. (1991). Paths of information flow through the visual cortex. *Science, 251,* 1249–1251.

Mikulincer, M. (1995). Attachment style and the mental representation of the self. *Journal of Personality and Social Psychology, 69,* 1203–1215.

Milgram, S. (1963). Behavioral study of obedience. *Journal of Abnormal and Social Psychology, 67,* 371–378.

Milgram, S. (1965). Some conditions of obedience and disobedience to authority. *Human Relations, 18,* 57–76.

Milgram, S. (1970). The experience of living in cities. *Science, 167,* 1461–1468.

Milgram, S. (1974). *Obedience to authority.* New York: Harper & Row.

Milgram, S. (1977, October). Subject reaction: The neglected factor in the ethics of experimentation. *Hastings Center Report,* pp. 19–23.

Milgram, S., & Jodelet, D. (1976). Psychological maps of Paris. In H. M. Proshansky, W. H. Itelson, & L. G. Revlin (Eds.), *Environmental psychology.* New York: Holt, Rinehart & Winston.

Mill, J. S. (1874). *A system of logic* (8th ed.). New York: Harper.

Millar, S. (1994). *Understanding and representing space theory and evidence from studies with blind and sighted children.* New York: Oxford University Press.

Miller, G. A. (1956). The magical number seven, plus or minus two: Some limits on our capacity to process information. *Psychological Review, 63,* 81–97.

Miller, G. A., Heise, G. A., & Lichten, W. (1951). The intelligibility of speech as a function of the text and the test materials. *Journal of Experimental Psychology,* 329–335.

Miller, J. G. (1994). Cultural diversity in the morality of caring: Individually oriented versus duty-based interpersonal moral codes. *Cross-cultural Research, 28,* 3–39.

Miller, J. G., & Bersoff, D. M. (1992). Culture and moral judgment: How are conflicts between justice and interpersonal responsibilities resolved? *Journal of Personality and Social Psychology, 62,* 541–554.

Miller, J. G., & Bersoff, D. M. (1994). Cultural influences on the moral status of reciprocity and the discounting of endogenous motivation. *Personality and Social Psychology Bulletin, 20,* 592–607.

Miller, J. G., & Bersoff, D. M. (1995). Development in the context of everyday family relationships: Culture, interpersonal morality, and adaptation. In M. Killen & D. Hart (Eds.), *Morality in everyday life: A developmental perspective* (pp. 259–282). Cambridge, Eng.: Cambridge University Press.

Miller, J. L., & Eimas, P. D. (1995). Speech perception: From signal to word. *Annual Review of Psychology, 46,* 467–492.

Miller, K. F., Smith, C. M., Zhu, J., & Zhang, H. (1995). Preschool origins of cross-national differences in mathematical competence: The role of number-naming systems. *Psychological Science, 6,* 56–60.

Miller, L. T., & Vernon, P. A. (1992). The general factor in short-term memory, intelligence, and reaction time. *Intelligence, 16,* 5–29.

Miller, M. G., & Teates, J. F. (1985). Acquisition of dietary self-selection in rats with normal and impaired oral sensation. *Physiology and Behavior, 34*(3), 401–408.

Miller, N., & Davidson-Podgorny, G. (1987). Theoretical models of intergroup relations and the use of cooperative teams as an intervention for desegregated settings. In C. Hendrick (Ed.), *Group processes and intergroup relations.* Newberry Park, CA: Sage.

Miller, N. E. (1959). Liberalization of basic S-R concepts: Extensions to conflict behavior, motivation, and social learning. In S. Koch (Ed.), *Psychology: A study of science: Vol. 2.* New York: McGraw-Hill.

Miller, N. E., Bailey, C. U., & Stevenson, J. A. F. (1930). Decreased hunger but increased food intake resulting from hypothalmic lesions. *Science, 112,* 256–259.

Miller, N. T., Brewer, M. B., & Edwards, K. (1985). Cooperative interaction in desegregated settings: A laboratory analogue. *Journal of Social Issues, 41,* 63–75.

Miller, S. M., Brody, D. S., & Summerton, J. (1988). *Journal of Personality and Social Psychology, 54,* 142–148.

Miller, T. Q., Heath, L., Molcan, J. R., & Dugoni, B. L. (1991). Imitative violence in the real world: A reanalysis of homicide rates following championship prize fights. *Aggressive Behavior, 17,* 121–134.

Millon, T. (1981). *Disorders of personality. DSMIII: Axis II.* New York: Wiley.

Milner, B. (1962). Les troubles de la memoire accompagnant des lesions hippocampiques bilaterales. In *Physiologie de l'hippocampe.* Paris: C.N.R.S., pp.

257–272. [English translation in P. M. Milner & S. Glickman (Eds.), *Cognitive processes and the brain.* Princeton, NJ: Van Nostrand, 1965, pp. 97–111.]

Milner, B. (1965). Visually-guided maze learning in man: Effects of bilateral hippocampal, bilateral frontal, and unilateral cerebral lesions. *Neuropsychologia, 3,* 317–338.

Milner, B. R. (1966). Amnesia following operation on temporal lobes. In C. W. M. Whitty & O. L. Zangwill (Eds.), *Amnesia.* London: Butterworth.

Milner, D. (1983). *Children and race.* Beverly Hills, CA: Sage.

Minimi, H., & Dallenbach, K. M. (1946). The effect of activity upon learning and retention in the cockroach. *American Journal of Psychology, 59,* 1–58.

Minshew, N. J., Payton, J. B., & Sclabassi, R. J. (1986). Cortical neurophysiologic abnormalities in autism. *Neurology, 36*(Suppl. 1), 194.

Minuchin, S., & Fishman, H. (1981). *Family therapy techniques.* Cambridge, MA: Harvard University Press.

Mischel, W. (1993). *Introduction to personality.* New York: Harcourt Brace.

Mishkin, M., & Ungerleider, L. G. (1982). Contribution of striate inputs to the visuospatial functions of parieto-preoccipital cortex in monkeys. *Behavior and Brain Research, 6,* 57–77.

Mitchell, D. B. (1991). Implicit memory, explicit theories. *Contemporary Psychology, 36,* 1060–1061.

Mitchell, J. E., Pyle, R. L., Eckert, E. D., Hatsukami, D., et al. (1990). Bulimia nervosa in overweight individuals. *Journal of Nervous and Mental Disease, 178,* 324–327.

Miyake, K., Chen, S., & Campos, J. J. (1985). Infant temperament, mother's mode of interaction, and attachment in Japan: An interim report. In I. Bretherton & E. Waters (Eds.), Growing points of attachment theory and research. *Monographs of the Society for Research in Child Development, 50*(1–2, Serial No. 209).

Moergen, S., Merkel, W., and Brown, S. (1990). The use of covert sensitization and social skills training in the treatment of an obscene telephone caller. *Journal of Behavior Therapy and Experimental Psychiatry, 21,* 269–275.

Mogenson, G. J. (1976). Neural mechanisms of hunger: Current status and future prospects. In D. Novin, W. Wyrwicka, & G. Bray (Eds.), *Hunger: Basic mechanisms and clinical applications.* New York: Raven.

Mogg, K., Bradley, B. P., Williams, R., & Mathews, A. (1993). Subliminal processing of emotional information in anxiety and depression. *Journal of Abnormal Psychology, 102,* 304–311.

Moghaddam, F. M., Taylor, D. M., & Wright, S. C. (1993). *Social psychology in cross-cultural perspective.* New York: W. H. Freeman.

Mohr, D. C. (1995). Negative outcome in psychotherapy: A critical review. *Clinical Psychology: Science and Practice, 2,* 1–27.

Molloy, D. W., Guyett, G. H., Wilson, D. B., Duke, R., Rees, L., & Singer, J. (1991). Effect of tetrahydroaminoacridine on cognition, function and behaviour in Alzheimer's disease. *Canadian Medical Association Journal, 144,* 29–34.

Monahan, J. (1993). Limiting therapist exposure to *Tarasoff* liability. *The American Psychologist, 48,* 242–250.

Monane, M., Leichter, D., & Lewis, O. (1984). Physical abuse in psychiatrically hospitalized children and adolescents. *Journal of the American Academy of Child and Adolescent Psychiatry, 23,* 653–658.

Money, J., Schwartz, M., & Lewis, V. G. (1984). Adult erotosexual status and fetal hormonal masculinization and demasculinization: 46,XX congential virilizing adrenal hyperplasia and 46,XY androgen-insensitivity syndrome compared. *Psychoneuroendocrinology, 9,* 405–414.

Monroe, S., Thase, M., & Simons, A. (1992). Social factors and psychobiology of depression: Relations between life stress and rapid eye movement sleep latency. *Journal of Abnormal Psychology, 101,* 528–537.

Monteith, M. J., Zuwerink, J. R., & Devine, P. G. (1994). Prejudice and prejudice reduction: Classic challenges and contemporary approaches. In P. G. Devine, D. L. Hamilton, & T. M. Ostrom (Eds.), *Social cognition: Impact on social psychology* (pp. 324–346). San Diego, CA: Academic Press.

Montemayor, R. (1983). Parents and adolescents in conflict: All families some of the time and some families most of the time. *Journal of Early Adolescence, 3,* 83–103.

Montgomery, K. C. (1953). Exploratory behavior as a function of "similarity" of stimulation situations. *Journal of Comparative and Physiological Psychology, 46,* 129–133.

Monti-Bloch, L., & Grosser, B. I. (1991). Effect of putative pheromones on the electrical activity of the human vomeronasal organ and olfactory epithelium. *Journal of Steroid Biochemistry and Molecular Biology, 39,* 573–582.

Moon, C., Cooper, R. P., & Fifer, W. P. (1993). Two-day-olds prefer their native language. *Infant Behavior and Development, 16,* 495–500.

Moore, R. Y., & Bloom, F. E. (1979). Central catecholamine neuron systems: Anatomy and physiology of the norepinephrine and epinephrine systems. *Annual Review of Neuroscience, 2,* 113–168.

Moreland, R. L., & Beach, S. R. (1992). Exposure effects in the classroom: The development of affinity among students. *Journal of Experimental Social Psychology, 28,* 255–276.

Morgan, C. D., & Murray, H. A. (1935). A method for investigating fantasy: The thematic apperception test. *Archives of Neurology and Psychiatry, 34,* 289–306.

Morgan, J. I., & Curran, T. (1991). Stimulus-transcription coupling in the nervous system: Involvement of the inducible proto-oncogenes *fos* and *jun. Annual Review of Neuroscience, 14,* 421–451.

Morgenthaler, J., & Dean, W. (1990). *Smart drugs and nutrients.* Santa Cruz, CA: B & J Publications.

Morin, C. M., Kowatch, R. A., Barry, T., & Walton, E. (1993). Cognitive-behavior therapy for late-life insomnia. *Journal of Consulting and Clinical Psychology, 61,* 137–146.

Morisse, D., Batra, L., Hess, L., Silverman, R., & Corrigan, P. (1996). A demonstration of a token economy for the real world. *Applied and Preventive Psychology, 5,* 41–46.

Morris, C. D., Bransford, J. D., & Franks, J. J. (1977). Levels of processing versus transfer appropriate processing. *Journal of Verbal Learning and Verbal Behavior, 16,* 519–533.

Morris, M. W., & Peng, K. (1994). Culture and cause: American and Chinese attributions for social and physical events. *Journal of Personality and Social Psychology, 67,* 949–971.

Morrison, A. M., & Von Glinow, M. A. (1990). Women and minorities in management. *American Psychologist, 45,* 200–208.

Morrison, F., Holmes, D. L., & Haith, M. M. (1974). A developmental study of the effects of familiarity on short-term visual memory. *Journal of Experimental Child Psychology, 18,* 412–425.

Mortimer, R. G., Goldsteen, K., Armstrong, R. W., & Macrina, D. (1988). *Effects of enforcement, incentives, and publicity on seat belt use in Illinois.* University of Illinois, Dept. of Health & Safety Studies, Final Report to Illinois Dept. of Transportation (Safety Research Report 88–11).

Moscovici, S. (1985). Social influence and conformity. In G. Lindzey & E. Aronson (Eds.), *The handbook of social psychology: Vol. 2* (3rd ed.). New York: Random House.

Mowbray, C. T., Herman, S. E., & Hazel, K. L. (1992). Gender and serious mental illness: A feminist perspective. *Psychology of Women Quarterly, 16,* 107–126.

Moyer, D. M. (1995). An opposing view on prescription privileges for psychologists. *Professional Psychology: Research and Practice, 26,* 586–590.

Mueller, E., & Lucas, T. (1975). A developmental analysis of peer interaction among toddlers. In M. Lewis & L. A. Rosenblum (Eds.), *Friendship and peer relations.* New York: Wiley-Interscience.

Mueser, K. T. (1993). EMDR: Caveat emptor! *The Behavior Therapist, 16,* 218–219.

Muir, D., & Field, J. (1979). Newborn infants orient to sounds. *Child Development, 50,* 431–436.

Mukherjee, S., Sackheim, H. A., & Schnur, D. B. (1994). Electroconvulsive therapy of acute manic episodes: A review of 50 years' experience. *American Journal of Psychiatry, 151,* 169–176.

Mulder, H. E., Van Olphen, A. F., Bosman, A., & Smoorenburg, G. F. (1992). Phoneme recognition by deaf individuals using the multichannel nucleus cochlear implant. *Acta Otolaryngology, 112,* 946–955.

Mullen, B. (1986). Atrocity as a function of lynch mob composition: A self-attention perspective. *Personality and Social Psychology Bulletin, 12,* 187–197.

Munroe, R. H., & Munroe, R. L. (1994). Behavior across cultures: Results from observational studies. In W. J. Lonner & R. S. Malpass (Eds.), *Psychology and culture.* Boston: Allyn & Bacon.

Murphy, G. E., Wetzel, R. D., Robins, E., & McEvoy, L. (1992). Multiple risk factors predict suicide in alcoholism. *Archives of General Psychiatry, 49,* 459–463.

Murphy, K. R. (1993). *Honesty in the workplace.* Pacific Grove, CA: Brooks/Cole.

Murr, A., & Rogers, A. (1995, March 27). Gray matters. *Newsweek,* pp. 48–54.

Murray, B. (1995, June). Head Start sharpens focus on mental health. *APA Monitor* (p. 39).

Murray, B. (1996, Feburary). Psychology remains top college major. *APA Monitor,* (pp. 1, 42).

Murray, E. A., & Mishkin, M. (1985). Amygdalectomy impairs crossmodal association in monkeys. *Science, 228,* 604–606.

Murray, H. A. (1938). *Explorations in personality.* New York: Oxford University Press.

Murray, H. A. (1971). *Thematic Apperception Test.* Cambridge: Harvard University Press.

Murstein, B. I., & Fontaine, P. A. (1993). The public's knowledge about psychologists and other mental health professionals. *American Psychologist, 48*(7), 839–845.

Murthy, C. V., & Panda, S. C. (1987). A study of intelligence, socio-economic status and birth order among children belonging to SC-ST and non-SC-ST groups. *Indian Journal of Behaviour, 11,* 25–30.

Musick, J. (1987, September 14). Press conference concerning the Ounce of Prevention Project, Chicago, IL.

Mussen, P. H., & Eisenberg-Berg, N. (1977). *The roots of caring.* New York: W. H. Freeman.

Myers, B. J. (1987). Mother-infant bonding as a critical period. In M. H. Bornstein (Ed.), *Sensitive periods in development: Interdisciplinary perspectives.* Hillsdale, NJ: Lawrence Erlbaum Associates.

Myers, D. G., & Diener, E. (1995). Who is happy? *Psychological Science, 6,* 10–19.

Myers, P. I., & Hammill, D. D. (1990). *Learning disabilities: Basic concepts, assessment practices, and instructional strategies.* Austin, TX: Pro-ed.

Naëgelé, B., Thouvard, V., Pépin, J.-L., Lévy, P., Bonnet, C., Perret, J. E., Pellat, P., & Feuerstein, C. (1995). Deficits of cognitive functions in patients with sleep apnea syndrome. *Sleep, 18*(1), 43–52.

Naglieri, J. A., Das, J. P., Stevens, J. J., & Ledbetter, M. F. (1991). Confirmatory factor analysis of planning, attention, simultaneous, and successive cognitive processing tasks. *Journal of School Psychology, 29,* 1–17.

Narayanan, L., Menon, S., & Levine, E. L. (1995). Personality structure: A culture-specific examination of the five-factor model. *Journal of Personality Assessment, 64,* 51–62.

Nash, M., Drake, S., Wiley, S., Khalsa, S., & Lynn, S. (1986). Accuracy of recall by hypnotically age-regressed subjects. *Journal of Abnormal Psychology, 95,* 298–300.

Nathanson, J. A., Hunnicutt, E. J., Kantham, L., & Scavone, C. (1993). Cocaine as a naturally occurring insecticide. *Proceedings of the National Academy of Sciences of the United States of America, 90,* 9645–9648.

National Advisory Mental Health Council. (1996). Basic behavioral science research for mental health: Vulnerability and resilience. *American Psychologist, 51,* 22–28.

National Computer Systems. (1992). *Catalog of assessment instruments, reports, and services.* Minneapolis: NCS.

National Institute on Drug Abuse. (1991). *National household survey on drug abuse.* Washington, DC: NIDA.

National Joint Committee on Learning Disabilities (1994). *Collective perspective on issues affecting learning disabilities.* Austin, TX: Pro-ed.

National Science Foundation (1994). Characteristics of doctoral scientists and engineers in the United States: 1991. NSF Publication #94-307, Arlington, VA.

Neath, I. (1993). Contextual and distinctive processes and the serial position function. *Journal of Memory and Language, 32,* 820–840.

Needleman, H. (1996). Bone lead levels and delinquent behavior. *Journal of the American Medical Association, 275,* 363–369.

Neeper, S. A., Gomez-Pinilla, F., Choi, J., & Cotman, C. (1995). Exercise and brain neurotrophins. *Nature, 373,* 109.

Neher, A. (1991). Maslow's theory of motivation: A critique. *Journal of Humanistic Psychology, 31,* 89–112.

Neimark, E. D. (1982). Adolescent thought: Transition to formal operations. In B. B. Wolman & G. Stircler (Eds.), *Handbook of developmental psychology.* Englewood Cliffs, NJ: Prentice-Hall.

Neims, D. M., McNeill, J., Giles, T. R., & Todd, F. (1995). Incidence of laxative abuse in community and bulimic populations: A descriptive review. *International Journal of Eating Disorders, 17*(3), 211–228.

Neisser, U. (1991). A case of misplaced nostalgia. *American Psychologist, 46,* 34–36.

Neisser, U., Boodoo, G., Bouchard, T. J., Boykin, A. W., Brody, N., Ceci, S. J., Halpern, D. F., Loehlin, J. C., Perloff, R., Sternberg, R. J., & Urbina, S. (1996). Intelligence: Knowns and unknowns. *American Psychologist, 51,* 77–101.

Neitz, M., & Neitz, J. (1995, February 17). Numbers and ratios of visual pigment genes for normal red-green color vision. *Science, 267,* 1013–1016.

Nelson, D. L., Schreiber, T. A., & McEvoy, C. L. (1992). Processing implicit and explicit representations. *Psychological Review, 99,* 322–348.

Nelson, K. (1986). Event knowledge and cognitive development. In K. Nelson (Ed.), *Event knowledge: Structure and function in development.* Hillsdale, NJ: Lawrence Erlbaum Associates.

Nelson, K. (1993). Developing self-knowledge from autobiographical memory. In T. K. Srull & R. S. Wyer (Eds.), *The mental representation of trait and autobiographical knowledge about the self: Advances in social cognition: Vol. V.* Hillsdale, NJ: Lawrence Erlbaum Associates.

Nelson, K. (1993). The psychological and social origins of autobiographical memory. *Psychological Science, 4,* 7–14.

Nelson, L. L., & Christie, D. J. (1995). Peace in the psychology curriculum: Moving from assimilation to accommodation. *Peace and Conflict: Journal of Peace Psychology, 1,* 161–178.

Nelson, R. J., Demas, G. E., **Huang, P. L.**, Fishman, M. C., Dawson, V. L., Dawson, T. M., & Snyder, S. H. (1995). Behavioral abnormalities in male mice lacking neuronal nitric oxide synthase. *Nature, 378,* 383–386.

Neuberg, S. L. (1988). Behavioral implications of information presented outside of conscious awareness: The effects of subliminal presentation of trait information on behavior in the Prisoner's Dilemma Game. *Social Cognition, 6,* 207–230.

Neugarten, B. L. (1977). Personality and aging. In J. E. Birren & K. W. Schaie (Eds.), *Handbook of the psychology of aging.* New York: Van Nostrand Reinhold.

Neugarten, B. L., Havighurst, D. J., & Tobin, S. S. (1968). Personality and patterns of aging. In B. L. Neugarten (Ed.), *Middle age and aging.* Chicago: University of Chicago Press.

Neumann, C. S., Grimes, K., Walker, E. F., & Baum, K. (1995). Developmental pathways to schizophrenia: Behavioral subtypes. *Journal of Abnormal Psychology, 104,* 558–566.

Neves, D. M., & Anderson, J. R. (1981). Knowledge compilation: Mechanisms for the automatization of cognitive skills. In J. R. Anderson (Ed.), *Cognitive skills and their acquisition.* Hillsdale, NJ: Lawrence Erlbaum Associates.

Neville, H. A., Heppner, M. J., Louie, C. E., Thompson, C. E., Brooks, L., & Baker, C. E. (1996). The impact of multicultural training on white racial identity attitudes and therapy competencies. *Professional Psychology: Research and Practice, 27,* 83–89.

Newcomb, A. F., & Bagwell, C. L. (1995). Children's friendship relations: A meta-analytic review. *Psychological Bulletin, 117,* 306–347.

Newcombe, N., & Fox, N. A. (1994). Infantile amnesia: Through a glass darkly. *Child Development, 65,* 31–40.

Newell, A., & Simon, H. A. (1972). *Human problem solving.* Englewood Cliffs, NJ: Prentice-Hall.

Newman, J. H. (1993). A structural investigation of intellectual development and epistemological style in young adults. *Dissertation Abstracts International, 54*(5), 2786B.

Newman, J. H., & Martin, J. E. (1989, June). *Cognitive development and collegiate conversation.* Poster presented at the convention of the American Psychological Society, Alexandria, VA.

Newman, J. H., & Martin, J. E. (1996). *Modelling adult intellectual development: Confirmatory factor analysis of the epistemic process.* Unpublished manuscript.

Newman, J. P., & Kosson, D. S. (1986). Passive avoidance learning in psychopathic and nonpsychopathic offenders. *Journal of Abnormal Psychology, 95,* 252–256.

Newsweek (1994, August 14). A week in the death of America, pp. 24–32.

Nicassio, P. (1985). The psychological adjustment of the Southeast Asian refugee: An overview of empirical findings and theoretical models. *Journal of Cross-Cultural Psychology, 16,* 153–173.

NICHD Early Child Care Network (1994). Child care and child development: The NICHD Study of Early Child Care. In S. Friedman & H. C. Haywood (Eds.), *Developmental follow-up: Concepts, domains, and methods.* New York: Academic Press.

Nichols, D. E., & Oberlender, R. (1990). Structure-activity relationship of MDMA and related compounds: A new class of psychoactive drugs. *Annals of the New York Academy of Sciences, 600,* 613–625.

Nichols, R. (1978). Twin studies of ability, personality, and interests. *Homo, 29,* 158–173.

Nicholson, A. N., Pascoe, P. A., Spencer, M. B., Stone, B. M., Roehis, T., & Roth, T. (1986). Sleep after transmeridian fights. *Lancet, 2,* 1205–1208.

Nicholson, C. D. (1990). Pharmacology of nootropics and metabolically active compounds in relation to their use in dementia. *Psychopharmacology, 101,* 147–159.

Nicholson, I. R., & Neufeld, R. W. J. (1993). Classification of the schizophrenias according to symptomatology: A two factor model. *Journal of Abnormal Psychology, 102,* 259–270.

Nicholson, R. A., & Berman, J. S. (1983). Is follow-up necessary in evaluating psychotherapy? *Psychological Bulletin, 93*(2), 261–278.

Nickell, J. (1994). *Psychic sleuths: ESP and sensational cases.* Amherst, NY: Prometheus Books.

Nickerson, R. A., & Adams, M. J. (1979). Long-term memory for a common object. *Cognitive Psychology, 11,* 287–307.

Niedenthal, P. M., Setterlund, M. B., & Wherry, M. B. (1992). Possible self-complexity and affective reactions to goal-relevant evaluation. *Journal of Personality and Social Psychology, 63,* 5–16.

Nielson, E. B., Ginn, S. R., Cunningham, K. A., & Appeal, J. B. (1985). Antagonism of the LSD cue by putative serotonin antagonists: Relationship to inhibition of in vivo (-suo-3H) spiroperidol binding. *Behavioral Brain Research, 16*(2–3), 171–176.

Nielson Media. (1990). *1990 report on television.* New York: Nielson Media, Inc.

Nietzel, M. T., & Bernstein, D. A. (1987). *Introduction to clinical psychology.* (2nd ed.). New York: Prentice-Hall.

Nietzel, M. T., Bernstein, D. A., & Milich, R. (1991). *Introduction to clinical psychology* (3rd ed.). Englewood Cliffs, NJ: Prentice-Hall.

Nietzel, M. T., Bernstein, D. A., & Milich, R. (1994). *Introduction to clinical psychology* (4th ed.). Englewood Cliffs, NJ: Prentice-Hall.

Nietzel, M. T., Guthrie, P. R., & Susman, D. T. (1990). Utilization of community and social support resources. In F. H. Kanfer & A. P. Goldstein (Eds.), *Helping people change* (4th ed.). New York: Pergamon Press.

NIH (Technology Assessment Conference Panel) (1992). Methods for voluntary weight loss and control. *Annals of Internal Medicine, 116,* 942–949.

Nijhawan, R. (1991). Three dimensional Muller-Lyer illusion. *Perception and Psychophysics, 49,* 333–341.

Nilsson, N. J. (1995). Eye on the prize. *AI Magazine, 16,* 9–17.

NIMH (National Institute of Mental Health). (1985). *Electroconvulsive therapy: Consensus development conference statement.* Bethesda, MD: U.S. Department of Health and Human Services.

Nishikawa, T., Tsuda, A., Tanaka, M., & Nishikawa, M. (1994). Naloxone attenuates drinking behavior in psychiatric patients displaying self-induced water intoxication. *Progress in NeuroPsychopharmacology and Biological Psychiatry, 18*(1), 149–153.

Nolan, R. P., Spanos, N. P., Hayward, A. A., & Scott, H. A. (1995). The efficacy of hypnotic and nonhypnotic response-based imagery for self-managing recurrent headache. *Imagination, Cognition, and Personality, 14*(3), 183–201.

Nolen-Hoeksema, S. (1990). *Sex differences in depression.* Stanford, CA: Stanford University Press.

Nolen-Hoeksma, S., Morrow, J., & Fredrickson, N. (1993). Response styles and the duration of episodes of depressed mood. *Journal of Abnormal Psychology, 102,* 20–28.

Noll, R. B. (1994). Hypnotherapy for warts in children and adolescents. *Journal of Developmental and Behavioral Pediatrics, 15*(3), 170–173.

Norman, D. A. (1988). *The psychology of everyday things.* New York: Basic Books.

Nottebohm, F. (1985). Neuronal replacement in adulthood. *Annals of the New York Academy of Science, 457,* 143–161.

Novak, M. A. (1991, July). Psychologists care deeply about animals. *APA Monitor,* p. 4.

Nowak, M. A., May, R. M., & Sigmund, K. (1995). The arithmetics of mutual help. *Scientific American, 272,* 76–81.

Nugent, F. (1994). *An introduction to the profession of counseling.* Columbus, OH: Merrill.

Nurnberger, J. (1993). Genotyping status report for affective disorder. *Psychiatric Genetics, 3,* 207–214.

Nyamathi, A., Stein, J. A., & Brecht, M.-L. (1995). Psychosocial predictors of AIDS risk behavior and drug use in homeless and drug-addicted women of color. *Health Psychology, 14,* 265–273.

Nygren, R., & Levine, E. L. (in press). Leadership of work teams: Factors influencing team outcomes. In M. Beyerlein & D. Johnson (Eds.), *Advances in interdisciplinary study of work teams.* Greenwich, CT: JAI Press.

O'Brien, T. L. (1991, September 2). Computers help thwart "groupthink" that plagues meetings. *Chicago Sun Times.*

O'Connor, J. (1943). *Structural visualization.* Boston: Human Engineering Laboratory.

O'Dell, T. J., and Kandel, E. R. (1994). Low-frequency stimulation erases LTP through an NMDA receptor-mediated activation of phosphatases. *Learning and Memory, 1,* 129–139.

O'Farrell, T. J., & Murphy, C. M. (1995). Marital violence before and after alcoholism treatment. *Journal of Consulting and Clinical Psychology, 63,* 256–262.

O'Hare, D., & Roscoe, S. (1991). *Flight deck performance: The human factor.* Ames: Iowa University Press.

O'Leary, K. D., Malone, J., & Tyree, A. (1994). Physical aggression in early marriage: Prerelationship and relationship effects. *Journal of Consulting and Clinical Psychology, 62,* 594–602.

O'Reilly, K. R., & Higgins, D. L. (1991). AIDS community demonstration projects for HIV prevention among hard-to-reach groups. *Public Health Reports, 106,* 714–720.

Oakland, T., & Glutting, J. J. (1990). Examiner observations of children's WISC-R test-related behaviors: Possible socioeconomic status, race, and gender effects. *Psychological Assessment, 2,* 86–90.

Oatley, K. (1993). Those to whom evil is done. In R. S. Wyer & T. K. Srull (Eds.), *Toward a general theory of anger and emotional aggression: Advances in social cognition, Vol. VI.* Hillsdale, NJ: Lawrence Erlbaum Associates.

Oden, M. H. (1968). The fulfillment of promise: 40-year follow-up of the Terman gifted group. *Genetic Psychology Monographs, 17,* 3–93.

Offenbach, S., Chodzko-Zajko, W., & Ringel, R. (1990). Relationship between physiological status, cognition, and age in adult men. *Bulletin of the Psychonomics Society, 28*, 112–114.

Offerman, L. R., & Beil, C. (1992). Achievement styles of women leaders and their peers: Toward an understanding of women and leadership. *Psychology of Women Quarterly, 16*, 37–56.

Ofshe, R., & Watters, E. (1994). *Making monsters: False memories, psychotherapy, sexual hysteria.* New York: Scribners.

Ogles, B. M., Lambert, M. J., & Sawyer, J. D. (1995). Clinical significance of the National Institute of Mental Health treatment of depression collaborative research program data. *Journal of Consulting and Clinical Psychology, 63*, 321–326.

Ohira, H., & Kurono, K. (1993). Facial feedback effects on impression formation. *Perceptual and Motor Skills, 77*(3, Pt. 2), 1251–1258.

Öhman, A., Dimberg, U., & Ost, L. G. (1985). Animal and social phobias: A laboratory model. In S. Reiss & R. R. Bootzin (Eds.), *Theoretical issues in behavior therapy.* Orlando, FL: Academic Press.

Öhman, A., Erixon, G., & Lofberg, I. (1975). Phobias and preparedness: Phobic versus neutral picture as conditioned stimuli for human autonomic responses. *Journal of Abnormal Psychology, 84*, 41–45.

Öhman, A., & Soares, J. F. (1994). "Unconscious anxiety": Phobic responses to masked stimuli. *Journal of Abnormal Psychology, 103*(2), 231–240.

Olds, J. (1973). Commentary on positive reinforcement produced by electrical stimulation of septal areas and other regions of rat brain. In E. S. Valenstein (Ed.), *Brain stimulation and motivation: Research and commentary.* Glenview, IL: Scott, Foresman.

Olds, J., & Milner, P. (1954). Positive reinforcement produced by electrical stimulation of septal areas and other regions of the rat brain. *Journal of Comparative and Physiological Psychology, 47*, 419–427.

Oliner, S. P., & Oliner, P. M. (1988). *The altruistic personality: Rescuers of Jews in Nazi Europe.* New York: Free Press.

Olio, K. A. (1994). Truth in memory. *American Psychologist, 49*, 442–443.

Olness, K., & Ader, R. (1992). Conditioning as an adjunct in the pharmacotherapy of lupus erythmatosus. *Developmental and Behavioral Pediatrics, 13*, 124–125.

Olpe, H. R., Steinmann, M. W., & Jones, R. S. G. (1985). Electrophysiological perspectives on locus coeruleus: Its role in cognitive versus vegetative functions. *Physiological Psychology, 13*, 179–187.

Olson, G. M., & Sherman, T. (1983). Attention, learning, and memory in infants. In P. H. Mussen (Ed.), *Handbook of child psychology: Vol. 2. Infancy and developmental psychobiology.* New York: Wiley.

Olson, J. M. (1992). Self-perception of humor: Evidence for discounting and augmentation effects. *Journal of Personality and Social Psychology, 62*, 369–377.

Olson, J. M., & Zanna, M. P. (1993). Attitudes and attitude change. In L. W. Porter & M. R. Rosenzweig (Eds.), *Annual review of psychology* (Vol. 44, pp. 117–154). Palo Alto, CA: Annual Reviews Inc.

Ones, D. S., Viswesvaran, C., & Schmidt, F. L. (1993). Comprehensive meta-analysis of integrity test validities: Findings and implications for personnel selection and theories of job performance. *Journal of Applied Psychology, 78*, 679–703.

Orbell, J. M., van de Kragt, A. J. C., & Dawes, R. M. (1988). Explaining discussion-induced cooperation. *Journal of Personality and Social Psychology, 54*, 811–819.

Organ, D. W., & Konovsky, M. (1989). Cognitive versus affective determinants of organizational citizenship behavior. *Journal of Applied Psychology, 74*, 157–164.

Orlinsky, D. E., Grawe, K., & Parks, B. K. (1994). Process and outcome in psychotherapy—Noch Einmal. In A. E. Bergin & S. L. Garfield (Eds.), *Handbook of psychotherapy and behavior change.* New York: Wiley.

Orme-Johnson, D. (1992). Personal communication, April 20.

Orne, M. T. (1977). The construct of hypnosis: Implications of definition for research and practice. In W. E. Edmonston, Jr. (Ed.), *Conceptual and investigative approaches to hypnosis and hypnotic phenomena. Annals of the New York Academy of Sciences, 296*, 14–33.

Orne, M. T., & Evans, F. J. (1965). Social control in the psychological experiment: Antisocial behavior and hypnosis. *Journal of Personality and Social Psychology, 1*, 189–200.

Orne, M. T., & Holland, C. H. (1968). On the ecological validity of laboratory deceptions. *International Journal of Psychiatry, 6*, 282–293.

Orne, M. T., Sheehan, P. W., & Evans, F. J. (1968). Occurrence of posthypnotic behavior outside the experimental setting. *Journal of Personality and Social Psychology, 9*, 189–196.

Ornitz, E. M. (1989). Autism: At the interface of sensory and information processing. In G. Dawson (Ed.), *Autism: Nature, diagnosis, and treatment.* New York: Guilford.

Oskamp, S. (1991). *Attitudes and opinions.* Englewood Cliffs, NJ: Prentice-Hall.

Öst, L.-G. (1978). Behavioral treatment of thunder and lightning phobia. *Behaviour Research and Therapy, 16*, 197–207.

Öst, L.-G. (1992). Blood and injection phobia: Background and cognitive, physiological and behavioral variables. *Journal of Abnormal Psychology, 101*, 68–74.

Öst, L.-G., Hellström, K., & Kåver, A. (1992). One- versus five-session exposure in the treatment of needle phobia. *Behavior Therapy, 23*, 263–282.

Öst, L.-G., Salkovskis, P. M., & Hellström, K. (1991). One-session therapist-directed exposure vs. self-exposure in the treatment of spider phobia. *Behavior Therapy, 22*, 407–422.

Oster, H. (1981). "Recognition" of emotional expression in infancy? In M. E. Lamb & L. R. Sherrod (Eds.), *Infant social cognition.* Hillsdale, NJ: Lawrence Erlbaum Associates.

Ostrom, T. M., Skowronski, J. J., & Nowack, A. (1994). The cognitive foundations of attitudes: It's a wonderful construct. In P. G. Devine, D. L. Hamilton, & T. M. Ostrom (Eds.), *Social cognition: Impact on social psychology* (pp. 196–258). San Diego, CA: Academic Press.

Ottati, V. C., Riggle, E. J., Wyer, R. S., Schwarz, N., & Kuklinski, J. (1989). Cognitive and affective bases of opinion survey responses. *Journal of Personality and Social Psychology, 57*, 404–415.

Overton, D. A. (1984). State dependent learning and drug discriminations. In L. L. Iverson, S. D. Iverson, & S. H. Snyder (Eds.), *Handbook of psychopharmacology* (Vol. 18). New York: Plenum.

Oyserman, D. (1993). The lens of personhood: Viewing the self and others in a multicultural society. *Journal of Personality and Social Psychology, 65*, 993–1009.

Padilla, A. M., Lindholm, K. J., Chen, A., Duran, R., Hakuta, K., Lambert, W., & Tucker, G. R. (1991). The English-only movement: Myth, reality and implications for psychology. *American Psychologist, 46*, 120–130.

Paik, H., & Comstock, G. (1994). The effects of television violence on antisocial behavior: A meta-analysis. *Communication Research, 21*, 516–546.

Paivio, A. (1986). *Mental representations: A dual coding approach.* New York: Oxford University Press.

Paivio, S. C., & Greenberg, L. S. (1995). Resolving "unfinished business": Efficacy of experiential therapy using empty-chair dialogue. *Journal of Consulting and Clinical Psychology, 63*, 419–425.

Palmer, F. H., & Anderson, L. W. (1979). Long-term gains from early intervention: Findings from longitudinal studies. In E. Zigler & J. Valentine (Eds.), *Project Head Start: A legacy of the war on poverty.* New York: Free Press.

Palmer, R. L. (Ed.). (1981). *Electroconvulsive therapy: An appraisal.* New York: Oxford University Press.

Palmer, S. E. (1975). The effects of contextual scenes on the identification of objects. *Memory & Cognition, 3*, 519–526.

Palmer, S. E. (1992). Common region: A new principle of perceptual grouping. *Cognitive Psychology, 24*, 436–447.

Palmisano, M., & Herrmann, D. (1991). The facilitation of memory performance. *Bulletin of the Psychonomic Society, 29*, 557–559.

Pan, H. S., Neidig, P. H., & O'Leary, K. D. (1994). Predicting mild to severe husband-to-wife physical aggression. *Journal of Consulting and Clinical Psychology, 62*, 975–981.

Paoletti, M. G. (1995). Biodiversity, traditional landscapes and agroecosystem management. *Landscape and Urban Planning, 31*(1–3), 117–128.

Papp, L., Klein, D., Martinez, J., Schneier, F., Cole, R., Liebowitz, M., Hollander, E., Fryer, A., Jordan, F., & Gorman, J. (1993). Diagnostic and substance specificity of carbon monoxide–induced panic. *American Journal of Psychiatry, 150*, 250–257.

Pardo, J. V., Fox, P. T., & Raichle, M. E. (1991). Localization of a human system for sustained attention by positron emission tomography. *Nature, 349*, 61–64.

Parke, R. D., Berkowitz, L., Leyens, J. P., West, S. G., & Sebastian, R. J. (1977). Some effects of violent and nonviolent movies on the behavior of juvenile delinquents. In L. Berkowitz (Ed.), *Advances in experimental social psychology: Vol. 10.* New York: Academic Press.

Parker, J. G., & Asher, S. R. (1987). Peer relations and later adjustment: Are low-accepted children "at risk"? *Psychological Bulletin, 102*, 358–389.

Parkes, C. M. P., & Weiss, R. S. (1983). *Recovery from bereavement.* New York: Basic Books.

Parkin, A. J., & Walter, B. M. (1991). Aging, short-term memory, and frontal dysfunction. *Psychobiology, 19*, 175–179.

Parnas, J., Cannon, T., Jacobsen, B., Schulsinger, H., Schulsinger, F., & Mednick, S. (1993). Lifetime DSM-III-R diagnostic outcomes in the offspring of schizophrenic mothers. *Archives of General Psychiatry, 50*, 707–714.

Parrott, R. F. (1994). Central effects of CCK ligands in pigs making operant responses for food. *Pharmacology, Biochemistry, and Behavior, 49*(3), 463–469.

Parten, M. B. (1932). Social participation among preschool children. *Journal of Abnormal and Social Psychology, 27*, 243–269.

Parten, M. B. (1971). Social play among preschool children. In R. E. Herron & B. Sutton-Smith (Eds.), *Child's play.* New York: Wiley. (Reprinted from *Journal of Abnormal and Social Psychology, 28* (1933), 136–147.)

Pascarella, E. T. & Terenzini, P. T. (1991). *How college affects students: Findings and insights from twenty years of research.* San Francisco, CA: Jossey-Bass.

Patrick, C. J., Craig, K. D., & Prkachin, K. M. (1986). Observer judgments of pain: Facial action determinants. *Journal of Personality and Social Psychology, 50,* 1291–1298.

Patrick, C. J., Cuthbert, B. N., & Lang, P. J. (1994). Emotion in the criminal psychopath: Fear imaging processing. *Journal of Abnormal Psychology, 103,* 523–534.

Patterson, F. G. (1978). The gestures of a gorilla: Language acquisition in another pongid. *Brain and Language, 5,* 72–97.

Patterson, G. R. (1974). Intervention for boys with conduct problems: Multiple settings, treatments, and criteria. *Journal of Consulting and Clinical Psychology, 42,* 471–481.

Patterson, G. R., DeBaryshe, B. D., & Ramsey, E. (1989). A developmental perspective on antisocial behavior. *American Psychologist, 44,* 329–335.

Pattie, F. A. (1935). A report of attempts to produce uniocular blindness by hypnotic suggestion. *British Journal of Medical Psychiatry, 15,* 230–241.

Pauk, W., & Fiore, J. P. (1989). *Succeed in college!* Boston: Houghton Mifflin.

Paul, G. L. (1969). Behavior modification research: Design and tactics. In C. M. Franks (Ed.), *Behavior therapy: Appraisal and status* (pp. 29–62). New York: McGraw-Hill.

Pauls, D. L., Alsobrook, J. P., II, Goodman, W., Rasmussen, S., & Leckman, J. F. (1995). A family study of obsessive-compulsive disorder. *American Journal of Psychiatry, 152,* 76–84.

Paulus, P. B. (1988). *Prison crowding: A psychological perspective.* New York: Springer-Verlag.

Paunonen, S., Jackson, D., Trzebinski, J., & Forsterling, F. (1992). Personality structure across cultures: A multi-method evaluation. *Journal of Personality and Social Psychology, 62,* 447–456.

Pavkov, T., Lewis, D., & Lyons, J. (1989). Psychiatric diagnosis and racial bias: An empirical investigation. *Professional Psychology: Research and Practice, 20,* 364–368.

Payami, H., Bernard, S., Larsen, K., Kaye, J., & Nutt, J. (1995). Genetic anticipation in Parkinson's disease. *Neurology, 45,* 135–138.

Payne, J. W., Bettman, J. R., & Johnson, E. J. (1992). Behavioral decision research: A constructive processing perspective. *Annual Review of Psychology, 43,* 87–131.

Peck, J. W. (1978). Rats defend different body weights depending on palatability and accessibility of their food. *Journal of Comparative and Physiological Psychology, 92,* 555–570.

Pederson, P. (1994). A culture-centered approach to counseling. In W. J. Lonner & R. S. Malpass (Eds.), *Psychology and culture.* Boston: Allyn & Bacon.

Pelleymounter, M. A., Cullen, M. J., Baker, M. B., Hecht, R., Winters, D., Boone, T., & Collins, F. (1995). Effects of the *obese* gene product on body weight regulation in *ob/ob* mice. *Science, 269,* 540–543.

Penfield, W., & Rasmussen, T. (1968). *The cerebral cortex of man: A clinical study of localization of function.* New York: Hafner.

Pennebaker, J. W. (1985). Traumatic experience and psychosomatic disease: Exploring the roles of behavioural inhibition, obsession, and confiding. *Canadian Psychology, 26,* 82–95.

Pennebaker, J. W. (1990). *Opening up: The healing power of confiding in others.* New York: Morrow.

Pennebaker, J. W., & Chew, C. H. (1985). Deception, electrodermal activity, and inhibition of behavior. *Journal of Personality and Social Psychology, 49,* 1427–1433.

Pennebaker, J. W., Colder, M., & Sharp, L. K. (1990). Accelerating the coping process. *Journal of Personality and Social Psychology, 58,* 528–537.

Pennebaker, J. W., & O'Heeron, R. C. (1984). Confiding in others and illness rate among spouses of suicide and accidental death victims. *Journal of Abnormal Psychology, 93,* 473–476.

Penner, L. A., & Craiger, J. P. (1992). The weakest link: The performance of individual group members. In R. W. Swezey & E. Salas (Eds.), *Teams: Their training and performance* (pp. 57–74). Norwood, NJ: Ablex.

Penner, L. A., Fritzsche, B. A., Craiger, J. P., & Friefeld, T. R. (1995). Measuring the prosocial personality. In J. Butcher & C. D. Spielberger (Eds.), *Advances in personality assessment* (Vol. 10, pp. 147–163). Hillsdale, NJ: Lawrence Erlbaum Associates.

Pepeu, G. (1994). Memory disorders: Novel treatments, clinical perspective. *Life Sciences, 55,* 2189–2194.

Perdue, C. W., Dovidio, J. F., Gurtman, M. B., & Tyler, R. B. (1990). "Us" and "Them": Social categorization and the process of intergroup bias. *Journal of Personality and Social Psychology, 59,* 475–486.

Perkins, K. A. (1993). Introduction to special section: Clinical research in smoking cessation. *Journal of Consulting and Clinical Psychology, 61,* 715–717.

Perls, F. S., Hefferline, R. F., & Goodman, P. (1951). *Gestalt therapy.* New York: Julian Press.

Peroutka, S. J. (1989). "Ecstacy": A human neurotoxin? *Archives of General Psychiatry, 46,* 191.

Peroutka, S. J., Newman, H., & Harris, H. (1988). The subjective effects of 3, 4-methylenedioxymethamphetamine in recreational users. *Neuropharmacology, 1*(4), 273–277.

Perris, E. E., Myers, N. A., & Clifton, R. K. (1990). Long-term memory for a single infancy experience. *Child Development, 61,* 1796–1807.

Perry, W. G., Jr. (1970). *Forms of intellectual and ethical development during the college years: A scheme.* Troy, MO: Holt, Rinehart & Winston.

Pervin, L. A. (1993). *Personality: Theory and research* (6th ed.). New York: Wiley.

Pervin, L. A. (1994). A critical analysis of current trait theory. *Psychological Inquiry, 5,* 103–113.

Peterson, A., Compas, B., Brooks-Gunn, J., Stemmler, M., Ey, S., & Grant, K. (1993). Depression in adolescence. *American Psychologist, 48,* 155–168.

Peterson, A. C. (1987, September). Those gangly years. *Psychology Today,* pp. 28–34.

Peterson, C. (1995, April). *The preschool child witness: Errors in accounts of traumatic injury.* Paper presented at the biennial meeting of the Society for Research in Child Development, Indianapolis.

Peterson, C., Maier, S. F., & Seligman, M. E. (1993). *Learned helplessness: A theory for the age of personal control.* New York: Oxford University Press.

Peterson, C., & Seligman, M. E. P. (1984). Causal explanations as a risk factor for depression: Theory and evidence. *Psychological Review, 91,* 347–374.

Peterson, C., Seligman, M. E. P., & Vaillant, G. E. (1988). Pessimistic explanatory style is a risk factor for physical illness: A thirty-five year longitudinal study. *Journal of Personality and Social Psychology, 55,* 23–27.

Peterson, L. R., & Peterson, M. J. (1959). Short-term retention of individual verbal items. *Journal of Experimental Psychology, 58,* 193–198.

Peterson, S. E., Snyder, A., Fox, P. T., & Raichle, M. E. (1990). Activation of extrastriate and frontal cortical areas by visual words and word-like stimuli. *Science, 249,* 1041–1044.

Petitto, J., Folds, J., Ozer, H., Quade, D., & Evans, D. (1992). Abnormal diurnal variation in circulating natural killer cell phenotypes and cytotoxic activity in major depression. *American Journal of Psychiatry, 149,* 694–696.

Petrie, T. A., & Diehl, N. S. (1995). Sport psychology in the profession of psychology. *Professional Psychology: Research and Practice, 26,* 288–291.

Pettigrew, T. F. (1979). The ultimate attribution error: Extending Allport's cognitive analysis of prejudice. *Personality and Social Psychology Bulletin, 5,* 461–476.

Petty, R. (1995). Attitude change. In A. Tesser (Ed.), *Advanced social psychology* (pp. 195–257). New York: McGraw-Hill.

Petty, R., Cacioppo, J., & Goldman, R. (1981). Personal involvement as a determinant of argument-based persuasion. *Journal of Personality and Social Psychology, 41,* 847–855.

Petty, R., Cacioppo, J. T., & Schumann, D. (1983). Central and peripheral routes to advertising effectiveness: The moderating role of involvement. *Journal of Consumer Research, 10,* 134–148.

Petty, R. E., & Cacioppo, J. T. (1986). *Communication and persuasion: Central and peripheral routes to attitude change.* New York: Springer-Verlag.

Petty, R. E., Priester, J. R., & Wegener, D. T. (1994). Cognitive processes in attitude change. In R. S. Wyer & T. K. Srull (Eds.), *Handbook of social cognition* (2nd ed.). Hillsdale, NJ: Lawrence Erlbaum Associates.

Petursson, H. (1994). The benzodiazepine withdrawal syndrome. *Addiction, 89*(11), 1455–1459.

Peuskens, J. (1995). Risperidone in the treatment of patients with chronic schizophrenia: A multi-national, multi-centre, double-blind, parallel-group study versus haloperidol. *British Journal of Psychiatry, 166,* 712–726.

Pevernagie, D. A., Stanson, A. W., Daniels, B. K., & Shephard, J. W. (1995). Effects of body position on the upper airway of patients. *American Journal of Respiratory and Critical Care Medicine, 152*(1), 179–185.

Phares, E. J. (1991). *Introduction to personality* (3rd ed.). New York: HarperCollins.

Phelps, B. J., & Exum, M. E. (1992, Spring). Subliminal tapes: How to get the message across. *Skeptical Inquirer, 16,* 282–286.

Phelps, M. E., & Mazziotta, J. C. (1985). Positron emission tomography: Human brain function and biochemistry. *Science, 228,* 799–809.

Phillips, A. P., & Dipboye, R. L. (1989). Correlational tests of predictions from a process model of the interview. *Journal of Applied Psychology, 74,* 41–52.

Phillips, D. P. (1983). The impact of media violence on U.S. homicides. *American Sociological Review, 48,* 560–568.

Phillips, D. P., & Cartensen, L. L. (1986). Clustering of teenage suicides after television news stories about suicide. *New England Journal of Medicine, 315,* 685–689.

Phinney, J. S. (1990). Ethnic identity in adolescents and adults: A review of research. *Psychological Bulletin, 108,* 499–514.

Piaget, J. (1952). *The origins of intelligence in children.* New York: International Universities Press.

Pierce, G., Sarason, I., & Sarason, B. (1991). General and specific support expectations and stress as predictors of perceived supportivness: An experimental study. *Journal of Personality and Social Psychology, 63,* 297–307.

Pike, A., McGuire, S., Hetherington, E. M., Reiss, D., & Plomin, R. (in press). Family environment, adolescent depressive symptoms, and antisocial behavior: A multivariate genetic analysis. *Developmental Psychology.*

Piliavin, J. A., Dovidio, J. F., Gaertner, S. L., & Clark, R. D., III (1981). *Emergency intervention.* New York: Academic Press.

Pillard, R. C., & Bailey, J. M. (1995). A biologic perspective on sexual orientation. *Psychiatric Clinics of North America, 18*(1), 71–84.

Pillemer, D. B., & White, S. H. (1989). Childhood events recalled by children and adults. In H. W. Reese (Ed.), *Advances in child development and behavior* (Vol. 21). New York: Academic Press.

Pi-Sunyer, F. X. (1994). The fattening of America. *Journal of the American Medical Association, 272*(3), 238–239.

Plomin, R. (1986). *Development, genetics, and psychology.* Hillsdale, NJ: Lawrence Erlbaum Associates.

Plomin, R. (1989). Environment and genes: Determinants of behavior. *American Psychologist, 44,* 105–111.

Plomin, R. (1994). Nature, nurture and social development. *Social Development, 3,* 37–53.

Plomin, R. (1994a). The Emanuel Miller memorial lecture 1993: Genetic research and the identification of environmental influences. *Journal of Child Psychology and Psychiatry, 35,* 817–834.

Plomin, R. (1994b). *Genetics and experience: The developmental interplay between nature and nurture.* Newbury Park, CA: Sage.

Plomin, R. (1995). Molecular genetics and psychology. *Current Directions in Psychological Science, 4,* 1–4.

Plomin, R., & Bergeman, C. S. (1991). The nature of nurture: Genetic influence on "environmental" measures. *Behavioral and Brain Sciences, 14,* 373–427. (With Open Peer Commentary)

Plomin, R., Chipuer, H. M., & Loehlin, J. C. (1990). Behavioral genetics and personality. In L. A. Pervin (Ed.), *Handbook of personality: Theory and research* (pp. 225–243). New York: Guilford Press.

Plomin, R., & Daniels, D. (1987). Why are children in the same family so different from each other? *Behavioral and Brain Sciences, 10,* 1–16.

Plomin, R., DeFries, J. C., & McClearn, G. E. (1990). *Behavior genetics: A primer.* New York: W. H. Freeman.

Plomin, R., & McClearn, G. E. (Eds.). (1993). *Nature, nurture and psychology.* Washington, DC: American Psychological Association.

Plomin, R., & Neiderhiser, J. M. (1992). Genetics and experience. *Current Directions in Psychological Science, 1,* 160–163.

Plomin, R., Owen, M. J., & McGuffin, P. (1994). The genetic basis of complex human behaviors. *Science, 264,* 1733–1739.

Plomin, R., Reiss, D., Hetherington, E. M., & Howe, G. W. (1994). Nature and nurture: Genetic contributions to measures of the family environment. *Developmental Psychology, 30,* 32–43.

Plous, S. (1993). *The psychology of judgment and decision making.* New York: McGraw-Hill.

Poland, R. E., Rubin, R. T., Lesser, I. M., Lane, L. A., & Hart, P. J. (1987). Neuroendocrine aspects of primary endogenous depression. *Archives of General Psychiatry, 44,* 790–796.

Pollack, I. (1953). The assimilation of sequentially coded information. *American Journal of Psychology, 66,* 421–435.

Pollack, V. (1992). Meta-analysis of subjective sensitivity to alcohol in sons of alcoholics. *American Journal of Psychiatry, 149,* 1534–1538.

Polusny, M. A., & Folletee, V. M. (1995). Long-term correlates of child sexual abuse: Theory and review of the empirical literature. *Applied and Preventive Psychology, 4,* 143–166.

Polusny, M. A., & Follette, V. M. (1996). Remembering childhood abuse: A national survey of psychologists' clinical practices, beliefs, and personal experiences. *Professional Psychology: Research and Practice, 27,* 41–52.

Polyakov, V. V., Posokhov, S. I., Ponomaryova, I. P., & Zhukova, O. P. (1994). Sleep in space flight. *Aviakosmicheskaya I Ecologicheskaya Meditsina, 28*(3), 4–7.

Pomerleau, C. S., & Pomerleau, O. F. (1992). Euphoriant effects of nicotine in smokers. *Psychopharmacology, 108,* 460–465.

Poole, D. A., Lindsay, D. S., Memon, A., & Bull, R. (1995). Psychotherapy and the recovery of memories of childhood sexual abuse: U.S. and British practitioners' opinions, practices, and experiences. *Journal of Consulting and Clinical Psychology, 63,* 426–437.

Poon, L. W., & Fozard, J. L. (1978). Speed of retrieval from long-term memory in relation to age, familiarity, and datedness of information. *Journal of Gerontology, 33,* 711–717.

Pope, H. G., & Yurgelun-Todd, D. (1996). The residual cognitive effects of heavy marijuana use in college students. *Journal of the American Medical Association, 275,* 521–527.

Pope, K. S., & Vetter, V. A. (1992). Ethical dilemmas encountered by members of the American Psychological Association. *American Psychologist, 47,* 397–411.

Pope-Davis, D. B., Reynolds, A. L., Dings, J. G., & Nielson, D. (1995). Examining multicultural counseling competencies of graduate students in psychology. *Professional Psychology: Research and Practice, 26,* 322–329.

Porges, S. W., Doussard, R. J. A., & Maita, A. K. (1995). Vagal tone and the physiological regulation of emotion. *Monographs of the Society for Research on Child Development, 59*(2–3), 167–186, 250–283.

Porter, R. H. (1991). Human reproduction and the mother-infant relationship. In T. V. Getchell et al. (Eds.), *Taste and smell in health and disease.* New York: Raven Press.

Porter, R. H., Cernich, J. M., & McLaughlin, F. J. (1983). Maternal recognition of neonates through olfactory cues. *Physiology and Behavior, 30,* 151–154.

Posner, M. I. (1978). *Chronometric explorations of the mind.* Hillsdale, NJ: Lawrence Erlbaum Associates.

Posner, M. I., Nissen, M. J., & Ogden, W. C. (1978). Attended and unattended processing modes: The role of set for spatial location. In H. L. Pick & I. J. Saltzman (Eds.), *Modes of perceiving and processing information.* Hillsdale, NJ: Lawrence Erlbaum Associates.

Posner, M. I., & Peterson, S. E. (1990). The attention system of the human brain. *Annual Review of Neurosciences, 13,* 25–42.

Pousset, F. (1994). Cytokines as mediators in the central nervous system. *Biomedicine and Pharmacotherapy, 48,* 425–431.

Powell, G. J., Nabers, K., & Knight, M. (1992, June). Journal editors' attitudes toward statistical criteria for publication of manuscripts. Paper presented at the 4th annual convention of the American Psychological Society, San Diego.

Powell, R. A., & Boer, D. P. (1994). Did Freud mislead patients to confabulate memories of abuse? *Psychological Reports, 74,* 1283–1298.

Powell, T. J. (Ed.) (1990). *Working with self-help.* Silver Spring, MD: NASW Press.

Power, T. G., & Parke, R. D. (1983). Patterns of mother and father play with their 8-month-old infant: A multiple analysis approach. *Infant Behavior and Development, 6,* 453–459.

Powley, T. L., & Keesey, R. E. (1970). Relationship of body weight to the lateral hypothalamic syndrome. *Journal of Comparative and Physiological Psychology, 70,* 25–36.

Pratkanis, A. R. (1992). The cargo-cult science of subliminal persuasion. *Skeptical Inquirer, 16,* 260–273.

Pratkanis, A. R., & Aronson, E. (1991). *Age of propaganda: The everyday use and abuse of persuasion.* New York: W. H. Freeman.

Pratkanis, A. R., Eskenazi, J., & Greenwald, A. G. (1994). What you expect is what you believe (but not necessarily what you get): A test of the effectiveness of self-help audiotapes. *Basic and applied social psychology, 15,* 251–276.

Preciado, J. (1994). The empirical basis of behavior therapy applications with Hispanics. *The Behavior Therapist, 17,* 63–65.

Predmore, S. C. (1991). Micro-coding of cockpit communications in accident analyses: Crew coordination in the United Airlines flight 232 accident. In R. S. Jensen (Ed.), *Proceedings of the 6th International Symposium on Aviation Psychology.* Columbus: Ohio State University, Department of Aviation.

Preece, J., Sharp, H., Benyon, D., Holland, S., & Carey, T. (1994). *Human-computer interaction.* Reading, MA: Addison-Wesley.

Premack, D. (1965). Reinforcement theory. In D. Levine (Ed.), *Nebraska symposium on motivation.* Lincoln: University of Nebraska Press.

Premack, D. (1971). Language in chimpanzees? *Science, 172,* 808–822.

Prentice-Dunn, S., & Rogers, R. W. (1989). Deindividuation and the self-regulation of behavior. In P. B. Paulus (Ed.), *Psychology of group influence* (2nd ed.). Hillsdale, NJ: Lawrence Erlbaum Associates.

Pressey, S. L. (1926). Simple apparatus which gives tests and scores and teaches. *School and Society, 23,* 373–376.

Pressey, S. L. (1964). Autoinstruction: Perspectives, problems, and potentials. In E. R. Hilgard (Ed.), *Theories of learning and instruction.* Chicago: University of Chicago Press.

Price, B. K., & McNeill, B. W. (1992). Cultural commitment and attitudes toward seeking counseling services in American Indian college students. *Professional Psychology, 23,* 376–381.

Price, R. (1992). Psychosocial impact of job loss on individuals and families. *Current Directions in Psychological Sciences,* 1–11.

Prinzmetal, W. (1992). The word superiority effect does not require a T-scope. *Perception and Psychophysics, 51,* 473–484.

Prochaska, J. O. (1994). Strong and weak principles for progressing from precontemplation to action on the basis of twelve problem behaviors. *Health Psychology, 13,* 47–51.

Prochaska, J. O., & DiClemente, C. C. (1992). Stages of change in the modification of problem behaviors. In M. Hersen, R. M. Eisler, & P. M. Miller (Eds.), *Progress in behavior modification.* Sycamore, IL: Sycamore Press.

Prochaska, J. O., DiClemente, C., & Norcross, J. (1992). In search of how people change: Application to addictive behaviors. *American Psychologist, 47,* 1102–1114.

Prochaska, J. O., & Norcross, J. C. (1994). *Systems of psychotherapy: A transtheoretical analysis* (3rd ed.). Pacific Grove, CA: Brooks/Cole.

Prochaska, J. O., Velicer, W. F., Rossi, J. S., Goldstein, M. G., Marcus, B. H., Rakowski, W., Fiore, C., Harlow, L. L., Redding, C. A., Rosenbloom, D., & Rossi, S. R. (1994). Stages of change and decisional balance for 12 problem behaviors. *Health Psychology, 13,* 39–46.

Proctor, R. & Van Zandt, T. (1994). *Human factors in simple and complex systems.* Boston: Allyn & Bacon.

Pruitt, D. G., & Carnevale, P. J. (1993). *Negotiation in social conflict.* Pacific Grove, CA: Brooks/Cole.

Pruitt, D. G., Pierce, R. S., Zubek, J. M., Mcbillicuddy, N. B., & Welton, G. L. (1991). Determinants of short-term and long-term success in mediation. In S. Worchel & J. A. Simpson (Eds.), *Conflict between people and groups.* Chicago: Nelson-Hall.

Pryor, T. (1995). Diagnostic criteria for eating disorders: DSM–IV revisions. *Psychiatric Annals, 25*(1), 40–45.

Purcell, D. G., & Stewart, A. L. (1991). The object-detection effect: Configuration enhances perception. *Perception and Psychophysics, 50,* 215–224.

Qian, Z., Gilbert, M. E., Colicos, M. A., Kandel, E. R., & Kuhl, D. (1993). Tissue-plasminogen activator is induced as an immediate early gene during seizure, kindling and long-term potentiation. *Nature, 361,* 453–457.

Quay, H. C. (1979). Classification. In H. C. Quay & J. S. Werry (Eds.), *Psychopathological disorders of childhood* (2nd ed.). New York: Wiley.

Quintana, S. M., & Bernal, M. E. (1995). Ethnic minority training in counseling psychology: Comparisons with clinical psychology and proposed standards. *The Counseling Psychologist, 23*(1), 102–121.

Rabbitt, P. (1977). Changes in problem solving ability in old age. In J. E. Birren & K. W. Schaie (Eds.), *Handbook of the psychology of aging.* New York: Van Nostrand Reinhold.

Rachman, S. J. (1990). *Fear and courage* (2nd ed.). San Francisco: W. H. Freeman.

Rachman, S. J., & Hodgson, R. J. (1980). *Obsessions and compulsions.* Englewood Cliffs, NJ: Prentice-Hall.

Rada, J. B., & Rogers, R. W. (1973). *Obedience to authority: Presence of authority and command strength.* Paper presented at the annual convention of the Southeastern Psychological Association.

Radecki, T. E. (1990, April–June). Cartoon monitoring. *National Coalition on Television Violence News,* p. 9.

Raeff, C., Greenfield, P. M., & Quiroz, B. (1995, March). *Developing interpersonal relationships in the cultural contexts of individualism and collectivism.* Paper presented at the biennial meeting of the Society for Research in Child Development, Indianapolis.

Raguram, R., & Bhide, A. (1985). Patterns of phobic neurosis: A retrospective study. *British Journal of Psychiatry, 147,* 557–560.

Raine, A., Brennan, P., & Mednick, S. (1994). Birth complications combined with early maternal rejection at age 1 year predispose to violent crime at age 18 years. *Archives of General Psychiatry, 51,* 984–988.

Raine, A., Buschbaum, M. S., Stanley, J., Lottenberg, S., Abel, L., & Stoddard, J. (1994). Selective reductions in prefrontal glucose metabolism in murderers. *Biological Psychiatry, 36,* 365–373.

Raine, A., Venables, P., & Williams, M. (1990). Relationships between central and autonomic measures of arousal at age 15 years and criminality at age 24 years. *Archives of General Psychiatry, 47,* 1003–1007.

Rakowski, W., Dube, C., Marcus, B., Prochaska, J. O., Velicer, W., & Abrams, D. (1992). Assessing elements of women's decisions about mammography. *Health Psychology, 11,* 111–118.

Ramachandran, V. S. (1988, August). Perceiving shape from shading. *Scientific American,* pp. 76–83.

Ramey, C. T. (1992). High-risk children and IQ: Altering intergenerational patterns. *Intelligence, 16,* 239–256.

Ramey, C. T. (1995, June). *Biology and experience codetermine intellectual development: Beyond additive models.* Paper presented at the convention of the American Psychological Society, New York.

Ramey, C. T., Bryant, D. M., Wasik, B. H., Sparling, J. J., Fendt, K. H., & LaVange, L. M. (1992). Infant health and development program for low birth weight, premature infants: Program elements, family participation, and child intelligence. *Pediatrics, 89,* 454–465.

Ramey, C. T., & Ramey, S. L. (1992). Effective early intervention. *Mental Retardation, 30,* 337–345.

Randi, J. (1987). *Flim Flam!* Buffalo, NY: Prometheus Books.

Randles, J., & Hough, P. (1993). *Spontaneous human combustion.* New York: Dorset Press.

Rao, K. R., & Palmer, J. (1987). The anomaly called Psi: Recent research and criterion. *Brain and Behavior Sciences, 10,* 539–643.

Rapee, R., Brown, T., Antony, M., & Barlow, D. (1992). Response to hyperventilation and inhalation of 5.5% carbon dioxide-enriched air across DSM-III anxiety disorders. *Journal of Abnormal Psychology, 101,* 538–552.

Raskin, D. C. (1986). The polygraph in 1986: Scientific, professional and legal issues surrounding applications and acceptance of polygraph evidence. *Utah Law Review 1986,* 29–74.

Rasmussen, J., Pejtersen, A. M., & Goodstein, L. (1995). *Cognitive engineering: Concepts and applications.* New York: Wiley.

Ratcliff, R., & McKoon, G. (1989). Memory models, text processing, and cue-dependent retrieval. In H. L. Roediger & F. I. M. Craik (Eds.), *Varieties of memory and consciousness.* Hillsdale, NJ: Lawrence Erlbaum Associates.

Ratner, C. (1994). The unconscious: A perspective from sociohistorical psychology. *Journal of Mind and Behavior, 15*(4), 323–342.

Ray, D. W., Wandersman, A., Ellisor, J., & Huntington, D. E. (1982). The effects of high density in a juvenile correctional institution. *Basic and Applied Social Psychology, 3,* 95–108.

Raynor, J. O. (1970). Relationships between achievement-related motives, future orientation, and academic performance. *Journal of Personality and Social Psychology, 15,* 28–33.

Reason, J. (1990). *Human error.* Cambridge, Eng.: Cambridge University Press.

Reber, A. S. (1992). The cognitive unconscious: An evolutionary perspective. *Consciousness and Cognition: An International Journal, 1*(2), 93–133.

Redd, M., & de Castro, J. M. (1992). Social facilitation of eating: Effects of social instruction on food intake. *Physiology and Behavior, 52,* 749–754.

Redd, W. H. (1984). Psychological intervention to control cancer chemotherapy side effects. *Postgraduate Medicine, 75,* 105–113.

Reder, L. M., & Ritter, F. E. (1992). What determines initial feeling of knowing? Familiarity with question terms, not the answer. *Journal of Experimental Psychology: Learning, Memory, and Cognition, 18,* 435–451.

Ree, M. J., & Earles, J. A. (1992). Intelligence is the best predictor of job performance. *Current Directions in Psychological Science, 1,* 86–89.

Reed, G. M., Kemeny, M. E., Taylor, S. E., Wang, H.-Y. J., & Visscher, B. R. (1994). "Realistic acceptance" as a predictor of decreased survival time in gay men with AIDS. *Health Psychology, 13,* 299–307.

Reed, M. A., & Derryberry, D. (1995). Temperament and response processing: Facilitatory and inhibitory consequences of positive and negative motivational states. *Journal of Research in Personality, 29*(1), 59–84.

Reed, S. K. (1992). *Cognition: Theory and applications* (3rd ed.). Pacific Grove, CA: Brooks/Cole.

Reedy, M. N. (1983). Personality and aging. In D. S. Woodruff & J. E. Birren (Eds.), *Aging: Scientific perspectives and social issues* (2nd ed.). Monterey, CA: Brooks/Cole.

Reeves, R. A., Baker, G. A., Boyd, J. G., & Cialdini, R. B. (1991). The door-in-the-face technique: Reciprocal concessions vs. self-presentational explanations. *Journal of Social Behavior and Personality, 6,* 545–558.

Regan, D., Kaufman, L., & Lincoln, J. (1986). Motion in depth and visual acceleration. In K. Boff, L. Kaufman, & J. Thomas (Eds.), *Handbook of perception and human performance.* New York: Wiley.

Regier, D. A., Narrow, W., Rae, D., Manderschied, R., Locke, B., & Goodwin, F. (1993). The de facto U.S. mental and addictive disorders service system: Epidemiologic catchment area prospective 1-year prevalence rates of disorders and services. *Archives of General Psychiatry, 50,* 85–94.

Reicher, G. M. (1969). Perceptual recognition as a function of meaningfulness of stimulus material. *Journal of Experimental Psychology, 87,* 275–280.

Reinisch, J. M., Ziemba-Davis, M., & Sanders, S. A. (1991). Hormonal contributions to sexually dimorphic behavioral development in humans. *Psychoneuroendocrinology, 16,* 213–278.

Reisenzein, R. (1983). The Schachter theory of emotion: Two decades later. *Psychological Bulletin, 94,* 239–264.

Reisman, J. M. (1976). *A history of clinical psychology.* New York: Irvington.

Reiss, A. J., & Roth, J. A. (1993). *Understanding and preventing violence.* Washington, DC: National Academy Press.

Renfrey, G., & Spates, C. R. (1994). Eye movement desensitization: A partial dismantling study. *Journal of Behaviour Therapy and Experimental Psychiatry, 25,* 231–239.

Reno, R. R., Cialdini, R. B., & Kallgren, C. A. (1993). The transsituational influence of social norms. *Journal of Personality and Social Psychology, 64,* 104–112.

Repetti, R. L. (1994). Short-term and long-term processes linking job stressors to father-child interaction. *Social Development, 3,* 1–15.

Rescorla, L. A. (1981). Category development in early language. *Journal of Child Language, 8,* 225–238.

Rescorla, R. (1988). Pavlovian conditioning: It's not what you think it is. *American Psychologist, 43,* 151–159.

Rescorla, R. A. (1968). Probability of shock in the presence and absence of CS in fear conditioning. *Journal of Comparative and Physiological Psychology, 66,* 1–5.

Rescorla, R. A., & Gillian, D. J. (1980). An analysis of the facilitative effect of similarity on second-order conditioning. *Journal of Experimental Psychology: Animal Behavior Processes, 6,* 339–352.

Rescorla, R. A., & Wagner, A. R. (1972). A theory of Pavlovian conditioning: Variations in the effectiveness of reinforcement and nonreinforcement. In A. H. Black & W. F. Prokasy (Eds.), *Classical conditioning II.* New York: Appleton Century Crofts.

Revkin, A. C. (1989, September). Crack in the cradle. *Discover,* pp. 63–69.

Reynolds, B. A., & Weiss, S. (1992). Generation of neurons and astrocytes from isolated cells of the adult mammalian central nervous system. *Science, 255,* 1707–1710.

Reynolds, D. V. (1969). Surgery in the rat during electrical analgesia induced by focal brain stimulation. *Science, 164,* 444–445.

Rhee, E., Uleman, J. S., Lee, H. K., & Roman, R. J. (1995). Spontaneous self-descriptions and ethnic identities in individualistic and collectivistic cultures. *Journal of Personality and Social Psychology, 69,* 142–152.

Rheingold, H. (1991). *Virtual reality.* New York: Summit Books.

Rheingold, H., & Cook, K. (1975). The contents of boys' and girls' rooms as an index of parents' behavior. *Child Development, 46,* 459–463.

Rhodewalt, F., & Zone, J. B. (1989). Appraisal of life change, depression, and illness in hardy and nonhardy women. *Journal of Personality and Social Psychology, 56,* 81–88.

Ribeiro, S. C. M., Tandon, R., Grunhaus, L., & Greden, J. F. (1993). The DST as a predictor of outcome in depression: A meta-analysis. *American Journal of Psychiatry, 150,* 1618–1629.

Richardson, P. H., & Vincent, C. A. (1986). Acupuncture for the treatment of pain: A review of evaluative research. *Pain, 24,* 15–40.

Richardson-Klavehn, A., & Bjork, R. A. (1988). Measures of memory. *Annual Review of Psychology, 39,* 475–543.

Rickels, K., Schweizer, E., Weiss, S., & Zavodnick, S. (1993). Maintenance drug treatment of panic disorder. II: Short- and long-term outcome after drug taper. *Archives of General Psychiatry, 50,* 61–68.

Riedy, C. A., Chavez, M., Figlewicz, D. P., & Woods, S. C. (1995). Central insulin enhances sensitivity to cholecystokinin. *Physiology and Behavior, 58*(4), 755–760.

Riegel, K. F. (1975). Toward a dialectical theory of development. *Human Development, 18,* 50–64.

Riese, M. L. (1986). Temperament stability between the neonatal period and 24 months in full-term and preterm infants. *Infant Behavior and Development, 9,* 305. (Special issue: abstracts of papers presented at the Fifth International Conference on Infant Studies.)

Riger, S. (1992). Epistemological debates, feminist voices: Science, social values, and the study of women. *American Psychologist, 47,* 730–740.

Riggio, R. E. (1989). *Introduction to industrial/organizational psychology.* Glenview, IL: Scott, Foresman.

Rinn, W. E. (1984). The neuropsychology of facial expressions: A review of the neurological and psychological mechanisms for producing facial expressions. *Psychological Bulletin, 95,* 52–77.

Rips, L. J. (1994). *The psychology of proof: Deductive reasoning in human thinking.* Cambridge, MA: MIT Press.

Rittenhouse, C. D., Stickgold, R., & Hobson, J. A. (1994). Constraint on the transformation of characters, objects, and settings in dream reports. *Consciousness and Cognition, 3*(1), 100–113.

Robertson, J., & Robertson, J. (1971). Young children in brief separation: A fresh look. *Psychoanalytic Study of the Child, 26,* 264–315.

Robin, N., & Holyoak, K. J. (1995). Relational complexity and the functions of prefrontal cortex. In M. S. Gazzaniga (Ed.), *The cognitive neurosciences.* Cambridge, MA: MIT Press.

Robins, L. N., & Helzer, J. E. (1986). Diagnosis and clinical assessment: The current state of psychiatric diagnosis. *Annual Review of Psychology, 37,* 409–432.

Robins, L. N., Helzer, J. E., Weissman, M. M., Orvaschel, H., Gruenberg, E., Burke, J. D., Jr., & Regier, D. A. (1984). Lifetime prevalence of specific psychiatric disorders in three sites. *Archives of General Psychiatry, 41,* 949–958.

Robinson, J. H., & Pritchard, W. S. (1992). The role of nicotine in tobacco use. *Psychopharmacology, 108,* 397–407.

Robinson, J. H., & Pritchard, W. S. (1995). "The scientific case that nicotine is addictive": Reply. *Psychopharmacology, 117*(1), 16–17.

Rock, I. (1978). *An introduction to perception.* New York: Macmillan.

Rock, I. (1983). *The logic of perception.* Cambridge, MA: MIT Press.

Rockett, I. R., & Smith, G. S. (1989). Homicide, suicide, motor vehicle crash, and fall mortality: United States' experience in comparative perspective. *American Journal of Public Health, 79,* 1396–1400.

Rodin, J., & Langer, E. J. (1977). Long-term effects of a control-relevant intervention with the institutionalized aged. *Journal of Personality and Social Psychology, 35,* 879–902.

Rodin, J., & Salovey, P. (1989). Health psychology. *Annual Review of Psychology, 40,* 533–580.

Roediger, H. L., III. (1990). Implicit memory: Retention without remembering. *American Psychologist, 45,* 1043–1056.

Roediger, H. L., III, & McDermott, K. B. (1995). Creating false memories: Remembering words not presented in lists. *Journal of Experimental Psychology: Learning, Memory, and Cognition, 21,* 803–814.

Roffwarg, H. P., Hermann, J. H., & Bowe-Anders, C. (1978). The effects of sustained alterations of waking visual input on dream content. In A. M. Arkin, J. S. Antrobus, & S. J. Ellman (Eds.), *The mind in sleep.* Hillsdale, NJ: Lawrence Erlbaum Associates.

Roffwarg, H. P., Muzio, J. N., & Dement, W. C. (1966). Ontogenetic development of the human sleep-dream cycle. *Science, 152,* 604–619.

Rogers, A. G. (1987). Gender differences in moral reasoning: A validity study of two moral orientations. Unpublished doctoral dissertation, Washington University, St. Louis, MO.

Rogers, C. R. (1942). *Counseling and psychotherapy.* Boston: Houghton Mifflin.

Rogers, C. R. (1951). *Client-centered therapy.* Boston: Houghton Mifflin.

Rogers, C. R. (1961). *On becoming a person.* Boston: Houghton Mifflin.

Rogers, C. R. (1970). *Carl Rogers on encounter groups.* New York: Harper & Row.

Rogers, C. R. (1980). *A way of being.* Boston: Houghton Mifflin.

Rogers, J., Madamba, S. G., Staunton, D. A., & Siggins, G. R. (1986). Ethanol increases single unit activity in the inferior olivary nucleus. *Brain Research, 385,* 253–262.

Rogers, M., & Smith, K. H. (1993). Public perceptions of subliminal advertising: Why practitioners shouldn't ignore this issue. *Journal of Advertising Research, 33*(2), 10–18.

Rogers, S. M., & Turner, C. F. (1991). Male-male sexual contact in the U.S.A.: Findings from five sample surveys, 1970–1990. *Journal of Sex Research, 28,* 491–519.

Rogers, T. B. (1995). *The psychological testing enterprise.* Pacific Grove, CA: Brooks/Cole.

Rogers, Y. (1989). Icon design for the user interface. *International Review of Ergonomics, 2,* 129–154.

Rogoff, B., & Waddell, K. J. (1982). Memory for information organized in a scene by children from two cultures. *Child Development, 53,* 1224–1228.

Rokeach, M., & Mezei, L. (1966). Race and shared belief as factors in social choice. *Science, 151,* 167–172.

Ronen, S. (1986). *Comparative and multinational management.* New York: John Wiley & Sons.

Rook, K. S. (1987). Social support versus companionship: Effects on life stress, loneliness, and evaluations by others. *Journal of Personality and Social Psychology, 52,* 1132–1137.

Roper Organization (1992). *Unusual personal experiences: An analysis of data from three national surveys.* Las Vegas, NE: Bigelow Holding Co.

Rosch, E. (1975). Cognitive representations of semantic categories. *Journal of Experimental Psychology: General, 104,* 192–223.

Rosch, E., Mervis, C. B., Gray, W. D., Johnson, D. M., & Boyes-Braem, P. (1976). Basic objects in natural categories. *Cognitive Psychology, 8,* 382–439.

Rose, D. T., Abramson, L. Y., Hodulik, C. J., Halberstadt, L., & Leff, G. (1994). Heterogeneity of cognitive style among depressed inpatients. *Journal of Abnormal Psychology, 103,* 419–429.

Rosen, B. C., & D'Andrade, R. (1959). The psychosocial origins of achievement motivation. *Sociometry, 22,* 188–218.

Rosen, R. (1991). *The healthy company.* Los Angeles: J. P. Tarcher.

Rosenbaum, M., & Bennett, B. (1986). Homicide and depression. *American Journal of Psychiatry, 143,* 367–370.

Rosenbaum, R. (1995, January 15). The great Ivy League nude posture photo scandal. *New York Times Magazine,* pp. 26–31, 40, 46, 55, 56.

Rosenberg, M. B., Friedmann, T., Roberston, R. C., Tuszynski, M., Wolff, J. A., Breakefield, X. O., & Gage, F. H. (1988). Grafting genetically modifed cells to the damaged brain: Restorative effect of NGF expression. *Science, 242,* 1575–1578.

Rosenfarb, I. S., Goldstein, M. J., Mintz, J., & Nuechterlein, K. H. (1995). Expressed emotion and subclinical psychopathology observable within the transactions between schizophrenic patients and their family members. *Journal of Abnormal Psychology, 104,* 259–267.

Rosenfeld, J. P. (1995). Alternative views of Bashore and Rapp's (1993) alternatives to traditional polygraphy: A critique. *Psychological Bulletin, 117*(1), 159–166.

Rosengarten, F. (1969). *The book of spices.* Wynewood, PA: Livingston Publishing Co.

Rosenthal, R. (1994). Science and ethics in conducting, analyzing, and reporting psychological research. *Psychological Science, 5,* 127–134.

Rosenthal, R. (1994). Interpersonal expectancy effects: A 30-year perspective. *Current Directions in Psychological Science, 3,* 176–179.

Rosenthal, R. R. (1966). *Experimenter effects in behavioral research.* New York: Appleton-Century-Crofts.

Rosenthal, R. R., & Jacobson, L. (1968). *Pygmalion in the classroom.* New York: Holt, Rinehart & Winston.

Rosenzweig, M. R. (1992). Psychological science around the world. *American Psychologist, 47,* 718–722.

Ross, C., Joshi, S., & Currie, R. (1990). Dissociative experiences in the general population. *American Journal of Psychiatry, 147,* 1547–1552.

Ross, C., Miller, S., Reagor, P., Bjornson, L., Fraser, G., & Anderson, G. (1990). Structured interview data on 102 cases of multiple personality disorder from four centers. *American Journal of Psychiatry, 147,* 596–610.

Ross, C. A., Anderson, G., Fleisher, W. P., & Norton, G. R. (1991). The frequency of multiple personality disorder among psychiatric inpatients. *American Journal of Psychiatry, 148,* 1717–1720.

Ross, L., & Nisbett, R. E. (1991). *The person and the situation: Perspectives of social psychology.* New York: McGraw-Hill.

Ross, S. I., & Jackson, J. M. (1991). Teachers' expectations for black males' and black females' academic achievement. *Personality and Social Psychology Bulletin, 17,* 78–82.

Ross, S. M., & Ross, L. E. (1971). Comparison of trace and delay classical eyelid conditioning as a function of interstimulus interval. *Journal of Experimental Psychology, 91,* 165–167.

Rothbart, M., & Lewis, S. (1994). Cognitive processes and intergroup relations: A historical perspective: In P. G. Devine, D. L. Hamilton, & T. M. Ostrom (Eds.), *Social cognition: Impact on social psychology* (pp. 347–382). San Diego, CA: Academic Press.

Rothbaum, B. O., Hodges, L. F., Kooper, R., Opdyke, D., Williford, J. S., & North, M. (1995). Effectiveness of computer-generated (virtual reality) graded exposure in the treatment of acrophobia. *American Journal of Psychiatry, 152*(4), 626–628.

Rothblum, E. D. (1994). "I only read about myself on bathroom walls": The need for research on the mental health of lesbians and gay men. *Journal of Clinical and Consulting Psychology, 62*(2), 213–280.

Rothman, R. B. (1994). PCP Site 2—A high-affinity MK-801-insensitive phencyclidine binding site. *Neurotoxicology and Teratology, 16,* 343–353.

Rotter, J. (1982). *The development and application of social learning theory.* New York: Praeger.

Rotter, J. B. (1990). Internal versus external control of reinforcement: A case history of a variable. *American Psychologist, 45,* 489–493.

Rotton, J., & Frey, J. (1985). Air pollution, weather, and violent crimes: Concomitant time-series analysis of archival data. *Journal of Personality and Social Psychology, 49,* 1207–1220.

Rotton, J., Frey, J., Barry, T., Mulligan, M., & Fitzpatrick, M. (1979). The air pollution experience and physical aggression. *Journal of Applied Social Psychology, 9,* 397–412.

Rotton, J., & Kelly, I. W. (1985). Much ado about the full moon: A meta-analysis of lunar-lunacy research. *Psychological Bulletin, 97,* 286–306.

Rouéché, B. (1986, December 8). Cinnabar. *The New Yorker.*

Rovee-Collier, C. (1993). The capacity for long-term memory in infancy. *Current Directions in Psychological Science, 2,* 130–135.

Rowe, W. F. (1993). Psychic detectives: A critical examination. *Skeptical Inquirer, 17,* 159–165.

Rozanski, A., Bairey, C. N., Krantz, D. S., Friedman, J., Resser, K. J., Morell, M., Hilton-Chalfen, S., Hestrin, L., Bietendorf, J., & Berman, D. S. (1988). Mental stress and the induction of silent myocardial ischemia in patients with coronary artery disease. *New England Journal of Mecicine, 318,* 1005–1012.

Rozin, E. (1983). *Ethnic cuisine: The flavor principle cookbook.* Brattleboro, VT: Stephen Greene Press.

Rozin, P. (1982). "Taste-smell confusions" and the duality of the olfactory sense. *Perception and Psychophysics, 31,* 397–401.

Rozin, P. (1990). Getting to like the burn of chili pepper: Biological, psychological, and cultural factors. In B. G. Green, J. R. Mason, & M. R. Kare (Eds.), *Chemical irritation in the nose and mouth.* New York: Marcel Dekker.

Rozin, P. (1996). Towards a psychology of food and eating: From motivation to module to model to marker, morality, meaning and metaphor. *Current Directions in Psychological Science, 5,* 18–24.

Rozin, P., & Schiller, D. (1980). The nature and acquisition of a preference for chili pepper by humans. *Motivation and Emotion, 4*(1), 77–101.

Rozin, P., & Shenker, J. (1989). Liking oral cold and hot irritant sensations: Specificity to type of irritant and locus of stimulation. *Chemical Senses, 14*(6), 771–779.

Rubin, E. (1915). *Synsoplevede figure.* Copenhagen: Gyldendalske.

Rubin, J. Z., Pruitt, D. G., & Kim, S. H. (1994). *Social conflict: Escalation, stalemate, and settlement.* New York: McGraw-Hill.

Rugg, M. D., & Coles, M. G. H. (Eds.). (1995). *Electrophysiology of mind.* New York: Oxford University Press.

Rumbaugh, D. M. (Ed.). (1977). *Language learning by a chimpanzee: The Lana project.* New York: Academic Press.

Rumelhart, D. E., & McClelland, J. L., with the PDP Research Group. (1986). *Parallel distributed processing: Vol. 1. Foundations.* Cambridge, MA: MIT Press.

Rumelhart, D. E., & Todd, P. M. (1992). Learning and connectionist representations. In D. E. Meyer & S. Kornblum (Eds.), *Attention and performance XIV: Synergies in experimental psychology, artificial intelligence, and cognitive neuroscience* (pp. 3–30). Cambridge, MA: MIT Press.

Rusbult, C. E., Verette, J., Whitney, G. A., Slovik, L. F., & Lipkus, I. (1991). Accommodation processes in close relationships: Theory and preliminary empirical evidence. *Journal of Personality and Social Psychology, 60,* 53–78.

Rushton, J. P. (1990). Creativity, intelligence, and psychoticism. *Personality and Individual Differences, 11,* 1291–1298.

Rushton, J. P., Fulker, D. W., Neale, M. C., Nias, D. K. B., & Eysenck, H. J. (1986). Altruism and aggression: The heritability of individual differences. *Journal of Personality and Social Psychology, 50,* 1192–1198.

Russell, J. A. (1991). Culture and the categorization of emotions. *Psychological Bulletin, 110,* 426–450.

Russell, J. A. (1994). Is there universal recognition of emotion from facial expression? A review of the cross-cultural studies. *Psychological Bulletin, 155*(2), 102–141.

Russell, J. A. (1995). Facial expressions of emotion: What lies beyond minimal universality? *Psychological Bulletin, 118,* 379–391.

Russell, M. J. (1976). Human olfactory communication. *Nature, 260,* 520–522.

Russell, R. L. (1995). Introduction to the special section on multivariate psychotherapy process research: Structure and change in the talking cure. *Journal of Consulting and Clinical Psychology, 63,* 3–5.

Russo, N. F., & Denmark, F. L. (1987). Contributions of women to psychology. *Annual Review of Psychology, 38,* 279–298.

Rusted, J. M., & Warburton, D. M. (1992). Facilitation of memory by post-trial administration of nicotine: Evidence for an attentional explanation. *Psychopharmacology, 108,* 452–455.

Rutkowski, G. K., Gruder, C. L., & Romer, D. (1983). Group cohesiveness, social norms, and bystander intervention. *Journal of Personality and Social Psychology, 44,* 545–552.

Ryan, R. H., & Geiselman, R. E. (1991). Effects of biased information on the relationship between eyewitness confidence and accuracy. *Bulletin of the Psychonomic Society, 29,* 7–9.

Rymer, R. (1992, April 23). A silent childhood. *The New Yorker,* pp. 41–81.

Rymer, R. (1993). *Genie: A scientific tragedy.* New York: HarperCollins.

Rynders, J., & Horrobin, J. (1980). Educational provisions for young children with Down's syndrome. In J. Gottlieb (Ed.), *Educating mentally retarded persons in the mainstream* (pp. 109–147). Baltimore: University Park Press.

Sabolich, J. A., & Ortega, G. M. (1994). Sense of feel for lower limb amputees: A phase–one study. *Journal of Prosthetics and Orthotics, 6,* 36–41.

Sacerdoti, E. D. (1977). *A structure for plans and behavior.* New York: Elsevier North-Holland.

Sachdev, P., Hay, P., & Cumming, S. (1992). Surgical treatment of obsessive-compulsive disorder. *Archives of General Psychiatry, 49,* 582–583.

Sachs, J. (1967). Recognition memory for syntactic and semantic aspects of connected discourse. *Perception and Psychophysics, 2,* 437–442.

Sackeim, H. A. (1985, June). The case for ECT. *Psychology Today,* pp. 36–40.

Sackeim, H. A. (1988). Mechanisms of action of electroconvulsive therapy. In A. J. Frances & R. E. Hales (Eds.), *Annual Review of Psychiatry* (Vol. 7). Washington, DC: American Psychiatric Press.

Sackeim, H. A., Gur, R. C. J., & Saucy, M. C. (1978). Emotions are expressed more intensely on the left side of the face. *Science, 202,* 434–436.

Sackoff, J., & Weinstein, L. (1988). The effects of potential self-inflicted harm on obedience to an authority figure. *Bulletin of the Psychonomic Society, 26,* 347–348.

Sacks, O. (1985). *The man who mistook his wife for a hat.* New York: Summit Books.

Sacks, O. (1992, July 27). The landscape of his dreams. *The New Yorker.*

Sage, M. R., & Wilson, A. J. (1994). The blood-brain barrier: An important concept in neuroimaging. *American Journal of Neuroradiology, 15*(4), 601-622.

Sagi, A., van IJzendoorn, M. H., Aviezer, O., Donnell, F., & Mayseless, O. (1994). Sleeping out of home in a kibbutz communal arrangement: It makes a difference for infant-mother attachment. *Child Development, 65,* 992–1004.

Sakairi, Y. (1992). Studies on meditation using questionnaires. *Japanese Psychological Review, 35*(1), 94–112.

Sakmann, B. (1992). Elementary steps in synaptic transmission revealed by currents through single ion channels. *Science, 256,* 503–512.

Saks, M. J. (1992). Obedience versus disobedience to legitimate versus illegitimate authorities issuing good versus evil directives. *Psychological Science, 3,* 221–223.

Salovey, P., Mayer, J. D., & Rosenhan, D. L. (1991). Mood and helping: Mood as a motivator of helping and helping as a regulator of mood. In M. S. Clark (Ed.), *Review of personality and social psychology: Vol. 12. Prosocial behavior* (pp. 215–237). Newbury Park, CA: Sage.

Salthouse, T. A. (1990). Working memory as a processing resource in cognitive aging. *Developmental Review, 10,* 101–124.

Salthouse, T. A., Babcock, R. L., & Shaw, R. J. (1991). Effects of adult age on structural and operational capacities in working memory. *Psychology and Aging, 6,* 118–127.

Salthouse, T. A., & Prill, K. A. (1987). Inferences about age impairments in inferential reasoning. *Psychology and Aging, 2,* 43–51.

Samuelson, C. D., & Messick, D. M. (1995). When do people want to change the rules for allocating shared resources? In D. Schroeder (Ed.), *Social dilemmas: Perspectives on individuals and groups* (pp. 143–162). Westport, CT: Praeger.

Sanderson, W. C., Rapee, R. M., & Barlow, D. H. (1989). The influence of an illusion of control on panic attacks induced via inhalation of 5.5 carbon dioxide-enriched air. *Archives of General Psychiatry, 46,* 157–162.

Sandler, N. D. (1993). Panic gluttons: The cellular telephone scare shows what can happen when purveyors of junk science feed public fear. *Technology Review, 96,* 72–73.

Sanna, L. J. (1992). Self-efficacy theory: Implications for social facilitation and social loafing. *Journal of Personality and Social Psychology, 62,* 774–786.

Santucci, R., Terzian, D., & Kayson, W. A. (1989). Fear of success: Influence of sex, year, and program in college. *Psychological Reports, 64*(2), 551–555.

Sarason, I., Johnson, J., & Siegal, J. (1978). Assessing impact of life changes: Development of the life experiences survey. *Journal of Clinical and Consulting Psychology, 46,* 932–946.

Sarason, I. G. (1984). Stress, anxiety, and cognitive interference: Reactions to tests. *Journal of Personality and Social Psychology, 46*(4), 929–938.

Sarason, I. G., & Sarason, B. R. (Eds.). (1985). *Social support: Theory, research and applications.* The Hague: Martinus Nijhof.

Sarason, I. G., Sarason, B. R., Keefe, D. E., Hayes, B. E., & Shearin, E. N. (1986). Cognitive interference: Situational determinants and traitlike characteristics. *Journal of Personality and Social Psychology, 51,* 215–226.

Sarter, M., Berntson, G. G., & Cacioppo, J. T. (1996). Brain imaging and cognitive neuroscience: Toward strong inference in attributing function to structure. *American Psychologist, 51,* 13–21.

Sarter, N., & Woods, D. (1995). How in the world did we ever get into that mode? Mode error and awareness in supervisory control. *Human Factors, 37,* 5–19.

Sartorius, N., Jablensky, A., Korten, A., Ernberg, G., Anker, M., Cooper, J. E., & Day, R. (1986). Early manifestations and first-contact incidence of schizophrenia in different cultures: A preliminary report on the initial evaluation phase of the WHO Collaborative Study on Determinants of Outcome of Severe Mental Disorders. *Psychological Medicine, 16,* 909–928.

Satir, V. (1982). The therapist and family therapy: Process model. In A. M. Horne & M. M. Ohlsen (Eds.), *Family counseling and therapy.* Itasca, IL: Peacock.

Saudino, K. J., McGuire, S., Reiss, D., Heatherington, E. M., & Plomin, R. (1995). Parent ratings of EAS temperaments in twins, full siblings, half siblings, and step siblings. *Journal of Personality and Social Psychology, 68,* 723–733.

Saudou, F., Amara, D. A., Buhot, M. C., Dierich, A., Hen, R., Lemeur, M., Ramboz, S., & Segu, L., (1994). Enhanced aggressive behavior in mice lacking 5-HT1B receptor. *Science, 265,* 1875–1878.

Saufley, W. H., Otaka, S. R., & Bavaresco, J. L. (1985). Context effects: Classroom tests and context independence. *Memory & Cognition, 13,* 522–528.

Sauter, S., Murphy, L., & Hurrell, J. (1990). Prevention of work-related psychological disorders: A national strategy proposed by the National Institute for Occupational Safety and Health (NIOSH). *American Psychologist, 45,* 1146–1158.

Savage-Rumbaugh, E. S. (1990). Language acquisition in a non-human species: Implications for the innateness debate. *Developmental Psychobiology, 23,* 599–620.

Savage-Rumbaugh, E. S., McDonald, K., Sevcik, R. A., Hopkins, W. D., & Rubert, E. (1986). Spontaneous symbol acquisition and communicative use by pygmy chimpanzees (*Pan paniscus*). *Journal of Experimental Psychology: General, 115,* 211–235.

Savage-Rumbaugh, E. S., Murphy, J., Sevcik, R. A., Brakke, K. E., Williams, S. L., & Rumbaugh, D. M. (1993). Language comprehension in ape and child. *Monographs of the Society for Research in Child Development, 58*(3–4).

Savage-Rumbaugh, E. S., Pate, J. L., Lawson, J., Smith, S. T., & Rosenbaum, S. (1983). Can a chimpanzee make a statement? *Journal of Experimental Psychology: General, 112,* 469–487.

Savin-Williams, R. C. (1994). Verbal and physical abuse as stressors in the lives of lesbian, gay male, and bisexual youths: Associations with school problems, running away, substance abuse, prostitution, and suicide. *Journal of Consulting and Clinical Psychology, 62*(2), 261–269.

Savin-Williams, R. C. (1995). An exploratory study of pubertal maturation timing and self-esteem among gay and bisexual male youths. *Developmental Psychology, 31,* 56–64.

Savin-Williams, R. C., & Demo, D. H. (1984). Developmental change and stability in adolescent self-concept. *Developmental Psychology, 20,* 1100–1110.

Sayers, J. (1991). *Mother of psychoanalysis.* New York: Norton.

Sayers, S. L., & Baucom, D. H. (1991). Role of femininity and masculinity in distressed couples' communication. *Journal of Personality and Social Psychology, 61,* 641–647.

Scarborough, E., & Furumoto, L. (1987). *Untold lives: The first generation of American women psychologists.* New York: Columbia University Press.

Scarr, S. (1993). Biological and cultural diversity: The legacy of Darwin for development. *Child Development, 64,* 1333–1353.

Scarr, S., & Carter-Saltzman, L. (1982). Genetics and intelligence. In R. Sternberg (Ed.), *Handbook of human intelligence.* Cambridge, Eng.: Cambridge University Press.

Scarr, S., & Weinberg, R. A. (1976). IQ test performance of black children adopted by white families. *American Psychologist, 31,* 726–739.

Scarr, S., & Weinberg, R. A. (1978). The influence of "family background" on intellectual attainment. *American Sociological Review, 43,* 674–692.

Schachar, R., & Logan, G. (1990). Impulsivity and inhibitory control in normal development and childhood psychopathology. *Developmental Psychology, 26,* 710–720.

Schachter, S., & Singer, J. (1962). Cognitive, social and physiological determinants of emotional state. *Psychological Review, 69,* 379–399.

Schacter, D. L. (1987). Implicit memory: History and current status. *Journal of Experimental Psychology: Learning, Memory, and Cognition, 13,* 501–518.

Schacter, D. L., Chiu, C.-Y. P., & Ochsner, K. N. (1993). Implicit memory: A selective review. *Annual Review of Neuroscience, 16,* 159–182.

Schacter, D. L., Church, B., & Treadwell, J. (1994). Implicit memory in amnesic patients: Evidence for spared auditory priming. *Psychological Science, 5,* 20–25.

Schacter, D. L., & Cooper, L. A. (1993). Implicit and explicit memory for novel visual objects: Structure and function. *Journal of Experimental Psychology: Learning, Memory, and Cognition, 19*(5), 995–1009.

Schacter, D. L., Cooper, L. A., Delaney, S. M., Peterson, M. A., & Tharan, M. (1991). Implicit memory for possible and impossible objects: Constraints on the construction of structural descriptions. *Journal of Experimental Psychology: Learning, Memory, and Cognition, 17,* 3–19.

Schacter, D. L., & Tulving, E. (1982). Amnesia and memory research. In L. S. Cermak (Ed.), *Human memory and amnesia.* Hillsdale, NJ: Lawrence Erlbaum Associates.

Schaefer, J., Sykes, R., Rowley, R., & Baek, S. (1988, November). *Slow country music and drinking.* Paper presented at the 87th annual meetings of the American Anthropological Association, Phoenix, AZ.

Schafer, J., & Brown, S. A. (1991). Marijuana and cocaine effect expectancies and drug use patterns. *Journal of Counsulting and Clinical Psychology, 59,* 558–565.

Schaffer, C. E., Davidson, R. J., & Saron, C. (1983). Frontal and parietal EEG asymmetry in depressed and non-depressed subjects. *Biological Psychiatry, 18,* 753–762.

Schaie, K. W. (1989). Perceptual speed in adulthood: Cross-sectional and longitudinal studies. *Psychology and Aging, 4,* 443–453.

Schaie, K. W. (1993). The Seattle logitudinal study of adult intelligence. *Current Directions in Psychological Science, 2*(6), 171–175.

Schank, R. C., & Abelson, R. (1977). *Scripts, plans, goals, and understanding.* Hillsdale, NJ: Lawrence Erlbaum Associates.

Schank, R. C., & Hunter, L. (1985). The quest to understand thinking. *Byte, 10*(4), 143–144.

Scheerer, M., Rothmann, R., & Goldstein, K. (1945). A case of "idiot savant": An experimental study of personality organization. *Psychol. Monognomics, 58*(4).

Scheier, M. F., & Carver, C. S. (1987). Dispositional optimism and physical well-being: The influence of generalized outcome expectancies on health. *Journal of Personality, 55,* 169–210.

Scheier, M. F., Carver, C. S. & Bridges, M. W. (1994). Distinguishing optimism from neuroticism (and trait anxiety, self-mastery, and self-esteem): A reevaluation of the Life Orientation Test. *Journal of Personality and Social Psychology, 67,* 1063–1078.

Scheier, M. F., Matthews, K. A., Owens, J. F., Magovern, G. J., Lefebvre, R. C., Abbott, R. A., & Carver, C. S. (1989). Dispositional optimism and recovery from coronary artery bypass surgery: The beneficial effects on physical and psychological well-being. *Journal of Personality and Social Psychology, 57,* 1024–1040.

Schenck, C. H., & Mahowald, M. W. (1992). Motor dyscontrol in narcolepsy: Rapid eye movement (REM) sleep without atonia and REM sleep behavior disorder. *Annals of Neurology, 32*(1), 3–10.

Schieber, M. H., & Hibbard, L. S. (1993, July 23). How somatotopic is the motor cortex hand area? *Science, 261,* 489–492.

Schiff, M., Duyme, M., Dumaret, A., Stewart, J., Tomkiewicz, S., & Feingold, J. (1978). Intellectual status of working class children adopted early into upper-middle class families. *Science, 200,* 1503–1504.

Schildkraut, J. J. (1965). The catecholamine hypothesis of affective disorders: A review of supporting evidence. *American Journal of Psychiatry, 122,* 509–522.

Schindler, U. (1989). Pre-clinical evaluation of cognition-enhancing drugs. *Progress in Neuro-Psychopharmacology and Biological Psychiatry, 13*(Suppl.), S99–S115.

Schlenker, B. R., Phillips, S. T., Boniecki, K. A., & Schlenker, D. R. (1995). Championship pressures: Choking or triumphing in one's home territory? *Journal of Personality and Social Psychology, 68,* 632–648.

Schlesier-Stroop, B. (1984). Bulimia: A review of the literature. *Psychological Bulletin, 95,* 247–257.

Schlossberg, N. K. (1987, May). Taking the mystery out of change. *Psychology Today,* pp. 74–75.

Schmidt, H. (1969). Precognition of a quantum process. *Journal of Parapsychology, 33,* 99–108.

Schmidt, R. A., & Bjork, R. A. (1992, July). New conceptualizations of practice: Common principles in three paradigms suggest new concepts for training. *Psychological Science, 3*(4), 207–217.

Schmidt-Nowara, W., Lowe, A., Wiegand, L., Cartwright, R., Perez-Guerra, F., & Menn, S. (1995). Oral appliances for the treatment of snoring and obstructive sleep apnea: A review. *Sleep, 18*(6), 501–510.

Schnabel, T. (1987). Evaluation of the safety and side effects of antianxiety agents. *American Journal of Medicine, 82* (Suppl. 5A), 7–13.

Schnapf, J. L., Kraft, T. W., & Baylor, D. A. (1987). Spectral sensitivity of human cone photoreceptors. *Nature, 325,* 439–441.

Schneider, B. (1985). Organizational behavior. *Annual Review of Psychology, 36,* 573–611.

Schneider, D. J., Roediger, H. L., III, & Khan, M. (1993). Diverse ways of accessing self knowledge. In T. K. Srull & R. S. Wyer (Eds.), *The mental representation of trait and autobiographical knowledge about the self: Advances in social cognition: Vol. V.* Hillsdale, NJ: Lawrence Erlbaum Associates.

Schneider-Rosen, K., Braunwald, K. G., Carlson, V., & Cicchetti, D. (1985). Current perspectives in attachment theory: Illustration from the study of maltreated infants. In I. Bretherton & E. Waters (Eds.), Growing points of attachment theory and research. *Monographs of the Society for Research in Child Development, 50*(1–2, Serial No. 209).

Schneiderman, B. (1992). *Designing the user interface* (2nd ed.). Reading, MA: Addison-Wesley.

Schommer, M. (1990). Effects of beliefs about the nature of knowledge on comprehension. *Educational Psychology, 82*(3), 498–504.

Schopler, J., Lasko, C. A., Graetz, K. A., Drigotas, S. M., & Smith, V. A. (1991). The generality of the individual-group discontinuity effect: Variations in positivity-negativity of outcomes, players' relative power, and magnitude of outcomes. *Personality and Social Psychology Bulletin, 17,* 612–624.

Schreisheim, C. A., Tepper, B. J., & Tetrault, L. A. (1994). Least preferred co-worker score, situational control, and leadership effectiveness: A meta-analysis of contingency model performance predictions. *Journal of Applied Psychology, 79,* 561–573.

Schroeder, D. A. (1995). An introduction to social dilemmas. In D. Schroeder (Ed.), *Social dilemmas: Perspectives on individuals and groups* (pp. 1–13). Westport, CT: Praeger.

Schroeder, D. A., Penner, L. A., Dovidio, J. F., & Piliavin, J. A. (1995). *The psychology of helping and altruism: Problems and puzzles.* New York: McGraw-Hill.

Schultz, D. P., & Schultz, S. E. (1992). *A history of modern psychology* (5th ed.). Fort Worth, TX: Harcourt, Brace, Jovanovich.

Schultz, D. P., & Schultz, S. E. (1996). *Theories of personality* (6th ed.). Pacific Grove, CA: Brooks/Cole.

Schulz, R. (1978). *The psychology of death, dying, and bereavement.* Reading, MA: Addison-Wesley.

Schwartz, B., & Reisberg, D. (1991). *Learning and memory.* New York: W. W. Norton.

Schwartz, B., & Robbins, S. J. (1995). *Psychology of learning and behavior* (4th ed.). New York: W. W. Norton.

Schwartz, C., Kagan, J., & Snidman, N. (1995, May). Inhibition from toddlerhood to adolescence. Paper presented at the annual meeting of the American Psychiatric Association, Miami.

Schwarzer, R., & Leppin, A. (1991). Social support and health: A theoretical and empirical overview. *Journal of Social and Personal Relationships, 8,* 99–127.

Schweinhart, L. J., & Weikart, D. P. (1991). Response to "Beyond IQ in preschool programs?" *Intelligence, 15,* 313–315.

Schwenk, K. (1994, March 18). Why snakes have forked tongues. *Science, 263,* 1573–1577.

Scoggin, F., & McElreath, L. (1994). Efficacy of psychosocial treatments for geriatric depression: A quantitative review. *Journal of Consulting and Clinical Psychology, 62*(1), 69–74.

Scott, L. & O'Hara, M. W. (1993). Self-discrepancies in clinically anxious and depressed university students. *Journal of Abnormal Psychology, 102,* 282–287.

Scribner, S. (1977). Modes of thinking and ways of speaking: Culture and logic reconsidered. In P. N. Johnson-Laird & P. C. Watson (Eds.), *Thinking: Readings in cognitive science.* New York: Cambridge University Press.

Seab, J. P., Jagust, W. J., Wong, S. T. S., Roos, M. S., Reed, B. R., & Budinger, T. F. (1988). Quantitative NMR measurements of hippocampal atrophy in Alzheimer's disease. *Magnetic Resonance in Medicine, 8,* 200–208.

Seamon, J. G., Williams, P. C., Crowley, M. J., Kim, I. J., Langer, S. A., Orne, P. J., & Wishengrad, D. L. (1995). The mere exposure effect is based on implicit memory: Effects of stimulus type, encoding conditions, and number of exposures on recognition and affect judgements. *Journal of Experimental Psychology: Learning, Memory, and Cognition, 21*(3), 711-721.

Searle, L. V. (1949). The organization of hereditary maze-brightness and maze-dullness. *Genetic Psychology Monographs, 39,* 279–325.

Searleman, A., & Herrmann, D. (1994). *Memory from a broader perspective.* New York: McGraw-Hill.

Sears, R. (1977). Sources of satisfaction of the Terman gifted men. *American Psychologist, 32,* 119–128.

Secord, D., & Peevers, B. (1974). The development and attribution of person concepts. In T. Mischel (Ed.), *Understanding other persons.* Oxford: Blackwell.

Seeley, R. J., Kaplan, J. M., & Grill, H. J. (1995). Effect of occluding the pylorus on intraoral intake: A test of the gastric hypothesis of meal termination. *Physiology and Behavior, 58*(2), 245–249.

Segal, M., & Bloom, F. E. (1976). The action of norepinephrine in the rat hippocampus: III. Hippocampal cellular responses to locus coeruleus stimulation in the awake rat. *Brain Research, 107,* 499–511.

Segal, N. L. (1993). Twin, sibling, and adoption methods: Tests of evolutionary hypotheses. *American Psychologist, 48,* 943–956.

Segall, M. H., Dasen, P. R., Berry, J. W., & Poortinga, Y. H. (1990). *Human behavior in global perspective: An introduction to cross-cultural psychology.* Elmwood, NY: Pergamon Press.

Seidler, K., & Wickens, C. D. (1992). Distance and organization in multifunction displays. *Human Factors, 34,* 555–569.

Seiger, A., Nordberg, A., Vonholst, H., Backman, L., Ebendal, T., Alafuzoff, I., Amberla, K., Hartvig, P., Herlitz, A., Lilja, A., Lundquist, H., Langstrom, B., Meyerson, B., Persson, A., Viitanen, M., Winblad, B., & Olson, L. (1993). Intracranial infusion of purified nerve growth factor to an Alzheimer patient: the 1st attempt of a possible future treatment strategy. *Behavioral Brain Research, 57,* 255–261.

Selco, S. L., & Cohen, N. J. C. (1996). Processing operation–dependent priming in a symmetry detection task. Unpublished manuscript, University of Illinois.

Seligman, M. E. P. (1971). Phobias and preparedness. *Behavior Therapy, 2,* 307–320.

Seligman, M. E. P. (1975). *Helplessness: On depression, development, and death.* San Francisco: W. H. Freeman.

Seligman, M. E. P. (1991). *Learned optimism.* New York: Knopf.

Seligman, M. E. P. (1995). The effectiveness of psychotherapy: The *Consumer Reports* study. *American Psychologist, 50,* 965–974.

Seligman, M. E. P., Castellon, C., Cacciola, J., Shulman, P., Luborsky, L., Ollove, M., & Downing, R. (1988). Explanatory style change during cognitive therapy for unipolar depression. *Journal of Abnormal Psychology, 97,* 13–18.

Seligman, M. E. P., Klein, D. C., & Miller, W. R. (1976). Depression. In H. Leitenberg (Ed.), *Handbook of behavior modification and behavior therapy.* Englewood Cliffs, NJ: Prentice-Hall.

Seligman, M. E. P., & Maier, S. F. (1967). Failure to escape traumatic shock. *Journal of Experimental Psychology, 74,* 1–9.

Selkoe, D. J. (1991, November). Amyloid protein and Alzheimer's disease. *Scientific American,* pp. 68–78.

Sell, R. L., Wells, J. A., & Wypij, D. (1995). The prevalence of homosexual behavior and attraction in the United States, the United Kingdom, and France: Results of national population-based samples. *Archives of Sexual Behavior, 24*(3), 235–248.

Selman, R. L. (1980). *The growth of interpersonal understanding: Developmental and clinical analyses.* New York: Academic Press.

Selman, R. L. (1981). The child as a friendship philosopher. In S. R. Asher & J. M. Gottman (Eds.), *The development of children's friendships.* New York: Cambridge University Press.

Selye, H. (1956). *The stress of life.* New York: McGraw-Hill.

Selye, H. (1976). *The stress of life* (2nd ed.). New York: McGraw-Hill.

Senders, J. W., & Moray, N. P. (1991). *Human error.* Hillsdale, NJ: Lawrence Erlbaum Associates.

Serfaty, M., & Masterton, G. (1993). Fatal poisoning attributed to benzodiazepines in Britain during the 1980s. *British Journal of Psychiatry, 163,* 386–393.

Serpell, R. (1994). The cultural construction of intelligence. In W. J. Lonner & R. S. Malpass (Eds.), *Psychology and culture.* Boston: Allyn & Bacon.

Servan-Schreiber, E., & Anderson, J. R. (1990). Learning artificial grammars with competitive chunking. *Journal of Experimental Psychology: Learning, Memory, and Cognition, 16,* 592–608.

Service, R. F. (1994, October 14). Neuroscience: Will a new type of drug make memory-making easier? *Science, 266,* 218–219.

Sevcik, R. A., & Savage-Rumbaugh, E. S. (1994). Language comprehension and use by great apes. *Language and Communication, 14,* 37–58.

Shaffer, D., Gould, M., & Hicks, R. (1994). Worsening suicide rate in black teenagers. *American Journal of Psychiatry, 151,* 1810–1812.

Shaffer, D. R. (1973). *Children's responses to a hypothetical proposition.* Unpublished manuscript, Kent State University.

Shand, M. A. (1982). Sign-based short-term memory coding of American Sign Language and printed English words by congenitally deaf signers. *Cognitive Psychology, 14,* 1–12.

Shapiro, D. H., & Walsh, R. N. (Eds.) (1984). *Meditation: Classical and contemporary perspectives.* New York: Aldine.

Shapiro, F. (1989a). Eye movement desensitization: A new treatment for post-traumatic stress disorder. *Journal of Behavior Therapy and Experimental Psychiatry, 20,* 211–217.

Shapiro, F. (1989b). Efficacy of the eye movement desensitization procedure in the treatment of traumatic memories. *Journal of Traumatic Stress, 2,* 199–223.

Shapiro, F. (1991). Eye movement desensitization and reprocessing procedure: From EMD to EMD/R—A new treatment model for anxiety and related traumata. *The Behavior Therapist, 15,* 133–135.

Shapiro, F. (1994). EMDR: In the eye of a paradigm shift. *The Behavior Therapist, 17,* 153–156.

Shapiro, F. (1995). *Eye movement desensitization and reprocessing: Basic principles, protocols, and procedures.* New York: Guilford.

Shargill, N. S., Tsujii, S., Bray, G. A., & Erlanson, A. C. (1991). Enterostatin supresses food intake following injection into the third ventricle in rats. *Brain Research, 544*(1), 137–140.

Shaver, P. (1994, August). Attachment and care-giving in adult romantic relationships. Invited address presented at the annual meeting of the American Psychological Association, Los Angeles.

Shaver, P. R., & Brennan, K. A. (1992). Attachment styles and the "Big Five" personality traits: Their connections with each other and with romantic relationship outcomes. *Personality and Social Psychology Bulletin, 18,* 536–545.

Shaw, S. F., Cullen, J. P., McGuire, J. M., & Brinckerhoff, L. C. (1995). Operationalizing a definition of learning disabilities. *Journal of Learning Disabilities.*

Shaywitz, B. A., Shaywitz, S. E., Pugh, K. R., Constable, R. T., Skudlarski, P., Fulbright, R. K., Bronen, R. A., Fletcher, J. M., Shankweller, D. P., Katz, L., & Gore, J. C. (1995). Sex differences in the functional organization of the brain for language. *Nature, 373,* 607–609.

Shedler, J., & Block, J. (1990). Adolescent drug use and psychological health: A longitudinal inquiry. *American Psychologist, 45,* 612–630.

Shepard, C., Kohut, J. J., & Sweet, R. (1989). *News of the weird.* New York: New American Library.

Shepherd, C. (1994, March 31). News of the weird. *Daily Illini.*

Shepherd-Look, D. L. (1982). Sex differentiation and the development of sex roles. In B. B. Wolman & G. Stricker (Eds.), *Handbook of developmental psychology.* Englewood Cliffs, NJ: Prentice-Hall.

Shepperd, J. A. (1993). Productivity loss in performance groups: A motivation analysis. *Psychological Bulletin, 113,* 67–81.

Sher, K., Walitzer, K., Wood, P., & Brent, E. (1991). Characteristics of children of alcoholics: Putative risk factors, substance use and abuse, and psychopathology. *Journal of Abnormal Psychology, 100,* 427–448.

Sher, K. J., & Levenson, R. W. (1982). Risk for alcoholism and individual differences in the stress-response-dampening effects of alcohol. *Journal of Abnormal Psychology, 91,* 350–367.

Sheridan, T. B. (1993). My anxieties about virtual environments. *Presence, 2,* 141–142.

Sherif, M. (1937). An experimental approach to the study of attitudes. *Sociometry, 1,* 90–98.

Sherin, J. E., Shiromani, P. J., McCarley, R. W., & Saper, C. B. (1996). Activation of ventrolateral preoptic neurons during sleep. *Science, 271,* 216–219.

Sherman, S. J. (1980). On the self-erasing nature of errors of prediction. *Journal of Personality and Social Psychology, 39,* 211–221.

Sherwin, B. B., & Gelfand, M. M. (1987). The role of androgen in the maintenance of sexual functioning in oophorectomized women. *Psychosomatic Medicine, 49,* 397–409.

Sherwin, B. B., Gelfand, M. M., & Brender, W. (1985). Androgen enhances sexual motivation in females: A prospective crossover study of sex steroid administration in the surgical menopause. *Psychosomatic Medicine, 47,* 339–351.

Shiffman, S. (1993). Smoking cessation treatment: Any progress? *Journal of Consulting and Clinical Psychology, 61,* 718–722.

Shimamura, A. P., Berry, J. M., Mangels, J. A., Rusting, C. L., & Jurica, P. J. (1995). Memory and cognitive abilities in university professors: Evidence for successful aging. *Psychological Science, 6,* 271–277.

Shneiderman, B. (1992). *Designing the user interface* (2nd ed.). Reading, MA: Addison–Wesley.

Shore, M. F. (1992). Community mental health: Corpse or phoenix? Personal reflections on an era. *Professional Psychology: Research and Practice, 23,* 257–262.

Shortcliffe, E. H. (1983). Medical consultation systems: Designing for doctors. In M. E. Sime & M. J. Coombs (Eds.), *Designing for human computer communication.* New York: Academic Press.

Shweder, R. A., Much, N. C., Mahapatra, M., & Park, L. (1994). The "big three" of morality (autonomy, community, and divinity), and the "big three" explanations of suffering, as well. In A. Brandt & P. Rozin (Eds.), *Morality and health.* Stanford, CA: Stanford University Press.

Siegel, J. M., & Rogawski, M. A. (1988). A function for REM sleep: Regulation of noradrenergic receptor sensitivity. *Brain Research Review, 13,* 213–233.

Siegel, S., Hirson, R. E., Krank, M. D., & McCully, J. (1982). Heroin "overdose" death: The contribution of drug associated environmental cues. *Science, 216,* 430–437.

Siegler, R. S. (1994). Cognitive variability: A key to understanding cognitive development. *Current Directions in Psychological Science, 3,* 1–4.

Siegler, R. S. (1995). Children's thinking: How does change occur? In W. Schneider & F. Weinert (Eds.), *Memory performance and competencies: Issues in growth and development.* Hillsdale, NJ: Lawrence Erlbaum Associates.

Siegman, A. W., Dembroski, T. W., & Crump, D. (1992). Speech rate, loudness, and cardiovascular reactivity. *Journal of Behavioral Medicine, 15,* 519–532.

Siever, L. J., & Davis, K. L. (1985). Overview: Toward a dysregulation hypothesis of depression. *American Journal of Psychiatry, 142,* 1017–1031.

Siever, M. D. (1994). Sexual orientation and gender as factors in socioculturally acquired vulnerability to body dissatisfaction and eating disorders. Special section: Mental health of lesbian and gay men. *Journal of Consulting and Clinical Psychology, 62*(2), 252–260.

Sifneos, P. (1979). *Short-term dynamic psychotherapy: Evaluating and technique.* New York: Plenum.

Sigman, M. (1995). Nutrition and child development: More food for thought. *Current Directions in Psychological Science, 4,* 52–55.

Silbersweig, D. A., Stern, E., Frith, C., Cahill, C., Holmes, A., Grootoonk, S., Seaward, J., McKenna, P., Chua, S. E., Schnorr, L., Jones, T., & Frackowiak, R. S. J. (1995, November). A functional neuroanatomy of hallucinations in schizophrenia. *Nature, 378,* 176–179.

Silbert, M. H., & Pines, A. M. (1984). Pornography and sexual abuse of women. *Sex Roles, 10,* 857–868.

Sillito, A. M., Jones, H. E., Gerstein, G. L., & West, D. C. (1994). Feature-linked synchronization of thalamic relay cell firing induced by feedback from the visual cortex. *Nature, 369,* 479–482.

Silva, A. J., Paylor, R., Wehner, J. M., & Tonegawa, S. (1992). Impaired spatial learning in alpha-calcium-calmodulin kinsase-II mutant mice. *Science, 257,* 206–211.

Silver, B., Poland, R., & Lin, K.-M. (1993). Ethnicity and pharmacology of tricyclic antidepressants. In K.-M. Lin, R. Poland, & G. Nakasaki (Eds.), *Psychopharmacology and psychobiology of ethnicity.* Washington, DC: American Psychiatric Association Press.

Silver, R. L., & Wortman, C. B. (1980). Coping with undesirable life events. In J. Garber & M. E. P. Seligman (Eds.), *Human helplessness: Theory and applications* (pp. 279–340). New York: Academic Press.

Silverman, K., Evans, A. M., Strain, E. C., & Griffiths, R. R. (1992). Withdrawal syndrome after the double-blind cessation of caffeine consumption. *New England Journal of Medicine, 327,* 1109–1114.

Silverstein, L. B. (1996). Evolutionary psychology and the search for sex differences. *American Psychologist, 51,* 160–161.

Silviera, J. M. (1971). *Incubation: The effect of interruption timing and length on problem solution and quality of problem processing.* Unpublished doctoral dissertation, University of Oregon, Eugene.

Simmons, C. H., von Kolke, A., & Shimizu, H. (1986). Attitudes toward romantic love among American, German, and Japanese students. *Journal of Social Psychology, 126,* 793–799.

Simon, H. A. (1977). *Models of discovery and other topics in the methods of science.* Boston: Pallas Paperbacks.

Simon, H. A., & Gilmartin, K. (1973). A simulation of memory for chess positions. *Cognitive Psychology, 5,* 29–46.

Simpson, J. A., Rholes, W. S., & Nelligan, J. S. (1992). Support seeking and support giving within couples in an anxiety-provoking situation: The role of attachment styles. *Journal of Personality and Social Psychology, 62,* 434–446.

Sims, J. H., & Baumann, D. D. (1972). The tornado threat: Coping styles of the north and south. *Science, 17,* 1386–1392.

Sinclair, R. C., Hoffman, C., Mark, M. M., Martin, L. L., & Pickering, T. L. (1994). Construct accessibility and the misattribution of arousal. *Psychological Science, 5*(1), 15–19.

Singh, D. (1995). Female judgment of male attractiveness and desirability for relationships: Role of waist-to-hip ratio and financial status. *Journal of Personality and Social Psychology, 69,* 1089–1101.

Skinner, B. F. (1938). *The behavior of organisms.* New York: Appleton.

Skinner, B. F. (1958). Teaching machines. *Science, 128,* 969–977.

Skinner, B. F. (1961a). *Cumulative record* (3rd ed.). Englewood Cliffs, NJ: Prentice-Hall.

Skinner, B. F. (1961b). Teaching machines. *Scientific American* (November), pp. 91–102.

Skoe, E. E., & Diessner, R. (1994). Ethics of care, justice, identity, and gender: An extension and replication. *Merrill-Palmer Quarterly, 40,* 272–289.

Slamecka, N. J., & McElree, B. (1983). Normal forgetting of verbal lists as a function of their degree of learning. *Journal of Experimental Psychology: Learning, Memory, and Cognition, 9,* 384–397.

Slater, A., Mattock, A., Brown, E., & Bremner, J. G. (1991). Form perception at birth. *Journal of Experimental Child Psychology, 51,* 395–406.

Sleek, S. (1996, January). Psychologists build a culture of peace. *APA Monitor,* pp. 1, 33.

Sloan, J. H., Rivara, F. P., Reay, D. T., James, A. F., & Kellermann, A. L. (1990). Firearm regulations and rates of suicide: A comparison of two metropolitan areas. *New England Journal of Medicine, 322,* 369–373.

Sloane, R. B., Staples, F. R., Cristol, A. H., Yorkston, N. J., & Whipple, K. (1975). *Psychotherapy versus behavior therapy.* Cambridge, MA: Harvard University Press.

Slovic, P. (1984). *Facts versus fears: Understanding perceived risk.* Paper presented at science and public policy seminar sponsored by the Federation of Behavioral and Psychological and Cognitive Sciences, Washington, DC.

Small, I. F., Small, J. G., & Milstein, V. (1986). Electroconvulsive therapy. In P. A. Berger & H. K. H. Brodie (Eds.), *American handbook of psychiatry: Biological psychiatry* (2nd ed., Vol. 8). New York: Basic Books.

Smith, A., & Weissman, M. (1992). Epidemiology. In E. S. Paykel (Ed.), *Handbook of affective disorders* (2nd ed.). New York: Guilford.

Smith, A. C., III, & Kleinman, S. (1989). Managing emotions in medical school: Students' contacts with the living and the dead. *Social Psychology Quarterly, 52,* 56–69.

Smith, A. P., & Maben, A. (1993). Effects of sleep deprivation, lunch, and personality on performance, mood, and cardiovascular function. *Physiology and Behavior, 54*(5), 967–972.

Smith, C. A., & Ellsworth, P. C. (1987). Patterns of appraisal and emotion related to taking an exam. *Journal of Personality and Social Psychology, 52,* 475–488.

Smith, D., & Dumont, F. (1995). A cautionary study: Unwarranted interpretations of the Draw-a-Person test. *Professional Psychology: Research and Practice, 26,* 298–303.

Smith, D. E., Marcus, M. D., & Eldredge, K. L. (1994). Binge eating syndromes: A review of assessment and treatment with an emphasis on clinical application. *Behavior Therapy, 25*(4), 635–658.

Smith, E. R. (1990). Content and process specificity in the effects of prior experiences. In T. K. Srull & R. S. Wyer (Eds.), *Advances in social cognition: Vol. III. Content and process specificity in the effects of prior experiences.* Hillsdale, NJ: Lawrence Erlbaum Associates.

Smith, E. R. (1993). Social identity and social emotions: Toward new conceptualizations of prejudice. In D. M. Mackie & D. L. Hamilton (Eds.), *Affect, cognition, and stereotyping* (pp. 297–315). San Diego, CA: Academic Press.

Smith, E. R., & Henry, S. (1996). *An in-group becomes part of the self: Response time evidence.* Unpublished manuscript, Purdue University.

Smith, E. R., & Mackie, D. M. (1995). *Social psychology.* New York: Worth.

Smith, G. F., & Dorfman, D. D. (1975). The effect of stimulus uncertainty on the relationship between frequency of exposure and liking. *Journal of Personality and Social Psychology, 31,* 150–155.

Smith, G. R., Rost, K., & Kashner, T. M. (1995). A trial of the effect of a standardized psychiatric consultation on health outcomes and costs in somatizing patients. *Archives of General Psychiatry, 52,* 238–243.

Smith, H. S., & Cohen, L. H. (1993). Self-complexity and reactions to a relationship breakup. *Journal of Clinical and Social Psychology, 12,* 367–384.

Smith, J. (1993). *Understanding stress and coping.* New York: Macmillan.

Smith, K. D., Keating, J. P., & Stotland, E. (1989). Altruism reconsidered: The effect of denying feedback on a victim's status to empathic witnesses. *Journal of Personality and Social Psychology, 57,* 641–650.

Smith, M. (1988). Recall of spatial location by the amnesic patient HM. Special issue: Single case-studies in amnesia—Theoretical Advances. *Brain and Cognition, 7,* 178–183.

Smith, M. L., Glass, G. V., & Miller, T. I. (1980). *The benefits of psychotherapy.* Baltimore: Johns Hopkins University Press.

Smith, P. B., & Bond, M. H. (1993). *Social psychology across cultures: Analysis and perspectives.* Boston, MA: Allyn & Bacon.

Smith, S., & Freedman, D. G. (1983, April). *Mother-toddler interaction and maternal perception of child temperament in two ethnic groups: Chinese-American and European-American.* Paper presented at the meeting of the Society for Research in Child Development, Detroit, MI.

Smith, S. M., Glenberg, A. M., & Bjork, R. A. (1978). Environmental context and human memory. *Memory & Cognition, 6,* 342–355.

Smith, S. M., Vela, E., & Williamson, J. E. (1988). Shallow input processing does not induce environmental context-dependent recognition. *Bulletin of the Psychonomic Society, 26,* 537–540.

Smith, S. S., O'Hara, B. F., Persico, A. M., Gorelick, D. A., Newlin, D. B., Vlahov, D., Solomon, L., Pickens, R., & Uhl, G. R. (1992). Genetic vulnerability to drug abuse. The D_2 dopamine receptor *Taq* i B1 restriction fragment length polymorphism appears more frequently in polysubstance abusers. *Archives of General Psychiatry, 49,* 723–727.

Smith, T. W. (1992). Hostility and health: Current status of a psychosomatic hypothesis. *Health Psychology, 11,* 139–150.

Smith, T. W., & Frohm, K. D. (1985). What's so unhealthy about hostility? Construct validity and psychosocial correlates of the Cook and Medley HO scale. *Health Psychology, 4,* 503–520.

Smith, T. W., McGonigle, M., Turner, C., Ford, M., & Slattery, M. (1991). Cynical hostility in adult male twins. *Psychosomatic Medicine, 53,* 684–692.

Smyer, M. A., Balster, R. L., Egli, D., Johnson, D. L., Kilbey, M. M., Leith, N. J., & Puente, A. E. (1993). Summary of the report of the ad hoc task force on psychopharmacology of the American Psychological Association. *Professional Psychology: Research and Practice, 24*(4), 394–403.

Smythe, M. M., Collins, A. F., Morris, P. E., & Levy, P. (1995). *Cognition in action* (2nd ed.). Hillsdale, NJ: Lawrence Erlbaum Associates.

Snarey, J. (1987). A question of morality. *Psychological Bulletin, 97,* 202–232.

Sniezek, J. A. (1992). Groups under uncertainty: An examination of confidence in group decision making. *Organizational Behavior and Human Decision Processes, 52*, 124–155.

Snodgrass, S. R. (1994). Cocaine babies: A result of multiple teratogenic influences. *Journal of Child Neurology, 9*(3), 227–233.

Snow, R. E. (1995). Pygmalion and intelligence? *Current Directions in Psychological Science, 4*, 169–171.

Snowden, L. R., & Cheung, F. (1990). Use of inpatient mental health services by members of ethnic minority groups. *American Psychologist, 45*, 347–355.

Snyder, C. R., & Higgins, R. L. (1988). Excuses: Their effective role in the negotiation of reality. *American Psychologist, 104*, 23–35.

Snyder, D. K., & Wills, R. M. (1989). Behavioral versus insight-oriented marital therapy: Effects on individual and interspousal functioning. *Journal of Consulting and Clinical Psychology, 57*, 39–46.

Snyder, M., & Haugen, J. A. (1994). Why does behavioral confirmation occur? A functional perspective on the role of the perceiver. *Journal of Experimental Social Psychology, 30*, 218–246.

Snyder, M., & Haugen, J. A. (1995). Why does behavioral confirmation occur? A functional perspective on the role of the target. *Personality and Social Psychology Bulletin, 21*, 963–974.

Snyderman, M., & Rothman, S. (1987). Survey of expert opinion on intelligence and aptitude testing. *American Psychologist, 42*, 137–144.

Soetens, E., Casaer, S., D'Hooge, R., & Hueting, J. E. (1995). Effect of amphetamine on long-term retention of verbal material. *Psychopharmacology, 119*, 155–162.

Soken, N. H., & Pick, A. D. (1992). Intermodal perception of happy and angry expressive behaviors by seven–month–old infants. *Child Development, 63*, 787–795.

Sokoloff, L. (1981). Localization of functional activity in the central nervous system by measurement of glucose utilization with radioactive deoxyglucose. *Journal of Cerebral Blood Flow and Metabolism, 1*, 7–36.

Soloman, Z., Mikulincer, M., & Avitzur, E. (1988). Coping, loss of control, social support, and combat-related posttraumatic stress disorder: A prospective study. *Journal of Personality and Social Psychology, 55*, 279–285.

Solomon, R. L. (1980). The opponent-process theory of acquired motivation: The costs of pleasure and the benefits of pain. *American Psychologist, 35*, 691–712.

Solomon, R. L., & Corbit, J. D. (1974). An opponent-process theory of motivation: I. Temporal dynamics of affect. *Psychological Review, 81*, 119–145.

Solomon, R. L., Kamin, L. J., & Wynne, L. C. (1953). Traumatic avoidance learning: The outcomes of several extinction procedures with dogs. *Journal of Abnormal and Social Psychology, 48*, 291–302.

Solso, A. L. (1987). *Inside the Russian mind.* Unpublished manuscript.

Solso, A. L. (1991). *Cognitive psychology* (3rd ed.). Boston: Allyn & Bacon.

Sorce, J., Emde, R., Campos, J., & Klinnert, M. (1981, April). *Maternal emotional signaling: Its effect on the visual cliff behavior of one-year-olds.* Paper presented at the meetings of the Society for Research in Child Development, Boston, MA.

Spangler, W. (1992). Validity of questionnaire and TAT measures of need for achievement: Two meta-analyses. *Psychological Bulletin, 112*, 140–154.

Spanos, N. P. (1994). Multiple identity enactments and multiple personality disorder: A sociocognitive perspective. *Psychological Bulletin, 116*, 143–165.

Spanos, N. P., Burnley, M. C. E., & Cross, P. A. (1993). Response expectancies and interpretations as determinants of hypnotic responding. *Journal of Personality and Social Psychology, 65*(6), 1237–1242.

Spates, C. R., & Burnette, M. M. (1995). Eye movement desensitization: Three unusual cases. *Journal of Behaviour Therapy and Experimental Psychiatry, 26*, 51–55.

Spearman, C. (1904). General intelligence objectively determined and measured. *American Journal of Psychology, 15*, 201–293.

Spector, I. P., & Carey, M. P. (1990). Incidence and prevalence of the sexual dysfunctions: A critical review of the empirical literature. *Archives of Sexual Behavior, 19*(4), 389–408.

Speer, D. C., & Greenbaum, P. E. (1995). Five methods for computing significant individual client change and improvement rates: Support for an individual growth curve approach. *Journal of Consulting and Clinical Psychology, 63*, 1044–1048.

Spelke, E., & van de Walle, G. (1993). Perceiving and reasoning about objects: Insights from infants. In N. Eilan, W. Brewer, & R. McCarthy (Eds.), *Spatial representation.* Oxford: Basil Blackwell.

Spelke, E. S., Breinlinger, K., Macomber, J., & Jacobson, K. (1992). Origins of knowledge. *Psychological Review, 99*, 605–632.

Spencer, S. B., & Hemmer, R. C. (1993). Therapeutic bias with gay and lesbian clients: A functional analysis. *The Behavior Therapist, 16*, 93–97.

Sperry, R. W. (1968). Hemisphere deconnection and unity in conscious awareness. *American Psychologist, 23*, 723–733.

Sperry, R. W. (1974). Lateral specialization in the surgically separated hemispheres. In F. O. Schmitt & F. G. Wordon (Eds.), *The neurosciences third study program.* Cambridge, MA: MIT Press.

Sperry, R. W. (1993). The impact and promise of the cognitive revolution. *American Psychologist, 48*(8), 878–885.

Spielman, A. J., Saskin, P., & Thorpy, M. J. (1987). Treatment of chronic insomnia through restriction of time in bed. *Sleep, 10*, 45–56.

Spitz, H. H. (1991). Commentary on Locurto's "Beyond IQ in preschool programs?" *Intelligence, 15*, 327–333.

Spitzer, R., First, M., Williams, J., Kendler, K., Pincus, A., & Tucker, G. (1992). Now is the time to retire the term "Organic Mental Disorders." *American Journal of Psychiatry, 149*, 240–244.

Spitzer, R. L., Severino, S. K., Williams, J. B., & Parry, B. L. (1989). Late luteal phase dysphoric disorder and DSM-III-R. *American Journal of Psychiatry, 146*, 892–897.

Spitzer, R. L., Skodol, A. E., Gibbon, M., & Williams, J. B. W. (1983). *Psychopathology: A casebook.* New York: McGraw-Hill.

Sporer, S. L., Penrod, S., Read, D., & Cutler, B. (1995). Choosing, confidence, and accuracy: A meta-analysis of the confidence-accuracy relation in eyewitness testimony. *Psychological Bulletin, 118*, 315–327.

Sprafka, J., Folsom, A., Burke, G., Hahn, G., & Pirie, P. (1990). Type A behavior and its association with cardiovascular disease prevalence in blacks and whites: The Minnesota Heart Survey. *Journal of Behavioral Medicine, 13*, 1–13.

Sprecher, S., Hatfield, E., Anthony, C., & Potapova, E. (1994). Token resistance to sexual intercourse and consent to unwanted sexual intercourse: College students' dating experiences in three countries. *Journal of Sex Research, 31*(2), 125–132.

Sprecher, S., Sullivan, Q., & Hatfield, E. (1994). Mate selection preferences: Gender differences examined in a national sample. *Journal of Personality and Social Psychology, 66*, 1074–1080.

Springer, K., & Belk, A. (1994). The role of physical contact and association in early contamination sensitivity. *Developmental Psychology, 30*(6), 864–868.

Springer, S. P., & Deutsch, G. (1989). *Left brain, right brain.* San Francisco: W. H. Freeman.

Spruston, N., Schiller, Y., Stuart, G., & Sakmann, B. (1995, April 14). Activity-dependent action potential invasion and calcium influx into hippocampal CA1 dendrites. *Science, 268*, 297–300.

Squire, L. (1987). *Memory and brain.* New York: Oxford University Press.

Squire, L. R. (1986). Mechanisms of memory. *Science, 232*, 1612–1619.

Squire, L. R. (1992). Memory and the hippocampus: A synthesis from findings with rats, monkeys, and humans. *Psychological Review, 99*, 195–231.

Squire, L. R., & McKee, R. (1992). The influence of prior events on cognitive judgments in amnesia. *Journal of Experimental Psychology: Learning, Memory, and Cognition, 18*, 106–115.

Squire, L. R., & Zola-Morgan, S. (1991). The medial temporal lobe memory system. *Science, 253*, 1380–1386.

Squire, S. (1987, November 22). Shock therapy's return to respectability. *New York Times Magazine*, pp. 78–89.

St. Lawrence, J. S. (1993). African-American adolescents' knowledge, health-related attitudes, sexual behavior, and contraceptive decisions: Implications for the prevention of adolescent HIV infection. *Journal of Counsulting Clinical Psychology, 61*, 104–112.

St. Lawrence, J. S., Jefferson, K. W., Alleyne, E., & Brasfield, T. L. (1995). Comparison of education versus behavioral skills training interventions in lowering sexual HIV-risk behavior of substance-dependent adolescents. *Journal of Consulting and Clinical Psychology, 63*, 154–157.

Stacy, A. W., Sussman, S., Dent, C. W., & Flay, B. R. (1992). Moderators of peer social influence in adolescent smoking. *Personality and Social Psychology Bulletin, 18*, 163–172.

Stacy, A. W., Widaman, K. F., & Marlatt, G. A. (1990). Expectancy models of alcohol use. *Journal of Personality and Social Psychology, 58*, 918–928.

Staddon, J. E. R., & Ettinger, R. H. (1989). *Learning: An introduction to the principles of adaptive behavior.* San Diego: Harcourt Brace Jovanovich.

Staecker, H., Lefebvre, P., Malgrange, B., Moonen, G., & Vandewater, T. R. (1995, February 3). Regeneration and mammalian auditory hair cells: Reply. *Science, 267*, 709–711.

Standing, L., Conezio, J., & Haber, R. N. (1970). Perception and memory for pictures: Single-trial learning of 2500 visual stimuli. *Psychonomic Science, 19*, 73–74.

Stankov, L. (1988). Aging, attention and intelligence. *Psychology and Aging, 3*, 59–74.

Stankov, L. (1989). Attentional resources and intelligence: A disappearing link. *Personality and Individual Differences, 10*, 957–968.

Stanley, B. G., & Gillard, E. R. (1994). Hypothalamic neuropeptide Y and the regulation of eating behavior and body weight. *Current Directions in Psychological Science, 3*(1), 9–15.

Stanley, B. G., Willett, V. L., Donias, H. W., & Ha-Lyen, H. (1993). The lateral hypothalamus: A primary site mediating excitatory aminoacid-elicited eating. *Brain Research, 630*(1–2), 41–49.

Stansfield, S. A. (1994). A distributed virtual reality simulation system for situational training. *Presence, 3,* 360–366.

Staples, S. L. (1996). Human response to environmental noise. *American Psychologist, 51,* 143–150.

Starkey, P. (1992). The early development of numerical reasoning. *Cognition, 43,* 93–126.

Stasser, G. (1991). Pooling of unshared information during group discussion. In S. Worchel, W. Wood, & J. Simpson (Eds.), *Group processes and productivity.* Beverly Hills, CA: Sage.

Staubli, U., Perez, Y. Xu–Fb., Rogers, G., Ingvar, M., Stoneelander S., & Lynch, G. (1994). Centrally active modulators of glutamate receptors facilitate the induction of long-term potentiation in vivo. *Proceedings of the National Academy of Sciences of the United States of America, 91,* 11158–11162.

Stearns, C. Z., & Stearns, P. N. (1986). *Anger: The struggle for emotional control in America's history.* Chicago: University of Chicago Press.

Steblay, N. M. (1987). Helping behavior in rural and urban environments: A meta-analysis. *Psychological Bulletin, 102,* 346–356.

Steele, C. M. (1986, January). What happens when you drink too much? *Psychology Today.*

Steele, C. M., & Josephs, R. A. (1988). Drinking your troubles away II: An attention-allocation model of alcohol's effects on psychological stress. *Journal of Abnormal Psychology, 97,* 196–205.

Steele, T. D., McCann, U. D., & Ricaurte, G. A. (1994). 3,4-methylenedioxy-methamphetamine (MDMA, ecstacy): Pharmacology and toxicology in animals and humans. *Addiction, 89*(5), 539–551.

Stein, D. M., & Lambert, M. J. (1995). Graduate training in psychotherapy: Are therapy outcomes enhanced? *Journal of Consulting and Clinical Psychology, 63,* 182–196.

Steinberg, L. (1989). Pubertal maturation and parent-adolescent distance: An evolutionary perspective. In G. R. Adams, R. Montemayor, & T. P. Gullotta (Eds.), *Biology of adolescent behavior and development* (pp. 71–97). Newbury Park, CA: Sage.

Steinberg, L. (1990). Autonomy, conflict, and harmony in the family relationship. In S. S. Feldman & G. R. Elliott (Eds.), *At the threshold: The developing adolescent* (pp. 255–276). Cambridge, MA: Harvard University Press.

Steinberg, L., Dornbusch, S. M., & Brown, B. B. (1992). Ethnic differences in adolescent achievement: An ecological perspective. *American Psychologist, 47,* 723–729.

Steinberg, L., Lamborn, S. D., Darling, N., Mounts, N. S., & Dornbusch, S. M. (1994). Over-time changes in adjustment and competence among adolescents from authoritative, authoritarian, indulgent, and neglectful families. *Child Development, 65,* 754–770.

Steketee, G., & Goldstein, A. J. (1994). Reflections on Shapiro's reflections: Testing EMDR within a theoretical context. *The Behavior Therapist, 17,* 156–157.

Stemberger, R. T., Turner, S. M., Beidel, D. C., & Calhoun, K. S. (1995). Social phobia: An analysis of possible developmental factors. *Journal of Abnormal Psychology, 104,* 526–531.

Stepanski, E., Glinn, M., Zorick, F., & Roehrs, T. (1994). Heart rate changes in chronic insomnia. *Stress Medicine, 10*(4), 261–266.

Stephan, W. G. (1987). The contact hypothesis in intergroup relations. In C. Hendrick (Ed.), *Group processes in intergroup relations: Review of personality and social psychology* (Vol. 9, pp. 13–40). Newbury Park, CA: Sage.

Stephens, R. S., Roffman, R. A., & Simpson, E. E. (1994). Treating adult marijuana dependence: A test of the relapse prevention model. *Journal of Consulting and Clinical Psychology, 62*(1), 92–99.

Steriade, M., & McCarley, R. W. (1990). *Brainstem control of wakefulness and sleep.* New York: Plenum.

Stern, J., & Stern, M. (1992). Chiles (New Mexico). *The New Yorker,* p. 68.

Stern, Y., Burland, B., Tatemichi, T. K., Tang, M. X., Wilder, D., & Mayeux, R. (1994). Influence of education and occupation on the incidence of Alzheimer's disease. *Journal of the American Medical Association, 271,* 1004–1010.

Sternberg, R. J. (1982). Reasoning, problem solving and intelligence. In R. J. Sternberg (Ed.), *Handbook of human intelligence.* Cambridge, Eng.: Cambridge University Press.

Sternberg, R. J. (1985). *Beyond IQ: A triarchic theory of human intelligence.* Cambridge, Eng.: Cambridge University Press.

Sternberg, R. J. (1986a). A triangular theory of love. *Psychological Review, 93,* 119–135.

Sternberg, R. J. (1986b). Inside intelligence. *American Scientist, 74,* 137–143.

Sternberg, R. J. (1987). Liking versus loving: A comparative evaluation of theories. *Psychological Bulletin, 102,* 331–345.

Sternberg, R. J. (1988a). *The triarchic mind.* New York: Cambridge Press.

Sternberg, R. J. (1988b). *Triangulating love.* In R. J. Sternberg & M. L. Barnes (Eds.), *The psychology of love.* New Haven: Yale University Press.

Sternberg, R. J. (1989). Domain generality versus domain specificity: The life and impending death of a false dichotomy. *Merrill-Palmer Quarterly, 35,* 115–130.

Sternberg, R. J. (1993). The g-ocentric view of intelligence and job performance is wrong. *Current Directions in Psychological Science, 2,* 1–4.

Sternberg, R. J. (1994). Human intelligence: Its nature, use and interaction with context. In D. K. Detterman (Ed.), *Current topics in human intelligence* (Vol. 4). Norwood, NJ: Ablex.

Sternberg, R. J., & Gastel, J. (1989). Coping with novelty in human intelligence: An empirical investigation. *Intelligence, 13,* 187–197.

Sternberg, R. J., & Grajeck, S. (1984). The nature of love. *Journal of Personality and Social Psychology, 47,* 312–329.

Sternberg, R. J., & Lubert, T. I. (1992). Buy low and sell high: An investment approach to creativity. *Current Directions in Psychological Science, 1*(1), 1–5.

Sternberg, R. J., & Wagner, R. K. (1994). *Mind in context.* New York: Cambridge University Press.

Sternberg, R. J., Wagner, R. K., Williams, W. M., & Horvath, J. A. (1995). Testing common sense. *American Psychologist, 50,* 912–927.

Stevens, A. (1996). *Private myths: Dreams and dreaming.* Cambridge, MA: Harvard University Press.

Stevens, A., & Coupe, P. (1978). Distortions in judged spatial relations. *Cognitive Psychology, 10,* 422–437.

Stevens, D. G. (1995, July 29). New Doppler radar off to stormy start. *Chicago Tribune.*

Stevens, J. C., & Hooper, J. E. (1982). How skin and object temperature influence touch sensation. *Perception and Psychophysics, 32,* 282–285.

Stevenson, H. (1992). *A long way from being number one: What we can learn from East Asia.* Washington, DC: Federation of Behavior, Psychological and Cognitive Sciences.

Stevenson, H. W., Azuma, H., & Hakuta, K. (1986). *Child development and education in Japan.* New York: W. H. Freeman.

Stevenson, R. J., & Yeomans, M. R. (1995). Does exposure enhance liking for the chili burn? *Appetite, 24*(2), 107–120.

Stickgold, R., Pace-Schott, E., & Hobson, J. A. (1994). A new paradigm for dream research: Mentation reports following spontaneous arousal from REM and NREM sleep recorded in a home setting. *Consciousness and Cognition, 3,* 16–29.

Stickgold, R., Rittenhouse, C. D., & Hobson, J. A. (1994). Dream splicing: A new technique for assessing thematic coherence in subjective reports of mental activity. *Consciousness and Cognition, 3*(1), 114–128.

Stigler, J. (1992, March). Cultural differences in cognitive development and education. Paper presented at the Claremont Conference on Cognitive Development, Claremont CA.

Stiles, W. B., Shapiro, D. A., & Elliott, R. (1986). "Are all psychotherapies equivalent?" *American Psychologist, 41,* 165–180.

Stokol, D. (1995). The paradox of environmental psychology. *American Psychologist, 50,* 821–837.

Stolerman, I. P., & Jarvis, M. J. (1995). The scientific case that nicotine is addictive. *Psychopharmacology, 117*(1), 2–10.

Stone, W. F., Lederer, G., & Christie, R. (1993). *Strength and weakness: The authoritarian personality today.* New York: Springer-Verlag.

Strain, E. C., Mumford, G. K., Silverman, K., & Griffiths, R. R. (1994). Caffeine dependence syndrome: Evidence from case histories and experimental evaluations. *Journal of the American Medical Association, 272*(13), 1043–1048.

Strang, J., Andrew, J., & Caan, W. (1993). Cocaine in the UK: 1991. *British Journal of Psychiatry, 162,* 1–13.

Streissguth, A. P., Barr, H. M., Sampson, P. D., Darby, B. L., & Martin, D. C. (1989). IQ at age 4 in relation to maternal alcohol use and smoking during pregnancy. *Developmental Psychology, 25,* 3–11.

Streufert, S. (1986). *Complexity, managers and organizations.* Orlando, FL: Academic Press.

Strickland, B. R. (1989). Internal-external control expectancies: From contingency to creativity. *American Psychologist, 44,* 1–12.

Strickland, T., Ranganath, V., Lin, K–M., Poland, R., Mendoza, R., & Smith, M. (1991). Psychopharmacologic considerations in the treatment of Black American populations. *Psychopharmacology Bulletin, 27,* 441–448.

Strongman, K. T., & Kemp, S. (1991). Autobiographical memory for emotion. *Bulletin of the Psychonomic Society, 29*, 195–198.

Stroop, J. R. (1935). Studies of interference in serial verbal reactions. *Journal of Experimental Psychology, 18*, 643–662.

Strupp, H. H. (1989). Psychotherapy: Can the practitioner learn from the researcher? *American Psychologist, 44*, 717–724.

Stuber, M. L., Meeske, K., Gonzalez, S., Housekamp, B., Pynoos, R., & Kazak, A. (1994). Traumatic stress after childhood cancer I: Responses to treatment. *Psycho-Oncology, 3*, 305–312.

Stunkard, A. J., & Wadden, T. A. (1992). Psychological aspects of severe obesity. *American Journal of Clinical Nutrition, 55*, 524S–532S.

Suarez, E., Williams, R., Kuhn, C., Zimmerman, E., & Schanberg, S. (1991). Biobehavioral basis of coronary-prone behavior in middle-aged men. Part ii: Serum cholesterol, the Type A behavior pattern, and hostility as interactive modulators of physiological reactivity. *Psychosomatic Medicine, 53*, 528–537.

Subhan, Z., & Hindmarch, I. (1985). Psychopharmacological effects of vinpocetine in normal healthy volunteers. *European Journal of Pharmacology, 28*, 567–571.

Subrahmanyam, K., & Greenfield, P. M. (1994). Effect of video game practice on spatial skills in girls and boys. *Journal of Applied Developmental Psychology, 15*, 13–32.

Suchman, L. (1987). *Plans and situation action: The problem of human-machine communication.* New York: Cambridge University Press.

Suddath, R. L., Christison, G. W., Torrey, E. F., Casanova, M. F., & Weinberger, D. R. (1990). Anatomical abnormalities in the brains of monopsychotic twins discordant for schizophrenia. *New England Journal of Medicine, 322*, 789–794.

Sue, D. (1992). *Asian and Caucasian subjects' preference for different counseling styles.* Unpublished manuscript, Western Washington University.

Sue, S., & Okazaki, S. (1990). Asian-American educational achievements: A phenomenon in search of an explanation. *American Psychologist, 45*, 913–920.

Sue, S., Zane, N., & Young, K. (1994). Research on psychotherapy with culturally diverse populations. In A. E. Bergin & S. L. Garfield (Eds.), *Handbook of psychotherapy and behavior change.* New York: Wiley.

Suinn, R. M. (1995). Schizophrenia and bipolar disorder: Origins and influences. *Behavior Therapy, 26*, 557–571.

Sulin, R. A., & Dooling, D. J. (1974). Intrusion of a thematic idea in retention of prose. *Journal of Experimental Psychology, 103*, 255–262.

Sullivan, H. S. (1954). *The psychiatric interview.* New York: W. W. Norton.

Sullivan, J. W., & Horowitz, F. D. (1983). The effects of intonation on infant attention: The role of the rising intonation contour. *Journal of Child Language, 10*, 521–534.

Sullivan, K. T., & Bradbury, T. N. (1996). Preventing marital dysfunction: The primacy of secondary strategies. *The Behavior Therapist, 19*, 33–36.

Sullivan, L., & Stankov, L. (1990). Shadowing and target detection as a function of age: Implications for the role of processing resources in competing tasks and in general intelligence. *Australian Journal of Psychology, 42*, 173–185.

Suls, J., & Fletcher, B. (1985). The relative efficacy of avoidant and nonavoidant coping strategies: A meta-analysis. *Health Psychology, 4*, 249–288.

Suls, J., & Wan, C. K. (1993). The relationship between trait hostility and cardiovascular reactivity: A quantitative review and analysis. *Psychophysiology, 30*, 1–12.

Summala, H., & Mikkola, T. (1994). Fatal accidents among car and truck drivers: Effects of fatigue, age, and alcohol consumption. *Human Factors, 36*(2), 315–326.

Sundberg, N., & Sue, D. (1989). Research and research hypotheses about effectiveness in intercultural counseling. In P. Pederson, J. Draguns, W. Lonner, & J. Trimble (Eds.), *Counseling across cultures* (3rd ed.). Honolulu: University of Hawaii Press.

Suomi, S. J. (1991). Primate separation models of affective disorders. *Neurobiology of Learning, Emotion and Affect*, pp. 195–213.

Susser, E., & Lin, S. (1992). Schizophrenia after prenatal exposure to the Dutch hunger winter of 1944–1945. *Archives of General Psychiatry, 49*, 983–988.

Sutker, P. B., Davis, M. J., Uddo, M., & Ditta, S. R. (1995). War zone stress, personal resources, and PTSD in Persian Gulf War returnees. *Journal of Abnormal Psychology, 104*, 444–452.

Suzdak, P. D., Glowa, J. R., Crawley, J. N., Schwartz, R. D., Skolnick, P., & Paul, S. M. (1986). A selective imidazobenzodiazepine antagonist of ethanol in the rat. *Science, 234*, 1243–1247.

Suzuki, K. (1991). Moon illusion simulated in complete darkness: Planetarium experiment reexamined. *Perception and Psychophysics, 49*, 349–354.

Swaab, D. E., & Hofman, M. A. (1995). Sexual differentiation of the human hypothalamus in relation to gender and sexual orientation. *Trends in Neuroscience, 18*(6), 264–270.

Swaab, D. E., & Hofman, M. A. (1990). An enlarged suprachiasmatic nucleus in homosexual men. *Brain Research, 537*, 141–148.

Swann, W. B., Jr., De La Ronde, C., & Hixon, J. G. (1994). Authenticity and positivity strivings in marriage and courtship. *Journal of Personality and Social Psychology, 66*, 857–869.

Swann, W. B., Stein-Seroussi, A., & Giesler, R. B. (1992). Why people self-verify. *Journal of Personality and Social Psychology, 62*, 392–401.

Swanson, L. W. (1976). The locus coeruleus: A cytoarchitectonic, Golgi, and immunohistochemical study in the albino rat. *Brain Research, 110*, 39–56.

Sweat, J. A., & Durm, M. W. (1993). Psychics: Do police departments really use them? *Skeptical Inquirer, 17*, 148–158.

Sweller, J., & Gee, W. (1978). Einstellung: The sequence effect and hypothesis theory. *Journal of Experimental Psychology: Human Learning and Memory, 4*, 513–526.

Swets, J. A. (1992). The science of choosing the right decision threshold in high-stakes diagnostics. *American Psychologist, 47*, 522–532.

Swets, J., & Bjork, R. A. (1990). Enhancing human performance: An evaluation of "New Age" techniques considered by the U.S. Army. *Psychological Science, 1*, 85–96.

Swets, J., & Druckman, D. (1988). *Enhancing human performance.* Washington, DC: National Academy of Sciences Press.

Swets, J. A., & Pickett, R. M. (1982). *Evaluation of diagnostic systems: Methods from signal detection theory.* San Diego, CA: Academic Press.

Swithers, S. E., & Hall, W. G. (1994). Does oral experience terminate ingestion? *Appetite, 23*(2), 113–138.

Syzmanski, S., Lieberman, J. A., Alvir, J. M., Mayerhoff, D., Loebel, A., Geisler, S., Chakos, M., Koreen, A., Jody, D., Kane, J., Woerner, M., & Cooper, T. (1995). Gender differences in onset of illness, treatment response, course, and biologic indexes in first-episode schizophrenia patients. *American Journal of Psychiatry, 152*, 698–703.

Szasz, T. S. (1987). *Insanity: The idea and its consequences.* New York: Wiley.

Takayama, H., Ray, J., Raymon, H. K., Baird, A., Hogg, J., Fisher, L. J., & Gage, F. H. (1995). Basic fibroblast growth factor increases dopaminergic graft survival and function in a rat model of Parkinson's disease. *Nature Medicine, 1*, 53–64.

Takayama, Y., Sugishita, M., Kido, T., Ogawa, M., & Akiguchi, I. (1993). A case of foreign accent syndrome without aphasia caused by a lesion of the left precentral gyrus. *Neurology, 43*, 1361–1363.

Takei, N., Sham, P., O'Callaghan, E., Murray, G. K., Glover, G., & Murray, R. M. (1994). Prenatal exposure to influenza and the development of schizophrenia: Is the effect confined to females? *American Journal of Psychiatry, 151*, 117–119.

Takeuchi, A. H., & Hulse, S. H. (1993). Absolute pitch. *Psychological Bulletin, 113*, 345–361.

Talbot, J. D., Marrett, S., Evans, A. C., Meyer, E., Bushnell, M. C., & Duncan, G. H. (1991). Multiple representations of pain in human cerebral cortex. *Science, 251*, 1355–1358.

Tamis-LeMonda, C. S., Bornstein, M. H., Cyphers, L., Toda, S., & Ogino, M. (1992). Language and play at one year: A comparison of toddlers and mothers in the United States and Japan. *International Journal of Behavioral Development, 19*–42.

Tanaka-Matsumi, J., & Higginbotham, H. N. (1994). Clinical application of behavior therapy across ethnic and cultural boundaries. *The Behavior Therapist, 17*, 123–146.

Tannen, D. (1990). *You just don't understand: Women and men in conversation.* New York: Ballantine Books.

Tannen, D. (1994). *Gender and discourse.* New York: Oxford University Press.

Tanner, J. M. (1978). *Foetus into man: Physical growth from conception to maturity.* London: Open Books, 1978.

Tanner, J. M. (1992). Growth as a measure of nutritional and hygienic status of a population. *Hormone Research, 38*, 106–115.

Tarler-Benlolo, L. (1978). The role of relaxation in biofeedback training: A critical review of the literature. *Psychological Bulletin, 85*, 727–755.

Tartaglia, L. A., Dembski, M., Weng, X., Deng, N., Culpepper, J., Devos, R., Richards, G., Campfield, L. A., Clark, F. T., Deeds, J., Muir, C., Sanker, S., Moriarty, A., Moore, K. J., Smutko, J. S., Mays, G. G., Woolf, E. A., Monroe, C. A., & Tepper, R. I. (1996). Identification and expression cloning of a leptin receptor, OB-R. *Cell, 83*, 1263–1271.

Tasker, F., & Golombok, S. (1995). Adults raised as children in lesbian families. *American Journal of Orthopsychiatry, 65*(2), 203–215.

Tavris, C. (1992). *The mismeasure of woman.* New York: Simon & Schuster.

Taylor, R. L., & Richards, S. B. (1991). Patterns of intellectual differences of black, hispanic, and white children. *Psychology in the Schools, 28*, 5–8.

Taylor, S. E. (1989). *Positive illusions: Creative self-deception and the healthy mind.* New York: Basic Books.

Taylor, S. E. (1991). *Health psychology* (2nd ed.). New York: McGraw-Hill.

Taylor, S. E. (1995). *Health psychology* (3rd ed.). New York: McGraw-Hill.

Taylor, S. E., & Aspinwall, L. G. (1996). Mediating processes in psychosocial stress: Appraisal, coping, resistance, and vulnerability. In H. B. Kaplan (Ed.), *Perspectives on psychosocial stress*. New York: Academic Press.

Taylor, S. E., & Brown, J. D. (1988). Illusion and well-being: A social psychological perspective on mental health. *Psychological Bulletin, 103*, 193–210.

Taylor, S. E., Kemeny, M. E., Aspinwall, L. G., Schneider, S. G., Rodriguez, R., & Herbert, M. (1992). Optimism, coping, psychological distress, and high-risk sexual behavior among men at risk for acquired immunodeficiency syndrome (AIDS). *Journal of Personality and Social Psychology, 63*, 460–473.

Taylor, S. E., & Lobel, M. (1989). Social comparison activity under threat: Downward evaluation and upward contacts. *Psychological Review, 96*, 569–575.

Tecott, L. H., Sun, L. M., Akana, S. F., Strack, A. M., Lowenstein, D. H., Dallman, M. F., & Julius, D. (1995). Eating disorder and epilepsy in mice lacking 5-HT$_{2C}$ serotonin receptors. *Nature, 374*, 542–546.

Teghtsoonian, R. (1992). In defense of the pineal gland. *Behavioral and Brain Sciences, 15*, 224–225.

Teigen, K. H. (1994). Yerkes-Dodson: A law for all seasons. *Theory and Psychology, 4*(4), 525–547.

Teitelbaum, P. (1957). Random and food-directed activity in hyperphagic and normal rats. *Journal of Comparative and Physiological Psychology, 50*, 486–490.

Teitelbaum, P. (1961). Disturbances in feeding and drinking behavior after hypothalamic lesions. In M. R. Jones (Ed.), *Nebraska symposium on motivation*. Lincoln: University of Nebraska Press.

Telch, M. J., Brouillard, M., Telch, C. F., Agras, W. S., & Taylor, C. B. (1989). Role of cognitive appraisal in panic-related avoidance. *Behaviour Research and Therapy, 27*, 373–383.

Tellegen, A., Lykken, D. T., Bouchard, T. J., Wilcox, K. J., Segal, N. L., & Rich, S. (1988). Personality similarity in twins reared apart and together. *Journal of Personality and Social Psychology, 54*, 1031–1039.

Teplin, L. A., Abram, K. M., & McClelland, G. M. (1994). Does psychiatric disorder predict violent crime among released jail detainees? *American Psychologist, 49*, 335–342.

Ter Riet, G., Kleijnen, J., & Knipschild, P. (1990). Acupuncture and chronic pain: A criteria-based meta-analysis. *Journal of Clinical Epidemiology, 43*, 1191–1199.

Terenius, L. (1988). Significance of opioid peptides and other potential markers of neuropeptide systems in cerebrospinal fluid. *Progress in Brain Research, 77*, 419–429.

Terman, L. M. (1916). *The measurement of intelligence*. Boston: Houghton Mifflin.

Terman, L. M., & Oden, M. H. (1947). *The gifted child grows up: Volume 4. Genetic studies of genius*. Stanford, CA: Stanford University Press.

Terman, L. M., & Oden, M. H. (1959). *Genetic studies of genius: Vol 5. The gifted group at mid-life*. Stanford, CA: Stanford University Press.

Terman, L. M., & Oden, M. H. (1959). *The gifted group at midlife*. Stanford, CA: Stanford University Press.

Terrace, H. S., Petitto, L. A., Sanders, D. L., & Bever, J. G. (1979). Can an ape create a sentence? *Science, 206*, 891–902.

Tesser, A. (1988). Toward a self-evaluation maintenance model of social behavior. In L. Berkowitz (Ed.), *Advances in experimental social psychology* (Vol. 21, pp. 181–227). San Diego, CA: Academic Press.

Tesser, A. (1993). The importance of heritability in psychological research: The case of attitudes. *Psychological Review, 100*, 129–142.

Testa, B. M. (1994, Winter). Virtually walking in space. *Virtual Reality: Special Report, 1*(4), 67–74.

Tetlock, P. E. (1986). Psychological advice in foreign policy: What do we have to contribute? *American Psychologist, 41*, 557–567.

Tett, R. P., Jackson, D. N., & Rothstein, M. (1991). Personality measures as predictors of job performance: A meta-analytic review. *Personnel Psychology, 44*, 703–742.

Tharinger, D. J., Lambert, N. M., Bricklin, P. M., Feshbach, N., Johnson, N. F., Oakland, T. D., Paster, V. S., & Sanchez, W. (1996). Education reform: Challenges for psychology and psychologists. *Professional Psychology: Research and Practice, 27*, 24–33.

Thelen, E. (1992). Development as a dynamic system. *Current Directions in Psychological Science, 1*, 189–193.

Thelen, E. (1995). Motor development: A new synthesis. *American Psychologist, 50*, 79–95.

Theunisson, E. (1994). Factors influencing the design of perspective flight path displays for guidance and navigation. *Displays, 15*, 241–254.

Thibodeau, R., & Aronson, E. (1992). Taking a closer look: Reasserting the role of the self-concept in dissonance theory. *Personality and Social Psychology Bulletin, 18*, 591–602.

Thomas, A., & Chess, S. (1977). *Temperament and development*. New York: Brunner/Mazel.

Thomas, E. L., & Robinson, H. A. (1972). *Improving reading in every class: A sourcebook for teachers*. Boston: Allyn & Bacon.

Thomas, K. W., & Schmidt, W. H. (1976). A survey of managerial interests with respect to conflict. *Academy of Management Journal, 19*, 315–318.

Thompson, S. C., Sobolow-Shubin, A., Galbraith, M. E., Schwankovksy, L., & Cruzen, D. (1993). Maintaining perceptions of control: Finding perceived control in low control circumstances. *Journal of Personality and Social Psychology, 64*, 293–304.

Thompson, W. G. (1995). Coffee: Brew or bane. *American Journal of the Medical Sciences, 308*(1), 49–57.

Thomson, C. P. (1982). Memory for unique personal events: The roommate study. *Memory & Cognition, 10*, 324–332.

Thoresen, C., & Powell, L. (1992). Type A behavior pattern: New perspectives on theory, assessment, and intervention. *Journal of Clinical and Consulting Psychology, 60*, 595–604.

Thorndike, E. L. (1898). Animal intelligence: An experimental study of the associative processes in animals. *Psychological Monographs, 2*(Whole No. 8).

Thorndike, E. L. (1905). *The elements of psychology*. New York: Seiler.

Thorndike, E. L. (1914). *Educational psychology: Briefer course*. New York: Teacher's College, Columbia University.

Thorndike, R. L., Hagan, E., & Sattler, J. (1986). *Stanford-Binet* (4th ed.). Chicago: Riverside.

Thorne, B. (1986). Girls and boys together . . . but most apart: Gender arrangements in elementary school. In W. H. Hartup & Z. Rubin (Eds.), *Relationships and development*. Hillsdale, NJ: Lawrence Erlbaum Associates.

Thurstone, L., & Thurstone, T. (1941). Factorial studies of intelligence. *Psychological Monographs*, No. 2. Chicago: University of Chicago Press.

Tian, H.-G., Nan, Y., Hu, G., Dong, Q.-N., Yang, X.-L., Pietinen, P., & Nissinen, A. (1995). Dietary survey in a Chinese population. *European Journal of Clinical Nutrition, 49*, 27–32.

Tice, D. M. (1991). Esteem protection or enhancement? Self-handicapping motives and attributions differ by trait self-esteem. *Journal of Personality and Social Psychology, 60*, 711–725.

Tice, D. M., & Baumeister, R. F. (1990). Self-esteem, self-handicapping, and self-presentation: The strategy of inadequate practice. *Journal of Personality, 58*, 443–464.

Tiedemann, G. L., & Johnston, C. (1992). Evaluation of a parent training program to promote sharing between young siblings. *Behavior Therapy, 23*, 299–318.

Tiihonen, J., Kuikka, J., Bergstrom, K., Hakola, P., Karhu, J., Ryynänen, O.-P., & Föhr, J. (1995). Altered striatal dopamine re-uptake site densities in habitually violent and non-violent alcoholics. *Nature Medicine, 1*(7), 654-657.

Tiller, J., Schmidt, U., Ali, S., & Treasure, J. (1995). Patterns of punitiveness in women with eating disorders. *International Journal of Eating Disorders, 17*(4), 365–371.

Timberlake, W., & Farmer-Dougan, V. A. (1991). Reinforcement in applied settings: Figuring out ahead of time what will work. *Psychological Bulletin, 110*(3), 379–391.

Tinbergen, N. (1989). *The study of instinct*. Oxford: Clarendon.

Tinti, J. M., & Nofre, C. (1991). Design of sweeteners: A rational approach. In D. E. Walters et al. (Eds.), *Sweeteners: Discovery, molecular design, and chemoreception*. Washington, DC: American Chemical Society.

Tolin, D. F., Montgomery, R. W., Kleinknecht, R. A., & Lohr, J. M. (1996). An evaluation of eye movement desensitization and reprocessing (EMDR). In S. Knapp, L. VandeCreek, & T. L. Jackson (Eds.), *Innovations in clinical practice: A source book*. Sarasota, FL: Professional Resource Press.

Tolman, E. C., & Honzik, C. H. (1930). Introduction and removal of reward and maze performance in rats. *University of California Publication in Psychology, 4*, 257–275.

Tomarken, A. J., Mineka, S., & Cook, M. (1989). Fear-relevant selective associations and covariation bias. *Journal of Abnormal Psychology, 98*, 381–394.

Tomaso, H., Reisinger, E. C., Grasmug, E., Ramschak, H., & Krejs, G. J. (1995). Transmission of HIV. *Wiener Klinische Wochenschrift, 107*(3), 85–90.

Torgersen, S. (1983). Genetic factors in anxiety disorders. *Archives of General Psychiatry, 40*, 1085–1089.

Touchette, N. (1995). Anti-addiction drug ibogaine on trial. *Nature Medicine, 1*, 288–289.

Townsend, J. M., Kline, J., & Wasserman, T. H. (1995). Low-investment copulation: Sex differences in motivational and emotional reactions. *Ethology and Sociobiology, 16*(1), 25–51.

Trabasso, T. R., & Bower, G. H. (1968). *Attention in learning.* New York: Wiley.

Tracor, Inc. (1971). *Community reaction to aircraft noise: Vol. 1* (NASA Report CR–1761). Washington, DC: National Aeronautics and Space Administration.

Travis, J. (1994). Glia: The brain's other cells. *Science, 266,* 970–972.

Treffert, D. A. (1988). The idiot savant: A review of the syndrome. *American Journal of Psychiatry, 145,* 563–572.

Treisman, A. (1988). Features and objects: The 14th Bartlett memorial lecture. *Quarterly Journal of Experimental Psychology, 40,* 201–237.

Treisman, A., & Gelade, G. (1980). A feature integration theory of attention. *Cognitive Psychology, 12,* 97–136.

Treisman, A., Viera, A., & Hayes, A. (1992). Automaticity and preattentive processes. *American Journal of Psychology, 105,* 341–362.

Tremblay, A., & Bueman, B. (1995). Exercise-training, macronutrient balance and body weight control. *International Journal of Obesity, 19*(2), 79–86.

Tremblay, R. E., Pagani-Kurtz, L., Mâsse, L., Vitaro, F., & Pihl, R. O. (1995). A bimodal preventive intervention for disruptive kindergarten boys: Its impact through mid-adolescence. *Journal of Consulting and Clinical Psychology, 63,* 560–568.

Tremblay, R. E., Pihl, R. O., Vitaro, F., & Dobkin, P. (1994). Predicting early onset of male antisocial behavior from preschool behavior. *Archives of General Psychiatry, 51,* 732–739.

Triandis, H. C. (1964). Cultural influences upon cognitive processes. In L. Berkowitz (Ed.), *Advances in experimental social psychology.* New York: Academic Press.

Triandis, H. C. (1994). *Culture and social behavior.* New York: McGraw-Hill.

Triandis, H. C. (1995). *Individualism and collectivism.* Boulder, CO: Westview Press.

Triandis, H. C., Kurowski, L. L., & Gelfand, M. J. (1993). Workplace diversity. In H. C. Triandis, M. D. Dunnette, L. Hough (Eds.), *Handbook of industrial and organizational psychology.* Palo Alto, CA: Consulting Psychologists Press.

Tronick, E. Z. (1989). Emotions and emotional communication in infants. *American Psychologist, 44,* 112–119.

Tronick, E. Z., Morelli, G. A., & Ivey, P. K. (1992). The Efe forager infant and toddler's pattern of social relationships: Multiple and simultaneous. *Developmental Psychology, 28,* 568–577.

Trope, Y., Cohen, O., & Alfieri, T. (1991). Behavior identification as a mediator of dispositional inference. *Journal of Personality and Social Psychology, 61,* 873–883.

Trujillo, C. M. (1986). A comparative evaluation of classroom interactions between professors and minority and non-minority college students. *American Educational Research Journal, 23,* 629–642.

Trujillo, K. A., & Akil, H. (1991). Inhibition of morphine tolerance and dependence by the NMDA receptor antagonist MK–801. *Science, 251,* 85–87.

Trull, T. J., & Sher, K. J. (1994). Relationship between the five-factor model of personality and Axis I disorders in a nonclinical sample. *Journal of Personality and Social Psychology, 103,* 350–360.

Tryon, R. C. (1940). Genetic differences in maze-learning ability in rats. *Yearbook of the National Society for the Study of Education, 39,* 111–119.

Tryon, W. W. (1995). Resolving the cognitive behavioral controversy. *The Behavior Therapist, 18,* 83–86.

Tseng, W., Kan-Ming, M., Li-Shuen, L., Guo-Qian, C., Li-Wah, O., & Hong-Bo, Z. (1992). Koro epidemics in Guangdong China. *Journal of Nervous and Mental Disease, 180,* 117–123.

Tulving, E. (1979). Relation between encoding specificity and levels of processing. In L. S. Cermak & F. I. M. Craik (Eds.), *Levels of processing in human memory.* Hillsdale, NJ: Lawrence Erlbaum Associates.

Tulving, E. (1982). *Elements of episodic memory.* New York: Oxford University Press.

Tulving, E. (1988). Self-knowledge of an amnesic individual is represented abstractly. In T. K. Srull & R. S. Wyer (Eds.), *The mental representation of trait and autobiographical knowledge about the self: Advances in social cognition: Vol. V.* Hillsdale, NJ: Lawrence Erlbaum Associates.

Tulving, E., Hayman, C. A. G., & Macdonald, C. A. (1991). Long-lasting perceptual priming and semantic learning in amnesia: A case experiment. *Journal of Experimental Psychology: Learning, Memory, and Cognition, 17,* 595–617.

Tulving, E., & Psotka, J. (1971). Retroactive inhibition in free recall: Inaccessibility of information available in the memory store. *Journal of Experimental Psychology, 87,* 1–8.

Tulving, E., & Schacter, D. L. (1990). Priming and human memory systems. *Science, 247,* 301–306.

Tulving, E., Schacter, D. L., & Stark, H. (1982). Priming effects in word-fragment completion are independent of recognition memory. *Journal of Experimental Psychology: Learning, Memory, and Cognition, 8,* 336–342.

Tulving, E., & Thomson, D. M. (1973). Encoding specificity and retrieval processes in episodic memory. *Psychological Review, 80,* 352–373.

Turkington, C. (1987). Special talents. *Psychology Today,* pp. 42–46.

Turkkan, J. S. (1989). Classical conditioning: The new hegemony. *Behavioral & Brain Sciences, 12,* 121–179.

Turner, A. M., & Greenough, W. T. (1985). Differential rearing effects on rat visual cortex synapses: I. Synaptic and neuronal density and synapses per neuron. *Brain Research, 329,* 195–203.

Turner, J. C. (1987). *Rediscovering the social group: A self-categorization theory.* New York: Basil Blackwell.

Turner, J. C. (1991). *Social influence.* Pacific Grove, CA: Brooks/Cole.

Turner, M. E., Pratkanis, A. R., Probasco, P., & Leve, C. (1992). Threat, cohesion, and group effectiveness: Testing a social identity maintenance prospective on groupthink. *Journal of Personality and Social Psychology, 63,* 781–796.

Turton, M. D., O'Shea, D., Gunn, I., Beak, S. A., Edwards, C. M. B., Meeran, K., Choi, S. J., Taylor, G. M., Heath, M. M., Lambert, P. D., Wilding, J. P. H., Smith, D. M., Ghatel, M. A., Herbert, J., & Bloom, S. R. (1996). A role for glucagon-like peptide-1 in the central regulation of feeding. *Nature, 379,* 69–70.

Tversky, A. (1972). Elimination by aspects: A theory of choice. *Psychological Review, 79,* 281–299.

Tversky, A., & Kahneman, D. (1974). Judgment under uncertainty: Heuristics and biases. *Science, 185,* 1124–1131.

Tversky, A., & Kahneman, D. (1981). The framing of decisions and the psychology of choice. *Science, 211,* 453–458.

Tversky, A., & Kahneman, D. (1991). Loss aversion in riskless choice: A reference dependent model. *Quarterly Journal of Economics, 106,* 1039–1061.

Tversky, B., & Tuchin, M. (1989). A reconciliation of the evidence on eyewitness testimony: Comments on McCloskey and Zaragoza. *Journal of Experimental Psychology: General, 118,* 86–91.

Tyrka, A. R., Cannon, T., Haslam, N., Mednick, S., Schulsinger, F., Schulsinger, H., & Parnas, J. (1995). The latent structure of schizotypy: I. Premorbid indicators of a taxon of individuals at risk for schizophrenia spectrum disorders. *Journal of Abnormal Psychology, 104,* 173–183.

U.S. Bureau of the Census (1987). *U.S. suicides per 100,000 population (1985).* Washington, DC: U.S. Government Printing Office.

U.S. Bureau of the Census (1991). *Statistical abstract of the U.S.: 1991* (111th ed.). Washington, DC.

U.S. Bureau of the Census (1992). *Current population reports, Series P60, No. 181, Poverty in the United States: 1991.* Washington, DC: U.S. Government Printing Office.

U.S. Department of Commerce, Bureau of the Census. (1992). *Statistical Abstract of the United States* (112th ed.). Washington, DC: U.S. Government Printing Office.

U.S. Department of Health and Human Services. (1988). *Nicotine addiction: A report of the Surgeon General.* Office of the Assistant Secretary for Health, Office on Smoking and Health, Rockville, MD.

U.S. Department of Health and Human Services. (1990). *Healthy people 2000: National health promotion and disease prevention objectives.* Washington, DC: U.S. Government Printing Office.

U.S. Department of Health and Human Services. (1990). *Seventh annual report to the U.S. Congress on alcohol and health.* Rockville, MD: National Institute on Alcohol Abuse and Alcoholism.

U.S. Department of Health and Human Services. (1992). *NCPS AIDS community demonstration projects: What we have learned, 1985–1990.* Washington, DC: USDHHS.

U.S. Department of Health and Human Services, National Center for Health Statistics (1992). *Monthly Vital Statistics Report, 40,* 1.

U.S. Department of Health and Welfare. (1979). *Healthy people: The Surgeon General's report on health promotion and disease prevention.* Washington, DC: U. S. Government Printing Office.

Ullmann, L., & Krasner, L. (1975). *A psychological approach to abnormal behavior* (2nd ed.). Englewood Cliffs, NJ: Prentice-Hall.

USA Today (1995, October 9). Poll: A nation more divided.

Usher, J. A., & Neisser, U. (1993). Childhood amnesia and the beginnings of memory for four early life events. *Journal of Experimental Psychology: General, 122,* 155–165.

Vaillant, G. E. (1977). *Adaptation to life: How the best and brightest came of age.* Boston: Little, Brown.

Valenstein, E. S. (Ed.) (1980). *The psychosurgery debate.* San Francisco: W. H. Freeman.

Van Bezooijen, R., Otto, S. A., & Heenan, T. A. (1983). Recognition of vocal expression of emotion: A three-nation study to identify universal characteristics. *Journal of Cross-Cultural Psychology, 14,* 387–406.

Van Buskirk, R. L., & Erickson, R. P. (1977). Odorant responses in taste neurons of the rat NTS. *Brain Research, 135,* 287–303.

van den Boom, D. C. (1994). The influence of temperament and mothering on attachment and exploration: An experimental manipulation of sensitive responsiveness among lower-class mothers with irritable infants. *Child Development, 65,* 1457–1477.

Van de Ven, P. (1994). Comparisons among homophobic reactions of undergraduates, high school students, and young offenders. *Journal of Sex Research, 31*(2), 117–124.

van der Voort, T. H. A., & Valkenburg, P. M. (1994). Television's impact on fantasy play: A review of research. *Developmental Review, 14,* 27–51.

Van Essen, D. C., Anderson, C. H., & Felleman, D. J. (1992). Information processing in the primate visual system: An integrated systems perspective. *Science, 255,* 419–423.

van IJzendoorn, M. H. (1995). Adult attachment representations, parental responsiveness, and infant attachment: A meta-analysis on the predictive validity of the Adult Attachment Survey. *Psychological Bulletin, 117,* 387–403.

van IJzendoorn, M. H. (1995). Adult attachment representations, parental responsiveness, and infant attachment: A meta-analysis on the predictive validity of the Adult Attachment Interview. *Psychological Bulletin, 117,* 387–403.

van IJzendoorn, M. H., Juffer, F., & Duyvesteyn, M. G. C. (1995). Breaking the intergenerational cycle of insecure attachment: A review of the effects of attachment-based interventions on maternal sensitivity and infant security. *Journal of Child Psychology and Psychiatry, 36,* 225–248.

Van Sickel, A. D. (1992). Clinical hypnosis in the practice of anesthesia. *Nurse Anesthesiologist, 3,* 67–74.

Van Tol, H., Caren, M., Guan, H-C., Ohara, K., Bunzow, J., Civelli, O., Kennedy, J., Seeman, P., Niznik, H., & Jovanovic, V. (1992). Multiple dopamine D_4 receptor variants in the human population. *Nature, 358,* 149–152.

Vanderweele, D. A. (1994). Insulin is a prandial satiety hormone. *Physiology and Behavior, 56*(3), 619–622.

Vane, J. (1972). Intelligence and achievement test results of kindergarten children in England, Ireland and the United States. *Journal of Clinical Psychology, 29,* 191–193.

Vargha-Khadem, F., Isaacs, E., & Mishkin, M. (1994). Agnosia, alexia and a remarkable form of amnesia in an adolescent boy. *Brain, 117,* 683–703.

Vaughan, D. (1996). *The Challenger launch decision.* Chicago: University of Chicago Press.

Vaughan, K., Armstrong, M. S., Gold, R., O'Conner, N., Jenneke, W., & Tarrier, N. (1994). A trial of eye movement desensitization compared to image habituation training and applied muscle relaxation in posttraumatic stress disorder. *Journal of Behaviour Therapy and Experimental Psychiatry, 25,* 283–291.

Verfaellis, M., & Cermak, L. S. (1991). Neuropsychological issues in amnesia. In J. L. Martinez & R. P. Kesner (Eds.), *Learning and memory: A biological view* (2nd ed.). San Diego, CA: Academic Press.

Vernet, M. E., Robin, O., & Dittmar, A. (1995). The ohmic perturbation duration, an original temporal index to quantify electrodermal responses. *Behavioural Brain Research, 67*(1), 103–107.

Vernon, P. A. (1983). Speed of information processing and general intelligence. *Intelligence, 7,* 53–70.

Vernon, P. A. (1987a). New developments in reaction time research. In P. A. Vernon (Ed.), *Speed of information-processing and intelligence* (pp. 1–20). Norwood, NJ: Ablex.

Vernon, P. A. (Ed.) (1987b). *Speed of information-processing and intelligence.* Norwood, NJ: Ablex.

Vernon, P. A. (1993). Intelligence and neural efficiency. In D. K. Detterman (Ed.), *Current topics in human intelligence* (Vol. 3). Norwood, NJ: Ablex.

Viken, R. J., & McFall, R. M. (1994). Paradox lost: Implications of contemporary reinforcement theory for behavior therapy. *Current Directions in Psychological Science, 3,* 121–124.

Vincent, C. A., & Richardson, P. H. (1986). The evaluation of therapeutic acupuncture: Concepts and methods. *Pain, 24,* 1–13.

Vincent, K. R. (1991). Black/white IQ differences: Does age make a difference? *Journal of Clinical Psychology, 47,* 266–270.

Volkmar, F. R., & Greenough, W. T. (1972). Rearing complexity affects branching of dendrites in the visual cortex of the rat. *Science, 176,* 1445–1447.

Volpicelli, J. R., Alterman, A. I., Hayashida, M., & O'Brien, C. P. (1992). Naltrexone in the treatment of alcohol dependence. *Archives of General Psychiatry, 49,* 876–880.

von Bekesy, G. (1960). *Experiments in hearing.* New York: McGraw-Hill.

von Hippel, W., Hawkins, C., & Narayan, S. (1994). Personality and perceptual expertise: Individual differences in perceptual identification. *Psychological Science, 5,* 401–406.

Von Wright, J. M., Anderson, K., & Stenman, U. (1975). *Generalization of conditioned GSRs in dichotic listening.*

Vooijs, M. W., & van der Voort, T. H. (1993). Learning about television violence: The impact of a critical viewing curriculum on children's attitudinal judgments of crime series. *Journal of Research and Development in Education, 26,* 133–142.

Vorauer, J., & Ross, M. (1993). Exploring the nature and implications of functional independence: Do mental representations of the self become independent of their bases? In T. K. Srull & R. S. Wyer (Eds.), *The mental representation of trait and autobiographical knowledge about the self: Advances in social cognition: Vol. V.* Hillsdale, NJ: Lawrence Erlbaum Associates.

Voyer, D., Voyer, S., & Bryden, M. P. (1995). Magnitude of sex differences in spatial abilities: A meta-analysis and consideration of critical variables. *Psychological Bulletin, 117*(2), 250–270.

Vuchinich, R. E., & Sobell, M. B. (1978). Empirical separation of physiological and expected effects of alcohol on complex perceptual motor performance. *Psychopharmacology, 60,* 81–85.

Vygotsky, L. S. (1934/reprinted 1962). *Thought and language.* (E. Haufmann & G. Vaker, Eds. & Trans.) Cambridge, MA: MIT Press.

Waagenaar, W. (1986). My memory: A study of autobiographical memory over six years. *Cognitive Psychology, 18,* 225–252.

Waagenaar, W. A. (1989). *Paradoxes of gambling behavior.* Hillsdale, NJ: Lawrence Erlbaum Associates.

Wachs, T. D. (1992). *The nature of nurture.* Newbury Park, CA: Sage.

Wachs, T. D., & Gruen, C. E. (1982). *Early experience and human development.* New York: Plenum.

Wade, C. (1988, April). *Thinking critically about critical thinking in psychology.* Paper presented at the annual meeting of the Western Psychological Association, San Francisco, CA.

Wadsworth, S. (1994). School achievement. In J. C. DeFries, R. Plomin, & D. W. Fulker (Eds.), *Nature and nurture during middle childhood* (pp. 86–101). Cambridge, MA: Blackwell.

Wagner, E. F. A., Schutz, C. G., Chilcoat, H. D., & Anthony, J. C. (1994). Degree of acculturation and the risk of crack cocaine smoking among Hispanic Americans. *American Journal of Public Health, 84*(11), 1825–1827.

Waid, W. M., & Orne, M. T. (1981). Cognitive, social, and personality processes in the physiological detection of deception. In L. Berkowitz (Ed.), *Advances in experimental social psychology: Vol. 14.* New York: Academic Press.

Wainer, H. (1988). How accurately can we assess changes in minority performance on the SAT? *American Psychologist, 43,* 774–778.

Waite, B. M., Hillbrand, M., & Foster, H. G. (1992). Reduction of aggressive behavior after removal of Music Television. *Hospital and Community Psychiatry, 43,* 173–175.

Wakefield, J. C. (1992). The concept of mental disorder: On the boundary between biological facts and social values. *American Psychologist, 47,* 373–388.

Walberg, H. J. (1987). Studies show curricula efficiency can be attained. *NASSP Bulletin, 71,* 15–21.

Walker, L. (1991). The feminization of psychology. *Psychology of Women Newsletter of Division, 35,* 1, 4.

Walker, L. J. (1982). The sequentiality of Kohlberg's stages of moral development. *Child Development, 53,* 1330–1336.

Walker, L. J. (1989). A longitudinal study of moral reasoning. *Child Development, 60,* 157–166.

Walker-Andrews, A. S., Bahrick, L. E., Raglioni, S. S., & Dias, I. (1991). Infants' bimodal perception of gender. *Ecological Psychology, 3,* 55–75.

Wallace, A. F. C. (1959). Cultural determinants of response to hallucinatory experience. *Archives of General Psychiatry, 1,* 58–69.

Wallace, C., Liberman, R., MacKain, S., Blackwell, G., & Eckman, T. (1992). Effectiveness and replicability of modules for teaching social and instrumental skills to the severely mentally ill. *American Journal of Psychiatry, 149,* 654–658.

Wallace, R. K., & Benson, H. (1972). The physiology of meditation. *Scientific American, 226,* 84–90.

Wallen, K. (1989). Mate selection: Economics and affection. *Behavioral and Brain Sciences, 12,* 37–38.

Wallen, K., & Lovejoy, J. (1993). Sexual behavior: Endocrine function and therapy. In J. Schulkin (Ed.), *Hormonal pathways to mind and brain.* New York: Academic Press.

Waller, N. G., Kojetin, B. A., Bouchard, T. J., & Lykken, D. T. (1990). Genetic and environmental influences on religious interests, attitudes, and values. *Psychological Science, 1,* 138–142.

Waller, N. G., & Shaver, P. R. (1994). The importance of nongenetic influences on romantic love styles: A twin-family study. *Psychological Science, 5,* 268–274.

Wallerstein, J. S., & Blakeslee, S. (1989). *Second chances: Men, women and children a decade after divorce.* New York: Ticknor and Fields.

Wallerstein, R. S. (1989). The psychotherapy research project of the Menninger Foundation: An overview. *Journal of Consulting and Clinical Psychology, 57,* 195–205.

Wallman, J., Gottlieb, M. D., Rajaram, V., & Fugate-Wentzek, L. A. (1987). Local retinal regions control local eye growth and myopia. *Science, 237,* 73–76.

Walster, E., Traupmann, J., & Walster, G. W. (1978). Equity and extramarital sexuality. *Archives of Sexual Behavior, 7,* 127–141.

Walster, E., Walster, G. W., & Berscheid, E. (1978). *Equity: Theory and research.* Boston: Allyn & Bacon.

Walters, G. (1992). Drug-seeking behavior: Disease or lifestyle? *Professional Psychology, 23,* 139–145.

Wang, X., Merzenich, M. M., Sameshima, K., & Jenkins, W. M. (1995). Remodelling of hand representation in adult cortex determined by timing of tactile stimulation. *Nature, 378,* 71–75.

Warchol, M. E, Lambert, P. R., Goldstein, B. J., Forge, A., & Corwin, J. T. (1993). Regenerative proliferation in inner ear sensory epithelia from adult guinea pigs and humans. *Science, 259,* 1619–1622.

Ward, C. (1994). Culture and altered states of consciousness. In W. J. Lonner & R. S. Malpass (Eds.), *Psychology and culture.* Boston: Allyn & Bacon.

Ward, M. J., & Carlson, E. A. (1995). Associations among adult attachment representation, maternal sensitivity, and infant-mother attachment in a sample of adolescent mothers. *Child Development, 66,* 69–79

Warm, J. S., & Parasuraman, R. (1987). Vigilance: Basic and applied. *Human Factors, 29,* 623–740.

Warner, L., Kessler, R., Hughes, M., Anthony, J., & Nelson, C. (1995). Prevalence and correlates of drug use and dependence in the United States. *Archives of General Psychiatry, 52,* 219–229.

Warren, R., & Wertheimer, A. H. (1990). *Perception and control of self-motion.* Hillsdale, NJ: Lawrence Erlbaum Associates.

Warren, R. M., Obuseck, C. J., & Acroff, J. M. (1972). Auditory induction of absent sounds. *Science, 176,* 1149.

Warrington, E. K., & Weiskrantz, L. (1970). The amnesic syndrome: Consolidation or retrieval? *Nature, 228,* 626–630.

Wartburton, D. M. (1995). Effects of caffeine on cognition and mood without caffeine abstinence. *Psychopharmacology, 119,* 66–70.

Wartner, U., Grossmann, K., Fremmer-Bombik, E., & Suess, G. (1994). Attachment patterns at age six in south Germany: Predictability from infancy and implications for preschool behavior. *Child Development, 65,* 1014–1027.

Wasik, B. H., Ramey, C. T., Bryant, D. M., & Sparling, J. J. (1990). A longitudinal study of two early intervention strategies: Project CARE. *Child Development, 61,* 1682–1696.

Wasserman, E. A. (1995). The conceptual abilities of pigeons. *American Scientist, 83,* 246–255.

Wasserman, E. A., Hugart, J. A., & Kirkpatrick-Steger, K. (1995). Pigeons show same-different conceptualization after training with complex visual stimuli. *Journal of Experimental Psychology: Animal Behavior Processes, 21,* 248–252.

Waterman, A. S. (1982). Identity development from adolescence to adulthood: An extension of theory and a review of research. *Developmental Psychology, 18,* 341–358.

Watkins, C. E., Campbell, V. L., Nieberding, R., & Hallmark, R. (1995). Contemporary practice of psychological assessment by clinical psychologists. *Professional Psychology: Research and Practice, 26,* 54–60.

Watkins, M. J. (1989). Willful and nonwillful determinants of memory. In H. L. Roediger & F. I. M. Craik (Eds.), *Varieties of memory and consciousness.* Hillsdale, NJ: Lawrence Erlbaum Associates.

Watson, J. B. (1913). Psychology as the behaviorist views it. *Psychological Review, 20,* 158–177.

Watson, J. B. (1919). *Psychology from the standpoint of a behaviorist.* Philadelphia: Lippincott.

Watson, J. B. (1924). *Behaviorism.* New York: W. W. Norton.

Watson, J. B. (1925). *Behaviorism.* London: Kegan Paul, Trench, Trubner.

Watson, M. W. (1981). The development of social roles: A sequence of social-cognitive development. *New Directions for Child Development, 12,* 33–41.

Watson, R. I. (1963). *The great psychologists: From Aristotle to Freud.* Philadelphia: Lippincott.

Watt, N. F., & Saiz, C. (1991). Longitudinal studies of premorbid development of adult schizophrenics. In E. F. Walker (Ed.), *Schizophrenia: A life-course in developmental perspective.* San Diego, CA: Academic Press.

Weary, G., & Edwards, J. A. (1994). Social cognition and clinical psychology: Anxiety and the processing of social information. In R. S. Wyer & T. S. Srull

(Eds.), *Handbook of social cognition* (2nd ed.). Hillsdale, NJ: Lawrence Erlbaum Associates.

Weary, G., & Edwards, J. A. (in press). Causal uncertainty and related goal structures. In R. Sorrentino & E. T. Higgins (Eds.), *Handbook of motivation and cognition: Vol 3. The interpersonal context.* New York: Guilford.

Webb, W. B. (1968). *Sleep: An experimental approach.* New York: Macmillan.

Weber, R. J. (1992). *Forks, phonographs, and hot air balloons: A field guide to inventive thinking.* New York: Oxford University Press.

Wechsler, D. (1939). *The measurement of adult intelligence.* Baltimore: Williams & Wilkins.

Wechsler, D. (1949). *The Wechsler Intelligence Scale for Children.* New York: Psychological Corporation.

Weekes, J. R., Lynn, S. J., Green, J. P., & Brentar, J. T. (1992). Pseudomemory in hypnotized and task-motivated subjects. *Journal of Abnormal Psychology, 101,* 356–360.

Weeks, D., & Weeks, J. (1995). *Eccentrics: A study of sanity and strangeness.* New York: Villard.

Wehr, T. A., Sack, D., Rosenthal, N., Duncan, W., & Gillian, J. C. (1983). Circadian rhythm disturbances in manic-depressive illness. *Federation Practitioner, 42,* 2809–2814.

Weidner, G., Sexton, G., McLellarn, R., Connor, S., & Matarazzo, J. (1987). The role of Type A behavior and hostility in an elevation of plasma lipids in adult women and men. *Psychosomatic Medicine, 49,* 136–145.

Weinberg, J., & Levine, S. (1980). Psychobiology of coping in animals: The effects of predictability. In S. Levine & H. Ursin (Eds.), *Coping and health.* New York: Plenum.

Weinberg, R. A. (1989). Intelligence and IQ: Landmark issues and great debates. *American Psychologist, 44,* 98–104.

Weinberg, R. A., Scarr, S., & Waldman, I. D. (1992). The Minnesota transracial adoption study: A follow-up of IQ test performance at adolescence. *Intelligence, 16,* 117–135.

Weinberger, D. R. (1988). Schizophrenia and the frontal lobe. *Trends in Neuroscience, 11,* 367–370.

Weiner, B. (1980). *Human motivation.* New York: Holt, Rinehart & Winston.

Weiner, B. (1993). On sin versus sickness: A theory of perceived responsibility and social motivation. *American Psychologist, 48*(9), 957–965.

Weinstein, N. D. (1989). Effects of personal experience on self-protective behavior. *Psychological Bulletin, 105,* 31–50.

Weiskrantz, L. (1995). Blindsight—Not an island unto itself. *Current Directions in Psychological Science, 4,* 146–151.

Weisman, A., Lopez, S. R., Karno, M., & Jenkins, J. (1993). An attributional analysis of expressed emotion in Mexican-American families with schizophrenia. *Journal of Abnormal Psychology, 102,* 601–606.

Weiss, B., & Weisz, J. R. (1995). Relative effectiveness of behavioral versus nonbehavioral child psychotherapy. *Journal of Consulting and Clinical Psychology, 63,* 317–320.

Weiss, D. S., Marmar, C. R., Metzler, T. J., & Ronfeldt, H. M. (1995). Predicting symptomatic distress in emergency services personnel. *Journal of Consulting and Clinical Psychology, 63,* 361–368.

Weiss, S., & Moore, M. (1990). Cultural differences in the perception of magazine alcohol advertisements by Israeli Jewish, Moslem, Druze, and Christian high school students. *Drug and Alcohol Dependence, 26,* 209–215.

Weiss, V. (1986). From memory span and mental speed toward the quantum mechanics of intelligence. *Journal of Personality and Individual Differences, 7,* 737–749.

Weisskopf, M. G., & Nicoll, R. A. (1995). Presynaptic changes during mossy fibre LTP revealed by NMDA receptor-mediated synaptic responses. *Nature, 376,* 256–259.

Weissman, M., & Olfson, M. (1995). Depression in women: Implications for health care research. *Science, 269,* 799–801.

Weisstein, N., & Harris, C. S. (1974). Visual detection of line segments: An object superiority effect. *Science, 186,* 752–755.

Weisz, J. R., Weiss, B., Han, S. S., Granger, D. A., & Morton, T. (1995). Effects of psychotherapy with children and adolescents revisited: A meta-analysis of treatment outcome studies. *Psychological Bulletin, 117,* 450–468.

Weltzin, T. E., Bulik, C. M., McConaha, C. W., & Kaye, W. H. (1995). Laxative withdrawal and anxiety in bulimia nervosa. *International Journal of Eating Disorders, 17*(2), 141–146.

Weltzin, T. E., Fernstrom, M. H., & Kaye, W. H. (1994). Serotonin and bulimia nervosa. *Nutrition Reviews, 52,* 399–408.

Wenk, G. L. (1989). An hypothesis on the role of glucose in the mechanism of action of cognitive enhancers. *Psychopharmacology, 99,* 431–438.

Werker, J. F., & Desjardins, R. D. (1995). Listening to speech in the first year of life: Experiential influences on phoneme perception. *Current Directions in Psychological Science, 4*, 76–81.

Werner, E. E. (1995). Resilience in development. *Current Directions in Psychological Science, 4*, 81–85.

Wertheimer, M. (1987). *A brief history of psychology* (3rd ed.). New York: Holt, Rinehart & Winston.

Wesnes, K., Simpson, P. M., & Kidd, A. (1987). The use of a scopolamine model to study the nootropic effects of tenilsetam (CAS 997) in man. *Medical Science Research: Psychology and Psychiatry, 15*, 1063–1064.

West, R. L., Crook, T. H., & Barron, K. L. (1992). Everyday memory performance across the life span: Effects of age and noncognitive individual differences. *Psychology and Aging, 7*, 72–82.

Westen, D. (1991). Social cognition and object relations. *Psychological Bulletin, 109*, 429–455.

Westen, D. (1992). The cognitive self and the psychoanalytic self: Can we put ourselves together? *Psychological Inquiry, 3*, 1–14.

Wheeler, L., & Miyake, K. (1992). Social comparison in everyday life. *Journal of Personality and Social Psychology, 62*, 760–773.

Whimbey, A. (1976). *Intelligence can be taught.* New York: Bantam.

Whitam, F. L., Diamond, M., & Martin, J. (1993). Homosexual orientation in twins: A report on 61 pairs and three triplet sets. *Archives of Sexual Behavior, 22*(3), 187–206.

Whitbourne, S. K., Zuschlag, M. K., Elliot, L. B., & Waterman, A. D. (1992). Psychosocial development in adulthood: A 22-year sequential study. *Journal of Personality and Social Psychology, 63*, 260–271.

Whitbread, J., & McGown, A. (1994). The treatment of bulimia nervosa: What is effective? *Indian Journal of Clinical Psychology, 21*(2), 32–44.

White, D. E., & Glick, J. (1978). *Competence and the context of performance.* Paper presented at the meeting of the Jean Piaget Society, Philadelphia.

White, G. L., Fishbein, S., & Rutstein, J. (1981). Passionate love and the misattribution of arousal. *Journal of Personality and Social Psychology, 41*, 56–62.

White, K. M., Terry, D. J., & Hong, M. A. (1994). Safer sex behavior: The role of attitudes, norms, and control factors. *Journal of Applied Social Psychology, 24*(24), 2164–2192.

White, K. R., Taylor, M. J., & Moss, V. D. (1992). Does research support claims about the benefits of involving parents in early intervention programs? *Review of Educational Research, 62*, 91–125.

White, M. (1987). *The Japanese educational challenge: A commitment to children.* New York: Free Press.

White, R. K. (1984). *Fearful warriors: A psychological profile of U.S.-Soviet relations.* New York: Free Press.

Whitehouse, P. J., Struble, R. G., Hedreen, J. C., Clark, A. W., White, C. L., Parhad, I. M., & Price, D. L. (1983). Neuroanatomical evidence for a cholinergic deficit in Alzheimer's disease. *Psychopharmacology Bulletin, 19*, 437–440.

Whitley, B. E., & Hern, A. L. (1991). *Perceptions of vulnerability to pregnancy and the use of effective contraception.* Unpublished manuscript.

Whittington, M. A., Traub, R. D., & Jefferys, J. G. R. (1995, February 16). Synchronized oscillations in interneuron networks driven by metabotropic glutamate receptor activation. *Nature, 373*, 612–615.

Whorf, B. L. (1956). *Language, thought and reality.* Cambridge and New York: MIT Press and Wiley.

Wickelgren, W. (1977). Speed-accuracy tradeoff and information processing dynamics. *Acta Psychologica, 41*, 67–85.

Wickens, C. D. (1989). Attention. In D. Holding (Ed.), *Human skills.* New York: Wiley.

Wickens, C. D. (1992). Virtual reality and education. In *Proceedings of the IEEE International Conference on Systems, Man and Cybernetics.* New York: IEEE.

Wickens, C. D. (1992a). *Engineering psychology and human performance* (2nd ed.). New York: HarperCollins.

Wickens, C. D., Stokes, A., Barnett, B., & Hyman, F. (1992b). The effects of stress on pilot judgment in a MIDIS simulator. In O. Svenson & J. Maule (Eds.), *Time pressure and stress in human judgment and decision making.* New York: Plenum.

Wicker, F. W., Wiehe, J. A., Hagen, A. S., & . Brown, G. (1994). From wishing to intending: Differences in salience of positive versus negative consequences. *Journal of Personality, 62*(3), 347–368.

Wickrama, K., Conger, R. D., & Lorenz, F. O. (1995). Work, marriage, lifestyle, and changes in men's physical health. *Journal of Behavioral Medicine, 18*, 97–112.

Widiger, T., & Costa, P. (1994). Personality and personality disorders. *Journal of Abnormal Psychology, 103*, 78–91.

Widiger, T. A., Cadoret, R., Hare, R., Robins, L., Rutherford, M., Zanarini, M., Alterman, A., Apple, M., Corbitt, E., Forth, A., Hart, S., Kultermann, J., Woody,

G., & Frances, A. (1996). DSM-IV antisocial personality disorder field trial. *Journal of Abnormal Psychology, 105*, 3–16.

Widiger, T. A., & Kelso, K. (1983). Psychodiagnosis of Axis II. *Clinical Psychology Review, 3*, 491–510.

Widom, C. S. (1989). The cycle of violence. *Science, 244*, 160–166.

Widom, C. S. (1989). Does violence beget violence? A critical examination of the literature. *Psychological Bulletin, 106*, 3–28.

Wiebel, W. (1993). *The indigenous leader outreach model intervention manual.* Rockville, Maryland: National Institute on Drug Abuse.

Wiedenfeld, S., O'Leary, A., Bandura, A., Brown, S., Levine, S., & Raska, K. (1990). Inpact of perceived self-efficacy in coping with stressors on components of the immune system. *Journal of Personality and Social Psychology, 59*, 1082–1094.

Wiegersma, S., & Meertse, K. (1990). Subjective ordering, working memory, and aging. *Experimental Aging Research, 16*, 73–77.

Wiener, E., & Nagel, D. (1988). *Human factors in aviation.* Orlando, FL: Academic Press.

Wiertelak, E. P., Maier, S. F., & Watkins, L. R. (1992). Cholecystokinin antianalgesia: Safety cues abolish morphine analgesia. *Science, 256*, 830–833.

Wiley, M. G., & Crittenden, K. S. (1992). By your attributions you shall be known: Consequences of attributional accounts for professional and gender identities. *Sex Roles, 27*(5–6), 259–276.

Williams, G. V., & Goldman-Rakic, P. S. (1995). Modulation of memory fields by dopamine D_1 receptors in prefrontal cortex. *Nature, 376*, 572–575.

Williams, H. P., Wickens, C. D., & Hutchinson, S. (1994). Fidelity and interactivity in navigational training: A comparison of three methods. In *Proceedings of the 38th Annual Meeting of the Human Factors and Ergonomics Society.* Santa Monica, CA: Human Factors.

Williams, J. E., & Best, D. L. (1990). *Measuring stereotypes: A multination study* (Rev. ed.). Newbury Park, CA: Sage.

Williams, K. D., Jackson, J. M., & Karau, S. J. (1995). In D. Schroeder (Ed.), *Social dilemmas: Perspectives on individuals and groups* (pp. 117–142). Westport, CT: Praeger.

Williams, L. M. (1993). Recall of childhood trauma: A prospective study of women's memories of child sexual abuse. *Journal of Consulting and Clinical Psychology, 62*, 1167–1176.

Williams, M. H. (1992). Exploitation and inference: Mapping the damage from therapist-patient sexual involvement. *American Psychologist, 47*, 412–421.

Williams, R., Suarez, E., Kuhn, C., Zimmerman, E., & Schanberg, S. (1991). Biobehavioral basis of coronary-prone behavior in middle-aged men. Part I: Evidence for chronic SNS activation in Type As. *Psychosomatic Medicine, 53*, 517–527.

Williams, R. B., Jr., & Barefoot, J. C. (1988). Coronary-prone behavior: The emerging role of the hostility complex. In B. K. Houston & C. R. Snyder (Eds.), *Type A behavior pattern: Current trends and future directions* (pp. 189–221). New York: Wiley.

Williams, R. L. (1972). *The Black intelligence test of cultural homogeneity (BITCH)— A culture specific test.* Paper presented at the annual meeting of the American Psychological Association, Honolulu.

Willis, W. D., Jr. (1988). Dorsal horn neurophysiology of pain. *Annals of the New York Academy of Science, 531*, 76–89.

Wills, T. A. (1991). Similarity and self-esteem in downward comparison. In J. M. Suls & T. A. Wills (Eds.), *Social comparison: Contemporary theory and research* (pp. 23–50). Hillsdale, NJ: Lawrence Erlbaum Association.

Wilson, B. A. (1987). *Rehabilitation of memory.* New York: Guilford.

Wilson, G. T. (1985). Limitations of meta-analysis in the evaluation of the effects of psychological therapy. *Clinical Psychology Review, 5*, 35–47.

Wilson, S. A., Becker, L. A., & Tinker, R. H. (1995). Eye movement desensitization and reprocessing (EMDR) treatment for psychologically traumatized individuals. *Journal of Consulting and Clinical Psychology, 63*, 928–937.

Wimmer, H., & Perner, J. (1983). Beliefs about beliefs: Representation and constraining function of wrong beliefs in young children's understanding of deception. *Cognition, 13*, 103–128.

Winett, R. A. (1995). A framework for health promotion and disease prevention programs. *American Psychologist, 50*, 341–350.

Wing, K., Chiu, H. F. K., Ho, C. K. W., & Chen, C. N. (1994). Narcolepsy in Hong Kong Chinese—A preliminary experience. *Australian and New Zealand Journal of Medicine, 24*(3), 304–306.

Winkler, J., Suhr, S. T., Gage, F. H., Thal, L. J., & Fisher, L. J. (1995). Essential role of neocortical acetylcholine in spatial memory. *Nature, 375*, 484–487.

Winn, P. (1995). The lateral hypothalamus and motivated behavior: An old syndrome reassessed and a new perspective gained. *Current Directions in Psychological Science, 4*, 182–187.

Winokur, G., Coryell, W., Keller, M., Endicott, J., & Leon, A. (1995). A family study of manic-depressive (Bipolar I) disease. *Archives of General Psychiatry, 52,* 367–373.

Winson, J. (1990, November). The meaning of dreams. *Scientific American,* pp. 86–96.

Wise, R. A. (1988). The neurobiology of craving: Implications for the understanding and treatment of addiction. *Journal of Abnormal Psychology, 97,* 118–132.

Wise, R. A., & Rompre, P. P. (1989). Brain dopamine and reward. *Annual Review of Psychology, 40,* 191–225.

Witelson, S. (1994, November). Sex differences in numerical density of neurons in human auditory association cortex. Paper presented at the annual meeting of the Society for Neuroscience, Miami.

Witelson, S. F. (1992). Cognitive neuroanatomy: A new era. *Neurology, 42,* 709–713.

Wittchen, H. U., Zhao, S., Kessler, R. C., & Eaton, W. W. (1994). DSM-III-R: Generalized anxiety disorder in the national comorbidity survey. *Archives of General Psychiatry, 51,* 355–364.

Wogalter, M. S., Rashid, R., Clarke, S. W., & Kalsher, M. J. (1991). Evaluating the behavioral effectiveness of a multimodal voice warning sign in a visually cluttered environment. *Proceedings of the 35th Annual Meeting of the Human Factors Society* (pp. 718–722). Santa Monica, CA: Human Factors Society.

Woike, B. A. (1995). Most-memorable experiences: Evidence for a link between implicit and explicit motives and social cognitive processes in everyday life. *Journal of Personality and Social Psychology, 68,* 1081–1091.

Wolpe, J. (1958). *Psychotherapy by reciprocal inhibition.* Stanford, CA: Stanford University Press.

Wolpe, J. (1982). *The practice of behavior therapy* (3rd ed.). New York: Pergamon Press.

Wong, B. Y. L. (1986). Metacognition and special education: A review of a view. *Journal of Special Education, 20,* 9–29.

Wong, M. M., & Csikszentmihalyi, M. (1992). *Journal of Personality and Social Psychology, 60,* 154–164.

Wong, S. E., Martinez-Diaz, J. A., Massel, H. K., Edelstein, B. A., Wiegand, W., Bowen, L., & Liberman, R. P. (1993). Conversational skills training with schizophrenic inpatients: A study of generalization across settings and conversants. *Behavior Therapy, 24,* 285–304.

Wood, J. M., Nezworski, M. T., & Stejskal, W. J. (1996). The comprehensive system for the Rorschach: A critical examination. *Psychological Science, 7,* 3–10.

Wood, P. K. (1983). Inquiring systems and problem structure: Implications for cognitive development. *Human Development, 26,* 249–265.

Wood, W., Wong, F. Y., & Chachere, G. (1991). Effects of media violence on viewers' aggression in unconstrained social interaction. *Psychological Bulletin, 109,* 371–383.

Woodall, K. L., & Matthews, K. A. (1993). Changes in and stability of hostile characteristics: Results from a 4-year longitudinal study of children. *Journal of Personality and Social Psychology, 64,* 491–499.

Woodhead, M. (1988). When psychology informs public policy: The case of early childhood intervention. *American Psychologist, 43,* 443–454.

Woods, D. D. (1993). Process-tracing methods for the study of cognition outside of the experimental psychology laboratory. In G. A. Klein, J. Orasanu, R. Calderwood, & C. E. Zsambok (Eds.), *Decision making in action: Models and methods.* Norwood, NJ: Ablex.

Woodworth, R. S., & Schlosberg, H. (1954). *Experimental psychology.* New York: Holt.

Woody, G., & Frances, A. (1996). DSM-IV antisocial personality disorder field trial. *Journal of Abnormal Psychology, 105,* 3–16.

Wooley, J. D., & Wellman, H. M. (1993). Origin and truth: Young children's understanding of the relation of imaginary mental representations. *Child Development, 64,* 1–17.

Worchel, S., & Shackelford, S. L. (1991). Groups under stress: The influence of group structure and environment on process and performance. *Personality and Social Psychology Bulletin, 17,* 640–647.

Worchel, S., & Simpson, J. A. (Eds.) (1993). *Conflict between people and groups.* Chicago: Nelson-Hall.

World Health Organization. (1979). *Schizophrenia: An international follow-up study.* Geneva, Switzerland: World Health Organization.

Wortman, C. B. (1984). Social support and the cancer patient: Conceptual and methodological issues. *Cancer, 53,* 2339–2360.

Wright, E. F., Voyer, D., Wright, R. D., & Roney, C. (1995). Supporting audiences and performance under pressure: The home-ice disadvantage in hockey championships. *Journal of Sport Behavior, 18*(1), 21–28.

Wright, G. N., & Phillips, L. D. (1980). Cultural variation in probabilistic thinking:

Alternative ways of dealing with uncertainty. *International Journal of Psychology, 15,* 239–257.

Wright, R. (1995, March 13). The biology of violence. *New Yorker,* pp. 68–77.

Wright, W. F., & Bower, G. H. (1992). Mood effects on subjective probability. *Organizational Behavior and Human Decision Processes, 52,* 276–291.

Wu, J., Cohen, L. B., & Falk, C. X. (1994). Neuronal activity during different behaviors in aplysia: A distributed organization. *Science, 263,* 820–823.

Wucherpfennig, K. W., & Strominger, J. L. (1995). Molecular mimicry in T cell-mediated autoimmunity—Viral peptides activate human T cell clones specific for myelin basic protein. *Cell, 80,* 695–705.

Wurl, P. (1994). Acute caffeine intoxication after ingestion of a potentially lethal amount of coffee: A case report. *Wiener Klinische Wochenschrift, 106*(11), 359–361.

Wyer, R. S., & Srull, T. K. (Eds.). (1994). *Handbook of social cognition* (2nd ed.). Hillsdale, NJ: Lawrence Erlbaum Associates.

Wynn, K. (1992). Addition and subtraction by human infants. *Nature, 358,* 749–750.

Wynn, K. (1995). Infants possess a system of numerical knowledge. *Current Directions in Psychological Science, 4,* 172–177.

Xu, M., Hu, X. T., Cooper, D. C., Moratalla, R., Graybiel, A. M., White, F. J., & Tonegawa, S. (1994). Elimination of cocaine-induced hyperactivity and dopamine-mediated neurophysiological effects in dopamine D_1 receptor mutant mice. *Cell, 79,* 945–955.

Yahr, P., & Jacobsen, C. H. (1994). Hypothalamic knife cuts that disrupt mating in male gerbils sever efferents and forebrain afferents of the sexually dimorphic area. *Behavioral Neuroscience, 108*(4), 735–742.

Yakimovich, D., & Saltz, E. (1971). Helping behavior: The cry for help. *Psychonomic Science, 23,* 427–428.

Yalom, I. D. (1995). *The theory and practice of group therapy* (4th ed.). New York: Basic Books.

Yang, K., & Bond, M. (1990). Exploring implicit personality theories with indigenous or imported constructs: The Chinese case. *Journal of Personality and Social Psychology, 58,* 1087–1095.

Yantis, S. (1993). Stimulus-driven attentional capture. *Current Directions in Psychological Science, 2,* 156–161.

Yates, J. F., Lee, J. W., & Shinotsuka, H. (1992). *Cross-national variation in probability judgment.* Paper presented at the 33rd annual meeting of the Psychonomic Society, St. Louis.

Yates, J. F., Zhu, Y., Ronis, D. L., Wang, D. F., Shinotsuka, H., & Masanao, T. (1989). Probability judgment accuracy: China, Japan, and the United States. *Organizational Behavior and Human Decision Processes, 43,* 145–171.

Yeh, C., Shiell, M., Lamke, J., & Volpe, M. (1992). Physical therapy: Evaluation and treatment of chronic pain. In G. M. Aronoff (Ed.), *Evaluation and treatment of chronic pain.* Baltimore: Williams & Wilkins.

Yerkes, R. M. (Ed.) (1921). Psychological examining in the U.S. Army. *Memoirs of the National Academy of Sciences,* No. 15.

Yesavage, J. A., Leirer, V. O., Denari, M., & Hollister, L. E. (1985). Carry-over effects of marijuana intoxication on aircraft pilot performance: A preliminary report. *American Journal of Psychiatry, 142,* 1325–1329.

Yoder, J. D., & Kahn, A. S. (1993). Working toward an inclusive psychology of women. *American Psychologist, 48,* 846–850.

Yonas, A., Arterberry, M. E., & Granrud, C. D. (1987). Space perception in infancy. In R. Vasta (Ed.), *Annals of child development* (Vol. 4). Greenwich, CT: JAI Press.

Yonkers, K., Kando, J., Cole, J., & Blumenthal, S. (1992). Gender differences in pharmacokinetics and pharmacodynamics of psychotropic medication. *American Journal of Psychiatry, 149,* 587–595.

York, J. L., & Welte, J. W. (1994). Gender comparisons of alcohol consumption in alcoholic and nonalcoholic populations. *Journal of Studies on Alcohol, 55*(6), 743–750.

Young, A. W., Aggleton, J. P., Hellawell, D. J., & Johnson, M. (1995). Face processing impairments after amygdalotomy. *Brain, 118*(1), 15–24.

Young, A. W., & De Haan, E. H. F. (1992). Face recognition and awareness after brain injury. In A. D. Milner & M. D. Rugg (Eds.), *The neuropsychology of consciousness.* San Diego, CA: Academic Press.

Young, F. A., Leary, G. A., Baldwin, W. R., West, D. C., Box, R. A., Harris, E., & Johnson, C. (1969). The transmission of refractive errors within Eskimo families. *American Journal of Optometry, 46,* 676–685.

Young, M. (1966). Problem solving performance in two age groups. *Journal of Gerontology, 21,* 505–509.

Young, M. (1971). Age and sex differences in problem solving. *Journal of Gerontology, 26,* 331–336.

Youngstrom, N. (1992). Field of psychoanalysis undergoes resurgence. *APA Monitor, 23,* 24–25.

Youtz, R. P. (1968). Can fingers "see" color? *Psychology Today.*

Yukl, G., & Van Fleet, D. D. (1992). Theory and research on leadership in organizations. In M. D. Dunnette & L. M. Hough (Eds.), *Handbook of industrial and organizational psychology* (2nd ed., Vol. 3, pp. 147–198). Palo Alto, CA: Consulting Psychologists Press.

Yutrzenka, B. A. (1995). Making a case for training in ethnic and cultural diversity in increasing treatment efficacy. *Journal of Consulting and Clinical Psychology, 63,* 197–206.

Yutzy, S., Cloninger, C. R., Guze, S., Pribor, E., Martin, R., Kathol, R., Smith, G. R., & Strain, J. (1995). DSM-IV field trial: Testing a new proposal for somatization disorder. *American Journal of Psychiatry, 152,* 97–101.

Zahn-Waxler, C., Radke-Yarrow, M., Wagner, E., & Chapman, M. (1992). Development of concern for others. *Developmental Psychology, 28,* 1038–1047.

Zahrani, S. S., & Kaplowitz, S. A. (1993). Attributional biases in individualistic and collectivist cultures: A comparison of Americans with Saudis. *Social Psychology Quarterly, 56*(3), 223–233.

Zajonc, R. B. (1965). Social facilitation. *Science, 149,* 269–274.

Zaragoza, M. S., & Lane, S. M. (1994). Source misattributions and the suggestibility of eyewitness memory. *Journal of Experimental Psychology: Learning, Memory, and Cognition, 20,* 934-945.

Zatorre, R. J., Evans, A. C., Meyer, E., Gjedde, A. (1992). Lateralization of phonetic and pitch discrimination in speech processing. *Science, 256,* 846–849.

Zeki, S. (1992). The visual image in mind and brain. *Scientific American, 267,* 68–76.

Zelinski, E., Schaie, K. W., & Gribben, K. (1977, August). *Omission and commission errors: Task-specific adult lifespan differences.* Paper presented at the convention of the American Psychological Association, San Francisco.

Zhang, G., & Simon, H. A. (1985). STM capacity for Chinese words and idioms: Chunking and acoustical loop hypothesis. *Memory & Cognition, 13,* 193–201.

Zhou, J.-N., Hofman, M. A., Gooren, L. J. G., & Swaab, D. F. (1995). A sex difference in the human brain and its relation to transsexuality. *Nature, 378,* 68–70.

Zigler, E., & Seitz, V. (1982). Social policy and intelligence. In R. J. Sternberg (Ed.), *Handbook of human intelligence.* Cambridge, Eng.: Cambridge University Press.

Zigler, E., & Styfco, S. J. (1994). Head Start: Criticisms in a constructive context. *American Psychologist, 49*(2), 127–132.

Zigler, E., Taussig, C., & Black, K. (1992). Early childhood intervention: A promising preventive for juvenile delinquency. *American Psychologist, 47,* 997–1006.

Zillmann, D. (1984). *Connections between sex and aggression.* Hillsdale, NJ: Lawrence Erlbaum Associates.

Zillmann, D. (1988). Cognition-excitation interdependencies in aggressive behavior. *Aggressive Behavior, 14,* 51–64.

Zillmann, D., Baron, R. A., & Tamborini, R. (1981). Social costs of smoking: Effects of tobacco smoke on hostile behavior. *Journal of Applied Social Psychology, 11,* 548–561.

Zillmann, D., Katcher, A. H., & Milavsky, B. (1972). Excitation transfer from physical exercise to subsequent aggressive behavior. *Journal of Experimental Social Psychology, 8,* 247–259.

Zillmann, D., & Weaver, J. B. (1989). Pornography and men's sexual callousness toward women. In D. Zillmann & J. Bryant (Eds.), *Pornography: Research advances and policy considerations.* Hillsdale, NJ: Lawrence Erlbaum Associates.

Zimbardo, P. G. (1970). The human choice: Individuation, reason and order versus deindividuation, impulse and chaos. In W. J. Arnold & D. Levine (Eds.), *Nebraska Symposium on Motivation: (Vol. 17)* (pp. 237–307). Lincoln: University of Nebraska Press.

Zimbardo, P. G. (1973). The psychological power and pathology of imprisonment. In E. Aronson & R. Helmreich (Eds.), *Social psychology.* New York: Van Nostrand.

Zimmerman, M., Reischl, T., Seidman, E., Rappaport, J., Toro, P., & Salem, D. (1991). Expansion strategies of a mutual help organization. *American Journal of Community Psychology, 19,* 251–279.

Zinbarg, R. E., & Mineka, S. (1991). Animal models of psychopathology: II. Simple phobia. *The Behavior Therapist, 14,* 61–65.

Zorumski, C., & Isenberg, K. (1991). Insights into the structure and function of GABA-benzodiazepine receptors: Ion channels and psychiatry. *American Journal of Psychiatry, 148,* 162–173.

Zubin, J., & Spring, B. (1977). Vulnerability—A new view of schizophrenia. *Journal of Abnormal Psychology, 86,* 103–126.

Zuckerman, M. (1979). *Sensation seeking: Beyond the optimal level of arousal.* Hillsdale, NJ: Lawrence Erlbaum Associates.

Zuckerman, M. (1984). Sensation seeking: A comparative approach to a human approach. *The Behavioral and Brain Sciences, 7,* 413–471.

Zuckerman, M. (1990). Some dubious premises in research and theory on racial differences. *American Psychologist, 45,* 1297–1303.

Zuckerman, M. (1995). Good and bad humors: Biochemical bases of personality and its disorders. *Psychological Science, 6,* 325–332.

CREDITS

Credits (continued from copyright page)

Chapter 1: **p. 4:** *(top left)* Mark Richards/PhotoEdit.; *(top right)* Kaluzny/Thatcher/Tony Stone Images. *(bottom)* Frank Siteman/The Picture Cube. **p. 5:** *Figure 1.1* "Husband and father-in-law: Reversible Figure" by J. Botwinick, 1961, *American Journal of Psychology*, 7, 312–313. Copyright © 1961 University of Illinois Press. Reprinted by permission. **p. 6:** *(top)* Noboru Hashimoto/Sygma.; *(bottom)* F. St. Clair-Renard/Agence Vandystadt/Photo Researchers. **p. 7:** Archives of the History of American Psychology. **p. 8:** Archives of the History of American Psychology. **p. 9:** The Ferdinand Hamburger Archives of The Johns Hopkins University. **p. 10:** *(top)* Shaywitz, et al., 1995; NMR Research/Yale Medical School.; *(bottom)* Courtesy of Wellesley College Archives, photo by Partridge. **p. 11:** Courtesy of Wilberforce University, Archives and Special Collections. **p. 12:** *(top)* David Riecks.; *(bottom)* J. H. Robinson/Animals, Animals. **p. 13:** Bob Daemmrich/The Image Works. **p. 14:** Jay Freis/The Image Bank. **p. 15:** James King-Holmes/Science Photo Library/Photo Researchers. **p. 16:** *(top)* David Riecks; *(bottom)* Sylvial Johnson/Woodfin Camp. **p. 17:** Courtesy of Ross Parke. **p. 18:** *(top)* Gary A. Conner/PhotoEdit.; *(bottom)* Tom McCarthy/PhotoEdit. **p. 22:** Donna Binder/Impact Visuals.

Chapter 2: **p. 26:** © 1992 Watterson. Distributed by Universal Press Syndicate, reprinted with permission. All rights reserved. **p. 30:** Joe McNally/Sygma. **p. 31:** *(top)* David Young-Wolff/PhotoEdit.; *(bottom)* Tomas McAvoy, Life Magazine © Time Inc. **p. 32:** *(top)* Frank Siteman/The Picture Cube.; *(bottom)* John Elk/Stock Boston. **p. 36:** Ken Fisher/Tony Stone Images. **p. 39:** David Young-Wolff/PhotoEdit. **p. 42:** Meryl Joseph/The Stock Market. **p. 44:** Capital Features/The Image Works.

Chapter 3: **p. 52:** *Figure 3.4* Micrograph produced by John E. Heuser of Washington University School of Medicine, St. Louis, MO. Reprinted by permission. **p. 53:** *Figure 3.7* Max Planck Institute. **p. 55:** Astrid & Hans Frieder Michler/Science Photo Library/Photo Researchers. **p. 57:** Don Fawcett/Photo Researchers. **p. 61:** *(top)* Peter Fox M.D.; *(bottom)* D. N. Levin, H. Xiaoping, K. K. Tan, S. Galhotra, C. A. Pelizzare, G. T. Y. Chen, R. N. Beck, C-T. Chen, M. D. Cooper, J. F. Mullan, J. Hekmatpanah and J-P. Spire (1989). *The Brain:* Integrated three-dimensional display of MR and PET images. *Radiology*, 172: 783–789. By permission of the publisher. **p. 64:** *(left and center)* J. P. Seab et al. (1988), Quantitative NMR measurements of hippocampal atrophy in Alzheimer's disease. *Magnetic Resonance in Medicine* 8, 200–208, Copyright 1988, Academic Press. **p. 65:** Valina L. Dawson, Dept. of Neurology, Johns Hopkins University School of Medicine. **p. 67:** *Figure 3.17* Reprinted with permission of Simon & Schuster from *The Cerebral Cortex of Man*, by Wilder Penfield and Theodore Rasmussen. Copyright © 1950 Macmillan Publishing Company, Renewed @ 1978 Theodore Rasmussen. **p. 69:** *(top)* The Farside. Copyright 1986 Universal Press Syndicate. Reprinted with permission. All rights reserved.; *(bottom)* Fred McConnaughey/Photo Researchers. **p. 72:** Dan McCoy/Rainbow.; *Figure 3.21* J. L. Conel, *The Postnatal Development of the Human Cerebral Cortex*, Vols. I, VIII, Harvard University Press, 1939, 1967. Reprinted by permission. **p. 73:** Jim Wilson/Woodfin Camp. **p. 83:** Bard Wrisley/Gamma-Liaison.

Chapter 4: **p. 91:** *(bottom)* Courtesy of Noise Cancellation Technologies, Inc. **p. 93:** *(top right)* photo Lennart Nilsson/BEHOLD MAN, Little, Brown and Company. **p. 94:** *Figure 4.5* Adapted from *Experiments in Hearing* by G. von Bekesy. Copyright © 1960. Reprinted with permission of McGraw-Hill Book Company. **p. 95:** *Figure 4.6* G. L. Rasmussen and W. F. Windle, *Neural Mechanisms of the Auditory and Vestibular Systems*, 1960. Courtesy of Charles C. Thomas, Publisher, Springfield, Illinois. **p. 99:** J. Wallman. **p. 103:** *(bottom right)* Fritz Goro, Life Magazine © Time Inc. **p. 104:** *(top)* Peter L. Chapman. **p. 106:** Courtesy of Francoise Vienot. Photo by Jean Le Rohellec, MNHN, CNRS. **p. 109:** *Figure 4.22* "The Visual Image in Mind and Brain," by Semir Zeki. Copyright 1992 by Scientific American, Inc. All rights reserved. **p. 110:** *Figure 4.24* Leon B. Harmon and Bela Julesz (1973). *Science*, 180: 1194–97. Copyright © 1973 by the AAAS.; *Figure 4.23* Hubel, D. H., & Wiesel, T. N. 1962; 1965; redrawn by Kuffler, S. W. and Nicholls, A., 1976, *From Neuron to Brain*, Sinauer Associates, Inc. Reprinted by permission. **p. 113:** Francois Gohier/Photo Researchers. **p. 114:** Omikron/Photo Researchers. **p. 115:** Charles Kennard/Stock Boston. **p. 118:** *(top)* J. D. Sloane/The Picture Cube.; *(bottom)* Alain Evrard/Photo Researchers. **p. 119:** Peter Southwick/Stock Boston. **p. 121:** M. Grecco/Stock Boston. **p. 126:** Galanter, E. (1962). "Contemporary Psychophysics," in R. Brown (Ed.). *New Directions in Psychology*. New York: Holt, Rinehart & Winston. Reprinted by permission of the author.

Chapter 5: **p. 132:** Dan McCoy/Rainbow. **p. 134:** *(top)* The Far Side cartoon by Gary Larson is reprinted by permission of Chronicle Features, San Francisco, CA. All rights reserved. **p. 136:** *(bottom)* AP/Wide World Photos. **p. 137:** *(bottom)* Ira Kirschenbaum/Stock Boston. **p. 139:** The Farside © 1990 Farworks, Inc. Reprinted with permission of Universal Press Syndicate. All rights reserved. **p. 140:** *(top)* Jim Anderson/Woodfin Camp. **p. 144:** *Figure 5.16* Hudson, W. (1960). "Pictorial Depth Perception in Subcultural Groups in Africa." *Journal of Social Psychology*, 52, 183–208. Reprinted with permission of the Helen Dwight Reid Educational Foundation. Published by Heldref Publications, 1319 18th Street, N. W., Washington, DC 20030-1802. Copyright © 1960. **p. 146:** *Figure 5.21* Romelhart, D. E., and McClelland, J. L. (1986) Parallel Distributing Processing, Volume 1: Foundations. Cambridge, MA: MIT Press. Copyright © 1986 by the Massachusetts Institute of Technology. Reprinted by permission. **p. 147:** *(bottom)* Esbin/Anrs/The Image Works. **p. 148:** *Figure 5.24* Weisstein & Harris, *Science*, 1974, 186, 752–755. Copyright © 1974 by The American Association of the Advancement of Science. **p. 150:** *Figure 5.26* Johnson, M. A., Dziurawiec, S., Ellis, H., and Morton, J. (1991). "Newborns' Preferential Tracking of Face-Like Stimuli and Its Subsequent Decline." *Cognition*, 4, 1–19. Reprinted by permission of Elsevier Science Publishing. **p. 151:** Mark Richards/PhotoEdit. **p. 153:** *(top)* John Harrington/Black Star. **p. 155:** Martin Handford, *Find Waldo Now*, Little, Brown Publishers, 1988. **p. 156:** Larry Mulvehill/Rainbow. **p. 157:** James King-Holmes/W Industries/Science Photo Library/Photo Researchers.

Chapter 6: **p. 163:** © 1986, Washington Post Writers Group. Reprinted with permission.; *Figure 6.1* "Implicit Memory for Possible and Impossible Objects: Constraints on the Construction of Structural Descriptions" by Schacter, D. L., Cooper, L. A., Delaney, S. M., Peterson, M. A., and Tharan, M. from *Journal of Experimental Psychology: Learning, Memory, and Cognition*, 17, 3–19. Copyright © 1991 by the American Psychological Association. Reprinted by permission. **p. 169:** *(left)* T. Clark/The Image Works.; **p. 169:** *(right)* Lindsay Hebberd/Woodfin Camp. **p. 170:** Charles Gupton/Tony Stone Images. **p. 171:** *Figure 6.4* Reprinted with the permission of Macmillan Publishing Company from *Sleep: An Experimental Approach* by W. B. Webb. Copyright © 1968 by Wilse B. Webb. **p. 171:** *Figure 6.5* Adapted from Cartwright, *A Primer of Sleep and Dreaming*, Reading Mass: Addison-Wesley, 1978. Reprinted by permission. **p. 172:** *Figure 6.6 Science*, Vol. 152, page 606, 29 April 1966, (revised 1969), "Ontogenetic Development of the Human Sleep Dream Cycle." Copyright © 1966 by the AAAS. Roffwarg et al., 1966. With author permission. **p. 174:** *(top)* Bob Daemmrich/Stock Boston. **p. 175:** *(bottom)* Patrick Ward/Stock Boston. **p. 176:** *(bottom)* Allan Hobson/Photo Researchers. **p. 177:** *Figure 6.10* From *Hypnotic Age Susceptibility* by Ernest R. Hilgard, copyright © 1965 by Harcourt Brace Jovanovich, Inc. Reprinted by permission of the author. **p. 178:** *(top)* David Parker/Photo Researchers.; *Figure 6.11* Pattie, F. A. (1935). "A Report at Attempts to Produce Unoicular Blindness by Hypnotic Suggestion." *British Journal of Medical Psychiatry*, 15, 230–241. Reprinted by permission. **p. 181:** The William H. Helfand Collection, New York. **p. 182:** *Figure 6.14* From "Effects of Alcohol on Aggression in Males." A. R. Lang, D. J. Goeckner, V. J. Adesso & G. A. Marlett, *Journal of Abnormal Psychology*, #84, pp. 508–516. Copyright © 1975 by the American Psychological Association. Adapted by permission; and also from Kolata, G. (1986), "New drug counters alcohol intoxication," *Science*, 234, 1198–1199. Photo by Jules Asher at NIMH.; *(bottom)* Kenneth Murray/Photo Researchers. **p. 185:** Andrew Lichtenstein/Impact Visuals.

Chapter 7: **p. 196:** Great Brands of Europe, Inc. **p. 197:** Renee Lynn/Photo Researchers. **p. 199:** *(top)* Tom Stack & Assoc. **p. 201:** *(left)* Archives of the History of American Psychology.; *(right)* Ken Heyman/Black Star. **p. 202:** *(top)* Richard Wood/Picture Cube.; *Figure 7.8* From: *The Psychology of Learning and Memory* by Hintzman. Copyright © 1978 W. H. Freeman and Company. Used with permission. **p. 203:** *Figure 7.9* Adapted from "Teaching Machines" by B. F. Skinner. Copyright © 1961 by Scientific American, Inc. All rights reserved.; *Fig. 7.10* Frank Lotz

Miller/Black Star. **p. 204:** Jack Kurtz/Impact Visuals. **p. 205:** Rick Smolan/Stock Boston. **p. 206:** Courtesy of The Lincoln Electric Company. **p. 208:** Dan Walsh/Picture Cube. **p. 210:** J. Hillis Miller. **p. 212:** Lawrence Migdale/Stock Boston. **p. 215:** *Figure 7.15* Kohler, W. 1976. *The Mentality of Apes.* London: Routledge and Kegan Paul Plc. **p. 216:** Paul Chesley/Tony Stone Images. **p. 217:** Albert Bandura/Stanford University. **p. 222:** Marc Pokempner/Impact Visuals. **p. 224:** Frank Siteman/The Picture Cube. **p. 225:** Hank Morgan/Rainbow.

Chapter 8: **p. 230:** *(top)* Elizabeth Crews/Stock Boston.; *(bottom)* Bob Daemmrich/Stock Boston. **p. 234:** *Figure 8.5* From "Contextual Prerequisites for Understanding: Some Investigations of Comprehension and Recall" by Bransford and Johnson. *Journal of Verbal Learning and Verbal Behavior,* 61, pp. 717–726, 1972. **p. 237:** *Figure 8.6* Reprinted with permission of Macmillan Publishing Company from Cognitive Psychology: Memory, Language, and Thought by Darlene V. Howard. Copyright © 1983 by Darlene V. Howard. **p. 238:** Chip Hires/Gamma-Liaison. **p. 239:** *Figure 8.8* From "Long-Term Memory for a Common Object," by R. S. Nickerson and M. J. Adams. *Cognitive Psychology,* 1979, 11, 287–307. Reprinted by permission. **p. 240:** *(left)* Franco Magnani; *(right)* Susan Schwartzenberg/The Exploratorium. **p. 247:** *Figure 8.12* From *Cognitive Psychology: A Neural Network Approach* by C. Martindale. Copyright © 1991 Brooks/Cole Publishing, Pacific Grove, CA 93950, a division of Thomson Publishing Inc. By permission of the publisher. **p. 242:** Joe McNally/Matrix. **p. 243:** Jeff Dunn/The Picture Cube. **p. 246:** William F. Brewer. Originally appeared in *Cognitive Psychology,* 1981, 13, p. 211, published by Academic Press. **p. 248:** *(top)* AP/Wide World Photos. **p. 249:** Paul Conklin. **p. 251:** David Strickler/The Image Works. **p. 255:** *Figure 8.17* "Retroactive Inhibition in Free Recall: Inaccessibility of Information Available in the Memory Store" by Tulving and Psotka. *Journal of Experimental Psychology,* 87, pp. 1–8, 1971. Copyright © 1971 by the American Psychological Association. Adapted by permission.

Chapter 9: **p. 265:** *(bottom)* Lawrence Migdale/Stock Boston. **p. 269:** *(left)* Steven Starr/Stock Boston.; *(right)* Joe Sohm/Chromosohm/Stock Boston. **p. 270:** Steve Starr/Stock Boston. **p. 272:** NASA/Science Source/Photo Researchers. **p. 273:** A. Tannenbaum/Sygma. **p. 274:** James Lemass/The Picture Cube. **p. 276:** Calvin and Hobbes copyright 1992 Watterson. Distributed by Universal Press Syndicate. Reprinted with permission. All rights reserved. **p. 278:** Smithsonian Institution. **p. 283:** Hank Morgan/Science Source/Photo Researchers. **p. 284:** David Welcher/Sygma. **p. 285:** Jeff Topping/Gamma-Liaison. **p. 287:** Matthew Borkoski/Stock Boston. **p. 290:** *Figure 9.12* From *Cognitive Psychology and Information Processing* by Lachman/Lachman/Butterfield, p. 513, figure 13.4, 1979. Copyright © 1979 by Lawrence Erlbaum Associates. Reprinted by permission. **p. 291:** Eastcott/Momatiuk/The Image Works. **p. 292:** Joe McNally/Sygma. **p. 295:** Jeff Greenberg/Rainbow. **p. 296:** Herbert Terrace/Columbia University. **p. 299:** © Lawrence Migdale/Stock Boston.

Chapter 10: **p. 306:** Dan McCoy/Rainbow. **p. 307:** *Figure 10.1* Simulated items similar to those in the Wechsler Intelligence Scales for Adults and Children. Copyright © 1949, 1955, 1974, 1981, 1991 by the Psychological Corporation. Reproduced by permission. All rights reserved. **p. 311:** Peter Sibbald/Sygma. **p. 313:** *Figure 10.3* From Robert L. Williams, "Black Intelligence Test of Cultural Homogeneity," 1972. Reprinted by permission of the author.; *Figure 10.4* From the *Dynamic Assessment of Retarded Performers* by Reuven Feuerstein. Copyright © 1979 by Scott, Foresman and Company. Reprinted by permission of the author. **p. 314:** Leo Cullum 1987. **p. 315:** *Figure 10.5* From "Familial Studies of Intelligence: A Review," T. Bouchard et al., *Science,* Vol. 212, #4498, pp. 1055–9, 29 May 1981. Copyright © 1981 by the AAAS. **p. 317:** Andy Sacks/Tony Stone Images. **p. 318:** Bob Daemmrich. **p. 322:** Stephen Collins/Photo Researchers. **p. 324:** *(bottom)* Wayne Hot/The Picture Cube. **p. 326:** William Strode/Woodfin Camp. **p. 327:** Jim Daniels/The Picture Cube. **p. 329:** James Schnepf/Gamma-Liaison. **p. 331:** W. Hill/The Image Works. **p. 333:** Lawrence Migdale/Photo Researchers.

Chapter 11: **p. 339:** Frans Lanting/Minden Pictures. **p. 341:** *(bottom)* Fred Sponholtz. **p. 342:** *(bottom)* Okonieewski/The Image Works. **p. 345:** *(bottom)* Richard Howard. **p. 346:** Peter Menzel/Stock Boston. **p. 347:** Kopstein/Monkmeyer. **p. 348:** Reuters/Kansas City Star/Archive Photos. **p. 351:** *Figure 11.6* Adapted from W. H. Masters and V. E. Johnson. *Human Sexual Response,* p. 5 (Boston: Little, Brown and Company, 1966). **p. 354:** James Wilson/Woodfin Camp. **p. 357:** Reprinted by permission of the publishers from Henry A. Murray, *Thematic Apperception Test,* Cambridge, Mass.: Harvard University Press, copyright 1943 by the President and Fellows of Harvard College, © 1971 by Henry A. Murray. **p. 359:** Kevin Horan/Stock Boston. **p. 363:** Joe Hoyle/*The Daily Illini.* **p. 364:** *(bottom)* From *The Neurological Examination* 4th ed., by R. N. DeJong. New York: Lipincott/Harper & Row, 1979. **p. 365:** *Figure 11.12* From "Pathophysiology of emotional disorders associated with brain damage" by K. Poeck, in P. J. Vinken and G. W. Bruyn (Eds.) *Handbook of Clinical Neurology,* Vol. 3. New York: American

Elsevier, 1969. **p. 369:** *Figure 11.15* Figure 3 from "Voluntary Facial Action Generates Emotion-Specific Autonomic Nervous System Activity," by R. W. Levenson, P. Ekman, and W. V. Friesen, *Psychophysiology,* 1990, 24, 363–384. Copyright © 1990 the Society for Psychophysiological Research. Reprinted with permission of the author and the publisher from Levenson, Ekman, and Friesen, 1990. **p. 370:** *Science Magazine,* Volume 221. **p. 371:** Dan McCoy/Rainbow. **p. 372:** G. Veggi/Photo Researchers. **p. 375:** *(left)* Eastcott/Momatiuk/Woodfin Camp.; *(center)* Rick Smolan/Stock Boston.; *(right)* Jonathan Blair/Woodfin Camp. **p. 376:** *Figure 11.17* From "The Recognition of Threatening Facial Stimuli" by Aronoff, J., Barclay, A.M., and Stevenson, L. A. 1988. *Journal of Personality and Social Psychology,* 54, pp. 647–655. Copyright © 1988 by the American Psychological Association. Reprinted by permission.

Chapter 12: **p. 383:** James Wilson/Woodfin Camp. **p. 386:** John Chiasson/Gamma-Liaison. **p. 388:** Reproduced, with permission, from Nelson, C.A. (1987). The recognition of facial expressions in the first two years of life: Mechanisms of development. *Child Development,* 58, 889–909. **p. 389:** Petit Format/J. Da Cunha/Photo Researchers. **p. 391:** *(all four)* George Zimbel/Monkmeyer. **p. 392:** *(top)* Joe McNally/Sygma.; *(bottom)* Courtesy of Carolyn Rovee-Collier. **p. 395:** Reprinted with special permission of King Features Syndicate. **p. 397:** Michael Newman/PhotoEdit. **p. 400:** From *Genie,* © 1993 by Russ Rymer. Reprinted by permission of HarperCollins Publishers, Inc. All rights reserved. **p. 401:** Laima Druskis/Stock Boston. **p. 402:** Amy C. Etra/PhotoEdit. **p. 404:** AP/Wide World Photos. **p. 405:** Harlow Primate Library, University of Wisconsin. **p. 406:** Kevin Forest/Image Bank. **p. 410:** Nathan Nourok/PhotoEdit. **p. 411:** Bill Aron/PhotoEdit. **p. 412:** Wanstall/The Image Works. **p. 414:** *Figure 12.7* Tanner, J. M. (1978). *Foetus into man: Physical growth from conception to maturity.* **p. 415:** Reprinted with special permission of North America Syndicate. **p. 419:** *Figure 12.8* Colby, A., Kohlberg, L., Gibbs, J., & Lieberman, M. (1983). "A Longitudinal Study of Moral Judgement." *Monographs of the Society for Research in Child Development,* 48 (Whole nos. 1 & 2), (pp. 476, 477). **p. 421:** *(top)* The Farside © 1992 Farworks, Inc. Reprinted with permission of Universal Press Syndicate. All rights reserved. **p. 422:** *(top)* Delfina Colby/The News-Gazette.; *(bottom)* Bob Daemmrich/Stock Boston. **p. 423:** © 1990 Newsweek, Inc. All rights reserved. Reprinted by permission. **p. 424:** Paul Conklin/Monkmeyer.

Chapter 13: **p. 430:** Michael Newman/PhotoEdit. **p. 432:** *Table 13.2* Crandall, C. S., Preisler, J. J. & Aussprung, J. (1992). "Measuring life event stress in the lives of college students: The undergraduate Stress Questionnaire (USQ). *Journal of Behavioral Medicine,* 15, 627–662. **p. 433:** Stacy Rosenstock/Impact Visuals. **p. 434:** *Figure 13.2* "The General Adaptation Syndrome" from *Stress Without Distress* by Hans Selye, M.D., Copyright © 1974 by Hans Selye, M.D. Reprinted by permission of HarperCollins Publishers, Inc. **p. 436:** *(top)* L. Azerud/Sygma.; *(bottom)* © 1991 King World. **p. 438:** © 1984, Washington Post Writers Group. Reprinted with permission. **p. 439:** *Figure 13.4* Adapted from Lazarus, Opton, Nornikos, and Rankin, *Journal of Personality,* 33:4. Copyright © 1965 Duke University Press. Reprinted with permission. **p. 441:** *(bottom)* Lauren Greenfield/Sygma. **p. 442:** Dennis Brack/Black Star. **p. 446:** Boehringer Ingelheim International GmbH/photo Lennart Nilsson, *The Incredible Machine,* National Geographic Society. **p. 447:** Tony Freeman/PhotoEdit. **p. 449:** Huntly Hersch/The Picture Cube. **p. 452:** *Figure 13.5* Prochaska, W., DeClementi, C., and Norcross, J., "In Search of How People Change: Application to Addictive Behaviors," *American Psychologist,* 47, 1102–1114. Copyright © 1992 by the American Psychological Association. Reprinted by permission. **p. 454:** *(top)* Leslie O'Shaughnessy/Medical Images.; *(bottom)* Farley/Monkmeyer.

Chapter 14: **p. 459:** Bettmann Archive. **p. 460:** *(top)* Mary Evans Picture Library.; *Figure 14.2* Adapted from *Personality: Strategies and Issues,* by Robert M. Liebert and Michael D. Spiegler. Copyright © 1990 by Wadsworth, Inc. Reprinted by permission of Brooks/Cole Publishing Company, Pacific Grove, CA 93950. **p. 463:** Harriet Russell Stanley Fund, New Britain Museum of American Art. **p. 466:** *Figure 14.3* Reproduced by special permission of the publisher, Psychological Assessment Resources, Inc., Odessa, FL 33556. From the "NEO Personality Inventory" by Paul Costa and Robert McCrae. Copyright © 1978, 1985, 1989, 1991 by PAR, Inc. **p. 467:** *(top)* Barbara Alper/Stock Boston. **p. 467:** *Figure 14.4* Eysenck, H. J., Rachman, S.: "The Causes and Cures of Neurosis: An Introduction to Modern Behavior Therapy Based on Learning Theory and the Principle of Conditioning." 1965. Edits. Reprinted with permission. **p. 470:** Reuters/John McCoy/Archive Photos. **p. 472:** *(top)* The Far Side, copyright 1990 Farworks, Inc., reprinted with permission of Universal Press Syndicate. All rights reserved.; *(bottom)* Elena Rooraid/PhotoEdit. **p. 473:** *Figure 14.5* Material taken from the *Personality Research Form Manual, Second Edition.* Copyright © 1989, Douglas N. Jackson. Reproduced with permission of the Sigma Assessment Systems, Inc., Research Psychologists Press Division, Port Huron, MI.; *Figure 14.6* Reprinted from *Journal of Behavior Therapy and Experimental Psychiatry,* 13, "The Assessment and